The Personal Rule of CHARLES I

The Personal Rule of CHARLES I

KEVIN SHARPE

YALE UNIVERSITY PRESS
NEW HAVEN AND LONDON · 1992

For Gerald Aylmer

Set in Bembo by Best-set Typesetter Ltd., Hong Kong
Printed and bound in Great Britain by The Bath Press, Avon

Library of Congress Cataloging-in-Publication Data

Sharpe, Kevin.
The personal rule of Charles I / Kevin Sharpe.
p. cm.
Includes bibliographical references and index.
ISBN 0–300–05688–5
1. Charles I, King of England, 1600–1649. 2. Great Britain – Politics and government – 1625–1649. I. Title.
DA396.A2S48 1992
941.06′2 – dc20 92–16271
CIP

A catalogue record for this book is available from the British Library.

CONTENTS

LIST OF ILLUSTRATIONS

ACKNOWLEDGEMENTS

During the decade or more that I have worked on this study, many have made different contributions, without which it would never have been completed. First, the staff of the numerous libraries and record offices I visited in Great Britain, the United States of America and Australia all offered such generous assistance that it would be as inappropriate to single some out as it is impossible to name them all. I should, however, like to thank especially, along with the keepers of the public repositories, those custodians of private collections who generously made available to me important manuscripts in their possession. I am most grateful to the Marquess of Lothian for placing the invaluable Coke papers then at Melbourne Hall on temporary deposit at Derbyshire record office and to the staff there, especially Mr Andrew George, for facilitating my study of them. (These manuscripts are now in the British Library.) I should also like to thank the Duke of Buccleuch and Queensbury and Northamptonshire Record Office for access to the Montagu papers; the Duke of Norfolk and the late Dr Francis Steer for admission to see Arundel Castle manuscripts; the Marquess of Anglesey and Phillips for an opportunity to study the Anglesey manuscripts; the Marquess of Downshire and Berkshire Record Office for permission to cite the Trumbull papers; the Earl Fitzwilliam, his trustees and the staff of Sheffield Central Library for access to the Wentworth Woodhouse manuscripts; Nottingham University Library for admitting me to read the Clifton and Portland manuscripts; and Mr J.T.L. Jervoise and Hampshire Record Office for granting me access to the extensive Jervoise of Herriard collection.

Travel to English and foreign archives and libraries has become an expense few individuals can bear alone. And over the last decade or so scholarly research has – not entirely regrettably – become more of a business whose practitioners have to make a case for funding and who are evaluated and accountable for their productivity. From the beginning I have been most fortunate to have been supported with funding and time for research – and I can only hope that the completed study will be seen as some return on that investment. I am most grateful to the British Academy, the Wolfson Foundation, the Fulbright Foundation and the Committee for Advanced Studies at the University of Southampton for assistance with the costs of travel to archives; and to friends and colleagues who provided bed, board and cheer during visits to record repositories, especially Simon and Susie Adams for hospitality and friendship during a prolonged stay in Edinburgh. I should also like to express my thanks to the Provost and Fellows of Oriel College where I first thought about the 1630s during the delicious freedom of a research fellowship, and the Institute for Advanced Study, Princeton, for providing a year for reading seventeenth-century books in the most stimulating intellectual community in the world.

It is a sad comment, I think, on the pressures of time in English academic life that every word of the text that follows was written on other continents. A year at the Huntington Library and Stanford Humanities Center enabled me first to pull my researches together in lively and critical company; most recently, a fellowship at the Humanities Research Centre of the Australian National University in Canberra made possible the completion of the text. I would like to thank warmly Martin Ridge, Bliss Carnochan and Ian Donaldson for all their kind support and friendship that made those years as pleasurable as they were productive, and those colleagues at Southampton who made it possible for me to take leave. During both years the isolation of months of daily writing was greatly alleviated by the good cheer and warm companionship of friends old and new – in America, Dave Gutierrez, Kathryn Henry, Stephen Orgel, Michelle Pridmore-Brown and especially David Riggs and Steve Zwicker; in Australia, Bruce Coram, Ian and Grazia Donaldson, Harriet Guest, Hazel Rowley, Nicolaas Rupke and Greg Walker.

Whilst a historian has his first important dialogue with his sources, it is through conversation with other scholars that we refine and reformulate the questions we ask of the documents. Over the last ten or more years I have benefited, more than can easily be expressed, from numerous discussions with other early modern historians – formally in seminars and conferences, and informally through conversation and correspondence. To all those who will recognize a question asked or a suggestion posed that finds no specific acknowledgement, I express my thanks. For all the emphasis some would place on the historiographical controversies in Stuart studies, it is important always to remember that over the last years we have all been led to ask new questions and to review our first conclusions, and never to forget that many of the most stimulating exchanges are those that end in disagreement. Certainly much of what I have written owes a great deal to those with whom I have not concurred, and I would like to thank them for sending me back into the archives and for making me think again.

A full list of all who have helped this work in some way would include very many early modern historians in England, several in the USA and Australia, and not a few scholars of other periods and disciplines. But I would especially like to express my warm gratitude to Keith Baker, Christopher Brooks, John Elliott, Peter Lake, the late Brian Lyndon, Geoffrey Parker, Conrad Russell, Paul Seaver, Lawrence Stone, Keith Thomas, Greg Walker and Anne Whiteman, not only for all their generous advice, but for criticism and encouragement, both in good measure, over the years. To Hugh Trevor-Roper I owe more than can here be expressed for his inspiration, illumination and friendship over two decades. George Bernard and John Morrill added to all their earlier counsel and support the very great kindness (and labour) of a close and critical reading of the text for which I express my warm gratitude – as I do to the anonymous reader for Yale University Press who also saved me from a number of errors. Mark Stoyle not only displayed the sharp eye for a sloppy thought or phrase that I remember from his undergraduate days, he also assisted with checking the final scripts, as did Tim Wales who also offered some helpful advice, especially on the question of poor relief. The book is dedicated to a scholar who has not only made this period his own but who, amid sometimes bitter historiographical controversy, has stood as an example of scholarship, openness to debate and a generosity with time and advice, from which I have greatly benefited and for which I am deeply grateful.

At successive stages Alison Hamlin, Dee Marquez, Pearl Moyseyenko and Jean Wilson have valiantly battled to decode the private cypher that I hesitate to call handwriting. Thanks to them I have been able to keep my distance from the wordprocessor and the endless mysterious discussions of machines and software. Finally while an author breathes a sigh of relief at the completion of a project, for others it is the beginning of considerable labour and effort to transform a bare typescript into a book. Few authors can be better served than I have been by my agents Andrew Best and Peter Robinson of Curtis Brown, or by my publisher Dr Robert Baldock and the production team at Yale University Press.

In thanking them all, and the many more unnamed, I am only too aware how little *The Personal Rule* is a personal achievement. For its failings, however, the author must stand alone on the scaffold.

PREFACE

On 10 March 1629 Charles I dissolved the parliament that had been adjourned amidst stormy scenes the week before. He was not to call another until April 1640 when the war against the Scots made a grant of parliamentary taxation essential. Historians have not felt it necessary to explain why no parliaments were called for eleven years. Charles, it has been agreed, was possessed of an autocratic temperament. If he had any regard for parliaments at all he valued them only as ciphers to execute his commands. During the 'eleven years' tyranny', both the king's policies and methods of government, it is said, demonstrated his preference for rule by prerogative and his aspiration towards the absolutism then developing in France. But the experiment in personal rule not only failed, it was, many historians have argued, doomed to failure from the start. Opposition to the regime, strong we are told from the beginning, mounted steadily; the Scots war presented the opportunity to organize it. When members of parliament reassembled in the spring of 1640 they (allegedly) came to Westminster determined to dismantle the machinery of personal government and to prevent permanently rule by the royal prerogative. The political power struggle began; two years later it transferred to the battlefields of the English civil war.

Once this sketch of the decade of the 1630s was part of a larger historical mural with which all students of the English past were familiar. The seventeenth century had a special place in the story of English (and indeed American) history, as the century in which the champions of law and liberty, property and Protestantism triumphed over absolute monarchy and popery and laid the foundations for parliamentary government. From the mid-1970s, however, a group of historians began, from a variety of perspectives, to question this Whig interpretation of English history and to undermine its orthodoxy.

Seventeenth-century parliaments, Conrad Russell and others argued, were not the obvious heralds of their nineteenth-century namesakes. They met occasionally and were summoned to do the king's business; MPs, primarily concerned with their localities, did not seek to govern from Westminster. Most of all, parliaments neither sought, nor were able, to be an opposition to the monarchy. The constituents of parliament – king, Lords and Commons – endeavoured to work in harmony for the good governance of the commonweal. These so-called 'revisionist' scholars were far from agreed as to why things, or indeed what, went wrong in early Stuart England. Some attributed the problems of early Stuart government to the strains and demands of war, to a failure of 'counsel', or to mounting tensions between the centre and the localities. But these historians largely agreed that the problems of the early seventeenth century were problems for the king *and* parliament rather than one of an inevitable conflict between them.

By no means did these revisions meet with universal agreement. But the challenge to the established view certainly led many – as had been hoped – to (often the first) detailed investigation of the records and diaries of the Commons and Lords, to studies of individual counties and MPs and to investigation of the broader political contexts of parliamentary enactments and debates. For all the different interpretations, we now know a vast amount more about what happened in early Stuart parliaments. Moreover, whatever else divides them, most revisionist historians and their critics have tended to concur on one thing: that however serious the problems of the early Stuarts and their relations with parliaments, they were made a great deal worse by Charles I than by his father.

Indeed in recent historical writing James I has enjoyed a considerable rehabilitation. Where once the accession of a Scot to the English throne after the 'brilliant' reign of Elizabeth was taken as the beginning of the troubles, James is now depicted as an astute politician who ruled successfully in difficult circumstances. He overcame the problems of governing three kingdoms from London; he wisely avoided involvement in continental conflicts; most of all he maintained peace and equilibrium in the church. Though he had been guilty of failings and weaknesses, especially his susceptibility to favourites, when James I died, it is now more or less agreed, the English polity had not been shaken by any major tremors. And James's last parliament, that of 1624, had, arguably, been the most harmonious of his reign. The rehabilitation of James therefore has naturally focused both attention on the period after 1625 and blame on the reign of his son. Charles I was a very different character to his father: less malleable, more rigid, less approachable, more reserved. In three or four years, several historians have recently suggested, he transformed the political landscape and damaged the very foundations of the monarchy. Charles, it is argued, took a rigid stand on his prerogative and showed scant respect for the law or for parliaments. Still worse, his own preferences for ceremonial worship and patronage of churchmen like William Laud aroused fears for the safety of the church. By 1628 the king had so eroded the trust of his people that parliament demanded the acceptance of a Petition of Right as the guarantee of their liberties. In response, Charles abandoned the traditional courses of consent for the 'new politics' of rule without parliaments and so began the conflict which ultimately led to civil war. 'If Charles I had not succeeded to the English throne,' a scholar recently argued, 'the troubles of his reign would have been avoided'.

That judgement cannot be accepted until we have asked some questions it does not ponder and considered circumstances that it neglects. Because Charles succeeded to the throne of a realm at war, it is hard to determine whether politics after 1625 was altered more by the king's character and attitudes, or by the massive strains of the war effort on a commonweal that had for long been insulated from foreign engagements. The necessities of war led many in government to take measures they thought 'extraordinary' courses and, if we are to place any trust in his words, Charles I was one of them. New circumstances rather than new attitudes to his prerogative may have shaped the early years of Charles's reign. As for religion, the divisions in the church, always latent, came to the surface in the last years of James's reign and were a problem bequeathed *to* his son. In general there has been too little study of the extent to which Charles followed or abandoned his father's principles or policies; and perhaps too little recognition that the differences between father and son lay more in their styles of governing than in their political programmes or values.

Such an observation underlines the want of good political biographies of both kings. For all the extensive and fruitful research on early Stuart history in recent years, there have been no really satisfactory scholarly studies of James I and Charles I. Moreover, for all the revisionists' arguments that the importance of parliaments has been exaggerated, their work has continued to focus on parliaments rather than the crown, the court or the Council. In both respects it is significant that there has been no full study of the personal rule of Charles I since Samuel Rawson Gardiner wrote over a hundred years ago. A recent book helpfully sketches reactions to the Caroline regime, but fails to study in depth the aims and policies of Charles I and his ministers to which they were a response. Yet the 1630s offer us the rich opportunity to study Charles I as a king at peace, to understand his values and ideology of kingship and his priorities for the church. And they open a new perspective on the importance of parliaments in early Stuart England by enabling us to investigate the process of government during the only decade without them. A new history of the personal rule is therefore a, perhaps now the, vital chapter in the story of the origins of the English civil war.

From the outset the historian of the 1630s discerns serious problems with the traditional picture of inevitable and steadily escalating conflict. Though often frankly critical of Charles I, Edward Hyde, Earl of Clarendon, historian of the Great Rebellion he experienced, singled out the eleven years of non-parliamentary government as a period of the 'fullest calm and greatest measure of felicity'. Not only did other contemporaries concur in their praise of England's halcyon days; Charles from 1629 ruled a country that, unusually in Europe, enjoyed a decade of peace and the prosperity that came in its wake. Moreover, since he had no standing army nor independent bureaucracy, no intendants like the French kings to impose the will of Whitehall in the shires, Charles also ruled with the co-operation of the county gentry. Indeed as JPs and deputy lieutenants, as collectors of levies and fines, former MPs themselves made possible this decade of non-parliamentary government. Evidently a complete breakdown in relations between the king and the political nation did not result from the collapse of parliament in 1629. The history of the parliaments of the 1620s, as has been shown, offers few pointers to allegiances in or explanations of the English civil war.

Did, then, the breakdown occur during the 1630s? Was it the eleven years of government without parliaments that convinced the political nation that Charles had absolutist intentions that must be resisted? Was it the decade of personal rule that projected England towards civil conflict? The answers to these questions require a full study of the 1630s – of politics and religion, of foreign policy and finance, of the court and the counties, of attitudes and ideas. They require a study of the making of policy, the enactment of programmes, of the responses these measures excited and the opposition they aroused. This book attempts the first such study since Gardiner's narrative appeared in 1877.

Our first purpose will be to attempt to explain Charles I's decision to rule without parliaments. While several narratives have traced parliaments' growing disappointment with the new king, none has attempted to understand how a monarch who, in his first years on the throne, had summoned more parliaments than his predecessors for a century, came to regard it as impossible to govern with them. Charles I's early years as prince and monarch, his personal development, his relationship with the Duke of Buckingham, most of all the experience of fighting wars, will be shown to be central to that decision and to an understanding of the policies of the 1630s.

Part II will investigate the consequences of the break with parliaments, the personalities of the king and his ministers and their aims and ideals in the reform of state and church. We shall examine the extent to which Charles himself determined policy and the influence of his various advisers and court factions. Special attention will be paid to the court and its culture as Charles's public image of his kingship and as his model for the reformation of the realm. The Privy Council will be studied as the principal organ of government for transmitting the ideals of Whitehall to the gentry governors of the provinces. A full examination of Archbishop William Laud's and the king's programmes for the reformation of the Church of England belongs, we shall argue, in that broader quest for (and idealization of) an earlier order that informed and drove all Charles's values and policies during the first half of the personal rule.

Though those aims and policies remained and continued, and we shall pursue some of them to the end of the decade, Part III will start from what I shall argue were the very different circumstances of 1635. For with the death of Lord Treasurer Weston, the launching of the ship money fleet, the Peace of Prague and the entry of France into the Thirty Years War, Charles's priorities shifted very much to European considerations. The biggest item on the domestic agenda, ship money, was a consequence of that change of focus. I shall chart the diplomatic course that nearly took England into war against the Habsburgs and plot the rise of new men in the king's counsels at home as foreign policy reshaped the patterns of domestic and factional politics.

The summer of 1637 sharply checked the flow of events, when the Scots rose in resistance against the new Prayer Book devised for the kirk. The Scottish problem redirected foreign and domestic policy and ultimately brought about the collapse of the personal rule. It is important therefore that before we follow its course, we take stock of the situation in England. What had been the experience of non-parliamentary government? How had local governors, counties and towns responded to the personal rule? How freely could men voice opinions and dissent? What degree of opposition (especially legal and constitutional opposition) was there to the regime? If the greatest discontent arose from religion what was the cause of that discontent? How revolutionary was the puritan opposition? Were the puritans numerous and popular or a beleaguered minority? Did the events of the 1630s drive moderate men into more radical positions, and if so how and when?

1637, apparently the high point of the personal rule, also saw the dawn of its collapse: the rebellion in Scotland. Part IV will examine Charles's government of Scotland, the coronation of 1633 and the origins of the Prayer Book crisis. It will trace the prevarications, negotiations and decision to proceed militarily against the Covenanters. Throughout emphasis will be placed on English reactions to and perceptions of events in Scotland. We shall examine the organization of war, the burdens it imposed and the resentments it created or exacerbated. Was, it will be asked, the Scots war an occasion for the expression of long-felt antagonism, or the cause of a new opposition? Here I will suggest that military failures and the Scots' propaganda campaign greatly damaged the government. Moreover events in Scotland sounded the end of the Anglo-French treaty and contributed to a reorientation of the power balance at court that was dangerously to isolate powerful figures.

The final part of the book will seek to explain why those who had assisted Charles to rule for eleven years without parliaments now insisted that they could not govern in their localities without them. I shall sketch the first history of the Short Parliament since the publication of its debates and examine the importance of its failure for the king's second campaign in Scotland and for the political climate at home. With the defeat at Newburn and the decision to summon the Long Parliament our main story of non-parliamentary government comes to an end. In conclusion we shall look back at the nature of Charles's personal rule and glance forward to the origins of the English civil war, and assess the place of the 1630s in the conflict.

The parts of the book therefore will, basically, follow chronologically. But within the basic chronological parameters we shall pursue subjects across chronological boundaries, for where foreign affairs often demand careful narrative, other matters – religion, finance, local government – are better treated thematically. And whilst the making of policies, their enactment and reactions to them were in continuous dialogue, we shall examine them to some extent discretely for the sake of clarity.

Throughout this book an attempt has been made to draw on fresh archival material, for the study of secular and religious government, domestic and foreign affairs. For the localities work has been concentrated on counties that have not been studied and private collections that have not been exploited. The reader may find fewer references than expected to the familiar printed collections – like Rushworth or Nalson. This is because in researching this study I became increasingly aware of the extent to which seemingly innocent collections of texts constructed a narrative and imposed a thesis by selection, ordering and gloss – and even invention. The respective frontispieces of Rushworth's *Historical Collections* and Nalson's *Impartial Collection*, the one representing Charles I against divine justice, the other Britannia subjected by Janus-faced Scots, announce their polemical purpose (see Figure 1). If, as Nalson charged, Rushworth was 'a better advocate

1 Frontispiece to J. Nalson, *An Impartial Collection of the Great Affairs of State*, 1682.

than a historian', Nalson himself did not hesitate 'to tie up the loose and scattered papers with the circumstances, causes and consequences of them'. I have also made less use of the printed literature of the decade than I expected or than I hoped, given the vast time I spent with it. Contemporary pamphlets and tracts offer excellent evidence of what was read, expected, desired and idealized, and so we should use them. But they are far less reliable as a guide to what was going on, or even what was typically thought. The sermon provides a good example. Printed sermons tended to be official (court or assize sermons for instance) or puritan, illicitly published. They set up polarized positions which may have concerned only few and give little flavour of the typical sermon delivered, doubtless impromptu, in the country parish. Similarly treatises on the role of sheriffs or JPs present invaluable portraits of ideals but little guide to the practical conduct of business in the localities. Whatever use we make of such material we must read it in the context of court records, the letter dashed off on the day, the conversation overheard by an ambassador, the gossip reported by the newsmonger, the doggerel verse that circulated in the tavern or the camp.

Far from a shortage of archival material, there is more for the history of the 1630s than could be mastered in a lifetime. Whilst what follows is the fruit of what I have been able to study over a decade, no reader will be more aware than the author of how much more research might be done. Indeed though it is usual to apologize for a book of this length, I have become increasingly aware that each of my chapters is worthy of a monograph. Given, however, that my purpose is to capture some sense of the whole, I can only hope that others will be stimulated to closer examination of the parts.

Finally, as any student of the period will know, the historiography of early seventeenth-century England has itself in recent years been characterized more by civil war than halcyon calm. In this work I have taken my agenda less from the debates of historians than from the issues that emerged from the archives. So whilst my disagreements with others are sometimes marked, and the book has a case (indeed number of cases) to argue, I have eschewed polemical jousts for an account which may, it is hoped, add broadly to our knowledge and understanding not only of the personal rule, but of the nature of government and politics in early modern England.

The text of this book was completed, in Australia, in September 1990. I have attempted here and there to draw attention to works published after then but not to revise my own account. During the months of completing references, checking and tidying, Conrad Russell's long-awaited and important *The Fall of the British Monarchies* (and its epitome *The Causes of the English Civil War*) appeared in print. Because my account ends with the battle of Newburn we overlap but little. Where we do our stories are, for the most part, complementary. In so far as our accounts of the Short Parliament (slightly) differ, they should be read as written from the different perspectives of authors for whom 1640 is in one case the end, in the other the beginning of a story. Where we disagree substantially is over religion, not least because I cannot join Professor Russell in taking as 'read' what we now are beginning to see is a controversial and partisan account of the Caroline church. I hope my Chapter VI may help to explain why.

PART I

'ALL THE SHAME ON US': WAR AND DISHONOUR

I
'THE FUNERAL OF OUR PARLIAMENT': THE ORIGINS OF PERSONAL RULE

Love and diplomacy

It is ironic that Charles I is remembered as the king who sought to rule without parliaments. For the reputation of the young monarch who succeeded to the throne in 1625 could not have been more different. Charles I, as Sir Benjamin Rudyerd described him, was 'a prince bred up in parliaments'.[1] It was in the parliament of 1621 that the hitherto faltering prince had made his public political début and received a political education. In 1621 the prince who had just reached adulthood attended regularly in the House of Lords and heard and participated in debates on privileges, patents and, of broader import, foreign policy.

1621, the year of the prince's majority and political maturity, was a year crucial to the fortunes of the royal family, and to the course of English politics and international affairs. In 1621 the Twelve Years Truce negotiated between Spain and the Netherlands expired, and renewed war was expected. Of more immediate dynastic concern, news had come that Charles's sister and brother-in-law, Elizabeth and Frederick, who had in 1619 taken the throne of Bohemia, had been defeated in battle and driven from their ancestral lands in the Rhinish Palatinate by the army of Maximilian of Bavaria, acting on behalf of the Habsburg emperor, and by the Spaniards. These events threw into question the whole course and orientation of James I's diplomacy. Since the 1604 peace with Spain, James had pursued a Spanish marriage for his son – first Henry, then Charles – and had adhered to that policy (not least as a balance to the Palatine match) despite the criticisms of those who in Privy Council, parliament and pulpit had urged him to espouse the cause of Protestantism in Europe. The plight of Frederick

1. C. Russell, *Parliaments and English Politics* (Oxford, 1979), p. 212.

and Elizabeth, however, could not be ignored and James convened the second session of the parliament of 1621 specifically to discuss it.[2]

For his own part, James appears to have remained committed to the policy of a match with Spain, not least because he (correctly) suspected that military engagement in Germany would present insurmountable difficulties and impose unsustainable burdens on England. But the policy of a Spanish match had now to embrace the issue of the Palatinate. Indeed it took on a greater urgency as a potential means of solving the Palatine crisis by diplomacy, by, that is, incorporating the restoration of Frederick by Spanish means into the negotiations for the marriage between the Infanta and Prince Charles.

It is hard to determine in what ways his experience of these debates and issues over the summer and autumn of 1621 was related to another first experience that Prince Charles, somewhat belatedly, underwent soon after: the experience, for the first time at the age of twenty-one, of falling in love. Certainly then for the first time, though by no means the last in his life, private and public matters, love and politics, became indistinguishably intertwined. Some time before 1623 Charles fell in love with the Spanish Infanta Maria daughter of Philip IV. He dreamt of her; he cherished her portrait; he yearned to woo her. As has so often been the case, the fleet foot of Cupid overtook the slower, more measured paces of diplomacy. While James I continued the slow and cautious process of negotiations with Spain (to the frustration of the zealous Protestants and self-styled 'patriots' of the realm),[3] Charles, revealing, as he was frequently to do, a complete contrast of style to his father, acted on impulse and resolved to take the initiative. The prince determined to go to Madrid – if not with his father's blessing then in the stealth of the night, incognito, on a romantic mission which might (as he saw it) satisfy the honour of the nation as well as requite the passion of its prince.[4]

These experiences of love and diplomacy were powerful influences on the prince's early adult years. But they were not the only influences nor the only recent changes in Charles's life. Another was his relationship with his father's favourite George Villiers, Marquis of Buckingham. At first it had undoubtedly been an unhappy relationship for the prince. Villiers, handsome, athletic and confident, eight years Charles's

2. Cf. *ibid.*, ch. 2, esp. pp. 121–44; *idem*, 'The foreign policy debate in the House of Commons in 1621', *Hist. Journ.*, 20 (1977), pp. 289–309; R. Zaller, *The Parliament of 1621* (Berkeley and London, 1971).
3. T. Cogswell, 'England and the Spanish match', in R. Cust and A. Hughes (eds) *Conflict in Early Stuart England: Studies in Religion and Politics, 1603–1642* (1989), pp. 107–33; T. Cogswell, *The Blessed Revolution: English Politics and the Coming of War 1621–1624* (Cambridge, 1989), esp. p. 85.
4. S.R. Gardiner, *History of England from the Accession of James I to the Outbreak of the Civil War 1603–1642* (10 vols, 1883–4), IV, pp. 334, 368, 387; V, pp. 1, 19. R. Lockyer, *Buckingham: The Life and Political Career of George Villiers First Duke of Buckingham 1592–1628* (1981), pp. 134–5.

senior, seemed all that the shy prince was not. As James's bedfellow as well as favourite, as counsellor, 'gossip' and '*son*' he took the place in the king's affections that was more naturally due to the prince.[5] Charles, however, outgrew his jealousy and came to admire and love Buckingham, who took on the role of the charismatic elder sibling Charles had lost after the death of his radiant brother Henry and the marriage of his beloved sister Elizabeth. With James often sickly, capricious and unpredictable, the prince's proffer of friendship was something that Villiers could not afford to ignore. As Charles matured into adulthood, the two became closer. In 1621, co-operating in the House of Lords, Buckingham and Charles began to be seen by contemporaries as a political partnership.[6] Along with the new experiences of love and diplomacy, Charles's entry on to the stage of public affairs was marked by a close personal and political friendship that was never to be repeated throughout his life.

All three experiences fused in Charles's journey with Buckingham to Madrid in 1623. Contemporaries spoke of the escapade as a 'romance' but, as that term itself implied in seventeenth-century usage, it was no mere private courtship.[7] Though Charles may at times have embarrassed the Spaniards by his passionate but highly undiplomatic behaviour (climbing over walls to see the Infanta, smuggling himself into her presence), his visit was soon treated by his unwitting hosts (and others) as a major diplomatic event.[8] The prince's passion was integral to the struggle for power – in the Netherlands, in Germany, and throughout the Habsburg empire. It was also to be interwoven with English domestic politics. For in Madrid Charles and Buckingham cemented their friendship into an inseparable bond, and so ensured that those enemies of Buckingham in England who plotted the downfall of the duke had also, perhaps unknowingly, earned the hostility of the prince.

The journey to Madrid, Charles's first personal and public venture, ended in personal rejection and public failure. Charles returned without a bride and England was left without a Spanish match, or a diplomatic solution to the plight of Frederick and Elizabeth of the Palatine. For all that the populace celebrated his return as a bachelor and escape from the popish whore with an orgy of bonfires and bell-

5. D.H. Wilson, *King James VI and I* (1956), p. 384. We might also note that both James and Villiers referred to the prince as 'Baby Charles'.
6. Lockyer, *Buckingham*, p. 103; K. Sharpe (ed.) *Faction and Parliament* (Oxford, 1978), pp. 212–17; Russell, *Parliaments and Politics*.
7. P. Hardwicke (ed.) *Miscellaneous State Papers* (2 vols, 1778), I, p. 399; and K. Sharpe, *Criticism and Compliment: The Politics of Literature in the England of Charles I* (Cambridge, 1987), p. 296.
8. J. Howell to Thomas Porter, 10 July 1623, in J. Jacobs (ed.) *Epistolae Hoelianae* (1890), p. 169; Gardiner, *History of England*, V, p. 52.

ringing, the failure to secure the Infanta's hand delivered a mortal blow to Charles's honour and, as he saw it, the honour of the nation.[9] Private and national honour demanded satisfaction and Charles, supported by the now Duke of Buckingham, returned determined to lead England into a war with Spain.

There were obstacles to that design: many of the Privy Councillors and King James I himself. Charles and the duke turned therefore to parliament. It was a natural course of action: parliaments were customarily called before important decisions concerning war and peace were concluded and parliaments were the traditional source of supply for war. Moreover, parliaments, as Charles had seen, had clamoured for action against the Habsburgs. The prince and Buckingham prepared carefully for the parliament of 1624: they used their patronage at the hustings; they presented detailed reports on Spanish duplicity; they lobbied for a suspension of the treaty of 1604 and a declaration of war. Moreover they employed parliament as a political instrument for putting pressure on councillors, courtiers and the king and for attacking their enemies, encouraging the impeachment of Lord Treasurer Cranfield who remained committed to peace. Charles and Buckingham became the darlings of the House of Commons, leading the crusade against the Habsburg Antichrist that some had advocated for years.[10] If in 1624 Charles staked the satisfaction of his own and the nation's honour on co-operation with parliament, that did not appear to him then a risky gamble. Basking in the adulation of patriots, pamphleteers and MPs, the prince's honour and parliament appeared, in 1624, to be natural partners.

It was, however, as James I acutely discerned, an illusory and unnatural alliance. Where the prince had gone to Madrid fired with love for the Infanta and had there been attracted by the elaborate ceremonies of the Spanish court and even fascinated by the ordered rituals of the Spanish church, for many members of parliament Spain exemplified absolutism in government and the popish whore in religion. Secondly, where Charles sought through war to redeem his honour, such MPs pursued a religious crusade. And where for Charles war involved a dynastic battle between the regiments of princes, probably a massive military expedition against the forces of Philip IV, for many, indeed most, MPs the model for a Protestant crusade came from the years of Queen Elizabeth and the legendary defeat of the Spanish Armada.[11] Though many Elizabethan campaigns had been

9. See D. Cressy, 'The Protestant calendar and the vocabulary of celebration in early modern England', *Journal of British Studies*, 29 (1990), pp. 31–52; and *idem*, *Bonfires and Bells: National Memory and the Protestant Calendar in Elizabethan and Stuart England* (1989), ch. 6.

10. Russell, *Parliaments and Politics*, ch. 3; and R.E. Ruigh, *The Parliament of 1624* (Cambridge, Mass., 1971).

11. Cogswell, *Blessed Revolution*, pp. 14, 73.

conducted on the continent, it was, as Professor Cogswell puts it, the memory of the sea-dogs that dominated.[12] Naval warfare had been successful and cheap. Many MPs dreamed again that privateers operating at their own expense might, by preying on Spanish treasure ships, sap the Spaniards of strength in Europe whilst they enriched the coffers of Englishmen. Such a war would not drain the counties of money or men. But such was not the war that would redeem the prince's honour. In the euphoria of 1624, such differences were not aired and may not have been comprehended. But behind the harmonious rhetoric of war lay not only 'improperly deciphered signals from both sides' but fundamentally discordant attitudes to strategy, war and the conduct of foreign affairs.[13]

There were, King James perceived, domestic dangers too in the prince's love affair with parliament. In inviting parliaments to discuss *arcana imperii*, the most intimate of royal concerns, the match and foreign policy, Charles and Buckingham had unwittingly established them as a principal Council of War. In using parliament to put pressure on Councillors and the king they had taught a lesson in confrontation which would not easily be forgotten; in employing the device of parliamentary impeachment as the instrument to destroy their critics, the prince and the duke had made a rod, James put it, for their own backs.[14] Most of all in using parliament to break the Spanish match, they were also making themselves dependent on the Commons' readiness to finance a war.

It was such reservations, among other considerations, that inclined James to adhere to a policy of peace and reject parliament's counsel and his son's pressure to go to war. In the happy summer of 1624, however, James's sensible doubts appeared to both Charles and the Commons as obstructive and pusillanimous caution.[15] After tense sessions of parliament in 1614 and 1621 the partnership of prince and parliaments in 1624 seemed to augur well for both their futures. In March 1625 when the prince bred up in parliament at last succeeded his father, he became a king who was expected, and who expected, to call them often.

On both parts those expectations were sooner frustrated (and James I's misgivings sooner proven well founded) than either could have anticipated. The failure of the Spanish match and Charles's yearning for a bride pointed to the need for a royal marriage that would not compromise the Stuarts' honour. The breach with Spain also implied the need for a major ally, especially when the Dutch proved less

12. *Ibid.*, p. 14.
13. *Ibid.*, p. 301.
14. E. Hyde, Earl of Clarendon, *The History of the Rebellion and Civil Wars in England*, ed. W.D. Macray (6 vols, Oxford, 1888), I, p. 28.
15. Cogswell, *Blessed Revolution*, pp. 118–34.

compliant than expected. For both reasons, in May 1625 Charles was betrothed to the fifteen-year-old Princess Henrietta Maria, of France. The marriage treaty was to expose many of the misunderstandings behind the partnership between prince and parliament. In order to secure the marriage Charles, though he had at first hoped to avoid doing so, signed articles promising not only the free exercise of her religion for his wife, but some toleration for Catholics in England. To all members of parliament this would be anathema; in the godly it would, dangerously, plant seeds of mistrust. Moreover, Charles entered into an alliance with France at the very time that Louis XIII and his chief minister Cardinal Richelieu were proceeding to eradicate the privileges and attack the autonomous position of their own recusant subjects, the Protestant Huguenots. The differences between Charles's personal foreign policy and that advocated by the Commons and the inconsistencies of the royal marriage with the partnership of parliament would soon become apparent.

When Charles called his first parliament, however, in 1625, there was a more immediate problem to contend with: the failure of the first military ventures, the military expedition to the Palatinate of the mercenary Count Mansfeldt and the abortive assault on the Spanish treasure fleet at Cadiz. These failures and the post-mortem debates about them initiated what was to become the recurrent dialogue of the next few years. On the one side a conviction by the House of Commons that the military expeditions were ill supplied as a consequence of corrupt government and ill led by the incompetent command of Buckingham. On the other, the king's frustration that supplies necessary for the conduct of war were either not forthcoming, or inadequate, or provided too late to be of effect. To members of the House of Commons military failures over the next three years progressively proved the incompetence of royal counsels and the need to remove the king's favourite. To Charles the failure of supply added to the loss of honour experienced in Spain a personal guilt at the nation's betrayal of his trusted friend the duke and the public shame of defeat. Much of this controversy stemmed from different interpretations of what had been 'agreed' in 1624.[16] Thereafter, as events revealed the problems of the royal marriage, as the persecution of the Huguenots and quarrels about the marriage treaty plunged England into a disastrous war with France as well as Spain, as military failures were repeated, as Buckingham increasingly became the Commons' scapegoat for those defeats, finally as the sheer burdens of war on local society mounted, parliamentary sessions became tense and

16. *Ibid.*, p. 122. To be fair to him, Charles tried to clarify. When the Commons offered to assist the war in a parliamentary way, he enquired 'what parliamentary way they mean' (*ibid.*, p. 189).

strained.[17] During the war years 1625 to 1629 the prince bred up in parliaments fell out of love with them, as in turn the Commons' expectations of the new king turned sour. To look forward to 1629, however, is to run ahead of ourselves. The inclination to rule without parliaments did not begin when Charles succeeded his father.[18] If we are to understand the shift to non-parliamentary government in 1629, we must examine the king's experience of the war years which both explain the origins of Charles's personal rule and determined so many of its courses.

The sinews of war: finance

The principal problem of the war years was financial. Behind that simple generalization, however, lay a whole series of complex problems that were to reveal not only the difficulties in raising adequate sums for war supplies when they were needed, but more fundamental weaknesses in both central and local government the revelations of which were to have a profound effect on Charles I. The most immediate problem arose from the inadequacy of parliamentary supplies. Though the grant of subsidies and fifteenths in 1624 was 'the greatest aid which was ever granted in parliament to be levied in so short a time',[19] it fell, even by James I's underestimated calculations, far short of the costs of Mansfeldt's expedition, let alone the subsidies to Christian of Denmark. 'Generous though the 1624 parliament was the fact remains that it was not generous enough to underwrite the full expense of warfare.'[20] The unhappy circumstances of Charles's first two parliaments as king, cut short to stifle attacks on his favourite, meant that only two more subsidies were voted before 1628. Inadequate though the number of subsidies was, the situation was worsened by the decline in their real value. The problem was not new: 'The subsidies had ceased to approximate to a true valuation of a man's lands and goods as far back as the accession of Edward VI, and it was openly said in the 1590s that no one was assessed at above a tenth of his true wealth and some at a thirtieth or less.'[21] Thereafter the decline accelerated. Chichester paid over a third less for the subsidy

17. The central thesis of Professor Russell's *Parliaments and Politics* is that the burdens of war underlay the growing troubles between Charles and his parliaments.
18. Though Richard Cust would trace that inclination back to 1626 at the latest ('Charles I's declarations', paper delivered at the Institute of Historical Research, Oct. 1987), I do not find his arguments persuasive; cf. below, pp. 36–7, 705.
19. Ruigh, *Parliament of 1624*, p. 387.
20. Cogswell, *Blessed Revolution*, p. 311.
21. W.G. Hoskins (ed.) *Exeter in the Seventeenth Century: Tax and Rate Assessments 1602–1699* (Devon and Cornwall Record Soc., new series, Vol. II, 1957), pp. xiii–xiv.

in 1624 than it had in 1610.[22] Where even in Elizabeth's reign a subsidy was worth over £70,000, by the 1620s it was yielding only £50,000 – a decline even more dramatic in real terms across these last decades of a century of inflation unparalleled in English history.[23] The Privy Council was certainly aware of the problem. In February 1626 the Council informed the subsidy commissioners of Leicestershire that they had paid only £775 16s.6d. in 1621 compared to £1,276 9s.9d. in 1559![24] The fall of course had resulted from scandalous under-assessment, for which the subsidy commissioners were most to blame. As those of Leicestershire were reminded, 'if you who be great possessors would begin to heighten yourselves in some good proportion' an example of responsibility might be set to others.[25] After the grant of five subsidies in 1628 the Council renewed its efforts to improve their yield to the Exchequer.[26] Detailed instructions were issued to the subsidy commissioners to ensure that the generous grant of the Commons should not 'by ill handling and remissness of those who are trusted with assessing and levying of the same become rather greater in name than in truth and more in sound than in substance which hath appeared in former subsidies of later years (being found far less in proportion than in the times of the late Queen Elizabeth of blessed memory).'[27] The commissioners were ordered to set an example to others by fair assessment of themselves and to assess JPs at no less than £20. Strict enquiries were to be made into the wealth and abilities of freeholders and sheriffs' books were to be examined to ensure that none was omitted; the subsidy roll for 5 Elizabeth was sent to assist the commissioners.[28] But the Council's attempts came to little. If the Venetian ambassador's mention of an anticipated yield of £400,000 was a reliable guide to expectations, they were to be greatly frustrated.[29] The five subsidies brought in little over £275,000, and the larger

22. A.J. Fletcher, *A County Community in Peace and War: Sussex 1600–1660* (1976), p. 202.
23. C. Russell, 'Parliamentary history in perspective, 1604–1629', *History*, 61 (1976), p. 11; F.C. Dietz, *English Public Finance 1558–1641* (2 vols, 1964), II, pp. 391–3. In 1636, Nicholas estimated that a subsidy might be worth £54,000 (PRO, SP 16/325/16).
24. Huntington Library, Hastings MS 4221.
25. *Ibid.*
26. The rebuke evidently had little effect. In 1628, the Privy Council again blamed the Leicestershire subsidy commissioners for their neglect of the service: 'in lessening the rates they were formerly assessed at . . . thereby the subsidies intended . . . to the general service of the kingdom and other public occasions are very much fallen' (Hastings MS 4247).
27. Hampshire Record Office, Herriard MS 021: Privy Council to commissioners for subsidy, 30 June 1628. The instructions echo those of 1589.
28. The rot had set in already by then. Lord North told Lord Burleigh in 1589 that every man assessed 'is known to be worth at least ten times as much as he is set at and six times more in land'. I owe this reference to J. Taylor, 'Population, disease and family structure in early modern Hampshire' (Southampton University PhD thesis, 1980), p. 15.
29. *Calendar of State Papers Venetian* [*Cal. Stat. Pap. Venet.*], *1628–9*, p. 45. The government, more accurately but still over-optimistically, anticipated a yield of £300,000. *Calendar of State Papers Domestic* [*Cal. Stat. Pap. Dom.*], *1627–8*, p. 437.

problems remained. In 1640 one Staffordshire hundred was paying less than in 1327.[30]

It is hard to determine how far these problems for the government were appreciated in the country. The size of the black economy in our own age enables us to understand those who under-assessed themselves without any sense that they were thereby undermining the government of the country. Complaints in parliament about the burden of subsidies on the poor indicate a concern about the inequity of assessments.[31] Evidently there were some who were scandalized by the abuses in local assessment and collection and determined to reform them. On 5 February 1626 Thomas Milward of Hampshire wrote to Sir Thomas Jervoise informing him that he had earlier become a subsidy commissioner – not out of ambition but from anger at the 'ignorance, malice and injustice' of those who abused the office. Milward catalogued the corrupt practices whereby the least able to pay were 'most pinched and the strongest horses carried the lightest load', and exposed 'some others their miscarriages thwarting his Majesty's and the parliament's express instructions and absolute directions'. Milward had tried to effect reforms, but in consequence only found himself left out of the commission. His successors meanwhile continued their lax and corrupt practices, working in a small cabal, even omitting completely from the books substantial gentlemen worth as much as £5,000. Milward told the commissioners that there was no good reason why the subsidy should fall short of Elizabethan receipts; rather, he believed, the books could be raised by a quarter 'and no man just cause to complain and the weakest less cause to grudge'.[32] The evidence we have bears him out, but Greaves, one of the commissioners, 'made me answer I had not need to make such motions, the country would curse me for it' being 'high enough already charged'. Doubtless Greaves was more popular than Milward with his neighbours. The figures themselves suggest that his attitude was far more typical than Milward's. Subsidy commissioners continued to under-assess themselves and their friends and to over-assess those less able to pay.[33] Subsidies in no way reflected the capacities or wealth of the counties. As their yield dropped, their value to the crown in relation to other sources of revenue declined.[34] When it later turned to those other

30. 'S.H.A.B.', 'A subsidy roll of 1640' (Staffordshire Record Soc., 3rd series, 1941), p. 152.
31. Hastings MS 4250: Privy Council to subsidy commissioners of Leicestershire, 31 March 1629.
32. Thomas Milward to Sir Thomas Jervoise, 5 Feb. 1626, Herriard MS F. 10.
33. Milward was removed from the subsidy commission. Cf. Fletcher, *County Community*, appendix 5 and pp. 202–5. See also M.J. Braddick, 'Parliamentary lay taxation, circa 1590–1670: local problems of enforcement and collection with special reference to Norfolk' (University of Cambridge PhD thesis, 1987), pp. 17, 33–4, 40; and chs 1–3 on the failure of government attempts to improve the yield of subsidies.
34. Russell, 'Parliamentary history', p. 16.

means of raising money the Council would determine upon other means of assessment.

As a source of war finance subsidies presented problems other than their disappointingly low yield. The sums granted came in slowly, often years after their parliamentary grant and too late to finance the campaigns for which they were given and required. In small part this problem lay in the procedure for granting them: the subsidy bill required three readings and did not pass until the end of the session even when urgent circumstances had prompted an immediate vote of supply weeks (or months) earlier. But the delay in passing the bill was only the beginning of the problem. The local machinery for assessing and collecting moved tardily and the actual payment by individuals dragged on longer still. The subsidies granted in 1628 were, according to the Venetian ambassador, supposed to come in especially quickly and the Privy Council certainly stressed the urgency of need.[35] On 31 March 1629, however, the Council felt the need to renew the sense of urgency by reminding the commissioners of Leicestershire that 'half the last subsidy . . . payable the tenth of December last' was 'not yet received'. Immediate action was required 'so that the time for reasonable preparation for his Majesty's great occasions may not be spent before the means to set them forward may be had'.[36] When campaigning seasons were short and money, supplies, ships and troops had to be co-ordinated, delays could be fatal to any enterprise – especially when an impoverished government found it hard to raise credit. Yet despite the urgent circumstances of war, the pace of collection and payment remained slow, and those who being most aware of the urgency might have most been expected to pay promptly, scarcely set a good example. By November 1628 the Earl of Huntingdon had paid nothing of the £80 assessed on him in July for subsidies granted in June.[37] In 1636, the Earl of Suffolk still owed subsidies for which he had been assessed in the 1620s.[38] Ironically the war itself, far from quickening payment, may actually have delayed it, as the business and local costs of raising, billeting and transporting soldiers detracted from the attention that local officers could give to subsidy collection and blunted the willingness of those assessed to pay. In July 1628 Sir Edward Alford of Sussex told Sir John Coke that the sums spent on billeting troops and coat and conduct money had adversely affected the payment of subsidies.[39] When the crown lawyers in the ship

35. *Cal. Stat. Pap. Venet., 1628–9*, p. 156.
36. Hastings MS 4250.
37. Hastings MSS 13789, 13791.
38. Melbourne Hall, Coke MS, 54: petition of the Earl of Suffolk, 4 July 1636; calendared in *HMC Cowper*, II, pp. 123–4.
39. Coke MS 35: Edward Alford to Coke. The important point is not mentioned in the calendar of this letter (*HMC Cowper*, I, p. 359).

money case of 1638 played down the utility of subsidies as war finance on account of the long delays in receiving the money, they were not merely indulging in special pleading; they accurately described the fiscal crisis of the late 1620s.[40] Experience bore out the French ambassador's sense that subsidies were not a major factor in the effectiveness of the English war effort.[41] The lesson was well learned at home.

The failure, that is the poor yield and slow receipt, of subsidies drove a government in the midst of war to other means of raising money. Measures for both the short- and long-term enhancement of royal revenues were examined in the late 1620s, some of which were to lay the foundations for the fiscal programmes of the 1630s. In January 1628, for example, Sir John Borough, Keeper of the Tower records, presented to the Master of the Rolls a report based on extracts from Chancery records in the Tower on means by which kings of England had used to raise money. Borough's list ranged over the sale of wardships, better management of demesne lands, sale of fish taken from the king's ponds, the exploitation of vacant bishoprics, fines for encroachment on royal forests and fines on those of £40 land who failed to present themselves at the coronation to be knighted.[42] While some of these precedent courses set an agenda for long-term improvements and for the 1630s, they offered little solution to the pressing problems of war finance. As well as desperate expedients being taken – the pawning of the royal jewels and the extensive sale of crown lands – various emergency measures were contemplated: the raising of rates on imports, an excise, and a tax on inns among them.[43] Most significantly the Council proceeded with two experiments which were to transform the politics of the next decade: ship money and the forced loan.

In the summer of 1626 the Council had issued a demand for ship money from the coastal towns of England. The demand had sound precedent: the Elizabethan fleet that had taken Cadiz had been financed by such a levy.[44] With war with Spain exposing merchant shipping to privateering and tense relations with France, the coastal towns may not have been blind to the need for naval protection and defence. Despite some murmurings and complaints about inability to meet assessments the money was paid. But it was woefully inadequate to finance a major

40. J. Rushworth, *Historical Collections* (7 vols, 1659–1701), II (1680), pp. 571ff. Argument of Attorney Bankes; below, pp. 722–3.
41. PRO, French transcripts, 31/3/66, f.241; cf. *Cal. Stat. Pap. Venet., 1628–9*, pp. 45, 64, 70 for evidence that the Dutch, Venetians and others shared this view.
42. British Library [BL] Add. MS 34234, f.169 (extracts taken from the Tower Records by Borough for the Master of the Rolls).
43. *Cal. Stat. Pap. Dom., 1625–49*, p. 240; *1627–8*, pp. 537, 540–4; Dietz, *English Public Finance*, II, p. 234.
44. Gardiner, *History of England*, VI, p. 132.

fleet. In October 1627 it was reported that 'Such a rotten, miserable fleet set out to sea no men ever saw. Our enemies seeing it may scoff at our nation.'[45] By the end of the year arrears due to the navy exceeded a quarter of a million pounds and, it was estimated, £110,000 was needed to fit out fifty sails for the next spring.[46] Charles desperately needed to finance the fleet to be commanded by the Earl of Denbigh for the relief of La Rochelle. Over the winter of early 1628 therefore the decision was taken to extend ship money from the ports to the realm. On 11 February royal letters were directed to the JPs, deputy lieutenants and sheriffs of the counties pointing to the need to succour Denmark in the Sound, to threats posed by France and Spain, the inadvisability of waiting on parliament and the need to raise a fleet swiftly – a burden too heavy to be borne by the port towns alone.[47] The amounts to be levied on each county towards a total of £173,411 were prepared.[48] Local officers were urged in assessing their counties for such sums to rate as they saw fit 'yet in such sort as you will not make the uneven rate of subsidy your only rule of proportion, but proceed according to the true worth of men's lands and estates within the county that so the poor may be eased and yet the business done'.[49] It is likely that there were doubts about the efficacy of such a demand. Despite the undoubted emergency, only the previous year the deputy lieutenants of Essex had questioned the legality of a warrant requiring them as a coastal county to assist their port towns with the payment of ship money and had referred the request to the Grand Jury, which could find no precedent for the demand.[50] The responses from the other counties and towns were all but universally negative. Lincolnshire refused to pay the 'unusual and unexpected charge'; Somerset asked to be excused, fearing 'it will be a precedent of a charge which neither they nor their predecessors did ever bear'.[51] Coastal towns like Totnes and Norwich made excuses; the JPs of Devon warned that an attempt to levy ship money would prejudice the payment of the loan.[52] It may have been such considerations that led Charles to withdraw the letters for a national levy of ship money within days of issuing them. On 16 February, laying aside the demand, the king announced his decision

45. *Cal. Stat. Pap. Dom., 1627–8*, p. 409.
46. *Ibid.*, pp. 477, 555; Gardiner, *History of England*, VI, p. 220.
47. Gardiner, *History of England*, VI, pp. 226–7; R.J.W. Swales, 'The ship money levy of 1628', *Bull. Inst. Hist. Res.*, 50 (1977), pp. 174–6.
48. *Cal. Stat. Pap. Dom., 1627–8*, p. 555; Swales, 'Ship money', p. 168.
49. Bodleian, Firth MS C.4, pp. 451–2; Swales, 'Ship money', p. 175.
50. Firth MS C.4, pp. 321–4: deputy lieutenants of Essex to Privy Council, 6 April 1627; *Cal. Stat. Pap. Dom., 1627–8*, p. 128.
51. *Cal. Stat. Pap. Dom., 1627–8*, p. 138.
52. *Ibid.*, pp. 143, 156. Both Totnes and Norwich threatened that ship money would impede the loan.

'wholly to rely on the love of our people in parliament'.[53] With a session of parliament imminent, the ship money writ of 1628 was a scheme that was never put into action. Years later, in different circumstances, it was to loom large in the history of personal rule.

The success story of 1620s war finance was, for all its political cost, the forced loan. The dissolution of the 1626 parliament in June without a grant of subsidies necessitated some extraordinary source of revenue for the war. When in July the City refused a loan, the king and Council resolved on a demand, or request, for a free gift or benevolence like those raised by James I in 1614 and 1622.[54] Letters were sent out to JPs commanding them to exhort the counties, in the emergency prevailing, to supply the king voluntarily with the four subsidies which the Commons, before its precipitate dissolution, had judged necessary. The letters combined the rhetoric of affection with a threat that urgent need required no justification: 'And although no ordinary rules can prescribe law to necessity and the common defence and safety and even the subsistence of the whole might justly warrant if out of our royal prerogative and power we should take any way more extraordinary . . . yet we desiring nothing more than the love of our people . . .'.[55] The combination proved ineffective. Within weeks the Council was forced to soften its tone and to stress the voluntary nature of the gift requested. Still the benevolence failed: as most counties protested their inability or simply refused, only four responded positively and less than a thousand pounds was collected.[56]

The defeat of Christian of Denmark in August at Lutter – in large part attributable to the failure of promised English subsidies – exacerbated the international dangers and domestic fiscal crisis. From both, in September, the scheme for a forced loan emerged. The loan, the king's proclamation of 7 October explained, was a measure for the 'common defence', 'enforced upon us by that necessity to which no ordinary course can give the law' when time did not permit the summoning of a parliament. It was not to be a regular course, nor 'to be drawn into any example, nor made a precedent for after times'. The loan was an emergency expedient until the next grant of subsidies, and

53. Firth MS C.4, p. 454. The king explained the decision to rescind the levy in a proclamation announcing the assembly of a parliament issued the same day. J.F. Larkin (ed.) *Stuart Royal Proclamations II: Royal Proclamations of King Charles I, 1625–1646* (Oxford, 1983), no. 86, pp. 187–8.
54. Gardiner, *History of England*, VI, p. 124; R. Cust, *The Forced Loan and English Politics 1626–28* (Oxford, 1987), pp. 32–9, 153–8.
55. Hastings MS 1340: Charles I to JPs of all counties, 7 July 1626; *Acts of Privy Council June-Dec. 1626*, p. 167.
56. Gardiner, *History of England*, VI, p. 131; Cust, *Forced Loan*, pp. 33, 37–9, 91–9; Hastings MS 4226: Privy Council to JPs of Leicestershire, 26 July 1626.

assessments were based on the subsidy rolls.[57] The appeal to necessity in the state of emergency and the king's moderate language did not fall upon deaf ears. Just over a month after the commission for levying the loan (dated 20 October), on 26 December, Edward Reade informed Secretary Conway that on the Isle of Wight 'the loan money is gathering and the payments are willingly made'.[58] Other areas less immediately vulnerable to foreign invasion or attack also responded favourably and promptly. The Earl of Suffolk at Blandford in Dorset 'found the commissioners and people very inclined to lend'.[59] Abingdon started well, and in Oxford both the university and city 'accommodate themselves to the loan with much alacrity'.[60] In general, the speed of payment was impressive. By July 1627, £240,000 in loan money had been paid, more than the yield of four subsidies which had been expected from the 1626 parliament and on which the Council's calculations had been based.[61] For all that it gave rise to some fear of new ways of government, both in the amount raised and the promptness of payment the loan was a success that was to be important in the origins and shaping of the personal rule.

Successful though it was, the loan was by no means free of problems. Based on the subsidy rolls, the assessments for the loan obviously suffered from the same deficiencies as the subsidy – under-assessment or exclusion of many wealthy men, a disproportionate burden on those of modest means, an outmoded record of the economic and social changes that altered the conditions of individuals and owners. Even the diligent Hampshire commissioners signed several certificates of inability to pay on account of plague, decayed estates, large families and simple poverty, as well as returning reports of those on the subsidy roll who had since departed the county or died.[62] As with the subsidy, one weak link in the collection of the loan was the commissioners themselves. In the case of Essex the Privy Council specifically blamed the commissioners for the loan, rather than those assessed, for the county's shortcomings: 'those that are to lend . . . have showed good affections in paying and promising, but there hath been much slackness in the calling for and collection of the monies'.[63] Not least, some commissioners themselves had failed to pay.[64] The patterns of response to duty were as diverse as the personalities involved. In Hampshire, while Sir Thomas Jervoise worked hard, gathering

57. Larkin, *Stuart Royal Proclamations*, II, no. 55, pp. 110–12; Gardiner, *History of England*, VI, p. 144; Cust, *Forced Loan*, pp. 99–102.
58. Cust, *Forced Loan*, p. 47; *Cal. Stat. Pap. Dom., 1625–49*, p. 176.
59. *Cal. Stat. Pap. Dom., 1627–8*, p. 16.
60. *Ibid.*, p. 25.
61. *Ibid.*, p. 258; Cust, *Forced Loan*, p. 47.
62. Herriard MSS, Box 021: 'Certificates of inability to pay'.
63. Firth MS C.4, pp. 371–2.
64. *Ibid.*, p. 372.

information, receiving payments, keeping accounts and chivvying his colleagues, John Savage, one of the collectors for Kingsclere hundred, evidently did not pay his own assessment.[65] Had it not been for the careful oversight of the loan collection by the Council, it is likely that such inertia or footdragging would have frustrated its success. Conciliar pressure, most particularly the Privy Councillors' individual visits to their counties to urge subscription and payment, obviously counted for much.[66]

The loan not only met with the usual administrative inefficiencies and difficulties of local government and the laxity of local officials, it also encountered resistance and outright opposition to what were perceived to be uncustomary and improper courses. As we shall have cause to remark later in this study, dissatisfaction could be manifest in several ways and degrees. Sometimes disapproval of the loan was covert: several assessed simply refused to appear; or claimed to have paid in other divisions or counties; or shifted from one place to another to avoid payment.[67] Others, like those in Sherfield Loden in Hampshire, promised to pay all their assessments in the second instalment and offered nothing for the first – presumably in the hope that the loan would be recalled or superseded by the summoning of another parliament.[68] It is hard in such cases of evasion to determine how far principles and how far a simple reluctance to pay the money was operating.[69] The many instances of those who paid but refused to subscribe, like Sir Henry Wallop, suggest some scruples about endorsing the project with what Holles called a 'badge of lending'.[70] Similar reservations (as well as a healthy sense of precaution) may have lain behind Nottinghamshire's recording in its sessions roll the king's promise that the loan was not to set a precedent.[71] Others were more direct in their refusal or denunciation. One defaulter warned to appear at Basingstoke sessions replied that he was 'not able to pay this loan according as it is expressed in the warrant'.[72] In Dorset, Sir John Strangeways made a 'handsome refusal'.[73] Nottinghamshire, though

65. Herriard MSS, Box 021.
66. Hastings MS 10543: 'all the Council are gone but my Lord Duke who is to go into Buckinghamshire'; D. Hirst, 'The Privy Council and problems of enforcement in the 1620s', *Journ. Brit. Stud.*, 18 (1976), pp. 46–66; Cust, *Forced Loan*, ch. 2, esp. pp. 112–14.
67. Herriard MSS, Box 12, Box 021; Firth MS C.4, p. 372; Hastings MS 4235.
68. Herriard MSS, Box 021 (Jan. 1627).
69. Cust in my view too readily assumes that non-payment was evidence of principled opposition (*Forced Loan*, chs 3, 5).
70. Herriard MSS, Box 021; Bodleian, Rawlinson MS D.666, f.42; P.R. Seddon (ed.) *Letters of John Holles 1585–1637*, Vol. I (Thoroton Soc., 31, Nottingham, 1975), p. lxii.
71. A.J. Fletcher, *Reform in the Provinces: The Government of Stuart England* (1986), p. 366.
72. Herriard MSS, Box 12 (quarter sessions records, loan warrants to constables).
73. PRO, C.115/N3/8541 (Chancery Masters exhibits, Duchess of Norfolk deeds): Sir Henry Herbert to Viscount Scudamore, 2 Feb. 1627.

it paid, expressed concern at the manner of the levy as not being 'concluded in parliament'.[74] Individuals with strong ideological commitments clearly influenced their countrymen of less sophisticated or more mercenary natures. In Suffolk, the attorney Valentine Coppin's refusal to lend or authorize any others to subscribe carried weight with 'that common sort' who were 'ready to be led by so lewd an example'.[75] In Doncaster, Sir John Jackson's tenants could not have treated lightly his threat to hang any of them who paid.[76] In Worcestershire, Edward Hall of Hallow's 'openly refusing to lend or be bound' stymied the 'good success' of the first few days as 'those called after him so generally refuse that not three of a hundred would lend'.[77] Widespread refusals in some hundreds of Essex have been attributed to the example or lead of godly magistrates such as Sir Francis Barrington.[78] In Lincolnshire, an anonymous pamphlet, attributed by Dr Cust to Theophilus Clinton, Earl of Lincoln, circulated in manuscript, mobilized a protest and disrupted the collection of the loan.[79] Later a servant of the Earl was presented in Star Chamber for distributing letters to the freeholders exhorting them to have regard to their ancient privileges and warning them that none would have a security in his goods if the king could claim to take them at will.[80] The decision not to confine the ranks of the county commissioners to the 'well apportioned', indeed the probably deliberate inclusion of likely opponents meant that, dangerously, resistance to the loan emerged from the very officers responsible for its collection.[81] Some nominated refused to serve: like Barrington in Essex, or, in Leicestershire, Sir Roger Smith who, as he informed the Earl of Huntingdon, found himself 'unfitted for the place . . . (my conscience being stricter than other men's) and altogether unable to do what I would or should'.[82] Others of more malleable consciences or weaker spirits took office only in name, absenting themselves from sittings, neglecting to forward the name of recalcitrants to the Board, or hiding behind the protest that 'it exceedeth the ability of persuasion or other power which we have to prevail'.[83]

In the early months of 1627 the Council acted swiftly against recalcitrants, summoning refusers to the Board, confining them

74. *Cal. Stat. Pap. Dom., 1627–8*, p. 65.
75. *Ibid.*, p. 29: commissioners for loan to Council, 23 Jan. 1627.
76. *Ibid.*, p. 32: William Viscount Ayr to Charles I, 27 Jan. 1627.
77. *Ibid.*, p. 118: commissioners for loan to Council, March 1627.
78. *Ibid.*, p. 91; *Cal. Stat. Pap. Dom., 1625–49*, p. 151; Cust, *Forced Loan*, p. 277.
79. Cust, *Forced Loan*, pp. 170–4.
80. BL, Lansdowne MS 620, f.38.
81. Cust, *Forced Loan*, p. 53.
82. Hastings MSS 4325, 10978: Sir Roger Smith to Huntingdon, 15 Feb. 1627.
83. Hastings MS 4235; Firth MS C.4, p. 373.

without trial, sending the Earl of Lincoln to the Tower.[84] Later, especially after the rupture with France, however, the Council appears to have shown more concern with getting the loan money in than with proceeding against those of tender consciences – a course which was anyway proving of limited effect and great practical and political difficulty.[85] Commissioners were instructed to take the money from, and otherwise ignore, those who offered payment but had scruples about subscribing;[86] several who refused to subscribe, like Sir Henry Wallop of Basingstoke (whose refusal much retarded the service), remained unmolested in office as commissioner and JP.[87] During the summer of 1627 some refusers detained in London were sent home to a form of house arrest – with the famous exception of the five knights who, refusing to leave London, appealed to King's Bench for a habeas corpus.[88] By Christmas, all committed for refusing were released, only those who had actually stirred resistance being pursued to trial.[89] The foreign situation, a mounting sense of the need for delicate rather than confrontational dealings, perhaps most of all the inflow of money, steered the Council away from harshness or the opening of fundamental issues.

But the loan and the reactions to the loan undoubtedly raised problematic issues and constitutional questions which could not be ignored and which caused Councillors as well as recalcitrants evident concern. Amid all the debates, pamphlets and sermons,[90] perhaps the most revealing insight into those broader issues is to be found in the manuscript 'Relation of the occurrences that passed between the Lords of the Privy Council and [William] Coryton Knight concerning the affair of the loan'.[91] Coryton was examined on his refusal to pay when summoned by the commissioners of Cornwall. Unlike many who had avoided such a question Coryton was frank: the loan he had 'conceived to be the greatest business that ever moved in the commonwealth'.[92] Doubtful of the right course of action, he informed his examiners, he had followed his practice of consulting God and the statutes. As a

84. PRO, C.115/N3/8541: Herbert to Scudamore, 2 Feb. 1627; *Cal. Stat. Pap. Dom., 1627–8*, p. 81; Cust, *Forced Loan*, p. 60.
85. T.D. Whitaker (ed.) *The Life and Correspondence of Sir George Radcliffe* (1810), pp. 137–44; Cust, *Forced Loan*, p. 58ff.
86. *Acts of the Privy Council, June–Dec. 1626*, p. 388: letters to commissioners for loan, 29 Nov. 1626.
87. Herriard MSS, Box 021 ('The names of those who promised to lend and did not subscribe at Winchester . . .', 7 Dec. 1626); Cust, *Forced Loan*, p. 241.
88. Cust, *Forced Loan*, pp. 59–61.
89. Firth MS C.4, p. 383.
90. See Gardiner, *History of England*, VI, pp. 205–13; Cust, *Forced Loan*, ch. 3.
91. I first came across this MS in the Huntington Library MSS, HM 45148, ff.21–30v. Other copies are in BL, Harleian MS 39, ff.451–7; and Harleian MS 737, ff.159–65.
92. Huntington Library, HM 45148, f.22v.

consequence he found himself unable in conscience to pay. For all his desire to serve the king, he could not disobey what he understood to be the law governing this case: the statutes of 25 Edward I Caps 5, 6 and 33 Edward I Cap 6 which had decreed that no aids, taxes or tallages should be levied without consent.[93] The Council heard him and then asked how he thought the king's wants should be provided. To this Coryton had no specific answer. The king, he acknowledged, might from particular subjects by Privy Seal raise loans that were voluntary – as the forced loan was not. More generally, and unhelpfully, 'I said I was of the mind some were of in the parliament, that the king could never want'.[94] The Lords protested 'that whilst the parliament was sitting the kingdom might have been ruined' if all had been of that mind. Coryton continued to speak freely: he reasserted the illegality of the loan. The Council detained him no further, but in his own words, 'gave me leave to depart with fair respect'.[95] The interview must have left the Council with much to think about. Some, such as the Earls of Pembroke and Manchester, Lord Coventry and Secretary Coke, had expressed their discomfort at the highly unusual proceedings of a forced loan that was justified only by necessity; for them there was no answer to Coryton's stand on custom and law ('good laws as anywhere in the kingdom and of force, not made for that time only . . . but for ever').[96] On the other hand, to their questions about supply Coryton had been able to offer no practical solution, whereas the forced loan had shown that substantial sums could be raised outside of parliament. In the end, Coryton's interview encapsulated the dilemma: parliamentary subsidies were the only legitimate, regular course for war finance yet parliamentary subsidies had proved woefully inadequate as a means of financing the war. At some point the full comprehension of that dilemma was bound to lead to radical courses.[97]

For all its success, the forced loan by no means resolved the government's financial problems. Though over £240,000 was paid in loan money by the end of 1627, the cost of the soldiers and seamen raised for the defeated Rhé expedition alone amounted to £200,000 and an estimated £600,000 was required to prepare another fleet.[98] In part, too, what had facilitated the success of the loan had also circumscribed

93. *Ibid.*, f.23.
94. *Ibid.*, ff.24–27v.
95. *Ibid.*, f.30v.
96. *Ibid.*, f.26v; Cust, *Forced Loan*, pp. 51–4.
97. Dr Cust wishes to argue that Charles had already resolved on these courses in 1626. Episodes like Coryton's examination seem to me to support the view (that best fits the evidence of other royal pronouncements) that the king was still grappling with a problem and trying to find a solution.
98. Gardiner, *History of England*, VI, pp. 219–20; Dietz, *English Public Finance*, II, pp. 243–7; Cust, *Forced Loan*, pp. 75–6.

its value. Charles's promise that it was an extraordinary measure that would not be repeated effectively ruled out a second levy – despite some rumours to the contrary.[99] Moreover by a concession to the localities, necessary to secure their co-operation, about one-third of the loan paid never reached the Exchequer but was employed to defray the local costs of billeting and transporting troops.[100] For the counties and towns of England, faced with defence and war costs which they had not experienced in living memory, expected such expenses to be met by the central government. Whilst the king promised, and genuinely intended, to repay billet money, the Council had not expected to have to meet this from scarce immediate resources in the midst of war: local expenditure was a major source of central government credit.[101] Pressure to deduct such expenses from the loan came from local collectors and magistrates who were, of course, themselves often responsible for the other local charges, and who at times had personally to finance them. Sir Peter Temple of Stowe in Buckinghamshire complained to the Earl of Marlborough that because he had been unable in time to raise coat and conduct money in the county, a London draper Mr Reddell who had supplied the troops was suing him personally for his unpaid bill. Temple asked for the bill to be settled out of the loan money;[102] the Council gave order to that effect.[103] Similarly the Essex deputy lieutenants, who had themselves to pay the pressed men, requested their expenses and coat and conduct money be met from the loan.[104] At Portsmouth, reimbursement was sought by the commissioners, who took up £100 on their own bonds when Sir Piers Crosby's regiment arrived 'for preventing the spoil of the country in case the soldiers should be without means'.[105] The problems mounted: whole hundreds in Essex refused to contribute to the billet; and even protested at financing a county magazine of gunpowder.[106] Conciliar reminders, warnings and deputations overcame some difficulties.[107] But coercion had to be joined with concession to

99. T. Birch (ed.) *The Court and Times of Charles I* (2 vols, 1848), I, pp. 297, 303.
100. *Cal. Stat. Pap. Dom., 1627–8*, p. 437 (accounts of 16 Nov. 1627).
101. For examples, see *Acts of the Privy Council, June–Dec. 1626*, pp. 186, 216–17, 223, 309, 357. Similarly with the loan money, Charles required full accounts, 'that the country may have reallowance of what hath been paid . . . as we have promised . . .' (PRO, Signet Office (Irish Letter Books), S0/1/1, ff.212–212v).
102. Huntington Library, Temple of Stowe MSS, Box 6, STT 2270.
103. Temple of Stowe MS STT 577. The Council's agreement was reported in June: see Temple of Stowe MS STT 585: Sir Thomas Denton to Sir Thomas Temple, 1 June 1627.
104. Firth MSS, C.4, p. 332: deputy lieutenants to Council, 4 April 1627.
105. Firth MS C.4, p. 432. Bristol reported similarly: see Bristol Record Office, Common Council Books, 3, 1627–42, ff.6–6v.
106. Firth MS C.4, pp. 399, 401, 404, 429. The deputies had to assure their countrymen that the powder paid for would not leave the county (p. 405).
107. *Ibid.*, pp. 435, 444.

secure local cooperation. Faced with pressure from deputy lieutenants and JPs who confessed their inability to force local payment (and who feared loss of local standing) the Council bowed to the inevitable and permitted the loan money to be used to meet the costs of billeting and equipping troops.[108] In the case of Buckinghamshire even purveyance money was deducted from the loan.[109] In Hampshire, Jervoise's careful accounts of loan monies received and disbursed locally reveal the entire sums raised being deployed within the county.[110] In Dorset in April 1627 the loan money was not even adequate to discharge the billet of troops.[111] Complaints about and demands for reimbursement of billeting costs echoed loudly into the 1630s.[112] The use of loan money only just cooled to safety level a dangerously heated situation in the localities. To the centre, however, the price was high. Across the country, Dr Cust estimates, over £82,000 of the total loan money paid was spent in the shires rather than paid into the Exchequer.[113]

The loan, valuable as it was, made only a limited contribution to the costs of war. Debts mounted, more crown lands were sold (so reducing the crown's annual receipt); payment of royal household salaries and pensions was suspended.[114] In the summer of 1627, Secretary Sir John Coke told Viscount Conway that when he approached the Lord Treasurer for money, Marlborough answered 'in his usual phrase that tomorrow they will take that into consideration'.[115] By September Sir Robert Pye reported gloomily to Buckingham, 'we are upon the third year's anticipations, land much sold, credit lost'.[116] With the failure of the Rhé expedition in October, the revenues were anticipated to the extent of £319,728.[117] The situation was becoming impossible. In Sir John Coke's poignant words, 'money is the elixir which till it be fixed will never produce the philosopher's stone'.[118] A few in the localities

108. Cust, *Forced Loan*, pp. 123–6.
109. *Ibid.*, p. 119.
110. See Herriard MSS, Box 021 (A declaration of Sir Thomas Jervoise's accompts of money received and issued). The 'remain' after disbursements of £1,918 4s. 2d. for conduct money, armourers etc was 'nil'.
111. *Cal. Stat. Pap. Dom., 1627–8*, p. 151: deputies to Lord Treasurer Marlborough, 26 April 1627.
112. See, for example, the complaint of the mayor of Petersfield in 1635 (PRO, PC 2/44/649). Richard Joliffe was still petitioning for the payment of monies owed over the Isle of Wight in 1638 and had spent £500 'out of his own purse in following this business on behalf of the said isle' (*Cal. Stat. Pap. Dom., 1638–9*, p. 254).
113. Cust, *Forced Loan*, p. 123.
114. Gardiner, *History of England*, VI, p. 220; *Cal. Stat. Pap. Dom., 1627–8*, p. 353; *1625–49*, pp. 36–7; *Acts of the Privy Council, March 1625 to July 1626*, p. 441; *Sept. 1627 to June 1628*, pp. 207–8.
115. *Cal. Stat. Pap. Dom., 1627–8*, p. 225. The meaning was clearly that of the sign in my local pub: 'free beer tomorrow'.
116. *Ibid.*, p. 353.
117. *Ibid.*, p. 481.
118. *Ibid.*, p. 225.

may have understood the problem. In Hampshire, Thomas Long described the desperate financial plight that had led to ship money, privy seals, the melting of royal plate, the sale of crown land, the expulsion of the queen's servants, a scheme to debase the coinage – and still left an empty Exchequer.[119] But if there was a wider understanding of the fiscal problems it was not transformed into action or cash. When Weston succeeded to the Treasury, he inherited an empty Exchequer. It is small wonder that, in these circumstances, he argued that the king's affairs required 'rest and vigilancy'.[120]

The logistics of war: soldiers

For all that the shortage of money crippled the war effort, it was by no means the only problem revealed during the war years. Efforts to levy troops, supply them and transport them for service overseas or the attempt to put the local militia in a state of readiness to defend the country against invasion presented innumerable difficulties for central and local government, and exposed weaknesses that questioned the ability of England to fight a war or preserve its security. Some of these difficulties, of course, were related to shortage of money: soldiers in Dorset would not march on until they had shirts, shoes and pay.[121] But even when there was money to pay them troops presented a myriad of problems. Not since the 1590s had the English counties been required to levy men for service overseas, mainly in Ireland. Not since the reign of Henry VIII had troops been required, on the scale demanded in the 1620s, for battle on the continent – against France and the legendary tercios of the Habsburgs. For those pressed or conscripted, the prospects of returning unmaimed and in health were bleak. Conditions on board ship with rotten provisions and disease – at times even before leaving harbour – were hazardous enough. Attack, capture or shipwreck faced them next. Finally battle itself left many fatalities – all the more so when there was a shortage of surgeons.[122] The prospects for a wounded man who, on his return, could not sustain himself by his labour were hardly less bleak. If any dreamed of glory to be won in service overseas it was not the common soldier for whom, as large-scale desertions and instances of suicide bear witness, the awful reality was all too obvious.[123]

119. Hampshire Record Office, Sherfield MS XLII.
120. *Cal. Stat. Pap. Dom., 1628–9*, p. 258.
121. *Cal. Stat. Pap. Dom., 1627–8*, p. 148: Sir George Blundell to Buckingham, 24 April 1627.
122. *Cal. Stat. Pap. Dom., 1627–8*, p. 205.
123. For example, Herriard MS XLVIII; Firth MS C.4, pp. 314–15, 345; *Cal. Stat. Pap. Dom., 1627–8*, p. 286.

None but the most desperate men volunteered for service. And in conscripting troops local officials sought to pass over married men and fathers who might leave, possibly permanently, their dependants as a charge on the parish and to spare, too, substantial yeomen who contributed to the local rates. Men of property and influence manoeuvred and colluded to protect their relatives, friends and tenants. Thomas Duncombe wrote to the deputy lieutenants of Buckinghamshire asking them to spare the son of a widow who depended on his support.[124] Sir William Andrewes pleaded on behalf of his 'poor tenant', the husbandman William Chapman.[125] In Leicestershire, Thomas Everard, taking advantage of the constables' instructions to spare husbandmen, claimed his hundred had none else.[126] James Skipwith similarly protested there were but married men in the small hamlet where he dwelt.[127] From all considerations of convenience, able-bodied bachelors provided the best recruits. It is therefore hardly surprising that, failing to concur, they made themselves scarce at the time of the press. The deputy lieutenants of Leicestershire were obviously right in suspecting, as they told the Privy Council on 10 September 1627, that 'it is not in this place alone where as soon as there is a fame of levying men for the king a great part of them that it may concern do secretly transport themselves into other counties and places, absenting basely from their dwelling until they get assurance that the service without them is both furnished and finished'.[128] Local communities often closed ranks to protect their members. In Essex, Sergeant Andrewes, in pursuit of nineteen runaways, found that 'in most parts of the country they are more ready to hide them from me than to assist me'.[129] Constables responsible for aiding the press, often close in social status to the conscripts, clearly connived at much dodging.[130]

When local interests protected the more substantial members of the community and those quick-witted and able enough ran away, the press inevitably recruited the dregs of society. Sometimes they presented a very sorry spectacle. From Derbyshire, Michael Grenne told Sir John Coke that 'the able and sufficient' having 'hid themselves out of the way that they could not find them', those conscripted were more fit for a hospital than the king's service.[131] Sir George Blundell

124. Temple of Stowe MS, Box 6, STT 712.
125. Temple of Stowe MS, STT 39.
126. Hastings MS 2884: Thomas Everard to Earl of Huntingdon, 14 May 1625.
127. Hastings MS 10855: James Skipwith to Earl of Huntingdon, 16 May 1625.
128. Hastings MS 8536: deputy lieutenants of Leicestershire to Council, 10 Sept. 1627.
129. Firth MS C.4, p. 337.
130. Hastings MS 8536: T.G. Barnes, *Somerset 1625–1640: A County's Government during the Personal Rule* (Oxford, 1961), p. 113; J. Kent, *The English Village Constable 1580–1642* (Oxford, 1986), pp. 277–8.
131. Coke MS 35: Michael Grenne to Coke, 11 Aug. 1628.

complained to Buckingham that the men sent him by the deputy lieutenants of Hampshire (sixty short of their contingent) were 'half of them such creatures as he is ashamed to describe'.[132] Even the ranks of such a motley crew could not be sustained, for often those who had not succeeded in dodging the press ran away after being recruited – sometimes, as did the conscripted mariners of Essex in March 1627, while in the king's pay.[133] In April the Privy Council acknowledged that 'the mischief of the running away of men pressed' had grown 'so desperate' that urgent action was required.[134] But little could be done except the harsh punishment of those who were caught and whom the processes of local justice convicted as deserters.[135] The Council recognized the local obstacles to effective prosecution when it urged JPs to take especial care 'for the returning of a discreet jury' so that 'the mischief be not rather confirmed than prevented'.[136] The mass desertions continued.

Meanwhile the troops who were kept together presented no fewer headaches – from the moment of their assembly in the county of conscription to their delivery to a captain at Portsmouth. Many of them men who had lived on the fringes of or outside the law, they did not easily succumb to military discipline. In Essex they were reported 'clamorous' and mutinous;[137] across the country they threatened local inhabitants as well as their commanders.[138] The provost marshal, even when a county raised the money to pay one, could not, as Lord Maynard pointed out, be in all places at once.[139] Those responsible for the conduct of soldiers, then, must often have feared for their lives. At Harwich, discontented soldiers kidnapped their captain and threatened to throw him overboard; stories of attacks and violence were told and repeated.[140] As troops moved further from their home counties into communities with different dialects and customs, resentful and fearful of their presence, the tensions and clashes mounted. The famous riot at Witham in Essex on St Patrick's day 1628 was evidently sparked off by the Irish Catholic soldiers taking offence at the red crosses tied

132. *Cal. Stat. Pap. Dom., 1627–8*, pp. 154–5; Sir George Blundell to Buckingham, 30 April 1627.
133. Firth MS C.4, p. 314; cf. Sherfield MS XLVII.
134. Firth MS C.4, p. 345; *Acts of the Privy Council, Jan.–Aug. 1627*, p. 216: letter of 10 April 1627.
135. Kent, *Village Constable*, pp. 279–80, 291; cf. more generally C. Herrup, *The Common Peace: Participation and the Criminal Law in Seventeenth Century England* (Cambridge, 1987).
136. Firth MS C.4, p. 346.
137. *Ibid.*, p. 347.
138. *Cal. Stat. Pap. Dom., 1627–8*, pp. 178, 488, 519; *1628–9*, pp. 2, 79, 111. As the mayor of Canterbury put it, 'there is continual fear of rapine, robbery and bloodshed' (*Cal. Stat. Pap. Dom., 1628–9*, p. 145, 2 June 1628).
139. Firth MS C.4, p. 314.
140. *Ibid.*, p. 341.

to whipping posts and dogs' tails in the town. Doubtless the Irish nationality of the soldiers was as much a factor as their Catholicism.[141] Such incidents, of course, only worsened relations, and made communities even more reluctant to feed and billet troops. Like other local charges, the burden of billeting did not fall evenly. The 'persons of ability absolutely refusing to receive them into their houses', the burden of maintaining the soldiers was thrown on to the poor, who were least able to feed their unwanted guests, especially when the daily allowance fell short of the cost.[142] In turn, hungry soldiers became even more querulous. There were complaints in abundance, skirmishes aplenty and fights at the ports between landmen and sailors over inadequate supplies of victuals.[143] Once the troops were at last embarked, the local communities and officers doubtless breathed a sigh of relief at having escaped the worst outrages. But there was little cause for the Council to take comfort in the ramshackle and unruly bands that on various occasions between 1625 and 1628 sailed out of harbour for Denmark or Cadiz, La Rochelle or the Ile de Rhé.

There was no more reason for optimism about the conditions of local defence: that is the members, equipment and training of the county militia. The impetus to the formation and development of the county militia had been the threats to England occasioned by the break from Rome and the fear of invasion from France and Spain.[144] During Elizabeth's reign, amid threats from abroad and insurrections at home, attempts were made to make musters more frequent, to improve equipment and in general to turn the militia into, in Dr Boynton's phrase, 'a citizen's army'.[145] In 1573, shortly after the papal bull excommunicating the queen, the government ordered the establishment of 'trained bands' of selected men from each county who were to be, theoretically, in a constant state of trained readiness. The evidently mounting tensions in relations with Spain in the 1580s increased government activity and the willingness of localities to see the need for improved defences. Just how effective the militia became it is not possible to determine, since it was never put to the test of battle. But Geoffrey Parker's judgement that it would have been very ill prepared to offer much resistance had the Armada landed Parma's troops is probably not over-pessimistic.[146] After 1588 it was

141. See G.E. Aylmer, 'St Patrick's Day 1628 in Witham, Essex', *P&P*, 61 (1973), pp. 139–48; PRO, SP 16/96/39; Firth MS C.4, pp. 455–6.
142. Firth MS C.4, p. 431; cf. BL Add. MS 21922 (letterbook of Sir Richard Norton), f.133; *Cal. Stat. Pap. Dom., 1628–9*, p. 2.
143. Coke MS 35: Sir Gylford Slingsby to Coke, 18 Nov. 1628.
144. On the origins and development of the militia, see L. Boynton, *The Elizabethan Militia, 1558–1638* (1967).
145. *Ibid.*, p. 62.
146. G. Parker 'If the Armada had landed', *History*, 60 (1976), pp. 358–68, and cf. G. Parker and C. Martin, *The Spanish Armada* (1988), esp. ch. 14.

hard to sustain the momentum occasioned by crisis, despite the persistent rumours of a reformed armada and sporadic coastal raids. With the smooth succession of James I, the peace with Spain of 1604 and the illusory calm of the Pax Hispanica in Europe, the Council's attentiveness to muster attendance waned and the militia went into decline – what the Earl of Hertford in 1612 called a 'long vacation and rest'.[147] Not until the outbreak of the Thirty Years War did circumstances provide the motive for renewed action. When James I died, however, little had been done. After thirty years of peace and relative security the county militia had fallen far short of even their Elizabethan standards.[148]

The basic barometer of decline was the poor attendance at musters. In October 1627 the deputy lieutenants of Essex confessed to the Council 'the general refractoriness which we perceive daily to increase upon all musters and trainings and matters of charge whatsoever . . . which concern the safety and defence of the kingdom' – and this in time of war.[149] The following September Charles I himself acknowledged that there were the abuses and neglects in the trained bands of the counties.[150] Muster rolls had not been kept up, so as men had died, moved or sold property, their obligations to furnish men and arms had lapsed and new purchasers had not been charged to replace them.[151] Ironically the failure to revise the subsidy books so that they adequately reflected changing patterns of local wealth and ownership meant, since militia rolls used the subsidy books as their base, that men of ability often dodged their contributions to local defence as well.[152] After years of peace and lax enforcement, there were numerous questions and doubts concerning the obligations of individuals and areas. A diligent deputy lieutenant like Sir Thomas Temple in Buckinghamshire had to enquire whether clergy were included in the musters, whether soldiers could be pressed, and who had the responsibility for executing the letters to muster.[153] The less diligent probably did not bother. But Temple's questions raised real problems about the very foundation of militia payments and obligations. In 1604 parliament repealed the statutes of 1558 (4 and 5 Philip and Mary Caps 2, 3) which were

147. Boynton, *Elizabethan Militia*, p. 212 and ch. 7, *passim*; H.R. Trevor-Roper, 'Spain and Europe 1598–1621', in J.P. Cooper (ed.) *The Decline of Spain and the Thirty Years War 1609–1648* (New Cambridge Modern History, IV, Cambridge, 1970), pp. 260–82.
148. Boynton, *Elizabethan Militia*, pp. 237–43.
149. Firth MS C.4, p. 407.
150. PRO, Signet Office SO/1/1, f.173v: Charles I to Viscount Conway, 21 Sept. 1628. The king announced his intention to take on the oversight of the militia himself.
151. For example, BL Add. MS 21922, f.43; *Cal. Stat. Pap. Dom., 1625–49*, p. 79.
152. *Cal. Stat. Pap. Dom., 1625–49*, pp. 321–2 (petition of Humphrey Mawdett, 1628); 'by reason that men of ability are kept out of the subsidy book, no captain can have his complement . . .'.
153. Temple of Stowe MSS, Personal Box 8 (note on deputy lieutenancy, May 1626).

the legislative basis of the obligations to muster and keep arms and horses.[154] Their repeal 'gave rise to genuine confusion over the precise nature and extent of military obligations'; and it left the lord-lieutenants, in practice the resident deputy lieutenants, with only the authorization of the prerogative and Privy Council for their actions and orders.[155] Temple seriously doubted his authority to issue warrants, press soldiers or lay charges for powder and coat and conduct money, and it is clear his doubts were shared by others. In 1627, for example, Sir Charles Cornwallis, deputy lieutenant of Suffolk, urged on the Council the need for orders that would authorize deputies to coerce muster defaulters 'without pursuit in law or in parliament' for illegal action.[156] As the parliament of 1628 was to reveal, the deputy lieutenants' fears about their legal security were real.[157] Such fears undoubtedly in some instances undermined their willingness to act.

If the mustering of infantrymen had been sorely neglected, the horse were in a sorrier state still. The deputies of Buckinghamshire found all the horse due at Aylesbury's muster in August 1626 either absent or defective.[158] Sir Thomas Jervoise apologized 'for our horse, I am ashamed to speak of them'.[159] Social and economic changes in local society had a greater impact on the horse than the foot. The Privy Council itself recognized that as the principal manor houses that used to find the county horses were increasingly occupied by 'mean tenants' the numbers of horse listed on the muster roll became a fictitious ideal.[160] Even those due to appear with or provide horses did not find it difficult to default with impunity. For these men were gentlemen, the social equals, perhaps the relatives and friends, of the deputies who were responsible for cajoling them or reporting them to the Council. Not surprisingly the horse remained seriously defective.

The problems of decline and deficiency in the numbers of troops and horses were exacerbated by their inadequate training, equipment and supplies. During the years of peace the money to pay a muster master or professional soldier to train the militia and bands had doubtless appeared an unnecessary expenditure.[161] Conciliar pressure to enforce

154. Boynton, *Elizabethan Militia*, p. 209; cf. A. Hassell Smith, 'Militia rates and militia statutes, 1558–1663', in P. Clark, A.G.R. Smith and N. Tyacke (eds) *The English Commonwealth, 1547–1640* (Leicester, 1979), pp. 93–110.

155. Boynton, *Elizabethan Militia*, pp. 7, 9–11.

156. *Cal. Stat. Pap. Dom., 1627–8*, p. 198.

157. M. Cole, R.C. Johnson, M.F. Keeler and W. Bidwell (eds) *Commons Debates, 1628* (New Haven and London, 1977–1983), vols. II, p. 260: Speech of Sir Robert Phelips, 2 April 1628.

158. Temple of Stowe MSS, Military Box.

159. *Cal. Stat. Pap. Dom., 1625–49*, p. 94, 2 Jan. 1626.

160. BL Add. MS 21922, f.43. See L. Stone, *The Crisis of the Aristocracy* (Oxford, 1965), ch. 5. *Acts of the Privy Council, March 1625 to May 1626*, pp. 296–7.

161. Some counties used pensioners. See Boynton, *Elizabethan Militia*, pp. 99–107, 178–81, 210, 246–8.

their appointment (and pay) during the war years met with resentment and resistance. The deputy lieutenants of Rutland informed the Earl of Huntingdon in May and August 1626 that the charge of experienced soldiers to train the troops was quite unnecessary and 'very distasteful and burdensome to the country'.[162] Similar letters and protestations came in from most counties of England. But local claims that the militia could receive adequate training without professional instructors do not hold up. Most muster records reveal defective equipment and skills as well as absentees, and even these records probably concealed as many problems as they reported. The borrowing of arms by one area from another when, as often, musters were held in different parts of the county on different days is just one abuse on which the muster roll is silent. Men with faulty, archaic or borrowed muskets, pikes and arrows were unlikely to be well drilled in their use, and were, of course, ignorant of the modern weapons they were supposed to carry.[163] Attempts to improve local equipment and supplies also met with difficulties and resistance. After years of peace it may have been in the late 1620s, as it was in the late 1630s, hard to find suitable and speedy supplies.[164] John Browne may well have been telling the truth when he asked the Earl of Huntingdon to excuse him the musters, he having never been defective before, because he had, according to the new directions, ordered a complete new 'furniture' of armour which would not be ready in time.[165] A more common reaction to the novel costs of equipping and supplying the militia was resentment. In Leicestershire in 1626, in what was to be the opening round of a fifteen-year-long feud, Sir William Faunt protested against the unnecessary efforts of the Earl of Huntingdon to improve the local defences and the costs these improvements imposed. Over twenty years, Faunt claimed, £2,000 had been 'drawn out of the county by ten shillings and nine shillings and seven shillings at several times and the project hath always been to furnish the county with powder, match and bullet and is it so unfurnished now . . . that there is need of two thousand pounds at one clap in a time of peace?' As for the horses, 'I shall prove that my Lord's ancestors hath ever thought seven score horses a sufficient charge . . . and now in time of peace twelve score and ten . . . is now too few'. Faunt closed with a threat: that 'upon a complaint to a parliament, it will not give way that a whole county should be impoverished' by such taxations.[166] Faunt's lack of a sense of

162. Hastings MSS 10615 (4 May 1626), 10617 (6 Aug. 1626). And this in the midst of a war.

163. Boynton, *Elizabethan Militia*, pp. 238–41, 259–62, 267–71; cf. below, pp. 32, 487–90; Larkin, *Stuart Royal Proclamations*, II, no. 88, pp. 190–2; BL Add. MS 21922, f.129.

164. *Cal. Stat. Pap. Dom., 1627–8*, p. 205.

165. Hastings MS 13380.

166. Hastings MS 3148: Sir William Faunt to Sir Wolstan Dixie, 17 Nov. 1626.

reality extended beyond his failure to discern the states of peace and war. For Sir Wolstan Dixie, one of the deputies, in a polite reply, informed Faunt that after powder consumed in training the bands, there had been 'but the small remainder of one barrel', to replenish which a thousand pounds was levied on the county. With regard to the horse and Faunt's fanciful numbers, Dixie announced that the 'whole list in charge will not come to a hundred' and doubted whether the county was 'able to set out fourscore'. As Lord-Lieutenant, Huntingdon, Dixie reminded Faunt, was not out to wrong the county but to prepare responsibly for its defence.[167] It is not likely that his reply convinced a man who could regard his country as seemingly at peace in the autumn of 1626.

Some local officers themselves exhibited as little responsibility or sought rather to protect their communities from costs than to enforce orders for defence. Temple's reservations with respect to levies for powder and soldiers – 'whether new precedents will not be dangerous' – doubtless affected his willingness to proceed against recalcitrants and may have reflected a wider sense of obligation to protect the locality.[168] The deputy lieutenants of Rutland, championing the protests, petitioned the Earl of Huntingdon to be the county's spokesman at the Council Board for relief from their 'disproportionable charge'.[169] The deputy lieutenants of Essex who, we recall, had referred the demand for ship money to the grand jury, reported to the Council a county petition against the muster master and even acknowledged, in a letter to the constables about muster attendance, that 'our former remissness in this kind has been a great prejudice to his Majesty's service'.[170] Their remissness was both widespread and understandable. The deputy lieutenants had to reconcile their positions in local society with the execution of Conciliar directions, a feat difficult enough in ordinary times and nigh impossible in war. As the Essex deputies put it, 'such is our misfortune that these employments which in former times have added a power and credit unto men in their country do in these times make us neglected and disrespected of our neighbours'.[171] Even forceful deputies such as Sir Thomas Jervoise or Sir Richard Norton in Hampshire, where there was evidently less articulated protest at their activities, had to work endlessly to effect some improvements; and even then success depended ultimately upon local constables who could be, as the deputies of Leicestershire put it,

167. Hastings MS 2294: Sir Wolstan Dixie to Sir William Faunt, Nov. 1626.
168. Temple of Stowe MSS, Personal Box 8.
169. Hastings MS 13380.
170. Above, p. 14; Firth MS C.4, pp. 407–8: deputies to Council, 9 May 1627; p. 417: deputies to constables, 13 Nov. 1627.
171. Firth MS C.4, p. 421: deputy lieutenants of Essex to Chancellor of the Exchequer, 17 Dec. 1627.

'confident of their impunity by experience'.[172] Faced with unwilling subordinates and local communities there were limits to what the most active deputy lieutenants could do – especially without the full support of the Lord-Lieutenant or the Privy Council.

From 1625 the king and Council turned to the problem with a renewed energy characteristic of the new reign. The Council issued new orders and drill books and required the counties to report; professional soldiers (often men who had served in the Low Countries) were appointed as instructors.[173] Charles I wrote personally to lord-lieutenants indicating that he believed the militia to have been neglected and admonishing them carefully to oversee it.[174] In the summer of 1626 the king issued orders for constant practice with weapons and bodily exercise 'for the settling of a perfect militia'.[175] Reserve bands were to be developed from the untrained men and private arms were to be found for them; all aged sixteen to sixty who were fit and able were to be listed as potential reserves; the counties were to equip themselves with modern weapons. Improvements, however, did not occur at the pace demanded by the state of war with both France and Spain. Indeed the organization of troops for overseas service distracted the deputies from attention to the militia and heightened local resentments at military costs and services.[176] The Essex deputies who in 1627 had reported the increasing 'refractoriness' over charges and musters confessed the following summer that attendance had been poor on account of bad weather.[177] The repetition of royal letters and Council instructions for arming and training the militia itself offers as much evidence of the government's limited success as of its vigilance. Charles I himself prefaced new orders sent to Conway in September 1628 with the statement that 'The abuses and neglects of the trained bands of the several counties are by connivance and want of due care grown so customary as the directions of the state for reformation are commonly received as matters of form only.'[178] Announcing his intention to take strict account himself the king ordered lord-lieutenants to assess landowners, 'whether the owner be resident or not', and to

172. Herriard MSS, Box 021; Sherfield MS XLVIII; BL Add. MS 21922; Boynton, *Elizabethan Militia*, pp. 231–6, 250–2; Hastings MS 8536; deputy lieutenants to Council, 10 Sept. 1627; Fletcher, *Reform in the Provinces*, p. 301.

173. Boynton, *Elizabethan Militia*, p. 245; Hastings MS 1336; Temple of Stowe MSS, Box 6, STT 39 (26 Jan. 1626), STT 2456 (Buckingham to deputies, 24 Jan. 1626), STT 2468 (Buckingham to deputies, 30 June 1626); *Acts of the Privy Council, March 1625 to May 1626*, pp. 321–2, 484, 496–8.

174. PRO, SO 1/1/173v.

175. *Acts of the Privy Council, June 1626 to Dec. 1626*, pp. 71–4; cf. *Cal. Stat. Pap. Dom., 1627–8*, p. 214: deputy lieutenants of Northumberland to Earl of Suffolk, 13 June 1627.

176. For example, Hastings MS 8536; Coke MS 35.

177. Firth MS C.4, pp. 407, 461.

178. PRO, SO 1/1/173v.

charge the more substantial and stable members of society; to recruit resident householders to the trained bands, and to permit no changing of trained men without licence. Most important, in a gesture that was to typify his belief that tighter bureaucracy led to greater effectiveness, Charles commanded the lieutenants to pay close attention to the muster certificate and not simply to transcribe the last one 'without observing present defects'. No longer, the king concluded, would he rest content with mere formalities 'but require realities and effects'.[179] In addition to such general admonition, Charles endeavoured to deal with specific abuses and to assist improvements. He issued proclamations to stop the purloining of weapons and requiring the marking of arms with C.R. and a county stamp, to prevent arms being borrowed from other places or individuals for musters;[180] he granted some powder, amidst the shortages of the war years, to some boys of Chichester who exercised in arms 'for their encouragement and in the hope that the youth in other places may be stirred up'.[181] As we shall see, the hopes of some long-term improvements were not entirely misplaced.[182] But during the war years 1625–8 there is little evidence of greater effectiveness. Some deputies like Jervoise and Norton undoubtedly did their best. When a lord-lieutenant was resident to oversee the business the likelihood of success increased.[183] William Cavendish, Viscount Mansfield, boasted from Nottinghamshire in August 1627 that his trained bands were 'completely furnished every way after the modern fashion'.[184] In other counties the deputies acknowledged the many problems and defects 'to which we are not able to apply any remedy without troubling the Board with perpetual complaints'.[185] Often it was only when the Privy Council closely oversaw the implementation of orders and dealt with defaulters that things got done.[186]

The experience of war: government

The greater involvement, or interference, of the Privy Council in local business was one of the important consequences and developments of

179. Firth MS C.4, p. 475: Charles I to lord-lieutenants of Essex, 21 Sept. 1628; PRO, SP 16/117/46.
180. Larkin, *Stuart Royal Proclamations*, II, no. 88, pp. 190–2.
181. *Cal. Stat. Pap. Dom., 1627–8*, p. 336.
182. Below, pp. 487–90, 541–5.
183. Cust, *Forced Loan*, pp. 198–9.
184. *Cal. Stat. Pap. Dom., 1627–8*, p. 284; cf. J. Dias, 'Politics and administration in Nottinghamshire and Derbyshire 1590–1640' (Oxford University D. Phil. thesis, 1973).
185. Firth MS C.4, p. 431.
186. Hirst, 'Privy Council'.

the war years 1625 to 1628. Ship money, the loan, the reformation of the militia, the levying and transport of troops and supplies meant regular missives, orders, examinations and Council hearings which to a greater extent than before made the presence and power of the central government felt in the localities. Councillors went down into their own counties to urge subscription to the loan; Privy Council messengers were sent into Essex to assist the deputy lieutenants to collect money for troops.[187] This greater involvement led many Councillors to an increased awareness of the failings and deficiences of local government and to a sense of a greater need for responsibility and accountability. That new sense is articulated in the changing language of Council orders. The deputy lieutenants of Essex who had protested the absence of any precedents for ship money were told sharply that 'the occasions of states and defence of kingdoms in time of extraordinary dangers are not tied to ordinary and continued precedents'.[188] And they were censured for referring the business to the Grand Jury 'as if they and you at a public sessions had a controlling power over the acts of state'.[189] By no means all Privy Councillors approved of such language or its implications. The Earl of Dorset, not one of those regarded as unsympathetic to the prerogative, told Alderman Gerwaie of the Levant Company, 'I am sorry that the [Council] Board will intermeddle in matters of meum and tuum. Your most speedy and safe way will be, in all humble and mannerly terms, to discover to their lordships that the word "State" is only used to bolster out the business, and that the verity of their demand cannot appear but by a legal examination.'[190] But in general during the late 1620s the language of necessity entered into common usage and was significantly employed by those whom Dr Cust would categorize as the 'moderate' Councillors attached to traditional modes of government. In notes on the forced loan, Coke attempted to answer the view (held strongly by the Earl of Clare for instance) that the loan was a new departure that signalled a new style of rule without parliaments.[191] The justification for the loan, he reflected, was necessity: 'for the necessity breaketh stone walls, it maketh the earth to tremble, and to preserve the whole dissolveth the parts, and this necessity concerned the safety of the kingdom'.[192] Coke grappled to reconcile necessity with 'such ways as

187. Cust, *Forced Loan*, p. 112ff; Firth MS C.4, p. 444.
188. Firth MS C.4, p. 325, 12 April 1627.
189. *Ibid.*, p. 325.
190. *Cal. Stat. Pap. Dom., 1625–49*, p. 268, 8 Aug. 1628. For Dorset, see Cust, *Forced Loan*, pp. 29, 45, 55–6, 58, 77 and D.L. Smith, 'The political career of Edward Sackville, Fourth Earl of Dorset (1590–1652)' (University of Cambridge PhD thesis, 1989), ch. 2, esp. pp. 88–9. I am most grateful to David Smith for lending me a copy of his thesis.
191. Seddon, *Letters of John Holles*, I, p. lxiii.
192. PRO, SP 16/527/55; *Cal. Stat. Pap. Dom., 1625–49*, pp. 244–5; Cust (*Forced Loan*, p. 69) omits this sentence from his quotation from Coke's speech.

come nearest to consent' but in the end experience taught him the need to justify those courses to parliament.[193] The experience of the war years was similarly to teach other Councillors the need for greater direction of and authority over local government.

In the counties both the experience of war and greater Council interference in local affairs were unwelcome. Whilst the king and Council were often frustrated at the tardiness of local officials in implementing government orders, the provinces felt acutely the imposition of novel, expensive and disruptive burdens – burdens that strained local relationships and divided local communities. The billeting of soldiers was the greatest disruption. The burden, both in numbers lodged and duration of stay, was inevitably uneven, falling heaviest in areas where soldiers were led to embark on ships such as Portsmouth, Harwich or Plymouth. A small town like Romsey in Hampshire, for example, billeted 210 soldiers for fourteen weeks at a cost of £178 in the winter of 1626–7, and another company of ninety in April.[194] The small villages of North and South Stoneham lodged fifty-two soldiers of Captain Pelham's company in January 1628.[195] Not only was the cost considerable – equivalent, the deputies of Essex claimed, to 'two or three subsidies at the least every week' – the soldiers were invariably a cause of trouble.[196] Often lodged in villages far from where a JP lived, the unruly troops were at times virtually unpoliced. The Irish regiments, as we have seen, proved the worst, 'of a contrary religion and many of them ready to offer injury to such as are of our religion',[197] but skirmishes, the theft of food, and worse were far from rare.[198] Sir John Oglander graphically recalled the 'murders, rapes, robberies, burglaries, getting of bastards . . .' that were 'almost the undoing of the whole island' of Wight.[199] Martial law compounded rather than ameliorated the problem. For though it may have helped to quell the violence of the soldiers, martial law was also applied to the civilians who billeted them and to those who refused to receive the soldiers in their homes.[200] Thomas Grove told Sir Richard Grenville that in Wells

193. PRO, SP 16/527/55; Cust, *Forced Loan*, p. 69.
194. Herriard MSS, Military Box 029 (billeting accounts); Sherfield MS XLVII/12; Taylor estimates Romsey's population at a maximum of 1,500 by the mid-seventeenth century (see 'Population, disease and family structure', p. 71).
195. Herriard MSS, Box 029; North and South Stoneham were villages of low population density (see Taylor, 'Population, disease and family structure', p. 176).
196. Firth MS C.4, p. 442: deputies to Privy Council, 10 Feb. 1628.
197. Above, pp. 25–6; Firth MS C.4, p. 442.
198. For example, *Cal. Stat. Pap. Dom., 1628–9*, p. 145 (mayor of Canterbury to Council, 2 June 1628): 'The soldiers threaten to take the meat from the butchers' shops and others take away men's wares, and break open the doors of the billeters; yea, some of the officers would have killed their billeters in their own houses. The inhabitants . . . stand in fear of their lives.'
199. W.H. Long (ed.) *The Oglander Memoirs* (1888), p. 37.
200. See L. Boynton, 'Martial law and the Petition of Right', *Eng. Hist. Rev.*, 79 (1964), pp. 255–84. See also East Sussex Record Office, LCD/EWI; Herriard MSS, Box 029.

the people did not understand martial law nor would tolerate it.[201] For weeks and months at a time English localities, used to their own interpretation of the processes of law and justice, must have felt that they lived in a state of siege.[202]

The JPs and deputy lieutenants could not but protest at the burdens imposed on their counties and on themselves when they contrasted their circumstances with the comforts of the court or their fortunes with those who enjoyed the rich fruits of patronage.[203] Sir George Blundell complained to Buckingham that the duke made of him 'a pack horse while others live at court still getting either sergeants or baronets to put money in their purses'.[204] It was a common complaint, not without foundation when, during the years of Buckingham's hegemony, many were called upon to serve in the counties without the rewards of patronage at court. It is not surprising, therefore, that local officials usually felt greater sympathy for the sufferings of their neighbours than for the difficulties experienced by the Council. In June 1627 the deputies of Dorset informed the Council that they had impressed the required soldiers 'but with what difficulty and what lamentable cries of mothers, wives and children'; they petitioned for their release.[205] The mayor of Canterbury complained that in his city 'there is continual fear of rapine, robbery and bloodshed'.[206] The return of wounded men from campaigns abroad brought home the physical horrors of war and threw more men on the poor rate. The JPs of Wiltshire and Hampshire claimed they had more pensions to pay to casualties of the Cadiz and Rhé expeditions than could be met from the total poor law receipts of their counties.[207] As a consequence of all these experiences those governing in the localities, like those they governed, came to see the court and Council as remote from their world, alien, even opposed to their local interests and well-being. Whilst the language and fundamental beliefs were still shared, such tensions were threatening dangerously different attitudes to the commonweal.[208] As Colonel Goring frankly told Buckingham in

201. *Cal. Stat. Pap. Dom., 1628–9*, p. 79, 18 April 1628.
202. A.J. Fletcher and J. Stevenson (eds) *Order and Disorder in Early Modern England* (Cambridge, 1985), introduction; Herrup, *Common Peace, passim*.
203. Buckingham's failure to woo and win such figures through patronage exacerbated their frustrations and his problems. Cf. K. Sharpe, *Politics and Ideas in Early Stuart England* (1989), pp. 82–3.
204. *Cal. Stat. Pap. Dom., 1627–8*, p. 171, 10 May 1627.
205. *Ibid.*, p. 208, 8 June 1627.
206. See note 198.
207. *Cal. Stat. Pap. Dom., 1629–31*, p. 229, 6 April 1630; *1631–3*, p. 371, 4 July 1632.
208. See Cust and Hughes, *Conflict in Early Stuart England*, pp. 3–4, 19–21, and cf. Sharpe, *Criticism and Compliment*, pp. 11–20; P. Zagorin, 'The court and the country: a note on political terminology in the earlier seventeenth century', *Eng. Hist. Rev.*, 77 (1962), pp. 306–11.

November 1627, no man would lend money 'if they think it will go the way of the court which is now made diverse from the state'.[209]

For the king and Privy Council on the one hand, then, and the counties and local magistracy on the other, the war years were a period of problems, difficulties and frustrations which, on both parts, had profound effects on attitudes to government. Fearful for the very safety and survival of the commonweal, the Council came to believe that greater direction and important reforms were needed in the government of the localities, and to argue that necessity overrode customs and justified unusual courses.[210] In the counties of England, however, the demands and instructions of the Council were progressively regarded as novel, untraditional and even unconstitutional. Sir William Fleetwood reported one recalcitrant as saying 'the word "billet" [is] not, in any of our laws'.[211] Sir John Oglander was convinced that it was 'contrary to the law and liberty of freemen'.[212] Sir John Holles feared the new courses led 'to the overthrow of parliament and consequently to that of the state'.[213] Both the Council's and the counties' reactions are understandable. In modern societies there is no shortage of opposition to taxes or measures implemented for the defence of the realm. In early modern England genuine local ignorance of dangers facing the country and of the costs of war, and central ignorance of the consequences of war demands for ordinary householders, made mutual understanding even less likely. The structure of early modern English society and government, however, assumed the very harmony and co-operation that the war years disrupted. The local magistrates were expected by the Council to enact its orders and by clients and neighbours to safeguard local interests. When they had assembled in parliament in 1624 they had joined with Buckingham and Prince Charles in the common objective of persuading James I to break with Spain. Four years later when, after experiencing the realities of war, they proceeded to Westminster for the last parliament that Charles I was to summon for a decade, their sense of the interests of the country had become very different from the king's.

War, law and parliament

On 28 January writs were issued for another parliament to meet in March. As Dr Cust has demonstrated, the king's reluctance to

209. *Cal. Stat. Pap. Dom., 1627–8*, p. 422, 5 Nov. 1627. Goring's use of the word 'state' in this context repays careful pondering.
210. Below, pp. 59–60.
211. *Cal. Stat. Pap. Dom., 1627–8*, p. 551, 8 Feb. 1628.
212. Long, *Oglander Memoirs*, p. 38.
213. Seddon, *Letters of John Holles*, I, p. lxiii; and Seddon, *Letters of John Holles*, II (Thoroton Soc., 35, Nottingham, 1983), pp. 334–5: Holles to Viscount Saye and Sele, 12 Sept. 1626.

resummon a parliament was overcome by arguments in Council, which commanded a majority.[214] Many Councillors had expressed concern about the extraordinary courses of the previous years, the loan, the imprisonment of refusers, ship money and the like, and were anxious to see a return to normal courses of supply and government. Charles himself put forward counter-proposals for other fiscal expedients and expressed reservations about the speed with which parliament would supply him and the possibly truculent mood of the Commons. To Dr Cust such reservations suggest that Charles had come to see the Commons as a forum for a '"popular" assault on the very foundation of monarchy' and to regard 'the very idea of a parliament' as 'unpalatable'.[215] Yet despite his frustrations and doubts, we should not too hastily conclude that Charles I had as yet determined to live without parliaments. As Professor Russell has argued, the long session of 1626 was due more to Charles's commitment to traditional courses – especially his desire to have tonnage and poundage put on a statutory basis – than to optimism about supply.[216] And even after the experience of a parliament which had impeached his favourite and, as the king saw it, made offensive references to himself (including veiled hints that he had murdered his father), Charles blamed the dissolution not on the parliament, nor even the Commons as a body, but on the 'malicious practices of wicked spirits' who had subverted it.[217] It is excessively cynical to dismiss Charles's statement as rhetoric. The language of his proclamation for the loan and his later justification of such measures suggest that Charles regarded extraordinary financial expedients as sanctioned only by the immediate emergency, not as a permanent alternative to parliamentary supply. The king (as he was to say in a draft memorandum of 1628) loved the old ways of the kingdom, not novel modes of government.[218]

But in Charles I's mind his attachment to the traditional course of a parliament implied a reciprocal recognition by parliament of its responsibility to supply in wartime – especially for a war which, in his view, it had counselled. It is not clear how much the king hoped for from the Commons that assembled in the spring. Bishop William Laud drew up notes of subsidies voted by parliaments from the reign of Henry II, right up to those of James and Charles.[219] With Denbigh about to put to sea for La Rochelle, large sums were urgently needed.

214. Cust, *Forced Loan*, pp. 72–90.
215. *Ibid.*, pp. 87–8.
216. Russell, *Parliaments and Politics*, pp. 269–70, 283, 290, 304.
217. Gardiner, *History of England*, VI, pp. 106, 108, 109; Larkin, *Stuart Royal Proclamations*, II, pp. 92–5; R. Cust, 'Charles I's declarations', paper delivered at Institute of Historical Research, 19 Oct. 1987.
218. Temple of Stowe MSS, Parliament Box 1 (1373–1648), item 13, 'Answer in response to a Remonstrance'. See below, pp. 42–3.
219. *Cal. Stat. Pap. Dom., 1628–9*, p. 23. (The editor dates the note 17 March 1628.)

But it is unlikely that Charles could seriously have expected the grant of eleven subsidies which one intercepted letter alleged he desired.[220] The Venetian ambassador accurately predicted that the Commons would grant five, but less accurately and more optimistically estimated their yield at £500,000, nearly double what was received. Even that, he judged, 'will barely suffice for more than a slight reinforcement of the fleet'.[221] Whatever the amount there were clearly those, the king among them, who doubted whether parliament's generosity would finance the war without further resort to extraordinary measures.[222] John Hope, writing at the end of January, doubted whether 'they will give the king more than will do his work by halves'.[223] If his sentiments were right, his sums were wrong. The five subsidies were about a quarter of what Charles needed.[224]

While the king and Council tried to prepare Denbigh's fleet and made calculations on the supply to be voted, the elections to parliament showed a country concerned with very different priorities. Though the elections do not indicate a clear split, of the sort Goring had feared, between 'court' and 'country' they were, across the country, dominated by the issues and grievances of the war years: the loan, the imprisonment of refusers without due process of law, still more by the press, the billeting of troops and the imposition of martial law.[225] Many of those who as JPs and deputies had with difficulty, and sometimes loss of standing, implemented royal orders for raising men and money, now came to Westminster as MPs to represent and articulate the grievances of their counties. For them, the first business of the parliament, the newswriter Ralph Starkey informed Viscount Scudamore, would be the reassertion of the rights and liberties of the subject.[226] Francis Michell expressed the same hopes of the parliament to the Earl of Arundel: 'all wounds given by or by reason of non-parliament actions shall be healed'.[227]

On the day Michell wrote his letter, the different priorities of the king and the Commons were starkly revealed. In response to Secretary Coke's outline of the government's financial predicament they passed

220. *Ibid.*, p. 60: translation of an intercepted letter of 1 April 1628.
221. *Cal. Stat. Pap. Venet., 1628–9*, p. 45: Contarini to Doge and Senate, 5 April 1628.
222. Cust, *Forced Loan*, pp. 46, 48, 49. Dr Cust, in my view, too much plays down Charles's economic (as opposed to ideological) doubts about the value of parliaments.
223. *Cal. Stat. Pap. Dom., 1627–8*, p. 537, 31 Jan. 1628.
224. Dietz, *English Public Finance*, II, p. 245; Gardiner, *History of England*, VI, p. 239; PRO, SP 16/96/67.
225. S.P. Salt, 'Sir Thomas Wentworth and the parliamentary representation of Yorkshire, 1624–1628', *Northern Hist.*, 16 (1980), pp. 130–68.
226. 'And a plain exposition of Magna carta and other laws to this purpose as also an examination of the proceedings upon the habeas corpus handled in the King's Bench the last term' (PRO C.115/N4/8579: Ralph Starkey to Scudamore, 2 Feb. 1628).
227. BL, Cotton Titus MS B. VII, f.196: Francis Michell to Earl of Arundel, 26 March 1628.

a resolution condemning non-parliamentary levies.[228] And almost unanimously they expressed the conviction that their liberties and properties needed to be secured before they would proceed to supply. Such actions do not indicate that members of parliament had no sense of the crown's financial difficulties or the obligation to supply. Nor does their making supply conditional on the reform of abuse, provide evidence of a struggle for authority with the king. It is worth recalling that a leading spokesman for the (large) grant of five subsidies was also the most insistent voice for the redress of local grievances. Sir Thomas Wentworth desired neither to clip the king's prerogative nor to impede the government.[229] The course he promulgated, bills for supply and the liberty of the subject, expressed not only his personal need to meet his obligations to his king and his county; they fulfilled the very purpose of parliaments as occasions for reconciling the needs and wishes of the centre and the locality.[230] Like his fellow MPs he doubtless anticipated a successful and happy parliament.[231]

To the king, however, Wentworth's proposals offered no immediate solution to the problems of wartime government. And during the course of debates on the liberties of the subject, Councillors who had warmly advocated the resummoning of parliament developed a clearer sense of the difficulties of reconciling its demand for traditional courses with the realities of continuing the war. It is significant that during the course of the parliament Sir John Coke and others who had disliked the extraordinary courses, and even acknowledged their illegality, came to defend, as necessary to government, powers that a bill, subsequently the Petition of Right, was intended to limit.[232] 'Make what law you will,' Coke told the house, speaking as a secretary of state, 'if I discharge the place I bear I must commit men and not discover the cause to any jailer or judge'.[233] Coke and Attorney-General Heath endeavoured in the Commons to advance an argument which their experience of war enabled them to see with stark clarity. Government required emergency powers and these could not be rigorously defined but must be entrusted to the executive authority – the king – who was

228. Gardiner, *History of England*, VI, pp. 240–1; *Commons Debates 1628*, II, pp. 121, 125.
229. *Commons Debates 1628*, II, pp. 60–1, 250, 300, 415. Cf. Wentworth's own speech notes, in Sheffield Central Library, Wentworth Woodhouse MSS, WW 21/210.
230. Compare these remarks with D. Hirst, 'Court, country and politics before 1629' in Sharpe, *Faction and Parliament*, pp. 105–38; and C. Russell 'The nature of a parliament in early Stuart England', in H. Tomlinson (ed.) *Before the English Civil War* (1983), pp. 123–50. Much obfuscation has resulted from some historians' inability to distinguish between criticism and opposition.
231. See his opening words of 22 March, *Commons Debates 1628*, II, p. 60.
232. Russell, *Parliaments and Politics*, p. 346; M.B. Young, *Servility and Service: The Life and Work of Sir John Coke* (1986), pp. 171–6.
233. *Commons Debates 1628*, III, p. 189. I owe this reference to J.P. Somerville, *Politics and Ideology in England 1603–1640* (1986), p. 171.

responsible for the safety and protection of the realm.[234] Whilst some, including Holles, recognized the need for a power beyond the law in 'emergent occasions', the lawyers in the house, Sir Edward Coke, Serjeant Glanville, John Selden, Edward Littleton and William Noy, were more reluctant to do so. Horrified at revelations of the Attorney's attempt to alter the King's Bench record in the Five Knights Case so as to imply a decision in favour of the royal power of imprisonment without cause, they took a stand in the Commons against Heath's arguments for the prerogative.[235] A correspondent of Sir William Trumbull on 1 April described all Heath's '*suppositions and reasons of state* which he had made the day before being undeniably answered'.[236] They proceeded to secure them by a reaffirmation, indeed a tighter reinterpretation, of the law.

Given their experience of the war years and the revelations of governmental malpractices the MPs' preoccupation with liberties is perfectly understandable. But in insisting on redress of their grievances before supply they also prolonged the very situation which had produced the abuses of law in the first place. As Sir Francis Nethersole wrote to Elizabeth, queen of Bohemia, the king could do nothing about billeting without subsidies and the Commons would not vote subsidies until something was done about grievances like billeting.[237] The impasse was clear to Charles I, as were the difficulties he faced in resolving it. On the 28th he attempted to settle the matter by the offer of a promise to rule 'according to the laws and statutes of the realm'.[238] This left unresolved the question of interpretation of the law. As Laud's notes to proposals of Bishop Harsnett's indicate, the king had not abandoned his view that while subjects had fundamental rights they could be deprived of goods and liberty 'upon just cause'; nor his belief that 'in such extremities Necessitas est lex temporis'.[239] In practice he could not abandon that belief and continue to govern.[240] The king's promises, however, did not satisfy the Commons. They proceeded to draw up and secure the support of the Lords for a Petition of Right outlawing billeting, martial law and imprisonment without cause shown. When, in the end, Charles accepted the Petition, his answer was heralded with joy – because it was believed that king

234. *Commons Debates 1628*, II, pp. 524–5.
235. Seddon, *Letters of John Holles*, I, p. lxviii, p. 189: 'In emergent occasions, no law can hinder what is necessary to be done for the safety of us all'; *Commons Debates*, II, pp. 525–34; J.A. Guy, 'The origins of the Petition of Right Reconsidered', *Historical Journal*, 25 (1982), pp. 289–312.
236. Berkshire Record Office, Trumbull MS XVIII, f.111: Daniel Bedingfield to Sir William Trumbull, 18 April 1628.
237. *Cal. Stat. Pap. Dom., 1628–9*, p. 85, 22 April 1628.
238. Gardiner, *History of England*, VI, p. 263.
239. PRO, SP 16/102/14.
240. *Commons Debates 1628*, III, pp. 372–3, 12 May 1628.

and parliament had come to a common understandin...
celebration of an illusion, for the Petition of Right ...at was the
all the doubts and disagreements. Experience had sho... resolve
that, whatever the status of the law, in certain emergencies Charles
justified extra-legal action and that he, as custodian of the real...sity
to be judge of that necessity. Reluctantly he accepted the Petition – ...d
only because he desperately needed subsidies, but also because the judges had assured him that it did not occlude imprisonment at the king's command.[242]

The illusory nature of an accord between king and parliament was exposed even before Charles had given his final answer to the Petition of Right. In 1628 the immediate grievances of billeting and martial law had overshadowed other concerns that had ruptured the parliament of 1626, and which were of particular concern to Sir John Eliot.[243] On 3 June, the day following the king's first answer to the Petition, Eliot expounded on the woeful state of the nation at home and abroad: on the threats to true religion, on the ill-advised war with France, on the failure of military enterprises, on the mismanagement of finances and campaigns. At all points he alluded to the cause he did not name: the man who he believed had usurped royal patronage, the king's favourite and friend, the Duke of Buckingham.[244] In preparing for the parliament moderate Councillors had, as they believed, negotiated a deal with the leaders of the Commons whereby Buckingham, whose impeachment had disrupted the last session, would be immune from attack. Under Eliot's guidance, however, over the following week the Commons prepared a Remonstrance of grievances which now named Buckingham as 'the principal cause' of the 'evils and dangers' that faced the realm.[245] For the king, coming after the concessions he had made, the Remonstrance represented an unpalatable interference with 'points of state', a direct challenge to his right to appoint his ministers and to govern.[246] This spelled the end of the session of a parliament which, despite the grant of five subsidies, had done little to convince the king that it appreciated the problems that faced the government.[247]

241. Cf. J.G.A. Pocock, 'The Commons debates of 1628', *Journ. Hist. Ideas*, 39 (1978), pp. 329–34.
242. D. Parsons (ed.) *The Diary of Sir Henry Slingsby* (1836), p. 319; *Cal. Stat. Pap. Dom., 1628–9*, p. 142: Sir Arthur Ingram to Slingsby, 22 May 1628: 'in my opinion, they trench very deep on the king's prerogative which I admire the king will suffer, but I see not clemency is the cause'; J. Reeve, 'The legal status of the Petition of Right', *Hist. Journ.*, 29 (1986), pp. 257–77, esp. pp. 259–60.
243. J.N. Ball, 'Sir John Eliot and parliament: 1624–9', in Sharpe, *Faction and Parliament*, pp. 184–99.
244. *Commons Debates 1628*, IV, pp. 60–2.
245. Gardiner, *History of England*, VI, p. 317; and *Commons Debates 1628*, IV, p. 257.
246. *Commons Debates 1628*, IV, pp. 351–2.
247. Charles told the Commons on 17 June, 'You do not understand so much as I thought you had done.' (Quoted in Russell, *Parliaments and Politics*, p. 385.)

It is eas… ympathize with his view when one recalls that whilst the Com… had debated, Denbigh's fleet had sailed and failed in its mis… leaving the Protestants of La Rochelle starving and at the m… of Cardinal Richelieu.

We need not speculate on the state of the king's mind in the immediate aftermath of the parliamentary session of 1628. For though in the end he evidently decided not to publish it, Charles instructed Laud (with Weston's assistance) to draft a reply to the Commons' Remonstrance with 'a purpose to publish it'.[248] While the draft is in Laud's hand, Charles may well have overseen it, for it echoes at several points his language and may be taken as a reliable expression of his sentiments. Eliot's fears for the safety of religion, Charles took as a personal affront. The accusation that papists and Arminians were countenanced was 'a great wrong to ourself and government . . . our people must not be taught by a Parliament remonstrance . . . that we are so ignorant of truth'. No action or intention of the king undermined the religion of the nation. Nor, Charles continued, would he have the people misled into fears of innovation in secular government. The loan he confessed an 'undue course' – 'But we doubt not but our loving people will understand that necessity was then our law, that that course might then have been prevented if in the parliament before supplies had been given in the ordinary way'. As for billeting, Charles pointed out, as had Nethersole, that subsidies could have removed that grievance had they been granted sooner. Troops had not been retained to overawe, as some feared, the nation; funds were awaited to pay them off. Blaming the government (and the duke) for military disasters abroad ignored the misfortunes of war and glossed over the lack of supply which had contributed to failure. In general by so traducing the government the Remonstrance further weakened the king abroad. In naming Buckingham as the cause of all ills, it implied that the king had been led, having no judgement of his own. As we read through Charles's answers to the charges contained in the Remonstrance we may not only be struck by their force; we may also be tempted to conclude that in the summer of 1628, not entirely without reason, the king had given up with parliaments.[249] But such was not the conclusion of the draft response. Though Charles expressed his irritation

248. Temple of Stowe MSS, Parliament Box 1, item 13. On dorse, probably in Laud's hand: 'These I made by the king's command who had then a purpose to publish it in print. The then Chancellor of the Exchequer Sir Richard Weston was joined with me to make the preface. When I had done this he had it to frame the preface. But the king's mind altered not to publish it . . . who altered the king's mind in this God knows' (cf. *Cal. Stat. Pap. Dom., 1628–9*, p. 185).

249. As does Cust, *Forced Loan*, pp. 331–3; L.J. Reeve, *Charles I and the Road to Personal Rule* (Cambridge, 1989), pp. 12, 24. In so far as it attempts to understand Charles's view of things, my account is intended as a balance to Reeve.

at assemblies that 'forgetting their ancient and fair way of proceedings have swelled till they break themselves', he affirmed that 'we would be glad hereafter to see such moderate parliaments that we might love them and make them frequent'. 'Let us,' he concluded, 'see moderation and the ancient parliamentary way and we shall love nothing more than parliaments.'[250]

Though they presented his own selective view of events, passing over the Five Knights Case for example, there is no reason to doubt the sincerity of these remarks. There are other indications that, for all the session of 1628 had caused frustrations, Charles had not yet come to despair of governing in conjunction with parliaments. The prorogation, which allowed for reassembly at short notice without new elections, suggests at least that another session in the near future had not been ruled out. Other pointers to Charles's plans are the appointments and promotions made and reconciliations effected during the summer and autumn after the prorogation. The Earls of Bristol and Arundel were restored to favour; Richard Weston was promoted to Lord Treasurer.[251] Most remarked, Wentworth was raised to the peerage and promised the Lord Presidency of the Council of the North. Wentworth's appointment is important. It has often been read as an attempt by Charles and Buckingham to buy off their critics. But it is likely too, given how careful he was over the grant of favour or office, that Charles recognized that the Wentworth who had championed the Petition of Right was not an opponent of effective monarchical government. If he realized that there were such men, Charles had no need to give up on parliaments.[252]

The summer of 1628 was a time of reconsideration of the foreign situation and the wars. Honour demanded another expedition to relieve La Rochelle, but it was increasingly believed that it would mark the end of a war with France that many had regarded as an unnatural rupture.[253] Of greater significance were moves, for the first time since 1623, towards conciliation with Spain. There were sound reasons for this in the course of events in Europe. Given the failure of the Protestant cause in Germany, Spain appeared to offer the best hope for a diplomatic solution to the problem of the Palatinate. The Mantuan

250. Temple of Stowe MSS, Parliament Box 1, item 13.

251. *Cal. Stat. Pap. Dom., 1628–9*, p. 218: Sir Robert Aiton to Earl of Carlisle, 18 July 1628. Dudley Carleton was also made Viscount Dorchester and, in December, secretary of state. On Dorchester see L.J. Reeve, 'The Secretaryship of State of Viscount Dorchester: 1628–1632' (Cambridge University PhD thesis, 1984). I am grateful to John Reeve for permission to see his thesis and for many stimulating discussions of this period.

252. See P. Zagorin, 'Did Strafford change sides?', *Eng. Hist. Rev.*, 101 (1986), pp. 149–63. The article presents a useful survey of attitudes, but its conclusion fails to convince. Cf. *Dictionary of National Biography* [*DNB*], Wentworth, for Gardiner's more subtle evaluation.

253. Gardiner, *History of England*, VI, p. 333.

succession crisis too induced Spain to make overtures and concessions, so that it could concentrate on affairs in Italy. But there can be no denying that the domestic problems of the war years ultimately dictated the moves to peace. Charles told his sister that he *could* not decline offers of peace from Spain.[254] To the Prince of Orange he explained that he was negotiating for peace, 'being unable to bear the burden of war against two such great kings'.[255] Part of the blame for that inability the king could not but lay on parliament's failure to supply.

The retreat from war was for Charles more necessity than desire. In his view the failures of the years 1625–8, military failures and failures to fulfil promises to allies and friends, stained with dishonour and shame his first actions as king. The words dishonour and shame come naturally on to the page because Charles often employed them during these years and evidently more often experienced them.[256] When news came in, as it did almost daily, of shortages of victuals or men, Charles took the blame (as he often took the responsibility for an action) upon himself.[257] Those who went to fight campaigns abroad wrote back pathetically and bitterly of lack of adequate support. Sir Edward Conway told his father Secretary Conway of the inadequacy of his men and engineers at St Martins: 'if we lose this island it shall be your faults in England.'[258] Buckingham's officers 'give themselves for men neglected and forgotten in England'.[259] For Charles I, England's neglect was his neglect. Sovereignty, the proclamation for the loan declared, bestowed on the monarch as well as authority a bond, a duty to defend the realm; it placed responsibility at his feet.[260] 'If Buckingham should not be supplied,' Charles wrote to his Treasurer Marlborough in August 1627, 'it were an immeasurable shame to the king and the nation.'[261] The acute sense that a failure of supply had not only reneged on a public responsibility but also let down a close friend added greatly to Charles's personal sense of dishonour. There is an unusual tone of self-abnegation in Charles's letters to Buckingham

254. *Cal. Stat. Pap. Venet., 1628–9*, p. 183: Soranzo (Venetian envoy in the Netherlands) to Doge and Senate, 24 July 1628.
255. Gardiner, *History of England*, VI, pp. 333–4.
256. For example, *Cal. Stat. Pap. Dom., 1627–8*, p. 280: Charles I to Marlborough, 1 Aug. 1627; Harleian MS 6988, f. 76; Parsons, *Diary of Sir Henry Slingsby*, p. 319. J. Russell, the author of *The Spy: Discovering the Danger of Arminian Heresy and Spanish Treachery* (1628, STC 20577), sig. E2, urged 'let our state/Gaine once again what rate/so'ere it cost/if possible the honour it hath lost.'
257. Harleian MS 6988, ff.42, 76, 80.
258. *Cal. Stat. Pap. Dom., 1627–8*, p. 331, 4 Sept. 1627.
259. *Ibid.*, p. 35, 19 Sept. 1627.
260. Cf. 'A Declaration of his Majesty's clear intention in requiring the aid of his loving Subjects' (Larkin, *Stuart Royal Proclamations*, II. no. 5, pp. 110–12). Charles's sense of that responsibility cannot be overestimated.
261. *Cal. Stat. Pap. Dom., 1627–8*, p. 280, 1 Aug. 1627.

during these years.[262] Repeatedly he urged the duke not to blame himself: 'I must say this with my own hand that in this action you have had honour; all the shame must light on us.'[263] Through the early setbacks the young king found comforting hope in the future; in one splendid victory which would redeem honour and eradicate the stain of defeat. 'Thou and I are young enough,' he consoled Buckingham, after La Rochelle 'to redeem this misfortune.'[264] But the problems of supply continued; the misfortunes were not redeemed. When clear news came of the loss of Denbigh's ships Charles 'was never seen to be so moved'.[265] The king claimed, Arthur Ingram told Sir Henry Slingsby, that he was 'never so dishonoured'.[266] The French ambassador reported Charles in June to be so upset that he neither ate nor drank for two days, thinking of nothing but another attempt on La Rochelle.[267] Buckingham was assassinated in August before the launch of the fleet that was to restore his, the king's and the nation's honour. Charles's orders to the Earl of Lindsey, 'that you take care of our honour, the honour of our nation and your own honour' could not prevent the fall of La Rochelle or secure a posthumous vindication of Buckingham.[268] Charles's desperate desire, as the Venetian ambassador described it, for 'some honour, after so many dishonours and losses', was not to be fulfilled.[269]

This loss of honour was to have an enduring influence on Charles, and on his attitude to monarchy and to government. As he saw it his own and the nation's honour, his capacity to carry out his deeply felt duty to protect the realm, had been compromised by the failure of parliaments and local magistrates to fulfil their obligations.[270] Among the state papers for 1628 we find notes of questions arising from the king having been engaged in wars at the entreaty of parliament. Was it not, the memorandum asked, to go against God to deny aid for defence? If the people refused such aid, was it not the king's duty to make assessments of men's estates and goods to pay for it? And in such circumstances might not the king be justified in breaking (the admission is clear) the fundamental laws of the realm?[271] We do not

262. Harleian MS 6988, ff.42, 76, 80; *Cal. Stat. Pap. Dom., 1627–8*, p. 280.
263. Harleian MS 6988, ff.76–7.
264. *Ibid.*, f.78.
265. Gardiner, *History of England*, VI, pp. 291–3; *Cal. Stat. Pap. Dom., 1628–9*, p. 120, 21 May 1628.
266. Parsons, *Diary of Sir Henry Slingsby*, p. 319.
267. PRO, French transcripts, 31/3/65, f.108, 20 June 1628.
268. Gardiner, *History of England*, VI, pp. 368–9.
269. *Cal. Stat. Pap. Venet., 1628–9*, p. 394: Contarini to Doge, 18 Nov. 1628.
270. R.M. Smuts puts it well: 'Charles had staked his honour and the security of his kingdom on active and continuing parliamentary support': see *Court Culture and the Origins of a Royalist Tradition in Early Stuart England* (Pennsylvania, 1987), p. 37.
271. *Cal. Stat. Pap. Dom., 1628–9*, p. 533, April 1629.

know who drafted the questions, but we may be confident they were asked by Charles himself.[272] As his debts mounted, as maimed soldiers who had 'faithfully served the allies of their prince and country' struggled back, as petitions from the wounded and widowed flooded in over the following months and years, they were reflections that Charles would not forget.[273]

The king and his minister

Charles's first act as king, his entry into war with Spain, had arisen from an alliance forged in 1624 between the then prince, the Duke of Buckingham and parliament. Failure of supply strained that alliance and questioned the value of parliaments. But Charles did not dissolve or prorogue parliaments because they failed to supply: he terminated them because and when they proceeded, by impeachment or Remonstrance, to attack a trusted adviser and friend (see Figure 2). The relationship between Charles and Buckingham is crucial to our understanding not only of the years 1625 to 1628 – the history of those parliaments, the king's relations with his people, the development of his own character and world view – but of the decision to rule without parliaments and indeed of the rest of the reign. Though complex, it is clear that the relationship was both a political alliance and an emotional union, which was not to be repeated in Charles's reign. Historians have dwelt on the intense and almost certainly homosexual relationship between King James I and the duke; the letters to 'Steenie' from his 'dear dad' and 'gossip' have attracted much attention.[274] The love and admiration of Charles for the duke, not physically expressed, has been much less studied. Yet Charles's letters to Villiers are uncharacteristically intimate. 'No man,' the king wrote in July 1627, when Buckingham was in France, 'ever longed so much for anything as I do to hear some good news from you.'[275] 'No distance of place nor length of time,' he assured him the next month, 'can make me slacken much less diminish my love to you.'[276] Military expeditions added the pain of absence to that of dishonour. In November, anticipating

272. And even other 'moderate' Councillors. Sir John Coke evidently contemplated a scheme for a Loyal Association to aid the crown, on the lines of Olivares's plan for a Union of Arms: see *Cal. Stat. Pap. Dom., 1627–8*, p. 491.
273. Larkin, *Stuart Royal Proclamations*, II, pp. 250–1 (proclamation of 27 Dec. 1629 ordering soldiers to return to their dwelling places); *Cal. Stat. Pap. Dom., 1627–8*, p. 444 (Bagg's description of soldiers returned from Rhé); BL, Egerton MS 784 (William Whiteway's diary, 1618–34), p. 130.
274. Most successfully in R. Lockyer's fine biography, *Buckingham*.
275. Harleian MS 6988, f.27, 27 July 1627.
276. *Ibid.*, f.37, 25 Aug. 1627.

2 *George Villiers, Duke of Buckingham* by Daniel Mytens, 1626. The painting was placed in the Bear Gallery at Whitehall.

Buckingham's return, Charles expressed 'one of my greatest griefs . . . that I have not been with you in the time of suffering, for I know we would have much eased each other's griefs.'[277] The troubled early months of his marriage to the petulant Henrietta Maria (added to Charles's unease with the opposite sex) intensified his intimacy with Villiers. Charles discussed his marital problems with the duke and, revealingly, contrasted his relationship with his friend to that with his wife.[278] With Henrietta Maria he still feared in February 1628, 'we shall not agree: which I am sure cannot fall out between us'.[279] In Buckingham Charles found what he had lacked in his youth, 'the greatest riches and now hardest to be found, true friendship'.[280]

True friendship is a relationship of equals. And it is important that whatever the historical truth – on which in the end it is impossible to conclude – Charles saw his friendship with Buckingham in that way.[281] Whatever others might think, the duke, Charles protested in his draft reply to the Commons' Remonstrance, did not lead or govern him.[282] After Villiers's death he was to reiterate the point.[283] The two men, monarch and minister, agreed on most things.[284] The king made up his own mind and found his resolutions in happy harmony with those of the duke. The parliaments (and court factions) that attacked Buckingham therefore, in Charles's eyes, not only struck in wartime at the Lord Admiral of England and the commander-in-chief of the campaign, they challenged the king himself.[285] It is the nature of his relationship with Buckingham that helps explain Charles's refusal to follow the convention that criticism of his ministers did not imply criticism of himself. Because Buckingham and Charles were inseparable, attacks on Buckingham were, for Charles, threats to monarchy.

The national rejoicing at Buckingham's assassination, then, had as powerful an effect on Charles's attitudes to his people as the Commons' impeachment of the duke had on his attitude to parlia-

277. *Ibid.*, f.53, 6 Nov. 1627.
278. Charles referred to a letter from Henrietta Maria as a 'dry, ceremonious compliment' which he had 'answered accordingly' (*ibid.*, f.60, 23 Feb. 1628).
279. *Ibid.*
280. *Ibid.*, f.37.
281. Cf. M.A. Gibb, *Buckingham 1592–1628* (1935), esp. ch. 9; and Lockyer, *Buckingham*, pp. 466–72.
282. Temple of Stowe MSS, Parliament Box 1, item 13.
283. Birch, *Court and Times of Charles I*, I, p. 359, J. Mede to M. Stuteville, 20 Sept. 1628: 'whereas it was commonly thought he ruled his Majesty, it was clear otherwise, having been his Majesty's most faithful and obedient subject in all things; as his Majesty would make hereafter sensibly appear to the world.'
284. Harleian MS 6988, f.60, 23 Feb. 1628. Charles noted that they disagreed 'but seldom'.
285. Gardiner, *History of England*, VI, pp. 99, 117. Cf. Charles's remarks on the opposition to the duke in his later 'Declaration of the Causes which led him to Dissolve Parliament', *Bibliotheca Regia, or the Royal Library* (1659), p. 414.

ments. Indeed the two were connected: John Felton, Buckingham's assassin, claimed the parliamentary Remonstrance as his inspiration and authority;[286] leading parliamentarians were connected with Felton and thinly veiled their support for his act;[287] the son of one MP, Hugh Pyne, had even proclaimed that 'it can never be well with England until there be means made that the Duke's head may be set fall from his shoulders.'[288] Charles himself clearly blamed parliament's remonstrances, their 'much endeavours to demolish him', for misleading the country into thinking that Buckingham was 'the wall of separation' between king and people.[289] After all, popular pamphlets, doggerel verse and ballads branding Buckingham a coward, an enemy to the constitution and an Arminian vulgarized what had in substance been parliamentary charges.[290] The day after his assassination Sir Francis Nethersole told the Earl of Carlisle that while 'the base multitude in this town drink healths' (and 'there are infinitely more cheerful than sad faces of better degree'), the king 'took the duke's death very heavily, keeping his chamber all that day'.[291] Buckingham's funeral, which the king had wished to mark with a monument, was characterized instead by further demonstrations of popular contempt. A correspondent related to Henry Sherfield how:

> the Hamlet soldiers with the Lieutenant of the Tower commanded to be there to accompany the hearse instead of trailing their pikes, which is ordinary upon such occasions, and that to mean men, advanced them and the drum beat a march, and before they came unto the place appointed most of them ran away without giving any volley of shot at all and so left him almost to be buried in the dark, everyone running away with his torch.[292]

In their different reactions to Buckingham's death, there is a gulf between Charles, his parliaments and his people. In some sense, it was never quite bridged thereafter.[293]

With the death of Buckingham in August 1628 there is a very real sense in which the *personal* rule of Charles I may be said to have begun. Certainly contemporaries saw it so. Within a week of the assassination

286. *Cal. Stat. Pap. Dom., 1628–9*, p. 271: letter of Viscount Dorchester, 27 Aug. 1628.
287. Sir Robert Cotton and the Earl of Arundel were both thought to be linked with Felton. K. Sharpe, *Sir Robert Cotton: History and Politics in Early Modern England* (Oxford, 1979), p. 214; Birch, *Court and Times of Charles I*, I, p. 449. Arundel was related to Felton.
288. *Cal. Stat. Pap. Dom., 1627–8*, p. 213.
289. *Bibliotheca Regia*, p. 414.
290. Huntington Library, HM 742 (songs on the Duke of Buckingham); and HM 213, f.375: 'The Coppie of the Duke's Graces most excellent Rodomontades'. Cf. the articles of impeachment in *Lords Journals*, III, pp. 593–624.
291. *Cal. Stat. Pap. Dom., 1628–9*, p. 268, 24 Aug. 1628.
292. Sherfield MS XLII: Timothy Wade to Sherfield, 26 Sept. 1628.
293. Cf. Reeve, *Charles I*, p. 36.

of the king's chief minister, the Earl of Pembroke described the sun of the commonweal emerging from the clouds: 'the king our master,' he joyfully reported to Carlisle, 'begins to shine already.'[294] Though none could deny Charles's anguish and mourning at the duke's death, Lord Percy felt sure that by early September the king's 'secundae cogitationes were more judicial and resolute'.[295] A sense of change and renewed action were articulated by others. The Venetian ambassador obviously echoed general court gossip in expecting a major change of direction.[296] The Earl of Dorset predicted that with a king excellent in 'rare virtues', 'this kingdom shall flourish notwithstanding all our last seven years unfortunate undertakings'.[297] Joseph Mede reported to Sir Martin Stuteville what was running as current news: 'The king, they say, in fourteen days after the duke's death dispatched more business than the duke had done three months before.'[298] Whatever his earlier claims concerning his independence during Buckingham's lifetime, Charles was perceived now to be emerging as master of his own affairs. Contarini wrote to the Doge and Senate of Venice that the king 'declared his intention to undertake the affairs of the government'.[299] Over the weeks and months that followed, the royal control of patronage and appointments bore him out. As Secretary Dorchester put it at the end of September, the 'total directory' was henceforth to be in Charles's own hands.[300]

Though the death of Buckingham marks in one sense the beginning of Charles I's personal rule, that is his personal direction of affairs, it did not spell the end of parliaments. On 26 June Charles did not dissolve the parliament that had assembled in March; he prorogued it to 20 October.[301] The session had ended more hastily than planned ('so suddenly' as Charles put it in his prorogation speech) on account of the Remonstrance attacking Buckingham and a proposed second remonstrance condemning the receipt of tonnage and poundage without parliamentary consent as a 'breach of the fundamental liberties of this kingdom'.[302] The Venetian ambassador thought another session was

294. *Cal. Stat. Pap. Dom., 1625–49*, p. 290, 31 Aug. 1628.
295. *Ibid.*, p. 291: Percy to Carlisle, 3 Sept. 1628.
296. *Cal. Stat. Pap. Venet., 1628–9*, p. 262: Contarini to Doge, 2 Sept. 1628.
297. *Cal. Stat. Pap. Dom., 1625–49*, p. 302: Dorset to Carlisle, 2 Nov. 1628.
298. Birch, *Court and Times of Charles I*, I, p. 396. Mede to Stuteville, 20 Sept. 1628.
299. *Cal. Stat. Pap. Venet., 1628–9*, p. 283, 12 Sept. 1628.
300. *Cal. Stat. Pap. Dom., 1628–9*, p. 339: Dorchester to Carlisle, 30 Sept. 1628.
301. *Lords Journals*, III, p. 879.
302. Gardiner, *History of England*, VI, pp. 323–5; among the papers of Henry Sherfield (Sherfield MS XXXIX, no. 19) is a 'complete' copy of the Remonstrance of 25 June (not delivered) in which the Commons explained that time prevented them from enacting various measures. 'Among other things they have taken into especial care the preparing of a bill for the granting to your Majesty such a subsidy of tonnage and poundage as might uphold the profit and revenue . . .'.

unlikely.[303] After the grant of five subsidies further supply could not be expected from another session. As we have seen, however, both Charles's words and actions indicate that he always intended to recall it; if it were not for supply we need to ask what were his other reasons. Charles was anxious to have tonnage and poundage which he had collected without statutory authority since 1625 granted for life, as was customary, by parliament.[304] Such a bill had been read in the Commons in April and Charles was concerned to see it become law.[305] He was concerned, that is, still to pursue traditional courses: to govern with the co-operation of parliaments rather than without them. There was no move to personal, non-parliamentary government in the autumn of 1628.

Indeed the death of Buckingham, some argued, facilitated the recall of parliament. If there was no doubt in June about whether to summon another session, there were considerable questions and differences within the Council about *when* it should be called. The hasty dissolution had led to widespread dissatisfaction in the localities and among the gentry. Conway advised Sir John Coke in July that 'I conceive the time to be very improper for the king to come into the country when there is like to be much clamour and not that joy and cheerfulness which should appear in the hearts and faces of the people upon his Majesty's coming amongst them.'[306] The assassination of Buckingham the following month removed a hated figure, on whose behalf two sessions of parliament had been brought to a precipitate end and presented, as some unsympathetic to the duke quickly perceived it, an opportunity to clear the air. Sir Francis Nethersole was optimistic that the duke's death had transformed the situation: 'The stone of offence being now removed by the hand of God, it is to be hoped that the king and his people will come to a perfect unity.'[307] In the weeks after Buckingham's death arguments were aired in the Council chamber concerning the timing of the next session of parliament. On 30 September Secretary Dorchester informed the Earl of Carlisle that after 'much discourse', 'the appointed time is not resolved'. Many, he wrote, 'are of opinion the present opportunity is not to be let slip' for MPs to demonstrate that 'their former distempers were rather personal than real'.[308] Others, less sure that Buckingham had been the only

303. *Cal. Stat. Pap. Venet., 1628–9*, p. 188: Contarini to Doge, 25 July 1628.
304. Russell, *Parliaments and Politics*, pp. 390, 395.
305. *Commons Debates 1628*, II, pp. 244, 296–7; III, pp. 447–8. Cf. *Cal. Stat. Pap. Dom., 1628–9*, p. 183: Nethersole to queen of Bohemia, 30 June 1628. Reeve, *Charles I*, p. 58 points to Charles's necessities but this is to miss the point that Charles sought legitimation for what he was already successfully collecting.
306. Coke MS 35, 11 July 1628; *HMC Cowper*, I, pp. 357–8.
307. *Cal. Stat. Pap. Dom., 1628–9*, p. 268: Nethersole to Carlisle, 24 Aug. 1628.
308. *Ibid.*, p. 339, 30 Sept. 1628.

issue, countered that there was need for a period of settlement and reform before another session was called in the spring. Dorchester himself saw the need to get it right: 'it imports more than anything else that the next meeting should be without the late disorders.'[309] In the end it would appear that a compromise was reached: Charles declared his intention to recall parliament on 20 January 1629. Dorchester, who favoured co-operation with parliament, was yet glad of a period of respite, thinking that 'surely . . . the wisest, for the aegritudo in men's minds requires time to take it away and the medicine of a constant and settled government is like to be applied'.[310] We shall have occasion to consider Dorchester's language. For now it is important to observe that a belief in the need for some reformation of government, the guiding principle behind the orders and proclamations of the 1630s, predates the breach with parliaments. Rather the reforms, the rectifying of 'some things both in religion and government' were intended, Sir Robert Aiton informed Carlisle, 'to sweeten things for the parliament'.[311]

A last session?

For all the difficulties of 1628, many at court, and probably Charles I himself, approached what was to be this last session of parliament with high expectations.[312] Certainly there were some attempts to defuse criticism of the government. New commissions were established to investigate abuses at court and economies were embarked upon. Though the elevation of William Laud to the see of London cannot have been popular, former enemies of Buckingham were restored to favour. Moreover, Montagu's controversial *Appello Caesarem* was called in by proclamation and Charles reissued Queen Elizabeth's injunctions with a preface forbidding disputes over contentious points of theology.[313] Laws against papists were more strictly enforced. Archbishop Abbot was recalled to his office as were the judges who had refused to support the loan.[314] Charles evidently intended to convince MPs of his commitment to traditional ways in church and state.

309. *Ibid.*
310. *Cal. Stat. Pap. Dom., 1628–9*, p. 340.
311. *Ibid.*, p. 410: Sir Robert Aiton to Carlisle, 19 Dec. 1628; *ibid.*, p. 339. The desire for reform was, of course, a recurring rhetoric, but the writer clearly had particular measures and strategies in mind.
312. See Gardiner, *History of England*, VII, p. 30.
313. *Ibid.*, pp. 21–4; *Cal. Stat. Pap. Dom., 1628–9*, pp. 346, 396, 451; Larkin, *Stuart Royal Proclamations*, II, no. 105, pp. 216–18; *Articles Agreed Upon by the Archbishops and Bishops . . . 1562*, 'reprinted by his Majesty's Commandment with his royal declaration prefixed thereunto' (1628, STC 10051).
314. *Cal. Stat. Pap. Dom., 1628–9*, p. 414; *Cal. Stat. Pap. Venet., 1628–9*, p. 563; Larkin, *Stuart Royal Proclamations*, II, no. 96, pp. 203–6. Reeve, *Charles I*, p. 62 calls these 'token measures', given the religious issues and differences, but significantly the Calvinist Dorchester was optimistic.

Some thought that he would succeed. By November the Earl of Pembroke was expressing his hopes and expectations of 'the success' of a parliament which would mark 'the beginning of the raising again of our lost honour'.[315] Just before Christmas the Venetian envoy Contarini, who had earlier doubted the news of a reassembly, reported Privy Councillors 'preparing for a good harmony'.[316] Others, however, were less optimistic that important differences could be so easily settled. On the day that Contarini wrote his dispatch, Sir George Goring, predicting that tonnage and poundage (collected without parliamentary grant) and religion would dominate the session, expressed his concern 'that all evil spirits are not laid'; Sir Francis Nethersole also feared that the Petition of Right and religion were the great businesses that jeopardized the passage of a tonnage and poundage bill.[317] There was indeed concern at the printing of the Petition with only the king's first answer and despite Charles's declaration on religious controversy, there were, as we shall see, puritans who saw the religious issue as parliament's first business.[318] If Bulstrode Whitelocke's memory is reliable there were other Privy Councillors who, doubtful of success, resolved that 'if the parliament did not pass the bill for tonnage and poundage then to break it'.[319] For all the careful preparations and high hopes, it was the doubts and reservations of the sceptics that were rapidly borne out.

This is not the place for another narrative of the session of parliament held from 20 January to only 2 March 1629. Those brief weeks have recently been the subject of several substantial accounts.[320] As Goring had predicted, the issues of tonnage and poundage and religion dominated the session and could not be resolved. Some historians have argued that they were insoluble: that the differences between Charles and his subjects over the collection of extra-parliamentary revenues and over the theology and liturgy of the Church of England were fundamental and allowed of no settlement.[321] It is important therefore to note that many contemporaries – both in and out of parliament – did not see things that way and appeared to view the session as a failure precisely because it did not reach an accommodation.

315. *Cal. Stat. Pap. Dom., 1628–9*, p. 391: Pembroke to Carlisle, 26 Nov. 1628.

316. *Cal. Stat. Pap. Venet., 1628–9*, p. 444, 22 Dec. 1628.

317. *Cal. Stat. Pap. Dom., 1628–9*, p. 413, 22 Dec. 1628; Nethersole to queen of Bohemia, 24 Jan. 1629, *ibid.*, p. 456. See J. Reeve, 'The legal status of the Petition of Right'; E.R. Foster, 'Printing the Petition of Right', *Hunt. Lib. Quart.*, 38 (1974–5), pp. 81–3.

318. A. Searle (ed.) *Barrington Family Letters 1628–1632* (Camden Soc., 4th series, 28, 1983), p. 50: Robert Barrington to Joan Barrington, 28 Jan. 1629.

319. Bulstrode Whitelocke, *Memorials of the English Affairs* (1682 edn), p. 11.

320. Most substantially, C. Thompson, 'The divided leadership of the House of Commons in 1629', in Sharpe (ed.) *Faction and Parliament*, pp. 245–84; Russell, *Parliaments and Politics*, ch. 7; and Reeve, *Charles I*, ch. 3.

321. See, for a recent example, Reeve, *Charles I*, ch. 3; or D. Berkovitz, *John Selden's Formative Years* (Washington, 1988), ch. 11, esp. pp. 227–30.

The response at court is probably predictable. On 28 February a newsletter sent to Mr Damville at Liège predicted the break-up of the parliament in terms very sympathetic to the king. 'Hitherto,' he wrote, 'the king hath the patience to suffer them to traduce their own clergy and to fall upon his officers of his customs, his lords of the Council, his judge and his counsel at law in so high a kind as if the lower house of parliament were supreme head and governor of the church, king and people.'[322] With the advice of his Privy Council, the writer added, the king had urged them to 'fall upon his business', to deal with tonnage and poundage, for with nothing in the Exchequer and as yet no peace concluded, his situation was desperate. More interesting are the comments of independent observers. Contarini for one was clearly impressed by Charles's change of tactics. 'His Majesty,' he wrote home on 9 February, 'spoke very mildly' and his 'honied words' won applause.[323] The Commons, however, proceeded very slowly.[324] By 23 February he had identified 'rigid individuals who would like to abolish all the king's prerogatives'; their religious debates he thought ill suited to a time of war.[325] In the end parliament was dissolved 'without deciding anything' and Contarini did not expect another.[326] This feeling of a lost opportunity was shared even by those who had sat in the parliament. Bishop Davenant of Salisbury could not understand why the king's explanation of his past necessity and his anxiety to have tonnage and poundage only in the legal manner did not settle the issue. 'I must needs say,' he confided to Samuel Ward, 'I verily conceived that upon the fair declaration which the king made concerning the business, it would have been presently settled to the contentment of all.'[327] As for the religious controversies and the attempts to settle a definition of orthodoxy, Davenant, though himself a Calvinist, felt the Commons achieved little. 'For the points of doctrine controverted, I see not how the House of Commons can of themselves do any good in settling of them.'[328] Davenant portrayed a session that squandered time over two issues with little result.

One cannot read the debates of the 1629 session without sharing a

322. Coke MS 36: letter to Monsieur Damville, 28 Feb. 1629; *HMC Cowper*, I, p. 380.
323. *Cal. Stat. Pap. Venet., 1628–9*, p. 528.
324. *Ibid.*, p. 536.
325. *Ibid.*, pp. 551, 566.
326. *Ibid.*, pp. 579, 584.
327. Bodleian, Tanner MS 290, f.84: Davenant to Ward, 27 Feb. 1629. Cf. *Cal. Stat. Pap. Dom., 1628–9*, p. 183: Nethersole to queen of Bohemia, 30 June 1628. Gardiner compared parliament's refusal to grant tonnage and poundage to a modern monarch's exercise of the veto (*History of England*, VII, p. 58).
328. Tanner MS 290, f.84. See below, p. 298. This may be interpreted as Davenant's usual clericism, but his letter makes clear that overall his sympathies in this session were with the king.

sense of confusion and lack of direction. As different groups in the Commons vied for the leadership and the house swung from discussions of secular concerns to religious issues, there appeared little sign of order or progress towards some conclusion. Robert Barrington expressed his frustrations at his colleagues' failure to settle on any priority: 'general wisdom I am sure justifies the rather saving the best goods than by an untimely striving for all to let fall that which is most precious.'[329] The unruly scene at the close of the parliament, when the speaker was forcibly held in his chair while Sir John Eliot passed resolutions condemning innovations in religion and payment of customs duties, epitomized the disorder and futility of the session.[330] When the Speaker had delivered the message to adjourn, many were ready to obey. But after Eliot threw down his paper desiring it be read out, 'the confederates called and cried out to have it read but some others of the house spake to the contrary. The house thereupon was much troubled, many pressing violently and tumultuously . . .'.[331] In the mêlée Coryton struck Mr Winterton, who had wanted to leave.[332] And so the parliament came to its desperate end. No bill had been passed; no definition of orthodoxy arrived at; no resolution to the tonnage and poundage issue found. It is an understatement to say that the session frustrated those at court who had prepared for it with optimism.[333] Attorney-General Heath wrote to Carlisle on 7 March: 'The untoward disposition of a few ill members of the House of Commons has given such just occasions for dissolving the parliament' that he was sad to report.[334] The sorrow and anger, however, were not confined to the court. Barrington described the fracas of 2 March as a 'distraction . . . so sudden and so great'.[335] Clarendon recalled many good men 'scandalized at those distempers'.[336] Years later in Kent gentlemen still spoke of a parliament which had been 'much to blame in their carriage towards his Majesty'.[337] Sir Simonds D'Ewes thought the cause of the dissolution 'immaterial and frivolous' and condemned

329. W. Notestein and F.H. Relf (eds) *Commons Debates for 1629* (Minneapolis, 1921), *passim*. Also Searle, *Barrington Letters*, p. 59; Thompson, 'Divided leadership'; and *HMC, 13th Report, Appendix VII*.
330. I. Fraser, 'The agitation in the Commons, 2 March 1629, and the interrogation of the leaders of the anti-court group', *Bull. Inst. Hist. Res.*, 30 (1957), pp. 86–95; Thompson, 'Divided leadership', pp. 270–84.
331. Sherfield MS XXIII, item 17 (note on charges against Sir John Eliot).
332. Sherfield MS XXIII; BL Add. MS 12511, f.76 (information in Star Chamber, May 1629).
333. See Reeve, *Charles I*, pp. 87–8.
334. *Cal. Stat. Pap. Dom., 1628–9*, p. 489.
335. Searle, *Barrington Letters*, p. 59: Sir Thomas Barrington to his mother, 2 March 1629.
336. Clarendon, *History of the Rebellion*, I, p. 84.
337. Kent Archives Office, Twysden MS U47/47 Z2, p. 108. Cf. K. Fincham, 'The judges' dicision on ship money in February 1637: the reaction in Kent', *Bull. Inst. Hist. Res.*, 57 (1984), p. 233. See below, pp. 720–21 for a discussion of this document.

'divers fiery spirits in the House of Commons' who 'were very faulty and cannot be excused'.[338] The greater and better part, he believed, would have voted tonnage and poundage and found a religious accommodation with the king.[339] Sir Thomas Roe agreed that 'the zeal of the Commons was vented with more passion than wisdom'; that instead of taking the occasion for a settlement with 'a good prince' they were 'thrust upon a good work that hath shipwrecked all'.[340] Both D'Ewes and Roe had no doubt that a parliament which had been given an opportunity had thrown it away. The 'tumultuary' day of its dissolution D'Ewes recorded in his diary as 'the most gloomy, sad and dismal day for England that happened in five hundred years'.[341] Roe made what was for him an equally sad prediction: the 'parliament doors' he accurately foresaw 'sealed for many years'.[342]

On 2 March, then, the personal rule of Charles I, the eleven years of government without parliaments, began. It was evident that the dissolution after that final violent scene had closed more than just another session. Roe's sense that it had marked 'the funeral' of parliament was shared by others. After consulting his usual sources, the Venetian ambassador judged that 'it will never reassemble during the present king's life.'[343] Though the Council was divided, Contarini felt sure that the king's mind was clear: Charles, he reported, had returned from the Lords after the dissolution in high spirits. Never partial to parliaments, he had resolved now to rule by will.[344] Before we accept that judgement, however, we should pay careful attention to Charles I's own words. On 4 March Charles issued a proclamation for the dissolution of parliament.[345] In it he made a clear distinction between the 'ill-affected' whose 'malevolent dispositions' and 'seditious carriage' had wrecked the parliament and the 'greater number of sober and grave persons' desirous of unity. A week later Charles issued a fuller declaration of the causes which led him to dissolve the assembly, in which he defended his right to take tonnage and poundage and underlined the reforms he had enacted in preparation for a harmonious

338. J.O. Halliwell (ed.) *The Autobiography and Correspondence of Sir Simonds D'Ewes* (2 vols, 1845), I, p. 402.
339. *Ibid.*, p. 403. Cf. A. Ar., *The Practise of Princes* (1630, STC 722), p. 7: 'I know some lay great fault in the knights and burgesses for delaying the grant of the subsidy of tonnage and poundage considering the king's wants'.
340. L.J. Reeve, 'Sir Thomas Roe's prophecy of 1629', *Bull. Inst. Hist. Res.*, 56 (1983), pp. 120–1. In *Charles I* (p. 112), Dr Reeve plays down Roe's criticism of the MPs. This seems a less persuasive reading of Roe's words.
341. D'Ewes, *Autobiography*, I, p. 402.
342. Reeve, 'Sir Thomas Roe', p. 121; PRO, SP 16/139/21: letter of Roe to Lord Vere, 20 March 1629.
343. *Cal. Stat. Pap. Venet., 1628–9*, p. 584.
344. *Ibid.*, pp. 580–1, 584; Reeve, *Charles I*, pp. 99–100; Gardiner, *History of England*, VII, p. 78.
345. Larkin, *Stuart Royal Proclamations*, II, no. 108, pp. 223–4.

parliament.[346] The king's frustrations, his sense that aggressive inroads had been made on his authority, come over strongly. Over the years the Commons by setting up committees had sought to extend their jurisdiction; now they claimed to bind the judges and question Councillors, swelling, the king put it, 'beyond the rules of moderation'.[347] Yet for all this characterization, Charles reaffirmed that he did not impute the disruption to the whole house, 'knowing that there were amongst them many religious, grave and well-minded men'.[348] The distinctions made in these two declarations provide the important context for reading Charles's proclamation for suppressing false rumours concerning parliament, published on 27 March.[349] For the central thrust of that proclamation was the separation of Sir John Eliot and his faction ('an outlawed man, desperate in mind and fortune') from 'the wisest and best affected' who had disavowed his propositions.[350] Amid the stop of trade by merchants who followed Eliot's injunction to refuse tonnage and poundage, and rumours about the possibility of a parliament, Charles issued a statement of intent.[351] 'We have showed,' Charles reminded, 'by our frequent meeting with our people our love to the use of parliaments.'[352] The late abuses had driven him 'unwillingly' out of that course. But 'we shall be more inclinable to meet in parliament again,' the king announced, 'when our people shall see more clearly into our intents and actions, when such as have bred this interruption shall have received their condign punishment and those who are misled by them . . . shall come to a better understanding of us and themselves.'[353]

The proclamation made it clear that no parliament was to meet imminently, but it was not a renunciation of parliamentary government.[354] Far from being a new norm, a period of government without parliaments was seen as an 'interruption' to usual courses. Events had

346. *Bibliotheca Regia*, pp. 394–417.
347. *Ibid.*, p. 409.
348. *Ibid.*, p. 415.
349. Larkin, *Stuart Royal Proclamations*, II, no. 110, pp. 226–8. Here I dissent from Reeve (*Charles I*, p. 105) who, dismissing Charles's own words, argues 'The king had come to accuse the *entire* House of Commons' (my italics).
350. Larkin, *Stuart Royal Proclamations*, II, p. 227; cf. the language used in the trial: BL Add. MS 12511, f.76ff.
351. Gardiner, *History of England*, VII, pp. 81–3; Reeve, *Charles I*, pp. 109–12; W.J. Jones, *Politics and the Bench: The Judges and the Origins of the Civil War* (1971), pp. 75–6.
352. Larkin, *Stuart Royal Proclamations*, II, p. 228.
353. *Ibid.*
354. Dr Reeve argues that the conciliatory words were added 'almost certainly at Dorchester's suggestion' (*Charles I*, p. 11). There is no need, however, to believe that they did not reflect Charles's own beliefs faithfully; they certainly concurred with his practice. And for some evidence that Dorchester was fully behind the need for 'condign punishment' of the MPs, see his letter to Oliver Fleming of 3 March 1630 (*Cal. Stat. Pap. Dom., 1629–31*, p. 203).

shown that time was needed still to dispel what Dorchester, who helped draft the proclamation, had described as a mental disturbance in the body politic.[355] That is evidently how the situation was regarded in court circles. Lord Poulet felt sure that given time the people would become sensible of the happiness they enjoyed under Charles's government.[356] By May, Bishop John Williams was expressing his pleasure that the merchants were returning to their trade and 'ad saniorem mentem'.[357] But the mistrust and miscomprehension of the government, acknowledged by the king himself, could not be denied. The elderly Lionel Sharpe told Dorchester of the distance between Charles and his subjects.[358] Lord Poulet and the archbishop of York referred to 'fatal misapprehensions' of alterations;[359] Clarendon recalled an 'opinion . . . that there was really an intention to alter the form of government both in church and state'.[360] A libel pinned to Paul's Cross in May claimed that the king had lost the hearts of his people.[361] If the fears, the mists of misunderstanding, were to be dispelled, not only was a considerable time to pass, much was to be done. The Council had drawn up a memorandum of bills that had failed to become acts.[362] Heath, early in the year, outlined a set of reform propositions by enacting which 'there will be no doubt but his sacred Majesty as he is already by his good subjects shall be both loved, honoured and feared. And the aggravations of fears and jealousy will be soon dispelled.'[363] The personal rule commenced not just with the dissolution of a parliament, but with a sense of the need for reforms in church and state to support government and secure harmony. As Heath put it on 7 March: 'Now is the time to put brave and noble resolutions into acts' that the people may see more clearly 'his Majesty's religion and just government'.[364]

Personal rule

After four years on the throne, the prince bred up in parliaments had resolved to govern for a time without them. Recently historians have

355. Above, p. 52.
356. *Cal. Stat. Pap. Dom., 1628–9*, p. 557: Poulet to Dorchester, 24 May 1629.
357. *Ibid.*, p. 537. On the prevalence of the medical metaphor, see below, pp. 61–2.
358. *Cal. Stat. Pap. Dom., 1628–9*, pp. 541–2: L. Sharpe to Dorchester, 8 May 1629.
359. Wentworth Woodhouse MS 12/104: Archbishop Harsnett to Wentworth, 9 March 1630; *Cal. Stat. Pap. Dom., 1628–9*, p. 557.
360. Clarendon, *History of the Rebellion*, I, p. 84.
361. *Cal. Stat. Pap. Dom., 1628–9*, p. 550; PRO, SP 16/142/92, 93, 17 May 1629, endorsed by Laud.
362. Bodleian, Bankes MS 22/1–2; Russell, *Parliaments and Politics*, pp. 405–6.
363. PRO, SP 16/178/3; L.J. Reeve, 'Sir Robert Heath's advice to Charles I in 1629', *Bull. Inst. Hist. Res.*, 59 (1986), pp. 215–24.
364. *Cal. Stat. Pap. Dom., 1628–9*, p. 489: Heath to Carlisle, 7 March 1629.

again argued that the breakdown in relations was the consequence of Charles's implementation of 'new politics' in the government of church and state, and of an inherent aversion to parliaments. But the king's decision was not the natural consequence of an autocratic temperament nor the outcome of a careful plan or programme.[365] It had been taken, he put it, 'unwillingly'. Let us then reconsider why Charles was led to what he described as an 'interruption' of the normal courses of government in March 1629.[366] The failure of parliamentary supply is crucial to the answer. As we have seen, Charles blamed the failure of supply for military defeats, the loss of national and personal honour and for the impossible difficulties faced by his friend, the Duke of Buckingham. A calculation of the sums raised by extra-parliamentary levies, notably the loan, and the relative speed of its collection must also have raised questions about the value of parliamentary subsidies – especially if they had to be bought by a renunciation of other fiscal benefits or measures. Disarmingly, Sir John Holles himself acknowledged that 'the way by privy seals and benevolence is so easy and that of parliaments so conditional'.[367] As Conrad Russell observed, rather than pondering whether he could afford to govern without parliaments, Charles must have questioned whether he could afford to rule with them.[368]

Yet the figures and calculations do not get to the heart of the matter. The king called parliaments frequently between 1625 and 1629 because he then believed it customary to consult with the community of the realm in time of emergency or war.[369] To Charles those parliaments failed to meet their responsibility and so undermined his capacity to fulfil his royal obligation to protect the realm. During the period 1626 to 1629 we hear increasingly a new language: the language of necessity, and of public safety contrasted with private interests. Such language informed instructions to subsidy commissioners to assess their neighbours responsibly; it prefaced the letter sent by Charles to JPs justifying the loan.[370] 'No ordinary rules,' the king proclaimed, 'can prescribe law to necessity . . . the common defence and safety and even the very subsistence of the whole might justly warrant us.'[371]

365. See Cust, *The Forced Loan*; Reeve, *Charles I, passim*. Also see below, pp. 193–6, 705, on the issues of Charles's autocratic temperament and attitude to parliament.
366. Larkin, *Stuart Royal Proclamations*, II, p. 228. The importance of the king's use of this word cannot be overestimated.
367. Seddon, *Letters of John Holles*, I, p. lxiii.
368. Russell, 'Parliamentary history in perspective', pp. 14–16; *idem*, 'The nature of a parliament', p. 144; *idem*, *Parliaments and Politics*, pp. 49–53; and Dietz, *English Public Finance*, II, p. 246.
369. Russell, 'The nature of a parliament', pp. 145–6, 148.
370. *Acts of the Privy Council, July 1628 to April 1629*, pp. 377–8.
371. Hastings MS 1340.

Necessity, his secretary of state argued, 'to preserve the whole dissolveth the parts and this necessity concerned the safety of the whole kingdom'.[372] It was this extraordinary threat to the very existence of the state, and a powerful sense of his duty to defend the commonweal which, more than an autocratic temperament, led Charles to personal rule. For, as he saw it, those MPs who granted inadequate supplies or raised scruples about extraordinary levies in such circumstances were oblivious to necessity: they preferred their private interests and purses to the public good.[373] Though this was a selective view of recent events, it was not an unreasonable one. Moreover, many who did not concur with Charles's policies, shared his frustration with parliaments.

In 1628 the puritan satirist George Wither castigated his countrymen:

War threatens us, and we of want complaine,
Not knowing how our safeties to maintaine:
Yet we do nothing want that may conduce
In warre or peace, to serve a needfull use
Armes, victualls, men and money, we have store;
Yet shall we falsely cry that we are poore
We are so greedy that we will not spare
To save the hogge, one farthing worth of tarre.[374]

Whilst his subjects pursued, as Charles saw it, their private interests, they unkinged the monarch upon whom God had placed the responsibility for protection of his people. Few monarchs have had a greater sense of their duty and accountability to God than Charles I. The defence of the realm was a duty 'we are tied to do by that bond of sovereignty which under God we bear over you'.[375]

It is in the context of Charles's belief that parliaments were threatening his fulfilment of his duty to his people that the debates on the liberty of the subject in 1628 should be read. The king's willingness to declare that he would uphold the law *and* his insistence on the right to imprison without cause shown were neither contradictory positions nor sleight of hand.[376] To Charles such extra-legal powers, the prerogative, were essential for the preservation of the common good. Wither again took the point:

They who deny the king free pow'r to do
What his Republikes weal conduceth to

372. *Cal. Stat. Pap. Dom., 1625–49*, p. 244.
373. PRO, SP 16/138/45. I am grateful to Richard Cust for a transcript of this document.
374. G. Wither, *Britain's Remembrancer* (1628, STC 25899), f.239. Wither's remarks are all the more forceful coming from a figure sometimes labelled an 'opposition poet'. I am preparing a paper on this important work.
375. Larkin, *Stuart Royal Proclamations*, II, no. 55, p. 111.
376. As Gardiner acknowledged, *History of England*, VI, p. 248.

Because some law gainsayes; ev'n those deprive
Their Sov'raigne of a due prerogative;
Since for the common good it just may be
That some injustice may be done to me.[377]

Eliot's attempts to stop the collection of tonnage and poundage threatened in the midst of war to deprive the king of a revenue specifically given for the defence of the seas, a 'thing', as he put it, 'I cannot want', 'one of the direct maintenances of the crown'.[378] When Charles controversially recalled the printed copies of the Petition of Right with his second answer and reissued it with his first, it was because he feared that further 'interpretation' of what he had assented to would threaten his very capacity to govern.[379] As Sir James Bagg had warned at the time of Eliot's petition against the loan, Magna Carta was 'now made a chain to bind the king from doing anything'. That was to expose the realm to all evils, 'to admit the rascal to everything'.[380]

The failure of parliament was not the only threat to the stability of the country during the late 1620s. Attempts to raise and equip troops had exposed serious flaws in local government and in the Council's capacity to enforce its orders. Once again the language of official documents betrays a fear of the collapse of authority: the directions of the state were 'commonly received as matters of form only'.[381] In the localities private interests were a canker that was rotting the commonweal – part of the illness that Dorchester and others diagnosed in the ailing state. A sense of weakness and decline, the consequence of military failure and domestic tension, pervades the political literature of 1628 and 1629. The author of *The Spy* feared 'All symptoms of a kingdom that hath beene/Declining long may be in England seen.'[382] Wither felt that 'The world against our state doth now conspire/ Intestine dangers too.'[383] Both, for all their different diagnoses, called for unity and reform at home as the necessary condition of renown abroad.[384] The personal rule began amid a sense at court as well as in the country of the need for the 'medicine of a constant and settled government'.[385] As Bishop Harsnett put it to Sir Henry Vane: 'The

377. Wither, *Britain's Remembrancer*, f.236v.
378. *Lords Journals*, III, p. 879.
379. *Bibliotheca Regia*, pp. 395–6; Jones, *Politics and the Bench*, p. 74; E.R. Foster, 'Printing the Petition of Right', pp. 81–3.
380. *Cal. Stat. Pap. Dom., 1627–8*, p. 473: J. Bagg to Buckingham, 20 Dec. 1627.
381. PRO, SO 1/1/173v.
382. Russell, *The Spy*, sig.E.2.
383. Wither, *Britain's Remembrancer*, f.236; cf. ff.219–20.
384. So Wither 'we in concord should united be/And to supply the kingdomes wants agree' (f.236).
385. *Cal. Stat. Pap. Dom., 1628–9*, p. 340. From very different perspectives, several writers associated the plague and military failure with the social and political ills of the realm.

gallant ancient composition of our glorious state is much declined and is like a body without blood and sinews. How the vital spirit should be restored, hic labor, hic opus est.'[386] It was a labour and work to which the king and Council were to devote themselves for a decade.

See, for example, A.Ar., *Practise of Princes*, p. 19; H. Burton, *The Christian's Bulwark Against Satan's Battery* (1630, STC 4140), p. 3; R. Bernard, *The Bible-Battells* (1629, STC 1926); W. Prynne, *The Church of England's Old Antithesis to New Arminianism* (1629, STC 20457), sig. C2v; J. Dyke, *A Sermon Preached at the Publick Fast to the Commons House of Parliament, April 5th 1628* (1628, STC 7424), p. 19. The combination of circumstances and attitudes recalls the situation in Spain described in J.H. Elliott, 'Self-perception and decline in early seventeenth century Spain', *P&P*, 74 (1977), pp. 41–61. I am very grateful to John Elliott for stimulating discussions of these comparisons.

386. *Cal. Stat. Pap. Dom., 1629–31*, p. 167.

PART II

'THE MEDICINE OF A SETTLED GOVERNMENT': PEACE AND REFORMATION 1629–35

II
PAX CAROLANA: PEACE AND DIPLOMACY

The treaties with France and Spain

The first priority of personal rule was peace. In 1629 England was still at war with the two mightiest nations in Europe, with an empty Exchequer and massive debt. Even with parliamentary subsidies it had not proved possible to sustain the war. Without parliamentary supply it could not be continued. In February 1629, as Charles's last parliament procrastinated over a grant of tonnage and poundage, a newswriter reported 'it is hoped [the king] will think no more of war until he have his people in better order'.[1] Moves towards peace with France had commenced in the summer of 1628; with the capitulation of La Rochelle in October there was little left to fight for.[2] England had drifted into war, not least as a consequence of the Duke of Buckingham's personal quarrels with Cardinal Richelieu. The death of the favourite in August further reduced the friction between the nations whilst the close relationship that developed between Charles and his wife almost immediately after Buckingham's death facilitated negotiations. Henrietta Maria's pregnancy, it was said in January 1629, allayed the king's fury with France and made him 'very forward to have a peace'.[3] Privy Councillors sympathetic to France and attached to the queen, the Earl of Holland for example, and Scottish courtiers such as Hamilton, as well as those anxious to continue the war against Spain, pressed for a settlement.[4] For his part Richelieu, embroiled as a

1. Melbourne Hall, Coke MS 36: letter to Monsieur Damville, 28 Feb. 1629; cf. *Calendar of State Papers Venetian* [*Cal. Stat. Pap. Venet.*], *1628–9*, p. 581.
2. S.R. Gardiner, *History of England from the Accession of James I to the Outbreak of the Civil War 1603–1642* (10 vols, 1883–4), VI, pp. 361–70.
3. Coke MS 36: letter to Damville, 10 Jan. 1629; calendared in *HMC Cowper*, I, p. 378.
4. Coke MS 37: letter to Damville, 5 June 1629; *HMC Cowper*, I. p. 386.

consequence of the Mantuan succession crisis with Spain in Italy, was no less anxious for peace, and if possible desired an English alliance. Richelieu had forwarded propositions for a peace in October, during the last days of the siege of La Rochelle.[5] The question of the Huguenots delayed progress during the winter. In February 'the high carriage' of the French king, and his insistence on the performance of the marriage articles, was said to be threatening a settlement.[6] But with the king and queen in domestic harmony, and the Venetian ambassador mediating, negotiations reached a successful conclusion in a treaty of peace signed at Susa on 14 April and published in England a month later.[7] In England the treaty was generally welcomed;[8] in France 'the king and cardinal rejoiced about it without ceasing'.[9] Charles was forced to abandon the Huguenots, who were granted toleration in the Grâce de Alais.[10] Otherwise nothing was lost: Louis XIII did not insist on toleration for Catholics and, as it turned out, the queen's household servants, dismissed in 1626, were never re-established despite the terms of the marriage treaty.[11] For all England's weakness, France had too many other ambitions and divisions to prolong conflict in the Channel, and was especially anxious – be it by alliance or neutrality – to keep Charles from the bosom of the Habsburgs.[12]

With Spain, the problems were greater. Charles's sense of wounded honour had initiated the conflict and so reoriented the course of English foreign policy. And the war had been proclaimed as a campaign for the recovery of the Palatinate. On both counts this was a war which it was more difficult to conclude, and it is evident that it was some time before Charles became inclined to peace. Despite Buckingham's initiation of peace feelers, there are indications that the king was less enthusiastic.[13] In November 1628 Sir Robert Anstruther was sent to promise aid to Denmark against the Habsburgs. In

5. *Calendar of State Papers Domestic* [*Cal. Stat. Pap. Dom*] *1628–9*, p. 345; PRO, SP 16/118/28: propositions for peace from Richelieu, Oct. 1628.
6. Coke MS 36: letter to Damville, Feb. 1629.
7. Gardiner, *History of England*, VII, pp. 99–100; *Cal. Stat. Pap. Venet., 1628–9*, pp. 266, 273, 308, 313. L.J. Reeve, *Charles I and the Road to Personal Rule* (Cambridge, 1989), pp. 51–2. Also *The Articles of Peace Agreed upon Betwixt the two Crowns of Great Britain and of France*, published in both languages in 1629 (STC 9250).
8. Coke MS 36: letter to Damville, 5 June 1629.
9. *Cal. Stat. Pap. Venet., 1629–32*, p. 34: dispatch of Soranzo and Zorzi, ambassadors in France to Doge, 28 April 1629.
10. Even Dorchester 'had not wished the Huguenots to obstruct the treaty' (Reeve, *Charles I*, p. 51).
11. Gardiner, *History of England*, VII, p. 100. For the terms of the marriage treaty, see Huntington Library MS, HM 82.
12. PRO 31/3/65, f. 131; Coke MS 37: letter to Monsieur Damville, 5 June 1629; H. Lonchay (ed.) *Correspondance de la cour d'Espagne sur les affaires de Pays Bas au XVII siècle*, Vol. II (Brussels, 1927), p. 459: Rubens to Olivares, 30 June 1629.
13. *Cal. Stat. Pap. Venet., 1628–9*, p. 195; Gardiner, *History of England*, VI, p. 333.

December the appointment as secretary of Dudley Carleton, a champion of the Spanish war, lends strength to the suggestion that Charles had not abandoned it.[14] A correspondent reporting to Mr Damville the moves towards peace in January 1629 wrote that the king's 'heart is not quite of it', and that he was 'cold in that business'.[15] Whatever the king's heart and temperature, the war could not be sustained, especially after the dissolution of parliament in March. At least the bitter pill of necessity was sweetened. Spanish defeats in the Low Countries removed any Habsburg threat to England.[16] They also prompted the Archduchess Isabella to 'sweet carriage' towards England, 'which gained much upon the king's disposition'.[17] There was no doubting the desperate need for peace in Antwerp and Madrid. Isabella informed Philip IV of the mounting difficulties she faced in fighting the Dutch war.[18] From Spain the Venetian envoy reported that 'peace with England is so necessary to them that they would pay any price for it'.[19]

The price that Charles hoped to extract was the restoration of his sister and brother-in-law for which, in large part, the war had been waged. In May Isabella, making an astute choice of her envoy to a connoisseur king, dispatched Peter Paul Rubens to Charles I to negotiate for a peace with England and, through English mediation, with the Dutch.[20] In June, on receiving Rubens's proposals, Charles consulted with his Treasurer, Weston, and the Earl of Pembroke.[21] The outcome was a decision to involve in the negotiations the Chancellor of the Exchequer, Sir Francis Cottington, a known Hispanophile and former envoy to Spain. Court gossips read Cottington's departure for Madrid as a sure indicator of an imminent peace, 'a very great sign of our good meaning here . . . otherwise he would not so willingly undergo the employment'.[22] Charles's 'good meaning', however, was not yet a capitulation. Rubens was informed by Cottington that England was insisting that Spain surrender its fortresses in the Palatinate, and use its offices to pressure the emperor and Bavaria to restore theirs.[23] So instructed, Cottington departed in the autumn.[24]

14. Gardiner, *History of England*, VI, p. 372; Reeve, *Charles I*, pp. 53–7. On the significance of Dorchester's appointment, see *ibid.*, p. 40.
15. Coke MS 36: letter to Monsieur Damville, 10 Jan. 1629; *HMC Cowper I*, p. 378.
16. Reeve, *Charles I*, p. 239; J.H. Elliott, *The Count Duke of Olivares* (New Haven and London, 1986), pp. 357–8, 365, 379.
17. Coke MS 36: letter to Damville, Feb. 1629.
18. Lonchay, *Correspondance*, II, p. 452, 3 June 1629.
19. *Cal. Stat. Pap. Venet., 1629–32*, p. 145: Mocenigo to Doge, 28 July 1629; cf. Elliott, *Olivares*, pp. 368–9, 394.
20. Reeve, *Charles I*, pp. 238, 242–3.
21. Coke MS 36: letter to Damville, 5 June 1629; *HMC Cowper I*, p. 387.
22. Coke MS 37: letter to Damville, 26 June 1629.
23. Gardiner, *History of England*, VII, p. 103.
24. *Cal. Stat. Pap. Venet., 1629–32*, p. 163.

It was not a hopeless mission. In December, shortly after Cottington's arrival, the Venetian ambassador in Spain, Mocenigo, reported that Philip IV had informed the emperor of his intention to surrender the Lower Palatinate; he believed that Spain genuinely wished to see England satisfied.[25] The rub was the interests of the Duke of Bavaria, who occupied the Upper Palatinate and the Electoral dignity. If Olivares was to risk alienating allies in the empire, he needed peace not only with England but with the Dutch.[26] Cottington became convinced that there was scant hope of incorporating the Palatinate and saw his embassy as aborted.[27] In England, the Spanish agent Coloma was urging that peace precede any settlement of the Palatine's affairs, arguing that Spain could not bind itself to war against Bavaria and the emperor if they did not restore the lands and dignity.[28] Failing to draw imperial ambassadors to treat with Cottington at Madrid, Olivares could only offer to refer all to the forthcoming diet at Ratisbon [Regenuburg] at which he would promise Spanish intercession.[29] By April negotiations had reached an impasse. During the summer there were rumours of an interim truce, but by August it was clear that England had renounced its insistence on restitution as a precondition of peace.[30] The fate of the Palatinate now rested on Spain's vague promises of assistance. The alternatives were to accept it or go to war.[31] Charles was not inclined to war; neither the French nor the Dutch would commit themselves to a war for the Palatinate.[32] On 5 November a treaty of peace between England and Spain was signed in Madrid.[33] The treaty made no reference to the settlement of the Palatinate, which now rested on a mutual understanding worked out between Cottington and Olivares. In return for English pressure on the Dutch to make peace with Spain, Spain would work for Frederick's restitution. If the Dutch proved unwilling to come to terms, Cottington, probably acting more on his own initiative than on direct instructions, proposed an offensive alliance with Spain against them in return for the Palatinate.[34] With these vague promises and secret agreements known to few, the Peace of Madrid, ending five years of war, was published in England on 5 December.

25. *Ibid.*, p. 253: dispatch of 15 Dec. 1629; *ibid.*, p. 307; 30 Dec. 1629.
26. *Ibid.*, p. 307.
27. *Ibid.*, p. 327: Soranzo to Doge, 26 April 1630; PRO, SP 94/34, f.169.
28. *Cal. Stat. Pap. Venet., 1629–32*, pp. 327–8.
29. Gardiner, *History of England*, VII, p. 173; Reeve, *Charles I*, p. 250.
30. *Cal. Stat. Pap. Venet., 1629–32*, p. 357.
31. Reeve, *Charles I*, p. 250.
32. Gardiner, *History of England*, VII, p. 172.
33. PRO, SP 16/175/23; *Articles of Peace, Entercourse and Commerce . . . in a Treaty at Madrid* (1630, STC 9251).
34. *Cal. Stat. Pap. Venet., 1629–32*, pp. 439, 449; Gardiner, *History of England*, VII, pp. 172–3; Reeve, *Charles I*, ch. 7, esp. pp. 253–4.

Most historians have seen the peace with France and Spain as marking the end of any effective English role in Europe. Without parliaments, it is said, England could not afford a foreign policy. Gardiner characterized the 1630s as a return to the era of James I and Gondomar, to years of 'futile diplomacy'.[35] Dr Reeve is even harsher: Charles I, he claims, 'showed no . . . aptitude for politics abroad'; he 'could cut no ice' in Europe.[36] It is far from clear however that the treaties of 1629 and 1630 rendered England less effective than had her participation in war; and far from certain that the option of renewed conflict had been closed. Though envoys commented on Charles's and Weston's reluctance to call a parliament as an obstacle to English military engagement, the French and Venetians took the view that, in terms of war finance, subsidies were of limited significance.[37] Charles himself evidently did not equate the dissolution of parliament with a necessity for peace. The continuation of the committee for war and commissions for the manufacture of saltpetre suggest that the possibility of war was not discounted.[38] The history of Caroline diplomacy bears out that suggestion. It is not a story of disengagement from Europe; still less did England chart its course as a 'satellite of Spain'.[39] Though Charles maintained good relations with Spain, he simultaneously negotiated with and offered favours to her enemies and he remained receptive to proposals for anti-Habsburg leagues that might restore the Palatinate by force.[40] Often, it is true, such negotiations were intended to put pressure on Olivares. But the events of 1636–7, when Charles signed a treaty with France that would have aligned England against the Habsburgs, demonstrate that they were always more than a diplomatic bluff.[41] Indeed, for all their sense of England's impoverishment, the ambassadors of Europe, of Spain, France, Sweden and the Netherlands never dismissed England as lightly as have historians. Between 1628 and 1641 nearly one hundred ministers came to Whitehall to offer alliances and propositions.[42] For all England's incapacity to mount a major campaign, she had, as they recognized, a navy which could – as events were to show – facilitate or obstruct communications in the Channel and North Sea that were crucial to

35. Gardiner, *History of England*, VII, ch. 70.
36. Reeve, *Charles I*, pp. 227, 229; see p. 256 for a verdict that rings with Gardiner's nineteenth-century values.
37. For example, PRO, 31/3/66, f.241; PRO, 31/3/68, ff.114–17; *Cal. Stat. Pap. Venet., 1629–32*, p. 177; PRO, 31/3/66, f.231.
38. *Acts of the Privy Council, June 1630 to June 1631*, pp. 110, 369; *Cal. Stat. Pap. Dom., 1631–3*, p. 81.
39. Reeve, *Charles I*, p. 256.
40. *Cal. Stat. Pap. Venet., 1629–32*, pp. 163, 438.
41. Below, pp. 525–30.
42. A.J. Loomie (ed.) *Ceremonies of Charles I: The Note Books of John Finet, Master of Ceremonies 1628–1641* (New York, 1987), p. 4.

France, Spain, Flanders and Holland.[43] Ambassadors came, negotiated, manoeuvred and eyed each other anxiously because English neutrality could never be completely relied upon and because none of the major powers could afford to have England join their enemies. As the navy was strengthened in 1634 and especially from 1635 by ship money, England's importance in Europe became the greater and diplomatic activity involving her more feverish. When in 1630, then, Charles signed a peace, he did not remove England from glorious war to pusillanimous isolationism, he continued to pursue by diplomacy what he had failed to secure through conflict: the security and prosperity of England and the restitution of the Palatinate.

England and Spain 1630–5

Until 1635 Charles focused his hopes on Spain. Though he had been unable to secure the Palatinate in advance of the Peace of Madrid, Charles believed he had a firm understanding with Philip IV that Spain would work for its restitution. The object of diplomatic relations with Spain from the signing of the treaty was to translate that understanding into effective action. Cottington's last act before departing for England was to sign a secret treaty for the partition of the Netherlands, if the Dutch could not be brought to peace.[44] His secretary, Arthur Hopton, remained as England's agent to oversee the Spanish side of the bargain which Cottington had worked out with Olivares. On 5 February 1631 Hopton was sent his formal instructions: 'You are to observe that this peace is . . . principally grounded upon a promise conceived in writing and signed by the king of Spain for restitution and satisfaction to be procured and given unto the Prince Palatine now the King of Bohemia.'[45] Hopton was told to press for the performance of that promise and to co-ordinate with Anstruther in Vienna and Balthazar Gerbier in Brussels in a triangle of negotiations with the house of Habsburg. In his early dispatches he found cause for optimism: 'I conceive,' he wrote to Cottington, 'his Majesty's friendship is so much desired and so necessary for this crown.'[46] He professed himself 'in great hope that his Majesty may see his days crowned with the blessing of settling that business'.[47] Other envoys concurred that for the value of English assistance Spain would willingly yield the Palatinate; and

43. See, for example, the instructions of Châteauneuf (PRO, 31/3/65, f.117). The Battle of the Downs in 1639 was to bring the point home.
44. Reeve, *Charles I*, pp. 256–7; Bodleian, Clarendon MS 5, nos 294, 295. Cf. Charles's comments to the Spanish ambassador (Gardiner, *History of England*, VII, p. 177).
45. British Library [BL] Egerton MS 1820, ff.1v–2: instructions to Hopton, 5 Feb. 1631.
46. *Ibid.*, ff.42v–43, dispatch of 15 June 1631.
47. *Ibid.*, f.43.

Philip IV said so himself in a letter to the abbé Scaglia, his agent in Brussels.[48] The obvious obstacle to the total restoration of Frederick the Elector's estates was the Duke of Bavaria to whom the emperor had granted the Upper Palatinate in return for military assistance against the Bohemian rebels. But 'neither the interests nor opinions' of Spain, Hopton believed, 'have ever been in favour of the duke of Bavaria'.[49] For in so far as Bavaria stood in the way of peace, he threatened Spanish interests in the Netherlands which were at the centre of Olivares's concerns. Hopton came to trust in Olivares's sincerity. The two men evidently became close; they discussed religious differences and Olivares dropped formality to talk to Hopton even from his bed.[50] Hopton gained confidence 'both by the Condé's words as also by his manner of speaking (wherein he discovers his inclination as much as any man) that he is very thorough in his desire to give his Majesty satisfaction.'[51] The envoy had only one cautionary reservation: the interests of Spain, he pointed out, were in Flanders not Germany. Where the Palatinate was concerned action must emanate from Vienna; only words could come from Madrid.[52]

During the winter of 1631, however, Hopton became less optimistic. From Vienna, Anstruther wrote casting doubts on Spain's sincerity;[53] the transport of troops from the Low Countries to the Lower Palatinate confirmed growing suspicions of Spain's unwillingness to surrender its fortresses there.[54] Hopton began to see that the delays blamed on the emperor proceeded as much from Spain.[55] Talk of a future treaty between Spain and the emperor, the newswriter John Pory put it, 'for the King of Bohemia's profit may be concluded ad Calendas Graecas'.[56] In Madrid, Hopton felt the diplomatic climate chill. Olivares was personally cool, claiming English aid to the Swedes and Dutch disrupted the prospects of settlement.[57] In December he put the situation starkly to the English envoy: 'Let the King of Great Britain, said he, make us a good peace in Flanders, or let him make a general peace in Germany and let him take the Palatinate with a good will.'[58] Otherwise Spain had to look more to its friends in Germany than to

48. *Cal. Stat. Pap. Venet., 1629–32*, pp. 307, 500; and Lonchay, *Correspondance*, p. 579, 22 May 1631.
49. Egerton MS 1820, f.50, 11 July 1631.
50. *Ibid.*, ff.59v, 126v.
51. *Ibid.*, f.59v.
52. *Ibid.*, ff.65v (12 Oct. 1631), 70v (2 Nov. 1631).
53. *Ibid.*, f.81.
54. Gardiner, *History of England*, VII, p. 187; T. Birch (ed.) *The Court and Times of Charles I* (2 vols, 1848), II. p. 142: J. Pory to T. Puckering, 17 Nov. 1631.
55. Egerton MS 1820, f.104v, 1 Dec. 1631.
56. Birch, *Court and Times of Charles I*, II, p. 142.
57. Egerton MS 1820, f.115, 20 Dec. 1631.
58. *Ibid.*, f.109, 10 Dec. 1631.

England. The position, though far from encouraging, was not devoid of hope. In Spanish eyes there was something of vital importance that Charles could offer. The Dutch, Hopton rightly discerned, were 'the thorn that pricks them most of all others and for which they have no hope left but by his Majesty's credit and power'.[59] It was not an unreasonable assessment of the position. As Geoffrey Parker has pointed out, the hand of the Dutch was found to be behind every anti-Habsburg coalition.[60] Gustavus Adolphus's victories in Germany cut off prospects of imperial assistance and of a general peace. Spanish defeats in the Low Countries, culminating in the loss of Maastricht to the Dutch in the summer of 1632, brought the war to a crisis which threatened revolt and the secession of Flanders from Spain.[61] Olivares, through the embassy of the abbot of Scaglia, endeavoured to secure English aid to Germany and against the Dutch in return for the surrender of the Lower Palatinate.[62] He was pressing, that is, for the enactment of the secret treaty proferred by Cottington. As he went to successive audiences with the Condé Ducque at which allusions to such a deal were made, even Hopton was ignorant of the precise nature of that arrangement.[63]

In the winter of 1632, two events dominated diplomatic negotiations. The death of Frederick, the Elector Palatine, and the succession of his son, Charles's nephew, re-emphasized the urgent need to settle the Palatinate and increased Charles's responsibility for the Palatines. As the newswriter John Pory put it, 'upon that king's death our king and state are obliged to do more for a nephew than for a brother in law and more likewise for a widow than a wife'.[64] Cottington felt that it should be easier to restore the young Charles Louis who was not, like his father, tainted with the crime of rebellion against the emperor.[65] The month of Frederick's death, however, was also marked by an event of greater import. In November, Gustavus Adolphus, King of Sweden, was killed at the battle of Lutzen. Though the victory had been the Swedes', the loss of their brilliant and charismatic general who had become the champion of the Protestant cause in Europe rallied Habsburg spirits and, for the moment, eased their difficulties. Hopton

59. *ibid.*, f.139v, 12 Feb. 1632.
60. G. Parker, *The Thirty Years War* (1984), p. 103.
61. Gardiner, *History of England*, VII, p. 209.
62. *Ibid.*, VII, p. 190; Egerton MS 1820, ff.115, 176.
63. See Egerton MS 1820, ff.68, 313v. Windebank did not put Hopton fully in the picture until 1634.
64. Birch, *Court and Times of Charles I*, II, p. 206: Pory to Lord Brooke, 6 Dec. 1632. Hopton concurred that the business of the Palatinate 'now concerns' the king 'one degree nearer than it did' (Egerton MS 1820, f.240).
65. Egerton MS 1820, f.237; cf. Clarendon MS 5, no. 333, printed in R. Scrope and T. Monkhouse (eds) *State Papers Collected by Edward, Earl of Clarendon* (3 vols, Oxford, 1767–86), I, pp. 79–80.

reported that the Spaniards reacted 'as if they were restored from death to life'.[66] The death of Gustavus exposed the Lower Palatinate, which he had liberated from Spanish occupation, to attack from Bavaria and Hopton counselled the calling of a parliament in England to consider the Elector's safety.[67] Whilst he had not moved so far as to advise a war against the Habsburgs, 'I cannot,' he wrote in the spring of 1633, 'commend a friendship wherein we may lose much and gain little.'[68] But Spain's troubles were by no means over. The death of Gustavus was to lead to France taking a more prominent part in the conflict in Germany than hitherto she had done. Richelieu offered aid to the German Protestant princes of the League of Heilbronn; in September he sent French armies into the duchy of Lorraine in Alsace. Hopton saw the dangers for Spain: 'if a war should break out in Italy or a rupture should succeed with France before the business of Germany or Flanders be settled, they would be put to as hard a shift as any kingdom has been put at any time'.[69] If the troops of the League of Heilbronn held southern Germany and the French took the Rhine valley, the only route for Spanish troops to Flanders would be that of the dangerous passage by sea.[70] Fears of just such a possibility inspired the next diplomatic initiative, of which Hopton in Spain had been ignorant.

On 16 February 1634, Sir Francis Windebank, the principal secretary handling Spanish affairs, wrote to inform Hopton of these recent negotiations. The abbé Scaglia had made proposals along the lines of Cottington's secret treaty for an alliance between England and the Spanish Netherlands to invade and partition the Dutch republic.[71] Necolalde, the envoy from Spain, had complemented these proposals by an invitation to England to join in a league with Spain and to bring in the Elector Palatine on the Habsburg side.[72] In return, Charles I sought the revocation of the imperial ban, the restoration of the Lower Palatinate, now held by Swedish forces, through war, and negotiation with Bavaria for the Upper Palatinate. To 'stop the current of the States' conquests', Windebank and Cottington, possibly without Charles's full knowledge, had discussed with Necolalde the equipping of a fleet, partially financed by Spain, to secure the coast of Flanders and provide Spain with an open channel of communication.[73] Hopton's

66. Egerton MS 1820, f.218.
67. *Ibid.* f.225, 30 Dec. 1632. See below, p. 703.
68. Egerton MS 1820, f.254v, 12 April 1633.
69. *Ibid.*, f.290v, 26 Oct. 1633.
70. Gardiner, *History of England*, VII, p. 348; and see G. Parker, *The Army of Flanders and the Spanish Road 1567–1659* (Cambridge, 1972), pp. 254–60 and *passim*.
71. Egerton MS 1820, f.313v; *Clarendon State Papers*, I, pp. 74–7.
72. Egerton MS 1820, ff.313v–15.
73. *Ibid.*, ff.316–316v. Windebank told Hopton on 31 May that, concerning the proposition

task was to pursue these proposals in Spain. Cottington wrote the same week to assure him that 'the king's heart is now so right as nothing can hinder some good resolutions but the jealousy and incredulity of the Condé Ducque.'[74] After audiences with Olivares and Philip IV, Hopton reported, offering strong advice to Windebank. If England, he argued, were to set out a fleet for Flanders with Spanish money, it would be impossible for Charles to act independently or to mask, as was intended, his hostility towards the Dutch. Moreover, as paymasters, the Spanish would 'presume on the partnership' rather than be in obligation to England.[75] Instead, Hopton counselled – and in so doing, as we shall see, initiated the debates that led to the first writ of ship money – Charles should put a fleet to sea at his own cost.[76] An English fleet which the king could employ as he saw fit would keep his options open: it could be used to pressure the Dutch into a peace; Spain would have to offer the Palatinate rather than just money for its assistance. The envoy reaffirmed in other words what he had long advocated: that in dealing with Spain England must bargain from strength, 'think of some course to oblige them absolutely'.[77] The Council of War considered Hopton's dispatch, but by May the treaty was in abeyance.[78] While negotiations for a maritime treaty dragged on through the summer and winter of 1634, writs were issued in October for the first levy of ship money to equip an English fleet.[79] Though Hopton was sent detailed articles, and in January 1635 formal powers to conclude the agreements, the negotiations for the treaty became bogged down in Madrid as they had in London.[80] Necolalde delayed discussions by a number of pretexts; Olivares sought minor changes in the articles for which Hopton had no commission.[81] By April when it was becoming clear that the difficulties would not be resolved, Hopton explained that the Spaniards were reluctant to break with Bavaria and that Olivares strongly preferred the secret partition treaty to the maritime agreement which threatened to supplant it.[82] The interminable delays led in England to mounting frustrations with Spain at a time when France had occupied the Lower Palatinate and was urging

for putting a jointly financed fleet to sea, he and Cottington agreed, but 'His Majesty knows nothing of this nor shall by me' (*ibid.*, f.352v).

74. *Ibid.*, f.325, 13 Feb. 1634.
75. *Ibid.*, ff.330–5, esp. ff.333–333v, 8 April 1634; *Clarendon State Papers*, I, pp. 83–4. This advice was consistent with the counsel he had given since 1632 (Egerton MS 1820, f.120).
76. Below, pp. 548–50.
77. Egerton MS 1820, f.335.
78. *Ibid.*, f.352v and see below, pp. 509–19.
79. Gardiner, *History of England*, VII, p. 369.
80. Egerton MS 1820, f.400v–404v; *Clarendon State Papers*, I, pp. 109–13.
81. Egerton MS 1820, f.405v, ff.413–17, 7 Dec. 1634; see *Clarendon State Papers*, I, pp. 120–2, 173–7.
82. Egerton MS 1820, ff.453–457v, 7 April 1635.

Charles into an alliance.[83] The effective breakdown of the maritime treaty in May marked the end of an era and the failure of the principal strategy of Caroline diplomacy. Cottington was clearly surprised and disappointed; Windebank told Hopton (and John Taylor, envoy to Germany) that he would 'never set my heart on anything proposed by them hereafter'.[84] Even the Spanish faction had been disillusioned into thinking of other options. With the death of Weston in March, the very principle of Caroline policy, peace, was also called into question.[85]

England and the Dutch 1630–5

To some the failure of negotiations with Spain had always been a foregone conclusion. The growing evidence of Spanish duplicity seemed only to vindicate criticism of the peace that they had voiced since 1630. The most powerful articulation of such criticism came from the Hague, from Charles's own sister, Elizabeth of Bohemia, and from her agents in England, Sir Thomas Roe and Sir Francis Nethersole. To Roe and Nethersole the natural allies of England were the Dutch, who were fellow Protestants and since the 1560s champions of the war against the Habsburg Antichrist. In June 1632, Roe outlined the case for a Dutch alliance in 'A Discourse Concerning the Allies of England', presented to the Earl of Holland.[86] The decay of England's reputation abroad since the great days of Queen Elizabeth he attributed to neglect of the navy, peace with Spain and the dissolution of the international Protestant league. Because the best allies were friends in religion, he argued, 'he is no good Englishman that is either Spanish or French in faction'. England needed therefore to court the Dutch, in order to keep them from joining with France. Since the Catholics united, it was imperative for the Protestant princes to do so and central to any such confederation was an Anglo-Dutch agreement. Whilst he admitted that in matters of trade the Dutch had been 'insolent enough', the hand of friendship would again return them to their former 'obsequiousness'. 'There is no nation,' Roe concluded, 'so fit to unite unto us in respect of their power at sea and situation of their country and ports, their settled enmity with the great enemy and their little assurance from France.' While Roe hoped to win his case by persuasion, Nethersole tried to force matters by first committing Charles to a collection on behalf of the Palatinate without proper authorization from the king and secondly by threatening that, without the support

83. Below, p. 94.
84. Egerton MS 1820, f.438, 481, 488.
85. Below, p. 537 ff.
86. PRO, SP 16/218/29.

of an Anglo-Dutch alliance, the Elector Palatine would be thrown upon French protection.[87] Nethersole was dismissed from Elizabeth's service, under pressure from her brother. Roe, though he became chancellor of the Order of the Garter, failed to secure the post of secretary or to wield the influence he sought.[88]

The option of an offensive alliance with the Dutch was never closed in the 1630s. The treaty of Southampton of 1625, though strained, was never rescinded; negotiations between the countries were never broken;[89] Charles permitted the Dutch to recruit English troops to fill up the regiments in Holland, just as he permitted the Spaniards to levy men for Flanders.[90] But Roe's proposals for an Anglo-Dutch league never won favour with Charles. The king's personal prejudices cannot be discounted. Charles, like his father, felt little sympathy towards a republic or rebels against an anointed king; one newswriter believed he regarded the Dutch as 'the chief encouragers of his people against him', a nation which might be 'the ruin of him and his monarchy'.[91] There were, however, other good reasons to doubt some of Roe's arguments. Charles saw that the religious issue was now more complex than those who carried the banner of the old Protestant cause were ready to allow. It was naive to regard the wars in Europe as a primarily religious conflict when the emperor's own troops included Protestant regiments, or when, as Hopton put it, 'the Catholic cloak . . . hath so many holes in it'.[92] The United Provinces were themselves divided over religion, the Arminian Remonstrant party being more favourably disposed to peace than the counter-Remonstrants.[93] The Dutch commitment to the cause of Protestantism seemed to many less apparent than their pursuit of self-interest. Sir John Suckling, on a visit to Leyden in 1629, thought them a mean and *irreligious* race: 'religion they use as a stuff cloak in summer more for show than for anything else, their summum bonum being altogether wealth'.[94] Even discounting his prejudices, Suckling had put his finger on the inherent

87. *Cal. Stat. Pap. Dom., 1633–4*, pp. xxviii–xxxiv; also pp. 337, 393, 406; Coke MSS 44, 46; *Cal. Stat. Pap. Dom., 1633–4*, pp. 198, 404; Bodleian, Rawlison MS D.392 (at end).
88. Roe was considered, *Cal. Stat. Pap. Dom., 1631–2*, pp. 211–12.
89. Here I dissent from Reeve (*Charles I*, pp. 241, 260–2), who speaks emotively of 'betrayal'.
90. Egerton MS 1820, f.311.
91. Coke MS 91, 9 May 1630: newsletter. Style should not be discounted. The Dutch envoy, with a clumsiness believed typical of his race, took one of the queen's dwarfs for the young Prince Charles, causing derisive laughter at court (see *Cal. Stat. Pap. Venet., 1632–6*, p. 251).
92. Egerton MS 1820, f.357v, 7 July 1634.
93. Coke MS 39: Nicholas to Coke, 7 Sept. 1630; J. Israel, *The Dutch Republic and the Hispanic World* (Oxford, 1982), pp. 60–3 and *passim*.
94. Bodleian, Ashmole MS 826, f.102, 18 Nov. 1629. The slander is all the more powerful when we note that Suckling was himself accused of irreligion. Cf. J. Suckling, *An Account of Religion by Reason* (1646).

dilemma in England's relations with the Dutch: as well as potential allies, they were successful rivals for trade and dominance of the seas. Longstanding rivalry had sharpened in the 1620s, with crisis in the cloth trade and the massacre by the Dutch of an English trading post at Amboyna, an old question, as the Venetian envoy recognized in 1631, which 'still remains undecided'.[95] In the New World and the East Indies commercial rivalry had stopped little short of war. In Europe Dutch control of the carrying trade had provoked in 1621 the first of a series of navigational ordinances that were ultimately to lead to conflict.[96] The vast profits from Dutch fishing in English and Scottish waters created great ill-feeling, which in 1632 inspired the formation of a society for fishing to take the trade into British hands.[97] From Holland the Privy Council received regular and woeful complaints from the Merchant Adventurers regarding breach of agreements and imposts on English cloth laid and then raised to ruin their trade. The company's warehouses were broken open; the Dutch, they claimed, 'do tacitly seek to banish our cloth out of their countries'.[98]

Perhaps of even more significance than trade rivalry was the mounting Dutch strength at sea and military victories in Flanders. Since the sixteenth century English security had depended upon no power establishing overall dominance in the Low Countries.[99] The Dutch revolt brought fortunate relief for Elizabeth from the threat of a massive Spanish (and Catholic) military presence over the North Sea. A Dutch hegemony was no more welcome, especially given their superiority over the English navy and near dominance of the Baltic trade, the primary source of masting timber, hemp and copper.[100] One of Charles's interests in forming an English fishing company was the development of a commercial fleet as a counter to the Dutch.[101] His concern to strengthen the navy stemmed directly from fears of a more aggressive Dutch presence in the narrow seas. The fear was not misplaced. In October 1630 three Holland ships chased a Dunkirker into

95. *Cal. Stat. Pap. Venet., 1629–32*, p. 552; C. Wilson, *Profit and Power* (1957), pp. 25–47.
96. J. Larkin (ed.) *Stuart Royal Proclamations I: Proclamations of James I, 1603–1625* (Oxford, 1973), no. 228, pp. 543–5; B. Supple, *Commercial Crisis and Change in England, 1600–1642* (Cambridge, 1959); Coke MS 49, 23 Aug. 1634.
97. *Cal. Stat. Pap. Venet., 1629–32*, p. 530; below, pp. 250–52.
98. *HMC Cowper II*, p. 150: complaint of Merchant Adventurers in Holland; Coke MS 55.
99. Cf. R.B. Wernham, *Before the Armada* (1966), *passim*; R.B. Wernham, *After the Armada* (Oxford, 1984), pp. 23–25, 521; and C.H. Wilson, *Queen Elizabeth and the Revolt of the Netherlands* (1970).
100. R.W. Hinton, *The Eastland Trade and the Commonweal in the Seventeenth Century* (Cambridge, 1959), pp. 1–66; cf. R.H. Tawney, 'The Eastland trade', *Eng. Hist. Rev.*, 12 (1959–60), pp. 280–2.
101. Below, pp. 250–52; PRO, 31/3/67, ff.37ff; *Cal. Stat. Pap. Dom., 1634–5*, p. 390. Sir Nicholas Halse claimed that the Dutch took profit of £4–6 million annually at England's expense.

English waters in an 'act of great boldness'.[102] Similar incidents continued to assault English pride.[103] In 1635 Dutch men-of-war even pursued a Dunkirker into Scarborough, drove it aground, and chased the crew for two miles – to the alarm of the local inhabitants.[104] Windebank instructed the Earl of Lindsey, Admiral of the Fleet, to arrest the culprits and prosecute them in the Admiralty court, reminding him that if England waited for justice from Holland, they would wait as long as they had tarried for recompense for Amboyna.[105] Such episodes, far from commending Roe's plea for a Dutch alliance, drove Charles closer to the United Provinces' enemies. Windebank informed Hopton that one of Charles's main objectives in the maritime treaty discussed with Necolalde was 'to carry a jealous and watchful eye over the growing greatness of the States', and to find some means that 'may stop the unrest of the States' conquests'.[106] Under the pretence of freeing the seas from pirates, the fleet was to secure Flanders, protect merchant shipping and maintain English sovereignty of the seas. English efforts to strengthen its navy or aid the enemies of the Dutch served in turn to make suspicions of Dutch aggression into a reality. In July 1631 Captain Plumleigh, following orders to ply westward, reported that 'the Hollanders grumble extremely at us and reckon us their enemies almost in as high degree as the Spaniards'.[107] In 1633 George Goring believed 'the Hollanders never more sharply inclined towards us'.[108] In April 1634, not least on account of worsening relations with England, the Dutch signed a treaty with Louis XIII for a partition of the Spanish Netherlands, raising Charles's concern to alarm.[109] Throughout the early 1630s, tensions fuelled rumours of a breach between England and the United Provinces.[110] If the Dutch were co-religionists, economic and strategic considerations, as the puritan Commonwealth was to reveal, made them far from natural allies.

England and Sweden 1630–35

The supporters of a league with the Dutch were also advocates of an alliance with the figure who from his landing on the Baltic coast in

102. *Cal. Stat. Pap. Dom., 1629–31*, p. 365.
103. For example, the taking of one of Lord Maltravers's herring busses in 1632 (see PRO, C.115/M30/8103).
104. Coke MS 51: account of incident by bishop of Durham, 27 Aug. 1635.
105. Coke MS 51: Windebank to Coke, 6 Aug. 1635.
106. Egerton MS 1820: f.316–316v, 26 Feb. 1634.
107. *HMC Cowper I*, p. 436, 30 July 1631.
108. Coke MS 46, 9 June 1636.
109. J. Du Mont, *Corps Universal Diplomatique*, VI (Amsterdam, 1728), pp. 68–9; Gardiner, *History of England*, VII, pp. 366–7.
110. *Cal. Stat. Pap. Venet., 1629–32*, pp. xliv, 495, 499; *1632–6*, pp. 19, 132, 307; Larkin, *Stuart Royal Proclamations*, II, no. 182, pp. 418–20; Gardiner, *History of England*, VII, pp. 384–5; Reeve, *Charles I*, pp. 259, 367–8.

June 1630 literally took Europe by storm – Gustavus Adolphus, king of Sweden. Over the next two years, and beyond the gave, Gustavus represented the Protestant cause of the seventeenth century, as had Sir Philip Sidney that of the sixteenth century. In the verse of the poet Aurelian Townshend, Gustavus was the lion of the north, the apocalyptic figure who would be victor over the snakes of the bottomless pit.[111] To many, it was a deep mark of shame on England that while the Swedish sword laid low the Habsburg Antichrist – at Breitenfeld or at Nordlingen – Charles maintained a feeble neutrality or, worse, abetted Sweden's enemies. Pamphlets and corantos printed weekly avidly followed the victories of Gustavus and hagiographically reported his miraculous escapes from death.[112] The Council, feeling the smart of their criticism, tried to censor the publication of news.[113] But in verse and ballads, newsletters and sermons, Gustavus Adolphus continued to be worshipped as the hope for Protestantism, for Germany and for the cause of the Elector Palatine (see Figure 3). In response to a Swedish embassy to London in 1630, Charles permitted the Marquis of Hamilton to levy 6,000 troops to join the Swedish forces.[114] In his letter to the lord-lieutenants of the counties he described Hamilton's volunteers as 'for that king [of Sweden] in a war just and honourable . . . not undertaken for a private ambition . . . but for the re-establishing of such princes his allies as have been wrongfully dispossessed of their ancient dignities and estates of which sort the distressed case of our dear brother and only sister cannot but come near unto our heart'.[115] The following summer Sir Henry Vane was appointed to go as ambassador to Gustavus.

To the frustration of his subjects and many of his Council, Charles contributed no more to the Swedish campaigns. His peace with Spain and refusal to consider a parliament, it is argued, forced England into inactivity and deprived Charles of the opportunity to share in Swedish victories.[116] Though there is some truth in such arguments, there were considerations other than pure incapacity that questioned the wisdom of a Swedish alliance. Charles did not early on rule it out. At the very

111. 'Elegy on the death of the king of Sweden, sent to Thomas Carew', in C. Brown (ed.) *The Poems and Masques of Aurelian Townshend* (Reading, 1983), p. 48; cf. K. Sharpe, *Criticism and Compliment; The Politics of Literature in the England of Charles I* (Cambridge, 1987), pp. 174–6.
112. For example, *The Reasons for which Gustavus Adolphus was at length forced to march . . . into Germany* (1630, STC 12535); *The Swedish Intelligencer* (1632, STC 23522); *The Continuation of our Weekly News* (1632, STC 25201c), and cf. A. Searle (ed.) *Barrington Family Letters 1628–1632* (Camden Soc., 4th series, 28, 1983), pp. 230–41.
113. Below, pp. 646–7.
114. See Bodleian, Firth MS C.4, p. 518; Hampshire Record Office, Herriard MSS, Box 029: letter of Lord Treasurer Weston, 23 July 1631; *Acts of the Privy Council, June 1630 to June 1631*, p. 376.
115. Firth MS C.4, p. 518; PRO, SO 1/2/54.
116. Reeve, *Charles I*, pp. 263, 278–9.

VSTAVVS ADOLPHVS D . G . SVECORVM REX etc
Psal. 45. 4 & 5.
Gird thee with thy ſword vpon thy thigh, etc.
Good lucke haue thou with thine honour:
ride on, becauſe of the word of trueth,
For Nathaniell Butter & Nich. Bourne.
Ge Mountin ſculpsit

3 Equestrian portrait of Gustavus Adolphus. Frontispiece to *The Swedish Intelligencer*, 1632.

time of the peace with Spain, he informed Coloma, who attempted to prevent Hamilton's levies, that he would assist Sweden and any other enemies of the emperor 'so long as the interests of the Palatinate were not accommodated'.[117] The news of Gustavus's victories over Count Tilly he received in October 1631 as 'of the best' and 'hoped it would constantly be better'.[118] In Sptember, frustrated at the progress of negotiations in Vienna, he dispatched Vane to pursue the Swede with propositions for an alliance.[119] There was pressure in England for a treaty and rumours of a parliament to finance intervention.[120] Though he stopped short of recalling parliaments, Charles offered financial support to Gustavus in exchange for a commitment to restore the Palatinate. Vane's meetings with Gustavus, however, convinced him that there was little prospect of an alliance with Sweden that would be of benefit to England. Gustavus gave a cold reception to the ambassador of Frederick, Elector Palatine; he negotiated with the Catholic League and the Duke of Bavaria. In January he bluntly advised Vane to treat with Bavaria for the Palatinate; 'for what he held himself he was ready to render the same, so as I would show him a way how it might be defended against his enemies'.[121] When Gustavus did propose terms for an alliance, Vane thought them so 'exorbitant and extravagant' that they were not intended as a serious basis of negotiation but only to put pressure on Bavaria.[122] Charles himself told Hamilton the Swedish terms were as severe as the emperor's.[123] The Swedish king refused to allow the prince Palatine to make levies of troops saying he had already placed too much power with the princes of Germany. Vane prognosticated that 'if this king gets the Palatinate, it will be hard fetching it out of his hands'.[124] During the course of 1632, Gustavus went on from victory to victory. Charles I forwarded proposals for an English subsidy of £10,000 a month and, in expectation of an agreement, sent an envoy to Louis XIII to announce his intents and invite French assistance.[125] Vane feared that in response to these proposals Gustavus merely delayed; by the end of June, after

117. *Cal. Stat. Pap. Venet., 1629–32*, p. 438, also p. xxxviii; S.R. Gardiner (ed.) *Letters Relating to the Mission of Sir Thomas Roe to Gustavus Adolphus, 1629–30* (Camden Miscellany, 1875).
118. *Cal. Stat. Pap. Venet., 1629–32*, p. 556.
119. Clarendon MS 5, no. 305: papers relating to negotiations with Gustavus Adolphus.
120. Below, p. 703.
121. Clarendon MS 5, no. 305: 'Sir Henry Vane's relation of his embassy to the King of Sweden'.
122. *Ibid.*
123. G. Burnet, *Memoirs of the Lives and Actions of James and William, Dukes of Hamilton* (1677), p. 21, 31 Dec. 1631.
124. Gardiner, *History of England*, VII, p. 189; cf. PRO, SP 81/38, f.85 (the Earl of Carlisle's agreement); Clarendon MS 5, no. 305.
125. Gardiner, *History of England*, VII, pp. 204–5.

audience at Nuremberg, he judged 'that he intended not to conclude the treaty nor embrace the Palatine's interests'.[126] In the end, Gustavus offered only that the Elector should hold the Palatinate as a donative of Sweden, on condition of granting cautionary towns and a commitment to enter no league with any others.[127] Angry at such conditions, Vane left, with nothing concluded.[128] As a client of Weston, Vane has been described by Gardiner and Reeve as a candidate little suited to bring home a Swedish alliance. It is difficult, however, not to concur with the envoy in his suspicion that Gustavus's own ambitions in Germany and his dealings with Bavaria, France and Saxony made him, as even former supporters came to see, an unreliable champion of the Palatine's interests.[129] When Gustavus Adolphus met his end at the battle of Lutzen in November 1632, his death may have been mourned by the populace as that of a Protestant saint; for others it ended the threat of uncontrolled Swedish ambitions.

England and France 1630–5

The death of Gustavus Adolphus led to greater French involvement in the affairs of Germany. While Richelieu's armies had entered Lorraine in May, on the pretext of the duke's harbouring Louis's rebel brother, the cardinal had left the Swede to do his fighting for him in Germany.[130] After Gustavus was killed, Richelieu was quick to offer the weakened Protestant league his protection. It was, as both Richelieu and Olivares were aware, only a matter of time before they came to blows;[131] then, as Hopton had predicted, 'a rupture between these two crowns would cause a war for many years in Europe'.[132] More active French involvement in Germany presented to those who disliked any dealings with the Habsburgs a new hope for the cause of the Palatinate. Since the breach with Spain and match with France in 1625, the logic of English diplomacy had been an alliance with the Bourbons. That logic had been ruptured by the war in 1627. With the return to peace,

126. Clarendon MS 5, no. 305. Cf. *ibid.*, no. 305 for Coke's recapitulation of Vane's negotiation, 28 Sept. 1632.
127. Clarendon MS 5, no. 305; Gardiner, *History of England*, VII, p. 196; J. Rushworth, *Historical Collections*, II (1680), p. 166, July 1632.
128. *Cal. Stat. Pap. Venet., 1632–6*, p. vii.
129. Cf. Gardiner, *History of England*, VII, pp. 179, 196; *Cal. Stat. Pap. Venet., 1629–32*, p. 627. Even Roe recognized the argument that Gustavus might be 'overambitious' and an unreliable protagonist of the Palatine's interest: see SP 16/218/29. Also Clarendon MS 5, no. 305: Coke to Vane, 28 Sept. 1632; Reeve (*Charles I*, pp. 279–88) takes too rosy a view of Gustavus's value to England.
130. Gardiner, *History of England*, VII, p. 198.
131. *Ibid.*, p. 209.
132. Egerton MS 1820, f.205, 26 Aug. 1632.

those at court close to the queen, the Earl of Holland chief among them, worked to re-establish close relations.[133] From 1629 too a series of envoys was sent by Richelieu to endeavour to persuade England into a French alliance and to frustrate English negotiations with France's enemies, the Habsburgs. When he left for England in May 1629, the Marquis de Châteauneuf was instructed to bring England into a league with France, to procure the assistance of her navy and to persuade her to a war on the coasts of Spain, with offers of assistance for the recovery of the Palatinate.[134] The same principles underlay the orders to the Marquis de St Chaumont two years later. Chaumont pointed to the progress of the Swedes and urged England to enter a league with Gustavus and Richelieu.[135] The propositions were reiterated by Boutard in September 1633 and by Pougny in July 1634.[136] As the probability of outright conflict between France and Spain increased, Richelieu's concern to secure an English alliance intensified. Rumour of a revived maritime treaty between England and Spain led to the urgent dispatch of the Marquis de Senecterre with a brief to win England to alliance with the French and Dutch – or at least ensure her neutrality.[137]

A French alliance, however, for all its attractions as an alternative to negotiations with the Habsburgs, was problematic on a number of counts. The commitment of France to the cause of the Palatinate was far from clear. Secretary Sir John Coke informed Sir Thomas Herbert, who was writing a history, that one of the real causes of the war with France had been Richelieu's failure to help the Elector and the seizure of Mansfeldt's ships and goods at Bordeaux, when his company was en route to Germany.[138] Where religion was concerned, though Protestant Englishmen curiously closed their eyes to the fact, France was no more a natural ally to the Elector or England than was Spain. Indeed the *dévot* party at the French court which conspired against Richelieu were fanatical supporters of denominational alliances. There were more important considerations still. England and France were historically old enemies and for all that 1588 and its aftermath had given prominence to the threat from Spain, centuries-old hostility between England and France had not been eradicated. Indeed it had been fanned by the war. The 'high carriages' of the French during the

133. The Peace of Susa bound both powers 'to endeavour mutually to give aid and assistance unto their allies and friends'. See *The Articles of Peace . . . 1629* (STC 9250).

134. PRO, 31/3/66, ff.117ff; cf. M. Avenal, *Collection de documents inédits sur l'histoire de France: Lettres, instructions diplomatiques et papiers d'état du Cardinal Richelieu*, IV (Paris, 1863) pp. 559–64, 663.

135. PRO, 31/3/67, ff.42–4.

136. *Ibid.*, ff.92, 114–18.

137. PRO, 31/3/68, ff.138–43, 25 Feb. 1635.

138. Coke MS 38 (*HMC Cowper I*, p. 398, dates this document 'about 1629').

negotiations for the peace of Susa, we recall, had 'much disgusted' Charles, as indeed the French display of captured English ensigns in Notre Dame continued to affront English honour.[139] For his part Richelieu had vowed never to forget the Isle de Rhé.[140] Châteauneuf spoke of a 'mauvaise volonté naturelle vers la France' in England; a Venetian ambassador described the 'natural antipathy' between the countries.[141] Such ingrained sentiments were not easily overcome by the needs of diplomacy.

The tensions between the countries, however, were not just the legacy of history. Under Henri IV and Louis XIII France had begun to develop a navy that posed a challenge to English sovereignty of the seas, and to expand its commercial activities in Europe and the New World in a manner that threatened English companies.[142] Quarrels over captured prize ships, over colonial possessions in Canada, especially Quebec and Port Réal, continued throughout the 1630s.[143] More importantly, because closer to home, the naval rivalry intensified. At times it flared into belligerent incidents. On 23 September 1631 Captain Plumleigh related to Coke an episode in the Channel when the French had failed to lower their flags to the English ensign, as was customary. Shots were exchanged. 'I think it were better that both I and the ship under my charge,' Plumleigh bragged, 'were in the bottom of the seas than that I should live to see a Frenchman . . . wear a flag aloft in his Majesty's seas.'[144] Such incidents fuelled rumours of larger conflict. In May 1631 Secretary Dorchester took seriously intelligence of a French invasion.[145] As both France and, especially from 1634 onwards, England, developed their fleets, the risk of clashes over supremacy of the seas escalated. In December 1634, Captain Pennington reported that in France 'there is no speech . . . among the common people but of wars between us'.[146]

Uneasiness about the developing strength of the French navy was exacerbated by the French alliances with the Dutch. Anglo-French negotiations floundered on several occasions over Charles I's (correct) suspicions of a French agreement with the Dutch to partition the Spanish Netherlands (ironically not unlike his own secret negotiations

139. Above, pp. 43–5, 65–6; Coke MS 36; PRO, 31/3/66, f.168, 7 Oct. 1629.
140. Coke MS 46: Goring to Coke, 9 June 1633.
141. PRO, 31/3/66, f.232; *Cal. Stat. Pap. Venet., 1632–6*, p. 368.
142. In 1628 Dudley Carleton had declared that the French must give up 'the idea of making themselves masters of the sea' (*Cal. Stat. Pap. Venet., 1628–9*, p. 340). See G.D. Avenal, *Richelieu et la monarchie absolue*, III (Paris, 1895), pp. 157–226.
143. For example, PRO, 31/3/66, ff.243, 257–9; 31/3/67, f.40.
144. *HMC Cowper I*, pp. 442–3.
145. *Cal. Stat. Pap. Dom., 1631–3*, p. 32.
146. *Cal. Stat. Pap. Dom., 1634–5*, p. 339, 2 Dec. 1634. Sir Henry Herbert described Richelieu in 1631 as 'the greatest enemy that ever England had' (PRO, C.115/N3/8547).

with Spain to partition the United Provinces).[147] Such an agreement presented the threat not only of a combined French and Dutch fleet, but the greater menace of a French military presence in the Low Countries which historically it had been the aim of English diplomacy to prevent. Seen in this context the French involvement in Europe in the 1630s was not an entirely unmixed blessing. The French ambassadors were right to see England as wary of the growth of French power;[148] Richelieu felt it necessary to send an ambassador to explain France's entry into Lorraine.[149] There were doubts too about whether the growing might of France would be of benefit to the Elector Palatine. Both the queen of Bohemia and Nethersole were distrustful of French intentions and the persistent refusal of the French envoys to address the young Charles Louis as 'Elector' confirmed suspicions at the Hague and in England.[150] The suspicions were more than well founded. In August 1631, distrustful of the Habsburgs, Maximilian of Bavaria had sent an envoy to Richelieu and concluded a treaty by which they agreed to uphold each other's territories, so placing the Upper Palatinate under French protection.[151] French ambitions were, and were seen to be, quite different from the interests of the Elector and so of England. John Dinley reported from the Hague that the French were quite prepared to see a peace without the restitution of the Palatinate, and as they entered Alsace it was feared they would happily embark on war without it.[152] Roe thought the French pursued only their own interests and desired to 'swallow' the Rhineland.[153] His friend John Durie, responding to the French resolution to take Udenheim or Phillipsburg, so as to have a passage over the Rhine, feared that French armies would march through the Palatinate 'and tread it under foot when it is beginning to recover'.[154] Experience had taught Viscount Conway the need to be suspicious of the French embroilment in Germany: 'God hath forbid me to trust in princes,' he told Sir Robert Harley.[155] Sir John Coke watched the French anxiously: like his master he was sorry to see Lorraine fall to Louis in April 1634;[156] by the end of the year he was saying openly that they desired no less than dominion of the world.[157]

147. Du Mont, *Corps universal diplomatique*, V, pp. 522, 605–6; VI, pp. 68–9. Cf. Israel, *The Dutch Republic*, pp. 250–4.
148. PRO, 31/3/66, f.161v, 24 Sept. 1629; *Cal. Stat. Pap. Venet., 1632–6*, p. 191.
149. PRO, 31/3/67, f.92.
150. *Cal. Stat. Pap. Dom., 1633–4*, pp. 394, 398.
151. Gardiner, *History of England*, VII, p. 179; Du Mont, *Corps universal diplomatique*, VI, p. 14.
152. *Cal. Stat. Pap. Dom., 1633–4*, p. 58.
153. *Ibid.*, p. 430.
154. *Ibid.*, p. 417, 16 Jan. 1634.
155. BL, Loan MS 29/172, Harley Papers II, f.73, 2 Feb. 1634.
156. *Cal. Stat. Pap. Venet., 1632–6*, pp. 197, 209.
157. *Ibid.*, p. 304.

The expression of such suspicions by those known to be critical of a pro-Habsburg policy indicated that alliance with France was by no means an obvious course. For much of the early 1630s, Charles's negotiations with Louis, even his enthusiasm, as reported by Fontenay to Richelieu, 'd'unir la puissance et de se joindre entièrement à vous' were intended as much to put pressure on Madrid and Vienna as to align with France.[158] Growing Franco-Dutch amity and co-operation made the maritime treaty with Spain even more attractive to Charles.[159] Even when the prince Palatine threatened to place himself under French protection, Charles, after consulting with the foreign committee, resolved not to conclude with France.[160] Only the failure of the maritime treaty with Spain and the news of the Peace of Prague were to draw England closer to France.[161]

Interests and diplomatic objectives

Our sketch of England's relations with Spain, the United Provinces, Sweden and France provides a brief overview of the options open to Charles, the considerations he had to weigh and a bald summary of some of the arguments put forward at court, in Council and in the country. At bottom, of course, the options were two: war or peace. But within each there was a range of possibilities: war against Spain or against the Dutch, war in alliance with Spain or with Sweden, or France. Similarly, peace could be based on completely inactive neutrality or secured through defensive alliances which bound England and her allies to go to each other's aid in the event of incursion by an enemy.[162] Charles I and his Lord Treasurer, Weston, evidently preferred to avoid war; the experience of the 1620s, the failure of campaigns, the repercussions in England, were alone sufficient to explain that preference. Financial difficulties and a reluctance to resummon parliament were widely held to be prime considerations. We should not, however, exaggerate their importance in determining policy. Councillors and ambassadors felt free to advise recalling a parliament and there were widespread expectations of an assembly in the winter of 1631.[163] Though Charles then decided against it, Hopton for one did not believe the king's antipathy to parliaments so strong that it would stand in the way of his foreign policy.[164] The absence of

158. PRO, 31/3/67, f.74; *Cal. Stat. Pap. Venet., 1632–6*, p. 191.
159. See the instructions to Senecterre, 25 Feb. 1635 (PRO, 31/3/68, f.138).
160. Egerton MS 1820, ff.396v–397v; and 399v (17 Oct. 1634).
161. Below, pp. 509–19.
162. This important distinction is often not made.
163. Below, pp. 703–5.
164. Egerton MS 1820, f.225.

parliaments too did not guarantee that England would remain at peace. They had been of only limited help in fighting the wars of the 1620s; when Charles, as we shall see, signed an offensive and defensive alliance with France in 1637, no parliament was called. The Scots war was fought without one. Nor was financial weakness a greater restraint on foreign policy in the 1630s than in the 1620s. At a time when Charles was contemplating involvement in Germany and the question of money arose Weston promised that 'if the king might be engaged with honour that should not be wanting'.[165] As we shall see, even without subsidies Charles's income rose considerably during the personal rule, even taking no account of the large sums raised by ship money for the navy. By the mid-1630s, though England was weak in military terms, she had an important fleet. During the 1630s, still more so after 1635, war, as several ambassadors appreciated, was not ruled out; Charles raised with his foreign committee the possibility of fighting on several occasions.[166] Peace was not completely forced on England; it was a choice.

The preference for peace, however, did not result in complete withdrawal from European affairs. The many foreign envoys who commented on England's preference to remain neutral seemed aware from the beginning that their own security could not depend upon an English neutrality that might at any point be abandoned for more belligerent courses. Secretary Sir John Coke put it thus: 'as we are friends to all sides and enemies to none, so we will not tie ourselves to any neutrality which may hinder us from treating with any party that shall offer best conditions'.[167] Accordingly, despite peace with Spain, Charles sent Hamilton to Gustavus Adolphus; Cottington's secret maritime treaty with Spain committed England to war against the Dutch. Charles was prepared to make similar commitments in negotiations with Necolalde and, later, with France. Had English neutrality been guaranteed, envoys from Holland, France and Spain would not have manoeuvred so anxiously to secure it. For the point is that even neutrality was a bargaining position, and, in that respect, a counter on the gambling table of European diplomacy. In 1628 Contarini had reminded Charles I that his predecessors had 'always kept the balance between the great powers in Europe'.[168] At times, as Charles hinted to the Dutch envoy Joachimi, that role was best fulfilled by English neutrality.[169] Even whilst staying formally neutral, however, England could tilt the balance in permitting bullion to flow from

165. *Cal. Stat. Pap. Dom., 1633–4*, p. 254: J. Dinley to Roe, 29 Oct. 1633.
166. Reeve, *Charles I*, p. 279; Egerton MS 1820, f.399v.
167. PRO, SP 84/149, f.234.
168. *Cal. Stat. Pap. Venet., 1628–9*, p. 153.
169. *Cal. Stat. Pap. Venet., 1632–6*, pp. 286–7, 13 Oct. 1634.

Spain to the Netherlands, or offering the 'favour' of its fleet. When the Rhineland passage to the Low Countries was closed in 1634, and the importance of Dunkirk was thrown into sharp focus, both France and Spain were anxious to secure English support and even prepared to pay to preserve her neutrality. When we look with hindsight over the early years of personal rule, we conclude that Charles adhered consistently to a policy of peace and friendship with Spain. But the *possibility* of war was always a dimension of his diplomacy.[170] Was that then the 'futile diplomacy' of Gardiner's description? Or was Caroline policy, in returning essentially to Jacobean principles, the most sensible course in the Europe of 1629 to 1635?

Any answer to such a question must begin with a careful consideration of Charles I's objectives. Gardiner had no doubt about what they were: 'The one thing which he cared for was the re-establishment of his sister in the Palatinate.'[171] Recently this has been questioned. Dr Haskell has suggested that the king's priorities lay elsewhere: 'a substantial part of the foreign policy of the 1630s was not dominated by Charles I's interest in securing reinstatement for his nephew in the Palatinate. If any area of Europe emerges as being of particular interest to England, it is Flanders rather than the Palatinate.'[172] Dr Haskell sees the desire to liberate Flanders and Gerbier's negotiations for an independent Belgian state as a central tenet of diplomacy in 1632, the threat of a Franco-Dutch blockade of Flanders as the inspiration for the maritime treaty of 1634, and the desire to protect Flanders as the principal purpose of the ship money fleet.[173] The Palatinate, she concludes, though kept on the negotiating table, ranked low in the practicalities of diplomacy. We cannot fully accept this re-evaluation; for the prominence of the Palatinate in Charles's foreign policy evidence abounds. Nicholas wrote to Coke in 1630 that nothing was of greater importance to his master.[174] Hopton, whose instructions made clear that the Palatinate was 'his greatest business', told Philip IV of Spain directly 'That the king my master had esteemed the business of the Palatinate to have been his greatest misfortune and *so* his greatest business'.[175] Charles was very close to his sister and her family (in 1631 he paid the large sum of £210 for a Honthorst painting of her, the

170. *Ibid.*, p. xxi.
171. Gardiner, *History of England*, VII, p. 169.
172. P. Haskell, 'Sir Francis Windebank and the personal rule of Charles I' (University of Southampton, PhD thesis, 1978), p. 282. I am grateful to Pat Haskell for many stimulating discussions about Caroline foreign policy.
173. Haskell, 'Windebank', chs 5, 6; cf. Gardiner, *History of England*, VII, pp. 345–6.
174. Coke MS 39, 7 Sept. 1630.
175. Egerton MS 1820, ff.1, 125. The juxtaposition is worthy of note.

Elector and their children);[176] he clearly felt throughout a responsibility in honour for her welfare.[177] With the death of her husband and the succession of his nephew, the business, as Hopton had put it, 'concerns him one degree nearer than it did'.[178] In almost every dispatch the Palatinate is mentioned as the central objective.

Yet if Dr Haskell underplays the importance of the Palatinate in Caroline foreign policy, she is right to draw attention to other considerations that could not be ignored, and in the context of which the negotiations for the Elector had to be conducted. The first consideration was, naturally, the security of the realm. England was a small country surrounded by powerful neighbours. In 1629, when Charles embarked upon his personal rule, the situation in Europe was potentially menacing. The Edict of Restitution of March 1629, seizing Protestant bishoprics and abbeys, marked the height of the Habsburgs' power and indeed of Catholic hegemony. With the defeat of Denmark, there seemed no check on their sway in Germany. Since the revival of war with Spain in 1621, the Dutch had been winning major victories, but there was mounting uneasiness about their maritime strength and control of world trade. France, torn by civil war, had for long seemed weak. With the capitulation of the Huguenots, however, there dawned greater stability at home and Richelieu's strengthening of royal finances and the navy equipped him for influence abroad.[179] Potentially the ambitions of all these powers threatened England. Both Spain and the Dutch vied for total control of the Low Countries. Dutch and French naval power threatened to dwarf England's and end the control of the narrow seas on which her security depended. As one adviser put it to the king, in 1629, 'if the French proceed herein as he begins to be furnished with 100 sail of warlike ships, he will either be master of the narrow seas . . . or else by your Majesty must be constrained'.[180] Since England could not compete with these powers, her security depended upon their mutual hostility, upon ensuring that no one power controlled in Flanders or at sea, depended, in other words, on what we would now call a balance of power.[181] Sometimes the maintenance of that balance cut across or obstructed other objectives. Sir John Coke, no Hispanophile, came round to the view that there was 'better reason to maintain the Spaniards [in the Low Countries] than to

176. *Cal. Stat. Pap. Dom., 1629–31*, p. 558; cf. the prices paid for Van Dycks, PRO, SP 16/404/4. 'Le Roi à la chasse' cost £100.
177. Cf. Charles's speech to the Long Parliament on 5 July 1641 (Rushworth, *Historical Collections*, II, p. 365).
178. Egerton MS 1820, f.240.
179. See A.D. Lublinskaya, *French Absolutism: The Crucial Phase 1620–1629* (Cambridge, 1968).
180. Herriard MSS, Box 06: 'Affairs in the time of Charles I'.
181. *Cal. Stat. Pap. Venet., 1628–9*, pp. 153, 224.

let the French in'.[182] Even the ardent puritan Sir Thomas Barrington entertained the argument that 'reason of state' suggested the French and Dutch as 'so near . . . neighbours' might be worse than the Spanish.[183] Whatever his other objectives, the Palatinate first among them, Charles had always to keep his eye on the European scales and as events, battles and negotiations tipped the pans first this way then that, he had to strive to restore the equilibrium on which England's security was pivoted.

Another consideration of foreign policy was trade. Trade was directly related to security in seventeenth-century Europe. A manuscript among the papers of Sir John Coke, dated December 1629, makes the connection well. Headed 'The particular decay of navigation, mariners and merchants', the paper outlined the cost to England of trade in others', principally Dutch, ships.[184] The author catalogues the transportation of herrings, pilchards and sea coal in foreign bottoms, and the loss of employment, revenue and custom in consequence. The Hollanders, he observed, 'have the whole trade of Ireland' and traded with friends and enemies alike. Most seriously, their dominance of trade, especially in tallow, wax, timber and ordnance, made them 'the builders and furnishers of all nations for ships'. Indeed 'they strengthen our enemies with ships and ordnance' and so undermined England's security. The Dutch came to dominate in the Baltic. In addition, what our author did not observe, the Dutch control of the important East Indies trade in spices led them to amass bullion which other nations had to expend to purchase these essential preservatives. In Charles's reign considerable concern was expressed about bullion leaving the kingdom.[185] Bullion financed campaigns, paid mercenaries and bought friends. In the prevailing economic thinking of seventeenth-century Europe, these profits from trade and colonies were a principal source of power and security. Trade, of course, was also directly related to the king's own coffers, and the wealth was an important aspect of the strength of the monarchy. In a period of a diminishing royal demesne and the falling value of subsidies, customs duties were one of the most valuable and one of the few expanding sources of royal revenue.[186] The expansion of trade passing through English ports benefited not only the merchant but the king. All these considerations were in play in the conduct of diplomacy. England had to attempt to ensure a balance of powers in the Baltic;[187] the rivalry in the New World, as

182. M.B. Young, *Servility and Service: The Life and Work of Sir John Coke* (1986), p. 249; cf. Clarendon MS 5, no. 334: Windebank to Hopton, 16 Feb. 1634.
183. Searle, *Barrington Letters*, p. 244: Sir Thomas Barrington to Joan Barrington, 21 May 1632 – though he doubted it.
184. Coke MS 38 ('The particular decay of navigation, mariners and merchants').
185. *Ibid.*; and Herriard MSS, Box 06.
186. Coke MS 48: R. Mason to Coke, 19 July 1634.
187. *Cal. Stat. Pap. Venet., 1629–32*, p. 119.

Emmanuel Downing wrote to Coke, put England at odds with the Dutch and the French;[188] England and Holland contested not only for the herrings off the coasts, but for the purchase of French salt for curing them.[189]

If calculations of trade put England at odds with her near neighbours, they undoubtedly pushed her closer to Spain. In the early seventeenth century, the importance of Spanish markets had increased greatly; moreover Spanish wool was a valued import for the Wiltshire woollen manufacturers and Spanish bar iron a source of supply for the metal-working industry.[190] Peace and neutrality brought to England these benefits – and more. From the arrangement that Cottington made with Olivares, to bring Spanish bullion to London to be minted and transported to the Low Countries, emerged a larger carrying and re-export trade which laid the foundations of future commercial policy and success.[191] With the Dutch embroiled in war, Dover became for a decade an 'international entrepôt' and 'an unprecedentedly large share of the international carrying trade fell into English hands'[192] – the trade between Portugal and her colonies, the coastal trade between Spanish ports, the trade between France and Spain and the Low Countries and Spain. The massive rise in customs revenues is the barometer of the expansion of English trade.[193] Nor were the benefits of coining Spanish bullion negligible. In 1630, John Flower reported to Viscount Scudamore that twenty cartloads of silver had arrived at Cottington's house 'and it is said that he will send over a million every year to be coined here'.[194] The next year he (accurately) predicted that it would be a source of considerable profit to the king; two-thirds of the shipment was minted in England bringing, in return for bills of exchange, valuable bullion and the profits of the coining.[195] Though obviously beneficial, the profits of Spanish trade and bullion also complicated, some thought they constrained, English foreign policy. On several occasions Hopton expressed his fear that the Spaniards felt no need to make concessions to England over the Palatinate, resting confident that the commercial benefits secured them England's friendship.[196] Only warily did he counsel on one occasion diplomatic

188. Coke MS 49, 23 Aug. 1634.
189. PRO, C.115/M32/8185: J. Flower to Scudamore, 26 Feb. 1631.
190. C. Clay, *Economic Expansion and Social Change Vol. II: Industry, Trade and Government* (Cambridge, 1984), pp. 148–51, 161–2.
191. PRO, C.115/M30/8068, 8077; *Cal. Stat. Pap. Venet., 1629–32*, p. 491; J.S. Kepler, *The Exchange of Christendom: The International Entrepôt at Dover, 1622–1641* (Leicester, 1986); Young, *Servility and Service*, p. 251; Clay, *Economic Expansion*, II, pp. 165–6.
192. Clay, *Economic Expansion*, II, p.165.
193. *Cal. Stat. Pap. Venet., 1629–32*, p. 502; see below, pp. 126–9.
194. PRO, C.115/M30/8068, 28 March 1630.
195. *Ibid.*, M30/8077.
196. For example, Egerton MS 1820, f.254v; cf. PRO, 31/3/68, f.165; *Cal. Stat. Pap. Venet., 1629–32*, p. 275.

action which 'would be no small diminution to his Majesty's revenue in his customs, besides the interruption of one of the most considerable commerces we have'.[197] Successive Venetian ambassadors attributed the direction of Caroline diplomacy to the magnet of profit.[198] The French envoy Senecterre concluded that England opted for neutrality because it drew the trade of Europe to them.[199] In each case they exaggerated. Economic and commercial considerations seldom determined foreign policy. In 1637 the prospect of losing trade with Spain did not prevent Charles I from contemplating an anti-Habsburg war. But on several counts, domestic and international, bullion and trade were factors that could not be ignored.

English diplomacy and the Palatinate

The issue of the Palatinate could not be seen in isolation. The recovery of Frederick's ancestral lands and dignity was pursued within the broader context of the need to preserve English security and trade in a difficult and ever volatile situation. The problem was compounded by the fact that the Palatinate was embroiled in several different European conflicts which it proved impossible to untangle. Frederick's troubles began when, in 1619, he accepted the crown of Bohemia from rebels against the authority of the emperor Ferdinand II. Because imperial forces were not adequate, Ferdinand called upon the Spanish Habsburgs and Catholic Duke Maximilian of Bavaria to aid him. In return for defeating Frederick's army in 1620 at the battle of the White Mountain near Prague, they were permitted, as the Elector fled to the Hague, to occupy his lands in the Lower and Upper Palatinate. To Ferdinand, interest in the future of the Electorate was bound up with the strength of Catholicism and Habsburg authority in Germany. Frederick was a Calvinist and his vote in the electoral college balanced between Catholics and Protestants jeopardized the election of a Habsburg as king of the Romans, successor to the imperial dignity. Maximilian's interest lay in the aggrandizement of his own position by lands and through securing the Electoral dignity. To Spain, the main concern was in part family loyalty to the Habsburgs, but in larger part the strategic importance of the Palatinate to its fifty-year-old war with the Dutch which was about to resume, with the expiry of the Twelve Years Truce in 1621. The Palatinate lay on a vital line of communication for troops and supplies from Spain through Italy to Flanders, the only route if the passage through the narrow seas was jeopardized

197. Clarendon MS 16, no. 1255, 6 June 1639.
198. *Cal. Stat. Pap. Venet., 1629–32*, pp. 275, 611; *1632–6*, pp. 45, 357, 369.
199. PRO, 31/3/68, f.165.

by Dutch shipping or a hostile England or France.[200] From 1621 therefore the restoration of Frederick depended on satisfying the interests of Spain which occupied the Lower Palatinate, Bavaria which held the Upper, and the emperor who alone could revoke the ban and restore the Electoral title. Or it could be regained in battle. The collapse of Mansfeldt's expedition and the defeat of the Danes saw the failure of campaigns in Germany; the English war against Spain proved a fiasco. The fate of the prince Palatine was thrown back on diplomacy. It was difficult to know how best to negotiate. There was little pressure England could exercise in Germany. Moreover, as Sir Robert Anstruther observed in the autumn of 1631, the objectives of the interested parties, Ferdinand and Bavaria, were not the same: 'To rely upon the one, we incense the other, to deal with both at once they being in affection and interests so different, to reject both upon hope that their private emulation will turn to our advantage . . . I cannot propound.'[201] Anstruther posed the dilemma clearly; it is small wonder then, as Cottington admitted to Hopton, that the foreign committee had been troubled by it.[202] The only solution appeared to be negotiation with Spain in the hope that Philip IV and Olivares would not only surrender their own interests, but apply pressure on the emperor and he in turn on Bavaria to yield theirs. 'We are pacified,' Cottington told Hopton, 'out of confidence that the Condé Ducque will remedy it.'[203] That confidence subsequent events proved to be unfounded. Even in 1630 there were those, Anstruther among them, who doubted whether Spain was able or willing to dictate a settlement in Germany when the interests of the German princes, the Duke of Bavaria and the emperor were so different – to each other's and to Spain's.[204] Yet the Spanish option appeared the best diplomatic course. In October 1630 the Elector himself, according to the Venetian ambassador, 'seemed not altogether without hope that by means of England the Spaniards might find some way of restoring his fallen fortunes'.[205] In 1630 England had nothing to offer the Duke of Bavaria or the emperor. Spain, however, desperately needed peace with the Dutch and in return for such peace mediated by England, it could afford at least to surrender its own territory in the Palatinate.[206]

Events after 1630, however, served only to compound rather than clarify the dilemmas. The entry of Sweden into the war may have made the emperor more anxious to settle a peace in Germany, but it

200. See Parker, *The Army of Flanders and the Spanish Road.*
201. Egerton MS 1820, f.84v.
202. *Ibid.*, f.97v.
203. *Ibid.*
204. *Ibid.*, ff.81–3.
205. *Cal. Stat. Pap. Venet., 1629–32*, p. 426.
206. Cf. Lonchay, *Correspondance*, II, p. 579, no. 1752.

also complicated diplomacy. Gustavus Adolphus entered into alliance with the Protestant princes and with France, and so brought other interests into play.[207] When Sweden captured strongholds in the Lower Palatinate, the focus of English diplomacy drifted necessarily from Spain; with Bavaria drawing ever closer to the emperor, negotiations with Ferdinand were stymied and Anstruther was recalled from Vienna.[208] In April 1632 Gussoni reported from England: 'Now all their hopes are based on the sole foundation of supporting the arms of Sweden.'[209] Gustavus, however, could not bind himself to restore the Palatinate when France, with whom he was in league, had signed an agreement with the Duke of Bavaria to protect his claim to it.[210] And to pursue his ambitions in Germany, he had also to court Protestant princes such as the Lutheran John George of Saxony who was far from well disposed to Frederick. English negotiations with Sweden in turn damaged any possibility of Spanish assistance or the Emperor's co-operation. Olivares often alluded to this in discussions with Hopton.[211] In an interview with Windebank the Spanish resident Necolalde put the point bluntly: 'the truth is . . . you pull down as fast with one hand as you build up with the other, and my treaty with the Emperor and Sir Robert Anstruther's negotiating with the Protestant princes, the Swedes and the French in Germany are diametrically opposite and what appearance can there be of success when you fix upon nothing . . . and seeking to please both you are sure of neither.'[212] Whilst Necolalde stated the facts fairly, it was not clear what alternative course would be more effective. After Gustavus's death, Wallenstein and Feria won victories for the Habsburgs and threatened the Swedish tenure of the Lower Palatinate.[213] Richelieu sent French troops in to check the Habsburg recovery and shore up the Protestant league. By the end of 1634, while the imperialists held Heidelberg, France had taken most of the rest of the Palatinate 'and now by that means more out of the power of the king of Spain to restore than ever'.[214]

From 1630 to 1635, then, involved in the question of the Palatinate were the often contradictory interests of Spain, Bavaria, the Swedes and the French, as well as the emperor and the Protestant princes. As

207. And we must recall that the Lutheran princes were little inclined to Frederick's cause; cf. Coke MS 45: Nethersole to Coke, 27 May 1633.
208. *Cal. Stat. Pap. Venet., 1629–32*, p. 567.
209. *Ibid.*, p. 605.
210. Du Mont, *Corps universal diplomatique*, VI, p. 14; Scottish Record Office, GD 406/1, Hamilton MS 209.
211. For example, Egerton MS 1820, f.115–115v.
212. *Cal. Stat. Pap. Dom., 1633–4*, p. 76: Windebank to Weston, 31 May 1633.
213. *Cal. Stat. Pap. Venet., 1632–6*, p. 170.
214. Egerton MS 1820, ff.313v, 419; Gardiner, *History of England*, VII, p. 374.

Hopton disarmingly put it in June 1633, the best hope – he might have said the only hope – for the Palatinate was 'a composition wherein everybody must be contented to forgo his interests to fit us, which is hard to believe'.[215] Three years later, in his relation of the state of England, the Venetian ambassador Correr still saw things the same way: 'it is to be feared that the Palatine will remain disinherited for ever, having against him three great powers, the emperor, Spain and Bavaria, while the allied forces not being interested for themselves . . . but only for common interests which do not constrain them so much as they ought. The chief attention of each of the parties is directed elsewhere.'[216] Gardiner was highly critical of the flux of Caroline policy, of Charles I's 'offering aid to one or the other', his 'habit of making profuse and often contradictory offers to each bidder in turn'.[217] But it is hard to see, with the rapid changes of military and political fortunes, what else he could have done.

Amid the rapid changes in territorial control, there was one constant. The restoration of Frederick, then Charles Louis, to the Electoral title rested in the hands of the emperor. The imperial envoy to Madrid, Stromberg, told Hopton therefore that England needed to 'gratify' the emperor as well as Spain.[218] For much of the early 1630s, it was not clear how England could do so. Besides that, Hopton, through all his shifting moods of optimism and pessimism, persisted in the view that 'though the interests of Germany must colour that business, the interest of Spain must carry it'.[219] The justification for Charles's diplomacy therefore is that Spain held out the best hope for the revocation of the imperial ban as well as, for much of the time, the best prospect for the recovery of the Palatine's lands. Though fraught with problems, it was not a hopelessly naive course. Ferdinand had before depended on Spanish troops and the end of the Dutch war might again make them available to assist him. The entry of Sweden and France into the war underlined the value of Spanish armies and made the case for not alienating England more obvious. Stromberg specifically suggested an agreement whereby in return for the aid of an English fleet against the French, the emperor might surrender the Palatinate and compensate Bavaria by other lands.[220] Though the proposal was to prompt Charles to send an ambassador to the emperor, by the time he arrived, the Duke of Bavaria had married, and with heirs in prospect was less inclined to surrender his acquisitions

215. Egerton MS 1820, f.267v, 6 June 1633.
216. *Cal. Stat. Pap. Venet., 1636–9*, p. 307: Correr's relation, 24 Oct. 1637; cf. Egerton MS 1820, f.65v.
217. Gardiner, *History of England*, VII, p. 170.
218. Egerton MS 1820, f.432.
219. *Ibid.*, f.457v.
220. *Ibid.*, f.432.

or dignity.[221] Before that outcome, however, within months of Stromberg's proposal, and while negotiations for the maritime treaty with Spain were still dragging on, the emperor, faced with the threat of France, concluded a peace with the leading Protestant prince, John George of Saxony.[222] The Peace of Prague, signed in May 1635, alleviated some of Ferdinand's problems. For England it came as a fatal blow: the peace, while providing toleration for Lutherans, failed to recognize Calvinism; it established the Duke of Bavaria as Elector of the Palatinate.[223] Spain had failed to fulfil its promise and half a decade of diplomacy had proved a failure. In consequence, Charles reoriented his diplomacy and turned to France.

During the first half of the personal rule, Caroline diplomacy had failed to secure Charles's first objective: the Palatinate. But it should not be discounted as empty and futile. To preserve English security and to expand trade were real achievements. It may be that whatever Charles had done England would have remained safe and, as a neutral, prospered. But 'as the experience of Queen Elizabeth in the 1580s showed', England could not count on being able to remain at peace.[224] During the early 1630s, fears of invasion, talk of war and threats to English commerce were often expressed. Spain never discounted the possibility of war with England, and skirmishes over the flag and sovereignty of the seas made wars with either the Dutch or French, worse still against them both, a real possibility.[225] It has been suggested that Charles I showed considerable foresight in seeing the threat to England presented by the growing might of France at a time when most Englishmen were more troubled by inherited fears of Habsburg Spain.[226] The language of royal orders, instructions to ambassadors and Councillors' position papers, lends support to the suggestion.[227] In February 1634, Windebank was concerned to stop the Dutch casting themselves on France 'considering the vast designs and growth of that state'.[228] Poigny believed England favoured Spain by a maritime treaty largely out of 'jealousy', as he put it, of France.[229]

221. Below, pp. 519–23.
222. A newsletter had mentioned rumours and fears of such a peace from the spring of 1633. See Flower to Scudamore, 11 May 1633 (PRO, C.115/M31/8751) in which Flower cast doubts on Saxony's 'constancy'. Cf. *Cal. Stat. Pap. Venet., 1629–32*, p. 633.
223. Gardiner, *History of England*, VII, p. 388. The Venetian ambassador in London was reporting the negotiations for the peace in January (*Cal. Stat. Pap. Venet., 1632–6*, p. 322).
224. Clay, *Economic Expansion*, II, p. 206.
225. Egerton MS 1820, f.254v.
226. D. Coke, *The Last Elizabethan: Sir John Coke, 1563–1644* (1937), p. 188.
227. Coke himself warned the Marquis of Hamilton that 'when the French have settled their distractions at home they will again look towards the Rhine and towards the Low Countries' (Hamilton MS 276, 27 Sept. 1632).
228. Clarendon MS 5, no. 334, 16 Oct. 1634.
229. PRO, 31/3/68, ff.114, 116v, July 1634.

Whatever his prescience of future clashes with France or Holland, Charles I, it is clear, believed that England's security could not be taken for granted. Acting on that belief, he endeavoured, as we shall see, the reform of the militia and the development of a more powerful navy.[230]

The navy

Clearly Charles I regarded a strong navy as essential to the maintenance of English security and the preservation of England's and his own authority. He had taken great interest in the navy as a young prince and he applied himself personally to naval affairs as king.[231] From the very beginning of Charles's reign, it would seem, the Council pursued a project for equipping a fleet of a hundred ships (of 400 tons) with munitions and victuals to police the narrow seas and protect commercial traffic from the Dunkirkers.[232] The proposal envisaged half the cost being met by the king, half by the House of Commons. The scope of the project and the expectation of such funding turned out to be little more than wishful thinking. But the basic aim of developing a more effective fleet, after years of neglect, remained a priority not only for Charles but for the Duke of Buckingham. As Roger Lockyer has demonstrated, Buckingham took his duties as Lord Admiral seriously.[233] Having experienced the problem of rotten beef and biscuit, unsuitable men and unreliable ships and equipment, Buckingham endeavoured to reform abuses in naval administration, in the provision of supplies and construction of ships. Notes by Edward Nicholas, secretary to the Admiralty commissioners, reveal that Buckingham increased the fleet from 26 to 53 vessels (from 11,070 to 22,122 tons), repaired Chatham, Deptford and Portsmouth dockyards and encouraged the private building of larger trading vessels that might form, as they did for the Dutch, a naval reserve.[234] Buckingham, Nicholas reported, spent his own money on the navy 'and evidenced his zeal by motions made to the Council for means to maintain a fleet to guard the coast'.[235] Charles's own commitment to the programme did not slacken with Buckingham's death or the end of the wars with France and Spain. On 4 September 1628, only days after

230. Cf. Birch, *Court and Times of Charles I*, II, p. 123: Pory to Puckering, 16 June 1631.
231. See Coke MS 40: Nicholas's report on the office of Lord Admiral, Aug. 1631. Also, B.W. Quintrell, 'Charles I and his navy', *The Seventeenth Century*, 3 (1988), pp. 159–79.
232. Huntington Library, Ellesmere MS 7004.
233. R. Lockyer, *Buckingham: the Life and Political Career of George Villiers, 1st Duke of Buckingham, 1592–1628* (1981), pp. 91, 197, 301–2, 317, 340–2, 359–68.
234. *Cal. Stat. Pap. Dom., 1633–4*, p. 123.
235. *Ibid.*

the duke's assassination, the Earl of Haddington wrote of the king's immediate concern for the navy.[236] Charles may have intended to present a revised version of the 1625 project to his last session of parliament in 1629. Among the papers of Sir John Coke, one of the commissioners for the navy, we find a proposition dated 12 January 1629, for a fleet of five squadrons to be set out in the north sea, the east sea, the narrow seas, the Irish coast and St George's Channel, in order to secure trade, guard the coasts and maintain the English sovereignty of the seas. The charge was estimated at £66,438.[237] But the parliamentary session of 1629, far from voting supply, withheld the grant of tonnage and poundage traditionally given to the monarch in order to protect trade and shipping. It was not only Charles who regarded this as a dangerous abnegation of responsibility and lack of realism in the European circumstances of 1629. A newswriter told Monsieur Damville that 'it was thought fit by your late parliament . . . that since tonnage and poundage was denied by the merchants that formerly gave it for maintaining a fleet for defence of the narrow seas and that the king, in respect of his want of money, was not able to defend them, our narrow seas should be committed to the guard and keeping of the Hollanders'.[238] The facetious letter was very close to an uncomfortable truth. Without money the king could not safeguard the seas. A small fleet of seven vessels was put out to guard the coasts, but this was a woefully inadequate number when the returning Spanish plate fleet and a Dutch fleet lying in waiting for it made a major sea battle likely.[239]

Shortage of money limited action in the immediate aftermath of 1629, but Charles determined to continue efforts to reform the navy. The king took personal overall responsibility for the Admiral's position, to which, in 1638, he appointed his second son James, who was to execute the office when he came of age.[240] The Privy Council's letter to the JPs of Hampshire thanking them for their efforts in naval matters which 'his Majesty takes most to heart' was, as well as rare praise, more than rhetoric.[241] Kenrick Edisbury, a commissioner for the navy, felt certain that the king's personal involvement facilitated reform and improvements.[242] Charles went frequently to the docks to inspect his ships: in the summer of 1631 he toured Woolwich,

236. National Library of Scotland, MS 3134, f.109: Earl of Haddington to James Primrose, 4 Sept. 1628.
237. *HMC Cowper I*, pp. 378–9, 12 Jan. 1629.
238. Coke MS 91, 9 May 1630.
239. *Ibid.*
240. Coke MS 40; Gardiner, *History of England*, VIII, pp. 338–9; Bodleian, Bankes MS 42/74: order to prepare grant to Prince James.
241. Coke MS 42, 18 Aug. 1632.
242. Coke MS 48: K. Edisbury to Coke, 10 March 1634.

Portsmouth and Chatham,[243] going on to every ship 'and almost into every room in every ship', as well as inspecting the docks and storehouses.[244] The king issued proclamations against the sale of ships and for preserving shipping timber,[245] he forbade the cutting for building of timber that was suitable for the navy.[246] He also tried to enforce proclamations against the consumption of meat in Lent and fostered the project for a fishing association in order to promote shipbuilding and navigation.[247] The years 1628 to 1634 also saw a campaign by the king and Council to improve the condition of coastal castles, fortresses and docks. In November 1630 the commissioners for the navy commenced an investigation of the state of the forts at Milton and Tilbury near Gravesend.[248] Sir Thomas Culpeper was spurred to vigorous action as governor of Dover Castle.[249] In January 1635 a new dry dock was ordered to be built at Portsmouth and improvements were made to Chatham and Deptford dockyards.[250] As the situation in Europe grew more unstable, the condition of coastal defences became more pressing. In the summer of 1635 Sir Arthur Hopton advised the king that being 'compassed about by nations warlike by land and sea whose countries are all fortified' he needed urgently to attend to 'fortifying his coast'.[251] 'It is thought,' he added by way of comment on the navy, 'to be too uncertain a defence that which is subject to wind and weather.'

As an effective wall of defence, the English navy was compromised by more than the uncertainties of the elements. The naval campaigns of the war years had revealed serious deficiencies. In October 1628, for example, in the wake of the failure to relieve La Rochelle, a Captain Hackwell reported to Sir John Coke the problems of leaky ships and inadequate victuals.[252] Corrupt pursers, whose books came in 'very late', connived at reduced supplies and took a share of the profit.[253] In October 1630 the commissioners of the navy concluded a full enquiry into the problems. Their report did not make for encouraging reading. The five-week delays in getting victuals on board had led to rotting

243. PRO, C.115/M30/8079: Flower to Scudamore, 27 April 1631; PRO, C.115/N3/8547, 1 July 1631; C.115/M31/8136, 13 June 1631.
244. *Cal. Stat. Pap. Dom., 1631–3*, p. 90: Nicholas to Pennington, 25 June 1631.
245. Larkin, *Stuart Royal Proclamations*, II, no. 119, pp. 244–6, 12 July 1629.
246. PRO, SO 1/2/132.
247. Larkin, *Stuart Royal Proclamations*, II, pp. 251–2, 336–7, 354–5, 701–2; PRO, SO 1/2/134; below, pp. 250–52.
248. *HMC Cowper I*, p. 417: commissioners of navy to Coke, 24 Nov. 1630.
249. *HMC Cowper II*, p. 96.
250. *Cal. Stat. Pap. Dom., 1634–5*, pp. 449–50.
251. Egerton MS 1820, f.511v: Hopton to Windebank, 19 July 1635.
252. Coke MS 35, 20 Oct. 1628.
253. Coke MS 35: Sir G. Slyngsby to Coke, 18 Nov. 1628. Coke wrote margin headings to this letter such as 'books lame', perhaps as a reminder of abuses to be investigated.

and waste at the harbour; ships had sailed without their full complement of sailors (even the Admiral's own ship was twenty-eight short!); powder and munitions had been unaccountably 'expended' when no fighting had occurred. While some ships were short of victuals, others were oversupplied and the captains, it was suspected, turned the surplus to their own profit.[254] In order that 'your Majesty's navy royal may not only recover in short time the ancient reputation, but also grow to greater power and respect', the commissioners issued a series of recommendations that might effect the necessary reforms. Officers in particular, they urged, should attend to their duties in person, not appoint servants and clerks while they idled often far from their ships. They should meet weekly, oversee accounts and estimates personally and respond more quickly to correspondence. It was an ominous sign that the commissioners associated the problems with the very men, the officers, who were responsible for supervising their ships; and worse still that they repeated many of the ills catalogued by the Jacobean commissions of enquiry of 1608 and 1618.[255] It is not surprising, then, that the 1630 recommendations appear to have had little more effect. The following year, in May 1631, Captain Plumleigh (who alone had been commended in the report) complained of the inordinate delays in getting supplies on board and of the 'snail-paced people' responsible.[256] In January 1632 Kenelm Digby feared that even new ships being built fell short of acceptable standards.[257] Moreover, there were difficulties in getting cannon, and men were in short supply.[258] The last was a perennial problem. As Edisbury informed Nicholas, with the French and Dutch paying better wages, many English sailors preferred service abroad and those who stayed at home opted often to serve in the merchant fleets rather than the king's navy.[259] There were still complaints in 1636 that the merchants had the pick of the best sailors; 'no terror of punishment will restrain mariners from abandoning his Majesty's service'.[260] The press failed to work well and when it worked brought the dregs of society into the fleets.[261] Corruption remained rife, for all the king's watchfulness. Edisbury frankly acknowledged that little good would come of the reforms, 'for notwithstanding that Mr Secretary Windebank had delivered his Majesty's

254. Coke MS 39: 'Account for sea services', 30 Oct. 1630.
255. *Ibid.*, Coke MS 39, only briefly and inadequately calendared in *HMC Cowper I*, pp. 414–15; see A.P. McGowan (ed.) *The Jacobean Commissions of Enquiry, 1608 and 1618* (Navy Records Soc., 116, 1971).
256. Coke MS 39; MS 40: Plumleigh to Coke, 24 May 1631.
257. *HMC Cowper II*, p. 1: Digby to Coke, 2 Jan. 1633.
258. Coke MS 47: Sir John Heydon to Coke, March 1634.
259. *Cal. Stat. Pap. Dom., 1633–4*, p. 508, 15 March 1634.
260. *Cal. Stat. Pap. Dom., 1635–6*, p. 332: Sir Henry Palmer to the Lords of the Admiralty, 28 March 1636.
261. *Cal. Stat. Pap. Dom., 1633–4*, pp. 539, 541.

pleasure that all the delinquents over 15 prepare their answers in writing against his Majesty's return . . . yet the general voice amongst them is that there will be no further mention of the matter'.[262] He was probably right. Nicholas thought that even the Admiralty commissioners met too seldom.[263] Many of the problems continued even after the building of the substantial ship money fleets from 1634. In April 1635 Goddard complained to Coke of ships that were worm-eaten or in danger of sinking if they were not calked.[264] Captain Sir John Pennington endorsed general complaints about the poor standard of shipbuilding and repeated the old lament about the tardy provision of victuals.[265] What he could have effected in a week, he told Nicholas, the officers of the navy have been 'six or seven weeks about . . . and still not done'.[266] In November 1635 the ships due to put to sea had, he thought, 'but the name of a fleet as yet'.[267]

Whilst problems persisted, the need for an effective navy became more and more apparent. The threat to trade from pirates and marauders increased. In the spring of 1632, a Turkish landing on the west coast was feared;[268] pirates continually infested the waters off the coast of Ireland.[269] Plumleigh, ever assiduous, struggled to contain them. 'Never,' he reported in November 1633, 'was poor country so scourged by swarms of villains as Ireland has been this year by Biscayners to whose insolencies, if timely opposition had not been given, the utter ruin and decay of trade must of necessity have followed.'[270] Nearer to home, in October 1634 Ralph Conway wrote to Coke: 'the people on the coast were glad at the sight of the king's ships, having already received a great benefit as if they had been rescued from slavery by chasing away the Turks'.[271] The West Country fishermen were especially overjoyed. But the small flotilla of the king's coastal guard could not be everywhere; the challenges were too many to contain. In addition to Turks, Dunkirkers and Biscayners, English commercial shipping was challenged by Dutch and French men of war whose impudence knew no bounds.[272] The Dutch who fished in English waters even had the effrontery to dry their nets on

262. Coke MS 48: Edisbury to Coke, 10 March 1634.
263. *Cal. Stat. Pap. Dom., 1628–31*, p. 290.
264. Coke MS 50: H. Goddard to Coke, 22 April 1635.
265. Cf. *Cal. Stat. Pap. Dom., 1635*, pp. 438–9; cf. *1635–6*, p. 158: Sir William Monson's propositions, 12 Jan. 1636.
266. *Cal. Stat. Pap. Dom., 1635*, p. 465: Pennington to Nicholas, 5 Nov. 1635.
267. *Ibid.*
268. *HMC Cowper I*, p. 452: Richard, Earl of Cork, to Coke, 19 March 1632.
269. Coke MS 45: C. Walley to Coke, 17 May 1633.
270. Coke MS 47: Plumleigh to Coke, 14 Nov. 1633; *HMC Cowper II*, p. 36.
271. *Cal. Stat. Pap. Dom., 1634–5*, p. 222, 3 Oct. 1634. These 'Turks' were actually North Africans from Algiers and Morocco.
272. Cf. Coke MS 38: 'The particular decay of navigation'.

the English shore.[273] The deficiencies of normal policing left English ships to the mercy of marauders or forced them to take their own initiatives. The Merchant Adventurers of York, having lost ships to the Dunkirkers, kept their goods at home.[274] Bristol Common Council voted to finance the cost of ships to protect the city's vessels in the Irish seas.[275] As well as the assaults on merchant men, it became increasingly clear during the early 1630s that England needed a strong navy to check the mounting sea power of the French, as well as the Dutch, and to safeguard security through a strong presence in the narrow seas. Hopton counselled such a course from 1631.[276] Heath's propositions of 1629 had referred to the need to maintain the English sovereignty of the seas.[277] As the challenges grew, Charles, probably with the advice of Sir John Coke, determined to reassert his authority.[278] During the winter of 1633 to 1634 Sir John Borough, Keeper of the Tower records, researched the precedents and asserted the claim to sovereignty of the seas to be inherent in the English crown.[279] The following year John Selden's *Mare Clausum*, written in the reign of James I, was published and deposited with the Court of Admiralty and Privy Council as the most 'faithful and strong evidence for the dominion of the British seas'.[280] As Gardiner summarized it, 'the assertion of the sovereignty of the seas meant nothing less than an assertion that the whole of the English channel to the shores of France, and of the North sea to the shores of Flanders and Holland was completely under the dominion of the King of England'.[281] For all its boldness, it was, as the ambassadors of France and the United Provinces recognized, a claim to which Charles attached great importance.[282] The king reminded Châteauneuf that Queen Elizabeth had once warned an ambassador of Henri IV not to build strength at sea.[283] Five years later Senneterre was warned that the English had made even the ships of Philip II of Spain lower their flags to the ensign.[284]

273. Coke MS 52: instructions for the fleet, 1635.
274. York City Record Office, House Books, 35, f.79.
275. Bristol Record Office, Common Council Books, 3, f.3v, 3 July 1628.
276. Egerton MS 1820, f.120v.
277. Coke MS 36.
278. Kenelm Digby identified Coke as the moving force behind the reissue of Selden's *Mare Clausum* (Coke MS 51, 27 Aug. 1635).
279. Gardiner, *History of England*, VII, p. 358. It is no mere coincidence that it was at this time that the French and Dutch were entering into a close alliance and, in April 1634, a treaty for the partition of Flanders.
280. Rushworth, *Historical Collections*, II, p. 320.
281. Gardiner, *History of England*, VII, p. 358.
282. Cf. Rossingham's newsletter of 28 March 1635 (Huntington Library, Hastings MS 9598); PRO, 31/3/68, f.175v.
283. PRO, 31/3/66, f.161, 24 Sept. 1629.
284. PRO, 31/3/68, f.187.

It was in order to make good these claims that the first ship money fleet put to sea. Hopton, we recall, had emphasized the value of a fleet financed entirely in England for the favour of which Spain and others would have to bargain.[285] An independent fleet would enable England to preserve her neutrality whilst protecting shipping and keeping the seas open off the coast of Flanders. When it set out, the newswriter Edward Rossingham, with an ear to court gossip, suspected another purpose: 'peradventure our fleet hath another aim: to preserve the sovereignty of the narrow seas from the French king who hath had a design long to take it from us and therefore he hath provided a very great navy'.[286] Viscount Conway endorsed Rossingham's opinion. The first duty of Vice-Admiral Lindsey, he wrote, was 'to show the fleet to France'.[287] 'I think that if the French merchants could be brought to take convoys from us, it would advance much the king's mastery of the seas.'[288] The instructions to the fleet make it clear that this was central to its purpose. In addition to ridding the seas of pirates and protecting English merchantmen, the fleet was ordered to counter any actions 'tending to the denial or impeachment of that sovereignty which we and our progenitors time out of mind have had and enjoyed'.[289] The fleet was to protect England's allies as well as native shipping and to prevent any from passing without 'performing the due homage of the seas', by lowering their colours to English flags. English security was to be protected by forcing all other nations to recognize the sovereignty of the seas.

Gardiner was not impressed by the ship money fleet or its ability to carry out these objectives, and most historians have been no less sceptical.[290] At forty-two ships the fleet was not large by comparison with the total shipping the Dutch had at their command. But Nicholas, who knew his business, believed it to be 'the strongest fleet in *force* (though their number be small) that has been set out from hence these ten years'.[291] Windebank's praise was more extravagant: 'It is the most complete for goodness of ships and furniture of munition and in all other respects that hath been set out in the memory of any man.'[292] Given its objectives, the first ship money fleet was by no means ineffective.[293] The Dutch men-of-war began to do obeisance to the

285. Above, p. 74.
286. Hastings MS 9598.
287. *HMC Cowper II*, p. 92: Conway to Coke, 9 Sept. 1635.
288. *Ibid.*
289. Coke MS 52.
290. Gardiner, *History of England*, VII, pp. 385–90.
291. *Cal. Stat. Pap. Dom., 1634–5*, p. 377, 6 Dec. 1634.
292. Egerton MS 1820, f.482v, 27 May 1635.
293. Bulstrode Whitelocke seems to have been impessed: *Memorials of the English Affairs* (1682), pp. 23–4.

English flag and their fishing vessels were forced to buy licences to fish in English waters.[294] The Spaniards negotiated for the aid of the fleet; the French went to lengths to avoid encountering it so as to side-step the whole issue of acknowledging English sovereignty of the seas.[295] Gardiner viewed Lindsey's operations in the summer of 1635 as a 'mere display of naval force': 'to compel a few passing vessels to dip their flags was hardly a result worthy of the effort'.[296] That is to miss the point. It was, as Conway had recognized, the mere *showing* of the fleet that was central to its purpose: the reassertion of English naval power and sovereignty was a guarantee of English security and influence. The Venetian ambassador Gussoni was clearly impressed by the display of strength;[297] in August Sir William Monson reported the French 'wondering at the force of the English fleet, which will hereafter as much daunt them as the name of Talbot in former times'.[298] Gardiner, writing in the age of great British naval victories, looked for action and saw none.[299] Sir Kenelm Digby perceptively described to Coke how a mere naval presence could secure objectives. Charles I, he wrote, could hold the balance of power in Europe, 'if he keeps a fleet at sea and his navy in that reputation it now is in; for I assure your honour that is very great. And although my Lord of Lindsey do no more than sail up and down, yet the very setting of our best fleet out to sea is the greatest service that I believe hath been done the king these many years.'[300] When we consider the part the fleet played in relaxing the Dutch blockades and checking a Franco-Dutch assault on Flanders it is hard not to concur with Digby's assessment.

294. Coke MS 54: Conway to Coke, 1 Aug. 1636; calendared in *HMC Cowper II*, p. 144; *Cal. Stat. Pap. Dom., 1635*, p. 157.
295. Below, p. 510; Gardiner, *History of England*, VII, p. 385.
296. Gardiner, *History of England*, VII, pp. 384–5.
297. *Cal. Stat. Pap. Venet., 1632–6*, pp. 365–6; cf. Correr, *ibid.*, p. 372.
298. *Cal. Stat. Pap. Dom., 1635*, p. 348: Sir William Monson to Windebank, 23 Aug. 1635.
299. A different perspective is offered by the editor of *Cal. Stat. Pap. Venet., 1632–6*, p. xliii.
300. Coke MS 51: Digby to Coke, 29 Sept. 1635, fairly fully calendared in *HMC Cowper II*, pp. 94–5.

III
THE SEARCH FOR THE KING'S 'MINES': REVENUE AND FINANCE

Traditional revenues

Peace did not fundamentally diminish England's position in Europe. It was, however, a major benefit to the new regime at home, an opportunity to check the spiralling debt of the war years and attend to the desperate state of royal finance. The financial situation had been in near crisis when Charles succeeded to the throne. The costs of the abortive campaigns to Germany and against Cadiz had more than consumed the parliamentary grant of 1624.[1] In 1626 Charles found it necessary to suspend all payments to the officers of the royal household.[2] Arrears mounted; the crown jewels were pawned in Holland. Over the years 1626–30 there were vast sales of crown lands, which further reduced the king's annual income.[3] If tonnage and poundage had not been levied, government would have been impossible. When Weston became Lord Treasurer it was said that he succeeded to £2 million of debts.[4] The king by 1629 could not even pay for household provision;[5] Henrietta Maria, it was reported, was so ashamed of the dilapidated state of her apartments and effects that she was forced to receive the Duchess of Tremouille in the dark.[6] With the reserve pledged to the end of 1630, it was not clear how the king could go on governing at home, let alone fight a war.[7] A newswriter reported in

1. F.C. Dietz, *English Public Finance 1558–1641* (1964), ch. 10.
2. *Acts of the Privy Council, 1625–6*, pp. 441, 501.
3. Dietz, *English Public Finance*, pp. 243–4.
4. T. Birch (ed.) *The Court and Times of Charles I* (2 vols, 1848), II, p. 138: T. Gresley to T. Puckering, 27 Oct. 1631.
5. *Calendar of State Papers Venetian* [*Cal. Stat. Pap. Venet.*], *1629–32*, p. 297.
6. S.R. Gardiner, *History of England from the Accession of James I to the Outbreak of the Civil War 1603–1642* (10 vols, 1883–4), VII, p. 175; *Cal. Stat. Pap. Venet., 1629–32*, p. 359.
7. *Cal. Stat. Pap. Venet., 1628–9*, p. 581.

June 1629 that even with peace and parsimony, he could not see how to settle the king's debts.[8] In the months after the dissolution of parliament, the Venetian ambassador wrote, 'Everyone is looking to see from what quarter money may be raised for so many necessities.'[9]

Yet though the financial position was desperate at the beginning of the personal rule, it is not obvious that the decision to rule without parliament greatly worsened it. Subsidies were not granted for the expenses of ordinary peacetime government (the king was still expected to 'live of his own'), nor usually for the repayment of royal debts – especially when it was believed that those debts had arisen in part from the corruption and rapaciousness of favourites.[10] Moreover, parliaments often demanded in return for subsidies the suspension of those extraordinary courses by which the crown raised money – monopolies, additional impositions and loans, for example. For all the difficulties, the forced loan had brought in nearly as much as the five subsidies voted in 1628. The prospect of such large grants in the future was slight. The parliamentary votes of supply in 1624, 1625 and 1628, though inadequate for the war, had been unprecedentedly generous. From the beginning of Charles's reign over £600,000 in subsidies was paid into the Exchequer.[11] It is worth noting that by 1634, without subsidies, the king's annual revenue had reached that figure.[12]

But if the suspension of parliaments did not greatly add to the king's financial problems, it was not easy to see any solution to them. Perhaps since the sale of the monastic lands to finance Henry VIII's wars with France, the English monarchy had been unable in practice to live of its own. Under Edward, Mary and Elizabeth, more crown lands were sold to pay for campaigns in Scotland and Ireland. More drastically, the great inflation of the sixteenth century had eaten away the value of fixed rents and receipts from crown lands which had been granted on long leases – a political favour all the more necessary during the decades of rapid religious changes and the greater need of the crown to buy support. By the beginning of the seventeenth century, the annual income from crown estates was only £87,000.[13] During the first decade of Charles's reign, and mostly during the first five years, an additional £640,000 worth of crown lands and woods was sold,

8. Melbourne Hall, Coke MS 37: letter to Monsieur Damville, 26 June 1629. (Not calendared in *HMC Cowper I*, p. 388.)
9. *Cal. Stat. Pap. Venet., 1628–9*, p. 581.
10. Cf. G.L. Harriss, 'Medieval doctrines in the debates on supply', in K. Sharpe (ed.) *Faction and Parliament* (Oxford, 1978), pp. 73–104.
11. Above, pp. 9–11; *Calendar of State Papers Domestic* [*Cal. Stat. Pap. Dom.*], *1634–5*, p. 611; F.C. Dietz, *Receipts and Issues of the Exchequer during the Reigns of James I and Charles I* (Northampton, Mass., 1928), pp. 144–5.
12. *Cal. Stat. Pap. Dom., 1634–5*, p. 586: Windebank's notes of business conducted by the Lords of the Treasury.
13. Dietz, *English Public Finance*, p. 296.

mainly to pay war expenses.[14] There does seem to have been some attempt to ensure that monies owed from crown lands were paid. In what Gerald Aylmer has described as an 'early Tudor approach', receiverships and a surveyor-general of crown lands were appointed to improve the collection of revenue.[15] But since those in arrears with rents were often, like the Earl of Huntingdon, himself a receiver, among the most powerful magnates of the realm, there were political limitations to reform.[16] The inadequacy and erosion of crown lands had for some time been recognized as a problem. The more historically minded MPs had searched precedents for an act of resumption of alienated crown lands in 1625 and 1626, a course Charles himself pursued, with limited success, in Scotland.[17] But no action had been taken – not least because a figure like the Duke of Buckingham was one of the very culprits from whom, in the eyes of the Commons, the royal lands should be 'resumed'.[18] The long-term problem of a royal estate inadequate to finance peacetime government was exacerbated by the succession of Charles I and his personal circumstances. Where Mary and Elizabeth had both ruled childless, where James I after 1613 had only one son to provide for, Charles and Henrietta Maria were to produce five children in the first ten years of their married life. As the Lord Steward's records reveal, each of the royal children had to have their own establishment.[19] This obviously became a cause for concern. In November 1635 propositions were put forward for the erection of a council to provide revenue and an estate for the royal issue.[20] They included grants of reversions of crown lands currently leased, but also of concealed lands and 'flowers of the crown' that had been misplanted – presumably some revived form of the bills for resumption. Nothing came of the proposals. In 1640, the hope was still being expressed that 'it may in suceeding ages come to pass that a parliament may help the crown with an act of resumption'.[21] A royal demesne, from which the king might live of his own, was never established.

14. *Ibid.*, p. 299.
15. G. Aylmer, 'Studies in the institutions and personnel of English central administration' (University of Oxford, D. Phil. thesis, 1954), p. 580. I am most grateful to Dr Aylmer for permission to see his thesis and for many invaluable discussions of the 1630s. I often cite the thesis rather than *The King's Servants: The Civil Service of Charles I* (1961), because there is so much valuable information in the former which constraints of length excised from the latter.
16. Huntington Library, Hastings MS 7997: Juxon to Hastings, 28 April 1640.
17. Bodleian, Tanner MS 276, f.80; J.N. Ball, 'The parliamentary career of Sir John Eliot: 1604–1629' (Cambridge University, PhD thesis, 1953), p. 134; Cambridge University Library, MS Dd, 12.20.22, I, ff.65–66v.
18. J.N. Ball, 'Sir John Eliot and parliament, 1624–1629', in Sharpe, *Faction and Parliament*, pp. 180, 185.
19. See British Library [BL], Harleian MS 7623, for lists of diet and wages for the households of the royal children.
20. *Cal. Stat. Pap. Dom., 1635*, p. 515.
21. Huntington Library, Ellesmere MS 7826: Castle to Bridgewater, 3 March 1640.

Other traditional sources of royal revenue proved capable of more successful exploitation. One was wardships. The function of the Court of Wards and Liveries was not only or even primarily financial. Wardship was a feudal right of the crown to supervise the estates of minors (who in feudal law held them of the king) and to entrust their management to another until the heir came of age.[22] As Charles told his Master of the Court of Wards, Sir Robert Naunton, 'The charge we have lain upon you for the government of our wards much concerneth both our service and the good of of our people and chiefly our nobility upon whom our grace doth most reflect.'[23] The profit, however, either directly from the ward's lands or, more usually, from grants of wardship could, if exploited, be considerable. Sir Robert Naunton raised the annual yield of wards from £45,000 to over £53,000, and may have suggested further enhancements.[24] In October 1634 the newswriter Edward Rossingham told Viscount Scudamore that he had heard that with the next master's succession all wards would have to pay to the crown the full value of their estates according to their licences, which, he added, 'will very much advance the king's revenues'.[25] The next master, appointed in 1635, Sir Francis Cottington, certainly fulfilled the last prediction. He raised the yield of wardship to an annual £84,000 by 1640 and got the money in twice as quickly as his predecessor – an achievement that was quite 'exceptional'.[26] Such exploitation of a feudal incident was not without its political cost. Henry Slingsby described wardship in his diary as an abuse whereby 'young children may be bought and sold not unlike that law for bondmen which gives liberty to use them as one list'.[27] More generally, Clarendon recalled that Cottington's sharp increase made the gentry and nobility determined to abolish wardships – which they did in 1646.[28] Yet, as the historian of Somerset wardships has shown, for all the grumbling there is no evidence of lax payments;[29] and when he succeeded Cottington as master, Viscount Saye and Sele maintained the high profits of wards.[30] When, in a period of falling real income and expanding government business, the crown was expected to live

22. See J. Hurstfield, *The Queen's Wards* (1958).
23. Bodleian, Clarendon MS 5, no. 290, 12 June 1631.
24. R.E. Schreiber, *The Political Career of Sir Robert Naunton, 1589–1635* (1981), pp. 97–128, 163–4.
25. PRO, C.115/M36/8436, 3 Oct. 1634.
26. Dietz, *English Public Finance*, p. 303; M. Hawkins (ed.) *Sales of Wards in Somerset 1603–1641* (Somerset Record Soc., 67, Frome, 1965), pp. xxii–xxiv.
27. D. Parsons (ed.) *The Diary of Sir Henry Slingsby* (1836), pp. 17–18.
28. E. Hyde, Earl of Clarendon, *The History of the Rebellion and Civil Wars in England*, ed. W.D. Macray (6 vols, Oxford, 1888), I, pp. 198–9; W.J. Jones, *Politics and the Bench: The Judges and the Origins of the English Civil War* (1971), p. 103.
29. Hawkins, *Sales of Wards*, p. xxv.
30. Jones, *Politics and the Bench*, p. 102.

from traditional feudal revenues, there was little alternative to maximizing their value.

Purveyance provides another example of that harsh truth. Purveyance was a traditional right of the crown to take provisions for the royal household at below market cost. It originated as a form of tribute to a monarch on almost perpetual progress; it included labour and services – carting, for example – as well as commodities. During the early seventeenth century the actual provision of goods had been commuted to a monetary composition, by which the counties paid the difference between the market price of goods and the 'king's price'. With the king no longer peripatetic, and the household established largely in Whitehall, or one of the royal lodges within a closed southern circle, the payment of money doubtless seemed more convenient than the transportation of provisions.[31] Such an arrangement, however, did not render the charge more acceptable. Purveyance became a source of mounting irritation and frequently voiced complaints in Elizabethan and Jacobean parliaments. In 1610, in his scheme known as the Great Contract, Sir Robert Cecil, Earl of Salisbury, and Lord Treasurer, had been prepared to surrender purveyance as part of a package of feudal revenues in exchange for a fixed annual sum. When that scheme failed, an impoverished monarchy was forced to exploit purveyance along with other feudal privileges. In 1625 the Board of Greencloth, the Lord Steward's department, ordered a reversion to the practice of providing goods instead of money on account of 'diverse inconveniences' – perhaps because the value of goods was better protected against inflation.[32] Certainly the levy had led to innumerable disputes over assessments. In Essex and Somerset complaints were brought to quarter sessions and the assizes.[33] But the switch back to the direct provision of goods created at least as many problems as it solved. Essex complained in 1631 that poultry was taken beyond the fixed proportion and that the clerk of the market priced goods to the prejudice of the county.[34] Leicestershire failed in 1635 to provide the numbers of oxen and sheep due and the royal household officers were left to buy in the market and recover the monetary payment due.[35] It would seem that in different counties and at different times both methods of purveyance – by direct supply or composition – were in operation.[36] Whatever the method, purveyance met with widespread

31. See G.E. Aylmer, 'The last years of purveyance, 1610–1660', *Econ. Hist. Rev.*, 2nd series, 10 (1957), pp. 81–93.
32. Hastings MS 4134; PRO, LS (Lord Steward's department) 13/169, f.202.
33. Bodleian, Firth MS C.4, pp. 520–1; E.H. Bates Harbin (ed.) *Quarter Sessions Records for the County of Somerset, II, 1625–1649* (Somerset Record Soc., 24, Frome, 1908), pp. 2–3.
34. Firth MS C.4, p. 535; PRO, LS 13/169, f.179.
35. Hastings MS 4135: Lord Steward's department to Huntingdon, 19 Jan. 1635.
36. PRO, LS 13/169, f.202; cf. Aylmer, 'Last years of purveyance' and Aylmer, 'Studies in the central administration', p. 143.

resistance. At the end of 1629 Middlesex and Surrey were considerably in arrears on compositions due in 1624–5.[37] In Dorset one of the collectors, Mr Phelps, claimed that it had cost him £80 to chase up payments, with several persons and places claiming exemption.[38] Some individuals tried to claim exemption on the ground that they were royal servants – leading the Privy Council to issue an order that none was exempt from the charge.[39] Banbury corporation records show several refusals to pay in 1628;[40] in 1630 the city of Bristol sent a delegation to London to claim that their charter exempted them from payment.[41] More frequent were petitions for the amelioration of a disproportionate or unequal burden, either by individuals or whole counties. Such protests were not entirely without foundation. Coastal counties, Hampshire for example, bore an unusually heavy charge for carrying naval supplies, as did a county like Oxford with woods that supplied shipping timbers. Workers in Hampshire, who were frequently dragooned into public works, in August 1632 refused to labour for purveyance wages.[42] During the Scots war Nottinghamshire bore a large burden of the costs of horses and carts for the conveyance of men and supplies north.[43] At the March assizes of 1629, the Grand Jury of Essex protested that their charge for wood alone had amounted to £3,000, and that in addition new purveyance charges were levied for oats and hay for horses, poultry for the king's hawks and even for the carriage to court of Essex oysters. The burden had risen, they threatened, 'in so much that the county will in no ways be able to hold the former composition agreed upon unless they may be freed from these new charges'.[44] A similar presentment was made at the Epiphany assizes the next year, and the complaints grew.[45] Constables refused office because they were reluctant to be responsible for purveyance.[46]

But many of the novelties against which the Essex Grand Jury protested (the carriage of oysters among them!) were in fact long-established

37. PRO, LS 13/169, f.89.
38. Dorset County Record Office, quarter sessions orders 1625–37, ff.273v, 294.
39. PRO, PC 2/42/363, 22 Dec. 1632.
40. J.S.W. Gibbons and E.R.C. Brinkworth (eds) *Banbury Corporation Records* (Banbury Historical Soc., 15, 1977), p. 148.
41. Bristol Record Office, Common Council Books, 3, f.3.
42. For example, Bodleian, Rawlinson MS D.666, f.85; Coke MS 42, 18 Aug. 1632; Hampshire Record Office, Herriard MS 013; below, pp. 615–16.
43. Nottingham University Library, Clifton MSS, Cl/C 682: Earl of Kingston to Sir Gervase Clifton, 14 June 1639.
44. Firth MS C.4, pp. 520–1.
45. *Ibid.*, p. 523.
46. *Ibid.*, p. 535; cf. J. Kent, *The English Village Constable 1580–1642* (Oxford, 1986), pp. 42–4.

charges.[47] And it was such charges that, as the costs of the royal household increased, the Board of Greencloth ardently defended and steadily raised. A manor in Dorset that tried to claim exemption was firmly informed 'that purveyance is such an inseparable incident to the crown that no grant can exempt from it'.[48] In 1634 the Earl of Arundel, lord-lieutenant of Northumberland, Cumberland and Westmorland, was informed by a signet letter that the increasing charge of the royal establishment compelled the king to charge purveyances on these counties which had hitherto been exempt on account of their old obligation of border service.[49] With the union of 1603 and peace with the Scots, Charles explained, border service was redundant and so the north was to contribute to purveyance; ironically, a few years later, border service was being revived against the now rebellious Scots.[50] Across the country the costs of purveyance were rising and the protests multiplied in ever greater proportion. At the Michaelmas sessions of 1640, the gentry of Kent complained of a shilling rise in the composition in 1637.[51] The following August at the assizes Twysden recalled that 'the county was now much discontented at their so often raisings'.[52] The office of treasurer for the composition money they found in no statute and therefore argued that no one could be compelled to serve. It was decided to refer the grievance to parliament.[53] Indeed it became increasingly common to hear purveyance, an established right of the crown, described as a grievance. By the commissioners who examined the state of the king's revenues in 1641 it was listed as an 'illegal' revenue.[54] Purveyance was another of that catalogue of the 'ills' of Charles I's government published as the Grand Remonstrance.[55] Clearly the extensions and increases in purveyance had fuelled a mounting opposition to what had long been seen as an irritating burden. Whilst we cannot calculate the value of services or goods provided, the amounts raised seem small in proportion to the fuss. From 1630 to 1635, purveyance brought in just over £30,000 per annum; by 1640 it had risen to nearly £38,000.[56] For all that they were needed, such amounts did little to alleviate the king's financial difficulties or even the costs of the royal household.

47. Firth MS C.4, p. 538.
48. PRO, LS 13/169, f.62.
49. PRO, SO 1/2, f.185; cf. PRO, LS 13/169, f.240.
50. Below, pp. 798, 885.
51. Kent Archives Office, Twysden MS U47/47/01, p. 15.
52. *Ibid.*, p. 16.
53. *Ibid.*
54. Clarendon MS 20, no. 1539: 'A calculation of His Majesty's ordinary yearly revenue', 16 Aug. 1641.
55. S.R. Gardiner (ed.) *Constitutional Documents of the Puritan Revolution* (Oxford, 1899), p. 212.
56. PRO, Treasury Books, T56/2; Aylmer, 'Last years of purveyance', p. 85.

Knighthood and forest fines

During the war years, as we have seen, the king and the Council were desperately exploring alternative sources of revenue. Sir John Borough was sent to search the Tower records for ways by which past monarchs had legally raised money. Many of Borough's precedents involved the financial exploitation of feudal levies or of feudal rights which, though not originally intended as a means of raising money, could be turned to that end.[57] One obvious case was the commission for defective titles. By a proclamation of 27 May 1630, subjects who could not prove their titles to lands once held of the crown were invited to compound or risk legal process for recovery of the property.[58] In August 1635 a second proclamation renewed the commission.[59] Though Dr Larkin charts a 'dramatic rise' in the compositions paid, from £1,320 in 1634 to £4,840 in 1636, in terms of overall royal revenue, and still more of needs, the sums were small.[60] Whilst, as Dr Aylmer has argued, the commission for defective titles was a respectable means of preventing the evasion of taxes and feudal dues, it was clearly unpopular.[61] When, however, parliament had shied away from tackling the underlying problems of royal finance and the king was still expected to live of his own, it was imperative for the crown to exploit to the full its feudal rights. Penry Williams has estimated that by 1628 Charles had raised them to six times their Elizabethan levels.[62] In the course of doing so, as Clarendon perceptively put it, 'obsolete laws were revived and rigorously executed wherein the subject might be taught how unthrifty a thing it was by too strict a detaining that was his to put the king to enquire what was his own'.[63]

Of the 'obsolete laws' revived for their fiscal benefits, the most famous – perhaps one should say infamous – were those that led to knighthood and forest fines. Fines for not appearing to be knighted at the king's coronation were mentioned in Borough's list of precedents for raising money.[64] Precedents from the reign of Henry II showed fines imposed on those worth £10 or £15 in lands who had omitted to take the order, with the qualification rising by Henry VII's time to £40.[65] Since then, of course, inflation of at least 400 per cent had made

57. Above, p. 13.
58. J.F. Larkin (ed.) *Stuart Royal Proclamations II: Proclamations of King Charles I 1625–1646* (Oxford, 1983), no. 130, pp. 268–70.
59. *Ibid.*, no. 203, pp. 470–2.
60. *Ibid.*, p. 471, note 2.
61. Aylmer, 'Studies in central administration', p. 356.
62. P. Williams, *The Tudor Regime* (Oxford, 1979), pp. 72–3; cf. J. Hurstfield, 'The profits of fiscal feudalism, 1541–1602', *Econ. Hist. Rev.*, 2nd series (1955–6), pp. 53–61.
63. Clarendon, *History of the Rebellion*, I, pp. 84–5.
64. BL Add. MS 34324, f.281v.
65. PRO, SP 16/155/49; *Cal. Stat. Pap. Dom., 1629–31*, p. 147.

nonsense of this sum as a fiscal measurement of those suitable for elevation to knighthood. Moreover, the Jacobean orgy of creations made additions to the numbers of knights undesirable. Lord Keeper Coventry evidently reminded Charles I in December 1625 of the custom of creating knights at the coronation, but the king had replied: 'he is prevented there being more knights already than are necessary and therefore he is resolved not to make any'.[66] In the early years of Charles I's reign there was no thought of actually inducing men to present themselves for knighthood.[67] Fining them for not doing so, however, was another question. The device of distraint as a source of revenue had last been employed in the early Tudor years.[68] Since the usual occasion of the general summons was a coronation, or a state occasion such as the marriage of a prince, there was no instance of distraint of knighthood after the succession of Elizabeth I. The queen, it has been suggested, regarded the practice as obsolete.[69] It would appear that by the beginning of the seventeenth century it had become a matter of form. A proclamation for a general summons was issued prior to James I's coronation and the names of those worth £40 in freehold land for the last three years were returned into Chancery, but no attempt was made to fine any for their not presenting themselves.[70]

It is not clear when in Charles's reign a decision was made to resume the fines. Dr Leonard has suggested the date of November 1627 when the sheriffs' lists of the gentry qualified to be knighted were sent from Chancery to the Exchequer.[71] Some suspicion, however, that the idea had been mooted earlier arises from the proclamation of 30 January 1626, which summoned all eligible to appear in London before the 31st of the month – so making it impossible for any to attend and be knighted.[72] The proclamation provoked no reaction at the time, presumably because like James I's it was thought to be a formality. Whatever the date of the decision, the procedure was put into operation by the appointment of the Earl of Marlborough and others as commissioners to assess fines in May 1628.[73] Still no action was taken,

66. *Cal. Stat. Pap. Dom., 1625–49*, p. 79.
67. Charles knighted only 67 men in 1625 compared with over 600 raised by his father within weeks of succeeding to his throne; see H.C. Grazebrook, 'Obligatory knighthood temp. Charles I' (William Salt Archaeological Soc., II, 2, 1881), p. 6.
68. H.H. Leonard, 'Distraint of knighthood: the last phase, 1625–41', *History*, 63 (1978), pp. 23–37.
69. W.P. Baildon, 'Compositions for not taking knighthood at the coronation of Charles I', *Miscellanea* (Yorkshire Archaeological Soc., 41, 1920), p. 85.
70. Leonard, 'Distraint of knighthood', p. 23.
71. *Ibid.*, p. 24.
72. Baildon, 'Compositions', p. 86. This may, of course, have been intended to avoid the creation of more knights whilst preserving the formal summons; Charles elevated no one to knighthood between December 1625 and April 1626 (Grazebrook, 'Obligatory knighthood', p.6).
73. T. Rymer (ed.) *Foedera, Conventiones, Litterae* (20 vols, 1704–35), XVIII, pp. 1020–1.

however, and it was not until after a second and larger commission (headed by Lord Keeper Coventry) was appointed in January 1630 that gentlemen began to appear to answer for their delinquency.[74] On 29 February the newswriter John Flower informed Viscount Scudamore: 'There is a commission on foot to call up and compound with such as at the coronation should have come and been fined for not being made knights. Some think the composition will amount to as much as a subsidy.'[75] In March, Secretary Dorchester seemed pleased with the progress of the commission: 'the business of no knights,' he told the English envoy to the Swiss, 'goes roundly forward, no man disputing the legality of it in general, so as by this and other lawful but extraordinary ways some good sums are likely to be raised.'[76] If Dorchester's hopes, however, matched Flower's prediction, they were, at least initially frustrated. By the end of June 1630 the compositions paid totalled £11,767.[77] The Council therefore in July took the novel step of extending the commissions for compounding into the counties, so, the proclamation put it, that subjects might be spared the 'chargeable and troublesome' travel to London.[78] The 'ease of the subjects' was not the only consideration. By instructions issued in August, the commissioners were ordered to inform themselves by subsidy rolls, muster rolls and poor books, of all worth the £40 in land that made them liable to the fine.[79] Men's entire estates in lands and goods were to be taken into account; and constables and bailiffs were to bring information on individuals' means. Assessments were then to be made at a rate of at least two and a half times that in the subsidy book; no JPs were to pay less than £25. The following May another commission ordered instructors 'to take three times and a half as much as they were sessed in the subsidy . . .'.[80]

The commissioners appear to have acted promptly on their orders, but they encountered considerable difficulties. As we shall see, knighthood fines met with some direct opposition.[81] More generally, those who did not deny the legality of the fine grumbled at the amounts or claimed that they had not in 1626 been worth the £40 that made them liable to pay it. Sir Thomas Gerard told the Leicestershire commissioners that his freehold had come to him only in the last year of

74. Birmingham Reference Library, Doquets of Letters Patent, Coventry MS 602204/213, 28 Jan. 1630.
75. PRO, C.115/M31/8122.
76. *Cal. Stat. Pap. Dom., 1629–31*, p. 203: Dorchester to Fleming, 3 March 1630.
77. Leonard, 'Distraint of knighthood', p. 25.
78. Larkin, *Stuart Royal Proclamations*, II, no. 135, pp. 279–80.
79. Rawlinson MS C.674, f.74v; cf. Firth MS C.4, pp. 513–15.
80. Chester Record Office, Earwaker MS CR 63/2/19, ff.72v–73: 'A copy of the strange commission which came down into Cheshire the 26 of May 1631'.
81. Below, Chapter 11, p. 715.

James I's reign, not, as was the qualification, three years prior to the coronation.[82] Francis Coke in 1630 excused himself to Secretary Sir John that much of his estate had only come to him through his recent marriage.[83] In Kent Sir Edward Dering faced a range of ingenious excuses. Apart from the usual claims to have had less than £40, we find Richard Dancey of Adersham who 'maketh answer that at the coronation he had no estate of freehold, though about one month after he had';[84] George Wattle of 'Shipwey' protested 'he hath not £40 per annum clear above all charges'; James Dunmore at Maidstone claimed he 'doth not certainly know his estate'.[85] John Prick who suspiciously, if also understandably, went under an alias, claimed he had compounded in London; Edward Hadden said he had a tally from the Exchequer for his fine – but had left it at Lincoln's Inn in London.[86] Several pleaded that there had been no summons of men from the Cinque Ports; Richard Godfrey, Edward Lambe and several others all asked to be excused on the grounds that they had carried the canopy at the coronation.[87] The commissioners, often already hard-pressed JPs and deputy lieutenants, were put to enormous pains to ascertain who was liable for the fines and the amounts they should pay. Dering kept careful and full notebooks with the names of those who had paid, those who compounded in London, those who had not appeared and those who made excuses whom he required to put a signature or mark to their excuse. Such diligent labour by commissioners around the country produced results.[88] Most in Kent compounded at the rate of £10; in Northamptonshire Montagu's list of 104 names shows only twelve defaulters.[89] By January 1631 Thomas Carleton was reporting to Secretary Dorchester that 'Cumberland and Westmorland have paid in those fines above thirty subsidies'.[90] From Nottinghamshire the commissioners had by April raised £2,369, 'a greater proportion than by any other way could have been raised out of that county'.[91]

The king and the Council, however, were not satisfied. Signet letters in March 1631 informed commissioners that the service 'took not that effect which we expected'.[92] In July the king's announcement of his preference for 'sweet and gentle means' over 'rigour and con-

82. Hastings MSS, Legal Box 5.
83. Coke MS 39: Francis Coke to Sir John Coke, 14 Oct. 1630.
84. Kent Archives Office, Dering MS U1364/01.
85. Dering MSS U1256/01; U1311/02.
86. Dering MS U1256/01.
87. Dering MSS U1311/02; U1256/01; U1364/01.
88. Cf. J. Dias, 'Politics and administration in Nottinghamshire and Derbyshire 1590–1640' (Oxford University, D. Phil. thesis, 1973), p. 350.
89. Dering MS U/1364, 01; Northants Record Office, Montagu MS 27, f.76.
90. *Cal. Stat. Pap. Dom., 1629–31*, p. 486, 19 Jan. 1631.
91. *Cal. Stat. Pap. Dom., 1631–3*, p. 23.
92. PRO, SO 1/2, ff.44v–45, 22 March 1631. Cf. Hastings MS 1347.

straint' was accompanied by a warning that those who did not compound now would be summoned to the Council.[93] Personal royal letters sent to noblemen who headed the commission in their counties expressed the king's disappointment and urged them to greater effort.[94] The king's attorney was instructed to proceed against sheriffs who impeded the service by 'partial and negligent returns'.[95] For July 1633 we find in the state papers a list of non-compounders against whom proceedings were to be instituted.[96] Such pressure undoubtedly helped to overcome difficulties and local foot-dragging. In Yorkshire, the stage of an attempted resistance by David Foulis, over 800 gentlemen paid over £12,600.[97] What William Whiteway recorded about compositions for knighthood in his diary – 'it raised little money' – turned out to be false.[98] By April 1635 knighthood fines had brought in £173,537 to the Exchequer: the equivalent of over three subsidies and 'the largest single source of extraordinary revenue' other than the loan and the sale of crown lands.[99] Distraint of knighthood could not be a regular source of revenue. But as a measure to alleviate the fiscal crisis in the aftermath of the parliaments of 1629 it was an unqualified success.

Another precedent cited by Borough in his list of past measures for increasing royal revenue was that of fines levied for encroachments on or abuses in the royal forest of Dean.[100] At about the same time, Sir Miles Fleetwood was suggesting that disafforestation could 'exceedingly improve' the king's revenue.[101] Significantly, when Edward Stephens brought the case of knighthood fines to the Exchequer court in 1631, Baron Trevor compared them to the crown's rights in the forests which, he added, had once been of greater extent than they now were.[102] There was no doubting the accuracy of his legal opinion. An early seventeenth-century 'Treatise of the Forest Laws' noted that before the Great Charter for the Forest, the king had made forest, that is a preserve for hawks and game, whatever land he would; and still, the author continued, 'At the common law always the king may make a forest in all woods.'[103] Once an area came under forest law, it was an offence to kill deer or keep dogs, keep guns, hunt foxes, to fence,

93. PRO, SO 1/2, f.64v, 25 July 1631.
94. PRO, SO 1/2, f.26; Herriard MS 013.
95. *Cal. Stat. Pap. Dom., 1629–31*, p. 356.
96. *Cal. Stat. Pap. Dom., 1633–4*, p. 139.
97. Baildon, 'Compositions', p. 89.
98. BL, Egerton MS 784 (William Whiteway's diary, 1618–34), p. 158; see below, p. 696.
99. Leonard, 'Distraint of knighthood', p. 35.
100. BL Add. MS 34324, f.269v.
101. *Cal. Stat. Pap. Dom., 1627–8*, p. 372: Fleetwood to Conway, 4 Oct. 1627.
102. BL Add. MS 11674, f.86.
103. Rawlinson MS D.670: 'A treatise of the forest laws', a series of readings in one of the Inns of Court, f.9.

destroy bushes, fell wood, pasture cattle, build or in any way encroach upon it. Officers of the forest could be fined in the Swanimote court for not fulfilling their duties or for appearing improperly dressed or equipped. Others who inhabited the forest, or exploited its timber for iron forging, could be offered the opportunity to pay to have their land disafforested, and so removed from forest jurisdiction, or could be fined for their encroachment.[104] Like other aspects of medieval administration, however, the forest laws and courts and especially the once important forest eyres carried out by two chief justices for the forests (one north, one south of the Trent) had become little more than a formality.[105] In his treatise of forest laws, written in 1598, John Manwood regarded them as having gone 'clean out of knowledge in most places' and 'grown into contempt with many'.[106] The forest came to be regarded as common ground, both for humble folk who grazed a few animals and scratched a living from its land and for those who enclosed or emparked large areas for recreation or commercial exploitation. During the late sixteenth century the crown showed an increased concern in the forests and woods, as the value of land soared and royal fiscal problems mounted.[107] In 1597 the Privy Council ascribed to the collapse of the justices' eyres the decay of royal forests and the crown's rights in them.[108] In James's reign, perhaps as part of the larger schemes for trading feudal rights for money, Sir Julius Caesar proposed disafforestation as a source of revenue.[109] During the early years of Charles's reign, the needs of war finance probably explain the disafforestations of Selwood, Feckenham and Galtres, for there was clearly a growing sense of the need to preserve the woods and the 'honour and power', as Secretary Coke put it, that the king derived from royal forests.[110]

It is not clear by whom or exactly when the decision was taken to exploit royal rights for fiscal purposes, by reviving the justices' eyres, reasserting ancient forest boundaries and fining those who had encroached on them. Gardiner and others attribute the scheme to the Earl of Holland's attempts in 1634 to unseat Lord Treasurer Weston by exposing his abuse of royal woodland in the forest of Dean.[111] However, the inhabitants there had themselves earlier presented a

104. Rawlinson MS D.119; G. Hammersley, 'The revival of the forest laws under Charles I', *History*, 45 (1960), pp. 85–102.
105. P.A.J. Pettit, *The Royal Forests of Northamptonshire: A Study in their Economy, 1558–1714* (Northamptonshire Record Soc., 23, 1968), pp. 20–6; Leonard, 'Distraint of knighthood', pp. 85–8.
106. J. Dias, 'Politics and administration', p. 159.
107. Pettit, *Royal Forests*, pp. 26–8.
108. *Ibid.*, p. 41.
109. *Ibid.*, p. 52.
110. *Ibid.*, pp. 66–7.
111. Gardiner, *History of England*, VII, pp. 362–3.

petition of grievances and John Broughton, surveyor of Dean, acting on a commission issued out of the Council of the Marches, had embarked on a series of reforms and examinations in Dean before Holland kept his justice seat there.[112] Nearly two years before, in September 1632, an eyre had been held in the forest of Windsor.[113] The initial impetus for the revival of forest laws then may genuinely have been, as I shall argue, a desire to prevent the decay of woods.[114] Broughton's correspondence with Coke certainly reveals more concern with reform of abuses than with fines. It was evidently in 1634 that the full fiscal potential of the eyres was first seized on, and contemporary newswriters clearly associated the scheme to enrich the king with the competition for the Attorney's place on the death of William Noy in August. On 2 September Edward Rossingham informed Viscount Scudamore that all the shortlisted candidates for the place – Bramston, Littleton and Bankes – had laboured in the Tower until sunset searching for 'a great book of records taken from Sir Edward Coke'.[115] Their purpose was a mystery to him. By the 19th, however, all had become clear:

> That great search of the records of the Tower was to find out the ancient bounds of the forest of Waltham, which I hear did sometime extend beyond Chelmsford, but being then some great grievance to the county some deeds were made that concluded this forest in a narrower circuit. The deeds are like to be produced at the justice seat; if they be not lost where they are and not defective in law they may be useful, but I do hear the end of this justice seat will be to draw good compositions from such as have nothing to show to exempt their lands from the forest if now their lands were within forest bounds.[116]

Sir John Bankes became Attorney-General; among his own papers we find 'notes and observances' concerning a commission to enquire into the forests as a legal source of profit.[117]

On 1 October the Earl of Holland went to hold his justice seat in Essex. The next day, the newly appointed Lord Chief Justice, John Finch, produced a record of Edward I's reign showing a vast extent to the forest.[118] Rossingham thought that extending as it did from Catford bridge to Stratford by Bow, 'it is not any longer to be called

112. Berkshire Record Office, Trumbull Add. MS 37: petitions and grievances of the inhabitants of the forest of Dean; Coke MS 48: Broughton to Coke, 11 April 1634.
113. PRO, SO 1/2, f.116, 19 Sept. 1632; Rawlinson MS D.399.
114. Below, pp. 242–5.
115. PRO, C.115/M36/8432.
116. PRO, C.115/M36/8434.
117. Bodleian, Bankes MS 16/7 (undated).
118. Gardiner, *History of England*, VII, p. 365.

the forest of Waltham' but the 'forest of Essex'![119] The landowners of the county were asked to answer the case and their encroachment and the eyre was then adjourned. The following April, the county presented its own evidences (some sent by Finch himself) in answer to the case. The king's Solicitor-General, however, produced a staggering array of records to prove that no limitation had been set to the boundaries of Waltham forest since the Great Charter of the forest. The county 'acknowledging that they have a fair hearing', judgment was then given and the court proceeded to fine offenders.[120] The following year, Holland's eyre was extended into the New Forest and Northamptonshire;[121] in 1637 it was the turn of Rockingham forest, the boundaries of which were extended from a circumference of six to sixty miles.[122] It is likely that there were plans to conduct the eyre around the country. Among the papers of Sir John Coke is a list of thirty-nine 'forests and chases within the view of the Exchequer on the South side of the Trent';[123] it was also rumoured that all but three counties would be declared forest.[124] Whilst the purpose of the eyres was never purely fiscal, there can be no doubt that the revival of forest laws was 'prompted by undeniable financial motives'.[125] The poor who found themselves trespassers were fined only shillings, but large fines were adjudged against the gentry and aristocracy who were delinquent. In Northamptonshire, Sir Christopher Hatton was fined £7,000, the Earl and Countess of Westmorland £19,000.[126] Fines imposed in Rockingham forest totalled £67,000.[127] Such figures, however, bear no relation to the sums paid into the Exchequer. Fines were often imposed, as in Star Chamber, for example's sake and mitigated, at times drastically, for a mixture of practical and political reasons. So, in Gloucestershire Sir John Winter fined at £20,230 had his reduced to only £4,000; Sir Basil Brooke and George Mynne who had cut 178,000 cords of wood (valued at £59,400) had their fine commuted from the value of what was stolen to £12,000 – and were pardoned that on surrender of their iron works.[128] Forest fines then did not bring large sums into the Exchequer: the eyre in Dean evidently yielded nearly £18,000 and Exchequer accounts show a total of

119. PRO, C.115/N9/8851: Rossingham to Scudamore, 10 Oct. 1634.
120. Rawlinson MS C.722: 'Proceedings and arguments at an enquiry into the boundaries of the forest of Waltham'.
121. Gardiner, *History of England*, VII, p. 86.
122. *Ibid.*, p. 282.
123. Coke MS 87; this was a document orginally drawn up in 1616.
124. Pettit, *Royal Forests*, p. 84.
125. *Ibid.*, p. 46.
126. *Ibid.*, p. 88.
127. *Ibid.*
128. Hammersley, 'Revival of the forest laws', pp. 97–9.

less than £25,000 for the years 1636 to 1638.[129] The benefits to the crown of the recovered forest eyres may have been greater in other ways: renegotiated leases, improvement of wastes and preservation of timber, for instance. As a means of improving royal revenue, they made but a small contribution which could 'hardly have compensated for the indignation engendered'.[130]

Projects and patents

As well as the exploitation of traditional feudal rights, Charles I and his Council turned to more novel schemes to raise money. In many cases of projects propounded and patents granted, the motive was not solely nor even primarily financial; they emerged from genuine inventiveness, a governmental desire to regulate a trade or to protect a new manufacture. To this aspect of the projects of the 1630s we must return.[131] For now, it is the financial benefits that concern us, benefits that were often, perhaps usually, one among a number of considerations. Contemporaries clearly saw as financially motivated the commissions to grant licences for the sale of tobacco and to investigate the abuses of buildings in London. The Reverend Garrard informed Lord Wentworth that they were expected to raise substantial sums.[132] A letter to Secretary Coke was explicit about their purpose:

> Here at home we are most busy about raising of money to fill the king's coffers. There are committees of the lords appointed to compound with all such as will take licences to sell tobacco throughout England, as likewise with all those who have built homes hereabout London since the first of King James upon new foundations which as some compute amount to the number of 60,000. These two ways it is held will for the present bring in a very considerable sum by way of fine and also make large increase of the king's yearly revenue.[133]

It is likely that both proved a disappointment. By 1635, the commission for buildings was yielding only £8,547 a year and tobacco licences just over £10,000;[134] in the second half of the decade the tobacco licence was calculated to be worth £13,000 per annum.[135]

129. Clarendon MS 20, 1539; Dietz, *Receipts and Issues*, tables.
130. Pettit, *Royal Forest*, p. 92.
131. Below, pp. 257–62.
132. W. Knowler (ed.) *The Earl of Strafford's Letters and Despatches* (2 vols, 1739), I, p. 205, 27 Feb. 1634. Garrard disliked them; see below, pp. 121, 707.
133. Coke MS 48, 10 March 1634.
134. Harleian MS 3796, f.21; *Cal. Stat. Pap. Dom., 1635*, p. 160; cf. *1635–6*, p. 551.
135. Clarendon MS 20, no. 1539: this is likely to be an overestimate; cf. Harleian MS 3796, f.76.

There was in addition, however, a myriad of other schemes and projects which together brought a worthwhile sum into the Exchequer. Proposals to make salt from seawater,[136] to revive copper mining in Cornwall,[137] to manufacture turf 'after the Dutch manner', out of moorland waste,[138] schemes for the manufacture of sea coal, or soft iron or clay pipes or white writing paper were all supported for their yield to the crown as well as their promised benefits to the country.[139] Listing several, in March 1637, Garrard commented to Wentworth that 'discontinuance of parliaments brings up this kind of grain which commonly is blasted when they come.'[140] Usually the reality fell short of the promise: the profits made at the expense of the consumer lined private pockets more than the royal coffers.[141] The salt works at Newcastle on Tyne were expected to bring in £30,000 and the royal alum works yielded £12,500 a year during the late 1630s, but other projects – the copperas farm – and patents, such as those for dice and playing cards, brought only hundreds into the Exchequer.[142] This was a small return for the irritation such schemes provoked and royal ministers and courtiers at times protested loudly their dislike of such projects. Wentworth described them as 'the very scandal of his Majesty's affairs and the reproach of all his upright and well-meaning ministers'.[143] In 1639, sensitive to criticism, the Privy Council called in many of the licences and commissions granted.[144] Whatever the blow to the patentees, the loss to the crown was not great. Though they loomed large in criticism of Charles I's regime, monopolies played a small part in the king's financial survival during a decade of no parliaments.

That is true even of, perhaps especially of, the most notorious projects of the 1630s: the scheme to drain the Fens and the patent for the manufacture of 'new' soap. Both have been studied almost entirely as the cynical measures of an impoverished government to raise revenue at the expense of its subjects. Both, as we shall see, belong to a discussion of well-intentioned efforts to reinvigorate the English

136. Bankes MS 11/32.
137. PRO, SO 1/2, f.204.
138. Bankes MS 11/63.
139. Bankes MS 11/33, 42; *Cal. Stat. Pap. Dom., 1629–31*, p. 382.
140. Knowler, *Strafford Letters*, II, pp. 55–6, 23 March 1637.
141. As the Earl of Strafford put it to Windebank on 1 February 1636: 'Projects resemble the getting of the philosopher's stone; many fair hopes yet no assurance until it be fixed'. (*Cal. Stat. Pap. Dom., 1635–6*, p. 203); cf. W.R. Scott, *The Constitution and Finance of English, Scottish and Irish Joint Stock Companies to 1720* (3 vols, Cambridge, 1910–12), II, ch. 11.
142. Clarendon MS 20, no. 1539; Scott, *Joint Stock Companies*, I, pp. 209–12. The salt works folded soon after incorporation. A new company was established in 1639.
143. Knowler, *Strafford Letters*, II, pp. 76–7: Wentworth to Northumberland, 25 May 1637.
144. Coke MS 60: Windebank to Coke, 5 April 1639; PRO PC 2/50, p. 209; Larkin, *Stuart Royal Proclamations*, II, no. 283, pp. 673–6.

economy which had originally inspired the projects movement. One should not be cynical about reiterations of the good of the commonweal in orders and proclamations concerning the draining of the Great Level in Lincolnshire.[145] For all the corruption and incompetence that bedevilled the scheme, its origins did not lie solely or perhaps even primarily in the crown's quest for profit. Though the king reserved for the crown thousands of acres of the land to be reclaimed, any pecuniary benefit lay far in the future. Of the local taxes paid for the costs of the works, nothing came to the crown.

If the soap patent was to prove a different experience, it was not by the way at first intended. The grant of a patent for the manufacture of a new soap was one of the most scandalous episodes of the personal rule. It led to bitter squabbles at court, anger in the country and outrage among those involved in the trade. Once again the origins of the scheme (in the reign of James I) lay in a commendable enterprise to manufacture an English soap that dispensed with the need for imported potash.[146] The king maintained all along that his primary concern was to foster an English manufacture that would set the poor on work.[147] Some financial benefit to the crown, however, was envisaged from the beginning: the new company promised, as well as purchasing the patent, to pay the king £4 per ton of new soap sold.[148] The soap, as we shall see, won few converts and so the expected benefit to the crown did not materialize. By 1635, the Treasury commissioners calculated the profit to the crown over two years at only £6,000 or £7,000.[149] In that year, the independent soapmakers challenged the new company for the control of manufacture by offering to double the tonnage to £8, promising the king an annual revenue of £40,000 on an estimated sale of 5,000 tons.[150] The new company then retained its position by matching the offer.[151] But in 1637, the old soapmakers were incorporated – in return for a payment of £43,000 and the £8 per ton earlier promised.[152] The popularity of the traditional soap at last ensured that promises materialized into money. Soap was worth over £30,000 to

145. Below, pp. 252–6.
146. Dietz, *English Public Finance*, p. 265; see Gardiner, *History of England*, VII, pp. 71–7.
147. Larkin, *Stuart Royal Proclamations*, II, no. 176, pp. 395–408, esp. 396–7.
148. Scott, *Joint Stock Companies*, I, p. 211.
149. *Cal. Stat. Pap. Dom., 1634–5*, p. 592.
150. W. Scott and J. Bliss (eds) *The Works of William Laud* (7 vols, Oxford, 1847–60), VII, p. 140: Laud to Wentworth, 12 June 1635; Gardiner, *History of England*, VII, pp. 74–5.
151. Gardiner, *History of England*, VII, pp. 75–6.
152. Larkin, *Stuart Royal Proclamations*, II, no. 250, pp. 582–8; Patent Rolls 13 Ch. I, part 39, no. 10, cited in Gardiner, *History of England*, VII, p. 284, note 3.

Charles I in the closing years of the personal rule.[153] Alone of all the projects, it was a worthwhile if not massive contribution to the overall receipts of the Exchequer.

Other, more novel and radical courses to bring in revenue continued to be countenanced during the 1630s, as they had been during the desperate war years. 'They are always,' the Venetian ambassador reported in 1634, 'devising ways to supply the ordinary and extraordinary expenses of this crown.'[154] There were proposals for an income tax of 2 per cent on all worth in excess of £125 per annum;[155] for a tax on lawyers; for a mortuary tax or death duty;[156] and for an excise.[157] Some appear to have contemplated the sale of offices. In 1633 a duty on beer was mooted but – mercifully in the eyes of this author – was then dropped.[158] Indeed it is significant that none of the most radical proposals was enacted (and a mark of the fundamental conservatism that characterized the government of the personal rule). For all his understanding of the inadequacy of traditional sources of revenue to fund even peacetime government, Charles I was, like his contemporaries, trapped in a set of attitudes that dictated that the king should live of his own. Ironically it was to be one of Charles's leading opponents, John Pym, who was (in the 1640s) to effect the radical measure of an excise to finance government. It took the civil war to establish in England the idea of regular taxation. Before 1642, the *taille* and the *gabelle* which provided Louis XIII with massive revenues and freedom from calling the estates, or the *millones* and *sisa* which financed the Spanish *tercios*, Charles and his ministers could only look upon with envy.[159] Hopton could only wonder as he observed how 'the Cortes do every year give more and it is strange to see how patiently the people bears being laid on by this insensible way of *sisa*'.[160] Because, in this as in so many aspects of his rule, Charles looked not forwards or across the seas to continental practice but backwards to the English past, he was restricted to exploiting for fiscal purposes the 'obsolete laws' that had governed feudal relations. But the political costs were high and the fundamental problems of royal finance remained. The Venetian ambassador, with his strong grasp of the basis of power in Europe, used appropriate language when he described

153. Dietz, *English Public Finance*, p. 286; cf. Clarendon MS 20, 1539.
154. *Cal. Stat. Pap. Venet., 1632–6*, p. 195.
155. *Cal. Stat. Pap. Dom., 1628–9*, p. 435.
156. PRO, SP 16/89/17.
157. Dietz, *English Public Finance*, p. 264.
158. *Cal. Stat. Pap. Dom., 1631–3*, p. 506.
159. Cf. J.H. Elliott, *Richelieu and Olivares* (Cambridge, 1984), pp. 136ff.
160. Clarendon MS 18, no. 1349: Hopton to Windebank, 7 Feb. 1640.

Caroline fiscal expedients such as knighthood fines: 'All these may be called false mines for obtaining money, because they are good for once only.'[161]

Credit

One short-term solution to financial crisis was the most traditional of solutions: borrowing. All early modern monarchies lived on deficit financing, on borrowing and anticipating future revenue. Professor Ashton has shown how James I struggled to finance a mounting debt, on the ordinary and extraordinary account, by further borrowings that postponed the day of reckoning.[162] Charles therefore inherited large debts to which the war years added massively, a burden which had to be carried by the already inadequate ordinary revenue, or further postponed (and exacerbated) by yet more borrowing. After 1629, moreover, the opportunities for royal credit were fewer than usual. The end of parliaments meant that imminent subsidies could not be put up as security. During the late 1620s even the crown jewels had been pawned in the Netherlands, and there was discussion of schemes to compel merchants, who knew a bad bet when they saw one, to lend to the government.[163] During the personal rule, crown borrowing perforce became restricted to a narrower circle. Many of the old Jacobean lenders – Sir Baptist Hickes for example – had died; and their Caroline successor, Philip Burlamachi, went bankrupt.[164] The king's relations with the city of London were often strained: royal interference with the organization of city companies, the scandal of the soap monopoly, disputes over the colony of Londonderry and Conciliar demands and pressures made the great mercantile magnates less than willing lenders.[165] The king became dependent on private creditors, especially the customs farmers and Sir William Russell, treasurer of the navy.[166] This was to prove a source of weakness in the last years of personal rule when the crown could not secure loans from the city to finance the Scots war.[167] For most of the 1630s the arrangement presented few problems, not least because the government was more concerned with reducing the debt than with more

161. *Cal. Stat. Pap. Venet., 1629–32*, p. 298.
162. R. Ashton, 'Deficit finance in the reign of James I', *Econ. Hist. Rev.*, 2nd series, 10, (1957–8), pp. 15–29; *idem*, *The Crown and the Money Market* (Oxford, 1960).
163. BL Add. MS 34324, f.284.
164. Ashton, *Crown and Money Market*, p. 173.
165. R. Ashton, *The City and the Court, 1603–1643* (Cambridge, 1979).
166. *Ibid.*; and Ashton, *Crown and Money Market*, p. 191.
167. See below, pp. 888–9, 904.

borrowing. Richard Weston as Lord Treasurer performed two feats in this respect. First, by 1635 he had almost balanced the ordinary account, so that the running debts were not constantly increasing. Secondly, he acted to begin to pay off accumulated debts and thereby reduce the interest burden on the ordinary account. In May 1634 the Venetian envoy reported that Weston had paid off £800,000 worth of debt which had been charged at 10–12 per cent.[168] By 1636 Charles was in a position to start repaying Jacobean debts and to redeem the pawned crown jewels from the Netherlands.[169] In 1635, the debt as calculated by the commissioners for the Treasury stood at £1,163,655, including £370,000 of anticipated revenue.[170] Though the figure was still large, much of the debt existed on paper only: many of the obligations to officials for arrears of fees and wages (£199,900), to individual lenders (£160,000) or to counties for remaining billet money were probably not going to be met 'and consequently worried no one but the individual crown creditors'.[171] The figure too was only £160,000 higher than the debt in 1624, despite the £2 million spent on the wars.[172] Extraordinary sums received into the Exchequer from reprisal goods (£217,468), the queen's dower (£163,803) and most of all sale of lands and woods (£651,474) had kept the debt within bounds.[173] Most importantly, in favourable contrast to earlier years or continental regimes, the effective debt was well below a year's revenue.

Indeed by 1635, though no radical courses had been taken, the Exchequer had recovered from financial sickness to reasonable health. Weston achieved, as we shall see, some reforms and economies: pensions were kept under control; most years the Cofferer of the Household and Master of the Wardrobe kept within their assignments.[174] As well as the extraordinary benefits of knighthood fines and the like, the Lord Treasurer also raised the ordinary revenues by nearly £50,000 to £618,000 a year.[175] In the last full year of his office receipts actually exceeded expenditure.[176] In the year of his death, the deficit on the ordinary account was only £18,000.[177] Considering the situation he

168. *Cal. Stat. Pap. Venet., 1632–6*, p. 223.
169. *Cal. Stat. Pap. Dom., 1636–7*, pp. x, 227.
170. Dietz, *English Public Finance*, p. 270; cf. Harleian MS 3796, f.27 and *Cal. Stat., Pap. Dom., 1634–5*, pp. 579, 586.
171. Harleian MS 3796, f.27; and Dietz, *English Public Finance*, p. 270.
172. Dietz, *English Public Finance*, p. 272.
173. Harleian MS 3796, f.21.
174. Below, pp. 237–9; Dietz, *English Public Finance*, p. 260; cf. Aylmer, 'Studies in the central administration', p. 285.
175. Dietz, *English Public Finance*, p. 269, citing PRO, E 407/78/5; *Cal. Stat. Pap. Venet., 1632–6*, p. 195.
176. *Cal. Stat. Pap. Dom., 1634–5*, p. 586.
177. PRO, Treasury Books, T56/2; Harleian MS 3796, f.76; Bankes MS 5/45, 46.

inherited in 1628, the position could, as Dr Aylmer concluded, have been 'a good deal worse'.[178]

Trade and customs revenues

What rescued the Caroline regime from crisis and funded a decade of personal rule was, as Weston had foreseen, peace and, what he may not have been able to predict, the expansion of trade. The customs duties levied on imported and exported goods were the only regular source of royal income that increased. They had been a controversial matter since 1625 when tonnage and poundage, traditionally granted for life, had been voted for only one year.[179] With the failure of the parliament of 1628–9 to legalize what the king was taking in practice the situation could have become desperate. After Sir John Eliot's denunciation of any who paid tonnage and poundage, merchants had ceased trading and customs revenues slumped from £500 to only £1–2 a day.[180] The Council had to take action. At least one newswriter believed that the proclamation forbidding rumours of a future parliament, published in March, was 'intended by putting them [the merchants] out of all hope of a parliament to draw them on to resume trade'.[181] The king sent for some of the leading merchants and, in William Whiteway's words, 'used many motives' to persuade them to trade.[182] No motive perhaps was more powerful than the opening of the French trade that led many to concentrate on profits more than parliaments. Those who had been 'terrified at Sir John Eliot's *brutum fulmen*' were by May returning, in Bishop Williams's phrase, to sanity.[183] Peace with Spain as well as France, and the English entry into the profitable carrying trade, saw leaps in the yield of customs to the Exchequer. Not all the due benefits of expanding trade came to the crown. In January 1632 the Privy Council appointed a commission to enquire into evasions and frauds perpetrated by landing goods at night in 'improper places', smuggling them in far from the customs house.[184] Proposals were discussed to establish in every port an office

178. Aylmer, 'Studies in the central administration', p. 726.
179. This was a consequence less of any constitutional struggle than of confusion over technicalities. See J.P. Cooper, 'The fall of the Stuart monarchy', in Cooper (ed.) *The Decline of Spain and the Thirty Years War* (Cambridge, 1970), pp. 553–8.
180. *Cal. Stat. Pap. Venet., 1629–32*, p. 8.
181. Bodleian, Tanner MS 72, f.1; cf. Jones, *Politics and the Bench*, p. 87.
182. BL, Egerton MS 784, p. 147; Tanner MS 72, f.1.
183. *Cal. Stat. Pap. Dom., 1628–9*, p. 524: Lake to Vane, 20 April 1629; *ibid.*, p. 537: Williams to Dorchester, 5 May 1629; *Cal. Stat. Pap. Venet., 1629–32*, p. 19.
184. *Cal. Stat. Pap. Dom., 1631–3*, p. 253.

for entering bills of landing which could be compared with customs house books, to ascertain whether duty had been paid.[185] For their part some merchants advocated free trade and low customs to establish England as a rival staple to the Dutch and further increase trade.[186] Because the crown did not have the administrative resources to collect the duties itself, the customs continued to be farmed, which meant, of course, that a large slice of the profits went to the syndicates that farmed them. Buoyant funds, however, enabled Weston to renegotiate the rent of the Great Farm and to raise that of the petty farms (of currants, French wines and sweet wines) from £44,000 to £60,000.[187] Judiciously, in December 1634 the customs farmers paid well over the rent due and lent substantial sums to the crown.[188] More importantly, those duties not farmed, the yield of which came to the Exchequer directly, increased dramatically: the 'new impositions' of 1608 were worth nearly £54,000 by the mid-1630s, and over £140,000 by 1640.[189] In July 1635, the value of all customs was estimated at £358,000, well over half the total receipts of the Exchequer.[190]

The 'balance of His Majesty's Receipts and Payments by a medium of five years' drawn up by the Treasury commissioners in December 1635 enables us to examine the details and check Dietz's figures.[191] The king's costs (from assignations of revenue and direct payments from receipts) included sums to the cofferer of the household of the king and queen, payments for the royal children and the queen of Bohemia, expenses of the wardrobe, chamber, jewelhouse, guard, ordnance, castles and garrisons, payments for ambassadors, secretaries, judges, the posts, keepers of royal houses, annuities and pensions and fees to a host of minor officials. Of the total of £636,536 the largest expenditure was on pensions (£131,099) and fees (£41,628) and on the maintenance of the royal households of the king, queen and princes (over £135,000, not including wardrobe expenses of more than £26,000). The Exchequer, we note, also dispensed £40,000 a year to the Treasurer of the Navy, as it continued to do during the years of the levy of ship money. Defalcations, that is deductions for debts, amounted to nearly £54,000 and an additional £20,000 a year (averaged over the ten years since Charles's succession) was paid in interest on monies advanced by Philip Burlamachi. In the big picture of Caroline finance, the annual

185. *Cal. Stat. Pap. Dom., 1633–4*, p. 338.
186. See Herriard MS, Box 06.
187. Dietz, *English Public Finance*, pp. 268–9. See also *ibid.* Chapter 15, *passim*.
188. *Cal. Stat. Pap. Dom., 1634–5*, p. 368.
189. Dietz, *English Public Finance*, p. 284.
190. *Cal. Stat. Pap. Dom., 1635*, p. 279.
191. Treasury Books, T56/1; cf. Harleian MS 3796.

sums spent on the allegedly profligate expense of masques (£1,310 a year) cannot be said to loom large.

On the receipt side of the balance, the income from the receivers-general of crown lands yielded £90,696 and the profits from the Duchies of Cornwall and Lancaster a further £25,735. Purveyance was valued at £30,330; wardship brought in a valuable £54,000; fines on recusants over £13,000. The imposts on tobacco and alum amounted to £29,000. But all other sources of revenue were now dwarfed by the income from customs, the Great Farm (at £150,000) and petty farms (at £60,000) alone amounting to twice the revenue from crown lands. In addition, the new impositions (totalling over £53,000), praetermitted customs (£17,677) and other duties brought the total close to the estimate made in the summer. Where during Elizabeth's reign the monarchy had still derived 40 per cent of its revenue from crown lands, the figure for Charles's reign was more like 15 per cent of the total £618,379.[192] If the monarchy was now funded by trade rather than estates, it at least had the benefit that customs duties were a revenue that was expanding. The Treasury commissioners looked to further enhancements.[193] To those Councillors who remembered the dark days of 1626–9, it must have seemed that the English monarchy had at last found its 'mines'.[194]

The following years were indeed to see substantial increases in revenue. In July 1635 the Treasury commissioners, appointed in March, implemented the further increases in customs duties planned by Weston before he died, and added further impositions on merchants alien and wines.[195] Together these enhanced the royal revenue by over £30,000 within a year, taking the Exchequer into surplus. When he was finally appointed Treasurer in March 1636, Juxon sought for yet further raises and levied a new duty on wines which brought in an additional £13,000.[196] But the most important increases after 1635, still more than before, came from inactivity as much as action. England's unique position as a country at peace in the midst of war and the emergence of Dover as an entrepôt port saw a great expansion in the carrying trade and re-export trade, which led to further climbs in customs revenues.[197] The rises are dramatic: by the end of the 1630s

192. *Ibid.*; cf. C. Clay, *Economic Expansion and Social Change, Vol II: Industry, Trade and Government* (Cambridge, 1984) p. 252.
193. Treasury Books, T56/1 lists some 'Expected Improvements', for example from new impositions.
194. *Cal. Stat. Pap. Venet., 1628–9*, p. 298.
195. *Cal. Stat. Pap. Dom., 1634–5*, pp. 594–5; PRO, PC 2/44, p. 573; Dietz, *English Public Finance*, p. 276.
196. Dietz, *English Public Finance*, pp. 281–3.
197. See above, pp. 90–91; and J.S. Kepler, *The Exchange of Christendom: The International Entrepôt at Dover, 1622–1641* (Leicester, 1976).

the new impositions of 1608 (which had yielded £54,000 in 1635) were bringing in over £141,000; the praetermitted customs more than doubled in value (to £36,512) by 1640.[198]

No wonder the weekly balances during the later 1630s often show a 'remain'. In addition to redeeming the pawned crown jewels, Vane in 1638 foresaw the prospect of paying off Jacobean debts.[199] In January 1639, it seems, the anticipations on the revenue were down to £307,000 and the next year had fallen to £221,763.[200] The king, as we shall see, was able to afford to fight the first campaign against the Scots without recalling a parliament. Dietz claims that even at the end of the fiscal year Michaelmas 1640 the Exchequer accounts show the ordinary, just, in credit.[201]

We do not need to rely on Dietz. The balances drawn up by the parliamentary commissioners for the Treasury, appointed in May 1641 after Juxon's resignation, offer some details and present an interesting comparison with the figures for 1635.[202] By 1641 the Great Farm was yielding £172,500 (an increase of 15 per cent) and the petty farms £72,500 (a 20 per cent improvement). The new impositions had risen to £120,000 and the customs yield in total was over £482,000 – perhaps a 50 per cent increase on their value in 1635. Interestingly, these sums were accounted separately from other revenue in the commissioners' calculations, perhaps on account of the questionable legality of levies taken without parliamentary grant since 1626. Certainly the king's other revenues were delineated quite distinctly under heads of those 'esteemed legal' and those 'means held illegal'. In the first list, revenue from crown lands had actually declined. The receivers–general brought in £13,964 and the Duchy of Cornwall receipts had plummeted from £14,880 to £3,435. Of the traditional feudal revenues only that from the Court of Wards had risen significantly, from £54,000 to £75,000. It is worthy of note that on the 'illegal side' the most significant yield (now £36,237) came from purveyance, one of the traditional revenues of the crown. Overall the king's income was now £899,482, nearly half as much again as in 1635. Given that the expenses of the crown had not risen correspondingly the improvement in the real fiscal position was even better than that.[203] Where Elizabeth in her later years had a deficit

198. Dietz, *English Public Finance*, p. 284.
199. *Cal. Stat. Pap. Dom., 1637–8*, p. 226. Weekly balances are in *Cal. Stat. Pap. Dom., passim*.
200. *Cal. Stat. Pap. Dom., 1638–9*, p. 388; *1639–40*, p. 39.
201. Dietz, *English Public Finance*, p. 285.
202. Clarendon MS 20, no. 1539.
203. Cf. Dietz, *English Public Finance*, ch. 18; Aylmer, 'Studies in the central administration', for example p. 239.

of £100,000 on the ordinary, the royal revenue, at least during the second half of the decade of personal rule, was sufficient for the expenses of peacetime government.[204] 'Never since the accession of the Stuart dynasty,' Gardiner wrote accurately, 'had the finances been in so flourishing a condition.'[205] Had Charles not fought two campaigns against the Scots, and lost, whatever his desires, he would have faced no fiscal necessity to call a parliament.

204. Dietz, *Receipts and Issues*, p. 133.
205. Gardiner, *History of England*, VIII, p. 281.

IV

PORTRAITS OF POWER: PERSONALITIES AND FACTIONS

The assassination of George Villiers, Duke of Buckingham, marked a fundamental change in court politics and the nature of government. Since 1623 Buckingham had dominated the political stage, excluding his rivals from access to the king and all but eclipsing the Privy Council as the principal source of advice. His monopoly of patronage and royal counsel had forced natural allies of the crown into the political wilderness or, worse, led them to vent their frustrations by non-cooperation with the government in their counties or criticism of it in parliaments. His elevation of often landless clients – many of his own family – to titles and offices had alienated many of the old aristocracy, had dangerously narrowed the court's contact with the powerful men of the localities and had greatly added to the political tensions of the war years 1624 to 1628.[1] With Buckingham's death, as we have seen, there was widespread hope of new counsels and an expectation that the king would himself come to prominence.[2] Neither hope was to be frustrated. Charles sorely grieved the duke's death and remained, throughout the 1630s, loyal to his family, continuing to honour past promises and grant new favours. As late as 1636 the king granted the profits of Hatfield Chase to Buckingham's younger son.[3] But John Pory was wrong in thinking that, with the duke's death, Charles determined on 'nothing so much . . . as the advancement of his friends and followers' and that any other who 'seek to catch at his offices . . . will find themselves deceived'.[4] Even before Villiers's death,

1. Cf. K. Sharpe, 'Crown, parliament and locality: government and communication in early Stuart England', *Eng. Hist. Rev.*, 101 (1986), pp. 321–50, esp. pp. 329, 334; K. Sharpe, *Politics and Ideas in Early Stuart England* (1989), pp. 82–8.
2. Above, pp. 48–52.
3. PRO, SO 1/3, f.19.
4. T. Birch (ed.) *The Court and Times of Charles I* (2 vols, 1848), I, p. 396. But cf. *Calendar of State Papers Domestic* [*Cal. Stat. Pap. Dom.*], *1628–9*, p. 270: Dorchester to Elizabeth of Bohemia, 27 Aug. 1628.

both the king and favourite appeared to have grasped the need to broaden patronage and counsel. Buckingham was prepared to surrender some of his many offices – the wardenship of the Cinque Ports to the Earl of Suffolk for example – and even to court old rivals and enemies.[5] The elevation of Wentworth to the peerage signalled an important switch from the duke's patronage of Wentworth's Yorkshire rivals, the Saviles, and must have aroused hope in others who had for years languished outside the warmth of his favour. Such hopes were raised by the news of Buckingham's death, which opened up not only the avenues of patronage and influence but also major positions in the administration. Algernon Lord Percy captured the excitement within days of Villiers's assassination: 'The eyes of all men,' he told the Earl of Salisbury, 'are now upon the king to see how he will dispose of those places that are fallen into his hands, with expectation and hopes that he will confer them upon more deserving men.'[6] The Venetian ambassador echoed court gossip that anticipated major changes in policy as well as place: 'a change will doubtless follow as he ruled everything single-handed, nor were his politics in accord with the views of the entire ministry'.[7] Former parliamentary critics (as well as Wentworth, William Noy and Sir Dudley Digges) came into the government. Former enemies of the duke were fully restored to favour: in October 1628 the Earl of Arundel returned to the Privy Council.[8] Richard Weston, who, but for the death of the duke might have been 'cashiered',[9] further patronized Wentworth and Arundel and brought in his 'great friend', Sir Francis Cottington.[10] But with the Admiralty and the Mastership of the Horse vacant, and the king's inclinations unknown, it was by no means clear who would emerge as the new brokers of patronage and power.

Wentworth and Laud

In the traditional textbook accounts of the personal rule two men emerge, after the uncertain months that followed Buckingham's death, to dominate the king's government and counsels: Thomas Wentworth

5. *Ibid.*, pp. 270, 222–4.
6. *HMC Salisbury MSS, XXII*, p. 246, 27 Aug. 1628.
7. *Calendar of State Papers Venetian* [*Cal. Stat. Pap. Venet.*], *1628–9*, p. 262.
8. S.R. Gardiner, *History of England from the Accession of James I to the Outbreak of the Civil War 1603–42* (10 vols, 1883–4), VI, p. 371; K. Sharpe, 'The Earl of Arundel, his circle and the opposition to the Duke of Buckingham', in K. Sharpe (ed.) *Faction and Parliament* (Oxford, 1978), p. 236.
9. E. Hyde, Earl of Clarendon, *The History of the Rebellion and Civil Wars in England*, ed. W.D. Macray (6 vols, Oxford 1888), I, p. 61.
10. *Cal. Stat. Pap. Dom., 1625–49*, p. 293; *Cal. Stat. Pap. Venet., 1628–9*, p. 394; Sir Philip Warwick, *Memoirs of the Reign of King Charles I* (1701), pp. 109–10.

4 *Thomas Wentworth, 1st Earl of Strafford* by Anthony van Dyck, 1633. Wentworth was a patron of the artist. This full-length portrait was inspired by a portrait of Charles V by Titian.

and William Laud, the partners in what they called 'Thorough'. Raised to the peerage in July 1628, Wentworth gained rapid promotion to the Lord Presidency of the Council of the North in December and, the following year, membership of the Privy Council Board. Only months before, he had been committed for refusing the loan and had emerged in parliament as a leading proponent of the Petition of Right. Yet while Wentworth's fortunes had been transformed, his principles were not. A figure imbued with a strong sense of order and authority, he was always an unnatural critic of the crown (see Figure 4). His frustrations at bad counsel and his own exclusion from power and favour doubtless go some way to explaining his behaviour in 1627–8.[11] But we should not doubt the devotion with which he represented the grievances of his county as MP, or the sincerity of his speeches on the liberty of the subject. Nor should we assume that he cynically abandoned them after his promotion to the court and Council. For in Wentworth's understanding of order the good of the country and court, the king and the subject, were not in opposition; rather he believed, his friend George Radcliffe put it, that regal power and the privileges of the people maintained each other.[12] In his own summary of his speech on the Petition of Right, Wentworth had emphasized: 'we desire no new thing for the subject, we intend not to diminish the just prerogative of the crown . . . cannot we do this without prejudice to the king or people? If not God has taken away our understanding.'[13] The need, he advised his fellow MPs, was 'to carry ourselves even betwixt prince and people that so the streams of sovereignty and subjection may run still and smoothe together in the worn and wonted channels'.[14] In 1628 the threats to property and liberty had seemed to him to loom larger than any to the prerogative. But to Wentworth the resolution of things amiss went reciprocally in hand with a proper regard for the needs of government. He was a man who believed in action and quickly lost patience with those who wasted time on words.[15] If the experience of parliament, after the Petition of Right, and especially in 1629, sharpened that impatience with the Commons that he had exhibited earlier, the assumption of responsibility more clearly focused his vision on the need for strong and stable government.[16]

In his first famous speech to the Council of the North, while

11. S.P. Salt, 'Sir Thomas Wentworth and the parliamentary representation of Yorkshire, 1614–28', *Northern History*, 16 (1980), pp. 130–68.
12. W. Knowler (ed.) *The Earl of Strafford's Letters and Despatches*, (2 vols, 1739), II, p. 434 (appendix).
13. Sheffield Central Library, Wentworth Woodhouse MS, WW 21/210.
14. J.P. Cooper (ed.) *Wentworth Papers 1597–1628* (Camden Soc., 4th series, 12, 1973), p. 293.
15. Sharpe, *Faction and Parliament*, pp. 7–8.
16. Gardiner, *History of England*, VI, pp. 335–7.

he reasserted the harmony, the 'mutual intelligences of love' between king and people, Wentworth stressed how order and the common good rested on the maintenance of and respect for regality: 'The authority of a king is the keystone which closeth up the arch of order and government, which contains each part in due relation to the whole and which, once shaken and infirmed, all the frame falls together into a confused heap . . .'.[17] As Lord President, he emerged as a vigorous upholder of the authority of the Council of the North, not least because, as he put it to Sir John Coke, 'the king's government and authority are so deeply at stake'.[18] The tone of his letters, to the mayor of York for instance, was sharp and authoritarian. He insisted on daily accounts of actions taken on his orders; he warned that the negligent would smart.[19] The experience of government, however, showed him that all did not bow to the king's (or his) authority. Wentworth reacted with a mixture of naive incredulity and outrage to the arrogance, as he termed it, of an age when 'every ordinary man must put himself in balance with the King, as if it were a measuring cast who were like to prove greater losers upon the parting'.[20] 'Nowadays,' he lamented, 'the uttermost that all his Majesty's ministers can do scarcely restrains the people within the bounds of respect and obedience.'[21] The challenge by David Foulis to the authority of the Council of the North exemplified to Wentworth the need for greater respect for authority. 'My lord,' Wentworth wrote to Carlisle as if discovering an unpalatable truth, 'you best know how much the regal power is become infirm by the easy way such have found who with rough hands have laid upon the flowers of it . . . and how necessary examples are (as well for the subject as the sovereign) to retain licentious spirits within the sober bounds of humility and fear.'[22] If Wentworth's natural concern for order and authority hardened into an obsession, it was because experience taught him that the arch of government was in danger of collapse.

Wentworth's mounting concern for authority did not, however, lead him to believe in the need for fundamental changes in government. He was a reformer, but not a radical. The aims and ideals which were conveyed in his favourite term 'Thorough' involved the reformation of existing government, not a revolution in the nature of government. 'Stare super antiquas vias' was, he told Sir John Coke, his axiom.[23] Wentworth's conservatism stemmed from a conviction that

17. *Ibid.*, VII, pp. 25–6.
18. Melbourne Hall, Coke MS 42: Wentworth to Coke, 1 Oct. 1632.
19. Though he signed the letter 'your very loving friend'; York City Record Office, House Books, 35, f.115v.
20. *Cal. Stat. Pap. Dom., 1631–3*, p. 429.
21. *Ibid.*, p. 450.
22. Gardiner, *History of England*, VII, p. 233.
23. 'Stick to old ways', Knowler, *Strafford Letters*, I, p. 269, 24 June 1634.

nothing was fundamentally wrong with the institutions of government that could not be put right. He thought in terms of personalities rather than of institutions. The best ministers he conceived to be aristocrats who brought their wealth and standing to the service of the crown, rather than lesser men who sought to take from it.[24] Governors and subjects alike needed to be brought to an understanding of the public good, then all would co-operate for the commonweal. A man given to axioms, the mark of those who believe that human nature itself is subject to order and rule,[25] Wentworth delivered once as an aphorism 'that if friends gave themselves time to understand one another, it is impossible honest men should fall out'.[26] If he and Laud understood each other, Cottington was told by Wentworth, they could not but be friends because they were partners in the king's service.[27] The optimism that led him to believe that ministers might all co-operate in government led him to a confidence that parliaments too, in time, would work in harmony with the king. And in time, by a combination of reward and service, all subjects might become 'new men', devoted to king and commonweal.[28] Though we think of him as a hard-headed man of affairs, Wentworth's optimism in the gradual revitalization of government through the reformation of men and manners never left him. On more than one occasion, it was an optimism that exasperated William Laud. As the bishop, who always had a firmer grasp of the realities of power and government, once wrote in reply to his friend's ambitions: 'first, if the common lawyers may be contained within their ancient and sober bounds; if the word Thorough be not left out . . . if we grow not faint . . . if others will do their parts . . . Now I pray with so many and such ifs as these, what may not be done and in a brave and noble way.'[29]

William Laud identified a characteristic central to Wentworth's personality and to his limitations as a statesman: his idealism.[30] Imbued with the most profound respect for royal authority himself, Wentworth could never understand why the royal word, once uttered, was not sufficient to secure execution. He never appreciated, that is, the gap between the public utterances of government and the response of localities and individuals that is central to the political process in any age – and especially in those centuries of personal government before

24. *Ibid.*, II, pp. 41–3.
25. Cf. below, p. 193; and Wentworth Woodhouse MS WW 13/65.
26. Wentworth Woodhouse MS WW 12/270.
27. Knowler, *Strafford Letters*, I, p. 163, 24 Nov. 1633.
28. *Ibid.*, p. 419; see below, p. 704; Gardiner, *History of England*, VIII, pp. 196–8.
29. Knowler, *Strafford Letters*, I, p. 155.
30. C.V. Wedgwood argues that both Laud and Strafford were idealists (*Thomas Wentworth, First Earl of Strafford, a Revaluation, 1593–1641*, 1961, p. 89). This and other letters, however, underline a distinct difference. Cf. below, pp. 142–3.

the development of bureaucracy and a professional civil service. That failure of comprehension stemmed from another characteristic: a tendency to believe that men were, or should be, like himself – or as he perceived himself to be. Wentworth saw himself, not unreasonably, as a devoted servant of the public weal who had subordinated his private interests to public duties. He served not out of ambition, but out of duty. He coveted neither wealth nor power; he claimed to hanker for a rural retreat from business – and when we view him on Van Dyck's canvas as the country lord with his hunting dogs we are brought almost to believe him.[31] Royal service, however, he viewed as a calling. 'A life of toil and labour,' he told his cousin Clifton, 'is and must be . . . my portion of this earth and be it so as I may attain heaven for a conclusion all things else are unto me become wondrous indifferent.'[32] Wentworth was a self-professed stoic because (though not perhaps his natural temperament) 'I judge it the best morality and duty of a man in employment'.[33] Committed to hard work and public duty to the point of jeopardizing his health, he expected no less of others.[34] Sir Gervase Clifton's wish to resign the cares of office shocked him by its selfishness. 'When you think better of it, less inwards upon your own ease, more outwards upon the duties we owe the public, I assure myself you will not desire it.'[35] The people of Ireland he reported, shortly after arriving as Lord Deputy, to be a strange people because 'their own privates [are] altogether their study without any regard at all to the public'.[36] In Ireland, as the king's representative, he saw it as his role to protect the commonweal from considerations of self. Suitors for land or favour were firmly reminded of the need to subordinate their purses and interests to those of the king and public. Even promises, he sternly told the powerful Earl of Arundel, were made always subject to a condition: 'if it be good to the service of king and kingdom'.[37]

We should not doubt Wentworth's sincerity even though contemporaries rightly observed that he had not failed to further his own interests or gild his own pockets. His claim that his personal profits were never more than the legitimate perquisites of devoted service was not disingenuous in the political morality of the age. Charles I, who appointed Wentworth as 'a man whose virtues and abilities are so well known to us', never came to doubt them and exonerated his minister

31. Knowler, *Strafford Letters*, I, p. 419.
32. Nottingham University Library, Clifton MS Cl/C 486, 30 Nov. 1636.
33. Knowler, *Strafford Letters*, II, p. 39: Wentworth to Sir George Butler, 30 Nov. 1636; cf. Wedgwood, *Strafford*, p. 118.
34. Clifton MS Cl/C 473, 475; cf. *Cal. Stat. Pap. Dom., 1640*, p. 447.
35. Wedgwood, *Strafford*, pp. 89–90.
36. Wentworth MS 8, f.11: Wentworth to Arundel, 19 Aug. 1633.
37. *Ibid.*, ff.168–72, 18 Dec. 1634.

from any charge of corruption.[38] Other testimonies endorse the king's confidence. A correspondent of Lord Hastings mentioned 'the good report of his uprightness and goodness';[39] Sir Thomas Roe thought him 'violently jealous in his master's ends';[40] the Earl of Pembroke commended his zeal and faith in the king's service.[41] Lord Poulett reported the amazement of the Irish that he did not take bribes – 'that he refuseth and rejecteth their gifts and presents which is a rare example in this kingdom'.[42] Though a 'terrible judge' (in Roe's words),[43] Wentworth won the affection of the Irish for his fairness, 'in so much,' Rossingham wrote, 'that when he comes abroad the poor Irish people do fall down upon their knees and pray to God to bless him, saying where hast thou been all this while that thou never comest hither till now to do us right and justice.'[44] As the Deputy's unrelenting labours for 'advantage to the crown . . . without the curses of the subject' visibly aged a once upright frame,[45] Christopher Wandesford, Master of the Rolls in Ireland, expressed in letters to Clifton his fear that Wentworth's devotion to duty threatened to break his health.[46] Wentworth's sense of himself as a man of discipline and duty was not self-deception; he set himself high standards of honesty and service and expected no less of others.

It was, along with his idealism, this self-righteousness that made Wentworth so reluctant to compromise or tolerate the foibles of others. As a consequence, while some admired his earnest labours for just government, many were alienated by his pride and hectoring. Even friends, who knew him 'sweet in private conversation', described him as 'severe' in business.[47] Those who knew him less well concluded that 'Nature hath not given him generally a personal affability.'[48] The French ambassador Poigny characterized him as 'fier et redoubté';[49] Clarendon recalled his 'predominant pride'.[50] Philip Warwick, secretary to Juxon and clerk of the signet, regretted that his considerable talents were 'lodged in a sour and haughty temper, so as it may probably be believed he expected to have more observance paid to him

38. PRO, SO 1/2, f.119v.
39. Huntington Library, Hastings MS 1229.
40. *Cal. Stat. Pap. Dom., 1634–5*, p. xxxix: Roe to Elizabeth of Bohemia, 10 Dec. 1634.
41. Wentworth MS WW 14/197.
42. Bristol Record Office, Smyth of Ashton Court MS 30674/125: Poulett to Smyth, 8 Sept. 1633.
43. *Cal. Stat. Pap. Dom., 1634–5*, p. 350.
44. PRO, C.115/M36/8427, 1 Aug. 1634.
45. Wedgwood, *Strafford*, p. 191; Clifton MS Cl/C 473.
46. Clifton MS Cl/C 475.
47. As did Roe; see note 43.
48. Wedgwood, *Strafford*, p. 105.
49. PRO, 31/3/68, f.216v.
50. Clarendon, *History of the Rebellion*, I, p. 342.

than he was willing to pay to others'.[51] Wentworth's sense of his own difference and isolation also distanced and isolated him.[52] He had few friends at court and perhaps no kindred spirit. In Clarendon's words, 'he wholly relied upon himself, and discerning many defects in most men, he too much neglected what they said or did'.[53] Though 'like a king' as Lord Deputy of Ireland, and a man of imagination and vision in all his master's affairs, Wentworth remained too isolated from his fellow ministers to exercise a major influence on the government of the personal rule.[54]

For most of the 1630s, of course, Wentworth was physically distanced from other courtiers and absent from the centre of influence and power. His commitment to his Lord Presidency meant that after 1628 he was only occasionally in London. When, in January 1632, he was appointed Lord Deputy of Ireland, the French ambassador did not know who he was.[55] After his departure in the summer of 1633 to take up his office, Wentworth was to return to England only once (in 1636) before his recall in 1639.[56] His absence did not mean that he did not count in the political calculations of anxious courtiers. There were rumours of Wentworth's taking Weston's place as Lord Treasurer in the summer of 1629,[57] and they persisted throughout the 1630s,[58] Wentworth feeling the need to assure Weston that he had no designs on his office.[59] Clearly many at court thought 'the best place is not too good for him' and that he wielded great influence.[60] His own regular letters to the king contained frank counsel which was evidently respected and appreciated.[61] But Wentworth always doubted his influence and feared for his standing.[62] And though his fears proved to be ill-founded, his doubts were not invalid. Far away from court, the Lord Deputy was, as his correspondence with Laud and others makes clear, dependent on others: for the king's reactions, the latest news, even common gossip. Absent in Ireland, he was also vulnerable to his enemies, for as Edward Nicholas put it, 'never was there as yet such an

51. Warwick, *Memoirs*, p. 110.
52. G. Bankes, *The Story of Corfe Castle* (1853), p. 55.
53. Clarendon, *History of the Rebellion*, I, p. 342.
54. Roe's description, quoted in Wedgwood, *Strafford*, p. 155.
55. PRO, 31/3/67, f.83: Fontenay to Bouthillier, 8 April 1633, 'celui qui est destiné Vice-Roy d'Irlande'.
56. For an account of his affairs in Ireland, see Bodleian, Tanner MS 114, f.110.
57. Birch, *Court and Times of Charles I*, II, p. 19: Dr Laney to Cosin, 25 June 1629.
58. For example, Wentworth MSS WW/22, f.109; WW/14, f.330; Knowler, *Strafford Letters*, I, p. 418; PRO, 31/3/68, f.216v; PRO, C.115/N3/8555.
59. Knowler, *Strafford Letters*, I, p. 79, Oct. 1632.
60. PRO, C.115/N3/8555: Herbert to Scudamore, 9 Aug. 1634.
61. For example, Knowler, *Strafford Letters*, II, p. 60; Wentworth MS WW3.
62. For example, Wentworth MS WW/8, ff.11, 94–5; Wentworth asked Arundel, a member of the Irish Committee, to protect his interests for he was in need of friends in England.

officer that lost not ground at court through his absence and the envy of malign persons'.[63] Wentworth's desperate quest for an earldom from 1634 was a mark of his insecurity and of the need for some recognition that would silence critics and 'set me right again . . . in the opinion of others'.[64] For all his greatness, his position was insecure: as Roe put it, he 'will either be the greatest man in England or much less than he is'.[65] As Lord Deputy of Ireland, Wentworth as well as attracting the hostility of court rivals and frustrated suitors earned the king's respect. But in other than Irish affairs, he was not before his return in 1639 a major influence in the king's counsel nor in shaping the policies and programmes of personal rule.

It is traditional to pair with Sir Thomas Wentworth as his partner in the programme of 'Thorough' Bishop William Laud. The two men became firm friends, albeit through correspondence more than personal contact, and Laud shared many of Wentworth's values. Like Wentworth he was a man of sincere intent and uprightness. Clarendon, who had mixed feelings about Laud, could not but praise his 'good conscience', 'sincere worthy intentions' and 'integrity';[66] Sir Thomas Roe told Elizabeth of Bohemia in December 1634 that the archbishop was 'very just, incorrupt . . . a rare counsellor for integrity'.[67] Even the Earl of Dorset (who as the queen's chamberlain was a leading figure in a rival faction) praised Laud as 'so faithful towards the king and so upright in his place.[68] Like Wentworth, Laud was personally an indefatigable worker of immense self-discipline, and even greater self-denial.[69] (See Figure 5.) Zealous, methodical and attentive to business, he was possessed, like his friend, of a strong sense of self-righteousness and little sympathy for those who, through laziness or self-interest, fell short of his standards. He waged a crusade against corruption at court and in the country: in a Star Chamber trial for the exaction of excessive fees he urged that 'it is high time that exaction and extortion be looked into'.[70] Like Wentworth, he was sure that reward and punishment were the means to bring all to a proper sense of public

63. *HMC Denbigh, V*, p. 8: Edward Nicholas to Fielding, 13 Dec. 1631. Cf. Sharpe, 'Crown, parliament and locality', pp. 325–6.
64. Knowler, *Strafford Letters*, I, p. 302; Wedgwood, *Strafford*, pp. 193–4; Sir C. Petrie (ed.) *The Letters, Speeches and Proclamations of Charles I* (1935), pp. 95–6.
65. *Cal. Stat. Pap. Dom., 1634–5*, p. 350, 10 Dec. 1634.
66. Clarendon, *History of the Rebellion*, I, p. 82.
67. *Cal. Stat. Pap. Dom., 1634–5*, p. xxxviii.
68. Tanner MS 67, f.91. Dorset made the remark at the trial of Williams in Star Chamber.
69. For an instance of his diligence, see *HMC De Lisle and Dudley, VI*, p. 240: Hawkins to Leicester, 2 April 1640; H.R. Trevor-Roper, *Archbishop Laud 1573–1645* (1940), p. 35. Hawkins delivered Laud a letter as he was going home after a long day. But 'he returned in again and said he would read it to see if it required an answer'.
70. British Library [BL], Harleian MS 4022, f.59v (Mynne's case).

5 *William Laud* by Van Dyck, 1638. There is no evidence that this was commissioned by Laud. It stands out as Van Dyck's most austere portrait.

service: 'fear,' he opined at the trial of Thomas Conisby, 'is the beginning of wisdom.'[71] As well as devotion to royal authority and to duty, Laud shared with Wentworth a sharp manner that alienated him from his fellows. Bulstrode Whitelocke, while acknowledging him as just and good, thought him 'too full of fire';[72] Cottington, who knew from personal experience, observed that 'he can never be reconciled where once he takes displeasure';[73] he could not argue in Council without losing his temper.[74] A common feeling of alienation and isolation was as much the cement of Laud's friendship with Wentworth as was their quest for reform and efficiency.

What Laud did not share was Wentworth's illusions and ideals. Where Wentworth was a visionary, Laud was a more practical man of affairs. He had no illusions that men would come to place the public good before their private interest. He recognized that ambition and particular ends were inevitable in public life. Early in their correspondence he had to explain to the new Lord Deputy, 'indeed my Lord I am for "Thorough" but I see that thick and thin stays somebody where I conceive it should not . . . private ends are such blocks in the public way'.[75] Aims and goals, Laud saw, had always to be geared to what was possible. 'By your lordship's leave,' he warned Wentworth, 'the conceit which you express, of all able and all hearty, and all running one way, and none caring for any ends so the king may be served is but a branch of Plato's Commonwealth which flourishes this day nowhere but in Utopia.'[76] There was no point, he similarly counselled Bishop Bedell, building castles in the air.[77] Experience confirmed Laud's sense of harsh practicalities: by 1637 he had, he confessed, 'done expecting of "Thorough".'[78] Though he shared Wentworth's aims, he never indulged in the fantasy that they could all be fulfilled. The church, he told his friend, alone would occupy all his energies and even for the church 'it is not possible for me or for any man to do that good which he would'.[79]

71. *Ibid.*, f.17.
72. Bulstrode Whitelocke, *Memorials of the English Affairs* (1682), p. 32.
73. *Cal. Stat. Pap. Dom., 1635*, p. ix.
74. Clarendon, *History of the Rebellion*, I, p. 132.
75. J. Blisse and W. Scott (eds) *The Works of William Laud* (7 vols, Oxford, 1847–60), VI, part I, p. 310: Laud to Wentworth, 9 Sept. 1633.
76. *Ibid.*, p. 320, 14 Oct. 1633; cf. *ibid.*, p. 330, 15 Nov. 1633. Laud wrote to Wentworth, 'you are upon so many "ifs" that by their help you may preserve any man upon ice, be it never so slippery. As first, if the common lawyers may be contained within their ancient and sober bounds; if the word "thorough" be not left out (as I am certain it is); if we grow not faint . . . if others will do their parts. Now I pray with so many, and such "ifs" as these, what may not be done, and in a brave and noble way? But can you tell when these "ifs" will meet, or be brought together?'
77. *Ibid.*, p. 286, 11 Sept. 1630.
78. *Works of Laud*, VI, part 2, p. 496, 26 Aug. 1637.
79. Knowler, *Strafford Letters*, I, pp. 110–11, 9 Sept. 1633.

Laud's sense of the limitations to what he could effect undoubtedly stemmed from the older man's long personal experience of checks to his own advancement and ambitions. Held back from appointment to an episcopal see until 1621, Laud did not really come into prominence until after the death of James I, by which time he was over fifty. Thanks to Buckingham's patronage, the new king asked Laud to advise him concerning the clergy eligible for promotion and raised him to the bishopric of Bath and Wells in 1626, with the promise of still higher honours.[80] In June 1628 he succeeded to London, with the archbishopric of Canterbury in prospect. Clearly Laud enjoyed Charles I's trust and rapidly became the principal royal adviser on religious affairs. He aided the king with the declaration prefixed to a new edition of the Thirty-Nine Articles;[81] he drafted for Charles considerations concerning the better government of the church that became the royal orders issued to Archbishop Abbot in 1629.[82] Yet despite his rapid rise, Laud's power and control, even in church affairs, may (as I shall argue below) have been exaggerated; he may have been less the architect of ecclesiastical policy than the executor of the king's own plans. In matters other than religion, there is little evidence that Laud was a principal figure in the government of the early 1630s. In the parliament of 1628 he had kept careful notes of the proceedings on the liberty of the subject and Charles, as we have seen, asked him to draft a royal reply to the Commons' Remonstrance.[83] But, especially after his elevation to London, Laud appears to have concentrated his energies, as he had told Wentworth, on the pressing concerns of the church.

The compartmentalized nature of government that became established after Buckingham's death helped to restrict Laud's influence to his own sphere. As a Privy Councillor he attended assiduously and evidently frequently contributed to debate;[84] in Star Chamber he was present and spoke often, sometimes suggesting broader reforms of state as well as church – not least that that court should 'as well remedy offences as punish offenders'.[85] But it is important to note that, as he informed Sir Thomas Roe, Laud was not a member in the early 1630s of any of the important committees of Council and few contemporaries

80. Gardiner, *History of England*, V, pp. 363–4.
81. P. Heylyn, *Cyprianus Anglicus or the History of the Life and Death of William Laud* (1668), part I, pp. 186–7.
82. J. Rushworth (ed.) *Historical Collections*, II (1680), p. 7; Lambeth Palace MS 943, f.91; Heylyn, *Cyprianus Anglicus*, pp. 188–9.
83. *Cal. Stat. Pap. Dom., 1628–9*, p. 88; Huntington Library, Temple of Stowe MSS, Parliament Box 13; above, pp. 42–3.
84. Laud's attendance was one of the highest. He attended over 80 per cent of all Council meetings from 1632 to 1640.
85. Harleian MS 4022, f.59v.

regarded him as prominent in the determination of secular affairs.[86] There is no need to doubt the truth of Laud's statement to Williams in September 1633 that the king 'had given me leave to move him in any business of the church whatsoever, but a charge withal that I should not be earnest in temporal causes'.[87] Only after 1634 did this change. In February and March 1635, during the weeks of the Earl of Portland's fatal illness, Laud was appointed to the committees for trade, the Exchequer, and foreign affairs.[88] Then the Venetian envoy described him as an old man with only a 'scant knowledge of the interests of state'.[89] And the French ambassador, Senneterre, thought that even then Laud would continue 'selon sa coustume pour attendre plûtot à faire le Pope sur le clergé d'Angleterre qu'aux affaires d'état'.[90] As Laud told Bishop Bramhall, the highest ecclesiastical office was already a great 'trouble'.[91] Though the notes and papers in his study in 1634 contain some material on foreign affairs, they are dominated by material on the Elizabethan church and foreign churches, on church courts and metropolitical visitations, on popery and puritanism – a testimony to Laud's labours in his mission to reform the church.[92] If his rivals and enemies at court suspected that Laud was ambitious to rule over affairs secular as well as clerical they may have been mistaken.

That is not to say that Laud was uninterested in power. His own fortunes had shown him that the promotion of policies depended on the advancement to place and that for the protection of the church it was necessary that clerics secure positions of honour and influence. Court life showed him clearly the 'envy and malice which must and will accompany all men which live in any place of eminence'[93] and, curiously, office exacerbated that paranoid insecurity which runs through his dreams.[94] Fearful that others plotted to supplant him in the king's affections, Laud in turn manoeuvred to embarrass his enemies and promote his friends.[95] Concerned that he did not have the king's ear he had William Juxon sworn Clerk of the Closet in 1632 'that

86. *Cal. Stat. Pap. Dom., 1633–4*, p. 562, 22 April 1634; *Cal. Stat. Pap. Venet., 1632–6*, p. 488.
87. *Works of Laud*, VI, part 1, p. 315, 16 Sept. 1633. Despite their relations, this appears to be more than special pleading; for Laud's insecurity about his standing with the king, see below, pp. 145, 284 ff.
88. *Works of Laud*, III, p. 223, diary for Feb. and March 1635.
89. *Cal. Stat. Pap. Venet., 1632–6*, p. 488.
90. PRO, 31/3/68, f.216v, 5 Sept. 1635.
91. Huntington Library MS, HA 15172 (Bramhall letters), 11 March 1633; *Cal. Stat. Pap. Dom., 1631–3*, p. 353: Laud to Windebank, 13 June 1632.
92. Tanner MS 88, f.20.
93. Huntington Library MS, HA 15172, xviii: Laud to Bramhall, Oct. 1638.
94. See Laud's diary, *Work of Laud*, III *passim*, for these dreams. Also C. Carlton, 'The dream life of Archbishop Laud', *History Today*, 36 (Dec. 1986), pp. 9–14.
95. See, for example, *Works of Laud*, III, p. 218.

I might have one that I could trust near his majesty'.[96] Similarly Windebank, according to Laud's biographer, was promoted that the bishop might have 'the king's ear on one side and the Clerk of the Closet on the other'.[97] Moreover Laud learned how to play the courtier: he went abroad in a coach of six horses;[98] he built a stone gallery – one of the fashionable home improvements of the age.[99] To celebrate his elevation to Canterbury he entertained the Privy Council to an elaborate banquet.[100] Yet when all that is said, there remains a strong impression that the court was not Laud's natural milieu. Aristocratic fashions and pastimes were not for him; pastorals and plays he had no time for;[101] Van Dyck's paintings he dismissed as 'vanity shadows'.[102] Unlike his contemporaries, he had not travelled; he could not partake of their cosmopolitan wit and banter. In his dislike of Cottington's 'Spanish tricks' and 'making of legs to fair ladies', we may discern, beyond the personal jar, Laud's deeper antipathy for the superficiality of court life.[103] Laud's natural home was elsewhere. He was, as Professor Trevor-Roper argued, always at heart a don.[104] 'More than anything else,' Laud's latest biographer writes, 'Oxford shaped him.'[105] Acerbic, pious, donnish and insular, Laud was not the personality suited to dominate the court nor even the king's affections.[106] Though later events were to cast him in a leading role, Laud did not shape the plot of personal rule. As late as 1637, he told the queen of Bohemia what he had earlier told Bishop Williams: 'his Majesty is not pleased I should trouble him with anything but Church business and indeed I have enough of that'.[107]

Weston and Cottington

While historians have traditionally elevated Laud and Wentworth to the first places of influence in the king's counsels, contemporaries knew better those who were closer to the king and wielded power. Looking back, Clarendon recalled that it was Richard Weston, the

96. *Ibid.*, p. 216.
97. Heylyn, *Cyprianus Anglicus*, I, p. 212.
98. C. Carlton, *Archbishop William Laud* (1987), p. 141.
99. *Works of Laud*, VI, part 2, p. 367: Laud to Scudamore, 29 March 1634.
100. *Cal. Stat. Pap. Venet., 1632–6*, p. 152.
101. Trevor-Roper, *Laud*, p. 34; Knowler, *Strafford Letters*, II, p. 56.
102. Carlton, *Laud*, p. 128.
103. *Works of Laud*, VI, part 2, p. 377; see below, pp. 234, 385.
104. Trevor-Roper, *Laud*, p. 37.
105. Carlton, *Laud*, p. 7.
106. Cf. Clarendon, *History of the Rebellion*, I, p. 82. Clarendon points out that Laud showed 'the least condescension to the arts and stratagems of the court'.
107. *Cal. Stat. Pap. Dom., 1637*, p. 308, 11 July. See above, p. 144.

Lord Treasurer, who rose to prominence after the uneasy and uncertain months that followed Buckingham's death.[108] Whilst many expected and desired to see James Hay, Earl of Carlisle, return to succeed Villiers as the king's favourite, others predicted, within days of the duke's death, that the 'greatest power' would be with Weston.[109] As the dust settled, Lord Percy's prognostication was rapidly confirmed. By mid-September Lord Goring was informing Carlisle: 'our Treasurer is the most potent man in this state'.[110] Two months later it was common talk. On 1 November it was reported, with a newswriter's typical exaggeration, 'my Lord Treasurer is dominus factotum, unto whom the residue, they say, are but ciphers'.[111] The move towards peace, to a period of 'rest and vigilancy' which Weston had advocated in Council and recommended to Buckingham, focused attention on the Treasurer rather than the warhawks.[112] The desperate financial situation offered no alternative to his sage counsel for 'a constant care . . . by lessening charge and increasing revenue'.[113] By July 1629, the French ambassador was describing Weston as not only the most powerful Councillor, but the only figure who had his master's confidence.[114] Sir Tobie Matthew observed him consolidating his position: 'My Lord Treasurer is daily greater and greater and whoever loves him least is the most forward to speak him fair.'[115] In the summer of 1631 John Pory reported the rumour that Weston was to be made Lord Admiral as well as Lord Treasurer, a combination of offices which would have bestowed on him greater power than any minister since the days of Henry VIII.[116] The attempt by his enemies in 1632 to topple the Treasurer, rather than coming near to success, served only to strengthen his position.[117] In the summer of 1634, even after the Earl of Holland's renewed efforts to supplant him, the French envoy, Poigny was told that it was Weston who possessed 'la confiance entière de son maistre et toute la conduite de ses affaires entre les mains'.[118]

Weston's prominence owed much to his office. During the early

108. Clarendon, *History of the Rebellion*, I, pp. 62–3, and on his earlier life, pp. 59–62. See also M.V.C. Alexander, *Charles I's Lord Treasurer: Sir Richard Weston, Earl of Portland, 1577–1635* (1975).
109. *Cal. Stat. Pap. Dom., 1625–49*, pp. 292–3: Percy to Carlisle, 3 Sept. 1628.
110. *Ibid.*, p. 294: Goring to Carlisle, 16 Sept. 1628.
111. Birch, *Court and Times of Charles I*, I, p. 419: Mede to Stuteville, 1 Nov. 1628.
112. See Coke MS 36: letter to Damville, 10 Jan. 1629; *HMC Cowper I*, p. 378.
113. Quoted in F.C. Dietz, *English Public Finance 1558–1641* (New York, 1964), p. 250.
114. PRO, 31/3/66, f.126: dispatch of 23 July 1629.
115. *Cal. Stat. Pap. Dom., 1625–49*, p. 367: letter to Vane, 3 March 1630.
116. Birch, *Court and Times of Charles I*, II, p. 123: Pory to Puckering, 16 June 1631.
117. As Tobie Mathew put it, 'His enemies by their witless envy and rage erected certain steps whereby he has risen so high . . .' (*Cal. Stat. Pap. Dom., 1631–3*, p. 437, 15 Nov. 1632).
118. PRO, 31/3/68, ff.114–115v; below, pp. 176–7.

years of personal rule peace and the ordering of finance were the most pressing concerns and Weston worked hard to reduce expenditure and raise the royal revenue. He had been a respected Chancellor of the Exchequer whom many had tipped for the treasurership when the Earl of Marlborough had secured the post in 1624. As well as honesty and learning he brought to his office considerable experience so that Charles 'received no other advice in the large business of his revenue'.[119] Unlike Wentworth, or Laud, he articulated no philosophy of state nor advocated any grandiose programme. His quiet caretakership of the Treasury offended the bustling Laud who characterized him, in letters to Wentworth, as the Lady Mora but for whose delays, caution and corruption so much more could have been achieved in reforming administration and government.[120] Historians have tended to endorse Laud's condemnation. Gardiner rather sneeringly concluded that his 'recipe for every ill was to leave matters alone'. 'Scarcely anything . . . was done by him . . . to place the finances on a sounder basis'.[121] Echoing the charge of his enemies, historians have judged Weston's ambitions to be only personal and negative. As a Hispanophile and suspected Catholic who had been attacked in the parliamentary session of 1629, the Treasurer, it is said, thought only of a pusillanimous withdrawal from the Protestant cause and of enabling the king to rule without parliaments.[122] Such a characterization does Weston less than justice. While he achieved no miracles as Treasurer, and the commissioners for the Treasury were to criticize sharply his management of finance,[123] his achievements should not be discounted.[124] As we have seen, the economies he instituted and the repayments of debts he embarked upon pulled the Exchequer back from crisis. If he stopped short of further reform, or revenue-raising schemes, that may have been as much from a sense of the political limitations to reform as laziness or lack of imagination. As Weston's biographer Professor Alexander concluded, the Lord Treasurer had an 'enviable record of government service'.[125]

Nor should statements of Weston's Hispanophilia or hostility to parliaments be taken uncritically. Despite the attacks on the Treasurer in 1629, Hopton had no reservations about recommending a parliament to him;[126] and in the autumn and winter of 1631 Weston himself

119. Clarendon, *History of the Rebellion*, I, p. 62.
120. *Works of Laud*, VI, part 2, pp. 385, 399.
121. Gardiner, *History of England*, VII, p. 377; cf. *Dictionary of National Biography* [*DNB*].
122. See Gardiner, *History of England*, and *DNB*.
123. PRO, 31/3/68, f.158; *Cal. Stat. Pap. Dom., 1635*, pp. 11, 110; Alexander, *Charles I's Lord Treasurer*, p. 208.
124. See *Cal. Stat. Pap. Venet., 1632–6*, pp. 223–4.
125. Alexander, *Charles I's Lord Treasurer*, p. 220.
126. BL, Egerton MS 1820, f.225.

said one would be summoned.[127] His support for negotiations with Spain owed more to his conviction of the need for peace than to affection for any country. The French ambassadors were advised that Weston espoused no nation's interests but those of England and was most of all anxious to keep his master out of a war for which there was no money.[128] Within that context, they regularly reported him to be a friend to France; Poigny feared his death would jeopardize France through the succession of more Spanish councillors.[129] Charles I himself was clear: his Treasurer was neither Spanish nor French, but 'bien Anglais'.[130] Even Weston's commitment to Catholicism needs to be treated with caution. For much of his life, he attended the services of the Church of England. And though he died in the Catholic faith and was married to a declared Catholic, 'he never had reputation and credit with that party who were the only people of the kingdom who did not believe him to be of their profession'.[131] Rather than Hispanophile or papist, Weston was first what Charles I considered him to be: his master's servant and the executor of the king's wishes.

Many of Weston's contemporaries did not share Laud's dislike for him. Though James I had once quipped that he spoke ill of all men ('no man need fear damnation if Sir Richard Weston went to heaven'),[132] and Clarendon thought his 'imperious nature' 'disobliging', even 'offending', Weston had both admirers and friends.[133] The Treasurer was travelled, learned and cultivated, which helps to explain his longstanding friendship with the likes of the Earls of Arundel and Bristol.[134] Cottington held him 'very dear'.[135] And Wentworth, for all his collusion in Laud's jokes about Lady Mora, described Weston as the 'very principal' of his friends.[136] The French ambassador regarded him as clever; the Venetian envoy, Gussoni, thought him a man of 'deep and sagacious intellect'.[137] Sir George Goring and Tobie Matthew attested to his honesty, ability and wisdom;[138] Ben Jonson praised his discernment and energy.[139] The greatest tribute came from Sir Henry Wotton. Wotton, one of the most powerful intellects of his age, lauded

127. PRO, C.115/M35/8386.
128. PRO, 31/3/68, ff.114–18: instructions to Poigny.
129. *Ibid.*, f.145.
130. PRO, 31/3/66, f.158v, 24 Sept. 1629.
131. Hastings MS 9598: Rossingham's letter, 28 March 1635; Clarendon, *History of the Rebellion*, I, p. 63.
132. W.H. Long (ed.) *The Oglander Memoirs* (1888), p. 124.
133. Clarendon, *History of the Rebellion*, I, p. 64.
134. He also collected paintings; see C. Brown, *Van Dyck* (1982), p. 137.
135. *Cal. Stat. Pap. Dom., 1631–3*, p. 294: T. Mathew to H. Vane, 25 March 1632.
136. Knowler, *Strafford Letters*, I, p. 79: Wentworth to Weston, Oct. 1632.
137. *Cal. Stat. Pap. Venet., 1632–6*, p. 367.
138. *Cal. Stat. Pap. Dom., 1625–49*, p. 294; *1631–3*, p. 437.
139. I. Donaldson (ed.) *Ben Jonson: Poems* (Oxford, 1975), p. 409. I am grateful to Ian Donaldson for many stimulating discussions of Jonson's poetry and politics.

Weston's 'searching judgement', 'indubitable integrity' and 'evident moderation' and the dignity, charity and hospitality of a man 'conversant with liberal studies'. He praised the most skilful management of the king's finances since the days of Burleigh.[140] Cynicism may lead us to suspect any praise of a Treasurer who paid the pensions and dispensed patronage at the early Stuart court. But it is clear that Weston inspired friendship, affection and respect – not least of all in Charles I himself. Not only did the king stand by his Lord Treasurer when enemies and the envious sought to discredit him, he twice paid off Weston's debts, and in addition to an earldom bestowed on him the whole of Chute forest in Hampshire 'and much other land belonging to the crown'.[141] Weston had the entire confidence and esteem of his master; the 'great favour' Charles showed him lasted literally to the grave. When during the last days of Weston's illness Sir Robert Pye, Remembrancer of the Exchequer, refused a request for £5,000 in the name of the Treasurer (because he believed him already to be dead) Charles I sent an express personal command that he should pay it.[142] Days later, the king went to him in person and sorrowed for his death.[143]

For all the trust and esteem he inspired, however, Weston perhaps never became intimate with Charles I and certainly never emerged as another royal favourite. Foreign envoys looked for a successor to Buckingham; English observers feared one. Clarendon claimed that, dissatisfied with his place, Weston wished to establish himself as sole favourite.[144] But Weston never enjoyed the personal access to the bedchamber nor the personal friendship that had been the foundation of Buckingham's power with two kings. He was evidently frustrated at the limits to his influence and insecure at times in his standing with the king. Contemporary references to the king's 'confidence' in Weston and 'graciousness' towards him convey a sense of a relationship that was formal rather than close; references to others as 'favourites', a term never applied to Weston, underpin that impression.[145] Unlike Buckingham, Weston never controlled the reins of patronage or built a party dependent upon himself. Though he was able to smoothe the way to favours, few appear to have owed their advancements or places purely or largely to his support. And while he arranged a powerful marriage for his son to the daughter of the Duke of

140. Tanner MS 299, f.84.
141. Clarendon, *History of the Rebellion*, I, pp. 62–3.
142. Hastings MS 9598.
143. Gardiner, *History of England*, VII, p. 378; *Cal. Stat. Pap. Venet., 1632–6*, p. 350, 23 March 1635: 'His Majesty is certainly deeply afflicted by this loss. He shows the greatest sorrow because he loved him cordially.'
144. Clarendon, *History of the Rebellion*, I, p. 62.
145. *Cal. Stat. Pap. Dom., 1631–3*, p. 437.

Lennox, he failed to secure for him a place at court, despite grooming him as a future secretary of state or Master of the Court of Wards.[146] Weston was powerful in the court of Charles I, and as Lord Treasurer the king's most important minister. But, unlike the Buckingham years, there were now rivals for the king's ear and affections and none enjoyed a monopoly of power.

The absence of a favourite in the years after Buckingham's death opened the court to a large number of men, making Whitehall a vortex of personalities who in their various ways and to different degrees influenced the course of politics and the style of government. After 1628 the court re-emerged as the junction of politics where all attitudes to domestic and foreign, secular and religious affairs could be expressed and exchanged. Laud and Wentworth, as exponents of 'Thorough', Weston as Lord Treasurer dominate the history books as they were often the subjects of court intrigue and gossip. But if we are to understand Caroline court politics and the debates and disagreements which were a characteristic of Caroline government, we must meet some of the other, less famous figures who acted on the public stage. Some we must envisage bent over their papers by the flickering light of candles late into the night; others in discussion with the king coming from the hunt or going to dine. Let us then, for a while, before we pry into the Council chamber or committee room, take an amble through the long gallery at Whitehall and as we pass the portraits of Councillors and courtiers – we shall group them as 'men of business' and 'courtier peers' – let us pause to make an acquaintance with a few of them more closely.

In a court dominated during the early 1630s by financial crisis, next to Weston one of the most important figures was the Chancellor of the Exchequer, Francis Baron Cottington. Traditional historiography has not characterized Cottington as a serious man of business. From Laud's correspondence he emerges as 'the Lady Mora's waiting maid' who 'would pace a little faster than her mistress did, but the steps would be as foul',[147] who was an unreliable wag and trickster rather than a figure of principle or integrity. Laud's criticism, however, may tell us more about the archbishop himself than about Cottington. The dark, ascetic figure of William Laud, whom alone of the Carolines Van Dyck's brush could not romanticize, was not one to appreciate a man of Cottington's obvious wit and gaiety. Cottington was a courtier *par excellence*. A gentleman, a horseman, the builder of a good estate who loved his hawks and sports, he was also an accomplished linguist and

146. PRO, C.115/M36/8436: Rossingham to Scudamore, 3 Oct. 1634; Knowler, *Strafford Letters*, I, p. 389: Garrard to Wentworth, 17 March 1635.
147. *Works of Laud*, VII, p. 145.

traveller who 'could not be said to be ignorant in any art of learning'.[148] In contrast to the sombre attire of others, Laud among them, Cottington evidently delighted in flamboyance: the Reverend Garrard reports him visiting the Earl of Salisbury 'bravely horsed in a white beaver with a studded hat band';[149] at the Earl of Northumberland's institution as Knight of the Garter, he attended rich in jewels and feathers 'in the Spanish way'.[150] Laud's famous sneer that he could not trust him 'for anything but making of legs to fair ladies' suggests, as well as fashionable gallantry, an ease with the fairer sex with which the misogynist bishop was not graced.[151] Cottington clearly had an easy manner; his 'natural temper was not liable to any transport of anger'; he did not react personally to disagreement or criticism.[152] His distinguishing trait – one that little endeared him to the humourless Laud – was his mirth and ready wit. Sometimes that wit was exercised at others' expense. When Wentworth from Ireland referred to the distempers of earlier parliaments, Cottington could not resist the quip at the Council Board 'quorum pars magna fui'.[153] But where Laud leapt to interpret the jest in the worst way and solemnly reported it to the Lord Deputy, others appear to have greatly appreciated Cottington's humour. The Reverend Garrard spoke of the 'jollities' he enjoyed with the Chancellor,[154] and even Wentworth (who obviously took no long-term offence at the earlier jibe) welcomed Cottington's return, in the summer of 1635, from his recent grave demeanour to his natural 'jovial strain . . . which humour becomes you better; I like it wondrous well'.[155] Cottington's banter need not be read, as Laud interpreted it, as the badge of a malicious or superficial character. Cottington took delight in language; he was graphic and forthright: 'I am stuck here,' he wrote to Wentworth from his country estate in 1633, 'like a turd upon a wall.'[156] But, Clarendon tells us, 'he never used anybody ill' and was a man of substance as well as style.[157]

In the affairs of state, Cottington was also a figure 'of great and long experience . . . in business of all kinds'.[158] Twice an envoy to Spain, several times an MP, a former clerk to the Privy Council and secretary to the Prince of Wales, Cottington brought to the government of the

148. Clarendon, *History of the Rebellion*, V, pp. 155–6; see M. Havran, *Caroline Courtier: The Life of Lord Cottington* (1973).
149. *Cal. Stat. Pap. Dom., 1636–7*, p. 75: Garrard to Conway, 26 July 1636.
150. Bankes, *Corfe Castle*, p. 54.
151. *Works of Laud*, VI, part 2, p. 377: Laud to Wentworth, 14 May 1634.
152. Clarendon, *History of the Rebellion*, V, p. 155.
153. 'In which I played a great part', Knowler, *Strafford Letters*, I, p. 253.
154. *Ibid.*, p. 267.
155. *Ibid.*, p. 441.
156. Wentworth MS WW/13, f.37.
157. Clarendon, *History of the Rebellion*, V, p. 156.
158. *Ibid.*, p. 155.

personal rule a broad knowledge of government and diplomacy. His judgement as a diplomat was greatly respected: when he was about to go to Spain to negotiate the peace it was reported that 'as he will be of great use there for furtherance of the business so will he be much wanted here where . . . he hath not left one so able . . . as he is'.[159] Cottington's obvious affection for Spain and things Spanish never blinded his judgement. He dismissed Weston's naive optimism that peace with Spain and the restoration of the Palatinate may be 'both on a day', telling Wentworth: 'what hereupon my own conjecture is may not be expressed in a letter'.[160] During the negotiations for a peace, frustrated at Spanish proceedings, he counselled his recall; it was Charles who ordered him to proceed.[161] From 1630 onwards, Cottington managed the delicate negotiations with Madrid for a secret partition treaty and maritime treaty as much the agent as architect of royal policy. 'Reason of state', however, always remained the basis of his inclination towards a Spanish alliance.[162] When it failed of its purpose, Cottington remained a vigorous member of the foreign committee that negotiated a French alliance, and in the later 1630s was thought to be anti-Spanish and pro-French.[163] For all Laud's wish to deny it, devotion to his master's rights and service characterized Cottington's public career. He chid those who were negligent in 'stopping the spoils of the forest';[164] in Star Chamber his sentences were severe against disturbers of the state; he attended regularly the Privy Council in which, next to the Treasurer, he is said to have wielded most influence.[165] Promoted to the mastership of the Wards, he raised, as we have seen, the revenue of that court 'to be much greater than it had ever been before his administration'.[166] Whatever the judgement of historians, his services as Chancellor of the Exchequer did not go unappreciated by the king or the court. Most tipped Cottington to succeed Weston as Treasurer because, as Edward Rossingham told Lord Clifton, he 'knows the business best'.[167] Though Laud accused him of unbridled ambition and grasping for the place, Cottington, after failing of success, congratulated Juxon, announcing with his usual good humour, that he would live longer than if he had

159. Coke MS 37: letter to Damville, June 1629.
160. Knowler, *Strafford Letters*, I, p. 51, 5 Aug. 1629.
161. Gardiner, *History of England*, VII, p. 171; L.J. Reeve, *Charles I and the Road to Personal Rule* (Cambridge, 1989), pp. 250–1.
162. See Egerton MS 1820, ff.114, 164.
163. See below, pp. 539–40.
164. Coke MS 48: Broughton to Coke, 11 April 1634.
165. *Cal. Stat. Pap. Venet., 1632–6*, p. 56.
166. Clarendon, *History of the Rebellion*, I, pp. 198–9.
167. Clifton MS Cl. C/376; cf. Huntington Library, Ellesmere MS 6540: Thomas Davies to Bridgewater, 18 Sept. 1635; Gardiner, *History of England*, VIII, p. 88 and note 2; *Cal. Stat. Pap. Venet., 1632–6*, p. 466; *Cal. Stat. Pap. Dom., 1635*, pp. 128, 413.

secured it.[168] Cottington continued to serve on the foreign and Irish committees and his central position in the king's counsels was re-affirmed by his appointment to the Scottish committee in 1638. His ambitions, however, may well have waned with the years or never reached the heights to which his rivals thought he aspired. It is evident that he contemplated retirement, for Lord Hopton in February 1640 wrote to persuade him 'that the present times are not for your lordship to be at rest, nor for his Majesty to spare . . . a counsellor of your Lordship's importance'.[169] Hopton's letter was not mere flattery. Cottington left with most who encountered him a great 'esteem of his parts'.[170]

Men of business

The principal men of business in Caroline government were the secretaries of state. In a non-bureaucratic, personal government, much of the responsibility for translating the king's wishes into orders or actions was theirs.[171] Their range of duties and breadth of correspondence, their co-ordination of Council business and communication between all 'departments' of government made them central in the administration, and so in the politics, of the personal rule. Central but not colourful. Unlike the aristocratic Weston or Wentworth or the flamboyant Cottington, the secretaries by their function and social status served rather than led, and left the limelight to others. As a result they are in danger of being buried beneath the paper that deluged them. Yet because so much was left to them, the secretaries could and did refine and even shape policies laid down by their betters. Since the personal style they brought to even routine labour – the way a discussion was summarized, a letter phrased – could affect their course, we need to observe them both at work and at leisure. The senior secretary, Sir John Coke, was appointed the year of Charles's succession and remained in office until near the end of personal rule when, in 1639, he retired to Derbyshire where until very recently his voluminous papers remained. While Clarendon disparaged him and history has drawn him as a rather colourless figure, of relatively little import or weight at the Caroline court, an examination of his manuscripts suggests a rather different picture.[172] For one thing, private correspondence introduces us to Coke the country gentleman as well

168. Knowler, *Strafford Letters*, I, p. 523: Garrard to Wentworth, 15 March 1636.
169. Bodleian, Clarendon MS 18, no. 1350, 7 Feb. 1640.
170. Clarendon, *History of the Rebellion*, I, p. 157.
171. See F.M.G. Evans, *The Principal Secretary of State* (1932).
172. Clarendon, *History of the Rebellion*, I, p. 80.

as grey administrator, enthusing over the delights of his hawks, falcons and dogs.[173] And it introduces us to a Coke consulting with his tailor over the colour of his ribbons and stockings, the cut of his suits, and what styles 'are all in fashion'.[174] Though Clarendon described him as a man of 'narrow education', 'unadorned with vigour and quickness', and the French envoy referred to his 'suffisance mediocre',[175] it is worth recalling that Coke had been a lecturer in rhetoric at Cambridge and was well read in the classics and Italian.[176] In 1636 Charles I entrusted him with an important speech to the University of Oxford on the presentation of their new code of statutes, a speech in which Coke lucidly outlined not only his sense of the interrelationship of learning and government, but an encomium of monarchical authority.[177] Though his papers support the view that he administered rather than made policy, Coke clearly had a vision of government and perhaps a more important place in it than he has been credited with. Wentworth for one saw him as 'a servant that goes the same way to my master's ends that I do'.[178]

The bureaucratic efficiency, for which Coke had earned his place, itself made him an important figure. He drafted letters and papers with care; he carefully arranged and indexed his correspondence,[179] often summarizing the contents of an item on the dorse;[180] he kept full notes of meetings of the navy commission, of committees and of the Council. When we review the 'staggering amount of business' that he dealt with, even on a day, we come to see that such efficiency was necessary for survival.[181] But it also established him in a powerful position. For in the early seventeenth century, though attitudes were changing, the archives of an office were the private property of its incumbent. Coke made the point clearly to the Earl of Northumberland when the latter was taking over his Whitehall chambers in 1639: 'His Majesty's letters, treaties, negotiations with foreign princes and states . . . are in my charge . . . The trunks, baskets and presses full of papers, if your lordship shall but look in at the windows, you will see so many and so mingled that the sorting and removing cannot be done in my absence.'[182] Coke's unique knowledge of his papers gave him a near unrivalled acquaintance with precedents and arguments and

173. Coke MS 49: Coke to his son, 20 Aug. 1634; Coke MS 53.
174. Coke MS 47, 4 Sept. and 13 Dec. 1633.
175. Clarendon, *History of the Rebellion*, I, p. 80; PRO, 31/3/67, f.38.
176. *HMC Cowper II*, p. 249.
177. *Works of Laud*, V, pp. 126–32.
178. M.B. Young, *Servility and Service: The Life and Work of Sir John Coke* (1986), p. 214.
179. *HMC Cowper II*, p. 234 (the original of this letter is missing from Coke MS 62); Coke MS 35.
180. Coke MS 46; and compare Coke MS 47: Heydon to Coke with *HMC Cowper II*, p. 46.
181. Young, *Servility and Service*, p. 205.
182. *HMC Cowper II*, p. 234.

a storehouse of information to support proposals.[183] It was Coke who was responsible for issuing Selden's *Mare Clausum* and so for reaffirming the English claim to sovereignty of the seas;[184] it was he who laid out the plans for a fishing association of Great Britain;[185] he was also behind the establishment of a domestic letter post;[186] his experience of the Jacobean navy commissions placed him in the fore of attempts to reform the navy;[187] it was Coke on whom Wentworth and Laud relied for careful attention to Irish affairs.[188] Experience of the Treasury commission and his own natural efficiency led him to recommend strongly the better keeping of receipts, issues and accounts which became a feature of Caroline reform.[189] His biographer even suggests that Coke through his personal practice was 'among the first of the great civil servants to build up the foundations of the different government departments'.[190] His long tenure of his office must have meant that he determined many of the administrative practices through which in any government concepts are turned into actions.

Those who have minimized Coke's role have pointed to his exclusion from crucial foreign negotiations for which, as secretary of state, he was technically responsible.[191] Cottington and Weston specifically ordered Hopton to report to Coke nothing but the formalities of his embassy and to say nothing of the secret negotiations for the partition of the Netherlands or of the purposes of the fleet to be jointly set out by England and Spain.[192] Undoubtedly, as the French envoy recognized, the decision to leave Coke in ignorance of these intrigues was based not on his ability to handle foreign correspondence, but on a recognition of his sympathies with the Dutch.[193] Far from sinister, however, such a course marked a return to Jacobean practice of a demarcation of responsibility and a balance of factions even in the secretariat.[194] Before his death, Dorchester had taken overall responsibility for foreign affairs, Coke for domestic. After Windebank's appointment in 1632, responsibilities began to be divided, Spain, Italy and Flanders passing to the junior secretary (with a reputation for

183. Cf. my remarks in *Sir Robert Cotton: History and Politics in Early Modern England* (Oxford, 1979), pp. 74, 78, 146.
184. Above, p. 102; Coke MS 51: Digby to Coke, 25 Aug. 1635.
185. D. Coke, *The Last Elizabethan: Sir John Coke, 1563–1644* (1937), p. 211ff.
186. *Ibid.*, p. 217. See K. Sharpe, 'Sir Thomas Witherings and the reform of the foreign posts', *Bull. Inst. Hist. Res.*, 57 (1984), pp. 149–63.
187. For example, Coke MS 39.
188. *Works of Laud*, VI, part 2, pp. 384, 403, 466; Coke, *The Last Elizabethan*, p. 199.
189. Coke MS 54: Coke to Laud, 19 July 1636; *HMC Cowper II*, p. 127.
190. Coke, *The Last Elizabethan*, p. 204.
191. *Ibid.*, p. 196; and Young, *Servility and Service*, p. 204.
192. Egerton MS 1820, f.325; cf. f.343.
193. PRO, 31/3/67, f.38; and 31/3/71, f.142v.
194. See R. Schreiber, *The Political Career of Sir Robert Naunton 1589–1635* (1981), p. 17.

discretion), while Coke handled the German, French and Dutch correspondence just as Lake and Winwood, Calvert and Naunton had earlier divided them.[195] Certainly we should not conclude from these arrangements that Coke's staunch Protestantism and commitment to a Protestant foreign policy compromised his standing at a court oriented to Arminianism and friendship with Spain. Whilst he favoured a war against Spain, Coke was not blind to the threats posed by the Dutch against whom, among others, he was anxious to reassert England's sovereignty of the seas.[196] There is no doubt that Coke was a man of strong Protestant convictions; the French envoy, with his usual insensitivity to the nuances of religious taxonomy, called him 'un des plus zèles Puritains'.[197] Yet Coke forcefully defended the Church of England, its liturgy and episcopacy, and there is no evidence that his beliefs caused any offence to the king.[198] In the late 1630s, it was the puritan magnates Northumberland and Leicester who conspired to remove him from his post; Laud and Wentworth supported him.[199]

Coke may not have established a close relationship with the king – few ministers got close to Charles I during the decade of personal rule – but there is little to suggest that the relationship between them was determined by ideological differences. It would seem that Coke's sense of the need for strong monarchy developed over the decade, whilst Charles I rose personally in his estimation as a result of the Scots war.[200] For his part Charles placed the utmost confidence in his secretary.[201] Manuscripts at Melbourne Hall show that Coke drafted many royal letters, instructions and proclamations and that often, even when he personally amended them, Charles let Coke's words pass, largely unaltered, as the expression of his own mind.[202] When Charles went on progress to Scotland in 1633, it was Coke he took with him as his personal secretary, leaving Windebank to handle business in London. In 1636, Wentworth informed him of the 'gracious intendments his Majesty hath towards you' and of the king's desire to reward him with Irish lands.[203] Coke played an important role on the Treasury commission in 1635–6, and, after the outbreak of the Scottish trouble, on the Council of War. Even when his enemies manoeuvred to oust him from office (to secure his job for Leicester)

195. *Cal. Stat. Pap. Dom., 1639–40*, p. 322.
196. Above, pp. 78, 98, 102.
197. PRO, 31/3/67, f.38.
198. *Cal. Stat. Pap. Dom., 1631–3*, p. 554; see below, pp. 362–3.
199. Ellesmere MS 7819; Clarendon, *History of the Rebellion*, I, p. 165; below, p. 840.
200. For example, Coke MS 63: Coke to Digby, [1639]; see *HMC Cowper II*, p. 247.
201. *HMC Cowper II*, p. 242.
202. For example, Coke MS 39; cf. below, pp. 200–202; *HMC Cowper II*, p. 176; Coke MS 46, 8 July 1633; Coke MS 54: instructions to Northumberland.
203. Coke MS 53, 25 March 1636 (transcribed in *HMC Cowper II*, p. 111).

Charles for long stuck by him. In September 1639 his own secretary, George Weckherlin, told Coke that the king 'eagerly' desired his return to business.[204] Clarendon claims that he was dismissed in 1640 as a sacrifice after the failure of the Scots war.[205] But Coke did not interpret his own removal as a mark of disfavour. Announcing to his son his 'retirement', he implied that he had been a not unwilling collaborator in that decision: 'no offence is taken against me and so much expression of good opinion and goodwill towards me both in Court and City that I would never withdraw myself with more favourable aspect'.[206] Coke *may* have been putting a brave face on his situation. But it is worth remembering that he was eighty years of age in 1640 and that his retirement had for long been mooted. Edward Rossingham whispered it to Scudamore in 1634;[207] in 1636 both the Venetian envoy and Reverend Garrard heard talk that Coke was too old to continue and would be removed.[208] He was getting slower at answering correspondence.[209] Though his constitution continued to be robust – he passed cheerfully amidst the tents in the cold night air of Berwick 'sans cloak' in 1639[210] – more and more of his letters after 1638 are penned by the hand of his clerks, and more responsibilities were deputed to his secretaries.[211] Perhaps the 'staggering amount of business', especially in wartime, had become too much. Coke died four years later. Never one of the great policy-makers, a figure who never attained what we would now call a 'high profile', Coke was characteristic of those early modern servants whose labours were yet vital to the course of politics as well as administration, in an age that did not distinguish the two. Only days before his retirement Edward Nicholas informed Sir John Pennington of Coke's going: 'who is much decayed, and albeit I cannot commend him for anything, yet I wish we have not a worse in his room *for seldom comes the better*'.[212] From another indefatigable royal servant and bureaucrat, it was not an unappreciative epitaph.

The historiography that has subordinated Coke has tended morally to condemn his fellow secretary Sir Francis Windebank. Whilst Coke is thought to have suffered for his Protestant commitments, Windebank is often described as emerging from obscurity to office on no better

204. *HMC Cowper II*, p. 242.
205. Clarendon, *History of the Rebellion*, I, p. 165.
206. *HMC Cowper II*, pp. 250–1.
207. PRO, C.115/M36/8436, 3 Oct. 1634.
208. *Cal. Stat. Pap. Venet., 1632–6*, p. 515; Knowler, *Strafford Letters*, I, p. 508.
209. See P. Haskell, 'Sir Francis Windebank and the personal rule of Charles I' (University of Southampton, PhD thesis, 1978), p. 134.
210. *Cal. Stat. Pap. Dom., 1639*, pp. 162–3: Norgate to Read, 12 May.
211. Young, *Servility and Service*, p. 254.
212. *Cal. Stat. Pap. Dom., 1639–40*, p. 158, 12 Dec. 1639.

qualifications than Catholicism and sympathy for Spain. The usually judicious Gardiner wrote of him 'Morally and intellectually timid . . . [he] was thoroughly alarmed at the progress of puritanism'.[213] Sir Thomas Roe, whom Windebank defeated for the post, disparaged him and damned him as 'a new secretary brought out of the dark . . . preferred by my Lord of London'.[214] Clearly Windebank neither advanced Roe's schemes for a Dutch alliance nor accorded with Gardiner's Victorian nonconformity. But his alleged Catholicism and Hispanophilia should neither stand in the way of an analysis of his secretaryship, nor be accepted uncritically. Though the Long Parliament was to prepare charges against him for discharging seminary priests and issuing letters of grace to recusants,[215] Windebank insisted, even from the safety of exile in Paris in 1641, that 'he never did anything concerning papists that he had no immediate order for from the king'; and that the release of priests had always been on written royal instructions.[216] Though he converted to Rome, whilst in France, just before his death in 1646, his commitment to Catholicism during the 1630s is far from clear. Panzani, the papal envoy, did not believe he was a Catholic and Windebank's defence of the oath of allegiance made him certain he was a Protestant.[217] Windebank expressed strong displeasure at his daughter's conversion to Rome.[218] In his personal worship, he followed Cosin's *Devotions*, which leads his biographer to conclude that he was an Arminian.[219] Laud's patronage of him from his early student days at St John's suggests an affinity between them and certainly indicates that the archbishop did not then suspect him of popery. The date of Windebank's conversion and the spiritual distance he had to travel to Rome must remain uncertain. But it may well be that when in 1641 he wrote to the Earl of Pembroke that he was a solid member of the primitive apostolic Church of England in which he had been baptized ('and I know nothing in the church of Rome that can win me from that church') he was simply stating the truth.[220]

Whatever his affinity to Rome, Windebank's devotion to the cause of Spain has certainly been misrepresented. Senecterre suspected that the secretary was believed to be pro-Spanish because of his friendship with Cottington and responsibility for the correspondence with

213. Gardiner, *History of England*, VIII, p. 133.
214. *Ibid.*, VII, p. 200, citing Roe to Elizabeth of Bohemia, 1 July 1632 (State Papers German).
215. Tanner MS 65, f.226.
216. Clarendon MS 19, no. 1490.
217. J. Berington (ed.) *The Memoirs of Gregorio Panzani* (Birmingham, 1793), pp. 142–5.
218. Haskell, 'Windebank', p. 518.
219. *Ibid.*, pp. 364, 550.
220. J. Nalson (ed.) *An Impartial Collection of the Great Affairs of State from the beginning of the Scotch Rebellion in 1639 to the Murder of Charles I* (2 vols. 1682–3), I, p. 652.

Hopton.[221] But for himself he did not believe it: for Windebank 'me vint dire en plein conseil que pour bien conserver le Palatinat il fallait ruiner la maison d'Autriche'.[222] Throughout his correspondence with Hopton, Windebank displayed distinct scepticism about Spanish intentions, finally declaring of the maritime treaty, 'I am of opinion it will come to nothing'.[223] Always a staunch advocate in Council of the need for a strong fleet to protect England against the Dutch and especially the French, Windebank's inclination to Spain was based on his belief in the need to offset the power of England's maritime rivals.[224] As we shall see, the disappointment of the Peace of Prague and the very different circumstances of 1635–7 were to convert Windebank into an advocate of the French connection and even of action against the Habsburgs to recover the Palatinate. His friendship with Spain went no further than their service to his master's interests.

Service, rather than Catholicism or Hispanophilia, explains Windebank's rise to office and place of importance in the government of Charles I. As well as to the patronage of Laud, Weston, Cottington and Arundel, Windebank owed his elevation to a king who 'saw and observed men long before he received them' and who knew his work as clerk of the signet.[225] As a new secretary, Windebank displayed the qualities that had secured him the post: care, thoroughness and efficiency. Even more than those of Coke (whom we regard as the quintessential bureaucrat), Windebank's papers and letters are models of clear organization and brisk, lucid reporting. Each item from the missive to which he is replying is isolated; each point receives a separate paragraph; each issue (even when several have been confused by others) is separated and neatly outlined.[226] In corresponding with Hopton he synthesizes the contents of several letters so as to address the items common to them.[227] When Sir John Coke joined the king on progress to Scotland or through his summer hunting lodges, Windebank fully but economically conveys Council business and carefully acknowledges receipt of, and responds to, Coke's dispatches.[228] His minutes of Council business transacted (and not completed) hint at the incisive skill of the committee man in capturing the essence of a

221. PRO, 31/3/68, f.162v; cf. Haskell, 'Windebank', p. 169.
222. PRO, 31/3/68, f.162v.
223. Egerton MS 1820, f.488v.
224. For example, *Cal. Stat. Pap. Dom., 1633–4*, pp. 488–9; cf. above, pp. 73–4, 78.
225. Clarendon's comment is cited in N. Carlisle, *An Enquiry into the Place and Quality of the Gentlemen of His Majesty's most Honourable Privy Chamber* (1829), p. 116.
226. While the bulk of these are in the state papers, a ready impression may be gleaned from the printed selections from the Clarendon MSS in R. Scrope and T. Monkhouse (eds) *State Papers Collected by Edward Earl of Clarendon* (3 vols, Oxford, 1767–86).
227. Egerton MS 1820, *passim*; see, for example, *Clarendon State Papers*, I, pp. 154–8.
228. Coke MS 45 (for example, 27 May 1633); Coke MS 46 (25 June 1633); Coke MS 49 (16 Aug. 1634); Coke MS 51 (20 Aug. 1635).

meeting;[229] his long, careful notes of Star Chamber cases (thirty-five pages on Pell *v.* Bagg) show sharp attention and a painstaking concern with record.[230] After 1635 when the Treasury commissioners reinstituted the running monthly Exchequer balances, the task of compiling or reporting them fell to Windebank. To all his responsibilities, Windebank brought not only efficiency, but devotion to duty. 'Times of freedom and liberty,' he once wrote to Lord Aston, in the depths of the summer of 1637, '[belong] as justly to friends as those of employment do to the public.'[231] Yet even on his vacation he never let up. That same summer while Coke joined the progress, Windebank took the chance to go home but, he explained to Northumberland, there were 'post stages laid to my house in the country and such letters as are addressed to me come thither in very good diligence'; thence he corresponded daily with the king.[232] Such diligence brought no vast rewards of wealth. Apart from the official income of his place, Windebank amassed no lands, nor titles, nor fortunes.[233] Peculation he spurned. When Bishop Bridgeman sent him £100 in gratitude for the secretary's part in bringing a case to a fair outcome, Windebank politely refused it: 'The golden way is not mine, neither have I hitherto trod it.'[234] Windebank's letters, as his biographer observes, are to a historical eye wearied by begging letters, refreshingly free of preoccupation with his own ambition.[235] Those he penned to his sovereign may strike us at times as discomfortingly obsequious.[236] But they offer a clue, I suggest, to the unfashionable impetus behind Windebank's unceasing labours: a devotion to sovereignty and the service of his king.

In such service, Charles I clearly placed the greatest confidence from Windebank's appointment in 1632 to his flight in 1640. The younger secretary was entrusted immediately with the sensitive Spanish negotiations, not least on account of his tact.[237] During much of the 1630s Charles entrusted to him the supervision of Council matters in which the king had himself taken an interest. When in Scotland, Charles placed on him the responsibility for all, and left him blank papers signed with the royal sign manual for Windebank to send out

229. See *Cal. Stat. Pap. Dom., 1631–3*, p. 427; *1633–4*, p. 488; Coke MS 42.
230. *Cal. Stat. Pap. Dom., 1637–8*, p. 399; *1635–6*, p. 192, Haskell, 'Windebank', p. 118.
231. Clarendon MS 12, no. 966: Windebank to Aston, 25 Aug. 1637.
232. *Cal. Stat. Pap. Dom., 1637*, pp. 366–7.
233. Nalson, *Impartial Collection*, I, p. 652.
234. B. Quintrell, 'Lancashire ills, the king's will and the troubles of Bishop Bridgeman', *Trans. Hist. Soc. of Lancashire and Cheshire*, 132 (1983), p. 84.
235. Haskell, 'Windebank', p. 536.
236. See, for example, National Library of Scotland, Advocates' MS 7/1/19, f.106, 16 July 1639.
237. Haskell, 'Windebank', p. 168.

under the king's hand.[238] His secretary's ever carefully organized dispatches Charles took full advantage of, briefly annotating those clear paragraphs in the margin, or at the foot.[239] The correspondence of 1639 (in the Clarendon State Papers) shows Windebank as the linchpin that held the various parts of government together during the long months of the king's absence in the north. For all their humble language and tentative tone in advancing a personal view, they also demonstrate that Windebank's service transcended the simply bureaucratic conduct of business. Windebank was frank in his counsel: as in 1632 he had told Charles a parliament was 'passionately longed for',[240] so in 1639 he advised the king not to cast himself on the French or Spaniard, and in 1640 to admit the Earl of Essex to his counsel.[241] In response, Charles confided all in his secretary, even entrusting him to pen a letter to Henrietta Maria asking her to instruct Cardinal Rosetti to leave.[242] The secretary 'brought out of the dark' had risen to the greatest responsibilities. For all his critics, Windebank had merited his charge.

Magnates and 'courtiers'

The priorities of modern government lead historians to concentrate on those, Treasurer, Chancellor, secretaries and the like, who conducted administrative business. Contemporaries paid more attention to social rank and style than to function. And many officers whose duties we think of as ceremonial rather than governmental – the Lord Chamberlain, the Master of the Horse, the Groom of the Stool – wielded more political influence than administrative officials. Their positions and domestic duties brought them into frequent contact with the king in a world at Whitehall in which the private household of the monarch and the public business of the realm were not clearly distinguished. As, then, we turn down the other side of the Long Gallery, we shall stand and pause before some of the great aristocratic officers of the royal household.

The position of Lord Chamberlain of the king's household had been with the Herbert family since 1615. Despite his reputation for puritanism, and his long personal antagonism towards Buckingham, William Herbert, third Earl of Pembroke, had held his position and

238. *Cal. Stat. Pap. Dom., 1639*, p. 447.
239. *Clarendon State Papers*, II, pp. 32–4, 39–40, 43, 46–7, 49, 53–4, 61–3, 97–8, 110–13, 117–19, 128.
240. Clarendon MS 5, no. 321.
241. *Clarendon State Papers*, II, pp. 49, 95–7; Clarendon MS 16, no. 1248.
242. *Clarendon State Papers*, II, p. 113.

retained a familiarity with James. His younger brother, Philip, entered the court in 1600 as a young man of sixteen and 'by the comeliness of his person' rapidly became a favourite of the king, who recommended him, on his deathbed, to his son.[243] Charles I continued his father's favours to the family: he entrusted Philip to go to France to convey Henrietta Maria back to England, and honoured him with the privilege of bearing the spurs at the king's coronation. In August 1626, when William was raised to the senior position in Council of Lord Steward of England, Philip succeeded to his place as Lord Chamberlain of the royal household. This was an office of considerable importance to a king who, as we shall see, never distinguished ceremony and power and who intended that his court should become a model for the reform of the commonweal. In the circumstances of the new reign, it was a position too which effectually gave Philip, Lord Montgomery, overlordship of the whole household, since the chief of the king's bedchamber, Sir James Fullarton, was of too lowly a status to vie for the supremacy with a peer of the realm.[244] In 1630, further honours were added in Philip's appointment as Lord Warden of the Stannaries. The elevation of Herbert poses questions which the absence of the family archive make it difficult to answer. In many of his sympathies and characteristics, Montgomery (who succeeded his brother William as fourth Earl of Pembroke in 1630) had little in common with Charles I: he was associated with puritanism and New England colonial ventures; he dallied with mistresses; he had a querulous disposition that was prone to erupt in violence; the queen disliked him. But for all that, for all that Clarendon claimed Charles valued him little, he evidently struck some chord with the king.[245] It may be that Charles, who loved hunting, delighted in the company of one who did 'understand dogs and horses very well'.[246] Clarendon's disdainful sketch of the earl, however, passes over more important and more intellectual interests. Charles and his Lord Chamberlain shared a passion for art and architecture; at the king's suggestion, Pembroke commissioned Inigo Jones for the magnificent Cube Room at Wilton House; he had, according to Aubrey, the greatest collection of Van Dycks 'of anyone in the world'.[247] When a consignment of pictures from Rome arrived in London in January 1637, Pembroke was one of those whom Charles

243. Clarendon, *History of the Rebellion*, I, p. 73–4.
244. Cf. K. Sharpe, 'The image of virtue: the court and household of Charles I 1625–1642', in D. Starkey (ed.) *The English Court from the Wars of the Roses to the Civil War* (1987), p. 245.
245. *DNB*; Clarendon, *History of the Rebellion*, II, pp. 538–40.
246. Clarendon, *History of the Rebellion*, I, p. 74.
247. T. Lever, *The Herberts of Wilton* (1967), pp. 100–1; Petrie, *Letters, Speeches and Proclamations of Charles I*, p. 83; and *DNB*.

6 *The Family of Philip Herbert, 4th Earl of Pembroke* by Van Dyck. This, the largest portrait group painted by Van Dyck, celebrates the marriage of Charles Herbert to Mary Villiers, Buckingham's daughter.

roused to join him in opening the cases.[248] Herein lies the explanation of the king's delight in stopping every year at Wilton while on summer progress.[249] (See Figure 6.) A common passion for the arts meant that Charles found there a relaxed intimacy, not often apparent in his relations with his peers.

Aesthetic affinities, as well as the earl's ancient lineage, may also help explain the standing at court of Thomas Howard, Earl of Arundel. Though Earl Marshal since 1621, and next in seniority on the Council Board to the most senior officers of state, Arundel found himself in disgrace with Charles from the beginning of his reign, on account of his opposition to the war with Spain and machinations against the royal favourite. It was not until after Buckingham's death that he was re-established fully at court and evidently began to win the king's regard.[250]The monarch and Earl Marshal had much in common: an obsession with order and formality, a gravity of bearing, a sense of history and antiquity, an interest in science and mathematics as well as a passion for collecting – curiosities, statues and paintings. Arundel was Charles's only serious rival, probably superior, in the narrow circles of English connoisseurship, and the two were, not infrequently,

248. C. Carlton, *Charles I: The Personal Monarch* (1983), p. 145.
249. *DNB*.
250. Sharpe, 'Earl of Arundel', pp. 236–7.

competitors for the same pieces. Whilst the two – both of rather rigid and austere bearing[251] – never became close, Arundel rose high in the king's estimation: in 1632 he was sent on embassy to the Hague to invite (and, it was expected, escort) Elizabeth of Bohemia to England; in 1636 he went as ambassador to the emperor; in 1638 he was given command of the king's army against the Scots, with vice-regal powers of life, death and reward.[252] The Venetian ambassador regarded him as of the greatest repute in Council;[253] Charles himself praised his 'wisdom, fidelity, valour and great abilities'.[254] As the premier earl of the realm, Arundel's presence counted for much. If the record does not show his regular involvement in the politics of personal rule, that was not least because 'he is given up to pictures and statues around which he would like us to pass all our time'.[255]

Perhaps the most ambitious of the aristocratic courtiers of Caroline England was Henry Rich, Earl of Holland. Rich had been appointed by James I in 1617 as a gentleman of the bedchamber to Prince Charles. But it was as a client of Buckingham's that he rose to an earldom in 1624 and was entrusted to take the king's proxy for the marriage treaty to France. The year of Charles's succession saw him rewarded with the Garter. Though during the years of Buckingham's hegemony, Holland undertook important embassies to the Low Countries as well as France and commanded the fleet sent to the Ile de Rhé, he was elevated to no office. Never slow to proffer himself, however, on Buckingham's death Holland endeavoured to succeed to his place and the Venetian ambassador, for one, thought that he would emerge as chief favourite.[256] Certainly there were few marks of favour that did not come Holland's way. He succeeded Buckingham as chancellor of the University of Cambridge; he was appointed in September 1628 Master of the Horse, a position which guaranteed him familiar access to a king who loved to hunt. In 1631 he was created chief justice in eyre of the forests south of the Trent. During the 1630s, Holland was the beneficiary of several royal grants and patents.[257] A favourite of the queen's and king's, he, in Clarendon's words, 'received every day new obligations from the king and great bounties, and continued to flourish above any man in the court'.[258] His income,

251. *Cal. Stat. Pap. Venet., 1632–6*, p. 256.
252. Below, pp. 519–23; BL Add. MS 11406, f.77.
253. *Cal. Stat. Pap. Venet., 1632–6*, p. 256.
254. BL Add. MS 11406, f.77.
255. Conn to Barberini, 5 Jan. 1638, cited in M.F.S. Hervey, *The Life, Correspondence and Collections of Thomas Howard, Earl of Arundel* (Cambridge, 1921), p. 398.
256. *Cal. Stat. Pap. Venet., 1628–9*, p. 262; cf. *Cal. Stat. Pap. Dom., 1625–49*, p. 291.
257. *DNB*; I owe this information to Dr Ronald Asch; cf. his 'The revival of monopolies: court and patronage during the personal rule of Charles I', in R.G. Asch (ed.) *Princes, Patronage and the Nobility* (forthcoming).
258. Clarendon, *History of the Rebellion*, I, p. 80.

not least from such favours, has been estimated at a massive £10–13,000.[259] Holland's proximity to the king was both confirmed and established by his appointment in 1636 as Groom of the Stool and chief gentleman of the bedchamber – a position of great importance to a monarch who took such care over his intimate domestic arrangements. The summation of all these honours and gifts brought him as close as anyone at the Caroline court to succeeding Buckingham as a favourite.

Yet for much of the decade Holland's ambitions were checked and his power limited. Though Charles esteemed him for his labours on the forest eyres, there is little evidence that Holland, for all his efforts, wielded great political influence.[260] Before 1637 he proved unable to persuade Charles to an anti-Spanish foreign policy; his many coups to unseat his opponents, mainly Lord Treasurer Weston, ended in embarrassing failure.[261] Holland failed to secure the Lord Admiralty that would have crowned his bid to follow Villiers and which he always believed his due.[262] The younger brother of the Earl of Warwick, with whom he shared an interest in the Providence Island colonization, Holland himself had a reputation as a champion of puritanism[263] – a reputation that is not entirely supported by his renown as a womanizer.[264] In truth his principles were perhaps always subordinate to his ambitions, and it was as much 'his private interests for his own advancement in favour' as any committed ideology that made him the enemy of Weston, then Laud.[265] Holland was first and foremost a courtier who had aspirations to become, like Buckingham, a minister. Wentworth was contemptuous of him. While Charles I showed no inclination to appoint him to major offices of state, the king, like the queen, found him an attractive companion, 'a very handsome man, of a lovely and winning presence and gentle conversation'. Holland particularly ingratiated himself with the vivacious Henrietta Maria;[266] they exchanged letters, papers and intimacy,[267] Holland composed verses about her.[268] It was only with the queen's rise to prominence in the second half of the decade that Holland began to acquire more power. Through Henrietta Maria's patronage he was

259. B. Donogan, 'A courtier's progress: greed and consistency in the life of the Earl of Holland', *Hist. Journ.*, 19 (1976), pp. 317–53; p. 331.
260. Ellesmere MS 6514: Savage to Bridgewater, 4 Oct. 1634; *Cal. Stat. Pap. Dom., 1634–5*, p. 310.
261. See below, pp. 176–7.
262. Donogan, 'Courtier's progress', p. 324.
263. *Ibid.*, pp. 340, 343.
264. *DNB*; Donogan, 'Courtier's progress', p. 340.
265. *Cal. Stat. Pap. Venet., 1629–32*, p. 160.
266. Clarendon, *History of the Rebellion*, I, p. 79.
267. Anglesey MSS, seen at Phillips' auction room: letters from Henrietta Maria.
268. Wentworth MS WW/17, f.282.

made General of the Horse[269] and by her means he hoped for the Lord Deputyship of Ireland.[270] During the civil war, the central traits of Holland's character – his desperation to rise by all parties rather than adhere to any one – cut short not only his ambitions but his life. After switching allegiances several times, he was beheaded in March 1649, only weeks after the king.

Holland's companion on the scaffold was a Scottish peer who alone perhaps could have vied with Rich for the title of royal favourite: James, Marquis of Hamilton (see Figure 7). Another client of Villiers, who married Buckingham's niece, Hamilton was the son of the second marquis, a favourite of James I's and one of the king's most powerful allies in the government of Scotland. James had attended Charles and Buckingham to Spain in 1623, but spent much of the next years in Scotland.[271] On his succession to the throne, Charles showed favour to his father's Scottish courtiers in general, and in particular to Hamilton. Within a month of Buckingham's death, Hamilton was tipped to succeed the duke as Master of the Horse and secured the post in November, after Holland's brief tenure.[272] He also became Gentleman of the King's Bedchamber and, in 1633, a Privy Councillor in England as well as Scotland. A critic of the peace with Spain, Hamilton determined to raise an army for the service of Gustavus Adolphus in 1631. Charles issued letters supporting his levy of volunteers and granted him the customs of wines in Scotland, said to be worth in excess of £10,000 per annum.[273] Though he continued to disagree with the drift of royal diplomacy, advocating a French alliance against the Habsburgs, Hamilton declined neither in Charles's favour nor esteem. The fruits of several projects – of wine and iron, and the licence for hackney coaches – were bestowed on him, together with other marks of the king's affection.[274] Hamilton, Clarendon believed, 'had the greatest power over the affection of the king of any man at that time'.[275] Again cultural affinities helped to foster their closeness. Hamilton was a major collector who prevailed upon ambassadors to keep a weather eye for choice pieces. More importantly, unlike Arundel, he knew well the king's tastes, co-operated in acquiring for Charles what he most coveted and was generous in his gifts to the

269. PRO, 31/3/71, f.19v; *HMC Cowper II*, p. 279.
270. Clarendon MS 19, no. 1476; *HMC De Lisle and Dudley, VI*, pp. 375, 386, 388.
271. G. Burnet, *The Memoirs of the Lives and Actions of James and William, Dukes of Hamilton* (1677), pp. 1–4.
272. *Cal. Stat. Pap. Dom., 1625–49*, p. 296. Significantly, it was said that, in order to secure the post, he would have to return to his wife.
273. PRO, C.115/M32/8185: Flower to Scudamore, 26 Feb. 1631.
274. *DNB*; I owe this information to Dr Ronald Asch; Clarendon, *History of the Rebellion*, I, p. 199.
275. Clarendon, *History of the Rebellion*, I, p. 57.

7 *James Hamilton, 3rd Marquis and later 1st Duke of Hamilton.* This portrait by Van Dyck was probably painted in 1640.

king. His relative, Lord Fielding, reporting the forthcoming sale of four Veronese paintings, added that those 'I hear is not very acceptable to the king and *therefore* not much to be esteemed by your lordship'.[276] But there were ties closer still, of nation and blood. Hamilton was more than the most powerful of Scottish magnates; he was next in line to the Scottish throne after the descendants of James VI. Despite rumours circulated by his enemies that Hamilton pursued treasonable plans to seize the Scottish crown, Charles placed his entire confidence in his principal counsellor for Scottish affairs.[277] With the outbreak of the Prayer Book rebellion, the king appointed him as commissioner to Scotland and entrusted the resolution of the problems that shook his throne solely to his 'true friend and loving cousin'.[278] For most of the 1630s, Hamilton was important in English counsels for the weight he added to that faction which advocated a French alliance: Richelieu's envoy Bellièvres described him as 'de bonnes qualités, il a grand coeur, esprit hardi'.[279] Such sympathies attached Hamilton, along with Holland, to the circles of the queen.

Henrietta Maria

Though Holland and Hamilton enjoyed an intimacy with the king experienced by few, the principal successor to the Duke of Buckingham's place in Charles's affections belonged to his wife, Henrietta Maria.[280] (See Figure 8.) The early years of their marriage had been far from happy. Quarrels over the queen's domestics (Charles had expelled 300 of them in 1626), the war with France, most of all Charles's relationship with Villiers, all added to the tensions natural in the early years of a marriage between a rather formal, shy twenty-five-year-old male and a headstrong teenage bride, for the first time away from home. Religion inevitably presented problems: Charles was a devoted member of the Church of England; Henrietta Maria, brought up in the increasingly intolerant Catholicism of the French court of the 1610s and 1620s, had sworn at her marriage to carry out any instructions sent her by the pope.[281] The king and queen too were of very different characters as well as faiths. Henrietta Maria was

276. Scottish Record Office, GD 406/1, Hamilton MS 9589, 1 May 1637.
277. *DNB*; Burnet, *Memoirs of . . . the Dukes of Hamilton*, p. 10; *Cal. Stat. Pap. Dom., 1631–3*, p. 437.
278. Hamilton MS 10476.
279. PRO, 31/3/68, f.135; PRO, 31/3/71, f.109.
280. We await a good political study of the queen; cf. Q. Bone, *Henrietta Maria: Queen of the Cavaliers* (Urbana, 1972).
281. E. Veevers, *Images of Love and Religion: Queen Henrietta Maria and Court Entertainments* (Cambridge, 1989), p. 75.

8 *Henrietta Maria* by Van Dyck. The portrait was painted in 1638 as a model for a bust of the queen by Bernini.

possessed of a natural gaiety, humour, innocence and Princess-Diana-like skittishness. She could be delightfully informal as well as regal. Weeks after her arrival in England, Sir John Davies wrote to the Earl of Huntingdon that the new queen, 'is much delighted with the River of Thames and doth love to walk in the meadows and look upon the haymakers and will sometimes take a rake and fork and sportingly make hay with them'.[282] (The pastoral the queen loved on the stage clearly represented some deep yearning for rural simplicity which runs through all the court culture of early Stuart England.) On another occasion, Henrietta, visiting the garden of the Duchess of Buckingham, 'challenged another to race over a long course of the Thames and won'.[283] The queen took delight in curiosities and, evidently, in potentially embarrassing situations. The Venetian envoy reported her much enchanted by her dwarf; the *faux pas* of the typically gauche Dutch envoy Joachimi in mistaking the dwarf for Prince Charles caused her much laughter.[284] Henrietta Maria brought to the court a naturalness, charm and vivacity that were otherwise lacking. Despite her religion, she was obviously much liked by courtiers who came often in contact with her. She loved plays, masques and feasts; she enjoyed acting, dressing up and games; she sang divinely well.[285] No wonder Lord Jermyn, one of her favourites, reported it a rather dull Christmas, in 1632, when Henrietta suffered an eye infection.[286] Certainly Charles could not make up for her absence: rather like his modern namesake, the king was never at home in his wife's informal little supper gatherings, where he 'behaved with a gravity which spoiled the conversation'.[287] In terms of natural disposition the royal marriage was one of opposites.

And yet, it would seem, an example of the axiom that opposites attract, Henrietta's French gaiety became a perfect complement to Charles I's Spanish gravity. For almost immediately after the death of Buckingham Charles and his wife genuinely fell in love. The queen's pregnancy, it was said, smoothed the way to peace with France and certainly symbolized the new relationship between king and queen.[288] As early as November 1628, Thomas Carew (who as gentleman of the bedchamber saw the royal couple in their more private moments) reported to the Earl of Carlisle, 'we find their master and mistress at

282. Hastings MS 1931, 21 July 1625. Marie Antoinette was not the first French queen to indulge in fantasies of rural simplicity.
283. *Cal. Stat. Pap. Venet., 1632–6*, p. 127.
284. *Cal. Stat. Pap. Venet., 1629–32*, p. 315; *1632–6*, p. 251.
285. A.J. Loomie (ed.) *Ceremonies of Charles I: The Note Books of John Finet, Master of Ceremonies 1628–1641* (New York, 1987), p. 167.
286. *Cal. Stat. Pap. Dom., 1631–3*, p. 249: Jermyn to Vane, 3 Jan. 1632.
287. PRO, 31/3/65, f.49.
288. Above, p. 65.

such a degree of kindness as he would imagine him a wooer again and her gladder to receive his caresses than he to make them'. Charles, he went on, had become the gallant knight in pursuit of his amour, this time more happily than the débâcle of his journey to Spain. 'Yesterday her birthday was solemnized by him on horseback where he took the ring offered and is resolved to grow "galan" every day more and more.'[289] Love was developing the king's confidence and sense of identity; and as the months and years of personal rule passed both continued to develop. By the end of 1628, Carew began to see the broader significance of the king's and queen's happiness, for Charles had 'so wholly made over all his affections to his wife that he dare say that they are out of danger of any other favourite'.[290] Instead Privy Councillors began to complain about the amount of time Charles and Henrietta spent in privacy together, as their new-found passion settled into a loving partnership.[291] The two could not bear to be apart. When Charles left in May 1633 to be crowned king of Scotland, he parted from the queen 'with much heaviness'.[292] 'Since our blessed master left our incomparable mistress,' Goring told Coke days after, 'she is sad in extremity.'[293] Her natural gaiety left her; she sat sewing and musing; a month later she was described as 'disconsolate'.[294] For his part, in August, Charles could not hurry back fast enough to surprise her by an 'almost flying journey'.[295] His queen was also 'my heart', the 'jewel', as he described her to the Earl of Northumberland, of his own crown.[296] Remarkably, as Gussoni observed, for all their religious differences, their love went on increasing.[297] Charles named ships after her.[298] When in 1637, she was expecting their fifth child, 'the king dines and sups with her and sits by her the greatest part of the day'.[299] In Van Dyck's paintings of the king and queen with their children, Charles's formality and melancholy are suspended; there is a warmth and affection in the subjects that encapsulates all that contemporary observers report and which shows too, as we shall see, how Charles's

289. *Cal. Stat. Pap. Dom., 1628–9*, p. 393.
290. *Ibid.*, p. 412.
291. When some nobles expressed their desire to be present on the king's birthday, 'the queen withstood it saying she should be less happy than any common country gentlewoman if she would not make one meal in a year without the presence of unknown faces' (Loomie, *Ceremonies of Charles I*, p. 75).
292. PRO, C.115/M31/8153; Finet to Scudamore, 12 May 1633. The king sent seven letters over the next two weeks; Coke MS 45: Goring to Coke, 3 June 1633.
293. Coke MS 44: Goring to Coke, 18 May 1633.
294. Coke MS 45: 3 June 1633; Coke MS 46, 22 June 1633.
295. *Cal. Stat. Pap. Venet., 1632–6*, p. 131.
296. *Cal. Stat. Pap. Venet., 1636–9*, p. 69; *Cal. Stat. Pap. Dom., 1638–9*, p. 622.
297. *Cal. Stat. Pap. Venet., 1632–6*, p. 363: Gussoni's relation of 1635.
298. *Cal. Stat. Pap. Dom., 1637–8*, pp. 159–60.
299. *HMC De Lisle and Dudley, VI*, p. 98: Countess of Leicester to Leicester, 30 March 1637.

marriage (the fulfilment of his self) became central to his perception of his kingship.[300] After some early years of misery and turmoil, Charles I and Henrietta Maria enjoyed the first happy and fertile royal marriage in over a century.

The incontrovertible evidence of the king's and queen's mutual love and affection has seduced most historians into arguing that after 1628 Henrietta Maria became Charles I's most influential adviser. Such a conclusion is erroneous. While Henrietta Maria 'concentrates in herself the favour and love' that were the Duke of Buckingham's she did not succeed to his power.[301] There were those that hoped she would. The Venetian envoy predicted that she would wield great authority 'if she knows how to use it' and thought a skilful French ambassador could educate the young queen into a greater role.[302] Yet while a whole series of French ambassadors were to take on precisely that task, they were to fail. Throughout the 1630s, one envoy after another urged the queen to take a more active part in promoting her religion and the interests of her native country. In almost every dispatch they bemoaned her reluctance or lack of interest in doing so.[303] A news-letter of 26 June 1629 described the queen as concerned little with matters of state.[304] In December of the same year, the Marquis de Châteauneuf called her 'timide et craintifre'.[305] Even in the personal matters of her right to a Catholic doctor and dame of honour, as agreed by the terms of the marriage treaty, Henrietta was less than assertive and referred the envoy to her husband. Domestic happiness appears to have made such issues of little significance to her. Châteauneuf summarized the position regretfully when he reported to Richelieu that the king lived with the queen in 'love, intimacy and privacy, but neither gives nor allows her any part in affairs'; for her part, enjoying freedom of religion, she refused to importune him for anything else.[306] It would appear that, for some years at any rate, Henrietta was happy with her position: keeping close to her husband, she confided to the Earl of Holland, was all she wanted.[307] Gradually, however, either through her own maturity or the influence of others, the queen began to assert herself more and establish an independent influence. In the court plays she patronized and collaborated in producing, modern critics have detected a feminism which may have

300. O. Millar, *The Tudor, Stuart and Early Georgian Pictures in the Collection of Her Majesty the Queen* (1963), plate 66; see below, pp. 183–8.
301. *Cal. Stat. Pap. Venet., 1628–9*, p. 310.
302. *Ibid.*, p. 286; *1632–6*, p. 169.
303. PRO, 31/3/65–68, *passim*.
304. Coke MS 37: letter to Damville, 26 June 1629.
305. PRO, 31/3/65 f.213.
306. *Ibid.*, f.121v.
307. Anglesey MSS.

expressed Henrietta's frustrations and aspirations: the women in the plays who reveal such good sense may be pleading for a greater role for the highest woman of the realm.[308] Henrietta Maria tried her strength in backing cabals intended to bring down the Spanish faction and especially Weston. To her political manoeuvrings, Charles reacted with firmness: he resisted, as we shall see, the conspiracy against his Treasurer and vindicated Weston in a manner that caused the queen considerable embarrassment and loss of face.[309] But after some tearful scenes and tantrums, the affection between them seemed unabated. Charles left the queen in nominal charge during his progress to Scotland, and the Council waited on her weekly, but Henrietta wielded little direct political power.[310] Rather her court took on an importance as an alternative home for those whose policies or persons were not in favour. In 1634 Sir Thomas Roe described, with only slight exaggeration, her majesty as 'the most gracious and needy sanctuary of those who have no other support'.[311] Circumstances in 1635, the death of Weston and the failure of negotiations with Spain, were to bring her to the front of the political stage. For most of the early 1630s, the king's script for personal rule did not assign his queen a leading part in the drama of politics and government.

Factions

The queen's portrait brings us to the end of our short amble through Whitehall. Later we shall encounter other courtiers who rose to prominence in the second half of the decade. For now we have at least some impression of the very different personalities that came to the fore after Buckingham's death and the various (often contradictory) sympathies and policies they espoused. After 1628, as a wide variety of men manoeuvred to secure a place and promote policies, factional politics returned. That Weston, Holland, Hamilton and Carlisle could all regard themselves or be perceived as potential favourites demonstrates the volatility of the political scene in the autumn and winter of 1628–9. As the months passed, the situation began to stabilize: no one figure emerged as Buckingham's successor; but among the powerful contenders working relationships were established, friendships were made and alliances were entered into.

It is tempting when we view with hindsight to schematize the factional politics of the early 1630s: to identify clear groups and to

308. Veevers, *Images of Love and Religion*, p. 65.
309. See below, pp. 176–7.
310. *Cal. Stat. Pap. Venet., 1632–6*, p. 117; *HMC Cowper II*, p. 20.
311. *Cal. Stat. Pap. Dom., 1633–4*, p. 543: Roe to Goring, 8 April 1634.

delineate coherent religious or political values.[312] Contemporaries themselves did so. Weston, Arundel, Bristol and Cottington were seen as a caucus. Lord Percy described Weston's as a popish faction;[313] in January 1629 a newsletter informed Mr Damville that 'the great favour the king showeth to his Lord Treasurer is much envied by the puritan party who take him for a great enemy to their projects'.[314] These alleged religious sympathies and inclinations were usually directly associated with attitudes to foreign policy – with preferences for war or peace, for a Spanish, French or Dutch alliance. Should we then think of court factions in the 1630s as coherent blocs united by shared ideologies as well as personal ties? English newswriters and court correspondence certainly reveal that contemporaries used the terms 'Spanish', 'French' and 'Dutch' to describe individuals and groups.[315] Foreign ambassadors were particularly given to delineating by such terms. At the most general level such language accurately represented reality. Weston, Cottington, Arundel and Windebank were associated and known to favour negotiations with Spain; Coke and Roe were opposed to that course. Holland and Hamilton attached themselves to Henrietta Maria's court and pressed for military intervention on behalf of the Elector Palatine, in alliance with France, and perhaps the Dutch. The groups vied for supremacy. 'There is a great competition in Court,' Lord Montagu was told, 'for the Admiralty between the French and the Spanish faction; Holland . . . is assisted by the Queen and French ambassador against Carlisle.'[316] Such affiliations undoubtedly survived the treaties with France and Spain.

However, it is to oversimplify to see the Spanish and French factions as solid ideological blocs, or parties, irresolubly bound together and antagonistic to each other. For one thing, many different interests and circumstances temporarily bound ministers to each other or a policy. Weston, as we have seen, favoured a Spanish alliance more because he desired peace than on account of any friendship with Spain. In 1632, Chaumont, the French envoy, reported that Weston was ready to serve the interests of France;[317] two years later, Poigny probably more accurately estimated that the Treasurer no more espoused the interests of one country than another, or any – except his own.[318] In 1631, the

312. There was perhaps too much schematization in K. Sharpe, 'Faction at the early Stuart court', *History Today*, 33 (Oct. 1983), pp. 40–6.
313. *Cal. Stat. Pap. Dom., 1625–49*, pp. 292–3.
314. *HMC Cowper I*, p. 378.
315. For example, *HMC Buccleuch-Whitehall, III*, p. 346.
316. PRO, SP 16/218/29.
317. PRO, 31/3/67, f.46.
318. PRO, 31/3/68, f.114ff.: instructions to Poigny; and cf. f.145.

Earl of Arundel, though supposedly the aristocratic figurehead of the Spanish faction, expressed his delight at the success of the Swedes in Germany and his hope that they would facilitate the restitution of the Elector Palatine.[319] On the other side, Sir Thomas Roe, accused of partiality towards the Dutch and Swedes, asserted that he was 'neither Swede, nor Spaniard, Dutch nor French, but a good Englishman'.[320] And, writing to Holland, he felt sufficiently sure of the earl's independence to generalize 'he is no good Englishman that is either Spanish or French in faction'. Significantly, Weston defended his supposed antagonist Secretary Coke as 'solely English' when the secretary was charged with too great an affection for the Hollanders.[321] The labels French, Spanish or Dutch should not be read too literally as commitments to the interests of those countries.

In the case of the 'French' faction, the tag itself conceals a more complicated content. Henrietta Maria was the daughter of Marie de Medici, the widow of Henri IV. Marie de Medici had vied with Richelieu for influence over her son, Louis XIII. When the coup to unseat the royal minister failed in 1630, on the so-called Day of Dupes, she had been forced to flee France for the refuge of the Spanish Netherlands, where she plotted against the cardinal. Henrietta Maria herself was won, probably with little difficulty, to her mother's cause and recruited as an antagonist of Richelieu's by the chevalier de Jars and Madame de Vantelet, who were members of her household. The Marquis de Châteauneuf, who had been converted to Marie de Medici's support by the Duchess of Chevreuse (herself exiled for conspiring against Richelieu), laboured to strengthen the Queen Mother's faction during his embassy to England in 1629.[322] The Earl of Holland, who had attached himself closely to Henrietta Maria's court, and some suspected to her person, befriended de Jars and Châteauneuf. Together with the queen they manoeuvred to bring the Queen Mother to England, so as to create difficulties for Richelieu from over the Channel. In the early 1630s, therefore, the queen's faction was not 'French' in any way that served the interests of Richelieu and Louis XIII. Marie de Medici and the Duchess of Chevreuse were seen as 'Spanish'. The English adherents of the faction Richelieu's loyal envoys regarded as a group committed only to their own self-interest. Holland and others, the Marquis de Fontenay reported in 1631, attached themselves to the queen from lack of favour elsewhere. With that exaggeration fostered by bitterness he wrote: 'il

319. *Cal. Stat. Pap. Dom., 1631–3*, p. 205: William Murray to Vane, 18 Dec. 1631.
320. *Ibid.*, p. 250: Roe to Holland, 9 June 1632.
321. *Ibid.*, pp. 397–8: Digby to Coke, 3 Aug. 1632.
322. PRO, 31/3/68, ff.114–18: instructions to Poigny; Gardiner, *History of England*, VII, p. 186.

les faut considérers commes gens perdus du credit et ruinés en leurs fortunes privés qui cherchent non pas à servir la France mais à se servir d'elle'.[323] Because they conspired against him too, Weston offered his services to Fontenay. In turn, the ambassador came to view the 'Spanish' Lord Treasurer as a greater friend to Richelieu and the French government than the so-called 'French' party in the queen's household. The labels had become very confused. If the queen's faction was not straightforwardly 'French', nor was it united by religion. For along with the court peers of strongly Protestant, even puritan reputations (Holland, Hamilton and Northumberland)[324] there were those Catholics or converts to Rome, such as Henry Lord Jermyn or Wat Montagu (younger son of the Earl of Manchester) who enjoyed the queen's favour and were entrusted with sensitive political and diplomatic roles. The Countess of Arundel too, though her husband was head of the Spanish faction, was described as 'the greatest with the Queen of all English ladies'.[325] The queen's court, then, was the home of a very heterogeneous group. It reminds us – as does Arundel's warm friendship with Archbishop Abbot – that the factional politics of the 1630s are too complicated to be reduced to the taxonomy of 'popish' or 'French', even though contemporaries were not averse to using such terms.[326]

To suggest that factions cannot be associated simply with ideologies is not to deny that there were sharp contentions and violent clashes that were sparked by very different attitudes as well as interests. The rivalry between Holland and Weston provides a good example of that blend of personal animosity, policy difference and intrigue that escalated into violence. Holland's anti-Spanish stance originated in his personal rivalry for the position of favourite with the Hispanophile Earl of Carlisle; the rise of Weston on a Spanish ticket was not the least of Holland's reasons for affiliation with the queen.[327] Personal hostilities then merged into larger struggles of power, and almost led to violence between Holland and Weston's son in March 1633. Jerome, Lord Weston (whom his father was promoting for high office), was sent to France in February of that year as a special envoy to Richelieu. Returning, he encountered a messenger conveying a packet from Holland to a French minister, which Weston brought back and delivered to Charles. Holland (and the queen), compromised by the contents, challenged the young Weston to a duel – which only the

323. PRO, 31/3/67, ff.16–17.
324. Charles I himself suspected the cabal in the queen's court, see PRO, 31/3/67, ff.85–6.
325. Katherine Gorges to Sir H. Smyth, 7 Dec. 1625, cited in J.H. Bettey (ed.) *Calendar of the Correspondence of the Smyth Family of Ashton Court* (Bristol Record Soc., 1982), p. 73.
326. See Hervey, *Arundel*, p. 298.
327. *Cal. Stat. Pap. Venet., 1629–32*, p. 264.

king's direct command prevented. Holland was committed to his house in Kensington.[328] Thereafter he conspired constantly to embarrass Treasurer Weston, with some success the next year when Portland's servant was found guilty of offences in the forest.[329] There was an enduring personal edge too between Laud and Cottington, in which each used every opportunity to diminish the standing of the other. Clarendon relates a story of Cottington completely reversing his position on the enclosure of Richmond Park in order to trick the archbishop into publicly denouncing him for what had been the king's own policy.[330] In the competitive world of court intrigue, it was not surprising that men tried to make capital out of any incident that might discredit a rival in the eyes of the king. As William Murray of the bedchamber wrote to Sir Henry Vane, 'The court is like the earth, naturally cold, and reflects no more affection than the sunshine of their master's favour beats upon it.'[331]

Yet, for all the intrigue and back-stabbing, those who disagreed with each other, disliked each other or were in competition with each other had still to live together in the confines of Whitehall and co-operate for the king's service. All was not contest and dispute. Court life was characterized by rituals of community and harmony – the exchange of New Year's gifts,[332] the participation in masques and festivals[333] – that should not be forgotten. And ministers of very different personalities and attitudes clearly did in the 1630s work constructively together. Windebank and Coke, for example, formed a successful partnership as secretaries, despite differences over religion and foreign policy. Weston excused Coke from the error of giving the Dutch ambassador a warrant to alter as he saw fit as a slip which 'the Secretary having the foreign affairs so lately might mistake in'.[334] For all their supposed dislike for each other, Holland gave freely to a kinsman of Laud a post for which he had been offered £1,500.[335] Wentworth remained on good terms with Cottington, and Juxon befriended him despite Laud's contempt for him.[336] Laud conducted

328. Bodleian, Rawlinson MS D.392: diary of 27 March 1633 to 18 Nov. 1635. Cf. Gardiner, *History of England*, VII, pp. 217–19.
329. *Ibid.*, pp. 362–3.
330. Clarendon, *History of the Rebellion*, I, pp. 132–6.
331. *Cal. Stat. Pap. Dom., 1631–3*, p. 205, 18 Dec. 1631.
332. See, for example, BL, Harley Roll, T2. Poets evidently wrote their poems as 'A New Year's Gift', see R. Dunlap (ed.) *The Poems of Thomas Carew* (Oxford, 1949), pp. 89–90.
333. It is worth noting here that puritan peers and many future parliamentarians danced in the masque.
334. *Cal. Stat. Pap. Dom., 1631–3*, pp. 397–8.
335. Hastings MS 9598: Rossingham to Huntingdon, 28 March 1635.
336. Knowler, *Strafford Letters*, I, p. 354; Anne Cottington asked Wentworth to be godfather to her child (Wentworth MS WW/13, f.105); above, pp. 136, 151; T. Mason, *Serving God and Mammon: William Juxon 1582–1663* (Newark, NJ, 1985), p. 43.

the service for the marriage of Weston's son to the daughter of the Duke of Lennox;[337] the queen stood as godmother to Lord Weston's daughter the month after his interception of her and Holland's letters.[338] No one was forced out of office by court intrigue in the 1630s, as they had been in the previous decades. Weston (whose five predecessors were still alive when he succeeded) was the first Lord Treasurer to die in office since Cecil – a remarkable feat during an era of retrenchment. Despite the well-publicized clashes, some contemporary observers began to remark on the relative peace at court. On 2 November 1630, Sir Robert Aiton advised Vane: 'In court he will find none of those jars between great ones that either were when he went away or have been begun since; all are quieted.'[339] The next March, Tobie Matthew was struck that 'all the world came good friends from Newmarket' where the court had been on progress.[340] Even weeks after the clash between Weston and Holland, Goring was able to report to Wentworth 'All our court here never at such peace and amity'.[341] The Countess of Devonshire told the Earl of Newcastle that from 'the news I have received from court, it appears that there is a great calm'.[342]

For that peace and calm Charles I himself was in no small measure responsible. The king, when making appointments, was 'very secret and retired in discovering which way he inclineth' and so cooled the heat of speculation.[343] He moved quickly and forcefully to stifle incipient conspiracy and to prevent factional warfare. In 1630 he brought Weston and the queen to a reconciliation;[344] he made Holland apologize to his Treasurer in 1633.[345] When in 1634 Weston complained he was traduced by Laud and Coventry, the king refused to countenance the quarrel and 'said he would reconcile the difference at some other time more privately'.[346] Laud was rebuked for his attempt to discredit Cottington.[347] 'Our court squabbles,' Roe accurately observed in 1634, 'are appeased by the king's prudence.'[348] Where in James I's reign those out to unseat ministers at times found the king with a willing ear, Charles acted to protect his servants. He advised Wentworth, Weston and others to place their confidence not in the support of factions, nor in rumours about their standing, but in his

337. *Works of Laud*, III, p. 215.
338. PRO, C.115/M31/8152: Flower to Scudamore, 4 May 1632.
339. *Cal. Stat. Pap. Dom., 1629–31*, p. 372.
340. *Cal. Stat. Pap. Dom., 1631–3*, p. 293.
341. Wentworth MS WW13, f.53, 23 Sept. 1633.
342. *HMC Portland, II*, p. 126.
343. BL Add. MS 33936, f.15: P. Moreton to T. Moreton, March 1632.
344. *Cal. Stat. Pap. Dom., 1625–49*, p. 381: Powys to Vane, 5 Nov. 1630.
345. Rawlinson MS D.392 (at end); *Cal. Stat. Pap. Dom., 1633–4*, pp. 14–15.
346. PRO, C.115/M36/8436: Rossingham to Scudamore, 3 Oct. 1634.
347. Clarendon, *History of the Rebellion*, I, p. 135.
348. *Cal. Stat. Pap. Dom., 1633–4*, pp. 36–7: Roe to Oxenstiern, 30 April.

own royal word and estimation of his own servants.[349] It was sound advice for them to follow. For at the centre of all the overlapping circles of networks and factions was the dominant figure in the government of the personal rule: Charles I himself.

Charles I

In a personal monarchy, the personality of the king was still the most important determinant of the course of politics and government. It is then unfortunate that Charles I still seems to elude his biographers, even when they attempt to study him prostrate on the psychoanalyst's couch.[350] One of the difficulties in penetrating the royal personality is a paucity of the most obvious documentation. Though we have the rich source of the *Eikon Basilike*, some doubts about the extent to which its language is the king's, still more perhaps its late composition, require we use it with caution.[351] And though there is more written evidence – annotations to letters, marginalia on papers, personal correspondence – than has hitherto been used, it remains that Charles, by the standards of his father (and many of his predecessors), was a taciturn figure.

There is no doubt that Charles could and did upon occasions speak lucidly and forcefully. Dean Fell had described him as prince as a 'master of English rhetoric'.[352] The king cared about language: he corrected those who misrepresented his meaning;[353] he praised his secretary Dorchester for bringing 'my own sense in my own words';[354] he set up a commission to establish a standard grammar for schools.[355] Charles's corrections to Coke's (and others') drafts and orders demonstrate that he loved plain and direct speech. He evidently enjoyed philosophical discussions at his dinner table.[356] For all the famous stutter, contemporaries testify to his clarity in expounding a position. Both Secretary Vane and the Earl of Bridgewater were impressed by

349. Knowler, *Strafford Letters*, II, p. 32; *Cal. Stat. Pap. Dom., 1634–5*, p. 194: Portland to Vane, 22 Aug. 1634.
350. Cf. Carlton, *Charles I, passim.*
351. H.R. Trevor-Roper, '*Eikon Basilike*: the problem of the king's book', *History Today* (Sept. 1951), pp. 7–12; J.P. Kenyon, 'Charles I and the *Eikon Basilike*', unpublished paper. I am very grateful to John Kenyon for his allowing me to see this important paper, which argues powerfully that the *Eikon Basilike* is a faithful record of the king's words.
352. R. Ollard, *The Image of the King: Charles I and Charles II* (1979), p. 38.
353. When, for example, Secretary Coke answered a departing Swedish envoy in Latin on the king's behalf, 'he did not report it in accordance with the king's intent, although corrected more than once, and his Majesty himself took it up from the beginning and explained it to the ambassador' (*Cal. Stat. Pap. Vanet., 1632–6*, p. 233).
354. Warwick, *Memoirs*, p. 71.
355. *Cal. Stat. Pap. Dom., 1637*, p. 530.
356. *Works of Laud*, III, p. 168.

his succinct summation of the situation at the Council of Peers at York; 'I have not known his Majesty,' Vane told Windebank, 'express himself better.'[357] The king was said to have weighed well and clearly outlined the pros and cons of the Treaty of Oxford in 1643.[358] His speeches on the eve of battle in the civil war roused his troops.[359] Few who have read Charles's powerfully dramatic speech at his own trial can doubt his capacities to choose words or grip an audience. Yet when all that is said, it remains clear that Charles I, unlike his father, took no delight in long or revealing speeches or discussions. Contemporary court observers referred to the king's 'reserved silence'.[360] The Venetian envoy noted in 1630 that even on the joyous occasion of the birth of a prince, the king had little to say: he 'is usually a prince of few words and even on this great and extraordinary occasion he was as reserved as usual'.[361] In July 1634, Thomas Viscount Wentworth prefaced his speech to the Irish parliament with the promise that 'I shall as near as I can speak in the style of my royal master which is to be with brevity and clearness'.[362] His promise virtually echoed Charles's own statements about himself: 'I shall not trouble you long with words,' he was to tell his parliament in 1640, 'it is not my fashion.'[363] As he said in a personal letter to Louis XIII, Charles was a man of few words.[364] Given his rhetorical capacity, his tendency to taciturnity may itself be a revealing characteristic. Speech is the art of persuasion; the orator participates in the political process and uses words to gain supporters. Charles I saw the royal word as the end not beginning of the processes of command and obedience. Rhetorical embellishment, verbal artistry were clouds before the clear beam of sovereignty. The king who spoke little was not the helpless victim of a debilitating stutter; he was a monarch who believed that 'majesty need not talk, so much as simply be'.[365]

If Charles revealed little of himself in public speeches or on paper his reign is rich in other documents that we may learn to read as expressions of the royal mind: court plays, festivals and ceremonies, masques and entertainments, to all of which Charles devoted considerable personal attention, most of all the paintings which were his love.

357. Ellesmere MS 7740; P. Yorke, Earl of Hardwicke, *Miscellaneous State Papers* (2 vols, 1778), II, pp. 186–7, 24 Sept. 1640.
358. R.W. Harris, *Clarendon and the English Revolution* (1983), p. 112.
359. J. Bowle, *Charles I* (1975), p. 233.
360. *Cal. Stat. Pap. Dom., 1629–31*, p. 464.
361. *Cal. Stat. Pap. Venet., 1629–32*, p. 350.
362. Tanner MS 70, f.18.
363. E. Cope (ed.) *Proceedings of the Short Parliament of 1640* (Camden Soc., 4th series, 19, 1977), p. 198.
364. Huntington Library MS, HM 20365.
365. P. Thomas, 'Charles I of England', in A.G. Dickens (ed.) *The Courts of Europe 1400–1800* (1977), pp. 191–212, esp. p. 195.

James I had a sharp sense of the word as the medium for the projection of his kingship; the *Basilikon Doron* is his political testament. Charles was preoccupied with visual representation, with the authority of images (and images of authority); he is most remembered from the canvases of Van Dyck.[366] Charles's passion for collecting and commissioning paintings, his designs for a new palace of Whitehall and involvement in other architectural projects were not merely the manifestation of a refined aesthetic sensibility. They were the personal articulations by the first monarch since the Middle Ages to have travelled the continent, of the Renaissance belief in the didactic nature of the visual, the heuristic potential of pictorial representations to lead one to a knowledge of the higher truths they mirror.[367] Van Dyck's portraits of the king and his family were, as we shall see, the highest documents of his authority to rule. Like James's speeches they offer glimpses into the nature of the royal person and sovereignty but soon become authorities themselves, reordering the observer's own universe so as to bring it into accord with the king's own mind. Charles's painstaking care with the dissemination of his image, for him synonymous with his authority, ranged far wider than an attention to the canvases strategically hung at Whitehall.[368] The king altered the royal seals to depict himself brandishing the sword of knighthood.[369] In May 1638 he wrote personally to the Lord Keeper expressing concern about the royal picture that was attached to letters patent: 'some such letters patents passing our great seal of England as were formerly accustomed to be lymned, flourished and set forth with our royal picture, arms or other imagery in borders have been lately done in that rude and unskilful manner as is not fit for record of that quality, being the lasting monuments remaining to posterity'.[370] The image of the king was, along with the word, what gave the document authority. That was because the king in turn was himself a representation on earth of the higher authority which he mediated. As Bishop Henry King put it: 'every king . . . is a medal cast in Christ's own mould'.[371] His language, his imagery is significant not least because it is not uncommon. At his elevation as Earl of Strafford in the royal Presence Wentworth announced: 'Kings on the throne are sacred

366. Cf. my remarks in 'A commonwealth of meanings, languages, analogues, ideas and politics', in Sharpe, *Politics and Ideas*, pp. 47–8.
367. I was reminded of the importance of this by R.M. Smuts, *Court Culture and the Origins of a Royalist Tradition in Early Stuart England* (Pennsylvania, 1987), p. 2.
368. The king rejected even commissioned works that did not please him; see *Cal. Stat. Pap. Dom., 1636–7*, p. 325.
369. R. Strong, *Charles I on Horseback* (1972), p. 51.
370. PRO, SO 1/3, f.77, May 1638.
371. H. King, *An Exposition Upon the Lord's Prayer* (1628, STC 14965), p. 109.

pictures of divine Majesty.'[372] Pictures of kings therefore were icons. When we turn to examine the values and ideology of the court, the paintings of Charles I, his family and courtiers will offer invaluable insights into kingship and government.

Some of Charles I's other intellectual pursuits are less well known. The king collected coins and medals, and employed the royal librarian Patrick Young and Inigo Jones to arrange them in order.[373] He danced, unlike his father, in the masques performed at court. He composed music.[374] His fascination extended to the mechanical arts. As a prince, Charles had paid a Dutchman to teach him the workings of model engines of war.[375] After attending a mass at the queen's chapel in which angels appeared to raise the host from the altar, he could not resist leaping up after the service to examine the machine that had effected the illusion.[376] Richard Delamain was retained by the king as a tutor in mathematics and made up several instruments, including a special sundial, for his master.[377] Charles evidently became sufficiently fascinated to himself invent some navigational instrument.[378] Oddities of the natural world no less commanded the king's attention, be they human (a woman who gave birth to quads) or mineral.[379] To a man who found in the sea in 1632 a lump of ambergris weighing 200 pounds, Charles gave £50.[380] In the case of the curious spring and rock discovered at Road Enstone, near Woodstock, the king rewarded Thomas Bushell who had found it with the farm of the royal mines in Wales.[381] And to the Earl of Danby who looked after the site he wrote that 'having viewed the place of that natural curiosity [he] not only thinks fit that the rock ought to be preserved but ornated with groves, walks, fish ponds, gardens and water works'.[382] Charles's suggestion might be fruitfully juxtaposed with the scenes both of wilderness and rural peace sketched by Inigo Jones for the masques.[383]

The king's artistic, scientific and naturalistic interests, I would suggest, all relate to each other and are a trait central to his personality and politics. The arts and sciences are the systems through

372. Tanner MS 67, f.122; cf. my *Politics and Ideas*, pp. 44–6.
373. PRO, SO 1/2, f.39.
374. A.L. Rowse, *Reflections on the Puritan Revolution* (1986), p. 119.
375. *Cal. Stat. Pap. Dom., 1611–18*, pp. 383, 385, 398. I owe this reference to Dr T.V. Wilks.
376. Birch, *Court and Times of Charles I*, II, pp. 310–14.
377. *Cal. Stat. Pap. Dom., 1637–8*, p. 282; *1638–9*, p. 243.
378. PRO, SP 16/407/86. I owe this reference to the kindness of Malcolm Smuts.
379. Rawlinson MS D.49.
380. BL, Egerton MS 784 (William Whiteway's diary, 1618–34), p. 172.
381. *DNB*.
382. *Cal. Stat. Pap. Dom., 1635*, p. 366, 3 Sept. 1635.
383. See my *Criticism and Compliment: The Politics of Literature in the England of Charles I* (Cambridge, 1987), pp. 199–202.

which men order the chaos of experience. In all his pursuits we may discern that striving for, that obsession with ordering that was the dominant feature of Charles as man and monarch. As a child, the prince had experienced great disorder: a brother dead, a sister lost to exile, parents estranged, a father's natural affections diverted. The royal family did not establish the context in which Charles could see (and learn) how personal habits and social relations could be ordered and harmonized. No more did the royal household: James was personally slovenly and unkempt, his court was licentious and decadent; the young Charles, according to Burnet, was 'much offended' with his father's 'light and familiar way'.[384] At a time of adolescent turmoil the prince was left to find his models of personal and political order outside his domestic environment. His unease with the dislocation of his adolescent experiences may well be a factor in his instant attraction towards the formality and gravity of the Spanish court. The masque progression from chaos to ordered calm, as indeed the development in portraiture from Mytens's faltering prince to Van Dyck's controlled sovereign, plot the development of the king's personality, his gradual discovery of a personal order that became the mould of a social order.[385] (See Figures 9 and 10.) The masques' theme and the subject of many of the paintings also point to the time and means of that personal maturity. Marital love and the celebration of family were to be the recurring motifs of royal representation in the 1630s.[386] In falling in love, at last, with Henrietta Maria, at about the time England settled at peace with France and Spain, Charles found peace and tranquillity for the first time in his reign, and his life.

The royal family was obviously central to Charles's sense of self. He not only spent much time (too much his Councillors believed) closeted with his wife, he was devoted to his children; on his deathbed he commended his wife for having blessed him with so many hopeful children.[387] Courtiers' letters give us glimpses of charming occasions when the king, queen and their children went 'a maying into St. James's Park'[388] or when in July 1633 Charles returned from his long progress to Scotland and 'The princes . . . welcomed him home with the prettiest innocent mirth that can be imagined'.[389] So reluctant was the king to part from his family that he evidently exposed his son

384. Quoted in M. Lee, *The Road to Revolution* (Urbana, 1985), p. 6.

385. This is not simply a change of artist. Van Dyck's borrowing from Titian began only after his arrival in England and was almost certainly in accordance with the tastes of Charles I, who (unlike Van Dyck) had seen and admired the paintings in Spain. Cf. M. Whinney and O. Millar, *English Art 1625–1714* (1957), pp. 69–70.

386. For the masques, see Sharpe, *Criticism and Compliment*, ch. 6, *passim*.

387. *Eikon Basilike* (1876 edn), p. 205.

388. Clifton MS Cl/C 310.

389. Coke MS 46: Windebank to Coke, 25 July 1633.

9 *Charles as Prince of Wales* by Daniel Mytens. The portrait was painted in 1623, probably on the return of the prince from Spain.

10 *Charles I* in *Garter Robes* by Van Dyck, 1636.

to a fever contracted 'the night before your Majesty departed from London, in which he was,' the doctor discreetly put it, 'a little too late with your Majesty in the park.'[390] The king kept a silver staff on which he recorded each of his children's growth.[391] When we stand before the Van Dyck paintings of Charles, Henrietta and the royal children, we cannot but be struck by the warmth and tenderness that softens the majesty of the artists' other works.[392] The subtle emphasis upon touch (Prince Charles's arm on his father's knee, his giving his hand to his infant brother James for support, Princess Elizabeth's cradling her baby sister) suffuses the canvases with a delicacy and unites the subjects into a physical and loving community (see Figures 11–13). The presence of dogs, nuzzling close to the children, not only adds to the domesticity, it hints – especially in the 1637 painting of the five children with Charles leaning on an enormous mastiff – that even in infancy the royal offspring exercise authority over the potential anarchy of nature[393] (see Figure 12). Their young faces are composed and their composure reflects and effects the composure of the world around them. The seemingly casual backdrops make the same point. The column, inscribed 'Regis Magnae Britanniae Proles Princeps', against which the prince leans (as in infancy he had leant on his father's knee) stands for the pillar of sovereignty which is his inheritance (see Figure 13). The silver basin filled with fruit (in the picture of the five children) reflects the fecundity of the royal family and the abundance the realm too derives from it. The calm landscapes in two of the paintings, one with Westminster in view on the king's right, take the observer's eye from the domestic harmony of the sitters to a contemplation of a larger social order and of government (in which incidentally the royal crown and parliament house are associated). Charles had the painting of himself, his wife and two eldest children placed at the end of the Long Gallery at Whitehall.[394] The representation of his family was the representation of his government.

'Never,' Lord Goring wrote to Secretary Coke in July 1633, 'was there a private family more at full peace and tranquillity than in this glorious kingdom.'[395] The language he used to describe the king's domestic life interestingly echoes that which Clarendon and others employed to describe the experience of personal rule: peace and tranquillity were the marks of the decade as well as of the royal

390. Coke MS 45: Dr Chambers to Charles I, 22 May 1633.
391. J.E. Shepphard, *Memorials of St James' Palace* (2 vols, 1894), II, p. 43. The staff is in the Ashmolean Museum in Oxford.
392. Cf. Millar, *Tudor, Stuart and Early Georgian Pictures*, plate 66; and O. Millar, *Van Dyck in England* (1982), p. 60.
393. Cf. below, pp. 226–7 and Sharpe, *Politics and Ideas*, pp. 51–2.
394. Millar, *Van Dyck in England*, pp. 46–7.
395. Coke MS 46, 2 July; *HMC Cowper II*, p. 25.

11 *Charles I with Henrietta Maria and Prince Charles and Princess Mary* by Van Dyck, 1632. The observer's gaze is directed from the royal family to the orb and sceptre of state and beyond to the Parliament House. The 'great peece' hung in the Long Gallery.

12 *The Five Eldest Children of Charles I* by Van Dyck, 1637. The painting was placed in the King's breakfast Chamber at Whitehall. Prince Charles's position at the centre of the group of his siblings underlines his right of inheritance and command.

13 *The Three Eldest Children of Charles I* by Van Dyck, 1635.

family.[396] It was as a father, Roy Strong has brilliantly demonstrated, that the Victorians most perceived and represented Charles I, especially in the tender depiction of the king with his children (*An Interview between Charles I and Oliver Cromwell*) (see Figure 14), but also even on a canvas from which the king himself is absent.[397] *And When Did You Last See Your Father?* (see Figure 15) is not only an emotional and dramatic scene; it gives to the boy prince alone (raised as if on a dais before his inquisitors) a calm that contrasts with the agitation of the figures who surround him, and a position which imbues him with some of the majesty that is literally in quest. In Victorian England the paterfamilias stood as not only a domestic but a public model of governance. Sir Henry James Maine, the jurist, wrote in his *History of Institutions* (1875) that 'the authority of the patriarch or paterfamilias over his family . . . is the element . . . out of which all permanent power of man over man has been gradually developed'.[398] It was no accident that Charles I was the historical figure selected to stand as that model. The king's own attitudes to government and authority often read like an extension to the commonweal of the government of the family. To his subjects, he told his son, he was a 'political parent'.[399] The rhetoric of patriarchalism of course was common; James I had often spoken of being the father of his people. But it was the happy circumstances and practice of domestic government in Charles's reign that empowered the representation with reality.[400] Charles was the first English king to be painted frequently with his family. The king's domestic rule was clearly patriarchal: 'I will,' he quipped with the Earl of Carlisle, 'expect no certainty in women's determinations.'[401] Charles insisted on controlling the staff and government of his wife's household; he allowed her no place in government.[402] He drew up elaborate rules for the ordering of his own and the prince's entourage.[403] In this, as in other respects, Charles's sense of personal order determined his attitude to public order and government.

In his personal conduct and morality, Charles was an ascetic figure of great personal control. He dressed unostentatiously, he ate moderately, he drank little alcohol.[404] The king organized his day

396. Clarendon, *History of the Rebellion*, I, p. 93; cf. R. Anselment, 'Clarendon and the Caroline myth of peace', *Journ. Brit. Stud.*, 23 (1984), pp. 37–54; below, pp. 608–11.
397. R. Strong, *And When Did You Last See Your Father? The Victorian Painter and British History* (1978).
398. *Oxford English Dictionary* [*OED*], 'paterfamilias'.
399. Petrie, *Letters, Speeches and Proclamations of Charles I*, p. 239.
400. Charles I's was the first happy royal marriage since Henry VII.
401. *Cal. Stat. Pap. Dom., 1627–8*, p. 276, 29 July 1627.
402. BL, Stowe MS 561, f.12: orders for the queen's household.
403. F. Steer (ed.) *Orders for the Household of Charles, Prince of Wales* (Lichfield, 1959).
404. Warwick, *Memoirs*, p. 64; T. Herbert, *Memoirs of the Last Two Years of the Reign of Charles I* (1873), pp. 24–5.

14 *Charles I, King of England, and His Children Before Oliver Cromwell* by Daniel Maclise, 1836.

15 '*And When Did You Last See Your Father?*' by W.F. Yeames, 1878.

carefully around duties and devotions; he adopted the rigid routine of the controlled personality, from his early rising when he donned his badge of St George to winding his watch last thing at night.[405] Not only was Charles one of the few monarch who did not take a mistress or lover, his disapproval of others' lapses was clearly made known. The king set an example of decorum, upright behaviour and self-control which he expected to see emulated by others. When the news of Buckingham's death was brought to him while he was attending prayers, Charles maintained his composure until the service had finished, when he withdrew to his chamber for two days.[406] It may be that such self-regulation had been learned rather than naturally inherited. His impulsive behaviour in going to Spain, and while he was there, do not suggest a complete absence of passion.[407] As Charles was to tell his son in his last hours, 'we have learnt to own ourself by retiring into ourself'.[408] But whether learned or not, Charles clearly attached great importance to self-control and morality, particularly among the leaders of society and government. His response to the scandals of the reign, especially since they were few and innocuous by Jacobean standards, are revealing of Charles's values. When, for example, in 1632 the laird of Lusse was prosecuted for incest, Charles was greatly concerned that 'the maintenance of his wife and children . . . be provided for', but would show him no mercy.[409] In the case of the *cause célèbre* of the decade, the trial of the Earl of Castlehaven for sodomy and rape, Charles went to the length of having a proclamation cried at the court gates 'prohibiting all women . . . to be present at it upon pain of ever after being reputed to have forfeited their modesty'.[410] Perhaps most revealingly, when the queen's favourite Henry Jermyn impregnated her maid Eleanor Villiers, Charles I pressed him to marry her or be banished from the court.[411] The king, as we shall see, endeavoured to reform a licentious court into a moral community. He placed such an emphasis upon morality because, as the iconography of paintings and masques evidences, he believed the regulation of the passions to be the foundation of order.

Throughout his life, Charles identified disorder with unbridled passions in the body politic. The failure of more than one parliament he ascribed to 'the disorder and passions of some members' who had

405. *Cal. Stat. Pap. Venet., 1625–6*, p. 21; Herbert, *Memoirs*, pp. 94, 145–6.
406. Above, pp. 48–9.
407. Above, pp. 4–5.
408. Petrie, *Letters, Speeches and Proclamations of Charles I*, p. 240.
409. National Library of Scotland MS 74, f.52, 13 Sept. 1632.
410. Hastings MS, Legal Box 5.
411. *HMC Cowper II*, pp. 40–1.

ruptured the natural harmony of king and parliaments.[412] Charles attached so much importance to the new statutes at Oxford because he believed that university learning taught self-regulation and disposed students to obedience and service.[413] His father-in-law, Henri IV, he informed the university in the summer of 1636, faced with a turbulent state (after the wars of religion) had made it his chief care to restore the collapsed discipline of the University of Paris.[414] The king's personal example too was one from which all might learn. Charles's dress and behaviour were didactic as well as personal. The famous royal countenance painted many times by Van Dyck was not sad or prescient of doom, as popular myth would have it; it announced, as did other visual motifs, that meditative control of the self that qualified the king to rule as head of the commonwealth.[415] It is a face which displays melancholy only in Milton's sense of the word in 'Il Penseroso':

> Sweet Bird that shunnst the noise of folly,
> Most musicall, most melancholy![416]

The preoccupation with ordered self-control is undoubtedly connected with Charles I's formality. The king was not incapable of familiarity or even humour. He evidently laid aside ceremony with his closest servants in the bedchamber,[417] and was familiar with those with whom he competed in sport – at tennis or bowls or cards for example.[418] Charles could at times put off the cloak of majesty to display a common touch: Sir John Oglander was clearly warmed by the king's intimacy with him when Charles came to the Isle of Wight in 1628;[419] on progress to Scotland Charles won the hearts of many who came to see him and was even capable of the kind of gesture that has been praised in Elizabeth I, that monarch of legendary popularity.[420] His humour could be wry and esoteric. When in 1630 at his reception the envoy Coloma announced that his master would not have chosen him, being only half-Spanish, had he intended to deceive, Charles 'was observed to have burst into a roar of laughter' – which, as the Venetian ambassador who clearly did not appreciate the humour

412. East Sussex Record Office, LCD/EW1, f.31: the king's letter concerning the loan, 7 July 1626.
413. Cf. *Works of Laud*, V, pp. 126–32.
414. Oxford University Archives, Convocation Register, R24, ff.125v–126.
415. Warwick tells us that Charles meditated daily (*Memoirs*, p. 67).
416. *OED*, 'melancholy'.
417. See R. Perrinchief, *Royal Martyr* (1676), p. 237. I owe this reference to Smuts, *Court Culture*, p. 199.
418. K, Sharpe, 'The image of virtue', pp. 246–8; *Cal. Stat. Pap. Dom.*, *1637*, p. 47; *1639–40*, p. 474; J.E. Shepphard, *The Old Palace of Whitehall* (1902), pp. 84–5.
419. Long, *Oglander Memoirs*, p. 40.
420. Below, p. 779.

added, 'is supposed to have been because of such an argument'.[421] Surprisingly he could also, albeit clumsily, venture a coarse jest, as the Countess of Leicester discovered to her cost in 1637, when at court. 'I found,' she wrote to her husband then in Paris, 'an inclination to show me some kindness, but he could not find the way; at last he told me that he perceived I was too kind to my husband when he was with me, which kept me lean, for he thought me much fatter than I use to be.' At this sexual innuendo the countess 'blushed' and 'all the company laughed at me'.[422] There were not many such humourous moments at the Caroline court. But such episodes, like Charles's enjoyment of some bawdy plays,[423] his love for his playful wife, his fondness for poets like Carew and Suckling, suggest that the austerity of the king's public personality was not simply the outward face of a staunchly puritanical nature, but a gravity self-imposed and donned as an essential garment of majesty.

The product, perhaps, of a dislocated youth and strict self-discipline, Charles developed into a rather rigid personality. He came to trust people slowly but his confidence, once placed, was unshakeable. We have had occasion to observe his support for Buckingham in the face of parliamentary hostility and popular hatred and of Weston in the face of court intrigue. His desertion of the Earl of Strafford in 1641 Charles came to regard as his greatest sin, which he repented to his death.[424] The corollary to the loyal support for trusted friends was the difficulty with which he overcame distrust or forgave an enemy. Bishop Williams and the Earl of Bristol for long paid the price of crossing the prince in 1624 by opposing the war with Spain; with quite unforgivable pettiness Charles demanded back from Lionel Cranfield, Earl of Middlesex, another critic of the war policy, a jewel given him by James I.[425] To those who had once displeased him the king's remarkable memory and recall of names and situations was a permanent block to favour. This tendency for the judgement once made to become fixed was as true for policies as personalities. Charles certainly listened to a wide range of opinion; and he revitalized the Privy Council as the major organ of advice.[426] He came to decisions slowly, distrusting precipitate resolution: 'though second thoughts sometimes may come too late,' he wrote to Windebank from Holyrood in 1633, 'yet for the most part they are the best.'[427] Once, however, Charles

421. *Cal. Stat. Pap. Venet., 1629–32*, p. 269.
422. A. Collins, *Letters and Memorials of State . . . Collected by Sir H. Sidney* (2 vols, 1746), II, p. 472: Countess of Leicester to Leicester, 14 March 1637.
423. See Sharpe, *Criticism and Compliment*, pp. 44–8.
424. *Eikon Basilike*, pp. 5–10.
425. *HMC Cowper II*, p. 11; cf. p. 67.
426. Below, pp. 262–74.
427. Clarendon MS 5, f.317, 22 June 1632.

had made up his mind, just as once he had taken a minister into his trust, a decision all but hardened into an inviolable resolution. In 1629 the Venetian ambassador Contarini observed, concerning the dispute over the queen's servants, 'there is further the king's tenacity which no argument can shake in a matter of this kind'.[428] Poigny, the French envoy, captured the same trait well in a sentence, in his dispatch of September 1634: 'l'humeur de sa Majesté estant de ne se relascher point du tout aux choses qu'il a une fois résolues'.[429] Decisions became, in other words, principles to which the king adhered tenaciously even through changing circumstances. Interestingly in this context, Charles was given to composing and passing on to others axioms and rules for the conduct of personal and public business. They came to his mind as he read Bacon's *Advancement of Learning* and he scribbled them in the margin.[430] 'A wise man,' he advised Lord Herbert, 'should never begin to accuse himself';[431] it was evidently more than the off-chance citation of an adage, for Charles repeated the counsel to both Weston and Wentworth.[432] He also drew up axioms, the *Eikon Basilike* would suggest, as a guide of conduct for himself. When in December 1640 the Earl of Northumberland put forward Leicester's name for secretary, the king replied that Leicester's aristocratic status rendered him too great for that office: 'that was a rule he had set to himself which he resolved not to alter'.[433] Once again the royal fondness for rules and adages speaks to a desire to order the chaos of society and even of human nature. Charles I viewed the process of government not, as his father had, as a series of manoeuvres, adjustments and compromises, but as the devising of the right rules and the implementation of them.

Charles was drawn to Neoplatonic philosophy because he regarded the business of government as the ordering by higher reason of the potential anarchy of human nature and society. This, together with the king's rigidity and devotion to rules, has led historians to describe Charles as the classic authoritarian personality.[434] There are certainly contemporaries who endorsed this assessment. Charles's language was often authoritarian. He spoke of 'our prerogative royal which we will

428. *Cal. Stat. Pap. Venet., 1628–9*, p. 485.
429. PRO, 31/3/68, f.124, 29 Sept. 1634.
430. F. Bacon, *Of the Advancement of Learning* (London, 1640). The BL copy (6, 46 V I) bears extensive annotation in Charles's hand.
431. *Cal. Stat. Pap. Dom., 1640*, p. 338.
432. Knowler, *Strafford Letters*, II, p. 32; above, pp. 178–9. Charles also cited Scottish proverbs (Petrie, *Letters, Speeches and Proclamations of Charles I*, p. 103).
433. Collins, *Letters and Memorials*, II, p. 664.
434. Carlton (*Charles I*, p. 159) and D. Hirst (*Authority and Conflict: England 1603–1658*, 1986, p. 375) use the term. Cf. J. Sommerville, *Politics and Ideology in England 1603–1640* (1986), pp. 127–31, 237; and R. Cust and A. Hughes (eds) *Conflict in Early Stuart England: Studies in Religion and Politics, 1603–1642* (1989), pp. 187, 227–8, 249.

not have argued and brought into question'.[435] He advocated sharp punishments 'to the terrifying of others from committing the like offences'.[436] 'It appears,' he once wrote to Wentworth of the Irish, 'that oftentimes force and terror do more restrain such people than law or religion.'[437] In that last comment, however, we may also see why we must question the description 'authoritarian'. Law and religion, which are seen to be the normal modes of restraint and rule, are not the expressions of any royal, or human, will; they express and prescribe orders and codes given to man by God.[438] Because the king is God's lieutenant on earth it is his duty to accord with, exemplify, enact and enforce those codes. If Charles's language sounds authoritarian, it was because he saw it as his duty to see that his subjects (as well as himself) obeyed God's authority; the royal prerogative being entrusted to him, in order to carry out that duty. If being a king, he told his son, meant breaking God's trust, it was an empty thing 'not worth taking up'; but fulfil that trust and 'you shall never want a kingdom'.[439]

Whether or not we regard him as authoritarian, Charles was neither autocratic nor tyrannical. Aristotle (whose ideas dominated Renaissance theories of kingship) defined a tyrant as one who ruled for his own and not the public good; an autocrat is one who elevates his will above the law. Charles by contrast, saw himself as the custodian of the common good and the common law. The king's power was given him to support not undermine the laws. The prerogative, he counselled his son, should *not* be exercised as a 'legal tyranny' nor 'to gratify any faction with the perturbation of the laws'.[440] Rather the prerogative was part of the laws 'in which is wrapped up the public interest and the good of the community'.[441] Neither the king nor his family were 'private'; they belonged to the body of the realm.[442] Even the birth of his first son Charles announced as for the good of the kingdom, 'whose welfare we will ever preserve before any other blessing that can befall us in this life'.[443] The most princely of all employments, Charles wrote, was to 'intend the welfare of those over whom God shall place you'.[444] Charles believed it the duty of all, the subjects as the king, to

435. PRO, SO 1/3, f.43.
436. E.H. Bates-Harbin (ed.) *Quarter Sessions Records for . . . Somerset, II, Charles I, 1625–39* (Somerset Record Soc., 24, 1908), pp. 239–41: letter of Charles I, 6 July 1635.
437. PRO, SO 1/2, f.119v, 16 Oct. 1632.
438. Cf. my *Politics and Ideas*, pp. 14–17, 41.
439. *Eikon Basilike* (1876 edn), p. 205.
440. *Ibid.*, p. 197.
441. *Ibid.*
442. Coke MS 46: Goring to Coke, 2 July 1633.
443. Larkin, *Stuart Royal Proclamations*, II, no. 132, p. 273.
444. *Eikon Basilike* (1876), p. 192.

subordinate their private interests to the public good. That belief pervades the language of royal letters, decrees and orders, and especially the signet letters which perhaps most directly express the king's mind. Orders or proclamations, for draining the Fens, for erecting a society of fishing, for commanding the nobility to their country estates or for the preservation of episcopal lands, re-echo the discourse of 'common good' and the need to subject 'private ends'. It was more than rhetoric. The king expected in 1633 that those who inhabited houses adjacent to Durham cathedral might willingly have them demolished so as to enhance the view![445] To help with the provision of saltpetre he asked his subjects to store their urine for a year![446] That extraordinary attitude only becomes explicable when we note that Charles was willing for the saltpetre men to dig up his own house at Woodstock.[447] Royal authority was, he saw it, subordinated to the common good and granted for preserving it. Challenges to authority were therefore threats to the commonweal. 'Disobedience to sovereignty,' the king wrote to the Earl of Pembroke, 'hath been a principal cause of many inconveniences lately crept in and still growing in this state.'[448] Sovereignty, Secretary Coke argued, did not challenge but co-operate with the law: 'it is upon the duty of a king and of the ministers of his justice for the preservation of government, without which men's lives and estates cannot be preserved'.[449] There is a staunchly legalistic strain to Charles's theory and practice of kingship, which has not been sufficiently emphasized. It is evident in his enquiries as to the legality of imprisonment on royal command, knighthood fines and ship money; in the genuine detestation he expressed for Thomas Harrison who upbraided Justice Hutton after the ship money trial, and for his view that the prerogative overrode all law.[450] 'The settled laws of these kingdoms to which you are rightly heir,' the *Eikon Basilike* tells Prince Charles, 'are the most excellent rules you can govern by.'[451]

The language of law, public good and commonweal point to the conservatism central to Charles's personality. Where some historians have depicted him as looking longingly to France and the 'absolutism' of the Bourbons, and forward to its alleged zenith under the monarchy of Louis XIV, Charles I, as we shall often have occasion to observe, looked backwards: to an idealized past of social order, harmony,

445. G. Ornsby (ed.) *The Correspondence of John Cosin* (2 vols, Surtees Soc., 52 & 55, 1869–72), I, p. 216.
446. Larkin, *Stuart Royal Proclamations*, II, no. 58, p. 119.
447. *Cal. Stat. Pap. Dom., 1635–6*, p. 448.
448. PRO, SO 1/2/108, June 1632.
449. Young, *Servility and Service*, pp. 174–8; Coke MS 37, 9 Aug. 1629; cf. PRO, SP 16/138/45.
450. Tanner MS 70, f.164; Tanner MS 299, f.173.
451. *Eikon Basilike* (1876), p. 196.

community and respect for authority and law.[452] Through all the frustrations and problems of the 1620s Charles seems never to have contemplated fundamental changes in the nature of English government – the establishment of English intendants for example. Though Buckingham had suggested doing away with parliaments the king had rejected the idea.[453] As Professor Carlton astutely observed, 'for Charles's reign the records contain no vast collection of papers of great innovators such as those of Thomas Cromwell or the Cecils'; ministers, like the king, displayed a 'deference to medieval institutions'.[454] A Venetian ambassador was advised by the Lord Chamberlain that Charles was 'very averse from altering things long practised'; 'they told me that the king greatly disliked innovations'.[455] When he thought of reform, Charles thought not in terms of institutions but of men – of finding 'honest and able ministers' and 'persons of quality and merit'.[456] And because he believed that in the past harmony had prevailed, he concurred with Attorney-General Bankes that 'precedents are the chief guide to the world's actions'.[457] Even in the recent Tudor past, perhaps especially in the reign of Henry VIII, Charles believed he saw what he sought for his own reign: uniformity, order, stability. The first adult Englishman to succeed to the throne since Henry VIII, he often consulted Henrician precedents; he named one of his ships the *Mary Rose*.[458] If the commonweal had since been threatened by interest, dissension and disobedience, no radical changes in government were required, but a renovation of old practices and attitudes. Once again the metaphors of Charles's political discourse reveal the traditionalism of his thinking. The king refers to 'malevolent' and ill-affected men, to a realm beset by illness or disease. It was then for the king not to innovate, but to purge the 'peccant humour' and apply 'the medicine of a constant and settled government.'[459] As Roe put it, 'It is only the great temper, justice and wisdom of his Majesty that corrects ill humours.'[460] During the personal rule of the 1630s, Charles followed no Gallican model nor aimed at an absolutist rule. As the good physician of the commonweal, he set out to restore the health of the body politic.

Men of conservative values are not always perceived as conservative; nor are their methods always traditional. Reformation and renovation

452. Dr L.J. Reeve uses the term 'absolutism' in his *Charles I*, p. 24.
453. PRO, 31/3/36, ff.131ff, 6 Aug. 1629.
454. Carlton, *Charles I*, pp. 62, 83.
455. *Cal. Stat. Pap. Venet., 1636–9*, pp. 434–5.
456. PRO, SO 1/1, ff.208–209v.
457. Bodleian, Bankes MS 65/8.
458. *Cal. Stat. Pap. Dom., 1635–6*, p. 358.
459. Above, p. 52.
460. *Cal. Stat. Pap. Dom., 1634–5*, p. 338.

can, as we know, be perceived as innovation, especially when they are neither adequately explained nor communicated. Charles himself recognized that 'the beginnings of any reformations will seem strange and by some refractory and jealous spirits receive opposition and disputes though they apparently tend to their preservation'.[461] But he did not do enough to make them less strange, to dispel fears, to win over jealous spirits; he did not proceed with patience and caution. For all his traditional values there was an important trait in Charles's character that could make his style appear both novel and radical: his energy. As Conrad Russell put it, 'Charles, unlike James, *suffered* from energy'.[462] There was a physical dimension to that trait which is often underemphasized by biographers who dwell too much on his weakness as a prince and aesthetic sensibilities. Charles was of 'robust vigour', 'well proportioned and strong', a keen and excellent hunter who spent the whole day in the saddle, a rider at the ring and a frequent and competitive tennis player.[463] He was a monarch quick to take action and, in 1642 as in 1638, to take up arms. No *rex pacificus*, Charles told Hamilton that when his army was assembled against the Covenanters, he would be able to 'show myself like myself'.[464] Actions spoke louder than words; it was no use to 'grin like the little bear showing our teeth and not then be able to bite'.[465] Charles, as he told Louis XIII, showed himself not by words but 'toute ma vie par mes actionnes'.[466] His then was an impatient style, that would not rest content with formalities, generalities or delays. 'The resolution which we have hereby intimated unto you,' the Lord-Lieutenant of Essex was warned, was 'not to be any longer satisfied with formalities but require realities and effects.'[467] It was a sentence that might have become Charles's motto. For as he turned to the reformation of church and state, he exhibited a zeal and vigour which he demanded of others at court and in the country. Conservative aims and a radical style were to characterize the government of the personal rule.

A man obsessed with order and morality, a character formal and rigid, devoted to rules and axioms, a monarch with almost a sense of mission and the energy to put his principles into practice, Charles I proved a radical change of style to his father. Educated in the blunter environment of the Scottish court where the art of kingship was the direct skill in managing men, James remained in England the

461. PRO, SO 1/3, f.34.
462. C. Russell, *Parliaments and English Politics, 1621–1629* (Oxford, 1979), p. 422.
463. *Cal. Stat. Pap. Venet., 1632–6*, p. 362; *1636–9*, p. 1; *Cal. Stat. Pap. Dom., 1637*, p. 97; *1625–6*, p. 577.
464. Hamilton MS GD 406/1, 10527.
465. Hamilton MS 555.
466. Huntington MS, HM 20365.
467. Bodleian, Firth MS C.4, p. 476.

quintessential politician.[468] He argued, he persuaded, he manoeuvred, but knowing too that politics is the art of the possible, he compromised, waited or drew back. James tolerated men's foibles and was sufficiently lazy (or astute) to leave things alone. Charles, by contrast, was a man of principle. Because he knew that he ruled for the good of his subjects, he expected that it be obvious to them too; he felt little need to explain his actions or the benefits of his policy. Once the king's decision had been made and the royal word delivered, the political process, as far as Charles was concerned, was over. Like others of strong principles, he tended to see things in black and white. While he was open to counsel, he could be angered by criticism. Where, in the heat of debate James could pass over the Presbyterian Melville calling him 'God's silly vassal', faced with criticism Charles's face hardened: 'without saying a word, he paced the room, giving every indication of being much moved and angered'.[469] The culture of the reigns may tell us much about the kings. The Jacobean drama, the city comedy, addresses a king who delighted in humour, bawdy informality, most of all in words, debate, discussion. When we think of Caroline culture, we think first of the visual arts – of the statements of values made eternal on canvas or in stone.[470] Charles's policies were not profoundly different from those of James. But as Burnet so aptly put it, 'What his father begun out of policy was prosecuted by him out of conscience'.[471]

The character and style of Charles I were obviously of general import in the politics and government of the decade. But, we must go on to ask, to what extent did the king determine the course of affairs? How involved was Charles personally in the administration of the 1630s? These are important questions which we must examine in some detail, if only because Charles I's most recent biographer has presented the king as a lazy man who, leaving the business of government to others, delighted in the escapist pleasures of his pictures and plays. 'The king,' Professor Carlton writes, 'did not wish to work very hard preferring to spend his energies on the world of the court'; his 'clerical interventions were noteworthy only for their rareness and a pettifogging concern for trivia . . . Charles's impact on broader policy matters was almost as slight'.[472] As a consequence, 'a high proportion of acts done in Charles's name were done either without his knowledge or

468. Cf. J. Wormald, 'James VI and I: two kings or one?', *History*, 68 (1983), pp. 187–209.
469. *Cal. Stat. Pap. Venet., 1636–9*, p. 111. The occasion was a letter presented to Charles I in December 1636 by the Earl of Danby. See below, pp. 713–14.
470. I shall be exploring this interaction further in a study of representations of authority in the English Renaissance.
471. Burnet, *Memoirs of . . . the Dukes of Hamilton*, p. 29; cf. Gardiner, *History of England*, VIII, pp. 299–300.
472. Carlton, *Charles I*, pp. 157–8.

initiative'.[473] The conclusion comes as a surprise, not least because Carlton depicts the boy prince as a swot and the adult Charles in the parliament of 1621 as an 'assiduous freshman member of the Upper House' who 'soon won a reputation for diligence'.[474] Professor Carlton's judgement on the monarch cannot be endorsed. In the first year of his reign, Charles dispensed with the sign manual and personally signed all his papers.[475] Contemporary commentators far more often identify the king as swot than as slouch. It is true that Châteauneuf the French envoy reported in 1629 that Charles dealt only with minutiae and left the big decisions to his ministers; but he was most concerned to identify Buckingham's successor and in general overestimated Weston's power.[476] Charles's own admission to Hamilton that he was 'lazy enough in writing' referred to the brevity (rather than infrequency) of his missives – which are found in plenty in Hamilton's papers.[477] The first Viscount Falkland claimed, in 1631, that the king seldom read petitions himself, leaving them to his 'secretary's relation', but it is far from clear that he was right.[478] For we know that Charles received petitions personally: Delamain presented his tract and suit 'in the room next to the gallery, which the king took and liking the subject read in till he came to the chapel'.[479] Similarly in 1635 Sir John Heydon intercepted Charles in the stone gallery where he requested the royal signature on a contract to disafforest Selwood and Roche forests in Somerset.[480] This was evidently a standard way of catching the king's attention – so common that two gentlemen ushers were appointed to go before the king on state days to see that none thrust petitions into his hand.[481] Books of petitions in the state papers also offer plentiful evidence of royal attention. Though at the foot of each suit the king declared his pleasure usually by referring the matter to appropriate Privy Councillors, in some cases he answered personally.[482] Moreover his recall of detail – in the cases of Gregory Hockmore or Bridget Rosister for example – was impressive.[483] In March 1637 Charles instructed the masters of requests that no petitions delivered to them for royal consideration should be viewed by anyone until the king had

473. *Ibid.*, p. 158.
474. *Ibid.*, pp. 10, 31.
475. P. Gregg, *King Charles I* (1981), p. 122.
476. PRO, 31/3/66, f.139, 22 Aug. 1629.
477. Burnet, *Memoirs of . . . the Dukes of Hamilton*, p. 21, 31 Dec. 1631. Cf. below, p. 791 ff.
478. *Cal. Stat. Pap. Dom., 1631–3*, p. 128: Falkland to Dorchester, 3 Aug. 1631.
479. Ellesmere MS 6521: Delamain to Bridgewater, Dec. 1634.
480. *Cal. Stat. Pap. Dom., 1635*, pp. 432–3.
481. Stowe MS 561, f.7.
482. For example, PRO, SP 16/403.
483. *Ibid.*, ff.96–7, 142.

seen them.[484] While he left the details of petitions to others, Charles was far from ignorant of the suits that came to his in-tray, and in some cases decided their outcome.

More generally, contemporaries, like Philip Warwick, who knew Charles well describe him as a monarch who spent much time alone in his privy quarters, reading, writing and amending letters and papers.[485] Though Secretary Coke charged Buckingham with neglecting his correspondence, he never complained of Charles's lack of diligence.[486] The contrast struck others. Joseph Mede reported the news at court in September 1628 that 'the king, they say, in fourteen days after the duke's death despatched more business than the duke had done three months before'.[487] The Venetian ambassador described Charles in the 1630s closeted, writing dispatches;[488] and Thomas Roe informed Elizabeth of Bohemia, on 1 August 1636, that 'his Majesty on Sunday the 24th of last month at Apethorpe wrote all the afternoon shut up in his own chamber two long letters'.[489] Interesting as they are, there is no need to rely on these contemporary perceptions for we have abundant evidence of Charles's reading, correcting and writing papers, much of it ignored or unexamined by his biographers. From almost every department of government business we find documents that demonstrate the king's personal involvement. Charles read Bishop Bramhall's letters from Ireland;[490] all state dispatches from Ireland but revenue business, the king had sent directly to himself.[491] While he had some of the vast foreign correspondence abstracted, he perused them all;[492] packets from Boswell at the Hague and Hopton in Madrid 'his Majesty reserved for himself';[493] Taylor's letters from Vienna Charles carefully read through and commented on.[494] Other packets of foreign correspondence were periodically delivered personally to the king, even when he was on progress at Oatlands.[495] The letters, amended drafts, proclamations and apostiled papers in the royal out-tray flesh out the picture of the king's involvements. We know that Charles

484. PRO, PC 2/47/212.
485. Warwick, *Memoirs*, p. 70.
486. D. Hirst, 'The Privy Council and problems of enforcement in the 1620s', *Journ. Brit. Stud.*, 18 (1978), p. 55.
487. Birch, *Court and Times of Charles I*, I, p. 396.
488. *Cal. Stat. Pap. Venet., 1636–9*, p. 51.
489. *Cal. Stat. Pap. Dom., 1636–7*, p. 83.
490. See Laud to Bramhall, 13 Jan. 1635 (Huntington MS, HA 15172).
491. BL, MS 29/172, f.50; cf. Coke MS 42, 10 Aug. 1632.
492. Coke MS 59: Weckherlin to Coke, 8 Aug. 1639; Berkshire Record Office, Trumbull MS 543/2, *passim*.
493. Coke MS 51: Windebank to Coke, 4 Aug. 1635.
494. Clarendon MS 12, no. 952.
495. For example, Coke MS 42: Weston to Coke, 28 Aug. 1632; Coke MS 51: Windebank to Coke, 27 Aug. 1635.

wrote fully and regularly to Wentworth in Ireland; less well known are his letters to the Earl of Lindsey and to the Earl of Northumberland, commanders of his fleet, to Hamilton in Scotland, or to Windebank when Charles led his army to York in 1639.[496] There is too in the royal outpost a multiplicity of papers bearing Charles's marginalia and interlining in a clear and careful hand. Detailed annotations are found, for example, on Laud's metropolitan reports,[497] on the draft constitution for the Association for Fishing,[498] on instructions to raise a levy for the Palatinate,[499] on letters to the commissioners for sewers,[500] on petitions of nobles concerning precedency;[501] and on Admiralty papers concerning forts and castles.[502] In general a large proportion of the letters and documents in the Clarendon state paper collection, the Hamilton archive and, still more, in Secretary Coke's manuscripts at Melbourne Hall bears Charles's emendations (see Figures 16a and 16b). The king corrected Coke's draft of a letter to Davenant, bishop of Salisbury over the case of Henry Sherfield, dispatches concerning Scots ministers in Ireland and papers concerning ship money.[503] The last particularly commanded Charles's attention; the king's hand is found on Sir William Russell's accounts, and the state papers contain some holograph figures and calculations of his own.[504] Most of the letters from Windebank bear Charles's point-by-point margin notes (see Figure 17).

What the archives suggest is that Charles indicated his general purpose, left his secretary to draft a letter or discussion papers according to the appropriate form, but then reviewed the draft or plan carefully, correcting content and expression.[505] The secretary then finalized copy, as Windebank told Charles he had done concerning the maritime treaty, 'with your alterations'.[506] The interlinings make it clear that the royal review of papers was far from a cursory reading. The papers of George Weckherlin, German secretary to the Council, leave the same impression: sometimes the king went with him over letters to be sent out; at other times Weckherlin, as his diary informs us, 'having drawn an answer his Majesty in the morning perused and

496. As well as the letters printed in Knowler, see Wentworth MS 40, ff.3–41; *HMC Cowper II*, pp. 142–3, 175; *HMC 3rd Report*, p. 75; Coke MS 54; Hamilton MSS, *passim*; *Clarendon State Papers*, II, *passim*.
497. *Works of Laud*, V, Part II.
498. Coke MS 41: Noy to Coke, 7 March 1632.
499. Clarendon MS 4, no. 315: amendment by Charles I.
500. Coke MS 49, 25 Sept. 1634.
501. Coke MS 36.
502. *Cal. Stat. Pap. Dom., 1635–6*, p. 555.
503. Coke MS 44, 15 Feb. 1633; Coke MS 42, 10 Aug. 1632; *HMC Cowper II*, pp. 142–3.
504. *Cal. Stat. Pap. Dom., 1636–7*, p. 376; *1637–8*, p. 197.
505. For example, Coke MS 42, 31 Aug. 1632; Coke MS 49, 25 Sept. 1634.
506. Clarendon MS 4, no. 371.

corrected the same'.[507] What we can discover of the procedure in issuing proclamations confirms Professor Larkin's belief 'that Charles himself was the primary author of the most important ones'.[508] Some clearly began with his conception; some had their first draft from his own hand.[509] But in all cases drafts by others evidently came back to the king for final approval and signature.[510] We have seen enough evidence to know that neither the approval nor the signature was a matter only of form.

The multiplicity of examples of royal emendations and corrections must lead us to refute the contention that Charles I was ill-informed and lazy. We must instead place the king prominently at the centre of government. For as well as evidence of his writing and correcting documents we gain a clear impression of his directing affairs – even when his personal hand was neither used nor necessary. Letters written by Windebank, to take a case, were dictated verbatim by Charles.[511] Amidst the flurry of business in the summer of 1639 he similarly used Sir Henry Vane and explained to Hamilton: 'Having no time myself to write so much I was forced to use his pen, therefore I shall only say that what is here written, I have directed, seen and approved.'[512] The Earl of Northumberland as Admiral took his instructions directly from the king and made account to him personally.[513] Northumberland's reports were delivered to Charles even while he was on summer vacation at Woodstock, whither the commissioners for the Admiralty were also summoned to discuss naval business.[514] Charles, as we shall see, attended the Privy Council fairly regularly and after 1634 sat with his Councillors every Sunday to receive accounts from the ship money sheriffs.[515] He personally decided at times on business to be debated at the Board and kept up to date with what passed when he was absent.[516] When the Council was dismissed in August 1639 for a holiday until Michaelmas, Charles summoned Weckherlin daily to hear an account of news.[517] As well as the full Council Board, the king made appearances at its various committees: he was a diligent member of the Committee for Trade, for example in February and March of

507. Trumbull MS 453/2, 14 Feb. 1637 and 27 June 1638.
508. Larkin, *Stuart Royal Proclamations*, II, p. xx.
509. PRO, PC 2/41/246.
510. For example, Coke MS 53: Bankes to Coke, 7 April 1636.
511. *Clarendon State Papers*, II, p. 14.
512. Hamilton MS 1179.
513. Coke MS 54, 8 July 1636; Coke MS 55, 6 Oct. 1636.
514. *Ibid.*; and Coke MS 54, 23 Aug. 1636.
515. Below, pp. 263–4, 583.
516. *Cal. Stat. Pap. Dom., 1634–5*, p. 45; *1635–6*, p. 555; cf. Coke MS 42: Windebank to Coke, 22 Oct. 1632; *HMC Cowper II*, p. 175.
517. Coke MS 63: Weckherlin to Coke, 15 Aug. 1639.

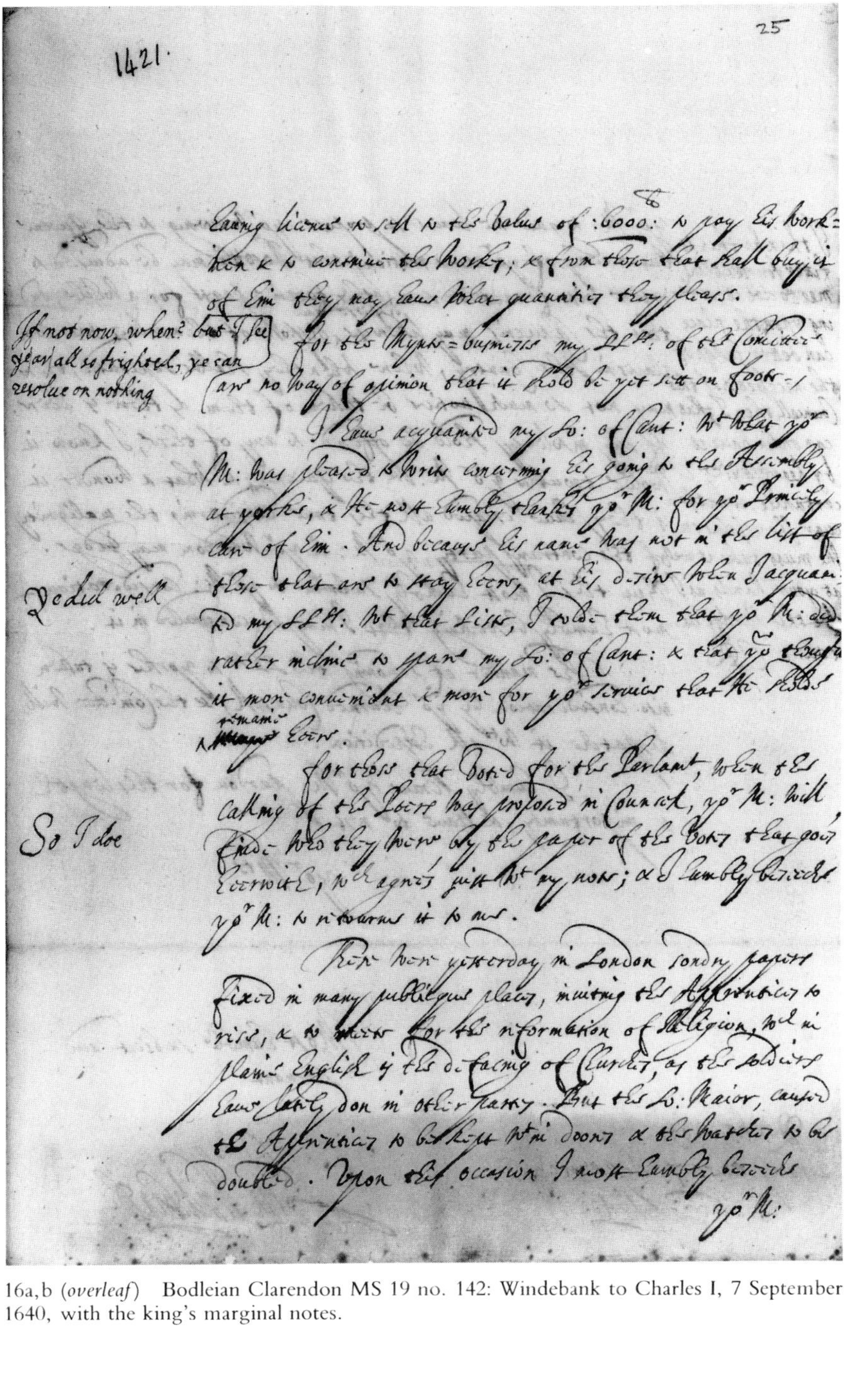

1421.

25

hauing licence to sell to the value of :6000li: to pay his workmen & to continue the worke; & from those that shall buy
of him they may haue what quantitie they please.

If not now, when? but I see ye ar all so frighted, ye can resolue on nothing

For the Mynt=businesse my LLds: of the Committee
are no way of opinion that it should be yet sett on foote.

I haue acquainted my Lo: of Cant: wth what yor
M: was pleased to write concerning his going to the Assembly
at Yorke, & he most humbly thankes yor M: for yor Princely
care of him. And because his name was not in the list of
those that are to stay heere, at his desire when I acquainted my LLds: wth that list, I tolde them that yor M: did
rather incline to haue my Lo: of Cant: & that you thought
it more conuenient & more for yor seruice that he should
remaine heere.

Ye did well

For those that voted for the Parlamt, when the
calling of the Peeres was proposed in Councell, yor M: will
finde who they were by the paper of the votes that goes
herewith, wch agrees just wth my notes; & I humbly beseech
yor M: to returne it to me.

So I doe

There were yesterday in London sondry papers
fixed in many publique places, inuiting the Apprentices to
rise, & to meete for the reformation of Religion, wch in
plaine English is the defacing of Churches, as the soldiers
haue lately don in other partes. But the Lo: Maior, caused
the Apprentices to be kept wthin doores & the watches to be
doubled. Upon this occasion I most humbly beseech
yor M:

16a,b (*overleaf*) Bodleian Clarendon MS 19 no. 142: Windebank to Charles I, 7 September 1640, with the king's marginal notes.

I thinke this is fitter for you, then mee to doe it, as being vpon the place can better judge of the necessitie of this Councell then I that can onlie haue it by heresay; & certanlie, whatsoever she resolue on she must take it well at your hands, as I doe this lardge account CR

yor M: to give me leave to propose yor writing to the Queene but meerly of yor owne motion, that Rosetti may be advised to retire into France or some other remote part for a while, and that the Capucins may likewise disperse and dispose of themselves into some places in the Country, where when they shalbe seperated, there may not so much notice be taken of them as there is here. If any mislikeing should be offered to any of them, I know it would trouble yor M: & the Queene, & what a wonder it is they have escaped all this time considering the malignity of the contrary party, yor M: in yor wisdom may judge. But this I most humbly submitt to yor M: consideration, most humbly beseeching that I may be concealed in it.

The manner of somoning the LLds to Yorke is taken into consideration by yor learned Counsell, & the Committee will dispatche it wth all Expedition.

I humbly crave yor M: pardon for this length & importunity, & crave to rest

yor Mts

Most humble subiect and servant

Fran: Windebanke

Yorke :9:

Drury lane: 7: Septem: 1640:

1635 when victualling licences to vintners were under discussion.[518] During 1636 and 1637, Weckherlin's diary records Charles working daily: signing, reading and returning papers. The turnaround time should not pass without comment. A dispatch sent by Windebank to his master on 23 January was returned apostiled by Charles on the 24th.[519] Another – a long report from Taylor delivered to the king on 15 August – was back to Windebank two days later.[520] The date not only confirms the impression of Charles's daily attention to business; it indicates an efficiency in dealing with correspondence that the present writer can only describe as enviable and admirable.

Clarendon recalled that Charles paid careful attention to the selection of his officers and domestic servants, privy chambermen and bedchambermen. Not trusting to recommendation, he observed men long before placing his trust in them.[521] Thomas Carew of the bedchamber was his personal choice against strong Scottish competition;[522] the king reserved to himself the appointment to seemingly minor posts, such as captain of the artillery garden and the clerkships in Chancery;[523] he intervened in the appointment of a clerk to the court of Star Chamber to advance his candidate.[524] Sir Thomas Herbert, writing to Viscount Scudamore in 1632 about the appointment of a new secretary, clearly believed the (slightly surprising) choice Charles's own: 'the king is pleased to reach men by his choice wheresoever they are and rather to fit men for places than places for men'.[525] It was an astute observation with which others concurred. For though Roe had been favoured for the post, on account of support from the Swedish lobby, one writer wryly predicted that a grain of Charles I's support was worth more than an ounce of anyone else's.[526] Henry Percy gave the same advice to the Earl of Leicester in 1637 when he was seeking the secretaryship or some other major office. Public speculation, he warned, would only ruin Leicester's chances: 'our master loves not to hear other people give what is only fit for him'.[527] In appointments to place as well as in matters of policy, Charles exercised close personal supervision.

Charles I was not another Philip II of Spain, of whom it was said 'no secretary uses more paper than his Majesty'.[528] His attention to

518. *Cal. Stat. Pap. Dom., 1635*, pp. 520, 556, 598.
519. *Cal. Stat. Pap. Dom., 1635–6*, p. 179.
520. Clarendon MS 12, no. 952.
521. Sharpe, *Politics and Ideas*, p. 163.
522. E. Hyde, Earl of Clarendon, *The Life of Edward Earl of Clarendon* (Oxford, 1761), p. 36.
523. PRO, PC 2/42/385; *Cal. Stat. Pap. Dom., 1635*, p. 251.
524. *Cal. Stat. Pap. Dom., 1635–6*, p. 57.
525. PRO, C.115/N3/8549, 23 June.
526. *Cal. Stat. Pap. Dom., 1631–3*, p. 212, anonymous.
527. Collins, *Letters and Memorials*, II, p. 156, 20 Sept. 1637.
528. See G. Parker, *Philip II* (Boston, 1978), pp. 26–9, 30–5, 70.

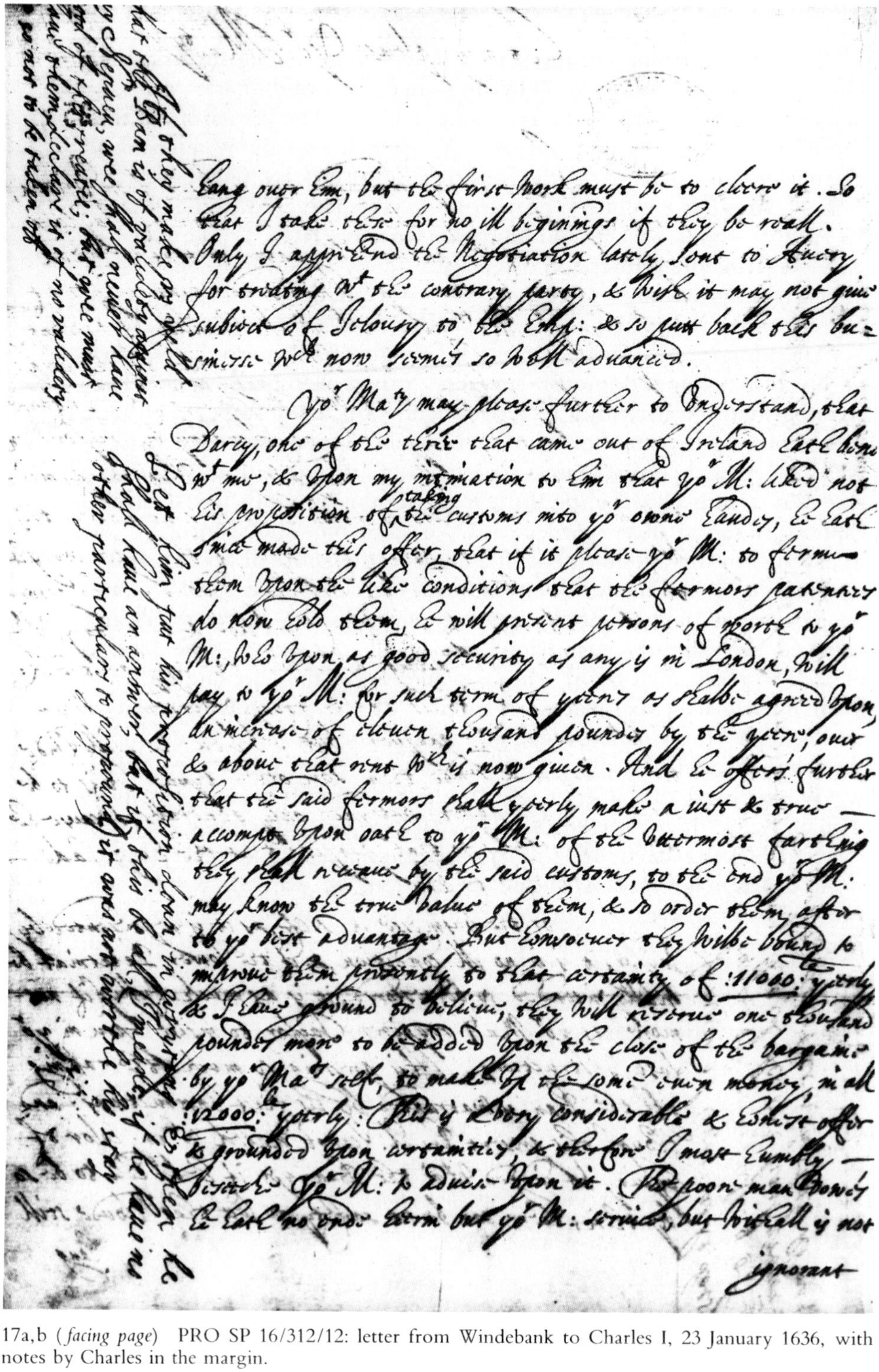
hang over him, but the first work must be to cleere it. So that I take these for no ill beginings if they be reall. Only I apprehend the Negotiation lately sent to Hungary for treating wth the contrary party, & wish it may not giue subiect of Jelousy to the Emp: & so putt back this businesse wch now seemes so well aduanced.

Yor Maty may please further to understand, that Darcy, one of the three that came out of Ireland hath bene wth me, & upon my intimation to him that yor M: liked not his proposition of taking the customs into yor owne handes, he hath since made this offer, that if it please yor M: to farme them upon the like conditions that the fermors at present do now hold them, he will present persons of worth to yor M:, who upon as good security as any is in London, will pay to yor M: for such term of yeers as shalbe agreed upon, an encrease of eleuen thousand poundes by the yeere, over & aboue that rent wch is now giuen. And he offers further that the said fermors shall yeerly make a iust & true accompt upon oath to yor M: of the uttermost farthing they shall receaue by the said customs, to the end yor M: may know the true value of them, & so order them after to yor best aduantage. But howsoever they wilbe bound to improue them presently to that certainty of :11000: yeerly & I haue ground to belieue, they will procure one thousand poundes more to be added upon the close of the bargaine by yor Maty selfe, to make up the some euen money, in all 12000: yeerly. This is a very considerable & honest offer & grounded upon certainties, & therfore I most humbly beseech yor M: to aduise upon it. The poore man vowes he hath no other ayme but yor M: seruice, but withall is not ignorant

17a,b (*facing page*) PRO SP 16/312/12: letter from Windebank to Charles I, 23 January 1636, with notes by Charles in the margin.

ignorant what hazard he shall run hereby of being utterly ruined if my L: Dep: ever com to know such an offer came from him. And therfore he most humbly craves yor Ma^ts protection, that being a Lawyer by profession he may live here & follow his studies in one of the Innes of Court, as never daring to appeare again in Ireland. He likewise makes all the vowes that a Christian can, that he was so farr from the least imagination of disserving yor M: in the parlament in Ireland, that he will make it appeare upon perill of his life, that no man was more forward in yor service.

I lyke not this

What he did may easilie be seen by his imploiment with his fellowes; but his intentions must bee left to God

Here is another busines concerning Burlamacchi who was employed into France to receive the remainder of the moneys due for the Queenes mariage, & to pay such tickets as were appointed by the Commissioners for satisfaction of the French officers of the Queenes household, divers of wch officers mistrusting they should not receave their moneys, petitioned the Fr: King that they might remayne in the handes of the Tres^r of the Espargne, wch was agreed unto accordingly. But som of these moneys remayning yet unpaied upon som pretences of one Claude Voyse, against Burlamacchi, the said Voyse hath staied these moneys in the handes of the Tres^r of the Espargne, and hereupon a great clamor being raised to yor Ma^ts honor & disservice, Burlamacchi is an humble suitor to yor Ma^ty to recomend the hearing & accomodation of this businesse to yor Amb^r: in France, who being upon the place, will be best hable to discover where the abuse lyes. If yor Ma^ty so please, I will give order to this purpose to the Lo: Scudamor.

J. Coke

It is a reason: therfor recomend his Busines accordinglie

documents did not confine him to his study. It was neither expected, nor desirable, nor perhaps by the seventeeth century possible, for the king to deal with everything personally. Already good delegation was of the essence of good government. As Viscount Conway remarked to the Reverend Garrard, 'Great statesmen that are held in estimation for their wisdom most commonly attain to it by having business prepared, for they make the work no more than the midwife makes the child.'[529] Sometimes, that is, others conceived policies or developed the seed of an idea planted by the king, nurtured proposals and brought them to life. In Dorchester, Coke and Windebank Charles found industrious and able secretaries who would often interpret the king's own mind and translate his intentions into letters and decrees that could pass through the Signet Office without alteration.[530] Such delegation is not neglect. There is enough evidence of Charles's checking and amending to indicate that what went out unaltered should not be seen as passing without his knowledge. Sometimes the king skilfully adapted an existing letter or one drafted by his secretaries, changing only a word or two for its new recipient; secretaries were left to take initiative, subject to final royal review.[531] Such practices were efficient, not neglectful. Very shortly after Buckingham's death, the Venetian ambassador had reported that the king 'declares his intention to undertake the affairs of the government.'[532] What he meant by his intention was explained by Secretary Dorchester weeks later: 'Everyone walks within the circle of his charge, and his Majesty's hand is the chief and, in effect, the sole directory.'[533] Business was discussed in Council, delegated to the appropriate individuals and came back to the Board and to the king for final decision. The administrators who researched precedents, refined proposals, filled in details and drew up options clearly had an important influence on policy. But, *pace* Professor Carlton, contemporaries were in no doubt who ultimately governed. As Sir Thomas Roe put it in 1636: 'Everything is but discourse until His Majesty give his consent.'[534]

529. BL Loan MS 29/172, f.153: Conway to Garrard, 31 July 1637. Charles himself said that 'he would willingly make his own dispatches but that he found it better to be a cobbler than a shoemaker' (Warwick, *Memoirs*, p. 70).
530. Cf. Warwick, *Memoirs*, p. 71 on Charles's attitude to Dorchester and Falkland.
531. For example, Coke MS 52, 8 Nov. 1635.
532. *Cal. Stat. Pap. Venet., 1628–9*, p. 283, 12 Sept. 1628.
533. Birch, *Court and Times of Charles I*, II, p. 2: Dorchester to Carlisle, 19 Dec. 1628.
534. *Cal. Stat. Pap. Dom., 1636–7*, p. 250: Roe to Elector Palatine, 31 Dec. 1636.

V

'A RULE OF ORDER IN HIS OWN HOUSE': THE REFORMATION OF THE COURT AND ADMINISTRATION

The court

A monarch who was obsessed with order and decorum and of a strong moral stance, who attached great importance to the domestic realm and who was a vigorous reformer, it was natural for Charles I to turn to the reformation of his larger household, that is his court. Reform of the court was not, of course, a purely domestic concern. The court had always been the seat of government as well as the home of the king; from perhaps the reign of Henry VIII Whitehall had emerged as the focus and the image of personal monarchy, as more emphasis was placed on magnificence and display. During the later sixteenth century most aristocrats and many gentlemen (and increasingly, with the invention of the spring carriage, women) came to court. News of the court, copies of court sermons, accounts of festivals and plays percolated back to the country. To the court, too, men and women began to look for models – of dress, behaviour and values. This was not just a matter of fashion. Renaissance courtesy literature required the court to stand as an example of virtue for the realm. Practical evidence that it did not always do so, the Overbury scandal and other instances of debauchery and corruption, far from undermining the ideal invested it with greater importance and urgency.[1] It was, Nicholas Faret wrote in *The Art to Please in Courts* (1632), for the courtier to present 'an idea of that which is possible'; to pursue in his own life decorum, discretion and self-regulation that he might represent the possibility of human self-perfection.[2] The Spaniard Juan de Santa Maria's *Christian Policie*, translated into English the same

1. See K. Sharpe, *Criticism and Compliment: The Politics of Literature in the England of Charles I* (Cambridge, 1987), ch. 1, esp. pp. 19–21.
2. N. Faret, *The Art to Please in Court* (1632, STC 10686), p. 400.

year, reinforced Faret's argument: at court the king set an example of manners and moderation 'to teach and instruct the people by his virtues'.[3] Those around him, his nobles and counsellors, learned from his example and disseminated courtly values to the country; from the court 'is diffused all the good or ill'.[4] The English preacher William Struther in the very title of his *A Looking Glass for Princes and People* depicted the court as the mirror which reflected the person of the king to his subjects, as well as the glass in which the king viewed himself. 'The court of kings,' he wrote, shifting the metaphors, 'is an abridgement of their kingdoms and the circle of the subjects nearest to them. It is a proof of the government of their persons and an image of the ruling of their states.'[5] The importance of the court then could not be exaggerated: 'As is the prince, so is his court . . . as the court is so the country will be.'[6] It is no coincidence that these values were asserted in the early 1630s. For, unlike his father, Charles I had an acute sense of the importance of the court as an example for the government of the country. Just as he believed that 'every man should be a rule of order and abstinence in his own house', so he intended 'to establish government and order in our court which from thence may spread with more order through all parts of our kingdoms'.[7] The masque *Coelum Britannicum*, written by Charles's gentleman of the bedchamber Thomas Carew, takes as its theme the reform of the court as the foundation of the reformation of society, manners and government.[8] In the changes he effected in the domestic arrangements at court then, we may not only see the stamp of Charles's character and personal morality; we may also begin to discern his ideals for the government of the country.

Charles's impact upon the style of the court had been felt within days of his succession. On 25 April 1625, the Venetian ambassador reported, 'the king observes a rule of great decorum. The nobles do not enter his apartments in confusion as heretofore, but each rank has its appointed place and he has declared that he desires the rules and maxims of the late Queen Elizabeth . . . The king has also drawn up rules for himself, dividing the day from his very early rising, for prayers, exercises, audiences, business, eating and sleeping. It is said that he will set apart a day for public audience and he does not wish

3. J. de S. Maria, *Christian Policie* (1632, STC 14831), pp. 361, 371–2.
4. *Ibid.*, p. 372.
5. W. Struther, *A Looking Glass for Princes and People* (1632, STC 23369), p. 70.
6. *Ibid.*, pp. 70–1.
7. J.F. Larkin (ed.) *Stuart Royal Proclamations, II: Proclamations of King Charles I, 1625–46* (Oxford, 1983) no. 37, p. 80; PRO, Lord Chamberlain's books, LC 5/180, p. 1.
8. S. Orgel and R. Strong (eds) *Inigo Jones: The Theatre of the Stuart Court* (2 vols, Berkeley and London, 1973), II, pp. 567–98. For a discussion, see Sharpe, *Criticism and Compliment*, pp. 232–43.

anyone to be introduced to him unless sent for.'[9] With the establishment of peace with France and Spain, Charles turned promptly to drawing up the 'rules and maxims' that might effect his desired reformation of the court. It would seem that commissioners met in early 1629 to investigate the best way to restore the court to its ancient splendour.[10] In 1630 the reform began with the promulgation of rules for proper behaviour in the royal chapel and privy chambers and for the government of the Great Wardrobe.[11] We may probably date to the same time the parchment book of orders for the royal household in the Lord Chamberlain's department of the Public Record Office, which is annotated and signed by the king himself.[12] These comprehensive regulations prescribe behaviour at court and qualifications for admission from the entrance gate through the public rooms to the innermost sanctum of the royal bedchambers. The Knight Marshal and porter at the gate were ordered to scrutinize carefully those entering the precincts of the court and to check all names against a list to be kept at the lodge. The porters were to have 'special regard that no ragged boys nor unseemly persons be suffered to make a stay in any of the courts' and royal servants were reminded that their own domestics should be 'comely and seemly persons' well apparelled and behaved.[13] The king's personal sense of morality echoes throughout the orders. In order that 'our house may be a place of civility and honour', standards of behaviour were to be rigorously enforced. If any domestic was 'noised to be a profane person or outrageous rioter or ribald, a notorious drunkard, swearer, railer or quarreller', he was to be ousted from his place. Similarly any royal servant or courtier found 'so vicious and unmannerly that he is unfit to live in virtuous and

9. *Calendan of State Papers Venetian* [*Cal. Stat. Pap. Venet.*], *1625–6*, p. 21.
10. *HMC Cowper I*, p. 382.
11. Huntington Library, Hastings MSS, Miscellaneous Box: orders for proper behaviour upon entering the royal chapel and privy chamber; National Library of Scotland MS 191: orders for His Majesty's Great Wardrobe, 15 April 1630.
12. I so dated them in 'The image of virtue: the court and household of Charles I, 1625–1642', in D. Starkey (ed.) *The English Court from the Wars of the Roses to the Civil War* (1987)), p. 231. Since then, Dr Cuddy has suggested to me that the book is more likely to be the product of the reforms of 1637 and that the dating '1630' (in a late hand on the parchment book) is erroneous. There are problems about dating the book, but I incline to an earlier date than Dr Cuddy because contemporaries later referred to reforms in the sixth year of the king's reign (*Calendar of State Papers Domestic* [*Cal. Stat. Pap. Dom.*], *1637–8*, p. 467) and newsletters referred to 'new orders' in 1631 (PRO, C. 115/M31/8140: Flower to Scudamore, 24 Dec. 1631). In 1637, Coke referred to an earlier set of Caroline orders with which the Eltham ordinances were to be compared by the committee for household reform (PRO, SP 16/375/1). Also, orders signed by the king and queen for the government of Henrietta Maria's household in 1631 (British Library [BL], Stowe MS 561, ff.12, 18) closely echo PRO, LC 5/180. For the purposes of my discussion, the date is not crucial. I am most grateful to Neil Cuddy for correspondence on this subject.
13. PRO, LC 5/180.

civil company' was to be banished the verge, the boundary of the royal household.[14] In 1630, to give teeth to these orders, Charles re-established the court of the marshal of the household;[15] two years later he made enquiries of the judges concerning settling a court for the palace of Westminster with jurisdiction for twelve miles around.[16] Though it was almost impossible to enforce on the hundreds of individuals who made up the court the king's own strict codes of behaviour, Charles reacted firmly to public breaches of morality and decorum.[17] When Jermyn and Mistress Villiers (who was clearly generous with her favours)[18] were committed to the Tower for their adultery, the newswriter Flower expected they would remain there a long time, having greatly displeased the king.[19] William Crofts and Peter Apsley were banished the court for misdemeanours in 1636; in 1635 privy chamber gentlemen lost their places for swearing.[20] The Marquis of Hamilton was thought to be a strong candidate for Master of the Horse only 'if he will cohabit with his wife'.[21] Charles set, as some contemporaries complained, a very different moral tone for his court to that of his father: orgies, sexual dalliance and adultery were less in evidence, or at least less public;[22] even ribaldry and innuendo were not tolerated.[23] Though the wife of the Cromwellian Colonel Hutchinson of the New Model army and therefore an enemy to Charles, Lucy Hutchinson, a lady of strict puritan disposition, praised the second Stuart for his purging the vices of his father's court: 'The face of the court was much changed in the king, for King Charles was temperate, chaste and serious, so that the fools, and bawds, mimics and catamites of the former Court grew out of fashion.'[24]

As well as an insistence on morality and civility, the household orders were concerned to re-establish a strict hierarchy of rooms and persons. Believing that the order of classical architecture might best order the world of the court, Charles from his accession to the throne

14. *Ibid.*
15. J. Rushworth, *Historical Collections* II (1680), p. 104.
16. PRO, SO 1/2, f.82v: Charles I to the judges of King's Bench, Feb. 1632; *Cal. Stat. Pap. Dom., 1631–3*, p. 266.
17. See the satire on the licentiousness of the Caroline court, Bodleian, Ashmole MSS 36–7 (bound together), f.264.
18. She had affairs with Lords Newport and Fielding as well as Jermyn. Melbourne Hall, Coke MS 47: Jermyn to king, 1633; *HMC Cowper II*, pp. 40–1.
19. PRO, C.115/M31/8151: Flower to Scudamore, 11 May 1633.
20. PRO, PC 2/46/452.
21. *Cal. Stat. Pap. Dom., 1625–49*, p. 296.
22. As Robert Reade put it to Windebank, 'We keep all our virginities at court still, at least we lose them not avowedly' (*Cal. Stat. Pap. Dom., 1639–40*, p. 364).
23. Cf. *Coelum Britannicum*, lines 208–18, in Orgel and Strong, *Inigo Jones*, II, p. 572.
24. L. Hutchinson, *Memoirs of the Life of Colonel Hutchinson*, ed. C.H. Firth (2 vols, New York, 1885), I, pp. 119–20.

dreamed of having Inigo Jones build a new palace at Whitehall; he was still planning in 1638; 'even in captivity in 1647 he sat scrutinizing plans for a palace at Whitehall twice the size of the Escorial'.[25] (See Figures 18 and 19). Denied the new fabric he dreamed of, Charles could only endeavour to impose on the rambling anarchy of Whitehall's rooms, closets and backstairs, a structured order of use. The king reaffirmed that the passage from the court gates to the Presence Chamber be through the Great Hall, in which on Sundays and Offering Days the chief officers of the household were to take their meals. In the Great Chamber the yeomen of the guard were to attend in person, and to ensure that no footmen or other servants of courtiers pass through without escort. In the Presence Chamber, in which the throne represented the majesty of the monarch even in his absence, the Gentlemen Ushers' daily waiters were instructed to keep a watch on all, to ensure comely behaviour and due reverence for the state (see Figure 20). The Gentlemen Pensioners, chosen from the best families of the realm, were ordered to be in attendance with their axes by ten o'clock. In the royal chapel, separate stalls were delineated for men and women and seating was differentiated by rank, none under the degree of baron being permitted to sit opposite the dean's place; officers of the household below stairs were not permitted to occupy any of the stalls.[26] Though the Privy Chamber, once the inner sanctum of the court, had ceased by the early seventeenth century to be the private domestic quarters of the king, Charles seems concerned to reassert its significance as the first step inside the privy lodgings. Only noblemen and sworn gentlemen of the Privy Chamber were permitted to enter the room and none was permitted there to relax over a game of cards or chess.[27] In royal houses where there was only one chamber which had to serve as a Presence Chamber and Privy Chamber, the king insisted on a distinction being preserved, decreeing that 'the said chamber shall be avoided and become the Privy Chamber after warning given to cover the table there for our meals and also at other times when our pleasure shall be to have the same private'.[28] Such distinctions were important to Charles; the absence of formal accommodation at Royston and Newmarket made them less popular as residences.[29]

Strictest of all were the rules governing entrée to the royal bedchamber. Since its importation by James VI and I from Scotland, this was the king's most private quarters in which he slept, dressed and

25. See K. Sharpe, *Politics and Ideas in Early Stuart England* (1989), p. 361, note 18; Coke MS 58; P. Thomas 'Charles I: the tragedy of absolutism', in A.G. Dickens (ed.) *The Courts of Europe, 1400–1800* (1977), p. 193.
26. PRO, SP 16/375/2.
27. Sharpe, 'The image of virtue', pp. 233–4; PRO, SP 16/375/2.
28. PRO, LC 5/180, p. 24.
29. I owe this information to Dr Arthur Macgregor of the Ashmolean Museum.

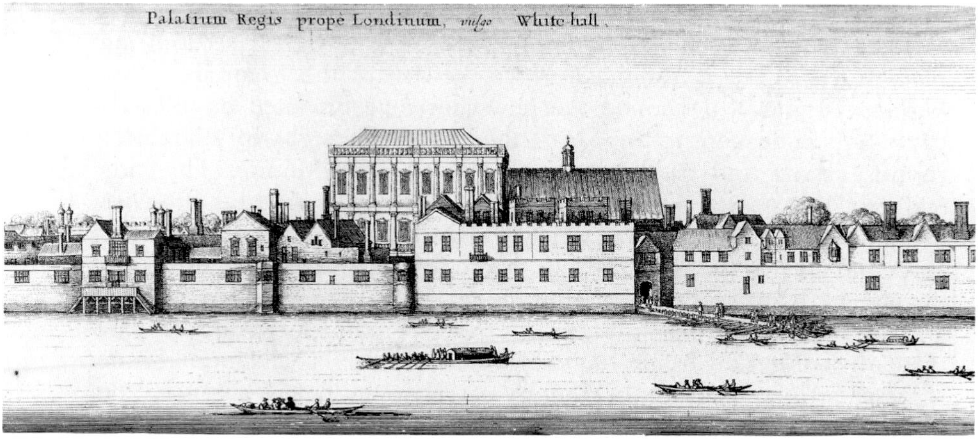

18 *Whitehall Palace from the River*, etching by Wenceslaus Hollar, 1647, showing Inigo Jones's Banqueting Hall.

19 *Design for a New Palace at Whitehall*, drawing by John Webb after Inigo Jones, *c.* 1637–9, showing park and river elevations.

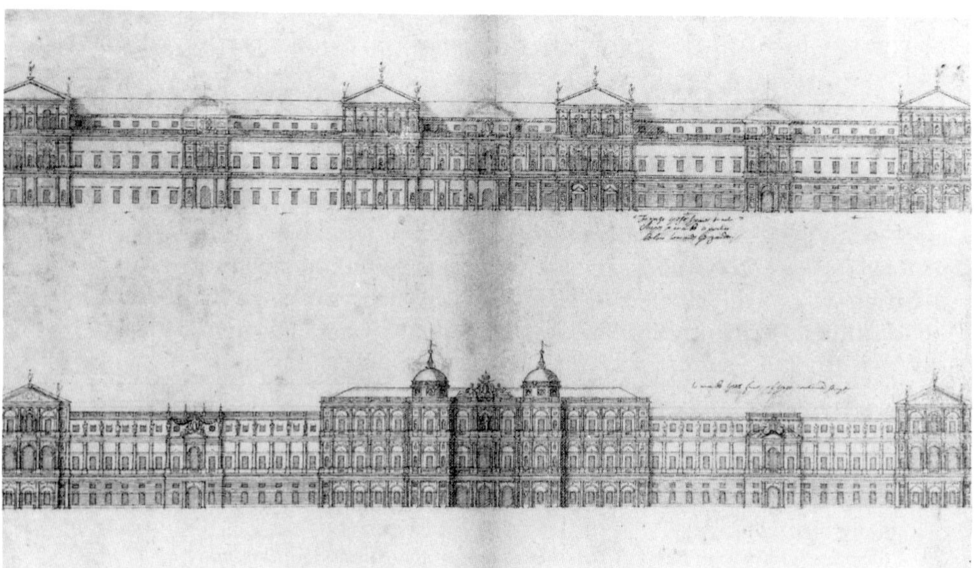

LE CERCLE DE LEVRS MAGESTES DANS LA CHAMBRE DE
PRESENCE A S. IAMES

20 Presence Chamber, St James's Palace from Puget's *Histoire de l'Entrée* . . . , 1639. The king, queen and queen mother are seated in a circle of courtiers.

was attended by his personal body servants. Apart from princes of the blood, Charles ordered that none have access to the bedchamber but the gentlemen of that chamber and those, such as doctors or barbers, who necessarily attended the king on particular occasions. All others, including Privy Councillors who were not bedchambermen and secretaries of state, had to attend the king in the outer withdrawing room, between the Privy Chamber and bedchamber.[30] The right of entry therefore to each room at Whitehall became more restricted, the closer one approached the majesty of the king. In order to overcome some of the architectural deficiencies of Whitehall, the orders firmly forbade any alternative passage to the king via backstairs or privy galleries: 'all accesses generally shall be made through the rooms of state'.[31] Indeed in order to secure his privacy and prevent unauthorized or indiscriminate access to rooms, the king ordered new

30. See N. Cuddy, 'The revival of the entourage', and my 'Image of virtue', in Starkey, *The English Court*, pp. 173–260.
31. PRO, LC 5/180.

treble locks to be fitted to the privy lodgings, for which the keys were entrusted to only a select few.[32] In contrast to the easy familiarity of Jacobean Whitehall, Charles drew up rules in order to fashion what Sir Philip Warwick called 'the most regular and splendid court in Christendom'.

As the 1630s progressed the royal establishment consisted not of one court but of several. From the early days of his marriage Charles had insisted on the governance of his wife's household. In 1627 he evidently drew up for the queen's court orders which were revised and signed by Charles and Henrietta Maria in November 1631.[33] The household of Charles Prince of Wales was formally established in 1638 and a body of rules was issued along the lines of those for the king's own court.[34] The prince's governor, the Earl of Newcastle, was entrusted to supervise the officers of the prince's household and to implement the ordinances.[35] During 1637 and 1638, the king appointed a commission for further reform of his own household. Secretary Coke and others transcribed the Eltham ordinances, issued by Henry VIII for his court in 1526, and after comparison with those earlier signed by Charles, made recommendations that a new book be drawn up.[36] It seems likely that many of their wide-ranging proposals for reform were lost in the distractions of the Scots war.

Neither the commissioners' proposals nor the various orders promulgated were novel. They drew on earlier Jacobean orders for the chapel and Privy Chamber, on Elizabethan precedent, most of all at Charles's own direction they closely followed the Eltham 'statutes', as Coke called them, of Henry VIII.[37] John Flower, describing the household reforms to Viscount Scudamore in December 1631, observed, 'there be nothing new in them but that which concerns the gentlemen pensioners'.[38] In 1638 the Reverend Garrard wrote to Wentworth concerning the work of the commissioners, 'they look back to Henry the Seventh, Henry the Eighth and Queen Elizabeth's time'.[39] As in other aspects of his government, Charles sought the reformation of his household through the renovation of old practices and rules that had been allowed to lapse. In one of his first proclamations after succeeding to the throne the king, confirming Burnet's claims about his dislike for the familiarity of James's reign, stated: 'Whereas, out of our own

32. PRO, LC 3/31, p. 3.
33. Stowe MS 561, ff.12–18.
34. F. Steer (ed.) *Orders for the Household of Charles, Prince of Wales* (Lichfield, 1959).
35. *Ibid.*, p. 3; cf. BL, Harleian MS 7623; Bodleian, Bankes MS 54/53.
36. PRO, PC 2/48/403; PRO, SP 16/375/1; *Cal. Stat. Pap. Dom., 1637–8*, pp. 49, 142.
37. PRO, SP 16/375/1; PRO, PC 2/48/403; Harleian MS 589. I owe this last reference to Neil Cuddy.
38. PRO, C. 115/M31/8140.
39. W. Knowler, *The Earl of Strafford's Letters and Despatches* (2 vols, 1739), II, p. 140.

observance in the late reign of our most dear and royal father, we saw much disorder in and about his household by reason of the many idle persons and other unnecessary attendants following the same; which evil, we, finding to bring much dishonour to our house, have resolved the reformation thereof'.[40] In all aspects of court life Charles insisted on the letter of formality. The king himself unlike his father, but like Queen Elizabeth, kept the board of state in the Presence Chamber. He required the Lord Chamberlain and others to dine in the Great Chamber and when absent to appoint a deputy to keep their place; he enjoined his Treasurer of the household to eat at festival times with the below-stairs officers in the great hall ('at which he mutinies').[41] Envoys were no longer sat at the king's table but, as in Spain or France, entertained by the officers of the household. Royal progresses were carefully supervised and ordered. In the ceremony of touching for the king's evil, it was proclaimed, 'order is to be observed and fit times are necessarily to be appointed'.[42] Both English observers and foreign ambassadors were quick to sense a change. Sir John Finet, Master of Ceremonies, was rather dismayed when escorting an ambassador to the king to find himself stopped at the door of the Privy Chamber whence a gentleman of that chamber assumed his charge; the Venetian ambassador was pleasantly surprised to find himself attended to his audience by a Privy Councillor and a knight of the Garter.[43] Though most of these requirements were not new, to contemporaries whose memories did not go back to Elizabeth, let alone Henry VIII, the change effected at court by Charles evidently appeared as a major shift from familiarity to formality.

Along with a renewed formality the Caroline court was coloured by a hue very much taken from the king's own palette: an emphasis upon ceremony and ritual. James Wadsworth's *The Present Estate of Spain* would suggest that in this, as in other aspects of court reform, Charles had found in Madrid a model of the manners that attuned with his tastes.[44] When, like Philip IV, he dined in state in the Presence, Charles was attended with the most elaborate ceremony. The cupbearers and carvers were ordered

40. Larkin, *Stuart Royal Proclamations*, II, no. 14, p. 37.
41. Sharpe, 'Image of virtue', p. 239; *HMC Denbigh V*, p. 8; PRO, LS 13/169, f.221; *Cal. Stat. Pap. Dom., 1631–3*, p. 206.
42. T. Birch, *The Court and Times of Charles I* (2 vols, 1848), II, p. 24; Larkin, *Stuart Royal Proclamations*, II, no. 17, p. 44; T. Rymer (ed.) *Foedera, Conventiones, Litterae* (15 vols, 1704–35), XIX, p. 449.
43. J. Finet, *Finetti Philoxenis* (1656), p. 145; *Cal. Stat. Pap. Venet., 1625–6*, pp. 524–5; cf. Sharpe, 'The image of virtue', pp. 228, 240.
44. J. Wadsworth, *The Present Estate of Spayne* (1630, STC 24929). Wadsworth describes the Order of the Golden Fleece, the ceremony of the king's dining and going to chapel and his manner of receiving ambassadors.

> before they give their attendance upon the king's person to wash their hands; the while they are with the Gentlemen Ushers in washing every man in the chamber is to be uncovered; after the Gentleman Usher is to call for a bowl of sack . . . and to drink to one of the gentlemen that have washed. After the carver hath his towel upon his shoulder, he and the Gentlemen Usher goeth together in the Presence Chamber where they make three congés at three several parts of the chamber and so come to the board.[45]

Such rituals publicly emphasized the reverence due to the king's body and the mystical majesty of monarchy. The orders at all points stress the need to maintain distance from the royal persons, the king, queen and children. The Gentlemen Ushers were commanded to see that 'no man of whatsoever degree he be of be so hardy to come to the king's chair nor stand under the cloth of state . . . nor to stand upon his carpet'.[46] The towel used by the king in washing, the Gentlemen Usher was to raise above his head as he walked from the Presence.[47] The Maundy ceremony of washing the poor's feet was similarly characterized by rituals which stressed the symbols of majesty whilst distancing the king, who was represented by the bishop almoner, from physical contact.[48] Even those coming to court to be touched for the king's evil had to produce a certificate to show that they had not been touched before.[49] At all times 'both noblemen and their ladies' were admonished to use 'great distance and respect to the royal persons'.[50]

Such concern with reverence and ritual in the daily round of court life became an obsession on public occasions, when the court was on display to the kingdom. When the king went to chapel, the Gentlemen Ushers warned nobles in town to resort to court to attend him. The greatest nobles went arm in arm with any ambassador present while the rest in the procession were commanded to progress in orderly ranks 'and not break them with pretences of speaking one with another', 'that being one of the most eminent and frequent occasions whereby men's ranks in precedence were distinguished and discerned'.[51] The service in the chapel, especially the offering by the king, was marked by elaborate ritual. The king's donation brought by a groom of the chamber was delivered to a Gentleman Usher, who in turn handed it on to the most eminent nobleman, 'who shall kiss it and deliver it to the king immediately before the offering when the king is

45. Stowe MS 561, ff.6–7.
46. *Ibid.*, f.5.
47. BL, Sloane MS 1494, ff.12–12v.
48. *Ibid.*, ff.24–24v.
49. Larkin, *Stuart Royal Proclamations*, II, no. 126, p. 257.
50. Hastings MSS, Miscellaneous Box 1.
51. Sloane MS 1494, f.86; PRO, LC 5/180, p. 16.

set on his knees'. The king then received the coin (a noble) from the nobleman kneeling on his right and offered it to the cleric officiating.[52] On Candlemas day (the day of the purification of the Virgin) even more ceremony accompanied the king's offering of seven nobles.[53] At the christening of Prince Charles everything was planned to the last detail to make for a magnificent as well as duly pious occasion.[54] Detailed preparations were made to ensure that major royal progresses maintained such solemnity and dignity when the household went abroad. When Charles and Henrietta were invited to dine with the Lord Mayor, they went, William Whiteway recorded, 'in great estate'.[55] Such ceremonies and processions did not only reflect Charles's personal preferences; they expressed the royal mind. They communicated, as Charles was acutely aware, an image of royalty, what we might even call a monarchical ideology.

The festivities of the Garter provide a splendid example. Charles I clearly attached enormous importance to the Order of the Garter, and perhaps desired that it should emulate the Habsburg Order of the Golden Fleece, the festival of which he may have witnessed in Spain.[56] Herbert, gentleman of the bedchamber, informs us that the king put on his George first thing in the morning and never failed to wear it.[57] On the reverse, significantly, was a picture of his wife.[58] When we view Rubens's painting of St George slaying the dragon and rescuing the princess, we quickly discern the association (see Figure 21). In his letter to his son, at the prince's inauguration into the order, Charles referred to the 'emulation of chivalry' and 'the glory of heroic actions' which the knights swore to uphold.[59] Rubens's picture, however, is also an apocalyptic drama: the slaying of the dragon of evil and the triumph of innocence. Charles changed the Garter badge to enhance the religious imagery by adding 'a huge aureola of silver rays copied from the French order of the holy spirit' to the holy cross of St George.[60] (See Figure 22). As Peter Heylyn, the chaplain of the order, wrote in his history of St George, the badge symbolized 'how bravely he repelled the Devil, how constantly he persevered in the profession of his faith'.[61] The Garter symbolized for Charles, as Roy Strong

52. Sloane MS 1494, f.10.
53. *Ibid.*, f.17.
54. Bodleian, Eng. Hist. MS E28, f.1.
55. BL, Egerton MS 784 (William Whiteway's diary, 1618–34), p. 180.
56. Cf. Wadsworth, *Present Estate of Spayne*, p. 39ff.
57. Herbert, *Memoirs of the Last Two Years of the Reign of Charles I* (1873), p. 146; Sharpe, 'The image of virtue', pp. 245–6 and note 120.
58. E. Ashmole, *The History of the Most Noble Order of the Garter* (1715), p. 182.
59. *Ibid.*, p. 273.
60. Thomas, 'Charles I: the tragedy of absolutism', p. 197.
61. R. Strong, *Van Dyck: Charles I on Horseback* (1972), pp. 61–2.

brilliantly expounded it, manliness and chivalry, chastity, piety and self-regulation, honour and hierarchy, order and propriety. What needs to be emphasized is that the Garter also communicated these private virtues to the public realm. The king ordered all knights of the order always to wear their George; the badge is prominent in nearly all the paintings of Charles himself.[62] He exempted the Garter alone in the 1640s from the ban on ornaments to clothing.[63] He ordered it be added to a new seal for Ireland in 1632;[64] he minted the first money on which the emblem appeared.[65] Charles determined that the Order of the Garter and its festivals might, like his court in general, promulgate an image of ordered virtue.[66] Sir Thomas Roe, appointed Chancellor in 1637, described the king's passionate desire 'to restore his most noble order . . . to the primitive institution';[67] Elias Ashmole, the historian of the Garter, recalled that 'King Charles I designed and endeavoured the most complete and absolute reformation of any of his predecessors'.[68]

In 1629 the king revived the custom, long lapsed, of the sovereign proceeding to Windsor on the eve of St George's day.[69] The procession became more lavish; in the 1630s 'the gallantry of attendants began to increase and augment'.[70] The ceremony of the installation of the Earl of Northumberland was so sumptuous and magnificent that Garrard told Wentworth 'The Garter is grown a dear honour, few subjects will be able to follow this pattern.'[71] Though magnificent, the Garter feasts were also made 'more orderly' and the religious solemnities were observed in full; Charles supped publicly, with full ceremony in St George's Hall.[72] For the installation of his son in 1638, a major public cavalcade – of the sort rarely mounted by the Stuarts – was planned.[73]

62. Charles rebuked the Prince of Orange for not wearing his Garter and reminded him of his obligation to wear it daily (*Cal. Stat. Pap. Venet., 1632–6*, p. 557).
63. Larkin, *Stuart Royal Proclamations*, II, no. 422, p. 907.
64. PRO, SO 1/2, f.90v, April 1632. A new seal for England was ordered in 1637 (PRO, SO 1/3, f.55, 25 Oct.).
65. Ashmole, *History of the Garter*, p. 161.
66. The king's concern stretched to the re-edification of St George's chapel in Lisbon; see PRO, SP 16/255/1.
67. *HMC Salisbury XXII*, p. 294: Roe to Salisbury, 13 Jan. 1638.
68. Ashmole, *History of the Garter*, p. 148; see Knowler, *Strafford Letters*, I, p. 242; *Cal. Stat. Pap. Dom., 1631–3*, p. 230; and S. Bond (ed.) *The Chapter Acts of the Dean and Canons of Windsor* (1966), pp. 182–3.
69. Ashmole, *History of the Garter*, p. 444.
70. *Ibid.*, p. 438.
71. Knowler, *Strafford Letters*, I, p. 427.
72. PRO, C.115/N8/8804: Finet to Scudamore, 17 April 1637; Strong, *Van Dyck*, pp. 60–1; Ashmole, *History of the Garter*, p. 483.
73. Ashmole, *History of the Garter*, p. 320; cf. R.M. Smuts, 'Public ceremony and royal charisma: the English royal entry in London, 1485–1642', in A.L. Beier, D. Cannadine and J.M. Rosenheim (eds) *The First Modern Society* (Cambridge, 1989), pp. 65–93. The Venetian envoy, though, said that crowds 'usually attend' the Garter procession (*Cal. Stat. Pap. Venet., 1629–32*, p. 331).

21 *Landscape with St George and the Dragon* by Rubens, 1629–30. Oliver Millar writes: 'The saint is almost certainly a romantically conceived portrait of Charles I'. Lambeth Palace is recognizable in the distance.

22 *Portrait of Charles I as Garter Knight* by Van Dyck, 1632. The symbolic significance of the Garter to Charles I is strikingly displayed in this portrait.

23 *Charles I and the Knights of the Garter in Procession* by Van Dyck, 1638. A sketch for a projected series of tapest

After a ceremony in the old palace of Westminister, Prince Charles was to take the oath in Henry VII's chapel before being created knight of the Bath at Whitehall. He was then to ride, with all the knights in their robes, from Somerset House in the Strand to Windsor for his installation. A month before his inauguration, the 'public solemnity' was, John Burgh explained, abandoned for a 'private investiture' – perhaps because events in Scotland made the festival too expensive or inappropriate.[74] What remained of the plans is a sketch by Van Dyck of a feast day procession, which was intended to become a painting or tapestries for the walls of the Banqueting House.[75] (See Figure 23.) It was, as Ashmole claimed, the representation of a military triumph, a state entry and a religious thanksgiving.[76] The Garter festival was, we might say, the publicization of the king's person and conscience in a spectacular liturgy of state.

The politics of court culture

It is as documents of political ideology that we may fruitfully study the paintings and poems, masques and plays written and performed at the Caroline court. Historians are still reluctant to read paintings or poems as primary documents of social and political values.[77] Our own culture has tended artificially to delineate and elevate the 'aesthetic' as a

74. PRO, C.115/N4/8624: Burgh to Scudamore, 11 April 1638.
75. E. Shepphard, *The Old Palace of Whitehall* (1902), p. 20; C. Brown, *Van Dyck* (Oxford, 1982), p. 190.
76. Ashmole, *History of the Garter*, p. 552.
77. Though for a spectacularly illuminating recent study, see S. Schama, *The Embarrassment of Riches* (1987).

rating the history of the Garter.

separate sphere raised above the world of affairs.[78] The age of the Renaissance, however, did not make such a demarcation. Fictions were not seen as retreats from reality, but an engagement with it in order to mediate higher truths. Representations were not regarded as distortions of subjects but mirrors (to use their popular metaphor) in which men might perceive their own essence. The cosmos and the commonweal were themselves depicted as creative constructs, works of art; by corollary all artistic representations of that world were in the broadest sense political.[79] Images, signs, were not seen as separate from objects but, often, in Platonic terminology, as their true form. Names *were* things; external countenances announced inner qualities.[80] Whether words or pictures, images not only represented authority, they possessed authority. They did so because the artist shared a common purpose with the statesman: the inculcation and dissemination of virtue. In the representation, be it on canvas or on the stage, the beholder or reader discerned the higher principles which he should adopt as the governing statutes in the polity of his own person.

The culture of the Caroline court was characterized until recently as escapist, as withdrawal from harsh political reality into an ethereal world of ideals and illusions. We should study it rather as the most powerful and perhaps last manifestation of the Renaissance belief in the didactic power of images. At one level the paintings of Van Dyck

78. Cf. the introductory remarks in K. Sharpe and S. Zwicker (eds) *Politics of Discourse: The Literature and History of Seventeenth Century England* (Berkeley and London, 1987).
79. Cf. my *Politics and Ideas*, pp. 44–7.
80. Cf. B. Vickers, 'Analogy versus identity: the rejection of occult symbolism, 1580–1680', in B. Vickers (ed.) *Occult and Scientific Studies in the Renaissance* (Cambridge, 1984), pp. 95–164.

may be viewed as romanticized portraits of their subjects and celebrations of their advancements that pandered to personal vanity. Arundel is painted in his armour as commander of the army against the Scots, the apogee of his political honours. Northumberland commands the canvas with a fleet in the background as Lord High Admiral of England[81] (see Figure 24). But what the paintings have in common is what perhaps has made them endure, their capturing of the very essence of nobility. In all Van Dyck's canvases – of elder statesmen, gay adolescents or infant princes – the subjects radiate control, the self-regulation that comes from inner strength, from that innate virtue which was the essence of nobility and from which nobility derived its authority to govern. Their richness of dress never becomes indulgence; the record of their office never a blatant boast; their pose is one of 'psychic balance' rather than swagger.[82] The subjects appear, and this is the greatness of Van Dyck's achievement, natural, themselves. They are themselves because they have command of their own potentially unruly appetites and so have fulfilled their highest nature. And exercising command over themselves, they effortlessly command their worlds – of government, warfare, creative and intellectual endeavour, exploration. As Arundel, contemplating the colonization of Madagascar, rules over the globe with staff and compass (see Figure 25), so Percy rests lightly on the huge anchor of a ship under his command. The dramatist Sir John Suckling proclaims his being, his authority as a writer specifically: as he turns the pages of a folio Shakespeare, he rests upon a rock which bears the motto of his own stability: 'Do not look for yourself outside yourself'[83] (see Figure 26). Natural authority, the portrait of Wentworth with Sir Philip Mainwaring reminds us, drew after itself attentive admiration and emulation (see Figure 27). The representations on canvas of the Caroline courtiers were intended to do no less.

The paintings of Charles I himself of course subsume many of these ideas into the most powerful visual statements of the claim of virtue to exercise government. The man in domestic harmony with his family may rule harmoniously as the father of his people; the monarch in Garter robes is the quintessence of nobility and piety. The three most

81. Brown, *Van Dyck*, plate 204, p. 202; cf. D. Howarth, *Lord Arundel and his Circle* (1985), plate 115, p. 166.
82. The phrase is from R.M. Smuts, *Court Culture and the Origins of a Royalist Tradition in Early Stuart England* (Pennsylvania, 1987), p. 204.
83. Brown, *Van Dyck*, pp. 212–14; M. Rogers, 'The meaning of Van Dyck's portrait of Sir John Suckling', *Burlington Magazine*, 120 (1978), pp. 714–5. Rogers shows that the motto is from the stoic satirist Persius.

24 *Algernon Percy, 10th Earl of Northumberland* by Van Dyck, 1636–8. Northumberland, a patron of Van Dyck, was appointed Governor of the Fleet in 1636 and Lord High Admiral in 1638.

25 *Thomas Howard, 2nd Earl of Arundel, with Alethia, Countess of Arundel* by Van Dyck, *c.* 1639. Both figures point to Madagascar which the Earl devised a scheme to colonize.

26 *Sir John Suckling* by Van Dyck, *c.* 1637. The poet and courtier accompanied Charles I against the Scots arrayed in gorgeous clothes.

27 *Thomas Wentworth, 1st Earl of Strafford, with Sir Philip Mainwaring* by Van Dyck, 1639–40. Mainwaring was Wentworth's Secretary of State in Ireland. The painting was modelled on Titian's portrait of Georges d'Armagnac with his secretary.

famous paintings of Charles I, however, depict him on horseback or with his horse and attendants 'à la chasse' (see Figures 28, 29 and 30). Here we view, at first reading, the accomplished noble hunter, the horseman, the heir to emperors mounted *à l'antique*, the martial victor riding through the arch of triumph.[84] But as we read in the literature of Caroline England, we learn that the mastery of the great horse was recommended for young princes as an education in taming the passions.[85] Specifically Sir Henry Wotton in *Plausus et Vota* depicted the king's command of the great horse as symbolic of his taming of the furies.[86] In 'Le Roi à la chasse' the beast bows its head towards the king, who strives not as a hunter but commands the natural world he surveys. His triumph is not merely over himself; it is – note the gaze of St Antoine – that of Christ, over the sins that had thrown confusion into paradise.[87]

Van Dyck did not execute only portraits at the Caroline court. In the late 1630s the artist painted at royal command the spectacular *Cupid and Psyche* (see Figure 31). In the Renaissance the myth of Cupid and Psyche (Greek: the soul) was bound up with the Neoplatonic ideas of love as the means by which the soul reaches out for the highest good and establishes command over the basest appetites. In the England of 1630, the story of Cupid and Psyche was popular at court and the subject of a long 'moral poem' by Shackerley Marmion.[88] There was a design to have the ceiling of the Queen's House at Greenwich decorated with representations of the story.[89] It is an important comment on the recurring motifs of Caroline culture that the poem and the paintings might easily be thought to have come from the world of masque.

The court masque was once dismissed, and still is by some historians, as the most narcissistic and exclusive of genres, the ultimate gesture of escapism of a court that looked inward on itself. That a monarch as hard-working as Charles devoted much time to the entertainments, however, alerts us to their political significance. The staging in Whitehall, the vying for places by ambassadors, the dancing by courtiers, most of all by the king and queen, necessarily made

84. Strong, *Van Dyck*, *passim*, esp. p. 63.
85. See my *Politics and Ideas*, pp. 51–2.
86. Thomas, 'Charles I: the tragedy of absolutism', p. 200.
87. Cf. J.S. Held, 'Le Roi à la Chasse', *Art Bulletin*, 40 (1958), pp. 139–49; and R.M. Smuts, *Court Culture*, pp. 171–7.
88. For a discussion of the symbolism, see M. Summers (ed.) *The Complete Works of Thomas Shadwell* (New York, 1927), p. cxiii. I owe this reference – and valuable discussions of this subject – to Ian Donaldson.
89. J. Harris and G. Higgot, *Inigo Jones: Complete Architectural Drawings* (New York, 1989), p. 232.

28 *Charles I on Horseback* by Van Dyck, 1637.

29 *Charles I à la chasse* by Van Dyck, *c.* 1635.

30 *Charles I on Horseback with M. de St Antoine* by Van Dyck, 1633. This was the painting displayed at the end of the gallery at St James's, along with pictures of emperors on horseback by Giulio Romano.

the masques political liturgies.[90] What made them 'the high mass of Neo-platonic monarchy performed by the whole clerisy of court' was the meanings and mysteries they communicated and mediated.[91] The theme of the masque was the imposition of order and peace on chaos and fury through the agency of the king and queen (see Figures 32 and 33). The love of the royal couple represented their ordering of their rebellious passions and hence their natural claim to rule over others.[92] The scenes of calm landscapes and classically ordered buildings in the final scenes associate, like the backdrops of Van Dyck's canvases, the command of self with more universal ideas of government. Conquering the furies of antimasques the dancers tread the orderly paces that choreograph the steps of their soul's progression to understanding that, as the preacher and playwright Thomas Goffe put it in his discussion of masque: 'he surely shall that conquers first himself sure conquer all'.[93]

It was, then, a political ideology that the masques performed at Whitehall communicated to those (courtiers, aristocrats and visitors) in positions of authority who might translate its ideals into practice within their own spheres of influence. They also reached a wider audience: books of the masques were often sent by newswriters along with copies of speeches and gossip; in the case of one entertainment 3,000 copies were printed and sold to the country.[94] Masque-like entertainments were also staged when Charles went on progress to Scotland, at Bolsover and Welbeck.[95] The Earl of Bridgewater evidently hosted such entertainments at Ludlow; the austere Wentworth held them at Dublin; there may have been similar performances in other aristocratic households.[96] They were clearly viewed as political occasions; contemporary observers frequently describe the king and courtiers as 'busy' rehearsing for masques, with all the connotations of attendance to duty.[97] The language of masque often echoed (and was echoed by) the discourse of politics; the speech welcoming Charles I

90. A. Collins, *Letters and Memorials of State . . . Collected by Sir H. Sidney* (2 vols, 1746), II, p. 621; PRO, C.115/M31/8132; PRO, C.115/M35/8386; BL Add. MS 11045, f.92v; A.J. Loomie (ed.) *Ceremonies of Charles I: The Note Books of John Finet, Master of Ceremonies 1628–1641* (New York, 1987), p. 119.
91. The phrase is from Thomas, 'Charles I: the tragedy of absolutism', p. 224.
92. Sharpe, *Criticism and Compliment*, ch. 6.
93. Thomas Goffe, *The Couragious Turke* (1632, STC 11977), sig.E.
94. Newswriters sent out copies of the masques (PRO, C.115/M31/8132: Flower to Scudamore, 15 Jan. 1631). *The Triumph of Peace* sold 3,000 copies; see G.E. Bentley, *The Jacobean and Caroline Stage* (7 vols, Oxford, 1941–68), VII, p. 1162.
95. See C.H. Herford and P. Simpson (eds) *Ben Jonson* (11 vols, Oxford, 1925–53), VII, pp. 787–814. I hope to study the politics of these two entertainments.
96. *Comus* was staged at Ludlow Castle Howarth, *Lord Arundel*, p. 114; cf. *HMC 3rd Report*, p. 83; C115/M35/8390 and below, p. 780.
97. Collins, *Letters and Memorials*, p. 621: Northumberland to Leicester, 5 Dec. 1639.

31 *Cupid and Psyche* by Van Dyck, 1639–40. This is the only mythological work Van Dyck is known to have painted at the court of Charles I.

to York in 1639 for example praised the 'eminent virtues, sublime gifts and illuminations' of the monarch that filled 'the whole universe with splendour', from a throne established on columns of piety and justice.[98] Most of all, experience and the representation of experience, play and politics, were not rigidly distinguished. When the campaign against the Scots was being prepared, Sir Henry Slingsby reflected: 'At such time we need not go to theatres to understand by fabulous representations the tragic recollections of human fortunes, ourselves shall be the actors.'[99] The following year, in *Salmacida Spolia* Charles and Henrietta Maria danced with the Scottish Duke of Lennox a masque lauding obedience and union. Masques and festivals were not, what Graham Parry and Robert Ashton have argued, distractions from

98. York City Record Office, House Books, 36, f.29. See below, pp. 642–3.
99. D. Parsons (ed.) *The Diary of Sir Henry Slingsby* (1836), p. 13.

32 The masque, *Salmacida Spolia*, scene 1: 'a horrid scene . . . of a storm and tempest'. Inigo Jones, 1640.

33 *Salmacida Spolia*, scene 2: 'the sky serene, afar off zephyrs appeared breathing a gentle gale; in the landscape were cornfields and pleasant trees . . .'. Inigo Jones, 1640.

government; they 'were not evasions of kingship but of its essence'.[100] In an era of non-bureaucratic government, in a realm that lacked a standing army, in a system of patronage, the communication of ideas and principles was a principal art of politics. The highest mysteries of cosmic harmony, and their interrelation with the government of the commonwealth and the regulation of the self, were the politics of Caroline art.

Whilst the culture of the Caroline court undoubtedly mediated an ideology, some scholars have argued for its address to narrower and more partisan concerns. Literary scholars have employed labels such as 'Cavalier drama' and 'Cavalier poetry' to categorize a uniform courtly style and aesthetic.[101] Historians have argued that the cultural divisions between 'court' and 'country' presaged and helped to shape the later divide into Cavalier and Roundhead.[102] There are serious problems with such a thesis, as I have argued elsewhere.[103] Many of those labelled 'Cavalier' dramatists and poets died before the king raised his standard, indeed before the world divided into ideological camps. The court of Charles I was a heterogeneous world, in which lived Catholics and puritans, Hispanophiles and Francophiles, the pacific and the belligerent, English and Scots. Future parliamentarians such as Warwick, Wharton and Northumberland sat for Van Dyck, along with future royalists. Holland and Lennox and the Egertons, Wharton, Fielding and Carlisle danced together in the masques. The word 'cavalier' itself conveyed no specific political sympathies in the 1630s, and its usage corresponds little to the alignments of 1642. The Venetian ambassador called the Earl of Warwick 'that cavalier' and employed the word in the plural to describe the resisters of ship money;[104] Roe described the Earl of Leicester as a gallant cavalier;[105] Arundel praised the 'brave cavallata' of the Inns who had staged the *Triumph of Peace*.[106] Clearly the word meant little more than gallant or gay blade.

In so far as there was a pre-existing ethos or style at the Caroline

100. Thomas, 'Charles I: the tragedy of absolutism', p. 199; R. Ashton. *The English Civil War* (1978), pp. 30–1; G. Parry, *The Golden Age Restor'd: The Culture of the Stuart Court* (Manchester, 1981).
101. For example, A. Harbage, *Cavalier Drama* (New York, 1936 and 1964); C.V. Wedgwood, *Poetry and Politics under the Stuarts* (Cambridge, 1960). These were important pioneering studies, for all that they now appear too schematic.
102. P. Zagorin, *The Court and the Country* (1969); P. Thomas, 'Two cultures? Court and country under Charles I', in C. Russell (ed.) *The Origins of the English Civil War* (1973), pp. 168–96. These works became textbook orthodoxy, for example in L. Stone, *The Causes of the English Revolution* (1972 and subsequent edns).
103. Sharpe, *Criticism and Compliment*, ch. 1.
104. *Cal. Stat. Pap. Venet., 1629–32*, p. 380; *1632–6*, p. 325.
105. *Cal. Stat. Pap. Dom., 1636–7*, p. 336: Roe to Exeter, 2 Jan. 1637.
106. Sheffield Central Library, Wentworth Woodhouse MS, WW/13, f.201: Arundel to Wentworth, 22 Feb. 1634.

court, it is far from obvious that it should be described as Cavalier. The swaggering young gallants of popular romance we may recognize in some contemporary comment.[107] Viscount Conway wrote to George Garrard from the court vacation at Newmarket in 1638: 'When we do not hunt we hawk . . . the rest of the time is spent in tennis, chess and dice, and in a word we eat and drink and rise up to play; and this is to live like a gentleman, for what is a gentleman but his pleasure.'[108] But there is more than a hint that Conway's tone was ironic and critical rather than congratulatory. His lively humour was often sardonic and he was after all the son of a father who had 'ever conceived honour to be active virtue employed in service'.[109] Certainly Lord President Conway's axiom was more typical of the statesmen of the personal rule. Archbishop Laud, one of nature's ascetics, perhaps predictably condemned as 'an unhappy and ungodly life' that which 'too many gentlemen do lead, to spend all their time in hunting or hawking'.[110] But he was by no means isolated at court in his puritanism. The king and queen, the papal envoy Panzani observed, were 'strictly virtuous and professed enemies to immodesty and *gallantry*'.[111] Charles for long 'earnestly wished' to establish an academy of nobility for 'the virtuous education of their children at home in safety and their preservation from the too frequent vices of the times by a diversion of their minds from idleness and vanity to noble and better employment'.[112] In default of such an academy at home, Windebank thought it best to send his son abroad to remove him from English hawking, hunting 'and worse idle courses'.[113] The Senecanism from which Arundel and Wentworth and others drew their philosophy was totally averse to the frothy gaiety we associate with the gallant.[114] William Trumbull, envoy to Brussels, advised his son to read Seneca's *De Ira* to the choleric young lad Paget with whom he was travelling in France.[115] The popularity of Justus Lipsius' edition of Seneca and his own *De Constantia* suggest (as again perhaps do the Caroline Van Dycks) that stoicism was a fashionable aristocratic pose of the age.[116] Yet it was still more a philosophy of service to the state. Trumbull

107. And, ironically, in the portrait of the Presbyterian Lord Stuart (Brown, *Van Dyck*, plate 194, p. 193).
108. *HMC Portland III*, pp. 51–2, 26 Feb.
109. For his humour, see BL, Loan MS 29/172, pp. 117, 147; *Cal. Stat. Pap. Dom., 1629–31*, p. 126. Cf. Coke MS 38: Conway to Wake, 7 Dec. 1629.
110. Quoted in R.H. Whitelocke, *Memoirs Biographical and Historical of Bulstrode Whitelocke* (1860), p. 80.
111. J. Berington (ed.) *The Memoirs of Gregorio Panzani* (Birmingham, 1793), p. 188.
112. PRO, SO 1/3, f.8v.
113. Egerton MS 1820, f.543: Windebank to Hopton, 3 Sep. 1635.
114. Howarth, *Lord Arundel*, pp. 85, 87; above, p. 137.
115. Berkshire Record Office, Trumbull Add. MS 52; cf. Trumbull MS 50, f.67.
116. See G. Oestreich, *Neo-Stoicism and the Early Modern State* (Cambridge, 1982).

had recommended Seneca to his son as part of that body of reading necessary 'towards some profession in the commonwealth'.[117] William, who learned his lesson well, quoted him back to his father: 'as saith Seneca . . . we are all members of this universe and so should conspire for the advancement of the public good'.[118] Wentworth was less out of fashion than he thought when he described to Sir George Butler his philosophy of devotion to public good: 'This you will say is Stoicism, a philosophy antiquated and grown out of fashion long ago and the practice of it for the most part an unregarded poverty . . . yet I judge it the best morality and duty of a man in employment.'[119]

Devotion to duty as well as pleasure was very much an aspect of the culture of the Caroline court. Such a commitment to duty and service was what Charles wanted to disseminate throughout the administration and the realm. The king, the Earl of Danby put it, wanted to restore the commonwealth, the public good.[120] Order required the subjection of private interests to the governance of reason. Believing that the government of the whole stood on the well-ordering of the parts, Charles and his ministers embarked on a wide variety of reforms, at the centre and in the localities, in church and state, society and economy 'to the end that there may be one uniform course of government in and through all our whole monarchy'.[121] As the king was to tell his son, 'No glory is more to be envied that that of due reforming either church or state.'[122]

The household below stairs

The campaign to regulate and reform began with the central administration. Through the various departments of the royal household attempts were made to impose below stairs that same order that was being enacted in rooms of state above. Often the need for economies provided the spur for reform but always the king's concern for order shaped its course. The household establishment had presented a problem from Charles's succession to the throne: the staff was swollen to a large number as Charles had brought to the crown his own former servants as Prince of Wales (the first since Henry VIII) and inherited those of his father. Perhaps hundreds held offices as supernumeraries and had bouge of court at the king's expense.[123] A commission of

117. Trumbull Add. MS 52, 19 Sep. 1629.
118. Trumbull MS 50, f.67.
119. Knowler, *Strafford Letters*, II, p. 39, 30 Nov. 1636.
120. *Cal. Stat. Pap. Dom., 1628–9*, p. 388: Danby to Carlisle, Nov. 1628.
121. *Cal. Stat. Pap. Dom., 1629–31*, p. 40; Larkin, *Stuart Royal Proclamations*, II, p. 10.
122. *Eikon Basilike* (1876 edn), p. 149.
123. Sharpe, 'The image of virtue', p. 236.

enquiry into the household was appointed in 1626 but little was done during the war years.[124] In 1629, however, it was reported that the horde of attendants was to be reduced to the level of Queen Elizabeth's reign.[125] The records were studied and the number of places in each department was specified; none was to be admitted into any place until the household had been reduced to its earlier establishment. Economies were ordered, in matters large and small. The number of servants allowed to royal officials was limited – presumably from fear that they dined at the king's expense.[126] Where possible, men were deprived of the right of diet and put instead on the more fixed and more accountable system of board wages.[127] The Groom of the Stool was told to purchase at the cheapest price rather than take his provisions automatically from the Great Wardrobe – an early instance of competitive tendering.[128] The numbers of carts assigned to each department on progress were listed.[129] In the royal household, Professor Aylmer concluded, the year 1629 to 1630 was the year of maximum economy as the new impetus to reform and Weston's influence made themselves felt.[130] The cost of diet fell by £12,524 to £47,196 per year where it stayed for most of the 1630s.[131] For all Weston's efforts at other reforms, little was achieved. The costs of the household, partly on account of the growing royal family, continued to rise.[132] In 1637 a commission was established to effect further economies. 'The King,' the Countess of Leicester told her husband, 'is in a greater humour of thrift than you can imagine.'[133] The commissioners sat for a day a week and there was talk of reducing those entitled to dine at court tables to the establishment of Henry VIII.[134] Little emerged from their labours and the Scots were soon distracting the Council with more pressing business. Greater success with reform would have necessitated a fundamental assault on established practices and privileges on which neither the king nor his ministers were radical enough to embark.[135]

Some efforts were made to deal with blatant corruption – not least

124. Rymer, *Foedera*, XVIII, p. 768; cf. *Cal. Stat. Pap. Dom., 1625–6*, pp. 360, 398.
125. Birch, *Court and Times of Charles I*, II, p. 36: Gresley to Puckering, 15 Nov.
126. PRO, SP 16/386/97.
127. G.E. Aylmer, 'Studies in the institutions and personnel of English central administration' (University of Oxford, D.Phil. thesis, 1954), p. 306.
128. Stowe MS 563, f.16v.
129. PRO, LS 13/30; LS 13/169, f.196.
130. Aylmer, 'Studies in the central administration', p. 285.
131. *Ibid.*, p. 286.
132. F.C. Dietz, *English Public Finance 1558–1641* (New York, 1964), p. 416.
133. PRO, PC 2/48, p. 403; *HMC De Lisle and Dudley*, VI, p. 72.
134. *HMC De Lisle and Dudley*, p. 139.
135. Cf. G.E. Aylmer, 'Attempts at administrative reform, 1625–1640', *Eng. Hist. Rev.*, 62 (1957), pp. 229–59, esp. pp. 256–7.

through an insistence upon more efficient accounting. Accounting systems had evidently been slack enough to allow many to purloin provisions without any risk of detection other than the occasional scrutiny of the porter at the gate. In November 1628 it was ordered that arrears in any department should be reckoned within fourteen days of the end of the accounting month.[136] But it is clear that accounting remained slack. In 1638 the household commissioners ordered an investigation of all accounts since 17 Henry VIII.[137] They learned that there were three modes of accounting: between the purveyors and the cofferer, the officers of the Greencloth and the sergeants of each household department and the cofferer and the king. As a consequence there was considerable room for irregularities.[138] In general the figures for valuations and sales were shown to be chaotic and corrupt, permitting royal goods to be sold off at well below their market price to the king's servants.[139] As for the cofferer's records, 'he doth not make it appear what he hath paid or left unpaid'.[140] The commissioners recommended major changes in accounting procedures; clerks of the kitchens were required to submit bills for all meals over ten dishes.[141] In the prince's household, it was ordered that the weight of beef and mutton be recorded daily and all provisions checked as they came in.[142] We cannot know what impact the atmosphere of enquiry and reform had on levels of corruption, but it is unlikely much was achieved. In 1639 it was still the porter at the gate who was entrusted to see that visitors to court 'do not purloin or carry forth provisions . . . nor suffer any silver or pewter dishes to be carried out of the court gates'.[143] Thefts, losses and corruption continued. But it may be significant that the worst figures in household finances were recorded for the first two years of the reign, 'at which time the household was unsettled and many occasions of waste and losses'.[144] At least after 1628 the situation did not get much worse.[145]

Special attention was paid to the reform of the royal wardrobe. With a new monarch and a new queen who had to be fully supplied, the costs of the Wardrobe mounted sharply early in the reign.[146] In 1628 a

136. PRO, LS 13/169.
137. *Ibid.*, f.317; *Cal. Stat. Pap. Dom., 1637–8*, p. 256.
138. *Cal. Stat. Pap. Dom., 1637–8*, p. 312.
139. PRO, LS 13/169, f.314.
140. *Ibid.*, f.320.
141. *Ibid.*, f.342; *Cal. Stat. Pap. Dom., 1637–8*, p. 520.
142. Harleian MS 7623, f.18.
143. *Ibid.*, f.15v. For instances of pilfering, see BL, Harley Roll, T2; Sharpe, 'The image of virtue', pp. 238–9, notes 69 and 71; PRO, PC 2/41/235.
144. PRO, LS 13/169, pp. 34–5.
145. Aylmer, 'Studies in the central administration', p. 154.
146. From £13,000 per annum in the later 1620s to over £27,000 in 1630–1; see Aylmer, 'Studies in the central administration', p. 296.

commission was granted to investigate abuses and settle the Wardrobe in better order.[147] A detailed report was made in 1630 on the basis of which the king and Privy Council issued orders in April.[148] A fixed sum of £16,000 per annum was assigned to the department plus £5,000 for the wardrobe of robes, and all expenditures were to be strictly accounted for.[149] The money issued by the Treasurer to the Master of the Wardrobe was to be locked in a chest and not issued without the consent of both the Master and the Clerk. The Clerk was ordered to be present at all deliveries to record the quality and quantity of goods received, in particular to check that all hangings were made with linings. The court tailors had received allowances for regular repair yet many hangings were 'in great decay and little reparation done'; all such allowances were to be scrutinized and certified by the Clerk.[150] Payment of wages and debts due prior to April 1630 was temporarily suspended so as to restore the Wardrobe finances on a sounder footing.[151] Henceforth, it was ordered, creditors' bills should be brought in immediately for settlement. The figures for wardrobe expenditure, over £27,600 for the year 1630–1, indicate that the attempted reforms had little effect. In 1631 further propositions were advanced for regulating the Wardrobe.[152] It is clear that the major problems were not solved, for in 1632 Sir Bevis Thelwall, the Clerk of the Great Wardrobe, the officer directly responsible for supervision, was himself charged with misconduct and irregular ways of making payment that had cost the king double.[153] On 17 December 1633 a commission under the great seal to investigate the Wardrobe was issued to Weston, Cottington, Pembroke, Coke and others.[154] The king, reciting the earlier orders, admitted that they had not been observed and urged a full enquiry.[155] The commissioners found the persistence of old 'scams' – tailors' bills, for instance, had been grossly inflated by the unauthorized addition of travel costs; they advised that over £6,000 a year might be saved if the officers bought not at the inflated credit prices but on fairer terms for cash.[156] Their boast that the annual charge might thereby be reduced to £20,000 was not fulfilled, but there were evidently some results. From 1634, the

147. *Cal. Stat. Pap. Dom., 1628–9*, p. 396, 26 Nov. 1628.
148. *Cal. Stat. Pap. Dom., 1629–31*, p. 235; Rymer, *Foedera*, XIX, p. 482; National Library of Scotland MS 191.
149. National Library of Scotland MS 191; *Cal. Stat. Pap. Dom., 1629–31*, p. 235.
150. National Library of Scotland MS 191.
151. Coke MS 40: draft order for Wardrobe.
152. PRO, SP 16/195/42.
153. *Cal. Stat. Pap. Dom., 1631–3*, p. 485.
154. Birmingham Reference Library, Docquets, of Letters Patent, Coventry MS 602204/319.
155. *Cal. Stat. Pap. Dom., 1633–4*, p. 325.
156. *Ibid.*, p. 454; *1631–3*, p. 589.

Wardrobe was spending an average of £22,000, a fall of £5,000 a year from the beginning of the reign – not least perhaps because once Charles 'had built up a large wardrobe of suits and cloaks in the early years of his reign, he appears to have kept them longer and to have been content with fewer replacements than his father.[157] Still in 1639, on a renewed economy drive, the king directed that the orders of the 1633 commission (themselves based on directives of 1630) were not being observed and should be reissued.[158]

Early attempts were also made to reform the procedures of the Exchequer. In October 1628 a royal signet letter to the Chief Barons asked them to investigate the pipe rolls of sheriffs' accounts which had been falsified, it was suspected, to conceal funds detained.[159] The king referred specifically to frauds by clerks of the Exchequer and instructed the barons to collect past debts and remove abuses. Ominously, one Arthur Jarvis who had been guilty of falsifying accounts was still handling them.[160] There were other inefficiencies: the king was told, for example, that it was not possible for a strict account of loan monies to be kept by the Exchequer of receipts, which he insisted on as a record that the counties might in future be repaid.[161] A book of warrants and instructions addressed by the Lord Treasurer and Chancellor of the Exchequer to the auditors offers some evidence of attempts to improve procedures and remedy abuses: requests for accounts to be hastened, for overdue rents neglected by the auditors to be collected, for better records of royal tenants and the rents they paid, for payment of copyhold fines and a prompter payment of fee farm rents.[162] Clearly, however, accounts were not properly kept up. In May 1633 financial affairs were in such a state of uncertainty that a special commission had to be established to ascertain whether Philip Burlamachi owed the king money or whether Charles owed it to him![163] Evidently transactions with Burlamachi had operated without regular procedures or warrants and the Treasury commissioners in 1635–6 after much labour still could not reduce his accounts to a proper state.[164] Sir John Coke expressed his disgust at the lapses: 'whoever will reduce a king to any other than legal accounts doth not only open a way to deceit . . . but brings confusion into the govern-

157. Aylmer, 'Studies in the central administration', pp. 201, 296.
158. *Ibid.*, p. 306; *idem*, 'Attempts at administrative reform', p. 253.
159. PRO, SO 1/1, f.178v.
160. Huntington Library, Ellesmere MS 7927.
161. PRO, SO 1/1, f.212.
162. Bodleian, Rawlinson MS C.431, ff.32, 34, 38, 48, and *passim*.
163. PRO, SO 1/2, f.141; see A.V. Judges, 'Philip Burlamachi', *Economica*, 6 (1926), pp. 286–300 and R. Ashton, 'The disbursing official under the early Stuarts: the cases of Sir William Russell and Philip Burlamachi', *Bull. Inst. Hist. Res.*, 30 (1957), pp. 162–73.
164. Coke MS 54: Coke to Juxon, 3 Aug. 1636.

ment of the revenue of the crown, the consequence whereof is worse than any particular loss'.[165] Some improvements were made as a result of the commissioners' investigations. In 1635 Charles required that all accounts since 1603 be called in and checked;[166] the same year the Treasury commissioners asked the household for a certificate of all fees and annuities paid 'together with a medium of all the receipts and the payments in your said office cast up for the five years last past'.[167] Orders were also issued to the clerk of the pipe and auditors of the Exchequer requiring them to investigate the accounts of sheriffs' bailiffs.[168] That similar requests were to be made in 1641 suggests that the 1635 reforms met with limited success. Debts were discovered then by the parliamentary commissioners – 'which we conceive if it had not been through neglect of the officers might have been before this brought in for the supplying of his Majesty's necessitous occasions'.[169] Though partisan, they were probably right. For those called upon to economize or keep strict accounts so that dishonesty would not go undetected were the very men who gained from extravagant expenditure and loose practices – what we might now call 'creative accounting'. As Viscount Wimbledon wrote to Sir Edward Nicholas, expressing no doubt a not uncommon attitude: 'what should I trouble myself to husband his Majesty's money . . . more men prosper with spending and getting the king's money than by saving it. For I see all will away and he is the wisest that getteth his part'.[170]

The commission for fees

Reform was concerned not only with those who illicitly got and spent the king's money, but also with those guilty of extorting the public's. In June 1627 Charles I renewed the commission for fees, appointed in 1610 and renewed in 1622 in response to parliamentary agitation.[171] The brief of the commission was to investigate fees charged by officials in courts of justice, administrative offices, ecclesiastical bodies and corporations, to ensure that only the prescribed sums were levied and

165. *Ibid*,; cf. Coke MS 54: Coke to Laud, 19 July 1636.
166. Aylmer, 'Studies in the central administration', p. 577.
167. PRO, LS 13/169, f.256.
168. PRO, SO 1/2, f.251v; see Aylmer, 'Studies in the central administration', p. 607.
169. Rawlinson MS C.431, f.59. See also Scottish Record Office Hamilton MS GD 406/1, 866; *Cal. Stat. Pap. Dom., 1640–1*, p. 566.
170. *Cal. Stat. Pap. Dom., 1627–8*, p. 160.
171. Rymer, *Foedera*, XVIII, p. 844; J.S. Wilson, 'Sir Henry Spelman and the royal commission on fees 1622–40', in J.C. Davies (ed.) *Studies presented to Sir Hilary Jenkinson* (1957), pp. 456–570; G.E. Aylmer, 'Charles I's commission on fees, 1627–40', *Bull. Inst. Hist. Res.*, 31 (1958), pp. 58–67.

to proceed against those who extorted higher charges. Dr Aylmer has suggested that since in January 1627 all officers were forgiven past offences in return for a payment of £1,000 each, the revival of the commission months later was 'from the first in part at least a revenue or loan raising device as well as a concession to popular discontent'.[172] There is contemporary comment to support this view. The newswriter Rossingham was later to inform the Earl of Huntingdon that 'the clerk to the commission for extortion of fees saith that he doubted not but to bring into the king's coffers above 800 thousand pounds by the way of Star Chamber fines for extorting'.[173] Since Star Chamber fines in total brought to the crown only £2,000 a year it is clear the claim was wildly exaggerated.[174] More importantly, we should not study the commission for fees as only a fiscal measure, or even as primarily one. The commission's investigations proceeded thoroughly over a wide range of offices, in London and the provinces, against favoured officials and men of little weight. In one year they met ninety times.[175] The antiquary Sir Henry Spelman was recruited to research precedents and claimed to do the bulk of the work, after a new commission issued in 1629; in 1633 he suggested they meet daily.[176] In 1632 the six clerks of Chancery came under the commissioners' examination and some found a bill against them in Star Chamber.[177] John Pory told Viscount Scudamore, 'it is thought that all the ministerial offices of any worth here about London must pass through the same purgatory, it being a fruit of the commission which hath been on foot these three years to make a scrutiny into them'.[178] Two years later Sir George Mynne, the clerk of the Hanaper in Chancery, was presented for taking higher fees than those anciently established.[179] Mynne lost his office.[180] Moreover the speeches of the Councillors in Star Chamber point strongly to concerns wider than the perennial need to raise money. Fees, the Privy Seal reminded Mynne, were for work and pains, not the automatic right of persons because they held a place;[181] Heath condemned all such 'oppressors of his Majesty's subjects'.[182] Laud, typically, wanted

172. Aylmer, 'Studies in the central administration', p. 670.
173. Hastings MS 9597, 14 Feb. 1635.
174. Below, p. 679.
175. Aylmer, 'Commission on fees', pp. 61–2; Wilson, 'Spelman and the royal commission on fees', p. 462.
176. BL Add. MS 34601, f.268; Wilson, 'Spelman and the royal commission on fees', p. 462.
177. Birch, *Court and Times of Charles I*, II, pp. 189–90: Pory to Scudamore, 1 Nov.
178. *Ibid.*, p. 190.
179. Harleian MS 4022, f.32.
180. Bankes MS 54/63. Mynne was also in trouble as an ironmaster for wrongful felling of trees. See G.E. Aylmer, *The King's Servants: The Civil Service of Charles I, 1625–42* (1961), pp. 118–19.
181. Harleian MS 4022, f.58. Often, of course, the offices were executed by a deputy; Wilson, 'Spelman and the royal commission on fees', p. 465.
182. Harleian MS 4022, f.54.

to devise a rule that would prevent the offence, not just punish the offender.[183] It is impossible to measure the results of the commission, but its thoroughness (the commissioners required a permanent clerk to organize investigations)[184] is impressive, and its well publicized activities may well have worried many into honesty.[185] Moreover Spelman's suggested reforms concerning wasteful writing and excessive clerks may have increased efficiency. It was still at work in the spring of 1640.[186] Even if there was a financial gain to the crown, there is no need to doubt Cottington's belief that 'the subject hath more reason to thank his Majesty for the service of the commissioners for exacted fees than any which hath been done this long time'.[187]

Reform and regulation

Too often the measures taken by the crown and the Council to regulate and reform have been studied only as devices for raising money. This is not to deny that in many cases desire for financial gain was an acknowledged motive. But it is worth remembering that such fines contributed little to the royal revenues during the 1630s and the fiscal motive does not itself explain why some abuses were prosecuted rather than others. Fines, in Caroline England, as today, were more a form of punishment than a source of revenue; indeed in the 1630s large fines were usually imposed for example's sake and considerably mitigated in payment.[188] Often the fiscal and reforming aspects were connected, in measures intended to restore to the crown lost rights and jurisdictions as well as lost benefits and revenue.

An obvious example is presented by the investigations into the condition of the royal forests. We have already discussed the fines arising from the renewal of forest eyres as a source of royal revenue – rightly so for contemporaries were quite aware of the financial benefit to the crown. Commenting on the eyre conducted in the forest of Dean, Edward Savage informed the Earl of Bridgewater, 'they are most of them like to pay their fines which *adds much* to the service'.[189] Savage's language makes our point: fiscal gain was an important plus,

183. *Ibid.*, f.59v.
184. Bankes MS 37/27.
185. It was renewed in 1637 (Bankes MS 54/16) and was at work in Chester that year (PRO, PC 2/48, p. 373).
186. Aylmer, 'Commission on fees', p. 66, and note 5, but note that the commission's agenda for February 1640 is in PRO, SP 46/82, f.181.
187. Harleian MS 4022, f.53, though the commission was cited as a grievance in the Grand Remonstrance. See below, pp. 928–9.
188. Below, p. 679.
189. Ellesmere MS 6514, 4 Oct. 1634.

but not the basis of the revival of forest laws. The Earl of Manchester put it even more clearly in one of his frank letters to his brother, Sir Edward Montagu, in 1630: 'We have been in the forest, not to get money [though] our charge is so great, but to put it in a state of a forest, all was so out of order.'[190] The preservation of trees was clearly of great importance to a king concerned to strengthen the navy. There was a shortage of the right sort of timber for shipbuilding and large expanses of forest were needed to maintain a supply.[191] In the forest of Dean John Gibbon was proceeded against specifically for cutting down 3,000 trees that had been selected and marked for shipbuilding, and it is evident that such abuse was common.[192] When shipwrights were authorized in 1636 to select timber in Sherwood forest it was acknowledged that those responsible for aiding them were guilty of spoliation; 'most of the officers of this forest would rather keep their custom in stealing his Majesty's wood than have it put to so profitable and honourable use'.[193] The contract with Sir John Winter concerning his lease of woods for iron works had attempted to reserve shipping timber for the crown; but the reservation was clearly not honoured and Winter was, in addition to his large fine, ordered to dismantle his furnace.[194] During the years of ship money and the strengthening of the fleet, preservation of timber was an important consideration: even in June 1641, the commissioners for the navy, recalling Winter's abuse, were arranging precise procedures for the selection and preservation of trees for the navy.[195] More generally, the casual appropriation or sale of timber meant a loss of profit to the crown at a time of a diminishing demesne and, still more important, a loss of jurisdiction and rights. Sir John Coke had adamantly expressed the view that sale of forest lands made the crown 'necessarily grow less both in honour and power', and the maintenance of both was clearly an important aspect of the programme of the 1630s.[196] The articles administered to the jury at the Windsor eyre in 1632 stress both the order of the forest, its officers, inhabitants and rules, and the need to preserve intact the king's woods, belongings and game.[197] In 1634 Chief Justice Bridgeman was instructed by signet letter that his brief was 'for

190. *HMC Buccleuch-Whitehall, I*, p. 270, 28 Oct. 1630.
191. Coke MS 40: Edisbury to Coke, 17 Aug. 1631; Trumbull Add. MS 37; PRO, PC 2 41/104.
192. Rawlinson MS D.119, ff.12, 20.
193. Arundel Castle Letters, no. 358: Newcastle to Arundel, 23 Feb. 1636.
194. Rawlinson MS D.119, f.14; Winter's contract is in PRO, SO 1/2, f.176v.
195. Bristol Record Office, Smyth of Ashton Court MS 36074/136e: Throckmorton to Smyth, June 1641.
196. P.A.J. Pettit, *The Royal Forests of Northamptonshire: A Study in their Economy, 1558–1714* (Northamptonshire Record Soc., 23, 1968) p. 66.
197. Rawlinson MS D.399, f.90ff.

redressing the great abuses which through the neglect and discontinuance of the forest laws and government there are grown so high that the said forest is thereby in danger to be utterly ruined'.[198] Justice Broughton, 'chid soundly' by Cottington 'for being negligent in stopping the spoils of the forest', proceeded to call miscreants weekly to answer on oath and even commit them to St Brevill's castle.[199] In these proceedings the protection of the forests seems more in evidence than the pursuit of fines. Sir Henry Vane astutely (and rightly) believed that it would advance his petition to secure lands in the forest of Teesdale if he offered to keep it stocked with deer.[200] The maintenance of the king's game and pleasures was still an important 'flower of the crown'.

Forest laws, however, protected not only royal privileges. The clothiers of Essex complained that the destruction of woods threatened their supplies of dye.[201] The mayor of Bristol took the initiative in petitioning the Earl of Holland, pointing out the dangers to his city and all the ports in the Severn if Dean forest were destroyed.[202] The inhabitants themselves, perhaps as early as 1630, presented to the Privy Council grievances including the spoil of timber by coal producers, the unauthorized enclosure of lands by gentlemen and the excess of cabins and cottages in the forest.[203] Their petition reminds us that the forest had sheltered many who, living on the margins of poverty, depended upon their environment, its legitimate waste and common land, for an existence. Gentry enclosure threatened that existence, as did the entrepreneurial exploitation of forest lands for manufactures. The revival of forest laws provided some protection. The jury at Windsor in September 1632 was told specifically to present oppressions of inhabitants by unjust exaction, bribe or unlicensed enclosure.[204] In negotiating enclosures with lessees, the king, as Buchanan Sharp has shown, endeavoured to secure for the inhabitants some few acres in lieu of the lost benefits of the common.[205] Justice Finch's claim that the forest laws were implemented 'without the least distaste or disaffection or complaint or clamour of his people' and the king's own expressed belief that the forest laws were for the benefit of his subjects as well as himself should not be read as disingenuous.[206] The riots in the forests

198. PRO, SO 1/2, ff.175v–176, 12 April 1634.
199. Coke MS 48: Broughton to Coke, 11 April 1634.
200. Bankes MS 43/6: file on Vane's petition, 29 June 1635.
201. *Cal. Stat. Pap. Dom., 1635–6*, p. 465.
202. Bristol Record Office, Common Council Books 3, ff.50–5.
203. Trumbull, Add. MS 37: 'Grievances of the inhabitants of the forest for Dean [1630?]'.
204. Rawlinson MS D.399, ff.90–2.
205. B. Sharp, *In Contempt of all Authority: Rural Artisans and Riot in the West of England, 1586–1660* (Berkeley and London, 1980), p. 145.
206. Rawlinson MS C.722, ff.56v–7; see Coke MS 62: Broughton to Coke, 2 June 1639.

arose from popular resistance to aristocratic encroachments on a way of life that the forest laws did more to preserve than destroy.[207] Those most incensed by the eyres were men like Sir John Winter who had developed not only manufactures but enclosed parks and estates on what were royal lands. It is of significance that despite the grievances of such as Winter being echoed in the Grand Remonstrance, the forest laws were not repealed by the Long Parliament and their value, especially with regard to preserving ship timber, was appreciated at the Restoration.[208] In reconfirming those laws, in reordering the chaos of the forests, in preserving timber and reducing waste, and in doing something to protect customary rights, as well as those of the crown, the forest eyres belong within the programme of reformation that characterized the personal rule.

Another aspect of reform were the efforts to tighten the control of trades and commodities during the 1630s. The proclamations and Council registers of the 1630s are dominated by orders regulating processes of manufacture, merchant companies and incorporations. Again historians have not been slow to point out the financial benefits to the crown of greater government control. The king exacted fees and fines for granting charters and derived customs and rents from particular trades and commodities. Some measures, the regulation of playing-card and dice manufacture for example, seem largely inspired by financial motives. In 1638 the Privy Council investigating a dispute between the brickmakers and bricklayers stipulated 'that his Majesty's duty arising from the corporation of brickmakers be not impeached in any settlement'.[209] The tobacco trade provides an obvious example of royal interest. The ban on tobacco growing in England stemmed not least from the financial benefits deriving from American tobacco that came to the Customs House in London.[210] But – even in the use of tobacco – it would be cynical to assume that only fiscal considerations motivated the desire to regulate and control. For James I's dislike of tobacco and the habit of smoking was one of the few preferences Charles I inherited from his father. In letters of 1633 to the JPs of England, informing them in what towns tobacco might be sold, the king warned that even in licensed places it should not be taken 'for wantonness and excess, provoking them to drinking and other inconveniences to the great impairing of their health and depraving of

207. Sharp, *In Contempt of all Authority*, pp. 143–5, 250.

208. S.R. Gardiner (ed.) *Constitutional Documents of the Puritan Revolution* (Oxford, 1906), p. 211 art. 21, cf. art. 25; W.J. Jones, *Politics and the Bench: The Judges and the Origins of the English Civil War* (1971), p. 96. Forest fines, as they had been levied, were condemned by the parliament. Cf below, p. 926.

209. PRO, PC 2/49/438, 30 Sept. 1638.

210. Larkin, *Stuart Royal Proclamations*, II, no. 144, pp. 307–10.

their manners'.[211] The regulation of trades and corporations was never simply a fiscal device, but a means of stabilizing and regulating, of guaranteeing rights and investments, of promoting efficiency, perhaps most of all in Caroline England of ordering through royal control. Particular trades were obviously linked to considerations of security. Charles issued proclamations tightly restricting the Eastland trade to members of that company not least on account of England's dependence on the Baltic for naval supplies, 'to maintain and increase the trade of our merchants and the strength of our navy as principal veins and sinews for the wealth and strength of our kingdom'.[212]

But even in the purely domestic realm, the king and Council equated the reformation of trade and manufacture with greater regulation. The 1630s was a decade of incorporations, often as a result of small organizations splitting off from larger to form their own companies, like the butchers, the glovers, the spectacle-makers, the felt-makers and the hatband-makers.[213] In several cases, as Professor Ashton has demonstrated for London, such government 'interference' in the organizations of the city companies was bitterly resented.[214] In 1637, similarly, the city of York was to complain that the proposed incorporation of brewsters and maltsters infringed its Elizabethan charter and the rights of its citizens to brew their own beer.[215] But not all attempts at regulation met with discontent. Often the impetus for greater control came from merchants themselves or from the consumers. Protection against foreign competition was one obvious area in which governmental control could be beneficial and was sought. A signet letter to the judges of the Court of Record in London in 1634 requiring them to take legal action against foreign tailors trading against the law clearly acted on the complaints of the 'poor handicraftsmen of the said company of Merchant Taylors' who were 'not able to maintain themselves and their families' on account of such interloping.[216]

In the sphere of wages, prices and standards, government regulation was regarded in the seventeenth century as necessary for social as well as commercial stability. The crisis of the late 1620s clearly sharpened the Council's sense of its obligation. In what was in the time of slump clearly an employers' market, the Privy Council instructed JPs to force clothiers to pay at normal rates: 'it were a great shame if for want of due care in such as are specially trusted with the execution of

211. *Ibid.*, no. 173, pp. 387–9.
212. *Ibid.*, no. 124, pp. 252–4; cf. R.W. Hinton, *The Eastland Trade and the Commonweal in the Seventeenth Century* (Cambridge, 1959).
213. PRO, PC 2/48/127; PC 2/49/347; PC 2/51/28; PC 2/50/110.
214. R. Ashton, *The City and the Court 1603–1643* (Cambridge, 1979), ch. 2, esp. pp. 72–81.
215. York House Books, 35, f.332.
216. PRO, SO 1/2, f.217v.

these laws the poor should be punished in these times of scarcity and dearth'.[217] Throughout the 1630s, too, the king and Council issued proclamations attempting to control the prices of goods. That of 1634, for example, prescribed the prices of a standard shopping list of foodstuffs and household goods for London and forbade anyone 'upon any colour or pretext whatsoever to sell . . . at higher or greater rates'.[218] The efforts to defy the market were then, as in modern economies, of little effect. The Reverend Garrard told Wentworth that as a consequence of the proclamation, producers 'will not bring [their goods] to London as heretofore, so that housekeeping in London is grown much more chargeable than it was before these proclamations were published'.[219] The government, however, persisted. In 1637 proceedings in Star Chamber were instituted against the starch-makers for illegally enhancing prices.[220] In 1636 detailed directions were issued to the clerk of the market ordering him to supervise the payment of proper wages, to end the deceits of false weights and sizes by which the consumers were abused and to punish those responsible.[221] The attention paid to such courses underlines the extent to which in the economic sphere, as in so many other branches of government, the greater regulation of the 1630s was entirely conservative in its aims. The king's insistence on closing all shops in Lombard Street, London that were not goldsmiths may offer an insight into the royal mind.[222] For it suggests as well as a concern with order above the free flow of commerce, a medieval attitude to trade, a perception of a world still held in harmony by fair prices and wages, clearly delineated streets and guild regulation, a world in which the economic preoccupations with profit, interest and competition were to be subordinated for the order of the commonweal.

What we may call the guild mentality (itself an idealization of the past) also lay behind the Caroline drive to regulate standards – in processes of manufacture and in the professions. Though again there was nothing novel about the policy, the degree of attention and energy devoted to its implementation is a characteristic of the personal rule. Proclamations were issued to prevent frauds through the false making and packing of butter casks,[223] to proscribe the use in silk manufacture of dyes that artificially increased the weight of the cloth,[224] to prohibit

217. Bodleian, Firth MS C.4, p. 533; cf. p. 507.
218. Larkin, *Stuart Royal Proclamations*, II, no. 177, pp. 408–12.
219. Knowler, *Strafford Letters*, I, p. 206, 27 Feb. 1634.
220. *Cal. Stat. Pap. Dom., 1637*, p. 240.
221. Larkin, *Stuart Royal Proclamations*, II, no. 223, pp. 519–28; cf. *ibid.*, no. 228, pp. 683–6.
222. PRO, PC 2/48/504.
223. *Cal. Stat. Pap. Dom., 1634–5*, p. 290; Larkin, *Stuart Royal Proclamations*, II, no. 189, pp. 436–9.
224. Larkin, *Stuart Royal Proclamations*, II, no. 138, pp. 289–92, and *ibid.*, no. 157, pp. 344–9.

mixing other materials with beaver in the production of beaver hats[225] – and a host of other such illicit lapses from standards.[226] In several cases grants of incorporation were given primarily to assist with control over standards. The silk manufacturers obtained an incorporation in 1631 on the basis of their promise that they would be able to reform abuses;[227] the glaziers were incorporated on the understanding that they would maintain standards.[228] The brick and tile makers, formed into a chartered company in 1632, were granted powers to set down rules for manufacture 'as may work reformation therein for the future'.[229] The policy did not always work: by 1636 the silkmen were found to be the worst offenders in the malpractices they had bonded to end.[230] The government therefore kept a watchful eye. In 1633 Charles I wrote personally to the mayor and aldermen of London complaining of the lack of skill shown by the quality controllers whose task it was to inspect the hides used by tanners, many of which had proved unfit.[231] The Privy Council set up a commission to investigate the observance of clothing standards in the West Country manufactures and to review processes of inspection.[232] Orders were sent to Oxfordshire, Gloucestershire and Wiltshire for the reformation of the manufacture of white cloths.[233] Perhaps most effective, the court of Star Chamber was used frequently to prosecute offenders. Andrew Arnold, Joseph Waybourne and others were proceeded against for the fraudulent corruption of beaver,[234] Andrew Coleman for counterfeiting seals and passing off cheap backing cloth as good Colchester stuff,[235] one Gerson for mixing earth and water to make his wood, sold by weight, heavier.[236] Other miscreants were prosecuted for mixing hartshorn with cochineal, for blending coarse wool with silk and for false packing wool to defraud purchasers.[237] The judges drew particular attention in the court to such instances of the adulteration of commodities. Similarly they proceeded against those who breached professional codes, as the Council endeavoured to enforce apprenticeship laws and to regulate the practices of attornies, apothecaries and

225. *Ibid.*, no. 293, pp. 695–7.
226. For example, proclamations no. 165, 241, 277 and 278.
227. *Cal. Stat. Pap. Dom., 1636–7*, p. 302.
228. *Cal. Stat. Pap. Dom., 1637*, p. 68.
229. Bankes MS 52/4.
230. *Cal. Stat. Pap. Dom., 1636–7*, p. 302.
231. PRO, SO 1/2, f.157v.
232. C. Clay, *Economic Expansion and Social Change Vol. II: Industry, Trade and Government* (Cambridge, 1984), pp. 247–8.
233. PRO, PC 2/42/257.
234. *Cal. Stat. Pap. Dom., 1639–40*, p. 414. Cf. H.E. Phillips, 'The court of Star Chamber' (University of London, MA thesis, 1939), p. 278.
235. Phillips, 'Star Chamber', p. 278.
236. *Ibid.*, p. 281.
237. Rawlinson MS C.827: Star Chamber, 25 April 1639.

the like. In 1638 Richard Edwards was fined for compounding ill medicines, being one of the doubtless many self-appointed apothecaries who was not a member of the College of Physicians.[238]

The impetus for the campaign for improved standards came at times from manufacturers whose reputations suffered from the malpractices of their less honest fellows. It was the Merchant Adventurers who first suggested an enquiry into the West Country cloth trade;[239] the merchants trading to France in March 1635 petitioned for the better supervision of the Welsh cottons because poor standards had compromised their commerce.[240] In 1639 the Company of Pinmakers claimed that shoddy pins stamped with a counterfeit seal of quality were undercutting their superior product; they petitioned the Council to investigate.[241] But to others, not all of them offenders, the extent of government supervision was a cause of great irritation.[242] Sir Francis Seymour, for instance, argued that the commission for the reformation of cloth manufacture was an affront to the dignity of the JP, an implication that he did not know what was for the good of his county.[243] Other reactions were more extreme. At Bradford in April 1632 Anthony Wither, one of the commissioners, was thrown in the River Avon which, as he ruefully recalled, 'was twenty feet deep'.[244] Such complaints and responses may indicate, along with other evidence, that the commission was beginning to have an effect that had not been felt before. In the regulation of standards of manufacture, as in so much else in Caroline England, conservative programmes were enacted with radical vigour.

Reform and enterprise

Reformation embraced, as well as the regulation, the expansion and improvement of trade and manufacture, and in particular efforts to increase the proportion of European commerce in English hands. As throughout the early modern period, the government did not want for advice from (often self-appointed) pundits who proffered sensible schemes along with pipe dreams, and promised vast profits more of which were illusory than real. An advice paper in the Herriard manuscripts urged the Council to establish a silk-finishing industry, to

238. Phillips, 'Star Chamber', p. 278. Cf. (for attornies) PRO, PC 2/45/268.
239. Clay, *Economic Expansion*, II, pp. 247–8.
240. *Cal. Stat. Pap. Dom., 1635*, p. 307.
241. *Cal. Stat. Pap. Dom., 1638–9*, p. 531.
242. As the patentees had been a principal grievance in the 1620s, not least on account of their interference in local affairs.
243. *Cal. Stat. Pap. Dom., 1634–5*, p. 3.
244. *Cal. Stat. Pap. Dom., 1631–3*, p. 212.

dye and dress all cloth at home (evidently the Cockayne project had not dampened this idea), to produce beer for export, and to restrict the export of iron so as to impede French and Dutch shipbuilding and expand the English share of the carrying trade.[245] The Council itself evidently commissioned detailed enquiries into the trade and manufacture in foreign hands and calculated the loss to England at over £620,000 a year.[246] In most cases the rival identified was also the model recommended: the Dutch. The author of the Herriard manuscript advised as the solution to several problems the emulation of Dutch practice. In a packet of measures, one of his suggestions was the need for a government-sponsored company to vie with the Dutch in the profitable fishing trade. 'Never was there more cause than now,' the paper argued, 'for your Majesty to set forward this blessed work in causing your subjects with others to fish in your own seas and in your own coasts which lie more properly for the purpose than Holland.' The idea was not new: the Dutch herring trade, their 'chiefest goldmine', had long been the subject of envy; from the 1610s onwards Sir Walter Raleigh, and the economic theorists Thomas Mun and Edward Misselden, had advocated a rival British enterprise.[247] But in the later 1620s the idea very much came to the fore in several different proposals promoting what was one common purpose. In November 1629, Sir William Monson put to the Council suggestions for establishing a fishing business around the isles of Orkney, Shetland and Lewis;[248] a scheme for the fishing of pilchards to be underwritten by private investors has also survived dated that year.[249] The following year, 1630, the pamphlet *Britain's Busse*, first published in 1615, was reissued as *England's Royal Fishing Revived*.[250] Sensing the moment, the author set down the exact costs of equipping, manning and provisioning a fleet of busses and ended with a plea to his fellow countrymen to finance them and to the king to incorporate them into a joint stock company which would grow as profits flowed in.[251]

In 1630 the first official steps were taken, when a commission was established to enquire into the fishing off the coasts of England and Scotland. During July the king acquainted the Lord Chancellor of Scotland with his design and in November the Scottish commissioners were appointed and given a copy of the brief sent to their English

245. Hampshire Record Office, Herriard MSS, Box 06: 'Affairs in the time of Charles I'.
246. Coke MS 38: 'Considerations concerning navigation, trade and merchants'.
247. W.R. Scott, *The Constitution and Finance of English, Scottish and Irish Joint Stock Companies to 1720* (3 vols, Cambridge, 1910–12), II, p. 361.
248. *Cal. Stat. Pap. Dom., 1629–31*, p. 109.
249. *HMC Ancaster*, pp. 403–5.
250. S.E., *Britain's Busse* (1615, STC 21486 and 1630, STC 21487).
251. *Ibid.*, sig. F1v.

counterparts.[252] Secretary Coke, an ardent exponent of the scheme, liaised between the commissioners of the two nations and forwarded to the Privy Council in Scotland the propositions approved in England for a fleet of 200 vessels of 30–40 tons.[253] The deliberations soon ran into difficulties. The Scots proved jealous to preserve the fishing off their lochs and isles to themselves and wanted the English debarred – much to the annoyance of the king, who would tolerate no 'hindrance to this general work which may so much import the good of all our kingdom'.[254] Private investors were also reluctant to come in until the fishing grounds had been chosen and there was a prospect of imminent activity.[255] The commissioners continued to discuss and exchange drafts, carefully read and interlined by Charles.[256] By the summer of 1632 steps were taken to form the company entitled the Society of the Fishery of Great Britain and Ireland.[257] Under the protectorship of the king, a council of twelve (six English, six Scots) was to administer the company and the subordinate organizations which were to be established in various provinces, towns and burghs.[258] A court was proposed to issue orders and resolve disputes.[259] In January 1633, in the hand of Edward Nicholas, we find the first list of adventurers with notes of their promises to purchase stock totalling £11,750.[260] The eventual failure of the society was sown here with its first planting. For it commenced with 'ludicrously insufficient capital' and many who had promised to buy stock backed off.[261] The tiny fleet set out was therefore too insignificant to compete seriously with the Dutch and too feeble to defend itself – from them and the Dunkirk pirates who preyed on them. What had begun as a blow against the Dutch ended up at their mercy.[262] In 1633 it was reported that the Dutch had taken over the fishing trade, 'which will not be recovered without some more vigorous enterprise, as causing the city of London to be engaged therein, to lead on others and to make a fair entrance into the work'.[263]

Initial disappointments, however, offered no incentive to investors: by 1635 less than £10,000 had been raised in capital and losses com-

252. National Library of Scotland MS 82; Advocates' MS, 31/2/16.
253. See D. Coke, *The Last Elizabethan: Sir John Coke, 1563–1644* (1937), pp. 210–14.
254. Advocates' MS 31/2/16, ff.16–69, esp. f.26, quotation f.37; cf. *Cal. Stat. Pap. Dom., 1631–3*, p. 237.
255. Scott, *Joint Stock Companies*, II, p. 363.
256. Coke MS 41: Noy to Coke, 7 March 1632; Advocates' MS 31/2/16.
257. The commission is PRO, SP 16/221/1.
258. PRO, SP 16/229/79, 80, 83.
259. PRO, SP 16/229/94.
260. *Cal. Stat. Pap. Dom., 1631–3*, p. 510.
261. Scott, *Joint Stock Companies*, II, p. 366.
262. PRO, 31/3/67, ff.40–40v, 9 April 1632; PRO, SP 16/229/79.
263. PRO, SP 84/146, f.74: E. Misselden to the Earl of Arundel.

pelled extra assessments on the 1633 subscribers.[264] In 1635 the king attempted to shore up the company by exempting it from the jurisdiction of any court other than the Privy Council.[265] Nicholas advanced the suggestion that all gentlemen of the bedchamber should be compelled to become adventurers.[266] Though the suggestion evidently came to naught, it points to the king's close involvement with the project. When the commissioners complained that they were disturbed by Highlanders when fishing the lochs, Charles wrote to the Scottish Council and the Earl of Seaforth to request their assistance.[267] A committee was set up to hear the company's grievances and the ship money fleets were directed especially to offer them protection from the Dutch and Dunkirkers.[268] In March 1637 the association was the subject of a full enquiry; the king himself in Council ordered an investigation of how stock had been employed, accounts of returns and losses and suggestions for better management.[269] Charles also wrote personal letters, such as that to the bishop of Durham in 1637, urging him to rally assistance for the society in his area;[270] a Council ban was imposed on fishing in the Thames from March to August to ensure a stock for the company.[271] Still the losses mounted.[272] In 1639, the king ordered another investigation.[273] Significantly on this occasion, the Earl of Pembroke claimed that, though there were serious losses to Dunkirkers and stock was still desperately needed to set out busses, the society was beginning to make a profit from the herring trade.[274] The Scots war, however, added to the difficulties and the company virtually ceased to trade. An effort was made in 1640 to revive it by means of a lottery, but it was not until the end of the century that the plans came to fruit.[275] The Society for the Fisheries of Great Britain bears witness to the near insurmountable obstacles to the promotion of grand schemes for the improvement of trade. But its history is also evidence of the king's personal attention to the promotion of a project 'which tends so much to the public good'.[276]

Another project that captured the king's attention also took impetus from the example of the Dutch: the attempts to drain and reclaim for

264. Scott, *Joint Stock Companies*, II, pp. 366–7.
265. *Cal. Stat. Pap. Dom., 1635*, p. 141.
266. *Ibid.*, p. 264.
267. *Ibid.*, p. 271; Bankes MS 37/14.
268. Bankes MS 37/14; below, pp. 596–7.
269. *Cal. Stat. Pap. Dom., 1636–7*, p. 489: order of 8 March 1637.
270. PRO, SO 1/3, f.32, 31 March 1637.
271. PRO, PC 2/46/40, 14 March 1636.
272. See the statement of losses 1637–8 in *Cal. Stat. Pap. Dom., 1637–8*, p. 579.
273. *Cal. Stat. Pap. Dom., 1639*, pp. 528–9, 28 Sept.
274. *Ibid.*, p. 533; cf. PRO, PC 2/50/655, Sept. 1639.
275. Scott, *Joint Stock Companies*, II, p. 372.
276. *Cal. Stat. Pap. Dom., 1635*, p. 271: Charles I to Earl of Seaforth, 13 July.

agriculture the flooded lands of the bleak Fens. The geography of the Fens had for long been seen as a special problem that required special jurisdictions. The low-lying land, many rivers and erosion of banks as boats were dragged over them and carts plied their trade made it essential to take action to prevent the waters claiming even more of the land. The commissions for sewers, first established by statute in 1427, collected special rates for the maintenance of walls, ditches and gutters and presented the names of those who damaged them. Their job was to maintain the status quo. Towards the end of the sixteenth century, that great age of projects in England, the more ambitious idea of draining the marshes attracted interest. James I, partly because the crown held extensive estates in the Fens, showed great interest: surveys were commissioned and several reports were made. Yet though a session of 1619 agreed that the rich soil might yield an abundance of benefits and James employed the Dutch engineer, Cornelius Vermuyden, to embark on the enterprise, nothing of substance occurred before the king's death in 1625.[277] Charles too, at first, seemed inclined to leave the business to local initiative.[278] In 1629, however, H.C.'s *A Discourse Concerning the Draining of the Fens and Surrounded Grounds* was published and drew attention to the project.[279] H.C. pointed to the potential wealth of what was 'a little kingdom itself: as much and as good ground . . . as the States of the Low Countries enjoy in the Netherlands.[280] He also reminded the king of the benefits that might accrue to the monarchy from the sixteen royal manors on the south side of Boston.[281] H.C.'s appeal to the need to undertake the work may have struck a chord. Certainly from 1629 the state papers show a marked increase in royal and Conciliar interest in the draining of the various parts of the Fens.

In March 1629, a contract was granted to Vermuyden to drain the marshlands of Yorkshire, Lincolnshire and Nottinghamshire.[282] The county assizes of Lincoln were ordered by royal letter to inform the county that the king regarded the work as for the benefit of the commonweal and would punish any who resisted it.[283] In the summer, a letter to the commissioners of sewers in Norfolk and

277. A.M. Kirkus (ed.) *The Records of the Commissioners of Sewers in the Parts of Holland, 1547–1603*, Vol. I (Lincolnshire Record Soc., 54, 1959), introduction; H.C. Darby, *The Draining of the Fens* (Cambridge, 1940), pp. 35–8; M E. Kennedy, 'Charles I and local government: the draining of the East and West Fens', *Albion*, 15 (1983), pp. 19–31.
278. Darby, *Draining of the Fens*, p. 37.
279. H.C., *A Discourse Concerning the Draining of the Fens and Surrounded Grounds in the Six Counties of Norfolk* (1629, STC 4270).
280. *Ibid.*, sig.A.3v.
281. *Ibid.*, sig.A.4v.
282. PRO, SO 1/1 f.204, 11 March.
283. *Ibid.*

Suffolk announced Charles's desire to see the work undertaken and ordered a tax be levied to finance it.[284] Typically not content with the slow pace at which such enterprises moved, Charles wrote again to the Lincolnshire commissioners in February 1630, commanding them quickly to conclude a bargain with the undertakers so that work might get under way that summer.[285] By the early 1630s, after years of discussion, work was commencing on the Great Level of the South Fens under the Earl of Bedford, the East and West Fens (led by Sir Anthony Thomas), the Eight Hundred Fen near Boston (entrusted by Charles to Sir William Killigrew) and the neighbouring area under the direction of the Earl of Lindsey.[286] The king continued to keep a watchful supervision over the various schemes: he advised Lindsey to increase the taxation he levied; he ordered resistance to be checked.[287]

The projects, however, ran into all sorts of trouble. There was resistance to the work from the beginning from local vested interests. The 200 foreigners brought to work on the draining project at Hatfield cannot have been welcome to the locals – especially as, according to Bishop Neile, they were willing to do more work for a groat than the English would do for sixpence.[288] Fear of the loss of the marshland as common aroused the hostility of the poor, who eked an existence gathering 'reeds, fodder, thaches, turves, flaggs, hassocks, segg, flaggweed for fleggeren coltors, mattweede for churches, chambers, beds and many other fen commodities', or taking the fish and fowl that were found in abundance.[289] Though compensation was allowed for, the people 'will not pay any considerable rent for what they say have been their common' and so the undertakers brought in French tenants, further sharpening local hostility to the venture.[290] Such tensions led to lawsuits, which Vermuyden claimed cost more than the value of the land.[291] They burst out in scenes of violence in which the populace, acting as forerunners of the Luddites, beat down the ditches and works which had been completed in the name of progress.[292] Such hostility produced a widespread reluctance to pay the rates necessary for the work, and led to disputes between the undertakers and the inhabitants over payments and obligations. Vermuyden himself spent

284. PRO, SO 1/1, f.227, June 1629.
285. PRO, SO 1/2, f.4v, 20 Feb.
286. Darby, *Draining of the Fens*, pp. 38–48.
287. PRO, SO 1/2, f.12, 12 Feb. 1633.
288. *Cal. Stat. Pap. Dom., 1636–7*, pp. 12–13: Neile to Laud, 23 June 1636. This is not an unfamiliar story in our own time.
289. Darby, *Draining of the Fens*, pp. 49–53, quotation p. 52.
290. PRO, SO 1/2, f.251; *Cal. Stat. Pap. Dom., 1637*, p. 195.
291. *Cal. Stat. Pap. Dom., 1637–8*, p. 12.
292. See K. Lindley, *Fenland Riots and the English Revolution* (1981), for a fine description (albeit unsatisfactory explanation) of riots; *Cal. Stat. Pap. Dom., 1637–8*, p. 503; *1639*, p. 232.

time in custody for his own refusal to contribute his proportion after tangled disagreements with the locality.[293] Worst of all, the undertakers quarrelled with each other and allegations were made by all sides of breaches of covenant.[294] Despite such obstacles and setbacks, the king remained committed to a scheme that he believed to be for the welfare of his subjects, even if they did not recognize it. The averseness of the owners of the land and others to contribute, Charles wrote to Lindsey in language that goes to the heart of his values, 'must not prejudice the public good'.[295] To scotch rumours that the whole scheme was a project of private men, the king wrote to the commissioners for King's Sedgemoor to announce his resolution to take a speedy course in the matter.[296] In 1637, frustrated at the lack of action, Charles announced to the commissioners for sewers his determination to take on himself the draining of the Great Fen.[297] Within days a commission ordered a taxation of 20 shillings an acre to finance the ditching and draining, 'to be paid by the said inhabitants . . . they being to receive benefits by the draining thereof'.[298] When complaints came in of work inadequately carried out, the king demonstrated that his protection of undertakers was matched by a concern to see that the draining was 'really and truly performed' by appointing commissioners to inspect alleged defects.[299]

How successful then was the drainage? In answering such a question it is difficult to plot a path between the exaggerated boasts of the undertakers and the complaints of those who were opposed to the undertaking from the beginning. There was confusion too about the expected level of dryness in winter and summer seasons.[300] Bedford's Great Level was not drained to the satisfaction of local inhabitants, despite the commissioners for sewers passing it, and Charles, removing the earl from his charge, accepted the complaints.[301] But by no means all met with failure. In 1634, one Charles Harbord, the king's Surveyor-General, surveyed the work carried out near Boston by Sir Anthony Thomas. The enterprise had been beset by many delays but the results in the end were not discouraging. Despite the locals' complaints, Harbord reported that Thomas and his consortium had fulfilled their contract. Only 3,000 acres of the whole East and

293. PRO, SO 1/2, f.127; Coke MS 45: Cottington to Coke, 4 June 1633.
294. PRO, PC 2/43/525.
295. PRO, SO 1/2, f.127.
296. Coke MS 43, 11 Oct. 1632.
297. Ellesmere MS 6748/43, 18 March.
298. *Ibid.*, 28 March.
299. *Cal. Stat. Pap. Dom., 1635–6*, p. 297; cf. Kennedy, 'Charles I and local government', pp. 23–4.
300. Darby, *Draining of the Fens*, pp. 53–4.
301. Gardiner, *History of England*, VIII, pp. 295–6.

West Fen remained under water and the undertakers even planned, beyond the initial bargain, to make the river navigable.[302] There were defects – no ground had been set aside to guarantee the perpetual maintenance of the work (1,500 acres had originally been agreed) and Harbord feared that insufficient defence had been provided against the winter floods from the uplands. But he believed that there were remedies for such ills and that the undertakers were willing to carry them out. In general the ground was judged 'fit for arable, or meadow, or pasture' and indeed was so used until the outbreak of civil war.[303] In October 1639, a petition to the Privy Council concerning the low prices of grain in Hatfield Chase referred to the abundance of the crop, 'where it is much increased by the draining of the level'.[304] In May 1640 Richard Ligon, reporting to Killigrew on the Eight Hundred Fen, wrote: 'Upon my arrival here I find but little water standing in the Fen, and I do believe in a few days all will be run off.' For all that, Ligon added, 'yet the country go on still to do us what mischief they may', denouncing fen drainers in elections to parliament.[305] Ligon was confident enough to invite commissioners appointed by parliament to inspect the works and see how free the land was of water. His confidence missed the point. In large part the opposition to the drainage of the Fens was an emotive resistance to change, to the erosion of a way of life potentially and actually threatened by common bog being transformed into agricultural land.[306] Some historians have been as emotional in their verdict on the scheme. Dr Clive Holmes writes passionately of 'the deployment of royal authority to crush a peasantry'.[307] There is no need to be so emotional or condemnatory. Charles entered personally and vigorously into the draining of the Fens because he believed it 'so good and so public a work', bringing the benefits of a 'rich and industrious life' of improved husbandry to wasteland.[308] In Gardiner's words, 'he desired both that the rich should be benefited and the poor should not be wronged'.[309] By the end of the century, the very real benefits of the policy were beginning to be seen.[310]

302. Coke MS 49: Harbord to Coke, 6 Sept. 1634, calendared in *HMC Cowper II*, p. 68.
303. Darby, *Draining of the Fens*, p. 46.
304. *Cal. Stat. Pap. Dom., 1639–40*, p. 24.
305. *Cal. Stat. Pap. Dom., 1640*, p. 111.
306. As H.C put it, some preferred 1,000 acres with nothing to 500 rich ones (*The Draining of the Fens*, sig.B.2v).
307. C. Holmes, *Seventeenth Century Lincolnshire* (Lincoln, 1980), p. 124; cf. Kennedy, 'Charles I and local government', p. 31.
308. Kennedy, 'Charles I and local government', p. 25; PRO, SP 16/187/76; cf. PRO, SO 1/1, f.207; SO 1/2, f.134; SO 1/3, ff.244, 272.
309. Gardiner, *History of England*, VIII, p. 299.
310. Darby, *Draining of the Fens*, ch. 3.

Projects and improvements

The scheme to drain the Fens was perhaps the greatest of what were hundreds of projects for improvement supported by the king and Council during the decade of personal rule. The very word 'project' has often been sufficient to suggest the worst facets of Stuart government – the promotion of dubious enterprises dedicated to the rapid gain of crown or courtiers at great cost to society. There can be no doubt that some fall into this category and that considerations of profit weighed heavily with an impoverished monarchy. But the projects of the 1630s should not all be judged by the critical speeches of the Long Parliament. As Dr Thirsk has splendidly demonstrated, projects had a long and respectable history. They took life during the 1540s and 1550s, the decades of the commonwealthsmen, and belong to the era of fertile ideas for the improvement of economy and society that produced pamphlets such as *The Discourse of the Common Weal*. Burghley patronized and issued patents of monopoly to protect many new ideas, inventions and processes and Henry Howard, Earl of Northampton, took a great interest in them during James's reign.[311] From the later years of Elizabeth's reign, the financial exploitation of the power to grant a monopoly tarnished the support of legitimate projects. Significantly, however, the support of new processes and companies was exempted from the restrictions of the Monopolies Act of 1624, perhaps because it was recognized that the development costs of new native manufactures required a monopoly.

Several of the projects proposed and supported in the 1630s belong in the best tradition of inventiveness for the improvement of the economy and society. Thomas Russell put forward proposals for the setting up of copper mines in Cornwall to furnish the realm with a metal much needed for shipping.[312] A patent was granted to James Vanderbrooke for making turves 'after the Dutch manner' from the wastes of moors.[313] A scheme to make salt from seawater attracted much interest on account of the English dependence on French supplies for the fishing industry.[314] Patents were issued for promoting more efficient ways of growing carrots,[315] and to Nathaniel Waterhouse and others for new methods of fertilizing arable ground.[316] Among the papers of Attorney-General Bankes we find a myriad of other schemes

311. J. Thirsk, *Economic Policy and Projects* (Oxford, 1978); K. Sharpe, *Sir Robert Cotton 1586–1631: History and Politics in Early Modern England* (Oxford, 1979), pp. 122–3.
312. PRO, SO 1/2, f.204.
313. Bankes MS 11/63.
314. Bankes MS 11/32.
315. Bankes MS 11/55.
316. *A Direction to the Husbandman in a New, Cheap and Easie Way of Fertilizing* (1634, STC 6902).

which were undergoing investigation and report: for making clay pipes and white writing paper, for new smiths' furnaces, watermills and laundry houses.[317] The enterprising David Ramsey alone boasted the discovery of new methods of raising water from deep pits, making hard iron soft and enabling boats to sail against strong winds.[318] Some projects, for all their chequered history, were forward-looking and remain with us today. The establishment of an overseas mail service and the erection of a domestic running post by Thomas Witherings were schemes of the loftiest ambitions and broadest vision.[319] William Ryley's petition for a patent to insure the homes of Londoners against fire at a cost of 12d. in £20 was perhaps ill-timed amidst the Scottish crisis of 1638.[320] Not for another half century, until after the Great Fire had razed the capital, was his scheme translated into practice. Mr Wolfen, who claimed, the same year, to have developed a smokeless fuel, had even longer to wait for a suitably ecologically-sensitive-market.[321]

Though in all these cases, the crown sought to benefit from the grant of a patent, the quality of the service or product to be offered was often to the fore in consideration of petitions and proposals. Petitions were usually referred to Privy Councillors. The grant to George Danby of a patent for the sole melting of copper into ingots was made on the proviso that 'if this grant prove prejudicial to the commonwealth then upon signification from his Majesty or the Privy Council it is to determine'.[322] The Council's ears were not closed to complaints. Lord Keeper Coventry, hearing when in Kent of the abuses of his patent by a licensed tobacco seller, reported the complaint to the Board.[323] Clearly, however, many grants of monopoly were cynically exploited by courtiers for their own profits and deeply unpopular with the people.[324] But such were condemned as much by royal ministers as by any other critics, Wentworth branding projectors as 'the very scandal of his Majesty's affairs and the reproach of all his upright and well-meaning ministers'.[325] In April 1637, according to the Earl of Northumberland, the king sitting with the committee for

317. Bankes MS 11, *passim*.
318. *Cal. Stat. Pap. Dom., 1629–31*, p. 382.
319. See K. Sharpe, 'Thomas Witherings and the reform of the foreign posts', *Bull. Inst. Hist. Res.*, 57 (1984), pp. 149–64.
320. *Cal. Stat. Pap. Dom., 1637–8*, p. 392; though an anonymous petitioner had tried before: *Cal. Stat. Pap. Dom., 1635–6*, p. 80.
321. *Cal. Stat. Pap. Dom., 1637–8*, p. 490.
322. *Cal. Stat. Pap. Dom., 1635–6*, p. 237.
323. Kent Archives Office, Dering MS U350/010 (a).
324. Aylmer, 'Studies in the central administration', p. 353. Professor Aylmer sees this as a feature especially of the second half of the decade.
325. Knowler, *Strafford Letters*, II, pp. 76–7: Wentworth to Northumberland, 25 May 1637; cf. Wentworth MS WW/10, ff.85–7.

trade investigated a large number of patents and 'fifty of them were damned'.[326] Evidently some of the most unpopular grants were those that had failed to meet the Council's expectations. In March 1639 the Council again reviewed patents granted on false assurances and promises;[327] the following month a proclamation announced the revocation of commissions or grants for licensing brewers, cottages and inmates, compounding with offenders touching tobacco, for transporting sheepskins and a horde of others.[328] The need to make concessions to popular feeling during the Scots war clearly influenced the timing of the proclamation: the committee for war had advised that unpopular patents be recalled before men were levied for the army to go against the Scots.[329] But there is no need to doubt the sincerity of the Council's claim that:

> Whereas divers grants, licences, privileges and commissions have been procured from his Majesty, some under his Great Seal of England and some others under his privy seal, signet or sign manual, upon *pretences* that the same would tend to the common good and profit of his subjects, which since *upon experience* have been found prejudicial and inconvenient to his people, contrary to his Majesty's gracious intention in granting the same . . . and in their execution have been notoriously abused, He is now pleased . . . to publish and declare [them] . . . utterly void.[330]

As Charles had once put it, ill success was not evidence of ill intention.[331] The failure of projects to fulfil their promises was an expression more of the weaknesses in, than cynical exploitation of power by, Caroline government.

Even the most notorious of all Caroline projects needs to be studied in the context of endeavours to improve the economy as well as bring money to the Exchequer. The scheme to manufacture soap by a process that required only native English commodities – olive oil and rape – as opposed to imported foreign potash had first been put forward in 1623.[332] The project was revived in December 1631 when a group petitioned to be incorporated for the manufacture of whitesoap 'of the materials of this kingdom only'.[333] In January 1632 the Society of Soapers was formed, 'his Majesty intending the advancement of

326. Knowler, *Strafford Letters*, II, p. 71: Northumberland to Wentworth, 28 April 1637.
327. *Cal. Stat. Pap. Dom., 1638–9*, p. 99; PRO, PC 2/50/209.
328. Larkin, *Stuart Royal Proclamations*, II, no. 283, pp. 673–6.
329. *Cal. Stat. Pap. Dom., 1638–9*, p. 99.
330. Larkin, *Stuart Royal Proclamations*, II, p. 674; my italics.
331. Huntington Library, Temple of Stowe MSS, Parliament Box 13: draft answer to Remonstrance.
332. Dietz, *English Public Finance*, p. 264.
333. *Cal. Stat. Pap. Dom., 1631–3*, p. 212.

the native commodities of this realm'.[334] Though they were given no monopoly, except over their own process of production, the company was authorized to test the quality of all soaps and prohibit the manufacture of those it deemed to fall short of standard. As well as promising £20,000 a year to the king, the soapers undertook to retail their superior and native product at the low price of 3d. the pound.[335] A royal proclamation of June 1632 confirmed the new company's privileges, announced the procedures for quality control and prescribed that only rape and olive oil be used in the manufacture.[336] The hope was that the new process might assist in 'setting on work the natives and people of this realm, whereby the subjects thereof have attained to great wealth and riches, and the same have always been of the more advantage and benefit when they have been made of materials arising within our own dominions'.[337]

For all the good intentions, however, the project ran into immediate difficulties and the new soap met with consumer resistance. The Newfoundland merchants who could not sell their oil were little pleased.[338] The old soap manufacturers who often used fish oil protested at the ban and at the power given the new company to judge the respective quality of the new and old product. Indeed they claimed 'that the soap made by the patentees washeth not so white nor so sweet nor goeth so far'.[339] Behind their protest was more than the special pleading of a vested interest: there was genuine dissatisfaction with the new product. In April 1633 a group of aldermen and commoners of London, having tested the new soap, reported to the mayor that for washing coarse linen it was satisfactory: 'but for goodness, sweetness and merchantableness it is far inferior to the best soft soap and not so fit to be used for washing fine linen'.[340] The Privy Council did not ignore the complaints. Faced with charge and countercharge, it ordered in December 1633 the Lord Mayor and aldermen to conduct an independent test. None of us brought up on the earliest and crudest of television commercials can read the account of what happened without humour. Two laundresses were asked each to wash a basket of dirty linen, one with the old, the other with the new soap. At the end of the trial it was found that the new soap lathered better, that clothes washed in it were 'as white and sweeter' than those laundered with the old soap, and that 'it goeth further'; it was even

334. Larkin, *Stuart Royal Proclamations*, II, p. 356.
335. Gardiner, *History of England*, VIII, p. 71.
336. Larkin, *Stuart Royal Proclamations*, II, no. 161, pp. 355–9.
337. *Ibid.*, p. 396.
338. *Cal. Stat. Pap. Dom., 1634–5*, p. 393.
339. PRO, PC 2/43/272.
340. *Cal. Stat. Pap. Dom., 1631–3*, p. 321.

gentler on the hands.[341] In support of their own findings, the mayor and aldermen also forwarded certificates from over eighty persons (including countesses!) to make the seventeenth-century equivalent of the claim that nine out of ten women preferred New Soap to brand X.[342] Complaints against the new product were dismissed as ignorant or malicious. Armed with the report, the Council wrote to the JPs of England in February recommending the new soap and issued a proclamation confirming all the company's privileges.[343] The complaints, however, did not subside, and the old soap continued to be manufactured.[344] Evidently the king continued to listen to grievances: in October 1634 Lord Savage informed the Earl of Bridgewater that 'his Majesty' in Privy Council did 'hear some complaints against the new soapmakers and London news is that [they] shall be put down'.[345] The newswriter Rossingham repeated the rumour: on summer progress the clamour of the poor against the new soap had led the king to discuss with the old soapmakers.[346] By January 1635 the old soapmakers were negotiating to recover their trade. Without the political support of Cottington for the new company they might have succeeded.[347] By May 1637 after bitter feuds in Council the old soapers got their business again promising the king 8d. a ton. 'Everybody,' reported William Gorges to Thomas Smyth, 'is like to go the sweeter for this in their lining.'[348]

The story of the soap patent undoubtedly casts light on some of the shadier aspects of Caroline England: factional intrigue, personal interest and the quest for gain. The crown itself derived over £29,000 per annum in payments and fines from the incorporation of the soapmen and the tonnage they offered.[349] But we should not forget the claim, repeated in letters and proclamations, that the project had won support not least from the king's care 'for the advancement of the native commodities of our kingdoms' and 'the employment of many of our poor people'.[350] Even when the old soapmen were reinstated in 1637, it was stipulated that no potash should be imported for the manufacture;[351] then as throughout mayors and JPs were instructed

341. Larkin, *Stuart Royal Proclamations*, II, p. 405.
342. Gardiner, *History of England*, VIII, p. 73.
343. PRO, SP 16/252/21; above, note 336.
344. See H.E. Matthews (ed.) *Proceedings, Minutes and Enrolments of the Company of Soapmakers, 1562–1642* (Bristol Record Soc., 10, 1940), p. 195 and PRO, C.115/N9/8851; C.115/N3/8555.
345. Ellesmere MS 6514, 4 Oct. 1634.
346. PRO, C.115/M36/8431: Rossingham to Scudamore, 29 Aug. 1634.
347. Gardiner, *History of England*, VIII, pp. 74–5.
348. Smyth of Ashton Court MS C.51/10: Gorges to Smyth, 29 May.
349. Bodleian, Clarendon MS 20, no. 1539.
350. Larkin, *Stuart Royal Proclamations*, II, pp. 356, 429.
351. *Ibid.*, pp. 582–8: 'A proclamation touching the Corporation of Soapmakers', 28 Dec. 1637.

to ensure that excessive prices were not charged.[352] Like the earlier Cockayne project, the patent for a new soap was placed in the wrong hands and proved unsuccessful, but the reasons and intentions behind it – a governmental desire to stimulate native manufactures – make it, like other projects, part of the story of attempted reforms of economy, society and government in early Stuart England.

The Privy Council

Central to all the programmes of reform – of the central administration, of trades and manufactures, and (as we shall see) of the localities – was the principal organ of government in Caroline England: the Privy Council. In 1628 the Council itself was in need of reformation. During the years of Buckingham's hegemony little heed had been paid to the Council's advice. Differences between Councillors had spilled from the chamber into factional rivalries; important decisions were taken in private, as contemporaries complained, rather than discussed at the Board. As an administrative and executive organ the Privy Council was weakened by being required to carry out policies in the determination of which it had had little say and, still more, by the removal from the Board of powerful Councillors, such as Arundel, with whom Buckingham had quarrelled. By the late 1620s there was a crisis of counsel which was seen to be part of the overall crisis of state.[353] The death of Buckingham, however, provided an opportunity for the resumption of normal courses and the decision to rule for a time without parliaments necessitated the restoration of the Council as an effective advisory and executive body.

Days after Buckingham's death, Lord Percy had pondered whether Charles would govern alone, rely on one or two confidants or entrust business to his Council.[354] Though the king involved himself closely in the business of government, after 1628 in emulation of Henry VIII's practice and in fulfilment of Heath's hopes he ruled in conjunction with his Privy Council rather than through secret advice.[355] Whilst Charles had strong views on aspects of policy, there is abundant evidence that he encouraged open and free discussion of important issues and that Councillors felt able to express themselves frankly. The

352. *Ibid.*, pp. 583–4.
353. Cf. K. Sharpe (ed.) *Faction and Parliament: Essays on Early Stuart History* (Oxford, 1978), pp. 37–42; and *idem*, 'Crown, parliament and locality: government and communication in early Stuart England', *Eng. Hist. Rev.*, 101 (1986), pp. 336–9.
354. *Cal. Stat. Pap. Dom., 1625–49*, p. 292: Percy to Carlisle, 3 Sept. 1628.
355. PRO, SP 16/178/3; J. Haywarde, *History of Henry the Eighth* (1632, STC 13088) reminded readers how Henry VIII frequented the Council often and took no decision before discussion (p. 19).

Venetian ambassador's early observation of the king's willingness to listen to advice is confirmed by Charles's own letter to the Earl of Marlborough in 1627: 'do not hide from me those rubs that hinder your business, ever putting me in false hopes till it be too late to help; but let me timely know your impediments . . .'.[356] The same exhortation was written into the oath of the Privy Councillor in 1632: 'you shall in all things to be moved, treated and debated in Council faitefully and truly declare your mind and opinion according to your heart and conscience'.[357]

Charles was involved with his Council almost on a daily basis. The evidence concerning the frequency of his personal attendance at the Board is beset by difficulties. When the king was present, it was ordered in 1630 that no clerks should attend, which makes the record perhaps less than reliable.[358] Other evidence suggests that Charles was in attendance for at least part of a meeting on more occasions than the Council register lists him as present.[359] As well as attending more frequently than his father,[360] Charles evidently participated fully in Council discussion.[361] Weckherlin refers to the king at the Board having 'moved' to grant the informers a large proportion of the fines on butchers who raised the price of victuals.[362] Sometimes the king went ahead with a course – 'against most of the Lords' opinion';[363] mostly he went with Council advice, especially unanimous counsel, even when, as with the decision to call the parliament of 1628 and the Short Parliament, it went against his inclinations.[364] Charles evidently prepared carefully for meetings – there are notes of Council business

356. *Cal. Stat. Pap. Venet., 1625–6*, pp. 26–7; cf. *Cal. Stat. Pap. Dom., 1625–49*, p. 302; *1627–8*, pp. 256–7.
357. PRO, PC 2/42/1.
358. *Cal. Stat. Pap. Dom., 1629–31*, p. 373; Lambeth Palace MS 943, p. 178, orders of 3 Nov. 1630.
359. For example, Bankes MS 42/33; PRO, PC 2/42/536. The king is not listed as present in the register, but is described as sitting in Council.
360. Charles sat almost daily in 1629 (*Cal. Stat. Pap. Venet., 1629–32*, p. 8); attended four of seven meetings in June 1636 (*Cal. Stat. Pap. Dom., 1635–6*, p. 525); four of six in August and September 1637 (*Cal. Stat. Pap. Dom., 1637*, p. 403); all the meetings of September 1638 (*Cal. Stat. Pap. Dom., 1638–9*, p. 2) and fifteen of twenty meetings in April 1640 (*Cal. Stat. Pap. Dom., 1640*, p. 103). These figures are more reliable than calculations from lists of attendance in the Council registers, for the reasons cited in note 359.
361. *Cal. Stat. Pap. Venet., 1625–6*, pp. 26–7; *1632–6*, p. 280.
362. Trumbull MS 54, 26 May 1630.
363. Trumbull MS 543/2, 5 Aug. 1638; cf. his annoyance at the Council's acting without him in the case of Bishop Bridgeman, when Charles made it clear that he 'liked not well that you interpose in a business not left to you, of which his Majesty hath a special care'. See B. Quintrell, 'Lancashire ills, the king's will and the troubling of Bishop Bridgeman', *Trans. Hist. Soc. of Lancashire and Cheshire*, 132 (1983), pp. 74–90.
364. R.P. Cust, *The Forced Loan and English Politics, 1626–1628* (Oxford, 1987), p. 72ff; below, pp. 851–2.

in his hand.[365] He even attended committees of the Council and communicated their resolutions to the full Board.[366] The presence and participation of the king in Council deliberation appears to have increased after Weston's death. With the Scottish crisis and preparation for war, his attendance became frequent. But throughout the 1630s Charles's presence was never a cause for surprise. As Weckherlin wrote to Secretary Coke in 1639, the king was 'as usual . . . at the board without any extraordinary affairs'.[367]

Even when the king was not in attendance, the Council acted as his principal consultative body: the junction box which brought together the various strands of information and where decisions were made and passed to the king for approval.[368] The resolution for suppressing the gazettes in 1632 was taken, for example, 'by general consent of the lords'.[369] On important matters, especially foreign affairs, the Council referred matters back to the king who often conferred with a smaller committee.[370] Even routine Council propositions were promptly reported to him.[371] The course that led to ship money, as we shall see, reveals what may have been the typical process in king–Council co-operation. Options, possibilities and precedents were searched, the Council analysed and summarized the pros and cons and left Charles to make the final decision.[372] For his part, there was little on which the king did not consult them. In 1636 the Venetian ambassador wrote that 'the king does nothing and decides nothing except after the most mature and weighty consultation'.[373] Professor Larkin has concluded that most of the royal proclamations of the 1630s were, as they claim, drawn up with the advice of Council. The decisions whether to ally with France or declare neutrality, whether to dissolve and summon parliaments, were put to the Council and its committees. Only the business of Scotland was not communicated to the Council Board – because the northern kingdom had its own separate Council, as government. When the Prayer Book rebellion made Scots affairs a concern in England too, Charles set up a committee of the English Council to deal with it and kept the Council informed of his dealings with the Covenanters.

365. For example *Cal. Stat. Pap. Dom., 1634–5*, p. 451.
366. *Ibid.*, p. 520; *Cal. Stat. Pap. Dom., 1635*, p. 11. Cf. Lambeth Palace MS 943, p. 193.
367. Coke MS 63, 25 Aug. 1639.
368. The French envoy Poigny said that Charles did nothing without his Council (*Cal. Stat. Pap. Venet., 1632–6*, p. 280). Cf. Charles's own remarks on the importance of counsel in *Eikon Basilike* (1876), p. 198.
369. Coke MS 42: Windebank to Coke, 22 Oct. 1632.
370. Coke MS 51; *Cal. Stat. Pap. Dom., 1635*, p. 402.
371. Coke MS 42: Windebank to Coke, 22 Oct. 1632.
372. Below, pp. 550–52.
373. *Cal. Stat. Pap. Venet., 1636–9*, p. 55.

Just as Charles was concerned to make the Council Board a body genuinely representative of the realm, so he regarded his Council as the 'representative body' of his own majesty.[374] Orders instructed Councillors to behave with the gravity that set an example and commanded authority, 'to be a rule and precedent of good order both to our court and kingdom'.[375] The king disliked quarrels between Councillors; in the wake of the feud between Holland and Weston, in April 1633, he ordered that any Councillor issuing or accepting a challenge to a duel should lose his place.[376] As representatives of royal majesty, when Councillors attended the royal chapel in the king's absence none present was to remain covered.[377] When he journeyed to Scotland in the spring of 1639, Charles commended the care of his wife and the prince to his Council, requiring them to attend the queen every Sunday.[378] While the Council was left to govern in the king's name, Windebank in Whitehall acted as the channel of communication daily with Coke and Charles I himself. Throughout the 1630s, quite unlike the previous decade, the process of decision-making in government involved a dialogue and partnership between the king and his Council.[379]

The business of the Council expanded greatly during the decade of personal rule. In part this arose from the suspension of parliaments: local grievances and petitions that might have been aired in the Commons came to the Council. Still more increased business stemmed from the king's own activity – from his determination to see a programme of reforms enacted. The responsibility for the administration, communication and enforcement of royal policies lay often with the Council alone. It was the Council's task to organize, receive and analyse the detailed reports, censuses and enquiries which, a feature of Caroline government, were requested in the process of framing and implementing royal programmes. Monthly returns from JPs required from 1630 by the Book of Orders,[380] censuses of aristocrats and gentlemen living in London and of all foreigners resident in the capital,[381] on top of the 'stacks' of routine letters and reports posed a nearly insurmountable problem of organization. The vast business, correspondence and supervision generated after 1634 by ship money

374. PRO, SP 16/375/1; Hastings MSS, Miscellaneous Box.
375. PRO, SP 16/375/1.
376. *Cal. Stat. Pap. Dom., 1633–4*, p. 14. For Charles's intervention to stop Holland and Newcastle duelling in 1639, see Coke MS 63: Weckherlin to Coke, 15 Aug. 1639.
377. PRO, SP 16/375/1.
378. PRO, PC 2/50/208.
379. Cf. G. Huxley, *Endymion Porter: the Life of a Courtier* (1959), p. 238; C. Roberts, *The Growth of Responsible Government in Stuart England* (Cambridge, 1966), p. 75.
380. *Acts of the Privy Council, 1630–1*, p. 213. Below, p. 459.
381. Bankes MS 14 62; PRO, PC 2/42/290; PC 2/43/65; PC 2/44/61, 317; PC 2/46/133.

turned difficulties into impossibilities. During the 1630s an energetic monarch of bureaucratic temperament placed the principal institution of a non-bureaucratic system of government under the greatest strain. It is only remarkable that for most of the time the small body of active Councillors, and their even smaller support staff, managed to bear it without breaking.

Little has been written about the procedures and politics of the principal organ of government in early modern England. Where for the parliaments of the early seventeenth century, in addition to the formal journals of the Houses of Commons and Lords, we have a wealth of diaries, copies of speeches, lists of precedents, evidence of debates, divisions, that is of the political process at work, the surviving Council documents that can be certainly identified are few in number. The Council registers are full and complete for Charles's reign. But we have no continuous set of clerks' notes, and no personal memoirs revealing of Conciliar discussions. The surviving private papers of secretaries of state Windebank and Coke, and of clerks such as George Weckherlin and Edward Nicholas ('the busiest man in the Caroline government')[382] offer occasional glimpses inside the Council chamber, but no correspondence still radiates, as does that of MPs and news-letters about parliament, the heat of debate. The political discourse and activity of the Council is largely closed to us. But, for all the deficiencies of evidence, we may learn more about the Council than has been written, and gain a clear sense of the reforms and developments in procedures enacted during the reign of Charles I.

The early Stuart Council was still more a branch of the medieval royal household than an organ of bureaucratic government. Though the Council met at times in the Star Chamber its usual place of meeting, the Council chamber, faced the king's bedchamber at Whitehall.[383] It also met at Greenwich, Oatlands and Hampton Court and other royal palaces when it followed the king on progress.[384] Committees of the Council, having usually no official meeting place, were convened most probably in the chambers of one of the prominent courtiers who was a member; the council of war, for instance, met in the Lord Chamberlain's lodgings.[385] When the king was absent for a long period – in Scotland in 1633 and 1639 – many Councillors went with him, underlining the sense of personal service and counsel from which the Privy Council took its origin and name. On such occasions those

382. Aylmer, 'Studies in the central administration', p. 371.
383. See Starkey, *The English Court*, p. vi. The Council often used Star Chamber days for its meetings. See too Trumbull Add. MS 36 and E.R. Turner, *The Privy Council of England* (2 vols, Baltimore, 1927), I, pp. 86–91.
384. BL Add. MS 34324, f.238.
385. *HMC Cowper II*, p. 210; cf. PRO, SO 1/2, f.51v.

who remained at Whitehall to govern in the king's name appear to have regarded themselves as the secondary limb of the body. In 1633, Windebank feared that if a circular letter (for a contribution to the Palatinate) were signed by the Councillors in London only it would carry less weight.[386] When Nethersole was examined for overstepping his authority in the matter, though the Council in London conducted the enquiry, the decision about the outcome was referred to those closer to the king in Edinburgh.[387] Similarly in 1639, Laud wrote to Coke acknowledging that he and his colleagues in London would be less in the picture than those in Scotland; he only petitioned that 'there should be strict correspondence and communication of affairs and occurrences' between the two – 'except such things as it shall please his Majesty to reserve from our knowledge'.[388] The Council was a body of servants of a personal monarch.

Indeed the Council was as important as a collection of powerful individuals as it was as a body; or perhaps it is better to say that the authority of the Board and of the individuals who comprised it was inextricably interwoven. During James I's reign (after 1612) and especially the years of Buckingham's rule, contemporaries complained of a Council of nonentities. Members of the Commons, as well as grand figures such as Arundel, called for the appointment of powerful aristocratic counsellors whose land, prestige and local influence might strengthen the Board.[389] After 1628, Charles appears to have paid careful attention to the constituency of his Council. The recruitment of the Lords Presidents of the North and the Marches and of the Secretary of State for Scotland made the Council more representative of the realm; the appointment of individuals like Wentworth, Newcastle and Northumberland added substantial landed influence (especially in the north) to the Council. Further consideration was had in 1640 'whether it will not be fit to call some of the country nobility to the Board'.[390] Such care and consideration suggest an acute awareness on the king's part that the Council was a broadly political body as well as a narrowly functional institution, that membership of the Board bound powerful individuals to the government, even if they had no formal office within it. Not all Councillors, especially such 'political' appointments, were expected to attend meetings: Sir Julius Caesar's note of 1625 on the Privy Council informs us that only those

386. *Cal. Stat. Pap. Dom., 1633–4*, p. 116.
387. *Ibid.*, p. 122; cf. Coke MS 51, 8 Aug. 1635.
388. *HMC Cowper II*, p. 223, 26 April 1639; cf. P. Haskell, 'Sir Francis Windebank and the personal rule of Charles I' (University of Southampton, PhD thesis, 1978), p. 435.
389. K. Sharpe, 'The Earl of Arundel, his circle and the opposition to the Duke of Buckingham, 1618–1628', in Sharpe, *Faction and Parliament*, p. 277; cf. Sharpe, 'Crown, parliament and locality', pp. 336–7.
390. PRO, PC 2/40/1; *Cal. Stat. Pap. Dom., 1640*, p. 634; below, pp. 946–9.

with lodgings in court were accustomed and expected to attend regularly.[391] However, when summoned by the Lord President or secretary to the Wednesday and Friday meetings, every Councillor was obliged to appear or send in his excuse.[392] And it is clear that during the 1630s the most important business was referred to the full Board; for when only a few Councillors were present various businesses – the posts, the punishment of a libeller, a response to the Dutch ambassador – were deferred.[393] The actual attendance of Councillors clearly fell short of what was required by orders drawn up in December 1630. Some meetings were attended by as few as four or five of about forty Councillors. But the average number present, a dozen or thirteen, usually included the principal officeholders or those who, other evidence indicates, were at the time wielding the greatest influence.[394] Laud, Windebank, Lord Keeper Coventry and the Earl of Manchester, Lord Privy Seal, were consistently among the most frequent attenders; Holland attended well below a third of the meetings except, significantly, in his bid for power and influence in 1636; the increasing attendance of Northumberland and Vane charts perhaps their rise to power towards the end of the decade. Overall the attendance of many with burdensome office and commitments elsewhere (we recall Windebank was on over thirty committees),[395] not to mention lands and families in the country, is not only an example of diligence; it is evidence itself of the revived importance of the Council as the principal organ of influence and government.

Council meetings were carefully prepared by the secretaries of state who, in the absence of a Lord President, acquainted the Council with the business of the day. Windebank's notes listing the '11th proposition' and the '14th and 15th proposition' (the city magazines) suggest an organized agenda and formalization of business.[396] Petitions were heard on Wednesdays and Fridays and only then 'if the greater occasions of state do not hinder'.[397] After 1635 the Council met on Sundays to review ship money payments and returns.[398] Thirteen or fourteen meetings a month were therefore quite common in the second part of the decade.[399] Ministers met privately in advance of Council meetings

391. BL Add. MS 34324, f.238.
392. Lambeth Palace MS 943, p. 177.
393. Trumbull Add. MS 54, 21 May 1630; PRO, PC 2/43/252; Coke MS 51: Windebank to Coke, 6 Aug. 1635.
394. These are my own calculations. Cf. Haskell, 'Windebank', appendix D (Privy Council membership and attendance).
395. Haskell, 'Windebank', p. 88.
396. Coke MS 43: Windebank to Coke, 22 Oct. 1632.
397. Lambeth Palace MS 943, p. 177.
398. *Cal. Stat. Pap. Dom., 1635*, p. xxiv.
399. For example *Cal. Stat. Pap. Dom., 1637*, p. 171, May.

to co-ordinate their discussions, as the Treasurer and Chancellor of the Exchequer appear to have done on Thursdays.[400] During the 1630s it became established practice at the end of a meeting to list the business unfinished or referred so that matters would not, as had often happened in the House of Commons, fall by default.[401] The list then often prescribed the agenda for the next assembly. For the dozen or so Councillors who formed the quorum of regulars the amount and range of business was colossal. On many subjects the Councillors could not themselves hope to have personal knowledge or expertise. The evidence for the decade, however, indicates an impressive thoroughness; the Council took pains to undertake full investigations and obtain expert advice before taking decisions. Prospective patentees were called to the Board to explain their schemes; the background to petitions presented was often carefully researched.[402] The judges were summoned in 1633 to advise on responses to the Book of Orders;[403] a question concerning the clergy's contribution to a rate was referred to legal counsel for consultation of the records and precedents.[404] Proclamations, it seems, were finalized for publication only after drafts had been referred to those knowledgeable or concerned in the matter: the Lords of the Admiralty, for example, checked the proclamation concerning the manufacture of saltpetre before it was issued in 1635.[405] Though the results of Conciliar investigations and efforts at times fell short of anticipation, the care taken over their proceedings is striking.

The principal means by which the Council coped with its vastly increased business was the development and refinement of the committee system. As Professor Elton has argued, though a large Council had political advantages, the daily business of government was more effectively handled by a smaller body.[406] Committees of the Council were not new to the personal rule. But under James I they appear to have been *ad hoc* assemblies formed to deal with an issue and then dissolved. During the 1630s they developed an institutional life of their own. Committees became permanent and regular: that for Ireland met on Wednesday mornings, the committee for war on Thursdays, that for the ordnance on Friday mornings before the full Board in the afternoon.[407] Moreover the committees themselves spawned subcommittees, both of temporary and longstanding duration. The

400. *Cal. Stat. Pap. Dom., 1633–4*, p. 351.
401. *Ibid.*, p. 266; *Cal. Stat. Pap. Dom., 1634–5*, pp. 378, 531.
402. Trumbull Add. MS 55.
403. Lambeth Palace MS 943, p. 185.
404. Trumbull Add. MS 55.
405. *Ibid.*, 16 Jan. 1635.
406. G.R. Elton, 'Tudor government: the points of contact II – the Council', *Trans. Royal Hist. Soc.*, 5th series, 25 (1975), pp. 195–212.
407. PRO, PC 2/41/1.

committee for the restoration of St Paul's cathedral was an offshoot of that for charitable uses;[408] in 1638–9 sub-committees for the militia, for the king's journey to York and for the business of government in his absence reported to the 'grand committee' at Whitehall every Thursday and Saturday.[409] Whilst it is clear that some of the most important committees kept a separate formal record (as the Council of War had its own 'committee book'), it is not clear that all did.[410] It may be that some proceedings of committees, especially those attended by a Council clerk, were recorded in the Council registers themselves; some are among the private papers of Windebank, Coke and Nicholas; most have not survived.[411] Certainly the proceedings of committees became increasingly formal. Windebank's notes for the committee for trade suggests that the procedure for reading and discussing propositions closely followed that of the Privy Council;[412] the sub-committee for St Paul's was formally thanked for its work at the Board.[413] Council chamber keepers attended on the committees as they did on the Council.[414] Payments to Council clerks for their extra duties attending committees are added evidence of their institutionalization and importance: Sir William Beecher received the large sum of £500 for his long attendance on the committee for Ireland;[415] Sir William Boswell served the committee for war for four years with his assistant.[416]

Increasingly, it seems, much of the preparation of important business was entrusted to the committees. When Laud told Roe in April 1634 that because he was not a member of the foreign committee, he had little to say in foreign affairs, he was not guilty of special pleading.[417] The committees were often where the influence was wielded. A mark of their enhanced importance is the order of 1630 for diligent attendance and the removal from membership of anyone who absented himself on three occasions.[418] By removing business from the full Board the standing committees for much of the decade prevented the Council from being paralysed by a myriad of particular and detailed problems and still enabled considerable attention to be given to such particular concerns. The Irish committee devoted five meetings

408. PRO, PC 2/42/144; PC 2/45/373.
409. *Cal. Stat. Pap. Dom., 1638–9*, p. 340.
410. *Ibid.*, p. 389.
411. Aylmer, 'Studies in the central administration', p. 50. Some of the seemingly poorly attended Council meetings may, in fact, be committee meetings.
412. For example, *Cal. Stat. Pap. Dom., 1634–5*, p. 513.
413. PRO, PC 2/42/144.
414. PRO, PC 2/43/542.
415. *Cal. Stat. Pap. Dom., 1635–6*, p. 340.
416. PRO, PC 2/42/50.
417. Above, pp. 143–5.
418. Lambeth Palace MS 943, p. 178.

between 1630 and 1632 to investigating the petition of the Earl of Nithsdale for a grant of the proceeds of some Irish rents.[419] The committee system placed massive burdens on the few men who sat on them, but the evidence suggests a remarkably painstaking attention to the business with which they were entrusted.

As well as the development of the committee system, business was greatly facilitated in the 1630s by improvements in the procedures and records of the Council. In November 1630 orders were drawn up for the conduct of Council business, formalizing and regularizing Sir Julius Caesar's observations of practice in 1625.[420] After the Lord President or secretary acquainted the lords with the business of the day, debate was to proceed with freedom and confidentiality. Discussion was to be ordered, respectful and to the point: 'everyone,' it was decreed in an admonition that might have been useful in parliament, 'is to speak with respect to the other, and no offence to be taken for any free advice, but as little discourse is to be used as may be for saving of time.' 'And when any Lord speaks [in] the Council he is to be uncovered and good attention is to be given without interruption by private conference and with regard that no more than one speak at once.' Secret business was conducted in closed court and not recorded in the register. Debate was forbidden in the presence of any petitioners or parties to a cause. If the Councillors could not agree then resolution was taken after voting. There was evidently even a proxy system of sorts: on the matter of sweet wines in 1633 Treasurer Weston, unable to be present, 'had left his vote unto my Lord Cottington'.[421] But, in order to maintain the prevalent ideals and norms of unity and 'consensus', votes were not published and majority decisions stood as the order of the whole Board.[422]

The 1630 orders also defined more closely the duties of the clerks of whom there were four ordinary and five or six extraordinary. Except when the king was present, a clerk was always to attend for a month's duty, aided for the first week of the month by the clerk of the previous month and for the last week by his successor for the next 'that so he may acquaint himself with the business depending against the time he comes to wait'. Subsequent orders to the clerks reveal a growing sophistication in the keeping of Council records. In November 1631 it was decreed that all Council orders should be entered in the register within a week (and letters within two weeks).[423] The following year

419. PRO, SO 1/2, f.99v.
420. Lambeth Palace MS 943, pp. 177–8, calendared in *Cal. Stat. Pap. Dom., 1629–31*, p. 373.
421. Hampshire Record Office, Sherfield MS, XXXV: letter of John Elzye, 23 May 1633.
422. Cf. M. Kishlansky, 'The emergence of adversary politics in the Long Parliament', *Journ. Mod. Hist.*, 49 (1977), pp. 617–40.
423. PRO, PC 2/41/218.

the clerks were instructed to keep a new book for each month, in which they were also to enter in the margin the subject of every order and for which they were to make an index of entries for ease of reference.[424] Former books were divided among the four clerks so that they too could be indexed. At the end of his period of attendance each clerk was to bring his book signed with his name for the inspection of the Board.[425] From 1634–5 Council decisions that created precedents for future consultation began to be listed at the back of the register.[426] Still further refinements in record-keeping were discussed. Among Windebank's memoranda of business pending in July 1635 we find 'better ordering of the Council books, more secrecy, the record to be better kept'.[427] Clerks began to keep lists of matters left unresolved at the end of their waiting month;[428] inventories were taken of books, records and manuscripts in the Council chest;[429] there is a reference to a keeper of the Council archives.[430] Increased demands for bureaucratically efficient records so increased the burdens on the four clerks that each took on two assistants.[431] But the clerks' assistants were not permitted to attend Council meetings and the burden of business mounted: the clerks were ordered to make an abstract of the returns to the commission for charitable uses.[432] Nicholas, though he continued in his regular duties as a clerk, must have found the organization of ship money writs and returns more than a full-time job. In 1636 the clerks were required to check and verify all orders before presenting them to a Councillor for signature.[433]

If we follow Wallace Notestein's criteria for the winning of the initiative by the House of Commons, we cannot but conclude that the elaboration and refinement of Council records and procedures bears witness to the dominance of the Council in the administration and government of Caroline England.[434] Certainly as the historian reads through the Council registers he is struck by a fullness, neatness and organization that were clearly the foundations of a more efficient institution.

How efficient, then, was the Privy Council as a consequence of the reforms of the personal rule? In the end, with this as other measures

424. PRO, PC 2/41/514.
425. *Cal. Stat. Pap. Dom., 1631–3*, p. 307.
426. PRO, PC 2/44, at end of book.
427. *Cal. Stat. Pap. Dom., 1635*, p. 296.
428. *Cal. Stat. Pap. Dom., 1634–5*, pp. 378, 513; *1637*, p. 580.
429. *Cal. Stat. Pap. Dom., 1637–8*, p. 482.
430. *Cal. Stat. Pap. Dom., 1636–7*, p. 319.
431. Chester Record Office, Brereton MS CR/63/2/702, f.66v.
432. PRO, PC 2/42/325.
433. PRO, PC 2/45/359.
434. See W. Notestein, *The Winning of the Initiative by the House of Commons* (1924).

taken, because Charles I effected no radical institutional changes, but invigorated and developed existing practices, success depended upon personalities. Manifold problems remained. A Privy Council order dealing with the abuses of a patentee for tobacco, 'happening in Mr Dickenson's waiting month, by reason of his sickness and since of his death, hath been hitherto laid by and unaffected'.[435] In 1635 ship money writs arrived late owing to the 'miscarriage' of Council messengers.[436] Even Windebank in 1640 held on to Council papers and so prevented their being entered in the register.[437] One Dymock who was in charge of keeping the Council chest sold the register of Edward VI's reign to a bookseller![438] Innovative plans to rationalize secretarial labour by putting one man, Edward Nicholas, in charge of ship money writs and dispatches floundered 'in regard it might have been an injury to the clerks of the Council'.[439] Occasional blanks in the registers suggest that the clerks did not always work to the high standards laid down. There were limits to the Councillors' own willingness to serve. In 1637 Sir Henry Vane complained to Wentworth, 'what labour it is even in the most important affairs to assemble a committee'.[440] Given human weaknesses, the logistical problems of moving around royal houses and the vast workload, the Council doubtless acted at times on too little information, proceeded too tardily, and failed to ensure the effective execution of its orders. But when this historian with only one office to look after and limited business to attend to reads that a man as deluged with paper as Nicholas could in 1638 dig out and forward immediately to Secretary Coke a paper he had prepared eight years before, it is hard to restrain admiration.[441] Whilst the very system of personal government was beset by limitations, the reforms of the 1630s enabled the Council to function impressively within them.

During the first half of the personal rule, the reformed Council was to act as the centre for the implementation of a broader programme of reform which was carried beyond Whitehall into local society and government. It was to receive thousands of petitions and enquiries. The Book of Orders and the quest for an exact militia were to add massively to the Council's burdens. The imposition and administration of ship money, especially after 1635, was to swamp the government and ultimately defeat the programme of domestic social reform. Yet

435. Dering MS U350/010 (a): Coventry to Dering, 19 Jan. 1635.
436. *Cal. Stat. Pap. Dom., 1634–5*, p. 563.
437. R. Scrope and T. Monkhouse (eds) *State Papers Collected by Edward, Earl of Clarendon* (3 vols, Oxford, 1767–86), II, p. 122: Windebank to Charles I, 25 Sept.
438. *Cal. Stat. Pap. Dom., 1636–7*, p. 449.
439. *Cal. Stat. Pap. Dom., 1634–5*, p. 243.
440. Knowler, *Strafford Letters*, II, p. 87, 1 Aug.
441. Coke MS 57, 7 March 1638.

until the different needs and priorities of the mid-decade diverted it, the success of the Council (as we shall see) in enacting the reform and renovation of the counties was by no means unimpressive. Before we leave Whitehall, however, to observe the government's programme in the shires, we must turn to a concern of the highest priority to Charles I: the reformation of the Church of England.

VI

'THE RIGHT ESTATE OF THE CHURCH': CHARLES I, WILLIAM LAUD AND THE REFORMATION OF THE CHURCH

The king and the church

For all the research on early modern England, the nature of the Church of England and the religion of the English laity remains one of the dark corners of the historical terrain. Where the ecclesiastical history of Charles I's reign is concerned, much recent scholarship has perhaps more obscured than clarified the policies of the king and his bishops. The historiographical consensus has it that the 1630s saw a revolution in the Church of England both in theology and liturgy. With the succession of the new king, the argument goes, a new party emerged to dominate the episcopal bench. The Arminians challenged the orthodox predestinarianism of the Elizabethan and Jacobean church; they pressed a rigid conformity to innovative ceremony and ritual; they ruptured the harmony and peace of the church which had been the achievement of the 1559 settlement.[1] In the religious revolution

1. The orthodoxy began to be established in N. Tyacke, 'Puritanism, Arminianism and counter-revolution', in C. Russell (ed.) *The Origins of the English Civil War* (1973), pp. 119–34. The argument is developed and modified in Tyacke, *Anti-Calvinists: the Rise of English Arminianism, c.1590–1640* (Oxford, 1987). The thesis has provoked a major controversy: see P. White, 'The rise of Arminianism reconsidered', *P&P*, 101 (1983), pp. 34–54; Tyacke and White, 'Arminianism reconsidered', *P&P*, 115 (1987), pp. 201–29; P. Lake, 'Calvinism and the English church 1570–1635', *P&P*, 114 (1987), pp. 32–76 and the correspondence in the *Times Literary Supplement* [*TLS*] August and September 1987, pp. 884, 899, 922, 955, 1017. See also P. Collinson, *The Religion of Protestants* (Oxford, 1982) and *idem*, *The Birthpangs of Protestant England* (1989) and for an invaluable contextualization, H.R. Trevor-Roper, *Catholics, Anglicans and Puritans* (1987), ch. 2. Despite the controversy, the Tyacke thesis is more or less taken as read by C. Russell. However, a major critique has appeared which has yet to be answered in S. Lambert's powerful 'Richard Montagu, Arminianism and censorship', *P&P*, 124 (1989), pp. 36–68. A full and persuasive new account is found in P. White, *Predestination, Policy and Polemic: Conflict and Consensus in the English Church from the Reformation to the Civil War* (Cambridge, forthcoming) and in J. Davies, *The Caroline Captivity of the Church* (forthcoming). The following chapter is based on my own research, but I am grateful to Peter White and Julian Davies for permitting me to see their important studies.

that was soon to cause a political conflagration, the chief protagonist was an ayatollah of rigid theological views and liturgical preferences which he set out to impose upon a reluctant nation through the agencies and power of the state. Archbishop William Laud was, in the judgement of Patrick Collinson, 'the greatest calamity ever visited upon the Church of England'.[2]

The thesis of an Arminian revolution rests upon some assumptions about the Elizabethan and Jacobean church which require further investigation or qualification. It is clear from the appeal made to the purity of the Elizabethan church by Charles and Laud and his chaplain Peter Heylyn on the one hand and their critics on the other that the character of the Church of England was open to more than one interpretation. The settlement of 1559 and the Thirty-Nine Articles of 1563 had indeed cleverly effected a compromise in difficult circumstances. Establishing a Protestant church and liturgy, the settlement left considerable room for tender Catholic consciences to manoeuvre. By the most general of phrases it was hoped to avoid complex theological controversies – not least among Protestants themselves. The Church of England as it was created in the early years of Elizabeth's reign was founded not on a narrowly defined and agreed theology, but on what was intended as a common mode of worship. Articles and constitutions, of course, especially in matters of the spirit, do not determine practice. During the course of Elizabeth's reign, not least because her bishops were, perforce in the absence of other candidates, appointed from the ranks of the Genevan exiles, the church became more pronouncedly Calvinist. In matters of liturgy prescribed practices were abandoned and modes of worship became diversified by the preferences of bishops, local clergy and gentry patrons to livings. Some, the queen among them, resisted both the departures from the Book of Common Prayer and the efforts to take the church closer to Geneva.[3] By the 1580s and 1590s there was a reaction to the Calvinists from a generation in the universities who had not sucked the milk of Genevan piety. In Oxford 'theologians gradually moved towards a distinctive "Anglicanism" which in line with Elizabeth's own policy rejected strict confessionalism and allowed hopes of comprehension' in the spirit of 1559.[4] In Lincolnshire William Williams who preached against the Calvinist theology of double predestination claimed the support of 'the best in Cambridge'.[5] In both the universities in the

2. Collinson, *The Religion of Protestants*, p. 90; cf. R. Ashton, *The English Civil War* (1978), p. 110.
3. Cf. White, 'Arminianism reconsidered', pp. 36–37; H. Hajzyk, 'The church in Lincolnshire, *c.*1595–1640' (Cambridge University, PhD thesis, 1980), pp. 222–4.
4. J. McConica (ed.) *The History of the University of Oxford, III, The Collegiate University* (Oxford, 1986), pp. 329–31.
5. Hajzyk, 'The church in Lincolnshire', p. 239.

1590s, a heated theological debate took place, which the queen and her archbishop, Whitgift, were anxious to cool. Richard Hooker's *Laws of Ecclesiastical Polity*, penned during that decade, was as well as a counterblast to the puritans and a justification of the liturgy, an attempt to reaffirm the comprehension of the 1559 settlement and to support a distinct Anglican church, independent from Geneva as Rome, to which all members of the English commonweal might belong.[6] The hope for unity was not fulfilled; the debates continued to be fervent. Though the controversies were not quelled, the Calvinists' takeover of the church was checked: a broad spectrum of beliefs and preferences in matters theological and liturgical was accommodated. At the local, and especially the popular, level it is unlikely that the arguments, especially the complex university debates over free will, had any relevance to the rhythms of religious life. Though it doubtless meant different things to different men, it is evident that the Church of England, even an Anglican piety, was established in the affections of the nation by the end of the century.

The disagreements and tensions in the church were held in balance and control for the first half of the reign of James I. What sharpened them for outright confrontation was less ecclesiastical disputes at home than the course of affairs in Europe.[7] In 1559, for reasons of foreign policy and security more than anything else, Elizabeth had wished to establish a national church, independent of the operational headquarters of religious war at Rome and Geneva. Archbishop Parker, aided by Elizabethan antiquaries, researched to establish the history of the British church from the days of Christ and the supposed mission of Joseph of Arimathea – to invent, we might say, an Anglican tradition.[8] But as battles raged in Europe between, as some oversimply viewed them, the armies of Catholic and Reformed, there was mounting pressure for the Church of England to affiliate itself more closely with the Protestant, that is the Calvinist, cause.[9] During the 1620s as during the 1560s and 1580s, as the cries for a crusade against the popish Antichrist reached a crescendo, questions and disagreements within the

6. It will be evident here that I remain unconvinced by Peter Lake's argument that Hooker invented Anglicanism (P. Lake, *Anglicans and Puritans? Presbyterianism and English Conformist Thought from Whitgift to Hooker*, 1988, ch. 4), not least because there is so little examination of his predecessors, cf. White, *Predestination, Policy and Polemic*, chs 3, 4 and 7.
7. Too often the debates over English theology have been narrowly isolated from broader European currents of ideas and politics. Now see H.R. Trevor-Roper, *Catholics, Anglicans and Puritans* (1987).
8. Cf. K. Sharpe, *Sir Robert Cotton: History and Politics in Early Modern England* (Oxford, 1979), pp. 8–9.
9. On which see S.L. Adams's splendid work, 'The Protestant cause: religious alliance with the Western European Calvinist communities as a political issue in England, 1585–1630' (Oxford University, D. Phil. thesis, 1973).

church which had for the most part been confined to scholarly debate or simmered without steaming boiled over and flowed into the broader political arena. Did the Thirty-Nine Articles ally England with the rigid predestinarian theology of the Calvinist churches of the continent? Was the liturgy and polity of the English church sufficiently purged of Romish practices and hierarchy? Where did England stand in the struggle for the defence and advance of international Calvinism?

During the years when England's security seemed to many (of various theological persuasions) to depend upon a closer identity with the Protestant cause, those who had always pressed for that closer affiliation – the predestinarians and the puritans – gained the ascendancy. But they never established an orthodoxy; nor did they ever control the Jacobean church. James I himself, though tutored by one of the hottest Protestants of the sixteenth century, never allowed them to establish a monopoly. Nor did he commit himself to their cause. James remained committed to bishops, to the Prayer Book and to the ceremonies of the church: in his private chapel he retained ornate images, and pictures of the apostles.[10] He showed little sympathy for puritans, Lucy Hutchinson even believing that he 'harboured a secret desire of revenge upon the godly in both nations'.[11] Concerning the contested questions of theology, though at the Synod of Dort he lent the support of the English church to the Dutch Calvinists in their struggle with the Arminians, he did so largely for diplomatic reasons and at home remained uncommitted.[12] In 1622 James issued directions to preachers that were intended to silence theological controversies.[13] Amidst the most public theological controversy of his reign – the quarrel over Richard Montagu's *New Gagg* – he was equivocal. The Montagu whom the hotter Protestants in the House of Commons wished to condemn as an Arminian, a papist and a traitor, James declared had written nothing that conflicted with the doctrine of the church. For his part Montagu, who was bidding for a bishopric, evidently expected the king's support.[14] Despite all the attempts of the Calvinists from the Hampton Court conference onwards, the Church of England in James I's reign still embraced a variety of different theological positions;

10. W. Hunt, *The Puritan Moment: The Coming of Revolution in an English County* (Cambridge Mass., 1983), p. 180.
11. M. Finlayson, *Historians, Puritanism and the English Revolution* (Toronto, 1983), p. 58.
12. Cf. J. Platt, 'Eirenical Anglicans at the Synod of Dort', in D. Baker (ed.) *Reform and Reformation: England and the Continent, c.1500–c.1750* (Studies in Church History 2, Oxford, 1979), pp. 221–43; and Platt, 'The British delegation and the framing of the second head of doctrine at the Snyod of Dort' (unpublished paper). I am grateful to Dr Platt for this paper and for much else besides. Cf. White, *Predestination, Policy and Polemic*, ch. 9.
13. E. Cardwell, *Documentary Annals of the Reformed Church of England* (2 vols, Oxford, 1844), II, pp. 198–203.
14. Lambert, 'Richard Montagu', pp. 43–50; White, 'Arminianism reconsidered', pp. 46–7.

it included bishops John Overall and Lancelot Andrewes (the latter tipped for Canterbury in 1611) as well as Morton, Davenant and Archbishop Abbot.

There was considerable speculation about the consequences for the church of the succession of Charles I – even before he came to the throne in 1625. When he was in the Tower in 1641, Bishop Wren recalled the growing interest in and anxiety concerning the religious views of the prince, as James's illness focused attention on the succession of his son. When Wren, chaplain to Prince Charles, returned from Spain with the prince in 1623, Andrewes, bishop of Winchester, summoned him to his London residence where he met Richard Neile, bishop of Durham and Laud then bishop of St David's. The gathering informed Wren that they had been discussing 'those things in foresight whereof we conceive will 'ere long come to pass' (the death of James) and were anxious to learn from him where the prince stood concerning the church. Wren gave his opinion that Charles's learning was not equal to that of his father, who, it must be said, was one of the most learned theological disputants in seventeenth-century Europe. 'Yet,' Wren continued, 'I know his judgement to be very right and as for his affections in these particulars which your lordship have pointed at, for upholding the doctrine and discipline and the right estate of the church, I have more confidence of him than of his father.[15] Much has been made of this account and meeting. For Dr Tyacke the 'Durham house' group constituted the van of the English Arminian movement. Wren, he argues, foresaw that the next king would be a champion of their cause and a ladder by which they might climb to ascendancy in the church.[16]

It is hard to know exactly how to interpret Wren's report, as indeed it is difficult to be clear about Charles's theology. But the reference to the 'estate' of the church and the coupling of 'doctrine and discipline' may, I think, be the most revealing of insights. To Charles the three were connected. Believing that external manifestations expressed and shaped sensibilities and beliefs he was committed to the maintenance of the fabric of the church and its ceremonies. Obsessed with order, he placed great stress on ordered ritual and uniformity of worship. These, more than fine theological distinctions, bring us close to what the church meant to Charles. Clarendon tells us that Charles was averse to Catholics (converts still more than those bred in the faith) and puritans because they went 'against the government established'.[17] The Church

15. Bodleian, Rawlinson MS D.392; C. Wren, *Parentilia, or Memoirs of the Family of the Wrens* (1750), p. 45ff.
16. Tyacke, *Anti-Calvinists*, pp. 113–14 and ch. 5 *passim*.
17. E. Hyde, Earl of Clarendon, *The History of the Rebellion and Civil Wars in England*, ed. W.D. Macray (6 vols, Oxford, 1888), I, p. 109.

of England he believed 'the nearest to the practice of the Apostles and the best for the propagation and advancement of Christian religion of any church in the world'.[18] That church Charles commended to his son as a church independent of others, one which charted 'the middle way between the pomp of superstitious tyranny and the meanness of fantastic anarchy'.[19] The king saw it as his duty not to change the church, but to sustain it, to protect it from encroachments and to strengthen it against criticism by the reform of abuses. The charges made by parliament in 1628 that the church was threatened by Arminianism and popery, Charles took as a personal affront.[20] 'Among the cares that attend the princely office', he believed the church should ever have 'the first place'.[21] It had been, he told the mayor of London, 'our care since we came to the crown . . . to defend the true faith'.[22] The 'chief honour and safety of the crown', he wrote to Neile, was bound up with 'the maintenance of true religion'.[23]

But wherein for Charles did 'true religion' lie? What did the Church of England, which meant different things to different men, mean to the head of the church? 'True religion,' Charles once told Bishop Bridgeman of Chester, 'must be planted and preserved by unity and good life.'[24] These were the hallmarks of Charles's personal faith. Though evidently effective and learned in religious debate, his faith did not rest on fine theological points.[25] He followed the Scriptures and the Fathers; he read therein of heaven and hell and strove to attain the one and avoid the other.[26] These were 'the true but and limit which we must not pass'; there need be no 'digging deeper into the secrets of God'.[27] Where Scripture was not self-evidently clear, it was for the practice of the church to determine. Rather than in theological disputes, Charles's faith was founded on devotions. From the very day of his coronation – the day of the purification of St Mary the Virgin, on which the king wore white rather than imperial purple – Charles

18. *Ibid.*
19. Sir C. Petrie (ed.) *The Letters, Speeches and Proclamations of Charles I* (1935), p. 269; *Eikon Basilike* (1649), p. 216.
20. Huntington Library, Temple of Stowe MSS, Parliament Box 13, above, p. 42.
21. *Calendar of State Papers Domestic* [*Cal. Stat. Pap. Dom.*], *1637*, p. 299: Charles I to Bishop Mainwaring of St Davids, 9 July.
22. PRO, SO 1/2, ff.55v–56, May 1631.
23. PRO, SO 1/2, f.73, 3 Nov. 1631.
24. G.T.O. Bridgeman (ed.) *The History of the Church and Manor of Wigan*, part 2 (Chetham Soc., new series, 16, 1889), p. 338.
25. *Bibliotheca Regia, or the Royal Library* (1659) pp. 65–103.
26. Bodleian, Eng. Hist MS E.28, ff.549–68, esp. f.561: 'The King of Great Britain's confession of his faith'. The date is '3 non Jan 1625'. The list on the flyleaf in a later hand attributes this to James I. Professor C. Carlton takes the manuscript as Charles's (*Charles I: the Personal Monarch*, 1983, p. 63). I am inclined to agree. The document reads much more like the king than his father and may even be in Charles's own hand.
27. *Ibid.*

attended assiduously to his devotions.[28] In his bedchamber he surrounded himself with devotional paintings and kept by his side the gospels and the apocalypse.[29] Unlike his father, he joined in prayers every Sunday at the royal chapel, which was adorned with religious hangings and a crucifix.[30] The king himself composed a form of prayer for relief of the realm from plague.[31] In fulfilment of his belief that even kings were men before an omniscient God and were 'by serious humiliation to implore the grace and favour' of God's majesty',[32] Charles regularly attended confession, and placed a confessor in his son's (as in his own) household.[33] In addition he unburdened his soul to his bishops, putting his 'great case of conscience' to Laud in 1631.[34] During the civil war years, Charles commanded his troops to attend divine service twice daily.[35] In all these personal devotions, the king followed prescribed prayers and practices. He attached importance to the set forms and calendar of worship, to the observation of Lent and fast days. The Venetian envoy described the king's fond attachment to the 'rites' of the church.[36] True religion meant for Charles the practice of worship in accord with the prescribed liturgy of a Church of England which in his view eschewed 'superstition' on the one hand and 'profanity' on the other.[37]

Whilst he sought to defend that church from challenges from without, within the body of the church Charles sought to eschew controversy and secure unity. He entered himself into disputes with the Marquess of Worcester, refuting the latter's defence of Catholicism;[38] he ordered Laud to publish his *Conference with Fisher* as a defence of the church against Rome.[39] He rigorously proceeded against puritans – less

28. C. Wordsworth (ed.) *The Manner of the Coronation of King Charles I of England* (Bradshaw Soc., 2, 1892), p. 6.
29. BL Add. MS 16112: Van der Dort's catalogue of pictures; New College Oxford MS 9502: diary of Robert Woodforde, 9 Oct. 1638: 'I was in the king's chamber where I saw the 4 gospels, the Acts of the Apostles and the Apocalypse'. On this diary, see below, pp. 694–5.
30. M. Fuller, *The Life of Bishop Davenant, 1592–1641* (1897), p. 305; cf. J. Bliss and W. Scott (eds) *The Works of William Laud* (7 vols, Oxford, 1847–60), III, p. 197.
31. J. Larkin (ed.) *Stuart Royal Proclamations II: Proclamations of King Charles I, 1625–46* (Oxford, 1983), p. 47; cf. *A Form of Common Prayer, together with an Order of Fasting* (1625, STC 16540).
32. Larkin, *Stuart Royal Proclamations*, II, no. 229. pp. 538–40: proclamation for a general fast, 18 Oct. 1636.
33. British Library [BL], Harleian MS 7623; PRO, LS 13/30; PRO, SP 16/154/76; *Calendar of State Papers Venetian* [*Cal. Stat. Pap. Venet.*], *1636–9*, p. xlvi.
34. *Works of Laud*, III, p. 213.
35. Larkin, *Stuart Royal Proclamations*, II, no. 424, pp. 909–11.
36. *Cal. Stat. Pap. Venet., 1636–9*, p. 125.
37. Cf. the king's note in his copy of Bacon's *The Advancement of Learning* (1640), p. 307: 'if a man by eschewing superstition grow to be profane, what hath he gotten?'
38. *Bibliotheca Regia*, p. 65ff.
39. *Works of Laud*, II, pp. viii–ix.

for what they believed in conscience than for their challenge to the commonweal of church and state. 'The neglect of punishing puritans,' he once wrote in the margin of Bishop Neile's reports, 'breeds papists.'[40] Otherwise, Charles did all he could to silence dispute and suppress difference. He was personally tolerant; sure of his own faith, he could befriend Catholics and Presbyterians and respect men's private consciences.[41] But the unity of the visible church had to be preserved from public contest. Accordingly, 'to take away all occasions of . . . offence', Charles suppressed two sermons of Roger Mainwaring that had caused offence to parliament.[42] In response to the controversy surrounding Richard Montagu, the king issued a proclamation, carefully worded and drafted by his own hand, for the peace and quiet of the church and the maintenance – let us note the coupling again – of its 'doctrine and discipline' against novelty.[43] A renewed attempt at unity and peace was made by Charles in his prefatory declaration to the edition of Elizabethan articles published in 1628.[44] Reaffirming his own belief that the articles 'contain the true doctrine of the Church of England', the king announced that since all clergymen willingly subscribed to them they must 'all agree in the true usual literal meaning of the said articles'. Since all could agree on a form of words, whatever their private interpretation, there was no need for 'further curious search.' It was therefore ordered that 'no man hereafter shall either print or preach to draw the articles aside *any way* . . . and shall not put his own sense or comment to be the meaning of the article'.[45] His desire, Charles told his parliament, was to see passions subside.[46] When the heat of controversy was still not cooled, he acted in January 1629 to suppress Montagu's defence, his *Appello Caesarem*, in which he had invoked the support of James I for his cause. The proclamation reiterated the king's 'care to conserve and maintain the church, committed to our charge, in the unity of true religion and the bond of peace, and not to suffer unnecessary disputes'. The articles of religion had been reissued the previous year 'for the establishing of consent in true religion', but the differences continuing the king had resolved to take away their cause, 'hoping thereby that men will no more trouble themselves with these unnecessary questions'.[47] In a typical Caroline compromise Mainwaring and Montagu were both promoted to place,

40. *Cal. Stat. Pap. Dom., 1633–4*, pp. 443–5.
41. Carlton, *Charles I*, p. 140; P. Gregg, *King Charles I* (1981), p. 266.
42. Larkin, *Stuart Royal Proclamations*, II, no. 92, p. 198.
43. *Ibid.*, no. 43, p. 92.
44. *Articles Agreed upon by the Archbishops and Bishops of Both Provinces and the Whole Clergie, Reprinted by his Majesties Command* (1628, STC 10051).
45. *Ibid.*, pp. 4–5.
46. Temple of Stowe MSS, Parliament Box 13.
47. Larkin, *Stuart Royal Proclamations*, II, no. 105, pp. 218–20.

but not permitted to publish views which might 'trouble the quiet' of the church.

Some have argued that Charles's injunctions to silence were intended to silence some rather than others.[48] But, as we shall see, the evidence suggests that the king was genuinely bent on stopping the publishing and preaching 'pro or contra concerning these differences' and genuinely and impartially committed to unity.[49] When in 1632, Henry Sherfield, the recorder of Salisbury, smashed a stained-glass window in a city church the incident threatened to become a controversy over the nature of church ornaments. Yet while Sherfield was prosecuted, for defying the bishop, Charles ordered that the window be replaced by plain glass, not the coloured glass that had offended by its 'popish' representations of God.[50] It is significant that the Earl of Dorset advised Sherfield that he would avoid further trouble if he abstained from speeches, that is if he allowed the matter to drop and avoided controversy.[51] The same preoccupations with peace seem to have governed Charles's behaviour when in 1629 Bishop John Davenant preached before the king at court on the subject of predestination. He was reprimanded – not for his views but for his public debating of disputed points: 'his Majesty declared his resolution that he would not have this high point meddled withal or debated either the one way or the other because it was too high for the people's understanding and other points which concern reformation and newness of life were more needful and profitable'.[52] Davenant continued to preach regularly before the king.[53]

As well as the maintenance of peace and unity Charles's priority as supreme governor appears to have been the upholding the estate of the church – the preservation of its fabric and of the status of the episcopacy and clergy. Signet letters show his attempts to encourage, as we shall see, the repair and re-edification of churches 'that respect being and outward reverence being . . . a clear evidence of true zeal'.[54] Charles vigorously upheld the privileges of cathedrals and ordered the civic magistracy 'to manifest your conformity', as he put it to the corporation of York, 'to the orders established'.[55] He endeavoured

48. Tyacke, *Anti-Calvinists*, p. 181. C. Russell, letter in the *TLS*, 21 Aug. 1987, p. 899; cf. p. 925 and the effective reply by I. Green, 4 Sept. 1987 (p. 955).
49. Larkin, *Stuart Royal Proclamations*, II, p. 219; below, pp. 296–7.
50. Melbourne Hall, Coke MS 44, 15 Feb. 1633, transcribed in *HMC Cowper II*, p. 2–3; see below, pp. 345–8.
51. Hampshire Record Office, Sherfield MS XLV: Dorset to Sherfield, 22 July 1632.
52. Boldeian, Tanner MS 290, f.86v.
53. Sherfield MS XLV, 5 March 1632; PRO, LC 5/132: lists of Lent preachers. Davenant was a regular.
54. PRO, SO 1/2, ff.55v–56: Charles I to mayor of London, May 1631.
55. York City Record Office, House Books, 35, f.336.

to secure better endowment for the clergy and their freedom from dependency on the laity. The strength of the church rested not only on its buildings and status; it was founded also on the good order and discipline of its clergy. Charles therefore personally drafted directives to his bishops. He ordered their residency in their sees; he commanded them to keep hospitality; he instructed them to ordain no minister without a title to a benefice.[56] The king examined carefully the bishops' annual reports on their dioceses;[57] he raised none to the episcopacy 'but such as he has some knowledge of himself as having been his own chaplain in ordinary or otherwise'.[58] The selection of Lent preachers and chaplains at court was Charles's own;[59] he intervened to improve the selection of ministers who preached the assize sermons;[60] he personally upheld the jurisdiction of the church courts against challenges and corrupt clergy.[61] The evidence of the king's own hand on proclamations, episcopal reports and declarations, the range of signet letters dealing with religious matters support the view of Davenant's biographer that Charles I assumed the role of 'universal bishop', and that the history of the church in the 1630s was written around the king's own preferences and concerns.[62]

Archbishop Laud

The role of 'universal bishop' is usually given in histories of the 1630s to William Laud. Historians almost unanimously describe Laud, who was elevated to the see of London in 1628 and the archbishopric of Canterbury in 1633, as the evil counsellor whose influence on Charles cost the king his crown. The traditional assumption, however, that Laud formulated the religious policy of the personal rule must be questioned. His relationship with the king is not easily captured. The two were not close personally, as Laud's constant insecurity and efforts to place confidants in the king's bedchamber make clear.[63] The king clearly valued and trusted his advice on ecclesiastical affairs, but did not take it exclusively or in full. Laud seems to have been more interested in John Dury's efforts to unite the Protestant churches in

56. PRO, SP 16/153/40–3.
57. His marginalia are on all Laud's metropolitical returns; see Lambeth Palace MS 943, pp. 251–7.
58. *Cal. Stat. Pap. Dom., 1635*, p. 376: Laud to Elizabeth of Bohemia, 11 Sept.
59. BL, Egerton MS 2978, f.47; PRO, LC 5/132; *Cal. Stat. Pap. Dom., 1637–8*, p. 235.
60. Tanner MS 71, f.142: Charles I to Abbot, 31 May 1632.
61. Lambeth Palace MS 943, pp. 545–7; Larkin, *Stuart Royal Proclamations*, II, no. 244, pp. 572–3.
62. Fuller, *Davenant*, p. 309.
63. K. Sharpe, 'The image of virtue: the court and household of Charles I, 1625–1642', in D. Starkey (ed.) *The English Court from the Wars of the Roses to the Civil War* (1987), p. 252.

Germany than was Charles, and may have been more committed to improving tithes and clerical stipends.[64] For his part, Charles clearly had his own ideas and priorities: he thought of reviving the Elizabethan injunctions against Laud's inclinations;[65] the Book of Sports was entirely Charles's policy;[66] and the king, as Julian Davies has demonstrated, attached more importance to railing altars at the east end than did his archbishop.[67] The tone of his letters and reports suggests that Laud saw himself very much as the executor rather than deviser of royal policy; the latest research – on the role of Pierce and Wren as well as the king himself – bears him out. On most matters, however, it is clear that the king and his archbishop worked in close agreement and co-operation. A draft of the king's instructions to the clergy, issued in January 1629, written partly in Laud's, partly in Charles's own hand, probably offers a nice insight into their working relationship: a relationship like that of Charles with his other ministers in which the 'directory' was the king's, but advice, the refinement, the implementation and administration of policy was left to his servants.[68]

Laud is one of those unfortunate historical figures whose biography has been penned largely from the writings of his enemies. He was especially unfortunate in attracting as his greatest enemy one of the most prolific and vitriolic polemicists of the seventeenth century, William Prynne.[69] Laud's enemies claimed that he aimed to suppress the gospel and promote idolatry as the means to bring in popery. Prynne asserted that the archbishop was ambitious for a cardinal's hat; and the scent of crypto-Catholicism has lingered round Laud's memory ever since.[70] It is a charge completely without foundation. Laud proceeded vigorously against recusants in the country and at court, and alienated the queen by his outspoken opposition to the attendance of English Catholics at her private chapel.[71] He showed little interest in the embassy of Gregorio Panzani which was intended to foster closer relations between England and Rome.[72] Most sig-

64. *Cal. Stat. Pap. Dom., 1633–4*, pp. 453, 562; *Works of Laud*, V, p. 327.
65. *Cal. Stat. Pap. Dom., 1629–31*, p. 119: Laud to Dorchester, 10 Dec. 1629.
66. I owe this point to the persuasive account by J. Davies, *The Caroline Captivity of the Church*, ch. 5. I am grateful to Julian Davies for his allowing me to read this important book in advance of publication and for many stimulating discussions. Our work on the Caroline church has proceeded independently to often quite similar conclusions. See below, pp. 351–9.
67. *Ibid.*, ch. 6; and see below, pp. 333–45.
68. Cardwell, *Documentary Annals*, II, p. 229ff.
69. Prynne is still too often read uncritically as evidence for Laud's designs and intentions.
70. *Cal. Stat. Pap. Dom., 1629–31*, p. 195; BL, MS 29/172, f.308; Tanner MS 299, ff.161–161v.
71. Below, pp. 305–6; *Works of Laud*, III, p. 229; W. Knowler, *The Earl of Strafford's Letters and Despatches* (2 vols, 1739), I, p. 426.
72. S.R. Gardiner, *History of England from the Accession of James I to the Outbreak of the Civil War, 1603–1642* (10 vols, 1883–4), VIII, p. 143.

nificantly, Laud penned one of the most lucid and complete answers to the Catholic challenge to the Church of England that the seventeenth century produced. The *Conference with Fisher the Jesuit* is still seldom read. To read, however, Laud's rebuttal of the claims of the papacy, of the doctrines of transubstantiation, communion in one kind, the invocation of saints and the adoration of images is to understand (for all his respect for its antiquity) how little inclined to the Catholic church he was.[73] Laud's treatise enables us to comprehend that when he said that he could contemplate no closer union till 'Rome were other than it was', the Catholic church would, to gain Laud as a member, have had to be very different indeed.[74]

But if Laud was not a papist, was he not clearly the spawn of a papist, an Arminian? To most historians Laud's 'Arminianism' is beyond question.[75] Not only did Prynne and other enemies call him an Arminian, his chaplain and first biographer Peter Heylyn maintained that in a sermon preached at Oxford in 1616 Laud supported Arminian tenets.[76] Neither can be taken as reliable evidence. Heylyn, writing in the 1660s, had his own reasons for wishing to recruit Laud to that cause. And it is significant that in drawing up the case against the archbishop in 1641, Prynne did not press the charge of Arminianism – largely because he failed to find sufficient proof to sustain it.[77] Laud's denial of the accusation during the 1630s and in his trial defence – 'I have nothing to do to defend Arminianism' – cannot of course be taken uncritically; though it is worthy of comment that he did not deny other charges which were as damning in his prosecutors' eyes.[78] But Thomas Crosfield's record that on Christmas day 1632 Laud preached against Arminius cannot be so easily dismissed.[79] Laud was evidently discomfited by the doctrine of reprobation, which, he told Viscount Saye and Sele, 'my very soul abominates'.[80] Concerning the controversy over predestination, however, he wrote to Wentworth and Matthew Brooke of Trinity College, Cambridge (who was composing a treatise on the subject) in almost identical words: that 'the truth whatsoever it be . . . is not determinable by any human reason in

73. *A Relation of the Conference between William Laud . . . and Mr Fisher the Jesuit*, in *Works of Laud*, II.
74. *Works of Laud*, III, p. 219.
75. Dr Tyacke appears, curiously, to regard the case as proven in *Anti-Calvinists*, appendix II. Cf. White, *Predestination, Policy and Polemic*.
76. P. Heylyn, *Cyprianus Anglicus or the History of the Life and Death of William Laud* (1668), part I, pp. 66–7.
77. K. Sharpe, 'Archbishop William Laud', *History Today*, 33 (1983), pp. 26–30; W. Lamont, *Godly Rule* (1969), p. 65.
78. *The History of the Troubles and Trial of William Laud* (1695), p. 353.
79. F.S. Boas (ed.) *The Diary of Thomas Crosfield* (1935), p. 63.
80. *Works of Laud*, VI, part 1, p. 133.

this life'.[81] A convincing case that Laud was a doctrinal Arminian has yet to be made.

There is little discussion of theological disputes or questions in Laud's writings or sermons. He obviously admired Lancelot Andrewes – and sent Andrewes's sermons as a gift to Queen Elizabeth of Bohemia.[82] But many admired Andrewes, one of the great preachers and theologians of his day, who did not espouse all his positions – James I (and perhaps Charles I, who gave Andrewes's sermons to his daughter) among them.[83] At least one contemporary critic, a doggerel balladeer, believed the archbishop's faith a curious amalgam of many ingredients.[84] Laud however had no doubts about his God or his church. He personalized the passages of Scripture he studied; his diary, ironically like so many puritan diaries, charts his spiritual struggles and joys. In the treatise penned so that 'the Christian world may see and judge of my religion', he set out his creed: 'I have lived and shall, God willing, die in the faith of Christ as it was professed in the ancient primitive church, and as it is professed in the present Church of England'.[85] That church Laud defended against challenges from Catholics and puritans. But concerning the nature of the church itself, he 'abhorred too rigid definition'.[86] Laud believed in the Hookerian doctrine of adiaphora – 'in and about things not necessary' for salvation, 'there ought not to be a contention to a separation'.[87] The Church of England did not deliver anathemas against those who dissented in some particulars; it was a broad church in which differences could be accommodated, if they were not publicly stirred.[88] Laud, like Charles, strove, as he said at his trial, for unity and peace rather than division and discord. 'I have resolved,' he declares in the *Conference with Fisher*, 'in handling matters of religion to leave all gall out of my ink.'[89] It was no empty claim. Concerning the adoption of the canons of the Church of England in Ireland, Laud advised Bishop Bramhall, 'tis better having them materially and in substance with peace than formally with heart burning among yourselves'.[90] A plan to publish a defence of bowing to the altar he disliked because it would provoke a reply and so 'beget bitterness and intestine contestations'.[91] His irritation

81. *Ibid.*, p. 292; VII, p. 275.
82. *Cal. Stat. Pap. Dom., 1631–3*, p. 196.
83. *Works of Laud*, II, p. xxvi.
84. Harleian MS 4931, f.8.
85. *Conference with Fisher*, in *Works of Laud*, II, pp. xxiii, 373.
86. W.H. Hutton, *Archbishop William Laud* (1895), p. 132.
87. *Conference with Fisher*, p. 218.
88. *Ibid.*, pp. 59–60.
89. *Ibid.*, p. 149.
90. Huntington Library MS, HA 15172, 11 May 1635.
91. Lambeth Palace MS 943, p. 97.

at the public disputation of religious questions by preachers at Chelsea College is evident in his endorsement of a letter recounting them – 'controversy college'.[92] When he encountered controversy, he tried to quell it. 'Hear all differences privately,' Laud instructed his vicar-general, Sir John Lambe, 'and make a peaceable end if you can.' [93] With regard to the sharpest dispute of all – that over predestination and free will – he had, he told his friend Gerard Voss in a personal letter of 1629, 'always moved every rock to see that those scruples and perplexing questions are not publicly debated before the people lest piety and charity be violated under the guise of truth. I have always counselled moderate ways.'[94] As archbishop, Laud was as good as his word: he counselled silence to those sympathetic to Arminian tenets as well as those critical of them.[95]

For Laud the unity of the church rested not on narrowly defined dogma but on the community and uniformity of worship. Attendance at the parish church and participation in a common service conducted according to the canons and Book of Common Prayer were for him the hallmarks of membership of the Church of England. The church, he wrote in his *Conference with Fisher*, was in the commonweal; to be a member of the commonweal was also to be of the church.[96] Laud disliked the imposition of long excommunications because it withdrew the excommunicated from the body of the church; he would not have it imposed lightly – against, for instance, the poor who could not afford church dues.[97] In High Commission Laud in May 1632 delivered a long speech on the importance of attending the parish church.[98] He could not accept immigrants worshipping according to different rites because there was no place for 'mongrels' in the parish.[99] The unity of the visible church required one set form of worship. In the departure from the canons and the diversity of local practice tolerated by some of his predecessors and especially by Abbot, Laud believed the decline of piety had its roots. 'No one thing,' he wrote in the preface to the *Conference*, 'hath made conscientious men more wavering in their own minds, or more apt and easy to be drawn aside from the sincerity of religion professed in the church of England than the want of uniform and decent order in too many churches of the kingdom.'[100] External

92. Tanner MS 142, f.55: George Cottington to Laud.
93. *Cal. Stat. Pap. Dom., 1637*, p. 355.
94. *Works of Laud*, VI, part 1, p. 259, 10 May 1629. Too little attention has been paid to this important letter. Cf. *ibid.*, p. 264.
95. For instance the silencing of Tooker of Oriel College; see *Works of Laud*, V, p. 15.
96. Conference with Fisher, p. 223.
97. *Works of Laud*, V, p. 358.
98. Rawlinson MS A.128.
99. W.J.C. Moens (ed.) *The Walloon Church of Norwich: its Registers and History* (Huguenot Soc., I, 1887), p. 91.
100. *Conference with Fisher*, p. xvi.

worship was to Laud the witness of the inner faith, and external worship could not be uniform without prescribed ceremonies. Ceremonies were not the essence of faith; men should not place 'the principal part of their piety in them'.[101] But they strengthened faith; they were necessary as 'the hedges that fence the substance of religion from all the indignities which profaneness and sacrilege too commonly put upon it'.[102] Whilst there was room in the church for difference of belief – salvation was not shut up in narrow conclaves – 'unity cannot long continue in the church where uniformity is shut out at the church door'.[103] Without some ceremonies it was not possible to 'keep any order'. 'They are small things but wilful contempt of them, and breach of public order, is no small offence before God.'[104]

It was this attachment to uniformity of worship rather than theological disputes that fired Laud's campaign against the puritans. In rejecting the common forms of worship they separated themselves from the community of the parish to become (James I had used the same term) a 'faction'.[105] In emphasizing private revelation they challenged the authority of the church. Laud said of those who worshipped apart from the parish church, 'these are dangerous men, they are a scattered company'. They were a danger to the authority of the monarchy as well as the church. In June 1632 Laud expressed his horror at having come upon a conventicle of separatists 'in the very brake where the king's stag should have been lodged for his hunting next morning'.[106] Prynne and his fellows he saw guilty of sedition as well as heterodoxy.[107] Because for Laud, as for Hooker, the church and commonweal were one community, those who could not subscribe to the church were exiled from the realm. In the case of literal exiles to New England, Laud wished them gone.[108] Good order in church and state could not accommodate puritan dissent. The Scots' rebellion only confirmed Laud's paranoia about the puritan threat: 'never did I see any man of that humour,' he wrote to Hamilton, 'yet but he was deep-dyed in some violence or other.'[109]

The unity and uniformity of the church, Laud believed, depended upon the maintenance of the authority of the church and of its bishops

101. *Ibid.*, p. 312.
102. *Ibid.*, p. xvi.
103. *Ibid.*, pp. xvii, 59; *Works of Laud*, IV, p. 60.
104. PRO, SP 16/308/38.
105. *Cal. Stat. Pap. Dom., 1639–40*, p. 515; *Works of Laud*, VI, part 2, p. 500.
106. *Cal. Stat. Pap. Dom., 1631–3*, p. 353.
107. See *Works of Laud*, VI, part 2, p. 500; J. Bruce and S.R. Gardiner (eds) *Documents Relating to the Proceedings against William Prynne in 1634 and 1637* (Camden Soc., new series, 18, 1877), appendix, p. 486ff.: Laud's speech.
108. Huntington Library MS, HA 15172: Laud to Bramhall, 27 June 1637.
109. A. Peterkin (ed.) *Records of the Kirk of Scotland, Vol. I* (Edinburgh, 1838), p. 123: Laud to Hamilton, 3 Dec. 1638.

and clergy. That authority, however, had been eroded. Lay endowments and subscriptions had created a class of preachers dependent upon lay support, who were chosen often to reflect the preference of their patrons rather than to uphold the articles and canons of the church.[110] Lecturers Laud particularly disliked because 'by reason of their pay [they] are the people's creatures'.[111] The lay control of advowsons, and the poverty of the church Laud regarded as his fundamental problems. As he confided to Wentworth in 1633 shortly after becoming archbishop, 'as for the church, it is so bound up in the forms of the common law that it is not possible for me or for any man to do that good which he would . . . they which have gotten so much power in and over the church will not let go their hold'.[112] Parliaments, Laud felt, had encouraged the alienation of church possessions and furthered the encroachment on church authority. He therefore, in Philip Warwick's words, 'endeavoured to preserve the jurisdiction which the church anciently exercised before the secular authority owned her'.[113] Bishop Bridgeman of Chester captured Laud's policy well: 'I know your intention is to benefit the church and to free it from the hands of corruption and sacrilege, with which oftentimes lay patrons seize on the fruits of . . . benefices'.[114] Within the bounds of the common law Laud worked to restore church properties in Ireland, and to better endow the church and clergy in England. He asserted to the full his powers of metropolitical visitation over the universities and dioceses of England; he reinvigorated the church courts; he secured the appointment of clergy and bishops to secular office – to the commission of the peace, even (his greatest triumph) to the Lord Treasurership of England. Indeed Clarendon argued, probably correctly, the principal cause of Laud's downfall was his desire to promote churchmen, to reverse, as it seemed to some, that triumph of the laity over the clergy which was a characteristic of the English Reformation.[115] Laud, however, saw little choice: appointments such as Juxon's to high office was one of the ways for the church to 'hold up themselves under God'.[116] The uniformity he sought required that the clergy and episcopacy enjoy economic independence and possess the status and authority to enforce subscription to the codes and canons of the church.

The authority of the bishop was central to Laud's programme

110. On the problems he faced, see C. Hill's magisterial work, *The Economic Problems of the Church from Archbishop Whitgift to the Long Parliament* (Oxford, 1956).
111. J. Rushworth (ed.) *Historical Collections of Private Passages of State* (7 vols, 1659–1721), II, p. 7.
112. Knowler, *Strafford Letters*, I, pp. 110–11, 9 Sept.
113. Sir Philip Warwick, *Memoirs of the Reign of King Charles I* (1701), p. 79; cf. *Cal. Stat. Pap. Dom., 1633–4*, pp. 232–3.
114. *Cal. Stat. Pap. Dom., 1638–9*, p. 523, 1 March 1639.
115. Clarendon, *History of the Rebellion*, I, p. 115.
116. *Works of Laud*, III, p. 226.

for uniformity of worship. As bishop of London and archbishop of Canterbury he himself issued long and detailed visitational articles that enquired as much into the behaviour of the parish clergy as of the laity.[117] He expected similar diligence from his colleagues on the episcopal bench; as metropolitan he demanded full reports on the dioceses, which he analysed with the king. The episcopate, he told Bishop Hall, was the foundation of the church; without it 'all . . . shall be democratical'.[118] In 1626 he recommended a bishop be appointed for every shire.[119] In order to uphold the authority of the episcopacy Laud insisted that they reside in their sees rather than, as had been common, flock to court or city. He required them to preserve the patrimony of their bishoprics and not to sell or lease lands in transactions that might impoverish their successors. In 1628 Laud wrote sharply to George Coke, bishop of Hereford, upbraiding him for using 'bishopric timber' for his own household purposes and for using his office to promote his son.[120] The bishops in the Laudian church were given considerable control and independence in their dioceses, but during the 1630s stricter account was required than had been expected by Laud's predecessor. The French envoy Senecterre exaggerated when he observed that it was Laud's aim 'à faire le Pape sur le clergé d'Angleterre';[121] as archbishop, Laud did not increase metropolitical power over the bishops. But his diligence and activity, his donnish hectoring, were felt throughout the dioceses of England.

The change of archbishop in 1633 was described by the editor of the state papers domestic as 'one from an Abbot who was disinclined to interfere' to a Laud who was 'active, zealous, singularly methodical and attentive to business . . . with the most definite notions of what he esteemed to be true and right'.[122] He continues to describe Laud's 'determination to propagate and establish his own opinions and to repress all opposition'. Laud's energy – satirized in Lambert Osbaldeston's description, the 'Little hocus pocus' – is undeniable;[123] but his reputation for repression and harshness is ill deserved. The archbishop did not ride roughshod over tender consciences: 'I had rather,' he wrote to Bramhall, 'there should be a charitable than a legal end.'[124] Even in the case of ceremonies he went to lengths to win rather than cajole men to conformity. The practice of kneeling at communion he believed would gain converts in time by the decency of

117. In *Works of Laud*, V.
118. *Cal. Stat. Pap. Dom., 1639–40*, pp. 87–8.
119. I owe this information to Julian Davies.
120. *HMC Cowper II*, p. 198, 27 Oct. 1638.
121. PRO, 31/3/68, f.216v.
122. *Cal. Stat. Pap. Dom., 1633–4*, p. xiii.
123. See C. Carlton, *Archbishop William Laud* (1987), p. 147.
124. Huntington Library MS, HA 15172: Laud to Bramhall, 5 April 1637.

the gesture itself.[125] He would not force Corbet in Oxford to bow to the altar;[126] he did not even enforce in his own diocese royal orders to place the communion table at the east end (he did not, as we shall see, order communicants to come up to the rails).[127] 'His grace,' Dr Holdsworth put it, 'delights in gentleness.'[128] With the foreign congregations at Canterbury even as late as 1638 Laud still believed it 'fitting to keep a moderate hand'.[129] Though he was himself examined by the High Commission, William Gouge (the puritan divine and future member of the Westminster Assembly) expressed his esteem for Laud's 'fair dealing' with him. More generally he acknowledged that 'concerning some ministers that refused to subscribe or conform' he would himself bear witness to 'the bishop's patient forbearing with them giving them time to consult conformable ministers and vouchsafing to confer with them himself'.[130] Gouge's testimony is powerful support to Laud's own claim that none but the most persistently obstinate of ministers were deprived of their benefices. 'Moderate ways' more than harshness or fanaticism characterized Laud's campaign for liturgical conformity as they had his attempts to secure doctrinal peace. That this is not the verdict of history is due in part to the power of his enemies' invective, in part to his own failure 'to make his designs and purposes appear as candid as they were'.[131] Most of all perhaps, Laud's commitment to enforcing the observance of the Prayer Book and canons, as had been intended by the queen and her archbishop in 1559, was seen in the 1630s as innovatory and controversial because it followed the long latitudinarian archepiscopacy of George Abbot during which conformity had been little pressed.[132] Laud did not create division in a church which was harmoniously united in consensus. Like Archbishop Bancroft, in his efforts to preserve the church as defined by its articles and canons he exposed differences and dissensions that were of long duration.

Theological wrangles

Some of those differences were undoubtedly theological. Montagu's *A Gagg for the New Gospel* publicized a debate that had for the most part

125. *Works of Laud*, V, p. 343.
126. *Ibid.*, p. 206.
127. Below, pp. 343–4.
128. *Cal. Stat. Pap. Dom., 1639*, p. 16.
129. *Works of Laud*, V, p. 356. See below, pp. 348–51.
130. *Cal. Stat. Pap. Dom., 1631–3*, p. 167: Gouge to Laud, 19 Oct. 1631.
131. Clarendon, *History of the Rebellion*, I, p. 25.
132. *Cal. Stat. Pap. Dom., 1633–4*, p. xiii; W.M. Abbot, 'The issue of episcopacy in the Long Parliament, 1640–48' (Oxford University, D. Phil. thesis, 1981), p. 103. I remain unpersuaded by recent efforts to rehabilitate Archbishop Abbot.

been confined to academic circles. When it was published in 1624, a year in which the religious temperature was raised by the prospect of a crusade against the Habsburgs, Montagu was seen to be the enemy from within. The Arminians were feared to be the fifth column through which the papists would insinuate themselves and corrupt the faith. Montagu not only publicized religious controversy, he politicized it. When he was attacked by the House of Commons as well as by other divines, he appealed to James for vindication and was permitted to pen his appeal, in which he defended his position. Amidst the mounting furore, James referred Montagu's work, his vindication of himself from the charge of Arminianism and popery, to be examined by Dr Francis White, dean of Carlisle, who had taken a prominent part in polemical controversy against Rome. White was ordered to examine Montagu's writings for orthodoxy according to the rules of antiquity. White concluded that Montagu rejected absolute predestination, but in doing so was no innovator. For on this matter, Hooker and Robert Abbot, bishop of Salisbury (elder brother of the archbishop) had both criticized Calvin's doctrine of reprobation as novel and perilous; and even the English delegates to Dort (who had supported the doctrine of election) had described the tenet of reprobation as 'horridas opiniones in Scripturis minus fundatas quae ad desperationem faciunt'. White concurred with them and Montagu that 'if God's predestination shall be suffered to be preached among Christian people according to Calvin's . . . dictates, it will cause the greatest part of people to abhor our religion'.[133] In general, he maintained, English divines took no such view, nor even concurred in all points with Dort. Rather they believed that the promises of the gospel ought to be proposed universally to all men – an emphasis different from Calvin's and not fundamentally at odds with the Catholic position 'concerning the co-operation of grace and free will in us'. Montagu, he concluded, on this issue had said nothing that conflicted with the doctrine and articles of the Church of England. On other matters – the place of images, the belief that Rome was a true church, his support for confession – White vindicated Montagu's claim to be orthodox. With his licence, *Appello Caesarem* appeared in print.[134]

Given White's later close affinities with Laud and Charles I and his promotion in the Caroline church, he may be suspected, even in 1624, being sympathetically inclined towards Montagu's position. It is of importance therefore that among the papers of the Egerton family we find another examination of the differences between 'Mr Montagu and

133. Rawlinson MS C.573. 'Horrid opinions with little foundation in Scripture that lead to desperation.'
134. *Ibid.*, Lambert, 'Richard Montagu', pp. 42–9; cf. F. White, *A Treatise of the Sabbath Day* (1635, STC 25383), p. 63.

informers'. In this case the anonymous commentator J.D., after a long and detached examination of the charges, displays some sympathy for the objections raised against the *Gagg* and *Appello Caesarem*.[135] Concerning the question of merit in salvation he concludes, 'I cannot absolutely acquit Mr Montagu in this place'. But in the main this report too maintains that when Montagu's words were not misrepresented or twisted by 'harsh misinterpretation', there was no ground for suspecting him of popery or for challenging his defence of himself: that what others called an Arminian stance on predestination was in fact a Lutheran position to which he consented 'no otherwise than he perceives the Church of England consents with them'. On this crucial question of free will, the examiner could only 'profess the question obscure' and place hope in the possibility of reconciling moderate men, even by some agreed formula taken from their own words.

Montagu's defence, however, served only to inflame his critics. Charles I, seeing that his plan to silence discussion by taking Montagu into his protection as a royal chaplain had failed, changed tack and arranged a public conference where the issues might be broadly aired. 'Many of the nobility being present', at the Duke of Buckingham's London residence, Bishop Morton and Dr Preston put the case against Montagu, and White defended him. The evidence suggests that the argument went White's (and Montagu's) way. Charges of popery were seen to be groundless and the attempt to prove that Montagu was unorthodox on the subject of predestination failed. Moreover Buckingham disliked what he heard from Morton on the subject and even the Earl of Pembroke, a political patron of the puritans, concurred that Calvinist predestinarianism was 'a most pernicious doctrine, and unfit for any people to hear'.[136] Montagu was cleared but given no occasion or cause for triumph. The king's proclamation of June 1626, carefully worded to avoid references to persons or 'Arminianism', enjoined silence and peace on all.[137] Thereafter Charles and the Privy Council went to lengths to quieten controversy: in addition to the preface to the Elizabethan articles, the king was reported as warning that if the Arminians did not conform to the articles their tenets would be condemned.[138] Even in the face of the House of Commons' provocative campaign against Montagu, the king acted with careful moderation. Whilst Montagu was raised to the bishopric of Chichester

135. Huntington Library, Ellesmere MS 6878: 'Mr Montagu & informers yae & nae'.
136. White, 'Arminianism reconsidered', pp. 49–50.
137. Larkin, *Stuart Royal Proclamations*, II, no. 43, pp. 90–3; Charles removed references to Montagu and changed that to Arminianism to 'schism' (PRO, SP 16/29/79).
138. T. Birch (ed.) *The Court and Times of Charles I* (2 vols, 1848), I, p. 439: Pory to Mede, 28 Nov. 1628.

and granted a royal pardon, Attorney Heath warned him to 'prevent occasions of strife' and to revise the style of his book in order to explain himself more clearly so that 'a stop be given to this unhappy difference and jealousy which otherwise may trouble the quiet of our church and occasion the disquiet of the Commonwealth'.[139] By a proclamation of January 1629 the *Appeal* that James I had licensed, Charles I suppressed, to take away what troubled 'the quiet of the church'.[140]

In January 1626 Laud had confided to his diary his fear that the issues surrounding 'the cause, book and opinions of Richard Montagu' constituted 'a cloud arising and threatening the church of England'.[141] He was right; the debate was not silenced. During the second half of the 1620s many works appeared challenging Montagu's arguments and asserting the doctrine of predestination. In *A Plea for Grace* William Pemble dismissed Arminianism as 'a silly shift devised to uphold the liberty of man's will and universality of grace'.[142] Nicholas Carpenter argued that the Arminians admitted God only as a servant of men.[143] I.R., the author of *The Spy Discovering the Danger of Arminian Heresies and Spanish Treachery* linked the two;[144] the vitriolic Prynne, in his usual colourful rhetoric, branded Arminianism as 'an old condemned heresy raised up from hell of late by some Jesuits and infernal spirits, to kindle a combustion in all Protestant states and churches'.[145] Clearly the spectre of Arminianism raised the largest fears. P.J. thought it 'a mere stirrup to help men into the saddle of popery', a device by which papists disguised themselves as conformable Protestants.[146] It was therefore a cause for alarm to him that Arminianism appeared to be the way to promotion in the church and that bishops White, Field, Buckeridge, Harsnett, Howson, Neile and Laud held some of the best sees and most powerful positions.[147] The fear of an Arminian takeover in England was linked not only to the threat of Catholicism (we recall the Edict of Restitution marked the height of Habsburg power in 1629), but also to reactions to rigid Calyinism in Europe. The Earl of Norwich wrote to the Earl of Carlisle in September 1628 that Arminius was grown famous 'and as greatly a favourite to the

139. *Cal. Stat. Pap. Dom., 1628–9*, p. 346, 7 Oct. 1628.
140. Larkin, *Stuart Royal Proclamations*, II, no. 105, pp. 218–20.
141. *Works of Laud*, III, pp. 179–80.
142. W. Pemble, *A Plea for Grace* (1629, STC 19592), p. 23.
143. N. Carpenter, *Achitopel* (1629, STC 4669), p. 30.
144. I.R. [J. Russell], *The Spy: Discovering the Danger of Arminian Heresie* (1628, STC 20577), sig. B1.
145. W. Prynne, *The Church of England's Old Antithesis to New Arminianism* (1629, STC 20457).
146. P.J., *Christ's Confession and Complaint Concerning His Kingdom and Servants* (1629, STC 19069), p. 48.
147. *Ibid.*, p. 60.

world . . . in so much that the whole Christian world is almost become Arminian . . .'.[148] In 1631 Thomas Gataker the puritan divine heard that Arminians were being appointed to chairs in Holland and feared that Arminian sermons were finding favourable hearing in England.[149] Bishop Davenant of Salisbury expressed his concern that unorthodox Arminian points were going unanswered; and got to the point of advising a canon against the doctrine.[150] In the cross bill against the bishops which they filed at their trial, Prynne, Burton and Bastwick decried those books which, they claimed, in abundance promoted innovation and the doctrine of free will: 'fiery Calvinism, once a darling in England, is at length accounted heresy'.[151]

As often with fears and phobias, the spectre of doctrinal Arminianism was out of all proportion to the reality. During the late 1620s after Montagu evoked so many responses, no defence of or apologia for him or the doctrine of free will was published. In 1633 a dictionary dedicated to Laud defined 'praedestinati' as heretics;[152] the following year O.N.'s *An Apology of English Arminianism* staged a debate between 'Enthusiastus' and 'Arminius' and gave the victory to the latter, for free will and against the doctrine of reprobation.[153] Francis White's *A Treatise of the Sabbath Day* (1635) maintained that Christ had redeemed all mankind 'and that upon the cross he made a full, perfect and sufficient sacrifice and satisfaction for the sins of the whole world'.[154] Most blatantly and powerfully Samuel Hoard's *God's Love to Mankind* subjected reprobation and damnation to rigorous criticism and branded them anathema to godliness.[155] But such apologiae were few and there is little evidence that they were officially sanctioned. Hoard, indeed, had held a living in the Earl of Warwick's patronage.[156] What evidence we have does not suggest that unpublished sermons in favour of Arminianism were any more frequent or widespread. The newswriter Rossingham reported an Oxford preacher denied his grace in 1634 for maintaining that good works justified;[157] the Northamptonshire puritan and attorney, Robert Woodforde, heard Dr Beale preach against supralapsarianism (the doctrine that election

148. *Cal. Stat. Pap. Dom., 1628–9*, p. 311, 2 Sept. 1628.
149. Tanner MS 71, f.68: Gataker to Ward, 17 Feb. 1631.
150. *Ibid.*, f.164: Davenant to Ward, 23 July 1633; E. Cope (ed.) *Proceedings of the Short Parliament of 1640* (Camden Soc., 4th series, 19, 1977), p. 111.
151. Tanner MS 299, f.156v.
152. Tyacke, *Anti-Calvinists*, p. 183.
153. O.N., *An Apology of English Arminianism* (1634, STC 18333).
154. White, *Treatise of the Sabbath Day*, p. 63.
155. S. Hoard, *God's Love to Mankind Manifested by Disproving the Absolute Decree for their Damnation* (1635, STC 13534).
156. *Dictionary of National Biography* [*DNB*].
157. PRO, C.115/M36/8426: Rossingham to Scudamore, 11 July 1634.

and damnation predated the fall) as well as in favour of confession.[158] Among the papers of Sir Edward Nicholas we find propositions to which the clergy of London were asked to assent, including a statement that all those baptized were regenerated, but the status of the document is not clear.[159] Even added together such scraps and incidents scarcely amount to an Arminian revolution worthy of the paranoia generated. They indicate rather that for the most part the king's injunctions to silence had, by the end of the twenties, at last begun to take effect.

For some, however, it was the imposition of silence itself which excited fear. To those for whom the Calvinist doctrine of predestination was the central tenet of faith the prohibition against preaching and publishing inflamed rather than ameliorated the situation. In *The Marrow of Divinitie* (1632) the Heidelberg minister reminded the English that 'the doctrine of predestination is not to be . . . concealed in the cloud of silence'.[160] Taking his cue, Henry Burton in *The Christian's Bulwark*, denouncing all 'pontifical Pelagians' and engaging specifically with Montagu's *New Gagg*, asserted the centrality of predestination to Christianity.[161] In 1633 John Prideaux, Regius professor of divinity at Oxford, presiding at Peter Heylyn's disputation for his doctorate of divinity, 'upon an occasion of the mentioning of the absolute decree . . . broke out into a great and long discourse that his mouth was shut by authority, otherwise he would maintain the truth contra omnes'.[162] The same year Mr Burton brought to a Hampshire JP (probably Sir Thomas Jervoise) a petition subscribed by twenty-two ministers of London complaining against 'the interpretation of the king's proclamation and declaration whereby said to be prohibited from preaching of sundry points of the Christian religion, naming election and predestination, whereby they are in a strait either to disobey God in forbearing to discover his whole counsel or to be questioned as contemners of his Majesty's royal command'.[163] Bishop Davenant's correspondence with Samuel Ward makes it clear too that, while he learned discretion well enough not to publish his views, he believed the question of predestination of central importance in the church.[164]

Yet it is important to appreciate that even some of those who were concerned about the issue of predestination were unsure how best to

158. New College Oxford MS 9502 (Woodforde's diary), 21 Oct. 1638.
159. *Cal. Stat. Pap. Dom., 1635–6*, p. 50.
160. J. Gerhard, *The Marrow of Divinitie* (1632, STC 11769), p. 81.
161. H. Burton, *The Christian's Bulwark* (1632, STC 4140), *passim* and p. 341.
162. Rawlinson MS D.353, ff.104–104v.
163. Hampshire Record Office, Herriard MSS, Box 07, 14 Feb. 1633.
164. For example, Tanner MS 67, f.160; Tanner MS 290, f.86.

settle it, and did not agree among themselves. Davenant for one may have looked forward to discussing the question with Ward, 'but to set down or define anything touching those diversa signa rationis I profess I cannot do it to satisfy myself and therefore much less to satisfy others. The thing is merely imaginary and therefore as men's imaginations are divers and sometimes quite contrary . . . so are all the delineations of priority and posteriority in God's inward and secret decrees . . . I know not two that agree in all points'.[165] (Here Davenant appears at no great distance from Laud, who thought the question 'unmasterable'.)[166] Others shared Davenant's difficulties: Bishop Henry King could not agree with the Arminians but maintained that God 'hath left some part of thine election to be made up by thyself'.[167] Archbishop Ussher, one of the bishops most respected by the godly, even expressed equivocal views on the question of salvation offered to man by God.[168] Given the difficulties, most divines, of different persuasions, preferred not to explore the controversy. Bishop Bedell, a pupil of William Perkins, told Ward that he thought it best not to press for exactness or tease out differences on the subject of man's conversion.[169] Bishop Joseph Hall, one of the delegates to Dort, recommended his readers to 'leave all curious disquisitions to the schools'.[170] Peter Smart, who attacked John Cosin for his introduction of ceremonies to Durham, wrote that 'We may not presume to enter into God's judgements and give sentence of election or reprobation upon any';[171] even the author of *The Spy* left the theological 'tenents' of the predestinarian controversy 'for the schools dispute'.[172] George Wither in *Britain's Remembrancer* advised no prying into God's secret counsels.[173] Such positions and language are not far removed from what Cornelius Burges, a royal chaplain, regarded as the declaration of a wise king who had checked those 'that are too bold in prying into the secrets of God'.[174] Silence did not please the zealots, but for many divines it ended sterile controversy and opened richer roads to piety.

If the learned divines equivocated or counselled silence, the parish clergy and the laity probably remained for the most part ignorant of, or displayed little interest in, the debates. There are examples of Arminian preachers in the parishes. Jeremiah Ravens, vicar of Chattisham in

165. Tanner MS 71, f.64: Davenant to Ward, 24 Jan. 1631.
166. *Works of Laud*, VI, part 1, p. 292; *Cal. Stat. Pap. Dom., 1629–31*, pp. 384–5, 396.
167. H. King, *An Exposition upon the Lord's Prayer* (1628, STC 14695), p. 152.
168. Rawlinson MS C.849, f.282.
169. Tanner MS 71, f.189.
170. J. Hall, *The Olde Religion* (1628, STC 12690), epistle dedicatory.
171. P. Smart, *A Sermon Preached in the Cathedral Church of Durham* (1628, STC 22640), p. 3.
172. Russell, *The Spy*, sig. A.1v.
173. G. Wither, *Britain's Remembrancer* (1628, STC 25899), p. 54.
174. C. Burges, *Baptismal Regeneration of Elect Infants* (1629, STC 4109), p. 276.

Lincolnshire was charged in 1644 with 'saying that man hath free will to be saved if he will, and that all should be saved that are baptized'.[175] Theodore Beale, vicar of Ash Bocking, 'once in the pulpit used this argument viz that Christ must save the greatest part of people, otherwise he can be no Saviour'.[176] At the other extreme ministers like Lapthorne are found 'preaching nothing but desperation to his parishioners and threatenings so that he made one hang himself, another to drown himself, and others to die through sickness through despair'.[177] For the most part, however, as the evidence of the committee for scandalous ministers and of visitations suggests, doctrinal differences were not often a real issue in the parishes. Even in the sophisticated environment of a city such as Coventry, the zealous Woodforde defending, as he saw it, God's truth in predestination 'found few here that favoured it'.[178] The logic of strict predestination did not square easily with the vocation of a preaching ministry,[179] so John Hansley's sermon that the names of the saved could be written in a ring found few emulators.[180] Those who preached on the theology of salvation therefore either softened the rigours of Calvinist double predestination or performed some tricky boxing of the compass.[181] One sermon on election in the Rawlinson manuscripts speaks, rather inconsistently, of wilful sin as the cause of reprobation;[182] those who argued that God must have foreseen and therefore forewilled their reprobation were admonished that it was not fit to argue in that manner. In Somerset a congregation was evidently told that the reprobate excluded themselves from grace by their wilful actions.[183] The less nimble or more pragmatic preachers preferred to avoid the issue altogether. John Swan advised his fellow ministers that to meddle with predestination was unwise: 'It is enough for us that we stir up our flocks to attend their salvation and to work it with fear and trembling; and not busy their heads with such thorny debates and wounding questions as torment their souls.'[184] In *The English Gentleman*, Richard Braithwaite counselled the laity to eschew all such disputes for the

175. C. Holmes (ed.) *The Suffolk Committees for Scandalous Ministers, 1644–46* (Suffolk Record Soc., 13, 1970), p. 39.
176. *Ibid.*, p. 43.
177. PRO, C.115/M36/8437: Rossingham to Scudamore, 18 Oct. 1634.
178. Woodforde's diary, 1 Nov. 1638.
179. Cf. G.E. Aylmer's comment that predestination was 'one of the least attractive dogmas ever formulated in any religion' (*Rebellion or Revolution?*, Oxford, 1986, p. 138).
180. *Cal. Stat. Pap. Dom., 1636–7*, p. 266.
181. J. Morgan, *Godly Learning; Puritan Attitudes towards Reason, Learning and Education* (Cambridge, 1986), p. 24; P. Collinson, *The Elizabethan Puritan Movement* (1967), p. 37.
182. Rawlinson MS C.585.
183. Somerset Record Office, Phelips MS DD/Ph/248.
184. J. Swan, *A Sermon pointing out the Chief Causes and Cures of such Unruly Stirs as are not seldom found in the Church of God* (1637, STC 23515), p. 16.

'ordinary means of attaining salvation'.[185] The ordinary means of salvation had more to do with belief in God than the theologies of election. Those who submitted their wills to God, one preacher told his flock, would be converted into the ranks of God's chosen.[186] Even in puritan Norwich the churchwardens of St Andrew's presented their incumbent, William Bridges, for denying that Christ died for all men.[187] Among the laity, even among the families known for their support of puritanism, the Calvinist doctrine of predestination may have been less central to their faith than some have supposed. The Earl of Huntingdon, for example, descendant of the great patron of Elizabethan puritanism, referred in his commonplace book to those 'that dare go down into the pit of predestination';[188] Lord Herbert, Sir Robert Harley told the preacher Robert Misley in 1631, 'says he loves a puritan, but not a predestinator'.[189] If the clergy and lay elites shunned nice theological points, the further one goes into the country parishes and down the social scale, the less were any solifidian doctrines held and the more, as Keith Thomas has brilliantly demonstrated, the heterodox equation of salvation and good works was still made.[190] The religion of most Protestants, as we shall see, had very little to do with quarrels about supralapsarianism.

The evidence suggests that with the end of England's involvement in the wars of Europe after 1630, some of the heat went out of the religious debate – at least until the trial of Prynne, Burton and Bastwick and the outbreak of the Prayer Book rebellion in Scotland. Montagu's name was little heard and the vitriolic wrangles of the late 1620s subsided. In April 1634 Dr Robert Baron, professor of divinity at Aberdeen, wrote to Laud congratulating him for his observations on Scripture in his *Answer* to Fisher, 'and still more for his having quieted the discord in the Church on the subject of predestination and the questions connected therewith by the royal prohibition of preaching on that subject'.[191] Baron's congratulations were not inappropriate. In 1636, Lucy Downing, wrote to her brother John Winthrop about the condition of the church at home: 'I cannot say that the doctrine of sanctification is now so frequently pressed and taught as we have known and could wish it . . . but the chief incitement of our stay here and that which justifies all others in that God doth now as graciously

185. R. Braithwaite, *The English Gentleman* (1630, STC 3563, p. 121. Braithwaite dismissed the 'ignorant laics familiarly disputing of the too high points of predestination'.
186. Tanner MS 65, f.46.
187. Tanner MS 68, f.79.
188. Huntington Library, Hastings MSS, Religious Box 1: commonplace book.
189. BL, MS 29/172, f.46: 8 Dec. 1631.
190. K.V. Thomas, *Religion and the Decline of Magic* (1971), esp. ch. 6.
191. *Cal. Stat. Pap. Dom., 1633–4*, p. 560, 20 April 1634. We should note that Baron was later to be condemned for heresy by the General Assembly.

and gloriously hold forth Christ and the word of reconciliation to us now here as hath been known in England.'[192]

The Catholics and Rome

The controversy over Arminianism and predestination was inextricably bound up with fears of Catholicism and the question of the Church of England's relations with Rome. During the mid- to late 1620s, fear of Catholics, always present but usually latent in English gentry society, burst into at times near hysteria. The discovery, shortly before the convention of the 1628 parliament, of a Jesuit meeting place at a house in Clerkenwell (belonging to the Earl of Shrewsbury) evoked fears of plots out of all proportion to the situation.[193] The Venetian envoy Contarini reports the fears of English Catholics that their children would be taken away from them, to be raised in Protestant households.[194] The panic did not die down; the reprieve of the captured Jesuits was one of the issues that dominated the parliamentary session of 1629. Like his father, Charles I did not join willingly in the parliamentary chorus that at times bayed for Catholic blood.[195] He did not, he told Contarini, 'approve of so much rigour . . . against the papists'; but, he added, 'it was necessary to keep them somewhat curbed, as they were sometimes seditious'.[196] In practice the king's curbs were rigorous. A proclamation of August 1628 commanded the detention of all Jesuits and the strict punishment of those who received them.[197] The children of nobles in seminaries abroad were ordered home.[198] In 1631 a commission of enquiry into the jurisdiction of the law courts ordered that a stop be put to the practice whereby lax prison-keepers let their charges go abroad 'and which is most insufferable priests and Jesuits are let loose to say masses . . . and to seduce our people in all places to the great and just offence both of God and our laws'.[199] In 1634 Captain William Rose of Queenborough, who ran a business shipping English subjects to seminaries on the continent, was seized and brought before the Council;[200] the next year the Jesuit tutors

192. *The Winthrop Papers* (Massachusetts Hist. Soc., 5th series, 1, 1871), p. 15; cf. W. Gouge's praise of 'a free use of all God's holy ordinances requisite for our spiritual edification' (*The Saints' Sacrifice*, 1632, STC 12125, p. 276).
193. Gardiner, *History of England*, VI, p. 238.
194. *Cal. Stat. Pap. Venet., 1628–9*, p. 167.
195. M. Havran, *The Catholics of Caroline England* (1962), pp. 69, 73.
196. *Cal. Stat. Pap. Venet., 1628–9*, p. 167.
197. Larkin, *Stuart Royal Proclamations*, II, no. 96, pp. 203–6.
198. *Ibid.*, no. 23, pp. 52–4.
199. Ellesmere MS 7928.
200. *Cal. Stat. Pap. Dom., 1634–5*, p. 297.

at a school at Stanley George in Derbyshire were discovered and apprehended.[201] One of the biggest problems of control was that of the priests who proselytized from the shelter of ambassadorial residences whither English Catholics in London flocked to mass. Charles, seeing that the practice caused scandal, attempted early on to check it, requiring 'the law to be observed with greater exactitude as far as his own household is concerned'.[202] In March 1629 guards were posted outside the Spanish, French and Venetian ambassadors' houses and the English Catholics 'on coming out of mass were immediately arrested'.[203] As the plentiful examples of the modern age of terrorism remind us, however, policing diplomatic quarters was difficult and thorny territory: incidents such as that in 1635, when a priest was forced out of the French ambassador's house where he had taken sanctuary, could easily spark major clashes.[204] As we shall see, the queen's household presented special problems. It is clear that Charles's efforts to prevent English attendance at mass in envoys' chapels was never fully successful, but it was not for want of effort. In 1633 Windebank drafted a proclamation forbidding any Englishman to attend public mass and any foreigner from endeavouring to draw the king's subjects from the Church of England.[205] Individual letters were sent to ambassadors to the same effect in 1635.[206] Two years later another proclamation was published, reinforcing the prohibition, 'under pain of the severest punishments'.[207] In 1640, recusants were forbidden to come within ten miles of London.[208]

Even those recusants who pursued their faith privately and quietly in the country were not left alone. Like his father, Charles I may, as Walter Montagu said, have been capable of distinguishing a Catholic from a traitor, but he was not prepared to treat recusancy lightly.[209] In March 1630, for example, the bishop of Chester was exhorted to discover the true value of recusant estates so that the king might pursue a course that 'may both contain them in their due allegiance unto us and also by degrees invite them to conformity in religion, or else give us cause to proceed to more severity'.[210] The judges of assize

201. *Cal. Stat. Pap. Dom., 1635*, p. 303.
202. *Cal. Stat. Pap. Venet., 1629–32*, p. 304.
203. *Ibid.*, p. 308.
204. A.J. Loomie (ed.) *Ceremonies of Charles I: The Note Books of John Finet, Master of Ceremonies 1628–1641* (New York, 1987), p. 182.
205. Bodleian, Clarendon MS 4, no. 329; for earlier orders, see PRO, C.115/M31/8125 and C.115/M30/8084.
206. PRO, PC 2/44/520.
207. PRO, PC 2/48/326; Larkin, *Stuart Royal Proclamations*, II, no. 249, pp. 580–2.
208. Larkin, *Stuart Royal Proclamations*, II, no. 315, pp. 736–8.
209. *Cal. Stat. Pap. Dom., 1635*, p. 497: Montagu to the Earl of Manchester, 21 Nov.
210. PRO, SO 1/2, f.9v, 21 March 1630. Cf. B. Quintrell, 'Lancashire ills, the king's will and the troubling of Bishop Bridgeman', *Trans. Hist. Soc. of Lancashire and Cheshire*, 132 (1983), pp. 67–102.

in 1632 were charged to ensure that the most substantial recusants did not escape.[211] Lists of recusants in the various counties were kept; the JPs of Cornwall, Kent and Somerset were ordered to seek out recusants who by the neglect of churchwardens and constables had not been presented at the assizes.[212] Obviously the benefits to the Exchequer were not negligible: recusancy fines which had averaged £6,000 a year in the 1620s were yielding over £20,000 in the mid-1630s,[213] but the fines were intended as punishment and disincentive as well as revenue. John Pory told Viscount Scudamore that the greatest recusants were being presented 'because they infected many both by example and persuasion'.[214] The increased fines must have hurt. Thomas Meynell of North Kilvington in the North Riding paid £1,000 to compound over the decade 1631 to 1640;[215] in Somerset the increased payments for all recusants averaged £84.[216] That such sums led several families to bankruptcy questions Dr Clifton's conclusion that fines were willingly paid for *de facto* toleration[217] – especially since 'in practice composition was not a guarantee against further fines'.[218]

Certainly the French ambassadors formed no impression of leniency in Charles's dealings with his Catholic subjects. Whereas, they observed, under James I on payment of a fine recusants were not troubled in the exercise of religion, under Charles they were hounded more than they had been by his two predecessors. None, the envoy observed, escaped.[219] Absentees from church over six months were closely monitored, reported and brought before JPs, who required them to take the oath of allegiance. Refusal resulted in a fine of 200 livres a month, the collection of which was strictly pursued. Failure to pay led to the confiscation of all goods. Complaints of English Catholics endorse the reputation of harshness. In 1636 the Norwich sessions presented more recusants than ever before (in response, Wren was told, to Laud's prompting) and the oldest families especially found themselves under scrutiny.[220] Two years later one obviously disgruntled

211. Rawlinson MS A.128, f.24v.
212. PRO, SP 16/171/76; *Cal. Stat. Pap. Dom., 1638–9*, p. 222; Kent Archives Office, Dering MS U350/010, 24 Nov. 1634; E.H. Bates-Harbin (ed.) *Quarter Sessions Records for . . . Somerset, II, Charles I 1625–39* (Somerset Record Soc., 24, 1908), p. 262.
213. S.R. Gardiner, *History of England from the Accession of James I to the Outbreak of the Civil War, 1603–42* (10 vols, 1883–4), VIII, p. 130.
214. PRO, C.115/M35/8384, June 1632.
215. H. Aveling, 'The recusancy papers of the Meynell family of N. Kilvington in the North Riding of Yorkshire, 1596–1676', in E.E. Reynolds (ed.) *Miscellanea* (Catholic Record Soc., 56, 1964), p. xxxvi.
216. J.A. Williams (ed.) *Post-Reformation Catholicism in Bath*, I (Catholic Record Soc., 65, 1975), p. 30.
217. R. Clifton, 'The fear of Catholics in England' (University of Oxford, D.Phil. thesis, 1967), p. 68.
218. Havran, *Catholics of Caroline England*, p. 92.
219. PRO, 31/3/66, f.226v.
220. Tanner MS 68, f.154.

recusant, Mrs Cole, was examined for exclaiming that if she were queen she would hang the king for dealing with Catholics so harshly.[221] It is not, then, surprising that the Catholic community responded with little enthusiasm to the call to support the king's campaign against the Scots in 1639; indeed the campaign to win their assistance concentrated more on threats of worse to come than on any record of what had been done for them.[222] It is one of the ironies of the seventeenth century that recusants fared better under the parliamentary regime of the 1640s and the Cromwellian protectorate than during the decade of personal rule when the suspicions of leniency bore little relation to the Catholics' experience.[223]

The strict treatment of recusants during the 1630s may seem hard to reconcile with widespread fears of Catholicism that reached a crescendo at the end of the decade in the hysteria over an alleged popish plot.[224] In part the answer lies in numbers. For all the government's efforts to check them, there were many more priests, seculars and regulars, resident in England during the 1630s than there had been in 1603 – perhaps well over seventy in London alone and several hundred in the country.[225] The number of recusants too had probably increased by 50 per cent and the ranks of all Catholics (that is including those not identified as recusants) may well have surpassed 300,000.[226] Yet since 'in general the county community managed to live in peace and even friendship with its Catholic members in the decades before the civil war', an explanation by numbers – even had they been perceived – is unlikely to take us far.[227] What was much more visible was a focus of Roman Catholicism in the household of Henrietta Maria. The young French queen was personally devoted to her faith, was attached to the dévot party at the French court and had sworn to the pope to promote Catholicism in her new kingdom.[228] The practice of her faith was guaranteed her by her marriage articles of 1624, and the protection of her English Catholic subjects who wished to practise theirs she regarded as a duty. In consequence the queen's household became a public place of worship, a refuge for metropolitan Catholics and a headquarters for a campaign of conversions. In 1632 work began on the building of a Catholic chapel at Somerset House, which, when

221. *Cal. Stat. Pap. Dom., 1637–8*, p. 521.
222. Rawlinson MS D.720; below, pp. 843–4.
223. J.C.H. Aveling, *Catholic Recusancy in the City of York, 1558–1791* (Catholic Record Soc. monographs, 2, 1970), p. 89; R. Hutton, *The Restoration: a Political and Religious History of England and Wales 1658–1667* (Oxford, 1985), p. 7.
224. Below, pp. 842–7, 909–11.
225. Havran, *Catholics of Caroline England*, pp. 79–80.
226. *Ibid.*, p. 83.
227. A. Fletcher, *A County Community in Peace and War: Sussex, 1600–1660* (1976), p. 101.
228. E. Veevers, *Images of Love and Religion: Queen Henrietta Maria and Court Entertainments* (Cambridge, 1989), p. 92.

complete, became the perfect stage for the celebration of the baroque mass.[229] There was a core of Catholic favourites, such as Jermyn and Montagu, in the queen's household and, it has recently been argued, the culture of the queen's court drew from ideas of beauty, light and love which were associated with the cult of the Virgin Mary.[230] Henrietta Maria's household therefore became the conspicuous headquarters of Catholicism. In 1638 she even planned a procession through the streets of London to Somerset House, to sing a *Te Deum* for the birth of the dauphin.[231] What caused most scandal were the conversions of leading aristocrats, especially ladies, effected by priests within the queen's court.[232] In 1636, George Conn, papal envoy, observed that 'whereas in the past the Catholics could only hear mass at the embassies with great risk of being arrested when they came out, now the chapels of the queen and the ambassadors are . . . frequented with freedom'.[233] Lord Boteler, Lady Newport and Lady Hamilton were only the most spectacular figures of a series of conversions which excited fear.

Contrary, however, to what many who heard the sensational news suspected, Charles I and Laud were as scandalized as any. In 1630 the king ordered English subjects not to attend mass at the queen's chapel at Denmark House and a gentleman usher of the queen's privy chamber was posted at the gate.[234] The prohibition was issued again the next year.[235] Laud wanted Lady Falkland debarred the court in 1634 because her daughters had become Catholic 'not without the practice of their mother'.[236] Walter Montagu, the queen's favourite, sacrificed the king's as well as his father, the Earl of Manchester's, favour when he converted to Rome; significantly, when he returned to London from France in 1637 it was only the Earls of Holland and Dorset, the queen's Lord Chamberlain, who were prepared to welcome him.[237] With the more public proselytizing that followed George Conn's embassy, Charles took further action. He was 'bitterly displeased' at Lady Newport's conversion and after Laud's speech against the freedom of worship at Denmark House and Conciliar discussion, he ordered the presentation of any English subject attending masses at

229. *Ibid.*, p. 136; R.M. Smuts, *Court Culture and the Origins of a Royalist Tradition in Early Stuart England* (Philadelphia, 1987), pp. 228–9.
230. Veevers, *Images of Love and Religion*, p. 92.
231. PRO, C.115/N8/8822: Finet to Scudamore, 5 Sept. 1638.
232. Knowler, *Strafford Letters*, II, p. 165: Garrard to Wentworth, 10 May 1638; *Works of Laud*, III, p. 229; see G. Albion, *Charles I and the Court of Rome* (1935), ch. 8.
233. *Cal. Stat. Pap. Venet., 1636–9*, p. 69.
234. PRO, C.115/M31/8125: Flower to Scudamore, 20 March 1630.
235. PRO, C.115/M30/8084: Flower to Scudamore, 20 Aug. 1631.
236. *Cal. Stat. Pap. Dom., 1634–5*, p. 159.
237. A.H. Mathew, *The Life of Tobie Mathew* (1907), p. 303; PRO, C.115/N4/8612: Burgh to Scudamore, 12 April 1637.

ambassadors' residences; he even reprimanded the Spanish ambassador for his too conspicuous passage to Somerset House.[238] The ban, according to John Burgh, 'much staggers the papists and makes them somewhat fearful'.[239] Heated discussions of these issues led to many of the few quarrels between Charles and Henrietta Maria. But there were limits to what the king could do – limits imposed not only by a desire, comprehensible to all husbands, to avoid the anger or sulks of his wife. He could not challenge the queen's right to practise her faith – or that of her 'servants'. Windebank's advice that all foreign priests be ordered out of London could not easily be followed.[240] Charles had required the queen's household servants to take the oaths of allegiance and supremacy but her large entourage was a group hard to define or police. The queen's own increasing maturity manifested itself in greater boldness, in religion as in politics. The scandalous conversions continued. In May 1638 the Reverend Garrard reported to Wentworth that Katherine Howard and Lady Maltravers, wife of the heir to the premier noble house of the realm, had joined the Catholic fold.[241] By the end of the decade, there were mounting fears that the marriage of Charles to Henrietta Maria might lead the Church of England itself to match with the whore of Babylon.[242]

Such a match was not beyond the hopes of Rome. Gregorio Panzani (who arrived at the end of 1634) and George Conn (who succeeded him in 1636) came to England with the purpose of exploring the ground for effecting a reconciliation. The papacy went to great lengths to woo Charles I with favours and presents that could not have been more precious to him: Bernini's bust of the king's head (for which the Van Dyck of the king in three positions was painted) is the most famous one.[243] (See Figure 34.) Panzani, if his memoirs may be trusted, was initially optimistic: Charles, he reported, was attracted to many tenets of Catholicism; he had declared that he would rather have lost a hand than see schism in the church; and, attending a service at the queen's new chapel, 'it was a satisfaction to him to observe the order and significancy of their ceremonies'.[244] Conn endorsed his predecessor's optimism: Charles believed in the decrees of the first four ecumenical councils and the theology of the church Fathers.[245] Bishop

238. *Cal. Stat. Pap. Venet., 1636–9*, pp. 319, 324; PRO, C.115/N.8/8817: Finet to Scudamore, 21 April 1638.
239. PRO, C.115/N4/8612.
240. Clifton, 'Fear of Catholics', p. 93.
241. Knowler, *Strafford Letters*, II, p. 165.
242. Cf below, p. 844.
243. J. Berington (ed.) *The Memoirs of Gregorio Panzani* (Birmingham, 1793), p. 195; on the missions in general, see Albion, *Charles I and the Court of Rome*; see also, O. Millar, *Van Dyck in England* (1982), p. 65.
244. Berington, *Memoirs of Panzani*, p. 137.
245. Havran, *Catholics of Caroline England*, p. 31; cf. Eng. Hist. MS E.28.

34 *Charles I in Three Positions* by Van Dyck, 1635. This was painted as a model for Bernini's marble bust. The Garter is prominent.

Richard Montagu suggested that, with the exception of Morton, Davenant and Hall, the episcopate might be won to the idea of reunification.[246] Both Panzani and Conn, however, were naive in their optimism. That Charles expressed a desire for the union of Christendom was neither significant nor a sinister step towards Rome. James I, as Hugh Trevor-Roper brilliantly demonstrated, emerged as the European hope for and champion of an ecumenical resolution to the religious schisms of Europe in the decade before the outbreak of the Thirty Years War.[247] Expressions of desire for an ideal are not propositions for the effecting of a reality. Windebank, who on one occasion told Panzani that without the extremists, the Jesuits at the one end, the puritans at the other, a union between England and Rome would be in prospect, on another occasion mentioned that Rome

246. Berington, *Memoirs of Panzani*, p. 246.

247. I was privileged to hear Hugh Trevor-Roper deliver the Wiles lectures on 'The ecumenical movement in Europe'. See also B. Patterson, 'King James I's call for an ecumenical council', in G.J. Cuming and D. Baker (eds) *Councils and Assemblies* (Cambridge, 1971), pp. 267–76.

would have to give up communion in one kind, the Latin liturgy and clerical celibacy.[248] Sir Arthur Hopton, in a rueful conversation with Olivares on the same subject, added papal supremacy to the list of conditions which would have involved the renunciation of the central tenets of the Catholic faith.[249] Laud too may have deeply regretted the rent of Christendom, but he showed little interest in Rome's negotiations.[250] Panzani hardly got to see him – or Juxon, bishop of London.[251] While Conn was in England, trying to keep the scheme of reconciliation alive, the bishop of Durham and John Cosin were writing against the popish doctrine of merit.[252] And in November 1637, William Chillingworth, under Laud's direction, published his *The Religion of Protestants* which, as Viscount Conway told Sir Robert Harley, scotched the prospects of a union: 'that which I have read of him is very sharp in gentle words, so that it seems we are not going to Rome, whither so ever else we are going'.[253] Undoubtedly the very presence of Panzani and Conn gave rise to concern. Panzani's reception at court was 'to the wonder of everyone', 'a thing that has not been seen before since the time of Queen Mary.'[254] The charge to the assize judges in 1638 acknowledged that rumours were circulating that the king was popishly inclined.[255] On the contrary, Charles was sure enough in his faith to discuss without fear of being seduced. Clarendon was sure 'no man was more averse from the Romish church than he was, nor better understood the motives of their separation from us'.[256]

The economic problems of the church

If Charles and Laud yearned at times for the age of the pre-Reformation church, it was a nostalgia for a church that, as they saw it, was united, strong and wealthy, rather than divided and dependent. The English Reformation, more than perhaps any other European reformation, had resulted in the plunder of church wealth and an assault on the clerical estate. With the dissolution of the monasteries and the sales of monastic lands (sometimes to *arrivistes*) much of the wealth that had maintained the benefices and parish churches of England passed into the hands of

248. Berington, *Memoirs of Panzani*, pp. 163–4.
249. Egerton MS 1820, ff.126v–128v.
250. *Troubles and Trial of William Laud*, p. 412; cf. Berington, *Memoirs of Panzani*, p. 135.
251. Heylyn, *Cyprianus Anglicus*, p. 386; Gardiner, *History of England*, VIII, p. 143.
252. *HMC Cowper II*, p. 156: Cosin to Coke, 4 March 1637.
253. W. Chillingworth, *The Religion of Protestants: A Safe Way to Salvation* (1638, STC 5138); BL, MS 29/172, f.172, 18 Nov. 1637; Gardiner, *History of England*, VIII, pp. 261–2.
254. *Cal. Stat. Pap. Venet., 1632–6*, p. 496; J. McCann and H. Connolly (eds) *Memorials of Father Augustine Baker* (Catholic Record Soc., 33, 1933), p. 271.
255. Rawlinson MS B.243.
256. Clarendon, *History of the Rebellion*, I, p. 109.

laymen, not all of whom were inclined to use it for pious purposes.[257]

By the 1580s Whitgift was arguing that only 600 of 9,000 livings in England were able to support a minister.[258] The growing demand for a preaching ministry in late sixteenth-century and early Stuart England exacerbated the problem. The graduate clergy who were preferred to 'dumb dogs' sought a proper maintenance, which lay control and the general poverty of the church denied them. Like the modern health service the early Stuart church was caught between the Scylla of rising expectations and the Charybdis of shrinking resources. An extract from Laud's archiepiscopal register for 1634–5 records his calculation that of 8,803 benefices in England, 3,277 were lay impropriations where it was difficult in law to interfere with the rights of the patron.[259] In some counties, Hampshire for example, by far the greater part of the parsonages were impropriate.[260] Moreover, Laud's notes reveal, over half the benefices (4,543) were worth less than £10 per annum, and a huge 8,659 were estimated at below £40 a year, probably the figure at which a tolerable living would have been enjoyed.[261] The figures present the economic facts starkly. But they mask an ever grimmer reality of stipends not paid by impropriators and tithes not paid by parishioners. Some ministers were undoubtedly the victims of old composition agreements which had not kept pace with inflation; some fell foul of estate transactions in which they were conveniently forgotten.[262] The parishioners of Bletchworth who petitioned Laud in 1634 on behalf of their vicar who could get no maintenance from the lessee of the impropriate parsonage were unusual perhaps only in their support for their incumbent.[263] In most of the parishes of England the clergy were a lowly group dependent on their patrons and parishioners for a meagre livelihood. The Earl of Bridgewater, known for his puritan sympathies, had to be cajoled to pay his share of the vicar's allowance at Rostherne.[264] In Bristol the parishioners of 'several parishes' were in arrears with payments for the maintenance of their preacher.[265] Several ministers were like Michael Evans of Merioneth, led by desperation to petition the Privy Council to order their tithes to

257. Cf. Hill, *Economic Problems of the Church*.
258. D. Hirst, *Authority and Conflict* (1986), p. 63.
259. *Cal. Stat. Pap. Dom., 1634–5*, p. 381.
260. *Cal. Stat. Pap. Dom., 1639*, p. 32.
261. *Cal. Stat. Pap. Dom., 1634–5*, p. 381; Rawlinson MS A.297, f.85v. It is not clear whether Laud's figures were tithe valuations or included glebe terriers. In 1604 the House of Commons had asked for all benefices worth less than £20 to be augmented (Hill, *Economic Problems of the Church*, p. 251).
262. C. Holmes, *Seventeenth Century Lincolnshire* (Lincoln, 1980), p. 56; M. Stieg, *Laud's Laboratory: the Diocese of Bath and Wells in the Early Seventeenth Century* (1983), p. 148.
263. *Cal. Stat. Pap. Dom., 1634–5*, p. 422.
264. Ellesmere MSS 6805, 6806.
265. Bristol Record Office, Common Council Books, 3, f.16v, Oct. 1629.

be paid them.[266] Cases like that of George Woodland, farmer of tithes at Wigston's hospital, Leicester against Arthur Hall, who had failed to pay them, show how difficult the recovery of clerical dues could be; Hall appealed successively to the Arches (the audience court of Canterbury) and then moved a prohibition to the Common Pleas, during all which time he did not pay his tithes.[267] The pathetic case of John Reinoldes was probably far from untypical. In 1629 he wrote to Lady Temple of Stowe, Buckinghamshire, that he was deeply in debt and enjoyed only £7 a year, 'a poor pittance to maintain the town's priest. My necessity hath been and is exceeding great. I protest before the Lord I have preached twice in one day at this church sundry times and fasted all the day not having wherewith to feed myself.' Not having had 12d. in as many months, Reinoldes denounced his parishioners as 'peevish', and 'void of Christianity'. He had little time for Sir Thomas Temple, whom he accused of taking the straw from the church and still demanding the bricks.[268]

The consequences of that degree of dependence are not hard to see: worry about money, Reinoldes pointed out, distracted the clergy from their duties. Money could also be used as a form of control. The parishioners of Stradbrooke in Suffolk were in possession of land worth £40 per annum which had been bequeathed for godly purposes. They were prepared to employ it in order to purchase a lease of the impropriated rectory to supplement the stipend of their vicar, James Bucke. Two parishioners, however, George Borrett and Francis Sancroft, took exception to Bucke's efforts to bring their parish to conformity and deprived him of the benefit.[269] This poverty and dependence of the clergy undermined the parochial structure and Laud's and the king's desire for uniformity; indeed they feared it threatened the very existence of the church. One report on the dilapidated parishes of the realm confirms their fears. Where there was a maintenance of less than £70, and often no curate, 'the parishioners are occasioned either to resort to foreign parish churches and leave their own, or else to provide for themselves such stipendiary lecturers as often times preach those parishes, sometimes those noble towns, into sects and factions to the great disquiet of the church'.[270]

Such fears underlay Charles I's and Laud's campaign against the feoffees for impropriations. The feoffees were a group of lawyers, clergymen and merchants who from the beginning of Charles's reign

266. *Cal. Stat. Pap. Dom., 1635*, p. 126.
267. *Ibid.*, p. 148.
268. Temple of Stowe MSS, Correspondence Box 7, STT 1664: John Reinoldes to Lady Temple [C.1629].
269. *Cal. Stat. Pap. Dom., 1635*, p. 528.
270. Rawlinson MS D.353, f.82.

combined to raise contributions for the purchase of lay impropriations and advowsons and the appointment of their chosen candidates to benefices and lectureships.[271] For some years they were left to their work, probably not least because their intention of improving the endowment of an impoverished church and clergy was officially commended, and there had been little close scrutiny of their appointments or activities.[272] John Browne, for example, informed the Earl of Huntingdon in March 1633 that he had agreed to the appointment of Mr Mould to a schoolmaster's place, being satisfied with his scholarly attainments, on the recommendation of the feoffees. Little had he known that Mould was a man 'publicly defamed'.[273] Laud may all along have had his suspicions, seeing the names of William Gouge, Richard Sibbes and John Davenport among the feoffees. But the whistle was blown on their activities, or so Peter Heylyn tells us, by a fellow of Magdalen College, Oxford (himself) resorting to a town in Gloucestershire where he noticed that the impropriation acquired by the feoffees remained in lay hands, and that the lecturer appointed was a nonconformist. On his return to Oxford, on 11 July 1630, the Magdalen don preached in St Mary's on the enemy who sowed tares amongst the wheat.[274] Soon after William Noy, whose biblical knowledge was obviously as good as his legal learning, began a prosecution of the feoffees in the Exchequer court. Notes by Laud that may have been taken in connection with the case, endorsed 'the feoffment of Norwich', mention twelve trustees in the city who had raised £200, which they forwarded to London, to 'prototrustees'. These then paid £20 per annum to one Bridges, 'an absurd and turbulent fellow', to preach.[275] Though the feoffees insisted publicly that all beneficiaries of their patronage were graduates and conformable to the Church of England, Laud believed this was 'only to the eye of the world'.[276] When we note that nearly all the feoffees were also adventurers in New England companies, we may conclude that on this occasion he did not react with excessive paranoia.[277]

In 1632 information was exhibited in the Exchequer against the feoffees for holding property without the consent of the crown. The court found that they had not employed the money raised as had

271. See Hill, *Economic Problems of the Church*, ch. 11 and I.M. Calder (ed.) *Activities of the Puritan Faction of the Church of England, 1625–1633* (1957). Calder lists their purchases, pp. xv–xvii.
272. Cf. Calder, *Activities of the Puritan Faction*, pp. 47, 59.
273. Hastings MS 1071: John Browne to Huntingdon, 4 March 1633.
274. Heylyn, *Cyprianus Anglicus*, p. 199; Gardiner, *History of England*, VII, p. 258.
275. *Cal. Stat. Pap. Dom., 1625–49*, p. 400.
276. *Ibid.*
277. V. Pearl, *London and the Outbreak of the Puritan Revolution* (Oxford, 1964), p. 164. Davenport left for America.

been intended by the donors. Impropriations had been purchased not to fund or augment the stipends of permanent incumbents; funds were deployed to pay lecturers who remained accountable to the organization.[278] Charles I learned that at Bunbury in Cheshire, the Haberdashers' Company appointed a preacher whom they claimed to displace at will. 'I will not,' he asserted, 'endure that any lay person (much less a corporation) have power to place and displace curates or beneficed prelates at their pleasure.'[279] The court ordered that the feoffees be dissolved, and there was evidently some consideration of criminal proceedings against them.[280] Laud expressed his relief in his diary: 'they were the main instruments for the puritan faction to undo the church'.[281] The feoffees' assets were confiscated to the crown and Charles decreed that they be bestowed in 'the right and best way' for the maintenance of incumbents.[282] Accordingly the rectory of Dunstable, purchased by the feoffees, was granted to the church there, that of Cirencester to its church; a £20 annuity was given to Beaulieu church in Hampshire; another annuity went to Marlow church in Buckinghamshire. The profits of the rectory of Aylesbury were bestowed on the free school of the town, the profits of wool in Rinver Whittington, Staffordshire on their school.[283] The feoffees did not all earn the king's displeasure: Richard Sibbes was appointed to a vicarage.[284] The contributions raised by the feoffees were employed for 'pious work' but appointments were taken out of puritan control.[285]

As well as the feoffees for impropriations there were more conservative, even official, programmes for improving the wealth of the church and the condition of the clergy. Among the Ellesmere manuscripts, dated September 1629, we find a document that advocates a scheme for restoring to the church impropriate parsonages and tithes (by purchase or by gift) and for securing to the crown perpetual annuities from the same. The proponent of the plan, Richard Day, son of William Day, bishop of Winchester, argued that the landed families of the realm would finance the scheme. He cited those, such as Sir Richard Anderson of Shropshire or Mr Hampden of Buckinghamshire, who had voluntarily donated to the church impropriations in their hands. The son of a knight who had thrown himself off a church steeple in London restored five or six impropriations (to atone for his

278. Calder, *Activities of the Puritan Faction*, pp. 50–61, 119–20. Calder prints Noy's speech and other documents pertaining to the case.
279. Bridgeman, *History of the Church and Manor of Wigan*, II, p. 369.
280. Calder, *Activities of the Puritan Faction*, pp. 109, 123.
281. *Works of Laud*, III, p. 216.
282. Rushworth, *Historical Collections*, II, p. 150.
283. PRO, SO 1/3, f.147v.
284. Gardiner, *History of England*, VII, p. 259.
285. Rushworth, *Historical Collections*, II, p. 150.

father's sacrilege and death) and, Day added, there were many others with consciences troubled by intermeddling with church property and tithes. All that was needed, he concluded, was royal encouragement and the issue of letters patent authorizing a national collection.[286] The language of contemporary discussion suggests that others thought that with Charles I, that most un-Erastian of monarchs, on the throne and parliamentary anticlericalism silenced, the time for the cause of the church was ripe. The author of *The Curse of Sacrilege* (1630) inveighed against laymen who took the tithes of the church as robbers of God and against Henry VIII, its greatest despoiler, as a beastly man.[287] Along with strong rhetoric came radical plans. Among Laud's papers at Lambeth palace is a set of propositions suggesting that *all* church lands should be restored to the church and their lay purchasers compensated only with leases for lives. The author propounded that when any nobleman made a suit to the king, it should be granted only on condition that the beneficiary show that he provided proper maintenance for the clergy; all grants of lands, pensions or annuities, he suggested, should be subject to a 20 per cent withholding.[288]

No national collection was in fact instituted, nor were such radical programmes implemented, but within the bounds of realism, the king did take action. In 1632 Charles ordered a systematic investigation of rectories formerly in the crown's patronage and alienated since 30 Elizabeth. A signet letter informed the archbishop of Canterbury that some in possession of royal manors had usurped a right to appoint incumbents on the false pretence that the advowson had been appended to their property. Henceforth, it was ordered, pending the enquiry, no presentation to a living was to be made until the king had reviewed it.[289] An instance from Heysham, Lancashire, suggests that the king took back the advowson when those who laid claim to it could not prove their title.[290] Doubtless Charles was inclined to do more: in the *Eikon Basilike* he declared his abhorrence for the usurpation of church property.[291] In Ireland forty or fifty advowsons were restored to the crown after William Murray's unrelenting campaign there to search out advowsons that had been usurped from the king.[292] In 1634 such royal impropriations in Ireland were handed over to the church.[293] Similarly the initial draft of the Act of Revocation of 1625 for Scotland

286. Ellesmere MS 6999.
287. B.E., *The Curse of Sacrilege* (Oxford, 1630, STC 1025), pp. 12, 20 and *passim*.
288. Lambeth Palace MS 943, p. 395.
289. PRO, SO 1/2, f.112v, 17 July 1632; Nottingham University Library, Clifton MS Cl/C 140.
290. Bridgeman, *History of the Church and Manor of Wigan*, II, p. 402.
291. *Eikon Basilike* (1649), p. 102.
292. PRO, SO 1/2, ff.85, 138; Lambeth Palace MS 943, p. 553.
293. Hill, *Economic Problems of the Church*, pp. 334–6.

mooted the restoration to the kirk of all lands that had fallen into lay hands since 1542.[294] Excited doubtless by the programme in Ireland and Scotland some churchmen in England began to fantasize 'that the king would take all ecclesiastical livings into his hands to dispose of . . . because of the many corruptions and abuses of laymen patrons'. The realistic knew, however, that 'this is supposed too good to be true'.[295] The common law limited the inroads that could be made on lay impropriations, even if, as we shall see, it did not always calm the fears of the laity that their property was under threat.[296] In practice, royal action was limited to incidents and gestures – Charles, for example, attached a fellowship at Eton to the underendowed vicarage of Windsor – and to making sure things did not get worse.[297] In 1638 the Masters of Requests were ordered to present no petitions relating to the church without full information so that the king could be sure to prevent prejudices to the clergy.[298] Beyond that, what was achieved was, as Christopher Hill demonstrated, an 'anti-climax'.[299]

However, whilst they could do little to recover impropriations, Charles and Laud did support the clergy in their efforts and actions to secure from reluctant lay patrons and local inhabitants the stipends and tithes that were their due. In the case of stipends, Laud endeavoured to revive the rights of pre-Reformation bishops to ensure that appropriators paid fair maintenance to the clergy.[300] In 1634, in a test case, the vicar of Preshute, Wiltshire brought a suit in the church courts against the impropriator for not allowing him adequate maintenance. The impropriator endeavoured by prohibition to remove the case to the common law courts but he was refused and was ordered by the ordinary, the bishop of Salisbury (Davenant) to augment the stipend.[301] Armed with legal precedent, Laud set out to improve others: the bishop of Ely was instructed to urge the Earl of Bedford to improve the living of a minister; Bishop Williams was told to review the stipends of vicars across his diocese. Charles I himself ordered a 100 per cent increase in the stipends of the ministers in St Giles (from £100 to £200 per annum).[302] But often bishops themselves were wary of upsetting powerful laity and as the 1630s progressed, any far-reaching

294. *Ibid.*, p. 332.
295. Boas, *Diary of Thomas Crosfield*, p. 82.
296. *Works of Laud*, VI, part 1, p. 310; below, pp. 392–3, 400, 776.
297. Tanner MS 314, f.75; cf. Bridgeman, *History of the Church and Manor of Wigan*, II, pp. 416–18.
298. Lambeth Palace MS 943, p. 639.
299. Hill, *Economic Problems of the Church*, p. 326.
300. *Ibid.*, p. 321.
301. *Ibid.*, pp. 322–3.
302. *Ibid.*, pp. 323–4, 329; *Cal. Stat. Pap. Dom., 1637–8*, p. 416.

plans that might have been entertained were curtailed by political considerations and the need to conciliate.

The same was true of tithes. In 1634 the clergy of London petitioned the king that many benefices in the rich capital were worth less than £40 and most under £100.[303] The reason, they complained, was that they had no way of discovering the true rent values of properties and that landlords often made two leases – one the legal transaction, the other to show the parson in order to deceive him by undervaluation out of his due tenth. They asked for the right of appeal over the head of the mayor to the Lord Keeper, 'to wage war with rich and powerful citizens' and petitioned for the 2s. 9d. in the pound decreed to them by 37 Henry VIII Cap 12.[304] The citizens who, it was acknowledged, paid most in tithes objected to any increase and, with the failure to secure a settlement by agreement, the case passed to the king and Council.[305] For three years nothing happened; then, in April 1638 the Council, bombarded by claim and counter-claim, ordered the civic authorities and ministers of each parish to make a return of their emoluments.[306] In January 1639 the king, still reviewing the case, granted that pending a settlement the clergy might sue for their tithes in the courts. Thereafter the issue was lost in the preoccupation with the Scots war.[307] The Norwich clergy fared better. Their petition to parliament for their maintenance in 1606 had failed as a result of the influence exerted by the city MPs.[308] Backed by Wren, however, in 1637 they petitioned the king who ordered that every citizen should pay 2s. in the pound, and that any refuser should be tried in Chancery.[309] The clergy however did not enjoy the fruits of their success for long: in 1641 the citizenry petitioned the Long Parliament against the settlement which, in Humphrey Prideaux's words was 'quashed . . . before it was ever thoroughly put in execution'.[310] Royal and archiepiscopal encouragement undoubtedly gave the spur to private clerical action: a study of the diocese of Bath and Wells has revealed a large number of tithe cases in the church courts during the 1630s.[311] But other than scattered successes, the action generally did more to fuel anticlericalism than greatly to improve the condition of the clergy.

303. Rawlinson MS D.353, f.87.
304. *Ibid.*, ff.87–8; PRO, SP 16/535/15; T.C. Dale (ed.) *The Inhabitants of London in 1638* (1931), pp. vi–vii.
305. PRO, SP 16/268/105; Dale, *Inhabitants of London*, pp. ix–x.
306. PRO, PC 2/49/128, 22 April 1638.
307. Dale, *Inhabitants of London*, pp. xi–xii; *Cal. Stat. Pap. Dom., 1638–9*, pp. 344–5.
308. Tanner MS 290, f.102.
309. Wren, *Parentilia*, p. 112.
310. Hill, *Economic Problems of the Church*, p. 286; Tanner MS 290, f.102; Tanner MS 220, f.130.
311. Stieg, *Laud's Laboratory*, pp. 132, 146.

In the programme to preserve and restore the wealth of the church, high among Charles's concerns was the maintenance of the bishoprics. 'How necessary and fit it is,' he wrote in 1631, 'for the maintenance of the church that bishoprics dispossessed by violent usurpations and reduced to poverty should by all fit and lawful means be favoured and supported.'[312] When occasion arose the king moved to improve the endowment of poor sees. He got the manor and farm of Horfield added to the bishopric of Bristol;[313] he showed interest in buying the advowson of Wigan to annex to the bishopric of Chester.[314] But preservation and improvement, the king stressed, were very much too the bishop's own responsibility. Accordingly, the dean and prebends of Peterborough were urged to husband their resources better when the manors of Castor and Sutton, which had been greatly undervalued in the last transaction, came up for re-lease.[315] The dean of Exeter was forbidden by royal order to exercise the power granted to him by the chapter to let lands and manors belonging to the church because, the king suspected, private ends might be preferred 'to the great hazard of the common good of the said church'.[316] The bishop of Hereford, we saw, was rebuked for using 'bishopric timber' for his own household purposes.[317] Generally bishops were ordered not to grant long leases of lands and those departing from a see were forbidden from entering into transactions that might impoverish a successor.[318] Similar concern was exhibited over preserving the livelihood of collegiate churches. In 1634 Charles wrote personally to the dean of Salisbury concerning the inconveniences arising from leasing church lands for lives. Though by ancient statute deans were authorized to let properties for twenty-one years or three lives, 'time and experience have made it apparent that there is a great deal of difference between them especially in church leases where men are commonly in years before they come to those places'.[319] To prevent avaricious deans from mortgaging the future the royal order prescribed grants for years only – 'all which we have done,' Charles told the dean and chapter of Canterbury, 'for the great good and advancement of the church.'[320] The fundamental economic problems of the church were beyond royal resolution; in the end the church depended on the charity and generosity of the laity. But within

312. PRO, SO 1/2, f.47v.
313. *Ibid.*, f.134v; *Cal. Stat. Pap. Dom., 1638–9*, p. 205: Charles I to Bishop Skinner [1638].
314. Bridgeman, *History of the Church and Manor of Wigan*, II, pp. 416–18.
315. PRO, SO 1/3, f.105, 9 Nov. 1638.
316. PRO, SO 1/2, f.33v, Sept. 1630.
317. Coke MS 59: Laud to Bishop Coke, 27 Oct. 1638.
318. Cardwell, *Documentary Annals*, p. 229: instructions to bishops, 1629; cf. Tanner MS 70, f.45: orders to bishops, 19 Jan. 1635; and *Cal. Stat. Pap. Dom., 1634–5*, p. 88: Charles I to Laud, 22 June 1634.
319. Rawlinson MS B.372, f.16: Charles I to the dean of Salisbury, 22 June 1634.
320. Tanner MS 128, f.41: Charles I to dean and chapter of Canterbury, 20 June 1634.

the limits of the law and his own means, Charles I endeavoured to improve the bishoprics and benefices of England; to ensure that they received their due and preserved their resources for the good of the church.

The fabric of the church

The king's and Laud's programme for religious uniformity focused attention on the parish church as the centre of worship and community. The parish churches of England, however, were themselves monuments not to the beauty of holiness but to the poverty of the church and years of neglect. In part the decay of many churches reflected a puritan preoccupation with the invisible church of the saints rather than the visible church of the parish. As two offenders in Somerset charged with damaging and profaning the church said in their defence, 'where is the church? The church is where the congregation is assembled, though it be at the beacon upon the top of the hill.'[321] But in larger part the neglect during the early Stuart years owed much, in Clarendon's words, to 'the remissness of Abbot and of other bishops by his example' who had allowed churches 'to be kept so indecently and slovenly . . . the rain and the wind to infest them'.[322] Clarendon did not exaggerate. Neglect and ruin had literally left some parishes without a church at all, forcing the inhabitants to attend services elsewhere. In no few parishes of England, as Sir Marmaduke Lloyd put it to the Earl of Bridgewater, 'iam seges est ubi Sion fuit' (There is now a cornfield where once was the house of God).[323] As alarming were the many more churches on the verge of imminent collapse. Wren's visitation of Norwich revealed churches where the roof was open to the thatch (at Stratton Strawless) or 'the roof is off' (as at Great Witchingham) and others (as at Horsey and Eccles) 'standing already within the sea'.[324] In May 1634 Bishop Morton reported the 'desperate desolation' of churches in Northumberland.[325] In 1633 the archbishop of York's visitation report confessed that in most places churches 'are very miserable and ruinous in the fabric'.[326] Laud's metropolitical visitation of 1634 listed numerous cases around the country of 'ecclesia desolat';[327] and the sorry story was repeated

321. Bates-Harbin, *Quarter Sessions Records for . . . Somerset*, II, p. xxvi.
322. Clarendon, *History of the Rebellion*, I, p. 126.
323. Ellesmere MS 7412: Sir Marmaduke Lloyd to Bridgewater, 16 Aug. 1637.
324. Tanner MS 68, f.209.
325. *Cal. Stat. Pap. Dom., 1634–5*, p. 39.
326. Bridgeman, *History of the Church and Manor of Wigan*, II, p. 368.
327. Canterbury Cathedral diocesan archives, bishops' registers, V7; call books V/V/45, esp. f.63v.

the next year in Nathaniel Brent's (Laud's vicar-general) catalogue of churches 'utterly decayed'.[328] Notes from the visitation of Buckinghamshire in 1637 suggest that no church was in a completely satisfactory state of repair, with damage ranging from broken seats and windows to falling steeples and decaying chancels.[329] At Bladon, Buckinghamshire, 'it rains in the West end of the church'; at Wyrandsbury it snowed in.[330] At Elm in Cambridge, it rained on the altar.[331]

Imminent collapse and serious decay were obviously the worst problems but by any standards even many of the churches of solid structure appear to have been unfit places for worship. William Pickering was prosecuted in Star Chamber in Trinity term 1638 for, among other offences, converting part of a consecrated church into a pigsty;[332] keeping pigs and other animals in the churchyard was common.[333] At St Mary's Bungay, Suffolk, the churchyard had been converted into an alehouse;[334] markets were held in churches on wet days in the diocese of York.[335] In Norwich, according to Wren's reports, from inns with back doors on to the churchyard inhabitants 'issued in the night at their back doors into the churchyard and there . . . buried the emptyings of their jakes'.[336] At Woodbridge the parishioners did not even have to make that unsavoury journey for on one side of the churchyard 'in open view did hang a privy house'.[337] Almost every diocesan report confirmed the impression that in many of the parishes of England churches were dilapidated, profaned or inadequately furnished for the solemnities of worship. Even judging by standards less elevated than those set by the Laudians, churches like Westhamprett in Sussex where they 'christen in a bucket' lacked some of the trappings of holiness.[338]

On 11 October 1629 Charles I, probably at Laud's prompting, issued a proclamation, the first of the century, 'for preventing the

328. *Cal. Stat. Pap. Dom., 1634–5*, pp. 204–5; PRO, SP 16/293/128.
329. PRO, SP 16/366/79. Cf. E.R.C. Brinkworth, 'The Laudian church in Buckinghamshire', *Univ. of Birmingham Hist. Journ.* 5 (1955–6), pp. 31–59, esp. 41–7.
330. PRO, SP 16/366/79.
331. W.M. Palmer (ed.) *Episcopal Visitation Returns for Cambridgeshire* (Cambridge, 1930), p. 59.
332. Rawlinson MS C.827, 30 May 1638.
333. For example, York City Records Office, quarter sessions, F.7, pp. 133–4; Hastings MSS, HAM, Box 26: Huntingdon's charge; PRO, SP 16/293/128; Tanner MS 68, ff.209–17.
334. Tanner MS 68, f.213.
335. Bridgeman, *History of the Church and Manor of Wigan*, II, p. 369.
336. Tanner MS 68, f.316.
337. *Ibid.*, f.317v.
338. Fletcher, *A County Community in Peace and War*, p. 86.

decays of churches and chapels'.[339] Archbishops, bishops and deacons were instructed to enquire into the condition of churches within their jurisdiction 'and therein not to rely upon the churchwardens' presentments who to save themselves and their neighbours from charge will easily omit to make known the decays of their churches and their own defaults'.[340] The responsibility for remedying the defects once noted was placed firmly with the parish, and bishops were urged to use the ecclesiastical courts to enforce payments of rates for repairs. The proclamation prompted close attention during episcopal visitations to the detection and correction of defects. Action began to be taken by ecclesiastical authorities even against gentlemen of substance who were often the worst offenders in neglecting to pay for repairs. Giles Fleming, author of *Magnificence Exemplified*, bitterly remarked that the average gentleman 'would be more liberal to a horse race than to a synagogue'.[341] Whilst there are some splendid exceptions – Lord William Howard of Naworth's household accounts show his generosity in maintaining churches – many gentry had been lax and were now charged for years of neglect.[342] Sir Thomas Temple of Stowe was prosecuted for non-payment of arrears for repair of the church at Lutterworth, Leicestershire, where he held between 400 and 500 acres.[343] The accounts of John Edwards, bailiff to Thomas Smyth of Ashton Court, show a payment in January 1636 to a glazier 'for mending high chancel windows *for which my Master was presented*'.[344] Sir Edward Dering in Kent was presented often by the churchwardens of Charing for allowing the aisle there to decay and was threatened with a citation by Nathaniel Brent if he failed to remedy it.[345] Wren reported Sir William Russell, Treasurer of the Navy, to the king in the account of his diocese of 1637 for allowing Lenwood church to fall into disrepair.[346] The records of Chichester registry show regular citations, of clergy as well as laymen, for failure to carry out maintenance work;[347] in Bath and Wells a high proportion of gentlemen were presented for failing to repair or pay rates for the church.[348]

339. Larkin, *Stuart Royal Proclamations*, II, no. 212, pp. 248–50.
340. *Ibid.*, p. 249.
341. G. Fleming, *Magnificence Exemplified and the Repair of St Pauls Exhorted Unto* (1634, STC 11052), p. 51.
342. G. Ornsby (ed.) *Selections from the Household Books of the Lord William Howard of Naworth Castle* (Surtees Soc., 68, 1878), pp. 319–20.
343. Temple of Stowe MSS, STT M, Box 19.
344. Bristol Record Office, Smyth of Ashton Court MS 36074/22.
345. Dering MS U275/C1/5: Brent to Dering, 27 Sept. 1633.
346. Works of Laud, V, p. 351.
347. BL Add. MS 39425: 'Extracts from Chichester registry'; cf. West Sussex Record Office, EP 1/22/1 and 1/26/2.
348. Stieg, *Laud's Laboratory*, p. 238.

The number of citations is evidence of course that the problem was not solved, but it is equally clear that close investigation and threats of citation also produced results. Dering promised to re-edify the chapel. In 1633 Thomas Morland, also of Kent, was forced to show a certificate that he had repaired Sutton church in order to avoid being jailed.[349] By 1637 Bishop Bridgeman was claiming that churches in his diocese had been placed in decent condition, thanks to the bequests of the laity.[350] Travellers round England – such as Sir William Brereton and a captain and lieutenant from Norwich – testify to real improvements in church buildings, furnishings and decoration.[351] More generally, as we shall see, parish records, in particular churchwardens' accounts, such as those of Ashhurst in Chichester, or Shorne in Kent, suggest increases in parish expenditure on repairs, windows, bell-ropes, tables, churchyards, gates and fences.[352] Doubtless in some places any improvements were carried out grudgingly and only under official pressure: Bishop Corbet of Norwich reported strong feelings in some places against the restoration of churches and there is no shortage of examples of those who clung tightly to their purses.[353] But it may be the case too that in *some* parishes, official action provided only an extra spur to parish initiatives. It would seem that in some areas local pride led to independent action to restore and improve the parish church. Alderman Aldworth of Bristol left £15 in his will to be paid to the churchwardens of St Michael's towards the work of repairing the Minster there.[354] In Hayes, Middlesex 'on the entreaty of the parishioners' John Page provided a new pulpit and pews.[355] The churchwardens of St Bartholomew's, Chichester replied proudly to a question about their furniture that they did not have a dean's book, but as they were beautifying their church and chancel they would provide one.[356] For parishes that took, or wished to take, action on their own initiative, official encouragement and supervision offered opportunities. William Godsell, for instance, petitioned Laud directly for help to

349. Kent Archives Office, QSO/W1, f.44.
350. Bridgeman, *History of the Church and Manor of Wigan*, II, p. 395.
351. E. Hawkins (ed.) *Travels in Holland, the United Provinces, England, Scotland and Ireland by Sir William Brereton* (Chetham Soc., 1, 1844); L.G. Wickham Legg (ed), *A Relation of a Short Survey of Twenty-Six Counties . . . in a Seven week Journey begun . . . August 11 1634 by a Captain, a Lieutenant and an Ancient* (1904) and *idem* (ed.) *A Relation of a Short Survey of the Western Counties made by a Lieutenant of the Military Company in Norwich* (Camden Miscellany, 16, 1936).
352. Below, pp. 390–92; Kent Archives Office, P336/5/1; and Brinkworth, 'Laudian church in Buckinghamshire'.
353. *Cal. Stat. Pap. Dom., 1633–4*, p. 574; speech of Corbet at synod of clergy, 29 April 1634.
354. Bristol Common Council Books, 3, f.78.
355. *Cal. Stat. Pap. Dom., 1635*, pp. 68–9.
356. BL Add. MS 39425: dean's book 1629–37, 5 Oct. 1633 (foliation confused).

repair the dilapidated chapel of Royden, Somerset, where the font stone was being used as a cheese press.[357] The next year a High Commission order compelled a local rate for its restoration.[358] In 1631 the parishioners of St Albans Wood Street petitioned the bishop of London to require the minister's assistance to restore their church.[359] Sympathy from on high made it easier for ordinary parishioners too to present not only recalcitrant ratepayers but neglectful clergy – as at Binderton, Chichester where Mr Biddulph the vicar was cited for not fencing in the churchyard.[360] Generous gifts – like Charles I's grant of a High Commission fine of £1,000 to York 'for repairing the ruins of the cathedral church' – probably set an example and primed the pump for other donations.[361]

Though more research needs to be done before we can conclude with confidence, the overall impression is that during the 1630s, in large part thanks to Laud's promptings, improvements were being made across England to parish churches that had long been in need of repair. In 1636 Neile claimed that over £6,000 was spent on such work in the East Riding of York alone.[362] Whilst the impetus to government action came in part from the importance Charles and Laud attached to the externals of worship and ceremony, it is also clear that the connection was not a necessary one. In Buckinghamshire, to take a case, Dinton and Shalstone churches were in very poor condition, but their altars were furnished properly.[363] More interestingly, some known for sympathies with puritanism actively supported the restorations of churches. On his tour of England Sir William Brereton noted with approval the fair churches of Bristol.[364] The Earl of Huntingdon during his travels showed great interest in the condition of churches and in particular praised those which were well maintained, with regular pews and even stained glass.[365] 'The beautifying and decoring of the Church,' Huntingdon wrote to Sir John Lambe, dean of the Arches, in 1634, 'all that are of impartial judgement must needs consent unto for the fittingness and decency thereof.'[366] In his address to the Leicestershire quarter sessions in 1638 he urged the importance

357. *Cal. Stat. Pap. Dom., 1637*, p. 491: Godsell to Laud, 21 Oct.
358. *Cal. Stat. Pap. Dom., 1638–9*, pp. 74–5.
359. PRO, SO 1/2, f.76, 2 Dec. 1631.
360. Canterbury Cathedral diocesan archives, 2/3/16, archdeacon's visitation of 1637; *Cal. Stat. Pap. Dom., 1635–6*, p. 307; West Sussex Record Office, EP 1/22/1: churchwardens' presentments, 1640, Binderton.
361. Note in York Minister chapter house, for Nov. 1632.
362. PRO, SP 16/312/84: Neile to Charles I, Jan. 1636.
363. PRO, SP 16/366/79: notes on visitation, 1637.
364. Hawkins, *Travels of Brereton*, p. 178.
365. Hastings MS, Personal HAP 18, and 5537: Huntingdon to Lambe, 8 Sept. 1634.
366. Hastings MS 5537.

of maintaining churches and churchyards.[367] While the costs and episcopal hectoring offended some, the programme to repair the churches did not necessarily arouse widespread antagonism, even from those who sympathized little with Laud's other preferences. 'The work,' according to Clarendon, 'sure was very grateful to all men of devotion.'[368]

St Paul's

The most public and most spectacular demonstration of the king's concern for the condition of churches was his ambitious scheme for the rebuilding of St Paul's cathedral in London. The poor, ruined state of the cathedral concerned Charles both because it was an eyesore in a metropolis that he wished to refashion as a capital of classical order and because St Paul's exemplified the neglect of cathedrals and churches around the country. Not only was the building decayed; it was marred by houses built illicitly on church property, some abutting its very walls. Moreover the cathedral and Paul's Walk had become, rather than a shrine of worship, an exchange where daily gathered a concourse of merchants, money-changers, newsmongers (like John Chamberlain and John Pory), conversationalists, idle loiterers, worse still pickpockets and whores who hung around its doors and meandered through the church itself.[369] One poor old gentleman up from the country who was arraigned for having defecated in St Paul's excused himself on the ground that he had not realized that he was in a church![370] His story was not incredible: the Privy Council itself reported in 1632 that St Paul's 'is used like a street for carriage through of all burdens, provisions and necessaries'.[371] In 1631, Gardiner suggests at Laud's prompting, Charles I visited the cathedral and instigated plans for its restoration. In June the king wrote to the mayor of London reminding the corporation of his general efforts to encourage the maintenance and re-edification of churches and urging the city to set a good example in the case of St Paul's, before contributions were requested from the country at large.[372] Money from the city came in slowly: by May 1633 only £5,400 had been collected[373] – just half the £10,000 that the commissioners for pious uses had deemed necessary as

367. Hastings MS, HAM, 26.
368. Clarendon, *History of the Rebellion*, I, p. 126.
369. PRO, PC 2/41/354; Gardiner, *History of England*, VII, pp. 245–6.
370. *Cal. Stat. Pap. Dom., 1635*, p. 234.
371. PRO, PC 2/41/354.
372. *Cal. Stat. Pap. Dom., 1631–3*, p. 95.
373. *Cal. Stat. Pap. Dom., 1633–4*, p. 65: Inigo Jones to committee, May 1633.

capital before work could be begun.[374] In December 1633 therefore the king issued commissions to the counties, usually to the JPs. The letter appointing them informed the commissioners of the decay of the church occasioned by the possessions that once supported it falling into lay hands; further neglect, they were told, might lead the cathedral to collapse. The bounty of the king and other individuals had proved insufficient. It was now for the commissioners to call the residents of their counties and to request their free aid, 'using to them such persuasions as to your wisdom shall be thought expedient'.[375] An enthusiastic and popular response was obviously anticipated: the meaner people, the commissioners were advised, not having time to attend upon them, should be permitted to pay their contributions to the churchwardens of their parishes. Ministers were to keep full accounts of payments and promises of payments in parish books, and the commissioners were instructed to record the names of all donors and the sums they advanced. The moneys received and the records kept were to be delivered to the chamber in London. Other than feeling the need to assure the commissioners that all moneys raised would truly be spent on St Paul's, the king and Council appear to have been confident that the necessity and piety of the work would be its own self-evident advocate.

Such confidence was not entirely misplaced. In Hampshire, the commissioners Henry Wallop and Sir Thomas Jervoise (though of puritan sympathies) embarked diligently on their task. They repeated the king's own language describing the collection as 'a work of that pious consequence that we doubted of no man's forwardness therein'.[376] They set an example by promising large sums themselves: Wallop £10 a year over three years, Jervoise £5.[377] They pressured gentlemen who did not voluntarily come forward to appear before them.[378] The response in Hampshire was uneven: of thirty summoned in March 1634 in Basingstoke, nine failed to appear.[379] In Micheldever, however, thirty-five inhabitants, most of modest means, offered £2 15s. and in Odiham seventy-nine parishioners contributed £12, some through gifts of pennies.[380] Doubtless some like William Willoway who in 1634 promised to pay 6d. in 1636 may have promised more than they hoped to be obliged to perform, but the sums paid and the numbers contributing in Hampshire suggest at least that the levy was

374. *Cal. Stat. Pap. Dom., 1631–3*, p. 528.
375. Herriard MS, Box 012: commission of 20 Dec. 1633.; cf. *Bibliotheca Regia*, pp. 265–6.
376. Herriard MS 44/M/69, Box 013 (quarter sessions), 26 March 1633.
377. Herriard MS, Box 012: file on repairs to St Paul's.
378. *Ibid.*, Box 013.
379. *Ibid.*, 26 March 1633.
380. *Ibid.*, Box 012.

not unpopular.[381] In Bristol, the clergy set the example. Payment of 40s. in three instalments by George Williamson, vicar of All Saints, initiated other donations and promises from the deanery and clergy.[382] Leading citizens such as Sir Ferdinando Gorges and Thomas Smyth offered 20s. a year for the years that it was projected the building work would take; others followed their lead with donations and pledges of 10s.[383] Once again payments by the lower orders, largely through collections in church, raised over £18. The corporation of York, within days of receiving the commission, summoned all citizens who were charged with payments for the relief of the poor to contribute to St Paul's.[384] In Kent, at Ashford and East Yalding, perhaps on account of the example of generosity set by Sir Roger Twysden and Sir Edward Dering, many contributed according to their assessment in the subsidy book;[385] across the county the response was less positive.[386] Our best evidence and fullest picture comes from the Marches, where the Earl of Bridgewater vigorously championed the collection and kept detailed records. There we see that over the thirty-seven parishes of the hundred of Oswestry of 367 souls summoned, 344 contributed and only 23 refused or failed to pay.[387] Across the country the initial response appears to have been encouraging. Though perhaps significantly in the heartland of puritanism near Colchester, as William Lynne complained to Laud, 'the best gave not so much as was spent in persuading them', there appears to have been no concerted puritan opposition to the collection.[388] John Bastwick's denunciation of the re-edification of St Paul's – 'making a seat for a priest's arse' – evidently struck little chord with godly gentlemen like Wallop, Dering, Jervoise, Bridgewater and others who laboured to further it.[389] By Michaelmas 1633 nearly £18,000 had been received into the chamber at London; by September the following year well over £30,000.[390]

The success was not evenly sustained. The king, Council and others tried to keep up the initial momentum and pressure. Charles himself took on the entire cost of building what was to become the splendid west portal of the cathedral (see Figure 35);[391] he also decreed that all

381. *Ibid.*
382. Bristol Record office, EP/A/30/1: 'The benevolence and contribution of the clergy within the city and deanery of Bristol'.
383. Smyth of Ashton Court MS 36214: collection for St Paul's, 1633.
384. York House Books, 35, f.188: 15 Jan. 1633.
385. Dering MS U570/01, f.109, 27 Aug. 1634 (Ashford); Kent Archives Office, Twysden MS U47/47/Z2, f.73, 8 Aug. 1634 (East Yalding).
386. Dering MS U350/C2/49.
387. Ellesmere MS 7422.
388. *Cal. Stat. Pap. Dom., 1634–5*, p. 252, 29 Oct. 1634.
389. Carlton, *Laud*, p. 95.
390. *Cal. Stat. Pap. Dom., 1633–4*, p. 442; *1634–5*, p. 220.
391. PRO, SO 1/2, f.177v: Charles I to Laud, May 1634; Lambeth Palace MS 943, p. 361.

35 *St Paul's from the West*, etching by Wenceslaus Hollar, 1656. The inscription on the Corinthian portico announces that it was paid for by Charles I.

fines in the court of High Commission should go towards St Paul's.[392] Giles Fleming, a vicar of Waddingworth, Lincolnshire, exhorted his fellow clergy and countrymen to contribute to an edifice that stood for the whole church of England.[393] Encouragement was accompanied by pressure: hints were given to the clergy that their career prospects might be affected by their response.[394] Names were kept of all who paid and did not pay, even though contributions were 'voluntary', and the committee for charitable uses perused records monthly.[395] The widow Mary More who refused to contribute was deprived on the king's own order of the favourable lease she held of St Paul's.[396] Despite example and pressure, however, between 1634 and 1637 the contributions waned. Even in counties that at first responded well payments dwindled. Micheldever, Hampshire, which had contributed

392. Bodleian, Bankes MS 43/63, 26 March 1636.
393. Fleming, *Magnificence Exemplified*, p. 49 and *passim*.
394. Gardiner, *History of England*, VII, p. 245, note 2.
395. PRO, PC 2/43/444; PC 2/45/373, 23 Jan. 1636.
396. *Cal. Stat. Pap. Dom., 1634–5*, p. 428.

£2 15s. in 1634 paid only 15s. in 1636.[397] As for Wiltshire, where some had promised substantial sums, Laud in June 1637 complained that over the last two years only 8s. 10d. had been collected.[398] The decline in payments is again best documented for the Marches. On 9 July 1637 the Council wrote to Bridgewater to reprimand him for the slow collection in the border counties, whence it appeared 'by the imperfect books sent by some of those parts to the chamber of London that many of known abilities have refused or very meanly contributed giving example thereby to the inferior sort'.[399] Bridgewater's own investigations confirmed the Council's pessimistic impressions. In Cirencester, he was informed, much of what was paid remained in private hands.[400] Sir Marmaduke Lloyd was more graphic: many, he declared, had pulled down churches rather than repair them; there were more men willing to rob Peter than to pay Paul![401] Though Gloucestershire had perfected its records, Bridgewater had by September 1637 received no account books from Worcestershire, Denbigh, Flint, Herefordshire, Montgomery or Pembrokeshire.[402] And although accounts from Merioneth show that the numbers of defaulters there were still few, in general the readiness to contribute had faded.[403] The years 1636 and 1637 saw just over £9,000 and £10,000 respectively paid into the chamber at London, not much more than half the sums raised in the first year.[404]

Some historians may be tempted to see the decline in response as evidence of mounting disenchantment with the Caroline regime in general and with Laud's archiepiscopate in particular. Certainly this explanation should not be discounted. In issuing the commission Charles had felt obliged to scotch 'rumours or imaginations of diverting the said monies to any other purpose' as 'but the fancies of men either grossly malevolent or causelessly jealous'.[405] In May 1634 he expressed to Laud his fear that enemies to the work were stirring up trouble by pretending that the Council planned to raise money under the pretence of a pious end 'and then to turn it to other uses'.[406] He repeated the same worry to Juxon in 1637.[407] It may be too – though there is little direct evidence – that the rebuilding of St Paul's suffered,

397. Herriard MS, Box 012.
398. Rawlinson MS B.372, f.15, 30 June 1637.
399. Ellesmere MS 7410.
400. Ellesmere MS 7411: Bridgeman to Bridgewater, 12 Aug. 1637.
401. Ellesmere MS 7412: Lloyd to Bridgewater, 16 Aug. 1637.
402. Ellesmere MS 7514: draft of Bridgewater's letter to Council, 28 Sept. 1637.
403. Ellesmere MS 7418.
404. Carlton, *Laud*, p. 95.
405. Herriard MSS, Box 012.
406. Lambeth Palace MS 943, p. 361: Charles I to Laud, 20 April 1634; PRO, SO 1/2, f.177v.
407. *Cal. Stat. Pap. Dom., 1637*, pp. 118–19, 24 Nov. 1638.

in some men's minds at least, from its association with Laud's programme for the beauty of holiness; there was an unfortunately direct link between them when the restoration necessitated the demolition of St Gregory's, the church where, as we shall see, the disputes over the position of the communion table became a test case.[408] But in general the record suggests that the fall-off in contributions has more mundane and less ideological explanations. Clearly there were some who thought charity ought to begin closer to home. Sir John Monson, for example, told Laud that the backwardness of his county expressed no lack of zeal for the rebuilding of St Paul's but a concern for Lincoln cathedral.[409] Bishop Wright of Lichfield informed Lambe that in Staffordshire the citizens saw no fruit for them in the adornment of St Paul's and spent the money instead on the church at Tutbury.[410] Localism was not the only check to continuing generosity. The mayor of Haverfordwest hinted to the Earl of Bridgewater in 1637 that the two former years' contributions made the raising of a third much more difficult.[411] Richard Herbert was more explicit. The towns of Caldicot and Abergavenny, he explained, contributed poorly now on account of other recent costs and charges – for bridges, the repair of sea walls, most of all the plague, which added substantially to the payments for poor relief.[412] He closed his letter with a plea to spare his area *annual* contributions to St Paul's. From the JPs of Pembroke came similar references to 'many late exactions' and the inability of inhabitants to pay more.[413]

The story may well have been the same around many parts of the country. Plague, military charges, most of all ship money, added to local burdens. And as other charges mounted, the suspicion that contributions to St Paul's might become annual made them, as it was to make ship money, less acceptable and more resisted. In December 1635, the JPs of York had warned the Privy Council that even subjects who had come forward freely to contribute would not be willing to continue paying large sums, 'much less to be tied to annual contributions'.[414] Such reluctance is not evidence of opposition to the Laudian programme. For in 1639, perhaps after some relaxing of official pressure since 1637, £16,000 was paid towards St Paul's – a figure which equalled the first year's contribution at a time when the government was in no position to bully the recalcitrant.[415] Perhaps the

408. Rushworth, *Historical Collections*, II, p. 411; below, p. 333 ff.
409. *Cal. Stat. Pap. Dom., 1637*, p. 512, 2 Nov.
410. *Cal. Stat. Pap. Dom., 1638–9*, pp. 118–19, 24 Nov. 1638.
411. Ellesmere MS 7414, 28 Sept. 1637.
412. Ellesmere MS 7517, 14 Nov. 1637.
413. Ellesmere MS 7420, 7 May 1638.
414. *Cal. Stat. Pap. Dom., 1635*, p. 568, 16 Dec. 1635.
415. Carlton, *Laud*, p. 95.

visible evidence of what had been achieved provided the final spur: by the end of the decade St Paul's had been cleared of houses; the long nave 'stood exposed to view in its unrivalled proportions';[416] Inigo Jones was far advanced in his work on the Corinthian west portal; and was evidently proud enough of his achievement to make the improved St Paul's the centrepiece of one of the scenes in his masque, *Britannia Triumphans*.[417]

There were evidently many in London, and perhaps beyond, no less proud of the work. Heylyn, who acknowledged that the project had many enemies, claimed also that it had much support.[418] The anonymous author of *The Jew's High Commendation of the Metropolitan Cathedral Church of St Paul* in 1638 supports him.[419] St Paul's sings:

As famous as I ever have bin
I now shall receive my high renown
And all my honours returned me agen
I am old Paul of London town,
Now God preserve our Gracious King
Lord Mayor and the aldermen
which have been pleased in this noble thing
To give old Paul a new trimming agen.

Ceremonies

The restoration and enhancement of churches was for Charles I and Laud part of a larger reformation of worship, a renewed concern for ritual and ceremony. Almost from the creation of the Church of England prescribed ceremonies and liturgical practices had been neglected in many parishes of England. Laud wished to restore and enforce them and took his stand on the canons of 1604 which Abbot had failed to press. As we have seen, Laud regarded ceremonies as essential to the unity of the church: 'without some ceremonies,' he wrote in 1635 among notes on the Elizabethan Act of Uniformity, ''tis not possible to keep any order or quiet discipline.'[420] He also regarded the *acts* of worship – taking communion, kneeling, standing at the creed, bowing to the altar – not only as ancient approved ceremonies of the apostolic church, but as important as hearing the word. The

416. Gardiner, *History of England*, VII, p. 246.
417. S. Orgel and R. Strong (eds) *Inigo Jones: The Theatre of the Stuart Court* (2 vols, Berkeley and London, 1973), II, pp. 668–70.
418. Heylyn, *Cyprianus Anglicus*, p. 209.
419. *The Jew's High Commendation of the Metropolitan Cathedral Church of St Paul* (1638, Bodleian, Wood 401/126).
420. PRO, SP 16/308/38.

altar or table, not the pulpit, was for Laud 'the greatest place of God's residence on earth' and he felt himself 'bound to worship with body as well as soul'.[421] Reverence in the worship of God was the outward expression and bulwark of the inner faith. Laud denied that in this he was an innovator: on his summer visitation of 1634 Brent, Laud's vicar-general, pointed out 'that the present Archbishop would require no more than hath been required ever since the Reformation'.[422] Nor did he press all his own preferences – he never insisted on bowing for instance.[423] But his attachment to the implementation of the canons did see in many of the dioceses of England a new emphasis upon liturgical ceremonies and in some cases a concern with ritual that far surpassed his own.

Most of the apologiae for ceremonies during the 1630s suggest little concern with theology, and certainly little evidence of a connection with the Arminian doctrine of free will. In a sermon of 1639, John Swan urged his congregation to worship with the knees and hands, as well as the ear: 'to prefer preaching before praying is to magnify the means before the end'.[424] But he in no way denigrated preaching and pressed for the church of the Fathers, who had found time to preach and worship. Robert Skinner, royal chaplain, in a court sermon of 1634 on the text of Psalm 96, praised the 'present times where in the beauty of holiness . . . seems to revive and flourish . . . It argues religion hath life in it.'[425] But he was at pains to emphasize the inner beauty of the soul over the place or manner of worship.[426] Samuel Hoard defended the church's authority in prescribing ceremonies – citing Perkins's and Calvin's defence of them – but described them as the circumstance rather than substance of religion.[427] Christopher Dow similarly defended the church against the charge of innovation by showing that all ceremonies were prescribed by the Elizabethan injunctions and the canons and were anyway only 'external'.[428] Ambrose Fisher explicitly argued in his *Defence of the Liturgy* (1630) that in ceremonies was 'not necessity of holiness but peaceable uniformity of order'.[429]

Indeed many of those who defended ceremonies were products less

421. Bruce and Gardiner, *Documents Relating to the Proceedings against William Prynne*; F. Hargrave, *A Complete Collection of State Trials* (11 vols, 1776–81), I, pp. 491–2.
422. BL, Egerton MS 784, p. 207.
423. *Works of Laud*, V, p. 206; Hutton, *William Laud*, p. 95; Wren thought it prescribed by injunction 52; see Wren, *Parentilia*, p. 80.
424. J. Swan, *A Sermon*, p. 15.
425. R. Skinner, *A Sermon Preached before the King* (1634, STC 22628), p. 35.
426. *Ibid.*, p. 30.
427. S. Hoard, *The Church's Authority Asserted* (1637, STC 13533), pp. 5, 12.
428. C. Dow, *Innovations Unjustly Charged upon the Present Church and State* (1637, STC 7090), p. 115.
429. A. Fisher, *A Defence of the Liturgy* (1630, STC 10855), p. 39.

of the Caroline than the Jacobean church, with established Calvinist credentials. Bishop Henry King, a former chaplain to James I, regretted the lapse of certain ceremonies: 'God's name must be sanctified as by our inward so also by our outward worship.'[430] Robert Sanderson's sermon first preached in 1619 and published in 1632 denounced Arminius's corrupt doctrine and showed some sympathy to puritans, but defended ceremonies as the key to orderly worship.[431] Joseph Mede, who was once thought to look 'too much towards Geneva', argued for bodily worship in general and bowing in particular.[432] Bishop Griffith Williams dedicated to the Earl of Pembroke, whose chaplain he was, a study of *The True Church* in which he argued that 'no exception against ceremonies can be any excuse for separation from the church'.[433] Bishop Bridgeman of Chester, though lenient to the puritans in his diocese, raised the communion table in his cathedral, had the east window glazed with the story of the Annunciation and gilded the organ there.[434] John Williams of Lincoln consecrated the chapel of Lincoln College, Oxford to the Virgin and favoured in his own diocese music, organs, plate and other elaborate ornament.[435] A fondness for ceremony crossed the whole spectrum of theological positions.

To those puritans committed exclusively to the propagation of the word and through it man's personal communication with God the defence of ceremony was, as it had been in Elizabeth's reign, anathema. To Peter Smart, John Cosin, the dean of Durham's, insistence on standing and bowing, his elaborate altar and 340 candles at evensong turned worship 'well near into a theatrical stage play'.[436] Alexander Leighton's diatribe, *Sion's Plea Against the Prelacie*, denounced ceremonies as the relics of Antichrist.[437] In the cross bill that they presented against the bishops at their trial in Star Chamber Prynne, Burton and Bastwick upbraided them for introducing 'popish' rites - standing at the apostles' creed, bowing, praying to the east, kneeling, altarcloths, crucifixes and the like.[438] Such loud denunciations clearly had fainter

430. King, *An Exposition upon the Lord's Prayer*, pp. 94–5.
431. R. Sanderson, *Twelve Sermons Preached* (1632, STC 21706), first sermon.
432. J. Mede, *The Reverence of God's House* (1638, STC 17769), for example pp. 47, 52; *DNB*. He was bitterly denounced for doing so by old friends like William Twisse, the millenarian and future prolocutor to the Westminster Assembly. I owe this point to John Morrill.
433. G. Williams, *The True Church* (1629, STC 25721), epistle dedicatory, pp. 94–5, 163.
434. Bridgeman, *History of the Church and Manor of Wigan*, II, p. 449; Cheshire Record Office, EDA/3/1, ff.192v–193.
435. H. Hajzyk, 'The church in Lincolnshire', p. 102.
436. Rawlinson MS D.821, ff.4–7; cf. W.H.D. Longstaff (ed.) *The Acts of the High Commission in Durham* (Surtees Soc., 34, 1858), pp. 198, 215, 225.
437. A. Leighton, *An Appeal to the Parliament; or Sion's Plea against the Prelacie* (1628, STC 15429), see p. 94.
438. Tanner MS 299, ff.148–60v, esp. ff.150v, 154v.

echoes among the godly laity. In Kent Sir Edward Dering criticized bowing as a Catholic gesture;[439] Sir Henry Slingsby of Yorkshire disliked it too – 'I thought it came too near idolatry.'[440] Simonds D'Ewes expressed his sympathy for tender consciences that stumbled at a ceremony.[441] But, having acknowledged puritan antagonism, there is no reason to believe, and recent research that leads us to doubt, that the Caroline emphasis upon ceremonies met with widespread resistance or unpopularity. Even some of godly connections and inclinations appear little concerned at the emphasis on ceremonies. Viscount Conway, brother to Lady Brilliana Harley, saw no harm in church music nor any idolatry in the royal chapel, for all its altar, candlesticks and ceremony.[442] The puritan Sir William Waller claimed he was not 'nor ever was against a modest dress of religion'.[443] In Somerset, James Ashe, a puritan, in 1634 denounced the churchwardens of his parish for allowing the curate to refrain from wearing his surplice, to omit reading the liturgy at prayer and to fail to bow at the name of Jesus.[444]

For most laymen ceremonies may well have been a matter of greater indifference than historians have believed. As a sermon delivered in Dorset in 1637 put it, 'though there have been according to the diversity and different condition of succeeding times some alterations in sacraments and ceremonies yet the same Jesus Christ and the same salvation through Christ is both shadowed and signified in all.'[445] When attitudes and reactions to ceremonies were strong they may well have been more affected by changes in circumstance and local custom than by any concerted position or opposition among the parishioners. Because episcopal practice had long varied, local reactions were quite different. In Northamptonshire, William Dodson cited Archbishop Whitgift against the practice of bowing;[446] others observed that it was a practice advocated by Hooker, or instigated by Lancelot Andrewes.[447] In Norwich some defended Bishop Wren against the charge of innovation by pointing out that Dr Norton had preached in scarlet and that Bishop Harsnett had enjoined kneeling at communion.[448] In

439. Dering MS U133/02/8.
440. D. Parsons (ed.) *The Diary of Sir Henry Slingsby* (1836), pp. 7–8.
441. J.O. Halliwell (ed.) *The Autobiography and Correspondence of Sir Simonds D'Ewes* (2 vols, 1845), II, p. 119.
442. BL, MS 29/172, f.14. Conway spoke of the 'false ground' of Smart's attack on ceremonies: Conway to Harley, 3 Aug. 1630.
443. J.T. Cliffe, *The Puritan Gentry: The Great Puritan Families of Early Stuart England* (1984), p. 27.
444. Stieg, *Laud's Laboratory*, p. 202.
445. Rawlinson MS C 764, f.30, 6 Jan. 1638.
446. *Cal. Stat. Pap. Dom., 1634–5*, pp. 22–3.
447. Clarendon MS 4, no. 152; Rawlinson MS C.573, p. 9.
448. Tanner MS 314, f.180v: Mapletoft's defence of Wren.

St Andrew's, Canterbury the churchwardens presented Mr Ferrier for failing to kneel when the cup came to him at communion;[449] others protested against it as an innovation.[450] In Suffolk the spectrum of sensibilities was even more interesting: the laity did not object to bowing *per se* – 'Mr Beale [vicar of Ash Bocking] did indeed bow prettily and decently, as if he went to begin a dance'[451] – but to the manner – as of parson Bucke of Stradbrooke who 'went to it like an idolator with three congés down to the very ground'.[452] They were, however, alienated by quite traditional practices. William Proctor of Standishall was presented for the very orthodox gesture of 'preaching in his surplice and hood'.[453] In other words what was traditional and what was perceived as innovative (what was liked and disliked) differed from place to place and, since individual memory of even shared experience could be selective, from person to person. As Wren said himself against the charge of novelty: 'Speaking . . . of the religion and ceremonies in the Church of England, in as much as new and old are terms of relation and are said but respectively to former or later things, he humbly conceiveth it necessary, first to design the times upon which the state of our church is bounded and to which we intend to refer.'[454]

Laud's emphasis on canonical ceremonies, then, won him odium in some places; in others it only affirmed the status quo. Yet even when his injunctions appeared novel we should not assume that they automatically aroused antagonism. On several matters of novel emphasis (such as bowing or coming to the rails to receive communion) Laud proceeded with caution in the belief that people might be won over by observation of the decency of the practice.[455] His optimism was shared by the author of notes on the issue of bowing, in the Rawlinson manuscripts:

> The truth is that pious ceremony (though established by canon yet) through long removing by ecclesiastical governors had been so generally disused . . . that the vicar's using of that gesture seemed at the first uncouth to sundry otherwise very conformable men which being now reduced to the ancient course again is offensive to none but such as will not be pleased [?but] with their own fancies.[456]

449. Canterbury Cathedral diocesan archives, 2/3/16: archdeacon's visitation, 1637.
450. Cf. Rawlinson MS D.353, f.141.
451. Holmes, *Suffolk Committees for Scandalous Ministers*, p. 45.
452. *Ibid.*
453. *Ibid.*, p. 86; this was one of his 'late innovations'.
454. Wren, *Parentilia*, p. 99.
455. Above, pp. 291–2.
456. Rawlinson MS D.353, f.141.

He may have been right: in Taunton only one man was presented for not kneeling at communion;[457] by the end of the 1630s, Laud reported that receiving at the rails was no longer contentious.[458] Time could persuade men to the decency of practices long lapsed. Recent research on the 1640s suggests there was a considerable attachment to the ritual of the Anglican church.[459] There may then be much truth in Clarendon's observation that though the expenses (of altarcloths, chalices, candlesticks and vestments) caused murmurings, Laud's ceremonial injunctions were acceptable to 'grave and intelligent persons'.[460]

The altar controversies

Clarendon included in his catalogue of 'acceptable' developments the removing of the communion tables to the upper end of the chancel and railing them, often against the east wall. Such has not been the verdict of historians who have described disputes over east end altars and rails as central issues in the religious polarization that presaged the divisions of the civil war. Undeniably, in the 1630s altars and rails generated debates and a number of clashes. But the complex issues and controversies, even in some cases the facts, have been misrepresented and misunderstood by historians – as they probably were by contemporaries. The first misconception concerns that much misunderstood figure, William Laud. Though he is usually portrayed as the architect of the policy, Laud in his diocesan or metropolitical visitation articles never enjoined that tables be placed at the east end of churches in an altarwise position, north–south against the wall. In his articles of 1628 for the visitation of the diocese of London he enquired whether the communion table was according to the Elizabethan injunctions 'placed in such convenient sort within the chancel or church as that the minister may be best heard in his prayer and administration and that the greater number may communicate?'[461] He repeated the same words in his first visitation as archbishop. Whilst he may have preferred an east end position (he had so moved the table in 1616 as dean of Gloucester), there is no evidence that he tried to force it on others.[462]

457. Stieg, *Laud's Laboratory*, p. 233.
458. *Works of Laud*, V, p. 360: Laud's account for 1638; cf. Tanner MS 68, f.331.
459. See J.S. Morrill's splendid essay 'The church in England, 1642–9', in J.S. Morrill (ed.) *Reactions to the English Civil War* (1982), pp. 89–114.
460. Clarendon, *History of the Rebellion*, I, p. 127.
461. *Works of Laud*, V, p. 405.
462. H.R. Trevor-Roper, *Archbishop Laud* (1940), pp. 45–6.

On the contrary, after the St Gregory's case, Laud told Bishop John Williams that though the king preferred altars at the east end, the church did not prescribe it, and for himself he regarded it as indifferent.[463] At his speech at the trial of Prynne, Burton and Bastwick, Laud restated that position: 'the standing of the table either way was a matter of indifferency'.[464] In practice he was as good as his word – and was, at least by some, seen to be. Bishop Davenant informed the parish of Aldbourn, Wiltshire that Laud had left the position of the table to be ordered 'by the only rule of conveniency'.[465] The people of Leigh in Essex used the article book of Laud's metropolitical visitation to support their claim 'to remove the table at the time of celebration' into the body of the church or chancel.[466] The argument that Laud instigated and rigidly enforced east end altars can no longer be sustained.[467]

If Laud's position has been misunderstood, the case of St Gregory's, which allegedly marked the triumph of his policy, has also been inaccurately reported. In the first place, though bishop of London, Laud had no authority over what was a decanal peculiar. The dean of St Paul's, Thomas Winiffe, a Calvinist of alleged puritan sympathies, and the chapter, acting as ordinaries of St Gregory's church which sat under the walls of the cathedral, ordered the removal of the communion table to the east end of the chancel. Five parishioners complained against the move and appealed to the dean of the Arches. In November 1633 Charles called the dispute to be heard at the Privy Council. At the Council Board on 3 November the king ruled in favour of the dean and chapter.[468] The decision has usually been taken as a general royal order, prompted by Laud, for the placing of tables altarwise at the east end. Whilst this was almost certainly the king's preference, it was not the outcome of the St Gregory's case. Charles determined not the position of the table but the power of the ordinary to decide on the conveniency of the position of the table, where that was disputed.[469] In so doing, he did not decree uniformity but effectively licensed a variety of diocesan practice since in most cases the bishop was the ordinary.

463. *Works of Laud*, VI, part 2, p. 350: Laud to Williams, 25 Feb. 1634; cf. *ibid.*, p. 351: Williams to Laud, 7 March 1634.
464. Hargrave, *State Trials*, I, pp. 491–2.
465. *Cal. Stat. Pap. Dom., 1637*, pp. 121–2, 17 May.
466. *Cal. Stat. Pap. Dom., 1636–7*, p. 29: Dr R. Aylett to Lambe, 29 June 1636.
467. This argument will be further substantiated by Dr Julian Davies. The preceding account is based on my own work, but I am extremely grateful to Julian Davies for his allowing me to see his important findings on this matter.
468. PRO, PC 2/43/304; Gardiner, *History of England*, VII, pp. 310–12.
469. PRO, SP 16/250/12; *Cal. Stat. Pap. Dom., 1633–4*, p. 273; Cardwell, *Documentary Annals*, II, p. 237.

Shortly after the case was heard, in February 1634, Charles issued further instructions that the tables should normally be railed at the east end, and that communion should be received at the rails there.[470] It is not certain whose mind was most behind the formulation of those instructions: Dr Julian Davies has suggested the influence of Bishop Pierce of Bath and Wells and/or Matthew Wren, Clerk of the Closet. Wren, however, was to deny enforcing it in his own diocese[471] and Pierce seems never to have required communicants to receive at the rail.[472] One is left therefore with the conclusion that the metropolitical order was Charles's own, a conclusion reinforced by its inclusion in the Irish canons of 1634. What is certain is that Laud was not behind it. We have seen that his own metropolitical articles were faithful to the Elizabethan rubric. Further, in private instructions to his vicar-general he ordered that none be prosecuted for breach of it.[473] There was clearly a difference between Charles and his archbishop over altars. When in 1636 a clergyman in Bedfordshire erected a stone altar and was ordered by Bishop Williams to remove it, Laud backed Williams; the king by contrast thought it 'a bold part in the bishop and the poor priest in no fault'.[474] Laud stuck to his guns; he never ordered east end altars. Other bishops and clerics more enthusiastically proceeded to put the royal order into effect. Wren, on his primary visitation as bishop of Norwich, required that 'the communion table in every church do always [stand] close under the east wall of the chancel, the ends thereof North and South', adding 'unless the ordinary give particular direction otherwise'.[475] Among other enthusiastic enforcers were the Calvinists Bishop Davenant of Salisbury, Archdeacon Holdsworth of Huntingdon, Archdeacon King of Colchester and Dean Balcanquhall of Durham.[476] There were differences over the position of the communion table, but they do not run parallel to the line that divided Arminians and Calvinists.[477] The differences were complex and personal, rather than theological and ideological.

The famous controversies – at Beckington, Somerset and between Laud and John Williams – reinforce such a conclusion. In the diocese of Bath and Wells, Pierce requested the removal of the table to the east

470. See J. Davies, *Caroline Captivity of the Church*, ch. 6; Laud's letter to Williams, cited in note 463.
471. Wren, *Parentilia*, p. 75.
472. Davies, *Caroline Captivity of the Church*; cf. Tyacke, *Anti-Calvinists*, p. 207.
473. Cf. Bulstrode Whitelocke, *Memorials of the English Affairs* (1682 edn), p. 24; *Works of Laud*, V, p. 418; *Cal. Stat. Pap. Dom., 1637*, pp. 121–2.
474. *Works of Laud*, V, p. 342.
475. Tanner MS 68, f.33.
476. Davies, *Caroline Captivity of the Church*, ch. 6; for Davenant see *Cal. Stat. Pap. Dom., 1637*, pp. 121–2; Fuller, *Davenant*, pp. 154–5.
477. As is at times assumed in Tyacke, *Anti-Calvinists* and 'Puritanism, Arminianism and counter-revolution'.

end at Beckington in 1634. The churchwardens refused to obey and petitioned Laud. Pierce excommunicated them for disobedience and sent his own explanation to the archbishop.[478] He preferred east end altars, he argued, because they more closely followed Elizabethan injunctions, were less open to profanity, and emulated cathedral churches; they also, he added, left more room in the chancel for communicants.[479] The last point very much suggests that Pierce's defence of his action arose very specifically from Beckington, rather than a generally rigid stand. There was no mention of altars in his visitation articles before 1636,[480] and the churchwardens themselves observed that they had been sworn to no article concerning them.[481] The circumstances at Beckington were peculiar. The table there stood on a raised stone chancel with trenches around it. Pierce enquired when such an alteration, which took up most of the space in the chancel, had been carried out and worried that the minister might not be heard.[482] There was an agreement that a levelled chancel would be more decent, and Pierce ordered the 'lanes' on each side to be filled and the table to be moved to the east end, to save room lost behind it where it stood in the middle.[483] The alteration was a great deal more costly than usual, and this may well have been a factor in the dispute. No other parishes in Somerset raised the issue: if Rushworth is to be trusted, one reason the Beckington petition to have the table restored met with little success was the fear that it might spark off others who had hitherto been conformable.[484] There were evidently troublemakers in the parish: Sir Robert Phelips blamed John Ashe, a 'puritan', for stirring 'a most violent opposition' and 'some foul riots in the church itself'.[485] Once it became a dispute over his authority, Pierce's position (not unlike Davenant's in his letter to the parishioners of Aldbourne) hardened and the dispute escalated.[486] In 1638 at the assizes the Beckington men were ordered to make public submission to Pierce at Wells.[487] What had begun perhaps as a practical improvement became a contest of will and power.

In the case of Williams, the distance between him and Laud – at least

478. See 'Documents of the Laudian period', in T.F. Palmer (ed.) *Collectanea, II* (Somerset Record Soc., 43, 1928), pp. 177–217.
479. Lambeth Palace MS 943, p. 475; Palmer, *Collectanea*, pp. 190–1.
480. Tyacke, *Anti-Calvinists*, p. 207.
481. Lambeth Palace MS 943, p. 481.
482. *Ibid.*, p. 491; Palmer, *Collecteana*, pp. 199–203.
483. Lambeth Palace MS 943, p. 499.
484. Rushworth, *Historical Collections*, II, p. 300.
485. E. Cope, *Politics without Parliaments, 1629–1640* (1987), p. 53.
486. Stieg, *Laud's Laboratory*, p. 300.
487. T.G. Barnes (ed.) *Somerset Assize Orders, 1629–1640* (Somerset Record Soc., 65, 1959), p. 37; cf. the submission of Thomas Holmes in 1640, p. 48.

on the position of the altar – has been much exaggerated.[488] Like Laud, Williams held to no hard line on the matter. His fondness for ornament and order inclined him to favour in his own residence at Buckden a table against the east wall, and the railing of altars to avoid profanity, but he was wedded to no sacramental position and, like Laud, was ready to compromise.[489] In 1628 he had to adjudicate a dispute at Grantham between the vicar, one Tytler, who removed the table to the east end of the church, behind the rood screen, and Alderman Wheatley and others who carried it back. Arguments about the risk of profaning the table and where the vicar was better heard were made and opposed. Williams acted with a studied discretion that spoke to his own position. He praised the vicar for his desire to emulate cathedral practice. 'But,' he went on, 'that you should be so violent for an altar at the upper end of the choir, that your table ought to stand altarwise, that the fixing thereof in the choir is canonical and that it ought not to be removed in the body of the church, I conceive to be in you so many mistakings.'[490] The bishop agreed that the upper end of the chancel was the right position, but denied that the altarwise north–south position against the east wall was ever the usual practice in country churches where the rural folk 'would think them dressers rather than tables'. Whilst he approved of altars at the east wall in cathedrals, and royal or bishops' chapels, 'where there are no people so void of instruction to be scandalised', in the parish church he preferred an east–west position for the table decently covered, at the upper end of the chancel. Most importantly, he concluded his letter to Tytler, 'whichever side, you or your parish, shall first yield in this needless controversy shall remain in my poor judgement the more discreet, grave or learned of the two'.[491]

Order rather than dogma remained Williams's rule. In 1633 he urged the mayor of Leicester, who was refurbishing the chancel of the church, to stand the communion table in the upper end 'fairly covered and adorned' – unless any complained that there it was inconvenient.[492] His advice was evidently followed across his diocese. On his journey through Leicestershire in January 1636, the Earl of Huntingdon described Cheekley church, where 'the communion table standeth in the middle of the chancel railed about with banisters, one

488. For one in H.T. Blethen, 'The altar controversy and the royal supremacy, 1627–1641', *Welsh Hist. Rev.*, 9 (1978), pp. 142–54.
489. Gardiner, *History of England*, VII, p. 17.
490. Rawlinson MS D.353, f.140; Bodleian, Ashmole MS, 826 ff.173–4.
491. Ashmole MS 826, f.174; also Tanner MS 378, f.79v.
492. Hastings MS 13330, 18 Sept. 1633; cf. *Cal. Stat. Pap. Dom., 1633–4*, p. 103: Williams to Burdin, surrogate of ecclesiastical court at Leicester, 19 June 1633.

step to go into it, the ends of the table stand east and west in the church'.[493] Controversy only attached itself to Williams's altar policy with the publication in 1637 of his *The Holy Table: Name and Thing*.[494] Written anonymously, *The Holy Table* attacked *A Coale from the Altar*, written by Laud's chaplain Peter Heylyn.[495] It annoyed Laud, whose personal quarrels with Williams had escalated, and he referred to it sardonically in his speech at Prynne's trial.[496] Doubtless he feared, especially in 1637, that such a work might create a controversy – and it is not fanciful to suggest that Williams had published out of personal pique. But Laud did not refute Williams's position because there was no need for him to do so. Williams's recommended compromise, though far from Charles I's metropolitical order, was close to Laud's own practice.

Across the country, as the practice of individual bishops varied concerning the placing, positioning and railing of the table, so did the response. At Hertford, the foreman of the grand jury presented the altar there as an innovation;[497] the parishioners of St Giles, Northamptonshire pulled theirs down.[498] At Coventry, it was Bishop Wright who required St Michael's church which had 'been at great charge in making a septum about the table' to bring it down into the chancel.[499] Wren permitted the parishioners of Lavenham and Yarmouth to move their tables outside the rails at time of communion.[500] Across London, under Juxon, the conversion of tables into east end altars appears to have proceeded smoothly: the churchwardens of Lambeth not only moved their table, but also voluntarily contributed to provide it with a 'decent gilt cup and two silver flagons'.[501] The town church of Northampton had an east end altar in 1637.[502] The episcopal visitation returns for Cambridgeshire in 1638 suggest many churches had east-end altars.[503] In Sussex there appears to have been acquiescence in the removal of the altar to the east until one Stapley raised it as a grievance at the Michaelmas sessions of 1639.[504] Even after the

493. Hastings MSS, Personal HAP, Box 18.
494. [J. Williams], *The Holy Table: Name and Thing* (1637, STC 25724).
495. P. Heylyn, *A Coale from the Altar* (1636, STC 13270).
496. Gardiner, *History of England*, VIII, pp. 253–4.
497. BL Add. MS 11045, f.135v.
498. New College Oxford MS 9502 (Woodforde's diary), 25, 31 Dec. 1637.
499. *Cal. Stat. Pap. Dom., 1636–7*, p. 525: Latham to Lambe, 27 March 1637.
500. Wren, *Parentilia*, p. 76.
501. C. Drew (ed.) *Lambeth Churchwardens' Accounts, Part II* (Surrey Record Soc., 44, 1943), p. 109; Tyacke, *Anti-Calvinists*, p. 208.
502. Woodforde's diary, 12 Nov. 1637.
503. Palmer, *Episcopal Visitation Returns for Cambridgeshire*, for example, pp. 6, 21, 27, 31, 32, 36, 37, 44.
504. *Cal. Stat. Pap. Dom., 1639–40*, pp. 386–7.

Caroline personal rule was toppled, attitudes to altars and local practice varied. Sir Edward Hyde, arguing in the Short Parliament that it was not contrary to the Elizabethan rubric that 'the communion table stand altarwise', did not want for support.[505] Mr Chalmley thought it mattered not how it stood;[506] Benjamin Rudyerd regretted that any trouble could have arisen over a 'metaphor', the altar.[507] Sir William Waller argued that it was a matter for the governors of the church: 'where the rubric leaves a latitude, somebody must prescribe a place else the parish divided among themselves'.[508] The issue was one not of theology, but 'regularity and uniformity'.[509]

The question of the position of the communion table is often confused with the related issue of altar rails. Many historians have assumed that altar rails were by definition placed north–south across the chancel before an altar at the east end. Thence they have concluded that the presence of rails expressed liturgical preferences and theological positions, demarcating a holy sanctum where the communion might be celebrated like a Catholic mass. But this is too simplistic. Williams disapproved of tables standing altarwise at the east wall but ordered rails; Laud who had placed no rails as president of St John's College, Oxford began to enforce what was an official metropolitical order only after 1637.[510] It is important to recognize that the presence of rails did not mean an altar at the east end. There is plenty of evidence in churchwardens' accounts that many tables were railed in the chancel or the body of the church, not at the east. In Chichester diocese we find a report from Chipley to the archdeacon that the table there was 'compassed about with a handsome rail';[511] at Ferring it was 'railed about', at West Grinstead 'compassed about'.[512] Amersham in Buckinghamshire had a wainscot 'round about the communion table'.[513] In general whenever we read of a table railed *about* (as opposed to *in* or *across*) we probably should assume a table in the chancel or church fenced on all sides. All Hallows, Barking had just such a table until they were ordered to move it to the east end, under

505. J. Maltby (ed.) *The Short Parliament Diary of Sir Thomas Aston* (Camden Soc., 4th series, 35, 1988), p. 88.
506. *Ibid.*, p. 91.
507. J. Nalson, *An Impartial Collection of the Great Affairs of State from the Beginning of the Scotch Rebellion in 1639 to the Murder of King Charles I* (2 vols, 1682–3), I, p. 49.
508. Maltby, *Aston Diary*, p. 91.
509. *Ibid.*, p. 96.
510. Lambeth Palace MS 943, p. 607; Wren, *Parentilia*, pp. 75–6; *Works of Laud*, VI, part 2, pp. 478–9. I owe the point about St John's to J. Davies, *Caroline Captivity of the Church*.
511. West Sussex Record Office, EP 1/22/1: archdeacon's visitation bill.
512. *Ibid.*
513. PRO, SP 16/366/79.

protest in 1637.[514] The people of Sherborne in Dorset evidently were required to new rail theirs; they used the 'old rails of the communion table' for timber for church repairs.[515] Even Beckington, as Prynne acknowledged, had had its table 'railed in with wainscott' before Pierce's order to move it 'from the place where it anciently stood . . . to rail it altarwise against the east end of the chancel'.[516]

Nor were altar rails an invention of the Laudians or of the 1630s. In many parts of the country rails had been in existence since the reign of Elizabeth, and the metropolitical order effected no change. Where they were no longer, they often had been, so could hardly be called an innovation. Assisting Wren to answer the charges against him, William Allanson told him that concerning St Edmund's, Norwich, 'I am credibly and certainly informed by one Mr William Paine (who commenced Master of Arts in Caius College A° 1582 . . . a man almost of fourscore years of age) that above three score years since when he lived in St Edmund's . . . that rails were then in that church and did compass in the communion table'.[517] Indeed the increased number of communicants was leading long before Laud's archiepiscopacy to the installation of rails in many parish churches. Strood in Kent had them from 1607,[518] Upwaltham's were 'decayed' by the 1630s;[519] Wren claimed they had long existed in Norwich churches;[520] St Giles, Cripplegate in London had them time out of mind;[521] All Hallows, Barking's predate the 1630s.[522] In Chichester in 1620 Mr Roger Jesson offered to bear the charge of a frame 'for the communicants to receive the communion in a more decent manner than heretofore'.[523]

This was undoubtedly the motive behind the Caroline drive for rails. Laud argued that if the table were not railed boys leant and wrote at it, workmen used it as a nailing bench, and dogs pissed against it.[524] The last was no rhetorical point: dogs were a regular nuisance in churches and Great St Mary's in Cambridge actually paid a dog man to keep them out.[525] All Laud's worst fears were realized in an

514. *Cal. Stat. Pap. Dom., 1637–8*, p. 67.
515. Dorset Record Office, Sherborne churchwardens' accounts, CW/109, p. 155 (1639).
516. Tanner MS 299, f.158.
517. Tanner MS 314, f.110.
518. H.R. Plomer (ed.) *The Churchwardens' Accounts of St Nicholas, Strood, Part II, 1603–1662* (Kent Archaeological Soc., Records Branch, 5, 1927), p. 93.
519. H. Johnstone (ed.) *Churchwardens' Presentments, Part I: Archdeaconry of Chichester* (Sussex Record Soc., 49, 1949), p. 104.
520. Wren, *Parentilia*, p. 77.
521. A. Fletcher, *The Outbreak of the English Civil War* (1981), p. 118.
522. Above, note 514; J. Hogg in his unpublished paper 'Arminianism in parochial London' (given at the Institute of Historical Research in June 1987).
523. Johnstone, *Chichester Presentments*, p. 219.
524. Heylyn, *Cyprianus Anglicus*, p. 289.
525. Palmer, *Episcopal Visitation Returns for Cambridgeshire*, p. 37.

incident at Tadlow, in the diocese of Ely in 1638. On Christmas day the congregation could not take communion

> for that in the sermon time the dog of William Staple came to the communion table (which stood without any rail or enclosure before it) and leaping up took the loaf of bread prepared for the sacrament and ran away with it in his mouth which although some of the parishioners took from the dog and set it again upon the table, yet the vicar . . . thought not meet to consecrate that bread.[526]

One did not have to be a devotee of the beauty of holiness to sympathize with him, or with Wren who tells the story. That such were genuinely the motives for railing cannot be denied. At the visitation of Buckinghamshire in 1637, Mentmore was instructed to have more 'barristers' between the rail spaces.[527] At Cheddington it was ordered that 'the feet of the rails be cut off, so that the frame of the rails may be set on the ground' – presumably in both cases not to elevate the table but to stop dogs sneaking through or under.[528] There was a wide variety of rails accepted – some with cupboards built in as at Datchett, Buckinghamshire.[529] As Wren said, those who accused him of railing off an area as too sacred for the parishioners to enter 'do account God's people as dogs: for so only were the words of this defendant's direction, that the rails should be so thick with pillars that dogs might not get in'.[530]

Some were offended by the orders to erect rails. Verses were written against the vicar of St Nicholas, Colchester for railing in the table there;[531] some in Norwich referred to them as pillars of popery.[532] Prynne, who thought them popish, tried to maintain that bishops had erected them against the king's wishes.[533] Robert Woodforde associated them with God's judgments on the land through plague: 'The rail in the chancel is now almost up and it is confidently reported that the sickness is in the town.'[534] These examples come from well-known centres and leaders of puritanism. The 1640s saw a more widespread assault on rails: Hatfield pulled theirs down; Frodsham in Cheshire paid to dismantle theirs; soldiers tore them down in Staffordshire and

526. Lambeth Palace MS 943, p. 616.
527. *Cal. Stat. Pap. Dom., 1637*, p. 398.
528. PRO, SP 16/366/79.
529. *Ibid.*
530. Wren, *Parentilia*, pp. 75–6.
531. *Cal. Stat. Pap. Dom., 1631–3*, p. 492.
532. Tanner MS 68, f.104.
533. Tanner MS 299, f.153.
534. Woodforde's diary, 17 March 1638.

across the country.[535] Whilst it is difficult to know exactly how to interpret the iconoclasm of the 1640s, we should not read it straightforwardly as pent-up hostility to rails.[536] The Long Parliament, after all, ordered their removal and called to account churches that did not obey their command. Similarly, few would have been prepared to defend their rails before a horde of marauding soldiers. However, the Earl of Warwick, for all his patronage of puritanism, sent to the houses of correction those who in the summer of 1640 pulled down rails in Essex.[537] Wimborne in Dorset appears to have erected a new rail in 1641 and there was widespread spontaneous replacement of them on the eve of the Restoration.[538]

The order for railing in the 1630s probably met with general acquiescence: across the dioceses of London and Chichester and in Buckinghamshire rails appear to have been the norm. Several were clearly erected as a result of parish rather than official initiative. It was at the petition of William Newton, one of the parishioners at St Maurice, Winchester that the table there was 'railed around in a decent manner'.[539] The rector of St Vedast's in London sought an order for a rail to avoid disorder;[540] Hitchingfield in Sussex railed the table 'to keep it from profanation'.[541] From Bury in 1636 Thomas Goad wrote to Bishop Wren that 'this day after sermon when we sat in the chancel such a throng crowded upon the communion table that we saw the necessity of rails'.[542] At Ware the churchwardens 'for avoiding disorder at the time of administration of the holy communion at a general meeting of the parishioners and with the consent of the greater part of them' agreed that the table should be set in the chancel and railed.[543] In many churchwardens' accounts, adjectives such as 'comely', 'handsome', 'neat', 'fine' applied to rails suggest that they could often be an object of pride. We should not let the diatribe of puritans stand as evidence of a universal condemnation of altar rails.

What was more contentious than the rails themselves were the orders of some bishops and clergy that parishioners come up to the rails and kneel there to receive communion. For some this perhaps

535. *Cal. Stat. Pap. Dom., 1640*, p. 580; Cheshire Record Office, P 8/13/2.
536. See J. Sharpe, 'Crime and delinquency in an Essex parish', in J.S. Cockburn (ed.) *Crime in England, 1550–1800* (1977), pp. 90–109, for the case of John Ayly of Kelvedon who destroyed altar rails but was also guilty of moral offences that suggest he was far from godly in his behaviour.
537. *Cal. Stat. Pap. Dom., 1640*, p. 517.
538. Dorset County Record Office, P204/CW42: Wimborne Minster churchwardens' accounts, 1641.
539. *Cal. Stat. Pap. Dom., 1635*, p. 133.
540. *Cal. Stat. Pap. Dom., 1635–6*, p. 47.
541. West Sussex Record Office, EP 1/22/1.
542. Tanner MS 68, f.45.
543. *Cal. Stat. Pap. Dom., 1635–6*, p. 123.

undermined the fellowship of the communion and placed emphasis on the sacrificial; to more it meant the inconvenience of leaving their seats and an enhancement of clerical status that was by no means always welcomed. In Norwich, a group of rebellious parishioners expressed their disapproval of the practice by entering the railed area and walking around the minister so as to disturb the service.[544] Again, however, the practice was not an innovation of the 1630s and may have been growing in response to the larger numbers taking communion. Old Mr Paine of Norwich recalled 'that above thirty years ago when he lived in London, he received communion at the rails in St Martin's church in the fields'; and at St Michael's in Norwich 'Mr King the rector and every communicant came up to the rails without the least scruple at all'.[545] Where, however, it was novel, it could, as Laud appreciated, disturb tender consciences. Much depended on the tact and style of the minister as well as the parishioners. Wren included kneeling at the rails in his visitation articles – in order, he claimed, to identify recusants and avoid lewdness – but molested none who refused.[546] Pierce and Neile insisted on it; Bishops Montagu and Bridgeman (who ordered railed altars at the east end) did not. Some ministers went to foolhardy lengths to enforce it. Thomas Bond, vicar of Debenham, Suffolk pressured his parishioners so much that some stayed away from communion for over a year.[547] In what sounds like a *Daily Mirror* story about the health service, it was reported that the vicar of Benhall made a lame man crawl to the rails.[548] Ministers were indicted at the Chelmsford assizes for refusing communion; others were indicted in Suffolk.[549]

Laud, though history has not told it so, never forced communicants to the rail and persistently counselled others to proceed with tact. As Laud told Williams, the requirement was not canonical and rather than being forced, 'I think . . . the people will best be won by the decency of the thing itself'.[550] When the parishioners of Wallsern, Lincolnshire complained that Dr Gorsuch would not give them communion except at the rails, the archbishop ordered him to behave 'in a peaceable and Christianlike way'.[551] He sent instructions to Mr Wilsher, minister at St Peter's Bread Street that 'none are to be compelled to come, save those that are willing'.[552] The parson of Welwyn, Hertfordshire he

544. Tanner MS 68, f.104.
545. Tanner MS 314, f.110.
546. Wren, *Parentilia*, pp. 83, 98.
547. Holmes, *Suffolk Committees for Scandalous Ministers*, p. 81.
548. *Ibid.*, p. 68.
549. *Works of Laud*, V, p. 364; *Cal. Stat. Pap. Dom., 1639*, pp. 438–9.
550. *Works of Laud*, V, p. 343.
551. *Cal. Stat. Pap. Dom., 1637*, pp. 484–5.
552. *Cal. Stat. Pap. Dom., 1639*, p. 16.

wrote to, asking him to administer communion to those kneeling 'in any part of the chancel'.[553] Rossingham the newswriter reported to Viscount Conway Laud's questioning 'the parson should exact their coming up to the rail to receive the sacrament, if so the pews be conveniently situated in the church to administer to them'.[554] Lambe, Laud's vicar-general, and Dr Richard Holdsworth, archdeacon of Huntingdon, followed his instructions to moderation.[555] Bishop Richard Montagu of Norwich put a stop to Wren's injunction – not least because there was no royal or archiepiscopal order for it.[556]

That such tact could have its rewards is well illustrated by a letter to Sir Robert Harley from Nathaniel Harrison in April 1637. Harrison told of going to celebrate Easter communion at his church where 'the communion table is altarwise newly ingirt'. The congregation came to receive the sacrament at the usual place in the chancel where 'ever before times it was given' and were served. One Mr Griffith and others, however, having scruples concerning the newly erected rails, asked Dr Coote the parson to come down from the chancel and administer communion to them in their seats: 'whereupon the said Dr Coote went immediately to him and the rest and there used some persuasive reasons to them to come up to the rails'. Most were won, 'but the said Mr Griffith refused . . . whereupon Dr Coote told him that he would pray for him' and then gave him communion, Griffith 'submissively kneeling' in his place.[557] In the case of ministers like Coote, Laud may have been right in believing that men would gradually be won by the decency of the practice. Despite puritan opposition, many were. At St Ives, Holdsworth reported in 1639, 'all the parishioners there, being about 800 had used for the space of almost three years with unanimous conformity to come up to the rails'.[558] At Welwyn, where Laud had ordered the vicar to refrain from force, most evidently accepted it for in 1635 the puritans were circulating a petition 'to draw men back again who were come to the cancelling'.[559] Wren claimed conformity in many parishes of Norwich; the bishop of Ely reported to Laud in 1638 that across more than 1,300 parishes not thirteen had been disciplined for refusing to come to the rail.[560] By

553. *Works of Laud*, VI, part 2, pp. 478–9; BL Add. MS 11045, f.14: Rossingham to Scudamore, 22 April 1639.
554. *Cal. Stat. Pap. Dom., 1639*, p. 71, 23 April.
555. *Cal. Stat. Pap. Dom., 1639–40*, pp. 365–6, 387.
556. Lambeth Palace MS 943, p. 631. Montagu clearly thought he had Laud's support.
557. BL, MS 29/172, f.138: Nathaniel Harrison to Sir Robert Harley, April 1637.
558. *Cal. Stat. Pap. Dom., 1639–40*, p. 365.
559. Temple of Stowe MSS, Correspondence Box 11, no. 1891: Sibthorpe to Lambe, 7 June 1639.
560. *Works of Laud*, V, p. 360.

1638 Laud was able to tell the king that receiving at the rails was practised 'almost everywhere' in the kingdom.[561]

The liturgical developments of the 1630s, like the programme to restore and enhance the fabric and furniture of parish churches, met with some opposition but certainly not with universal antagonism. Responses to particular initiatives varied from diocese to diocese, even from parish to parish; different reactions to, and perceptions of, changes may be explained as much by personal and regional factors – the preferences and tact of bishops and clergymen, the variety of local custom and practice – as by clearly defined theological alignments. Whilst the orders of, say, Neile or Wren or Pierce on the one hand and the views of Prynne and Burton on the other were fundamentally at odds, it is simplistic – no it is false – to see the disagreements over liturgy and ceremonies in the 1630s in terms of a polarization of Arminians and puritans, or Arminians and 'orthodox' Anglicans. There are too many less rigid stands and complex combinations of attitudes which do not fit such a model of confrontation. John Williams, though personally at odds with the king and the archbishop for much of the 1630s, shared many of their values and preferences. Bishop John Davenant of Salisbury, for all his concern over the issue of predestination, rigorously enforced in his diocese tables railed at the east end and standing altarwise. Laud, as we have seen, did not. Theological positions and liturgical preferences were not, as Dr Tyacke at times appears to argue, neatly related. Nor were they universally divisive. There may have been a war between the bishops and the puritans in the 1630s, but that should not be equated with a battle between Arminians and Calvinists or indeed ceremonialists and low churchmen, nor seen as a conflict that divided all the parishes of England. Examining some of the *causes célèbres* more closely, we have suggested that it is the complexity of the issues and differences that emerge. Grantham, St Gregory's and Beckington lend scant support to a thesis of simple polarization. The same may be said of the last notorious instance we shall examine: the case of Henry Sherfield.

Henry Sherfield: a case study in complexities

In October 1630, Henry Sherfield, recorder of the borough of Salisbury, deliberately broke with his stick a window of the parish church of St Edmund's. The window had represented in stained glass

561. *Ibid.*

the Creation and, most offensive to Sherfield, God 'in the form of an old man'. His act of iconoclasm has been reported in the textbooks as 'one of the best known cases of puritan religious protest in the years preceding the civil war'. His prosecution in Star Chamber is similarly seen as evidence of the Arminian bishops' determination to deal rigorously with such opposition.[562] In detail the story is less clear-cut. Sherfield had some sympathies with the godly, and had exhibited in 1629 serious reservations about Montagu's pardon, but he was by no means a staunch puritan; he had been accustomed to kneeling at communion and was active in punishing separatists.[563] He had also shown himself a painstaking magistrate, quick to 'suppress idleness and loose living' in a manner that might have commended him to a government that was drafting the Book of Orders.[564] Stained-glass windows were still common across the country and not all, even of godly sympathies, condemned them: Sir William Brereton, for one, was fascinated by some of their representations.[565] Sherfield's objection to the window at St Edmund's was fired by seeing a simple woman pay homage to it and by a broader suspicion that it bred superstition among the ignorant. His action in smashing it was not purely a personal whim. In January 1630 a meeting of the vestry had decided to replace the window with plain glass on the grounds, they said, that the offending window was 'somewhat decayed and broken and is very darksome, whereby such as sit near the same cannot see to read in their books'.[566]

The person incensed by Sherfield's action was not one of the noted Laudians, but the bishop of Salisbury, the Calvinist John Davenant. Davenant had forbidden the churchwardens of St Edmund's to replace the window and had questioned the authority of the vestry to make any such order. It was Davenant who determined to prosecute and who brought the action to the attention of the king, and the king who personally instructed Attorney Noy to bring the case in Star Chamber.[567] The mayor of Salisbury (and others) attempted to inter-

562. Gardiner, *History of England*, VII, p. 254ff; P. Slack, 'Religious protest and urban authority: the case of Henry Sherfield, iconoclast, 1633', in D. Baker (ed.) *Schism, Heresy and Religious Protest* (Cambridge, 1972), pp. 295–302. Neither account makes use of the Sherfield MSS in the Hampshire Record Office.

563. Slack, 'Religious protest and urban authority', p. 296; Sherfield MSS XXXIX/63, 67, 68; XLV (draft petition, 1632); Gardiner, *History of England*, VII, p. 255.

564. Sherfield MS XLII: Roger Knight to Sherfield, 24 March 1631.

565. Hawkins, *Travels of Brereton*, pp. 83, 176, especially the representation of a friar correcting a nun 'and turning down her bed-clothes to the middle'.

566. Herriard MS E77: mayor of Salisbury to Pembroke, 30 Jan. 1631; Slack, 'Religious protest and urban authority', pp. 295–6.

567. Dr Slack suggests that Davenant may have been half-hearted in the prosecution. But Sherfield was told that the bishop was his greatest enemy (Sherfield MS XLII: Knight to Sherfield, 24 March 1631) and Davenant pressed for damages (*Cal. Stat. Pap. Dom., 1633–4*, p. 19).

vene on Sherfield's behalf. In a letter to the Lord Chamberlain, he expressed surprise at Sherfield's prosecution and sued for a pardon. He praised the recorder's services to the city (in setting men to work and binding apprentices); he reaffirmed that at the vestry meeting eleven good men, all conformable to the church, had, with sound precedent, ordered the window replaced; he observed, accurately, that other stained-glass windows had been broken with less consequent fuss.[568] In a passage, subsequently crossed out in the draft, he intimated that private quarrels underlay the hounding of Sherfield – an intimation confirmed by a private letter sent by Roger Knight to the recorder. Evidently underlying the case were tensions between the cathedral and the corporation that were common in other cities.[569] Sherfield himself sought the aid of the Earl of Dorset in obtaining the favour of the king.[570] Dorset spoke to Charles and advised Sherfield to sue for pardon.[571] However, Sherfield's petition, protesting his loyalty to the church and distaste for puritans, presented at Beaulieu while the king was on progress, was 'all rejected without any answer'.[572]

The Star Chamber case went ahead. Noy, prosecuting, focused on the question of the vestry's right to order the alteration of the window without the consent of the bishop.[573] Gardiner suggests persuasively that 'it was evident from the language employed by Coventry and the Chief Justices . . . that they shared [Sherfield's] dislike of the representation'.[574] But this, as even the godly William Whiteway recognized, was not the issue.[575] Sherfield had challenged the bishop's authority – an authority which the Calvinist Davenant was as determined to preserve as Laud. Though Dorset and Coke spoke in mitigation of the punishment, Sherfield was fined £500 and ordered publicly to confess his fault in meddling with matters that were under the authority of the ordinary. He hoped to evade his fine, but, untypically, was made to pay it in full.[576] Moreover the king personally drafted the form of words to ensure Sherfield made a full, 'significant and humble' submission, 'that all may take notice that the sentence is fully executed'.[577] Significantly, Charles I ordered the window be repaired (at Sherfield's expense) with plain glass – even though the original glass was reparable.[578] For the king, as others, the Sherfield case was concerned

568. Herriard MS E77; *Cal. Stat. Pap. Dom., 1627–8*, p. 433.
569. Below, pp. 397–8.
570. Sherfield MS XLV: Sherfield to Dorset, 5 March 1632.
571. *Ibid.*: Dorset to Sherfield, 22 July.
572. *Ibid.*: draft petition.
573. The case is in Hargrave, *State Trials*, I, pp. 399–418.
574. Gardiner, *History of England*, VII, p. 257.
575. Egerton MS 784, p. 180.
576. Herriard MS E77: Sherfield to Lady Jervoise, 17 April 1633; Sherfield MS XXXV, F.
577. Coke MS 44: letter to Davenant, 15 Feb. 1633.
578. *Ibid.*

not with ceremonial disagreements, but with the authority of the episcopacy. On this occasion, as on others, Charles showed his determination to uphold the authority of the church.

Churches abroad and foreign congregations at home

The king's determination to establish the uniformity and authority of the church extended, as we shall see, to Scotland and beyond. Charles and Laud were concerned to ensure the conformity to the Church of England of English merchant communities dwelling abroad and to bring foreign congregations in England to attend their parish church and worship according to Anglican rites. The king's concern about the orthodoxy of the expatriate English was evidently not misplaced. John Ayschcombe reported that among the English settled in Holland all sorts of religious practices and beliefs were tolerated, even views (presumably Pelagian) condemned by the Synod of Dort. Some, he claimed, had even become Anabaptists.[579] While in matters of liturgy, the French and Germans in Holland conformed to their mother churches, the English did not, 'most of them serving God in their public assemblies without any set form of prayer at all'. In July 1632 Edward Misselden, deputy governor of the Merchant Adventurers at Delft, wrote to Secretary Coke to press the need for conformable ministers to be sent to the company there; their current minister, he wrote, had no affection for the Church of England, 'but is wholly for the Presbyterian kind of teaching and government of the church'.[580] At Rotterdam, the situation could hardly have been worse given that the minister to the English congregation there was Hugh Peter, the future radical chaplain to the Cromwellian New Model army.[581] The king and Council acted on such alarming information: in October 1633 the Merchant Adventurers were ordered to receive no minister in foreign parts without the approval of the king and certification under the hand of the bishop of London that the candidate was conformable to the discipline of the Church of England.[582] Peter Heylyn informs us that one Beaumont was sent to Holland to check on the conformity of the English congregations there and that Laud even turned his attention beyond – to the English merchant communities in Turkey and India.[583]

579. Tanner MS 395, ff.100–2: 'Account of the religion professed by the English settled in Holland'. See also Hutton, *William Laud* (1895), ch. 6.
580. Coke MS 42: Misselden to Coke, 26 July 1632.
581. *Cal. Stat. Pap. Dom., 1633–4*, p. 318.
582. *Ibid.*, p. 225.
583. Heylyn, *Cyprianus Anglicus*, p. 260.

Whilst the nonconformity of English subjects overseas was a matter of concern, the presence in England of foreign congregations worshipping according to different rites presented a greater affront to the quest for unity and uniformity. The 'stranger churches' had found refuge in England from persecution on the continent in the reign of Edward VI; more had immigrated and settled in the 1560s after the peace between France and Spain.[584] Whilst Elizabeth I had not granted the wide-ranging privileges and semi-autonomy allowed by Edward, a recognition of the economic benefits of skilled immigrants from Holland had secured them from serious molestation. To the hotter sort of English Protestants, the immigrants were both a reminder of the dark days of exile under Mary and a visible link with the continental Protestant churches. And they laboured to bring the half-reformed Church of England into closer liaison with their continental brethren. Laud saw things otherwise. The stranger churches in Kent, he believed, 'used irreverence at their communion' and 'sat together as if it were in a tavern or ale-house'.[585] More importantly, he abhorred their schismatic existence outside the body of the church. Whilst it was right that they had been given a home from persecution, it had not been intended that for generations they 'should live like an absolute divided body from the Church of England established' for that 'must needs work in their affections and alienate them from the state'.[586] The foreigners, he told Charles, were 'a church within a church, which in time grow to be a kind of another Commonwealth within this, and so ready for that which I hold not fit to express any further'. Inhabiting port towns, close to France and Holland, the strangers were, like Catholics, a potential fifth column: 'were occasion offered God knows what advantage they may take to themselves . . .'.[587]

In 1634 he presented a paper showing that, contrary to their charters, the French and Dutch churches admitted English subjects who did not conform and 'thereby breed a nursery of ill-minded persons to the church'.[588] Few arguments could have been more persuasive with Charles I, who urged Laud to bring the matter of stranger churches to the Council Board.[589] Laud issued injunctions requiring foreigners to apply themselves to learn the liturgy of the English church and ordering their children to separate themselves from their congregations

584. See A. Pettegree, *Foreign Protestant Communities in Sixteenth Century London* (Oxford, 1986).
585. F.W. Cross, *A History of the Walloon and Huguenot Church at Canterbury* (Huguenot Soc., 15, 1898), p. 105.
586. Moens, *Walloon Church of Norwich*, p. 271.
587. *Ibid.*
588. *Cal. Stat. Pap. Dom., 1633–4*, pp. 556–7.
589. *Works of Laud*, V, p. 323.

and attend their parish church.[590] The strangers, claiming exemption from metropolitical visitation, petitioned Charles I, reminding the king of their economic contribution to the nation. The London churches appealed for privileges that the king had confirmed at his succession; Laud's injunctions, they protested, would deprive their ministers and their poor of maintenance, and threatened the dissolution of their communities.[591] When the appeal to royal favour secured little response, representatives of the congregations at Canterbury, Maidstone and Sandwich in Kent arranged in January 1635 to meet with Laud. The archbishop was firm: 'I know your doctrine, parity of ministers'; he told them that most of all he disliked hearing of *churches* – 'there was but one church'.[592] The French ambassador Poigny reported in February that the French, Dutch and Flemish ministers complained about having to wear surplices and kneel at communion; he predicted that they would be forced to follow absolutely the English liturgy.[593]

Laud, however, compromised. He saw delegates from the churches again in March 1635 and granted permission for foreign-born strangers to continue their own liturgy provided those born in England (since it was unfitting that there be 'mongrels' among the king's subjects) became members of the parishes where they lived.[594] Once again Laud appears to have preferred moderation to rigid conformity. The French and Dutch ministers thanked the archbishop for 'his honourable and gracious usage of them' and promised to persuade their congregations to conform.[595] Laud, for his part, continued to hold it 'fitting to keep a moderate hand with them'.[596] The strategy produced some results. The English liturgy was translated into French and Dutch.[597] By April 1635 William Somner was reporting that some members of the Dutch church at Maidstone had broken from their congregation and were attending their local church.[598] Bishop Wren pressured the French settled in the Isle of Axholme to use the English liturgy and expressed hope that the Walloons would follow them.[599] Thomas Jackson was able to inform Nathaniel Brent that the churchwardens of St Alphege's

590. Cross, *Walloon Church at Canterbury*, p. 115; *Cal. Stat. Pap. Dom., 1635*, pp. 82–3.
591. Temple of Stowe MSS: religious papers, petitions; *Cal. Stat. Pap. Dom., 1634–5*, p. 380.
592. Moens, *Walloon Church of Norwich*, p. 89.
593. PRO, 31/3/68, f.136v.
594. Moens, *Walloon Church of Norwich*, p. 91.
595. *Cal. Stat. Pap. Dom., 1634–5*, p. 575.
596. *Works of Laud*, V, p. 356.
597. Moens, *Walloon Church of Norwich*, p. 92.
598. *Cal. Stat. Pap. Dom., 1635*, pp. 25–6.
599. Tanner MS 68, f.311.

Canterbury reported so many more foreigners coming to church that there were too few seats to hold them.[600] Laud himself in his metropolitical report for 1636 claimed that in Kent the Walloons came orderly to church and received the sacraments.[601] Doubtless, as Heylyn argued, the business of persuading the foreign congregations to conformity 'went forward more or less as the ministers and church-wardens stood affected in their several parishes'.[602] There was clearly resentment and opposition: petitions to the king continued;[603] stranger families left Norwich for Holland;[604] the troubles of the late 1630s saw foreigners in Canterbury who had conformed drifting away again from the parish church.[605] In 1643 Laud was to be charged, in language that echoed the 1634 petition, with having separated England from reformed Protestantism. Yet for all that, the membership of foreign churches fell from nearly 11,000 to just over 4,000 across the decade.[606] Given more time, Laud might have fulfilled his goal of securing the second generation of settlers as members of the English church.

The Book of Sports

A concern with the parish church as the focus of the social as well as religious community underlay what was probably Charles I's most contentious injunction: the reissue of the Book of Sports. Recreations and games on Sundays after church, on festival days and saints' days had been traditional features of the medieval church. During Elizabeth's reign, however, especially from the 1570s and in the early seventeenth century, there had been a move, led by the puritans, to impose upon the parish life of England a stricter observation of the sabbath which would have outlawed all festivities and sports, preserving the entire day for worship, attendance at afternoon sermons and meditation on the passages of Scripture. Such rigid Sabbatarianism was not to the taste of Queen Elizabeth, who allowed dice, cards, even a wrestling match in her chapel, and who encouraged Sunday games.[607] But it found some support among the propertied classes, of various religious affinities, who feared the drunkenness, debauchery and disorder which

600. *Cal. Stat. Pap. Dom., 1635*, pp. 588–9.
601. *Works of Laud*, V, p. 337.
602. Heylyn, *Cyprianus Anglicus*, p. 265.
603. *Cal. Stat. Pap. Dom., 1635*, p. 150; Moens, *Walloon Church of Norwich*, p. 93.
604. *Ibid.*, p. 94.
605. *Ibid.*, pp. 95–6.
606. Carlton, *Laud*, p. 88.
607. R. Greaves, *Society and Religion in Elizabethan England* (Minnesota, 1981), p. 431.

could so easily be the outcome of sports and wakes.[608] The issue was one that divided along class lines more than a religious axis. It also involved more than one concept of order. On his journey through Lancashire on his way back from Scotland in 1617, James I was informed that the magistrates' prohibition of all Sunday games alienated the common people, and in the dark corners of the north perhaps made the appeal of the old religion all the greater. In the *Basilikon Doron*, his political testament to his son, James had defended some lawful games. In 1617 he ordered the Lancashire JPs not to forbid them. The following year he extended his ruling in a declaration of sports which the clergy of all England were ordered to read from the pulpit.[609] The king's pleasure was that provided it be 'without impediment or neglect of divine service', the people should not be disturbed 'or discouraged from any lawful recreation, such as dancing, either men or women; archery for men, leaping, vaulting or any other such harmless recreation, nor from having of May-games, Whitsun-ales and Morris dances . . .'.[610] Such games were not without benefits: they improved the fitness and martial skills of the villagers who constituted the county militia; they provided a rare release from a life of toil and drudgery (and so a social safety valve); moreover they could foster a sense of neighbourliness and community which was essential to social stability.

The declaration was greeted with some noisy opposition and evidently was not pressed. But the issue and disagreements clearly did not go away: the godly and many magistrates pushed to suppress games; the populace claimed their pleasures; the clergy quarrelled. In 1628 H. Greenwood and Theophilus Brabourne bemoaned the profanation of the sabbath and called for its strict observation.[611] Griffith Williams in *The True Church* stressed the importance of sabbath observance;[612] Lewis Bayly, bishop of Bangor, argued in *The Practice of Pietie* (1630) that 'lawful sports . . . steal away our affections from the contemplation of heavenly things'.[613] The author of *The Campe Royall* (1629) called

608. K. Parker, *The English Sabbath* (Cambridge, 1988) is a useful recent discussion but it underestimates the differences over the observation of the sabbath and too simply equates differences over this matter with disputes over other theological and liturgical issues.

609. Gardiner, *History of England*, III, pp. 247–51; L. Marcus, *The Politics of Mirth* (Chicago, 1986), p. 3; J. Tait, 'The declaration of sports for Lancashire', *Eng. Hist. Rev.*, 32 (1917), pp. 561–8.

610. J.C. Tanner (ed.) *Constitutional Documents of the Reign of James I* (Cambridge, 1930), pp. 54–6.

611. H. Greenwood, *The Prisoner's Prayers* (1628, STC 12335), p. 58: 'No one shall enter thy sabbath and rest of glory but he that hath been strictly careful to keep thy sabbath on earth'; T. Brabourne, *A Discourse upon the Sabbath Day* (1628, STC 3474).

612. G. Williams, *The True Church* (1629, STC 25721), p. 293ff.

613. L. Bayly, *The Practice of Pietie* (1630 edn; STC 1609), p. 445; cf. pp. 403, 451–2. Greenwood, Brabourne, Williams and Bayly were otherwise of quite different religious sympathies.

on all magistrates to put an end to 'heathenish May Games and Whitsun ales'.[614] In the localities, as presentments demonstrate, games continued, but as the rapid rise in presentments also indicates, the campaign to suppress them went on unabated. Early in Charles I's reign, statutes had been passed for due observation of the sabbath, but as Michael Dalton observed in the 1630 edition of *The Country Justice*, games were 'not unlawful or evil of themselves . . . the king by his prerogative may tolerate and license the moderate use of all such games'.[615] Charles was perhaps even less disposed than his father to strict Sabbatarianism: he sat with his Council on Sundays; and he permitted court performances of plays on the sabbath.[616] But opposed to any profanity, he had passed the statutes forbidding bear-baiting, plays 'or other unlawful exercises' and against carting and selling victuals on the sabbath.

A controversy over the sabbath in Charles's reign was initiated not by the king but, as in James I's case, from a dispute in the localities. Church ales and wakes had long been held in the county of Somerset – and had also long been infamous as occasions of disorder, and worse. In 1615 two men had died as a result of a drunken foray and orders had been issued to suppress them. In 1632 Chief Justice Denham, on the western circuit, reissued the ban at the assizes, in response to complaints by local magistrates and ministers. The order came to Laud's and the king's notice either through the information of Sir Robert Phelips or from Bishop Pierce who jealously guarded his episcopal authority from lay encroachment.[617] Charles instructed Justice Richardson to revoke the orders at the next (Lent) assizes. The judge sought to ignore the royal instructions and was summoned to the Privy Council, where he was censured by the king. His famous remark to the Earl of Dorset as he left the Council chamber – 'I am like to be choked with the archbishop's lawn sleeves' – suggests that Richardson saw the issue less as a question of the legitimacy of Sunday sports, and more as a contention between lay and clerical authority.[618] It is evident that Charles I saw it in these terms. On 2 May 1633 the king wrote to Sir Robert Phelips, Sir Henry Berkeley and other Somerset JPs to ascertain whether former assize judges had made such

614. S. Bachiler, *The Campe Royall* (1629, STC 1107), epistle to the reader.
615. 1 Caroli I, Cap 1, Cap 23; 3 Caroli I, Cap 2; M. Dalton, *The Country Justice* (1630, STC 6209), pp. 63–4.
616. P. Thomas, 'Charles I: the tragedy of absolutism', in A.G. Dickens (ed.) *The Courts of Europe, 1400–1800* (1977), pp. 197–8. Elizabeth also encouraged Sunday festivities; see Wordsworth, *Coronation of Charles I*, p.v.
617. Gardiner, *History of England*, VII, pp. 319–20; T.G. Barnes, 'County politics and a puritan *cause célèbre*: Somerset churchales, 1633', *Trans. Royal Hist. Soc.*, 5th series, 9 (1959), pp. 103–32; *Cal. Stat. Pap. Dom., 1628–9*, p. 20.
618. Barnes, 'Somerset churchales', p. 118.

orders without warrant from the bishop. 'Our intention,' he assured them, 'in this business is no way to give a liberty to the breach or profanation of the Lords day, which we will to be kept with that solemnity and reverence that is due to it, but that the people after evening prayer may use such decent and sober recreations as are fit.'[619] Over the summer Phelips informed the king that Richardson had acted wrongly and that the traditional wakes might be held in Somerset without fear of chaos and insubordination. In October Laud reported to Bishop Pierce the king's discontent with Richardson's order: 'he conceives that disorders may be prevented by the justices of the peace and yet leave the feasts to be kept for the neighbourly meetings and recreations of the people.'[620] Charles, Laud added, had become convinced that the opposition to the wakes had stemmed less from widespread fears of disorder than from the machinations of the 'humourists' – the puritans. He required the bishop to test the opinion of the ministers of the county.

So tipped off, Pierce reported back to Laud, the following month, that he had made enquiry concerning the wakes among the 'better sort' of the clergy. From them he had discovered that far from impeding divine service, on feast days the churches were better attended. The ministers as well as people therefore desired their continuation 'for a memorial of the dedication of their churches, for the civilising of people, for their lawful recreations, for composing differences by meeting of friends, for increase of love and amity, as being feasts of charity, for relief of the poor, the richer sort keeping then open house and for many other reasons' – not least that they raised money for the maintenance of the church.[621] Some ministers had added that without such festivals and sports many of the people would have been inclined to frequent tippling houses, or, worse, conventicles. Only the 'preciser sort', enemies to all recreation on Sundays, disliked them. The king, however, received another petition, got up by Sir Arthur Hopton and signed, according to William Whiteway, by thirty-six justices, arguing that the church ales fostered disorder and riot. Whiteway claims that Charles conferred privately with Hopton at Woodstock 'and gave him such satisfaction that at his return he bound over 120 of the revellers'.[622] The claims and counter-claims, prompted by factional rivalries as much as religious preferences among the gentry, led Charles to take a course of action that might 'for the ease, comfort and recreation of our well-deserving people' permit the feasts and wakes to be held, whilst

619. PRO, SO 1/2, f.141.
620. Barnes, 'Somerset churchales', p. 114.
621. *Cal. Stat. Pap. Dom., 1633–4*, p. 231: Laud to Pierce, 4 Oct. 1633; and *Cal. Stat. Pap. Dom., 1633–4*, p. 275: Pierce to Laud, 5 Nov. 1633.
622. BL, Egerton MS 784 (William Whiteway's diary 1618–34), p. 185.

ensuring that 'all disorders there may be prevented or punished'.[623] It was to secure that middle position, not to authorize licence, that the king reissued verbatim the Jacobean Book of Sports on 18 October 1633.[624]

The Book of Sports, which was to be published in every parish of the realm, licensed dancing, May games, and archery, but prohibited bear- and bull-baiting and 'interludes' as well as all recreations before the end of divine service. It may well have been, in the most literal sense, popular. Though they have left little record of their attitudes, the humble poor of the parishes quite probably, as Pierce had claimed, valued village wakes and Sunday sports: indeed the large numbers of absentees caught tippling or at games *during* divine service suggest that many would have extended the royal licence to recreation further than the king wished. The reactions of the clergy and the propertied, however, were far less favourable. The puritan response is not surprising. Ignatius Jordan, a champion of the moral minority in early Stuart parliaments, tried to get Bishop Hall to persuade the king to recall the declaration.[625] Henry Burton in *A Divine Tragedy Later Acted* listed a series of spectacular calamities which he blamed on the licensing of profanity.[626] In Cambridge James Priest stormed against altars and organs and protested that 'some scurvy popish bishop hath got a toleration for boys to play upon the Sabbath day';[627] in Shaftesbury Edward Williams preached against the Book of Sports 'in a most high kind of terrification, as if it were a most dreadful thing and near damnable . . . to use any recreations on the Sabbath' (he was presented by the churchwardens of Holy Trinity as a nuisance to the parish).[628] Perhaps no less surprising than these examples of puritan denunciations are the official apologiae. Francis White was commissioned to answer Brabourne in *A Treatise of the Sabbath Day* (1635), a work which underpinned the royal contrast between lawful and unlawful sports and defended the former from Scripture.[629] Christopher Dow's *Innovations Unjustly Charged*, a response to Burton, denounced rigid Sabbatarianism as a hindrance to the conversion of papists.[630] A third edition of Prideaux's *The Doctrine of the Sabbath* (originally

623. Gardiner, *Constitutional Documents of the Puritan Revolution* (Oxford, 1906), pp. 102–3; the last caveat was more than rhetoric. It has been estimated that the 'effect of its enforcement on church discipline resulted in more presentments for sabbath breaking than usual' (R. Marchant, *The Church under the Law*, Cambridge, 1969, pp. 217–18).
624. Gardiner, *Constitutional Documents*, pp. 99–103.
625. John Earle, *Microcosmographie* (1628, STC 7439), p. 28; Whiteway's diary, p. 190.
626. Marcus, *Politics of Mirth*, p. 152.
627. *Cal. Stat. Pap. Dom., 1635*, p. 270.
628. *Cal. Stat. Pap. Dom., 1634–5*, p. 2.
629. White, *Treatise of the Sabbath Day*.
630. Dow, *Innovations Unjustly Charged*, p. 78.

delivered in the act at Oxford in 1622), defending the magistrate's power to determine such questions, appeared in 1635.[631]

Prideaux's name, however, is enough to suggest that the sabbath question did not divide divines neatly between Arminians and Calvinists, nor even between high and low churchmen. In his defence of Wren, Edmund Mapletoft maintained that as curate of Canfield his father 'though precise enough' had thought the book might be safely read.[632] As Julian Davies has shown, Joseph Hall, the delegate to Dort, was not a strict Sabbatarian; Cosin, however, was. Wren enforced the Book of Sports strictly; Laud for his part did not.[633] Sir John Lambe, commissary of the archdeaconries of Leicestershire and Buckinghamshire, enforced the orders to read the book to the letter. Laud, however, instructed him to give those of tender conscience, like Zachary Seaton, rector of Aspley, Bedfordshire, time to consider his response.[634] Thomas Valentine, rector of Chalfont St Giles, who had been suspended for not reading the declaration, petitioned Laud, who answered him 'that he would stand right in your opinion except some other matter appeared against him';[635] Laud ordered his suspension to be revoked. When one Herbert Palmer had resigned himself to suffering the loss of his place rather than read the declaration, he found, at the archbishop's visitation, 'rather a connivance at him, than an enforcement thereof'.[636] While the charge against Laud, like Palmer's surprise, suggests that others did not see him so, the archbishop was far from a strict enforcer of what was very much the king's book.

Around the country, the Book of Sports clearly caused concern and anguish in men and women who were not over-precise in their religion. In Whitelocke's words, it 'gave great distaste to many both others as well as those who are usually termed puritans'.[637] Some magistrates clearly harboured fears that, despite its wording, the declaration would become an invitation to unrestrained licence. In York the mayor, 'nothing repugning or contrary to what is commanded by his Majesty's declaration', took extra care to observe who took advantage of it to dodge church and head for the alehouse.[638] John Winthrop was informed in 1636 that 'masters of families complain exceedingly they cannot contain their servants from excursions into all

631. J. Prideaux, *The Doctrine of the Sabbath* (1634, STC 20348), pp. 38–9; *ibid.* (1635, STC 20350), p. 41.
632. Tanner MS 314, f.180v.
633. Davies, *Caroline Captivity of the Church*, ch. 5.
634. *Cal. Stat. Pap. Dom., 1636–7*, p. 182; *1637–8*, p. 377.
635. *Cal. Stat. Pap. Dom., 1637–8*, p. 560.
636. Cope, *Politics without Parliaments*, p. 89.
637. Whitelocke, *Memorials of English Affairs*, pp. 17–18.
638. York House Books, 35, f.333.

profane sports and pastimes on the Lords day'.[639] Thomas May even claimed that those 'who had before been loose and careless . . . were ashamed to be invited by the authority of the churchmen, to that which themselves could not have pardoned in themselves'.[640] Nicholas Estwick, rector of Workton, confessed his worries to Samuel Ward. Estwick was not sure whether in itself the book violated the sabbath but he was far from convinced that dancing, Whitsun ales and May games were lawful: 'I do vehemently suspect that some of those in our country towns are seldom or never used . . . without sin and many times with great disorder.' He wished therefore that they had died away with other Catholic rituals such as night vigils and that 'supreme authority would not have quickened men to practise them'. Estwick had the book published in his church, without himself reading it.[641] He was a moderate, indeed conservative, minister who subscribed to the view that 'if a godly Constantine commands me to publish his constitutions which are not condemned by the church . . . I may publish his pleasure'.[642] But, as his long letter announced in every line, he harboured reservations and confessed that had he been required personally to read the declaration:

> I would have run the same hazard with those which have refused to publish the book; for albeit I would be loathe to suffer for disobedience to man's laws in point of ceremony yet it would not trouble my conscience to suffer for matters of that great consequence which do so much concern God's glory and worship as the due sanctification of the Sabbath.[643]

The reservations of a figure like Estwick make it clear that concern over the profanation of the sabbath was felt far beyond the narrow (if noisy) circles of puritan Sabbatarianism. The magistrates of York presented to the petty sessions any who sold ale on the Sabbath;[644] in Chichester haymakers were presented for working on holy days;[645] the Northamptonshire quarter sessions records show indictments for playing games.[646] Binderton in Sussex, though a model parish in terms of its altar railed at the east, did not permit church ales.[647] In 1638

639. *The Winthrop Papers* (Massachusetts Hist. Soc., 4th series, 6, Boston, 1863), p. 408; *Winthrop Papers* III (*Massachusetts Hist. Soc.* 1943), p. 305.
640. T. May, *The History of the Parliament of England which Began November the Third 1640* (1812 edn), p. 16.
641. Tanner MS 71, f.186: Estwick to Ward, 23 Jan. 1634.
642. *Ibid.*, f.186v.
643. *Ibid.*, f.186. The importance of this letter can hardly be exaggerated.
644. York House Books, 35, f.174v.
645. BL Add. MS 39425, p. 2.
646. J. Wake (ed.) *Quarter Sessions Records of the County of Northampton* (Northampton Record Soc., 1, 1924), pp. 28, 64.
647. West Sussex Record Office, EP 1/22/1: churchwardens' presentments.

Richard Stent was cited in Chichester for ploughing on a holy day.[648] At Wimborne in Dorset several men were presented into the peculiar court for fishing on the sabbath.[649] Henry Sherfield regarded sabbath-breaking as one of the evils for which the realm had been chastised by plague;[650] in Buckinghamshire Sir Thomas Temple told his son Peter that of the two most important commandments of God one was not profaning the sabbath, 'which last will be a principal means that you shall keep the rest of the commandments'.[651] Dennis Bond of Dorset graphically records in his diary for 1639 the fate that met those who broke the sabbath: 'a maypole being fetched by some of Wilton near Sarum upon the 19th May the cart overturned within a mile of Sarum and did kill the carter. The woman at Wilton which was to give the entertainment for the drinking that same day scalded her child in a milk pan that it died: this was done on the Lord's day in the morning . . .'.[652] Men like Sherfield, Temple and Bond were not fanatical puritan zealots. There were others like them perhaps behind the argument made in 1640 that 'the people . . . need all curbs that may be not animations to spur them on to all profaneness and disorder'.[653]

It was then especially undiplomatic that for such figures the reading of the Book of Sports was made a test of obedience to authority. Estwick, though he managed to salve his conscience, had been forced to contemplate the possibility of a clash between the magistrate's command and the will of God. In the Rawlinson manuscripts we encounter the case of another clergyman, Humphry Chambers, who found himself even more anguished. His apology for refusing to read the king's declaration for using sports on Sunday is a learned, scholarly piece, devoid of puritan cant, a reasoned argument that places his reservations in sharp focus. Chambers cites in support of his case Prideaux, the church Fathers and Councils, Hooker and Lancelot Andrewes, as well as the statute 3 Charles I against 'travail' on the Lord's day. Chambers was not entangled by 'Judaical' obsessions; eating, dressing food, rescuing beasts in distress he was sure were permissible on the sabbath. Even sociability, exercising neighbourliness, modest recreation he could condone. But he feared that the mixed dancing and May games of the vulgar inflamed the lusts of the flesh and distracted them from God. Chambers was not a puritan killjoy, opposed in principle to such activities: 'I am not convinced,' he wrote, 'that modest persons may not with Christian moderation make

648. Johnstone, *Chichester Presentments*, p. 134; BL Add. MS 39425, p. 2.
649. Dorset Record Office, P/204, CP 13: Wimborne Peculiar court records.
650. Sherfield MS XXXVIII.
651. Temple of Stowe MS 8, STT 2326, 7 Aug. 1631.
652. Dorset Record Office, D413, Box 22, p. 52.
653. Rawlinson MS C.573, p. 8.

some lawful use of mixed dancing.' Yet when they were practised on the Lord's day, 'I yet stand in my conscience assured that God's name is dishonoured'.[654] Chambers could not read the declaration, but he was spared the dilemma of choosing between his duty to God and Caesar. For his bishop sent another to Chamber's church to read it and in such circumstances he submitted to its being read to preserve the peace, so that the 'distraction thereof may not afford ground for a Romish jubilee or schismatical triumph'.[655]

Such a manoeuvre enabled others to side-step an unwelcome choice. Archbishop Ussher noticed that 'there was no clause . . . commanding the ministers to read the book, but if it were *published* in the church by the clerk or churchwardens, the king's command is performed'.[656] Accordingly when the bishop of Bristol urged one of his clergy, Mr White, to read the book and he refused, 'the churchwardens in his absence procured Mr Holliday to read it on Friday morning . . . none being then at church but he and the clerk and the churchwardens'.[657] Others, however, confronted less tactful diocesans. Whilst Coke of Bristol, Laud and Juxon connived at others reading the declaration, Davenant of Salisbury did not.[658] In such cases refusal to read led to suspension and made a question of conscience a political showdown. Rossingham explained in September 1634 to Viscount Scudamore that those who continued obstinate would have to be deprived of their benefices: 'for upon the same grounds (which is only the party's dislike) other men may refuse to publish the king's will above the government of the commonwealth and the question will not be whether that sporting upon the Sunday be lawful yea or no, but whether they do not all to disobey the command of authority'.[659] Charles's intention in the Book of Sports had been first to preserve, not least against puritan assault, the rhythms and rituals of parish life which were central to his perception of the *ecclesia Anglicana*. But perhaps more than any other of his injunctions it raised opponents who were not natural enemies to the church and forced them to a radical choice that presaged the choice many were to have to make in 1642: that between conscience and obedience.

654. Rawlinson MS A.409, quotations ff.54, 61. Though not opposed to mixed dancing, Humphry Chambers was horrified by the wanton gestures demanded by 'Maid Marian's' part. We are left to guess what they might have been.
655. *Ibid.*, ff.72–72v.
656. Hawkins, *Travels of Brereton*, pp. 139–40.
657. Whiteway's diary, p. 206.
658. Davies, *Caroline Captivity of the Church*, ch. 5.
659. PRO, C.115/M36/8432: Rossingham to Scudamore, 2 Sept. 1634.

Perceptions of religious controversies

Arminianism and predestination, altars and rails, the Sherfield case and the Book of Sports. It has been customary to write the religious history of the reign of Charles I as a series of bitter contests between the innovating Laudians and the orthodox. We have suggested, however, that though there were questions and disagreements, attitudes to the various issues do not align men neatly into warring camps, nor were all of the measures widely opposed or contentious. The livery companies who championed puritan lecturers in London still contributed willingly to the refurbishment of St Paul's.[660] How then did contemporaries view the religious measures and controversies of the decade? When we turn one ear away from the noisy diatribes of puritan polemic (on which too often whole assessments of the church have been based) to listen to the language of more moderate and more typical clerics and laymen, what picture, to shift our senses, do we form? At certain times, mainly in and after 1637, contemporaries clearly discerned major religious confrontation. The appearance of books by Burton and Bastwick led Viscount Conway to write to Sir Robert Harley, on April of that year, 'there will be no war but between the bishops and the puritans which grows very hot'.[661] The next month Robert Lecke informed Sir Gervase Clifton, 'all the doings that I hear of is the civil wars amongst the clergy whose pens are their pikes and so they fight daily between the table and the altar'.[662] The Earl of Leicester's estate manager, William Hawkins, wrote to the earl in Paris concerning the same quarrel: 'so bitter are our churchmen now in their invectives one against another that it grieveth all good people to see it'.[663] In the year of the publication of *The Holy Table*, the trial of Prynne, Burton and Bastwick and the outbreak of troubles over the Prayer Book in Scotland, a contemporary sense of sharp confrontation is not surprising. What is more noteworthy is the laymen's irritated (or patronizing?) sense of the emptiness, perhaps absurdity, of what were squabbles amongst divines; and still more important is the very different picture given by contemporaries earlier in the decade.

Religious disagreements there undoubtedly were over the nature of the Church of England: in the Long Parliament Sir Nathaniel Fiennes was to acknowledge, 'it is doubtful what is meant by the discipline and what by the doctrine of the Church of England, for what some call superstitious innovations . . . others affirm to be consonant to the

660. Pearl, *London and the Outbreak of the Puritan Revolution*, p. 161.
661. BL, MS 29/172, f.138: Conway to Harley, 21 April 1637.
662. Clifton MS Cl/C 309: Lecke to Clifton, 3 May 1637.
663. *HMC De Lisle and Dudley VI*, p. 95: Hawkins to Leicester, 16 March 1637.

primitive Reformation.'[664] But since the inception of the Church of England it had always been so, as the Venetian envoy Correr appreciated in penning his relation of the state of England in October 1637: 'England has never been able to secure conformity to a single faith, or to avoid the difficulties caused by a multiplicity of factions.'[665] Yet such differences do not appear to have hardened into rigid parties, or prevented friendships between men of quite different views. Sir John Coke and Sir Kenelm Digby remained close friends after Digby's conversion to Rome;[666] Laud continued to be affectionate towards him.[667] The bishop of Durham, Thomas Morton, congratulated Samuel Ward on his tract on confession;[668] Herrick was a friend of John Williams.[669] Thomas Bedford of Cambridge, composing a treatise on the efficacy of the sacraments, called on the assistance of Samuel Ward, despite the latter's known antipathy to the case.[670] In the localities friendships overrode very different religious sympathies: in Herefordshire the model godly family, the Harleys, were on good terms with the ceremonialist Viscount Scudamore who, incidentally, appears to have been friendly with the puritan circles at Warwick House as well as with Laud.[671] Bishop Bridgeman remained a friend of Christopher Potter, for all the latter's puritanism.[672] In Warwickshire, as Dr Hughes has shown, Sir Thomas Lucy's friendship with the future Presbyterian Robert Harris 'was compatible with an earlier affection for John Donne and an eclectic library of divinity books, the Koran amongst them'![673] The Earl of Dorset's patronage of puritans, of Brian Duppa, Vice-Chancellor during Laud's chancellorship at Oxford, and of the poet John Suckling suggests that doctrinal considerations played little part in his distribution of favour.[674] In Lincolnshire, Dr Hajzyk concluded, differing opinions 'did not preclude the exchange of books, meals, loans, conversations and friends'.[675]

664. Nalson, *Impartial Collection*, I, p. 672.
665. *Cal. Stat. Pap. Venet., 1636–9*, p. 300.
666. Coke MS 49; for example 24 Aug. 1634, Coke to son.
667. Coke MS 56, 15 Feb. 1637; *HMC Cowper II*, pp. 154–5.
668. Tanner MS 67, f.31, 20 Jan. 1639.
669. Ashmole MS 36, f.298: Herrick's poem to Williams as a New Year's gift.
670. Tanner MS 70, f.101, 20 Oct. 1636.
671. Indeed, they intermarried. See J. Eales, *Puritans and Roundheads: The Harleys of Brampton Bryan and the Outbreak of the English Civil War* (Cambridge, 1990), pp. 11, 37–8; PRO, C.115/M35/8386 (Pory to Scudamore, 17 Dec. 1631) refers to all the Viscount's friends at Warwick House.
672. Bridgeman, *History of the Church and Manor of Wigan*, p. 455.
673. A. Hughes, *Politics, Society and Civil War in Warwickshire 1620–1660* (Cambridge, 1987), p. 71.
674. I owe this information to David Smith of Selwyn College, Cambridge. I am most grateful to him for allowing me to see his work on Dorset.
675. Hajzyk, 'The church in Lincolnshire', p. 218.

Indeed, aside from the king's injunctions to silence and peace, there appears to have been a willingness amongst most men to play down theological differences. Bishop John Davenant, after being involved in controversy in 1629, seems as anxious to secure peace as pursue polemic; he came round to the view, he told the ecumenist John Dury, that 'we ought not to make so much account of truth as to be altogether careless of peace'.[676] The tendency of controversialists to wish to label each other met with little approval. George Wither, despite his godly sympathies, rejected the labels puritan and Arminian which some 'mistermed' their enemies.[677] Bishop Griffith Williams too recognized that some were 'termed Zwinglians, Lutherans, Calvinists . . . and the like; names indeed, though perhaps revered in themselves, yet surely through the folly of their followers much derogatory to that glorious name of Christians'.[678] Similarly the Earl of Manchester told his son: 'we build upon Christ not Luther. We renounce all men alike as inventors of our religion and "hold only the apostolical doctrine of the ancient and primitive Catholic church".'[679] Such contemporary observations take us away from the heat of controversy, indeed bring us quite close to Laud's own desire, expressed at his trial, that men should pursue Christian unity rather than agonize over doctrinal tags.

Liturgical and ceremonial issues, the externals of worship, undoubtedly divided men more. Viscount Conway thought this the crucial difference between law and religion; in law 'if that foundation be preserved it is no matter what the differences be . . . but in religion the superstructure may be of different worth and to the ruin of the foundation'.[680] There were clearly differences between those, as Dr Browning put it to Laud, addicted to 'hearing the word', and those devoted to 'God's service and worship'.[681] Humphrey Ramsden found that the ceremonies he practised at St John's Cambridge led him to be maligned in his cure in Northampton.[682] Once again, however, we should not assume that the pamphlet wars over ceremonies describe a reality of widespread conflict. Bishop Joseph Hall, no Laudian, thought it 'a thousand times better to swallow a ceremony than rend a church'.[683] Secretary Coke, though sympathetic to the godly, expressed his conviction that: 'it is no small dishonour to his Majesty's government and also to our church and religion that in a country where way is given to all sorts of religions . . . we should make dif-

676. *Cal. Stat. Pap. Dom., 1633–4*, p. 351: Davenant to Dury [1633].
677. Wither, *Britain's Remembrancer*, f.245.
678. Williams, *The True Church*, p. 84; cf. p. 46.
679. *HMC De Lisle and Dudley VI*, p. 44: Manchester to Montagu, 20 May 1636.
680. BL, MS 29/172, f.172: Conway to Harley, 18 Nov. 1637.
681. *Cal. Stat. Pap. Dom., 1629–31*, p. 87: Browning to Laud, 3 Nov. 1629.
682. *Cal. Stat. Pap. Dom., 1638–9*, p. 587: Ramsden to Lambe, 20 March 1639.
683. J. Hall, *The Works of Joseph Hall* (1628, STC 12636), p. 316.

ficulty in using that liturgy which is prescribed to all good subjects, but is also most agreeable to that which was used in the primitive and best times of the church'.[684] Among the more moderate even of the godly such views were not uncommon. Conway, Lady Harley's brother, rejected Smart's accusations of idolatry and defended some ceremonies: 'our church liturgy have sufficiently allowed of priests, altar and sacrifice in a true and qualified sense'.[685] Bishop Howson of Durham, however, tried to make excuses for Smart.[686] Wither had little time for those so careful to let no superstition in 'That they have, almost, wholly banisht hence/All decency and pious Reverence'.[687] In the localities once again disagreements over ceremony were often softened if not dispelled by personal relationships – and time. In Yorkshire Henry Slingsby disapproved of the practice of bowing performed by Timothy Thurscross, a prebend of York. They discussed the matter and evidently agreed to differ – 'everyone may do as he is persuaded in mind'.[688] Thurscross preached at the christening of Slingsby's son and, admiring his piety, Henry in 1642 nominated him to his advowson at Knaresborough.[689] Hardliners there were in Caroline England, on the episcopal bench and among the hotter sort of Protestants, but as Clarendon put it, 'in truth none of the one side were at all inclined to popery and very many of the other were most affectionate to the peace and prosperity of the church'.[690] For most, at least until 1637, the lines were not clearly drawn.

The bishops and the dioceses

Nor, despite the quip that the Arminians held 'all the best bishoprics in England', was the episcopal bench the preserve of any one faction. As Dr Lambert has recently argued, the Jacobean episcopate was a mixed crew whose fortunes fluctuated, with those of a godly sympathy to the fore in the 1620s.[691] It is worth therefore reminding ourselves that after Laud's elevation to Canterbury though the likes of Montagu, Wren, Curle and Duppa were favoured by promotion, only five new appointments were made to English bishoprics. If there was a revolution in the Caroline church, it had to be effected largely by Jacobean bishops. There are also other indications that the path to

684. *Cal. Stat. Pap. Dom., 1631–3*, p. 554.
685. BL, MS 29/172, f.10.
686. *Cal. Stat. Pap. Dom., 1629–31*, p. 363: Howson to Laud, 20 Oct. 1630.
687. Wither, *Britain's Remembrancer*, f.254.
688. Parsons, *Diary of Sir Henry Slingsby*, p. 8.
689. *Ibid.*, pp. 19, 329.
690. Clarendon, *History of the Rebellion*, I, p. 124.
691. S. Lambert, 'Richard Montagu', p. 42.

favour did not follow rigid party lines. John Prideaux, long famous for making Exeter College, Oxford of which he was rector a haven for puritans, preached before the king at Windsor, and some thought 'he may peradventure carry back a mitre to Oxford'. He had to wait until 1641, but Laud entrusted him with the revision of Chillingworth's *The Religion of Protestants*.[692] During the 1630s John Dury and Richard Sibbes, the puritan divine, were appointed to benefices, and Samuel Fell, chaplain to James I, was made archdeacon of Worcester and dean of Lichfield.[693] In 1635, Ralph Brownbrigg, 'a learned man and no Arminian', as the Reverend Garrard described him to Conway, was appointed head of St Catharine's College, Cambridge; he became vice-chancellor of the university in 1637.[694] Across the country, only 144 clerical livings were in the archbishop's gift; between 1635 and 1638 he made appointments to 27 of them.[695] Moreover, as chancellor of Oxford, Laud made no attempts to establish the nursery of an Arminian clergy, nor even a high church party; rather he expended his energies in the university (as so often in the church) on securing discipline and good order.[696] As for the king, the list of preachers who delivered the Lent sermon at court (from whom the royal chaplains were often chosen) may be revealing.[697] For as well as Laud, Juxon and Pierce, we find the puritan Thomas Winniffe, Thomas Howell future bishop of Bristol who, Wood tells us, was regarded as a puritan, and Isaac Bargrave who quarrelled with Laud for much of the decade. John Williams of Lincoln, and John Davenant of Salisbury were regulars despite their differences with the king and archbishop. The hand of fortune, the paucity of deaths in the 1630s, would have made it difficult for Charles and Laud to build a party united in its view of the church. There is little evidence to suggest that they attempted it.

Indeed royal policy, in that it emphasized the jurisdiction and authority of the bishop, left room for a variety of practice in different dioceses. The king's instructions of 1629 made the episcopate the linchpin of the programme to reform the church: it was the bishops who were responsible for ensuring that divine service was diligently attended, that lecturers conformed and that catechizing took place in the afternoons. Bishops were ordered to reside in their houses because,

692. Berkshire Record Office, Trumbull Add. MS 52: Trumbull to son, 15 Sept. 1629; *DNB*.
693. *Cal. Stat. Pap. Dom., 1633–4*, p. 453; Gardiner, *History of England*, VII, p. 262; PRO, SO 1/1, f.229; SO 1/3, f.64.
694. *Cal. Stat. Pap. Dom., 1635*, p. 385.
695. Carlton, *Laud*, p. 107.
696. K. Sharpe, 'Archbishop Laud and the University of Oxford', in H. Lloyd Jones, V. Pearl and B. Worden (eds) *History and Imagination* (1981), pp. 146–64.
697. PRO, LC 5/132 (warrant books): lists of Lent preachers; BL, Egerton MS 2978, f.47: preachers for 1633.

like their secular counterparts the lord-lieutenants, Charles saw them as governors, as well as spiritual leaders – clerical overlords whose residences were centres of hospitality and who represented royal authority. When the bishop of Carlisle asked to be absent from his see, 'the king would not grant it because he thought it unreasonable that a main pillar of the country should be absent in such needful times'.[698] As we have seen, there were proposals to appoint a bishop for every county as well as a scheme to remove all particular jurisdictions in the diocese, settling total authority on the bishop.[699] With the endowment of power went responsibility: the bishops were required to send a report annually to their metropolitan, who passed his on to the king. Charles's instructions of 1634 required them also to give notice of any alterations in matters concerning doctrine and discipline in their dioceses.[700] They were subject to Laud's metropolitical visitation in 1635, to the investigations of his vicar-general and to the orders subsequently issued. In addition, there were in several dioceses those ready to send private information to Laud concerning things amiss. But overall it is the independence of the bishops that is striking. Bishop Matthew Wren acknowledged it too when he observed in his defence that none needed to be religious exiles from England when they could have moved to another diocese where the bishop was less inclined to harry nonconformists.[701] It was more than a rhetorical point. Bridgeman of Chester, Morton of Durham, Corbet at Norwich, Wright of Coventry were lenient in their treatment of puritans.[702] More generally it was, as Trevor-Roper put it, 'simple enough for easy going bishops to report *omnia bene*', as did Peterborough, Rochester, Exeter, Ely, Chichester, Oxford and Salisbury in 1635.[703] Some sent in no account at all. For all the talk of uniformity, the bishops were left considerable room to interpret royal orders and pursue their own priorities.

Until we have more studies of individual dioceses we cannot generalize confidently concerning the episcopal response to Charles's and Laud's injunctions nor assess the extent to which particular localities experienced official pressure to alter modes of worship. The quite different implementation of the injunctions for altars and the Book of Sports must lead us to suspect very different episcopal priorities and styles. Bridgeman concentrated on the beautification of

698. Boas, *Diary of Thomas Crosfield*, p. 31.
699. Lambeth Palace MS 943, pp. 395–6.
700. Tanner MS 70, f.45.
701. Wren, *Parentilia*, p. 102.
702. Bridgeman, *History of the Church and Manor of Wigan*, p. 453; R. Howell, *Newcastle upon Tyne in the Puritan Revolution* (Oxford, 1967), p. 84; Cliffe, *The Puritan Gentry*, p. 173; Hughes, *Politics, Society and Civil War*, p. 79.
703. Trevor-Roper, *Archbishop Laud*, p. 174; *Works of Laud*, V, p. 334.

his cathedral, the improvement of his episcopal endowments, and the careful preservation of bishops' evidences, registers and charters.[704] But very much concerned with his local base, he eschewed controversy with the civic authorities, and remained on cool terms with Archbishop Neile.[705] Though evidently inclined to ceremony himself, he did not press observance on others, so many were found by the archbishop of York in 1633 who 'observed not the book and orders prescribed'.[706] Neile by contrast was driven by an obsession for conformity to the canons and royal injunctions that surpassed Laud's own. His vigour led to a rise in presentments in the ecclesiastical courts from 3,250 in 1623 to over 5,000 by 1637.[707] His campaign, however, to purge his diocese of recusants ('the pope's traitorous agents') and puritans met with limited success: 'too many puritans were already dug into city incumbencies' to secure conformity.[708] As for Bath and Wells, while Laud once dolefully wished that all dioceses could emulate it, a full recent study has shown that Pierce had a limited impact and apart from 'petty, small-minded correction' little fundamentally changed.[709]

Certainly, Brent's report to Laud from the metropolitical visitation of 1635 indicates that many episcopal claims had been over-optimistic. Brent pointed out that for Shrewsbury the bishop's note had been mistaken: many things there were out of order, especially the communion table.[710] Where Godfrey Goodman of Gloucester had reported to Laud in 1634 that he thought there none non-conformable in his diocese, the vicar-general identified several 'believed puritanical' who were 'much given to straggle from their own parishes to hear strangers'.[711] At Peterborough, where the bishop had boasted all in order, Brent found churches governed by orders of their own making.[712] Ironically Coventry, which had sent in no report when Laud submitted his account for 1634, was found to be wholly conformable.[713] In general much was amiss. In Ipswich some had proved 'exceeding factious'; in Northampton there was opposition to bowing; there were conventicles in Guildford.[714] In Derby, Brent had to

704. Cheshire Record Office, EDA/3/1: Bridgeman's ledger, esp. ff.130–1, 192v–193.
705. B. W. Quintrell, 'Lancashire ills, the king's will and the troubling of Bishop Bridgeman', pp. 94–5.
706. Bridgeman, *Hitory of the Church and Manor of Wigan*, p. 367.
707. Marchant, *The Church under the Law*, p. 230.
708. *Cal. Stat. Pap. Dom., 1637–8*, p. 310; Aveling, *Catholic Recusancy in York*, p. 79.
709. *Works of Laud*, V, p. 325; Stieg, *Laud's Laboratory*, p. 287.
710. *Cal. Stat. Pap. Dom., 1635*, p. xxxvi.
711. *Works of Laud*, V, p. 330; *Cal. Stat. Pap. Dom., 1635*, p. xl.
712. *Cal. Stat. Pap. Dom., 1635*, p. xxxiii; *Works of Laud*, V, p. 330.
713. *Cal. Stat. Pap. Dom., 1635*, p. xxxviii.
714. *Ibid.*, pp. xxxii, xxxv, xliv.

suspend drunken ministers; at Stratford he disciplined the minister for keeping hogs in the chancel.[715]

Brent's catalogue of ills reads like an exhaustive examination of the dioceses of England. We should recall therefore that he visited each place for only a few days and was usually dependent on others for the information that he gleaned. Brent himself was fully aware of the limits to his knowledge: the ministers of Cirencester, he reported, professed conformity but were 'much suspected for inconformity'.[716] Similarly in Norwich there were clergy believed to be nonconformists 'but they carried themselves so warily that nothing could be proved against them'.[717] There were doubtless more cases where even Brent's suspicions had not been aroused. The impossibility of oversight made the enforcement of the orders issued to rectify ills little more than a pious hope. Miscreants such as 'Mr Hampden' of Beaconsfield may have given 'so much assurance of his willing obedience unto the laws of the church hereafter'; but Brent had little means of discerning whether he fulfilled his promise.[718] The orders to Winchester cathedral to reform services depended for their implementation on the co-operation of the dean and chapter: Dean Young, regarding bowing, standing at the creed and other recommendations as innovations, more likely proved obstructive.[719] Such situations were repeated in various parts of the country: as Dr Andrewes wrote to Sir John Lambe, 'The orders of Sir Nathaniel Brent enjoined at the metropolitical visitation are treated as if not seriously intended to be obeyed.'[720] Because Laud never had the opportunity of a second metropolitical visitation, his programme succeeded, as Heylyn put it, 'more or less as the bishops were of spirit and affection to advance the work'.[721]

There were limits to the effectiveness even of those bishops who were willing, indeed enthusiastic to co-operate in the implementation of metropolitical orders. Many bishops, Heylyn tells us, left the enforcement of orders concerning afternoon catechizing to their chancellors and allowed the position of the communion table to be decided by individual ministers.[722] Deans and chapters who exercised peculiar jurisdiction outside episcopal authority, Laud feared, 'suffer [the church] to be abused . . . and have no visitor'.[723] Especially in

715. *Ibid.*, pp. xxxviii, xl.
716. *Ibid.*, p. xli.
717. *Ibid.*, p. xxx.
718. *Cal. Stat. Pap. Dom., 1634–5*, p. 250.
719. *Cal. Stat. Pap. Dom., 1635*, p. 133; F.R. Goodman, *The Diary of John Young, Dean of Winchester* (1928), p. 109.
720. *Cal. Stat. Pap. Dom., 1635*, p. 26: Andrewes to Lambe, 14 April.
721. Heylyn, *Cyprianus Anglicus*, pp. 270–1.
722. *Ibid.*, pp. 294–5.
723. *Cal. Stat. Pap. Dom., 1634–5*, p. 215.

large dioceses, the bishop could have little personal knowledge of parish practices, so enforcement had very much to be entrusted to others. Uncooperative ministers could employ tactics and ruses which it was very hard to police. In response to the royal orders to catechize on Sunday afternoons instead of a sermon, 'many preachers sought to evade the king's declaration by seeming to conform thereunto, but utterly colluding therein as by demanding a question or two of a boy, and then falling into a large sermon'.[724] As one of Wren's commissioners, Dr Thomas Eden, observed, many unconformable ministers 'have scaped so many years and so many visitations'.[725] Powerful gentlemen protected nonconformist ministers under the guise of private chaplains and schoolmasters.[726] The problem was even greater with the laity. Dr Samuel Collins, Regius professor of divinity at Cambridge, defended himself to Arthur Duck, writing from Braintree in Essex in 1632 in response to Laud's displeasure with him over the nonconformity there: 'it is no easy matter to reduce a numerous congregation into order that has been disorderly these fifty years and for the last seven years has been encouraged in that way by all the refractory ministers of the country'.[727]

At the parish level, the enforcement of visitation orders and the presentment of recalcitrants depended upon the co-operation of the lay churchwardens who might well be unsympathetic to particular injunctions they were supposed to enforce or reluctant to present friends and neighbours who disobeyed them. The royal proclamation for the repair of churches acknowledged that churchwardens were unreliable in reporting the poor condition of parish churches – probably through fear of the cost that would be incurred as a consequence.[728] The archbishop of York in 1633 identified them as a fundamental weakness of the whole ecclesiastical system; 'it is,' he commented in a report on his dioceses, 'in a manner impossible for the bishops to know how the public service is performed in every church and chapel of his diocese. The bishop can but enquire but by the oath of churchwardens and sidesmen, who make no conscience of dispensing with their oath, and can hardly be brought to present anything, be things never so far out of order.'[729] The bishops depended on several subordinate officials, chancellors, deacons, churchwardens, 'and if they be negligent or corrupt it is not possible for the bishops to know and reform things that are amiss'. In some places – Ely for example –

724. Tanner MS 220, f.65.
725. Tanner MS 68, f.52.
726. Tanner MS 280, f.185.
727. *Cal. Stat. Pap. Dom., 1631–3*, p. 255: Dr Collins to Duck, 18 Jan. 1632.
728. Above, pp. 318–19.
729. Bridgeman, *History of the Church and Manor of Wigan*, p. 371.

puritans took advantage of the weakness of the system to get themselves elected churchwardens so that they could protect the nonconformity of the godly from being exposed.[730] Sometimes they corruptly took money for forbearing to report absentees from church or other unofficial practices.[731] More frequently they were lazy and anxious not to rock the parish boat. So at Aldrington in Sussex the churchwardens returned *omnia bene* when it appears the church had no font or bible and was much in need of repair.[732] In 1636, Bishop Montagu's survey of churches in Chichester diocese revealed 202 things amiss, only one of which had been reported.[733] The chancellor of Lincoln diocese was informed that the churchwardens there 'present usually *omnia bene* when there is almost nothing in order': the congregation, for example, sitting with their hats on, lying along the pews or absenting themselves altogether.[734] The perfunctory nature of the clerk's examination of churchwardens meant that their misdemeanours were often not discovered until much later (perhaps by more diligent successors) if at all. At Mortlake the man chosen churchwarden, Lionel Bostock, spent most of his time drunk.[735] Given parish officials such as him, Thomas Goad was not over-cynical in his belief that whatever a bishop did to reform or reduce men to conformity, 'when our backs are turned things will resolve in statum primum'.[736]

Matthew Wren and the diocese of Norwich

Goad expressed that belief to perhaps the most vigorous of all the Caroline bishops in his campaign for order and uniformity – Matthew Wren. Wren, chaplain to Charles as prince, and Clerk of the Closet to the king, was elevated from the see of Hereford to Norwich in 1635. Immediately he set out to make a model diocese of what had long been known as a centre of puritan nonconformity, with its strong commercial connections with Holland. Wren's visitation articles, consisting of over 130 questions, ranged with formidable detail over all areas of the religious life of the clergy and laity and the requirements of the canons of 1604 and royal orders of 1629. Did the minister adhere to the royal injunction to avoid controversy and teach obedience to lawful authority? Was the table placed conveniently and usually at the east

730. M. Spufford, *Contrasting Communities: English Villagers in the Sixteenth and Seventeenth Centuries* (Cambridge, 1974), p. 269.
731. *Works of Laud*, V, p. 408.
732. Fletcher, *County Community*, p. 83.
733. *Ibid.*, p. 85.
734. *Ibid.*; *Cal. Stat. Pap. Dom., 1634–5*, p. 64.
735. *Cal. Stat. Pap. Dom., 1634–5*, p. 560.
736. Tanner MS 68, f.45.

end, in a north–south position? Did any married live apart? Did parishioners attend for prayers and sacraments as well as sermons? Wren required a full answer to every distinct question; here no *omnia bene* would be accepted.[737] The 'little Pope regulas', as Prynne nicknamed him, intended to exercise a close jurisdiction which many of godly sympathies saw might flush out nonconformists who had escaped less diligent diocesans.[738] Lucy Downing told Mary Winthrop in May 1636, 'The bishop of Norwich . . . doth impose a hundred and thirty-two articles to the clergy in his diocese, some whereof they fear will put by both Mr Lea and divers others, which thought themselves very conformable men.'[739] Together with his articles of enquiry, Wren instructed his vicar-general Clement Corbet to see that catechizing and divine service were properly performed.[740] He ordered ministers to read the second service at the communion table, prayers to follow the form laid down in the 55th canon, no sermon to be delivered before the reading of the Nicene creed and the reverence of kneeling and standing at the prescribed points of the litany. His injunctions for his primary visitation, as well as rehearsing the above, added orders for rails and forbade pews which obscured sight of the congregation, 'tavern pots' which defamed the table and the ringing of bells to indicate to those who absented themselves from the full service that it was time for the sermon.[741]

The visitation of the diocese only confirmed Wren's fears about the extent to which things were amiss and reinforced his paranoia about the puritans. Corbet and others reported ministers who departed from the canons, parishioners who dodged prayers, absent clergy, the omission of the surplice, in general the problem of the dependency of the clergy on the laity and the obstructions of the Norwich aldermen.[742] Thomas Goad, dean of Bocking, told the bishop how even conformable clergy were being corrupted: at Bury the preacher, formerly not schismatical, 'upon his marriage in tribum puritannicum . . . thinks he must pipe so that they may dance at it'.[743] Corbet, as chancellor, discovered many conventicles where he feared 'they intend to overturn and evaporate our cultus of prayer and preaching'.[744] Such fears drove Wren to strive for even closer supervision and control. With Corbet's assistance he drew up 'particular orders, directions and remembrances'

737. *Ibid.*, ff.65–73; R.W. Ketton-Cremer, *Norfolk in the Civil War* (1969), ch. 4; *Cal. Stat. Pap. Dom., 1636–7*, p. 261.
738. W. Prynne, *Newes from Ipswich* (1636, STC 20469), p. 4.
739. *Winthrop Papers*, I, p. 11.
740. Tanner MS 137, f.7, 6 March 1636.
741. *Ibid.*, f.8.
742. Tanner MS 68, ff.1v, 2, 7, 10v, 11.
743. *Ibid.*, f.45: Goad to Wren, 5 April 1636.
744. *Ibid.*, f.1v.

which prescribed in detail the form of service to be used, the behaviour of the clergy and congregation, the forms of marriage, churching, baptism, communion, and the furniture of the church.[745] He also, after this primary visitation, appointed standing commissioners in the diocese with power to investigate how his directions were observed in every parish.[746] Throughout 1637 the commissioners continued to investigate and report. If bureaucratic effort and personal energy could have secured conformity, Norwich would have emerged as the model diocese.

The opposition Wren aroused may be taken, in one way, as a measure of his success in pressuring men to conformity. Thomas Allen, for example, rector of St Edmund's church in Norwich, condemned the visitation as a breach of royal supremacy and soon after fled to Holland.[747] The citizens also petitioned against Wren's injunctions and found support among city aldermen who were either sympathetic to puritanism or antagonized by the bishop's hectoring tone to the laity.[748] Orders for bowing, east end altars, reading the second service, it was claimed, had forced many to leave the city. In 1640 Wren was the bishop other than Laud whom the Commons were quick to impeach. In many details, as the Norwich petition recognized, Wren went further than Laud in his drive for conformity[749] – partly through personal inclination, partly because he believed, not as we shall see without reason, that some in his troubled diocese 'seeketh the subversion of all order and religion'.[750] But despite the charges later levelled against him, Wren did not seek to subvert preaching and sermons, nor conduct a purge of the clergy. Wren was not opposed to lecturers if they conformed to the church. As he wrote concerning the lectureship at Haverhill, 'preaching of the word is in itself most holy and good and shall ever find all encouragement and promotion at my hands', yet, 'I am resolved to let no man preach in any place where he is not also charged with the cure, thereby to put a straighter tie upon him to observe and justify the rites and ceremonies which the church enjoineth . . . for the preserving of unity in doctrine.'[751] Wren licensed, he told the king, several lectures by conformable divines and caused Sunday sermons to be delivered in thirty-four Norwich churches where at his coming to the diocese there had been only four.[752]

745. *Ibid.*, ff.24–5, 33–6.
746. *Ibid.*, f.219.
747. *Ibid.*, f.115.
748. *Ibid.*, ff.159, 160.
749. *Ibid.*, f.160, points out that the last metropolitical visitation 'settled all in quiet and peace'.
750. Tanner MS 68, f.219.
751. *Ibid.*, f.92.
752. *Ibid.*, f.316.

Preaching as well as prayer were part of Wren's culture of worship, as Dr King concluded: 'Wren took trouble to propose lecturers and to try and persuade them to conformity'.[753] Only the few intransigently recalcitrant were suppressed.

Nor is Prynne's claim (in his Star Chamber cross bill) that Wren suspended sixty ministers borne out by the evidence.[754] At his trial Wren claimed that few had been suspended, and of those who were, most were restored soon after – Robert Kent the same afternoon.[755] The bishop's papers for 1636 list those censured, in some cases with notes ('a very famous man for drunkenness') that indicate the cause.[756] Only Thomas Allen 'fled into Holland' leaving 'a protestation behind him against the ecclesiastical jurisdiction, much like Burton'.[757] Corbet's correspondence shows that others resigned, as did Mr Carter of St Peter's, who could not read prayers according to the 55th canon.[758] But in general such cases are not only few, they are outnumbered by the many examples of Wren's patient and tolerant efforts to win over ministers who had, often for years, failed to conform.[759] Thomas Warren, for example, minister of St Lawrence's church, though he admitted that he did not obey the canons or injunctions, was given time to conform.'[760] Robert Stansby, rector of Westhorpe, had never worn his surplice or conducted service according to the Book of Common Prayer, and even after his formal presentment by the commissioners, he continued in his nonconformity: Wren gave him two months to confer with learned men in order to satisfy his conscience.[761] With Nicholas Sherwood, rector of Earsham, Wren's patience appears remarkable: Sherwood had frequented alehouses, played dice, blasphemed, and verbally abused women from the pulpit, but Wren extended him a pardon if he acknowledged his fault and promised reformation.[762] The rector of St Clement's, Ipswich, Thomas Scott, though disciplined by Wren, acknowledged that 'your lordship's former gentleness in proceeding with me hath been such that I am sure it is rare . . . your lordship's sweet hand upon me hath so mollified my mind . . . that I have observed sundry your lordship's

753. See P. King, 'Bishop Wren and the suppression of the Norwich lecturers', *Hist. Journ*, 11 (1968), pp. 237–54, quotation p. 253.
754. Tanner MS 299, f.158v.
755. Wren, *Parentilia*, p. 94.
756. Tanner MS 314, f.120.
757. *Ibid.*
758. Tanner MS 68, f.7.
759. On the numbers, see King, 'Bishop Wren and the suppression of the Norwich lecturers', p. 252; *Works of Laud*, V, pp. 340, 341; *Cal. Stat. Pap. Dom., 1636–7*, p. 223; Tanner MS 68, ff.316, 332; Tanner MS 220, f.1.
760. Tanner MS 314, f.127.
761. Tanner MS 68, ff.129, 134.
762. *Ibid.*, f.252.

directions which formerly I thought I should not have done'.[763] Months later Scott thanked Wren for not proceeding legally against him but allowing him time. Though he had remained 'defective' in some points, he promised his reformation.[764] The bishop exhibited the same patience with the laity: Edmund Mapletoft testified that Wren for some time offered to take the communion to those who had scruples about coming to the rails to receive it.[765]

Despite a hard core of opponents, there is no doubt that Wren's campaign began to meet with success. The dean and prebendaries of Norwich were clear that though some few in the city got up a petition against it, they had 'found the people generally to take great liking in this reformation'.[766] Several Norwich clergy were to certify that Wren had increased piety in the diocese; in June 1637 the commissioners of the archdeaconry of Norwich could report that 'in most parishes . . . we have found the ministers and people very tractable and ready to perform what was enjoined by your lordship'.[767] In 1639 the diocese of Norwich was returned as quiet and conformable, but for some who balked at receiving at the rail.[768] Time might have won the parishioners of the diocese, other than committed puritans, to the reformation Wren sought. In May 1638, however, Wren was promoted to Ely. Corbet regretted the timing of the move before the diocese was perfected – 'which a year or two more would have reduced to a good pass by your lordship's indefatigable diligence and vigilancy'.[769] Wren was himself aware of the consequences of the news. 'The report of my removal,' he told Edmund Pierce, commissary of Suffolk, at the end of March, 'makes the factious people creep out and show themselves.' The 'holy brood' assembled to scoff and jeer at the devoted as they went to church.[770] Foulke Robartes, a minister in the diocese for thirty-six years, was even more pessimistic. In his time he had seen seven bishops before Wren, seven 'of your predecessors that have begun some reformation amongst us, but none of them attempted to bring things so full home to the primitive Christian devotion nor so really to reduce the pristine splendour of religion as your lordship hath done with good success'. Some, he reflected, had entered the see with the vigour of a storm, which had then blown over quickly; but you, he praised Wren, came in 'with less noise . . . but more efficacy to make the ground fruitful'. In 1638, Robartes knew that still 'there is much to

763. *Ibid.*, ff.287, 295, 297: Scott to Wren, 17 April 1637.
764. *Ibid.*, f.299: Scott to Wren, 12 Aug. 1637.
765. Tanner MS 314, f.180.
766. Tanner MS 68, f.167, Oct. 1636.
767. *Ibid.*, ff.164, 240, 9 June 1637.
768. *Works of Laud*, V, p. 364; Lambeth Palace MS 943, p. 615.
769. Tanner MS 68, f.11.
770. *Ibid.*, f.327.

be done in this diocese' which, with Wren's departure, 'I despair ever to see effected'. 'Withall my lord,' he closed, 'all that you have done I more than fear will be undone.'[771]

Robartes wrote not only the truth about Norwich but an epitaph on the Caroline and Laudian programme to reform the church. The time which Laud believed might accustom men to decency was not given. If Norwich never became the model diocese of Wren's intention, we must suspect that others where bishops neither shared Wren's goals nor emulated his vigour fell far short of the ideal. If the experiment did not succeed in Laud's laboratories, there could be no theological or liturgical revolution across the realm.

The court of High Commission

Our argument that there was no Arminian revolution in the England of the 1630s requires that we look critically at a surprisingly enduring myth: the myth that surrounds the court of High Commission. High Commission, we have been taught, was abolished in 1641, because it was one of the harsh instruments of control, an ecclesiastical Star Chamber, by which Charles I had sustained his eleven years' tyranny. 'This,' wrote Alexander Leighton in 1628, 'is like the lion's den out of which very few are delivered with their lives.'[772] In 1640 the court of High Commission was branded a bugbear worse than the notorious Spanish Inquisition.[773] Even over seventy years after a major study, the caricatures of 1641, the taint of oppression and tyranny have not been dispelled.[774] Some historians still see in the High Commission 'one of the chief causes of the revolution of 1640'.[775]

In every area, however, the records show the reality to be very different from the reputation. The statute 1 Elizabeth Cap I section VIII conferred on the crown the power to appoint commissioners to exercise jurisdiction over affairs ecclesiastical ('to visit, reform, redress, order, correct and amend all . . . heresies, errors, schisms, abuses, offences and contempts') and formed the basis from which letters patent were issued by Elizabeth and her successors.[776] Charles I's letter patent of 1625 virtually rehearsed those issued in 1601, but greatly increased the commissioners' numbers.[777] The increased numbers of

771. *Ibid.*, f.309: Robartes to Wren, 2 March 1638.
772. Leighton, *An Appeal to the Parliament*, p. 126.
773. BL, Harleian MS 4931, f.39.
774. R.G. Usher, *The Rise and Fall of the High Commission* (Oxford, 1913).
775. *Ibid.*, p. 5.
776. Printed *ibid.*, p. 336. The opponents of the court questioned from the beginning the nature of these letters patent and this jurisdiction. Cf. Hutton, *William Laud*, pp. 96–8.
777. *Ibid.*, pp. 241–2.

commissioners (108 in 1633) in practice facilitated the extension of the powers of the court into the localities.[778] But including as it did *all* the bishops, royal judges, many Privy Councillors and gentry, the Caroline High Commission was always representative of a wide range of opinions and preferences.[779] Accordingly the list of commissioners for causes ecclesiastical in 1631 includes noblemen of strong Protestant convictions – Viscounts Dorchester and Conway, the Earls of Manchester, Pembroke, and Holland – and bishops such as John Williams and Archbishop Abbot, as well as Laud, Pierce and Wren.[780] Similarly in the commission for 1633, the Earl of Bridgewater, the Marquis of Hamilton, Lords Wentworth and Coventry, Coke, Heath, Noy and Naunton sat alongside those of less obvious sympathies for the godly: Arundel, Cottington and Windebank. 'In the giving of every definitive sentence, every commissioner hath an equal voice one with the other and the most voices make the sentence.'[781] With such a heterogeneous body, therefore, and with such a constitution, it was intrinsically difficult for High Commission to become the instrument of a party. Moreover, High Commission could only deal with cases that came to its attention as a consequence of presentments by ecclesiastical officers, or ordinary parishioners. Laud did revive the visitorial powers that made the commission more effective in the diocese and the commissioners issued warrants to county magistrates for search of prohibited books, but even in the small number of official actions, prosecution depended upon local information and co-operation.[782]

The powers and procedure of the court have often been misrepresented. The accused was summoned to appear by letter and bound over to reappear; he was then examined under oath on the articles of the charge; a term was assigned for witnesses' depositions, for formal examination by the defence and prosecution, before judgment and sentence.[783] The written procedure and trial largely in private, though different from the common law, the commission shared with the Star Chamber, the Chancery, the Admiralty, the Court of Requests and the Councils of the North and Marches. It was often more efficient than that of the common law courts: flexible and quick, whilst allowing for thorough examination of the evidence – as the case of Robert Bradling in the court at Durham well demon-

778. *Ibid.*, p. 250.
779. Usher lists all the commissioners 1549–1641 in appendix II.
780. Ellesmere MS 7730.
781. *Ibid.*
782. Usher, *Rise and Fall of the High Commission*, pp. 242–3, 251.
783. *Cal. Stat. Pap. Dom., 1635–6*, pp. xxix–xxx; Usher, *Rise and Fall of the High Commission*, p. 275; Longstaff, *Acts of the High Commission in Durham*, p. 266.

strates.[784] Indeed what most struck the historian of the commission was the 'superabundance of evidence testifying to the consistent care and effort shown by the commissioners, that their powers should be exercised with equity, moderation and absolute fairness, and that their procedure should be free from undue delay, expense and vexation'.[785] It was the use of the oath *ex officio* that attracted odium to the procedure of the court. From Elizabeth's reign the court's examination by an oath under which a party accused might incriminate himself had raised, as well as puritan opposition, concern among common lawyers who anyway disliked jurisdictions outside the common law. In James I's reign, led by Sir Edward Coke, the common law judges threatened to stymie the operation of the court by issuing a large number of prohibitions which challenged the court's jurisdiction and transferred the case to common law.[786] In 1611, however, James I himself intervened, issuing a new commission which restated the court's authority to imprison and employ the oath *ex officio* and its wide powers to examine clergy and try any who challenged clerical authority or disrupted church services.[787]

Naturally inclined to uphold the authority of the clergy, Charles I, as the letters patent of 1625 indicate, was a staunch supporter of the court, and of its procedure by oath. In 1632 the jurisdiction of the court met with a serious challenge in the famous case of Peter Smart, who had been disciplined for his attack on the ceremonial practices in Durham cathedral. Though excommunicated and degraded from office by High Commission in 1630, Smart on St Peter's day 1632 took his old stall in the choir there, in contempt of authority. The common lawyers at York denied that the High Commissioners there could meddle with him for his insolency 'in regard that he is a prisoner of the King's Bench, removed by habeas corpus from York'. This, Archbishop Neile told Laud, 'seemeth to me a strange privilege'. 'If that be avowed for good we may give up the High Commission.' He urged Canterbury 'to move his majesty herein and to obtain some better resolution for our proceedings'.[788] It was just such a challenge, renewed in the pamphlet attacks on the ecclesiastical hierarchy in 1637, that moved the king to action. On 18 August 1637 Charles published a proclamation announcing the opinion of the judges that bishops might keep ecclesiastical courts 'and that the proceedings in the High

784. Usher, *Rise and Fall of the High Commission*, pp. 260–1; Longstaff, *Acts of the High Commission in Durham*, pp. 53–63, 105.
785. Usher, *Rise and Fall of the High Commission*, p. 267.
786. M.H. Maguire, 'The attack of the common lawyers on the oath *ex officio*', in *Essays in Honour of C.H. McIlwain* (Cambridge Mass., 1936), pp. 199–229.
787. Usher, *Rise and Fall of the High Commission*, chs 8, 9 and pp. 236–41.
788. Coke MS 42: Neile to Laud, 28 July 1632.

Commission . . . are agreeable to the laws and statutes of the realm'.[789] The following February a signet letter to the commissioners clarified their powers and procedures concerning the controversial oath, which obstinate sectaries had been refusing to take.[790] High Commission's proceedings, it declared, followed civil and canon law, and were analogous to those of Star Chamber, Chancery and Requests 'wherein defendants have always used to answer on oath in causes against themselves'. The king ordered accordingly that all brought before the court were to be enjoined to take the oath to answer articles and that those who refused should be held to have confessed. There could have been no clearer reassertion of the authority of the court at a time of mounting challenge.

Yet though the authority of High Commission was underpinned, it did not in the reign of Charles I become an instrument for the searching of tender consciences nor for the cruel and harsh repression of the heterodox. In the recent words of John Kenyon, 'the general impression then and later that it was a key weapon in Laud's campaign against the puritans is on the whole false'.[791] In the first place of all the cases heard between 1611 and 1640 80 per cent were brought not by ecclesiastical officials but by parishioners themselves against the clergy or each other. And of the 20 per cent officially prosecuted, about half were brought on behalf of the poor.[792] Very few cases indeed were concerned with theology or belief, and those that were defy any neat categorization.[793] So George Bardett of Yarmouth was prosecuted for preaching that the benefit of Christ's death was limited to the elect (as well as that clergy should be elected),[794] but Dr Everitt was proceeded against for claiming that damned spirits could find mercy, Bishop Montagu being 'smart' in condemning him.[795] Despite the claims of Prynne, Burton, Bastwick and others that the court hounded moderate ministers for their 'virtue and piety', it was only the most outrageous, blasphemous and anti-Christian tenets that were prosecuted.[796] Everitt (or Everard) had denied the resurrection of the human body and the existence of hell;[797] Andrew Lapthorne, rector of Tretire in Hereford, questioned whether Christ descended into hell;[798] John James of Northamptonshire was presented for preaching that all children,

789. Larkin, *Stuart Royal Proclamations*, II, no. 244, pp. 572–3.
790. PRO, SO 1/3, f.69, 4 Feb. 1638.
791. J.P. Kenyon (ed.) *The Stuart Constitution* (2nd edn, Cambridge, 1986), p. 159.
792. *Ibid.*
793. See the table in Usher, *Rise and Fall of the High Commission*, p. 279.
794. *Cal. Stat. Pap. Dom., 1634–5*, p. 537.
795. BL Add. MS 11045, f.37.
796. Hargrave *State Trials*, I, p. 495; Tanner MS 299, f.160.
797. Tanner MS 67, f.143.
798. *Cal. Stat. Pap. Dom., 1634–5*, p. 263.

whether baptized or not, were within the covenant of God and beneficiaries of His promise.[799] Such heterodox pronouncements cut across the disagreements about predestination that allegedly polarized the realm. Moreover they seldom met with harsh punishment. All the punishments – of fine, deprivation and imprisonment – laid on Everard were ordered to be taken off if he recanted.[800] In the case of Thomas Hubberd and the separatists of St Giles, the court enquired what hope there was of reclaiming them from their schismatical opinions;[801] even John Vaux, clerk of St Helen's Auckland, suspended for selling almanacs from the communion table and casting figures on it in order to prophesy, was restored to his place.[802]

High Commission does appear to have used its powers of search in order to discover conventicles and unlicensed books:[803] Richard Blagrave, for example, was imprisoned for importing libellous works from Geneva and Amsterdam.[804] But in this they enjoyed (as well as depended upon) the active co-operation of justices of the peace of various religious persuasions. In 1636, Nathaniel Brent thanked Sir Edward Dering of Kent, not one of the most Laudian magistrates of England, for his care in the business and his assistance with the prosecution of John Fenner.[805] Once again the number of cases is small (two in the year April 1634–5, two in 1640) and the court displayed at times remarkable leniency. In 1640 William Jackson, who had imported Amsterdam bibles in order to discharge his debts, was ordered only to take them back and sell them there.[806]

Nonconformity or refusal to comply with the Prayer Book and canons were, as we might expect, the subject of more cases. Along with his other offences Anthony Lapthorne had not read service according to the Book of Common Prayer, had failed to observe holy days and omitted the sign of the cross in baptism.[807] John James and George Bardett, whom we have encountered, denounced bowing;[808] Charles Chauncey, vicar of Ware, omitted to wear his surplice, condemned the changes in the church and praised the puritans and those preparing to go to New England out of conscience.[809] Several

799. *Ibid.*, p. 410.
800. BL Add. MS 11045, f.37.
801. *Cal. Stat. Pap. Dom., 1635–6*, p. 86.
802. Longstaff, *Acts of the High Commission in Durham*, pp. 34–5.
803. Dering MS U133/02/7; *Cal. Stat. Pap. Dom., 1633–4*, p. 538; *1635–6*, p. 242–3.
804. Rawlinson MS A.128, f.27; S.R. Gardiner, *Reports of Cases in the Courts of Star Chamber and High Commission* (Camden Soc., new series, 39, 1886), p. 274.
805. Dering MS U1275/C1/8.
806. *Cal. Stat. Pap. Dom., 1640*, p. 378.
807. *Cal. Stat. Pap. Dom., 1634–5*, p. 263.
808. *Ibid.*, pp. 410, 537.
809. *Cal. Stat, Pap. Dom., 1629–31*, p. 233.

such cases emerge from the records of the commissioners who met in London and in Durham. But what remains striking are both the relatively few examples from the 1630s when the liturgical preferences of Charles I and Laud are supposed to have been widely unpopular and the desire of the commissioners to persuade rather than repress nonconformists. In November 1634, Edward Lyneold, rector of Ealing, came before the court having long failed to conform to the rites and ceremonies of the church. Though he refused to conform before the commissioners, 'the court, to win him to conformity, gave him liberty for that purpose until the last session of next term'.[810] When we read such cases, we cannot but question the thesis that High Commission led a witch-hunt against nonconformists.

Neither matters of theology nor liturgy constituted the main business of the courts. In so far as the layman found himself before the Caroline commissioners it was for abuse of the clergy or church, or most often for moral offences. High Commission records offer rich evidence of the intrinsic anticlericalism of English lay society since the Reformation, as well as puritan antagonism to the church hierarchy. Richard Parry of Pembrokeshire was fined for proclaiming (probably at an 'if I ruled the world' party game) that if he were king, there would be no bishops in the land.[811] Bastwick called the bishops 'grolls' (fools) and denied there was any difference between them and ministers.[812] John Ekins of Northamptonshire was prosecuted for saying a ploughman was as good as a priest.[813] There were many tithe cases and prosecutions for failure to repair the church. In several such cases, however, the initiative came from the parish, and the High Commission was used as a support to parish authorities in maintaining peace and order. The same was even truer of the prosecution of moral offences which crossed religious differences and concerned all members of the parish elites who seem, in the early modern period, to have been preoccupied with the moral order. It is unlikely that many would have objected to the prosecution (in the diocese of Hereford) of one John Williams who in addition to having two wives was also accused of abusing a dead corpse in the grave![814] The many cases of incest and incontinency clearly relate to fears of vagrants as much as divine wrath. In general the high numbers of cases concerned with matters matrimonial, alimony and the reconciliation of estranged spouses, express a strong local need for an agency of moral enforcement to shore up moral

810. *Cal. Stat. Pap. Dom., 1634–5*, pp. 326, 328, 331.
811. *Ibid.*, p. 52.
812. *Ibid.*, p. 547.
813. *Ibid.*, p. 268.
814. Coke MS 54: George Coke to Sir J. Coke, 26 Aug. 1636.

norms. The extent to which such issues outnumber all matters more narrowly ecclesiastical is our best evidence that High Commission was more the tool of the parishioners of England than their persecutor.[815]

Indeed far from being only an instrument of clerical authority, High Commission provided an effective forum for the parish presentation of unworthy, corrupt or querulous clergy. The commissioners encouraged men so to use it. At the trial in May 1632 of a Mr Dod for attending a conventicle, the archbishop delivered a speech on the importance of attending the parish church, adding that if the clergy fell short of standards, it was for the parishioners to inform against them.[816] Several cases make it clear that they did. Stephen Dennison, clerk, was presented in November 1634 for so railing against the sins of his congregation that they stopped attending his services; his prosecutors motioned for his suspension, which the court at that time denied.[817] The parishioners of St Catherine's, Cree Church, having installed with great pride a stained-glass window of Abraham's offering Isaac, presented Dr Dennison who had lampooned it 'to the great affront of the parishioners'.[818] Francis Abbot, vicar of Poslingford, found himself in court after some sharp clashes with his parishioners in which he had denounced the wives as whores, pulled three men from their pews and told the churchwardens 'I care no more for you than the dirt on my shoes.'[819] In Leicestershire it was the Earl of Huntingdon who presented Thomas Pestell of Packington for his vexatious behaviour to his parishioners, the earl included. 'Vexatious' Pestell indeed was. Not content with telling Huntingdon he was his equal and claiming the calling of minister to be above that of king, he engaged in unseemly scraps with one of his congregation, Francis Stacy, kicked him 'and did bite him with your teeth through the ear'. One Sunday Pestell invited all the parish to holy communion, then, ordering the women to depart, he locked the men in 'and strictly examined them one after another upon their salvation . . . and did greatly terrify and perplex them'.[820] The failings of Joseph Harrison, a vicar from Suffolk, appear very ordinary by comparison. A regular at the alehouse, he was too drunk to read divine service, swore at his parishioners and christened bastards. We might be inclined to sympathize with those who questioned his suitability for the cloth when we learn that he was also 'a

815. Alimony, adultery and other marital cases constitute by far the largest proportion of suits in 1634–5 and 1640; see Usher, *Rise and Fall of the High Commission*, p. 279.
816. Rawlinson MS A.128, ff.29–31, 3 May 1632.
817. *Cal. Stat. Pap. Dom., 1634–5*, p. 318.
818. *Cal. Stat. Pap. Dom., 1635–6*, pp. 105–7.
819. *Cal. Stat. Pap. Dom., 1634–5*, p. 319.
820. Hastings MS, Legal Box 5: proceedings in High Commission between 'My Lord' and Mr Pestell, Trinity term 1632.

professor of the art of magic and in particular charming of pigs'.[821] That he failed to wear his surplice would seem a mere footnote to the catalogue of his sins, but significantly it reveals the High Commission's sensitivity to the danger that punishment even of such a figure could be misrepresented. The bishop of Rochester in condemning him was concerned that men 'know by his punishment that he is not sentenced for not wearing the surplice but for drunkenness, profaning of marriage and making men believe in perpetual adultery'.[822] His speech points more generally to the priorities of the court and to the distance between its practice and its reputation.

The High Commission has undoubtedly had a bad press. The attacks on the court in 1641 referred to arbitrary proceedings, biased judges, numerous suspensions and harsh fines. Petitions to the Long Parliament such as those of Sir Robert Howard and Lambert Osbaldeston protested against the illegal proceedings of the court and challenged its right to fine or imprison.[823] In November 1640 a mob broke into the 'round house' to destroy the court's records, as an emblem of oppression.[824] The court, however, had been far from a tool of clerical power: articles had been brought against senior ecclesiastical officers, such as Henry Jones, chancellor to the bishop of Gloucester, for extorting excessive fees.[825] The commissioners not only proceeded with scrupulous respect for the law, but took care to discover spurious accusations that arose from parish feuds. The charges of incest and false preaching against William Laing, vicar of Bradworthy in Devon, were dismissed for want of proof and from a suspicion that they were founded in 'mere malice'.[826] When George Long was presented by his minister for retaining parish funds and scoffing at the clergy, the court was persuaded by his defence that he had been unjustly prosecuted and ordered the minister to pay costs.[827] Punishments too were less severe than historical mythology would have it. The court could not order physical mutilation. It could and did imprison for refusal to take the oath but that, as Usher aptly put it, favourably compares 'with the pressing under lead weights, till the culprit pleaded or died, used at common law for the same purpose'.[828]

Large fines in High Commission, as in Star Chamber, were often imposed for example's sake and then reduced by three-quarters or,

821. Rawlinson MS A.128, f.27; others were charged with christening a cat!
822. *Ibid.*
823. Ellesmere MS 6936: petitions of Howard and Osbaldeston and proceedings thereon.
824. BL Add. MS 11045, ff.126, 129; *HMC Cowper II*, p. 262.
825. *Cal. Stat. Pap. Dom., 1635–6*, pp. 46–7.
826. *Cal. Stat. Pap. Dom., 1634–5*, p. 552.
827. Rawlinson MS A.128, ff.31–3, 3 May 1632.
828. Usher, *Rise and Fall of the High Commission*, p. 325.

after evidence of compliance with the court's orders, remitted.[829] Poorer offenders were often let off lightly. In the case of Richard Rookesby of Boston, who could not pay his expenses, the court ordered they be paid by the four co-defendants who had led him into error.[830] With one Lucett from Warwickshire, who profaned St Paul's with excrement, the commissioners saw fit to deal mercifully because he 'did this vile act merely through ignorance and necessity, being about four score years old'.[831] John South was excused doing penance for his incest because it was felt that it might jeopardize his forthcoming marriage;[832] others presented for living apart were simply ordered to return to their wives.[833] As with nonconformist clergy so with laymen, the court emphasized reformation rather than punishment.

Why then did High Commission attract such odium? The opposition from separatists and puritans is not hard to understand, but they did not constitute the majority of the House of Commons that voted its abolition. In part the answer belongs, as we shall see, to the emotive politics and fears of 1641. But Clarendon offers two valuable observations. In the first place, because the money from fines went to the fund for rebuilding St Paul's, some suspected that charges were trumped up in High Commission in order to sustain the income.[834] Secondly, and more importantly, the presentation and punishment of gentlemen greatly alienated the propertied classes. It was one thing for common folk to stand penitent in a white sheet for their adultery, incest, or other moral lapses. Such, even among the lower orders themselves, was one of the symbols of a complex semiotics of social control. But when Sir Robert Howard was fined £3,000 and publicly exposed for his adulterous liaison with Lady Purbeck,[835] when Sir Alex Cave of Rotherby was ordered to perform penance for his adultery with Amy Roe,[836] or when Sir William Hellwys was ordered to face the shame of penitence in a white sheet, the case was different.[837] Ironically in such cases the puritans were at one with the court that institutionalized the culture of discipline: Sir Thomas Barrington approved the £10,000 fine on Sir George Allington for his incestuous

829. *Ibid.*, p. 265; *Cal. Stat. Pap. Dom., 1635*, p. 130.
830. *Cal. Stat. Pap. Dom., 1635*, p. 199.
831. *Ibid.*, pp. 234–5.
832. *Ibid.*, p. 234.
833. *Cal. Stat. Pap. Dom., 1634–5*, p. 481. Poor William Cumbiford who had compelled his wife 'to lie at one end of the house while he lies at the other' was ordered to dwell with her (*Cal. Stat. Pap. Dom., 1635–6*, p. 90).
834. Clarendon, *History of the Rebellion*, I, p. 125; above, pp. 323, 326–7.
835. Ellesmere MS 6936; Gardiner, *History of England*, VIII, p. 145.
836. *Cal. Stat. Pap. Dom., 1634–5*, p. 325.
837. *Ibid.*, p. 553; cf. *Cal. Stat. Pap. Dom., 1635–6*, p. 500.

liaison as 'an excellent example'.[838] In general, however, such punishments made High Commission the object of gentry anticlericalism. In 1641 they decreed that 'no new courts shall be erected, ordained or appointed . . . which shall or may have the like power'.[839] As so often in the history of the civil war, experience cast a different light on perception. Even while the bill for abolition was being discussed, there were those who began to fear that 'without this tribunal the way to licence will stand open'.[840] Thomas Knyvett bemoaned that 'most fearful thing to see what books are daily printed, what sermons preached . . . for now no man fears the power of any ecclesiastical court'.[841] Newsletters reported the disgust of 'sober wise men' that the court was invaded by the mob.[842] After the Restoration, though the court was not restored, the agencies of moral control would be harsher than any High Commission. But then they would be safely under the control of a gentry who would wield them over their inferiors rather than be 'levelled' by them 'with the common people'.[843]

The religion of most Protestants?

When we step back from the controversies and *causes célèbres*, from the myths and misrepresentations, historical and contemporary, what picture may we paint of the church of England and the religious life of its people in the reign of Charles I? It is both remarkable and regrettable that too little work has been done for us to feel that we might paint to the life. Obsessed for too long by the small minority of the godly, historians have paid too little attention to the religion of most Protestants, to what Christopher Haigh has called 'parish Anglicanism'. His term is especially helpful because what is apparent from the sketches we have is that the picture will look different as we move not only from diocese to diocese, but from parish to parish. As Anthony Fletcher concluded from a study of Sussex, 'the conditions of local society remained the decisive influences on the form of worship employed from village to village'.[844] It is appropriate for us then

838. A. Searle (ed.) *Barrington Family Letters 1628–1632* (Camden Soc., 4th series, 28, 1983), p. 190: Barrington to his mother, 13 May 1631.
839. See the act for its abolition in Gardiner, *Constitutional Documents*, pp. 186–9; quotation p. 189.
840. *Cal. Stat. Pap. Venet., 1640–2*, p. 178.
841. Abbot, 'Issue of episcopacy in the Long Parliament', pp. 203–4.
842. BL Add. MS 11045, f.130.
843. Clarendon, *History of the Rebellion*, I, p. 125. See D.W. Bahlman, *The Moral Revolution of 1688* (New Haven, 1957).
844. Fletcher, *County Community*, p. 89.

fleetingly to tour some of the villages of England to catch a glimpse of religious life in some of its diversity.

There are examples of clergy whom doubtless Charles and Laud would have regarded as a model for other parishes. George Coke, bishop of Bristol, felt able to tell his brother the secretary in 1633 that the clergy in his diocese he found 'both able and painful'.[845] From Ashurst in Chichester, it was reported that the minister laboured to reclaim recusants, read divine service, with the litany on Wednesdays and Fridays, 'weareth a fine large surplice', preached in gown and cassock, used reverence at the name of Jesus, was 'careful in examining and instructing the youth of the parish', catechized in the afternoon, administered the communion to those kneeling, and was diligent in churching women and visiting the sick.[846] We do not know how many clergy there were like him. But we do know that at the other end of the spectrum there were those like Mr Constable of Derbyshire who had preached only five times in twelve years,[847] or the drunken Mr Hutchinson of Shadoxhirst in Kent who abused the constables of his parish with 'beastly' (and doubtless quite unclerical) language when they told him to stop drinking and go home.[848] Clearly many clergy were far from practising what they preached. Thomas Burleston, who cut up his surplice to make himself shirts, was often so drunk he could not conduct communion.[849] Nicholas Gamen, curate of Lamyatt in the diocese of Bath and Wells, was more blatant in his hypocrisy. At Wells cathedral he 'took occasion to speak much in his sermon against drunkenness in a very commendable manner'; but 'in the afternoon of the same day he was so drunk himself that he became a sick spectacle . . . when he was to take horse he was hardly able to lift over his leg to rise into the saddle'.[850] Drink was far from the only clerical failing. Thomas Stocke, clerk, asked his parish to find him a good wench, and, impatient of their assistance, he lasciviously kissed two in the full view of his congregation.[851] Thomas Newman, rector of Little Cornard in Suffolk, exchanged bawdy jests about the females' genitalia with the men in his congregation.[852] William Gibbons, rector of Great Beakings 'in a suspicious [sic!] and lustful manner' put his hands under the clothes of Susan Scott;[853] the curate of Aldeburgh took Elizabeth

845. Coke MS 47, 4 Sept. 1633.
846. West Sussex Record Office, EP 1/22/1. E.R.C. Brinkworth shows that the visitation of Buckinghamshire revealed a high standard of clergy, see 'The Laudian church in Buckinghamshire'.
847. Coke MS 49: Osborne to Coke, 18 Aug. 1634.
848. Dering MS U570/01.
849. Longstaff, *Acts of the High Commission in Durham*, p. 126.
850. Stieg, *Laud's Laboratory*, p. 205.
851. Longstaff, *Acts of the High Commission in Durham*, p. 131.
852. Holmes, *Suffolk Committees for Scandalous Ministers*, p. 61.
853. *Ibid.*, pp. 70–1.

Prettie, one of his flock, 'threw her over a chair and used her very uncivilly', crying 'tell not me of a benefice, give me a woman's belly'.[854] With such colourful characters we are a long way from Ashurst or the godly village of Terling,[855] but drinkers and womanizers like these were part of the Church of England and, quite probably, popular down-to-earth figures in the local community. Between the extremes there were 'the moderate majority of the early Stuart clergy' who, as Ian Green has argued, have been relatively neglected:[856] clergy like the vicar of Claverdon, Thomas Pilkington who, appointed in 1629, continued to administer to his flock, through many changes of ecclesiastical codes and establishments, well into the 1680s.[857] The Pilkingtons of early modern England remind us how far from the high controversies and conflicts of the church the typical parish clergyman was.

About lay religious belief and practice we may speak with even less certainty. Divines certainly discerned in the 1630s that, especially among the gentry, there was too little piety, too secular a culture and a fashionable scepticism and rationalism that even led to Socinianism. Laud thought the Socinians, who questioned the doctrine of the Trinity, the most dangerous sect to have emerged since the birth of Christianity and was sensitive enough about its dangers to snap at his friend Wentworth's fashionable taste for poetry and painting.[858] 'I fear,' Laud wrote in the *Conference with Fisher*, 'that atheism and irreligion gather strength.'[859] Preachers and clergy of very different persuasions, Richard James, Anthony Grosse, Joseph Hall and many puritans, feared that classical learning, the mark of the gentleman, was exalted above the teaching of the apostles.[860] There is evidence to suggest their fears were real. John Earle in his popular *Microcosmographie* described the fashionable young blade as one who 'distastes religion as a sad thing'.[861] Francis Lenton's young gallant went often to the theatre but seldom to church,[862] leading the author of *Austin's Urania* to quip that since divinity was forsaken for love poems it was time to

854. *Ibid.*, p. 117.
855. K. Wrightson and D. Levine, *Poverty and Piety in an English Village: Terling 1525–1700* (New York, 1979).
856. I. Green, 'Career prospects and clerical conformity in the early Stuart church', *P&P*, 90 (1981), pp. 71–115.
857. See P. Styles, 'A seventeenth century Warwickshire clergyman: Thomas Pilkington, vicar of Claverdon', in P. Styles, *Studies in Seventeenth Century West Midlands History* (Kineton, 1978), pp. 71–89.
858. Knowler, *Strafford Letters*, II, p. 170.
859. *Works of Laud*, II, p. xv.
860. R. James, *A Sermon Delivered in Oxford* (1630, STC 14443), sig.F.2; A. Grosse, *Death's Deliverance* (1632, STC 12393), sig.B; J. Hall, *Works of Joseph Hall*, p. 73.
861. Earle, *Microcosmographie*, p. 30.
862. F. Lenton, *The Young Gallant's Whirligig* (1629, STC 15467), p. 7.

teach Scripture in verse![863] The courtesy books for young gentlemen, such as Braithwaite's *English Gentleman* and Anthony Stafford's *The Guide of Honour*, counselled the young to mix divine with classical texts in their education,[864] blending the profane and sacred in a manner that caused Arminian divines such as Thomas Jackson as much concern as any puritan.[865] Lower down the social scale, as Keith Thomas has powerfully demonstrated, in popular culture orthodox Protestantism had to contend with the remnants of the old faith, myth and romance, ignorance and scepticism, superstition and magic.[866] Bishop Pierce had to order a father in his diocese to stop advertising his seventh son (in a line with no daughters) as possessed of miraculous curative powers.[867] Marjorie Stubbs told her friend Elizabeth Readshaw that she knew 'a tale . . . of Robin Hood worth four and twenty of . . . the catechism'.[868] In York the ecclesiastical commissioners presented John Benington, a local grocer, for reciting charms.[869]

For most, however, attendance at church and some simple belief in the gospel was a central part of life, and, in an age of low life expectancy, of preparation for death. Earle described the plain country churchgoer ('his hand guides the plough and the plough his thoughts') as one who took his religion from his landlord. He 'comes to church in his best clothes and sits there with his neighbours where he is capable of only two prayers, for rain and fair weather'.[870] Several preachers bemoaned the many who came to church, ill prepared, preoccupied with worldly concerns and little inclined to listen to sermons intently. Robert Bolton condemned those who had lived under a preacher twenty years yet 'scarce a man amongst them all able to give an account of his faith in any one article';[871] he thought most went to church for 'fashion and company'.[872] Doubtless many did, as they still do in rural parts, treat the church as the substitute for the youth club. During communion, in the diocese of Durham in 1634, the John Richardson who jested and asked the communicants the names of 'all the pretty wenches in this parish' is a recognizable figure.[873]

863. S. Austin, *Austin's Urania* (1629, STC 971), epistle dedicatory to Drayton.
864. R. Braithwaite, *The English Gentleman* (1630), p. 32; A. Stafford, *The Guide of Honour* (1634, STC 23124), p. 16.
865. G.E. Aylmer, 'Collective mentalities in mid-seventeenth-century England: IV cross currents: neutrals, trimmers and others', *Trans. Royal Hist. Soc.*, 5th series, 39 (1989), p. 12.
866. Thomas, *Religion and the Decline of Magic*, *passim*.
867. *Cal. Stat. Pap. Dom., 1637*, p. 548.
868. Longstaff, *Acts of the High Commission in Durham*, pp. 52–3.
869. York Record Office, quarter sessions minutes, F.7, pp. 28–9.
870. Earle, *Microcosmographie*, p. 28.
871. R. Bolton, *The Carnal Professor* (1634, STC 3225), pp. 28–9.
872. R. Bolton, *The Saint's Sure and Perpetual Guide* (1634, STC 3248), p. 146.
873. Longstaff, *Acts of the High Commission in Durham*, p. 82.

But the social and the religious blended in the customary calendar of the parish and even those only half attentive to the word might be devoted to the rituals of the church. Ancient customs, such as beating the bounds in Rogation week, and other events in the Anglican calendar, were part of the rhythm of parish life and fostered a sense of community that was centred on the church.[874] The Book of Sports and Laudian support for these rituals, the emphasis on hospitality and community, even the renewed emphasis on worship over hearing the word, may well have given the Caroline church a popular appeal.[875] The concern with being buried in the churchyard, with seats and places, and with the ringing of wedding bells is evidence of a growing commitment to and affection for the church. Dr Haigh has suggested that the regular taking of communion was becoming more popular at the very time puritan pamphlets acknowledged lay antipathy to the new religion of the book.[876] Even from areas renowned for puritanism came petitions against nonconformity. On his travels through Northamptonshire, Robert Woodforde was horrified by the frequency with which he came across railed altars and vicars who bowed at the name of Jesus and conducted prayers according to the canons.[877] Even in Harley's homeland, John Tombes, vicar of Leominster, found his congregation more prepared to maintain organists than sustain his preaching.[878] As Professor Collinson admitted, 'practitioners of commonplace prayer book religion, unlike the more strident minorities, do not pluck at the historian's sleeve.'[879] Their numbers should not be underestimated. As a ballad popular during the elections of 1640 advised: 'both papist shun and puritan'.[880] By 1640, whatever its foundation, there was already a considerable popular affection for the church, which was to survive the civil war.[881]

A clearer picture of parish religion requires a fuller study of the sermon as typically delivered in the country church. This may at first seem a strange suggestion. Historians have drawn heavily on the voluminous sermon literature in print, especially to document the theological and liturgical disputes of the age. Such printed sermons are important: both official and puritan they were intended to reach a wide

874. Cf. D. Cressy, *Bonfires and Bells: National Memory and the Protestant Calendar in Elizabethan and Stuart England* (1989).
875. J.J. Scarisbrick, *The Reformation and the English People* (Oxford, 1984), p. 187.
876. C. Haigh, 'The Church of England and its people', unpublished paper. I am extremely grateful to Christopher Haigh for stimulating discussions of his research on this subject.
877. Woodforde's diary, for example, 3 Sept. and 12 Nov. 1637, 19 Jan., 4 March and 12 March 1638.
878. BL, MS 29/172, f. 344.
879. Collinson, *The Religion of Protestants*, p. 192.
880. BL, Harleian MS 4931, f. 39v.
881. Morrill, 'The church in England 1642–9'; D. Underdown, *Revel, Riot and Rebellion: Popular Politics and Culture in England, 1603–1660* (Oxford, 1985), p. 68.

audience, often to press a polemical case. Similarly, sermons delivered at court, at visitations, at assizes, on major public occasions or days of commemoration (such as Powder day) found their way into print along with those of famous preachers, like Lancelot Andrewes, or of puritan champions, like Preston, collected after their death. What we need to keep in mind, however, is that none of these, perhaps very few printed sermons, were in any way typical of those normally heard by the parishioners of England. The typical Sunday sermon, of course, not only failed to get into print, it usually failed to survive. In most cases probably the minister (if anything like Earl's 'Raw Young Preacher') had no text but extemporized on a passage of Scripture either completely spontaneously or with a few notes.[882] But though only a small residue of the flood of pulpit oratory, some parish sermons have survived in manuscript, as well as the notes of many others. Together with other occasional references in correspondence and reports, they enable us to gain some idea of the experience of the weekly sermon.

Some clearly did deal with contentious issues, and even delicate political matters. William Bridges of Norwich preached against the doctrine that Christ died for all;[883] Nathaniel Barnard, lecturer of St Sepulchre's, delivered sermons against the popish practices of the age;[884] Ward at Ipswich preached against bowing and the Book of Sports.[885] In Leicestershire in 1631 Mr Beale evidently attempted some complicated theology (lost on its auditor);[886] at Winchester one Mr Hill preached against idolatry.[887] Peter Simon, curate of Newland, who had been involved in the riot in the forest of Dean, delivered radical sermons on the equality of man.[888] Complicated theological arguments, however, appear rarely to have been the stuff of sermons, and when they were they passed over the parishioners' heads. Theodore Beale claimed that if one enquired within half an hour of the congregation, 'whether the vicar preached this or that doctrine, they cannot tell, they have forgotten'.[889] It was not least for such practical reasons that the dean of Salisbury sent a directive to the clergy of his diocese, urging them not to 'turn the pulpit into the chair to dispute of modern divines'; for, he went on, that way 'you will rather teach than confute what you suppose error. These controversies are not known to the people and why should they be troubled with controversies that are

882. Earle, *Microcosmographie*, pp. 2–3.
883. Tanner MS 68, f. 79.
884. Rushworth, *Historical Collections*, II, p. 140.
885. *Ibid.*, p. 301.
886. Hastings MSS, Religious Box 1: notes on Beale's sermon, 4 March 1631.
887. Goodman, *Diary of John Young*, p. 126.
888. *Cal. Stat. Pap. Dom., 1631–3*, p. 36.
889. Holmes, *Suffolk Committees for Scandalous Ministers*, p. 43.

hardly capable of principles of religion.'[890] The clergy were advised to preach the basics of religion: Christ crucified, faith and repentance, as the bulwarks against atheism, popery and schism. There is little evidence of clergy preaching on the high points of Arminianism or predestination. At Pluckley in Kent, the parson Samuel Jemmet urged his flock not to wonder about such things;[891] preaching on 2 Kings IV, verse 7, Ralph Crane counselled no troubled soul should despair of God.[892] A sermon preached at Ludlow advocated vigilance against both Romanists and separatists who threatened the crown.[893]

More interesting than such individual examples is a set of notes from sermons preached in Dorset.[894] Among them we find visitation sermons – appropriately on the duties of pastors, bishops and magistrates; sermons urging men to bow 'in prayer and thanksgiving unto God thereby testifying that thou hast devoted thy heart unto him';[895] sermons on confession and good works as 'necessary consequents and effects of a lively faith'.[896] Most, however, appear to have been concerned with basic Christian virtues. As one sermon – on the sin of anger – put it, 'Though there hath been according to the diversity and different condition of succeeding times some alteration in sacraments and ceremonies, yet the same Jesus Christ and the same salvation through Christ is both shadowed and signified in all.'[897] Perhaps very few of the hundreds of sermons delivered in the 1630s engaged with theological controversies and differences. Those hundreds that the Earl of Huntingdon paid to have bound in 1628 included many by Lancelot Andrewes along with a collection of funeral sermons.[898] Even in that hotbed of puritanism, Chelmsford in Essex, we find a lecturer Mr South preaching against schism and nonconformity and in advocacy of Christian peace and charity. As Dr Aylett wrote to Laud, even in Essex 'such excellent sermons would bring again the people in love with conformity'.[899] Until more research has been undertaken we cannot be sure how the parish sermon shaped the religious consciousness of Caroline England. But if we may read anything back from the experience of the 1640s and 1650s, when the parishes remained tenaciously loyal to the Anglican church, it must be that the preaching of Arminians and puritans had made little impact.

890. Rawlinson MS C. 421, f. 27.
891. Dering MSS (ecclesiastical), Q4: articles objected against Samuel Jemmet.
892. Ellesmere MS 6870, p. 49.
893. Ellesmere MS 6873.
894. Rawlinson MS C. 764: 27 sermons preached in Dorsetshire.
895. *Ibid.*, f. 78v.
896. *Ibid.*, f. 110.
897. *Ibid.*, f. 30, 6 Jan. 1637–8.
898. Hastings MS, Financial Box 12.
899. *Cal. Stat. Pap. Dom., 1629–31*, p. 197.

Recently historians have begun to exploit another record for rich evidence of religious life at the crucial level of the parish: churchwardens' presentments and accounts. As the name suggests churchwardens' presentments were responses to visitation articles, with lists of those things defective or individuals recalcitrant in any point; the accounts are records of expenditure by churchwardens on the fabric and maintenance of the church and on the furniture of worship – fonts, basins, pulpits, altarcloths, surplices, bell-ropes, bibles, prayer books and the like. The records are not without interpretative problems: it was probably the diligent churchwardens who kept the fullest records and the most diligent may well have been those most inclined to order and decency. We do not have in many cases continuous records over decades for the same parish. Nevertheless these records are especially valuable because they initiate from the parish and (in the case of accounts) were drawn up not for ecclesiastical officers but for the parish itself, and so are less likely to idealize.

I have taken samples from Bristol, Banbury and Lambeth, and from Chichester, Cheshire, Dorset and Kent. The records from Chichester diocese suggest diligent ministers who wore their surplice, well-maintained churches and orderly services. They reveal parishes like East Whittering railing its table for the first time in the late 1630s and confession being given at Chipley and Warnham. Parishes such as Doneghton and Ashurst were boasting that their newly erected rails were handsome; at West Grinstead, East Whittering and Warnham communion was received kneeling.[900] This may be a less than surprising conformity in the diocese to which Richard Montagu had been appointed bishop in 1628. More interesting is the evidence from Cheshire, where Bridgeman was far from harsh against nonconformists and from Kent and Dorset where the magistracy were unsympathetic to many of Laud's priorities and programmes. Holy Trinity parish in Chester took evident pride in its church, buying communion cup and plate and spending heavily 'for the repair and beautifying of the church', throughout the 1630s. Regular washing of the surplice suggests that it was usually worn; the lavish preparation for festivals (buying holly and candles for Christmas, organizing a dinner for the day of perambulating the bounds) fulfilled all Charles I's hopes that the church be the focus of the parish community.[901] Chester St Mary, with its railed table and pulpit, fine gilding and carving, marbled pillars and hanging candlesticks, bought the Book of Sports – presumably in order to read it.[902] Frodsham, as well as undertaking a

900. West Sussex Record Office, EP 1/22/1: churchwardens' presentments 1636, 1637, 1640, 1641.

901. Cheshire Record Office, P1/11: Holy Trinity churchwardens' accounts, 1634–40.

902. Cheshire Record Office, P20/13/1: accounts of 1630–8.

full programme of works, imposed in 1636 an extra levy for 'ornaments and reparations' and paid for a new surplice, to accompany its fine communion utensils.[903] In Kent, the accounts for the parish of Shorne evidence regular expenditure on maintaining the church, reglazing the windows, mending the table and washing the surplice and suggest regular communion and a parish concern to give charity and hospitality to the wandering poor.[904] In Strood, the church was regularly cleaned and laid with rushes, the surplice washed frequently; moreover, devotion to the king went beyond the usual bell-ringing on the royal birthday – there were prayers for Charles on his journey to Scotland in 1638 and the royal arms were carved in 1640.[905]

The Dorset records are the fullest and most continuous. In Bere Regis extensive work on the church included in 1632 painting the king's arms. As well as mending and regularly washing the surplice, the parish required a new communion cloth in 1633.[906] The parish of Wimborne as well as annual repairs to walls and windows and payments 'for keeping pigeons from the organs by laying boards in the steeple' purchased candlesticks, a new prayer book or new surplices almost every year.[907] In 1633, evidently possessing several, they paid 'for making a rail to hang the surplices' and ordered new ones to be made for the choirboys. The mounting opposition to the ecclesiastical establishment detectable in some parts of the country after 1637 finds no manifestation here. In 1639, as well as yet more new surplices and altarcloths, Wimborne spent on a 'new rail and posts' for the communion table.[908] Three years later, after the iconoclastic riots of 1640–1, they purchased candlesticks and replaced 'one of the surplices being taken by a soldier'.[909] The records of the parish of Sherborne tell a not dissimilar story.[910] Payments for candles and washing church linen recur throughout the decade; in 1635 'a new surplice of Holland' cloth was bought.[911] 1638 saw the 'new railing in of the communion table'.[912] In 1642 the churchwardens ordered bars to be erected at the windows, presumably to save the church and its valued contents from plunder and pillage.[913] As for the city of Dorchester itself, the town of John White the promoter of colonization and a renowned centre of puritanism, the churchwardens' accounts for Holy Trinity offer little

903. Cheshire Record Office, P8/13/1.
904. Kent Archives Office, P 336/5/1: Shorne parish, 1630–81.
905. Plomer, *Churchwardens' Accounts of St Nicholas, Strood*, esp. pp. 157–88.
906. Dorset Record Office, P 213/CW 4–7.
907. Dorset Record Office, P 204/CW 41: Wimborne churchwardens' accounts, 1581–1636.
908. Dorset Record Office, P 204/CW 42, 1639.
909. *Ibid.*, 1643.
910. Dorset Record Office, P 155/CW 99–112.
911. Dorset Record Office, P 155/CW 105.
912. Dorset Record Office, P 155/CW 108.
913. Dorset Record Office, P 155/CW 112.

evidence of widespread antagonism or apathy towards the Church of England. Certainly the churchwardens were active in supervising repair, making new seats, presumably for a growing congregation, washing the surplice (unlikely to be washed if never worn) and in providing a book of canons and candles and basins for the communion table. Here, together with the new seats, the increasing expenditure on communion wine may well indicate an increased attendance at church services.[914]

Space prevents us visiting many other such parishes.[915] In general, churchwardens' records have still to be fully studied. The regular payments they list testify to widespread problems, especially the dilapidated state into which many churches had fallen. But they show in many places too a parish initiative and drive to improve and enhance the conditions of worship. They suggest that for all we hear of puritan and popular hostility to the high church liturgy of Laud, the congregations of many parishes were willing to pay for furnishings and for an order and decency that was not so far removed from Laud's beauty of holiness as some historians would like to believe.

The clergy and the laity

In recent years excessive concentration on theological and liturgical issues has diverted historians' attention from more common and more important tensions and conflict: that between the laity and the clergy. Such conflicts of course, as any who have read in English literature since Chaucer need no reminding, were not new. But in the late sixteenth and early seventeenth centuries the emergence of a graduate clergy with a growing sense of itself as an elite may have heightened tensions. Certainly there were clear signs of determination among the laity that the clergy should be confined to their own sphere: in most of the parliaments of the 1620s bills were promoted to exclude clergy from the commission of the peace.[916] Alexander Leighton was probably well aware of the appeal to laymen of less godly persuasions than himself when he argued in *Sion's Plea Against the Prelacie* (1628) that the clergy 'intrude upon secular offices due to the nobility and gentry' and 'the like may be said of ministers being justices of peace'.[917]

In the 1630s, then, Charles's and Laud's determination to promote

914. Dorset Record Office, P 173/CW ff. 41v–65 (1628–40); account for 1630 at other end of book out of foliation.
915. See, for example, Drew, *Lambeth Churchwardens' Accounts*, II. The parishioners of Lambeth annually washed church linen. They also purchased frankincense and a book of canons, as well as moving the altar and providing a gilt cup.
916. For example, *Commons Journals*, I. p. 599, 832–41, 884, 886, 891, 904.
917. Leighton, *An Appeal to the Parliament*, p. 129.

the independence and authority of the church and clergy, as the necessary means to a religious reformation, further strained historically uneasy relationships. The strong language in which the king and archbishop voiced their determination to free churchmen of any 'lay dependency' began to echo through the clerical establishment.[918] In 1630 Brian Duppa took delight in Laud's appointment as chancellor of Oxford University as a victory against the 'malice and envy of the age that thinks no honour well placed if conferred upon the clergy'.[919] Three years later, Corbet all but repeated Charles's words when he expressed his regret to Wren that 'the laic contribution and support hath made the ecclesiastical persons . . . wag and dance after their pipe'.[920] The provocative tone of such letters was not confined to correspondence or conversation with friends, or even to fellow clergy. At the assizes in Sussex, a bishop's son declaimed against those who had bought church lands as despoilers guilty of sacrilege;[921] on a visitation to Salisbury cathedral, Dr Chaffin added to the litany his own prayer: 'from all lay puritans and all lay parliament men good lord deliver me . . .'.[922] Across the country, during the 1630s, with a firm sense of support from above not evident during Abbot's archiepiscopacy, the clergy began to reassert their status in local society and government, in a manner that led to some sharp clashes.

We have a nice illustration of the tension that could be built up in an exchange that took place at the quarter sessions in Hampshire. The occasion was a message sent from the bishop of Salisbury to the recorder concerning the imprisonment of a clergyman, Mr Ashton. The bishop questioned the justice's right to commit a clergyman, claiming that the authority in such cases rested with the diocesan. On receiving the bishop's message from Mr Good, his chaplain, the recorder replied that the magistrates must confer. Good, however, insisted on an immediate answer and a heated exchange ensued: the recorder told Good to be civil; Good replied he had no need of a lesson in manners. When Good was reminded of the dignity of the sessions that he had interrupted, he responded with an assertion of the power of and respect due to his diocesan and then proceeded, with his companion, to march up and down in front of the judges, without removing his hat – walking 'short turns always in the face of the court almost an hour together without any reverence or respect of the court, but as it seemed to affront the same'.[923] Bishop Davenant, who had

918. *Works of Laud*, V, p. 321.
919. *Cal. Stat. Pap. Dom., 1629–31*, p. 243: Duppa to Laud, 26 April 1630.
920. Tanner MS 68, f. 2: Corbet to Wren, 3 June 1636.
921. *Cal. Stat. Pap. Dom., 1640*, pp. 520–1: Rossingham to Conway, 27 July.
922. G. Bankes, *The Story of Corfe Castle* (1853), p. 83; cf. below, pp. 937–8.
923. Sherfield MS XXXVIII: Salisbury sessions and assizes, 8 Oct. 1630.

not himself intended any offence, later wrote to calm tempers. But the episode offers a nice insight into the delicate church–state relations in a diocese where the bishop, although no Laudian, by his firm stand on his episcopal authority and desire to increase clerical representation on the commission of the peace, had taught the example of assertiveness to his subordinates. Other bishops and clergy were less tactful than Davenant. Chief Justice Richardson, bruised in his exchange with Pierce, was not the only justice to be humiliated by the 'lawn sleeves'.[924] In 1636 Bishop Wren gave instructions to Dr Thomas Eden, a commissioner of Norwich, to make arrangements for divine service at the Bury assizes. Eden was to inform the Lord Chief Justice that he should be early at the church or the service would commence without him: 'As also that his lordship will not be pleased to rise or depart after the sermon till the prayer for the church be said and the blessing given.' Eden, in giving Wren's message, was not likely to have been any more tactful in his tone, believing as he did that 'the King's common counsel . . . do so overbear all that we stand but for ciphers'.[925]

Whilst the clashes between laity and clergy were by no means provoked only by Laudians, there were other specific features of Laud's and Charles I's religious policy that led to disputes. The emphasis on the beauty of holiness and vestments elevated the clergy; the archbishop's support increased tithe suits; his directions led to better, and more expensive, maintenance of churches. And – of no small importance – his concern for the physical appearance of the church sparked a heated controversy over seats and places in church. In early modern England, we need to recall, attendance at church was the week's public occasion; a person's place or seat in the church, like a reserved box at the opera or privileged position at Wimbledon, was a visible statement of his rank in local society. Gentry or long-established parish families owned or were assigned (for a charge) specific boxes or seats closer to the pulpit and communion table, placing them nearer to God and at a remove from the common folk who competed for a place on the bench or, as often as not, stood. Understandably, leading laymen were particularly concerned to safeguard and ambitious families to secure this privilege. As the many entries for payments in churchwardens' accounts indicate, the competition for seats was hot: in Chichester it led to a fight.[926] In Wimborne, Dorset, Henry Bradstocke, in 1629, paid 6s.8d. to sit in the seat where Mr Swayne sat 'under the organs' and, in addition bought seats for his daughters

924. Above, pp. 353–5.
925. Tanner MS 68, f. 191.
926. West Sussex Record Office, EP 1/22/1; the fight was at Yaxton in 1637.

there.[927] Parish officials and clergy, anxious to shore up rank and preserve order, were usually careful to sustain established places. When the Earl of Huntingdon's claim to a pew in the church at Loughborough was opposed, though neither party had 'proof sufficient to maintain right of prescription', the ordinary used his authority to decide in favour of the earl and added that if Huntingdon desired to build a pew there, he would not be denied.[928] The parishioners themselves proved conservative on such matters of social rank. In July 1628 those of Sherborne in Dorset decided that no seat in their church should be sold or assigned without the consent of the churchwardens, 'and that men henceforth be placed in seats fit for their rank and place as may be for decency and comeliness'.[929] (The parish's own sense of decorum and order also led to an expression of 'our dislike of the rude and disorderly standing and sitting of women upon the said forms amongst the men'.)[930] Local conservatism and respect for rank and custom meant that on the matter of seats the laity and clergy were unlikely to come into disagreement.

What altered things was Laud's, and perhaps still more Charles I's, dislike of seats or pews that in any way marred the church, in particular those erected behind the pulpit or communion table. When the king or archbishop came across or heard of such, they ordered their removal, regardless of who owned them and insensitive to the consequences for local status. So in 1629 Sir Nicholas Gilbourne of Kent found his family pew threatened by the re-edification of his church ordered by Nathaniel Brent. Gilbourne heard that Brent was coming to view the church, but did not see that he could 'lawfully deface or pluck down any part of the church . . . to open a supposed and needless door'. Most of all he was greatly disturbed that as a result of the work he may 'be left out of those seats which were so long ago built at mine own charge and wherein I and my family have sat so many years together'.[931] Gilbourne's experience was repeated throughout the country and affected those of even higher social rank, as churches were restored and beautified in accordance with royal and metropolitical directions. The Earl of Huntingdon in 1638 was incensed to find that at the visitation of his diocese the seat that he had claimed as his own was occupied by clergy: 'I was,' he complained to Lambe, 'never so confronted, nor such an indignity offered to be put upon me.'[932] His

927. Dorset Record Office, P 204/CW 41, p. 223. Significantly, Bradstocke was one of the churchwardens at this time, perhaps an illustration of social climbing.
928. Hastings MSS, HAM, Box 26, 1 Feb. 1640.
929. Dorset Record Office, Sherborne vestry MS, P 155/V. E1, f. 13.
930. *Ibid.*, f. 13v.
931. Dering MS U275/C1/2: Gilbourne to Dering, 26 May 1629.
932. *Cal. Stat. Pap. Dom., 1637–8*, p. 577: Huntingdon to Lambe, July 1638.

visitor, Dr Roane, planned to remove from All Saints, Huntingdonshire seats, as the parishioners protested, used by passing strangers (the church was on the road to London), by local dignitaries – and even the seat occupied by James I when he worshipped there.[933] In Stoke Poges, Lady Winwood's seat was removed by order of the 1637 visitation.[934] In 1634 the Earl of Exeter expressed his concern to Lambe that his cousin and tenant Balguy, deputy recorder of Stamford, might lose his seat at St George's church after some work there on the church and pulpit. If the seats were 'not supplied by others as good', Exeter claimed, he and his family 'will suffer prejudice in his inheritance, the said seats being of long time used with the said house, wherein his ancestors sometimes inhabited'.[935] Such loss of face was very likely to enrage men like Exeter and his cousin who were in all other respects conformable and 'very forward to settle others in obedience'.

The quarrel over seats and status became particularly sharp in cathedral cities where large numbers of high-ranking clergy, archdeacons and deans among them, as well as mayors and aldermen, attended the service. Often this was a rivalry over who sat where, heightened in the 1630s by the clergy's bold assertion of their status. One Sunday in 1633 at York Minster, for example, Dr Wickham took a place two or three stalls in front of the Lord Mayor, 'which as yet was never seen before'. The city magistracy's suspicion that Wickham would not have claimed the place 'without the consent of some greater than himself' proved well founded.[936] The archdeacon explained that he had been instructed to sit there by Laud and offered the place to the mayor. His tact, however, was not emulated by his clerical colleagues: Dr Hodgson was 'very sharp' and asked 'if my Lord Mayor should take it well if they should send to him to know why he dwelt in *his* house'.[937] A potential quarrel was averted: Wickham generously surrendered, was rewarded with a citizenship and ended up sitting with the mayor! But not all such instances were so accommodated. In Worcester, Charles I personally ordered all the seats leading to the west window, in which the mayor and aldermen traditionally sat, to be removed. Though he permitted unfixed seats, the dean acknowledged that they little satisfied the bench, who still wanted 'their gay and lofty seats' as a sign of their status.[938] The king issued similar instructions to Durham, having visited the cathedral on his progress to Scotland in 1633.[939] Wren

933. *Cal. Stat. Pap. Dom., 1638–9*, p. 620.
934. PRO, SP 16/366/79.
935. *Cal. Stat. Pap. Dom., 1634–5*, p. 15: Earl of Exeter to Lambe, 19 May 1634.
936. York House Books, 35, f. 218v.
937. *Ibid.*, f. 224v.
938. S. Bond (ed.) *The Chamber Order Book of Worcester, 1602–1650* (Worcestershire Record Soc., new series 8, 1974), p. 46; *Cal. Stat. Pap. Dom., 1639–40*, pp. 129–30.
939. G. Ornsby (ed.) *Correspondence of John Cosin* (Surtees Soc., 55, 1872), I, pp. 215–16.

had them removed from Norwich cathedral, Laud from Salisbury.[940] After the visitation of Gloucester in 1635 the archbishop ordered the dismantling not of seats occupied by the mayor and aldermen but – a still greater affront to civic snobbery – those assigned to their wives.[941] Whilst it is true that private seats had grown up indiscriminately and doubtless increased in size and grandeur, so blocking the congregation's sight of worship (as important to the king as its sound), the orders for removal were provocative and aroused interminable controversy. As Neile tactfully warned Bishop Bridgeman in January 1635, 'to remove any from the place where they and their ancestors have time out of mind accustomed to sit will beget more brabbles, suits in law and prohibitions than either you or I would be contented to be troubled with.'[942]

'Brabbles' troubled most of the cathedral towns during the 1630s. In several cases tensions between the cathedral close and the aldermanic bench had a long history: Chichester cathedral had quarrelled with the mayor over his right to bear his mace in church since Elizabeth's reign;[943] under James I half of the cathedral towns witnessed disputes over jurisdiction; in many cases the civic dignitaries ceased to attend for worship.[944] What exacerbated longstanding tensions was Charles I's tendency, in all these cases, to reaffirm and press the rights and jurisdiction of the cathedral. In 1636 Charles ordered the mayor and aldermen of Chichester to attend cathedral service, not to challenge the precedency of the dean and not to carry the mace.[945] The following year the royal order was extended to all cathedrals and signet letters were addressed to the mayors of each city commanding their obedience.[946] In a world in which status and authority were expressed through symbols and processions, the prohibition on carrying the mace subjected the corporation (which as John Earle put it 'comes oft to church to make a show') to subordination and indignity.[947] There were protests and grumblings; the mayor and aldermen of Norwich even petitioned the king to be exempted from compulsory attendance at the cathedral, 'the inconveniences thereof being many and intolerable'. After pointing out that their presence was needed in their parish churches, the mayor and aldermen claimed that the low seats that were left to them in the cathedral exposed them to 'extreme winds and cold' – and to worse indignities:

940. Wren, *Parentilia*, p. 77; *Works of Laud*, V, p. 324.
941. Lambeth Palace MS 943, p. 443.
942. Bridgeman, *History of the Church and Manor of Wigan*, pp. 377–9.
943. Fletcher, *County Community*, pp. 235–7.
944. I owe this information to Dr. Kenneth Fincham.
945. Tanner MS 148, f. 18.
946. PRO, SO 1/3, ff. 29v, 41; *Cal. Stat. Pap. Dom., 1637–8*, p. 82.
947. Earle, *Microcosmographie*, p. 5.

> By reason that there be many seats over our heads we are oftentimes exposed to much danger as also to have many scorns and contempts as in the mayoralty of Mr Christopher Barrett a great Bible was let fall from above and missed very little of hitting him upon the head and broke his spectacles . . . And not long before the time of Mr Barrett's mayoralty some made water in the gallery on the aldermen's heads and it dropped down into their wives' seats . . . and also about the same time divers citizens of good account . . . had their gowns and cloaks cut and mangled as they sat at sermon and prayers in the said church. That in the time of the present mayor that now is upon that Sunday the day before the knights of the shire was chosen in October last alderman Shipdham Justice of Peace and sitting next the mayor, somebody most beastly did conspurcate and shit upon his gown from the galleries above and the Sunday immediately after some from the galleries let fall a shoe which narrowly missed the mayor's head and at one another time one from the said gallery did spit upon alderman Barrett's head . . .[948]

Whether this graphic protest masked a puritan antipathy to the cathedral services of Wren's diocese or the undignified reality of the magistrates' experience, their petition was to no avail and they were compelled to attend.

The aldermanic surrender of precedence to the cathedral clergy was more than symbolic. In cathedral and in university cities, Charles, often reversing a long-term trend, enhanced the authority of the clergy and altered city charters to exclude the close and colleges from civic jurisdiction. In 1634, the corporation of York wrote to the Lord Keeper to appeal against the dean and chapter's claim, in violation of the charter of 1632, 'to exercise the authority of justices of peace'.[949] Two years later the victory was won by the clergy.[950] The same year, in June, Chichester was made to surrender its charter and in the new grant lost control of the close.[951] In 1637 the Attorney and Solicitor adjudicating a local dispute in Salisbury, ruled that the bishop and dean, and all canons residentiary, should join the commission.[952] The Privy Council in 1638 extended the ruling to all cathedral cities.[953] Similarly, the new charter for Oxford granted the university extensive new powers of search and jurisdiction in the city.[954] All these clerical

948. Tanner MS 220, ff. 147–9; Cf. J.T. Evans, *Seventeenth Century Norwich* (Oxford, 1979), ch. 3.
949. York House Books, 35, ff. 242–3; Aveling, *Catholic Recusancy in York*, p. 77.
950. Aveling, *Catholic Recusancy in York*, p. 77.
951. *Cal. Stat. Pap. Dom., 1635–6*, p. 538, 4 June 1636.
952. *Cal. Stat. Pap. Dom., 1637*, pp. 4, 105.
953. PRO, PC 2/49/250.
954. Sharpe, 'Archbishop Laud and the University of Oxford', pp. 154–5; S. Gibson, *The Great Charter of Charles I to the University of Oxford* (1933).

triumphs fanned the smouldering tensions between lay and ecclesiastical authorities. In Worcestershire the city and the dean quarrelled throughout the later 1630s over the city lecturer's right to preach in the cathedral.[955] In Winchester, as in other cities, such tensions compromised the collection of ship money. The cathedral in 1636 refused to be rated by the city and insisted that it be independently assessed by the county sheriff; the quarrel escalating to the point where the mayor committed two 'singing men' as defaulters though the sheriff had already discharged them as having paid.[956] In York strained relations continued across the decade, Neile claiming that the mayor of York had maliciously introduced as lecturer at All Hallows John Shaw, largely to lead a party against him.[957] When the Short Parliament convened the corporation endeavoured to recover its charter rights and hired lawyers to advise them 'what reasons may best be given why the bishop and his chancellor may not be justice of peace within the city'.[958]

Though the clashes were most heated in the cathedral towns where lay and ecclesiastical authorities came most directly into contact, enhanced clerical status and power were felt throughout the counties of England. The check on prohibitions strengthened the ecclesiastical courts; in larger numbers than ever clergy were appointed to the commission of the peace. The bishops, ordered to reside in their dioceses, played a wider or more active role in local government. Bishop Wright of Coventry and Lichfield evidently played an important part in the organization of the Warwickshire militia;[959] in January 1636 the Privy Council asked the bishop of Bath and Wells to help settle a dispute between Sir Robert Phelips and the sheriff of Somerset over the ship money assessments for the parish of Northover.[960] Not all relationships were antagonistic: Bristol sent its Bishop Coke a piece of plate worth £20 as a token of their love.[961] The enhanced status of the clergy offered perhaps a renewed social opportunity to younger sons of the gentry to pursue a career in the church; Heylyn claims that during the 1630s the gentry began to be desirous to match their daughters with clergymen, 'the clergy grown to such esteem for parts and power that the gentry thought none of their daughters to be better disposed of'.[962] But for many gentlemen the enhanced pride of the clergy was a cause of considerable offence; and threatened, as they

955. Bond, *Chamber Order Book of Worcester*, p. 45.
956. Goodman, *Diary of John Young*, pp. 119–28.
957. C. Jackson (ed.), *The Life of Master John Shaw* (Surtees Soc. 65, 1877), p. 129.
958. York House Books, 36, f. 41.
959. For example, *Cal. Stat. Pap. Dom., 1635*, p. 437.
960. PRO, PC 2/45/348.
961. Bristol Common Council Books, 3, f. 41v.
962. Heylyn, *Cyprianus Anglicus*, p. 237.

saw it, to overturn the victory the laity secured at the time of the Reformation. As early as 1628 George Wither was complaining 'what imperious lords their doctorships are grown'.[963] In his address to the Grand Jury at the Oxford assizes in 1634, Justice Whitelocke observed that 'spiritual men were beginning to swell higher than ordinary';[964] for their claim at the trial of Bastwick that bishops held their power not of the crown but *iure divino*, he believed, 'they might have been censured themselves in Henry II's or Edward III's times'.[965] Sir Henry Slingsby considered the clergy 'covetous, contentious, proud, boasters, ambitious . . .'.[966] James Partridge denounced them for wearing 'beaver hats of great price . . . also cassocks and doublets of satin', adding 'their wives also go in loose gowns of silk, beaver hats, fans in their hands and many other vanities'.[967]

The appointment of Juxon to the treasurership in 1636 fanned the flames of such anticlericalism. His inauguration ceremony 'in more state and glory than any of his predecessors have done in our time', with 150 horse and bishops 'in their rochets and lawn sleeves and corner caps', publicly proclaimed the new clerical power.[968] James Howell (and even the Reverend Garrard) hearing of it did not hide from Wentworth their sense of surprise and perhaps resentment: ''tis news indeed it being now twice time out of mind since the white robe and the white staff marched together; we begin to live here in the Church triumphant and there wants but one more to keep the King's conscience (which is more proper for a churchman than his coin) to make up a triumvirate.'[969] The Venetian envoy heard several 'complain fiercely that the most conspicuous offices and the greatest authority in the royal council are falling by degrees into the hands of ecclesiastics, to the prejudice of the nobility'.[970] The resentment spread wide: in Wiltshire Edward Stockman told the congregation one Sunday in 1639 'that all the clergy in the land were too proud';[971] Brereton, on his travels, heard that in Scotland they were recovering the land of the abbeys and 'will in a short time possess themselves of the third part of the kingdom'.[972] With the Scots war and the resummoning of parliament, the laity took their opportunity to check clerical ambitions and pretensions. As Thomas Gorges wrote to Thomas Smyth of Ashton Court, 'you need not fear pride now in black coats, since the

963. Wither, *Britain's Remembrancer*, f. 192v.
964. R. Whitelocke, *Memoirs of Bulstrode Whitelocke* (1860 edn), p. 118.
965. Whitelocke, *Memorials of English Affairs*, (1682 edn), p. 22.
966. Parsons, *Diary of Sir Henry Slingsby*, p. 21.
967. J. Partridge, *The Letters Patent of the Presbyterie* (1632, STC 19420), p. 50.
968. PRO, C. 115/N4/8607: Burgh to Scudamore, 13 May 1636.
969. Knowler, *Strafford Letters*, I, pp. 522, 523.
970. *Cal. Stat. Pap. Venet., 1632–6*, p. 531.
971. *Cal. Stat. Pap. Dom., 1638–9*, p. 473.
972. Hawkins, *Travels of Brereton*, p. 100; cf. p. 182.

Scottish army hath made our General of the Horse with all his troops retreat . . . the cry goes nothing but a parliament will settle them and make the sacred function humble enough, I warrant you'.[973] The parliaments of 1640 bore out his prediction: soon after its meeting Pym urged the Short Parliament that they should 'follow the steps of our ancestors that they would not subject themselves to the power of the clergy'.[974]

Indeed the hostility to the bishops in 1640 and 1641, so often taken as evidence of widespread opposition to the theology or liturgy of the Laudian church, may well have represented rather a sharp anticlericalist reaction to the clerical pride of the 1630s. It was not their theology nor even their churchmanship that decided which bishops were the targets of vitriol; in the end all of them, godly sympathizers as well as Laudians, went down. Bishop Williams, at least initially, won affection, in part because he quarrelled with Laud, but also because he placed considerable emphasis on deference to the laity.[975] In his assertion of clerical authority Laud was more in the tradition of Whitgift and Bancroft than the Arminian Andrewes, who was praised in a funeral sermon for meddling 'little in civil and temporal affairs'.[976] Similarly Juxon, after an inauspicious start, avoided the odium of the parliamentary gentry on account of his unaggressive manner – and in part perhaps thanks to his love of hunting and renowned pack of hounds that won him (at least) Whitelocke's respect and admiration.[977] While Wren and Laud were impeached, Juxon was left to reside in peace at his London residence in Fulham; as Sir Philip Warwick observed, none complained of him to or in a parliament that was 'itching after such complaints'.[978] In 1660 he was chosen archbishop of a church that was to be much more subject to the laity. Such was not the church of Laud. As Clarendon observed, the archbishop 'did naturally believe that nothing more contributed to the benefit and advancement of the church than the promotion of churchmen to places of the greatest honour and offices of the highest trust'. This, he judged, more than any theological pretences, 'was the unhappy foundation of his own ruin, and of the prejudice towards and malice against, and almost destruction of the church'.[979]

973. Smyth of Ashton Court MS AC C51/4.
974. Maltby, *Aston Diary*, p. 51.
975. Hajzyk, 'The church in Lincolnshire', p. 136.
976. C. Hill, *Collected Essays II: Religion and Politics in Seventeenth Century England* (Brighton, 1986), p. 78; J. Buckeridge, *A Sermon Preached at the Funeral of Lancelot Andrewes* (1634, STC 4004), p. 19.
977. Whitelocke, *Memorials of English Affairs*, p. 23; *Cal. Stat. Pap. Venet., 1632–6*, p. 540: *Cal. Stat. Pap. Dom., 1639*, p. 146; *HMC Marquis of Bath, II*, p. 75; PRO, C. 115/N8/8799.
978. Warwick, *Memoirs*, pp. 94–5.
979. Clarendon, *History of the Rebellion*, I, p. 115.

A final evaluation of what has been too simply called the 'Laudian church', still more of the religious life of England in the 1630s, awaits a great deal more research. But there is already sufficient ground for suggesting that too much attention has been paid to polarization and confrontation, and to the sources most likely to present such a picture – puritan sermons, polemical tracts, hagiographic apologiae. The renewed emphasis on conformity to the Prayer Book and the canons undoubtedly, as we shall see, alienated the godly and drove some who had felt more comfortable during Abbot's archiepiscopate to separatism or exile.[980] But when we read gentry correspondence, parish sermons, and churchwardens' records we do not get the impression that the bulk of the propertied or populace were antagonistic to the church: even Sir Edward Dering thought Laud's 'intent of public uniformity was a good purpose', albeit, 'in the way of his pursuit thereof he was extremely faulty'.[981] Perhaps more than other aspects of the decade, the religious history of the 1630s has been obscured by later events – by the rumours of a popish plot, by the Long Parliament, by the trial of Laud, by the civil war and the emergence of the sects. It is currently fashionable to stress the role of religion in the causes of the English civil war and in our conclusion we will have occasion to return to it.[982] But during the 1630s, and especially before the outbreak of the Scots war, though the battle grew hot at times between the bishops and the puritans, and there were tensions between laity and clergy, most in the parishes remained devoted to *their* Church of England – to its fabric, customs and rituals.

980. Below, Chapter XII.
981. E. Dering, *A Collection of Speeches in Matter of Religion* (1642), p. 4; I owe this reference to the kindness of Kenneth Fincham. Cf. S.P. Salt, 'The origins of Sir Edward Dering's attack on the ecclesiastical hierarchy, 1625–1640', *Hist. Journ.*, 30 (1987), pp. 21–52.
982. J.S. Morrill, 'The religious context of the English civil war', *Trans. Royal. Hist. Soc.*, 5th series, 34 (1984), pp. 155–78; *idem*, 'The attack on the Church of England in the Long Parliament, 1640–42', in D. Beales and G. Best, *History, Society and the Churches* (Cambridge, 1985), pp. 105–24; cf. below, pp. 933–40.

VII

'ORDER THROUGH ALL PARTS OF OUR KINGDOMS'? THE GOVERNANCE OF THE LOCALITIES

In his preface to the orders for the government of his royal household, Charles had expressed his purpose 'to establish government and order in our court which from thence may spread with more order through all parts of our kingdoms'.[1] Far from being a retreat from the harsh realities of the world outside Whitehall, the court, as the masque *Coelum Britannicum* announces, was to be a model, an influence for the broader reform of government and society. Similarly the reformation of the church incorporated for Charles and Laud a reform of society: they sought to restore the parish church as the focus of a shared worship and also as the centre of fellowship, of the local community. They believed that the beauty of holiness might also bring to the parishes of England something of that force for civilizing and ordering which the masques, paintings and buildings performed at the centre of government. It is time then for us to turn to the broadest manifestations of the Caroline programme for order and reform: to the translation of ideals and policies articulated and shaped at court to the shires of England. We must examine the aims and measures of Caroline social policy, the agencies through which it was transmitted to the localities, and the instruments of supervision and enforcement. In fine, through close study of the Book of Orders and the programme for an exact militia, we shall endeavour to evaluate the extent to which ideals of reform were enacted in practice.

The imperial capital

The beam of influence from His Majesty's court (to use the language of masque) fell first upon his royal capital. Charles I undoubtedly differed

1. PRO, LC 5/180; cf. above, pp. 211–12.

from his predecessors in his perception of London and was perhaps the first English monarch to conceive of it as a capital, as 'our royal city, the imperial seat and chamber of this our kingdom'.[2] Within a few years of his succession, others were also beginning to see it in this way. London, the king was told in 1629, was 'the metropolis of England where . . . your actions are examples to other places'.[3] London, the author of *The Life of King Alfred* wrote in 1634, was 'the King's chamber, the heart of the commonwealth, and as it were a summary of the whole kingdom'.[4] Such a sense that London was the exemplum and heart of the realm made Charles determined to make the capital a model of order and civility. He propounded and supervised detailed measures in order to make it so. In July 1634 the king wrote personally to the mayor concerning his project to beautify the city 'being our royal chamber and the principal seat of our residence'.[5] He recommended a scheme for raising and levelling the streets, leaving a passage for coaches and horses – presumably demarcating a clear pedestrian pavement.[6] He also advised the installation of a system of lead pipes to carry a water supply for cleaning the streets 'for avoiding those unwholesome and contagious vapours which infest the city at all times'. In part such plans – like that for cleaning sewer filth from the area round Whitehall[7] – were prompted by a desire to rid the royal court of such unwholesome vapours and the concomitant risks of disease, but the king's plans for the city were larger and less narrowly centred than that. Charles and the Council commissioned Inigo Jones to investigate the means of providing the capital with a wholesome water supply;[8] they ordered more regular cleaning of streets and strict penalties for those who fouled them;[9] they issued a proclamation for the 'cleansing and conservation' of the River Thames;[10] they established a number of 'new water engines' as a fire brigade to be always on call.[11] Large building projects were also considered. As well as Jones's plans for a new Whitehall palace that would have dwarfed the Escorial,[12] the king and Council reviewed detailed plans for a new London Bridge, with drainage channels, and, at the king's request,

2. *Acts of the Privy Council, 1630–1*, p. 311.
3. J. Davenport, *A Royal Edict for Military Exercises* (1629, STC 6313), p. 14.
4. R. Powell, *The Life of King Alfred* (1634, STC 20161), p. 119.
5. PRO, SO 1/2, ff.186–7.
6. *Ibid.*
7. PRO, PC 2/43/275, 589.
8. PRO, PC 2/43/624; PC 2/42/305.
9. PRO, PC 2/43/311.
10. J.F. Larkin (ed.) *Stuart Royal Proclamations, II: Proclamations of King Charles I, 1625–46* (Oxford, 1983), no. 230, pp. 540–3.
11. PRO, PC 2/49/19, 7 March 1638.
12. See J. Harris, S. Orgel and R. Strong, *The King's Arcadia: Inigo Jones and the Stuart Court* (1973), pp. 147, 170.

rails between the footway and coaches.[13] A model was made and presented to the Board, where the king added his desire for arches and his opposition to houses that might impede the passage.[14] Though the king was anxious for work to start, the cost of the grandiose plan was estimated at £5,000 and, as Garrard informed Conway, the citizens who were left to finance it knew not where to raise the money.[15]

The rapid increase in private coaches and carriages and consequent congestion in the city also came under investigation. As early as 1633 the inconveniences of the crowding of coaches at the playhouse led to a Council decree that visitors to the Blackfriars theatre should travel by water or by foot.[16] But the problem was of large proportion and measures were taken to tackle it. In 1636 a proclamation restraining the use of coaches in London prohibited the use of a private carriage by anyone who did not keep four horses for the king.[17] Evidently the proclamation was enforced strictly, for when he came to London in the summer of 1636 Viscount Wentworth was given the services of a hackney coachman, so that he would not violate the recent order.[18] The hackney carriages were themselves subject to close regulation. In April 1634 the Council expressed concern at the excessive use of the hackney coaches, which numbered nearly 2,000 on one estimate.[19] Attorney-General Bankes considered plans to incorporate the London coachmen into a self-governing body with its own code of discipline, accountable to the Council.[20] In 1636 it was ordered that no taxis could be hired for distances below three miles out of London or Westminster.[21] Again, enforcement was strict. A few months after the proclamation, a group of a hundred coachmen offered £500 per annum for permission to run a service despite the order;[22] in February 1637 Sir Edmund Verney offered £1,000 to operate 200 coaches.[23] Both offers were rejected and the proclamation was reaffirmed. In November 1637 the Council licensed fifty hackney coachmen to operate with eight horses each, in green livery and at fixed rates.[24] Though market forces were inevitably to win in the end – 400 coaches were running in the

13. *Calendar of State Papers Domestic* [*Cal. Stat. Pap. Dom.*], *1635*, p. 385; PRO, PC 2/45/99.
14. PRO, PC 2/45/99.
15. *Cal. Stat. Pap. Dom., 1635*, p. 385, 18 Sept.
16. PRO, PC 2/43/267.
17. Larkin, *Stuart Royal Proclamations*, II, no. 210, pp. 494–6; Bodleian, Bankes MS 9/28; *Cal. Stat. Pap. Dom., 1634–5*, p. 8.
18. Bankes MS 64/27.
19. PRO, PC 2/43/605.
20. Bankes MS 5/77.
21. PRO, PC 2/46/270.
22. Larkin, *Stuart Royal Proclamations*, II, p. 495, note 2.
23. *Ibid.*
24. PRO, PC 2/48/359.

1660s – a measure of control was imposed on them in the 1630s.[25]

The rapid growth of London since the end of Elizabeth's reign had thrown up considerable problems of social control, which Caroline government endeavoured to tackle. In a series of demands that must have placed great strain on the resources of pre-bureaucratic municipal government, the Council requested of the mayor detailed lists of all the taverns in the city,[26] all strangers dwelling in Middlesex,[27] all lodgings in the city and all who had recently taken up residence there.[28] The censuses providing the accurate information base for policy, the Council ordered many taverns to be closed, forbade gentlemen to come up to dwell in the city unless they were required on the king's business and enacted measures to stem the expanding immigration and consequently deteriorating conditions.[29] Further censuses and returns enabled the government to check on the enforcement of its directives.[30] Those responsible for government in the city, the aldermen, were forbidden to leave for their country estates without the permission of the mayor.[31] Steps were also taken, as we have seen, to better order the trades and corporations of the city.[32] A proclamation of February 1637 forbade any to exercise a trade without being admitted to a corporation.[33] The strict requirement that Lombard Street be closed to all businesses but goldsmiths (who were all instructed to move there) expressed the king's 'offence' at the blemish on his vision of the ancient order of city trade and topography and his obsession with 'that uniform show which was an ornament to those places. . . .'.[34]

Efforts were even made to extend the order exemplified within the precincts of the City of London to the ever-growing, ever-menacing disorder of the suburbs outside. In this case the initiative may have come as much from the city as the crown. In *English Villainies* (1632) the city dramatist Thomas Dekker lamented, 'How happy . . . were cities if they had no suburbs sith wence they serve but as caves where monsters are bred up to devour the cities.'[35] In November of the same year the mayor presented a petition to the Council complaining against the injury done to the city by the enlargement of the suburbs, the multitude of the meaner sort who had immigrated there and, a silent

25. S. Pegge, *Curialia Miscellanea: or Anecdotes of Old Times* (1818), p. 294.
26. *Cal. Stat. Pap. Dom., 1633–4*, pp. 234–6; PRO, PC 2/43/292.
27. *Cal. Stat. Pap. Dom., 1635*, p. 283; PRO, PC 2/44/161; PC 2/50/150.
28. PRO, PC 2/44/317.
29. Bankes MS 49/8; PRO, PC 2/43/157; below, pp. 414–17
30. See, for example, I. Scouloudi, *Returns of Strangers in the Metropolis* (Huguenot Soc., 57, 1985), p. 98.
31. PRO, PC 2/48/122.
32. Above, pp. 245–9.
33. Larkin, *Stuart Royal Proclamations*, II, no. 234, pp. 549–52.
34. *Cal. Stat. Pap. Dom., 1634–5*, p. 288.
35. T. Dekker, *English Villainies* (1632, STC 6491), sig. F. 3v.

subtext, the competition for trade from those who were outside the constraints of corporations, apprenticeship regulations and entry fines.[36] Foreigners, claimed the rhetoric not unfamiliar to modern ears, were robbing native Londoners of their livelihood. The king and Council took the petition seriously, not least because the suburbs symbolized the disorder and danger of insurrection by the many-headed monster that preoccupied early modern authority. After a Privy Council investigation, therefore, the solution advocated – typical of Caroline government – was the incorporation of all citizens who had served an apprenticeship and were practising trades or manufactures within three miles of the city, so as to bring them under a government.[37] It was not easy to enforce the scheme. Foreigners refused to come into the corporation and continued to trade outside it.[38] In March 1638 the city was pressing the government to enforce a ban on all who had not served an apprenticeship there or taken the freedom of the city from trading.[39] In March 1639 the tense relations between the new corporation and the city were discussed at the Council Board.[40] The complaints make it clear that the incorporation of the suburbs was never more than a qualified success. The city resented the endorsement of a rival authority; entry fines and regulations deterred many from joining and it was impossible to police business carried on independently.[41] Nor were the suburbs reduced to that political order that was the king's intention. Significantly, in the court masques of the 1630s the suburbs are represented as the location of antimasque disorder, 'a horrid hell' in contrast to the peace, harmony and ordered proportions of the city.[42]

It is important that in the court masques of the 1630s the order of the city of London is represented as architectural harmony, for it enables us to understand the ideological importance of a Caroline programme that has too often been considered only as a fiscal expedient: the commission for the regulation of buildings. As we have seen, some contemporaries saw the commission for buildings as a means of raising money through fines on those who had built illicitly: the newswriters Garrard and Rossingham both thought that the delinquents 'will bring

36. *Cal. Stat. Pap. Dom., 1631–3*, p. 446, Nov. 1632.
37. J. Rushworth, *Historical Collections*, II (1680), p. 452; *Cal. Stat. Pap. Dom., 1635–6*, p. 359.
38. See *HMC De Lisle and Dudley VI*, p. 93: Hawkins to Leicester, 9 March 1637; V. Pearl, *London and the Outbreak of the Puritan Revolution* (Oxford, 1964), pp. 31–6; R. Ashton, *The City and the Court, 1603–1643* (Cambridge, 1979), pp. 166 ff.
39. PRO, PC 2/49/51.
40. PRO, PC 2/50/173.
41. Ashton, *City and Court*, pp. 166–7.
42. K. Sharpe, *Criticism and Compliment: The Politics of Literature in the England of Charles I* (Cambridge, 1987), pp. 205–7.

into the Exchequer a round sum of money'.[43] But when we examine the proclamation of 11 July 1630 it becomes clear that money was not the only or primary goal. The proclamation stipulated that any who erected new buildings within three miles of London were to be summoned to the Council Board; any aldermen who failed to report them were to lose their office. Henceforth, the proclamation decreed, no new structure was to be built except on an existing site, and of no material other than brick or stone. Detailed specifications were prescribed. Storeys were to be a minimum 10 feet in height, walls were to be at least $1\frac{1}{2}$ bricks thick, no windows were to be installed until the frames were seen to be strong, secure and flush to the building. Even building bricks were ordered to be of uniform (9 in $\times$ $4\frac{3}{8}$ in) size.[44] In its details the proclamation evokes relatively modern ordinances – and it probably aroused the same irritation and charges of bureaucratic interference. The proclamation, however, declared that it designed all for beauty and health 'tending to the public good of our people'.[45]

In the early years it may be that the effect of the proclamation was mainly fiscal. Those prepared to risk compounding contrived to build. In October 1632 the mayor and aldermen of London petitioned the Council concerning the indiscriminate erection of new dwellings which attracted hordes of migrants without proper provisions for their accommodation.[46] The following year, in November 1633, Secretary Coke drafted a Council order which drew attention to the ill consequences of inadequate control: an influx of foreigners outside of authority, blocked conduits and an enhanced risk of infection.[47] The Council decreed that new licences should not be granted and that those granted but not yet acted upon should be revoked. The commission for buildings was instructed to ensure that licences were not abused, to inspect and order the demolition of any that had breached the required standards. Weeks later the Earl of Dorset successfully moved at the Board that none be allowed to compound.[48] The receipt of fines gave way to reform. For the rest of the 1630s the Council and the commission appear to have kept a strict watch over developments. Many illicit buildings were demolished; sheriffs were reminded in 1635 to compound with none who had built since March 1634.[49] The

43. T. Birch (ed.) *The Court and Times of Charles I* (2 vols, 1848), II, p. 233; W. Knowler (ed.) *The Earl of Strafford's Letters and Despatches* (2 vols, 1739), I, p. 205; above, pp. 120–21.
44. Larkin, *Stuart Royal Proclamations*, II, no. 136, pp. 280–7.
45. *Ibid.*, p. 281.
46. Gardiner, *History of England from the Accession of James I to the Outbreak of the Civil War 1603–42* (10 vols, 1883–4), VIII, p. 288.
47. *Cal. Stat. Pap. Dom., 1633–4*, p. 285.
48. *Ibid.*, p. 428.
49. *Cal. Stat. Pap. Dom., 1635*, pp. 532–3, 4 Dec.; *1635–6*, p. 267: list of buildings demolished.

commissioners were told to take notice of *all* new structures, even sheds and stalls and other 'conversions' surreptitiously employed as accommodation.[50] Even aristocratic builders such as the Earl of Bedford, who had paid £2,000 for his licence to build Covent Garden, found their speculative ventures came under close scrutiny.[51] In December 1634, the commissioners expressed their dissatisfaction with the sewage arrangements of the Covent Garden development and ordered the earl to ensure that no filth spilled into the nearby Thames.[52] They continued to keep a close eye on his work. In March 1635 Bedford was questioned at the Council Board concerning some buildings erected without licence in Covent Garden, which suggests that his piazza was developed, as were other licensed projects, according to strict government guidelines.[53] For all the efforts, illicit building went on – as it still does in the modern age with its greater resources of supervision. But the commissioners and Council, when they discovered offenders, were uncompromising. In July 1637 they ordered the demolition of a number of buildings which had been hastily thrown up in the summer while the Councillors and commissioners were away![54]

Offenders against the proclamation were often prosecuted in Star Chamber and the cases there add strength to the suggestion that reform of the city overrode financial considerations. John More, a clerk of the signet, found himself under an *ore tenus* in Star Chamber for having built seventeen timber coach-houses, thirteen stables and seven houses on the plot of an orchard in St Martin-in-the-Fields which he had purchased. Though the buildings had been erected in James I's reign, More was fined £1,000 and ordered to pull them down by Easter, on pain of a further £1,000.[55] In March he appealed to the Council, only to meet with an unsympathetic response: the Earl of Arundel advised the Board, 'first execution of demolition, then consideration might be had of the fine'.[56] More, who had probably taken a calculated risk that at worst he would face a small fine, was taught the painful lesson that the Caroline regime was taking a tougher line. 'I never heard,' he protested, 'of any house yet demolished that was erected within a man's several freehold as all mine are, nor of the great fines of 500 marks and £500 in former times imposed [nor] any more

50. PRO, PC 2/43/81.
51. L. Stone, 'The residential development of the West End of London in the seventeenth century', in B. Malament (ed.) *After the Reformation* (Manchester, 1980), pp. 167–212, p. 197.
52. *Cal. Stat. Pap. Dom., 1634–5*, p. 347; cf. Melbourne Hall, Coke MS 56.
53. Knowler, *Strafford Letters*, I, p. 372; cf. PRO, SO 1/2, f.132v; SO 1/3, f.168v.
54. PRO, PC 2/48/157; *Cal. Stat. Pap. Dom., 1636–7*, p. 542.
55. British Library [BL] Harleian MS 4022, f.1–1v; PRO, C. 115/M31/8174.
56. Coke MS 48: John More to Coke, 6 March.

paid than 100 marks for any and that rather in respect of obstinate proceedings against warnings (which I never did) than *merely for building contrary to proclamation.*'[57] In July More and his co-speculator John Dickenson were bewailing the £1,000 fine imposed for their failure to dismantle their buildings by the stipulated time and the zeal of the sheriff who had demolished more than the commissioners had ordered.[58] Cottington told them that had they built for their own use, it might have extenuated their crime.[59] The court, however, was firm against speculators because 'increase of buildings causeth a conflux of people not easy to be governed, causeth dearth and pestilence and so consequently causeth the other parts of the kingdom to suffer'.[60]

The use of Star Chamber to enforce the proclamation against building had been, according to William Hudson who penned a treatise on the court, 'very necessary if anything would deter men from that horrible mischief of increasing that head which is swollen to a great bigness already'.[61] The swelling, however, was not due to new building alone. The commissioners for buildings were also briefed to investigate and proceed against those who divided the existing structures into smaller tenements which, in the Council's eyes, added to the numbers of loose people, vagrants and petty criminals.[62] In February 1637 the Council revived an Elizabethan decree that if landlords divided buildings into tenements the tenants might live there rent free, so removing the economic incentive to cash in on immigration to the capital.[63] In May the mayor was required to survey all houses built in and within three miles of the city, and their inhabitants – a survey which revealed the scale of the problem.[64] The Company of Freemasons had divided the common hall over their kitchen into three dwellings;[65] in Little All Hallows, Sir Francis Clarke's house was home to eleven married couples and fifteen single persons;[66] in the parish of St Alban in one property there were ten families dwelling in ten rooms 'divers of which have also lodgers' – all of whom received alms of the parish.[67] The environs of London faced the same pressures as the city. Dr Thomas Creighton reported from Greenwich: 'We have found so many conversions of houses into small tenements and many newly

57. *Ibid.* (my italics).
58. Berkshire Record Office, Trumbull Add. MS 37, 23 July 1634.
59. Harleian MS 4022, f.3.
60. *Ibid.*, f.2v.
61. Huntington Library, Ellesmere MS 7921; on Hudson, see below, pp. 667–9.
62. *Cal. Stat. Pap. Dom., 1629–31*, p. 308.
63. *Cal. Stat. Pap. Dom., 1636–7*, p. 443; Birch, *Court and Times of Charles I*, II, p. 282.
64. *Cal. Stat. Pap. Dom., 1637*, p. 68.
65. *Ibid.*, p. 178.
66. *Ibid.*, p. 180.
67. *Ibid.* See PRO, SP 16/359.

erected cottages all filled with people resorting to the town upon hope of preferment into one of the hospitals erected here, or to be set on work in ballasting ships, that the better sort of inhabitants find it too great a burden, the poor's book being risen within a few years from £30 to £60.'[68] Creighton, the vicar, sued on their behalf for a Star Chamber decree to reform the 'enormities about London'. The Council specifically exempted from any pardon of offence or composition for breaching the proclamation any who converted houses into tenements.[69] In 1638 they even ordered a search of the cellars around Long Acre, to check who had converted them into lodgings.[70] A judicial ruling that all inmates were the responsibility of those who lodged them shifted some of the social problems from the parish to the speculating landlord.[71] But from the highest social levels down the accommodation pressures on a swiftly expanding capital limited the achievements of social control. The Smyths found Bedford's new houses in Covent Garden 'so very little';[72] even Viscount Scudamore, returning from Paris, was warned of the 'so little conveniences of lodgings in the city'.[73] When the greatest of the land were having to compromise their standards, there was little hope of the lowly being rescued from squalor.

While social control remained at the core of the government's concern over buildings in London, there appears to have been, in Charles's reign, even more than James's, a strong aesthetic and even ideological dimension to the commissioners' work. Orders to demolish buildings near the hospital at Knightsbridge or St Paul's cathedral were intended to remove 'a great blemish' and reveal, in their proportion and majesty, great landmarks of the city.[74] Investigations of plasterers who overlaid stone with plaster suggests a concern with appearance as well as with safety;[75] regulations governing the size of bricks perfectly encapsulate the king's obsession with uniformity and his sense of the relationship of aesthetic to social order.[76] Architecture, after all, as the present Prince of Wales reminds us, is a branch of politics – of what we would now call social engineering. The Council ordered the removal of water steps and backstairs from inns and taverns by means of which rogues slipped away from justice, just as planners now avoid the back alleys and high walls that shelter muggers and burglars.[77] The licences

68. *Cal. Stat. Pap. Dom., 1637*, p. 111, 16 May.
69. PRO, PC 2/47/117.
70. PRO, PC 2/48/199.
71. Birch, *Court and Times of Charles I*, II, p. 282.
72. Bristol Record Office, Smyth of Ashton Court MS AC 1/C53/9.
73. PRO, C.115/N8/8827: Finet to Scudamore, 10 Jan. 1639.
74. PRO, PC 2/42/334; PC 2/41/470; *Cal. Stat. Pap. Dom., 1633–4*, p. 499; *1634–5*, p. 299.
75. PRO, PC 2/48/212.
76. Above, pp. 182–3, 193–4.
77. Trumbull Add. MS 36: Council order, 6 Nov. 1633.

to build granted during Charles I's reign excluded alehouses and tobacco shops, those solvents of the moral community.[78] Bedford's Covent Garden piazza with St Paul's church at the west end was designed around 'the concept of the local community in which residential housing was supplemented by a church and a market'.[79] The key figure in Covent Garden was also a leading and long-serving member of the buildings commission. And Inigo Jones, the king's architect, brought to his work there many of the values that informed his commissions for royal buildings and masques. The Earl of Arundel, a fellow commissioner, told Wentworth in January 1635 that it was Jones who pressed for the proclamation for buildings: 'he avows he did it out of his duty to propagate the arts'.[80] There is no reason to doubt him. The draft warrant for a grant of incorporation to the brick and tile makers was referred by the king to the commission because it was hoped the company might be 'the chief ornament for the beautifying of his magnificent and metropolitan city of London'.[81] The London Charles envisaged, with its amphitheatre, restored St Paul's, new Whitehall Palace, the London Jones represented (in default of its being built) in scenes for masques, was the classical capital of a Caroline empire.[82] Like the Roman capital that was its inspiration, it was in its architecture and planning as well as government to be a model and symbol of an order which, it was intended, would be replicated throughout the realm.

The communication of ideals

London might stand as the vision of order, but the principal medium for the communication of the king's values to the country during the 1630s was the royal word. In the absence of parliaments and hence of statutes the printed proclamation, read or posted in the market squares, offered the only means of disseminating an order widely. Proclamations could not change the law, but for the most part Charles had no desire to do so. They could, and were intended to, quicken the execution of the law and, as the author of *The Attourney's Academy* (1630) concluded, if a proclamation 'be in supplement or declaration of a law that hath been formerly made and been good it is to be obeyed as

78. *Cal. Stat. Pap. Dom., 1633–4*, p. 285.
79. L. Stone, 'Residential development of the West End', p. 206.
80. Sheffield Central Library, Wentworth Woodhouse MS WW/14, f.280: Arundel to Wentworth, 22 Jan. 1635.
81. Bankes MS 12/34.
82. Charles referred to London as his 'imperial city' (Larkin, *Stuart Royal Proclamations*, II, p. 85).

a law'.[83] Proclamations as well as dealing with *ad hoc* problems and emergencies – harvest failure or plague – shaped the priorities of law enforcement and local government. The recent edition of Charles I's royal proclamations has forced us to question some old assumptions about prerogative government and the personal rule. For, as Professor Larkin observes, in the period 1629–40 'what strikes one surprisingly is the comparatively small number of proclamations issued'.[84] Indeed the average of one a month compares almost exactly with that of the reign of James I. By contrast during the years before (1625–9) and after (1640–2) the personal rule, the average is two proclamations a month. Whereas the war years required the issue of regular decrees and instructions, the emphasis of the 1630s was on enforcement rather than alteration of the law. Many of the proclamations of the personal rule specifically refer to the statutes they reaffirm and in some cases earlier proclamations that had not taken effect. Few appear in the litany of complaints against the government in 1641.

Most of the proclamations of the 1630s are concerned with public order and welfare broadly conceived – with plague and poor relief, with the regulation of cottagers and inmates, with the supply of foodstuffs and provisions, the protection of fishing, with the pollution of the air by coal fumes – and with religion and morality: the observation of Lent and the prevention of profane swearing, for example. While proclamations against counterfeit jewels, against setting dogs to take partridges or against dressing venison in common inns were intended to preserve social hierarchy by upholding the privileges of the gentry, those for a letter service or for the restraint of heavy carriages that destroyed highways exhibited a concern for the 'public interest' in its broadest sense. Whilst many of the proclamations are conventional enough, that for 'lessening the great annoyance of smoke'[85] or that which, to prevent burglaries, ordered pawnbrokers to register all articles they accepted demonstrates a concern with detail and an attempt to prevent as well as respond to problems less in evidence before.[86] Because there are strong reasons to believe that the king's own pen was often at work in drafting them,[87] the list of such enactments is, as Professor Larkin claimed, very 'helpful to those attempting to measure the ability of King Charles I to govern England'.[88]

There is no reason to suppose that most of the proclamations were contentious. In 1639 the Council reviewed, along with projects and

83. T. Powell, *The Attourney's Academy* (1630, STC 20164a), p. 225; cf. p. 218.
84. Larkin, *Stuart Royal Proclamations*, II, pp. x–xi.
85. *Ibid.*, no. 185, pp. 426–8.
86. *Ibid.*, no. 134, pp. 276–8.
87. *Ibid.*, p. xx; see, for example, PRO, PC 2/41/246. Coke also drafted proclamations and submitted his drafts for the king's perusal. See, for example, *HMC Cowper II*, p. 176.
88. Larkin, *Stuart Royal Proclamations*, II, p. xx.

patents, some it believed to be unpopular and, probably with reluctance, recalled that prohibiting the accommodation of inmates.[89] The repetition of others – that against eating meat in Lent for example – suggests that some proclamations (not necessarily novel or even of political import) were never willingly obeyed nor easily enforced.[90] But in many cases proclamations met, and were seen to meet, a need or resolved a problem. This is obvious in the case of those dealing with food shortages or plague, to which JPs responded promptly, but proclamations concerning gold weights or gardeners, as well as those for the maintenance of standards, often arose from merchant petitions or consumer complaints.[91] It is easy (and humorous) to cite cases like that of Thomas Peynell who, true to his word, declared that he did not give a fart for the royal proclamation against swearing.[92] But we should not from such episodes conclude that in a decade of no parliaments and statutes, proclamations were viewed with suspicion, or not taken seriously. JPs' notebooks show plentiful examples of recognizances taken from those who had breached even routine proclamations – for example by dressing flesh in Lent.[93] In Westminster forty-two chief cooks and innkeepers were fined payments to the poor for their disobedience.[94] Proclamations were not lightly broken or ignored. In 1635 Lord Poulett wanted to come up to London to arrange credit for his son's journey abroad – but, he told Coke, 'I dare not adventure to . . . in regard of the proclamations'.[95] In 1632 the corporation of York decided to keep a file of proclamations so that it had a clear record of what the city magistrates were required to perform.[96] If the proclamations offer some guide to Charles I's values and aims, they suggest that in general these were neither radical nor contentious.

To one proclamation Charles attached especial importance as a measure central to his quest for reform of local society by a reinvigoration of traditional modes of government. The proclamation, first published in 1626 and reissued in 1627 and 1632, commanded the nobility and gentry to leave London within forty days and 'resort to the several counties where they usually resided and there keep their habitations and hospitality'.[97] It referred to the waste of gentry estates

89. PRO, PC 2/50/311.
90. And cf. PRO, PC 2/42/387.
91. Larkin, *Stuart Royal Proclamations*, II, no. 164, pp. 366–8; no. 190, pp. 439–41; PRO, SP 16/192/55; Larkin, *Stuart Royal Proclamations*, II, no. 164, pp. 376–80; see also Bankes MS 64/7.
92. Bankes MS 63/34.
93. For example, Kent Archives Office, Dering MS U570/01, f.21.
94. *Cal. Stat. Pap. Dom., 1629–31*, p. 397.
95. Coke MS 50, 8 March 1635.
96. York City Record Office, House Books, 35, f.162v.
97. Larkin, *Stuart Royal Proclamations*, II, no. 56, pp. 112–13; no. 77, pp. 170–2; no. 159,

in the capital (a popular theme of Jacobean and Caroline drama), to the desirability of their maintaining wealth and power in the localities, most of all to the need for resident gentry governors in the counties. All who were not Privy Councillors or personal attendants upon the king were forbidden to stay; if business brought them to London they were required to seek permission to come up and to leave their families at home. The king threatened the disobedient with a 'constant severity' and the court of Star Chamber. The proclamation was not new: the first had been issued by Elizabeth I in 1596 and there were several to the same purpose published by James.[98] What was different – and typical – in Charles I's was the effort during the 1630s to give the proclamation teeth. Not only did the king and Council instruct the mayor, aldermen and JPs of London closely to oversee it, the mayor was required on several occasions to return to the Board certificates of those, 'especially of noblemen and gentlement of quality', who lodged in London in defiance of the order.[99] And the Lord Keeper's charge to the assize judges explaining the hurt done to, and the king's desire to preserve, the commonweal urged their assistance with enforcement.[100] Those who claimed a need to come up evidently had to secure a formal licence – apparently through the agency of the Lord Chamberlain.[101] There are over 200 such warrants for the decade among the papers of Attorney-General Bankes.[102] But most were granted only temporarily; and the strictures of the proclamation evidently affected noblemen as mighty as the Earls of Clare and Northumberland (who was not a Councillor until 1636) as well as lesser men.[103] Offenders against the proclamation were rapidly prosecuted in Star Chamber: in November 1632 one William Palmer was fined £1,000 and newswriters predicted that many more would be prosecuted.[104] Two years later, when the Council was making another proclamation, it was reported that 'Mr Attorney doth first peruse all the answers of all those against whom Attorney Noy exhibited bills in the Star Chamber that so, by knowing

pp. 350–3. On the background, cf. F. Heal, 'The crown, the gentry and London: the enforcement of proclamation 1596–1640', in C. Cross, D. Loades and J. Scarisbrick (eds) *Law and Government under the Tudors* (Cambridge, 1988), pp. 211–26.

98. P.L. Hughes and J.F. Larkin (eds) *Tudor Royal Proclamations*, III (New Haven, 1969), pp. 169–71; Hughes and Larkin, *Stuart Royal Proclamations, I: Proclamations of James I, 1603–1625* (Oxford, 1973), pp. 21–2, 356–7, 369–71, 561–2. An instance of an Elizabethan prosecution in Star Chamber arising from breach of the proclamation is in Ellesmere MS 7921, f.36v.
99. Larkin, *Stuart Royal Proclamations*, II, p. 350; PRO, PC 2/42/242; PC 2/43/65; PC 2/44/161; cf. Bankes MSS 64/12 and 65/14.
100. Bodleian, Rawlinson MS A. 128, ff.24vff.
101. *Cal. Stat. Pap. Dom., 1631–3*, p. 369.
102. For example, Bankes MSS 64/12, 65/14 and 54/92.
103. Bankes MS 14/62 returns their names, along with others in breach of the proclamation.
104. BL Add. MS 42117 (at end); PRO, C.115/M30/8106: Flower to Scudamore, 10 Nov. 1632; PRO, C.115/M32/8205, 19 Jan. 1633.

their former pretences, he may fortify . . . against the like excuses hereafter.'[105] The king, Rossingham told Viscount Scudamore, 'is very zealous of his proclamation against town dwellers and therefore hath often charged his Attorney to prosecute against them'.[106]

It is not easy to judge the king's success. The reissues of the proclamations, the annual letters to the mayor and JPs, the lists of those prosecuted, indicate that it was not, at least initially, as successful as was hoped. The need to come up to London on business or to lobby – most of all the glittering attractions of what was emerging as a London season – were not easily resisted. The poet Thomas Carew joked that even when husbands stayed at home their wives could not resist the social magnet of the capital and the sparkling pleasures, not all licit, that it offered.[107] But Carew (and other poets) testify also to the effects of the royal order. In 1634 Sir John Strangeways was refused permission to keep Christmas in the capital.[108] Lord Poulett was not alone in his unease about being caught breaking the proclamation.[109] Sir Simonds D'Ewes, though at first complacent, decided to leave Islington.[110] Sir Gervase Clifton was warned that forty gentlemen had been summoned into Star Chamber for staying in the city;[111] in 1634 Robert Lecke told him of further prosecutions and their effects: 'few or none adventure . . .'.[112] Sir George Twisleton, Bt., even felt the need to obtain a licence (through the Earl of Kellie) to remain in the city while he recovered his health.[113] Similarly Viscount Chaworth asked Sir John Coke to move the king personally to grant him leave to bring his wife up to the doctor.[114] Significantly, in proffering his suit, he promised 'in obedience to the proclamation, we leave our son at one of my houses with a competent family for house-keeping in the country'.

As well as appreciating that the proclamation was strictly enforced, Chaworth properly perceived the king's purpose. Some have argued that the proclamation was yet another device to raise money; more

105. PRO, C.115/M36/8437: Rossingham to Scudamore, 18 Oct. 1634.
106. PRO, C.115/M36/8439: Rossingham to Scudamore, 31 Oct. 1634.
107. Carew referred to the wives leaving their husbands in the country while they went to the capital 'soliciting business in their own persons and leaving their husbands at home for stallions of hospitality' (*Coelum Britannicum*, lines 247–9, in Orgel and Strong, *Inigo Jones*, II, p. 572).
108. BL, Egerton MS 784, p. 217.
109. Coke MS 50; above, p. 414.
110. J.O. Halliwell (ed.) *The Autobiography and Correspondence of Sir Simonds D'Ewes* (2 vols, 1845), II, p. 79–80.
111. Nottingham University Library, Clifton MS Cl/C 59: Robert Butler to Clifton, 30 Jan. 1632.
112. Clifton MS Cl/C 307, 15 Nov. 1634.
113. Coke MS 50, 5 Nov. 1634; *HMC Cowper II*, p. 71.
114. *HMC Cowper I*, p. 485, 1 Dec. 1632.

recently historians have curiously claimed that it was intended to disperse a potential gentry opposition from gathering in the metropolis.[115] There is little evidence to support either suggestion. The measure responded to a widespread concern about the decay of hospitality. The author of a treatise on *Christian Hospitalitie* specifically praised James I's earlier proclamation of 1616.[116] Richard Braithwaite in his popular work *The English Gentleman* (1630) savagely criticized the gentry who gave up their country houses and responsibilities to the poor, for a mean retinue and life at court;[117] Henry Peacham in 1634 satirized their wives who departed 'flowery gardens sweet' and 'healthful county air' for the court and metropolis.[118] The populace lamented a 'phantastick age' in which all hospitality had declined.[119] Charles intended while controlling the spread of London that the gentry, as Wither versed it, 'may do good/Among their tenants, by their neighbourhood'.[120] It was not a forlorn hope. Within months of the proclamation, it was reported that 'new houses begin to be good cheap and I think victuals will not be the dearer for the proclamation. I presume more chimneys [in the country] are likely to smoke this Christmas than have been seen many years before.'[121] Gentry and nobility were ordered to their country seats, as bishops were commanded to their sees, as Irish nobles and officeholders were ordered to their country, and as aldermen were instructed to remain in London: because government in early modern England depended upon the presence of powerful local men.[122]

Although it may not have been welcome to many of them, the royal proclamation ordering the nobility and gentry to their country estates was related to Charles I's policy of sustaining and reinforcing the privileges and powers of the aristocracy. This is not the place to take up the question of the wealth, status and power of the nobility in early Stuart England – though, even after Lawrence Stone's magisterial study, it remains a question whether we should not think more of a

115. Larkin, *Stuart Royal Proclamations*, II, p. 351; M. Butler, *Theatre and Crisis, 1632–1642* (Cambridge, 1984), p. 118; T. Cogswell, *The Blessed Revolution: English Politics and the Coming of War, 1621–1624* (Cambridge, 1989), p. 34.
116. C. Dalechamp, *Christian Hospitalitie Handled Common-place-wise* (1632, STC 6192), pp. 123–7.
117. R. Braithwaite, *The English Gentleman* (1630, STC 3563), pp. 66–7, 332–3.
118. H. Peacham, *Thestylis Atrata: or a Funeral Elegie upon Francis, Countesse of Warwick* (1634, STC 19516), sig.C.
119. *The Phantastick Age* (1634, STC 197), a ballad.
120. G. Wither, *Britain's Remembrancer* (1628, STC 25899), p. 67.
121. PRO, C.115/N3/8550: Herbert to Scudamore, 8 Nov. 1632. At the Star Chamber trial of William Palmer, Justice Richardson lamented 'hospitality forgot in country'. On the theme of hospitality, see F. Heale's useful survey, *Hospitality in Early Modern England* (Oxford, 1990). This work appeared after my manuscript had been substantially completed.
122. See PRO, SO 1/2, f.204v.

change than a decline in the position of the nobles.[123] For all the alleged 'crisis of the aristocracy', they still dominated the society and government of the counties where they held their estates; they were still the military class. What had compromised the status of the nobility as much as any shift in their economic fortunes was the inflation of honours that had characterized the reign of James I and especially the decade after 1615. Between 1615 and 1628 the numbers of earls had risen from 27 to 65, and peers overall from 81 to 126; at Elizabeth's death the House of Lords had totalled 55. Between 1611, when the title was created to raise money, and 1628, 284 baronetcies were granted – or, rather, sold.[124] In addition, James raised over 2,000 men to knighthood, over 900 of them in the first months of his reign – a number far in excess of Elizabeth's creations over forty-five years.[125] The numbers, though bad enough, tell only part of the story. For many of those elevated were pure courtier peers, some Buckingham's relatives, with little land or local influence, who were granted Scottish or Irish titles. During the 1620s both the Houses of Lords and the Commons protested about the dilution and tarnishing of the nobility that resulted from an orgy of indiscriminate honours.[126] Sir John Oglander, for example, reflected on the creation of Lord Mountjoy as Earl of Newport, 'what success this new Earl may have who hath the title but no land or place therein after ages shall see'.[127] As for baronetcies, since for the La Rochelle campaign they were sold for £150 each, Oglander believed they were counted less than others of inferior rank and hoped that a future parliament would return them to 'dust'.[128] The landless knight, of little ability or worth, became a stock-in-trade of dramatic satire on the Jacobean stage.[129] In the end such expressions of derision dented the market for honours: in 1628 Stephen Smyth told Thomas Smyth, 'There are some Irish honours

123. L. Stone, *The Crisis of the Aristocracy, 1558–1641* (Oxford, 1965); cf. the review by J.H. Hexter, printed in *On Historians* (1979), pp. 149–226 and the incisive comments of J.P. Cooper in 'The counting of manors', *Econ. Hist. Rev.*, 2nd series, 8 (1956), pp. 377–85; 'The social distribution of land and men in England, 1436–1700', *Econ. Hist. Rev.*, 2nd series, 20 (1967), pp. 419–40; and in J.P. Cooper, *Land, Men and Beliefs* (1983), pp. 1–42.
124. Rawlinson MS B.18, f.169; Rawlinson MS B.68; T. Walkley, *A Catalogue of the Nobility of England, Scotland and Ireland* (1630, STC 24974); Stone, *Crisis of the Aristocracy*, ch. 3, see chart, p. 95.
125. Stone, *Crisis of the Aristocracy*, p. 74; Rawlinson MS B.18, f.2; 432 were dubbed on 23 July 1604 (Stone, *Crisis*, p. 76); cf. H.S. Grazebrooke, *Obligatory Knighthood temp. Charles I* (William Salt Archaeological Soc., II, 1881), p. 6.
126. K. Sharpe, 'Crown, parliament and locality: government and communication in early Stuart England', *Eng. Hist. Rev.*, 101 (1986), pp. 334–5.
127. W.H. Long (ed.) *The Oglander Memoirs* (1888), p. 14.
128. *Ibid.*, p. 48.
129. Examples abound, but see J. Shirley, *Changes: or Love in a Maze* (1632, STC 22437).

too conferred of late, but they are . . . things methinks which few men care for nowadays.'[130]

Evidently, from his succession to the throne, Charles shared a concern that the inflation of honours had depleted their worth. In December 1625 Viscount Conway reported to Lord Keeper Coventry that the king would create no new knights at his coronation because he believed there were too many already.[131] Yet, during the period of Buckingham's hegemony and, more importantly, the war years, when finances were desperate, the sale of titles continued: seventy-eight baronetcies were sold after 1625.[132] After 1628–9, however, the traffic in titles came to an abrupt halt. Only eight baronetcies were sold after 1628, only three were granted after 1630, until the crisis of 1641 saw a resumption of wartime expediencies.[133] Even the gifts of titles promised were revoked. Isobel Musgrave, wife of Lieutenant Francis Musgrave, had hoped to enjoy the profits of the nomination to a baronetcy that Buckingham had granted her husband, 'but since his [the Duke of Buckingham's] death, the king had told her that he would not grant any more of that kind'.[134] Similarly, Captain Henry Keys, who had been granted a blank for the making of a baronet in return for services at La Rochelle, 'in dutiful conformity to his Majesty's pleasure' resigned it.[135] Charles's determination to put a stop to the inflation of all honours soon became obvious by experience, for throughout the 1630s the king returned to an almost Elizabethan parsimony in the granting of titles. Charles created only five English peers between 1631 and 1640 and two Irish.[136] Even his most industrious minister, Viscount Wentworth, was forced to wait, impatiently, until 1640 for his elevation to an earldom. Though in 1636 the Earl of Kingston informed the hopeful Sir Gervase Clifton of 'constant reports that the list of nobility shall shortly be lengthened', by 1640 the peerage was slightly smaller than it had been at the beginning of personal rule.[137] Charles's tight policy in granting titles may, like Elizabeth's, have dangerously narrowed the support the court enjoyed in the country – as the Duke of Newcastle was later to suggest.[138] But it was clearly designed to reverse the excesses of the previous decade

130. J.H. Bettey, *Calendar of the Correspondence of the Smyth Family of Ashton Court, 1548–1642* (Bristol Record Soc., 35, 1982), p. 92, 18 Aug. 1628.
131. *Cal. Stat. Pap. Dom., 1625–49*, p. 79; cf. above, p. 113.
132. Rawlinson MS B.18, f.169.
133. *Ibid.*; Stone, *Crisis of the Aristocracy*, p. 96; and W.H. Black (ed.) *Docquets of Letters Patent* (2 vols, 1837), II, pp. 300–2, and *passim*.
134. *Cal. Stat. Pap. Dom., 1628–9*, p. 379.
135. *HMC Cowper I*, p. 397.
136. Stone, *Crisis of the Aristocracy*, pp. 98, 104, appendix III, p. 755.
137. Clifton MS Cl/C 660, 23 Jan. 1636.
138. S.A. Strong, *A Catalogue of Documents in the Library at Welbeck* (1903), p. 213.

and so to restore the esteem to titles which were now only sparingly bestowed.

As well as stemming the tide, Charles also endeavoured to repair some of the damage done by the Jacobean flood of creations. In June 1629, for example, the king, considering a petition in Council, ruled on the precedence of English over Irish or Scottish peers. Desirous, as he put it, to preserve the 'ancient lustre' of the English nobles and 'to encourage them with all alacrity to join the management of the affairs of the Commonwealth', he ruled that none with Irish or Scottish titles having no livelihood in England could be nominated to any commission – including, of course, the commission of the peace.[139] It was an important decision, the final draft of which was corrected in the king's own hand, and an early expression of a new attitude.[140] During the personal rule, the restoration of the privileges of the nobility and their traditional role in governing was a central characteristic of Charles's social policy. The king's 'principal care', as he told the Earl of Bath, to preserve honour is evidenced in a variety of enactments and decisions.[141] Charles forbade the killing and dressing of game by common folk in inns because 'we are careful to preserve the right appertaining to our nobility and gentry in their lawful and commendable pleasure and recreations . . .'.[142] He prohibited the purchase of 'counterfeit jewels' – costume jewellery – not least because it decked out lesser figures in the finery that was the mark of nobility.[143] He exempted English (but significantly not Irish or Scottish) nobles from showing arms at musters.[144] Sir John Finet, the king's Master of Ceremonies, desperately trying to find suitable housing for visiting ambassadors, found Charles determined not to require any nobleman to surrender his home.[145] In appointments to places of government and honour the king was careful of rank. The proportion of lay peers on the Privy Council increased from two-thirds to over three-quarters; nobles were more frequently appointed to commissions in central and local government.[146] Gentlemen of the Privy Chamber and gentlemen pensioners were selected from the most distinguished families 'that all our loving subjects of best rank and worth may find themselves

139. Ellesmere MS 6931; *HMC Cowper I*, p. 373. In some cases this principle was circumvented by conferring English titles on prominent Scottish and Irish peers.
140. See Coke MS 36 for the draft with Charles's corrections.
141. PRO, SO 1/2, f.116v.
142. *Ibid.*, f.248v; Dering MS U350/010 (6).
143. PRO, PC 2/46/53; Larkin, *Stuart Royal Proclamations*, II, no. 217, pp. 507–8.
144. *Cal. Stat. Pap. Dom., 1635*, p. 524.
145. A.J. Loomie (ed.) *Ceremonies of Charles I: The Note Books of John Finet, Master of Ceremonies 1628–1641* (New York, 1987), p. 229.
146. Stone, *Crisis of the Aristocracy*, p. 751, most were first generation peers; D.J. Wilkinson, 'The commission of the peace in Lancashire, 1603–1642', *Trans. Hist. Soc. of Lancashire and Cheshire*, 132 (1983), pp. 41–66.

interested in the trust and honour of our service'.[147] Under Charles more than James new appointments to the commission of the peace reflected ancestral connection;[148] in 1637 a docquet was issued to the heralds to visit all England so as to reform abuses that had arisen for want of regular visitations.[149] The king intervened personally on behalf of his nobility when men of lesser rank contested with them at law.[150] With privilege, however, in Charles's mind, went responsibility. He subscribed to the Renaissance ideal and convention that aristocracy (which literally means 'the best') drew its title from virtue as well as birth. At the creation of Wentworth as Earl of Strafford in the Presence Chamber in 1640, Charles praised the new earl: 'such is the propenseness of your goodness that the habit thereof acquired by long practice seems to be co-essential with your nature.'[151] In the personalities and education of the nobility the king took a close interest. He advised on their marriages.[152] Philip Warwick, Gentleman of the Bedchamber, tells us that Charles saw young noblemen personally, to pass on counsel and instruction, before they departed on the Grand Tour.[153] In December 1635, he granted £100 to Sir Francis Kynaston for his Museum Minervae, a college and finishing school for gentlemen, and interested himself for long in the establishment of an academy for young nobles on the model of Richelieu's in France.[154] In 1636 he personally commended to the bounty of the nobility and gentry a project to erect a building and appoint masters of faculties, to effect 'that which we have long earnestly wished, namely the virtuous education of their children at home in safety and their preservation from the too frequent vices of the times by a diversion of their minds from idleness and vanity to noble and better employments'.[155] As well as maintaining the privileges and standards of the nobility, Charles sought to reaffirm their close personal allegiance to the crown. Among the papers of Attorney-General Bankes we find notes 'for homage and fealty' arguing for their restoration, for 'by reason of the respiting of homage his Majesty's tenants have never used to swear their fealties and allegiance to his Majesty, whereby no small tie and means to bind

147. PRO, LC 5/180.
148. Wilkinson, 'Commission of the peace in Lancashire', p. 54.
149. Birmingham Reference Library, Docquets of Letter Patent Coventry MS 602756/151, 25 Dec. 1633.
150. PRO, SO 1/2, f.162v. The king disliked it that 'a man of mean quality shall prosecute against a nobleman for an offence of passion or heat only'.
151. Bodleian, Tanner MS 67, f.122.
152. For example, PRO, SO 1/2, f.116v: Charles I to Earl of Bath, 23 Sept. 1632.
153. Sir Philip Warwick, *Memoirs of the Reign of King Charles I* (1701), p. 72.
154. *Cal. Stat. Pap. Dom., 1635*, p. 550; PRO, SO 1/3, f.8; cf. R. Caudill, 'Some literary evidence of the development of English virtuoso interests in the seventeenth century' (Oxford University, D. Phil. thesis, 1975), esp. ch. 8 on academies.
155. PRO, SO 1/3, f.8, 3 June.

them to their obedience is left undone'.[156] In 1638–9, as Professor Stone revealed, 'a general resumption of honours' was discussed in Council, and it was agreed that all titles be granted only after an oath of personal loyalty and in return for personal service in war.[157] The king's emphasis on the duties as well as privileges of noblemen stemmed from the belief he shared with Wentworth that 'men of blood and estates' were the natural partners with the crown in government.[158] As he was to put it in a letter of 1640 from the Great Council called to York, Charles regarded his peers as 'a principal part of the representative body of this Kingdom'.[159]

The justices of assize

Proclamations expressed royal desires and policies for reform; the gentry and nobility, residing in their counties, were expected to govern in the king's name and according to his wishes. In early modern England there were no agents radiating from Whitehall to deliver royal commands to the counties and the personal rule saw no real scheme to implement them. Charles I did, however, in a decade of no parliaments, make full use of a traditional organ of government as an instrument for the communication of his priorities and policies to the magistracy of the counties: the justices of assize. Twice yearly, usually during the Lent vacation (late February and March) and the Trinity vacation (July and early August), the common law judges, dividing the realm into six circuits (the Home, the Midland, the Norfolk, the Oxford, the Western and the Northern) in pairs visited each of the counties of England to hold the county assizes.[160] The assizes formed the principal court for the trial of major crimes beyond the purview of the quarter sessions – murder, manslaughter or witchcraft; they tried all suspects bailed or held in gaol; they heard the presentments of the grand juries which could initiate process as well as act as a preliminary inquisition for crown proceedings.[161] Perhaps more important, as well as a forum of criminal justice the assizes were a major event in local government. The assizes were one of the most important administrative and social occasions in the calendar of the county gentry. In some counties, such as Lancashire, they provided

156. Bankes MS 5.
157. Stone, *Crisis of the Aristocracy*, pp. 117–19.
158. Knowler, *Strafford Letters*, II, pp. 41–3.
159. PRO, SO 1/3, f.196; cf. below, pp. 915–19.
160. J.S. Cockburn, *A History of English Assizes, 1558–1714*, (Cambridge, 1972), p. 24, prints a map of the circuits.
161. Cockburn, *History of the Assizes*, p. 111; J.S. Morrill, *The Cheshire Grand Jury, 1625–1659* (Leicester, 1975).

the only occasion at which the JPs (who met in different parts of the county for their sessions) came together to discuss the business of their whole shire.[162] In all counties the elaborate dinner for the judge, provided at the expense of the sheriff, offered not only a magnificent feast (sheriff Buxton of Norfolk spent nearly £500 in the summer of 1638)[163] but, rather like a dinner of the Round Table, an opportunity to mix, be seen, press a suit or whisper some malice about a rival in a powerful ear. Because he recognized the significance of the occasion, in March 1624 the Earl of Kingston, for all his pain and talk of being close to death, spoke of his 'extreme desire' to be at the Nottinghamshire assizes.[164] Moreover, in some cases sensitive political questions and grievances were referred to the full meeting of the county: in Kent, for example, complaints against raised purveyance payments came to the assizes.[165] More importantly the report of the judges' resolution in camera on ship money prompted (as we shall see) a full debate on the issue among the gentry assembled at the assizes.[166] With all justices expected to attend, and a high proportion present in practice, the judges presiding in their robes as symbols of the king's justice and autority, with men and women attending the trials as a public entertainment, the assizes were, in Charles I's own words, 'places and auditories, being assemblies of the principal persons of each county'.[167]

From the county's point of view, the arrival of the justices presented an opportunity for the resolution of difficult or controversial legal problems and for settling disputes between parishes and counties – over, for example, settlement of bastard children or bridge repairs.[168] At Exeter in 1636, in response to a petition from the mayor, the judges set down rules for regulating the trade of the city;[169] the corporation of York appealed to Justice Hutton to resolve the quarrel between the mayor and Dr Wickham over seats in the Minster – and later sent him a gift of wine for the pains he had taken to settle the matter.[170] Even powerful figures such as the Earl of Bridgewater, Lord President of the

162. B.W. Quintrell (ed.) 'Proceedings of the Lancashire justices of the peace at the sheriff's table during assizes week, 1578–1694', *Trans. Hist. Soc. of Lancashire and Cheshire*, 131 (1981), pp. 4–5, 12.
163. Cambridge University Library, Buxton MSS, Box 96. I am grateful to Clive Holmes for drawing these manuscripts to my attention.
164. Clifton MS Cl/C 658: Kingston to Clifton.
165. Kent Archives Office, Twysden MS U47/47, 01, p. 15.
166. Twysden MS U47/47, Z1, Z2; below, pp. 720–21.
167. Tanner MS 71, f.142: Charles I to Archbishop Abbot, 31 May 1632. By no means all the JPs in fact attended. Dr Herrup shows that half attended in Sussex (C. Herrup, *The Common Peace: Participation and the Criminal Law in Seventeenth Century England*, Cambridge, 1987, p. 61).
168. Cockburn, *History of the Assizes*, pp. 174, 178.
169. PRO, PC 2/45/460.
170. York House Books, 35, ff.218v–219v, 230.

Council of the Marches, valued the advice of the assize judges in reviewing candidates suitable for the shrievalty.[171] After 1635 the justices were frequently called upon to settle rating disputes arising from ship money assessments.[172] Most commonly, they were presented with questions concerning the administration of the poor law. At Norwich in 1633 they were asked about the settlement of single mothers and their bastards and whether taking apprentices was compulsory.[173] In this case the enquiry led to the promulgation by Justice Heath of thirty-eight 'resolutions' which were transmitted by the other judges to their circuits. These covered as well as apprenticeship and complex bastardy cases, property law, the powers of constables, lodgers, poor relief, service, and 'what is accounted a lawful settling in a parish and what not'.[174] Heath's resolutions were evidently a welcome guide to the JPs of the 1630s;[175] they were even included in the 1661 edition of the manual for magistrates, *The Complete Justice*.[176] The assize judges not only corrected procedural slips made by local JPs, they offered a welcome source of legal and administrative expertise to the amateurs responsible for the preservation of the peace.[177]

From the point of view of the king and Council, the judges provided a rare, indeed unique, occasion of direct contact between the centre and the locality – as Bacon put it, 'to represent to the people the graces and cares of the king; and again upon your return to present to the king the distastes and griefs of the people'.[178] The first of the functions was always more emphasized, the judges being used to convey, personally and directly, royal orders to the counties. So in 1630 the judges were instructed to order JPs to greater diligence in fining absentees from church;[179] in 1635 the king required the judges on the Western circuit to urge JPs to take more care to secure good sureties upon recognizances and to be cautious in discharging debts.[180] In 1630 a signed letter was sent to the Western Circuit asking the judges to summon to the assizes the commissioners appointed for draining King's Sedgemoor.[181] Judges devoted to the king's service

171. Ellesmere MS 7279.
172. For example, PRO, PC 2/49/241; *HMC Cowper II*, p. 153.
173. Tanner MS 288, f.266–270v.
174. T.G. Barnes (ed.) *Somerset Assize Orders, 1629–1640* (Somerset Record Soc., 65, 1959), pp. 63–70.
175. *Ibid.*, p. xxviii.
176. A.J. Fletcher, *Reform in the Provinces* (New Haven and London, 1986), p. 94.
177. Cockburn, *History of the Assizes*, pp. 170–1; cf. J.S. Cockburn (ed.) *Western Circuit Assize Orders, 1629–1648* (Camden Soc., 4th series, 17, 1976), for examples of orders resolving local difficulties and disputes over rates for repair of roads and bridges, poor relief and legal settlement, especially of bastards.
178. Quoted in Cockburn, *History of the Assizes*, p. 154.
179. Kent Archives Office, quarter sessions, QSO W1, f.29v.
180. PRO, SO 1/2, f.229v, 6 July.
181. PRO, SO 1/2, f.8.

could at times act like zealous intendants in executing government policy. In 1639 Finch told Laud how he nipped in the bud a protest against ship money at the Exeter assizes. Before the Grand Jury and assembly of justices he reminded Sir Richard Strode, a protagonist of the petition, of his Star Chamber fine 'and other symptoms of his unquiet spirit'. And from these he 'took my rise in general . . . to put them in mind how often their state had been abused by men who cloaked their own ambitions or malicious ends under pretext of zeal to the common liberty'.[182] Finch's strategy did the trick: the Grand Jury threw out Strode's protest to hear Finch expound on Charles I's happy government. But not all assize judges were like Finch, nor uncritical instruments of royal wishes. Justice Yelverton, we recall, at a meeting with the prebendaries of Durham in 1629 declared his support for Smart's controversial sermon and his personal objection to organs, church music and ceremonies favoured by the bishop (and the king).[183] Justice Richardson resisted royal instructions to permit church ales in Somerset and made his sympathy for those who opposed them publicly known.[184] Richardson, for his pains, was demoted to the less attractive Home Circuit.[185] Such cases apart, the judges and the assizes in general provided a valuable vehicle of communication to a county auditory. In part, the assize sermon offered a forum where homilies on obedience, justice and service might be delivered to the sheriffs, constables and others in the presence of 'lions under the throne'.[186] More importantly, the judges addressed the assizes on the priorities of government and received their brief before leaving for the circuits in their 'charge', an address usually delivered by the Lord Keeper in Star Chamber.

The historian of the assizes has argued that after the mid-Jacobean years charges declined in importance and resorted to generalities.[187] This is only partly true; for the period of personal rule when the use of the judges as administrators 'reached its fullest development', the charges may be read as a barometer of official emphases and preoccupations.[188] I have examined texts of the Lord Keeper's addresses to the judges for 1628, 1631, 1632, 1635, 1637, 1638 and 1640.[189] Together with notes by Coke from 1633 and by Windebank from the

182. *Cal. Stat. Pap. Dom., 1639*, p. 439, 8 Aug. 1639.
183. *Cal. Stat. Pap. Dom., 1629–31*, p. 15.
184. Above, pp. 353–4.
185. PRO, SP 16/269/55; Cockburn, *History of the Assizes*, p. 233.
186. See, for example, Robert Harris, *Two Sermons* (1628, STC 12853); Theophilus Taylor, *The Mappe of Moses* (1629, STC 23819).
187. Cockburn, *History of the Assizes*, p. 184.
188. *Ibid.*, p. 186.
189. The references for all these texts appear below; many have not been found or studied hitherto.

Trinity 1635 address,[190] they enable us to see how the priorities of royal policy, as delivered to the localities, shifted over the decade. The address for Trinity 1628 naturally reflects the circumstances of war in the Lord Keeper's urging vigilance with regard to musters, beacons, the careful keeping of watch and ward and the supervision of vagrants. The Lord Keeper's speech, however, opened with an announcement (to be reported to the county) of the king's particular concern at the increase of papists and sectaries, and an injunction to the judges to be strict in their prosecution of recusants and especially priests. The broader lessons learned from the war years, the sheer difficulties of organizing the localities for the war effort, may also lie behind the evident concern for the integrity of the state and commonwealth that permeates Coventry's speech. After general exhortations concerning the common good and the need for 'every particular man' to subjugate his interest to 'the whole commonwealth', the Lord Keeper, in language that would provide the script for the Book of Orders two years later, 'furthermore . . . signified that his Majesty's pleasure was that they should . . . certify his Majesty of the state of the several places of the kingdom and how they found the counties governed and that they should cherish such as they found diligent and careful in the execution of justice and certify the names of such as they found negligent and careless'.[191] The address makes clear that the role of the judges of assize as supervisors of the local magistracy, formalized as we shall see in the Book of Orders, began to be emphasized during the war years. By the summer of 1632, the very different priorities of peace and social reform were reflected in the charge, for along with the repeated injunctions (which alone give the lie to any claim that the government was soft on Catholics) to vigilance in the apprehension of recusants, the Lord Keeper emphasized the enforcement of Lent and fish days, the prevention of enclosures that led to depopulation and the execution of orders against rogues and vagrants. Most of all, the charge explained at some length the reasons behind the forthcoming proclamation, ordering the gentry to their country residences: 'justices of peace' – Coventry told them he took his words from the king – 'should be at home to do justice'.[192] In 1633, in addition to general exhortations to advance religion and justice, the judges were told to oversee more carefully the orders promulgated for providing employment, and regulating alehouses.[193] In other words, social reform, good justice and effective local government were the central concerns

190. *Cal. Stat. Pap. Dom., 1633–4*, p. 352; *1635*, p. 128.
191. BL, Lansdowne MS 620, f.74; cf. *HMC Buccleuch-Whitehall I*, pp. 270–1 and below, pp. 456 ff.
192. Rawlinson MS A.128, ff.24v–26.
193. PRO, SP 16/255/44.

of the Lord Keeper's charge during the first half of the personal rule – the period we have designated the years of peace and reformation.

1635 marked a departure. The traditional concerns with justice and social order were still manifest. Judges were told to look for the corruption of sheriffs and jurors, to see that men of power did not manipulate the course of justice. The need to check depopulation, punish vagabonds, bind apprentices and control alehouses was, traditionally, urged. Indeed a new awareness that in the end the implementation of these policies depended on the parish officers led to the requirement that the assize judges help ensure that constables, headboroughs and tithing men be chosen 'as they ought to be (not people of little wealth, and as little understanding) but that they were elected out of the better sort of yeomenry'.[194] This year, however, there were new circumstances abroad and specific initiatives to promote: there were rumours of war and the king had set in order his militia and embarked on the equipment of a fleet from ship money, which was soon to be extended throughout the country. Accordingly, the judges were told to inform the gatherings of county gentry at the assizes that the sovereignty of the seas was not just an ancient right of the English crown, but one necessary for the safety of the realm. Without the protection of a greater fleet, English commodities could not be sold, nor could any security be preserved. Therefore, in announcing the second writ of ship money, the judges were 'to let the people know his Majesty's care to preserve the ancient dominion' and 'how just it is the king should take this way seeing all are concerned in it'.[195] Not only does Coventry's speech signal a shift from domestic matters to the international situation, it has a justificatory tone less in evidence before and suggests that the government was becoming more sensitive to the need to explain unusual courses. By 1637 that tone may be heard more clearly. Recusants, justice, the need to persuade JPs to attend assizes and sessions are recurring topics, but a sense of the need to respond to the unease generated by ship money dominates the text. Whilst acknowledging that actions had been brought by some, the Lord Keeper informed the judges that Yorkshire had responded promptly to the demand for £12,000 ship money. He instructed them to inform the localities of this example and of the judges' own resolution, in response to the king's query, that when the good and safety of the kingdom was at stake, the king had a right to exact the levy: 'The judges in their circuits to report the same that all men may take knowledge thereof and inform themselves, and this case shows that justice and sovereignty kiss each other.'[196] From the charge to the judges, as from the register

194. Rushworth, *Historical Collections*, II, pp. 294–7.
195. *Cal. Stat. Pap. Dom., 1635*, p. 128; cf. Twysden MS U47/47, Z1, p. 54.
196. Rawlinson MS C.827, 14 Feb. 1637.

of the Privy Council, we may read how the concerns with domestic reform were becoming swamped, during the second half of the personal rule, by the need to place the realm in a state of defence and by the administration of ship money for the fleet.

Significantly, from 1638 the issue of ship money fades from prominence in the charge, lending support to the suggestion I shall venture that Hampden's case may have resolved many doubts.[197] The rating disputes that preoccupied the Council from 1635 are attended to in Coventry's speech of June 1638, but as part of the broader business of local government rather than specifically in connection with ship money. Observing that petitions against unequal taxes came daily to the Council Board, the Lord Keeper opined: 'It is a heavy thing that those that are rich should put off all from themselves and lay it upon the poor and friendless, that is the general case whether for the levying of men, providing of munition etc., generally I find the landlord finds a way to ease his own demesne and lays his burden upon his tenants.'[198] The concern for social justice and fair treatment of the poor also prompted the orders to the justices to examine complaints about prices, the devices of engrossers to raise them and the activities of the clerks of the market who were not without blemish in the execution of their business – 'it behoves you the justices of assize to take some pains to reform these cases'. In general the judges were reminded of the excellent rules issued eight years earlier and reprimanded for having 'failed to do as it was expected from you' in seeing them implemented. Hinting that he had often raised other particular matters with them, Coventry kept his speech to a few heads and left the rest to their wisdom. For the most part, his address seems to return to the social issues of the earlier 1630s. Several phrases, however, give this address a significant topicality. First, the reference to the provision of men and munitions points to the preparations for war against the Scots which, only days earlier, Charles I had told the Marquis of Hamilton he was making.[199] Secondly, commanding a vigilant watch over recusants to which 'you have been constantly and continuously called upon', Coventry's speech acknowledges directly the suspicion of some that the bishops and the king himself were tainted by popery. Accurately predicting that great peril might ensue from such rumours, the Lord Keeper informed the judges of the proceedings against one Pickering of Shropshire for perpetrating such scandal and urged them to advertise it on their circuits, to 'beat down those scandalous

197. Below, pp. 728–9. The amount requested in 1638 was also much smaller and it may therefore have been thought that payment required no prompting.
198. Rawlinson MS B.243, ff.17–20, 14 June 1638.
199. Scottish Record Office, GD 406/1, Hamilton MS 10485; below, pp. 794–5.

rumours that all men may know the sincerity of the king's heart and how he doth distaste all backsliding in religion'.[200]

The last of the charges we shall examine was the first given by the new Lord Keeper, Baron Finch, on 13 February 1640.[201] At first reading it appears conventional enough, urging the judges to ensure that sheriffs and JPs do their duty, to maintain the church against papists and puritans, to deal with the increasing number of highwaymen and the alehouses that often harboured them. But there was evidently a tone of strident urgency too in Finch's homilies on the danger of popularity (the 'insolence of the vulgar') and the necessity of prompt ship money payment ('God forbid we should stay for provision of naval power till our enemies be floating upon us').[202] William Hawkins wrote to the Earl of Leicester of Finch's address to the judges that 'he exhorted them to maintain the port of their places and not value the cringing of the people and popular applause; and that they should be earnest in the matter of the ship money, thinking no man so base as to think his Majesty would demand it if there were not need'.[203] If Hawkins reported accurately, a new era in the employment of assize judges as 'the great surveyors of the kingdom' may have been beginning.[204]

Throughout the 1630s the king placed great emphasis on the role of the justices as overseers of social policy and social order. Their responsibility for collecting quarterly reports from JPs and sheriffs, instituted by the Book of Orders 'proved to be the apogee of their administrative power'.[205] Charles regarded them as successors to the Angevin justices in eyre; he spoke of their circuits as 'one of the chiefest ways of peace and government'.[206] When, along with the abolition of the court of Star Chamber, the charge to the judges was terminated, Charles wrote a circular letter to be read at the assizes as a necessary substitution for an important line of communication.[207] It is not easy to assess how 'indispensable' (to use Professor Barnes's term) the circuit judges were as a 'nexus of communication between the Privy Council and local government'.[208] We do not know how closely individual judges echoed at the assizes the priorities of the Lord Keeper's charge – or how far they adapted their discourse to their local

200. Rawlinson MS B.243, f.18v.
201. Rawlinson MS D.720, f.51; J. Nalson, *An Impartial Collection of the Great Affairs of State from the beginning of the Scotch Rebellion in 1639 to the Murder of Charles I* (2 vols, 1682–3), I, pp. 286–9.
202. Nalson, *Impartial Collection*, I, p. 288.
203. *HMC De Lisle and Dudley, VI*, p. 231, 13 Feb. 1640.
204. Nalson, *Impartial Collection*, I, p. 289.
205. Cockburn, *History of the Assizes*, p. 186.
206. Rawlinson MS B.243.
207. Twysden MS U47/47, Zi, p. 155.
208. Barnes, *Somerset Assize Orders*, p. xx.

auditors.[209] The Long Parliament's anxiety to determine who went on circuit is suggestive.[210] It is clear that some judges like Finch pressed government policies with zeal, if not tact. In 1640 Justice William Jones told the Lord Keeper that in his charge at Abingdon he had argued that, in the name of defence, the king could claim a power over men's lands and goods.[211] But the divisions of the bench over the ship money case made it unlikely that others went so far. More generally, the repeated injunctions to enforce apprenticeship and vagrancy orders lends support to the view that 'the judges lacked the will and the inclination to become an intendancy'.[212] They could not have done so even had they wished to, for the circuit judges knew too little of the localities they rode to involve themselves in the details of local administration and politics. In the first place they did not remain on the same circuit. And whilst the frequency with which they were moved should not be exaggerated (Hutton rode the Midland circuit for twelve years, Jones the Oxford from 1621 to 1640), there were thirty-five changes of pairing between 1631 and 1640, which must have limited the development of local knowledge and connections.[213] More limiting still was the short time allowed for the assizes of each county and the number of criminal proceedings that had to be rushed through in the two or three days twice a year in order to clear the gaols.[214] Such a schedule must often have made little more than a pious hope Coventry's order that they should examine whilst in each county 'how the king's peace is kept, how the king's people is used, what oppressions or enormities and to find and apply the remedies'.[215] In a sense other than that intended by the Lord Keeper, the circuit judges were only 'visitors of the kingdom'. As Thomas Scott the elder put it in an assize sermon at Norwich, the judges might be the eyes of the state, but they in turn needed to see by the eyes of others, especially the justices of the peace.[216]

The commission of the peace

Scott's metaphor brings out sharply the unique nature of the English polity in which, for all the occasional visitor from Westminster, local

209. See, however, Rushworth, *Historical Collections*, II, p. 364.
210. Barnes, *Somerset Assize Orders*, p. xxii.
211. *Cal. Stat. Pap. Dom., 1640*, pp. 512–13.
212. Fletcher, *Reform in the Provinces*, p. 51.
213. *Ibid.*, p. 44; Barnes, *Somerset Assize Orders*, p. xv; See Cockburn, *History of the Assizes*, appendix 1. The average tenure was $1\frac{1}{2}$ to 4 years; on the Home circuit for example it was 3 years (Herrup, *Common Peace*, p. 57).
214. Cockburn, *History of the Assizes*, chs 6, 7; Barnes, *Somerset Assize Orders*, p. xvii.
215. *Cal. Stat. Pap. Dom., 1633–4*, p. 352.
216. I owe this information to Peter Lake. Cf. Lake, 'Constitutional consensus and puritan opposition in the 1620s: Thomas Scott and the Spanish match', *Hist. Journ.*, 25 (1982), pp. 805–25.

government remained in the hands of local men, most importantly the JPs. From its inception the commission of the peace contained a weakness. There was an inherent limitation to the effectiveness of a government placed in the hands of unpaid local gentry who were not without their own interests – interests which were not always harmonious with the directives of Whitehall. An enclosing JP, to cite a case, was unlikely to be a strict enforcer of the statutes and proclamations against enclosing. In general, however, the system (perhaps arrangement is a better term) worked well if only (perhaps especially) because of the central government's sense of the need at times to adjust its orders to local needs and circumstances. England may not have been an 'absolutist' state, but it remained remarkably free of the endemic local revolts that occurred in seventeenth-century France. However, if the inbuilt limitations to central control help explain the success of the commission of the peace, that very success in turn created a further problem: a vast increase in the business and burdens placed on the JPs' shoulders by the end of the sixteenth century. In his *Eirenarcha*, first published in 1581, William Lambarde had referred to the 'stacks' of statutes for the enforcement of which JPs were responsible. The many editions his treatise for magistrates went through in the early seventeenth century reflects the numerous additions to those stacks, and the increasing need of the amateur justice for some guide to them.[217] In 1630, in the fourth edition of *The Country Justice*, Michael Dalton listed some of those responsibilities conferred by statute, proclamation or Conciliar directive: enforcing fast days and attendance at church, binding apprentices, putting the poor to work, plague relief, the regulation of alehouses, the punishment of vagrants, relief of maimed soldiers and the impotent poor, the punishment of incontinence, the provision of corn, the maintenance of standards, weights, wages and prices, the repair of bridges, the conservation of rivers (and fish fry), the assessment of local rates and taxes, as well as all aspects of the presentation of felons: the taking of oaths and sureties, binding over, the referral to the assizes, commitment to gaol, whipping, branding, and confinement to the house of correction.[218]

The principal forum of local justice and administration was traditionally the quarter sessions, held four times yearly in each county. Whilst nominally the sessions were held in one place for the whole county (albeit in some counties such as Somerset and Dorset in different towns)[219] distance, topography and even custom meant that this was not always the case: in Lincolnshire because separate commissions

217. There were twelve editions by 1620.
218. M. Dalton, *The Country Justice* (4th edn, 1630, STC 6209).
219. E.H. Bates-Harbin, *Quarter Sessions Records for the County of Somerset, II, Charles I, 1625–39* (Somerset Record Soc., 24, 1908); Dorset Record Office, quarter sessions orders.

were issued for the ancient divisions of the shire, sessions were held in three different places.[220] Even where there was one session for the whole county, attendance was often sporadic and reflected the distance individuals had to travel. In Warwickshire during the 1630s, only three JPs from the north of the county attended the sessions held at Warwick.[221] The idea of the sessions as, like the assizes, an assembly of the county magistracy became less and less of a reality as pressure of business meant JPs had to do more and more of their work in smaller groups, individually and informally, within their immediate localities. In many parts of the country during the early seventeenth century, JPs increasingly began to meet, often monthly, in small groups of those who lived in proximity, in what became known as petty sessions. Indeed in some counties and towns this practice became formalized into a requirement.[222] In 1625, for example, the city of York ordered its JPs to convene in petty sessions once a month and required all justices and aldermen to reside in their charge; absentees from this sessions were also fined 20s. plus 5s. each day they failed to attend.[223] In Northamptonshire, according to Sir Edward Montagu, the justices met regularly (every three weeks) in petty sessions, in order to conduct business more efficiently.[224] In Essex there were petty sessions and smaller gatherings of two or three JPs.[225] The manuals for magistrates began to register these developments. Dalton's *Country Justice* contained, as its title announced, 'the practice of the justice of the peace and of their sessions' – because, Dalton acknowledged, in reality the bulk of the JPs' business was the daily administration of justice and affairs out of sessions.[226] *The Country Justice* explained therefore the powers of JPs acting in small groups or alone (new powers to convent, hear, attach) and a guide to the exercise of their jurisdiction within their vicinities. Another manual, *The Complete Justice*, offered an alphabetical 'compendium of the particulars incident to JPs either in sessions or out of sessions'.[227] The attitude of Whitehall to these developments was ambivalent. The king and Council recognized the desirability of more frequent and smaller meetings: in 1628 among state paper propositions to enlarge the powers of JPs we find a suggestion that each justice should take responsibility for a particular area.[228] And yet, Laud believed 'as most of the Lords do that the

220. C. Holmes, *Seventeenth Century Lincolnshire* (Lincoln, 1980), p. 83.
221. Fletcher, *Reform in the Provinces*, p. 109.
222. *Ibid.*, p. 123.
223. York House Books, 35, ff.68v, 86, 125.
224. *HMC Buccleuch-Whitehall I*, p. 271; cf. below, pp. 458–9.
225. B.W. Quintrell, 'The government of the county of Essex, 1603–42' (University of London, Ph.D. thesis, 1965), pp. 52–3.
226. Dalton, *Country Justice*, p. 19.
227. *The Complete Justice* (1638, Bodleian Antiq. fE. 1638, 15).
228. PRO, SP 16/89/17.

division of the counties into several divisions between the justices of the peace is the dividing and distracting of the king's service'.[229] The Lord Keeper agreed: 'that any Justice of Peace should appropriate to himself any part of the county is a thing intolerable'.[230] What the Council wanted was both active out of sessions service and diligent full attendance at the sessions, so as to co-ordinate activity and responsibility across the county. The Book of Orders, as we shall see, required all JPs to meet monthly in petty sessions and to report monthly to the sheriff, who was in turn to forward all reports to the justice of assize. Like other written directories, the orders attempted to reinvigorate individual JPs and to promote their co-operation for the effective government of the county.

Quarter sessions records for the 1630s reveal no radical changes in the nature of the business of the commission of the peace: apprenticeship, rogues and vagrants, alehouses, bastardy cases, sabbath breaching, inmates, highway and bridge repairs, petty theft, assault, recusancy, breach of the peace are the usual fare, together with some colourful characters and moral offences (chasing a buck in a West Riding park; in the North Riding, a man 'abusing himself in church at Rashelf, being drunk').[231] But the social pressures of the decade and the rising costs of supporting maimed soldiers and the poor do seem to have produced a larger number of disputes over parish rates and assessments, which vie with bastardy and alehouses as the most frequent cases at the sessions. In general, the Caroline records suggest a sharp upward turn in the graph of escalating business that had been rising steadily from the beginning of the century. In Cheshire, for example, the bench had issued 429 orders in the 1610s; by the 1630s the number had risen above 750.[232] The sessions were meeting longer – for two, three and even more days, rather than one – and there were signs of a recognition that more efficient procedures were required in order to cope with business. In October 1635 it was ordered at the quarter sessions in Kent that the clerk of the peace should enter in a ledger all the acts of the sessions so that it might be presented at the next meeting for perusal.[233] The North Riding of Yorkshire the same year instituted a special annual meeting to enquire into the activities of parish officers.[234] Still, the justice dispensed at the sessions was often rough: in Dorset

229. Harleian MS 4022, f.17, 7 May 1634.
230. *Ibid.*, ff.17v–18.
231. J. Lister (ed.) *West Riding Sessions Records II* (York Archaeological Soc., 54, 1915), p. 33; J.C. Atkinson (ed.) *Quarter Sessions Records* (North Riding Record Soc., 4, 1886), p. 52. Cf. J. Wake (ed.) *Quarter Sessions Records of the County of Northampton* (Northamptonshire Record Soc., 1, 1924).
232. Fletcher, *Reform in the Provinces*, pp. 87–8.
233. Kent Archives Office, QS OW1, f.78.
234. Atkinson, *North Riding Quarter Sessions*, p. 33.

responsibility for a bastard was pinned on Richard Genge for no other reason than that he had exchanged love tokens with the mother, Eleanor Chilcott, who had blamed another for her condition; Joanne Guy, who became a vagrant when her master died, was whipped and sent back to the parish of her birth.[235] And for all the developments in archives and procedure, the administration of the sessions by no means always ran strictly to form. In Leicestershire in 1631, the clerk of the peace boldly formed, on the direction of Sir John Skeffington, an order on a petition that the bench had rejected, and recorded it as an official order of the sessions. When he was discovered and challenged, he protested, probably truthfully, that those who complained had often asked him to do the same thing![236]

The quarter sessions, the incident reminds us, was a major forum of county politics as well as administration. For many the inducement to attend, as with the assizes, was as much the social gathering of the gentry as the business of the bench. Sir Francis Wortley, the Earl of Clifton was told, came up from London to Nottinghamshire to the sessions and sat on the bench for only an hour or so, 'and having according to his old custom a harsh passage or two with Sir Hardolphe Visse' departed on his journey towards York.[237] Attendance varied – with the attractiveness of the town, distance, the state of the roads, as well as personal interest such as Wortley's. In Warwickshire and Shropshire attendance was low, averaging only eleven in the latter case in the decade of personal rule; in Essex it was higher, usually well over twenty. 'In counties where the bench was peripatetic,' Professor Fletcher concludes, 'attendance averages around eight to twelve were typical.'[238] Averages, however, tell only part of the story. In the spring of 1639, in the midst of the Scots war, the Earl of Kingston wrote to Sir Gervase Clifton that 'I was conjured to the last . . . Sessions by my good neighbour Mr Moseley, lest it should have failed for want of a quorum'.[239] Clearly efforts to increase attendance met with only partial success. When in his 1637 charge to the assize judges, Lord Keeper Coventry described JPs who did not attend quarter sessions as guilty of wilful perjury, his extravagant language owed much to the scale of the problem.[240] It also manifested the importance the Council attached to the sessions (along with the assizes) as the central institution of county government. In the charge given by Henry Hastings, Earl of Huntingdon, as *custos rotulorum* of the county of Leicestershire in 1638

235. Dorset Record Office, quarter sessions orders, ff.195v, 311.
236. Huntington Library, Hastings MS 8538.
237. Clifton MS Cl/C 220: Thomas Hughes to Clifton.
238. Fletcher, *Reform in the Provinces*, p. 109.
239. Clifton MS Cl/C 272, 29 April 1639.
240. Rawlinson MS C.827.

we have a fine example of how important an occasion the sessions could be. In a language clear and lighthearted, Huntingdon addressed his fellow members of the bench and the freeholders of the grand jury, mixing personal touches with an encomium on the common law and a powerful exhortation to duty. He gave a model explanation of the process of criminal law and the role of jury presentments and trials; he then delivered his charge concerning the service of God, the quiet governing of the county and the diligent mustering of troops. Most importantly, he closed urging the county to 'give the King your hearts' and relieve him with supplies, adding 'The speediness of the performance adds much to the value of the thing whether it be either with ship money, loans or any other ways wherein we may express our dutiful and serviceable affections unto his Majesty, for all our happiness consisteth in his Majesty's welfare.'[241] Huntingdon's charge reminds us how in some cases, where the chairman of the bench was a devoted servant of king and Council, the sessions could provide another platform for the effective and sympathetic communication of royal aims and policies.[242] Other charges were doubtless more briefly formal and less sympathetic to the needs of the king. Indeed quarter sessions could become a forum of county discontent as well as a stage for the advertisement of the court's programmes. Nottinghamshire entered on its sessions rolls the king's promise to raise no more loans;[243] in Northamptonshire the 'honourable bench' was urged to champion the discontents of the county in the matter of ship money.[244] A collection of individuals varying in their diligence, political and religious attitudes, priorities and perspectives, the quarter sessions, whilst they could be a channel for the local execution of central orders, were also the most public manifestations of the autonomy of the English county magistracy.

Though the Caroline government endeavoured to improve the efficiency, it made no attempt on the authority or even autonomy of the justices of the peace. Whilst assize judges were instructed to watch over local magistrates, JPs in turn were encouraged to report on the judges. Though Conciliar commissioners responsible to Whitehall were evidently mooted in early drafts of the Book of Orders, they were never appointed.[245] Coventry's quest for improved efficiency focused on securing a smaller band of active JPs, rather than the large numbers of indolent and absentees. In Kent the commission which had

241. Hastings MS, HAM Box 26: copy of charge of Earl of Huntingdon, as custos at Epiphany sessions, Leicester, 1638.
242. Cf. Fletcher, *Reform in the Provinces*, pp. 166–75.
243. *Ibid.*, p. 366.
244. Northamptonshire Record Office, Montagu MS 27, f.23.
245. PRO, SO 1/2, f.141; see below, pp. 459–60.

numbered ninety-seven in 1608 was reduced to sixty-three by 1636. Lancashire saw a drop from sixty-two to fifty-three over the period 1630 to 1640.[246] Beyond that, however, little changed. Coventry's expressed intention to dismiss from the commission all who failed to attend the sessions was certainly not executed; and his threat to sack any JPs who took tobacco on the bench was even less likely to have been effective.[247] In some counties – Somerset, Sussex and Worcestershire for example – there was a definite increase in the clerical membership of the bench.[248] But for the most part the same families recur on the early Stuart commissions, ancestral connection being perhaps a particularly important criterion to Charles I.[249] There is little evidence of attempts at political manipulation and none of any purge of JPs. In August 1625, it had been suggested that all JPs who had opposed the grant of supplies in parliament should be removed from the commission of the peace, but nothing came of the suggestion.[250] In 1636 and 1637 justices of the peace were required to take at the assizes an oath that they would hazard their lives against all conspiracies and rebellions against the king ('and if it shall come veiled under pretence of religion I hold it more abominable before God').[251] However, the principal purpose of administering the oath appears to have been a test less of loyalty than of diligence, Coventry employing it to dismiss all who did not appear to swear – 'a systematic paring away of dead wood in the commissions of the peace', as Professor Barnes has described it.[252] As yet there is little evidence to indicate that lack of co-operation over knighthood and forest fines, ship money or the Scots war resulted in dismissal from office, as had occurred earlier with the forced loan.[253] Indeed the experience of the loan may well have delivered the lesson that certain local gentlemen were all but indispensable to effective government in the county and that their removal was 'counter-productive'. During the years of personal rule Charles left the justices of the peace as independent governors of their localities, who carried out their duties, more or less diligently, in the context of personal interests, relationships and changing circumstances which were the essence of county politics.

246. Fletcher, *Reform in the Provinces*, p. 31; Wilkinson, 'Commission of the peace in Lancashire', p. 43.
247. Rawlinson MSS A.128, C.827.
248. Wilkinson, 'Commission of the peace in Lancashire', p. 49; Fletcher, *Reform in the Provinces*, p. 31.
249. Wilkinson, 'Commission of the peace in Lancashire', p. 54.
250. *Cal. Stat. Pap. Dom., 1625–49*, p. 155.
251. See, for example, Hampshire Record Office, Herriard MS 013.
252. T.G. Barnes, *Somerset, 1625–40: A County Government during the Personal Rule* (Oxford, 1961), pp. 305–6. There is no evidence of a more directly political motive here.
253. Though see the bald statement in Fletcher, *Reform in the Provinces*, p. 10.

It would be wrong, however, to conclude from such an observation that JPs during the 1630s were lacking in diligence or willingness to serve. There were assiduous attenders of the sessions like John Harrington of Somerset or Sir William Brereton and Thomas Mallory of Cheshire.[254] In Essex Sir William Masham and his brother-in-law Sir Thomas Barrington formed an 'outstandingly successful partnership' in enforcing social legislation.[255] Some JPs' notebooks suggest almost indefatigable diligence. Such evidence is not without problems, for the justices who kept the fullest records may well have been the most active; but private notebooks, because they were not intended for any other than personal use, offer an invaluable record of the remarkable sense of duty and pains of some JPs who may not have been as few in number as the notebooks that have survived. The JP of Sussex, for example, whose notebook for the two years 1633–5 is now in the Rawlinson manuscripts, clearly took his duties very seriously, acquainting himself with the towns, hundreds and villages of the county, drawing up precedents of use to the execution of his office, taking detailed notes on procedure and the forms of various warrants (for impressing soldiers, for a search, to distrain for relief of the poor) and formulating rules for combating the spread of plague and precepts for routine local administration. The impression of diligence is confirmed by the attention he gave to watch and ward, the maintenance of beacons, the trained bands, the carriage of shipping timber and payments for St Paul's cathedral.[256] In Kent, Sir Edward Dering, though he probably already harboured reservations about some aspects of royal policy during the 1630s, stands as another model JP. His surviving papers include 'a remembrance of all recognizances taken, of all the principal warrants sent and other the most material business' he performed from 1632, together with some memoranda of his earlier years as JP.[257] Dering's concern with alehouses and bastards some historians might wish to attribute to his commitment to the culture of discipline that, it has been argued, bound magistrates of godly sympathies. But Dering's recording of assize orders, his efforts to see roads and bridges repaired, his concern with poor relief, his thoroughness in enforcing the Book of Orders and proclamations against inmates, his massive labours in connection with knighthood fines and payments for St Paul's all speak to a broader and willing obedience to Conciliar orders and directives. The thoroughness of the Kent magistracy descended to often small details: when Francis

254. *Ibid.*, p. 147; J.S. Morrill, *Cheshire 1630–1660: County Government and Society during the English Revolution* (Oxford, 1974), p. 16.
255. Fletcher, *Reform in the Provinces*, p. 145.
256. Rawlinson MS B.431.
257. Dering MS U570/01.

Jennifer, asked to give account why he lived idle with no employment, replied that he was a soldier at Deal castle, Dering was sent to the Earl of Suffolk (Lord Warden of the Cinque Ports) in order to check.[258] But as well as his energy and effort, notebooks like Dering's also reveal how difficult it was for the most active and willing of justices to carry out all their duties. The sheer numbers of recurring indictments for failing to repair roads and bridges or make payments for poor relief show how difficult it was, in a pre-bureaucratic age, to order local society. Even the offences of drunkenness and incontinence that preoccupied Dering could not be contained. And, as the minister John Bankes complained to Dering in January 1641, when there was, as in the case of Thanet, no JP within fourteen or fifteen miles, alehouses and drunkenness went undetected and beyond all control.[259] There were limitations to the effective government of even the most industrious JPs; even those who worked as hard as Dering, or Jervoise and Wallop in Hampshire, depended ultimately on the subordinate officers – constables, overseers and churchwardens – to whom they referred many cases and from whom they derived information.

The constables

Even more than the JP, the constable was the workhorse of local government, upon whom the effective implementation of Conciliar directives depended. The constables were responsible in the hundreds and parishes in which they dwelt for all policing and keeping the peace (dealing with drunkards, riots, executing warrants, raising the hue and cry); the enforcement of orders and proclamations concerning alehouses, inmates, recusants and poor relief; military affairs: musters, the press and the parish armour; and taxation both national and local – purveyance, payments for St Paul's, ship money and military charges, local rates for bridge and highway repair, the poor house and house of correction, relief of maimed soldiers and so on. In addition they often had the responsibility for local duties: guarding village crops, maintaining hedges and sheep dams, suppressing vermin.[260] It was their local knowledge that made them potentially so valuable to the Council and the justices. The constables, the Council told the county of Essex in response to a petition concerning purveyance payment, 'do best understand the state of the county to proportion the assessment'.[261] In 1635, in York, in just over one month (May–June) the constables

258. Kent Archives Office, QSO W1, f.78.
259. Dering MS U350 C2/88.
260. See J.R. Kent, *The English Village Constable, 1580–1642* (Oxford, 1986).
261. Bodleian, Firth MS C.4, p. 537.

were called in by the aldermen to give account of their dealings with beggars, inmates, ship money and to confer with the Council about a course for setting the poor on work.[262] If the importance of their place is not in doubt, the status, character and industry of the typical constable remains a subject of controversy. Most hundred or high constables were substantial freeholders and farmers. But the ranks of the parish or petty constables could contain husbandmen and tenant farmers of a wide range of wealth and local standing. Where Professor Barnes characterized the constables of Somerset as men of mean condition, illiterate, ignorant and negligent, Dr Kent defends them as often of substantial position (yeomen or even lesser gentry), experience of local office, dedication to duty and effectiveness.[263] Contemporary commentators were as divided in their assessments. 'A constable,' William Fennor wrote in *A True Description of a Compter* (1629), 'is the preserver of peace, the attacker of vice and the intelligencer of injuries';[264] his authority, Dalton reminded readers of *The Country Justice*, unlike the JPs, did not terminate with the death of the king.[265] 'As proud as a new made constable' was evidently a contemporary proverb and suggests a respect for and desire to attain such office.[266] However, assize sermons frequently exhorting constables to do their duty and not to tip off suspects so they might flee from justice suggest a rather different picture.[267] And the caricature in Earle's *Microcosmographie*, of the constable often drunk and caught napping, is a familiar figure on the early Stuart stage.[268] Clearly there was no typical constable, the holders of local office being as varied as the economies and structures of their hundreds and villages, most of all as the possibilities of human nature itself. Dr Kent's findings, however, do suggest that during the 1630s the constables were recruited from men of lower status and newer families as the burdens of the Book of Orders and ship money made the office less attractive.[269]

Certainly, the constables and the parish constables in particular did not, like the JPs, bring to their office a social rank and distance that endowed them with natural authority. In consequence, whilst in general they enjoyed more co-operation from their neighbours than

262. York House Books, 35, f.280.
263. Barnes, *Somerset*, p. 76; Kent, *Village Constable*, ch. 4, esp. pp. 89, 100, 140, 152; cf. K. Wrightson, 'Two concepts of order: justices, constables and jurymen in seventeenth-century England', in J. Brewer and J. Styles (eds) *An Ungovernable People: The English and their Law in the Seventeenth and Eighteenth Centuries* (1980), pp. 21–46.
264. W. Fennor, *A True Description of a Compter* (1629, STC 10786), p. 51.
265. Datlon, *Country Justice*, p. 12.
266. Fennor, *True Description of a Compter*, p. 13.
267. For example, Taylor, *Mappe of Moses*, p. 47.
268. J. Earle, *Microcosmographie* (1628, STC 7439), p. 20. Cf. Jonson, *Bartholomew Fair*, Act IV, scene v.
269. Kent, *Village Constable*, pp. 72, 109, 130; cf. *Cal. Stat. Pap. Dom., 1636–7*, p. 490.

some have assumed, the job could be a difficult one in a society where status counted for more than office. Francis Haycock who, when arrested in York at 11 p.m. by Francis Cotton for being drunk and disorderly, 'told the said constable he cared not for him a fart' may not have been untypical in his lack of deference.[270] Even a clergyman in Kent, Reverend Hutchinson, when told to stop drinking and go home, reviled the constable with 'beastly language'.[271] When it comes to arresting drunks, a policeman's lot has never been a happy one. Often it was a dangerous job. In Bristol in May 1636 it took three constables to arrest the soused Humphrey Coop and even then double-strengthened by (and like) the beer he had over-indulged in, he 'resisted the constables and gave them some blows and thumps in the breast.'[272] Even the fairer sex were no less troublesome: in Malton, in the North Riding of Yorkshire, three women appeared at quarter sessions for assaulting a constable;[273] in 1636 at Bristol Mary Aray struck the constable who was sent to bring her before the sessions.[274] Constables sent to distrain for ship money default, often, as we shall see, encountered pitchforks and other improvised weapons wielded by angry female hands.[275] Such challenges to the constable were often not strictly punished; Sir Thomas Walsingham, JP for Kent, only bound John Blanken to keep the peace 'for beating the constable'.[276] During the later 1630s little could protect them from threats and violence, as ship money together with military charges for the Scots war made them more and more unpopular.[277]

The constable's position was uncomfortable in other ways. Because he was intimately acquainted with the parishioners in his jurisdiction, because he usually held his office for only one year and then had to return to normal life in a small community, the exercise of authority, still more the infliction of punishment, was fraught with problems. There are several cases where constables allowed criminal friends, relatives or neighbours to slip away: in Dorset constables allowed one arrested for battery to escape and permitted the father of a bastard to leave so as to avoid maintenance.[278] When we encounter the chilling order to a constable of York to arrange the whipping of his son-in-law for stealing a pewter platter we see how close relationships could be and why the constable might not always have been zealous in the

270. York House Books, 35, f.118v.
271. Dering MS U570/01, f.74.
272. Bristol Record Office, QS 04446, f.57.
273. Atkinson, *North Riding Quarter Sessions*, p. 97.
274. Bristol Record Office, QS 04446, f.50v.
275. *Cal. Stat. Pap. Dom., 1637–8*, p. 198. Below, pp. 717–19.
276. Kent Archives Office, Dalison MS U522/04, f.21.
277. Kent, *Village Constable*, pp. 303–4.
278. Dorset Record Office, quarter sessions orders, 1625–37, f.214.

detection of crime.[279] Local communities had their own priorities and concerns when it came to law enforcement and often reacted less harshly to vagrants and alehouses than Councillors ever fearful of the many-headed monster. Several constables were presented at quarter sessions in the 1630s for not apprehending rogues, or for letting vagrants go unpunished.[280] Constables too were placed in a difficult, indeed ambivalent, position as collectors of unpopular rates and taxes – especially when the burden fell on their own parishes and themselves. In Somerset they were found negligent in organizing relief for the plague-ridden town of Taunton;[281] in April 1633 the JPs of Berkshire reported constables remiss in collecting monies for St Paul's;[282] many constables, particularly in the later 1630s, protested their inability to collect ship money when they could not secure the co-operation of their local communities in assessing.[283] Fearful of recriminations and lawsuits as well as violence, they became increasingly unwilling to distrain the goods of those who refused to pay.[284] In some instances, as local figures the constables championed the resistance to unpopular charges rather than trying to levy them from their neighbours.[285] The Earl of Bridgewater suspected that high constables in Shropshire had been movers behind the Grand Jury presentment there against payments for the muster master; his suspicions appear to have been well founded.[286] Many constables were branded 'refractory' by sheriffs and the Council; several were gaoled for outright refusal to perform their duties or outright opposition to orders.[287]

The unattractiveness of the job (as well as the risk of being out of pocket) prompted some refusals. Whilst this number should not be exaggerated (only three cases are found in Warwickshire)[288] there were more refusals, it would appear, in the 1630s than in any other decade of the late Tudor and early Stuart years.[289] In Essex in 1631 the burden of levying composition money led some of the more substantial freeholders to decline the office: 'by the extraordinary trouble and danger

279. York House Books, 35, f.217v.
280. Cf. Kent, *Village Constable*, p. 201; Wake, *Quarter Sessions Records of . . . Northampton*, p. 75; Bates-Harbin, *Quarter Sessions Records for . . . Somerset*, p. 274.
281. Barnes, *Somerset Assize Orders*, p. 3.
282. *Cal. Stat. Pap. Dom., 1633–4*, p. 9.
283. For example, Buxton MSS, Box 96: petition of Matthew Stevenson and Roger Reynolds.
284. Buxton MSS, Box 96: Council to Buxton, 30 June 1638.
285. E. Cope (ed.) *Proceedings of the Short Parliament of 1640* (Camden Soc. 4th series, 19, 1977), p. 287; *Cal. Stat. Pap. Dom., 1638–9*, p. 35; Bankes MS 42/46.
286. Ellesmere MSS 7660, 7667–9.
287. Many were called to the Board in September 1637. See, for exmaple, *Cal. Stat. Pap. Dom., 1637*, p. 437.
288. A. Hughes, *Politics, Society and Civil War in Warwickshire, 1620–1660* (Cambridge, 1987), p. 278.
289. Kent, *Village Constable*, pp. 77–8.

imposed on them . . . the ablest and fittest men refuse that office to the great prejudice of the country'.[290] In some counties, with the responsibilities for ship money, refusals to serve increased: in Somerset there were no fewer than twelve such cases between 1635 and 1638;[291] and the instances of refusal were growing in Kent.[292] Beyond exhortations to appoint the right men and threats against the refusers or negligent, there was little the justices or Council could do. In Kent in 1640 John Dyve, elected constable for Ashford, was bound over for his refusal to serve: 'for that such contempts as these and the like are very dangerous, of evil consequence tending much to the neglect of his Majesty's service'.[293] Dyve, like others reluctant – Chris Woolcott and William Markall of Somerset for instance – was ordered to serve.[294] But an unwilling constable was not likely to be zealous in the conduct of his office, and there were limits to the supervision and pressure that JPs could exercise over their subordinates. The JPs of Shropshire reported in 1634 that 'having fined the petty constables ten shillings a piece for the use of the poor of their parishes, their diligence has been so quickened that wandering beggars are despatched out of their parts and the true poor people abiding are better maintained'.[295] The corporation of York appointed two men in each parish to keep a check on the constables.[296] But such tactics were less successful in the late 1630s when the failings of the constables were the tip of a larger iceberg of discontent in their communities; and when the pressure they faced from below loomed even greater than the injunctions to duty from above.

Herein lay the strengths and weaknesses of the constabulary. Their office 'often required a rather careful balancing act if they were to attempt to satisfy both their superiors and their fellow inhabitants'.[297] For most of the decade, that equilibrium was more or less preserved. Probably most carried out their duties adequately and retained the goodwill of their communities. Pressure from justices of assize and JPs and the monthly meetings to which constables were called to account did produce in general greater vigour and activity in suppressing vagrants and providing for the poor.[298] There were model constables like William Cooke of Lancashire who was held in such esteem that the

290. Firth MS C.4, p. 535.
291. Barnes, *Somerset*, p. 241.
292. Kent Archives Office, QS OW1, for example, ff.115, 119v; *ibid.*, U522/04, f.33.
293. Kent Archives Office, QS OW1, f.115.
294. Bates-Harbin, *Quarter Sessions Records for . . . Somerset* p. 303; Barnes, *Somerset Assize Orders*, p. 36.
295. *Cal. Stat. Pap. Dom., 1633–4*, p. 524.
296. York House Books, 35, f.112v.
297. Kent, *Village Constable*, pp. 279–80.
298. *Ibid.*, pp. 202, 226–8.

bench wanted him to serve a third term.[299] Hugh Tresse of Offham in Kent was evidently equally well regarded; for having been three times churchwarden, twice surveyor of the highway, and twice constable, in 1637 he was chosen again.[300] On the other hand the eighty-year-old Gabriel Wright, constable of Little Smeaton in the West Riding, was not likely to have been very effective, being infirm and residing over a mile from town;[301] no more impressive was the constable of Gillinge, Yorkshire who appointed 'a poor old blind man, not able to see the light of a candle to watch the whole town';[302] or William Thompson, constable of Edgeware, who deserted his place with the onset of plague.[303] Beyond the examples of diligence and negligence, the safest generalization is that when it was impossible, as it increasingly became towards 1640, to balance central demands and local feeling, the constables were more inclined to tilt towards the latter not least because 'it was to their fellow inhabitants that they were obliged to render account at the end of their term'.[304] If the 'crux of reform in the parishes' depended upon 'the securing of proficient co-operation from the . . . constables' that may ultimately have involved securing the co-operation of the local communities themselves.[305]

The Privy Council and local government

Though JPs and their subordinates were local men and often spokesmen for their local communities, they were also accountable to the Privy Council for the exercise of their office. The Privy Council was responsible for the overseeing of all aspects of local government and for ensuring that local officials executed royal orders. After the promulgation of the Book of Orders it perused the reports of the JPs and took action on that (and other) information it received. Historians have tended to underestimate the importance of the Council in local affairs; though often distant, Whitehall could never be far from the mind of the local magistracy whose position depended on the Council's approval.[306] A summons to the Council Board for failure to execute an order was itself a major inconvenience and expense, beside the fear of

299. Quintrell, 'Proceedings of the Lancashire justices of the peace', p. 20.
300. Kent Archives Office, QS OW1, f.85v.
301. Lister, *West Riding Sessions Records*, p. 67.
302. Atkinson, *North Riding Quarter Sessions*, p. 69.
303. *Cal. Stat. Pap. Dom., 1629–31*, p. 375.
304. Kent, *Village Constable*, p. 63.
305. Fletcher, *Reform in the Provinces*, p. 117.
306. Cf. my 'Culture, politics and the English civil war', *Hunt. Lib. Quart.*, 57 (1988), pp. 122–4; and see C. Holmes's discussion of 'brokers' in *Seventeenth Century Lincolnshire*, ch. 6.

any punishment that might be inflicted there. For a JP or deputy lieutenant, being removed from his commission involved a loss of local prestige and probably dangerous subordination to a local rival. Often sharp words and the threat of summons quickened the indolent and blunted the nerve of the intransigent. The Earl of Manchester told the Duke of Buckingham in 1627 that the muster defaulters in Northamptonshire had been bound to appear at the Council Board, 'which was done in the face of the county and with demonstration of reproach and disgrace'.[307] During the collection of the forced loan, it is clear that many believed a summons to the Board sufficient to quell any opposition.[308] Throughout the 1630s it remained the Council's principal instrument of enforcement: constables, JPs, deputy lieutenants and particularly, as we shall see, ship money sheriffs were called to account for their failures or recalcitrance. From Shropshire, members of the Grand Jury were summoned.[309] Perhaps even more important, the gentry, it would appear, were conscious of the watchful eyes of the Council on their activities. Sir Edward Montagu was advised not to pursue any enclosures against Council orders: 'The state hath a severe eye upon all these', he was warned.[310] In Norfolk Sir John Holland advised his fellow deputy lieutenant Sir Thomas Hobart that, concerning the militia, 'the Lords I believe will listen after our diligence and there will be them at leisure to give intelligence'.[311] In the fierce competition for local honour and office, a black mark in the Council's books was not to be risked lightly.

At times the Council determined to make an example of an offender. In 1634, for example, the Board determined to proceed against Robert Ridley, a muster defaulter from Yorkshire, with harsh punishment.[312] But it would be wrong to view the Council during the 1630s as the organ of a reign of terror, examining scores of local officials and inflicting sharp punishments. Privy Councillors were themselves well aware that successful government in the localities depended ultimately upon co-operation rather than confrontation with the leading local families. When we read accounts of examinations at the Board, such as that of William Mallory for refusing the loan, we are struck by the frankness of the exchange and the moderation of the Council's proceedings.[313] In 1629, Mr Clarke, one of the Merchant Adventurers, was commended for his plain dealing in admitting to the Board that

307. *Cal. Stat. Pap. Dom., 1627–8*, p. 15.
308. *Ibid.*, pp. 233, 236.
309. Ellesmere MSS 7628, 7630.
310. Montagu MS 15, f.46.
311. Tanner MS 177, f.19v.
312. PRO, PC 2/43/489.
313. Above, pp. 19–20.

it was the House of Commons' declaration against tonnage and poundage that had deterred the company from shipping its cloth.[314] Other examinations reinforce the impression that the Council preferred to conciliate rather than terrorize. In February 1629 the Earl of Huntingdon referred to the Board one Mr Foreman, a minister, for his default at the musters. Foreman, however, produced a letter to his interrogators, easing him of that duty. Accordingly the Council dismissed him, explaining that it intended to deal only with the wilfully refractory: 'if the minister be none of that rank, but one that only seeks ease in an overcharge and submits himself to what may be proportionable to his poor means, we have no desire to detain him here to his trouble or charge'.[315]

The distinction between resistance and a protest against overassessment, as rating disputes over ship money were to reveal, could be a matter of interpretation, even a grey area of ambiguity in which the refractory could take refuge. But the Council appears to have remained committed to fairness, and respectful of law and precedent. Despite the sharp words to the deputy lieutenants of Essex for their 'confronting of the counsel and directions of his Majesty and this board . . . with the counsels and direction of a Grand Jury . . . as if they and you at a public session had a controlling power over the acts of state', when the JPs who were summoned explained that they had proceeded according to a precedent of 1596 they were dismissed.[316] Almost incredibly the constables of Banbury were discharged on no better excuse than that no such service as that of collecting ship money had ever been required of them before.[317] In general the priority of the Council appears always to have been securing future co-operation rather than punishing past offences. So in November 1635, Richard Knightley, a muster defaulter, was discharged on a promise of conformity, vouched for by the Earl of Exeter.[318] Some from Oxford who were summoned in 1637 for refusing to take on the shrievalty were spared any punishment on promising that they would perform their duties.[319] Wentworth and Laud often feared that the Council proceeded too tenderly.[320] It would seem that only the persistent and vocal recalcitrant felt the sting of punishment: in most cases firm words were mingled with mild courses – and praise with punishment.

314. Tanner MS 72, f.1.
315. Hastings MS 4248.
316. Firth MS C.4, pp. 325–6.
317. J.S.W. Gibson and E.R.C. Brinkworth (eds) *Banbury Corporation Records* (Banbury Historical Soc., 15, 1977), pp. 165–6.
318. PRO, PC 2/45/228.
319. PRO, PC 2/47/190.
320. J. Blisse and W. Scott (eds) *The Works of Laud* (7 vols, Oxford, 1847–60), VI, part 2, p. 553; Knowler, *Strafford Letters*, II, p. 413.

Such a mixture was not always effective: as the JPs of Leicestershire told the Council, 'terrifying, threatening . . . some for fear value, others not at all'.[321] But mildness and tact with firmness could also function to activate without upsetting that sense of loyalty and service on which the operation of local government was based. Sir John Melton advised the Council to respond to complaints about the price of gunpowder in Yorkshire with a direction that it be purchased at the prices set – adding, 'and the more mildly and sooner this were done the better'.[322] His advice may well have been astute.

The Privy Council could not function simply as an instrument of uncomprising central control over the localities. It lacked independent bureaucracy and agents and it depended upon others for local information. Moreover as well as an executive organ, the Council served as an investigative body and a tribunal of appeal to which local officials in difficulties, common subjects aggrieved or parties in contention could resort for assistance, redress or arbitration.[323] If this was a traditional function of the Council, its importance was enhanced in the 1630s by the absence of parliaments. In the exercise of these roles, it was vital that the Council should not be viewed by the provinces as an alien or hostile institution.[324] During the decade of personal rule, taking up a problem that had taxed parliament, the Council embarked on investigations into the decay of the cloth trade, the success of which depended upon the assistance of the JPs of Wiltshire and Somerset.[325] The Board also received a multitude of private suits, petitions and complaints, the investigation and resolution of which involved referral to local officials. Complaints against Cornelius Vermuyden (the fen drainer),[326] the maintenance dispute between Mrs Bennett (a former nurse to the royal children) and her husband,[327] quarrels between the Earl of Leicester and St Martin's parish, between the governor and bailiffs of Yarmouth and the scores of petitions against ship money requirements, underline the fact that the Council was viewed as a judicial body which could assist with the maintenance of local peace and order, as well as be an organ of central directives.[328] This was a necessary role. In Kent, Sir Roger Twysden reflected on the potential dangers when the only appeal against ship money sheriffs – to the

321. *Cal. Stat. Pap. Dom., 1629–31*, p. 406.
322. Coke MS 60, 12 Jan. 1639.
323. Cf. P. Lake, 'The collection of ship money in Cheshire: a case study of the relations between central and local government', *Northern History*, 17 (1981), pp. 44–71.
324. Cf. K. Fincham, 'The judges' decision on ship money in February 1637: the reaction of Kent', *Bull. Inst Hist. Res.*, 57 (1986), p. 235.
325. PRO, PC 2/41/77.
326. PRO, PC 2/43/30.
327. PRO, PC 2/49/541–2.
328. PRO, PC 2/41/367.

Council – was seen as 'so full of trouble as poor men had rather suffer much than that way receive benefit'.[329] The Council's openness to complaint helped for much of the decade to sustain stable government, but it also meant that at times in response to local suits the Council had to compromise and adjust the very orders that it had issued.

When we discuss the Privy Council as a body for the overseeing of local government, we should never forget that it was a collection of individuals who were themselves men of substance and standing in the localities. This was, from the king's point of view, desirable, necessary and, especially after Buckingham's death, promoted. The forced loan, we have seen, owed its success to Privy Councillors returning to their localities to activate it.[330] The Book of Orders was to formalize a traditional expectation in requiring Councillors to oversee the areas in which they held their estates or wielded influence. Councillors usually returned to their county seats for long periods of the summer; even Secretary Sir John Coke found time to participate actively in the affairs of Derbyshire.[331] Yet although this was a source of strength to the authority of the Board, it was also another limitation on centralization. Like any other patrons, Councillors intervened on behalf of their tenants and clients and advanced their own interests in ways that did not always harmonize with the directives of the Board. In September 1629, for example, the Earl of Manchester requested the Earl of Huntingdon to spare Sir Henry Hastings the charge for providing arms levied on lands he had purchased in Leicestershire.[332] Lord Weston endeavoured on several occasions to protect Hampshire from the burden of the Council's demands.[333] Whilst the Council proved ready to punish its lesser officers, messengers and pursuivants for neglect of duties, as individuals Councillors did not always themselves present a model of obedience. In December 1632 the officers responsible for clearing the streets and hanging lights in London had occasion to complain to the Council of recalcitrants. Ironically they found 'the greatest difficulties are for the houses of noblemen and Privy Councillors . . . whom the said officers by reason of the respect due unto them knew not how to compel to the observance of such orders'.[334] The incident nicely illustrates how even at the highest level local and personal interests compromised central government. Together with its lack of capacity, the dual role of the Council and Councillors meant that Conciliar supervision of the localities functioned less through

329. Twysden MS U47/47, Z2, p. 198.
330. R. Cust, *The Forced Loan and English Politics, 1626–1628* (Oxford, 1987), pp. 112–13.
331. Cf. J. Robertson, 'Caroline culture: bridging court and country?' *History*, 75 (1990), pp. 294–5.
332. Hastings MS 9342.
333. For example, Herriard MS XLIV, I5.
334. PRO, PC 2/42/342.

power and strict command and more through persuasion and co-operation. It is a testament to the general stability and health of the regime that for most of the decade co-operation was secured.

The Councils of the North and the Marches

In parts of the realm, an agency of central government had a permanent and powerful presence. And those areas, the north and the Marches of Wales, both enjoyed local access to royal seats of justice without recourse to the courts at Westminster. The jurisdiction of the Councils for the North and the Marches had arisen from their distance and, more especially, from the need for strong government and defence in outlying areas that bordered on once hostile neighbours, the Scots and the Welsh. The Councils brought not only the authority of the Privy Council to the locality; but in the person of the president a direct representative of the monarchy itself. Undoubtedly during the sixteenth century, the Council of the North played a crucial role in the gradual reduction of northern independence to royal authority. Charles I was anxious to maintain the privileges of the Council as a bastion of royal justice in his northern capital, York. In June 1629 the king wrote to Viscount Wentworth, who had been appointed president the previous year, requiring him to see his instructions and decree performed 'by such ways as are used in Chancery', notwithstanding the prohibitions filed by common lawyers who were antagonistic to the equity jurisdiction of the court.[335] In 1632 Charles renewed the commission for the president and Council authorizing them to hear causes as in Star Chamber according to the procedure of the court of Chancery. If, they were told, a writ of habeas corpus were granted the party was still not to be discharged until he had performed the orders of the Council. The authority of the Council to stay proceedings in other courts was reaffirmed and the king delivered his intentions to allow no prohibitions which removed cases from its jurisdiction.[336] Though Charles clearly expressed his determination to uphold its authority, opposition to the court's jurisdiction did not cease: in December 1632 Wentworth complained to the Privy Council that Sir Thomas Gower (for the apprehension of whom he had issued a commission of rebellion) had fled to London to lodge with other 'rebels of the North' and claim exemption from the jurisdiction of the court.[337]

335. *Cal. Stat. Pap. Dom., 1628–9*, p. 585; cf. PRO, SO 1/1, f.227v.
336. Rushworth, *Historical Collections*, II, p. 158. See R.R. Reid, *The King's Council in the North* (1921), pp. 404–35.
337. *Cal. Stat. Pap. Dom., 1631–3*, p. 450: Wentworth to Privy Council, 1 Dec. 1632; Gardiner, *History of England*, VII, pp. 232–8.

In 1634 Sir Edward Osborne, vice-president of the Council, stressed the need to support one of its officers, Mr Turner, who had an action for false arrest brought against him by one Askwith whom he had detained on order of the court. Direct intervention was required, Osborne told Secretary Coke, 'well knowing how backward the judges have been and ever will be to allow the acts of this court to be given in evidence at any trial, it being only established by commission and not by Act of Parliament . . .'.[338] The authority of the Council of the North, he reminded the secretary, was 'of mighty advantage . . . to his Majesty'.

In closing his letter, Osborne also referred to the court as of 'no less benefit to the subject in those parts'. It may be that historians have placed emphasis on the Council as an instrument of royal authority to the exclusion of its function as a fountain of royal justice. In 1629 Charles specifically described the purpose of the court as providing 'for the more speedy administration of justice' for those in remote parts, without drawing them to Westminster.[339] He disliked prohibitions because they impeded the course of justice; and he urged the Council to be punctual in its proceedings so that subjects seeking justice might not suffer the long delays of the Westminster courts. The king was not alone in his appreciation of the benefits of the court to the region. In 1639, when Charles visited York in order to organize his campaign against the Scots, the recorder of the city chose to dwell on the Council in his speech in praise of the king: 'Your Majesty maintains a lamp of justice in this city . . . which shines into five several counties at which each subject may light a torch by the brightness whereof he may see his own right'.[340] Subsequent events suggest that the recorder's speech articulated more than the formal rhetoric of compliment. When the Long Parliament was debating the abolition of the Council of the North, along with other prerogative jurisdictions, the corporation of York met, on 4 January 1641, 'to consider whether it be fit for the city to endeavour that the court before the Council (which is now in agitation to be taken away) may be still continued, if be then to show their reasons for the same'.[341] After the court, along with the Council, had been abolished, the city in September 1641 voted to petition the king and Commons urging that a special court be established at York.[342] Clearly the abolition of the court, which had acted as a magnet to bring hordes of suitors to the city, disrupted the economic life of the regional capital and those who were sent to London in

338. Coke MS 48: Sir Edward Osborne to Coke, 10 June 1634.
339. PRO, SO 1/1, f.227v.
340. York House Books, 36, f.29.
341. *Ibid.*, f.51v.
342. *Ibid.*, f.59v, 21 Sept. 1641.

February 1642 to press parliament for an act to restore a court spoke of 'the present deadness of trade for want of such resort to the city as formerly hath been';[343] Mr Triplett, writing to Sir Edward Hyde, predicted that 'above a hundred families will be utterly and instantly undone and . . . the whole town of York beggared'.[344] But economic interests were not the only consideration. The court had contributed 'to the general good of this city'.[345] Triplett criticized Hyde for over-passionate eloquence in damning a court which would have enabled him to deal effectively with Lilburne. The abolition of the court removed a jurisdiction which had been of genuine benefit in providing inexpensive and quick local justice, without the inconvenience of long journeys to Westminster.

Though an organ of central government and royal justice, the Council of the North was also very much a local institution. It did not breach that fundamental principle (and distinguishing feature) of English local government: that authority in an area was delegated to the most powerful local men. Wentworth was appointed president in 1628 because, frustrated by his inability to gain patronage from the Duke of Buckingham, he had not employed his local influence fully in the interests of the king and Council and because the value of his influence in the government of the region was obvious.[346] Yorkshire politics, however, like politics in most counties, was ridden by factions and under Wentworth's presidency the Council became embroiled in local rivalries and disputes.[347] Wentworth naturally attempted to employ his presidential authority, as his rival Lord Savile had used his influence with Buckingham, to defeat his enemies. His running campaigns against Viscount Fauconberg, against David Foulis and against Savile through much of the 1630s involved the Council of the North in the long and at times bitter history of county faction. In 1638 Osborne complained to Coke that though he and Savile had been friends, since Osborne's appointment as vice-president Savile 'hath always carried a disaffected heart, not only to me but my Lord Deputy . . .' and attempted always to mislead and obstruct the Lords of the Council there.[348] Such squabbles and wounded pride underlay some of the hostility to the Council in 1640. But they also remind us that the Council, because it by no means had a monopoly of local

343. *Ibid.*, f.67.
344. Bodleian, Clarendon MS 20, no. 1528, 7 May 1641.
345. York House Books, 36, f.67v.
346. See S.P. Salt, 'Sir Thomas Wentworth and the parliamentary representation of Yorkshire, 1614–1628', *Northern History*, 16 (1980), pp. 130–68.
347. Cf. G.C.F. Forster, 'Faction and county government in early Stuart Yorkshire', *Northern History*, 11 (1975), pp. 70–86.
348. Coke MS 59: Osborne to Coke, 4 Dec. 1638; partly calendared in *HMC Cowper II*, p. 204.

influence, could never easily secure local co-operation with central directives. Had Wentworth remained at York, Savile would still have stood as another source of patronage and focus of influence. In Wentworth's absence, after his appointment to the Lord Deputyship of Ireland in 1633, the authority of the Council was undoubtedly compromised. Retaining his presidency (on which he perceived his local power base depended) Wentworth from Ireland continued to devote considerable attention to the affairs of the north. He was a prompt and active correspondent with Osborne and the mayor of York; he used his influence with the king and Council to maintain the court's jurisdiction; when he returned to England, he spent some time consolidating his authority in the north.[349]

But there was, in a system of personal government, no substitute for a man's presence. Osborne himself complained that 'My lord being so remote tis impossible his hand, his commissions or directions should always come so speedily'; in consequence he feared 'no business carried with a fair hand since some of the deputy lieutenants will assume mastery of power over all the rest and follow their own wills'.[350] Osborne's bid for the powers of a Lord-Lieutenant was based on more than mere personal ambition. The vice-president was one important player on the chessboard of local politics; indeed local circumstances sometimes dictated that he fall in with local rather than central wishes. In 1639 Sir John Melton complained about the petition from York against the high price of gunpowder. Osborne, he told Coke, had not cast his vote for it, but once passed, he had been obliged, lacking the authority to contest it, to put his hand to it.[351] The next month Osborne found his authority inadequate to order a levy of money for the transport of shipping timber.[352] The authority of the Council of the North should not be underestimated. But like all agencies of authority in early modern England its effectiveness depended on the influence powerful individuals brought to it (as well as derived from it). The authority of the Council of the North was exercised in the arena of local politics. To recognize that is to appreciate that it was no instrument of centralization or 'absolutism'.

The story of the Council of the Marches is, in many respects, similar. The Council of the Marches, however, rested on firm statutory basis, as a consequence of the Henrician revolution in the government of

349. Cf. C.V. Wedgwood, *Thomas Wentworth, First Earl of Strafford 1593 to 1641: A Revaluation* (1961), pp. 103–16, 210–21.
350. Coke MS 59: Osborne to Coke.
351. Coke MS 60: Melton to Coke, 12 Jan. 1639.
352. Coke MS 60: Osborne to Coke, 2 Feb. 1639.

Wales between 1536 and 1543.[353] The instructions given to the Earl of Bridgewater as Lord President of the Council in May 1633 reaffirmed the powers of the court to examine all criminal cases, perjuries and false rumours, to hear complaints and petitions, to try civil cases, to issue proclamations, to administer oaths, examine witnesses, apprehend suspects, punish the convicted and award damages in suits between party and party.[354] Charles I required the careful keeping of records of fines and penalties and duplicates of bonds and recognizances.[355] Like the Council of the North, that for the Marches combined executive and judicial functions. The Lord President's residence at Ludlow castle where the Council also had diet was a representation of royal authority in what had been the unstable territory of the Marcher lordships. The Council had a supervisory role over the government of the shires in all aspects of local administration: the maintenance of highways and bridges, the regulation of inmates and alehouses, the punishment of moral offences: incest, adultery and fornication. Yet it was also a jurisdiction to which ordinary people could appeal, an equity court to which those aggrieved by local justice or administration could sue for retribution. We find a striking demonstration of this in the case of Marjorie Evans, which, it has recently been suggested, may have shaped some of the issues in Milton's *Comus*, performed at Ludlow in 1634.[356] The humble Marjorie Evans who claimed to have been raped, failed to get justice done against one Burghill, her violator, who was related to the JP to whom Evans presented her accusation. After two years of failing to get her case heard, Marjorie, with the support of her aunt, appealed to the Council of the Marches – to royal justice. Bridgewater's investigation of the petition and case fills scores of pages of his manuscripts at the Huntington Library, and offers splendid evidence of his exhaustive efforts to discover the truth of her allegations.[357] Ultimately Evans was vindicated. The availability to her of local justice, which incurred none of the expense of a suit in the Westminster courts, alone enabled her partial vindication.[358]

Bridgewater's care in keeping the court's casebooks during the 1630s enables us to see clearly the value of the Council's jurisdiction to local

353. See J. Dodderidge, *The History of the Ancient and Modern Estate of the Principality of Wales* (1630, STC 6982), p. 38; and P. Williams, *The Council in the Marches of Wales under Elizabeth I* (Cardiff, 1958).
354. Ellesmere MSS 7397, 7571.
355. Ellesmere MS 7571.
356. L. Marcus, 'The milieu of Milton's *Comus*: judicial reform at Ludlow and the problem of sexual assault', *Criticism*, 25 (1983), pp. 293–327. I am grateful to Leah Marcus for an offprint of this article and for stimulating discussions in 1982 at the Huntington Library when we were both working on the documents concerned with the Evans case.
357. See, for example, Ellesmere MSS 7382, 7391, 7394, 7399, 7400, 7402.
358. Marcus, 'Milieu of Milton's *Comus*', pp. 312–13.

society, as well as the crown. In the first place the court was clearly hearing a record number of cases – some 1,200 a year, compared with an average of only 50 a year in Star Chamber.[359] And whilst the court was still dealing with law and order offences which had been its original rationale – riot and affray, for example – and also in large numbers with alehouses and sexual incontinency, the vast bulk of the business (at least two-thirds) came from civil actions initiated by private individuals.[360] Dr Williams has shown that of 140 cases heard in the Marches in Michaelmas term 1633, only five were presented by the Attorney.[361] Examination of the casebooks for June and July 1632, and for Hilary term 1636–7 strengthens Williams's findings. In the first period, not performing agreements, wrongful imprisonment, personal assault, most of all debt causes dominate the 502 cases heard in just twenty-four days.[362] In the second sample of 284 cases only six were presented by the Attorney; again the bulk of the business, other than the odd case of contempt, was private disputes principally over debts and arrears of rent.[363] While it has been suggested that in the 1630s 'the court was imposing an extraordinarily large number of petty fines for minor breaches of regulations', the samples from 1632 and 1636–7 (£1904 and £880 respectively) suggest that the amounts imposed (always considerably higher than what was paid) were not increasing.[364] Moreover it would appear that a smaller proportion of criminal cases resulted in a fine – which frees the Council of any charge of conducting vigorous prosecutions only for financial gain, despite the fact that the salaries of the judges depended upon the income from fines.[365] In general, examination of the casebooks yields evidence to argue that the court provided efficient and effective justice, for which there was considerable local demand. 'It allowed free scope for the ordinary plaintiff. It convicted defendants in under one third of the cases. It was liberal in awarding costs to men wrongfully accused.'[366]

Why then was the Council of the Marches attacked by parliament and dissolved in 1641? In answering such a question, we face the difficulty of disentangling reasons from accusations. In an undated paper on 'the Court of the Marches' in the Hastings manuscripts that clearly belongs to the debates of the Long Parliament, we find a list of objections to the court: that it lost the crown thousands of pounds

359. P. Williams, 'The activity of the Council in the Marches under the early Stuarts', *Welsh Hist. Rev.*, 1 (1961), pp. 133–60, quotation p. 135.
360. *Ibid.*, p. 141.
361. *Ibid.*, p. 142.
362. Ellesmere MSS 7564–8.
363. Ellesmere MSS 7569–74; cf. Williams, 'Council in the Marches', table IV, p. 159.
364. Williams, 'Council in the Marches', p. 154.
365. *Ibid.*, pp. 143–5, 158–9.
366. *Ibid.*, p. 144.

yearly without any benefit, that it was grievous to the people of Wales and impoverished them with unnecessary suits and that there were in every county of Wales courts of great sessions (established by 34 and 35 Henry VIII) which (along with the Westminster courts) adequately provided justice.[367] 'Some remembrances of the mischiefs and inconveniences that the King's majesty's subjects have and do endure by the government of the Council in the Marches of Wales' added other complaints and more serious allegations: that the Council was in breach of the law, restrained subjects from prosecuting their suits at common law, raised excessive fees and imposed heavy fines to sustain its staff and judges, sold justice, imposed cruel punishments and forced men to incriminate themselves under oath.[368] Whilst the popularity of the court as judged by the number of suits would indicate there was little substance to many of these allegations, the language suggests the work of interest groups long antagonistic to the court. Common lawyers were opposed to the court, as to other equity jurisdictions (and to the examination by oath). Some Welsh doubtless resented what they had always regarded as a facet of English subjugation of them; some in the four English border counties objected to the extension to them of the Henrician acts that empowered the king to give the law to Wales. The high incidence of cases of sexual incontinence (often punished by the whip) may have attracted to the court some of that anticlerical sentiment earned by High Commission and other ecclesiastical courts which usually prosecuted such offences. More importantly, the fear and myth of Star Chamber with which the other prerogative courts were associated infected the Council of the Marches and clouded impartial consideration of its merits. One defender of the court clearly believed that most of the odium that adhered to it was really directed at Star Chamber, 'which being taken away the cause of complaint is removed'.[369] The Council, he argued, and its jurisdiction over the four English shires, had been necessary to prevent potential conspiracies and insurrections and to stop offenders fleeing justice across the borders. The arguments of the king's Solicitor and others that without the Council justice and government could not subsist in the Marches had some force.[370] In Wales, sessions were held only twice a year – in North Wales only once; large distances and travel, difficult in winter, threatened to deprive litigants of justice and to leave parties who had been the victims of mistakes in writs of execution without remedy until the next sessions.[371] 'The appeal to the Council by writs of error,'

367. Hastings MSS, Manorial Box 70.
368. Ellesmere MS 7492.
369. Clarendon MS 19, no. 1485.
370. Ellesmere MSS 7462, 7466.
371. *Ibid.*, 7466.

it was claimed, 'did prevent several mischiefs.'[372] Within weeks of the dissolution of the Council, Thomas Milward was reporting outrages in the Marches that could not be contained.[373] The itinerant justices told Bridgewater that arrested criminals were being violently rescued and taken across the border.[374] Such episodes added force to the arguments for the Council that, though 'envied' by some, it was neither broadly disliked nor oppressive, but a source of cheap local justice for the poor (at a quarter the cost of the Westminster courts) and essential for the maintenance of local stability.[375] As far as the poor and defenceless like Marjorie Evans were concerned, the Council of the Marches secured rather than perverted justice and represented not oppression, but some appeal beyond a local magistracy whose leaders would have permitted her violation to have gone unpunished.

Although Charles I had quite definite aims for the reformation of local society and government, he looked to the justices of the peace and the constables, the traditional officers of local government, to execute his programmes. There were evidently no thoughts of changing the structure of English local government, no proposals for the implementation of something like the intendants, increasingly deployed by Richelieu during the 1620s and 1630s as agents of central government. Charles, if anything, reaffirmed the privileges and authority of local magnates and magistrates. The supervision of local government was entrusted, as traditionally, to the justices of assize, the Privy Council and the Councils of the North and the Marches. Royal directives and reforms endeavoured to improve their procedures and systematize (often through enquiries and reports) their informal practices. But in the end they too of necessity depended upon local information; and they were bodies of individuals who themselves were not without local loyalties and interests. The arrangements of English local government, which the king kept intact, made it difficult, indeed impossible, for the central government to enforce programmes and policies to which the majority of the propertied classes who ruled in the shires was opposed. Our brief study of the mechanisms demonstrates how government in Caroline England rested not upon compulsion, but co-operation and consent.

During the first half of the decade of personal rule, when the king was preoccupied with domestic reform, two major plans dominated the royal programme: the Book of Orders and the revitalization of the county militias. In the context of what we have observed of the

372. *Ibid.*, 7539.
373. *Ibid.*, 7541: Milward to Bridgewater, 18 Sept. 1641.
374. *Ibid.*, 7543.
375. *Ibid.*, 7362.

structure of local government, we must turn to examine with what degree of support and success these plans were implemented and effected.

The Book of Orders

Recently historians have unravelled the tangled history of the Book of Orders and traced its emergence from Elizabethan and Jacobean antecedents to the particular role played in 1630 by Henry Montagu, Earl of Manchester, who a decade earlier had sat on an abortive commission for the reinvigoration and reform of local government. Paul Slack in particular has elucidated the long pedigree of the three books of orders dealing with poverty, famine and pestilence which were published in 1630 to 1631, culminating in the Orders and Directions together with a commission for the better administration of justice issued in January 1631.[376] And he and Brian Quintrell have demonstrated conclusively that the final shape of the orders owed nothing, as was once thought, to Laud, Wentworth and their policy of Thorough but emerged from the correspondence Manchester conducted with his brother, Edward Lord Montagu of Boughton, Northamptonshire, the leading justice of the peace in his half of his county.[377] To their accounts of the genesis of the Book of Orders we need only add more detailed information about the immediate context from which the directives emerged. For there is some suggestion that the Book of Orders, like so many aspects of the domestic reforms of the early 1630s, originated in the war years and the dislocations which they had revealed. In February 1628, for example, Charles issued a royal proclamation ordering the strict execution of statutes against rogues and vagabonds, which, especially with disbanded, hungry and potentially mutinous troops moving around the country, 'much concerneth the peaceable and happy government of this kingdom'.[378] Significantly, in view of the Book of Orders, the proclamation required that the JPs 'do once in every month give a certificate in writing to the Lord Lieutenant' of the county and that once in every two months the Lieutenant return these reports to the Council Board, 'that so we may fully understand what reformation doth follow upon this our admonition'.[379] Then in the summer of 1628, in his charge to the

376. P. Slack, 'Books of Orders: the making of English social policy, 1577–1631', *Trans. Royal Hist. Soc.*, 5th series, 30 (1981), pp. 1–22.
377. B.W. Quintrell, 'The making of Charles I's Book of Orders', *Eng. Hist. Rev.*, 95 (1980), pp. 553–72.
378. Larkin, *Stuart Royal Proclamations*, II, no. 85, pp. 185–6.
379. *Ibid.*, p. 186; cf. PRO, SP 16/89/17.

judges of assize, the Lord Keeper referred to 'his Majesty's pleasure . . . that they should . . . certify his Majesty of the state of the several places of the kingdom and how they found the counties governed and that they should cherish such as they found diligent and careful in the execution of justice and certify the names of such as they found negligent'.[380] Evidently, the need for mechanisms of closer supervision of JPs based on written reports, mooted by Lord Keeper Bacon in 1620, was again being urged in Council during the years of instability.[381]

In 1629 the collapse of the cloth trade and the simultaneous harvest failure posed an immediate crisis which exacerbated the danger of disorder and insurrection and, as importantly, brought an awareness of such dangers very much to the fore in the localities. Local communities began to appeal for assistance in tackling the crisis. In May 1629 the JPs of Leicestershire wrote to the Earl of Huntingdon to seek his support for their decision to ban all converting of barley into malt until the shortage of corn had ended.[382] The JPs of Durham wrote directly to the Privy Council reporting the high price of corn, their fear that it might rise higher and their conviction that the only solution was a ban on all grain exports.[383] From their Easter quarter sessions of 1629, the justices of the peace of Essex wrote in desperation to the Privy Council informing them of a petition presented to them by 200 weavers from Braintree and Bocking.[384] The petitioners were unemployed and followed the JPs menacingly from place to place. It was feared that if conditions did not improve 30,000 cloth workers and their dependants might be left hungry. Already the clothiers were laying off workers, 'which causeth the people to meet in multitudes to whom we shall never be able to give any satisfaction by any power or means we have as justices of peace'. The JPs called upon the Council to act and help. Their fears were seen to be well founded: in May rioters in the county attacked a corn ship.[385] When the rioters were hanged it was reported that 'the better sort of people were much pleased with the justices being before that time much dismayed with the insolency of these people'.[386] The borough of Dorchester in 1629, less afflicted with difficulties but endeavouring to apply preventative medicine, petitioned for extra authority to regulate traders 'the better to set the poor on work'.[387] Attorney-General Heath responded to their suit for a

380. Lansdowne MS 620, f.74.
381. Quintrell, 'Making of Charles I's Book of Orders', pp. 559–60.
382. Hastings MS 10355, 28 May 1629.
383. *Cal. Stat. Pap. Dom., 1628–9*, p. 450, 14 Jan. 1629.
384. Firth MS C.4, p. 484.
385. *Ibid.*, p. 501.
386. *Ibid.*, p. 503.
387. *Cal. Stat. Pap. Dom., 1625–49*, p. 349.

revised charter with enthusiasm: 'if other cities and towns,' he wrote to the secretary, 'would follow their example, it might with much advantage to the whole kingdom be easily affected.'[388] In May 1629 a proclamation commanded the 'due execution of the laws made for setting the poor on work', and charged the assize judges to 'take an exact account how these things have been and shall be from time to time observed'.[389] So in 1629, faced with a crisis of unemployment and food shortage, the county magistrates, fearful of popular insurrection, petitioned the Council for assistance and fused local initiative with central actions to tackle the threat of instability and disorder in a realm still at war.

It is in this context of local petitions and initiatives and Conciliar orders and directions of 1628 and 1629 that we need to place the correspondence between the Earl of Manchester, Lord Privy Seal and his brother Lord Montagu. During the course of 1630, Manchester and Montagu corresponded about the problems of grain supply, price-fixing, the regulation of the markets and means of setting the poor on work.[390] While the letters were being exchanged, Manchester was evidently reformulating plans which he had first advanced in 1620 for improved accountability among local governors. And, it would appear, his proposals were being discussed and refined in Council. On 9 September 1630, at a Council meeting to discuss, among other matters, the state of famine and the regulation of alehouses, 'Mr Treasurer' (presumably Sir Thomas Edmondes) advocated: 'Justices of peace to meet once in six weeks and see the constables execute their offices.'[391] On 15 September resolutions were taken, together with a suggestion that JPs who did not execute Council orders should be removed from the commission.[392] At the end of the month, a proclamation was published prohibiting the victualling of foreign ships, and commanding the strict keeping of the assizes of bread and beer and the observance of fish days and Lent.[393] Companies were ordered to forgo sumptuous feasts and recommended to donate the sums saved to the poor. Manchester continued to draw on his brother's knowledge and experience. It was 'ancient practice' in Northamptonshire, approved by the assize judges, that the JPs met every three weeks in their

388. *Ibid.*

389. Larkin, *Stuart Royal Proclamations*, II, no. 115, pp. 236–7.

390. *HMC Buccleuch-Whitehall I*, p. 272; *III*, pp. 354–5; Montagu MSS, vols 6, 16; Slack, 'Books of Orders', p. 14. I first saw these MSS before the publication of Dr Slack's article and my account varies somewhat from his.

391. Trumbull MS 55, 9 Sept. 1630. Neither Slack nor Quintrell notes this important discussion.

392. *Ibid.*

393. Larkin, *Stuart Royal Proclamations*, II, no. 141, pp. 298–304.

divisions.[394] Accordingly, Manchester, probably on 4 November, wrote to Montagu

> to desire from you the copy of those articles you inquire upon at your three weeks sessions. To know from you what were the best way to quicken all justices of peace, to put in execution the laws for punishing of rogues, relieving poor, suppressing of alehouses and drunkenness, putting forth apprentices and employing men to labour and other laws of this kind.[395]

On 22 November the sheriff of the county, Thomas Elmes, told Montagu of a request from the Privy Council that he 'speedily . . . certify unto the Lords the doings and proceedings . . . of all justices of the peace in this county'.[396] The response to these enquiries resulted in the making of the Book of Orders which, as Manchester told his brother in forwarding a draft, took its 'conceit' from his example in Northamptonshire.[397]

When the orders were published in January (1631) they required all JPs to meet monthly in petty sessions and to report quarterly on their administration of the laws. These reports were to be sent to the sheriff, who was to give them to the assize judges for examination by the Privy Council. A commission issued to the Privy Councillors divided them into six groups, each responsible for one of the six circuits of the realm and each composed of Councillors with influence in the counties of his circuit. So the archbishop of York, Wentworth, Viscount Wilmot, Lord Newburgh, Sir Henry Vane, Cottington and Sir William Alexander had responsibility for Yorkshire, Lancashire, Cumberland, Westmorland and Northumberland.[398] All Councillors, however, had equal power over all the shires, and authority to appoint deputies 'in every or any county, city . . . or town corporate' to exercise jurisdiction on their behalf.[399] When he received the printed book, Montagu expressed his surprise at and dislike of these last provisions. Whilst he was familiar with the chain of accountability through the sheriff and justices of assize, 'I do not,' he wrote to his brother, 'well understand the mystery of appointing deputies.'[400] Manchester explained, 'The power to appoint deputies is but in cases where we find negligence we may authorise some to be spies upon them to certify or quicken proceedings.'[401] Whatever the original intent, in the event

394. Wake, *Quarter Sessions Records of . . . Northampton*, p. 91.
395. Montagu MS 6; *HMC Buccleuch-Whitehall, I*, p. 271.
396. Montagu MS 27, f.11.
397. *HMC Buccleuch-Whitehall, I*, pp. 271–2; *ibid.*, p. 273.
398. Hastings MS 13333.
399. Quintrell, 'Making of Charles I's Book of Orders', p. 562.
400. Montagu MS 10, f.47, not calendared in *HMC Buccleuch-Whitehall III*, p. 355.
401. *HMC Buccleuch-Whitehall I*, p. 273, 27 Jan. 1631.

that power was never deployed. Other than Conciliar admonition and the obligation to send in certificates, the execution of the Book of Orders, like its genesis, was in practice left to co-operation between the localities and the centre.[402]

The initial response from the localities appears to have been one of swift concurrence with the court's directions. The city of York 'ordered that all the constables and alehouse keepers both in the city and Ainsty shall be warned to be at the Common Hall . . . to receive such directions as the justices assisted with Mr Recorder shall think fit concerning the proclamation and orders come from his Majesty for preventing the excessive expense of corn and victual'; moreover, it appointed aldermen to search maltsters' kilns for stocks of barley.[403] The JPs of Abingdon returned a full report by early April, describing their monthly meetings and action to deal with rogues and poor relief.[404] In Essex, the publication of the orders prompted a flurry of magisterial activity.[405] There were, of course, early problems. The justices of the peace of Leicestershire apologized for their delayed response, explaining that they had been prevented from holding sessions by the absence of their clerk of the peace whose father was a maltster.[406] Several counties were slow in sending in their certificates, only eighteen having submitted reports by 1633.[407] Some of those submitted proved defective in some points: whilst Dorchester fulfilled all expectations – 'a very good certificate and full in all points' – the commissioners noted that from Hampshire, Portsdown hundred omitted to mention the price of corn and Basingstoke failed to report on the state of the highways. Wiltshire returned only one certificate for the whole county.[408]

Yet though only a proportion of the reports due were returned, the task of reading and vetting them soon proved too much for the commission. In May 1631 the Council, acting rather like a parliamentary committee of the whole house, established itself as a committee for charitable uses, under the commission of 5 January.[409] By the end of 1632, however, it appears that only an abstract of the certificates

402. *Orders and Directions Together with a Commission for the Better Administration of Justice . . .* (1630, STC 9252). The commission is printed in Rymer, *Foedera, Conventiones, Litterae* (20 vols. 1704–35), XIX, pp. 231–5.
403. York House Books, 35, f.90.
404. Tanner MS 395, f.61v.
405. W. Hunt, *The Puritan Moment: The Coming of Revolution in an English County* (Cambridge, Mass., 1983), p. 71; Fletcher, *Reform in the Provinces*, p. 59; Firth MS C.4, pp. 528–9; Wrightson, 'Two concepts of order', p. 39.
406. *Cal. Stat. Pap. Dom., 1629–31*, p. 406.
407. Quintrell, 'Proceedings of the Lancashire justices of the peace', p. 44.
408. PRO, SP 16/259/88; cf. SP 16/205/25 and see E.M. Leonard, *The Early History of English Poor Relief* (Cambridge, 1900), appendix, pp. 342–66 for examples of certificates.
409. Quintrell, 'Making of Charles I's Book of Orders', p. 566.

from the counties was reported to the Board, as the committee for charitable uses became preoccupied with raising contributions for the rebuilding of St Paul's.[410] The Council, amid all its other business, simply did not have the resources to police the enforcement of its orders. And in the absence of local deputies it had no choice but to take the certificates returned on trust. The quality of information received from various counties differed greatly. Though the occasional certificate, such as that from Agbrigg and Morley in York, was nearly eight pages long, most were short summaries of business that the Council had to take on trust.[411] Undoubtedly vague statements that all had been done cannot be taken as accurate descriptions of local activity. When asked for the return of his certificate by the sheriff of Northamptonshire, Sir Rowland St John took the view that 'it is observed to be a rule of discreet policy in general businesses to make a general answer, lest by descending too far into particulars something should be fastened upon which may produce an unexpected prejudice'.[412] Because the Council did not have an independent source of local knowledge, the success of the Book of Orders depended upon the willingness of the localities to implement it. As the immediate harvest crisis subsided, the enthusiasm for what was an onerous task undoubtedly waned in some areas.[413] In January 1634 the Council upbraided the mayor of London for his remissness in making a return;[414] the following year Weston personally ordered the JPs of Kent to deliver their certificates 'fair written and subscribed as by the said printed books is directed'.[415] In May 1635, a general Conciliar letter was sent to all JPs reminding them of their duties to execute the orders.[416] In 1636 and 1638 the justices of assize were charged to quicken local activity.[417] A proclamation of 1640 for 'the due execution of the laws made for setting the poor on work' did little more than reaffirm the Book of Orders in this respect, 'spurring justices to greater efficiency' and urging judges to make stricter inspection.[418] Other than these general exhortations, preoccupation after 1635 with foreign affairs and especially ship money diverted the Council from close attention to the Book of Orders. Fewer certificates were returned after the early years; by the end of the decade perhaps only one-tenth

410. PRO, PC 2/42/325.
411. *Cal. Stat. Pap. Dom., 1635*, p. 175; *1634–5*, pp. 440–7.
412. Montagu MS 1, f.60: Rowland St John to Sir Oliver St John, 15 Dec. 1630.
413. Fletcher, *Reform in the Provinces*, p. 57.
414. PRO, PC 2/43/423.
415. Dering MS U350/010, 15 May 1635.
416. PRO, PC 2/44/555.
417. Rawlinson MSS B.243, C.827.
418. Larkin, *Stuart Royal Proclamations*, II, no. 302, pp. 712–14.

of the reports due had been sent into the Council or forwarded by the judges.[419] No county or hundred sent in its full quota.[420]

It would be wrong to conclude from such observations that the Book of Orders met with failure. In the first place certificates did continue to come in and sometimes went into detail beyond that required by the Council. Scray in Kent in 1637 listed by name the apprentices they had put out, their masters, all the alehouse keepers licensed, all rogues punished and all absentees from church.[421] Great Yarmouth returned the amount of its yearly levies for the poor (noting that last year, cold weather had led them to raise the sum by £125).[422] Abergavenny consistently returned detailed certificates;[423] in 1638 the Kendal JPs forwarded a mass of material, including notes they had received from all the churchwardens and overseers.[424] Lambeth churchwardens' accounts for 1637 show sums paid 'for writing our monthly certificate to the justices';[425] the JPs of Monmouth similarly sent notes of their monthly meetings.[426] Secondly, the absence of certificates cannot be simply read as a failure to implement the orders. Northamptonshire, which had provided the Council with its model, sent in few reports; in Essex and Warwickshire, also remiss in making returns, local government was much improved.[427] In Kent, though there is a gap in the county's certificates between 1634 and 1636, the sessions order books and especially Dering's notebooks show a vigorous activity which has led one historian to venture the suggestion that the county magistrates regarded the bureaucratic chore of returning the certificates as the least important part of the orders.[428] Lancashire, which sent in no return until Hilary term 1634 and then forwarded 'threadbare and unconvincing documents', continued to hold petty sessions every three weeks.[429] By the end of the decade, Dr Quintrell had shown, the JPs 'were now paying rather closer attention to the way parishes were implementing disciplinary and welfare statutes'. 'The county's ample, if belated, response to the 1631 Book of Orders showed what might occasionally be done.'[430]

The Book of Orders had emerged from local as well as central initiatives and in many instances local magistrates took advantage of it

419. Fletcher, *Reform in the Provinces*, p. 58. 970 certificates have survived.
420. Cf. Quintrell, 'Making of Charles I's Book of Orders', p. 569.
421. *Cal. Stat. Pap. Dom., 1636–7*, p. 330.
422. *Ibid.*, p. 531.
423. *Cal. Stat. Pap. Dom., 1637*, p. 271; *1636–7*, p. 331.
424. *Cal. Stat. Pap. Dom., 1637–8*, p. 546.
425. C. Drew (ed.) *Lambeth Churchwardens' Accounts* (Surrey Record Soc., 1943), p. 131.
426. PRO, SP 16/293/82.
427. Fletcher, *Reform in the Provinces*, p. 59.
428. Kent Archives Office, QSO, W1; I owe this point to Ken Fincham.
429. Quintrell, 'Proceedings of the Lancashire justices of the peace', pp. 34, 44.
430. *Ibid.*, pp. 44, 51.

to press their own reforms with official backing. In Kent in 1633, in a move that went beyond the requirements of the Council, the JPs called upon the constables to collect reports from ministers and overseers concerning, as well as the numbers of alehouses, cottages erected and inmates received, the names of unmarried men and women living out of service.[431] Elsewhere, the pressure of the Council directives led counties which had held no (or few) petty sessions to adopt them or hold them more regularly – as in Devon, Warwickshire and some of the rapes of Sussex.[432] Whilst historians are partly right to stress that the Book of Orders was 'not properly enforced' and so depended upon the whims of nearly autonomous local governors,[433] we should not forget that the Council's novel demand for continuous reporting required the magistrate to put his hand regularly to an account of his activity.[434] If this led most JPs to some greater sense of their duty and accountability, it may have fulfilled many of the king's and Council's intentions, and done much to alleviate some of the worst social problems of the decade.[435]

Dearth

The first and immediate intention behind the Conciliar orders of the 1630s was the alleviation of the worst consequences of the harvest failure and grain crisis of 1629 and 1630. Though the fear of food shortage was endemic in early modern England, the dearth of 1630 was especially severe. The diarist William Whiteway noted the price of grain rising from 4s. to 7s. a bushel between April and August, to 10s. 'and in the north country far dearer' by November and to 14s. a bushel in London by the spring of 1631.[436] In wartime it was particularly difficult to get grain supplies from abroad.[437] There were few places like Bristol that had with foresight provided a storehouse of grain.[438] The harvest failure threatened starvation on a scale that could not be alleviated by the half-dozen ships of corn that Charles I managed to

431. Kent Archives Office, QSO, W1, f.44.
432. Fletcher, *Reform in the Provinces*, pp. 127–8; Hughes, *Politics, Society and Civil War*, p. 57.
433. Fletcher, *Reform in the Provinces*, pp. 57, 123.
434. Anthony Fletcher, I think, underestimates this.
435. Cf. Quintrell, in 'Making of Charles I's Book of Orders', p. 570: 'The JPs certificates may . . . have been more useful . . . for what they represented . . . than for what they contained'.
436. Egerton MS 784, pp. 154, 157, 159, 162; cf. W.G. Hoskins, 'Harvest fluctuations and English economic history, 1620–1759', *Agric. Hist. Rev*, 16 (1968), pp. 15–31; and the table printed in Hunt, *Puritan Moment*, p. 244.
437. Hastings MS 4225.
438. Bristol Record Office, Common Council Books, 3, f.1v.

secure from the emperor of Russia.[439] Tumults were soon reported from several parts of the country:[440] there were food riots at Canterbury and Faversham in Kent and Sir Walter Roberts, a JP who purchased corn, was attacked.[441] In Hampshire one Sutton, a corn badger, narrowly escaped with his life 'notwithstanding the many charitable acts done by him to the poor of the country'.[442] The threat of disorder led to local action. In Leicestershire, William Potter and Edward Large were quick to recommend that one way to ease the shortage was to restrain the conversion of barley to malt for brewing.[443] And the Council was as quick to respond with orders forbidding the brewing of strong beer and regulating engrossing and forestalling.[444] Whilst the order probably met with acceptance in many parts of the country, the localism of early modern England still led the JPs of Dorset to exempt from the ban on malting 'such as are farmers of grounds and have corn sufficient growing on their own demesne'.[445] The order issued in September endeavoured traditionally to curb rising prices by forcing farmers to bring their corn to market and sell at fixed rates.[446] Some JPs quickly responded: 'the Huntingdonshire bench,' writes Mr Fletcher, 'carried out detailed enquiries in November . . . about the stores of corn held by farmers both in their barns and on the ground and about the deals they had made for buying grain for resale.'[447] In some areas the price of grain fell in weeks by 2s. 8d. the bushel.[448] The order, however, proved inadequate. In December the Council was writing to JPs requiring them to meet weekly to oversee measures to lower the price of corn.[449] As reports of desperate shortages and riots continued to come in over the winter, the Council took further action, including the issue in March 1631 of a proclamation prohibiting the export of any corn which awarded to informers half of any corn seized from delinquents.[450] The crude measures of the Council endeavouring to ensure a supply were neither completely effective nor always

439. PRO, SO 1/1, f.212v; Coke MS 41: Thomas Chamberlain to Coke, 17 Sept. 1631.
440. *Cal. Stat. Pap. Dom., 1629–31*, p. 386; *1631–3*, p. 40; *Acts of the Privy Council 1630–1*, p. 268; see J. Walter and K. Wrightson, 'Dearth and the social order in early modern England', *P&P*, 71 (1976), pp. 22–42.
441. P. Clark, 'Popular protest and disturbance in Kent, 1558–1640', *Econ. Hist. Rev.*, 29 (1976), pp. 365–81, p. 370.
442. Hampshire Record Office, Herriard MSS, Box 012, May 1631.
443. Hastings MS 10355; cf. J. Thirsk and J.P. Cooper (eds) *Seventeenth Century Economic Documents* (Oxford, 1972), pp. 35–8.
444. Hastings MS 4225; Firth MS C.4, p. 530.
445. Dorset quarter session orders, f.259.
446. Larkin, *Stuart Royal Proclamations*, II, no. 141, pp. 298–304.
447. Fletcher, *Reform in the Provinces*, p. 194.
448. Firth MS C.4, pp. 525–6.
449. *Acts of the Privy Council June 1630 to June 1631*, p. 152.
450. Walter and Wrightson, 'Dearth and the social order', pp. 37–8; *Cal. Stat. Pap. Dom., 1629–31*, p. 548; Larkin, *Stuart Royal Proclamations*, II, no. 146, pp. 312–14.

welcome. JPs at times protected powerful interest groups; in Suffolk, Sam Puckle secured a licence to transport corn on false pretences.[451] More importantly, some were to complain, in some cases not without good reason, that government interference with local economies actually did more harm than good. Because the Council was not familiar with all local circumstances, its directives for the common good sometimes jarred with local needs and conditions.[452] The JPs of Norfolk, for instance, argued that the compulsion to send corn to market did not best serve the economy of the sheep–corn county and offered their own local solutions to the problem of providing for the poor.[453] In Sussex the blanket ban on all transport of corn threatened to stop the coastal supply of Rye from the western rapes of the county.[454] The argument that attendance at market drew the poor from their labours was heard from several counties.[455] Moreover, it was claimed from some parts of the country that, rather like the famous (and apocryphal) modern crisis of a shortage of toilet rolls, rumour of dearth and action to contain it sometimes created the very problem it attempted to solve, by encouraging hoarding.[456] The JPs of Dorset complained to the Council in November 1631 that 'corn was raised to so high a price at the end of last year by the interference of the justices and the suspicion of want thereby excited'.[457] The Essex magistracy protested that a search for concealed corn would 'occasion a doubt of great scarcity' and raise the price of corn imported to the county.[458] Hertfordshire JPs told the Council that 'their still looking to markets is an occasion that the markets are smaller, the corn dearer'.[459] Despite such drawbacks, the combination of Conciliar orders and local adjustment to regional circumstances saw the country through the immediate crisis without widescale insurrection. The good harvest of the next year saw prices return to something like the level of the 1620s. By October 1631 Sir Walter Pye was able to inform the Earl of Bridgewater that corn in the area held a stable price;[460] the JPs of Sussex reported their harvest plentiful.[461] The following summer the justices of Somerset expressed their relief to the sheriff that 'God be

451. *Cal. Stat. Pap. Dom., 1629–31*, p. 545.
452. See R.B. Outhwaite, 'Dearth and government intervention in English grain markets, 1590–1700', *Econ. Hist. Rev.*, 34 (1981), pp. 389–406.
453. A. Fletcher, *A County Community in Peace and War: Sussex, 1600–1660* (1976), p. 150; cf. Thirsk and Cooper, *Seventeenth Century Economic Documents*, pp. 343–7.
454. Fletcher, *County Community*, p. 151.
455. Fletcher, *Reform in the Provinces*, pp. 197–9.
456. Cf. Outhwaite, 'Dearth and government intervention', p. 405.
457. *Cal. Stat. Pap. Dom., 1629–31*, p. 186.
458. Firth MS C.4, p. 540.
459. *Cal. Stat. Pap. Dom., 1629–31*, p. 539.
460. Ellesmere MS 7083.
461. *Cal. Stat. Pap. Dom., 1631–3*, p. 210, 28 Dec. 1631.

praised, the scarcity is now turned into plenty and the price of all manner of grain fallen well nigh to half.'[462] By January 1632 the Privy Council felt able to relax its ban on the sale of corn. The crisis had passed.[463]

With the immediate crisis over, it is usually argued, the dearth orders became a dead letter. The experience of 1630, however, was not forgotten – either by the localities or by the Council. The corporation of Bristol continued and extended its policy of maintaining a common storehouse; in 1635 the city ordered it be stocked with bread, butter, cheese, oats and pease (as well as corn), to be sold to the poor at reasonable rates.[464] Less enterprising authorities were chivvied to take similar action by the Council. The mayor of London received several Conciliar letters requiring him to ensure adequate stocks of grain and stable prices;[465] in August 1632 the JPs of Hampshire were alerted to the illegal shipment of grain from their coasts and were warned that the navy might be deployed to search coastal shipping;[466] the JPs of Chester were reminded in 1637 to keep a watchful eye for the abuses of engrossing corn.[467] In general, throughout the 1630s the Council remained vigilant to the danger of excessive malting. In 1636, with grain prices rising again, they resolved to regulate the trade. Letters in the king's name ordered that no brewers should convert grain to malt, nor any maltster during the months of June, July or August. The number of maltsters was to be limited and those licensed to malt were to be incorporated – after they had certified the volume of their cisterns.[468] The order remained in force until grain prices fell again in 1638.[469] Once again, well-intentioned orders created other unforeseen difficulties. The JPs of Hertfordshire pointed out that reducing the number of maltsters led many formerly so employed to add to the ranks of day labourers 'of whom many already want work'.[470] The sheriff of Buckinghamshire, Sir Alex Denton, complained that the restriction of maltsters also deprived some regions of the benefits derived from selling their grain.[471] Overall, however, as the long-established practice in some counties such as Cheshire testifies, regulation of maltsters eased the pressures on corn prices.[472]

462. *Ibid.*, p. 394, 30 July 1632.
463. PRO, PC 2/41/350; cf. Outhwaite, 'Dearth and government intervention', p. 405.
464. Bristol Common Council Books, 3, f.59v, 24 March 1635.
465. For example, PRO, PC 2/41/87 and PC 2/42/238.
466. Coke MS 42: Council to JPs of Hampshire, 18 Aug. 1632.
467. *Cal. Stat. Pap. Dom., 1636–7*, p. 406, 31 Jan. 1637.
468. Ellesmere MSS 6967, 6968: articles to be observed by all maltsters; Larkin, *Stuart Royal Proclamations*, II, no. 240, pp. 560–4.
469. Larkin, *Stuart Royal Proclamations*, II, no. 264, pp. 618–19.
470. *Cal. Stat. Pap. Dom., 1636–7*, p. 323.
471. *Cal. Stat. Pap. Dom., 1637–8*, p. 237, 8 Feb. 1638.
472. Cheshire Record Office, QJB, 1/5, f.268.

Concerning the other cause of dearth, engrossing, the Council could do little beyond urging the local magistrate and assize judges to be vigilant and severe against offenders. Some evidently responded. The city of York in April 1638 seized two ships of corn belonging to Thomas Lanthropp, a 'common engrosser', and ordered the grain to be sold to the local poor at reasonable prices.[473] Though there was no other harvest failure like that of 1630, it was a real achievement that there were no major problems concerning the provision of corn throughout the rest of the decade. No JP's certificate mentioned starvation, for all the fears that had been expressed. When prices began to rise in 1637 the Council was quick to take preventative action, and for the most part the localities were ready with their co-operation.[474] In the Short Parliament, a bill for the better preserving of corn expressed an awareness of the need to treat the long-term problem with preventive measures, but there was no immediate difficulty.[475] Indeed a petition from Hertfordshire was now protesting that the cheapness of grain made it difficult for local farmers to maintain their families.[476] If the 1630s was the decade when 'most Conciliar pressure was exerted' on the grain market, that pressure prevented the dearths of 1629–30 and 1637 escalating into a crisis of starvation.[477]

The employment of the poor

An adequate supply of corn, Sir Thomas Jervoise of Hampshire observed, was in itself of little use if the poor were unemployed and had no money to purchase it when it came to market.[478] The bad harvest of 1630 that had driven up grain prices came in the wake of a crisis in the cloth trade in 1629 which threatened to throw thousands on to poor relief.[479] In the spring of 1629 'A Brief Declaration concerning the State of the Manufacturers of Wools in the County of Essex' explained that 50,000 in the shire drew their livelihood thereby, 20,000 of them from the area around Colchester.[480] A prohibition by

473. York House Books, 36, f.6v.
474. Outhwaite, 'Dearth and government intervention', p. 398; B. Sharp, *In Contempt of all Authority: Rural Artisans and Riot in the West of England, 1586–1660* (Berkeley and Los Angeles, 1980), p. 57.
475. Cope, *Proceedings of the Short Parliament*, p. 83.
476. *Ibid.*, p. 277.
477. Outhwaite, 'Dearth and government intervention', pp. 398, 405 and *passim*.
478. *Cal. Stat. Pap. Dom., 1629–31*, p. 403: Jervoise to Conway, 6 Dec. 1630.
479. See Thirsk and Cooper, *Seventeenth Century Economic Documents*, pp. 224–32; C. Clay, *Economic Expansion and Social Change, England 1500–1700* (2 vols, Cambridge, 1984), I, pp. 221–2; B. Supple, *Commercial Crisis and Change in England, 1600–1642* (Cambridge, 1959), pp. 102–4.
480. Firth MS C.4, pp. 489ff.

Spain on the import of English bays had left by now £6,000 worth unsold, together with a further £6,000 worth of says, the finer serge-like stuff. The manufacturers of Coggeshall, Witham, Braintree, Bocking, Dedham and Langham, though operating on a smaller scale, shared the same fate: 'their poverty is exceeding great'. Tumultuous assemblies of unemployed were gathering. The JPs of Braintree informed the Council that they knew of no parish able to set their poor on work.[481] On 8 May a petition of 100,000 weavers to Charles I presented their plight after twelve years of decay of trade. Wages had fallen by 7s. in the pound, and though they sold their very beds to buy food they still had only 'so small a portion of bread as is hardly to keep life and soul together'.[482] Their masters, they explained, could not help, having no market for their product. From Berkshire came a similar lament, the JPs explaining to the Council that 'the poor of Newbury have their dependency on the clothiers who forbear to set them on work, having no vent for their cloth. They are at present in a miserable condition . . .'.[483]

Against the fluctuations of the market, the Council was powerless to act. In the summer of 1630 the king even recommended the army of volunteers being raised by the Marquis of Hamilton to go to Sweden for 'the benefit the kingdom will find in disburdening itself of so many unnecessary men that want employment'.[484] Other than such expedients, the government's answer to the crisis was a reaffirmation of 'all the laws heretofore made and now standing in force, for the relief of the indigent and impotent poor, for binding out apprentices, for providing of stocks and for setting the poor on work'.[485] A proclamation of May 1629 required the churchwardens and JPs in their divisions to take all into their consideration, the sessions to settle courses to resolve the problems, and the assize judges to review them.[486] These requirements were incorporated into the Book of Orders and constituted the brief given to the Council commission of 2 January. In particular the book reiterated the requirement of able masters to take on apprentices, and lists of the numbers put out and names became a regular feature of the reports filed by the JPs from their petty sessions. In some counties and cities, local initiative had already pre-empted Conciliar requirements. York, for example, in March 1629 had ordered all apprentices enrolled.[487] In May 1631 they

481. *Ibid.*, p. 493.
482. *Ibid.*, pp. 494–5.
483. *Cal. Stat. Pap. Dom., 1629–31*, p. 418, Dec. 1630.
484. *Cal. Stat. Pap. Dom., 1631–3*, p. 83, 19 June 1631.
485. Larkin, *Stuart Royal Proclamations*, II, p. 236.
486. *Ibid.*, no. 115, pp. 236–7.
487. York House Books, 35, f.80, 29 March 1629.

appointed four men in every ward with a budget of £10 to set the poor on work.[488] Across the country, however, the Book of Orders clearly quickened activity. By March 1631, the JPs of Kingsclere in Hampshire had bound over fifty apprentices.[489] In 1633 the assize judges ruled that journeymen could be legally compelled to take on an apprentice from another parish, if he was from the same hundred, and that those who refused might be committed to gaol.[490] From almost all counties there is evidence of vigour: in Kent Sir Edward Dering's notes for March 1633 alone include a three-page list of apprentices placed and a further list of 'names of such as are yet fit to take or to pay toward putting out'.[491] His papers show that his diligence in this regard remained unabated throughout the decade. In November 1634 the city of Bristol appointed a committee of aldermen to consider the best course for setting the poor on work and for providing employment for the 'hospital boys', to keep them from idleness 'which makes them unfit to be apprentices'.[492] In 1636 the Privy Council made it a requirement of all foreign traders resident in England that they take an apprentice and instruct him in their skill.[493]

There was some resistance. Some refused to take on an apprentice and Thomas Trevelyan of Somerset and John Potkins, churchwarden of Pluckley in Kent, were called to answer for their refusal at the Council Board.[494] Others, less openly defiant, acted half-heartedly: Wiltshire clothiers were reported to be sluggish and the churchwardens there neglected the business.[495] Interestingly too, given the scepticism expressed by some historians about affective family relationships in early modern England, we find mention of 'the unwillingness of foolish poor parents to part with their children'.[496] But despite such obstacles, Conciliar pressure meant that 'much more was achieved in the 1630s than had been previously'.[497] On 19 October 1633, the JPs of Somerset reported to Lord Chief Justice Richardson that they had bound out 400 poor children as apprentices;[498] the JPs of Arundel listed 100 apprentices in a year.[499] The early momentum was sustained: a certificate of 1635 from Bulmer in the West Riding cited 300 bound

488. *Ibid.*, f.106.
489. *Cal. Stat. Pap. Dom., 1629–31*, p. 526, 3 March 1631.
490. Tanner MS 288, f.266.
491. Dering MS U570/01, ff.28–30.
492. Bristol Common Council Books, 3, f.54v.
493. PRO, PC 2/46/322.
494. PRO, PC 2/43/71; PC 2/43/98. Below, p. 712.
495. *Cal. Stat. Pap. Dom., 1633–4*, p. 273.
496. *Ibid.*; cf. L. Stone, *The Family, Sex and Marriage in England, 1500–1800* (1977).
497. Fletcher, *Reform in the Provinces*, pp. 215–16.
498. *Cal. Stat. Pap. Dom., 1633–4*, p. 253.
499. *Ibid.*, p. 284.

apprentices;[500] in March 1638 Agbrigg and Morley in York claimed 118 new apprentices in their certificate for the quarter.[501] The division of Holland in Lincolnshire boasted besides that it found work for 200 weekly from utensils in the town stock.[502] Dr Quintrell has demonstrated that the surviving certificates returned from the JPs of Essex show over 1,000 apprentices bound during the period 1631–40;[503] for Sussex, Mr Fletcher concludes that 'during the 1630s apprenticeship of poor children was made systematic in every rape'.[504] The social stability of the 1630s may owe much to these figures.

The problem less easily solved – and possibly exacerbated by Council policy – was that of the conditions of apprenticeship. The cruel master and victim apprentice was part of a long history and larger literature, some of it fictional, some all too harshly real. The ideal of the extended family into which the child was placed 'apprendere' (to learn) and from which he might emerge to become a citizen and member of a livery company was an ideal which the relationship did not always live up to.[505] Those who had been forced to take on an apprentice against their wishes were not likely to be devoted masters. In Bristol, Elizabeth Chilton was deserted by her master Richard Case who left the parish, claiming that he could not afford to maintain her.[506] William Butler had his arm broken by his master and was rendered incapable of any work;[507] in York, John Leadley was left lame as a consequence of his master's cruelty.[508] JPs took seriously the duties of masters to their apprentices, but could often do little more than release the children from their bond; doubtless many cases of maltreatment failed to reach their attention. Modern society has not resolved the problems of cruelty and abuse within the family, or of detecting cases before they become tragedies. We cannot be sure how happy the lot of the typical apprentice was. What the Conciliar orders achieved was a greatly increased number of opportunities for the young to secure training in a craft, or in the case of girls in 'housewifery',[509] 'that is to say,' Edmund Bolton put it in *The Cities Advocate*, 'to the discipline and art of honest gain'.[510]

500. *Cal. Stat. Pap. Dom., 1635–6*, p. 136.
501. *Cal. Stat. Pap. Dom., 1637–8*, p. 545.
502. *Cal. Stat. Pap. Dom., 1636–7*, p. 43.
503. B.W. Quintrell, 'The government of the county of Essex 1603–1642' (London University PhD thesis, 1965), p. 220.
504. Fletcher, *County Community*, p. 158.
505. E. Bolton, *The Cities Advocate* (1629, STC 3219), for example, pp. 11, 27.
506. Bristol Record Office, QS, f.53v.
507. *Ibid.*, f.38.
508. York Record Office, F7, quarter sessions minutes, f.92.
509. Fletcher, *Reform in the Provinces*, p. 217.
510. Bolton, *Cities Advocate*, p. 51.

Enclosures and depopulation

Though the collapse of the cloth trade and the dislocation of trade in wartime were the principal reasons for rising unemployment, there was a longer-term contributing factor to which the king and Council paid renewed attention during the decade of personal rule. The enclosure of common land and the conversion of arable to pasture reduced the numbers both of those who eked a living from the soil and of those who could find wage-labour in the fields, and consequently multiplied the numbers of landless poor. Complaints against and government concern over enclosures, of course, go back to the sixteenth century (and before) but here, as in so many other respects, Caroline government sought to reinvigorate Tudor legislation. Though not specifically a clause of the Book of Orders published in January 1631, the Council's directives to prevent depopulating enclosures, as Dr Slack has argued, belong to the packages of social policy formulated in the early 1630s, which are usually (and rightly) associated with those orders.[511] In 1630 letters were sent to the JPs of the midland counties, urging them to check enclosures and return information of lands enclosed in recent years.[512] The commissioners for charitable uses discussed enclosure and apparently aired the possibility that the rebuilding of St Paul's cathedral might be financed from fines on enclosers and depopulators in Lincolnshire, Leicestershire and Northamptonshire.[513] A new campaign against them was obviously in preparation. Later in 1631, a warrant was delivered to the Attorney-General to prepare commissions of enquiry into such depopulation and conversions from arable to pasture that had taken place since Queen Elizabeth's time in Lincolnshire, Leicestershire, Gloucestershire, Wiltshire, Northamptonshire and Somerset.[514] In 1632 the justices on circuit to these shires were instructed in the charge to prevent any further enclosure that led to depopulation.[515] Since the magistrate class was that often involved in enclosing, the enforcement of Council directives was always problematic. But enclosing JPs could exhibit a sense of responsibility that rose above self-interest: evidently in Northamptonshire enclosers gave compensatory land to those they deprived of the common, and in Buckinghamshire Sir Peter Temple entered into similar negotiations when he embarked on a project.[516]

511. Slack, 'Books of Orders', p. 2.
512. *Cal. Stat. Pap. Dom., 1629–31*, pp. 451, 491.
513. *Ibid.*, p. 563.
514. *Cal. Stat. Pap. Dom., 1631–3*, p. 490; see Bankes MS 50/48, 49.
515. Rawlinson MS A.128.
516. Huntington Library, Temple of Stowe MSS, 8, STT 565; STT M, Oversize Box 2: petition of inhabitants of Stowe.

The Council commissioners went about their business thoroughly and clients, informants and aggrieved parties were quick to report to members of the Board. From Derbyshire, Gilbert Ward wrote to Sir John Coke that the JPs of his county were slow in certifying enclosers.[517] A few years later William Danvers of Derbyshire found himself certified to the Council for decay of tillage.[518] The sense of renewed government inspection began to affect those contemplating enclosing. In May 1634, Lawrence Tanfield advised Sir Edward Montagu of Boughton, Northamptonshire against the purchase of ground for that purpose: 'for that as I formerly intimated to your lordship by Mr Payne the state hath a severe eye upon all the new enclosures and as is thought will take some course for preventing future and punishing present offences of that nature as general nuisances to the commonwealth'.[519] Tanfield concluded his advice with a warning: 'there is an information in the Star Chamber against a Kentish knight for enclosure and depopulation'.

The case referred to was that of Sir Anthony Roper, who was presented in Star Chamber for depopulation and converting tillage to pasture contrary to statutes from Henry VIII's reign and after. Though Roper appeared in court in October, some months after William Noy's death, the late Attorney had, Windebank was told, determined 'to make some of these fellows exemplar in the Star Chamber'.[520] Roper was fined the large sum of £4,000 and was ordered to rebuild the cottages he had let rot.[521] His trial became something of a *cause célèbre* and must have sent a shiver down many a gentry spine. As the newswriter Rossingham wrote to Viscount Scudamore, 'this is a leading case, for many landed men have taken in some arable grounds to enlarge their parks or demesnes and have also pulled down some farm houses or cottages.'[522] Under Noy's successor, Attorney Bankes, active investigation and prosecution of enclosers continued.[523] In early 1636, John Burgh announced another investigation: 'much question here is throughout all the kingdom,' he told Scudamore, 'about depopulations and decay of tillage. Commissions have been sent into the country by way of enquiry and those that compound not with the lords that are here the commissioners for those compositions are to be proceeded against in the Star Chamber . . . few landed men are

517. *HMC Cowper I*, p. 426, 27 Jan. 1631.
518. Coke MS 52: Danvers to Coke, 18 Dec. 1635.
519. Montagu MS 15, f.46, 15 May 1634.
520. Ellesmere MS 7878; H.E. Phillips, 'The court of Star Chamber, 1603–42' (London University, MA thesis, 1939), p. 266; *Cal. Stat. Pap. Dom., 1634–5*, p. 279: John Phillipot to Windebank, 3 Nov. 1634.
521. Phillips, 'Star Chamber', p. 266; Rushworth, *Historical Collections*, II, p. 268.
522. PRO, C.115/M36/8437: Rossingham to Scudamore, 18 Oct. 1634.
523. See Bankes MSS 50/48, 9; 55/109.

free from payment.'[524] Even Lord Saye and Sele was presented by the commissioners for having depopulated three farms in Brumby, Lincolnshire and for having enclosed the common.[525] Whilst the benefit to the government of fines should not be discounted, the financial aspects of the commission were not the most important. Its activities encouraged local denunciations of those 'monsters of men, despoilers of towns, occasioners of beggars . . . cruel enclosers', as Joseph Bentham, rector of Boughton, Northamptonshire described them.[526] And it enabled men like Thomas Williamson to present charges even against powerful magnates.[527] The full extent of the commissioners' success in reversing illicit enclosures, more importantly in preventing more, must remain unknown. But the campaign continued right to the end of the personal rule; the king himself, having observed on his journey to Scotland the depopulation of the northern counties, expressed his determination to see the commission kept on foot.[528] In August 1639 Rossingham noted that its proceedings had brought £40,000 to the Exchequer. Just as importantly, he observed, 'the kingdom itself hath had a very great advantage – namely in this: that they have erected since this commission was afoot above two thousand farms which were formerly depopulated.'[529]

Poor relief

Finding work for the able-bodied was one facet of the Elizabethan campaigns against poverty revitalized by the Book of Orders. The other was the provision of relief for the old, sick and impotent, those unable to maintain themselves by labour. Caroline policy envisaged no change in Elizabethan legislation: for the impotent, the maimed or the fatherless a parish rate was assessed on parishioners who were deemed able to contribute.[530] The Elizabethan poor law had been, at least in theory, an enterprising enactment; and even in practice it may have contributed to the realm's emergence from the severe economic crises of the 1590s without massive popular insurrection. But, in many areas, there had been at best a slow response to the requirement of the 1597 statute to appoint overseers and establish a system of relief. And across the country the implementation of the procedures was often *ad hoc* and

524. PRO, C.115/N4/8608: Burgh to Scudamore, 24 Feb. 1636.
525. Coke MS 53: Thomas Williamson to Sir J. Coke Jnr, 26 April 1636.
526. P.A.J. Pettit, *The Royal Forests of Northamptonshire: a Study in their Economy, 1558–1714* (Northamptonshire Record Soc., 23, 1968), p. 147.
527. Coke MS 53.
528. BL Add. MS 11045, f.47: Rossingham to Scudamore, 20 Aug. 1639.
529. *Ibid.*
530. W.K. Jordan, *Philanthropy in England, 1480–1660* (1959), pp. 101–4.

spasmodic rather than regular and routine.[531] Time, a Council that had been less than vigilant in enforcing the code, and the unpopularity of regular parish rates led to lapses in the administration of the poor laws. In Buckinghamshire in 1627, tenants of royal estates at Lutterworth protested that Sir Thomas Temple refused to pay rates for the poor assessed on the pasture he leased there.[532] The Dorset quarter sessions records show several cases of refusal to pay poor rates in the 1620s; in Blandford, the churchwardens and overseers themselves failed to make their payments.[533] The wars of 1625–30 greatly exacerbated the problems: the cost of billeting and transporting soldiers dampened willingness and reduced ability to maintain the poor, whilst casualties of war added to the numbers of the impotent dependants upon relief and, in those cases where freeholders had served in the armies, lessened the ranks of those able to contribute. On top of the bad harvests and collapse of the cloth trade, the drift back to their parishes of wounded soldiers from La Rochelle and the Ile de Rhé subjected poor relief to severe strain. In 1629 the town of Aylesford in Kent was over £14 in arrears on its fund for the relief of maimed soldiers.[534]

Over the early 1630s, the situation worsened. At the April sessions at Sherborne in Dorset it was reported that in the parish of Allington the numbers of poor 'have of late so greatly increased and multiplied that the inhabitants of the said parish are no ways able to relieve them, notwithstanding they have been thereunto rated to the utter most of their abilities'.[535] Complaints about the rates were heard more frequently and quarrels about unequal assessments multiplied as JPs tried to levy higher sums. In Pluckley in Kent the inhabitants threatened legal action against those who proceeded to make assessments for poor relief whereby 'that service is much neglected and the poor thereby likely to be in very great distress'.[536] At Beaminster in Dorset, where there was widespread discontent over the rate, one John Hilary, a 'gentleman', tried to seize the book of rates from the hands of the overseer William Seaborne in church, 'but seeing the said Seaborne to hold the same so fast that he could not get it away from him . . . the said Hilary then delivered him a writ issuing out of his Majesty's court of King's Bench at Westminster directed to the said William Seaborne and others requiring them to surcease to execute the said office of. . . overseers of the poor'. Hilary also grabbed the money (11s. 8d.) gathered by Seaborne and refused to return it.[537]

531. Fletcher, *Reform in the Provinces*, pp. 183–4.
532. Temple of Stowe MS 6, STT 804.
533. Dorset Record Office, QS, ff.159v–162.
534. Kent Archives Office, QSO W1, f.21v.
535. Dorset Record Office, QS, f.313v.
536. Kent Archives Office, QSO W1, f.63.
537. Dorset Record Office, QS, f.355v.

It was in this context and to tackle these problems that the Council reaffirmed the Elizabethan requirement to provide relief for the poor and maimed soldiers. There can be no doubt that during the 1630s far greater sums were levied and raised both in the parishes and for the county funds for charitable uses and maimed soldiers. Moreover, though there were still counties like Northumberland where the poor laws remained totally unenforced, the decade of personal rule saw in many shires the establishment of the principle of regular rates for poor relief.[538] The overseer's accounts for the parish of Melbury Osmond, Dorset, for example, where some thirty-six inhabitants contributed payments, show a shift in 1637 from a twice-yearly to monthly rating, 'or oftener if need be' as the annual sums levied were falling far short of expenditure.[539] In Pluckley, Kent, the costs of poor relief rose sharply from £19 5s. 11d. in 1629 to £42 in 1642, as the numbers in receipt of relief increased from 20 in 1628 to 45 in 1641.[540] In 1631, the aldermen of Richmond in Yorkshire reported their need to double weekly payments from 16s. 3d. to 31s. 4d.;[541] Somerton in Somerset had doubled its rate over twenty years;[542] Taunton 'by reason of the many late presses' and the increase in maimed soldiers had in 1631 to raise £50 over and above its usual rate.[543] Banbury the same year doubled its assessments for the poor.[544] The parish of Holy Trinity, Chester, increased payments from £12 to £17 between 1635 and 1639.[545] The amount spent on the poor of Salisbury in the 1630s was double what it had been in the first decade of the century.[546] In Norwich expenditure on the poor rose from an average of £150 per annum in the 1620s to over £400 in the 1640s.[547] In Braintree Essex the payments for the poor rate climbed from £157 in the 1610s to over £1,000 in the 1630s.[548] Whilst such scattered figures and claims should not be used without caution, they do indicate a strong rise over the

538. Fletcher, *Reform in the Provinces*, p. 184.
539. Dorset Record Office, P 223/OV1: Melbury Osmond, account of overseers for poor.
540. Kent Archives Office, P 289/5/1 (1628–64).
541. *Cal. Stat. Pap. Dom., 1631–3*, p. 26.
542. Bates-Harbin, *Quarter Sessions Records for . . . Somerset*, p. 140.
543. *Ibid.*, p. 156.
544. Gibson and Brinkworth, *Banbury Corporation Records*, p. 152.
545. Cheshire Record Office, P1/11.
546. P. Slack (ed.) *Poverty in Early Stuart Salisbury* (Wiltshire Record Soc., 31, 1975), p. 15.
547. I owe this information to a paper given by Dr Paul Slack. See also P. Slack, *Poverty and Policy in Tudor and Stuart England* (1988). Tim Wales suggests most of the increase came in the 1640s. See T. Wales, 'Poverty, poor relief and the life cycle: some evidence from seventeenth-century Norfolk', in R. Smith (ed.) *Land, Kinship and Life Cycle* (Cambridge, 1984), pp. 354–7. I am grateful to Tim Wales for discussions of this point, as much else.
548. Hunt, *Puritan Moment*, p. 235.

decade, which was then again sharply accelerated by the dislocations of the 1640s.[549]

The major cities did most for their poor, as they probably always had. In 1632 the city of York was levying the colossal sum of £445 13s. 8d. which prudently was considerably in excess of sums disbursed in relief.[550] In May of that year it was able to abate the poor rate, there being 'a good stock of money to set the poor on work'.[551] The city, however, did not become complacent about the problem. In addition to the usual officers and a treasurer for maimed soldiers, the aldermen in 1634 appointed a man in each ward with responsibility for distributing money to the old and impotent, among other tasks.[552] The corporation of Bristol had been hard hit by the war demands of the 1620s. In July, and again in October 1629, they had had also to levy a special rate to maintain Irish beggars while they awaited a wind that would remove them from port.[553] During the early 1630s the city was active in efforts to provide food and secure work for the poor and had a good record of private donations to charity, alderman Aldworth leaving £1,000 to the poor of the city in his will.[554] In 1635 the Common Council received a report on its project for the provision of a storehouse for the poor, concluding that 'the benefit of this storehouse we think fit should extend as well to poor householders which have no relief from the parishes as to those which have allowance.'[555] The city sessions took action to ensure provision for orphans and deserted wives.[556] Whilst more research is needed, the impression we have is that though wandering beggars and those whom design or misfortune had transplanted from a 'foreign' parish were usually dispatched without aid (and often with lashes), the impotent poor were not left to starve. The rising numbers of dependants were matched by parish relief, which 'drifted steadily upwards' from 1630.[557]

Doubtless the success with which the poor laws bore the strains imposed on them was due most to local magistrates, and local charity.[558] The different records of the English counties show the extent to which

549. Cf. Jordan, *Philanthropy in England*, p. 136. It is not clear how this (probably very unreliable) graph was compiled.
550. York City Records, E70: books of assessment for relief of poor. In 1629 they abandoned civic feasts to donate the money saved to the poor. York House Books, 35, f.80.
551. York House Books, 35, f.168.
552. *Ibid.*, f.247, 15 Sept. 1634.
553. Bristol Common Council Books, 3, ff.13v, 27.
554. *Ibid.*, f.79.
555. *Ibid.*, insert in book.
556. Bristol Record Office, QS 04446, ff.2, 16v.
557. Though compare Leonard, *English Poor Relief* and A.L. Beier 'Poor relief in Warwickshire, 1630–1660', *P&P*, 35 (1966), pp. 77–100.
558. Fletcher, *Reform in the Provinces*, pp. 186–7; on the local mechanisms see Leonard, *English Poor Relief*, pp. 165–266.

poor relief was dependent on local initiatives. But Professor Fletcher goes too far in arguing that the establishment of the poor rate was 'a triumph of local initiative'.[559] The 1630s, it has recently been argued, was 'the only period when the central government made any consistent effort to ensure that the legislation [for poor relief] was fully implemented'.[560] That pressure not only 'quickened' sluggish JPs;[561] it enabled those magistrates who were besieged by local complaints to appeal to an authority outside the locality. The justices of assize were charged to pay particular attention to relief of the poor. At the Norwich assizes in March 1633, the judges, in response to questions arising from disputes over poor relief, ordered that whilst land ought to be the basis of assessment 'there may be an addition for the visible ability of the parishioners according to good discretion.'[562] In Kent, the sessions for Easter 1634 announced the ruling of Justice Heath concerning the assessments for the poor in the parish of Goudhurst. Heath ordered that all inhabitants were to be rated according to their lands and rents, annuities and other profits deriving therefrom, 'also their abilities', consisting of money, stock, household stuff and other personal estate.[563] He warned that refusers should be indicted and fined according to the quality of their offence. Such judicial pronouncements, as well as confirming the justices' statutory duties and power, may have made it possible to lift the growing burden of the poor rate from relatively humble landowners (several in Melbury Osmond were assessed at 1d.; John Speede of Dorset had two kettles distrained for his arrears) on to those of greater personal wealth.[564]

Over the course of the decade, direct royal and Conciliar directives continued to act as a spur. In 1632 for example the Lord Keeper, by royal command, sent a warrant to the sheriff of Leicester, ordering him to summon a jury to enquire into lands bestowed for charitable uses.[565] In 1635 Charles I ordered the strict enforcement of the statute of 21 James I which imposed a 12d. fine to the poor on all heard cursing or blaspheming, a measure which could have added much to the local coffers.[566] In 1638 a further royal proclamation commanded the establishment of a pension fund for maimed seamen and their widows.[567] The Council also intervened on particular occasions – to urge in 1636 greater attention to the plight of poor debtors in Norwich

559. *Ibid.*, p. 187.
560. Clay, *Economic Expansion*, I, p. 230.
561. Cf. Jordan's remarks about 'continuous pressure' (*Philanthropy in England*, p. 134).
562. Tanner MS 288, f.268v.
563. Kent Archives Office, QSO W1, f.65.
564. Dorset Record Office, P 223/OV1; QS, f.213.
565. Hastings MS, HAM 26.
566. *Cal. Stat. Pap. Dom., 1635*, p. 248.
567. Larkin, *Stuart Royal Proclamations*, II, no. 272. pp. 637–9.

gaol,[568] or in 1638 to request that corn from Devon, Cornwall and Somerset be made available for the relief of the poor in Gloucester and Worcestershire.[569] In the end it is impossible to conclude how much of the action that was taken to relieve poverty stemmed from a local recognition of need and how much from central direction and supervision.[570] The requirements to hold petty sessions and report on poor relief almost certainly reduced the numbers of JPs who felt they could shun this responsibility with impunity and led some to send precise details and figures of action taken and moneys levied.[571] But to whomever the credit is finally due, during the decade that witnessed in France regular uprisings by desperate and starving peasants, the poor laws in England functioned sufficiently well to maintain a period of social stability calmer than any since the Elizabethan legislation was introduced.[572]

Vagrancy and social order

Concern for poor relief not only reflected a genuine concern (about which it is possible to be too cynical) for the less fortunate members of society, it also expressed fears for the maintenance of the social order – at the level of the parish community and the realm. In the eyes of the king and Council indeed the two were closely associated. The vagrancy laws of 1598 were centred on the principle of the parish of domicile to which vagrants, after dire punishment, were to be returned.[573] In 1625, interestingly, Charles I endeavoured to institute the same system in Scotland, ordering all poor and idle beggars to be assigned a parish which might then become responsible for their entertainment through parish rates.[574] Wandering beggars in early modern England were often but one step from becoming cutpurses and highway robbers; they threatened local order and the peace of the realm. While local communities were able to make their own distinctions between the deserving poor (who were often given a bed and a few pence) and the potentially dangerous, the suppression and

568. PRO, PC 2/46/89.
569. PRO, PC 2/48/506.
570. Jordan, *Philanthropy in England*, pp. 135, 268; Leonard, *English Poor Relief*, p. 254.
571. *Cal. Stat. Pap. Dom., 1636–7*, p. 329; *1638–9*, p. 284.
572. Jordan, *Philanthropy in England*, p. 133; Leonard, *English Poor Relief*, ch. 8, esp. pp. 132, 163–4, 254; G.W. Oxley, *Poor Relief in England and Wales, 1601–1834* (Newton Abbot, 1974), pp. 17–18. The achievement is all the greater when placed alongside the difficult circumstances. See Clay, *Economic Expansion*, I, pp. 216–18.
573. Leonard, *English Poor Relief*, pp. 133–6; Jordan, *Philanthropy in England*, pp. 94–8; Fletcher, *Reform in the Provinces*, p. 204; Slack, *Poverty and Policy*, pp. 126–9.
574. National Library of Scotland, Advocates' MS 33/7/11.

punishment of vagrancy concerned local magistrates as much as the Council.[575] In 1629, with the bad harvest evoking fears, the Dorset quarter sessions ordered that all beggars should be punished in the house of correction with 'moderate whipping'.[576] What the Book of Orders did, in this respect as in others, was quicken both the enforcement of existing legislation for punishing vagrants, and the prohibition on subdividing houses into tenements, in which the wandering poor took refuge.[577] The names and numbers of 'inmates' and vagrants whipped were required of constables, overseers and JPs by the orders, and perhaps in consequence there were, as Professor Fletcher has concluded, 'more signs of determination in the attack on vagrancy during the 1630s than in the preceding or succeeding decades'.[578] In 1632 the JPs of Worcester reported 105 vagrants punished in Evesham and Pershore in the first three months of the year.[579] Evidently their zeal was not typical. For the charge to the judges in June 1632 referred to the failure of the late orders to deal with the vagrant problem: 'execution is made in one county and not in another. Now unless execution be done in all, it will but drive them from one county to another.'[580]

The Council blamed the failure on the justices of the peace and then, after more charges, on the justices of assize who, they maintained, had failed to admonish the magistrates.[581] In 1638 Coventry reminded the circuit judges of the printed orders 'wherein excellent rules are set down for the repressing and punishing of vagabonds', concerning which, 'you have failed to do as it was expected from you'.[582] The Council tried to maintain the momentum of the orders by writing directly to the JPs, as it did to those of Kent in 1634 about the vagrants known to be wandering the highways of the shire. The magistrates were put in mind of their duties and the frequent exhortations to fulfil them:

> sometimes we have observed some present amendment upon the same by the discharging of the highways and streets of those persons, yet it seemeth the care thereof is so much remitted as

575. Slack, *Poverty and Policy*, pp. 92–4; cf. P. Slack, 'Vagrants and vagrancy in England, 1598–1664', *Econ. Hist. Rev.*, 27 (1974), pp. 360–80; see esp. p. 368 and A.L. Beier, *Masterless Men* (1985).
576. Dorset Record Office, QS f.115v.
577. Fletcher, *Reform in the Provinces*, pp. 205–10.
578. *Ibid.*, p. 209.
579. *Cal. Stat. Pap. Dom., 1631–3*, p. 305.
580. Rawlinson MS A.128.
581. Rawlinson MS C.827; Bodleian, Ashmole MS 824, V1, f.56; cf. Temple of Stowe MS 9, STT 2315.
582. Rawlinson MS B.243; cf. PRO, PC 2/49/272.

> the streets and highways are as soon after as much pestered with them, as we do observe at this time an extraordinary confluence of rogues and beggars on the highways about London.[583]

Such exhortations to vigilance certainly spurred local governors to greater efforts: the thirty-seven counties which returned certificates listed a total over the decade of 26,000 vagrants apprehended and punished, 614 in the counties of Kent, Sussex and Surrey, 916 from Lancashire and Westmorland.[584] In April 1636, the hundred of Cashio, St Albans, claimed it had shipped 192 vagrants since its last certificate;[585] Chafford in Essex listed 169 punished in one quarter of 1637.[586] The 'failure' that the Council perceived needs to be set in the context of these figures of magisterial activity. Yet the fact remains that vagrants apprehended 'were only the tip of the iceberg'.[587] In part this was due to a leniency on the part of some humble local officers who evidently felt more sympathy for the homeless poor than did their superiors. 'Constables' accounts,' writes Dr Slack, 'show that less than one in ten of the migrants passing through a village were usually whipped.'[588] In Wiltshire in 1633 no fewer than thirty-three constables were indicted for their delinquency in apprehending vagrants.[589] But recent research on constables' activities has suggested that such remissness was not widespread, and that in the 1630s in particular, the JPs of several counties were testifying to the greater diligence of their subordinates.[590]

It may be therefore that the Privy Council interpreted as unwillingness what was the inability of the magistrates in this respect and failed to appreciate the difficulties faced in containing vagrancy even by JPs who were industrious and severe in dealing with the problem. A growing class of landless poor was clearly adding numbers to the body of migrants and rogues who wandered the highways in search of work or easier, illicit pickings.[591] Moreover, the class of vagrants (only vaguely defined in the poor laws) was a fluctuating group not always easily defined, let alone policed. In Dorset, for example, a group of day labourers imported into Holnest parish by some brickmakers and tilemakers lived 'loosely', frequenting alehouses and committing many

583. Dering MS U350/010, 19 March 1634.
584. Fletcher, *Reform in the Provinces*, p. 207; Slack, 'Vagrants and vagrancy in England', p. 361.
585. *Cal. Stat. Pap. Dom., 1636–7*, p. 44.
586. *Cal. Stat. Pap. Dom., 1637–8*, p. 135.
587. Slack, 'Vagrants and vagrancy in England', p. 361.
588. Slack, *Poverty and Policy*, p. 92. This is not to suggest that the statute intended that all should be whipped; rather it gave the constable the power of a threat to move on the vagrant.
589. Kent, *Village Constable*, p. 201.
590. Fletcher, *County Community*, p. 166; Kent, *Village Constable*, p. 202.
591. Beier, *Masterless Men*, ch. 2.

disorders – a reminder that then even more than now 'navvies' and homeless vagrants could not easily be differentiated.[592] The most criminal and violent, like the band that terrorized the neighbourhood of Horsted Keynes in Sussex, were not to be tackled lightly.[593] And the more engaging and colourful professional vagrants, Shakespeare's Autolycus and his like, did not lack for their pack of wiles and ruses by which they endlessly dodged the authorities. Disabilities were feigned; hard-luck stories were told to the gullible.[594] Passes and licences for begging were often forged. Sir John Coke, writing to the Earl of Huntingdon about the abuse of licences, remarked 'indeed of late the country hath been much abused with writings of this sort brought by divers pretending great losses in Ireland and annexing counterfeit subscriptions'.[595] Even when detected and taken away, Coke appreciated, such certificates could be renewed 'under every hedge'.[596] 'It is possible,' he acknowledged, 'to counterfeit a nobleman's name very near his own manner of writing.' This was more than mere rhetoric: one Salisbury vagrant had a certificate forged literally 'by a stranger under a hedge' and may well have paid the two or three shillings it cost from the proceeds of ill-gotten gains.[597] The problem of vagrancy exposed the weaknesses of local government even when Council orders and local interests were closely identified.

Measures continued to be taken at local and central level. In 1635 the governors of Grantham in Lincolnshire procured an order from the assize judges permitting them to punish those who took in lodgers.[598] In February 1637 a Star Chamber decree revived an earlier enactment of 40 Elizabeth that if landlords divided properties into tenements and let them to the poor, the tenants might live there rent free.[599] In 1635 more radical steps were proposed. Evidently the Council considered the appointment in each county of a provost marshal with responsibility for dealing with vagrants.[600] Counties like Sussex which had experimented with the system had found it efficacious and adopted it regularly.[601] But in other parts of the realm, provost marshals were disliked as a charge on and intrusion into local society, a rival jurisdiction to the commission of the peace. The Earl of Warwick argued in October 1635 that they were 'of very little benefit' in suppressing

592. Dorset Record Office, QS, ff.248–248v.
593. Fletcher, *County Community*, p. 167.
594. Slack, 'Vagrants and vagrancy in England', esp. pp. 364–5.
595. Hastings MS 1536: Sir John Coke to Earl of Huntingdon, 12 Oct. 1639.
596. *Ibid.*; cf. Slack, 'Vagrants and vagrancy in England', p. 364.
597. Slack, *Poverty and Policy*, p. 97.
598. C. Holmes, *Seventeenth Century Lincolnshire*, p. 37.
599. *Cal. Stat. Pap. Dom., 1636–7*, p. 443.
600. *Cal. Stat. Pap. Dom., 1635*, p. 417.
601. Fletcher, *Reform in the Provinces*, pp. 209–10.

vagabonds 'who resort by foot-paths and bye-ways to one end of the county when they know the provost marshal to be in the other'.[602] Essex asked to be free of them.[603] The problem of vagrants fell in the end on the constables of the parishes; enforcement of the laws against them was varying, partial and spasmodic. Vagrancy was an intractable problem that surpassed the capacities of early modern, as it has of modern, government.

The regulation of the alehouse

Closely linked to concern about vagrants and the wandering poor were efforts to regulate that assembly room of the lower orders, the alehouse. In part the desire to limit and control alehouses in the early 1630s sprang from the need to regulate brewing at a time of a dearth of grain.[604] But the suspicion of the alehouse, among Privy Councillors and local magistrates, perhaps too with the 'parish elite' of the 'middling sort', went further. Hostility to the tavern was not confined to the puritans: alehouses were often depicted as the havens of migrants, petty criminals, prostitutes, immoral liaisons, irreligion and sedition. More generally, the double-ale consumed in large quantities (six men were seen by the author of *A Monster Late Found Out* to drink one hundred pots)[605] and the dubious gambling at dice and slide groat were suspected for their corruption of innocent folk and as solvents of the moral community on which the fragile stability of the early modern locality rested.[606] Though the reality, as Peter Clark has shown, was less colourful and menacing than the image, the alehouse continued as a symbol of the fear of social decadence and disruption, even though in some parts of the country the lesser gentry and clergy were known to join their inferiors in a pickled herring and pot by a roaring fireside.[607] The uncontrolled growth in the number of premises, especially unlicensed houses, fuelled the fears and determination to control them.[608] Thomas Dekker the playwright claimed in 1632 that whole

602. *Cal. Stat. Pap. Dom., 1635*, p. 417.
603. See R.B. Manning, *Village Revolts: Social Protest and Popular Disturbances in England, 1509–1640* (Oxford, 1988), pp. 184–5.
604. For example, Bates-Harbin, *Quarter Sessions Records for . . . Somerset*, p. 144; Wrightson, 'Two concepts of order', p. 39; Hastings MS 4225.
605. R. Rawlidge, *A Monster Late Found Out* (1628, STC 20766), p. 18.
606. *Ibid.*, p. 20; cf. *Cal. Stat. Pap. Dom., 1631–3*, pp. 133–4.
607. P. Clark, 'The alehouse and the alternative society', in D. Pennington and K. Thomas (eds) *Puritans and Revolutionaries* (Oxford, 1978), pp. 47–72; *idem*, *The English Alehouse* (1983), ch. 7; cf. K. Wrightson, 'Alehouses, order and reformation in rural England, 1590–1660', in E. and S. Yeo (eds) *Popular Culture and Class Conflict* (Hassocks, 1981), pp. 1–27; and S.K. Roberts, 'Alehouses, brewing and government under the early Stuarts', *Southern History*, 2 (1980), pp. 45–71.
608. Clark, *English Alehouse*, ch. 3.

streets of the capital had become 'but a continued alehouse';[609] in 1637 Dean Fell reported to Laud that there were nearly one hundred unlicensed establishments in Oxford.[610] The aldermen of York complained that they were the resort of lewd company;[611] the JPs of Warwick told their sheriff that they were 'the true nurseries of almost all the disorders'.[612]

Legislation to control the growth had been established by the statute 5 and 6 Edward VI Cap 25, which had set up the licensing sessions and the requirement of recognizances backed by two sureties.[613] Dekker felt that 'if the acts against these enormities were severely executed and drunkards punished as the law does sentence them, then would London be a very sober city.'[614] Local authorities and communities therefore tried to restrict the number of licences: the Grand Jury of Northamptonshire in 1630 suggesting that half the alehouses that had sprung up be suppressed 'and that there may be not above one in a country town that is not a thoroughfare'.[615] Enforcement of the statutes and procedures, however, was more complicated. Alehouses suppressed by one JP were often able to secure a licence from another, especially when magistrates stood to gain from the licensing fee, themselves had an interest in the brewing business, or were very simply reluctant to close a popular establishment.[616] The Somerset quarter sessions in 1630 was still tackling the problem after a series of regulatory enactments.[617] The efforts of the North Riding to ban from alehouses all unlawful games, vagrants, bad characters and seditious or foul language were even less likely to have been efficacious.[618]

The Book of Orders gave an impetus to the system of licensing by requiring reports on alehouses as part of the quarterly returns made by the justices of the peace to the assize judges.[619] Dr Wrightson has argued that as a consequence the early 1630s saw one of the greatest purges of unlicensed establishments. The Council maintained the pressure;[620] in 1633 they ordered a survey of all alehouses in London;[621] in 1635 they required all clerks of the peace to certify recognizances to London.[622] There is clear evidence that central intervention had

609. Dekker, *English Villainies*, sigs K3–3v.
610. *Works of Laud*, V, p. 179, 15 Aug. 1637.
611. York House Books, 35, ff.82, 83v.
612. *Cal. Stat. Pap. Dom., 1631–3*, pp. 133–4.
613. Fletcher, *Reform in the Provinces*, p. 232.
614. Dekker, *English Villainies*, sig.K.4v.
615. Wake, *Quarter Sessions Records of Northampton*, p. 64.
616. PRO, PC 2/44/91; Fletcher, *Reform in the Provinces*, pp. 235–8.
617. Bates-Harbin, *Quarter Sessions Records for . . . Somerset*, p. 120.
618. Atkinson, *North Riding Quarter Session*, p. 33.
619. Clark, 'Alehouse and alternative society', p. 69.
620. Wrightson, 'Two concepts of order', p. 39.
621. PRO, PC 2/43/151, 157.
622. Fletcher, *Reform in the Provinces*, p. 233.

some effect: the JPs' certificates frequently list the numbers of licensed alehouses, the names of their keepers and fines imposed on those who ran illicit establishments. Skenfrith in Monmouth licensed fifty-six alehouses at one sessions in 1637 – and suppressed seventy-two;[623] Great Yarmouth collected £5 in fines in the summer of 1636.[624] However, checking the mushroom growth of the unlicensed house, often a modest room with free-flowing beer, was much more difficult than the regulating of licences. The Privy Council may have had some realistic chance of restricting the number of alehouses in Covent Garden to two, despite the complaints, but further from Whitehall such regulation was often literally no more than a pious hope.[625] For all the activities of Twysden and Dering in Kent, meetings in church with constables formulating an agreed list of desirable numbers, unlicensed alehouses continued to spring up.[626] John Edwards, estate manager to Thomas Smyth of Ashton Court, informed his master that though the JPs had issued warrants for the prosecution of brewers who supplied unlicensed houses, 'there is a way found to cosin the justice . . . they send for ale by pail fuls and fill their barrels that way and will sell in spite of any'.[627] In Bristol, Eleanour Westwood who set up an unlicensed alehouse to support herself when her husband was at sea typified a more general problem: that suppression of such small enterprises threatened to throw more on an overstrained poor rate.[628] Bristol records also reveal another popular ruse whereby wives took over the 'business' after their husbands had been convicted.[629] Even in that well-regulated second city of the realm the maintenance of an unlicensed tippling house was the most commonly recorded offence. In the North Riding of Yorkshire presentments of unauthorized tippling houses (some apparently maintained by keepers licensed elsewhere) rose from 87 in 1636 to over 200 in 1638.[630] The figures and frustrated efforts to reduce them demonstrate that timeless adage that where there is a market there will always be a ready supply. Whatever the sensibilities of their betters, for the lower orders the alehouse hearth, company and cup, licensed or unlicensed, provided that little cheer that made a life of hardship more durable.

If the circumscribing of numbers proved difficult, the regulation of behaviour at the alehouse must have been nigh impossible. Sir William

623. *Cal. Stat. Pap. Dom., 1637*, p. 275.
624. *Cal. Stat. Pap. Dom., 1636–7*, p. 331.
625. PRO, PC 2/43/508.
626. Twysden MS U47/47, Z1, p. 44.
627. Smyth of Ashton Court MS 36074/140 (c).
628. Bristol Record Office, quarter sessions 04446, f.4; Clark, 'Alehouse and alternative society', pp. 53–4; *idem*, *English Alehouse*, ch. 4.
629. For example, Bristol Record Office, QS 04446, f.6.
630. Atkinson, *North Riding Quarter Sessions*, pp. 63, 79, 106.

Bellenden's propositions that alehouses should not open at time of service, that no cards or 'shovegroat' be played nor any strong beer brewed there, that no unmarried couple be admitted nor any drinker permitted to remain after 9 p.m., make this writer less critical of modern licensing laws but sceptical of the likelihood of the enforcement of Bellenden's measures.[631] The king and Council, however, took them seriously. In 1634 the Board issued directives that only alehouses 'known by sufficient testimony to be of honest conversation' might continue;[632] in Yorkshire Wentworth, as Lord President, attempted to outlaw drinking beyond half an hour at a session.[633] Such strictures, if enforced, would certainly have placed on the record of offenders most of this writer's acquaintance, let alone the doubtlessly even more bibulous frequenters of the early modern alehouse. The point is that even if such proposals met with the sympathies of local JPs, their implementation at the parish level was never likely in a system of parish government that drew its officers from the local community, to which they returned after their term of office. For all the recent emphasis on the 'elite' status of many constables, there were at least as many quaffing with their neighbours;[634] and if they were not, there was none to know how long men made merry with their cups. As the Kentish minister John Bankes wrote to Sir Edward Dering, it was difficult to enforce laws against tippling, for prosecution required two witnesses and 'what witness that makes conscience of an oath dare swear that such company hath been in that house tippling for so long a time, unless he were there present with them'![635] Bankes had laboured, he said, to suppress drinking, but it required a coercive power from without. Complaints about the excessive number of and disorder emanating from alehouses continued through the Commonwealth and Protectorate.[636] But happily in most cases the desires of the local community overrode the denunciation of the moralists and the strict enforcement of the law.[637]

The Book of Orders: a review

Bankes's observation may serve as a fitting comment on the Book of Orders in general. Despite the appointment of the commission of

631. Bankes MS 66/12.
632. PRO, PC 2/43/542.
633. York House Books, 35, f.186.
634. Dekker, *English Villainies*, sig.K.3v; Kent, *Village Constable*, pp. 215–16; and see pp. 271–2; Wrightson, 'Two concepts of order', pp. 27–9.
635. Dering MS U350/C2/88.
636. Clark, *English Alehouse*, pp. 176–8; *idem*, 'Alehouse and alternative society', pp. 66–7.
637. Fletcher, *County Community*, pp. 153–4.

Councillors in 1631, there was no coercive power from without that had the knowledge and capacity to enforce the orders at the local level. The constable was accountable to the JP of course and the JP to the Council, but in the end both JPs and Councillors depended upon the most local official. And constables lived in a complex authority/consensus relationship with the communities in which they dwelt. The very different evaluations of the effectiveness of the Book of Orders by county historians themselves suggest that local circumstances were crucial in its implementation.[638] But to recognize that is not to go so far as to argue that it was largely irrelevant to the conduct of local government during the personal rule.[639] The Book was an important initiative in its attempts to spur local officials to carry out their duties and in its bureaucratization, through the quarterly reports, of their accountability for their actions. From many corners of the county, across a range of business there is clear evidence that it succeeded in, to use the Council's own term, 'quickening' the magistrate. Beyond that, we should be cautious of the excessive claims by some historians for the success and purpose of the Book. For it neither pre-empted the modern welfare state nor represented a bid by king and Council for centralization of the state.[640] It did nothing to change the policies or structure of local government and so was subject to the inbuilt inefficiencies of traditional courses and arrangements. Yet in all that it very much expressed the royal mind, whatever the king's part in its making. As we have remarked, Charles I was a conservative ruler with a strong sense that traditional Henrician and Elizabethan ways had worked and could be made to work again – through an obedience that would follow on a renewed royal injunction to duty. Within broad parameters, that optimism was not entirely misplaced. Though corruption, interests, idleness and opposition obstructed the establishment of the social harmony, order and paternalism that Charles idealized and represented in masques and pastoral landscapes, without the agencies of central authority developed on the continent a food supply was maintained and poor relief was provided (despite the rising costs). Social stability was preserved to a degree that was the envy of other European monarchies. The success of the Book of Orders of course owed much to the coincidence of the interest of the magisterial class with the programmes of central government. Our second case

638. For example, Barnes, *Somerset*, ch. 7; Morrill, *Cheshire*, p. 26; Hunt, *Puritan Moment*, pp. 71, 248–50; Hughes, *Politics, Society and the Civil War*, p. 111; P. Clark, *English Provincial Society from the Reformation to the Revolution* (Hassocks, 1977), pp. 350–3; B. Sharp, *In Contempt of all Authority*, pp. 55, 76–81. And see, more generally, the articles by Slack and Quintrell on the Book of Orders and Fletcher's *Reform in the Provinces*.

639. Fletcher comes too close to this conclusion in *Reform in the Provinces*, pp. 57–9.

640. As Leonard argued in *English Poor Relief*, for example, pp. 266, 297–300.

study of reform, therefore, must examine a project in which, it has been argued, the localities were less involved, to which they were often indifferent or antagonistic: the endeavours of the king and Council to establish an 'exact militia'.

The quest for an 'exact militia'

During the war years 1625–8 the county militia had often shown itself to be a ramshackle band, ill-equipped, poorly trained, deficient in numbers and hard to discipline.[641] The most active lieutenants and deputies had recognized and endeavoured to cure the problems. In Sussex, the Earl of Dorset acted to stop the borrowing of arms for musters, ordered the marking of each horse and harried the deputies to modernize weapons and equipment;[642] the deputy lieutenant of Cheshire improved the payments for the militia by a reassessment of local landowners to take account of changes of ownership and wealth.[643] In many parts of the country, however, musters, even in wartime, had been treated as matters of form only. The king and Council saw the need to take action. Some advocated monthly musters;[644] the deputy lieutenants of Devon suggested a thrice yearly meeting of all officers and some of the trained bands to accustom them to working together.[645] The Council Board discussed propositions for sending pursuivants to musters to haul defaulters directly back to Whitehall and for a biennial military review of the shire by deputy lieutenants.[646] They considered the appointment too of a special muster master for the notoriously deficient horse, as well as foot.[647] Wentworth, sounding a tune that he was to sing for the rest of the decade, stressed the need to deal firmly with those who failed persistently to attend musters or supply arms, telling Lord President Conway, 'unless there be a severe hand held . . . his Majesty's ministers shall never be able to effect this important service, there being a universal defection nay shaking off this duty almost in every corner of the Kingdom'.[648] As a result of its deliberations, in 1629 the Council issued orders for the training and equipping of the county bands in the

641. Above, pp. 23–32.
642. East Sussex Record Office, LCD/EW1, f.5v.
643. Chester Record Office, CR63/2/6, ff.45–46; cf. East Sussex Record Office, LCD/EW1, f.58.
644. For example, Norfolk Record Office, WLS, XVII/2, 410 X 5 (De Grey Letter Book): Maltravers to De Grey, 7 Aug. 1635.
645. *Cal. Stat. Pap. Dom., 1625–49*, p. 13: Francis, Lord Russell to Conway, 11 Jan. 1628.
646. PRO, SP 16/89/17.
647. *Cal. Stat. Pap. Dom., 1625–49*, p. 363.
648. *Cal. Stat. Pap. Dom., 1629–31*, p. 78: Wentworth to Conway, 14 Oct. 1629; cf. Knowler, *Strafford Letters*, II, pp. 411–13.

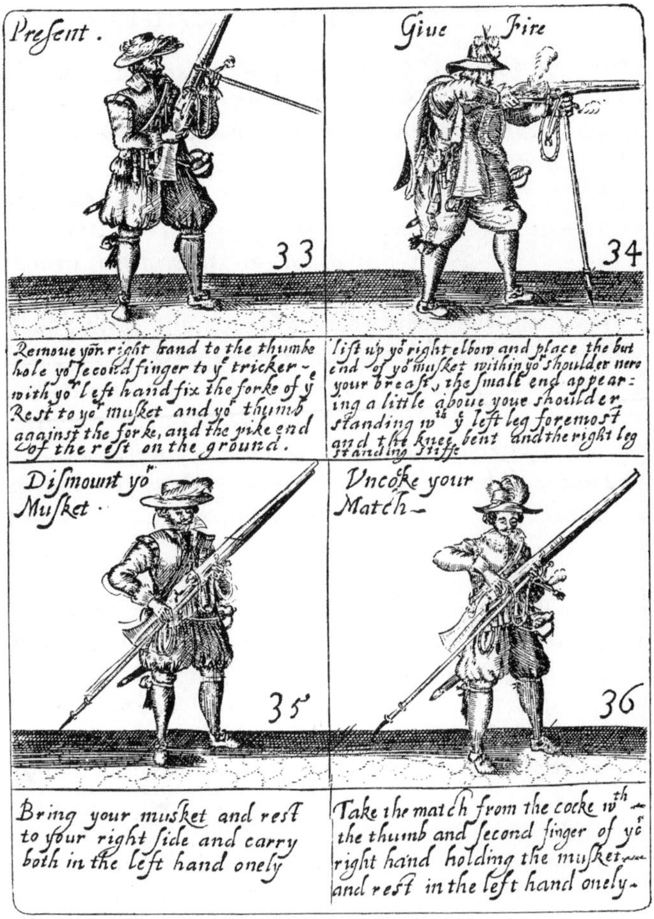

36 Order of drilling for the musket from *Directions for Musters . . . , 1638.*

modern fashion. They commanded that officers and soldiers be able and sufficient, and (in a year when the Edict of Restitution excited fears of Catholics) that they take the oaths of allegiance and supremacy. Once enrolled, none was to be permitted to avoid the service: if an enrolled soldier moved his dwelling, notice was to be given to a deputy lieutenant so that a replacement might be found to maintain the band. The counties were ordered to repair and maintain beacons, to store a supply of powder and match in magazines and to raise contributions for a muster master, responsible for ordering and training the bands.[649] (See Figure 36.) There was nothing novel about the orders: they reaffirmed the instructions of 1626 and attempted to remedy the deficiencies since catalogued. They endeavoured to deal

649. *Acts of the Privy Council, July 1628 to April 1629*, pp. 419–21, 30 April 1629; Ellesmere MS 7618.

with the long-term problem of social change which had eroded the very basis of the militia. Lord-lieutenants were instructed that in a case where a manor house, charged to supply arms, was divided among co-heirs or tenants, the charge was to be transferred to the new owners or occupiers, 'that no such alteration may diminish the bands which should rather be increased, especially the horse'.[650] The orders formed the basis of the Council's efforts to reform the militia during the first half of the decade.

They were not the only action taken. On 2 January 1630 a warrant was issued for a commission to survey the ordnance, which convened in March.[651] A committee of the Council for the ordnance met weekly during the 1630s, and ordered regular reviews of the stores of arms and munitions.[652] In 1630 the Council ordered the enforcement of the statute 33 Henry VIII whereby fathers were required to train their children in shooting with bows and arrows.[653] Charles I, to set an example, offered his protection to the company exercising at arms in the Artillery Yard.[654] Though peace was now concluded, the drive to refashion the militia continued. June 1631 saw the publication of a royal proclamation for the new making, repairing and stamping of armour.[655] As well as stressing the need for a national armoury to free the realm of dependence on foreign supplies, the proclamation provided for commissioners to go down to the localities where they would order the muster rolls, inspect the county's arms, order the alteration, repair, supply and stamping of the weapons and, incidentally, collect a levy for their expenses. Unusual in the degree of central interference it envisaged, the proclamation illustrates the king and Council's determination to raise the standards of the country's defences.

The problems and obstacles, however, were manifold. The effects of rapid social change and changes of land ownership were hard to counteract: in Staffordshire the county light horse had diminished from 99 to 31, by the gradual accumulation of land in the same hands; elsewhere the division of manors reduced the complement.[656] The natural rhythms of local life – harvest and bad weather – often disrupted training.[657] Natural indolence and reluctance to muster were

650. *Acts of the Privy Council, July 1628 to April 1629*, p. 420.
651. *Cal. Stat. Pap. Dom., 1629–31*, p. 158; Coventry MS 602204/222.
652. PRO, PC 2/41/1; the committee met on Friday mornings.
653. *Cal. Stat. Pap. Dom., 1629–31*, p. 465; cf. Larkin, *Stuart Royal Proclamations*, II, no. 150, pp. 329–30.
654. *Cal. Stat. Pap. Dom., 1631–3*, p. 284.
655. Larkin, *Stuart Royal Proclamations*, II, no. 149, pp. 321–8.
656. G. Wrottesley (ed.) *The Staffordshire Muster of AD 1640* (William Salt Archaeological Soc. 15, 1894), p. 203; Stone, *Crisis of the Aristocracy*, pp. 36–9, chs 4 and 5.
657. Herriard MS 029; Firth MS C.4, p. 461.

heightened by the security of peace and recession of foreign threats. In Sussex, efforts to exercise the bands on holiday ran up against their preference for drinking.[658] As for the auxiliaries, who were also obliged to attend at musters, according to Gervase Markham, 'having given in their names they depart away without any exercise or military instruction and so spend out the rest of the day in the alehouse . . . where they laugh at those which are taking pains'.[659] Doubt about the legal basis of the militia after the repeal in 1604 of 4 and 5 Philip and Mary Cap 3 may have strengthened the resolve of some defaulters.[660] Perhaps more importantly, together with the attack on their activities in the parliament of 1628, it undermined the authority of the deputies to proceed against the recalcitrant.[661] Those of east Sussex in 1631 'find still many defects in the due execution of our directions and some in two or three years have not returned any certificate at all'.[662] The deputy lieutenants of Rutland confessed to the Earl of Huntingdon their frustrations concerning those who 'have been found many times defective yet will not amend though often warned'.[663] Southampton refused to muster on the technical ground that the letters had been directed to the captains of the bands and not the mayor.[664] Hampshire admitted that some refractory of better quality had been omitted from a list of defaulters sent to the Council, lest the knowledge of their refusal become a bad example.[665] The Earl of Newcastle in 1633 echoed Wentworth's sense of the need to punish the refractory in order to bring others to conformity, but the threatening words were seldom followed by severity.[666] In 1632 a Council order banning levies of men for service abroad acknowledged that there were too few for the service of the realm at home.[667] Failure to establish an equitable militia rate added other problems.[668] The county powder magazines often fell far short of the standards anticipated in the orders of 1629: in December 1632, Sir Edward Dering confessed to the Earl of Suffolk that the 'proportion of powder in Dover Castle is so small that . . .

658. East Sussex Record Office, LCD/EW1, f.31.
659. G. Markham, *The Art of Archerie* (1634, STC 17333), p. 23.
660. L. Boynton, *The Elizabethan Militia* (1967), p. 209.
661. Above, p. 28.
662. East Sussex Record Office, LCD/EW1, f.74v.
663. Hastings MS 10620: deputy lieutenants to Huntingdon, 17 Sept. 1634.
664. Herriard MS XL/22.
665. Herriard MS XL/34.
666. *Cal. Stat. Pap. Dom., 1633–4*, p. 281: Newcastle to Council, 9 Nov. 1633. Cf. A. Hassell Smith, 'Militia rates and militia statutes, 1558–1663', in P. Clark, A.G.R. Smith and N. Tyacke (eds) *The English Commonwealth, 1547–1640* (Leicester, 1979), pp. 93–110, esp. p. 105.
667. Trumbull Add. MS 36.
668. Hassell Smith, 'Militia rates and militia statutes'; Herefordshire had no annual rate in 1635; Ellesmere MS 7674.

there will not be a corn of powder left'.[669] Arrears of payments of rates (Sir Arthur Haselrig owed nearly £5 in Leicestershire) meant, as well as poor supplies of powder and stock, that weapons and armour were neither maintained nor replaced with more modern equipment.[670] The Earl of Newport believed that many trained bands used old shot, 'which will be useless when there should be most occasion of employment', and antiquated muskets.[671] The Earl of Huntingdon endeavouring as Lord-Lieutenant of his county to replace old armour, some of it shot through with holes, met with protests that the new arms were no better and the old were still allowed elsewhere.[672] There have been enough debates in modern times about the costs of modernizing the country's weapons for us to appreciate that there were many in early modern England who preferred to keep their hands on their old muskets – and purses.

Some of the Council's desired 'improvements' threatened more than local purses. In particular the efforts to secure an adequate store of gunpowder in central and local arsenals were to subject many to considerable inconvenience and indignity. Gunpowder was made from saltpetre, which is produced where lime and decaying organic matter are found together. In seventeenth-century England the most obvious locations were houses, stables and, especially it would appear, dovecots. During the 1620s commissioners in search of saltpetre descended upon houses and proceeded to dig up the floors of stables and dovecots where the accumulated droppings of years and a lime soil had chemically combined to produce the nitrate. As a method of securing a regular supply, this was both inadequate and understandably unpopular.[673] In 1627 therefore Charles I had issued a proclamation for 'the better making of saltpetre within this kingdom'. Explaining the dangers of reliance on foreign supplies and acknowledging 'the trouble and grievance of our loving subjects by digging up of their dwelling houses', the proclamation concluded with the extraordinary command that all subjects were to preserve the 'stale' of their beasts and their own urine 'during the whole year' for the use of the gunpowder manufacturers.[674] Not surprisingly, the project did not meet with success. In July of the same year a further proclamation forbade

669. *HMC Cowper I*, p. 487, 23 Dec. 1632.
670. Hastings MSS, Military Box 1, 1637: 'A note of such money as Sir Arthur Haselrig Baronet is in arrear for the musters'.
671. *Cal. Stat. Pap. Dom., 1634–5*, p. 385.
672. Hastings MSS, Legal Box 7: papers re Star Chamber case, Huntington v. Sir William Faunt.
673. See, for example, Herriard MSS, Box 013 for Hampshire petitions against the petremen and Sir Thomas Jervoise's correspondence with the Lords Commissioners for the Admiralty concerning the grievance.
674. Larkin, *Stuart Royal Proclamations*, II, no. 58, pp. 116–20.

any to pave the floors of stables or dovecots which should 'lie open with good and mellow earth, apt to breed increase of the said . . . saltpetre'. The king ordered that none refuse access to the petremen nor bribe them 'for the sparing of any ground'.[675]

If the injunction acknowledged the grievances of the petremen's corruption and, still more, their brutal invasion of the domestic realm, it did little to palliate them. In March 1629 the Grand Jury of Essex formally protested at being 'oppressed by the late petremen'.[676] The following year a petition in Hampshire catalogued their abuses, including bribes of 5s. taken to spare some houses.[677] When one of the deputies, Sir Thomas Jervoise, invited the petitioners to present their case at Basingstoke, they showed the strength of their feelings by assembling in 'hordes'.[678] Jervoise heard of scandalous abuses: carts commandeered, due payments not made, pigeon-houses and stables damaged, even the very rooms where adults and children slept overturned and left unrepaired. Investigation over the next month revealed more misdemeanours: illicit charges, broken planks and boards, corruption, corn ruined when barns were dug up and, as the petitioners had claimed, digging in 'the very chambers and under the beds where they and their children lay that people knew not what to do nor how to follow their labour'.[679] If the list were not long enough, Jervoise observed that he could have added more charges but was determined to 'certify nothing . . . but what was clearly and fully proved'.[680] Similar laments were heard from other parts of the country. Sir Francis Seymour wrote from Somerset to complain to Secretary Coke that 'the saltpetremen care not in whose houses they dig, threatening men that by their commission they may dig in any man's house, in any room and at any time . . . if any oppose them they break up men's houses and dig by force'.[681] Seymour added that their taking of carriages at sowing and harvest time ranked among many other oppressions. Even Sir William Russell, treasurer of the navy, reported to the Lords of the Admiralty: 'there is no part of their commission which they have not abused'. The petremen, he explained, dug dovecots in breeding time, barns at harvest time, malthouses when the malt was green on the floor, even churches 'and in bedchambers placing their tubs by the bedside of the old and sick, even of women in childbed and persons on their death beds'.[682] Reading such graphic evidence, it is easy to see

675. *Ibid.*, no. 72, pp. 157–62.
676. Firth MS C.4, p. 521.
677. Herriard MSS, Box 013, 11 April 1630.
678. *Ibid.*, 11 March 1630.
679. *Ibid.*, 11 March 1630: Jervoise to commissioners for the Admiralty.
680. *Ibid.*, 18 May 1630: Jervoise to commissioners for the Admiralty.
681. *Cal. Stat. Pap. Dom., 1629–31*, p. 188: Seymour to Coke, 14 May 1630.
682. *Ibid.*, p. 245, 30 April 1630.

why the petremen were regarded as the hypocritical 'Pharisees' of the commonweal. 'I do not think there is any of [that] fraternity,' a correspondent told Coke, 'but abuse both King and people.'[683] The king and Council were not deaf to the grievances nor blind to the abuses: one Hillyard, one of the commissioners for the manufacture of saltpetre in Dorset and Gloucestershire, received harsh punishment for selling it rather than delivering the petre to the king's storehouse.[684] In February 1634 Thomas Helliard (perhaps the same offender), John Goodenough, Hugh Nicholls and others were prosecuted in Star Chamber for 'several misdemeanours and oppression of the gentry by colour of a bond for digging of saltpetre'.[685]

Oppressed gentlemen found it easier to seek amends than most. In general the policing of the saltpetremen was impossible. Gunpowder was urgently needed: as Viscount Wimbledon observed in 1635, 'it were better the Kingdom of England were without walls than powder . . . in time of peace provision must be made for war, for in time of war it is too late'.[686] Until the chemical production of sodium nitrate there was no alternative method of supply except East India Company imports from India.[687] While they heard and investigated complaints of abuses, the Lords of the Admiralty were asking Attorney Bankes to frame a proclamation requiring justices of the peace to assist the saltpetremen with their work.[688] The pressure of necessity then left room for the dishonest or over-zealous commissioners to continue to abuse their warrants. Some, like George Sparke at Chester, even posed as petremen in order to plunder.[689] Clashes continued: the pigeon-house of the rectory at Knoyle Magna in Wiltshire collapsed after the petremen had dug there;[690] in Norwich in 1635 the saltpetre workers threw a parish officer who questioned their activities down a 45-foot-deep well.[691] Thomas Bond was right to predict to Nicholas that whatever the complaints against them, the petremen would carry on as before; and he was as perceptive in his sense of the consequences: 'if the saltpetremen go down without redress of wrongs, it will strike despair into the heart of the country'.[692] Despair and resentment of the saltpetre manufacturers continued unabated throughout the 1630s. The author of *The Complete Justice* asserted that it was illegal for saltpetremen to dig in the mansion house of any subject

683. Coke MS 38: J. Rudhall to Coke, 4 Dec. 1629.
684. BL Add. MS 11764, ff.7–7v.
685. Phillips, 'Star Chamber', p. 264.
686. BL Add. MS 11764, f.8.
687. Clay, *Economic Expansion*, II, pp. 215–16.
688. *Cal. Stat. Pap. Dom., 1634–5*, p. 301, 22 Nov. 1634.
689. PRO, PC 2/46/38.
690. *Cal. Stat. Pap. Dom., 1637*, p. 187.
691. *Cal. Stat. Pap. Dom., 1635*, p. 533.
692. *Cal. Stat. Pap. Dom., 1629–31*, p. 219, 23 March 1630.

without his assent.[693] In 1638 the grand jury of Somerset presented them as a grievance.[694] But despite persistent efforts the king did not secure an adequate supply of gunpowder. In April 1639 the Council was forced to arrange the importation of saltpetre from abroad, for the king's campaign against the Scots.[695] Much antagonism had been generated for a relatively small return.

Another bone of contention was the Council order to each county to appoint and pay a muster master. The muster master was central to the Council's programme to attain regular professional training for the militia. In December 1629 the Privy Council prepared letters to the lord-lieutenants outlining the duties of muster masters and requesting certificates to show that they had been paid.[696] In some counties the muster master was a familiar figure at the assembly of the militia and in receipt of a regular stipend: in Lambeth and some Dorset parishes the churchwardens collected monies for his fee;[697] the Somerset quarter sessions in 1628 set his annual stipend at a handsome £50.[698] But such may well have been exceptional rather than typical, for complaints against the muster master were voiced loudly from the 1590s when the costs of his pay were shifted on to the shires.[699] In many parts of the country Council directives faced a longstanding antagonism to the muster master as an unnecessary expense and, often, an interfering foreigner in the affairs of the shire.[700] Captains of the trained bands resented a rival and more expert authority; any with experience of national service might sympathize with the conscript's lack of affection for his training officer.[701] That the post was sometimes sold to those less than well qualified, or exploited by lord-lieutenants as a source of patronage, only sharpened antagonism.[702] Many counties paid the muster master poorly or sporadically. In Chester, his fee was lowered from £50 under Elizabeth I to £30 during the more peaceful days of her successor;[703] Ipswich offered a mere £5.[704] The bishop of Durham reported in March 1630 that there had

693. *The Complete Justice*, p. 220.
694. Barnes, *Somerset Assize Orders*, p. 61.
695. PRO, PC 2/50/238.
696. Huntington MS, HM 7619; *Acts of the Privy Council, May 1629 to May 1630*, pp. 213–14.
697. Drew, *Lambeth Churchwardens' Accounts*, part II, p. 99; Dorset Record Office, Langton Long accounts, P 207/CW 1; Sherborne accounts, P155.
698. Bates-Harbin, *Quarter Sessions Records for . . . Somerset*, p. 61; cf. *Cal. Stat. Pap. Dom., 1629–31*, p. 188.
699. Fletcher, *Reform in the Provinces*, p. 314; P. Williams, *The Tudor Regime* (Oxford, 1979), p. 123.
700. There was never one in Durham (*Cal. Stat. Pap. Dom., 1629–31*, p. 200).
701. See, for example, Ellesmere MS 7646: JPs of Shropshire to Bridgewater, 26 May 1635.
702. Fletcher, *Reform in the Provinces*, pp. 314–15.
703. *Cal. Stat. Pap. Dom., 1629–31*, p. 191.
704. *Ibid.*, p. 188.

never been a muster master in his county;[705] the deputy lieutenants told the Earl of Huntingdon there was 'no memorial remaining with us of any money in particular usually required or levied and collected for the muster master . . . nor any command to certify an annual payment'.[706] Describing a practice that was probably quite common, they observed that 'those monies given them were never certain but as they deserved it by assisting the captains'. The deputy lieutenants of Rutland, even in the midst of war, informed the Earl of Huntingdon that though they had done their best to gather money for the muster master's fee they had gathered, slowly, only £8, 'which with much difficulty we have procured and by many is thought to be too much'.[707] Essex presented a petition, 'in the name of the shire at the Sessions', to be discharged of the burden.[708]

It was doubtless then as a result of the information it had received about the treatment of muster masters and of the poor response to its 1629 directive that the Council in 1631 instructed all lord-lieutenants to assess rates for the due payment of muster masters throughout the country.[709] The order was at best patchily implemented, as the decade of personal rule settled the realm at peace. Edward Burton, the muster master of Shropshire, was owed two years' pay in 1633;[710] Captain George Betts who was granted the position in Merioneth petitioned Bridgewater to also give him responsibility for Carnarvon, for though each county was supposed to pay a fee of £30, he had found it hard to raise £40 from the two.[711] Betts was already owed arrears for earlier service; and it would appear they were not paid. The gentry, justices of the peace and deputies, far from setting an example, were often unwilling to co-operate with the muster master whom they regarded (rather like the patentees of the 1620s) as an unwelcome intruder: 'any such new officer,' the deputies of Durham argued, was 'very distasteful to the country'.[712] In Leicestershire, Sir William Faunt promised his contribution to the muster master's fee and then failed to pay it, entering into a long dispute with the Earl of Huntingdon which ended up in Star Chamber.[713] Sir Arthur Haselrig of the same county abused Sir John Skeffington, one of the deputy lieutenants who demanded his contribution: 'If such gentlemen as you,' he told him, 'shall be justified to shark the country of their money, it will be a very pretty thing.'[714]

705. Above, note 700.
706. Hastings MS 10621: deputies of Rutland to Huntingdon, 25 July 1635.
707. Hastings MS 10619: deputies to Huntingdon, 14 June 1629.
708. Firth MS C.4, p. 408.
709. Rushworth, *Historical Collections*, II, p. 106.
710. Ellesmere MS 7625; see below, pp. 496–7, 520.
711. Ellesmere MS 7081: Betts to Bridgewater, 16 Sept. 1631; cf. Ellesmere MS 7094.
712. *Cal. Stat. Pap. Dom., 1629–31*, p. 200: bishop of Durham to Council, 1 March 1630.
713. Hastings MS 5543; Hastings MSS, Legal Box 5.
714. Hastings MSS, Legal Box 5.

With the support of such prominent figures of local society, it is easier to understand how a humble Northamptonshire attorney, brother to the chief constable of Towcester who was responsible for collecting the monies, could effectively mount an opposition to the muster master's fee.[715] 'In numerous counties including Buckinghamshire, Hampshire, Herefordshire, Hertfordshire, Leicestershire, Shropshire, Somerset and Suffolk,' Professor Fletcher found, 'the muster master's salary was a running sore . . .'.[716]

The best illustration of the resentment which the muster master aroused comes from a well documented and recently studied case in Shropshire.[717] On 15 April 1635 Richard Harris, clerk of the peace for the county, wrote to the Earl of Bridgewater to report an incident. At the sessions held there the week before the Grand jury had presented the muster master as a 'needless office in the county' and the assessments for his fee as a 'great grievance'. One Timothy Tourneur, a JP, had taxed the jury for their presentment arguing that 'the muster master was a necessary officer'. But he was countered by Sir John Corbet (another justice) who, appealing to the Petition of Right, impugned the legality of the assessment and, not surprisingly, found support among others.[718] News of the heated exchange spread quickly. On the 26th of the month, Edward Burton, the muster master in question, wrote to inform Bridgewater that the deputy lieutenants had issued warrants to fifteen hundreds of the county requiring from each a contribution of 10s. towards his fee. In response five had paid, six had asked for more time and three had 'absolutely denied payment'.[719] In the face of a possible collapse of payments and in character with his customary thoroughness, Bridgewater ordered an examination of the whole business.[720] On 28 May Tourneur gave a full account of his controversy with Corbet, who was related to the foreman of the Grand Jury, and his answer to Corbet's attack on the legality of the muster master's fee.

> I told him it could not be denied but that his Majesty by his prerogative might levy soldiers and much more command all his people to keep up the trained bands . . . and by like reason they are to bear the charge of all necessary dependents, as of officers to order

715. *Cal. Stat. Pap. Dom., 1631–3*, p. 278.
716. Fletcher, *Reform in the Provinces*, p. 315.
717. The story is told in E.S. Cope, 'Politics without parliaments: the dispute about muster masters' fees in Shropshire in the 1630s', *Hunt. Lib. Quart.*, 45 (1982), pp. 271–84. My account is based on independent study of the manuscripts.
718. Ellesmere MS 7632: Richard Harris, clerk of the peace, to Bridgewater, 15 April 1635.
719. Ellesmere MS 7337: Edward Burton to Bridgewater, 26 April 1635.
720. Ellesmere MS 7638: Bridgewater to Harris, 5 May 1635.

and regulate that business . . . the Muster Master was allowed in Queen Elizabeth's time.[721]

Tourneur's information was probably accurate, but the JPs' collective letter to Bridgewater better expressed local feeling. The muster master, they explained to the Lord President, had been presented as a grievance in his predecessor's time 'and never in our knowledge freely paid and yielded unto'.[722] Burton himself acknowledged that a decade earlier there had been opposition to paying and 'confesses he was as forward to oppose it as others' – because, unlike himself, the then muster master was a stranger to the county.[723] Others had argued that 'there is no reason nor law for it' and even the high sheriff had advised against paying the money.[724] Having gathered his intelligence, Bridgewater acted swiftly and effectively. The Council summoned the jurymen; Corbet was removed from the commission and imprisoned for six months in the Fleet for his outburst.[725] An annual fee of £50 was settled on Burton, and by July he had received his payment in full.[726] But the issue was not completely settled; ill feelings had by no means faded. Evidently difficulties in collecting the fee continued.[727] And in 1640 Corbet was to petition the House of Commons against the payments 'unlawfully settled' by which Bridgewater 'did unjustly oppress his Majesty's subjects'.[728] A grievance over the muster master had flared up into a constitutional issue and a battle for authority.[729]

During the Shropshire muster master's controversy, the deputy lieutenants, as Professor Cope observed, 'kept a low profile'.[730] Bridgewater's thoroughness and decisiveness was important in its resolution, as it was generally in his successful presidency of the Marches. The constant vigilance of a lord-lieutenant, he perceived, was essential for an effective militia. 'If these businesses,' he wrote to the deputies in May 1635, 'be never looked after nor cared for but when either the lords of the Council or myself do fall upon them, it is not to be imagined that they will ever be brought to that pass which is fit and his Majesty expecteth.'[731] Bridgewater's position was not typical: his position as Lord President of the Marches strengthened his authority as

721. Ellesmere MS 7647: Timothy Tourneur to Bridgewater, 28 May 1635.
722. Ellesmere MS 7646: JPs of Shropshire to Bridgewater, 26 May 1635.
723. Ellesmere MS 7651: deposition of Burton.
724. Ellesmere MS 7657: Jasper Heily to Henry Bowes, 5 June 1635.
725. Ellesmere MSS 7634, 7670.
726. Ellesmere MS 7673.
727. E.S. Cope, *Politics without Parliaments, 1629–40* (1987), p. 103.
728. Ellesmere MS 7670; Cope, 'Politics without Parliaments', p. 279.
729. Cope, 'Politics without Parliaments', pp. 275–81; cf. below, p. 712. As often, the incident illustrates a blend of local squabbles and higher principles.
730. Cope, *Politics without Parliaments*, p. 105.
731. Ellesmere MS 7639: Bridgewater to deputy lieutenants, 9 May 1635.

Lord-Lieutenant and required his frequent residence at Ludlow castle, where he might personally oversee the execution of Council orders and intervene directly in disputes.[732] For a variety of reasons other lord-lieutenants were not always present and personally influential in the counties of their charge. Several counties shared a lord-lieutenant and many lord-lieutenants, as officers in the royal household or Privy Councillors, were absent from their localities for much if not most of the year. Charles himself appears to have recognized this as a problem. During the later 1620s and 1630s he added to the number of lieutenants so that each county had its own, and many more than one. In some counties he included in the commission headed by a lord his eldest son (as Lord Maltravers joined his father Arundel) probably to deputize in his father's absence and to provide for continuity in the exercise of the office; lieutenants were required to reside in their counties.[733] Charles clearly appreciated that the personal influence wielded by landed magnates lent strength to the office of Lord-Lieutenant as in turn the aristocrat appointed derived further prestige from his commission. In 1640 he was to order lord-lieutenants to go down to their counties to quicken the levy of troops for the Scots war;[734] in the summer of 1642 he would condemn the militia ordinance not least on the ground that the Commons replaced the lord-lieutenants with men 'who have no interest in nor live near unto some of the counties to which they are nominated . . . whereby they cannot be properly serviceable to the counties wherewith they are entrusted'.[735] During the 1630s, however, when the Council was busier than usual and most lieutenants were Privy Councillors, they could not frequently attend in their counties to oversee their charge. Their authority, not constantly supported by their presence, depended largely upon their pen.

There were challenges to that authority, not least from powerful local gentlemen and justices who wanted no rival jurisdiction to the commission of the peace.[736] In 1629, as we have seen, the city of Southampton refused to muster because no letter to that end had been addressed to the mayor; the Lord-Lieutenant of Hampshire, Lord Weston, had to sort out the problem in the midst of illness and Council and Star Chamber business.[737] Disagreements about the power of lieutenancy divided the vice-president of the Council of

732. Though from his attendance in the Star Chamber it is also apparent that he was frequently in London.

733. See J.C. Sainty, *Lieutenants of Counties, 1585–1642, Bull. Inst. Hist. Res. Supplement*, 8 (1970); PRO, PC 2/50/208.

734. Hastings MSS, Military Box 1, 26 April 1640.

735. Hastings MS 1354: Charles I to Earl of Huntingdon, 12 June 1642.

736. See, for example, Coke MS 37: Powell to Coke, 8 June 1629.

737. Above, p. 490; Herriard MS XL/32.

the North and the mayor of York.[738] In Derbyshire the justices of the peace attempted to circumvent the Lord-Lieutenant's jurisdiction by requiring the constables to account to them for militia payments.[739] Such local disputes and challenges not only distracted the service but raised bigger issues and controversies. In Norwich the refusal of two aldermen to co-operate with Arundel and Maltravers in arranging the musters led to a direct questioning of the legal foundations of the lieutenancy. The aldermen's claim that the statute of Philip and Mary endowed them with authority as lieutenants for the city forced Arundel to a defence of his position: 'that the power of the Lord Lieutenants as the same is now given by his Majesty under the broad seal of England had no relation to the statute of Philip and Mary, but was given by the King's absolute and undoubted power of his prerogative royal for the safety and good of the kingdom, from which no city, shire or town corporate whatsoever had . . . any exemption'.[740] Though Arundel was vindicated at the Board, he had exposed the dependence of the commission on the prerogative.[741] The Earl of Huntingdon faced a longer and more acrimonious battle to assert his authority, the records of which dominate his papers for the decade. For Sir William Faunt not only refused his contribution to the muster master's fee, he slandered Huntingdon for oppressing the county and questioned whether the large sums paid were in fact being spent on military supplies.[742] As Huntingdon reported to the Council, Faunt endeavoured to use his power with his neighbours to stir up the people against paying rates or appearing at muster, 'out of a malignant humour to your Majesty's state and government . . . out of spleen and envy to your subject and in scandal and contempt of his honour, place and office'.[743] Huntingdon prosecuted Faunt in Star Chamber not only to secure his revenge, but also because it was necessary to clear himself of the aspersions cast upon him.[744] He had similarly felt the need to have satisfaction from Sir Henry Shirley, who had accused him of levying money on the pretence of providing carts for the militia.[745]

Such cases are poignant reminders that for all his authority over the county of his charge, the Lord-Lieutenant had to secure the co-operation of the substantial men of the shire.[746] His effectiveness

738. York House Books, 35, f.101.
739. Coke MS 37: Powell to Coke, 8 June 1629.
740. Bankes MS 42/63; PRO, PC 2/45/69.
741. PRO, PC 2/45/69.
742. Hastings MSS 3150, 5542, Legal Box 7.
743. Hastings MSS, Legal Box 7.
744. Above, pp. 29–30 and Hastings MSS, Legal Box 8.
745. Hastings MS 5519.
746. For an example, see Pembroke's letter of thanks to Lord Poulett, 7 March 1638 (Smyth of Ashton Court MS 30674/132 a).

depended on a reputation for fair dealing. And that, in turn, involved at times defending local interests against the very Conciliar orders that it was the Lieutenant's duty to see executed. On one occasion the Lord-Lieutenant of Hampshire urged the county to return a certificate quickly so that it looked as though they had acted prior to the Council's reminder.[747] 'Mutual trust and respect' between the Lord-Lieutenant and the county were the basis of the success of the commission.[748] It was here that the resident Lord-Lieutenant with an intimate knowledge and involvement in the politics of his county scored over absentees, however diligent. The second Earl of Portland appears in the later 1630s to have attended most of the meetings concerning the militia in Hampshire and developed a good working relationship with his deputies and the gentry.[749] Similarly the residence of the Earls of Suffolk and Newcastle appears greatly to have facilitated the effective organization of the militia in Suffolk and Nottinghamshire during the 1630s.[750] As Charles I's comment of 1642 reminds us, residence enabled the Lord-Lieutenant to be seen as serviceable to the county, as well as in it.[751] In the absence of a lord-lieutenant, as Sir Edward Osborne complained to Coke, matters were not ordered, disobedience was not dealt with and local factions were fomented.[752] With Wentworth, who exercised the commission of lieutenancy, absent, he predicted, 'some of the deputy Lieutenants will assume mastery over the rest and follow their own wills.'

The deputy lieutenants

In most counties of England, for much of the time, the responsibility for the militia rested on the deputy lieutenants. In their exercise of their office the deputies had advantages over the Lord-Lieutenant himself. Resident in the county, indeed in the area for which they were responsible, and almost always members of the commission of the peace, the deputies, three or four in number, were fully acquainted with local circumstances and families. In 1626 the Duke of Buckingham had consulted them concerning conditions in the county whence he took his title, because the deputies were 'such as best understand the

747. For example, Herriard MS XLIV/15.
748. Fletcher, *Reform in the Provinces*, p. 292.
749. See his 1637 statement of his intention to attend all musters (Herriard MS XLII/1).
750. Yale Center for Parliamentary History, film Y600 GC 45: letter book of Thomas Howard, 1st Earl of Suffolk; Huntington MS 22602; J. Dias, 'Politics and administration in Nottinghamshire and Derbyshire, 1590–1640' (Oxford University, D.Phil thesis, 1973).
751. Above, p. 498.
752. Coke MS 59: Osborne to Coke, 4 Dec. 1638.

state of the county'.[753] Charles I echoed his sentiments: when he ordered the bishop of Durham to increase the numbers of horse, he instructed him to take 'the advice of the deputy Lieutenants who best understand the estate of the county and men's abilities therein'.[754] In 1628 the Council discussed an extension of their jurisdiction over cities and corporate towns and to matters other than arms, evidently regarding them as the effective agents of government in the localities.[755] Yet while the deputies were possessed of more knowledge than their superior, they did not command his authority. Other than their commission, which was open to challenge on legal grounds, they had none of the power of elevated rank enjoyed by the aristocratic Lord-Lieutenant; they were the social equals of the gentry whom they were often called upon to chivvy and discipline. Recent events had further compromised their standing. During the war years, the role of the deputies in the unpopular measures of conscripting men, billeting troops on houses and enforcing martial law had eroded their respect from the local community. Questions and investigations in the Commons in 1628 had threatened their immunity from legal action.[756] As a consequence not only the authority but the desirability of the office was called into doubt. As the deputies of Essex complained to the Chancellor of the Exchequer, 'such is our misfortune that these employments which in former times have added power and credit unto men in their country do in these times make us neglected and disrespected of our neighbours.'[757] 'Indeed', they continued, 'all the corporations are grown to that head as they do scarce acknowledge themselves to be within the jurisdiction of lieutenancy'; one of their number resigned.[758] The experience of the war years and parliament were not soon forgotten. In July 1629, for example, the deputies of Northamptonshire forbore to levy money for the entertainment of the officers at muster because their warrants had been 'of late publicly impeached'.[759] In Rutland they doubted whether they had the authority to administer the oaths of supremacy and allegiance, as requested by the Council.[760] Sir Bernard Grenville of Tresmere expressed to Sir James Bagg his concern that the deputy lieutenants in general were as 'fearful' to do their duties as he was himself weary of

753. Temple of Stowe MSS 6, STT 2243.
754. PRO, SO 1/3, f.109: Charles I to bishop of Durham, 13 Dec. 1638.
755. PRO, SP 16/89/17.
756. *Cal. Stat. Pap. Dom., 1628–9*, p. 75; *1629–31*, p. 15; R.C. Johnson, M.F. Keeler and W. Bidwell, *Commons Debates, 1628* (New Haven and London, 1977–), II, pp. 41, 260, 564; III, pp. 33, 70, 422–424.
757. Firth MS C.4, p. 421, 17 Dec. 1627.
758. *Ibid.*, p. 443.
759. *Cal. Stat. Pap. Dom., 1629–31*, p. 20.
760. Hastings MS 10619: deputies to Huntingdon, 14 June 1629.

office.[761] The deputies depended upon the support of the Lord-Lieutenant. When he was preoccupied or indifferent, they often felt powerless and exposed. As Richard Norton wrote to Jervoise of the Lord-Lieutenant's duty to support them in their quarrel with the mayor of Southampton: 'if he will suffer his subordinate ministers . . . to sink into so base and like contempt with each mechanic poor corporation, for my part I will attend my plough'.[762]

The effectiveness of the deputy lieutenants as executors of Council orders was compromised not only by the limitations to their authority. What made them of such value to the Council – their involvement in local society and politics – also complicated their exercise of office. Because the interests of the deputies (family and friends, standing and estates) lay in the county and among their local communities there were limits to their willingness to disregard local sensibilities, especially to alienate their peers on the bench. As leading figures in county society they were expected to fulfil the role of patrons – to protect not violate local interests. Accordingly, when in 1629 the trained bands of Stratton in Cornwall petitioned to be released from the charge of providing arms, they asked the deputies to 'be patrons to your native county'.[763] In Durham, as we have seen, the deputies championed the Palatinate's resistance to the appointment and charge of a muster master.[764] The 'authoritarian tone' that, as Professor Fletcher points out, often worked wonders, had to be softened at times by a willingness to stand up for local customs and practices against the Council's relentless quest for uniformity.[765]

For all the inherent difficulties and ambiguity of their situation, however, it would be wrong to characterize the deputy lieutenants as unwilling or ineffectual in overseeing the Council's directives for musters, training and equipping the militia. The Council itself continued to attach great importance to having deputy lieutenants 'residing constantly' in their counties;[766] Bridgewater was advised that an increase in the number of deputies would see all better performed.[767] There is ample evidence of their diligence. The correspondence with the Earl of Huntingdon in the Hastings manuscripts shows the deputy lieutenants of Leicestershire and Rutland active, industrious and willing to present the refractory with a recommendation of exemplary punishment. In Hampshire the abundance, detail and order of papers on

761. *Cal. Stat. Pap. Dom., 1629–31*, p. 15, 19 July 1629.
762. Herriard MS 027/XL/31: T. Norton to Jervoise, 27 Nov. 1629.
763. *Cal. Stat. Pap. Dom., 1629–31*, p. 27.
764. Above, pp. 494–5; *Cal. Stat. Pap. Dom., 1629–31*, p. 200.
765. Fletcher, *Reform in the Provinces*, p. 310.
766. Firth MS C.4, p. 618.
767. Ellesmere MS 7656: Sir A. Corbett to Bridgewater, 4 June 1635.

military affairs bear testimony to the energy and pains of Sir Thomas Jervoise whose indefatigable labours effected considerable improvements. Sir Henry Slingsby of Yorkshire who usually did 'affect little business' was an active deputy.[768] The efficiency of Sir Wolstan Dixie, deputy lieutenant of Leicestershire, could be remarkable. His ability to forward to the Earl of Huntingdon within two or three days a letter he had received in 1626 can only be enviously admired by this author, as he surveys the chaos of his office and desk.[769] No less impressive Owen Wynn, receiving his Lieutenant's letter for musters at 9 a.m. had by noon forwarded it to his colleagues in Carnarvonshire.[770] The Council played its part in improving the performance of the deputies both by encouragement and admonition. Sir Richard Tichborne was granted by royal signet protection from his creditors in connection with his service as deputy lieutenant of Hampshire.[771] Sir John Holland of Norfolk sensed the watchful eye of the Council and accordingly advised his colleague: 'from sporting at Thetford I had rather put that off for a week longer than that it should be a means to retard the service or draw any just blame on us.'[772]

We cannot know how industrious most deputy lieutenants were, but that they usually co-operated in the execution of Council orders is strongly suggested by their unpopularity in 1640. At the election for the Short Parliament in Northamptonshire, for example, some declaimed against them: 'Away with deputy Lieutenants, we will have no deputy Lieutenants!'[773] In December 1640 a committee of the Long Parliament was appointed to investigate their misdemeanours and frame a bill to regulate their activities.[774] The deputy lieutenants were not devoted to the standards and order that Charles I sought in the militia, as all else. But in many counties, with (often necessary) regard for local circumstances, they worked hard to turn a reluctantly assembled home guard into a disciplined defence corps.

Their success should not be underestimated. Those historians who dismiss the programme for an exact militia as an inevitable failure from the beginning are mistaken. Though the Conciliar orders of 1629 required nothing new, peace freed the Council and lieutenancy from the preoccupation of preparing armies and fleets and so enabled them to concentrate on improved training for the militia at home. Local initiative suggests that some realization of the need for improved

768. D. Parsons, *Diary of Sir Henry Slingsby* (1836), p. 14.
769. Hastings MSS 2296, 3541.
770. *Calendar of the Wynn Papers, 1515–1690* (Aberystwyth, 1926), no. 1633, p. 261.
771. PRO, SO 1/3, f.108, 8 Dec. 1638.
772. Tanner MS 177, f.19v: Holland to Hobart, 2 Dec. 1638.
773. Bankes MS 42/55.
774. Ellesmere MS 7688.

defences was also permeating to the shires. In October 1630 Sir Edward Verney, one of the deputies of Buckinghamshire, wrote to tell his colleagues that it was 'high time to call to mind' that the Duke of Buckingham had taken the blame 'that we certified not up the forces of this county' and that it was now time to act: he requested a meeting within the fortnight.[775] The deputy lieutenants of Norfolk, passing on the Council's order to the captain of the foot, added an exhortation that all owners of lands should perform military service themselves rather than appoint deputies.[776] In March 1634, for the better instruction of the bands they ordered the appointment of a lieutenant, an ensign, three sergeants and a drummer.[777] The numbers of military manuals and instruction books such as James Acheson's *The Military Garden* (1629),[778] Cruso's *Militarie Instructions for the Cavallrie* (1632),[779] Barry's *Military Discipline* (1634)[780] or Gervase Markham's *Art of Archerie* (1634) suggest an increased interest in more up-to-date training methods.[781] Some of the works explore (and illustrate) continental military tactics and how to teach them in detail.[782] Great Yarmouth in Norfolk re-formed a military company in the town to provide instruction in the use of arms.[783] There were also improvements in military supplies and militia equipment.[784] York ordered a storehouse of powder and match to be established at the common hall, instituted a regular inspection and maintained a muster master to liaise with the mayor in a training programme for the city militia.[785] Worcester too instituted a powder store;[786] churchwardens' accounts for Lambeth show the parish purchasing new armour for the bands.[787] In Maldon, Essex, soldiers were required from 1630 to appear in advance of the musters and render account of the condition of their arms.[788] In Stockport, Cheshire, the constables raised a levy so as to give each trained soldier 4d. to prepare and repair his equipment.[789] Muster

775. Temple of Stowe MS 7, STT 2245: Verney and Sir Francis Goodwin to Temple, 14 Oct. 1630.
776. Tanner MS 177, ff.6–7v.
777. *Ibid.*, f.9v.
778. J. Acheson, *The Military Garden or Instructions for all Young Soldiers* (Edinburgh, 1629, STC 88).
779. J. Cruso, *Militarie Instructions for the Cavallrie* (Cambridge, 1632, STC 6099).
780. G. Barry, *A Discourse of Military Discipline* (1634, STC 1528).
781. Markham, *The Art of Archerie.*
782. See, for example, Acheson, Cruso and Barry for illustrations of tactics. Barry served in the Low Countries.
783. Norfolk Record Office, Yarmouth YC 18/6.
784. Norfolk Record Office, NRS 18034 41 D 1: Maltravers to De Grey, 7 Aug. 1635.
785. York House Books, 35, ff.190v, 273v, 282.
786. S. Bond (ed.) *The Chamber Order Book of Worcester, 1602–1650* (Worcestershire Record Soc., new series, 8, 1974), p. 237.
787. Drew, *Lambeth Churchwardens' Accounts*, pp. 85, 99.
788. Essex Record Office, D/B3/3/406. I owe this reference to the late Brian Lyndon.
789. Chester Record Office, CR.63/2/6, f.51.

certificates and reports from various parts of the country vaunt recent improvements.[790] From Glamorgan in October 1631 the deputy lieutenants reported all 'in good readiness';[791] the following year they boasted that all charged with arms performed military service in person and with modern weapons.[792] Staffordshire, in 1635, though acknowledging that the horse lacked modern pistols, reported that 'the foot companies were full and their arms good and serviceable'.[793] The deputy lieutenants of Cheshire informed their Lieutenant, the Earl of Derby, that though the numbers in the bands had not increased, 'the men are far more experienced', the deputies having 'assigned such to serve as are young and of the best ability and who taken delight in that service'.[794] To encourage them further, they had 'caused their arms to be fitted . . . to the best modern fashion'.

It would be naive to read all such reports uncritically.[795] But the optimism of deputies' letters and returns is often in marked contrast to the despair of their own earlier accounts. More particularly, in some counties we can compare the reports with independent evidence of improvements effected.[796] In Hampshire in 1629 the deputy lieutenants had painted a rather bleak picture of the state of the militia: officers had been careless of their command, musters were poorly attended, arms deficient. 'If,' they concluded, 'there be not a present course taken the service will fall to the ground.'[797] That sentence of despair may also have announced a resolution to act. And there is abundant evidence from Hampshire in the early 1630s that action was being taken. A great deal of paperwork was generated as Jervoise and others determined to secure accurate information about muster attendance and defaulters.[798] The deputies chivvied the colonels of the regiments and checked their returns, signing the dorse of the roll to indicate their validation.[799] They informed themselves promptly of deaths and departures that reduced the bands and acted quickly to remedy

790. See D.P. Carter, 'The "exact militia" in Lancashire, 1625–40', *Northern History*, 11 (1976), pp. 87–106, esp. pp. 87–92.
791. *Cal. Stat. Pap. Dom., 1631–3*, p. 175, 31 Oct. 1631.
792. *Ibid.*, p. 430, 25 Oct. 1632.
793. *Cal. Stat. Pap. Dom., 1635*, p. 344.
794. *Cal. Stat. Pap. Dom., 1631–3*, p. 170, 2 Oct. 1631.
795. Cf. Carter, '"Exact militia" in Lancashire', p. 89. It is also worth noting that in the civil war the militia companies often proved less effective than new recruits trained by Thirty Years War veterans, but this is not to dismiss the improvements in their utility as a local defence corps. I am grateful to John Morrill for this point.
796. *Ibid.*, pp. 90–1. In 1639 the Council sent its own agents into the northern counties to make an independent assessment of the condition of the militia.
797. Herriard MSS 027/XL/22: deputy lieutenants to Lord-Lieutenant [1629].
798. See, for example, Herriard MSS 025/XXX; Militia Box 026, 029.
799. Herriard MSS, Box 029: deputy lieutenants to Sir Thomas Jervoise, 20 May 1632; Herriard MSS, Box 025: muster returns.

defects.[800] By 1632, many of the muster books for the companies of foot list few or no absentees or deficiencies.[801] By the early 1630s the militia in Hampshire (as that in Berkshire, Cheshire and Lancashire) was already on its steady way to the improvement that was to be a characteristic of the decade.[802]

Circumstances, however, were before long to render steady improvements inadequate. The peace England had concluded with France and Spain had provided an uneasy security in an unsettled world. With the death of Gustavus Adolphus and the more active intervention of France in the war, the situation in Europe became more volatile and the position of England more precarious. In addition, as diplomatic dealings with the Habsburgs failed of their purpose, Charles I became persuaded of the need to negotiate for the recovery of the Palatinate with a more powerful hand and even to contemplate the possibility of English military involvement. Circumstances abroad and decisions at home then combined to necessitate renewed measures from 1635 for the further improvement of the militia, and indeed of the navy. Before we examine that second phase of the Caroline programme for an 'exact militia', we must turn to the circumstances and policies that not only made an effective English defence imperative, but turned the priorities of the government from domestic reforms to foreign engagements.

800. For example, Herriard MS, Box 025/XXX, 15, 25.

801. No absences were listed in 1632 for Basingstoke, the New Forest or Andover (Herriard MS, Box 025, XXXII). Similarly for 1633, at Andover, Romsey and Basingstoke (File XXXIII). Bishops Waltham was short of eight corslets and four muskets; Alton of one musket.

802. Below, pp. 541–5; Fletcher, *Reform in the Provinces*, pp. 289–93.

PART III

'A TURN OF ALL AFFAIRS': CHANGED CIRCUMSTANCES AND NEW COUNSELS

VIII

'A CHANGE OF POLICY' ENGLAND AND EUROPE 1635 TO 1637

The Peace of Prague

During the spring of 1635 events were unfolding – and not unfolding – in Europe in a manner that was to reorient the course of English politics for at least the next two years. The first consideration was the failure to conclude the maritime treaty with Spain. In January, sending Hopton the power to negotiate the treaty at Madrid, Windebank was already expressing his concern about the poor progress made with Necolalde in London.[1] As the weeks and months dragged on with no progress being made, the second factor in the reorientation of English policy had come into play. In May Lindsey commanded the first ship money fleet, financed by the writ issued in October the previous year.[2] The concurrence of these developments announced potentially radical changes in England's place in Europe. The frustrations of Anglo-Spanish negotiations opened a fissure, which others hoped might become a rupture, between powers which had acted in close alliance since Cottington had concluded peace. The ship money fleet many expected to worsen relations with the Dutch.[3] More importantly, renewed naval strength gave England an enhanced standing in the calculations made by other powers.[4] English neutrality could no longer be taken as a fact of life, the necessary consequence of her impotence; the favour, even the neutrality, of England had to be secured by

1. British Library [BL], Egerton MS 1820, f.435v: Windebank to Hopton, 23 Jan. 1635.
2. S.R. Gardiner, *History of England from the Accession of James I to the Outbreak of the Civil War, 1603–1642* (10 vols, 1883–4), VII, p. 384.
3. For example, Huntington Library, Hastings MS 9598: Rossingham to Huntingdon, 28 March 1635; PRO, 31/3/68, ff.146–7, 163.
4. *Calendar of State Papers Domestic* [*Cal. Stat. Pap. Dom.*], *1634–5*, p. 377; Egerton MS 1820, f.482v; PRO, 31/3/68, f.167.

diplomacy.[5] Moreover, if the failure of Anglo-Spanish negotiations posed the possibility, an English fleet which might strengthen Spain in the Low Countries suggested the desirability of drawing Charles I from alliance with the Habsburgs. In 1635 England became a focus of attention for all the major protagonists of the Thirty Years War.

France in particular watched the recent developments with interest. In April the French envoy, the Marquis de Senneterre learned directly from Charles I that England had neither concluded an agreement with Spain, nor engaged her ship money fleet to them. 'Il est libre,' he informed Richelieu.[6] Senneterre had no doubt that Spain had attempted to secure the aid of the English fleet for money and failed. He was clearly newly impressed by a monarch who had succeeded without Spanish assistance (and against French expectations) in raising the money and launching the fleet. He was also uneasy. The fleet was obviously a force to be reckoned with, but its intended purpose was unknown. Senneterre hoped it might be of advantage to France, but could predict nothing with confidence. The Spaniards, he knew, did all they could to keep Charles in their clutches; the king however 'a plus d'inclination à ne se commettre à rien du tout'.[7] Senneterre had good reason to be alert to the slightest move in any direction made by Charles I. For the third development which realigned the power politics of Europe, and raised England's importance in them, was the declaration of war on Spain by France. For some years Cardinal Richelieu had been offering and providing support to the enemies of the Austrian and Spanish Habsburgs: to the German Protestant princes, to the Duke of Bavaria, to the Danes and the Swedes. During the autumn and winter of 1634 French forces had crossed the Rhine and occupied the Palatinate.[8] However, in the early days of May, a French army entered Valencia and on the 9th a formal declaration of war against Spain was delivered by a French herald to Brussels.[9] From that day the conflict between France and Spain that was to outlast the battles in Germany and even the long struggle between Spain and the United Provinces became the central confrontation of the European wars.

Senneterre reported the joy in England at the news. Charles I, he wrote, now believed that he would be courted by all sides.[10] Even more seasoned diplomats were quick to see that the turn of

5. See *Calendar of State Papers Venetian* [*Cal. Stat. Pap. Venet.*], *1632–6*, p. 361 (Gussoni's relation, April 1635) and p. 383.
6. PRO, 31/3/68, ff.146–7, 4 April 1635.
7. PRO, 31/3/68, f.153, 12 April 1635.
8. Gardiner, *History of England*, VII, pp. 347–8.
9. *Ibid.*, p. 384.
10. PRO, 31/3/68, f.166, 16 May 1635.

events might be greatly to England's advantage. Sir Thomas Roe told Elizabeth, queen of Bohemia, that the wise course for England would be to 'look on a while and let these elephants waste their strength'. For 'in the meantime all parties will look upon his Majesty and he may take his opportunity to throw a little weight into the scale which may best profit him, and when both parties are out of breath sway the end and reap the benefit of war'.[11] If somewhat over-optimistic, England's joy was not entirely out of place. With Franco-Spanish hostilities, the Channel became of paramount importance: Spanish communications depended all the more on a friendly – or at least neutral – England. And an English alliance or neutrality was essential to French security if she were to wage war in Germany, Spain or especially Flanders. To both powers England could be a decisively effective ally; perhaps more significantly, to either Charles I could be a dangerous foe.

During May it was by no means clear what England would do. The frustration with Spain was mounting. Windebank declared he would 'never set my heart on anything proposed by them hereafter'. Spain, he told Hopton, went the right way to throw England into the arms of France.[12] The death of Weston in March had weakened the peace party.[13] With news of the French declaration of war, the Venetian envoy informed the Doge, 'even those who used most steadfastly to counsel neutrality now intimate that the altered state of affairs and the changed times must bring about a change of policy to meet the altered circumstances.'[14] Senneterre endeavoured to seize the moment to clinch an English alliance with France and made vague promises about the Palatinate.[15] An alliance with France, however, was a far from obvious benefit to Charles. Roe's and Elizabeth of Bohemia's disquiet over French self-interest and ambitions in the Palatinate, forcefully articulated during the winter of 1633 and 1634,[16] were reinforced by Charles's obtaining on 25 April 1635 a copy of the treaty between France and the Dutch, concluded in February.[17] By its terms, Louis XIII and the United Provinces agreed to partition the Spanish Low Countries and to continue to wage war until the Spaniards were evicted. Whilst provision was made for England to join, the agreement raised a dangerous spectre that Elizabethan diplomacy had endeavoured to exorcize: that of a powerful French presence in Flanders –

11. *Cal. Stat. Pap. Dom., 1635*, p. 41: Roe to Elizabeth of Bohemia, 23 April.
12. Egerton MS 1820, f.481, 27 May 1635.
13. See, for example, Roe's letter to Elizabeth of 5 April (*Cal. Stat. Pap. Dom., 1635*, p. 9); and *Cal. Stat. Pap. Venet., 1632–6*, p. 359.
14. *Cal. Stat. Pap. Venet., 1632–6*, p. 382, 11 May 1635.
15. PRO, 31/3/68, ff.166–8.
16. Above, pp. 85–6.
17. J. Du Mont, *Corps Universel diplomatique*, Vol VI (Amsterdam, 1728), p. 80; Gardiner, *History of England*, VII, pp. 380, 382.

a prospect even more unwelcome than that of continued Spanish occupation.[18] There were other causes for irritation and suspicion. The refusal of the French to agree to lower their flags to English ships both wounded English honour and threatened a challenge to English claims to supremacy in the narrow seas.[19] The reluctance of the French ambassador at the Hague to address the young Elector Palatine by his due title 'Electoral highness' confirmed English suspicions about the commitment the French had made to the Duke of Bavaria, and the sincerity of their promises for the Palatinate.[20] A French alliance by no means presented a solution to all the problems. But, with Senneterre offering articles for consideration, it was evidently a course worth pursuing – if only because negotiations with France, now it had declared war, might at last pressure Spain to conclude a restoration of Charles Louis.

'In the midst of the stirring events of the early summer,' however, 'Charles' hopes of regaining the Palatinate by negotiation had received an unexpected shock.'[21] On 20 May the Peace of Prague was signed between the Emperor Ferdinand and John George, Elector of Saxony. The leading Protestant prince in Germany laid down his arms, in return for the emperor's abandoning the Edict of Restitution. The gains were made only by the Lutherans. Calvinism remained outlawed; no provision was made for the restoration of the Palatinate.[22] The news of the peace did not reach England until late in July, and even then the details were not fully comprehended.[23] But the peace was to have a revolutionary effect on events in Europe and on English domestic and foreign policy. With the settlement in Germany, as Hopton predicted, the axis of power and conflict shifted to the Low Countries and so, for all it was bad news, to an arena in which England might play a larger role:

> For the matters of Germany . . . if things settle the Duke of Bavaria will be less considerable and the heft of this great war which so much concerns the house of Austria lying in Flanders and at sea, his Majesty comes to be as useful for these purposes as the other hath been for Germany and doubtless will be as much sought to as the other hath been.[24]

18. Cf. above, pp. 84–5.
19. For example, PRO, 31/3/68, ff.191–2, 13 July 1635.
20. *Ibid.*, f.183, 27 June 1635; cf. Gardiner, *History of England*, VIII, p. 92.
21. Gardiner, *History of England*, VII, p. 388.
22. Du Mont, *Corps universel diplomatique*, VI, pp. 89–108, 30 May 1635.
23. Egerton MS 1820, f.524; *Cal. Stat. Pap. Dom., 1635*, p. 280; *Cal. Stat. Pap. Venet., 1632–6*, p. 424.
24. Egerton MS 1820, f.524: Hopton to Windebank, 28 July 1635; R. Scrope and T. Monkhouse (eds) *State Papers Collected by Edward, Earl of Clarendon* (3 vols, Oxford, 1767–86), I, p. 301.

But a sense of possibilities was, at least in the short term, clouded by a feeling of anger and betrayal. On 24 July Windebank, who had been entrusted with the secret negotiations with Necolalde, wrote to Hopton, sending a copy of the articles of agreement between Ferdinand and Saxony. 'I assure you,' he told him commenting on the little hope they offered the Elector Palatine, 'we are much troubled at them here and I doubt they may awake other resolutions in his Majesty than he hath been hitherto willing to take, having given faith to the hopes and promises of more equal and peaceable ways.'[25] Though Necolalde was dismissing the Peace of Prague as 'imaginary', Windebank was all too sensible of its articles and their consequences. 'If there be any probability of better conditions from the French for the Palatinate than from you,' he told Hopton, 'as they offer very fair and you nothing at all, certainly we shall join heartily with them and then you are likely to have work enough.'[26] By mid-August, further news had deepened his despair and heated his anger: the contract of marriage between the emperor's daughter and (her uncle) the Duke of Bavaria presented the prospect of a permanent Bavarian succession in the Palatinate.[27] Even the rumours emanating from the Spanish ambassador in Venice that Charles Louis might marry a daughter of the emperor and become king of Bohemia Windebank dismissed as a mere distraction.[28] Charles I thought the proposals 'scarce worth the hearkening to'.[29] With the French armies entering Italy, Spain laboured by any means to keep discussions with England alive. But Windebank, rejecting their excuses, had come to the conclusion that the Peace of Prague had been concluded with the Spaniard's knowledge and approval.[30] To the secretary therefore their renewed offers of 'a chimerical electoral dignity with as imaginary an estate', like the scheme to endow the dispossessed Palatine prince with an estate in Linburg, 'are evident demonstrations that their only end is to feed us with fancies and to amuse us to gain time'.[31]

Senecterre worked to fan English anger at the marriage of Bavaria and Peace of Prague. He urged an alliance, tried to persuade Charles to put his nephew in charge of the English fleet and pressed for a licence for France to levy troops in Scotland.[32] Charles put his proposals to what was evidently a disputative Council meeting. During July

25. Egerton MS 1820, f.517v: Windebank to Hopton, 24 July 1635.
26. *Ibid.*, ff.516v–517, 518.
27. *Ibid.*, f.527, 13 Aug. 1635.
28. *Ibid.*, ff.527v–528.
29. *Ibid.*, f.541: Windebank to Hopton, 3 Sept. 1635; *Clarendon State Papers*, I, p. 524.
30. Egerton MS 1820, f.540.
31. *Ibid.*, f.541; *Clarendon State Papers*, I, pp. 295, 315.
32. PRO, 31/3/68, f.200.

the debate continued as contrary advice and pressure came from all sides. Spain renewed its attempts to placate Charles; denying any responsibility for the Peace of Prague, they urged him to approach the emperor directly for an explanation of its meaning and its implication for the future of the Elector Palatine.[33] Elizabeth of Bohemia made representations to Laud, sending copies of the peace, in the hope that they might open Charles's eyes to the need for action.[34] The Marquis of Hamilton and the queen spoke for a union with France.[35] Though the issue of the sovereignty of the seas continued to present obstacles, Senecterre pressed for an alliance, while doing his utmost to ensure that England be kept from the arms of Spain.[36]

The right course was by no means self-evident. If the duplicity of Spain now seemed transparent, suspicion of French aggrandizement was mounting. There was even more concern about the allies of France, the Dutch: in August a group of Dutchmen excited the greatest umbrage and fear when they pursued some Dunkirkers into English waters and even landed men on English soil at Scarborough.[37] The incident re-evoked bitter memories: as Windebank caustically commented to the Dutch envoy Joachimi, 'if his Majesty should stay and sue to them for justice perhaps he might expect as long as he has done in the business of Amboyna'.[38] With Weston dead and no dominant figure as yet emerging to succeed him, a variety of different arguments received an equal hearing.[39] While Holland and Hamilton advocated a commitment to France, Windebank delivered to the Council a warning that the French were only out to increase their territory and ultimately to secure the imperial dignity for the king of France. The French, he argued, invited England into 'this conjunction merely to make their own game and to draw on a peace to their better advantage from the Spaniard'.[40] The secretary reminded the foreign committee that the French had 'joined with the Hollanders in several articles to his Majesty's prejudice'; they challenged the king of England's right to sovereignty of the seas; they had 'strait intelligence' with the Duke of Bavaria and so refused to give the Elector Palatine his title; they had pretensions to all his territory west of the Rhine; in conclusion, they in no way wished to further the Palatine's cause, fearing that his restora-

33. Gardiner, *History of England*, VIII, p. 83.
34. *Cal. Stat. Pap. Dom., 1635*, p. 267, 20 July.
35. Gardiner, *History of England*, VIII, p. 85; PRO, 31/3/68, f.211.
36. PRO, 31/3/68, ff.204–206v.
37. *Cal. Stat. Pap. Dom., 1635*, p. 322: Windebank to Coke, 6 Aug.
38. *Ibid.*, p. 323.
39. Below, pp. 537–41.
40. *Cal. Stat. Pap. Dom., 1635*, p. 402, 29 Sept.: Windebank's notes of propositions submitted to the foreign committee.

tion might strengthen the Protestant party in France.[41] To these arguments against a French alliance, Laud (newly rising to prominence in Council for all his little experience of affairs) added his view that with Prince Charles Louis coming of age, it was appropriate to send an envoy formally to Vienna to request his restitution – if only to deprive the emperor of the excuse that he had never fulfilled legal requirements and demanded it.[42]

Amidst all these debates and proposals, it is not easy to discern Charles's own preferences. Roe told Elizabeth of Bohemia that he believed the king expected little from Vienna and was more inclined to action: 'I heard that if the cause had then had good seconds to have animated his Majesty's resolutions that the conjunction was fair . . .'. Laud, he wrote, being 'not used in foreign affairs' had been 'fearful to engage himself and his master in new ways', not least because he was unsure of his own support. Others, jealous of France and the Dutch, 'I fear cooled that brave warmth which appeared in his Majesty's heart'.[43] Roe's belief that Charles was inclined to a belligerent course may have been based on no more than his (not uncharacteristic) wishful thinking. But he may have been right: Charles's first inclinations to a French treaty may have surrendered to arguments put forward by Windebank and others, and especially to reservations about costs and resources. Roe hinted as much: 'They have an easy theme,' he lamented, 'who declaim against war whose expense hath no bounds and success no certainty.'[44]

In the end Charles decided to explore all options. What some have dismissed as a hopelessly contradictory diplomacy appears to have been founded on the belief, articulated by Kenelm Digby in a letter to Coke, that if Charles maintained a strong navy he might 'have a power to keep the balance open'.[45] Whilst he continued to listen to the overtures of Senneterre and the queen's faction for a French alliance, Charles dispatched Sir Walter Aston (Lord Aston of Forfar) as ambassador to Spain and sent John Taylor via the Spanish Netherlands to Ferdinand in Vienna. Aston was instructed to express England's dissatisfaction with the Peace of Prague and to explore further the tentative suggestions that the Elector Palatine might marry a princess of the house of Habsburg, and to revive the maritime treaty of the previous year.[46] Taylor was sent, as Laud had advocated, to request

41. *Ibid.*
42. *Cal. Stat. Pap. Dom., 1635*, p. 415: Laud to Elizabeth of Bohemia, 6 Oct.
43. *Ibid.*, p. 441: Roe to Elizabeth of Bohemia, 12 Oct.
44. *Ibid.*
45. Gardiner, *History of England*, VIII, pp. 83–5; Melbourne Hall, Coke MS 51: Digby to Coke, 29 Sept. 1635; calendared in *HMC Cowper, II*, pp. 94–5.
46. *Cal. Stat. Pap. Venet., 1632–6*, p. 454; *Clarendon State Papers*, I, p. 306: instructions to Aston, 15 Aug. 1635.

the investiture of Charles Louis, who was about to be eighteen, as Elector Palatine, and to offer English friendship for his full reinstatement to his lands and dignities.[47] To his sister Elizabeth, who thought 'this new sending to Vienna . . . to no other purpose but to lose time', Charles wrote to explain his strategy.[48] He wished to delay a little in order to force the French 'to unmask and deal plainly upon more equal terms'.[49] If nothing else, the new embassies succeeded in that. Though Senecterre, sensing Charles was playing for time, was all but inclined to suspend negotiations, Richelieu decided that he could not afford to risk England concluding with Spain.[50] He promised therefore that if Charles would engage not to assist the Habsburgs and give his nephew command of the bigger ship money fleet for which writs were being sent to the nation, France would undertake not to make peace without the restitution of the Palatinate. Charles wanted more. At the end of October he proposed to Senecterre that France should surrender Lorraine to the Habsburgs in return for the Palatinate.[51] In November he sent instructions to Viscount Scudamore, ambassador in Paris, to the same effect: if the emperor refused the deal, England would join with France in war.[52] With all these negotiations on the table, the young Elector Charles Louis arrived in England, on 21 November 1635.

Pougny, the extraordinary envoy from France, expected that with the arrival of the young Elector, pressure would mount on Charles to join in alliance with the French.[53] In fact Charles Louis's presence at his uncle's court presented a difficulty to the French ambassador – a difficulty of which the Spanish representative took full advantage (see Figure 37). Because of their commitment to Bavaria they could not, as we have observed, address the Elector by his title. Where this had been an irritation at the Hague, it was a greater affront in the English court at a time when the Elector was only weeks from his majority.[54] Necolalde, by contrast, showed no such reservation about greeting Charles Louis as 'your electoral highness'.[55] This was not just cynically strategical. Whatever Maximilian's friendly relations with the

47. *Clarendon State Papers*, I, p. 310: instructions to Taylor.
48. *Cal. Stat. Pap. Dom., 1635*, p. 368: Elizabeth of Bohemia to Laud, 15 Sept.
49. Gardiner, *History of England*, VIII, p. 83.
50. PRO, 31/3/68, ff.219–219v; Gardiner, *History of England*, VIII, p. 97.
51. PRO, 31/3/68, ff.243–246v; Gardiner, *History of England*, VIII, pp. 97–8.
52. Egerton MS 1820, ff.570v–571; *Clarendon State Papers*, I, p. 392.
53. PRO, 31/3/68, f.235: Poigny to Bouthillier, 24 Oct. 1635; *Cal. Stat. Pap. Venet., 1632–6*, p. 471.
54. Above, p. 512; PRO, 31/3/68, ff.257, 259, 263; *Cal. Stat. Pap. Venet., 1632–6*, p. 488; A.J. Loomie (ed.) *Ceremonies of Charles I: The Note Books of John Finet, Master of Ceremonies 1628–1641* (New York, 1987), pp. 188–90.
55. *Cal. Stat. Pap. Venet., 1632–6*, p. 489; Gardiner, *History of England*, VIII, pp. 99–100.

37 *Prince Charles Louis, Elector Palatine and Prince Rupert* by Van Dyck, 1637. Charles Louis arrived in London in November 1635 and was joined by his brother in February 1636.

emperor, Madrid had no obligations to Bavaria who, added to the other inconveniences he had caused Spain, was an ally of the Bourbons with whom Spain was now at war. Pougny, denied access himself, was concerned about the freedom with which the Spaniard visited the Palatine prince and the promises he made.[56] Senneterre worried the English might (naively in his view) be willing to separate their dealings with the Austrian and Spanish Habsburgs and exonerate Madrid from blame for the terms of the German peace.[57] By mid-December he was expressing his fear that if Spain agreed to the revocation of the imperial ban against the Elector they might control negotiations with England for the indefinite future.[58] The advantageous position seized by Necolalde in the winter was further strengthened by the first reports sent back from Taylor concerning the emperor's plans for the Palatinate.

56. PRO, 31/3/68, f.263.
57. *Ibid.*, f.243.
58. *Ibid.*, f.267.

Writing in December and January of the devastation that war had brought to Germany, he expressed his confidence that the Lower Palatinate would be restored; and that the ban would be taken off.[59] By February he was claiming the emperor's willingness to yield the whole Palatinate after Bavaria's death – predicted by 'a great astronomer' for the following August.[60] If the Peace of Prague had turned England sharply towards France in the summer, by the end of the year the Habsburg option was firmly back on the negotiating table – and appeared to promise as much.

Charles had not forgotten the Habsburgs' duplicity, nor was he fully ready to believe all Taylor wrote. In January he upbraided his envoy for taking too subservient a line – Taylor spoke too much 'of grace' rather than of right and was willing to concede more than he had instruction for.[61] Charles Louis, now joined in England by his younger brother Prince Rupert, and supported by Elizabeth and her agents, the queen, Holland and Hamilton, argued the futility of negotiation with the Habsburgs. The king, as Gardiner put it, 'was half-inclined to think that they were in the right'.[62] But circumstances had changed since the summer and it was not clear that a last effort to secure a resolution of the Palatine problem by diplomacy was more naive than an alliance with France. Hopton, perhaps the shrewdest of the envoys of the decade, presented the alternative realistically. Olivares, he told Cottington, had little inclination to the maritime treaty and was an unreliable bet for the restoration of the Palatinate. But, he added,

> in France I see not how it can be better, for if the recovery of the Palatinate shall be endeavoured by force your lordship knows how uncertain a thing it is, and we see how they deal with Mantua and Savoy who are their Benjamins. And withal I take it for a certain truth that both the French and Hollander do rather desire to continue the electoral dignity in the house of Bavaria than restore it to the prince Palatine, as the likeliest way to get the empire out of the house of Austria.[63]

It was not without reason, then, that Charles decided to keep his options open. Nor was England's position hopelessly weak. The flurry

59. *Clarendon State Papers*, I, pp. 369, 372, 375, 405, 425, 432.

60. *Ibid.*, p. 451.

61. PRO, SP 16/312/12; *Cal. Stat. Pap. Dom., 1635–6*, p. 179: Windebank to Charles I, 23 Jan. 1636, margin note by the king. Cf. *Clarendon State Papers*, I, pp. 428, 447: Windebank to Taylor, 16 Jan., 5 Feb. 1636.

62. Gardiner, *History of England*, VIII, pp. 101–2.

63. Egerton MS 1820, f.581v: Hopton to Windebank, 3 Feb. 1636. The reference to 'Benjamins' seems to refer to the strategic importance of Benjamin's lands for all their relatively small extent.

of diplomatic activity (there were two envoys from France resident and the Condé d'Onate was on his way from Spain) made observers 'begin to reason that the reputation of his Majesty is ascending'.[64] As Dinley wrote from the Hague to Roe, 'since he has taken his nephew and the seas into his care, the world looks upon him as an arbiter . . . As things are now sided, it is not improbable that his Majesty may do more with his reputation than heretofore with his armies.'[65]

The year of the three embassies: Arundel's mission to Vienna

In the spring of 1636, therefore, two special ambassadors extraordinary were appointed to journey, the one to Vienna, the other to Paris. On 1 April, Thomas Howard, Earl of Arundel, heir to the premier duchy of the realm, received his instructions for his embassy to the Emperor Ferdinand. The earl was formally to request the revocation of the imperial ban on Charles Louis, his restitution to his Electoral title, and the restoration of all his territory in the Palatinate. In return for 'a full restitution of our nephew's dignities and estates', Arundel was authorized to offer a league through which England would mediate a peace favourable to the emperor in Germany, intercede to bring the Swedes to 'reasonable contentment' and the United Provinces and France to truce with Spain. If any of the protagonists proved uncooperative, within the context of existing engagements England would assist the emperor with its fleets. If the emperor denied the 'total and absolute restitution' sought, he was to be warned that Charles would be 'forced to join with some other party' – namely with the French.[66] If the demands appear extravagant they were not inevitably doomed to be rejected. In March, Taylor had written to the effect that the Habsburgs were ready to offer entire satisfaction, albeit in time: the revocation of the ban and the Lower Palatinate immediately and the Upper and Electoral title on the death of the Duke of Bavaria.[67] Charles's agent with the German princes William Curtius was sent to Bavaria to inform him of Ferdinand's proposals and to urge him to consent to them.[68] The time seemed auspicious: with a diet about to convene at Ratisbon [Regensburg] Ferdinand was anxious

64. *Cal. Stat. Pap. Dom., 1635–6*, pp. 272–3: Dinley to Roe, 15 March 1636.
65. *Ibid.*, p. 273.
66. PRO, SP 80/9, f.105, 1 April 1636.
67. *Clarendon State Papers*, I, p. 447: Taylor to Windebank, 13 Feb. 1636; T. Birch (ed.) *The Court and Times of Charles I* (2 vols, 1848), II, p. 238: E.R. to Puckering, 30 March 1636; *Cal. Stat. Pap. Dom., 1635–6*, p. 314: Roe to Elizabeth of Bohemia, 22 March 1636; *HMC Denbigh, V*, pp. 20, 21.
68. *Clarendon State Papers*, I, p. 475.

to secure the election of his son, Ferdinand, king of Hungary, as king of the Romans (his successor to the imperial crown).[69] Even the queen of Bohemia, who had scathingly dismissed the venture, was pleased at Arundel's departure in April.[70] For all his reputation as a Hispanophile, Arundel had since the events of the previous year voiced his disenchantment with Spanish duplicity.[71] His embassy too would end all 'ambiguities'.[72] Since none was of greater status than the Earl Marshal, the emperor would no longer be able to delay on the excuse of awaiting an ambassador with plenipotentiary powers to conclude. The outcome of Arundel's embassy, as Elizabeth put it, would be 'tout ou rien'.[73]

Arundel set off in April towards the Hague, where he was warmly received by Elizabeth. The queen was relieved to see his commission and to have assurances that her son's rights would not be compromised.[74] Leaving from Utrecht, the Earl Marshal crossed Germany, arriving by mid-May at Nuremberg. There he learned the news that put into question the hopes for a full restitution of the Palatinate after Bavaria's death: the duchess was pregnant with an heir to Maximilian's estates.[75] Taylor, ever optimistic, felt confident in the Habsburgs' assurance that it would make no difference.[76] Arundel confided to Wentworth that he could hope only that in the current conjunction of circumstances the friendship of England would count for more than that of Bavaria.[77] Meeting Taylor at Nuremberg, Arundel learned that the emperor had arranged to meet with him at Linz, midway between Vienna and Ratisbon, where an imperial diet was due to convene in June.[78] A journey down the Danube brought the Earl Marshal to Linz on the 14th; two days later he was formally received; on the 18th he had his second audience, the first occasion of business after the ceremonies of welcome and delivery of letters of credence. The ambassador explained that he had come, in response to

69. G. Parker, *The Thirty Years War* (1984), p. 162.
70. Bodleian, Clarendon MS 8, no. 700.
71. See W.S. Knowler (ed.) *The Earl of Strafford's Letters and Despatches* (2 vols, 1739), I, p. 417: Arundel to Wentworth, 3 May 1635.
72. *Cal. Stat. Pap. Venet., 1632–6*, p. 538: Correr's dispatch of 4 April 1636.
73. *Cal. Stat. Pap. Dom., 1635–6*, p. 351: Elizabeth to Roe, 4 April 1636.
74. *Ibid.*, p. 367: Elizabeth to Roe, 14 April 1636. For a contemporary account of the Arundel embassy, see W. Crowne, *A true Relation of all the Remarkable Places and Passages Observed in the Travels of . . . the Earl of Arundel . . . Ambassador Extraordinary* (1637, STC 6097). Cf. M.F.S. Hervey, *The Life, Correspondence and Collections of Thomas Howard, Earl of Arundel* (Cambridge, 1921), ch. 26. Most reliable is 'A summary relation of the principal occurents happening in the embassage collected by Sir J. Borough' (PRO, State Papers German SP 80/10/55).
75. *Clarendon State Papers*, I, p. 529: Arundel to Windebank, 14 May 1636; *Cal. Stat. Pap. Venet., 1632–6*, p. 566; Gardiner, *History of England*, VIII, pp. 159–60.
76. *HMC Denbigh, V*, p. 26: Taylor to Fielding, 3 May 1636.
77. *Clarendon State Papers*, I, p. 529.
78. PRO, SP 80/10/55; Hervey, *Arundel*, p. 364.

Ferdinand's intimations to Taylor, to request the restitution of the Prince Palatine, on which the peace of the empire depended.[79] To his forceful and determined address, Ferdinand responded briefly that in time he would have his resolution. The Earl Marshal had not come to spend time. He waited only days before procuring another audience at which he pressed the king's need for 'present resolution'; commissioners were appointed to treat with him. Discussions quickly ran into difficulties over an alleged league offensive and defensive that Taylor, they claimed, had promised.[80] The commissioners offered nothing beyond the Lower Palatinate and the removal of the ban, terms, as Arundel put it to Windebank, 'which you see are ill enough'.[81] Soon they reached an impasse and with the emperor about to leave for Ratisbon, little progress was in prospect.[82] Arundel became convinced that the imperialists were trifling with him in order to spin out long delays. And he was equally suspicious that the Spaniards (Onate was at Vienna and took no notice of him) were ill inclined to assist the king. Before the end of the month, sensing that nothing was to be achieved beyond the earlier offer of partial restitution, he began to suggest that he be recalled.[83]

His request was not then granted, in part perhaps because others were less pessimistic, in part because Charles was not ready to announce the collapse of negotiations with the Habsburgs. Taylor was much more sanguine about the prospects in Germany than was Arundel. 'Our greatest certainty,' he told Lord Fielding in June, 'grows from the necessity they have here of making peace on any condition.'[84] He even believed that 'a restitution in integram is practicable', albeit 'not to be hoped for at once'.[85] The Venetian envoy in Germany, Ballarino, endorsed his opinion. With Arundel taking such a firm line, he reported, 'it is thought they will have to do something in earnest'.[86] From Spain, Lord Aston wrote of his growing confidence in the willingness of Olivares to satisfy England. 'They make here,' he told Viscount Scudamore, 'great professions of their desire . . . to give his Majesty satisfaction in the business of the Palatinate, and that we shall see good effects of their intentions.'[87] With an extraordinary leaving Spain for England, Aston held 'good hopes that the business of the

79. PRO, SP 80/10/55.
80. *Ibid.*, *Clarendon State Papers*, I, pp. 572–4.
81. Clarendon MS 9, no. 740: Arundel to Windebank, 22 June/2 July 1636.
82. PRO, SP 80/10/55.
83. PRO, SP 80/9, ff.181–92; Gardiner, *History of England*, VIII, p. 160.
84. *HMC Denbigh, V*, p. 29: Taylor to Fielding, 16/26 June 1636.
85. *Ibid.*, p. 30: Taylor to Fielding, 6 Aug. 1636.
86. *Cal. Stat. Pap. Venet., 1636–9*, p. 17, 5 July 1636.
87. PRO, C.115/N6/8674: Aston to Scudamore, 10 May 1636.

Palatinate . . . may at last come to have a fair and happy conclusion'.[88] The Spanish weakness and French power at sea disposed them, he opined, 'every day more . . . to a greater estimation of his Majesty's friendship'.[89] Arriving in England in July, Onate (formerly Philip IV's agent in Vienna) announced 'that the Palatinate shall be rendered suddenly, and affirms that he comes furnished with instructions to that effect'.[90]

In August, Arundel half-heartedly proceeded to Ratisbon, to which city all negotiations had been referred. He was not in good temper: he was angry at Taylor for having exceeded his instructions and, sensitive to any slight on his honour, was anxious to return home. The time had come, he felt, to heal the wounds inflicted on his master not with the salve of diplomacy but with iron and fire.[91] On 1 August he presented a formal written paper in Latin complaining of delays and insisting on total restitution as the necessary preliminary to any league between England and the Habsburgs.[92] By now he saw it as no more than a formality, not least because with Bavaria and Spain in possession of the Palatinate (and insisting on the advancement of their own interests), the emperor had little to grant.[93] By the end of August, Ferdinand delivered his formal response through Walderode, the secretary of the imperial Chancery. He would remove the imperial ban and, in return for some satisfaction of their interests, Spain would yield the Lower Palatinate. But the Electoral dignity and Upper Palatinate were legally invested on the Duke of Bavaria.[94] As Arundel described the paper to Windebank, it offered fair words but little satisfaction. Rumours of the restoration to his lands of the Landgrave of Hesse, who had allied with Sweden, added insult to the injury to England's honour: 'it may be observed how easily grace is offered to those that in person have been delinquents in the highest measure whilst his Majesty's mediation cannot prevail in the behalf of the guiltless princes his nephews'.[95] The emperor's commissioners claimed that his hands were tied by Spain's insistence on its *conveniencias*, on its desire to see England break with Holland and France before it would restore its part of the Palatinate.[96] Arundel, however, had no illusions about the game that was being

88. *Ibid.*, 8675: Aston to Scudamore, 31 May 1636.
89. *Ibid.*, 8677, 28 June 1636.
90. PRO, C.115/N6/8604: Northumberland to Scudamore, 14 July 1636.
91. *Cal. Stat. Pap. Venet., 1636–9*, p. 34; PRO, SP 80/10/85.
92. Clarendon MS 9, no. 786, 18 Aug. 1636.
93. PRO, State Papers Spanish, SP 94/38/145: Arundel to Aston, 29 Aug. 1636.
94. Clarendon MS 10, no. 786: Arundel's paper to the emperor; Clarendon MS 10, no. 791: Arundel to Windebank, 30 Aug. 1636; PRO, SP 94/38/145.
95. Clarendon MS 10, no. 791.
96. *Ibid.*

played. Nothing more was offered by Vienna than the terms of February 1635, now glossed with a justification of the Peace of Prague. As for Spain, which had long been promising intercession for the restoration of the Elector, it was for them to treat concerning this proposal directly in London, not by way of obstruction in Vienna. All, Arundel felt certain, was intended only to further discussion and prolong his stay to the detriment of the king's honour. On 13 September he requested his revocation.[97] Before the end of the month it was granted.[98]

As the report circulated that the earl had received his revocation, the Habsburgs, fearful of the consequences, moved frantically to delay his departure. In October, the king of Hungary came to see him several times at Ratisbon and offered his intercession.[99] Arundel however, realized that, though they expressed the Habsburgs' fear of adding to the ranks of their enemies, Hungary's solicitations held out no prospects of substance. Whenever he delayed his departure they became more non-committal about their promises.[100] The birth of a son to the Duke of Bavaria at the end of October snuffed the last flicker of hope through some accommodation after Maximilian's death.[101] At the beginning of November, Arundel asked for audience with Ferdinand, in order to take his formal departure.[102] On the 8th he set off to Nuremberg, where Colonel Leslie caught up with him, bringing letters from the emperor promising satisfaction.[103] They were worse than empty words for they referred to Elizabeth without her title Electress; Arundel returned them, remaining 'of opinion that nothing will be procured from them worth acceptance'.[104] Continuing through Frankfurt, where he heard the news of the election of the king of Hungary as king of the Romans, and Cologne, where his trumpeter was taken prisoner, Arundel arrived at the Hague in mid-December.[105] By the beginning of the New Year, he returned to court with, as Conway put it to Wentworth, 'very ill satisfaction'.[106]

97. Clarendon MS 10, no. 802, 13/23 Sept. 1636; *Cal. Stat. Pap. Dom., 1636–7*, p. 133; BL Add. MS 15970, f.36: Arundel to Petty, 8 Sept. 1636.
98. On 27 September 1636 (Berkshire Record Office, Trumbull MS 543/2).
99. PRO, SP 80/10/55, and 80/10/5: Arundel to Coke, 19 Oct. 1636; SP 80/10/11: Arundel to Coke, 25 Oct. 1636.
100. PRO, SP 80/10/55, 5.
101. PRO, SP 80/10/11: Arundel to Coke, 25 Oct. 1636.
102. PRO, SP 80/10/27: Arundel to Coke, 7/17 Nov. 1636.
103. PRO, SP 80/10/31; SP 80/10/55.
104. PRO, SP 80/10/33: Arundel to Coke, 13/23 Nov. 1636.
105. PRO, SP 80/10/37: Arundel to Coke, 20/30 Nov. 1636; SP 80/10/55; SP 80/10/48: Arundel to Coke, 19/29 Dec. 1636.
106. Knowler, *Strafford Letters*, II, p. 45: Conway to Wentworth, 4 Jan. 1637.

The year of the three embassies: Aston in Spain

While Arundel negotiated fruitlessly in Vienna and Germany, relations between England and Spain were steadily worsening. In January 1636 Lord Aston had arrived to a welcome in Madrid probably because his appointment as envoy promised to thaw the ice-cold relations that had followed the collapse of the maritime treaty and the Peace of Prague.[107] The political realities, however, remained unchanged. Sir Arthur Hopton, who stayed on and worked well with Aston, saw that though Spain did not greatly favour the Duke of Bavaria, they too required his retention of the Palatinate, at least until the election of a Catholic, Habsburg king of the Romans had been secured.[108] Beyond that, Hopton believed, Spain might offer something but he doubted whether they would ever restore the Elector Palatine to greatness.[109] Unable to offer anything tangible, the Spaniards sought only to spin out the time, in the hope of keeping England neutral. Onate, designated as Necolalde's successor as envoy to England, in the spring of 1636 delayed his departure, ostensibly on the grounds of illness, but, it was suspected, as much to play for time.[110] The realists expected little from his embassy: as Viscount Conway wrote to Secretary Coke in July, 'I believe that what the Spanish ambassador brings will be still in the clouds for he will never tell you plainly that the Palatinate shall not be restored.'[111] When in August he finally arrived, the truth of such prognostications became all too quickly evident: Onate proposed only a revival of the maritime treaty as a means to check the growth of France and the Dutch.[112] With news coming from Arundel in August and September that the Spaniards, far from facilitating, were blocks to his negotiations in Vienna, there was no inclination on Charles I's part to pick up the agenda of the previous year. The Venetian envoy in Paris was informing Scudamore that Spain was joined with the emperor and Bavaria in their design to ensure that the Elector Palatine never regained a foothold in Germany.[113] Even Aston, who had been optimistic of success, acknowledged that the Spaniards would not break with Bavaria.[114]

107. Egerton MS 1820, f.578: Hopton to Windebank, 12 Jan. 1636.
108. *Ibid.*
109. *Ibid.*, f.581: Hopton to Cottington, 3 Feb. 1637.
110. Clarendon MS 9, no. 692: Aston to Hopton, 5 April 1636; Clarendon MS 9, no. 707: Aston to Coke, 26 April 1636.
111. Coke MS 54: Conway to Coke, 14 July 1636.
112. PRO, C.115/N4/8604: Northumberland to Scudamore, 14 July 1636; Clarendon MS 9, no. 764: Aston to Windebank, 24 July 1636.
113. BL Add. MS 35097, f.17v.
114. Clarendon MS 12, nos 960, 976.

By the late summer of 1636, events began again to follow the course that had seemed logical the previous summer, with the news of the Peace of Prague. The so-called Spanish faction began to dissolve with the evidence of Spanish duplicity and disillusionment with their promises.[115] As Arundel wrote in November, 'I have been very sorry to be a witness of the offices of Spain coming so short which I have so much heretofore defended to their evil willers.'[116] Favours to Spain began to be withdrawn. Since Cottington's return Charles had permitted Spanish silver bound for Dunkirk to be convoyed via London, largely in order to rake off the profit of minting half the bullion into coin at the Tower mint or converting it into bills of exchange.[117] In July Charles ordered it stopped; when Windebank permitted a shipment to cross the Straits against the king's intentions he found himself in confinement.[118] The king's anger at his secretary was intended to make a public statement. The bullion sent to Flanders with English assistance was financing Spanish campaigns against the Dutch and the French. In June, a Spanish army crossed the frontier into Picardy and forced its way through to Corbie.[119] Far from wishing to assist a Spanish invasion of France, by July complete distrust of the Habsburgs was convincing Charles that an alliance with Louis XIII presented him with his best, indeed his only real, diplomatic option.

The year of the three embassies: Leicester in France

The Earl of Leicester received his instructions as extraordinary envoy to Paris in May.[120] His brief was to explain to Richelieu and Louis that Arundel had been dispatched to the emperor 'with more than a probable hope of good success'. But if the emperor offered no satisfaction 'we have engaged ourselves to join in arms with the furtherers and against the opposers of such a general peace'. Leicester was therefore to put the French in mind of the proposal made to Senneterre the previous year for exchange of the Palatinate for Lorraine as a means to that peace. Leicester's embassy was, as Gardiner suggested, undoubtedly

115. Below, pp. 537–41; A. Loomie, 'The Spanish faction at the court of Charles I, 1630–1638', *Bull. Inst. Hist. Res.*, 59 (1986), pp. 37–49.
116. PRO, SP 80/10/29: Arundel to Coke, 8/18 Nov. 1636.
117. *HMC 3rd Report*, p. 73; cf. *Cal. Stat. Pap. Dom., 1635*, p. 526.
118. Gardiner, *History of England*, VIII, p. 162.
119. *Ibid.*, p. 163.
120. The instructions are in PRO, State Papers French SP 78/101, ff.31–6; summarized in A. Collins, *Letters and Memorials of State Collected by Sir H. Sidney* (2 vols, 1746), II, pp. 374–8. A draft is in Coke MS 54, on dorse of letter, 1 May 1636; see *HMC Cowper*, II, p. 151. Leicester did not get on with the resident envoy, Viscount Scudamore; see *HMC De Lisle and Dudley, VI*, p. 74.

intended to put pressure on the emperor and on Spain.[121] But it would be wrong to conclude that this was its only purpose. The 'support' of England was out to tender in 1636 – on offer to whoever came up with the proposition most likely to aid the young Elector to the recovery of his rights.[122] Accordingly from the beginning the French negotiations were serious as well as strategic. Coke told Leicester in July that in return for a French promise not to make peace until the Palatinate had been restored, he might offer them the right to recruit troops from England and the aid of the ship money fleet.[123] There was no hope for England, the secretary added, in the Habsburgs' promises, though in order to get the best from France it was important to disguise their futility.[124] For his part, Leicester was confident that Richelieu was no less serious in his dealing with England: 'if they do not really desire and intend a strict and durable amity between these two crowns,' he reported, 'they are . . . the falsest . . . men of the world.'[125] For the Duke de Bouillon had assured him that 'if the King [of England] will join with us . . . he shall quickly have his Palatinates'.[126] The invasion of France and the threat to Paris raised Leicester's hopes to greater heights. 'If they have formerly been satisfied with neutrality it was when they needed no more than that.' Now they expressed their desire for England's friendship and if any doubted their sincerity, Leicester thought, 'their need of it at this time will argue for them'.[127]

By mid-August civil pleasantries were turning to concrete proposals: the French were asking how many men England could send to Germany and were pressing for Charles to send powers to conclude an alliance.[128] Louis's envoys in England, in confirmation of Leicester's news, were urging an offensive and defensive league in return for active aid in the recovery of the Palatinate.[129] By way of response Leicester was instructed to offer France the withdrawal of English favours from Spain, the right to levy volunteers and the assistance of the fleet, but not the offensive and defensive league that would quickly plunge England into war on the side of France. If the envoy could be sure not to engage Charles to a rupture, he was assured that he would be sent powers to conclude an agreement under the great seal.[130]

121. Gardiner, *History of England*, VIII, p. 160.
122. See *Cal. Stat. Pap. Venet., 1636–9*, p. 3, 6 June 1636.
123. Collins, *Letters and Memorials*, II, p. 393: Coke to Leicester, 20 July 1636.
124. *Ibid.*, p. 398, 29 July 1636.
125. *Ibid.*, p. 396: Leicester to Coke, 22 July 1636.
126. *Ibid.*, p. 399: Leicester to Coke, 29 July/8 Aug. 1636.
127. *Ibid.*, p. 403: Leicester to Coke, 8/18 Aug. 1636.
128. *Ibid.*, p. 406: Leicester to Coke, 16/26 Aug.1636.
129. Gardiner, *History of England*, VIII, p. 161.
130. Collins, *Letters and Memorials*, II, p. 415: Coke to Leicester, 20 July 1636.

Leicester protested that what was on offer was not enough to tempt the French, who were aware that the Duchess of Bavaria's pregnancy virtually put paid to any deal with the Habsburgs.[131] Coke's alterations to Bouillon's terms for a league he thought too ambiguous and too non-committal.[132] With considerable frankness he advised,

> they are not children who govern the affairs here and therefore will not be fed with shadows . . . They have a good opinion of their strength and think it sufficient for their own turn, at least to make their peace. But if you will make them do more and undertake the cause of others, who they know well enough are nearer to us than to them, you must help them or be assured they will do nothing.[133]

Over the following weeks while Bouillon considered the English alterations to his articles, Leicester's frustration at Coke's (or his master's) refusal to grasp the realities of his advice was matched by Coke's concern that Leicester should not exceed his instructions.[134] Events, however, staved off a possible impasse. Leicester's sense that the news of Arundel's rebuff by the emperor at Linz left a confederation with France the only option was clearly widely shared.[135] The Venetian ambassador in England reported in October that 'the court has been full this week of violent clamour and denunciation against the house of Austria' and thought that England was prepared to reconsider the terms of its treating with France.[136] The newswriter Rossingham predicted that a confederation would be formed;[137] even the Countess of Leicester told her husband that the king was 'well inclined to the French business'.[138] The earl himself, however, continued to doubt whether the English articles, with their offer of the fleet and 6,000 men (in addition to the future right to recruit), would satisfy Richelieu. Indeed he feared that the French were using the English terms only to extract better conditions from Austria:[139] as Leicester's estate manager was informed, 'I think it is an even lay here between their treaty with England and their peace of Cologne which of them they will incline

131. *Ibid.*, pp. 398–401: Leicester to Coke, 29 July/8 Aug. 1636; pp. 402–4, 8/18 Aug.; pp. 410–13, 23 Aug./2 Sept.; pp. 420–1, 9/19 Sept.
132. *Ibid.*, p. 415: Coke to Leicester, 30 Aug.; p. 419: Leicester to Coke, 6/16 Sept.; pp. 420–1, 9/19 Sept.; p. 425, 1/11 Oct. See also Charles Louis's letter to the queen of Bohemia, 11 Sept., in G. Bromley (ed.) *A Collection of Royal Letters* (1787), p. 82.
133. Collins, *Letters and memorials*, II, p. 435: Leicester to Coke, 23 Oct./2 Nov.
134. *Ibid.*, pp. 439–40, 441–2, 447, 448.
135. *Ibid.*, p. 434: Leicester to Coke, 23 Oct./2 Nov.
136. *Cal. Stat. Pap. Venet., 1636–9*, pp. 83–4: Correr to Doge, 17 Oct. 1636.
137. Birch, *Court and Times of Charles I*, II, p. 256: Rossingham to Puckering, 11 Oct. 1636.
138. Collins, *Letters and Memorials*, II, p. 444: Countess of Leicester to Leicester, 10 Nov. 1636.
139. *Ibid.*, pp. 447, 450: Leicester to Coke, 25 Nov./5 Dec., 16/26 Dec. 1636; *Cal. Stat. Pap. Venet., 1636–9*, p. 96.

to.'[140] If Leicester were right, the odds were soon changed – by the return of the Earl of Arundel at the very end of the year.

Arundel's return was important not only for his elucidation of the diplomatic situation, but also for his weight in English counsels. During the autumn and winter, whilst Holland and others had joined Leicester's plea for a greater English commitment to France, Windebank had aired his reservations and Laud had done his utmost to keep the king from an engagement that might lead to war.[141] As the senior nobleman of the realm, old ally of Weston and reputed Hispanophile, Arundel might have been expected to echo the reservations of those Councillors who feared any course that might end in conflict. Frustration and wounded personal honour, however, along with experience of diplomatic realities, led him to proffer very different counsels. On his way through Holland, Arundel had promised Elizabeth that he would be frank in telling the king that nothing was to be had from the Habsburgs.[142] Roe was uplifted by the news: 'if', he wrote to the Prince Elector, Arundel 'do not change in our cold and watery air, it is in his way to be the author of a turn of all affairs'.[143] The Earl Marshal had a long audience with the king within days of his return. He was warmly received by Charles who recognized, as the Countess of Leicester told her husband, that his ambassador had suffered 'an ill journey and scurvy usage'.[144] True to his promise, Arundel did not mask his 'ill satisfaction' nor mince words.[145] He affirmed that there was no point in continuing negotiations with the Habsburgs and declared himself in favour of an alliance with France and a breach with Spain.[146] Added to those of Holland and the queen, his voice was decisive. Correr, the Venetian ambassador, reported that the very day on which Arundel addressed the Council, England began to make preparations to equip a fleet and concluded on a new offer to France,

140. *HMC De Lisle and Dudley VI*, p. 72: Battière to Hawkins, 11/21 Dec. 1636.
141. Collins, *Letters and Memorials*, II, pp. 444, 452, 454; *Cal. Stat. Pap. Dom., 1636–7*, pp. 83, 98; Gardiner, *History of England*, VIII, p. 162; cf. J. Blisse and W. Scott (eds) *The Works of Laud William* (7 vols, Oxford, 1847–60) VI, part 2, p. 516; P. Haskell, 'Sir Francis Windebank and the personal rule of Charles I' (University of Southampton PhD thesis, 1978), p. 281.
142. *Cal. Stat. Pap. Dom., 1636–7*, p. 239: Elizabeth to Roe, 21/31 Dec. 1636; cf. Anglesey MSS, Elizabeth to Henrietta Maria, 10/20 Nov. 1636.
143. *Cal. Stat. Pap. Dom., 1636–7*, p. 249: Roe to Charles Louis, 31 Dec. 1636.
144. Collins, *Letters and Memorials*, II, p. 455: Countess of Leicester to Leicester, 10 Jan. 1637.
145. Knowler, *Strafford Letters*, II, p. 45: Conway to Wentworth, 4 Jan. 1637; pp. 48–9: Northumberland to Wentworth, 7 Feb.
146. *HMC Denbigh V*, pp. 45–7: Weckherlin to Fielding, 15/25 Feb. 1637; *Cal. Stat. Pap. Venet., 1636–9*, p. 133; cf. Elizabeth's memorandum to Arundel (PRO, SP 81/43/224, 31 Dec. 1636), and Arundel's letter to Aston (24 Jan. 1637), in Hervey, *Arundel*, pp. 403–4.

including a joint assault with the French and Dutch on Flanders.[147] At the news of the election of the king of the Romans, Charles instructed his nephew to issue a protestation against the invalidity of an election in which he had not taken his rightful part, and promised him a fleet to add force to his words.[148] The Countess of Leicester was quick to give her husband the good news of the turn of the tide: 'The busiest statesmen in the court,' she wrote with measured restraint, 'do now conceive more hope of a good conclusion in the French affairs . . .'.[149] The Earl of Northumberland told Wentworth that it was likely they would break with Spain.[150] The passing days only strengthened the king's resolve. On 1 February Rossingham reported Charles's anger at the imperial envoy's making no reference to Arundel's embassy;[151] on the 7th the Spanish ambassador was granted a short audience and came out 'cloudy'.[152] News was circulating that the French had abandoned their demand for an open declaration of war and that Charles was now personally disposed to open rupture. Arundel 'did not cease to advise it with all his might'; 'he really has,' Correr told the Doge and Senate, 'become a partisan in this cause.'[153]

Richelieu tacked nimbly to take advantage of the suddenly favourable change of wind. Aware of Charles's hesitancy about embroiling England in a full-scale war, he abandoned the demand for an immediate league offensive and defensive.[154] He offered instead terms by which England would permit the French to levy 6,000 volunteers and put to sea a fleet of thirty vessels to blockade the coast of Flanders. The package came close to what Coke had already been proposing. Accordingly Weckherlin recorded in his diary for 14 February that he perused with the king new instructions to be sent to Leicester and 'I did write fair both the treaty presently to be ratified and the assignation of an offensive and defensive league'.[155] The date was significant: on 14 February the Lord Keeper publicly read in Star Chamber the answer of the judges in reply to the king's question about his right to levy ship

147. *Cal. Stat. Pap. Venet., 1636–9*, p. 130, dispatch of 23 Jan. 1637.
148. *Ibid.*, p. 133; Birch, *Court and Times of Charles I*, II, p. 280; Gardiner, *History of England*, VIII, p. 204; *The Manifest of the Most Illustrious and Sovereign Prince Charles Lodowic Count Palatine* (1637, STC 5046).
149. *HMC De Lisle and Dudley VI*, p. 81: Countess of Leicester to Leicester, 21 Jan. 1637.
150. Knowler, *Strafford Letters*, II, pp. 48–9, 7 Feb. 1637; cf. Wentworth's own view in a letter to the Countess of Arundel, Sheffield Central Library, Wentworth Woodhouse MSS, WW/8, f.424.
151. Birch, *Court and Times of Charles I*, II, p. 271.
152. *Ibid.*, p. 275: Rossingham to Puckering.
153. *Cal. Stat. Pap. Venet., 1636–9*, pp. 146–7, 20 Feb. 1637.
154. Gardiner, *History of England*, VIII, p. 205.
155. Trumbull Miscellaneous MSS, LX1 (Weckherlin's diary, 1633–42), 13 Feb. 1637.

money.[156] Events at home as well as abroad were reorienting foreign policy to a course that might lead England into war. As the third ship money fleet was about to put to sea, the Prince Elector was put in command of fourteen vessels, in accordance with the treaty with France.[157]

The news of these rapid changes spread as swiftly around the country. A court correspondent, Sir John Beaumont, articulated the tense anticipation of February: 'Our chief news,' he wrote to Sir Gervase Clifton, 'is only expectation, for here are great preparations for a fleet . . . it is thought that though the peace be not absolutely broken . . . yet that we shall be upon cold terms with the house of Austria and Spain . . . it is much laboured that his Majesty should enter into a league with the cardinal offensive and defensive.'[158] Beaumont doubted it would be concluded through fear of 'too much overbalancing that side'. But as the ship money fleet prepared to sail, the real possibility of active English engagement in Europe began to dawn. Kenelm Digby writing from Paris assured Secretary Coke that there was no lack of respect for England: 'The world here is much more apprehensive of your sea preparations than you need be of theirs.'[159] With such a strong fleet, he added, the Dutch in particular would not step out of line. A certain patriotic fervour is audible in the correspondence of the spring. Ferdinando Gorges informed Thomas Smyth: 'There is like to be a great league betwixt us and the King of France. The Dutchmen stand off . . . 'Tis thought that Prince Rupert shall this summer open the war betwixt the Spaniard and his brother. Some think the Palsgrave himself will go to sea.'[160] Such reports reflected the talk at court where now almost no voice was heard in favour of further negotiation with Spain,[161] and most, including the Lord Chamberlain, perceived Charles himself to be determined to fight.[162] By May even Windebank, who had harboured most reservations about a break, wrote to Lord Aston in Spain to inform him of the

156. Gardiner, *History of England*, VIII, p. 208; *Cal. Stat. Pap. Dom., 1636–7*, pp. 416–7; below, pp. 719–20.
157. Anglesey MSS: Elizabeth of Bohemia to Henrietta Maria, 4/14 Feb. 1637; *Cal. Stat. Pap. Venet., 1636–9*, p. 141; *Cal. Stat. Pap. Dom., 1636–7*, p. 479, 1 March 1637: list of ships lent.
158. Nottingham University Library, Clifton MS Cl/C 227: Beaumont to Clifton, 5 Feb. 1637; cf. Gervase Clifton to his father Sir G. Clifton, 3 Feb. 1637 (*HMC Various VII*, p. 415).
159. Coke MS 56: Digby to Coke, 15 Feb. 1637.
160. Bristol Record Office, Smyth of Ashton Court MS AC1/C51/10: Gorges to Smyth, 29 May 1637.
161. Scottish Record Office, Hamilton MS GD 406/1, 9555: Hamilton to Fielding, 6 Feb. 1637; *Cal. Stat. Pap. Venet., 1636–9*, p. 146; *Cal. Stat. Pap. Dom., 1636–7*, pp. 249–50; Knowler, *Strafford Letters*, II, p. 53.
162. *HMC De Lisle and Dudley, VI*, p. 101.

Manifest of the Prince Elector calling for a league against the Habsburgs and the preparations made to give it teeth. 'The King of England must treat no more but act in earnest.'[163]

Only one voice continued persistently to question the wisdom of a league with France. When Arundel departed, disgruntled, from Vienna, he left John Taylor, at least formally, to conduct future negotiations. A half-Spaniard, with an attachment to the Habsburgs that seriously compromised his judgement, Taylor had been optimistic about the success of Arundel's mission.[164] During the Earl Marshal's visit, and even after his departure, that optimism never entirely left him.[165] Nor did his suspicion of France. While England awaited the completion of the treaty negotiations in Paris, and Windebank was informing Hopton that 'our intelligence with that crown grows into nearness and I doubt not but that it shall be for the good of Christendom', Taylor's dispatches began to express his concern forcefully.[166] If France were compelled to make peace, he argued, they would not bother about the restitution of the Palatinate, but would labour to secure the possessions they had gained in Italy. Contrarily, if their campaigns succeeded and they advanced to the Rhine, he believed it likely that they would make the Elector Palatine their pawn, much as Sweden had his father in 1632: 'and that both he and his country should lose their liberties aye and religion and for the infinite benefits which he hath received from England he should be compelled to be against us, if once we and the French should disagree'.[167] What France wanted, Taylor maintained, not inaccurately, was the ruin of Spain and conquest of the Low Countries, even though they often masked these ambitions with other rhetoric. In Italy and Germany, he reminded Windebank, Richelieu's forces 'enter with the title of protection but make more than half a conquest wheresoever they get a footing . . .'. Accordingly, he advised, Charles should recognize that he would gain nothing from France that he did not earn or take by his own forces. In a passage that Windebank (or the king?) underlined, he concluded: 'It is dangerous joining unless you have equal forces and of the same nature, for it is not enough to be superior at sea unless you can be at least equal at land.' France, he predicted, would emerge as another Sweden – only worse, for Gustavus at least 'was of our religion and had not those particular interests opposite to ours which

163. Clarendon MS 11, no. 928: Windebank to Aston, 29 May 1637.

164. Gardiner, *History of England*, VIII, p. 83; *Clarendon State Papers*, I, pp. 500, 524, 527, 581, 616, 620, 660, 700, 704; and *ibid.*, p. 662: Windebank to Taylor, 29 Sept. 1636.

165. *Clarendon State Papers*, I, p. 699.

166. Clarendon MS 12, no. 948, 14 July 1636.

167. *Ibid.*, no. 952: Taylor to Windebank, 26 July 1636.

the French have'.[168] If Taylor's warnings about French ambitions reveal an astute foresight of future dangers, his continued faith in the sincerity of the Habsburgs' assurances was little short of naive. Yet both his admonitions and his optimism comprised the two complementary parts of the refrain he repeatedly sang throughout the spring and summer of 1637. Taylor pressed for the resumption of negotiations in the other passage underscored by Windebank:

> the emperor inviteth you to continue your treaty; protesteth that he doth mean really to you to end this business so far as he may and is possible; assureth you that at Ratisbon there was a resolution taken what to do and how far to proceed in the restitution of the Count Palatines; that he holds well the same resolution and hath lessened nothing of his good intentions, that he will moderate the Spaniards' demands . . . and those of Bavaria.[169]

His hopes were raised even higher by the succession of the new Emperor Ferdinand in September.[170] In Vienna rumours began to circulate again of a possible match between the Palatine house and the Habsburgs – or even between the Prince of Wales and the emperor's daughter.[171] Taylor took them seriously and urged Windebank to do likewise. A concern fostered by the Danish ambassador (who had his own reasons for not wanting the Dutch and French further strengthened by a maritime alliance with England) that the German princes might settle agreements without taking account of the Palatine added fear and urgency to Taylor's belief in the need to reopen discussions.[172] Taylor was not alone in his doubts about the French. Viscount Fielding feared that from the alliance and war 'after the effusion of much blood and expense of treasure nothing may be gained but the sole burden thereof, the differences betwixt the other two crowns being the more easily to be accommodated when his Majesty turning the balance may force the Spaniards to seek, though upon disadvantageous terms, their reconciliation with France'.[173] The king, he counselled, needed to come to an agreement with the German and Italian princes to free himself of dependence upon the French who otherwise 'as a nation given much to undervalue others, and more particularly ours . . . may make use of his Majesty's resolution to gain for themselves an advantageous peace from the Spaniard and be after glad to leave the King engaged in those difficulties which they now so

168. *Ibid.*
169. *Ibid.*; cf. Clarendon MS 12, nos 963, 964, 19 Aug. 1636.
170. Clarendon MS 12, no. 985, 7 Oct. 1636.
171. *Ibid.*, no. 997, 4 Nov. 1636.
172. *Ibid.*, no. 994, 21 Oct. 1636.
173. Hamilton MS 9555: Fielding to (Hamilton), 6 Feb. 1637.

apparently suffer under'.[174] If others shared these reservations, they suppressed them in the mood of anger with the Habsburgs and hopes from France that characterized the weeks after Arundel's return. Indeed it was only the protraction of negotiations in Paris – and ultimately Charles's embroilment in domestic British concerns – that blocked the offensive and defensive alliance and England's likely entry into the Thirty Years War.

As early as March 1637 there were signs of impatience in England at the slow progress of the treaty: on the 27th Weckherlin dispatched a packet to Leicester containing orders to hasten the proceedings.[175] In France, however, the negotiations had met with obstacles.[176] Objections were raised to even the minor changes made by Charles. More seriously, Bouillon told Leicester that French diplomacy required that the treaty be referred to her allies, who were to meet in a diet at Hamburg.[177] The earl was evidently taken aback by this tack. The king of England, he argued, had never seen Hamburg as the place to conclude the treaty 'but for the reception of such confederates as would desire to enter into the treaty supposed to be already made between their Majesties'.[178] In response to Bouillon's protestations about the need to confer with the Dutch and the Swedes, the ambassador pressed for an immediate ratification. He met only with delays: the French gave him a paper of the 'differences' between their own and the English articles; the report of the emperor's death was said to hold up progress.[179] It may well be, as Gardiner argued, that Richelieu placed little hope in Charles and sought, like Spain, only to lock England into a safe neutrality, by playing for time.[180] But such an explanation is not entirely satisfactory. Senneterre and Pougny had laboured to obtain an English alliance in preference to neutrality; there was considerable advantage to be gained from the favour of the English fleet.[181] France, however, fighting a land war against the Habsburgs in Germany, Flanders and Italy, could not ignore her allies – the German princes, the Swedes and the Dutch. Their need to confer was real, not merely an excuse. Leicester worked to palliate English impatience and to

174. *Ibid.*
175. Trumbull MS 543/2, 27 March 1637.
176. Gardiner, *History of England*, VIII, p. 217.
177. Collins, *Letters and Memorials*, II, p. 473: Leicester to Coke, 17/27 March 1637.
178. *Ibid.*, p. 474. Charles Louis wrote similarly to his mother in May, 'tis true the King propounded the meeting at the Hague or Hamburg to draw in the States and the Swedes after the league was ratified between the two kings alone, which the French will not do without the approbation of all the confederates' (Bromley, *Royal Letters*, p. 86).
179. Collins, *Letters and Memorials*, II, pp. 481–3: Leicester to Coke, 29 March/8 April 1637; pp. 475–6, 21/31 March 1637.
180. Gardiner, *History of England*, VIII, p. 218.
181. Cf. M. Avenal, *Collection de documents inédits sur l'histoire de France: lettres, instructions diplomatiques et papiers d'état du Cardinal Richelieu*, V (Paris, 1863), p. 596.

keep the negotiations alive.[182] In May matters came to a head, as the campaigning season threatened to pass with nothing effected.[183] The French grumblings about England's unwillingness to declare war immediately found little support – even the Dutch, according to the Venetian envoy at the Hague, exonerated England from blame for the delays.[184] Charles again began to pay heed to Spanish overtures.[185]

Perhaps through fear of trying the king's patience so far as to incline him to Madrid, the French promulgated new proposals. They suggested sending to the Dutch and the Swedes to invite them to join an Anglo-French league and give answer at Hamburg. Charles I was then formally to make his demands of Austria and grant four to six weeks for them to be met. If the Habsburgs failed to satisfy him all the confederates would sign a league offensive and defensive and enter the war.[186] Though the new terms committed England further than his own earlier inclinations, Charles, as Coke replied swiftly to Leicester, 'is resolved to accept the treaty' and sent to his agents with the Swedes and the Dutch to advance the confederacy.[187] There were minor points to resolve (not least some inconsistencies between the Latin and French versions of the propositions), but these, Coke was confident, need 'neither delay time nor break the treaty'.[188] Throughout August and September, Coke wrote frequently to press Leicester to 'hasten the signing';[189] Windebank informed the envoy that 'both their Majesties are in some little disorder for the delay used by the French in the treaty'.[190] Despite the procrastination, many at the helm of affairs still expected a French alliance and a war. As late as November, the Earl of Northumberland told Wentworth that all would be concluded on the arrival of the new French ambassador, Bellièvres.[191] Laud, less pleased, predicted the same. 'As for war with Spain,' he wrote to the Lord Deputy, 'I can say no more of it yet but I fear it may come thither at last.'[192] Others, however, had begun to see the delays as interminable and indicative. In October Coke informed Leicester 'That those minis-

182. For example, Collins, *Letters and Memorials*, II, p. 486, 7/17 April 1637; pp. 492–3, 12/22 May 1637.
183. *Ibid.*, pp. 479, 492; *Cal. Stat. Pap. Venet., 1636–9*, pp. 183, 204, 215.
184. *Cal. Stat. Pap. Venet., 1636–9*, pp. 181, 204; cf. *Cal. Stat. Pap. Dom., 1636–7*, p. 504; *1637*, p. 82.
185. *Cal. Stat. Pap. Venet., 1636–9*, p. 209, 15 May 1637.
186. Collins, *Letters and Memorials*, II, pp. 497–9: Leicester to Coke, 6/16 June 1637.
187. *Ibid.*, p. 500: Coke to Leicester, 12 June 1637. He licensed Charles Louis to return to Holland to bring the states into the league (Bromley, *Royal Letters*, p. 91).
188. *Ibid.*, pp. 501–2: Coke to Leicester, 18 June 1637. Charles Louis agreed (Bromley, *Royal Letters*, p. 92).
189. *Ibid.*, p. 508, 1 Aug. 1637; cf. p. 513.
190. *Ibid.*, p. 515: Windebank to Leicester, 8 Sept. 1637.
191. Wentworth MS WW/17, no. 226: Northumberland to Wentworth, 15 Nov. 1637.
192. *Works of Laud*, VI, part 2, p. 516, 11 Nov. 1637.

ters can not be drawn to any assignment of time or place showeth, at least, that they are not so hot upon the treaty as they seemed at the first.' The Swedes, he now saw, sought their own settlement and the Dutch manoeuvred 'to hook into this treaty their pretensions against us for the sea'. 'It is hard, he concluded, to rectify all these oblique lines.'[193]

By the time he wrote, events were making it still harder, and it became clear that England would not be able to commit herself to any war or league. The riots that had greeted the introduction of the new Prayer Book in Edinburgh in July had escalated, as we shall see, into a widespread rebellion that preoccupied the government and ultimately led to a war between the king's British kingdoms.[194] 'How little occasion they have here to think of foreign affairs', Correr reported as the news of the riots spread.[195] The Scottish troubles were to disrupt the relations with France for other reasons. The Scots were traditional allies of the French and as hostilities with England intensified they were to appeal to their old allies for support. Richelieu, realizing that if domestic embroilments incapacitated England as an ally they at least guaranteed her impotent neutrality, was prepared to respond.[196] Some knowledge and greater suspicion of their aid to the Scots in turn exacerbated England's disillusionment with the French. When the congress much discussed in 1637 finally convened at Hamburg in 1638, disillusion had led to the destruction of the Anglo-French league. Richelieu would now give no undertaking not to make peace without the restoration of the Palatinate unless Charles would bind himself to join immediately in war – by land as well as by sea.[197]

The collapse of the French treaty ended a phase of diplomacy that had begun in the summer of 1635 with the news of the Peace of Prague. It is all too easy with hindsight to conclude from the failure of the negotiations the inevitability of their failure; and all too easy to assume that Charles would never go to war. With regard to the league it is difficult to judge. Would an agreement have been concluded before or at Hamburg if England had not become embroiled with the Scots?[198] And would such a confederation have plunged England into the Thirty Years War – perhaps until peace was concluded between France and Spain in 1659, or at least until the settlement of Germany in

193. Collins, *Letters and Memorials*, II, p. 520: Coke to Leicester, 18 Oct. 1637.
194. Below, Chapter XIII.
195. *Cal. Stat. Pap. Venet., 1636–9*, p. 259: dispatch of 28 Aug. 1637.
196. Below, pp. 827, 829, 833.
197. Gardiner, *History of England*, VIII, pp. 375–6.
198. The instructions to Bellièvres in October 1637 suggest that France was still serious. See BL Add. MS 45142, f.40v.

1648? There can be little doubt that whatever was adequate for his interest, Richelieu would have preferred an alliance with England to a neutrality that could not be relied upon. And, though suspicions of his pusillanimity may have remained, Charles, as his nephew himself acknowledged, had gone further in engaging himself in the spring of 1637 than at any point since the wars of the 1620s.[199] Charles I after all was not, like his father, a *rex pacificus*; Arundel's references to the Habsburgs' second slight on the king's honour may well have scratched at some old royal wounds from 1623.[200] The continuation of the Council of War and committee for the ordnance suggests that the possibility of war had never been closed;[201] in 1637 Charles himself wrote to Wentworth to warn him that he might break with Spain as a consequence of his treating with France.[202] The terms he accepted in June, if ratified by Richelieu, would have led to war.[203] There were, it must be said, English observers who remained doubtful that Charles would ever engage in a conflict.[204] But it is significant that they were not those powerful in the king's counsel. The best informed at home, along with the Venetian envoy, clearly read the king's mind as bent on belligerent courses. The Privy Council committee's search of the Tower rolls for precedents that proved the obligation of royal tenants holding by knight service to fight abroad gave them good reason to think so.[205] Windebank's shift of opinion is probably a good barometer of the general climate as well as the king's own condition. Laud, the senior Councillor, and Wentworth panicked at what they saw as an imminent conflict for which the realm was ill prepared, and at the 'distractions' and 'dangers' which threatened the security of England and Ireland.[206] Their 'fear' is strong evidence that had the French treaty been concluded in time for the fleet to sail in the spring of 1637, the halcyon days of Caroline peace might well have been then terminated.

199. Sir John Finet told Scudamore how a 'pasquil' at Brussels showing Charles sleeping in a chair with Spain piping behind him had stirred the king to action (PRO, C.115/N8/8805, 13/23 June 1637). Decisions to put the Elector to sea in July and license privateering in the West Indies meant, he reported, 'we may again be talked of in the style of the old world for brave Englishmen' (PRO, C.115/N8/8806, 5 July). As Master of Ceremonies, Finet was at the centre of court gossip.
200. Hervey, *Arundel*, p. 403.
201. The committee was revived in 1635 (PRO, PC 2/44/319; *Cal. Stat. Pap. Dom., 1637*, p. 87).
202. Knowler, *Strafford Letters*, II, p. 53.
203. Charles Louis thought in the summer of 1637 that his uncle 'is tied to break' with the Habsburgs (Bromley, *Royal Letters*, p. 92).
204. For example, BL, MS 29/172, f.139: Conway to Harley, 21 April 1637; Clifton MS Cl/C 27: Beaumont to Clifton, 5 Feb. 1637.
205. Birch, *Court and Times of Charles I*, II, p. 266: E.R. to Puckering, 17 Jan. 1637.
206. Knowler, *Strafford Letters*, II, p. 60 ff: Wentworth to Charles I, 31 March 1637; cf. p. 66; on Laud, see also *Cal. Stat. Pap. Dom., 1637*, p. 553.

IX

'THE DOMINION OF THE SEA'? FACTIONAL CHANGE AND FOREIGN PRIORITIES

The rise of the queen's men

Laud's fear that conflict was imminent owed as much to domestic, indeed personal, concerns as to events in Europe or the changes of diplomacy. For the real probability of war in 1637 reflected, as indeed it further effected, a reorientation of the factional alignments and politics at court, which had been shaken by the death of Richard Weston, Lord Treasurer and Earl of Portland on 13 March 1635. Though Weston had never emerged as another Buckingham, his death removed the prominent figure in the king's Council, in both foreign and domestic affairs. He was not immediately replaced as Treasurer. The king established an interim commission of five Privy Councillors – not least perhaps because there was no obvious candidate for the post.[1] While Laud, Manchester, Cottington and the secretaries Coke and Windebank were charged with the business of finance, another committee of six, consisting of the archbishop, Arundel, Carlisle, Holland and the secretaries, handled foreign affairs.[2] As the French ambassador Senneterre observed, the major Councillor on both committees, Laud, was the figure of most credit and authority in the king's counsels.[3] Laud, however, was completely inexperienced in foreign affairs and showed little interest in the complexities of European diplomacy beyond a general desire to keep Charles from foreign entanglements.[4] Of more significance for foreign policy was the rise to

1. Above, pp. 145–50; S.R. Gardiner, *History of England from the Accession of James I to the Outbreak of the Civil War, 1603–1642* (10 vols, 1883–4), VIII, pp. 68–70.
2. PRO, 31/3/68, f.146: Senecterre to Bouthillier, 4 April 1635.
3. *Calendar of State Papers Venetian* [*Cal. Stat. Pap. Venet.*], *1632–6*, p. 353.
4. *Calendar of State Papers Domestic* [*Cal. Stat. Pap. Dom.*], *1636–7*, p. 83.

prominence of Henry Rich, Earl of Holland. Since his unsuccessful attempt to discredit Weston, Holland had been confined to manoeuvring behind the scenes, in the base of his power and influence the queen's court, while the initiative lay with those negotiating the maritime treaty with Spain. His ascendancy from 1635 was a consequence not only of Weston's death, but of the collapse of the Spanish treaty, the increased attractiveness of a French alliance and the greater influence wielded by the queen. By the early summer of 1635 it was becoming clear that the dominance of that group committed to peace and friendly relations with Spain was giving way to more balanced counsels, in which the queen's faction was exercising more influence. While Arundel and Windebank perhaps were still inclined to Spain, they had begun to air their disillusionment with the sincerity of Habsburg promises; Laud, according to Roe, had little say.[5] With the queen acquiring a new authority, Laud and Windebank proceeded cautiously, anxious not to alienate Henrietta Maria, who alone of the contenders for power in 1635 was assured of the king's ear.[6]

The events of 1635 and the death of Weston did not only strengthen the queen; they led her to declare herself openly for France – and for support for the Cardinal Richelieu.[7] The death of the Treasurer helped to break Henrietta Maria's links with those who had supported her against him and who, led by Châteauneuf, had formed the opposition to the cardinal in France.[8] The queen wanted to re-establish good relations with Richelieu in order to secure her mother's return to France.[9] Perhaps most important, the outbreak of war between France and Spain not only weakened the Queen Mother's faction, it dictated the subordination of factional squabbles to the Bourbon struggle against the Habsburgs. In July Walter Montagu, one of Henrietta Maria's minions, was acting as go-between for the queen and French envoy who was pressing for an offensive and defensive alliance.[10] From 1635, the queen and her faction were openly committed to a treaty with France. As yet, however, it was by no means clear that they would emerge triumphant from the uncertainties and fluidities of court politics. The 16th of August saw heated discussions and disagreements in the Council over foreign affairs.[11] As well as Windebank, Cottington and Laud, Wentworth, Carlisle and Arundel

5. *Ibid.*; above, pp. 164–6; PRO 31/3/68, ff.170, 216v.
6. PRO, 31/3/68, ff.241–241v.
7. *Ibid.*, f.241.
8. Gardiner, *History of England*, VII, pp. 184–6, 217.
9. *Ibid.*, VIII, p. 98.
10. PRO, 31/3/68, f.176.
11. *Ibid.*, f.200; *Cal. Stat. Pap. Venet., 1632–6*, p. 424.

were thought to support the preservation of peace.[12] But the queen's faction was about to be strengthened by the arrival in England of Charles Louis, who hoped in person to persuade his uncle to champion his affairs. The stalemate in the counsels at home awaited the king's own resolution – or the appointment of a Lord Treasurer who might tip the balance. Senecterre observed with regret that both the leading candidates for the office – Wentworth and Cottington – were believed to be Spanish or inclined to neutrality.[13] But Henrietta Maria was more afraid of the proud Wentworth, and Cottington, whatever his reputation, was beginning to make noises concerning his willingness to serve France.[14] The final moves in foreign as well as domestic policy depended upon the appointment of a Treasurer. As the French ambassador wrote on 31 October, the councillors 'sont fort divisés entre eux et craignent que l'un vienne en plus de crédit que l'autre, et regardent à qui viendra la charge de Trésorier'.[15]

Though the French and Spanish factions (if we may so simplify them for the moment) were evenly balanced, there were important differences within them. Where the queen's party, Henrietta, Holland, Hamilton and the Prince Elector, were united, those inclined to peace were quarrelling among themselves. Wentworth and Cottington, for all their respective denials of any ambition for the place, were rivals for the treasurership;[16] Laud and Cottington had long been at odds and in August 1635 antagonism was sharpened by their dispute over the king's projected enlargement of Richmond Park.[17] During the summer of 1635, quarrels on the Treasury commission over the patent for the new soap divided Laud from his former client Windebank who, as the archbishop himself put it, 'forsook' his former patron and joined with Cottington.[18] Such personal differences, added to the failure of the maritime treaty and the news of the Peace of Prague, led to the fragmentation of the Spanish faction. And both may have made it easier for Cottington to gravitate towards the queen, promising his support

12. Above, pp. 514–15; PRO, 31/3/68, ff.114–18, 216; see also R. Schreiber, *The First Carlisle* (Transactions of the American Philosophical Soc., 74, Philadelphia, 1984). As we have seen, all such identifications were unreliable and fluid.
13. PRO, 31/3/68, ff.216–18, 5 Sept. 1635.
14. *Ibid.*, f.216v.
15. *Ibid.*, f.241, 31 Oct. 1635.
16. For example, *Cal. Stat. Pap. Venet., 1632–6*, pp. 353, 466, though it is evident that Wentworth genuinely did not covet the office.
17. W.S. Knowler (ed.) *The Earl of Strafford's Letters and Despatches* (2 vols, 1739), I, p. 478; on the dispute over Richmond Park see *Cal. Stat. Pap. Venet., 1632–6*, p. 436; and E. Hyde, Earl of Clarendon, *The History of the Rebellion and Civil Wars in England*, ed. W.D. Macray (6 vols, Oxford, 1888), I, pp. 132–6.
18. W. Scott and J. Bliss (eds) *The Works of William Laud* (7 vols, Oxford, 1847–60), III, pp. 223–4; *Cal. Stat. Pap. Dom., 1635–6*, p. viii; Gardiner, *History of England*, VIII, pp. 71–7.

for a French alliance in return for hers for his candidacy as Treasurer.[19] It was a shrewd move: the queen's opposition to Wentworth, not least on account of his dealings with Catholics, inclined her to the other contender and her support offset Laud's lobby for the Lord Deputy.[20] By the autumn all the news was that the white staff would be in Cottington's hands.[21] It was not to be. Wentworth's (evidently genuine) denial of any desire for the office seemingly cleared the way for the Chancellor.[22] But Laud's quarrels with Cottington made the archbishop determined to block him. He found an opportunity to compromise him; more importantly, he found a rival candidate: a former president, like himself, of St John's College, Oxford, his successor as bishop of London, a man of unimpeachable integrity whom he could rely on for support – William Juxon.[23] If the competition for the office had driven Cottington to intrigue with France, the appointment of Juxon over Wentworth deprived the Spanish faction of the advantage. Juxon showed little interest in politicking; he was not appointed to the committee for foreign policy. The way was still open for the queen's party to take control of foreign affairs.[24]

During the course of 1636, while Laud basked in his triumph in placing Juxon and was preoccupied with university and ecclesiastical affairs, those in the queen's household pressed ever more forcefully for a French alliance. They grew in influence and strength. In April the queen's party was not strong enough to secure for Holland or Hamilton the command of the fleet they desired;[25] Charles appointed the Earl of Northumberland who 'took care to keep himself aloof from the factions of the court'.[26] However, with Wentworth in Ireland, the Earl of Carlisle dead (in May) and Arundel en route to Vienna, there were few voices, other than Windebank's, to counter the French party. One newswriter (Finet) was even able to speak of the absence of 'apparent factions' in the summer of 1636.[27] Hamilton and especially

19. PRO, 31/3/68, f.216v; Gardiner, *History of England*, VIII, p. 85 and note 1.
20. *Works of Laud*, VI, part 2, p. 441: Laud to Wentworth, 16 Nov. 1635.
21. *Cal. Stat. Pap. Venet., 1632–6*, p. 466; Nottingham University Library, Clifton MS Cl/C 376: Rossingham to Clifton, 8 Aug. 1635.
22. Knowler, *Strafford Letters*, I, p. 410: Wentworth to Newcastle, 4 April 1635; Wentworth wrote to Sir George Butler in May 1635: 'I have an inward and obstinate aversion from it' (*ibid.*, I, p. 419).
23. Gardiner, *History of England*, VIII, pp. 89–91, 140–1; PRO, C.115/N8/8759: Finet to Scudamore, 10 March 1636. Finet spoke of Juxon's 'integrity and the opinion of his wisdom'. See T. Mason, *Serving God and Mammon: William Juxon 1582–1663* (Newark, NJ, 1985).
24. See Bodleian, Bankes MS 37/18.
25. Knowler, *Strafford Letters*, I, p. 478; Gardiner, *History of England*, VIII, p. 156.
26. Gardiner, *History of England*, VIII, p. 156; PRO, PC 2/49/41; Birmingham Reference Library, Docquets of Letters Patent, Coventry MS, 602204/442.
27. PRO, C.115/N8/8800: Finet to Scudamore, 30 June 1636.

Holland began to attend the Council assiduously.[28] In May the king and queen attended a banquet at Kensington House, Holland's London residence, after going 'a-Maying' with the earl in St James's Park. Newswriters – correctly – rumoured that Holland would succeed to Carlisle's place as Groom of the Stool and Chief Gentleman of the Bedchamber.[29] Arundel's gloomy prognostications from Vienna strengthened the French faction further. Holland began to work on Leicester and, by the end of the year, was thought to have had a major influence on Leicester's own ardent advocacy of the French alliance.[30] With Arundel's denunciation of the Spaniards, it looked as though Holland's goal would be attained. 'The majority of the ministers here,' the Venetian envoy told the Doge and Senate in February 1637, 'show themselves entirely French.'[31] The factional weathercock had turned through 180 degrees.

Events abroad, then, and factional manoeuvrings at home played together and combined to shape policy from the spring of 1635 to the winter of 1636–7. During those months when the maritime treaty with Spain collapsed, France entered the war, and Arundel's mission to Vienna failed, at home the queen and her followers were rising to a new prominence in the king's counsels. The old Spanish faction, divided in itself, all but disintegrated. At a time when much suggests that the king himself was undecided, the shift was of the greatest importance. For all his dogged determination, once his mind was made up, Charles listened carefully to counsel – perhaps especially in the realm of foreign affairs. As events abroad and manoeuvres at home combined so the growing influence of the French faction helped determine (as well as reflect) the king's own thinking. To Wentworth's and Laud's dismay, Charles resolved on a French alliance as the best means to the end of recovering the Palatinate – even if the logic of such a course was to lead England into war.

The defence of the realm: the militia

The entry of France into the Thirty Years War and the drift of English diplomacy towards a league against the Habsburgs combined to escalate the fears of possible invasion and to stimulate a new urgency in

28. See P. Haskell, 'Sir Francis Windebank and the personal rule of Charles I' (University of Southampton, PhD thesis, 1978), appendix D.
29. Clifton MS Cl/C, 310: Lecke to Clifton, 1 May 1636.
30. A. Collins, *Letters and Memorials of State . . . Collected by Sir H. Sidney* (2 vols, 1746), II, p. 452: Countess of Leicester to Leicester, 19 Dec. 1636.
31. *Cal. Stat. Pap. Venet., 1636–9*, p. 147. The testimony is no less powerful for the caveat that in many cases it was against their natural inclinations.

the Council's programme to forge an exact militia. Letters issued to the lord-lieutenants on 27 April 1635 mentioned the preparations being made by other countries, announced the launch of the first ship money fleet and informed them of the need for other military improvements to secure the realm at a time when England's neighbours were actively arming.[32] It has been suggested that the Conciliar letters were no more than a smokescreen, to mute the opposition to ship money by creating the appearance of an emergency.[33] But the dangers were real, not illusory or imagined. And the details of the April letters reveal the government's real anxiety rather than scaremongering. The orders required lord-lieutenants as usual to see musters dutifully attended and modern arms supplied; the oath of allegiance was required of all in arms. Now, however, the Council insisted that the trained men be ready at an hour's warning and that a list of all adult males (between the ages of sixteen and sixty) not in the trained bands be drawn up to form an auxiliary. Magazines were to be checked, beacons kept and arms confiscated from recusants repaired and maintained. All counties were commanded to appoint a provost marshal. In an effort to tackle the perennial weakness of the militia, all lord-lieutenants were exhorted to improve the numbers and quality of the horse: the Council were required to set an example, the Earl of Holland maintaining twelve, Laud eight and so on, that the rest of the nobility might follow.[34] The following month the Council required of the lord-lieutenants an account of all the monies levied for the militia, the muster master, the magazines and powder stores so that it might lay down rules permanently settling the charges throughout the counties.[35] In June, all captains of forts and castles were ordered to reside at their charges.[36] England was being placed in a state of readiness to defend her shores.

Lord-lieutenants, perhaps because many being Privy Councillors knew of the real menaces abroad, appear to have responded promptly to the Council's orders. The Earl of Derby, as Lord-Lieutenant of Cheshire, forwarded to his deputies by 30 April the letters he received on the 27th.[37] By the middle of May the constables of Buckinghamshire had received warrants authorizing them to compel all adult males to appear at the muster so as to be formed into companies.[38] In Norfolk, Lord Maltravers, who had already pre-empted the Council with local

32. PRO, PC 2/44/535; Chester Record Office MS CR.63/2/6, ff.51v–52v.
33. Gardiner, *History of England*, VII, pp. 382–4.
34. Knowler, *Strafford Letters*, I, p. 434.
35. Hampshire Record Office, Herriard MS, Box 026, file 41/6.
36. PRO, PC 2/44/607.
37. Chester Record Office, CR.63/2/6, f.52v.
38. Huntington Library, Temple of Stowe MS 9, STT 2315.

initiatives for training and exercising in arms, went beyond the formal requirements.[39] In order to ensure that the numbers were sustained he ordered a survey of the valuations of estates and insisted that freeholders themselves attend personally with their arms rather than devolving the obligation on their servants. Moreover, he required the captains to exercise the bands in squadrons once a month at least and to mark the arms of each company to check that they had a full complement of the required equipment.[40] Bishop Morton of Durham moved swiftly to see the militia increased and exercised, fit arms and powder provided and beacons manned by the summer.[41] In the Marches, Bridgewater acted with his usual efficiency; by July his deputies were able to report the spare men listed and defective arms repaired.[42] Within the counties, perhaps especially those furthest from the capital or the coast where the sense of urgency was less keenly felt, the old foot-dragging continued. Corbet, for example, confessed to Bridgewater in June that the horse of his county could not be called together at that time of year – and lacked a captain.[43] But there were real improvements, and, as important, an apparent desire to effect them. The deputies of Shropshire required the better sort 'to provide themselves with arms' and replaced old powder in the magazines.[44] Burton, the muster master, wrote to report that there were only ten defaulters at the musters; and though the corslets were still out of order, 'I find all the maintainers very willing to have everything complete according to your Lordship's directions.'[45] Most of the muster returns and reports for 1635 in the state papers present a picture of real improvements.[46] The lord-lieutenants of Bedford rebuked their deputies for their earlier 'connivance and remissness' and encouraged a large supply of arms.[47] In Dorset, the Earl of Suffolk not only saw the foot and bands mustered; he added to their numbers 600 men (taken from the old troop bands which did not usually muster) who were armed and trained to the same standards.[48] The deputies of Middlesex had 25,000 adults appear at their musters from whom they selected a thousand to be trained and equip themselves with arms to add to their

39. For example, Norfolk Record Office, Yarmouth YC/18/6.
40. Norfolk Record Office, WLS XVII/2 410, X 5: Maltravers to De Grey, 7 Aug. 1635; cf. Bodleian, Tanner MS 177, ff.8v, 10v.
41. *Cal. Stat. Pap. Dom., 1635*, p. 348.
42. Huntington Library, Ellesmere MS 7671.
43. Ellesmere MS 7656.
44. Ellesmere MS 7671.
45. Ellesmere MS 7673, 24 July 1635.
46. For example, *Cal. Stat. Pap. Dom., 1635*, pp. 411–12, 434.
47. *Ibid.*, pp. 411–12.
48. *Ibid.*, p. 434.

complement.[49] The Council itself was evidently optimistic that some steps had been taken to improve the defensive forces of the realm. Its orders of April 1635, reissued the following year, were to remain the basis of its militia programme for the rest of the decade.[50]

Again Hampshire offers an excellent case study of the improvements that were made, and not made. Here, as elsewhere, the insurmountable problem was the horse: the deputy lieutenants admitted that of 168 due to appear, they never saw more than half, 'and those for the most part base and unserviceable jades'.[51] The clergy showed a third at best of their proportion; the gentry were persistently refractory – the list of thirty names of defaulters in 1635 including many who had long been remiss. There were other problems: refusals to man beacons or to watch,[52] cases of the persistent defaulter, like William Wither who alone accounted for the shortfall of several weapons in the hundreds of Kingsclere and Overton.[53] But the deputies of Hampshire laboured enormously in response to the Council's orders of 1635, carefully checking the trained bands, listing all defaults and defects, returning the numbers of spare men and even arranging those auxiliaries into units according to the weapons it was thought they might, if called upon, best bear:[54] so Thomas Badd, captain for the town, listed 'the spare men resident within the hundred of Fareham and what arms they are fit to serve with' and gave them two weeks to find the requisite weapons.[55] Southampton listed corslets and muskets 'newly charged', evidently in an attempt to increase the city militia.[56] Across the county the number of men in arms was steadily increasing. Between 1627 and 1637 the county bands had been increased from 5,992 to 6,194, and there were, as well as fewer defaulters, more spare men in some state of training.[57] Nor was the impetus lost as the months passed. The Council's call in 1636 to sustain the effort demanded the previous year elicited the same diligent response from Hampshire. Though the Earl of Portland, Lord-Lieutenant, himself suspended the general musters on account of the plague, the deputy lieutenants laboured to see the muster master's fee collected and defects noted and dealt with.[58] In October they reported that 'the total of our forces will hold good with the same in the last year's certificate and that the trained bands are in a

49. *Cal. Stat. Pap. Dom., 1635–6*, p. 196.
50. L. Boynton, *The Elizabethan Militia* (1967), pp. 257–60.
51. Herriard MSS, Box 026/XLI.
52. *Ibid.*, Box 025/XXXV/5.
53. *Ibid.*, Box 025/XXXV/3.
54. *Ibid.*, Boxes 025, 026, *passim*; and see Box 026, XXXV/20.
55. *Ibid.*, Box 025/XXXV/15.
56. *Ibid.*, Box 025/XXXV/25.
57. *Ibid.*, Box 024/XXVIII/1; Box 026/XLIII/16; Boxes 027, 029.
58. *Ibid.*, Box 026/XLI.

usual readiness for the defence of the country'.[59] Even some of the horse troops, among which defects were still acknowledged to persist, had been 'lately increased'.[60] Portland's habit of attending musters in person obviously spurred his subordinates.[61] We do not have for most counties the detailed muster books and other military records that the Jervoise records provide for Hampshire, and so cannot be sure how typical it was.[62] A county on the south coast of England, close to the Isle of Wight and to the memories of the fears of invasion in the 1620s, Hampshire doubtless had a more immediate sense of the need to organize for defence than less exposed shires. However, the evidence – from Sussex, Cheshire and Lancashire for example – seems to suggest that the need for improved security was dawning on other parts of the realm.[63]

The defence of the realm: the origins of ship money

As the Council instructions for an improved militia went out, the first fleet financed by ship money was putting to sea. It belonged very much to the diplomacy of the first half of the decade. Consisting of forty-two vessels, nineteen over 500 tons, its brief was to clear the sea of pirates, protect English trading vessels, prevent the Dutch from fishing in English waters and, perhaps most importantly, 'preserve the sovereignty of the narrow seas from the French King who hath had a design long to take it from us and therefore he hath provided a very great navy'.[64] Conway, we recall, explained that the ships were ordered to sail across the Channel during summer 'purely to show the fleet to France'.[65] Though the scheme to share its cost with Spain had not borne fruit, the fleet was intended to benefit the Habsburgs and to convince them of the value of English assistance. The Earl of Lindsey, who commanded the ships in the Downs, convoyed vessels laden with men and money to Dunkirk and staved off the French and Dutch ships from a blockade of the Spanish supply lines to the Low Countries.[66]

59. *Ibid.*, Box 026/XLI/19.
60. *Ibid.*, Box 026/XLI/20.
61. *Ibid.*, Box 026/XLII/1.
62. Though cf. D.P. Carter, 'The "exact militia" in Lancashire, 1625–1642', *Northern History*, 11 (1976), pp.87–106.
63. A. Fletcher, *A County Community in Peace and War: Sussex, 1600–1660* (1975), p. 182; *idem.*, *Reform in the Provinces* (New Haven and London, 1986), pp. 286–91; *Cal. Stat. Pap. Dom., 1636–7*, pp. 240–1.
64. Temple of Stowe MSS, Ship Money Box; Melbourne Hall, Coke MS 52: instructions for the fleet; cf. *HMC Cowper, II*, p.104.
65. *HMC Cowper, II*, p. 92; above, pp. 103–4.
66. Gardiner, *History of England*, VII, p. 384; British Library [BL], Egerton MS 1820, f.482v.

Conflicts with France were expected; the French ambassador in London, as we have seen, was concerned at the new developments.[67] Charles took the opportunity to request of Spain not only the restoration of the Palatinate, but a share of the trade in Brazil.[68]

Then, as we know, events began to reorient English diplomacy; in turn they were to change the role of the fleet. The Peace of Prague ended the favour of the English fleet as an escort to the Spaniards. The entry of France into war, and the likelihood of intensified naval operations in the narrow seas, made it even clearer that a substantial fleet was necessary to guarantee England's security. In 1636 an even larger fleet set sail under the command of the Earl of Northumberland.[69] The discussions concerning England's entry into the war in alliance with France and the United Provinces assumed England's maintenance of a considerable navy until the conclusion of a peace in Europe. International events and diplomacy then, in this as in other ways, led to a measure that was to reshape the domestic priorities, policies and problems of the second half of the 1630s. For the means by which the necessary fleets were financed was the annual levy of a charge, commonly known as ship money.

The origins of the decision to levy ship money on the coastal towns of England in 1634, and the story of the extension of the levy to all the counties of the realm the following year, have curiously never been elucidated. Among the many myths about the levy perpetrated until recently, it has often been said that ship money was raised as a substitute for parliamentary subsidies for the funding of royal government. It was not. Ship money, as we shall later see in detail, was raised for and spent entirely on the navy.[70] The levies raised each year from 1634 to 1640 all emerged from the need for a stronger fleet, a need which in turn arose from domestic and foreign pressures. Charles, we recall, had as a prince shared his elder brother's interest in the fleet and shipbuilding;[71] on his succession to the throne, the war with Spain (then France) gave an immediacy to a long-felt sense of the need for naval security. Charles proposed to his last parliament in 1628 the furnishing of an annual fleet of twenty vessels.[72] Among the state papers for 1628 in the hand of a clerk to Secretary Conway we find propositions for every shire to contribute to the setting forth of a fleet, victualled for seven months.[73] A writ of ship money, we recall, was

67. Above, pp. 512ff.; PRO 31/3/68, f.187; Huntington Library, Hastings MS 9598.
68. *Cal. Stat. Pap. Venet., 1632–6*, p. 357.
69. See Coke MS 54, for his instructions.
70. Below, pp. 594–5.
71. B.W. Quintrell, 'Charles I and his navy', in *The Seventeenth Century, 3* (1988), pp. 159–79.
72. *Cal. Stat. Pap. Venet., 1628–9*, p. 62; cf. above, pp. 97–8.
73. *Cal. Stat. Pap. Dom., 1625–49*, p. 310.

issued – though the money was not in the end demanded.[74] The peace with France and Spain did little to lessen the concern. With Spain and the Dutch at war, English merchant shipping was constantly prey to pirates; some traders were brought to a virtual standstill. Devon merchants complained of attacks off the west coast and the mayor of Exeter told the Council that unless something were done 'the merchants will be undone'.[75] In March 1630 it was reported that the Newcastle colliers could not stir from port for fear of the Dunkirkers;[76] the price of coal soared and Newcastle became distressed for want of corn.[77] The bailiffs of Great Yarmouth the same month complained that 'by reason of the Dunkirkers the poor fishermen are so terrified that they are resolved not to go out', and prayed for the protection of a convoy.[78] Bristol and York, facing the same threats, petitioned for help whilst arranging some local defence of their own.[79] Trade was not the only consideration. Attorney Heath had represented to the king how important it was for a sense of security to provide an effective guard in the narrow seas.[80] Fears and rumours continued to haunt the south coast long after the conclusion of peace: the Isle of Wight sent a deputation to the Council to express its worries about the intentions of the French fleet and to ask for protection.[81] Charles was not deaf to these laments. In May 1630 the Council met to discuss the problems and in the summer a fleet of sorts put to sea.[82] Money, however, was in very short supply. Captain Plumleigh protested that his ships were woefully unequipped; Captain Ketelby 'never did see so defective a ship set to sea'.[83] The pirates continued to commit outrages off and on the coast.

Pressure for an improved navy was also coming, in a variety of ways, from abroad. Richelieu had been steadily building naval strength and, as was known, had entered into an alliance with the Dutch. For their part the Dutch, to add injury to their many recent insults, in 1632 took three busses belonging to the newly formed Society for Fishing which had been instituted to re-establish English rights over fishing waters.[84] Attempts to assert English sovereignty of the seas carried

74. Above, pp. 13–14.
75. *Cal. Stat. Pap. Dom., 1629–31*, pp. 44, 52, 233.
76. *Ibid.*, p. 206.
77. PRO,C.115/M31/8125: Flower to Scudamore, 20 March 1630.
78. *Cal. Stat. Pap. Dom., 1629–31*, p. 212.
79. Bristol Record Office, Common Council Books, 3, f.3v; York Record Office, York House Books, 35, f.79.
80. PRO, SP 16/178/3.
81. *Cal. Stat. Pap. Venet., 1629–32*, p. 283: dispatch of 8 Feb. 1630.
82. Berkshire Record Office, Trumbull MS 54, 11 May 1630; *Cal. Stat. Pap. Dom., 1629–31*, p. 276.
83. *Cal. Stat. Pap. Dom., 1629–31*, p. 276; *1631–2*, p. 76.
84. *Cal. Stat. Pap. Dom., 1631–3*, p.450.

little conviction without the hardware to back them up. As Captain Pennington put it to Nicholas, the Lords of the Admiralty may have instructed him to suffer no nation to fly a flag in the narrow seas, but twenty ships half-manned could not sustain such pretensions against larger, better-equipped fleets.[85] In 1632 Sir Robert Heath pressed the need for some action to check the boldness of the Dutch, arguing forcefully that England's security lay 'in our walls which is our shipping'.[86] In order to re-establish England's mastery of the seas, he advocated the provision not only of more ships, but of an adequate supply of iron ordnance and store of gunpowder. Pressure for a large fleet came not only from the strength of England's neighbours but from their desire – desire, that is, to see England strong at sea provided they could harness her as an ally. Châteauneuf had been advised that 'la plus grande force des Anglais consiste un grand numbre des vaisseaux et gens de mer'; and was instructed to persuade Charles to join in a naval war on the Spanish coasts.[87] Similarly Soranzo, the Venetian envoy, laboured to strengthen England as a potential ally against the Habsburgs. 'It was one of the ideas with which I came here', he wrote in 1630, to persuade Charles 'to send a good fleet to sea'.[88] At times Charles was inclined to listen to their overtures. Believing in May 1631 that little could be secured for the Palatine from negotiation, Charles, it was reported, 'has decided in good time to put naval affairs in some order so as to make good his cause in any event'.[89] In 1633 the king, reviving a decree of 1618, announced that two new ships would be built each year.[90] Though suspicion of the French and Dutch obstructed any likelihood of closer relations and drove England back to Madrid, diplomacy still suggested the benefits of negotiation from strength. Hopton, ambassador to Spain, argued early on that English neutrality meant nothing if it was seen as the want of power. The hope of Spanish aid for the Palatinate depended upon England being of assistance to Spain in Flanders – by 'making if his Majesty shall think fit some preparations by sea (which properly concerns them) so that they might see that his Majesty is provided to be of use to them'.[91]

All these influences came together during the course of 1633 as Dunkirk threatened to fall to the French and the Spanish negotiations made little progress. In February 1634 therefore, Windebank informed

85. *Ibid.*, p. 158: Pennington to Nicholas, 2 Oct. 1631.
86. *Cal. Stat. Pap. Dom., 1631–3*, p. 489. This appears to be an extract from his earlier propositions.
87. PRO, 31/3/65, f.117.
88. *Cal. Stat. Pap. Venet., 1629–32*, p. 374.
89. *Ibid.*, p. 502, 9 May 1632.
90. *Cal. Stat. Pap. Venet., 1632–6*, p. xxxviii; F.C. Dietz, *English Public Finance, 1558–1641* (1932), pp. 266–7.
91. Egerton MS 1820, f.120v: Hopton to Dorchester, 23 Dec. 1631.

Hopton that the king was conferring with the Spanish envoy Necolalde about putting a strong fleet to sea which might secure the coast of Flanders.[92] 'But,' the secretary concluded,

> howsoever his Majesty's own reason of state . . . doth chiefly move him to this course, yet is it so carried as the motion grows from Necolalde; unto whom it is represented that his Majesty is now at peace with all the world, that he shall hereby hazard a dangerous war with his neighbours, or at least enter into a great and insupportable charge; and therefore it will be necessary for the King of Spain to furnish money toward it; which doubtless he could no way spend more to his advantage.[93]

The thinking behind the project was reasonable enough: England could not afford the fleet and by this means the Habsburgs would help to finance it for them. In no way, however, did it satisfy Hopton. Taking Spanish money meant not, as he desired, negotiating for the Palatinate from strength, but a dependence upon Spain. Accordingly on 8 April he wrote to Windebank a reply that was to be crucial in the discussions that led to the first writ for ship money:

> I humbly propound to his Majesty as a matter of importance in his royal service that he should much advantage himself, oblige them more and remain at better liberty to alter his course as occasion shall serve if he would set out this armada at his own cost, and I think he should have a better hand with the Hollanders to oblige them to a truce being their enemy not in act but in possibility.[94]

Hopton's words may have found sympathetic ears: only weeks earlier, Windebank had personally advised the king that 'his honour and safety consist in his navy and money must be found for reparation of those walls, wheresoever else it be slowed'.[95] With Windebank's support, Hopton's letter initiated a flurry of discussion – in semi-secret among the foreign committee and in Council. At the beginning of June, at the king's special command, Secretary Coke delivered a report to the Board on the unsatisfactory state of foreign affairs.[96] The ancient respect for England was now at naught. English ships suffered pillage at the hands of the Turk, taxes from the Venetians, plunder by the Biscayners. In France English cloths were confiscated; Dutch ships insolently sailed up the Thames to cast anchor as high as Deptford –

92. R. Scrope and T. Monkhouse (eds) *State Papers Collected by Edward, Earl of Clarendon* (3 vols, Oxford, 1767–86), I, p. 76: Windebank to Hopton, 16 Feb. 1634.
93. *Ibid.*, p. 76.
94. Egerton MS 1820, ff.334–334v: Hopton to Windebank, 8 April 1634.
95. *Cal. Stat. Pap. Dom., 1633–4*, p. 488: Windebank to king, 5 March 1634.
96. PRO, SP 16/269/51, 8 June 1634.

under the very walls of the king's magazine. A means had to be found to redeem the realm from all such contempts, and to reassert English sovereignty of the seas. Coke therefore put his colleagues in mind of 'Mr Hopton's good advice': 'that there is no hope left of obtaining justice but by doing it yourself'.

It is likely that at that meeting a decision was made to investigate a levy for a fleet. Among the state papers for June 1634 we find notes by Secretary Coke (who had not been fully informed of Hopton's negotiations) concerning a project for setting forth a fleet and assessing a levy on the port towns.[97] The notes, suggestive of a Council meeting, indicate that Coke had himself been briefed to prepare an estimate of the cost, while Lord Treasurer Weston was to obtain from the Customs House a list of all the ports to be charged.[98] A number of ways of raising such a tax had evidently been aired and Attorney-General Noy was to attend the next meeting and advise on the precedents and manner of proceeding. Moving to Laud's papers at Lambeth palace we have a record of what took place at that meeting. On 21 July some of the Lords assembled at Whitehall 'concerning the great business'; they considered, with Sir John Bankes, Attorney-General to the Prince of Wales (who deputed for Attorney Noy then taking the waters for his sickness at Tunbridge), the forms of writs that might be directed to every sheriff and mayor for ship money.[99] From the debates, two schemes emerged: separate writs to the mayors of corporate towns and sheriffs, or writs to the sheriffs only. 'The Lords,' Laud noted, 'are of opinion that the first is fittest.'

There were other disputed propositions. Attorney Noy evidently expressed by letter his opinion that a levy for the whole six months' charge at once would be very heavy 'unless the maritime counties might be drawn into the contribution'. But this, Laud recorded, 'the Lords affirm is not legal nor warrantable by the . . . precedents. The Lords think fit that the payments be made more easy by making the levies from three months to three months by equal portions.' The next day, 22 July, Lord Coventry (who as Lord Keeper would be responsible for the issue of the writs) informed Coke (who had evidently not attended) of what had taken place and enclosed an account for the king. 'There was much time spent in the debate of that business,' he told the secretary, 'and several points treated of the substance of which . . . I have set down . . . not daring to trust any to copy it out'. Concerning Coke's own proposals, Coventry indicated that Noy had misliked the idea 'that so many towns so far distant one

97. *Cal. Stat. Pap. Dom., 1634–5*, p. 100, June 1634.
98. *Ibid.*
99. Lambeth Palace MS 943, pp. 187–8; Coke MS 48.

from another are charged jointly together', even though he had raised no objection earlier. Coke should therefore prepare to argue his case to the king.[100] To Charles I himself (who was on progress) Coventry sent a similar account of the meeting 'to prepare your Majesty's great business for guarding the sea'.[101] He outlined the debate over whether in towns the mayor or sheriff should make the assessment, informed the king that two types of writ had been drawn up so that he might decide on his preferred course, and put the pros and cons, as he saw them of each case, 'that your Majesty may digest them in your own thoughts at your best leisure and so at your return resolve the more maturely'.[102] Whilst, as had been argued, assessment by mayors involved the difficulty of co-ordinating towns that were far apart, it had clear political advantages:

> it is considerable if an assessment be made whether it will not be the more willingly undergone being made by themselves than if they be assessed by the sheriff of the county, for though it be not so in truth, yet it is not unlike that they will apprehend the sheriff's intromitting without them as an encroachment upon the franchise of their towns, which may perchance trouble them as much as the payment itself.[103]

Suggesting a compromise course whereby the towns were given some weeks to assess themselves before the sheriff intervened, Coventry closed his letter with what was to be an unhappily accurate prognostication of difficulties: it is worth asking, he wrote, 'whether the sheriff can have so good means to understand the ability of the towns as their head officers, and every little inequality (which in such a business cannot be avoided) being acted by the sheriff will minister cause of objection and grudging . . .'.[104]

Some months passed before the details were settled, not least because all were anxious to proceed with caution. Bankes and Sir John Borough, Keeper of the Tower records, researched the rolls for precedents;[105] lists of ships required or the money in lieu of them were prepared.[106] At the last minute, on 11 October, Bankes informed Coke that the writs for ship money contained some mistakes in the names of port towns, which were to be rectified when the king was present. 'This great business,' he half-excused himself, 'is proceeding with what

100. Coke MS 48: Coventry to Coke, 22 July 1634.
101. PRO, SP 16/272/36; see *Cal. Stat. Pap. Dom., 1634–5*, pp. xxvii–xxxi: Coventry to Charles I, 22 July 1634.
102. *Cal. Stat. Pap. Dom., 1634–5*, p. xxix.
103. *Ibid.*, p. xxviii–xxix.
104. *Ibid.*, p. xxix.
105. *Ibid.*, pp. 161, 234, 258; PRO, SP 16/276/65; Bankes MS 16/2.
106. *Cal. Stat. Pap. Dom., 1634–5*, p. 554.

possible expedition may be in a matter of so great importance.'[107] Caution may have prevented Windebank from apprising Hopton in October of the development prompted by his advice.[108] Soon after the middle of the month, however, the writs were ready. Coke issued a warrant for the writ with 'the postscript for his Majesty's hand'.[109] On 20 October the writs were issued to the maritime towns.[110] In early December Windebank at last felt able to tell Hopton that a fleet was being prepared: 'the work advances with great success which I hope will give his Majesty's counsels and affairs great reputation abroad'.[111] The king, he added, had sought Spanish money for the fleet not least as a barometer of Habsburg sincerity. Now he had chosen to finance it alone and so, Windebank wrote in an unacknowledged echo of Hopton's own words, 'is left free to take such a party as shall be most for his advantage'.[112]

Ship money had its distant origins in a long-felt sense of the need for a stronger fleet and took its impetus from the particular advice sent by Hopton in the spring of 1634. History has attributed the credit – or rather blame – for the decision to levy the tax to William Noy. When Clarendon and others so credit him, we should not doubt his role.[113] The newswriter Rossingham informing Viscount Scudamore of the issue of the writ described it as the Attorney's legacy.[114] But to see ship money as the project of one mind is too simple.[115] Rather the emergence of the scheme is, perhaps, indicative of how many strands intertwined in the making of Caroline policy. If a general sense of necessity was the mother of the plan, it was seeded by Hopton, nurtured by Windebank, Coke, Bankes and Coventry – as well as by Noy, who may have been the midwife of the writ itself. And though, as often, all the preparatory work was done by others – by Bankes and Borough in the archives, by Coke and Windebank in the Council chamber, by Noy and Coventry in Chancery – the final decision was taken by Charles I himself.

The ship money writs

The first writs of ship money then issued from the Lord Keeper on 20 October to the mayors, bailiffs and burgesses of the coastal corporate

107. *Ibid.*, p. 234.
108. Egerton MS 1820, ff.395–7: Windebank to Hopton, 16 Oct. 1634.
109. *HMC Cowper, II*, p. 70; the original is missing from the Coke MSS.
110. *Cal. Stat. Pap. Dom., 1634–5*, pp. 242–3.
111. Egerton MS 1820, f.419: Windebank to Hopton, 10 Dec. 1634.
112. *Ibid.*, f.440, 24 Jan. 1635.
113. Clarendon, *History of the Rebellion*, I, p. 92; Gardiner, *History of England*, VII, p. 356.
114. PRO, C.115/M36/8439: Rossingham to Scudamore, 31 Oct. 1634.
115. Whitelocke attributed it to Noy and Coventry jointly; see B. Whitelocke, *Memorials of the English Affairs* (1680), p. 22.

towns. At first, in accordance with suggestions made in the summer, it was thought 'requisite that the acts and dispatches concerning the same should pass through the hands of one man only' and 'the Lords thought fit that Edward Nicholas should be employed for making all directions and orders touching that service', entering into a book the writ and all subsequent papers related to it.[116] This in the end 'proceeded not in regard it might have been an injury to the clerks of the Council'.[117] Not until 3 December were the letters directed to the sheriffs of the counties authorizing them to rate and listing the ships to be provided.[118] The writ explained the purpose for which the money was demanded: Turks and other pirates seized the 'ships and goods and merchandises' of Englishmen and their allies. More seriously 'the dangers . . . which . . . in these times of war do hang over our heads . . . behoveth us and our subjects to hasten the defence of the sea and kingdom with all expedition . . . that we can'. Though, the writ continued, 'that charge of defence which concerneth all men ought to be supported by all', those who most derived the benefits of commerce by sea were now called upon to contribute for its defence. They were required to provide by 1 March at Portsmouth harbour a ship fitted and ready for six months' service, or a sum equal to the charge of maintaining ship and crew for that duration.[119] Gardiner was censorious of the language of the writ, which he branded as dishonest rhetoric fabricated to mask a quite different purpose: an unpopular Spanish alliance and possible assault on the Dutch.[120] But the disparity between the ship money writ and the proposals for a treaty with Spain should not lead us quickly to conclude the disingenuousness of the former. Though negotiations with Spain were still continuing, Hopton had dispatched his advice about the fleet previously to release England from any commitment to or dependence on Spain. When Necolalde was himself inclined to think the ship money writ a truer guide to Charles's intentions,[121] there is no need for us to doubt that its language expressed other than its purpose: to set out a navy that might protect commerce in pirate-infested seas and provide security against threats – whether they were perceived to come from the Dutch, French or Spaniard. It is worth pausing to make another observation and to correct an oft-repeated confusion. Technically ship money was not a tax but a service, or payment in lieu. The writ, that is, required a service (a ship) rather than a subsidy – London indeed provided a ship

116. *Cal. Stat. Pap. Dom., 1634–5*, p. 243: draft order of Lords of the Admiralty, 20 Oct. 1634.
117. Endorsement on document cited above, by Nicholas.
118. PRO, PC 2/44/261–2.
119. J. Rushworth, *Historical Collections*, II (1680), pp. 257–8.
120. Gardiner, *History of England*, VII, pp. 368–9.
121. *Ibid.*, p. 371.

not money – and the assessments made on the towns that opted not to follow London's example were similarly for the provision of a service.[122] They were sent to the Treasury of the Navy, not paid, like a tax, into the Exchequer. Noy, Bankes and Coventry had done their homework carefully: a good case could (and would) be made that because it was not a demand for an extra-parliamentary tax, ship money lay outside the anathemas of the Petition of Right.[123]

It seems most probable that at the time the first writ was issued the second, extending ship money to the whole country, was already envisaged – at least by some. Coventry had informed Charles in July 1634 that Noy had wanted the charge extended to the maritime counties as well as towns; those who had countered his proposal had advised it safest 'to begin with the towns'.[124] The principle enunciated in the first writ that 'the charge of defence which concerneth all men ought to be supported by all, as by the laws and customs of the kingdom of England hath been accustomed to be done' seems almost to announce the extension of the levy if need arose.[125] And it would seem that from the beginning contemporary commentators anticipated that ship money would become national. In October 1634, as the writs went out, the newswriter Rossingham reported an uncertainty over whether 'the money is only to be raised from the ports' or as 'other some say . . . levied throughout the whole kingdom'.[126] By February 1635 the younger John Coke in Derbyshire was being warned that 'a privy seal may reach you though you remain far from the seaside'.[127] We do not know whether his informant already had knowledge of a decision to extend the levy, or indeed when that decision was taken. In the state papers for 1 March 1635 we find a computation of the cost of equipping twenty ships, with 3,940 men, for six months, annotated by the king; it seems still to envisage the costs being borne by the coastal 'lands' only.[128] It therefore seems likely that the extension postdates the death of Weston and was a decision taken by the commissioners for the Treasury who reviewed the state of the king's finances over the following months.[129] The international pressures for a large fleet were mounting in 1635 and, moreover, the first levy of ship money, successful though it was, brought in less than the cost of equipping the

122. Cf. *ibid.*, p. 375.
123. Below, p. 724, and see H. Parker, *The Case of Ship Money Briefly Discoursed* (1640, STC 19215), pp. 40–2.
124. *Cal. Stat. Pap. Dom., 1634–5*, p. 162.
125. Rushworth, *Historical Collections*, II, p. 257.
126. PRO, C.115/M36/8439: Rossingham to Scudamore, 31 Oct. 1634.
127. Coke MS 50: J. Semple to Sir John Coke Jnr, 20 Feb. 1635.
128. *Cal. Stat. Pap. Dom., 1634–5*, p. 554.
129. Dietz, *English Public Finance*, pp. 274–5.

fleet. By June the resolution had been taken.[130] On the 18th,[131] Lord Keeper Coventry informed the assize judges going on their circuits. 'Christendom', he reminded them, 'is full of wars and there is nothing but rumours of wars' and in the unstable circumstances 'the dominion of the sea . . . is the best security of the land'. Accordingly, the king 'upon advice . . . hath resolved that he will forthwith send out new writs for the preparation of a greater fleet the next year; and that not only to the maritime towns, but to all the kingdom besides, for since that all the kingdom is interessed both in the honour, safety and profit, it is just and reasonable that they should all put to their helping hands'. The next month Laud, head of the Treasury commission, explained to Wentworth that the king had decided 'for the . . . defence of the kingdom to extend it to all counties and corporations . . . so that the navy may be full and yet the charge less as coming from so many hands'.[132] The extension of the levy was more significant, and potentially more contentious, than the original demand; it is clear that care was taken over the preparation of the second writ. On 6 August the Lords of the Council still in London signed the writs ready to go to the counties.[133] Windebank forwarded them to Coke (who was on progress with the king) so 'that the rest of their lordships may join the subscription, the business being of so great moment'.[134] This sense of need for a display of Conciliar unanimity meant that the writs, formally dated 4 August, went out several days later – but still nearly three months earlier than those of the previous year.[135]

The writ referred to the need for preparations to 'secure this realm against those dangers and extremities which have distressed other nations' and warned of the effects of war 'whensoever it taketh a people unprepared'. The writs were directed this time (a reversion to the option suspended in 1634) to the sheriff of each county, who was instructed to assess the hundreds, lathes, parishes – and the towns within his charge. In order to assist him, and doubtless in anticipation of a clash over jurisdiction with the mayors of corporate towns, the Council suggested sums which they deemed appropriate to be paid by the larger towns of each county – £350 by Westminster (of the £1,800 charged on Middlesex) for example, £100 for Dorchester and Weymouth, £60 for Poole in Dorset.[136] In instructions to the sheriffs on executing the writ, the Council, in an effort no doubt to allow for

130. *Ibid.*, p. 275.
131. Rushworth, *Historical Collections*, II, p. 294.
132. Knowler, *Strafford Letters*, I, p. 438: Laud to Wentworth, 6 July 1635.
133. Coke MS 51: Windebank to Coke, 6 Aug. 1635.
134. *Ibid.*: Windebank to Coke, 8 Aug. 1635.
135. *Cal. Stat. Pap. Dom., 1635*, p. xviii; Gardiner, *History of England*, VIII, p. 84.
136. Rushworth, *Historical Collections*, II, p. 260; *Cal. Stat. Pap. Dom., 1635*, p. 350.

local flexibility, issued advice that was to create a veritable chaos. 'But,' they wrote having reaffirmed the sheriff's power to assess, 'in case the major part of the corporations should agree upon any other rates and the sheriff should approve the same, the altered rate should stand.'[137] There were other potentially contradictory directives. The sheriff was instructed, with the help of discreet and sufficient men, to rate the lands and houses within each hundred or parish, 'as is accustomed in other common payments'. However, they were also urged to relieve poor cottagers of little means or land who lived by their labour and to assess in their stead 'men of ability by reason of gainful trades, great stocks of money or other personal estate who perchance have little or no lands and in ordinary landscot would pay nothing or very little'.[138] Finally, the Council letter acknowledged that with regard to the clergy it was unclear what privileges of exemption or reduction they had formerly been allowed, so it was left to the sheriff's discretion to tax them, having due respect to their dignities and callings.[139] If all these requirements were not already difficult enough to reconcile, the Council further commanded the luckless sheriff 'to have a more than ordinary care and regard whereby to prevent complaints of inequality in the assessment whereby we were much troubled the last year'. The letter closed with an admonition to the shrievalty to proceed 'roundly' and promptly against any who tried to block or delay the collection 'of what quality or condition soever they are'.[140]

It was an unenviable charge. The intentions behind the second writ and instructions for its execution were good and sound: to make one officer responsible for the whole county and its assessment; to assist him by suggesting rates for the major towns; to spare the poor, those with large families and debts; to tax a class that had notoriously escaped a due proportion of subsidy payments but had amassed personal wealth; in general, to offer central direction whilst leaving room for local initiative and circumstances. Yet in almost every clause there were loopholes and between each clause there were spaces through which and into which misunderstandings – genuine and fabricated – could emerge to impede the service. Was the charge on the towns that suggested by the Council, that set by the sheriff or that agreed by themselves? Was the method of assessment that of the common payments or the sheriff's own sense of what was fair (calculated one knew not how)? Were the clergy fully liable to pay-

137. *Cal. Stat. Pap. Dom., 1635*, p. 350: Council to sheriff of Dorset, 12 Aug. 1635; cf. Herriard MSS, Box 013.
138. *Cal. Stat. Pap. Dom., 1635*, p. 350.
139. *Ibid.*
140. Rushworth, *Historical Collections*, II, pp. 261–2.

ment according to their lands and means or not? Were the corporate towns now to send in their payments to the sheriff or direct to the Treasurer of the Navy? Such unresolved questions were soon to lead to a mass of letters from confused sheriffs to the Council, and to the need for further detailed instructions. The attempt to leave some initiative in local hands was to open the doors to local rivalries and interests. The second writ of ship money in fact was to generate correspondence, investigation and entanglement that swamped the officers of local government and overwhelmed the Privy Council for much of the rest of the decade. After 1635 preoccupation with the affairs of Europe and the business of ship money were to slow and impair that programme of domestic reforms that had characterized the early years of the personal rule.

For all its problems, the second ship money writ of 1635 was to remain the model for all the subsequent issues of 1636 to 1640. There were minor alterations. State paper notes by Nicholas for June 1636 show him tinkering with amounts to be assessed (in response to earlier complaints, noting that the writ for Peterborough should be directed to the dean and chapter rather than the mayor) and other observations.[141] More generally, he suggested a clause be inserted in the next writ for especial care to be taken over assessing equally and that sheriffs be instructed to sign assessments (separating the clergy's ecclesiastical and temporal estates) and certify them to the Board.[142] Other than that there was no change but for the issue of the writ in September 1636, a month later than its predecessor.[143] The following year, however, in response to mounting delays and problems, the Council accompanied the writs with further instructions to the sheriffs on how to deal with refractory payers, bailiffs and constables: they were advised to assess none who received alms, and on methods of assessing the clergy; most important they were admonished not to leave non-payers to the hope of their eventual conformity 'whereby all the trouble and burden was cast upon the end of the year' but to deal with them swiftly.[144] In 1638, on the king's personal instructions to Lord Keeper Coventry, the corporate towns were again given the authority to assess themselves for the sums charged on them, subject to the same principles of sparing poor cottagers and taxing personal wealth.[145] In 1639, the same amounts of money as 1637 were requested for ships of smaller tonnage, but a bribe – or carrot – appears to have

141. PRO, SP 16/329/73.
142. PRO, SP 16/329/74.
143. PRO, PC 2/46/378.
144. PRO, PC 2/48/236; cf. *Cal. Stat. Pap. Dom., 1637*, p. 46; Cambridge University Library, Buxton MSS, Box 96.
145. BL Add. MS 25040, f.2: Charles I to Coventry, 1638.

been dangled. Kent, for example, was normally charged £8,000 for a ship of 800 tons and was asked for the same payment for a vessel of 640 tons. However, the Council ordered that £6,400 would be accepted 'if the said sum was paid by the 20th February 1639 [i.e. 1640] but if it failed of being performed then the sum of £8,000 to be levied'.[146] Together with the 6d. in the pound offered now to sheriffs, the deal suggests that the Council was beginning to implement what we would now call an incentive scheme.[147] Clearly the writs indicate that the Caroline government attempted to learn from experience and refine its instructions in the light of earlier difficulties. In one sense it did not succeed: business, in the unwelcome shape of enquiries, complaints, disputes and investigations, continued to grow; delays mounted. But, as we shall see, ship money was paid. The discussions initiated by Hopton in the spring of 1634 resulted in perhaps the most successful extraordinary tax in early modern (perhaps in modern) British history.

The sheriffs

The writs for ship money projected into the spotlight of local, and indeed central, politics an official who had for decades (if not centuries) been cast in a subordinate role: the sheriff. In the earlier Middle Ages the sheriff had been the principal officer of the king in the shires. But the removal of indictments before the sheriff's tourn to trial at quarter sessions in the reign of Edward IV diminished his legal jurisidiction; and the development of the commission of the peace (on which he could not be active during his year of office) and of the lieutenancy eclipsed the sheriff as an officer of local government. That is not to say, however, that the sheriff was a negligible figure. The sheriff was the officer who received and was responsible for the execution of royal writs; he oversaw the collection of rents and debts due to the crown; he welcomed and arranged hospitality for the justices when they came on circuit to conduct the assizes; he organized the election of members of parliament; often he officially received the king in the event of a royal progress into the county. The shrievalty could be a costly and irksome job that detached the incumbent from the inner circles of county politics (focused on the sessions). But it could also, for some who had not yet entered those circles, provide an entrée into the

146. Kent Archives Office, Twysden MS U47/47/01, f.10; *Cal. Stat. Pap. Dom., 1639–40*, p. 89.

147. *Cal. Stat. Pap. Dom., 1640*, p. 251: Council warrant of 31 May. It was reported that the bribe was to be 12d. in the pound (BL Add. MS 11045, f.74: Rossingham to Scudamore, 19 Nov. 1639).

political networks. Michael Dalton, author of *Officium Vicecomitum*, the office and authority of sheriffs, insisted that it was an office not only for gentlemen, but for those worthy 'not only for the sufficiency of their estate, but also for their sincerity and honesty'.[148] It was a post to which many still attached great prestige.[149] Sir Hugh Cholmley of Yorkshire tells us that his father, Sir Richard, paid £1,000 for the shrievalty in 1625.[150] In Sussex in the 1630s, Sir Richard Evelyn, ancestor of the diarist John, was proud enough of his being chosen to ride with a large band of 116 retainers, in livery and plumage.[151] His pride was neither hubristic nor inappropriate. Sir Gervase Clifton's song in praise of the sheriffs of Derbyshire lists others who 'with sevenscore did appear/for gentlemen and braverie';[152] and the Earl of Kingston thanked his cousin Clifton in 1637 for having sent 'an exquisite description of the pomp of our several sheriffs' whom Clifton had joined in procession.[153] Evidently this was still an event. The list of those deemed suitable for the post in Shropshire in 1632 similarly indicates that the candidates were no mean men, but well able to support such display. The wealth of the thirty-three listed ranged from a very respectable £300 per annum to a rent in excess of £3,000 – a figure which surpassed that of many in the House of Lords.[154]

If the status of the shrievalty was uncertain, it is evident too that attitudes to the post varied greatly. Though Cholmley paid to secure it, others, well before the first levy of ship money, thought the office an undesirable burden. Sir Richard Cecil in 1630 thanked the Earl of Bridgewater for exempting him;[155] James Turbeville and Josia Godschalke wrote to the earl excusing themselves.[156] Sir Thomas Barrington's hope that he might avoid being pricked in 1631 was clearly shared by many of his Essex neighbours, for the king expressed his anger that 'the best men of the shires be not put into the bill'.[157] In York Leonard Hull, to avoid the office, willingly paid a £50 fine.[158] He

148. M. Dalton, *Officium Vicecomitum: the Office and Authoritie of Sheriffs* (1628, STC 6213), *passim* and epistle dedicatory. Cf. C.H. Karraker, *The Seventeenth Century Sheriff* (Chapel Hill, NC, 1930).
149. Heylyn for one described the sheriff as the chief official of the shire, *Microcosmos: A Little Description of the Great World* (Oxford, 1629, STC 13279), p. 474. In counties where there were separate sessions the sheriffs had a greater importance. I owe this point to John Morrill.
150. *The Memoirs of Sir Hugh Cholmley* (1787), p. 24.
151. Fletcher, *Country Community*, p. 142.
152. Clifton MSS, PWV/684: 'The Noble High Sherife March the 7th Anno 1636'.
153. Clifton MS Cl/C 670: Kingston to Clifton, 27 March 1637.
154. Ellesmere MS 7114, 10 Nov. 1632.
155. Ellesmere MS 6329: Sir Richard Cecil to Bridgewater, 26 Jan. 1630.
156. Ellesmere MSS 7196, 7197.
157. A. Searle (ed.) *Barrington Family Letters, 1628–32* (Camden Soc., 4th series, 28, 1983), pp. 217–18.
158. York House Books, 35, f.73v.

may not have made a bad bargain for the costs of the office (not least as Sheriff Buxton of Norfolk's accounts for the assize dinner make clear) could be high.[159] So Sir Richard Phillips in 1632 pleaded his debts, children and recent legal costs as his excuse for not serving;[160] and Sir Francis Coke asked Secretary Coke to spare his neighbour Edward Revell who was building a house, 'which you know will empty his purse'.[161] In 1632, John Griffiths, vice-admiral, urged the president of the Marches concerning the selection of a sheriff for Anglesey: 'I pray that whosoever the man be he may not be necessitous.'[162] To the expenses of the office must be added the burdens and inconveniences. The sheriff was obliged to reside in his county for the whole year of his office and had to secure a licence from the king for any exception. He had to deal with riots, distrain for debts, gather fines, forward warrants, make returns on writs, summon juries, brief the assize judges on local JPs and other officials, warn the bailiffs and constables to attend the sessions, summon the grand and trial juries, assist judges, JPs, commissioners for sewers, escheators, coroners, ecclesiastical officers, and make accounts into the Exchequer. Dereliction of any area of duty made him liable to a fine; only an under-sheriff assisted him.[163] Such a catalogue helps us understand why Hugh Ap William Prichard in 1633 requested exemption from office, being a man seventy-six years old who wished to enjoy his last days 'free from the tumultuous cares of such an office'.[164] Similarly, Henry Bulstrode was relieved that by succeeding as sheriff of Buckinghamshire a predecessor who had died in mid-term, he avoided serving a full year 'with all the attendant trouble, vexation, charge, and all the imposition of the King's officers of the Exchequer, not forgetting the bullying by the judges at the assize'.[165] The long lists of candidates for the shrievalty and the numerous letters of excuse and petitions for exemption found among the Bridgewater papers suggest that in the early seventeenth century the shrievalty was widely regarded as an unwelcome burden and expense.[166]

Perhaps the most interesting question for the history of the personal rule is how far ship money exacerbated the reluctance to serve and in general changed the nature of and attitudes to the office. Ship money

159. Buxton MSS, Box 97. I am grateful to Clive Holmes for this reference.
160. Ellesmere MS 7108.
161. Coke MS 39: Francis Coke to Coke, 29 Oct. 1630; *HMC Cowper, I*, p. 414.
162. Ellesmere MS 7110: John Griffiths to Bridgewater, 18 Oct. 1632.
163. Dalton, *Officium Vicecomitum*, *passim* and esp. pp. 93, 220, 256.
164. Ellesmere MS 7141: Ap. Prichard to Bridgewater, 18 Oct. 1633.
165. R.H. Whitelocke, *Memoirs of Bulstrode Whitelocke* (1860), p. 81.
166. For example, Ellesmere MSS 7061, 7093, 7099, 7101, 7114, 7125–9, 7135–6, 7166, 7180, 7193, 7239, 7275, 7279. The Treasury commission's decision to look into debts due from sheriffs to the crown added further reason to avoid the office. See G.E. Aylmer, *The King's Servants: The Civil Service of Charles I* (1961), ch. 4, esp. pp. 197–8.

necessitated one immediate change: on 20 December 1635 the king put to the Council the inconveniency of some counties (such as Sussex, Surrey and Huntingdonshire) having no sheriff of their own and the need to appoint them for the service.[167] Ship money also quickly brought the sheriff into a much closer relationship with the central government – indeed in the summer of 1636 the courtiers on progress even called on the sheriffs of the counties they travelled to quicken them in the service.[168] Historians have tended to assume that ship money made the burdens, costs, and ill-will associated now with the shrievalty unbearable and so greatly escalated reluctance to serve. Sheriffs were, after all, held responsible for any ship money not collected and were compelled, after their year of office, either to make good the shortfall from their own resources or/and accompany their successor around the county in a sometimes humiliating effort to make up (or recuperate) the sum.[169] (Though the surveyors of highways were often put to the same indignity and inconvenience, the stakes – both in terms of money and local status – were less high).[170] Sir Peter Temple of Buckinghamshire, for example, told his mother in July 1635 that he had paid £90 on behalf of his neighbours which he was now trying to recover;[171] in 1638 he was still being hounded by the Council for arrears.[172] There were several, as the French envoy Poigny reported in November 1635, who had not been able to recover the money they had advanced, and as the tax became more regular the numbers increased.[173] There was little the Council could do to help. Once a sheriff had made his assessment, he depended to a large extent on the under-sheriff, still more the head and high constables, to collect the money and ultimately on the willingness of gentry, yeomen and quite humble folk to pay it: chasing up arrears could involve a long and complex trek through the labyrinths of local politics.

Ship money too added hugely to the bureaucracy of the office: once the Council had sent the writ to the sheriff it left the tedious business of copying and dispatching the writs, making assessments, writing to constables and mayors, replying to correspondence to him alone – often literally alone since some sheriffs had no clerical assistants or personal amanuensis. Sir Peter Temple complained to his mother in

167. PRO, PC 2/45/294; cf. PRO 2/46/267.
168. *Cal. Stat. Pap. Dom., 1636–7*, p. 91.
169. J.S. Wilson, 'Sheriffs' rolls of the sixteenth and seventeenth centuries', *Eng. Hist. Rev.*, 47 (1932), pp. 31–45; Fletcher, *County Community*, p. 142; E.S. Cope, *Politics without Parliaments, 1629–1640* (1987), p. 107. See for example, Huntington Library MS HM 204.
170. For example, Dorset Record Office, quarter sessions orders, f.246.
171. Temple of Stowe MS 10, STT 2059: Temple to Lady Temple, 12 July 1635.
172. Temple of Stowe MS 11, STT 913: Council to Temple, Nov. 1638.
173. PRO, 31/3/68, f.251 v.

July 1635, 'I have been the director of writing some eighty warrants and letters since Friday night to Sunday night.'[174] He was fortunate that he did not personally have to write them. In addition if all (as often) did not go well the sheriff found himself in a time-consuming and sometimes uncomfortable correspondence with the Council and might face a summons to Whitehall to account for his service – so suffering an expensive journey to London and absence from his county, which only added to his difficulties in collecting arrears.[175] In the counties, the new emphasis on tax collecting was not likely to win the sheriff any popularity or respect – especially from those (and human nature tells us there will always be many) who believed themselves to be unfairly assessed. Ship money made it particularly hard for the sheriff to square the circle of central demands and local sensibilities. Elizabeth Pert expressed to her son-in-law, the sheriff of Norfolk, her 'hope that you will be careful to retain the King's favour and also keep the love of your countrymen' but this was, she acknowledged, 'a very hard task to be performed'.[176] The sheriff of Cheshire feared that diligence in executing Conciliar orders would mean he was 'accounted too officious and a pick-thank' at home.[177] At times the sheriff's own subordinates spurned his orders, either to court popularity or with the tacit support of social superiors among the gentry.[178] In Tintinhull hundred in Somerset (to which we shall have to return) Constable Napper in league with Sir Robert Phelips had no hesitation in telling sheriff Henry Hodges that he did not 'care a fart' for his warrant.[179] Not to mention his difficulties in collecting and indignity suffered at the hands of a subordinate, it must have discomforted Hodges to know that he was viewed as an enemy by the most influential gentleman of his county.[180] Perhaps as discomforting was a suspicion among some that appointment to the shrievalty should be seen as a royal punishment – an impression that may have derived from the king's decision in 1626 to prick Wentworth and others sheriffs to keep them out of parliament.[181] Sir George Chaworth complained bitterly to Secretary

174. Temple of Stowe MS 10, STT 2059.

175. In 1637, sheriffs from Hampshire, Herefordshire and Pembrokeshire asked to be excused attendance on the board because they would 'lose so much time in the collection' (*Cal. Stat. Pap. Dom., 1637*, p. 387).

176. Buxton MSS, Box 96: Elizabeth Pert to Buxton, 14 Aug. 1638.

177. *Cal. Stat. Pap. Dom., 1640*, p. 8: Sir Thomas Powell to Laurence Whitaker, 4 April.

178. Lord Coventry ruled that indentures between a sheriff and his under-sheriff did not absolve the former from responsibility for the latter's misdemeanours (J. Dias, 'Politics and administration in Nottinghamshire and Derbyshire, 1590–1640', Oxford University, D. Phil. thesis, 1973, p. 134).

179. *Cal. Stat. Pap. Dom., 1635*, p. 146; below, p. 582.

180. T.G. Barnes, *Somerset 1625–1640: A County's Government during the Personal Rule* (Oxford, 1961), pp. 216–17.

181. Gardiner, *History of England*, VI, p. 33; cf. Buxton MSS, Box 96.

Coke in 1638 that 'His Majesty hath pleased to make me his sheriff of a county, which the world . . . takes both as a mark of his displeasure and as a disparagement to me'.[182] Coke assured him that no such intention explained his selection, for the king 'chooseth none to be sheriffs whom he thinketh not well affected to his service'.[183] But Chaworth remained convinced, as he put it to Charles I himself, that 'I have the misfortune to have the worst inlet into the service that is possible, a prepossession of the whole country that I am in your Majesty's disfavour.'[184] He was not alone in this paranoia. Buxton's relatives thought that his enemies had conspired to get him appointed to a post that could only lose him friends.[185]

Not surprisingly, there are indications that, after 1635, it became more difficult to find able and willing candidates for the sheriff's office. Powerful patrons tried to obtain exemptions for their clients. The ever assiduous Bridgewater by 1637 encountered difficulty in finding sheriffs for Flint, Denbigh and Montgomery, not least because Lord Powys's 'interest prevaileth far' in securing pardons for his friends.[186] Even Edward Nicholas who was in charge of the collection helped a friend's son to evade the post.[187] The problem was obviously larger: in July 1636 the Privy Council sent letters to the justices of assize asking them to return from each county the names of four suitable candidates for the shrievalty and in September issued orders that none should be excused on the grounds of being a servant to the king or queen.[188] The difficulties encountered may have led to some less than suitable choices. One Anderson complained to Sir John Coke that he had been appointed sheriff of Northumberland though 'I have no land in that county nor place of habitation there to reside in, both which the law enjoins every sheriff of a county should have.'[189] As a stranger, he claimed not inaccurately, he would 'never be able to effect anything there'. In Suffolk, the candidate pricked, a Mr Baker, was discovered to be living abroad.[190] Probably the choices were narrowing. Though in Somerset the sheriffs remained for the most part JPs of gentry rank, studies of Sussex and especially Warwickshire have shown that many appointed in the 1630s were not of magisterial

182. *HMC Cowper, II*, p. 202: Chaworth to Coke, 6 Nov. 1638. For a possibly important background to Chaworth's fears, see also my *Faction and Parliament: Essays on Early Stuart History* (Oxford, 1978), pp. 222–3.
183. *HMC Cowper, II*, p. 203: Coke to Chaworth, 25 Nov. 1638.
184. *Ibid.*, p. 205: Chaworth to Coke, 18 Dec. 1638.
185. Buxton MSS, Box 96: Elizabeth Pert to Buxton, 14 Aug. 1638.
186. Ellesmere MS 7238: Bridgewater to Coventry, 22 Sept. 1637.
187. *Cal. Stat. Pap. Dom., 1639–40*, p. 551; cf. Ellesmere MS 7286.
188. PRO, PC 2/46/347, 370.
189. Coke MS 36: Anderson to Coke, 26 Dec. 1628.
190. Coke MS 52: Coventry to Coke, 30 Jan. 1636.

status.[191] If such was, or was perceived to be, the case it could make things worse, diminishing further the prestige of the office and the ranks of those who sought it.

It would be very misleading, however, to leap to the conclusion that as a consequence of the duties imposed by ship money, the office of sheriff had become despised or anathema – either to potential incumbents or to county society in general. For one, because the continuing success of ship money depended on the fact that the sheriff did not lack esteem, the king and Council, as Coke had told Chaworth, took great care over selections. In the state papers for 1638 we find Coventry conferring with Windebank over the choice of sheriffs for Berkshire. The care they took, their comments on the suitability of individuals, their research into past behaviour (even down to Sir Henry Willoughby's reaction to the king's suggestion of a match between his daughter and Suckling) all indicate their concern with finding the right men.[192] Secondly, beside the evidence of reluctance we must place the several cases of ready willingness to serve in the office. William Thomas's claim, in excusing himself for debt, that when able 'I shall not only be most readily willing but covetingly ambitious of so . . . eminent dignities' carries more conviction when we know that he served well as sheriff of Glamorgan.[193] John Bridgeman informed the Earl of Bridgewater that one John Newton, sheriff of Shropshire, wished to serve in the county of Montgomeryshire the following year; indeed he had 'given a special charge to his ploughmen for their liveries to keep them unspotted'.[194] In Suffolk, as Lord Keeper Coventry told Coke, one of the listed candidates 'is very willing to undergo the office and my Lord Chief Justice thinks him very able for it'.[195] His position last on the list may be revealing. It may be that some of those most willing were often men of lesser social status who saw their chance to rise. In Norwich the shrievalty was usually a step to higher things – a place on the aldermanic bench; in the counties it could be a ladder to the commission of the peace.[196] But the shrievalty on the whole was not in the 1630s staffed by men of lower status. The names of those who served in the border counties across the decade do not support any thesis of a change of class: Wynns in Anglesey and

191. Barnes, *Somerset*, pp. 132, 235–7; Fletcher, *County Community*, pp. 142–3; A. Hughes, *Politics, Society and Civil War in Warwickshire 1620–1660* (Cambridge, 1987), p. 105. Dr Hughes shows, however, that after 1635 there was an effort to choose men of higher standing.

192. *Cal. Stat. Pap. Dom., 1638–9*, p. 127: Coventry to Windebank, 27 Nov. 1638.

193. Ellesmere MS 7275: William Thomas to Bridgewater, 30 Sept. 1639.

194. Ellesmere MS 7203: John Bridgeman to Bridgewater, 13 Oct. 1635; Ellesmere MS 6976: Richard Harris to Bridgewater, 16 Oct. 1635.

195. Coke MS 52: Coventry to Coke, 30 Jan. 1636.

196. J. Evans, *Seventeenth Century Norwich* (Oxford, 1979), p. 51.

Denbigh, Vaughans in Camarthen, Lewises in Cardigan continued to monopolize the post.[197] What the shrievalty would be for some was a way to demonstrate loyalty and service. As the Reverend Garrard told Lord Wentworth at the pricking in January 1636, 'some there were that made suit to be sheriff which is not usual'.[198]

In some cases the motives for serving may have been less than noble. There is more than a suspicion that Norton, the sheriff of Lincolnshire in 1636, who retained money long in his hands, was backward in presenting accounts and uncooperative in assisting his successor, may have been exploiting his office for profit.[199] Other sheriffs, like Eare of Derbyshire who levied over £6 more than required and who distrained the animals of people who had paid the levy, may also have been more assiduous for their own gain than over-zealous in the public cause.[200] But there are more innocent explanations of why the shrievalty may have been desirable to some. We should not dismiss the most idealistic: a sense of duty to serve the king and commonweal – which in the seventeenth century was an important component of the ideal (and not a negligible one of the reality) of what it meant to be a gentleman. Those of talent, Michael Dalton remarked, dedicating his treatise on the sheriff to Sir Giles Alington, should employ it publicly for the good of others.[201] His call to duty did not fall entirely on deaf ears. Even the reluctant Thomas Smyth (of Ashton Court) promised to serve the next year if 'a more worthy and active name' could not be found.[202] Experience may have taught other reasons for taking the post. Since the sheriff was given sole responsibility for apportioning the county's assessment, in Twysden's words, 'an unlimited power from whom there was no appeal but the Council board', there was something to be said (in the interests of one's region as well as self) for wielding that authority rather than being subject to the arbitrary decisions of others.[203] Now of enhanced importance, the shrievalty became more embroiled in the regional and factional rivalries of county politics. Sheriffs could, and did, protect their own areas in making assessments and the opportunity to do so may have been an inducement to take office.[204]

Once a sheriff was pricked and in office, there was little point in his

197. Ellesmere MS 7328 tabulates them. For the county at large, see Coventry MS 602918 for 1629–33 and 1636–9 and *PRO Lists and Indexes*, no. 9 (1848).
198. Knowler, *Strafford Letters*, I, p. 509: Garrard to Wentworth, 25 Jan. 1636.
199. Coke MS 54: Coke to Lindsey, Aug. 1636; see *HMC Cowper, II*, p. 138.
200. Coke MS 55; *HMC Cowper, II*, p. 150.
201. Dalton, *Officium Vicecomitum*, epistle dedicatory to Sir Giles Alington.
202. Bristol Record Office, Smyth of Ashton Court MS 36074/150: Smyth to Thomas Meautys, 2 Oct. 1637.
203. Twysden MS U 47/47/Zi, p. 198.
204. Cf. below, pp. 576–7.

foot-dragging. Arrears at the end of his year meant not only (possibly) personal cost, but an indefinite prolongation of duty. Garrard wrote to Wentworth in December 1635, shortly after the new sheriffs had taken up office, that 'the high sheriffs to get themselves quick out of their offices bestir themselves apace in their several counties.'[205] The Council tended to take its standard from the best performers and ascribe any shortfall – slow payments or arrears – to lack of activity and diligence on the part of the sheriff; poor returns were always accompanied by the threat of Conciliar displeasure and summons, whatever the local obstacles. The best sheriffs – and there is no reason to believe them few in number – set about their charge vigorously, dutifully and scrupulously. Sir John Hotham, sheriff of York, took up hundreds of pounds on his credit, lest the service be 'foreslowed', and made suggestions for improving the collection.[206] The sheriff of Monmouth, George Milbourne, spent his own money.[207] In October 1636 John Frere, of Dorset, distrained the goods of his own son, 'that he would not seem partial'.[208] In 1635 the Council commended the sheriffs of Glamorgan, Devon, Cheshire and Lancashire for their pains.[209] The Council's commendation did not always mean the county's condemnation. In Kent, even Twysden who thought ship money illegal acknowledged that Sir George Sondes (sheriff for part of 1636 and 1637)

> did carry himself in that business of ship money with much moderation and temper, neither was there anything you would easily find fault with if it were not a desire too great of contenting all men which made him hearken to all complaints brought to him without hearing both parts together . . . in so much as there was in some places not less than six if not seven warrants or orders from him . . . each contradicting the other.[210]

Twysden's observation on Sondes is an apt comment on the difficulties faced by even the best-intentioned sheriffs; but it is also a testament to the industry and fairness that some brought to the task. Clifton's paper on 'the Noble High Sheriff March the 7th 1636' showered praise on the sheriff of Derbyshire who 'hath received the ship money and paid it to the Exchequer without arrest, distraint or toil'.[211] The prayers of the poor, the encomium closes, 'still to heaven

205. Knowler, *Strafford Letters*, I, p. 491.
206. *Cal. Stat. Pap. Dom., 1635*, p. 507.
207. *Ibid.*, p. 595.
208. *Cal. Stat. Pap. Dom., 1636–7*, p. 151.
209. *Cal. Stat. Pap. Dom., 1635*, pp. 594–5.
210. Twysden MS U 47/47/Zi, p.133.
211. Clifton MS PWV/684.

fly for him'. It would be naive to imagine prayers for the sheriff flying to heaven from most of the counties of England, jamming the precatory airwaves. But had there not been many able, for all the difficulties, to execute Council instructions without alienating the locality, the collection of ship money would have been a great deal less successful than it was.

Ship money: administrative problems and disputes

Though ship money in itself was no innovation, the decision to levy it in 1634, still more the extension of the rate to the inland counties and appointment of sheriffs to superintend it, created new administrative questions and difficulties. The instructions issued by the Council with the first writ produced confusion as to whether the sheriffs or the mayors of the corporate towns were to make their assessments.[212] One major problem was that foreseen in the Council discussions of the summer: the distance between the port towns and the difficulties of communication and co-operation between them.[213] The mayor of Dover, on receiving his orders, wrote to the Lord Warden of the Cinque Ports concerned about the instruction to meet and confer with other mayors. 'Such is the distance of these towns and cities,' he wrote, 'that [we] are at an exigent and know not where to begin or what to do.'[214] A good case study of the problems the writ presented comes from the Welsh marches. On 4 January 1635 John Bridgeman wrote to the Earl of Bridgewater and Secretary Coke pointing out that in dutiful response to the writ the sheriffs of Glamorgan and Monmouth and the mayors of Newport and Cardiff had sent to the sheriff of Camarthen to arrange a meeting at Ludlow where they might, if difficulties arose, also confer with the Council of the Marches. None, however, of the other sheriffs turned up there; indeed only the mayor of Chester replied – and then to claim that his own city would be the more appropriate place to meet.[215] Those magistrates who had bothered to make the journey were understandably annoyed – all the more so because with the thirty-day period for assessment after the receipt of the writ now expired, the right to assess now devolved on the sheriff alone.[216] Having lost the right to assess themselves, the mayors were at least anxious to make representations to the sheriffs so,

212. See Temple of Stowe MSS, ship money box C.73, Council to sheriff of Essex, 9 Dec. 1634.
213. Above, pp. 550–51.
214. *Cal. Stat. Pap. Dom., 1634–5*, p. 295, 17 Nov. 1634.
215. Coke MS 50; partly calendared in *HMC Cowper, II*, p. 73.
216. *Ibid.*

faute de mieux, they accepted a meeting at Chester 'although the place be very far distant from most parts of Wales'. The episode indicates how problematic was the first writ of ship money's requirement of a degree of local co-operation untypical of early modern England.

The extension of the writ to inland counties greatly complicated the problems – in towns and counties, for mayors and sheriffs alike. The city of York, for example, responded quickly to the writ but, apparently ignorant that a money payment was acceptable, was perplexed how and where to obtain a ship, whether to buy or hire one, how to get men to serve for six months and whether they had the right to press.[217] The sheriffs and mayors of the Marches similarly needed to be assured by Bridgewater that money was acceptable, 'there being no seasoned timber' in those parts.[218] In Kent, the second writ led to a multiplicity of questions. Were the justices of the corporate towns included in directions to justices of the county (and so to be present at the meeting)? How were Kent and Sussex, jointly charged with two ships, to co-operate in providing them? How were assessments to be made on the hundreds and parishes – according to the subsidies, by poll ('as in some places it is accustomed upon the watching of the beacons') or 'as the charge was laid upon the late setting out of soldiers'? Were noblemen and women or clergy to be assessed? If the assessment was challenged, who was to judge – 'it being impossible for the justices of peace to set down the assessments of every particular person, but must refer [it] to the constables and . . . such inferior officers who will undoubtedly favour their particulars and the abilities of divers . . . by means of their far distance cannot be known to the officers'? Finally, it was asked, if some refused to pay or be bound over to the Council what was to be done with them?[219]

Such queries were natural enough in a society that was governed as much by conventions as by institutions or officers. But these doubts and uncertainties delayed the making of assessments. Thomas Carter told Sir Peter Temple in December 1635 (four months after the issue of the second writ) that the Buckinghamshire town of Middle Claydon 'had short warning to gather up the said levy, having warning but one day to pay it in the next day'.[220] And even after the assessment was made there, tenants waited to consult their landlords – and Temple was expected to wait too until they heard. As well as those common to all, individual counties faced particular problems in implementing the writ. In some counties, Northampton especially, some hundreds had

217. York House Books, 35, f.257.
218. Coke MS 50: Bridgeman to Bridgewater, 4 Jan. 1635. A nice reminder that some saw ship money as a demand for a service.
219. Kent Archives Office, Darrell of Calehill MS U 386/05/8c.
220. Temple of Stowe MS 10, STT 189: Carter to Temple, 22 Dec. 1635.

been granted to private individuals who then had the right to place and remove bailiffs, so undermining the sheriff's authority.[221] In the Marches there was concern about the safe transportation of ship money;[222] in Sussex some uncertainty about how to dispose of it once collected.[223] The sheriff of Devon, Sir Thomas Drew, catalogued some of his difficulties in a letter of November 1635 explaining the delays in the service. The size of the county and the necessity to convene many meetings had held up assessments; then complaints of malice or favouritism by the constables had led to further delay. Examination of the assessments revealed the added complication of inequalities in the ancient local rates – the rectification of which required the assistance of JPs and deputy lieutenants, who were not formally empowered to make assessments. As a result of these problems Drew had encountered many refractory. The only surprise after his litany of problems is his concluding confidence that he had 'no doubt of the accomplishment of that service'.[224]

As a consequence of these difficulties – and of the need as always to adjust central requirements to local circumstances and practices – the methods of assessing and collecting ship money, and the impact of the levy, greatly varied: between county and county and even between different areas of the same county. In particular the Council's vague and general directions for assessing allowed for and resulted in very different practices. Edward Stephens, the sheriff of Gloucestershire, appears to have followed the writ to the letter, instructing the constables to meet with the 'discreet and sufficient men' of every parish to see how the money might be assessed, relieving the poor and those with large families and taxing those of little land and great personal wealth.[225] In Middlesex the sheriff and two or three leading inhabitants agreed to charge 'by the rule of the last subsidy' and calculated that a sum two and a half times the last subsidy assessment would be requisite.[226] The town of Cardigan and the ward of Walbrook in London also rated according to the subsidy but at six and five times the last subsidy payment respectively.[227] Gloucestershire assessed according to composition for purveyance;[228] the town of Banbury by

221. PRO, PC 2/51/109.
222. Coke MS 50: Bridgewater to Coke, 7 March 1635.
223. PRO, PC 2/47/144.
224. *Cal. Stat. Pap. Dom., 1635*, p. 478: Sir Thomas Drew to Council, 13 Nov. 1635.
225. Kent Archives Office, Sackville MS U 269/0267/8: Edward Stephens to constables of Deerhurst, 12 Oct. 1635.
226. *Cal. Stat. Pap. Dom., 1634–5*, p. 373.
227. *Ibid.*, pp. 376, 391.
228. *Cal. Stat. Pap. Dom., 1636–7*, p. 345. The rate was set at ten times the payment for purveyance.

hearths.[229] Essex implemented different rates across the county, some by land, some by ability.[230] Sir Thomas Aston, sheriff of Cheshire for 1636, raised one-third of the required sum on the basis of estates and the other two-thirds according to the mise rolls of payments usually made at the creation of a Prince of Wales which had become the basis of the county rates.[231] Across Kent there were varied methods of assessment in operation: for the village of Pluckley we find a table of payments correlated with 'acres', suggesting an assessment based on landholding.[232] In Charing, however, three columns headed 'acres', 'money' and 'ability' evidence a complex combination of principles in calculating assessments.[233]

The burden of ship money differed as greatly place to place as did the mode of assessment. Alongside Cardigan's claim that they paid the equivalent of six subsidies,[234] we have Colchester's, that their rate amounted to eleven, and the Isle of Purbeck's that they paid a sum equal to 'about twenty-five subsidies'.[235] Gloucestershire set the payment at ten times that for purveyance; the under-sheriff of Westmorland reported that to raise £500 in ship money he had to increase the 12d. in the pound rate for purveyance to 4s. 6d. in the pound.[236] More important than these figures of overall amounts is the clear evidence that ship money reached far deeper down into local society than the subsidies; and perhaps deeper than most local payments, for the poor for example. So, as Dr Hughes has shown, at Lea Marston, which formed one-sixth of the constabulary of Whitacre in Warwickshire, in 1637 thirty men paid the ship money charge of £4 10s., at a rate of 2s. ¾d. in the pound; for the subsidy of 1628 the whole constabulary's payment of £10 15s. was made by thirty-two people.[237] In the hundred of Titchfield, Hampshire, 71 individuals paid the subsidy of 1628 and 200 were assessed for ship money.[238] The Essex subsidy roll for 1640 lists 3,200 names; during the 1630s 14,500 peoples were assessed for ship money.[239] Mr Fletcher has suggested that in Sussex the weight

229. E.R.C. Brinkworth (ed.) *South Newington Churchwardens' Accounts, 1553–1684* (Banbury Historical Soc., 6, 1964), p. 48.
230. *Cal. Stat. Pap. Dom., 1638–9*, p. 231.
231. *Cal. Stat. Pap. Dom., 1636–7*, pp. 3–4. J.S. Morrill, *Cheshire 1630–1660: County Government and Society during the English Revolution* (Oxford, 1974), p. 28.
232. Kent Archives Office, Dering MS U 1107/03.
233. Darrell of Calehill MS U 386/05/5; cf. 4, 6 and 7.
234. *Cal. Stat. Pap. Dom., 1635*, p. 391.
235. *Cal. Stat. Pap. Dom., 1634–5*, pp. 464, 509.
236. Above, note 228; *Cal. Stat. Pap. Dom., 1635*. p. 556.
237. Hughes, *Politics, Society and Civil War*, p. 109.
238. P. Haskell, 'Ship money in Hampshire', in J. Webb, N. Yates and S. Peacock (eds) *Hampshire Studies* (Portsmouth, 1981).
239. J.S. Morrill, *The Revolt of the Provinces: Conservatives and Radicals in the English Civil War, 1630–1650* (1976), p. 27.

of the burden of ship money fell on the middle ranks of society, those who paid the poor rate.[240] It may well be that elsewhere, as was claimed, it fell on those still lower down the social scale. In Warwickshire, of 150 listed as defaulters on the first writ only twelve were recorded as gentlemen.[241] An assessment book for Essex dated March 1637, listing the sums charged on individuals, records several assessed at 2d. or 3d. Other names with '0-0-0' alongside them may suggest an unsuccessful attempt to cast the net even more widely.[242] In the village of Little Chart in Kent, several like Peter Bennett, Timothy Jennings or John Wood were assessed at 1d. in 1638.[243] In another parish, possession of one acre of land could apparently render Thomas Willen liable to payment of 1d..[244] Such charges imposed on some already on the margin of subsistence could make the difference between managing and not managing; small wonder that often humble household goods had to be distrained to make up for default. Even for those not on the poverty line, the perception of hardship should not be underestimated. In Dr Morrill's words, 'ship money was the first rate or tax ever paid by a majority of freeholders for a use outside the shire' and its methods of assessment 'unquestionably brought thousands of families into a national rating system for the first time'.[245] The 1637 ship money book for Essex shows 12,000 assessed for a tax for the first time.[246] It is hardly surprising that doubts and disputes followed in the wake of the ship writs.

Not only the differing methods of assessment between area and area, but the changes effected as one sheriff succeeded another led to the problems that were to consume most of the Council's, as well as many local officials', time and energy: disputes over rates and assessments. In almost every county we hear of disagreements between a sheriff and local boroughs, hundreds and parishes; from every corner of England complaints were sent to the Privy Council of unjust or even corrupt assessment by the sheriff. Sometimes the objection arose from a claim to exemption: the physicians of London claimed immunity;[247] in Cambridge some purchased the status of scholar servants and then sought privileged exemption from payment.[248] Sometimes complaints appear to have originated in the sheer size of the burden, as with the

240. Fletcher, *County Community*, p. 205.
241. PRO, SP 16/358.
242. Darrell of Calehill MS U 386/05/6.
243. *Ibid.*, U 386/05/7.
244. For example, *Cal. Stat. Pap. Dom., 1638–9*, pp. 121–2; cf. p. 2.
245. Morrill, *Revolt of the Provinces*, p. 27.
246. B.W. Quintrell, 'The government of the county of Essex, 1603–1642' (London University, PhD thesis, 1965), p. 320.
247. *Cal. Stat. Pap. Dom., 1635–6*, p. 8.
248. *Cal. Stat. Pap. Dom., 1635*, p. 372.

Isle of Purbeck in Dorset which was charged £550 in 1635.[249] In some cases confusion over jurisdiction produced misunderstandings. In Yorkshire various parishes of Clifton, Heslington, Roscliff and others were rated by both the city and the county sheriff;[250] Thomas Soame, the sheriff of Middlesex's, plan to use the overcharge on some parishes to make up the deficiency of others threatened massive trouble.[251] For most common was the belief, or claim, by a particular town, parish or hundred that they had been assessed disproportionately. On occasions comparisons were made – from what information it would be interesting to know – with other counties or corporations. Colchester reported in 1635 that the rate on their town 'amounts to eleven subsidies at least, whereas the charge of Southwark and Westminster amount to but three subsidies'.[252] Usually, however, reflecting the very local identities of seventeenth-century Englishmen, complaints arose from allegedly unequal assessments on adjacent hundreds. So the inhabitants of the southern part of the hundred of Basingstoke in Hampshire complained that they were assessed equally with the northern part of the hundred, 'when in truth we are not a full third part'.[253] Similarly the eastern part of the county of Northamptonshire contested an assessment that charged it £870 more than the west side.[254] In Lincolnshire, as well as the issue of how to assess the newly drained lands, there was a long-running dispute over rates between Kesteven and Holland.[255] Examples of disputes run into the hundreds. Where in some cases a new sheriff created the dispute by changing the rate, in others the same differences dogged each assessment and sheriff across the decade.

Many rating disputes originated in disagreements, rivalries and unresolved differences in county society that predated ship money, and often went far back into the past. The city of Chester and Sir William Brereton had been at loggerheads for years before his appointment as sheriff; disputes over ship money merely reflected and exacerbated those antagonisms.[256] Rating disputes were a normal consequence of any local charge: over poor relief in Hampshire and

249. *Cal. Stat. Pap. Dom., 1634–5*, p. 509.
250. *Cal. Stat. Pap. Dom., 1635–6*, p. 12; cf. York House Books, 35, ff.294v–295.
251. *Cal. Stat. Pap. Dom., 1635–6*, p. 549.
252. *Cal. Stat. Pap. Dom., 1634–5*, p. 464.
253. Herriard MSS, Box 012.
254. Northamptonshire Record Office, Montagu MS 3, f.220: Montagu to Sir Thomas Brooke, 16 Oct. 1635.
255. *Cal. Stat. Pap. Dom., 1637–8*, p. 267; C. Holmes, *Seventeenth Century Lincolnshire* (Lincoln, 1980), pp. 131–2; Morrill, *Revolt of the Provinces*, p. 26.
256. Morrill, *Cheshire*, p. 25; *HMC Cowper, II*, p. 153.

Dorset,[257] over highway and bridge repair in Oxfordshire and Kent,[258] over purveyance in Hertfordshire,[259] over the whole range of payments in Derbyshire and Somerset.[260] Those over ship money were loudest only perhaps because here the levy was largest and the sums paid were not deployed locally but sent to the Treasurer of the Navy. Ship money made some aware of the need to tackle longstanding inequalities. In April 1637 Sir Ferdinando Gorges wrote to Secretary Coke to tell him of a meeting of the JPs of his county to deal with complaints concerning the inequality of rates for all local charges. Something, he recognized, had to be done 'for the public service and his Majesty's great occasions'.[261] An instance from Somerset helps us to see why. In January 1637 Thomas Smyth wrote to the then sheriff of Somerset, William Basset, to tell him that several inhabitants had protested against Basset's assessments as they had the year before in Mr Hodges's shrievalty. In Somerset ship money assessments as other common payments were based on the Hinton rate, devised by commissioners for musters at Hinton St George in 1569 for levying soldiers for service in Ireland. By that measure, the two hundreds of Portbury and Redminster were liable for three men each. Over the last thirty or forty years, however, they had been charged as if for only two men in all local assessments – for bridges and roads as well as musters. Smyth was not sure how the abatement had come about; his father, he had been told, had arranged it at a sessions 'long since', where their reduction had been made up by an extra man being imposed on Winterstoke. Then the new arrangement had caused little controversy. But ship money changed things: 'now they would return him upon us again'.[262] Smyth had succeeded in protecting the hundreds as his father had. In 1636 Mr Hodges had been led to repeal his first warrants for £480 and reduce the assessment to £400, raising the other £80 by higher assessment elsewhere; now the question had come up again. Smyth requested of Basset a similar concession: 'by which means yourself may come the easier by the money . . . otherwise I fear you will find the people rude and addicted unto opposition'. The letter offers a nice example of old local skeletons in the cupboard

257. Herriard MS F.10; Dorset Record Office, quarter sessions orders, ff.330, 335 v.
258. Oxfordshire Record Office, Dillon MS XII, g.1; Kent Archives Office, quarter sessions orders, W1, f.14v.
259. *Cal. Stat. Pap. Dom., 1637*, p. 47.
260. Coke MS 56: Gorges to Coke, 18 April 1637; E.H. Bates-Harbin, *Quarter Sessions Records for the County of Somerset*, II (Somerset Record Soc., 24, 1908), pp. xxxi, 278, 308.
261. Coke MS 56.
262. Smyth of Ashton Court MS 36074/149: Thomas Smyth to William Basset, 15 Jan. 1637; Barnes, *Somerset*, pp. 213–14.

set rattling by ship money: a longstanding arrangement was thrown into dispute by the new financial implications for ship money; local peace could be disturbed as a result.

In many parts of the country relative inequalities in local assessments and contributions had arisen as the varied demographic and economic fortunes of particular regions had invalidated earlier arrangements. Worcestershire had ordered a new rating in 1632 out of an appreciation of the unfairness of the old assessments.[263] For much of the 1620s in Somerset Tintinhull hundred had been protesting its high rating, being 'but four or five small tithings with a multitude of poor people',[264] and Cheriton had denounced the county's inequality of 'all rates towards all taxes and payments'.[265] But in general when the charges were low, local and occasional, they led to no more than spasmodic grumblings; with a tax that was large, national and – as became clear by 1636 – of indefinite duration, disproportionate local rates became a major issue. Attempts to tackle the problem by re-rating, however, manufactured as many resentments as it settled. At Bradford in Somerset in 1636 a new rating was established based on estate rather than acreage, but it apparently produced only new complaints.[266] In the West Riding of Yorkshire, there was a rise in the number of disputed assessments for the poor rate in the later 1630s at Campsall, Crofton, Scalmanden, Todwick, Chappel, Haddsley and Thurnscoe.[267] The quarrels affected more than money and assessments; they threw into question regional affiliations. In 1638 the inhabitants of Linton in Kent complained about being taxed with Maidstone;[268] in 1638 the inhabitants of Tintinhull queried whether the Hescombe lands were part of the hundred.[269] The new charge had upset a lot of old agreements, in some cases reopened a lot of old sores.

As well as exacerbating existing tensions, ship money also created a multitude of new difficulties and disparities and spawned hundreds of new disputes. The disagreements that arose were inherent, as Lord Keeper Coventry had foreseen, in the writs: 'Every little inequality (which in such a business cannot be avoided) will minister cause of objection.'[270] In the first place the writs prescribed methods of assess-

263. *Cal. Stat. Pap. Dom., 1637*, pp. 64–5; S. Bond (ed.) *The Chamber Order Book of Worcester, 1602–1650* (Worcestershire Record Soc., new series, 8, 1974), p. 263.
264. Bates-Harbin, *Quarter Sessions Records for . . . Somerset*, p. 52.
265. *Ibid.*, p. 62.
266. *Ibid.*, pp. 256, 285.
267. J. Lister (ed.) *West Riding Sessions Records II: Orders 1611–1642* (York Archaeological Soc. Records Series, 54, 1915), pp. 127–8.
268. *Cal. Stat. Pap. Dom., 1634–5*, p. 473.
269. Barnes, *Somerset Assize Orders, 1629–1640* (Somerset Record Soc., 65, 1959), p. 44; cf. *Cal. Stat. Pap. Dom., 1638–9*, p. 232.
270. Above, p. 551.

ment that involved a departure from the traditional basis of taxation, and sought to tax personal as well as landed wealth. Secondly the inconsistencies gave the sheriffs no clear direction, but left the aggrieved room for complaint. As a former sheriff was to recall in 1660, 'they had neither rule nor precedent to walk by',[271] and, the sheriff of Flintshire agreed, 'it is very requisite to set down safe grounds for officers to walk in and rules'.[272] The writ implied assessments on land, money, by subsidies, other common payments or ability, and each sheriff appears to have adopted some one or combination of these according to ease, custom, fairness or interest. Whichever course was taken, after however much care, there were always aggrieved parties. The parish of Tonworth in Hampshire argued that in all contributions to the poor rate or church repair their 'ancient custom . . . time out of mind' was 'to rate every man according to the land which he holdeth'; with ship money threatening a different system, they petitioned 'to have this our ancient rate confirmed by this worshipful bench for the preservation and continuance of this our peace'.[273] Bristol, believing itself to suffer from an unfairness that made it the highest charged city in the west, petitioned that they might be rated 'proportionably with other cities and places according to the subsidy rate'.[274] Traditional methods, however, were not always the fairest. Sir Thomas Aston, sheriff of Cheshire, found the mise roll the most acceptable but not most equitable basis for rating: 'This is the rule most pleasing because accustomed, but is shown to be unequal in respect of the times since it was rated.'[275] Sir Grenville Verney, among his other problems, pointed out that the Council's instruction to rate according to other payments was abused: 'greatness has gained such advantage that he that has £500 per annum will pay no more than tenants that pay rack rents'.[276] Lloyd Pierce, sheriff of Montgomery for 1637, similarly informed Nicholas that he had rated by the traditional proportions 'though being made near thirty years ago it is no equal way to follow, many parishes being decayed and others improved'.[277] In such circumstances it was understandable that Sir George Stonehouse sheriff of Berkshire should ask for advice whether to base the tax on the traditional assessment, though known to be unequal, or attempt a radical re-rating which, though possibly fairer, would disadvantage some and attract the suspicion of novelty.[278]

271. Temple of Stowe MSS, ship money box: speech of Sir Peter Temple, *c.*1660.
272. *Cal. Stat. Pap. Dom., 1640*, p. 324.
273. Herriard MS F.10.
274. Bristol Common Council Books, 3, f.66v.
275. *Cal. Stat. Pap. Dom., 1636–7*, pp. 3–4.
276. *Cal. Stat. Pap. Dom., 1635–6*, p. 446.
277. *Cal. Stat. Pap. Dom., 1637*, pp. 64–5.
278. *Cal. Stat. Pap. Dom., 1637–8*, p. 348.

Recent controversies over local charges in England suggest there is no simple answer to his query in modern times. In the early seventeenth century, the sheriff met with many more obstacles. His duty to tax ability rather than simply land was compromised by his inability to make all the assessments himself. The limitations to his local knowledge compelled the sheriff to consult (as the writ acknowledged he should) JPs, constables and other principal householders of the parishes and hundreds. But such, as a Kent JP freely admitted, 'undoubtedly favour their particulars' and 'the abilities of divers by means of their far distance cannot be known to the officers'.[279] John Buxton, sheriff of Norfolk for 1639, complained to Nicholas that Blofield hundred would not even permit him to see the rules by which they calculated local payments.[280] Sheriff Cholmondley of Cheshire, in order to set his assessments, had to deal with over 400 local officials.[281] In general, the temptation was always strong to place a disproportionately high burden on strangers. Edward Darling's case was probably not untypical: rated high in Normanton, Nottinghamshire because he had trade in London, he was also assessed at a high rate in London on account of his house in Normanton.[282] Successive sheriffs of Hampshire were inclined to place a high burden on the garrison town of Portsmouth, inhabited largely by foreigners, and spare their own areas.[283] Overall the sheriff faced an unenviable task: as the sheriff of the notoriously divided county of Lincoln put it, 'without the help of the inhabitants it is not possible to assess the particular persons'; but with their assistance it was nearly impossible to settle any agreed rate.[284]

Those aggrieved at their assessment were quicker to charge the sheriff with wilful partiality than to recognize his problems. The city of Bristol in a petition to the Council referred to the 'unequal and partial dealing of the high sheriff of the counties of Somerset and Gloucester'.[285] Gervase Markham accused the sheriff of Nottingham of a 'vulture humour' on seeing his assessment.[286] The historian should not read this rhetoric as evidence of a corrupt shrievalty, when

279. Darrell of Calehill MS U 386/05/9.
280. *HMC Various II*, pp. 252–3.
281. See E. Marcotte, 'Shrieval administration of ship money in 1637: Limitations in early Stuart governance', *Bull. John Rylands Library*, 58 (1975), pp. 137–72. I am grateful to Elaine Marcotte (Hyams) for an offprint of this important article and for a helpful discussion of ship money in Cheshire.
282. *Cal. Stat. Pap. Dom., 1635*, p. 548.
283. P. Haskell, 'Ship money in Hampshire', in J. Webb, N. Yates and S. Peacock (eds) *Hampshire Studies* (Portsmouth, 1981), pp. 73–113, esp. pp. 92–4.
284. *Cal. Stat. Pap. Dom., 1639–40*, p. 556.
285. Bristol Common Council Books, 3, f.58.
286. *Cal. Stat. Pap. Dom., 1635–6*, p. 11.

even the most conscientious sheriffs faced the same charges. It was a genuine misunderstanding in Yorkshire in 1636 that led the town of Tadcaster to be assessed (differently) by both the city of York and the county sheriff, but the ensuing dispute sparked an act of vandalism in April when the city arms were thrown off Tadcaster bridge.[287] In Northamptonshire in 1635 Sheriff John Dryden appears to have taken great pains to arrive at a fair rating – consulting the purveyance roll, the list of the levies of fifteenths, the subsidy roll, all of which rated the east divisions of the county above the west; and he made real efforts to explain the basis of his rating, pointing out to Sir Edward Montagu that in the hundreds of the eastern part 'there are earls and lords of greater estate'.[288] He won little respect for his pains. His successor tried to be as accommodating and also ran into trouble. In March 1636 Charles Cockayne related how he had assessed Burton Latimer of the county at £25; receiving complaints from Thomas Bacon and others that it was unequal, he called constables, church-wardens and one of Bacon's tenants to make a new assessment. Bacon did not pay it; along with others he complained that it had not been made officially and instigated a third assessment: meanwhile the constables proceeded to collect according to the second.[289] Humphrey Chetham, sheriff for Lancashire in 1635, exhibited great care and scrupulousness: he met with the mayors, assessed the hundreds according to their customary book of rates, calling on the constables and consulting other assessors whose integrity had been affirmed. Still when his warrants went out, drawn up with 'good advice and great circumspection', there were complaints and delays.[290] In Kent, Edward Shute was clearly pained by the charges of partiality levelled at him after all his assiduous efforts to follow directions and secure a fair assessment. As he wrote, by way of self-justification to Sir Edward Dering:

> I am heartily sorry that so many of my respected friends and judicious neighbours should censure me and my proceedings in a business of this weight and consequences, or that any should tax me of partiality or inconsideration herein when I protest by the faith of a Christian and reputation of a gentleman I have in my judgement used all probable means to inform myself of the true worth of each hundred, and have imposed a tax upon them severally proportionable thereunto. Wherein I must confess I have not so much looked at the quantity of the land . . . as at the quality and ability of the

287. York House Books, 35, p. 318.
288. Montagu MS 15, f.66; *Cal. Stat. Pap. Dom., 1635*, p. 482.
289. *Cal. Stat. Pap. Dom., 1635–6*, p. 331.
290. *Cal. Stat. Pap. Dom., 1635*, p. xx.

> persons there resident . . . which course though it be not so pleasing unto some, yet it is, I am sure, most agreeable to the writ and the express directions in the Lords letters than to subject poor farmers and occupiers of land at racked rents to the payment of the greater part of this extraordinary imposition.[291]

Like Dryden trying to justify himself to Montagu, Shute felt isolated and spurned in the county of his charge. The lone sheriff is a familiar figure in the mythology of the wild west: ship money created many in the midst of the counties of England.

For even the Privy Council from whom the sheriff took his orders offered him little help. Indeed where rating disputes were concerned, the Council had two different, often contradictory, roles to play. On the one hand it was an executive body, issuing writs and instructions. On the other, traditionally and in the absence of parliaments all the more necessarily, the Council was also a tribunal of appeal, receiving suits, petitions and complaints from the English localities. It is clear that local magistrates and humbler men expected the Council to perform this role; recourse to the Council was both taken and threatened by those aggrieved at their assessments.[292] The city of Bristol in 1636 complained to the Council and commissioned its chamberlain to go to London to make representations to the Board;[293] Sir Edward Montagu threatened the sheriff of Northamptonshire that if his assessments were not amended, he would complain to the Lords.[294] When powerful corporations and well-connected individuals made such threats the sheriffs, as their many justificatory pleas to the Council evidence, were much troubled. In the case of Northamptonshire, the Earl of Manchester, Montagu's brother and a Privy Councillor himself, joined in the attack on the sheriff, accusing Dryden of overrating his tenants.[295] Personal interests were not absent from the Council Board. Even where no particular Councillor's interests were at stake, the Council felt bound to investigate all complaints and to seek an amicable solution. In so doing they bound their hands with years of painstaking investigations that diverted attention from the other business of government and the programme of reform.

As early as 1635 a large number of Council meetings were being taken up by ship money disputes.[296] At times the Council could

291. Dering MS U 1107/C.12, 30 Sept. 1635; cf. Twysden MS U 47/47, Zi, p. 133.
292. Cf. P. Lake, 'The collection of ship money in Cheshire during the 1630s: a case study of relations between central and local government', *Northern History*, 17 (1981), pp. 44–71, esp. pp. 54–7.
293. Bristol Common Council Books, 3, f.66v.
294. Montagu MS 3, f.220: Montagu to Sir Thomas Brooke, 16 Oct. 1635.
295. Montagu MS 33, Box B2/22: Manchester to Montagu, 31 Dec. 1635.
296. Trumbull Add. MS 55.

provide useful support: on 22 May 1637 Sir William Widdrington, sheriff of Northumberland, mentioned to Nicholas the inequalities between rural and urban parts in the county's rating, which threw a disproportionate burden on the poor.[297] A week later the Council instructed the assize judges on the northern circuit to deal with the problem at the assizes.[298] The sheriff of Kent in 1635 thanked the Council for its assistance in resolving a problem with Sandwich.[299] In 1636 Nicholas laboured to adjust charges in response to sheriffs' letters, local petitions and other information, lowering Hereford, for instance, and raising Leicestershire.[300] Too often, however, Council intervention served only to undermine the sheriff's authority and further frustrate the progress of collection. Sometimes the Council merely referred a petition back to the sheriff and urged him to act on it.[301] On other occasions, they brought in different local officials to adjudicate disputes. In January 1636 the assize judges were instructed to settle a disagreement over rates in Northamptonshire.[302] In Lincolnshire the lord-lieutenants and their deputies were called in to arbitrate.[303] In Somerset, Bishop Pierce of Bath and Wells was asked to resolve the difference between the sheriff and Sir Robert Phelips over the assessment of Northover.[304] Such courses often resulted in long delays and took from the sheriff his greatest advantage – his allegedly final authority over assessments – leaving him exposed to the power fluctuations of local politics.

What threw all into confusion was the Council's reassessments by its own authority. In November 1635, as a result of the Council's abatement of the assessment on Norwich from £1,100 to £774, the sheriff had to re-rate the whole county.[305] The same month the under-sheriff of Shropshire, Robert Madocks, warned Nicholas that any further reduction in Shrewsbury's assessment (already lowered from £780 to £450) would mean he would have to lay a 'second assessment upon the whole county which will beget great trouble'.[306] Richard Murden, sheriff of Warwick, countered Coventry's complaints about its charge with a similar warning: 'if there should be an alteration in the assessment, it would occasion fresh labour throughout the county and so prejudice the service . . . there would be such manifold complaints that

297. *Cal. Stat. Pap. Dom., 1637*, p. 139.
298. *Ibid.*, p. 167.
299. *Cal. Stat. Pap. Dom., 1635*, p. 426.
300. PRO, SP 16/329/73.
301. For example, PRO, PC 2/43/298; *Cal. Stat. Pap. Dom., 1635*, p. 407.
302. *Cal. Stat. Pap. Dom., 1635–6*, p. 188.
303. *Cal. Stat. Pap. Dom., 1636–7*, p. 149.
304. PRO, PC 2/45/348, Jan. 1636; cf. *Cal. Stat. Pap. Dom., 1636–7*, p. 401.
305. *Cal. Stat. Pap. Dom., 1635*, p. 478.
306. *Ibid.*, p. 480.

the service would be retarded'.[307] His admonition proved ineffective. In January 1636 Murden's successor, Verney, did have to re-rate on account of the Council's abatement of Coventry;[308] worse, two months later his calculations were again thrown into confusion by a Conciliar order in response to a petition from Birmingham. 'This,' he could only wail, 'produces a new retardation to the service as that of Coventry has done', adding the fear that Warwick and other towns were likely to follow suit with petitions that would retard all.[309] Still the next year, in response to such petitions, the Council 'eased' not only Birmingham but Colchester, Northampton, Maidstone, Camelford, Launceston and other towns.[310] In other words, whilst it continued to issue orders and letters chivvying and scolding sheriffs who were tardy in making their payments, the Council in its responses to local petitions and complaints was often responsible for those very delays. It could not act otherwise. The Earl of Bridgewater, who as president of the Marches was involved in many disputed cases, put the problem with stark accuracy. Writing to the Lord Keeper, he commented: 'unless some course may be taken for even and equal proportionable assessments I fear some difficulty, for your Lordship may remember how many complaints were presented the last time . . . and though some were relieved by the Board, yet divers found no ease.'[311]

Was there a solution to be found? For all the difficulties some contemporaries evidently thought so. Nicholas worked hard to take on board previous experience, complaints and information required in revising assessments; the Council reviewed position papers, like that of Sir Anthony Weldon which promised an end to or abatement of inequalities and disputes.[312] A sheriff like Shute appeared to believe that the Council might gradually settle his disagreements with other towns, as it had that with Sandwich.[313] More generally, and interestingly, at an important discussion of ship money at the assizes in Kent, some argued 'that for the inconveniences the inequalities did produce, a few years would so settle it that every city, town, hundred and parish should know what they were to pay and then there would be no great matter but what the high sheriff himself would easily redress'.[314] This optimism, though somewhat naive, was not entirely without

307. *Ibid.*, p. 405.
308. *Cal. Stat. Pap. Dom., 1635–6*, p. 145.
309. *Ibid.*, p. 278.
310. PRO, PC 2/48/363, Nov. 1637.
311. *Cal. Stat. Pap. Dom., 1635–6*, p. 6; *1637*, p. 46; PRO, SP 16/329/73, 74.
312. Ellesmere MS 7239: Bridgewater to Coventry, 20 Sept. 1636; *Cal. Stat. Pap. Dom., 1637–8*, pp. 233–4.
313. *Cal. Stat. Pap. Dom., 1635*, p. 426. He asked for the Council's help with Maidstone.
314. Twysden MS U 47/47/Zi, p. 198.

foundation. By the end of 1637 there is some impression that rating disputes were fewer in number and that the Council was beginning to emerge from under the burden of them.[315] Certainly, the fairness of ship money assessments, as opposed to earlier ratings, was beginning to dawn. In Warwickshire they became the basis for all other local levies, as they were to be the rule by which the levies of the 1640s were often assessed.[316] After the Restoration, Sir Peter Temple (whose testimony is the more powerful because he did not concur with it) recalled 'a generally received opinion that the ship rate was the most equal rate that ever was found out to measure the value of the kingdom by'.[317] However, if the situation was improving and perception changing, both happened too late. Sheriffs met with new as well as longstanding disagreements; the Council clerk had to number in a small signifying hand the writ from which the dispute had arisen, in order to keep track of quarrels as the years passed.[318] Disputes from 1635 were still being investigated in 1639;[319] sometimes the overworked clerk could not even discern for which writ an assessment was contested.[320] Ship money placed a colossal strain on the whole structure of government. Rating disputes came to dominate the records of the Council from 1634, as they did the levies of many officials, of central and local government, who had much other (and as they saw it more important) business to deal with.

Recently it has been argued that these rating disputes were more than just that. That they were in fact a strategy for opposing the tax, their purpose being to delay and stymie because it was dangerous to take a clear stand against the levy as an unconstitutional innovation. In letters to the Council especially, it is argued, opponents of the levy were more likely to pursue a practical petition for an abatement than the dangerous course of questioning the legality of the charge.[321] We shall have cause later to examine opposition to ship money in the context of reactions and resistance to the personal rule; but some remarks are appropriate here. The suggestion that rating disputes were a mask for more fundamental opposition to the tax is not entirely without credit. Before it became evident that ship money was to become a regular levy, any form of delay, in the hope that one might

315. This from reading through the Council register. Of course, not long after the resolution of Hampden's case, the Council was involved in preparations for the Scots war.
316. Hughes, *Politics, Society and Civil War*, p. 108; Morrill, *Revolt of the Provinces*, p. 59.
317. Temple of Stowe MSS, Ship Money Box: speech of Sir Peter Temple.
318. For example, PRO, PC 2/48/26.
319. PRO, PC 2/50/382.
320. PRO, PC 2/48/186 has the hand with '?2' written inside it.
321. Especially by P. Lake, in 'The collection of ship money in Cheshire'; R. Cust and A. Hughes (eds) *Conflict in Early Stuart England* (1989), pp. 13, 31. These take too little note of opponents who did take a stand. (See my discussion below, pp. 717–21)

not again be bothered, made sense: we do not need to go to great lengths to explain why people were not quick to open their purses. Others delayed in 1637 and 1639 in the hope that Hampden's case or parliament might terminate their duty to pay.[322] In some cases too it is clear that questioning an assessment could be the first step to a more principled challenge to the tax. At a public meeting at Hatfield, Hertfordshire in 1635, one Mr Taverner (who had already been examined by the Council for injudicious words) 'scornfully said, if any men were unequally rated, the Court of Requests was fit to relieve him'.[323] Those who were less outspoken *may* have been no less opposed to the levy. Behind the many disputes over the assesssment of Tintinhull hundred, Somerset, we may detect, and further suspect, the hand of Sir Robert Phelips who, as well as acting from personal interests and perpetrating personal rivalries and vendettas, may have been opposed in principle to the levy and determined to disrupt it.[324] The constables who deliberately made unequal assessments appear to have done so under Phelips's orders and protection – though Phelips himself was able to escape the blame and ire of the government.[325] However, the Council's declaration in November 1635 that Phelips had 'done nothing in the service of the shipping but what became a good subject and a well-affected person to his county' should make us cautious about too free an employment of the term opposition.[326] For even if they had their own shrewd reasons for not labelling Phelips as refractory, the Council's response to the differences in Somerest suggests that they drew a line between a rating dispute and a stand on principle.

It is clear, *pace* Lake and others, that they were right to do so. As we have seen, rating disputes had long occurred over other, less contentious levies – not least in Tintinhull hundred itself.[327] Those over ship money, even when manufactured, did not always evidence lofty principles: the deputy lieutenants of Derbyshire told the Earl of Newcastle in 1638 that one Mr Woodhouse of Glapwell, who represented several towns in their petitions to the Board, stirred unnecessary disputes because he had 'suits of his own which occasion almost his constant attending at London every term'.[328] More damaging to the argument, those who paid as well as those who collected

322. Below, pp. 587–8, 591.
323. *Cal. Stat. Pap. Dom., 1635*, p. 396.
324. Barnes, *Somerset*, pp. 214–19; cf. A. Fletcher, 'National and local awareness in the county communities', in H. Tomlinson (ed.) *Before the English Civil War* (1983), pp. 151–74, esp. pp. 157–9.
325. See *Cal. Stat. Pap. Dom., 1635*, pp. 119, 409, 502.
326. *Ibid.*, p. 502; *Cal. Stat. Pap. Dom., 1637*, p. 133.
327. Bates-Harbin, *Quarter Sessions Records for . . . Somerset*, p. 52.
328 *Cal. Stat. Pap. Dom., 1637–8*, pp. 494–5, 20 May 1638.

the levy often endeavoured to see that disputes did not disrupt collection. In Kent, for example, in 1635 the inhabitants of Linton complained that they had never been taxed before with Maidstone and petitioned against their assessment, meanwhile submitting 'themselves and the monies'.[329] From Nottinghamshire in 1637, Timothy Pusey wrote to Secretary Coke to inform him that he and other JPs had complained to the Council about the sheriff's abatement of his own hundred's charge at the expense of theirs, stressing: 'we are willing to pay and would not hinder the service, but loathe to have such a new precedent put upon us.'[330] Gloucestershire, protesting against its disproportionate assessment, placed its trust in the Council: 'This unequal proceeding would have hindered his Majesty's service but the chief inhabitants encouraged the payment rather than the service should be retarded, in hope they should be released by the Lords.'[331] The poor progress of the levy in Chynbury, Richard Harris told the Earl of Bridgewater, came from objections less to the tax than to the mode of assessment.[332] It would be naive to take all such statements at face value: in petitions to the Council, especially suits for redress, loyal rhetoric was more appropriate than grudging language. But not all expressions of loyalty were a rhetorical veil over the reality of opposition. Sheriffs themselves reported that fairer assessment could remove the blocks and lead to payment 'with contentment'.[333] In the end, actions speak louder than words – and still louder than silence. Even allowing that some expressed deep-felt resentment, rating disputes did not stop the payment of ship money into the Treasury of the Navy. Even while disputes continued, the money (albeit sometimes slowly) came in.

The payment of ship money

It did so not least because throughout the king and Council concentrated their energies on the collection. From the issue of the second writ, to the whole country, the king instituted regular Sunday meetings of the Council, over which he presided, to review the progress of the collection and the reports from the sheriffs.[334] Edward Nicholas was given special responsibility for keeping a record of all information arising from the writs, and was required to keep a book of all orders

329. *Cal. Stat. Pap. Dom., 1634–5*, p. 473.
330. Coke MS 56, 4 Dec. 1637.
331. *Cal. Stat. Pap. Dom., 1635*, p. 470.
332. Ellesmere MS 6976, 16 Oct. 1635.
333. *Cal. Stat. Pap. Dom., 1636–7*, pp. 3–4.
334. *Cal. Stat. Pap. Dom., 1635*, p. xxiv.

and letters relating to it.[335] As the problems arose, the Sunday meetings endeavoured to tackle them and refine procedure. In January 1637 the sheriffs were ordered to certify Nicholas fortnightly of their progress.[336] In addition each Saturday the Treasurer of the Navy sent him accounts of the monies paid and owed by each county.[337] After noting what was still in the hands of the sheriffs and calculating the remains, Nicholas presented the accounts, after burning the midnight oil, the next day. He kept the records of each writ in a separate book, and evidently a sort of filofax of reminders.[338] The labour was phenomenal. In 1636 Sir William Russell was asking for a 3d. in the pound commission on ship money to pay his clerks, as the £150 allowed him was proving inadequate.[339] The next year Nicholas's assistants were awarded an extra £30, 'having taken extraordinary pains in writing a large minute of letters to the sheriffs of England and Wales'.[340] With awe-inspiring efficiency, Nicholas even managed to rise above the detail of the daily administration and accounts. He wrote position papers on improving the mode of collection, and the Council took some sensible and imaginative steps to facilitate payment.[341] In 1635 it invited the sheriffs of all counties to send able representatives to Whitehall to peruse the ship money accounts, 'so that those who contributed may have the satisfaction to understand how those monies . . . have been issued'.[342] In 1637 they sent letters to inform the counties that the judges in camera had 'with one consent declared the legality of that service'.[343] As well as chivvying sheriffs and summoning them to the Board, the Council's review committee sent letters of praise and eventually offered a sweetener to its overworked agents.[344] At last, responding to suggestions that they be paid for their pains, the Council in May 1640 issued a warrant to the Treasurer of the Navy to pay 6d. in the pound to those sheriffs who paid their county's charge in full.[345] A newswriter told Viscount Scudamore that

335. PRO, PC 2/44/371; PC 2/45/207; *Cal. Stat. Pap. Dom., 1635*, p. 469. The treasurer of the navy signed two acquittances on receipt of payment, one to the payer, the other to Nicholas (*ibid.*, p. 452).
336. *Cal. Stat. Pap. Dom., 1636–7*, p. 379, order of king in Council, 22 Jan.
337. *Cal. Stat. Pap. Dom., 1637–8*, p. viii.
338. *Cal. Stat. Pap. Dom., 1637*, p. 457. That for 1637 he listed as 'my fourth book' (*ibid.*, p. 46); *1635–6*, p. 82; *1639*, p. 544.
339. *Cal. Stat. Pap. Dom., 1635–6*, p. 240. This was granted in June 1637 (*Cal. Stat. Pap. Dom., 1637*, p. 194).
340. *Cal. Stat. Pap. Dom., 1637*, p. 452.
341. *Cal. Stat. Pap. Dom., 1637*, p. 284; PRO, SP 16/329/73, 74; SP 16/363/34.
342. *Cal. Stat. Pap. Dom., 1635*, p. 407.
343. PRO, PC 2/48/136.
344. For example, PRO, PC 2/48/101, PC 2/49/354; examples of letters of congratulation are in PC 2/47/163 and PC 2/51/89.
345. *Cal. Stat. Pap. Dom., 1640*, p. 251: warrant of 31 May; cf. the rebuke five years earlier of the sheriff of Shropshire who had paid the 6d. on his own initiative (*Cal. Stat. Pap. Dom., 1635*, p. 545).

they would receive 12d. in the pound to cover their expenses.[346] Together with a remarkably efficient procedure of review and account, such tactics and sustained Conciliar pressure gradually ameliorated the difficulties and reduced the arrears on the writs as the months passed.

Ship money indeed, for all its problems, must qualify as one of the most successful taxes, indeed governmental enterprises, in early modern history. As Miss Gordon's figures revealed long ago, between 1634 and 1638 90 per cent of the ship money assessments was paid – what Dr Morrill has described as 'an extraordinary achievement by seventeenth century standards, and a far higher percentage than was later achieved by the parliamentary subsidies and poll tax [*sic*!]'.[347] As we shall see, corrections to Gordon's figures indicate that even more was paid than she calculated and the achievement was more extraordinary still.[348] The writ of 1635 imposed £218,500 on the whole country, a sum nearly equivalent to that raised by the grant of five subsidies in 1628. Though the amount was large – equal to the largest parliamentary grant given that century – and though the extension of ship money to the inland counties was unusual, the response was excellent both in the amount and speed of the return. Members of the Council and foreign committee were soon after the issue of the writ expressing their optimism. As early as 29 October (the writ had been issued in August) Windebank wrote to Hopton, 'the business of levying of monies for the next year's fleet goes on in the counties very cheerfully and some of them have already sent in their proportions of ready money'.[349] The king sat in Council inspecting the returns and 'discharges no sheriff till all the money of the county be paid in'.[350] There is little sign that coercion was necessary. At the assizes in Northamptonshire the justices announced the levy and its purpose and, Manchester told his brother Montagu, 'I hear it is well digested by the county.'[351] Twysden, who was himself doubtful about the legality of the tax, noted that in 1635 'there was not any in Kent that refused this peremptorily' and observed that when one Richard Spencer, son of Lord Spencer of Northamptonshire (whose family has in recent years risen closer to the throne), refused, a kinsman paid on his behalf.[352] In the end Kent paid £200 more than it was assessed, the surplus being allocated for repair of the county highways.[353] The picture appears to be the same across the country: the Reverend

346. BL Add. MS 11045, f.74: Rossingham to Scudamore, 19 Nov. 1639.
347. M.D. Gordon, 'The collection of ship money in the reign of Charles I', *Trans. Royal Hist. Soc.*, 3rd series, 4 (1910), pp. 141–62; Morrill, *Revolt of the Provinces*, p. 24.
348. Below, pp. 590–91.
349. Egerton MS 1820, f.55.
350. Montagu MS 33, Box B2/21: Manchester to Montagu, 21 Dec. 1635.
351. Montagu MS 6, f.71.
352. Twysden MS U 47/47, Z2, p. 189.
353. *Ibid.*

Garrard informed Wentworth, 'I do not hear of any numbers that are refusers so that it will prove a good business.'[354] The Council spoke of the service being 'cheerfully performed'; and were supported by the Venetian ambassador who believed that a desire to end the injuries they suffered at the hands of other nations fostered willing compliance.[355] Even 'the lesser folk,' he reported, 'agree to pay fairly readily, without waiting to be compelled.'[356] The returns bear out such optimistic prognostications and reports. Final accounts show the arrears at only £4,536.[357] More impressively, within a year of the issue of the writ over £180,000 (with London's contribution of ships, equal to over 90 per cent of the demand)[358] had come in;[359] and by the end of 1636 nearly £189,000 – about 95 per cent.[360] To say the least, it was a very encouraging beginning.

It may have been this very success that finally persuaded the Council to reissue the second writ the following autumn. This time £196,400 was demanded and again by the time of Russell's final account, the arrears were only £6,907.[361] But while the arrears were not significantly greater, the levy came in, as Coke told Juxon, more slowly.[362] The sheriff of Cambridgeshire reported in March that though none was refusing, payment was slow 'as men . . . are loathe to part with their money';[363] the sheriff of Dorset more dramatically described the poor 'who pay this like drops of blood'.[364] We may venture some explanations. Clearly the second assessment of the tax on the nation and the reiterated claim of an emergency caused some concern: the history of the loan illustrates that what men willingly pay as an extraordinary levy they may question as a regular tax. The writ of 1636 may have encountered the beginnings of a principled opposition.[365] But the large sum collected suggests there may be other explanations for the slower response. The writ itself was issued a month later and so lost the sheriff an important month of good weather and easy travel. The unresolved rating disputes of the previous year and the precedents to which they gave rise introduced complications.[366] The collection

354. Knowler, *Strafford Letters*, I, p. 491.
355. *Cal. Stat. Pap. Dom., 1635*, p. 544.
356. *Cal. Stat. Pap. Venet., 1632–6*, p. 325; cf. p. 434.
357. Rushworth, *Historical Collections*, II, p. 344: accounts signed May 1640.
358. Dietz, *English Public Finance*, p. 275.
359. *Cal. Stat. Pap. Dom., 1636–7*, p. 119.
360. *Ibid.*, p. 375.
361. BL, Lansdowne MS 232, p. 34; Rushworth, *Historical Collections*, II, p. 344.
362. Coke MS 54.
363. *Cal. Stat. Pap. Dom., 1636–7*, p. 487.
364. *Ibid.*, p. 150.
365. Below, p. 719.
366. See, for example, *Cal. Stat. Pap. Dom., 1636–7*, p. 488: sheriff of Shropshire to Nicholas, 17 Feb. 1637.

was impeded too by the plague, first identified in the spring of 1636, which became a major epidemic from the autumn through 1637 and into 1638.[367] Some towns like King's Lynn in Norfolk, though not disputing their assessment, petitioned to have it reduced on account of the effects of plague on their ability to pay.[368] A favourable response led, of course, to revised assessments elsewhere and hence to difficulties and delays. Windebank identified another problem, to which the Council was to become sensitive for the rest of the decade. Writing to Coke in the summer of 1636, he emphasized the urgent need for more effective action against pirates, 'that his Majesty's subjects . . . may be relieved and the service of the shipping the next year receive no impediment which is much to be feared it will if the clamours should continue'.[369] Though the navy achieved some successes – such as forcing the Dutch to take licences for fishing – the failure to eradicate the problem of piracy may have made some suspicious that the money was paid to little effect or, worse, diverted to other purposes. But if payments came in a little more slowly, their tardiness should not be exaggerated: within a year 85 per cent of the levy had been paid; within eighteen months over 95 per cent.[370] Things could hardly have been proceeding better.

The writ of 1637 met perhaps with the greatest foot-dragging of all. By March 1638 both secretaries were expressing their concern at the slow payment and sheriffs were summoned to the Board, as the season for setting out the fleet approached without the money to finance it.[371] It is traditional to attribute the sluggishness of this year to a mounting opposition fuelled by Hampden's challenge to the legality of the tax and the widespread publicity the case received. But once again, as we shall see, the story was more complicated.[372] Certainly while the case was pending, payments came in slowly as men delayed, awaiting the outcome of the legal decision. In June 1637 William Walter, sheriff of Oxfordshire, informed the Council that the case was affecting his collection: 'I find,' he wrote, 'many harbour an opinion that this case is depending in trial at the suit of some of their neighbours and they will first see the issue of that.'[373] Counties that had formerly paid quickly were reported as amassing arrears.[374] But once again we must note that

367. Cf. below, pp. 622–5; P. Slack, *The Impact of Plague in Tudor and Stuart England* (1985).
368. PRO, PC 2/48/101.
369. Coke MS 58, 24 Aug. 1638.
370. *Cal. Stat. Pap. Dom., 1637*, p. 455; *1639–40*, p. 551.
371. *Cal. Stat. Pap. Dom., 1637–8*, p. 297: Coke to Windebank, 7 March 1638.
372. Cf. below, pp. 728–9.
373. *Cal. Stat. Pap. Dom., 1637*, p. 196, 7 June.
374. *Cal. Stat. Pap. Dom., 1637–8*, pp. 243, 244, 246, 289, 337. Bedfordshire, which had paid well over 90 per cent of the first three writs, paid only just over a third in 1638. I

the figures will not sustain any argument for a collapse. The final yield was £178,599, leaving an arrear of £17,814.[375] The chronology of payments is revealing. In July 1638 the sum outstanding was £78,000, twice that of the year before;[376] but by October, when the case had been decided for the crown, they had fallen by £30,000, and the yield of ship money was only £23,000 less than the preceding year.[377] By the end of 1638 nearly 85 per cent of the levy had been paid.[378] In other words, the effect of Hampden's case had been to delay this proportion of the collection by three months. The delay led the collection to run into the next writ and may have impaired the subsequent levy of arrears, but the final yield still exceeded 90 per cent – hardly the beginning of the end.[379]

As well as Hampden's case, the collection of ship money in 1638 encountered other problems. The plague remained one: Sandwich was given longer to pay in April on account of the sickness in the town.[380] Hugh Nanney, sheriff of Merioneth, who heard 'of none that are refractory' nevertheless attributed delay to the 'scarcity of money among the meaner sort'.[381] Some defaulters in Surrey were found to have no goods to distrain.[382] Added to plague and hardship, the continuing problems of pirates blunted the willingness to pay. In August, Windebank expressed his fear to Coke that if the seas were not made safe 'it will give impediment to the levying of the ship money in arrear, which this service hath little need of at this time'.[383] There was also a new problem – the beginning of the troubles in Scotland, which undoubtedly diverted some of the government's attention and produced in the realm an atmosphere of uncertainty. Given these other impediments and the sums collected, there is no reason to conclude that Hampden's case made a major impact on ship money.

What was to impede and ultimately to all but wreck the collection of ship money was the war against the Scots.[384] The decision to lower the sum demanded to £69,750, a mere third of the earlier writs, was probably related to Charles's determination, during the summer of 1638, to enforce his will on the Scots.[385] For a war against the northern

would like to thank Michael Cole for a fruitful discussion of the regional patterns of ship money payments.

375. Dietz, *English Public Finance*, p. 280.
376. *Cal. Stat. Pap. Dom., 1637–8*, pp. 564, 578.
377. *Cal. Stat. Pap. Dom., 1638–9*, p. 64.
378. *Ibid.*, p. 295.
379. *Cal. Stat. Pap. Dom., 1639–40*, p. 527.
380. PRO, PC 2/49/89.
381. *Cal. Stat. Pap. Dom., 1637–8*, p. 328.
382. *Cal. Stat. Pap. Dom., 1638–9*, p. 2.
383. Coke MS 58, 24 Aug. 1638.
384. Cf. Morrill, *Revolt of the Provinces*, p. 28.
385. Lansdowne MS 232, p. 34.

kingdom would involve other charges, and the immediate necessity appeared to be on land rather than at sea. The smaller sum requested, however, did not secure, as may have been intended, speedy payment. In May the Privy Council wrote ordering the sheriffs to greater diligence, 'upon consideration of the slow coming in of ship money this year'.[386] Two months later, Windebank expressed to Coke his regret that 'the monies this year come in so slowly, the year being near expired and but half of the monies collected'.[387] This was more than pessimistic rhetoric: after a year only just over £40,000 had been paid in, under 60 per cent of the small total demanded.[388] The last months of 1639, however, saw a considerable improvement in the rate of collection, perhaps because the news of the Treaty of Berwick (concluded in the summer) spread back to promise the end of the burden of the Scots war. By December arrears had nearly halved from their October level and only £16,739 was still owing.[389] At the final assessment in the spring of 1640, £55,690 (80 per cent) had been raised.[390] The situation may have been even better than the bare sums signify, for it is clear that some ship money paid in 1639 was purloined for other, more pressing purposes and probably never reached the Treasury of the Navy. On 25 April, for example, the sheriff of Leicestershire explained to Nicholas:

> in regard of the many taxes that have lately been for soldiers and horses, most constables allege that they cannot get in the money although some had gathered part, but a tax coming for horses at four days' warning they were constrained to lay down that money having no time to gather other monies in so short a period. And truly I find that money is very scant for the present in regard of the late taxes, and that many which are well affected and willing to pay, yet do not for want of money, but desire a little respite.[391]

The sheriff of Anglesey concurred; poverty held up the collection.[392] Sir Thomas Powell of Denbigh met with similar experience of what university administrators would now call the 'virement' of funds: 'I am informed,' he told Nicholas in May, that 'some part being collected before it could be paid over to me has been used to pay conduct money for soldiers which, in regard of the present necessity for despatch in that service, the deputy lieutenants deemed a tolerable encroach-

386. PRO, PC 2/50/318.
387. Coke MS 62, 16 July 1639.
388. *Cal. Stat. Pap. Dom., 1639–40*, p. 16, 5 Oct. 1639.
389. *Ibid.*, p. 164, 14 Dec. 1639.
390. Dietz, *English Public Finance*, p. 280.
391. *Cal. Stat. Pap. Dom., 1639*, p. 81.
392. *Ibid.*, p. 84.

ment.'[393] He hoped – it was probably a pious hope – that the constables would make up what had been purloined. We cannot know how much ship money collected was diverted in this way. But we can be sure that they, along with other revisions, would have pushed the collection well beyond 80 per cent, far from a failure for the fifth levy of a tax raised amidst a myriad of other charges.

The collapse came the next – and final – year. It would appear that the Council originally had no intention to levy it. There is no reason to doubt Lord Keeper Finch's speech to the Short Parliament, in which he explained that only necessity had forced the king to change his mind and issue another writ.[394] For in November the Venetian ambassador reported a Conciliar debate on finances, at which it was '*decided at last*' to levy 'the *old* tax called ship money'.[395] Clearly the decision came as a surprise to many: Serjeant Godboult was to express his belief in the Short Parliament that 'ship money was a-dying . . .'.[396] An even greater surprise was the amount requested: £210,400. After the reduction of the previous year, it undoubtedly seemed a massive burden. If Rossingham's newsletter is to be believed, the Council and court were well aware of the resistance they were likely to encounter. It had been argued in Council, he told Viscount Scudamore, that the people would never be persuaded to pay. Though the judges had ruled the levy legal in a state of emergency, they had not authorized an annual tax and had shown reservations about imprisoning those who refused to pay. The distraint of the goods of some payers had proved ineffective when they could not be sold 'but lie rotting in the storehouses'. But on the other scale to such weighty argument, 'the King's great necessity overbalanceth all'. Moreover a cynical calculation had been made: even if many refused, two-thirds could realistically be expected, 'which is well worth the labour'.[397] In November 1639, in other words, the target the government set itself was midway between the official figure and last year's reduction: something around £140,000. Other factors were to prick the bubble even of that expectation. Only £53,000 or so was raised.[398]

Massive failure though the last writ was, it may have been less disastrous than is usually suggested, and certainly needs to be seen in context. First, there appears to be a serious error in Miss Gordon's calculations. Her tables list Cumberland and Westmorland as having

393. *Ibid.*, p. 113. For 'virement', see David Lodge, *Nice Work* (1989), p. 383.
394. J. Nalson (ed.) *An Impartial Collection of the Great Affairs of State from the Beginning of the Scotch Rebellion in 1639 to The Murder of Charles I* (2 vols, 1682–3), I, p. 325.
395. *Cal. Stat. Pap. Venet., 1636–9*, p. 596: dispatch of 25 Nov. 1639.
396. J. Maltby (ed.) *The Short Parliament Diary of Sir Thomas Aston* (Camden Soc., 4th series, 35, 1988), p. 41.
397. BL Add. MS 11045, f.43: Rossingham to Scudamore, 6 Aug. 1639.
398. Dietz, *English Public Finance*, p. 281.

paid nothing of their assessment. However, the author of the Lansdowne manuscript 'copy of the rates imposed on the several counties of this kingdom towards the providing and furnishing of ships' noted at the foot of his table: 'I suppose the counties of Cumberland and Westmorland might not be rated in the year 1640 [that is by the writ of 1639], or if it were rated not levied upon them in respect of the Scots army.'[399] More compelling evidence, Nicholas himself in his notes for November 1639 raised the 'query whether the four northern counties shall be exempted this year *as in the last*'.[400] If the four counties (as well as Cumberland and Westmorland, Durham and Northumberland) were so exempted, we must revise our returns for the writs of both 1638 and 1639 accordingly.

Secondly, the final writ commenced with an inbuilt disadvantage. The same sum of money as earlier levies was now demanded for ships of smaller tonnage.[401] There may have been respectable governmental reasons for the change, but to many (not surprisingly) it savoured of what, in modern argot, we would call a 'con'. By the beginning of February newswriters reported: 'some high sheriffs have been much troubled about the allocation of the ship writ this year as thus, whereas in some of the last years' writs the county of Suffolk was rated at £8,000 to provide 800 tons of shipping, this year that county is required by the writs to provide 640 tons of shipping but rated at the wonted sum of £8,000.'[402] Suffolk asked for an abatement. The Council's bribe that if all came in quickly they would accept £6,400 is unlikely to have struck many as fair dealing; in Kent, as we saw, it complicated the collection.[403]

The most important impedance in 1640, however, were the rumours of a parliament. Though they began to circulate by December (only weeks after the king's decision) they were initially distrusted – if only through fear that false hopes might be the more bitterly dashed.[404] But in February the writs went out for a parliament to assemble in April and thereafter ship money was perceived to be again on trial and by most condemned in anticipation of parliament's judgment. In several counties it is clear that the definite news transformed the pattern of payment. The mayor of Merioneth had collected his ship money by March;[405] Bristol was optimistic.[406] As for the maritime counties,

399. Lansdowne MS 232, p. 34.
400. *Cal. Stat. Pap. Dom., 1639–40*, p. 85.
401. *Ibid.*, p. 89.
402. BL Add. MS 11045, f.91.
403. Above, p. 558 and note 146; below p. 595.
404. For example, *Cal. Stat. Pap. Dom., 1639–40*, p. 158; cf. p. 420: extracts from letters to Cottington.
405. *Ibid.*, p. 586.
406. *Ibid.*, p. 530.

Cottington noted in February that 'the collection of ship money in Hampshire goes on so speedily that we conceive it will all be collected in very short time'.[407] In the west, 'we in Devonshire have news of a parliament, but no man believes it. The ship money we are sure of, for every man feels it already . . . yet there is no grudging . . .'.[408] In Sussex and Lancashire too most of the money had come in.[409] Within weeks the story was different: Hampshire's collection tailed off with the arrival of the writs and preparations for elections to parliament.[410] Towards the end of March, the sheriff of Berkshire told Nicholas, 'the main ground of the slackness at this present . . . is the expectation they have of the parliament that it will be represented to the King as a grievance, whereby they hope to obtain a remission.'[411] On 2 April Rossingham, who had earlier reported payment of ship money, told Scudamore, 'this parliament hath infinitely protracted this service'.[412]

There were other protractions. The renewed levies for war against the Scots after the breakdown of the peace stymied the collection in a variety of ways. Not least, the sheriff of Durham pointed out in May that some of the men assessed to pay were now in the trained bands that had been commanded out of the county![413] The costs of equipping soldiers for York everywhere reduced what little willingness there still was to pay.[414] The deputy lieutenants of Hampshire asked if they might use the ship money collected to levy horses for the supplies of the soldiers.[415] Others did so without asking. Even the Council seemed to condone such practices, ordering the sheriff of Durham to pay the money he had collected direct to the garrison at Berwick.[416] The Treasurer of the Navy, Russell, was promised a refund by the Board: it is unlikely that he received it. Around the country it was natural for nervous local communities to spend ship money feeding and moving on unruly soldiers. Some, like Bridgewater, may have been reluctant to send money up to London when wandering deserters and incidents of pillage and violence signalled that it might well not arrive safely.[417] The Council clearly believed that much more had been collected than had been received. As well as issuing a proclamation in

407. *Ibid.*, p. 420.
408. *Ibid.*
409. BL Add. MS 11045, f.92.
410. See C. Clifford, 'Ship money in Hampshire: collection and collapse', *Southern History*, 4 (1982), pp. 91–106; and P. Haskell, 'Ship money in Hampshire', pp. 73–113.
411. *Cal. Stat. Pap. Dom., 1639–40*, pp. 588–9, 26 March 1640.
412. BL Add. MS 11045, f.105.
413. *Cal. Stat. Pap. Dom., 1640*, p. 133.
414. *Ibid.*, p. 487: sheriff of Bristol to Nicholas, 17 July.
415. *Ibid.*, p. 123.
416. *Ibid.*, p. 368.
417. Coke MS 50.

August for the levy and payment of arrears, the Council, on 24 October, issued warrants to collect the sums (or their equivalent) taken by distress.[418] Sheriffs were instructed to pursue constables who had distrained goods but as yet made no account; and chief constables were ordered to enquire of parsons and curates who in each parish had paid ship money, how much and to whom. Less than a month after the issue of the warrant, however, Laud expressed the belief that 'ship money is laid aside, as a thing which will die of itself'.[419] The last attempt to gather it was abandoned. The Council never obtained the detailed information it requested, so the historian cannot gauge how much more was paid locally than reached London. It is unlikely that the totals ever reached over half what the Council expected.

It would be wrong to conclude a discussion of ship money payments on a negative note. Over the years 1634–40 nearly £800,000 was paid into the Treasury of the Navy, more than the value of all crown lands and woods sold and £200,000 more than all the subsidies received during Charles's reign.[420] Even including the last unsuccessful assessment that sum was 80 per cent of what the government demanded, and, as I have argued, more may actually have been paid than that. Payment was also – especially by the standards of the subsidy – remarkably swift. Until 1638, 90 per cent or more of ship money due on each writ was paid within a year: by comparison 'considerable' arrears on the subsidy of 1628 were still trickling into the Exchequer in 1631.[421] Where, for the military requirements of 1628, the subsidies of that year 'had only small value', each unit of ship money brought in money to pay for the fleet set out the following spring.[422] Such figures and observations must necessarily qualify the judgements of historians who see ship money sinking under mounting opposition. The geographical patterns of response and payment still await detailed exploration and more local studies. Where many counties paid the 1635 levy in full, only four were to do so in 1638.[423] But the history of local response is by no means easily categorized. Essex, the scene of an early attempt at questioning the legality of the tax, in the end paid above the national average. Hampden's county of Buckinghamshire had not been conspicuous for foot-dragging.[424] The generalization we can make is

418. J.F. Larkin (ed.), *Stuart Royal Proclamations, II: Proclamations of Charles I, 1625–1646* (Oxford, 1983), no. 311, pp. 728–30; BL MS 29/172, f.301.
419. *Works of Laud*, VI, part 2, p. 589.
420. *Cal. Stat. Pap. Dom., 1634–5*, p. 611; F.C. Dietz, *The Receipts and Issues of the Exchequer during the Reigns of James I and Charles I* (Northampton, Mass., 1928).
421. Dietz, *English Public Finance*, p. 246.
422. *Ibid.*
423. Gordon, 'Ship money', table B: Fletcher, *County Community*, p. 207. Curiously, there has been no overview of ship money since Gordon's article of 1910.
424. I am especially grateful to Michael Cole for discussions of this point.

hardly a surprising one: it was the coastal counties that had the best record of payment, a fact which may add to the suggestion that attitudes to ship money for most owed more to practical and local considerations than to high issues of principle. Overall the tax represents a triumph over thousands of particular difficulties and a successfully radical step in taxing, for the first time, some of the personal as well as landed wealth of the realm.

But it was not adequate for its purposes. The ultimate demolition of the (still repeated) myth that ship money kept Charles I solvent during the years of non-parliamentary government is the fact that it did not even pay for the navy. Philip Warwick, a clerk of the signet, tells us what the records themselves reveal: that Charles kept ship money strictly apart from his other revenue.[425] It was paid not into the Exchequer but the Treasury of the Navy where Sir William Russell kept the account; Nicholas kept a second record of the acquittances issued to those who had paid.[426] There were rumours from the beginning that ship money was not being used for the navy. To allay such fears, in February 1635 the Council ordered all expenditure arising from ship money to be kept separate from other naval finances and invited, as we saw, inspection of accounts.[427] It could do so with confidence because the rumours could not have been further from the truth. From early on there appears to have been a governmental realization that the money requested would be inadequate. In July 1635 Nicholas prepared estimates of monies needed over and above ship money to supply the ten ships that were putting to sea for three months.[428] Over the year the Exchequer contributed over £30,000 (and probably as much as £40,000) more than the sum raised by the 1634 writ (and this of course did not include the costs of ships at sea beyond the six months and through the winter).[429] Even with the great success of the first writ on the whole country, in 1636 'an overplus out of his Majesty's treasure' was still required to equip the fleet.[430] In July Russell expected to be over £16,000 short, which turned out to be over-optimistic, as the final deficit was double.[431] A costing in January 1637 of the expected expenses that spring made it clear that the writ of 1636 would not meet that year's needs, let alone, as had been hoped,

425. P. Warwick, *Memoirs of the Reign of King Charles I* (1701), p. 53.
426. Gordon, 'Ship money', pp. 141–2; *Cal. Stat. Pap. Dom., 1635*, p. 452.
427. PRO, PC 2/44/371; above, p. 584.
428. *Cal. Stat. Pap. Dom., 1635*, p. 258.
429. *Ibid.*, pp. 457, 590; *Cal. Stat. Pap. Dom., 1635–6*, p. 307. See also PRO, PC 2/50/382.
430. *Cal. Stat. Pap. Dom., 1635*, p. 407.
431. *Cal. Stat. Pap. Dom., 1636–7*, pp. 64, 351.

reimburse the last year's overplus.[432] By July £2,000 more had been spent than received, and future expenditure was set at £20,000 more than ship money arrears – assuming all the money was paid.[433]

With the writ of 1638 requesting only £69,750, the bulk of the cost of the fleet, as the Conciliar letters informed the sheriffs, was borne by the king.[434] Expenditure of royal resources, they added, had been an annual phenomenon. In May 1639 the accounts for the expenses of setting out a fleet were reviewed.[435] A realization that even the greatest sums hitherto paid had not met costs, together with an appreciation in 1639 that (especially after the previous year's reduction) yet more could not be demanded, led to the reduction in tonnage for the year's fleet. When faced with complaints about a constant charge for a smaller fleet, the Council was quick to explain, as it did to the sheriff of Kent: that

> by the experience of former years' services the proportion of £1,000 for 100 tons will not defray the charge of setting forth, manning and furnishing a ship for such time and in such manner as is required by His Majesty's writ which charge has been every year much increased through the slow payment of the monies required from the counties in as much as His Majesty has issued every year out of the Exchequer very great sums of money over and above what has been paid by the several counties for defraying the charge of such fleets . . . as by the accounts of the officers of the navy and ordnance appears.[436]

The king had, they concluded, abated the tonnage rather than increased the money. Rather than elaborate justification, it was an understatement. As Dr Aylmer demonstrated, ship money was not even sufficient to cover the expenses of the ordnance office, which received over £26,000 a year from the Exchequer in the late 1630s.[437] The ship money fleets of 1635–9, then, whatever they did to enhance England's reputation abroad, further drained the Exchequer at home. Charles I spoke honestly when he told the Short Parliament, 'for the ship money . . . he never made or intended to make any profit to himself of it, but only to preserve the dominion of the seas'.[438]

432. *Ibid.*, p. 341.
433. *Cal. Stat. Pap. Dom., 1637*, p. 319; cf. p. 500.
434. PRO, PC 2/50/532.
435. PRO, PC 2/50/382.
436. *Cal. Stat. Pap. Dom., 1639–40*, p. 308.
437. G.E. Aylmer, 'Studies in the institutions and personnel of English central administration, 1625–42' (University of Oxford, D. Phil. thesis, 1954), pp. 39ff.
438. *Bibliotheca Regia or the Royal Library* (1659), part II, pp. 341–2; cf. E. Cope (ed.) *Proceedings of the Short Parliament of 1640* (Camden Soc., 4th series, 19, 1977), p. 70, 24 April 1640.

The ship money fleets

Was the money well spent? Were the fleets effective? We have had cause to note and dissent from Gardiner's negative comments on the first ship money fleet, and we must qualify the 'practically nugatory' verdict on the effectiveness of its successors.[439] Assessment of the fleets, of course, requires consideration of their purpose, which is less simply described than might at first be thought, not least because it changed frequently. At times the Earl of Northumberland, Admiral of the Fleet, himself seemed unsure what was his role, and discontented at its limitations.[440] One rationale for the fleet had been protecting English commerce from pirates. Here its success was limited, but not negligible. During 1636 there were complaints about continuing attacks on packet boats, by French men of war in the Channel, by Dunkirkers off Ireland and by Turks off the coasts of Cornwall.[441] It may be such complaints that led Edward Read to remark to Coke in May, 'of our fleet I hear not anything is done by them'.[442] The problem was less that the fleet was redundant than that it was not big enough to be in several places at once. Though he knew his ships were needed elsewhere than the Channel in June, Northumberland could not go: 'I am doubtful,' he told the king, quite correctly, 'whether your Majesty will think fit to leave these seas without the whole fleet until the French designs be known . . .'.[443] When the next month he sailed north, he was just able to spare a couple of ships to secure the west coast from the Turks, but confessed 'it will not be in the power of a greater number of ships to keep them from coming in sometimes by stealth into those parts'.[444] As modern experience has shown, guerrillas can defy the most formidable of military opponents; in the 1630s, even with the ship money fleet, a guard could not be placed everywhere. After 1636, however, the complaints about pirates appear to be much reduced, as the fleet became a regular presence off the coasts.[445]

The second task was the protection of English fishing waters and the recently formed fishing company. As part of his claim to sovereignty of the seas, Charles required the Dutch who fished in 'English' waters to pay for a licence. Windebank instructed Northumberland that 'his

439. *Cal. Stat. Pap. Venet., 1632–6*, p. xliii; cf. Gardiner, *History of England*, VIII, p. 158.
440. For example, *Cal. Stat. Pap. Dom., 1635–6*, p. 346; cf. *1637*, p. 318: Roe to the Countess of Northumberland, 20 July; *1639*, p. 538.
441. Coke MS 53: 'Complaints of some English pillaged', 24 May 1636; J. Crewherne to Coke, 20 May 1636; *Cal. Stat. Pap. Dom., 1636–7*, p. 60.
442. Coke MS 53, 30 May 1636.
443. Coke MS 53: Northumberland to Charles I, 28 June 1636.
444. Coke MS 54: Northumberland to Charles I, 8 July 1636.
445. Coke MS 57: Windebank to Coke, 19 Feb. 1638.

Majesty is resolved they shall answer him in acknowledgement of his sovereignty and hereditary dominion in his seas, of which the fishing is a prime and principal target'.[446] A hundred licences were prepared, with a charge to the Dutch of 12d. a ton.[447] Some were doubtful of the capacity of Northumberland's fleet to enforce the claims. Conway believed that if they had to chase the Hollanders' busses, only the frigates would be fast enough to catch them.[448] Rossingham more cynically wrote that 'all the advantage . . . our fleet have of them is that they must fish in the night'.[449] Yet in August it was reported from the fleet that, though initially reluctant to pay, the Dutchmen 'when they saw they must lose their nets they found money' – one producing it from the sole of his shoe![450] One hundred and fifty busses all took licences that month, 'willingly' Secretary Coke was told.[451] And even Northumberland reported, 'I have now made them so to understand this business that the poor men now seek to us for licences and are willing to pay anything so they may have the King's protection.'[452] The Dutch, the Venetian envoy observed, were not strong enough to resist England along with their other enemies;[453] they were, Elizabeth of Bohemia told Roe, in 'a great alarm of the herring busses'.[454] Northumberland made them contribute a tenth of their catch.[455] What compromised this policy was not the inadequacy of the fleet but the change in diplomatic climate. With England entering into closer negotiations with France for an alliance against the Habsburgs, it was not easy to perpetrate aggression against French allies – the Dutch.[456] In July 1637 Windebank sent specific orders to Northumberland to go softly in the matter of the licences, if the Dutch proved unwilling: 'the truth is his Majesty in this conjuncture is not willing to proceed so roundly with them as he had done heretofore'.[457] The fleet, the secretary told Hopton, simply ceased to obstruct Dutch fishing.[458]

What it did do was raise England's standing and provide the bargaining counter that Charles could throw into one pan or another of

446. *HMC 3rd Report*, p. 72, 1 July 1636.
447. *Ibid.*: Lords of the Admiralty to Northumberland, 14 June 1636.
448. Coke MS 54: Conway to Coke, 1 Aug. 1636, aboard the *Triumph; HMC Cowper II*, p. 130.
449. T. Birch (ed.) *The Court and Times of Charles I* (2 vols, 1848), II, p. 254, 11 Oct. 1636.
450. Coke MS 54: Conway to Coke, 1 Aug. 1636.
451. *Ibid.*: Conway to Coke, 15 Aug. 1636.
452. *Ibid.*: Northumberland to Coke, 16 Aug. 1636.
453. *Cal. Stat. Pap. Venet., 1636–9*, p. 24.
454. *Cal. Stat. Pap. Dom., 1636–7*, p. 94, 15 Aug. 1636.
455. *Cal. Stat. Pap. Venet., 1636–9*, p. 52; cf. PRO, C.115/N4/8603: Northumberland to Scudamore, 14 Aug. 1636.
456. Above, pp. 525–36.
457. *Cal. Stat. Pap. Dom., 1637*, pp. 286–7, 6 July 1637.
458. *Clarendon State Papers*, II, p. 4: Windebank to Aston, 29 Dec. 1637.

the diplomatic scales. In the spring of 1637, at the time when the negotiations with France began in earnest, Kenelm Digby believed that the fleets greatly enhanced the respect of the French and Dutch for England. 'Nothing,' he opined to Conway, 'could have buoyed up the reputation of England so much as this has done.'[459] The English were, a discourse presented to the Cardinal Infant put it, 'maistres de la Manche'.[460] Most of all, the fleet continued to check any Franco-Dutch attempt on Flanders, at least until England was party to an alliance, and so preserved the security of the realm at a time when the theatre of war moved to the northern seas. A programme of shipbuilding was instigated which was to lay the foundation of the fleets with which Blake won his victories during the Commonwealth and Protectorate.[461] Because they entered into no major engagement, the ship money fleets should not be discounted. Though Northumberland began to wax discontent at his 'dull employment', the king believed his fleet 'will not be idle'.[462] In this case, the better judgement may well have been the king's.

New priorities

To sum up, the events of 1635 marked an important break in the history of Charles's eleven years of non-parliamentary government. In that year the balance of power in Europe was tilted and the diplomatic patterns rearranged by the entry of France into the war, England's disenchantment with Spain and the move towards alliance with France. From these developments emerged a renewed urgency to improve the militia and the first and second writs of ship money to equip a fleet. From the summer of 1635 until 1637 England faced the prospect (not just the possibility) of embroilment in Europe, and the risk of threats to her security. Historians of early modern France or Spain are accustomed to giving as much, or greater, prominence to foreign affairs as to domestic government. For England, little has been written – either on the making of foreign policy or on the attitudes of others to England's position. This is presumably because for most of the first half of that belligerent century England (with the exception of the fiasco of the mid-1620s) remained at peace. Yet, as modern times should make apparent, the fear of and preparations for war shape

459. *Cal. Stat. Pap. Dom., 1636–7*, pp. 378–9, 21/31 Jan. 1637.
460. H. Lonchay (ed.) *Correspondance de la cour d'Espagne sur les affaires des pays bas au XVII Siècle*, III (Brussels, 1930), p. 272: discourse on commerce.
461. D. Coke, *The Last Elizabethan: Sir John Coke, 1563–1644* (1937), p. 194.
462. A. Collins, *Letters and Memorials*, II, p. 472: Countess of Leicester to Leicester, 14 March 1637.

domestic politics, almost as much as actual engagement. And from 1635 there were major changes in the government of England at home as well as in its conduct of affairs with other nations.

Charles's values and long-term aims had not altered. The policy of reform through the reinvigoration of traditional institutions and practices was sustained and innovative projects were continued. Fen drainage programmes were extended; new statutes were devised for Oxford University; Laud used his authority to conduct a metropolitical visitation to add teeth to his efforts to reform the dioceses; assize judges continued to exhort JPs to execute diligently the Book of Orders. The reform of abuses at court continued to engage the king's and Council's attention. At the end of 1637 Charles instigated a thorough survey of his household; a commission perused the Eltham ordinances, drew up more regulations and further refined the rules of access to the various rooms at Whitehall. At the treasury, Juxon, following the work of the commissioners, began to organize the accounts and husband the king's revenue. As acting Admiral, Northumberland began an investigation into the problems in the administration of the navy and presented reports that were to lead in 1640 to the issue of detailed instructions to naval officers.[463] In the provinces, the commission of fees continued to meet; and individual JPs and deputies laboured diligently to put out apprentices, set the poor on work and muster the bands.

Yet for all these continuities, we must acknowledge that after 1635 the preoccupations and priorities of the king and Council shifted. After the death of Weston, Laud found himself on the foreign committee, alarmed by its discussions and distracted from his religious programme. New men, Holland for instance, whose priorities lay with foreign rather than domestic affairs, came to prominence. Charles I himself devoted hours to the careful perusal of dispatches from Hopton and Aston, Arundel and Leicester, to audiences with a large number of extraordinary ambassadors, and to penning personally letters to his envoys abroad. From 1635 the militia and most of all ship money dominate the Council register and push all else into the background. In the state papers we find fewer certificates returned from the Book of Orders – either because JPs were no longer pressured to send them in or because the Council no longer bothered to file them. 1635 was also, Gerald Aylmer observed, 'that year of inquiries and surveys', a year in which many aspects of domestic reform came under scrutiny.[464] Thereafter there was comparative silence: proposals for household

463. See Bodleian, Rawlinson MS A.462.
464. Aylmer, 'Studies in the central administration', p. 578; cf. pp. 112, 323, 706.

economies and reform, first promulgated in 1635, were not further discussed until the short-lived commission of 1637.

In making the decision to enter actively into the war against Spain, Richelieu (who had delayed the moment in order to gather strength) knew that he was sacrificing the programme of domestic reform that he had in mind for France.[465] Thomas, Viscount Wentworth feared that events were leading England the same way: war he knew would jeopardize all his achievements in Ireland (where the Habsburgs would seek to foment trouble). For England too he feared: 'I foresee nothing in it but *distractions* to his Majesty's affairs.'[465] Wentworth anxiously hoped that Charles would not prejudice what he had attained at home – it is clear he believed that time was healing and revitalizing – for only half-hopes and uncertain gains abroad. His plea for continued isolationism raised the rarely expressed disdain of Gardiner for a minister 'without care for the moral and spiritual interests of Europe as a whole'.[467] In the mid-1630s Wentworth's was a discordant voice in a chorus of counsels calling for action to recover the Palatinate. But it may be that in his conviction that war would jeopardize prosperity and stability at home, he was prophetic – although in the end it was to be a war against other British subjects not the Habsburgs in which Charles was to become embroiled. Despite Wentworth's fears, while tempests raged in Europe, in England the halcyon days, at least for a few more months, continued.

465. R. Bonney, *Political Change in France under Richelieu and Mazarin, 1624–1661* (Oxford, 1978), pp. 35–8; A.D. Lublinskaya, *French Absolutism: the Crucial Phase, 1620–29* (Cambridge, 1968), pp. 2, 299, 309 and *passim*; cf. J.H. Elliott, *Richelieu and Olivares* (Cambridge, 1984), ch. 3 and p. 97. I am grateful to John Elliott for stimulating discussions of this subject at the Institute for Advanced Study in 1982.

466. Knowler, *Strafford Letters*, II, p. 66: Wentworth to Laud, 3 April 1637; cf. his more muted tone in his letter to Charles I, pp. 60ff.

467. Gardiner, *History of England*, VIII, p. 215.

PART IV

CO-OPERATION AND CONFRONTATION: REACTIONS TO THE PERSONAL RULE 1629–37

X

'THE GREATEST MEASURE OF FELICITY'? CONDITIONS AND CIRCUMSTANCES

In 1637 Wentworth identified what he regarded as the achievements of the personal rule with the years of peace. Embroilment in war, he rightly foresaw, would destroy them all. It is fitting therefore that we stop to evaluate those achievements and more importantly the perceptions of the king's government before the Scots crisis threw all into turmoil. The years of Charles I's personal rule were less special, less different than traditional historiography has characterized them. In so far as they were distinctive, it was far from solely, or even primarily, because these were years without parliaments – for such there had been before.[1] Rather the 1630s were unusual years because they followed a period, rare in early modern history, of English warfare on the continent and of wars (even more rarely, patriotic historians would remind us) from which England scarcely emerged with glory. It was a decade too in which a monarch with a set of clear principles and an obsession with order endeavoured to shape his government to the blueprint of the ideals expressed at his court: represented on canvas, on the stage and in stone. The language of the government of personal rule, be it Charles's own or not, articulated the royal mind: a grammar of order, reform and efficiency – all for the good of the commonweal – underlay the communications between Whitehall and the counties. Royal and Conciliar proclamations and instructions were not innovative in their individual aims and purposes, but they were radical in their degree of coherence and sense of urgency, in their stress on the need for a renewed vigour and effectiveness in men and institutions if the fractured commonweal was to be repaired or reconstructed.

The success of the various governmental endeavours – the Book of Orders and social policy, the quest for an exact militia, Laud's pro-

1. From 1614 to 1621, for example, a period never referred to as the 'Seven Years Tyranny'.

gramme for reform of the church – we have seen to be varying and, whilst by no means negligible, limited. But was their success limited by the inherent problems and weaknesses of early modern government: by difficulties of communication, the absence of a bureaucracy, human weakness and ineptitude? Were the ambitions of those who made policy circumscribed by the laziness and indifference of local officials? Or were Charles's aims and programmes thwarted by the antagonism of deputy lieutenants and JPs, sheriffs and constables, and by the opposition of taxpayers and militia men?

Until recently, it was assumed that the answers to such questions were self-evident. Though, it was argued, censorship and fear of punishment prevented the widespread expression of outright resistance until later, during the 1630s the gentry and 'middling sort' of England impeded the attempts of the crown to refashion England into an absolutist state. The parliaments of 1640 presented them with the opportunity to dismantle what had been built. Now, we realize that the questions as well as the answers must be more complex. For in a society that lacked either a standing army to enforce its wishes or an independent paid bureaucracy to execute its policies the very terms 'compulsion' and 'resistance' (perhaps most of all that controversial word 'opposition') are fraught with complexities.[2] For in such a society, the very functioning (as well as power) of the government rested, to a large extent, on the attitudes and perceptions of its subjects – especially those nobles and gentry who were partners in ruling, but beyond, on the willingness of the lower orders to obey.[3] The authority of early modern government of course did not depend on the whims of subjects, or their like or dislike of particular courses. The Bible and the pulpit, the law and the courts, customs and habits of deference fostered a disposition to obey divinely ordained authority. But contained within the Tudor ideology of order were also other traditions and codes which could challenge it: traditions of civic independence, aristocratic conciliarism, and counsel, established codes of common law, precedent and history. (More subversively inhabiting the commonweal, if never accepted by it, were those imbued with values that had the potential to overturn the norms of society and government: puritans, atheists, and those who have been termed 'classical republicans'.)[4] In the end the authority of the government depended on

2. Cf. below, pp. 714ff.
3. Cf. A. Fletcher and J. Stevenson (eds) *Order and Disorder in Early Modern England* (Cambridge, 1985), introduction.
4. See my *Politics and Ideas in Early Stuart England* (1989), introduction; B. Worden, 'Classical republicanism and the English revolution' in H. Lloyd Jones, V. Pearl and B. Worden (eds) *History and Imagination* (1981), pp. 182–200; cf. *idem*, 'The Commonwealth kidney of Algernon Sidney', *Journ. Brit. Stud.*, 24 (1985), pp. 1–40.

men's willingness to accept it rather than on force or coercion. The degree of co-operation and confrontation depended therefore on a matrix of texts and attitudes drawn from official norms of a subject's duty, and these other codes (including individual religious convictions) and perceptions of customary modes of proceeding, in both local and national affairs.[5]

How then, we need to ask, did the English people of the 1630s perceive the government of Charles I? What were their attitudes to the suspension of parliaments? How did they react to the policies promulgated? What were the consequences for the localities of the Council's commands and how did the counties and hundreds view them? To what extent was there willing co-operation with, resentful compliance with or simmering opposition to the programmes of personal rule, or indeed to the Caroline regime in general?

Material conditions

Such questions themselves need to be placed in a broader context – that of the material and, we might say, psychological circumstances of the decade of personal rule. It is not easy to write with confidence about the economy and society of the 1630s. Historians tend to write about social and economic change over long periods that do not follow the chronologies of political history; we do not have the detailed evidence, especially statistics, to assess wealth, still less 'quality of life' at precise periods. Most of all, generalizations about the conditions of any group are subject to an infinite number of local and individual variables. Nevertheless, with such reservations in mind, we are able to sketch some outlines of the condition of the decade. Economic historians who do not always agree about very much do concur in seeing the period around 1630 as a turning point in the economic history of early modern England – and a turning point for the better.[6] For about that time the rapid population growth that had been a characteristic of the last century began to level off, and with that, the high inflation it had fuelled began to dampen and prices to stabilize. Compared with the period 1590–1630, which Dr Bowden described as 'among the most terrible years through which the country has every passed', the following decade saw the dawn of better days.[7] It saw too the

5. Cf. Sharpe, *Politics and Ideas*, pp. 21–3.
6. See, for recent surveys, K. Wrightson, *English Society, 1580–1680* (1982), pp. 125, 142–8; C.G.A. Clay, *Economic Expansion and Social Change: England 1500–1700* (2 vols, Cambridge, 1984), I, pp. 3–4 (and Fig.1), 31, 41, 44, 49, 50, 104; II, p. 187; and cf. J. Thirsk (ed.) *The Agrarian History of England and Wales, V, 1640–1750* (Cambridge, 1984); A.B. Appleby, *Famine in Tudor and Stuart England* (Liverpool, 1978), ch. 10.
7. Thirsk, *Agrarian History of England and Wales IV 1500–1640* (Cambridge, 1967), p. 621.

beginnings of improvements in the capacity of the country to feed itself and perhaps too, a slow improvement in real wages after a century of decline. The dearth of 1630 was the last of the decade, and one of the last of the century.[8]

This is by no means to suggest that problems had been solved. Indeed one of the problems bequeathed by the preceding century of rapid change was greater extremes in poverty and wealth, and a large class of landless poor. Whilst in a period of rapid inflation in grain prices, substantial yeomen and the better off (or more astute) husbandmen had been able to improve their lot (and, as contemporaries like Sir Thomas Smith or William Harrison observed, their lifestyles), those who could only scratch a subsistence from their smallholding, or worse depended entirely on wage labour at a time of an expanding labour force, saw their miserable existences descend to life-threatening (even fatal) conditions. Their numbers were increased by the tendency to larger holdings and enclosures not only, as was once thought, for pasture but for more productive arable production. Although enclosures might often take place by agreement, they still robbed the lowest orders of common rights, 'the importance of which to small tenants and cottagers might be incalculable'.[9] A farmer needed perhaps 30 acres to make a small profit in good years, and much more (50 is one estimate) to be safe from the vagaries of the market and the weather.[10] Beneath that were many smaller freeholders or leaseholders and cottagers who with a few acres 'eked out a living in good times, yet faced chronic distress in years of industrial depression'.[11] In one parish of Salisbury in 1635 well over one-third of the inhabitants were officially classified as poor.[12]

For this class of marginal people living at or below the level of subsistence, the 1630s did not obviously bring better days. The policies of disafforestation and the draining of the fens further eroded surviving areas of common land which had provided cottagers with a supplement or meagre alternative to labour. The clampdown on alehouses too robbed some of the urban and village poor of a popular sideline, which could make the difference between managing and not managing. All, however, was not negative: those who lost commons were granted a few acres and a reduced dependence on labour; government

8. Wrightson, *English Society*, pp. 143–4; Clay, *Economic Expansion*, I, p. 104.
9. Wrightson, *English Society*, p. 133 and see ch. 5 *passim*. See also W. Hunt, *The Puritan Moment: The Coming of Revolution in an English County* (Cambridge, Mass., 1983), p. 44; C. Holmes, *Seventeenth Century Lincolnshire* (Lincoln, 1980), ch. 2.
10. J.A. Sharpe, *Early Modern England: A Social History, 1550–1760* (1987), p. 132; K. Wrightson and D. Levine, *Poverty and Piety in an English Village: Terling 1525–1700* (New York, 1979), pp. 25–6.
11. Wrightson, *English Society*, p. 127.
12. *Ibid.*, p. 141.

policy, much more the weather, stabilized grain prices; a drive to put the poor on work and increase apprenticeships helped in the towns. Most of all the concentrated campaign to supervise and enforce the statutory provisions for poor relief appears to have meant that if life was poor and brutish, it was not cut short by actual starvation – as it was in Germany and France.

In general, for those above the level of the commonalty, the 1630s probably brought better times. Again this is by no means true across the country or for any class. Better harvests meant lower prices for those with a surplus to sell; individual yeomen quickly made and lost their fortunes. But along with better harvests, the decade saw great improvements in England's trade with other countries. The 1620s had been disastrous years: war, currency manipulations which made English goods expensive and Dutch competition had hit the English cloth trade, casting thousands into desperate unemployment.[13] The peace with France and Spain transformed the situation. It reopened the important Spanish market for English wool cloth. More generally, England benefited greatly through being for a decade alone among the European powers not at war. The country entered the re-export trade and muscled in on the carrying trade, conveying goods from Spain to the Low Countries and France and claiming entry into overseas markets. For a time Dover became a European entrepôt, as Antwerp had once been.[14] Though more research needs to be done, the availability of markets may well have stimulated rural industries; certainly peace introduced England to opportunities that it later became determined to take by belligerence. Ship money was important. Whilst, as we shall see, the burden of the tax could fall on those at times quite unable to bear it, it was not without its economic benefits – and not only in terms of protecting trade. Thanks to ship money a programme of royal shipbuilding took place which required labour and supplies in dockyard towns such as Chatham and Portsmouth and which gave some stimulus to the iron works which supplied ordnance as well as other materials.[15] Again regional differences may render hazardous any generalization, but Clarendon's memory of a decade of peace and prosperity was probably more than fanciful nostalgia.[16] As Professor Clark informs us, visitors to Kent during the decade described its prosperity 'in golden tones'.[17]

13. See B. Supple, *Commercial Crisis and Change in England, 1600–1642* (Cambridge, 1959).
14. J.S. Kepler, *The Exchange of Christendom: The International Entrepôt at Dover, 1622–1641* (Leicester, 1976); Clay, *Economic Expansion*, II, p. 187; see above, pp. 90–92.
15. Clay, *Economic Expansion*, II, pp. 186, 219–21.
16. E. Hyde, Earl of Clarendon, *The History of the Rebellion and Civil Wars in England*, ed. W.D. Macray (6 vols, Oxford, 1888), I, p. 93.
17. P. Clark, *English Provincial Society from the Reformation to the Revolution* (Hassocks, 1977), p. 354.

Halcyon days?

For most English people the 1630s may also have seen some easing of the fears and tensions of the previous decade. From 1618 and the outbreak of the Thirty Years War there was heightened anxiety concerning the seemingly irrepressible tide of Habsburg power and of popery; it permeated the speeches of MPs not usually thought of as the hottest Protestants; it underlay the concern about domestic religious quarrels and developments.[18] Fears of plots and invasions continued to circulate, rhythmically renewed by the celebration of Armada day and Powder day.[19] It was widely rumoured that James I had been poisoned; the new queen of England's father had recently been assassinated. The war years 1625–8 were regularly punctuated by scares and fears of invasion – of Ireland, on the south and west coasts, of the Isle of Wight. Even the peace brought little immediate comfort: the year of the Treaty of Susa with France saw also the issue of the Edict of Restitution and the height of Catholic power in the empire; the peace with Spain was regarded as a national shame by those who had grown up associating England's security with hostility to the Habsburgs. But the early 1630s saw a lowering of the temperature of paranoia. Gustavus Adolphus checked the swell of popery and there can be little doubt that the thirst for news and hagiographic celebration of his victories testify to a catharsis of indigenous insecurity as well as encomium of a new-found Protestant champion. After 1634 the ship money fleets fostered a greater sense of security and even some greater national pride. To some, courted by ambassadors from all the major powers, England could appear (whatever our view of the reality) strong and capable of tilting the balance in Europe. Certainly with the Habsburg fortunes on the wane, the French more respectful and the Dutch taking licences to fish, there was a new (if sometimes false) sense of security. It is no way better illustrated than by the government's failure to persuade its subjects (as part of its programme for the militia and ship money) of the existence of a state of emergency that threatened the survival of the realm.

During the 1640s, indeed, many were to look back on the decade of personal rule as a halcyon era for England in a Europe torn by strife. Clarendon in his *History of the Rebellion* was to recall that 'the like peace . . . and universal tranquillity for ten years was never enjoyed by any nation'.[20] In his *Memoirs* published at the end of the century, Sir

18. The European background to the fears of popery in England has been greatly underestimated by historians of English religious attitudes.
19. D. Cressy, *Bonfires and Bells: National Memory and the Protestant Calendar in Elizabethan and Stuart England* (1989), chs 7, 9.
20. Clarendon, *History of the Rebellion*, I, p. 84; cf. I, p. 93.

Philip Warwick, as he became in 1660, wrote: 'from the year 1628 unto the year 1638, I believe England was never master of a profounder peace, nor enjoy'd more wealth, or had the power and form of godliness visibly in it'.[21] Recently it has been suggested that in such panegyrics literary convention blended with recollections of reality into what was a mixture of history and romantic fiction.[22] Even during the 1630s, before the nostalgia induced by exile and harsher times, court poets had begun to sing of the peace and prosperity of halcyon days. Fanshawe in his 'Ode upon occasion of his Majesty's Proclamation in the year 1630' (ordering the nobility to their country estates) contrasted the miserable fate of Europe with England:

> White peace (the beautiful'st of things)
> Seemes here her everlasting rest
> To fix . . .

More famously (though more problematically), Thomas Carew replied to Aurelian Townshend's invitation to celebrate the victories of the deceased Gustavus Adolphus with an (apparent) paean to Charles's preference for peace.[23]

> Then let the Germans feare if Caesar shall,
> Or the United Princes, rise, and fall,
> But let us that in myrtle bowers sit
> Under secure shades, use the benefit
> Of peace and plenty, which the blessed hand
> Of our good prince gives this obdurate land.[24]

For the 'calm securitie' of England, the poem continued, the other powers of Europe would 'hang their armes up on the olive bough'.[25] Such passages have usually been read as the quintessence of false confidence, born of a naive and self-deluding isolation from political reality.[26] But it was an attitude widely shared by men of affairs – not

21. P. Warwick, *Memoirs of the Reign of King Charles I* (1703), pp. 62–3.
22. See R.A. Anselment, 'Clarendon and the Caroline myth of peace', *Journ. Brit. Stud.*, 23 (1984), pp. 37–54.
23. N.W. Bawcutt (ed.) *Sir Richard Fanshawe: Shorter Poems and Translations* (Liverpool, 1964), p. 6, lines 37–9.
24. R. Dunlap (ed.) *The Poems of Thomas Carew* (Oxford, 1949), p. 75, lines 43–8. See my discussion of this poem in K. Sharpe, *Criticism and Compliment: The Politics of Literature in the England of Charles I* (Cambridge, 1987), pp. 145–8. Anselment disagrees; he describes the poem as a 'provocation' ('Clarendon', p. 45). But Louis Marz long ago raised the interesting suggestion that the whole poem was ironic (*The Wit of Love*, Notre Dame, 1969, p. 78) and Professor Don Kennedy recently reminded me that, given the ban on the corantos celebrating Gustavus Adolphus, Carew's poem was an audacious venture. I am grateful to Professor Kennedy for discussions of this poem at Melbourne University in 1990.
25. Dunlap, *Poems of Carew*, p. 77, lines 102–4.
26. See especially C.V. Wedgwood, *Poetry and Politics under the Stuarts* (Cambridge, 1960).

only at court but beyond. In 1635, for example, the Earl of Carlisle wrote to Wentworth expressing his gratitude that 'in this universal combustion that threatens all Christendom, only our blessed master stands unshaken'.[27] Wentworth agreed: but for the Palatinate 'there was nothing left but honour and happiness for his Majesty to look upon reposing secure and quiet in his own interests whilst the two great neighbouring kings dispute their preferences each against the other in expense of treasure and blood'.[28] The Earl of Dorset, at the trial of Prynne for publishing *Histriomastix*, asked simply: 'when were our days more halcyon? When did the people of this land sing a more secure Quietus?'[29]

Even those critical of royal policies were no less ready to praise the benefits of peace. John Dinley wrote to Sir Thomas Roe, then at the Hague, that England was a land that 'flows in prosperity and peace'.[30] Lord Edward Montagu of Boughton, Northamptonshire, though known for his puritan sympathies, could still acknowledge that 'we hold ourselves . . . bound to be thankful to the Almighty that have received so much plenty and so many other blessings by the King's Majesty's high wisdom not only in the peaceable government of us under his own kingdom, but by settling of peace in all parts of Christendom which we pray long and long may continue.'[31] Such appreciative sentiments were more widely voiced. In the 1630 edition of the popular courtesy book, *The English Gentleman*, Richard Braithwaite, amidst advice on self-education to virtue, paused for patriotic praise of an island 'whose Halcyon days have attained that prerogative of peace which most parts of Christendom are at this day deprived of'.[32] Gyles Fleming thought the 'halcyon days' of Charles the right foundation on which the church might build;[33] and even the future member of the Westminster assembly, William Gouge, gave thanks to God for England's enjoyment of peace 'and a free use of all God's holy ordinances'. 'At this time,' he was well aware in 1632, 'this blessing ought to be the more highly esteemed because it is in a manner proper to us. For most of the parts of Christendom are now, or lately have been, exceedingly annoyed with bloody war.'[34]

As news circulated of the extent of devastation overseas appreciation of the blessing of peace permeated even circles whose rhetoric at least

27. Sheffield Central Library, Wentworth Woodhouse MS, WW/15, no. 49: Carlisle to Wentworth, 30 April 1635.
28. Bodleian, Clarendon MS 8, no. 667: Wentworth to Windebank, 3 March 1636.
29. Bodleian, Tanner MS 299, f.130v.
30. *Calendar of State Papers Domestic* [*Cal. Stat. Pap. Dom.*], *1634–5*, p. 512, 14/24 Feb. 1635.
31. Northamptonshire Record Office, Montagu MS 10/38.
32. R. Braithwaite, *The English Gentleman* (1630 ed, STC 3563), p. 298.
33. G. Fleming, *Magnificence Exemplified* (1634, STC 11052), p. 45.
34. W. Gouge, *The Saints Sacrifice* (1632, STC 12125), pp. 276–8.

had favoured more belligerent courses. Calibut Downing wrote to John Winthrop of Massachusetts in 1636 – evidently from report rather than experience – that 'Germany is now become a most desolate wilderness: there be many towns beautiful for buildings but neither man nor woman nor child in them. The country doth so swarm with rats.'[35] Arundel's embassy to Vienna with his entourage gave Englishmen direct experience of what they had heard.[36] And, as Geoffrey Parker observed, 'the account of William Crowne and the engravings of Wenceslaus Hollar, both of whom accompanied Charles I's ambassador to the electoral meeting at Regensburg in 1636, provide a horrifying picture of war-torn Germany.'[37] Such stories were told not only of Germany. From Paris Scudamore wrote of tumults, soldiers intimidating the people, robberies and insolencies by unpaid troops, the rising of over 5,000 *croquants* in desperation and rebellion against the burdens of war.[38] With such reports spreading abroad, we may suggest that the city of York's speech of welcome to Charles in 1633, praising the happy peace they lived under while other nations suffered the miseries of war, was more sincere than formal loyalist rhetoric.[39] With the rupture of that calm in 1639, even the Earl of Holland, who had long advocated a French alliance, could regret that the king was now faced with an army who had 'covered us all so many years under the wings of peace when all other princes have been laid open to the rage and calamities of war'.[40] Undoubtedly, there was criticism of English neutrality – especially from those for whom the contests in Europe were wars between the forces of light and darkness. To some the brilliant exploits of the Swedish king cast a spotlight of shame on the inactivity of England. But for many whose memories of the wars of the 1620s were lost husbands and sons, conscription and wounds, martial law and unruly troops, peace offered a real cause to praise the halcyon days England alone enjoyed.

Enduring problems

If a corrective is necessary to the excessive cynicism with which all celebrations of peace and plenty have been read, it would be just as

35. *The Winthrop Papers* (Massachusetts Hist. Soc, 4th series, 6, Boston, 1863), p. 45, 2 March 1636.
36. W. Crowne, *A True Relation of all the Remarkable Places Observed in the Travels of Thomas Lord Howard* (1637, STC 6097); cf. above, pp. 519–25.
37. G. Parker, *The Thirty Years War* (1984), p. 163. See too, A. Griffith and G. Kesmerova, *Wenceslaus Hollar: Prints and Drawings* (1983).
38. British Library [BL] Add. MS 35097, for example, ff.60v, 72, 80v, 127v; Add. MS 45142, ff.35, 37v, 41v.
39. York Record Office, York House Books, 35, f.209v.
40. *Cal. Stat. Pap. Dom., 1639*, p. 209: Holland to the Earl of Argyle, 22 May.

naive to accept the extravagant optimism of those like Sir Philip Warwick who wrote of an age when even cobblers had silver beakers – so rife were silver vessels among all conditions.[41] For as well as endemic economic and social problems, the early years of the 1630s, with troops returning from the wars, brought new ones. And for all that historians have tentatively seen the years around 1630 as the beginning of some improvements, it may have been several years before perceptions of better times caught up with reality. Certainly in many counties officials met with great difficulties in collecting even traditional and uncontentious levies for local purposes. In Dorset, for example, Thomas Yeatman, surveyor of the highways, found that what he collected during his year of office fell far short of the sum needed to carry out repairs; and he was forced to follow his successor to raise the arrears.[42] In Kent, in 1634, Sir Edward Hales told Sir Edward Dering that in his capacity as treasurer for Boughton highway he had had personally to contribute £10 to the monies raised, in order to pay the labourers.[43] Failure to pay contributions for the repair of highways and bridges contribute more entries to indictments at quarter sessions than any other misdemeanour. At Pluckley church in Kent, the inhabitants called by the constable and meeting to arrange the repair of a highway, refused to assess any charges and departed for home with nothing done.[44] It is not surprising that we learn of unfortunate labourers not reimbursed for their toils.[45]

Such examples of reluctance to pay local rates are not confined to the 1630s, nor indeed to the seventeenth century. But they do suggest that there was not in the local communities a perception of wealth. And if, as has been argued, the rich were beginning to get richer, it was far from clear that they were more ready to meet their share of local burdens. Sir Peter Temple of Stowe appears to have been remiss in his payments towards the maintenance of the house of correction,[46] and even Dering, we recall, was not free with his purse when it came to contributing to the repair of the church.[47] Indeed as many ship money sheriffs had discovered and revealed, local charges fell disproportionately on those least able to pay them and as the wealth gap widened so that disproportion became the greater. It was this realization that led the Council to consider settling local rates at Whitehall and meanwhile

41. Warwick, *Memoirs*, p. 63.
42. Dorset Record Office, quarter sessions orders, 1625–37, f.246.
43. Kent Archives Office, Dering MS U 350/C2/46, 2 Aug. 1634.
44. Dering MS U 570/01/19.
45. Dering MS U 350/C2/46; Kent Archives Office, West Kent quarter sessions, QSOW1, f.60 and *passim*.
46. Huntington Library, Temple of Stowe MS 8, STT 2251.
47. Above, p. 319.

to instruct the judges to keep a watchful eye. As the Lord Keeper Coventry told them in 1638, 'it is a heavy thing that in case of public service that those that are rich should put off all from themselves and lay it upon the poor and friendless, that is the general case . . . I find the landlord finds a way to ease his own demesne and lays his burden upon his tenants and the rich man upon his poor neighbours.'[48] Despite Conciliar injunctions to fairness, Coventry added, 'it is followed so slowly in the country as if it were a thing not fit for the undertaking'.

If (and more research is needed before we can conclude this with confidence) greater wealth were not permeating down through the local communities, there can be no doubt that greater costs were facing them. The long-term increase historians have identified in the class of dependent poor was clearly discerned by many localities during the 1630s. Somerton in Somerset complained in 1631 that the numbers of its poor had tripled in the last twenty years and that (we note the arithmetic) their poor rate had doubled, but was 'still scarcely sufficient to keep them alive'.[49] The problem was greatly exacerbated, Taunton protested, 'by reason of the many late presses of soldiers', which had necessitated a supplementary £50 per annum levy to the poor rate.[50] With pensions of £10 a head, that was not likely to go far; by 1633 one recipient's payments were £60 in arrears.[51] The next year the county, faced with costs desperately in excess of the rates, embarked on what was a social security check so as to reduce the numbers of claimants.[52] But the problems and costs mounted. As those wounded at Rhé grew older, they appear often to have become dependent on local support earlier than the usual age of 'retirement', as debilities or diseases shortened working lives. Aylesbury was too much in arrears in 1633 to pay the soldiers maimed in the 1620s.[53] Across the country, as payments for the poor rate were rising, so were complaints of the costs. The order of assize judges that assessments should be made on ability as well as land suggests again that often the most able got off lightly. The corporation of Banbury acted on its own initiative; 'we raised all the wealthier sort of inhabitants at twice as much or more weekly as they were before'.[54] But it is evident that this was far from usual. The inhabitants of Bearsted in Kent in 1636 reported that they

48. Bodleian, Rawlinson MS B. 243, f.19v.
49. E.H. Bates-Harbin, *Quarter Sessions Records for the County of Somerset*, II (Somerset Record Soc., 24, 1908), p. 140.
50. *Ibid.*, p. 156.
51. *Ibid.*, p. 200.
52. *Ibid.*, p. 210. All pensioners were ordered to appear at the sessions with their letters of recommendation.
53. Kent Archives Office, QSOW1, f.46.
54. J.S.W. Gibson and E.R.C. Brinkworth (eds) *Banbury Corporation Records* (Banbury Historical Soc., 15, 1977), p. 152.

were unable to pay for their poor, as did those of Allington in Dorset, 'notwithstanding they have been thereunto rated to the utter most of their abilities'.[55] In Yately, Hampshire, in 1636, 'by reason of some difference in that parish concerning the rates of the inhabitants there, the poor are now in great necessity'.[56] The bailiff of Buckingham told the sheriff that the inhabitants were complaining bitterly at the weekly cost;[57] in Trotiscliff, Kent they gave up collecting altogether.[58] The number of such protests suggests that in general, whatever the overall economic condition of the localities, the rising burdens were often falling on those least able to pay them. The 1d. contributions in the accounts for Melbury Osmond in Dorset support the suggestion.[59] Even without the extraordinary charges and levies of the 1630s, many parishioners, above the level of dependence and on the margin of subsistence, were facing serious difficulties.

New burdens

During the 1630s the localities were subjected to some untypical financial burdens. Wardship and purveyance, though traditional, were exploited to increase royal revenues; knighthood fines and forest fines were a more novel and unexpected imposition. Yet these affected primarily the gentry, or substantial propertied class who, since they were spared the payment of subsidies, may in the 1630s have paid no more on balance than in the previous decade. Other charges however, affected a broader spectrum of society. The contributions for the rebuilding of St Paul's, for example, appear in many places to have been assessed on the basis of those liable for the poor rate, so hitting those who were already faced with steeply rising payments for the poor and other charges.[60] In November 1637 Richard Herbert requested of the Earl of Bridgewater that the hundreds of Uske and Caldicott be excused monies for St Paul's given their high local expenses in repairing sea walls and bridges – Newport bridge alone having cost £1,500 in the last three years.[61] The rebuilding of St Paul's

55. Kent Archives Office, QSOW1, f.77; Dorset Record Office, quarter sessions orders, f.313v.
56. Hampshire Record Office, Herriard MSS, Box 013 (quarter sessions papers), 27 May 1636.
57. *Cal. Stat. Pap. Dom., 1631–3*, p. 25, 30 April 1631.
58. Kent Archives Office, QSOW1, f.70.
59. Dorset Record Office, F 223/OV1: Melbury Osmond, accounts of the overseers of the poor.
60. For example, Huntington Library, Ellesmere MSS 7410, 7418, 7420, 7421, 7517, 7524; York House Books, 35, f.188; Bristol Record Office, Smyth of Ashton Court MS 36214; Herriard MSS, Box 012.
61. Ellesmere MS, 7517.

involved the localities in expenses other than their fiscal contributions: counties with forests suffered the additional burden of the transportation cost of timber and stone for this, as for other royal building projects.[62] In 1632, to take a case, the county of Dorset reminded the Council that it had conveyed a thousand loads of Portland stone for work on the Banqueting House at Whitehall.[63] Churchwardens' accounts from almost every parish for which we have them bear testimony to the costs of repairing, enhancing and 'beautifying' parish churches and their furniture, often in response to the pressure of visitation orders.[64]

Ship money was, then, the largest of a number of charges but, importantly, it hit a class usually exempt from subsidy payments on whom many of the other burdens were falling. Moreover, though Council instructions ordered the sparing of poor men, some local assessments and indeed the basic domestic items (their beds and last remaining food) distrained for non-payment indicate that relatively humble folk were charged.[65] Even when the better off paid their share, there were repercussions for the community. Sir John Finet believed that the burden led masters to cut costs, reduce the numbers of their servants and so throw unemployed bands on to the highways.[66] Like St Paul's, ship money also involved high costs beyond the rates paid: namely, the expenses of cutting and transporting timber for the building and repairing of the ship money fleets from 1634 to 1640. The amounts and costs were not small. In one year the rape of Hastings paid £634 for carrying timber;[67] in 1635 the cost to the county of Northumberland for conveying 3,000 loads of ship timber was £1,190 'at least' – a charge they were unable to bear without the assistance of neighbouring counties.[68] The burdens, of course, were uneven. Hampshire necessarily suffered worst, with Portsmouth the main shipbuilding yard, but Kent, with Chatham dockyard, probably ran a close second. Complaints from both counties were common. In 1637 the JPs of Kent protested they were carrying at least 300 loads of timber annually, and at times over 500;[69] the following summer they again petitioned the Council for relief.[70] As for Hampshire, its forests were evidently in demand even before the building of ship money

62. See, for example, Rawlinson MS D.666, f.85: order to the JPs of Hampshire to provide building timber for the west end, 3 June 1639.
63. *Cal. Stat. Pap. Dom., 1631–3*, p. 381, 14 July 1632.
64. Above, pp. 390–92.
65. See, for example, *Cal. Stat. Pap. Dom., 1638–9*, pp. 121–2; *1636–7*, p. 150.
66. PRO, C.115/N8/8801: Finet to Scudamore, 11 Feb. 1637.
67. Rawlinson MS B.431 (justice's notebook for Sussex, 1633–9), f.39.
68. *Cal. Stat. Pap. Dom., 1635*, p. 156.
69. *Cal. Stat. Pap. Dom., 1636–7*, p. 462.
70. *Cal. Stat. Pap. Dom., 1637–8*, p. 550; cf. p. 479. And see Dering MS U 350/012.

fleets. In July 1631, Basingstoke, Kingsclere and Portsdown were excused the county charge of transporting building timber from Winchester to Reading on the grounds that they had already conveyed 400 loads that year![71] The following spring the county was asked to convey 1,500 loads at probably a third below the market costs of carriage.[72] Resistance to and disputes over the distribution of the charge mounted; in 1634 the Council wrote to the justices of the county upbraiding them for their slackness in providing carts.[73] The Council was not entirely unsympathetic to Hampshire's protests: they promised to ease the county 'with the help of the adjoining counties'; they also had the moulds of ships framed in the woods to reduce the need for carriage.[74] But as more was spent on the fleet, so the burden increased. Kenrick Edisbury, one of the navy commissioners, recognizing the 'great charge in carriage of timber' borne by Hampshire, urged that Wiltshire and Dorset give aid; there is no evidence his suggestion was followed.[75] A coastal county, with one of the best records for paying ship money, Hampshire was more able than inland counties (such as Oxfordshire or Staffordshire) to appreciate the need for shipbuilding.[76] Its exasperation over the costs of transporting timber were always more an expression of real hardship than special pleading. What finally led to outrage was the Council's demand, in the summer of 1639, for yet more timber – this time for St Paul's. The JPs somewhat curtly replied:

> That within four or five years last past the inhabitants of the counties of Southampton at their great charge have . . . carried and conveyed many thousand loads of timber and wood, some for his Majesty's navy, some for the repair of his Majesty's houses, some for fortification of the town of Portsmouth, besides the yearly purveyance of 333 loads of billet tallwood and faggots . . . for the provision of his Majesty's household. For the greatest part of all which carriages there hath been paid and allowed by the county seven or eight shillings the load beside His Majesty's price . . .[77]

Now they were asked for 244 loads of timber for the west end of St Paul's ('after the rate of seven shillings a load beside his Majesty's allowance') – having already 'contributed in a large proportion towards the repair of the said church upon his Majesty's commission'. They

71. Rawlinson MS D.666, f.84v.
72. Herriard MSS, Box 013: Council letter of 25 May 1632; cf. Hampshire Record Office, QS 44/M/69; Herriard MS E.77; and Hampshire Record Office, Sherfield MS XXXVII.
73. Herriard MSS, Box 013.
74. Melbourne Hall, Coke MS 42: Council to JPs of Hampshire, 18 Aug. 1632.
75. *Cal. Stat. Pap. Dom., 1636–7*, p. 9, 21 June 1636.
76. See *ibid.*, p. 408.
77. Rawlinson MS D.666, f.85–85v: response to demand of 3 June 1639.

were not spared the charge. The Council repeated its demand for carts it 'having been but such as other counties have with alacrity undergone'.[78] It was highly questionable whether other counties had borne Hampshire's charges, still more doubtful whether they had done so with 'alacrity'. But the shipbuilding programme had affected not only coastal counties. We are now familiar enough with the hidden costs of defence to sense that the halcyon days of the 1630s were not purchased cheaply.

Local difficulties

Financial costs were only the most tangible (or measurable) of the difficulties faced by the counties in meeting the Council's demands during the decade of personal rule. Others, differing in intensity from place to place, included the weather, difficulties of communication, the structure of particular local communities, the cajoling of friends and neighbours, and tense personal relationships. In Buckinghamshire, for example, Sir Thomas Temple found areas where decay of tillage had reduced the numbers of the militia and of subsidy payers.[79] The Earl of Huntingdon faced a similar shortage of husbandmen in Leicestershire.[80] In the Marches in the winter of 1636 frost and snow made it impossible to travel by horse or foot.[81] Frost and snow delayed ship money collection in Northumberland in 1638 and brought local meetings (over rates) to an end in Somerset.[82] Floods cost Staffordshire over £2,000 in damages in the winter of 1636–7, leading them to petition for an abatement of other charges.[83] Musters in Cumberland were impeded 'by reason of the remoteness' of some places 'and that they were in a stormy and mountainous country'.[84]

Administrative difficulties and anomalies exacerbated geography and the elements: some Huntingdonshire parishes paid with one town for rates for the poor and church repair, and with another for purveyance and other taxes.[85] In Dorset quarrels over the poor rate led to violence; in Oxfordshire the repair of the Blagrove Quainton highway was long a cause of contention.[86] In Kent there were several instances of

78. *Ibid.*, ff.85v–86: Council to JPs, 24 July and 2 Aug. 1639.
79. Temple of Stowe MSS, Personal Box 8.
80. Huntington Library, Hastings MS 2884.
81. Ellesmere MS 7224.
82. *Cal. Stat. Pap. Dom., 1637–8*, p. 330; Bates-Harbin, *Quarter Sessions Records for . . . Somerset*, p. 308.
83. *Cal. Stat. Pap. Dom., 1636–7*, p. 408.
84. *Cal. Stat. Pap. Dom., 1638–9*, p. 355.
85. *Cal. Stat. Pap. Dom., 1636–7*, p. 440.
86. Above, p. 474; Oxfordshire Record Office, Dillon MS XII, g.1.

administrative breakdown. No one, apparently, remembered who was responsible for the upkeep of East Peckham bridge;[87] with regard to the bridge in East Farleigh, confusion or disagreement led to a very unsatisfactory half-solution. For the parish repaired its side of the bridge up to the boundary stone 'and on the other side of the stone the speech was that the parish of Barming ought to repair, but they were so poor that they never did it . . . although the bridge on that side were in decay'.[88] There were endless squabbles between parishes, some arising from genuine problems, over responsibility for maintenance of wandering orphans and single mothers.[89] None of these disagreements were new; they were endemic to a pre-bureaucratic age when much was done by the 'rule' of differently and selectedly remembered – or at times forgotten – customs. They support Clive Holmes's cautionary remarks about excess emphasis on the county as the unit of local government and identity.[90] New or not, however, these difficulties and regional divisions form the backdrop to local responses to central demands. And with costs and burdens rising, it appears that they were exacerbated. Though as yet too little research has been done to conclude with confidence, it may be that local government became *more* difficult as communities and individuals sought more and more, as with ship money, to protect their hundred, parish or family, and pass the burden on to others. The sorts of problems and disputes that could arise are illustrated by the question raised in Kent about how to rate a gentleman who dwelt in one parish and had substantial estates in another. Twysden thought that

> if none were to be assessed but only for that they have in the parish there might be a great inconvenience for one hath £20 a year in the parish [where] his house stands and £1,500 per annum elsewhere, another hath only an £100 per annum and that in the same parish. If in the assessing to the poor there be no respect to be had to rents, he that is worth but an £100 might be rated much more than the other.

Yet, 'it was held a case of great difficulty' – and that not least because Justices Croke and Heath had disagreed in their rulings and the published judicial rulings of 1636 offered 'very little satisfaction'.[91] In early modern society there was infinite room for such confusions and insoluble questions which might impede the execution of a service or command.

87. Kent Archives Office, QSOW1, f.14v.
88. *Ibid.*, f.80.
89. For example, *ibid.*, ff.28, 70v.
90. C. Holmes, 'The county community in Stuart historiography', *Journ. Brit. Stud.*, 19 (1980), pp. 53–73.
91. Kent Archives Office, Twysden MS U 47/47/01, p. 17.

Personal and factional disputes (as well as reflecting) aggravated such difficulties. The historians of the Stuart counties have made us familiar with the longstanding family rivalries that coloured local politics and government: those of Grey and Hastings in Leicestershire, of Wentworth and Savile in Yorkshire, Sir Robert Phelips and Lord Poulett in Somerset.[92] In the hundreds and parishes, as the records of secular and ecclesiastical courts abundantly reveal, there was no shortage of similar quarrels among the orders below the gentry.[93] Such antagonisms could further encumber already difficult services. In Cheshire for instance, ship money assessments became entangled with quarrels between Sir William Brereton and the city of Chester; in Shropshire local disputes clearly underlay the controversies over the muster master's fee.[94] As vice-president of the Council of the North, Osborne at every turn found Savile's hostility to Wentworth directed against himself.[95] Such rivalries and clashes – of individuals, families and factions – permeated down the clientage networks into hundreds and villages that were quite capable of generating their own. In Terling, a third of the quarter sessions' business related to 'interpersonal disputes'.[96] Religious differences sharpened old and created new conflicts as villagers divided after church between the prayer meeting and the alehouse.[97]

It is ironic, then, that the new demands of the 1630s, such as payments for St Paul's and ship money, required more not less local cohesion and co-operation. Ship money especially necessitated meetings and consultations to agree assessments and proportions. Yet communication, even over short distances, presented considerable difficulties. Sheriff Dryden of Northamptonshire explained how hard it was to make assessments in a county fifty miles in length, and the increasing tendency of JPs to meet only in regional sessions would bear him out.[98] Travel was fraught with difficulties. For one, England evidently lacked a common standard for measuring distances. Kentish

92. G.C.F. Forster, 'Faction and county government in early Stuart Yorkshire', *Northern History*, 11 (1975), pp. 70–86; D. Hirst, 'Court, county and politics before 1629', in K. Sharpe (ed.) *Faction and Parliament*, (Oxford, 1978), pp. 106–37, esp. pp. 117–20, 125–7; Holmes, 'County community', pp. 61–3.
93. Wrightson and Levine, *Terling*, ch. 5; Wrightson, *English Society*, chs 2, 6, esp. pp. 61–5.
94. J.S. Morrill, 'Sir William Brereton and England's wars of religion', *Journ. Brit. Stud.*, 24 (1985), p. 313; above, pp. 496–7.
95. *HMC Cowper, II*, p. 204; above, pp. 450–51.
96. Wrightson and Levine, *Terling*, p. 117.
97. The Sibthorpe letters in the Temple of Stowe MSS offer striking testimony of the effect of religious differences on relationships in Northamptonshire; see below, p. 846. Since these letters begin in the 1630s, it is not clear how far we can take them as evidence of long-felt antagonisms. See too D. Underdown, *Revel, Riot and Rebellion: Popular Politics and Culture in England, 1603–1660* (Oxford, 1985), esp. ch. 3.
98. *Cal. Stat. Pap. Dom., 1635–6*, p. 166.

'miles' were longer than those elsewhere; similarly the distance between Uttoxeter and Newcastle under Lyme was 'accounted but twelve miles yet [they] are very long ones and may stand for 16 or 17 miles in the south'.[99] The roads there too were reported foul and narrow. In the winter much of England was effectively closed to travel as highways became mud tracks – a situation not much improved before the Turnpike Act of 1663.[100] Obstacles to travel were frequently, and not always disingenuously, cited as explanations for failure to attend at sessions or musters. Until the late 1630s the conveyance of orders was further impeded by the absence of a postal service. Before Thomas Witherings's establishment of running posts along the main arteries of communication from London, the Council was forced to rely on its own special messengers and sheriffs; deputy lieutenants and JPs presumably used their own servants.[101] As a consequence, ship money writs were delayed in 1634 on account of the 'miscarriage of the messengers'; and we often find weeks lost between the dispatch of Council instructions and the first evidence of local receipt.[102] If one of the inherent weaknesses of English local government was its general dependence upon local co-operation at a time when the physical (and psychological) obstacles to communication were great, the personal rule, with its drive for efficiency and novel levies, at times exposed those weaknesses more starkly.

Plague

Plague compounded all these problems as well as adding periodic crisis to a society neither knowledgeable enough nor equipped to cope with it. For some magistrates, especially those of godly leanings, plague could be a spur to greater diligence and activity. Henry Sherfield at a sessions in Hampshire in 1628 referred to the pestilence as a sign from God that the land was in need of reformation.[103] Even those less puritanically inclined, such as John Taylor the water poet, could regard plague as a purification of the land of sin and an opportunity for a new orientation.[104] But during the months, and even years, when disease

99. *Cal. Stat. Pap. Dom., 1633–4*, p. 69; Hastings MSS, Personal HAP, Box 18.
100. Sharpe, *Early Modern England*, p. 141. See B and S. Webb, *The Story of the King's Highway* (1913) and J. Crofts, *Packhorse, Wagon and Post: Land Carriage and Communications under the Tudors and Stuarts* (1967).
101. See C.R. Clear, *Thomas Witherings and the Birth of the Postal Service* (Post Office Green Papers, 15, 1935); cf. K. Sharpe, 'Sir Thomas Witherings and the reform of the foreign posts, 1632–40', *Bull. Inst. Hist. Res.*, 57 (1984), pp. 149–64.
102. *Cal. Stat. Pap. Dom., 1634–5*, p. 563.
103. Sherfield MS XXXVIII.
104. J. Taylor, *The Works of John Taylor* (1630, STC 23725), p. 62; cf. P. Slack, *The Impact of Plague in Tudor and Stuart England* (1985), pp. 236–42.

fell upon a city or county, the normal business of government, indeed of life, all but ground to a halt. In York in 1631, for example, as well as the infected, all children were confined to their houses.[105] Trade slowed down as fairs were banned and visitors from London (or elsewhere) were refused admission to the city. At times of great risk abroad, ships were not permitted to land nor any to come ashore for twenty days, so bringing supplies to a halt. Though magistrates attempted to enforce strict regulations concerning house confinements, authority often broke down. Men in fear of death do not quake at the prospect of a fine. In York in 1631 we read of several fined for 'dancing, drinking and revelling on the night time in these heavisome times of infection'.[106] Only the leniency of their punishment is surprising, and may express the magistrates' recognition of the potentially explosive tension in the city at this time. Even some of those responsible for order thought first of their own health and safety. Whilst in most infected towns 'some fragment of magisterial authority remained', there were doubtless many like William Thompson, constable of Edgware, who deserted his post and fled without appointing a deputy.[107] In October 1630, the Council had occasion to upbraid the JPs of Surrey for their failure to execute its orders for checking the spread of infection: 'such is found to be the remissness and negligence in the execution whether in you the justices of peace instructed therewithal or in the subordinate ministers and officers . . .'.[108] The assiduous magistrates who remained could not always guarantee to preserve control: in York, Alderman Lawne's family household was itself shut up, under suspicion of having been infected.[109] Moreover, in the short term the problems posed could be insurmountable. Lord Wentworth feared in 1631 that if the plague struck Leeds and Halifax, 'it would mightly distress and impoverish' all the West Riding of Yorkshire.[110] Preston in Lancashire claimed the same year that the pestilence or stop of trade had left 756 of its 887 inhabitants dependent on relief.[111] In Surrey, some of the neighbouring parishes assessed to help relieve those visited themselves became infected.[112] The poor rate, barely sufficient in normal times, could do little to alleviate such

105. York House Books, 35, f.115v.
106. *Ibid.*, ff.118v, 127v.
107. Slack, *Impact of Plague*, p. 259; *Cal. Stat. Pap. Dom., 1629–31*, p. 375. In Exeter, during the plague of 1625, all magistrates but the redoubtable Ignatius Jordan had fled the city. I owe this information to Mark Stoyle.
108. Temple of Stowe MSS, Box 7, STT 902.
109. Slack, *Impact of Plague*, p. 260.
110. *Ibid.*, p. 188.
111. *Ibid.*, p. 269.
112. Temple of Stowe MSS, Box 8, STT 1873.

circumstances. Mercifully, in 1630–1 the bout of plague was localized and short.

In these early years of personal rule, when the government exhibited 'great determination . . . to tackle many interrelated social problems', the plague encouraged some innovative thinking about how to prevent future recurrences.[113] In particular Charles I appears to have briefed his doctor, the Huguenot *émigré* Theodore de Mayerne, to report and the outcome was a series of inventive attitudes and proposals. To the list of traditional causes of plague – vagrancy, the alehouse and so on – Mayerne added, accurately we now believe, the diagnosis that it was carried by rats. And, in opposition to the traditional policy of house confinement, he advocated the erection of a series of hospitals on the lines of the Hôpital St Louis founded in 1607 by Henri IV.[114] In addition Mayerne stressed the need for a supervisory authority, a commission of health, to enforce all orders and measures rigorously, overriding, if need be, local jurisdictions. In words that could not but have appealed to the king, he argued 'Order is the life and soul of all things.'[115] But whatever their appeal to the king, his proposals never bore fruit and the urgent need for them appeared to recede with the plague itself.

A much worse outbreak, however, followed in 1636, and lasted into 1639. The Venetian ambassador was prophetically characterizing the outbreak in May 1636 as unusually severe;[116] Charles sent his family to the country and ordered that all royal residences be locked up until further notice.[117] During the spring the Council acted to check the spread of the infection in London: common chairs and sedans were prohibited;[118] rag traders were ordered to cease their business;[119] the legal term, the occasion of an influx of countrymen to London, was postponed;[120] the perambulations of the parish bounds, a festival customary during Ascension week, were banned.[121] In July all fairs were prohibited and, as the king and queen retreated to Hampton Court, all inmates within ten miles of the palace were ordered to move.[122] Paper mills (which used rags in their manufacturing process) were closed, as were all schools in the city.[123] The plague, however,

113. Slack, *Impact of Plague*, p. 217.
114. *Ibid.*, pp. 217–20. Hugh Trevor-Roper is currently completing a biography of Mayerne.
115. *Ibid.*, p. 315; cf. *Cal. Stat. Pap. Dom., 1637*, p. 397.
116. *Calendar of State Papers Venetian [Cal. Stat. Pap. Venet.], 1632–6*, p. 560.
117. *Ibid.*, p. 570; Coke MS 53: Weckherlin to Coke, 30 May 1636.
118. PRO, PC 2/46/140.
119. PRO, PC 2/46/147.
120. PRO, PC 2/46/187.
121. PRO, PC 2/46/170.
122. PRO, PC 2/46/347.
123. PRO, PC 2/46/454, PC 2/47/190.

had already taken grip on London and cities beyond. By October, the issue of a proclamation for a general fast perhaps acknowledged the inadequacy of the secular measures and the need to 'implore the grace and favour of that supreme offended Majesty who hath smitten the land and who only can heal it'.[124] Soon the London stages were bare, as for once the gentry remained in their country houses and shunned the capital.[125] The constant motion that was early Stuart London was stilled. On 30 June, Sir John Finch wrote to Viscount Scudamore that 'the better . . . part of London be already emptied into the country having with such haste and fear packed up bag and baggage as if some enemy had been immediately to besiege it'.[126]

From its garrison in London, however, the infection began a rapid conquest of the country, shattering the routines of rural and urban life and government. Hampshire abandoned its summer musters in 1636, fearing that the assembly of large numbers would add to the risks of contagion.[127] Bristol cancelled its summer fair and all but suspended trade: goods from London were denied passage beyond the city gate and no traveller or trader was admitted until he 'have aired himself without the gates by the space of twenty days'.[128] The city of York banned any who had arrived by water from lodging in the town's inns.[129] Still the plague continued its march and proved tenacious of the territories it had taken. While most epidemics lasted less than twelve months, through 1637 and 1638 emergency orders remained in force around much of the country. York increased its precautionary measures when the pestilence hit Hull in 1638.[130] In April of the same year Bristol, enacting a local version of Mayerne's proposals, designated a park and arranged the erection of some 'hovels' outside the city walls to quarantine its infected.[131] In May the Privy Council placed a blanket prohibition on all transportation of goods from infected places.[132]

The summer saw no improvement. Windebank informed Sir Arthur Hopton in September that few families in England were free from the distemper;[133] Thomas Smith wrote to Captain Pennington, 'the

124. J.F. Larkin (ed.), *Stuart Royal Proclamations, II: Proclamations of Charles I, 1625–46* (Oxford, 1983), no. 229, pp. 539–40. The language is a reminder (though we should not need one) that the king and Council were as inclined to see the hand of God in the attack of plague as was Henry Sherfield.
125. J.Q. Adams (ed.) *The Dramatic Records of Sir Henry Herbert* (1917), p. 57.
126. PRO, C.115/N8/8800, 30 June 1636.
127. Herriard MS 026/XLI/17.
128. Bristol Common Council Books, 3, f.68, 6 July 1636.
129. York House Books, 35, ff.318, 320, 348.
130. York House Books, 36, f.2.
131. Bristol Common Council Books, 3, ff.78, 84.
132. PRO, PC 2/49/182.
133. Clarendon MS 14, no. 1136, 30 Sept. 1638.

mortality decreases not; the country is worse than the city'.[134] They did not exaggerate: national mortality rates for 1638–9 were 35 per cent above the normal, the fifth worst figures over the period 1540–1660.[135] Burials in London in 1636 reached a high topped only by the major epidemics of 1603, 1625 and 1665.[136] In Essex, Dr Slack has shown, several parish registers record for 1638 mortality rates three or four times the norm, and that of Gestingthorpe over five times.[137] The figures present only the barest indication of the suffering and disruption. Together with the confinement of many to their homes, the stop in trade, fairs and markets and communications threw many into penury and impoverished cities and villages.[138] In November 1637, Bury St Edmunds petitioned the Council that it was trying to support over 3,000 persons and 103 families at the common charge.[139] Dr Samuel Clarke told Sir John Lambe that the sickness in Northampton was costing the town £40 a week in relief; the sheriff of the county claimed costs overall of £148 a week.[140] Some corporations were faced with an expenditure on relief of five or six times their annual income. In the year 1637–8 Norwich spent over £500 on a relatively small number of victims – more than the city's charge for ship money that year.[141]

Not surprisingly, these charges impeded the levy of ship money. By October 1636 Juxon and Cottington were already attributing the slower payment to the plague, and before the year was out counties were making suits to the Council for mitigation of their assessment on the grounds of the pestilence.[142] Sir Gervase Clifton was informed that the king was moved to reduce the sums paid, and it may be that, along with other factors, the plague influenced the reduction of ship money in 1638.[143] Not until early 1639 did the attorney Robert Woodforde declare the sickness gone from Northamptonshire;[144] in Hampshire 1639 remained one of the 'two . . . most sickly years in the early modern period'.[145] As well as the effect on ship money payments,

134. *Cal. Stat. Pap. Dom., 1638–9*, pp. 3–4, 4 Sept. 1638; cf. Nottingham University Library, Clifton MS Cl/C 309: Robert Lecke to Clifton, 7 May 1637.
135. Slack, *Impact of Plague*, p. 58.
136. *Ibid.*, p. 146.
137. *Ibid.*, p. 103.
138. *Ibid.*, pp. 186, 192; cf. J. Atkinson (ed.) *Quarter Sessions Records* (North Riding Record Soc., 4, 1886), p. 65.
139. *Cal. Stat. Pap. Dom., 1637*, p. 535.
140. *Cal. Stat. Pap. Dom., 1637–8*, p. 518, 17 June 1638; *1638–9*, p. 10, 10 Sept. 1638.
141. Slack, *Impact of Plague*, p. 281.
142. *Cal. Stat. Pap. Dom., 1636–7*, pp. 163, 286.
143. Clifton MS Cl/C 202: Thomas Hodges to Clifton, Feb. 1637.
144. New College Oxford, MS 9502 (Diary of Robert Woodforde), 22 May 1638.
145. J. Taylor, 'Population, disease and family structure in early modern Hampshire, with special reference to the towns' (University of Southampton, PhD thesis, 1980), p. 381.

plague disrupted musters, quarter sessions and other aspects of local administration. In Somerset it put an end to meetings and plans for the revision of local rates.[146] In places it led, in varying degrees of seriousness, to a breakdown of order. While the commissioners for buildings were out of town, to escape the infection, 200 illicit buildings were erected in London.[147] One correspondent described the capital in October 1636 as reduced to a 'state of want and lawlessness', with over 1,000 in the suburbs living by spoil and plunder.[148] Whilst trust should not be placed in all such stories, we know from experience that there are always elements of society ready to cash in on human misery when the forces of law and order are otherwise preoccupied.

The less tangible consequences of plague are even harder to assess. But in Dr Slack's fine analysis, tensions between figures of authority with their (as they were often regarded) inhumane rules and the infected and their relatives, divisions over responsibility for care of the sick and relief of the poor, desertion of duty by magistrate, friend or family all contributed to that 'divisive impact of plague on social ties', the erosion of the communal codes on which central as well as local government depended.[149] Its psychological impact for the most part we may only guess at. But there were no few, perhaps, ready to see the pestilence as a judgment on the land and, more dangerously for the government, on particular policies or enactments. So the puritan Robert Woodforde recorded in his diary for 17 March 1638: 'The rail in the chancel is now almost up and it is confidently reported that the sickness is in the town.'[150] And the plague was actually to blame for another occurrence for which the puritans were to find quite other explanations. For the plague in London drove many Norwich weavers out of business and into an exodus that the puritan aldermen of the city (and too many later historians) attributed to Bishop Wren's affliction of their conscience.[151] It was only one of the many ways in which the pestilence struck at the personal rule.

Co-operation or obstruction?

Our sketch of the financial burdens, occasional disasters, and the endemic difficulties (of communication, faction and so on) facing local governors provides the necessary background to the questions we

146. Bates-Harbin, *Quarter Sessions Records for . . . Somerset*, p. 308.
147. *Cal. Stat. Pap. Dom., 1636–7*, p. 542.
148. *Ibid.*, p. 120.
149. Slack, *Impact of Plague*, pp. 289, 308–10.
150. Woodforde diary, 17 March 1638.
151. Tanner MS 68, ff.147, 157; below, pp. 753–4.

must now foreground. To what extent did the localities of England co-operate in executing central orders and directives, during the years 1629 to 1640? Did relations between the localities and the central government worsen during these years? Is there evidence of strains between the Council and the counties that explain later events, the opposition in 1640, or even the divide of 1642? Our capacity to ask as well as begin to answer these questions is a tribute to the excellent scholarship that has elucidated English local history over the last twenty years or so. Yet it may be that the concentration on the county communities has led to an overemphasis on the antagonism between locality and centre and to oversimplification in our use of terms. When we talk of 'the centre' we presumably mean the Privy Council, which was usually the body issuing letters, orders and requests to local officials. The Council, however, as well as a corporate body, was a collection of individual men powerful in, and with estates, families and interests in their localities. Councillors – especially those whose offices did not require their daily attendance on the king – often returned to their localities during the summer, and when in London often reflected with rueful nostalgia on the joys of their country life.[152] No less than the county JPs, who were often also MPs, Privy Councillors wore two hats. It was essential for the functioning of English government that they did so. Charles I appreciated the need to recruit to the Council those with greatest influence in their localities and at the time of the loan and in early discussions on the Book of Orders foresaw using their influence directly to assist the implementation of policy. But wearing their other hat, Councillors as leaders of local society took their loyalties and responsibilities to their counties seriously. In May 1635, for example, Lord Weston wrote personally to the JPs of Kent to forewarn them that the Council had directed the assize judges to quicken the magistrates' execution of the Book of Orders.[153] Moreover, as the Earl of Manchester's involvement in a Northamptonshire ship money dispute evidences, Councillors had interests in and ties to regions below the level of the county and became, even in their absence, as Wentworth would not have needed reminding, involved in local rivalries and disputes.[154] And even as a body, the Council was as dependent upon the localities as it was placed in authority over them. Central policies, enactments and adjudications required detailed local knowledge which, of itself, the Council did not have. Other than the

152. Cf. J.S. Robertson, 'Caroline culture: bridging court and country?', *History*, 75 (1990), pp. 393–5. I am grateful to James Robertson for his showing me a copy of this article in advance of publication.
153. Dering MS U 350/010: Weston to the JPs of Kent. On this copy the date is given as 15 May 1635; this must be an error as Weston died on 13 March.
154. Cf. my remarks above, pp. 443–8.

serjeants at arms the Council had no messengers to or agents in the localities.[155] Accordingly local petitions or queries had usually to be referred back to local officials for information and even final resolution. When the Council received complaints about Sir Walter Norton, sheriff of Lincolnshire for 1636, they could not just 'believe reports without proof' and so commissioned the deputy lieutenants, local men, to investigate.[156] When the judges were asked at the Norwich assizes for a ruling on rating they acknowledged that they could not provide one for 'every particular'.[157] As for alehouses, they could only reply that the magistrates 'shall do very well to allow none but in places very fit' – and leave the choice of those places to local judgement. The Council was not and *could* not be simply an organ of central authority.

We have become more aware recently of the need for similar caution with regard to the use of terms such as 'county', or even more vaguely 'local'.[158] Though the county was a forum of administration and even a community with which its inhabitants identified, it was by no means the only, nor even the most important one. The governing classes of the gentry had wider horizons: their education, family and friendships, lawsuits and social life led them beyond the county boundaries. Their practice of government, on the contrary, with the growing importance of petty sessions, focused on the region rather than the shire. The contest of contiguous parishes over assessment for bridge and road repairs illustrates that there was no simple county or local interest that stood in confrontation to central wishes. More important, it is not the case that the gentry or substantial landowners and tradesmen of the counties and cities of England during the 1630s regarded the Council primarily as an alien body, tiresomely interfering in local affairs. As we saw, central enactments such as the Book of Orders often reflected local initiatives and needs and throughout the decade the localities looked to the Council to help resolve local problems: in 1637 Worcester petitioned the Privy Council for assistance in 'suppressing of the dividing of tenements within this city and against the receiving of inmates'.[159] Even with more contentious matters, local authorities did not approach the Council as an alien organ, but as the proper body (the representative body of royal justice) to which to petition and present a grievance. So, in the summer of 1634 Sir

155. G.E. Aylmer, 'Studies in the institutions and personnel of English central administration, 1625–42' (University of Oxford, D. Phil. thesis, 1954), p. 178.
156. *HMC Cowper, II*, p. 138.
157. Tanner MS 288, ff.268v–270v.
158. Holmes, 'County community'.
159. S. Bond (ed.) *The Chamber Order Book of Worcester, 1602–1650* (Worcestershire Record Soc., new series 8, 1974), p. 316.

Edward Dering made known to Lord Keeper Coventry the abuses of a tobacco patentee who had vexed the county of Kent; Coventry reported the grievance to the Council.[160] When the mayor and Dr Wickham of York quarrelled over their precedency in the cathedral, both petitioned the justices of assize, then the king.[161] In 1639 the city was to appeal to the Lord President of the Council of the North, a royal nominee, against its militia being conscripted for the Scots war.[162] The final appeal to the king was not an approach to an 'other'; the monarch was still seen as above interest, the fount of independent justice.

Counties and cities too were as careful as are corporations today to cultivate useful friends in high places. In 1628, for example, the Common Council of Bristol 'thought fit that Mr Trumbull, now one of the clerks of the Council, shall be employed as a friend and an agent at the Council table', with a fee of £20 per annum, to enhance his friendly disposition.[163] The city proffered sweeteners to those placed higher still, appointing Lord Treasurer Weston their high steward.[164] Those proved far-sighted appointments during a decade in which there was a whole variety of 'little businesses' which involved reference to the Council Board.[165] Bristol did not hesitate to exploit its contacts, resolving at the time of the knighthood fines 'to make use of my Lord Treasurer's favour if it be needful'.[166] The frequent delegations sent to Whitehall either by the mayor and aldermen or by interest groups within the city are evidence sufficient to conclude that any model of 'local'–'central' relations must be more complex than one of confrontation. In an age when government was founded on personal relationships, when ministers of the king retreated when possible to their counties and when the substantial men of the shires went frequently to London, there was no simple local interest defined in terms of antagonism to a central interest.[167]

The relationship between them was one of interdependency and reciprocity: its healthy functioning depended on a sense of balance of service and reward.[168] It may be that it was in this respect that English

160. Dering MS U 350/010: Coventry to Dering, 19 Jan. 1635.
161. Above, pp. 396, 423.
162. York House Books, 36, f.24v.
163. Bristol Common Council Books, 3, f.4v.
164. *Ibid.*, f.25; and Noy as recorder, ff.23–23v.
165. D.H. Sacks, 'The corporate town and the English state: Bristol's "little businesses", 1625–1641', *P&P*, 110 (1986), pp. 69–105. I had the opportunity to hear and discuss with Professor Sacks an early version of this paper at the Conference of British Studies at Yale University in 1982.
166. Bristol Common Council Books, 3, f.31v.
167. Cf. Sacks, 'Corporate town and the English state', p. 85.
168. Historians of England should carefully ponder the implications for English society of the brilliant analysis of service and reward in seventeenth-century Spain given in J.H. Elliott's *The Revolt of the Catalans* (Cambridge, 1963), esp. pp. 41ff. and 71–4.

monarchs from the 1590s to the end of the seventeenth century exhibited their greatest failings, and Charles I notable among them. The purpose of royal patronage was to support and reward diligent local servants and to tie powerful local figures to the interests of the crown and government. Elizabeth's failure to dispense patronage skilfully in her last years led to a rebellion and the dangerous isolation of her court.[169] Similarly, Buckingham's monopoly of patronage contributed greatly to the political instability of the 1620s and to the crown's difficulties with parliaments.[170] The decade of personal rule inherited some of these problems, but also contributed to them. For though Charles showed a renewed concern for the preservation of aristocratic privilege, not least because honours had been excessively granted, he raised few to peerages after the duke's death in 1628.[171] He was not, however, during the 1630s, reticent about making demands for service. The Book of Orders, the militia programme and ship money placed unimaginable burdens on local JPs, deputies and constables. Besides these were the interminable commissions and requests for surveys, responses and reports – only Charles could have asked the mayors of corporations to check that none wore brass buckles.[172] Such labours often earned officials local unpopularity. Many sheriffs could have echoed Buxton's lament that he 'is become the most odious despicable man to his country that can be imagined'.[173] Royal favour therefore was often hoped for not just out of ambition but because it was a stamp of approval that rescued the executors of unpopular measures from the assault of their enemies and even raised their prestige in their localities. Wentworth's desperation to obtain an earldom showed how such calculations operated at the highest levels of government. In Nottinghamshire, the Earl of Newcastle who worked assiduously on the king's behalf shared Wentworth's frustration: 'if,' he wrote to Wentworth, 'your Lordship and I lose our counties and have little thanks above neither, we have taken a great deal of pains in vain.'[174] In 1636 Edward Lord Herbert petitioned the king to restore the lieutenancies of Glamorgan and Monmouth to his father, the Earl of Worcester, who had supported the loan, but was now derided locally for being a 'jack out of office'.[175] Lower down the scale many

169. S.L. Adams, 'Eliza enthroned? The court and its politics', in C. Haigh (ed.) *The Reign of Elizabeth I* (1985), pp. 58–78; G.R. Elton, 'Tudor government: the points of contact, II: the Council', *Trans. Royal Hist. Soc.*, 5th series, 25 (1975), pp. 208–11; M.E. James, *Society, Politics and Culture: Studies in Early Modern England* (Cambridge, 1986), ch. 9.

170. Cf. K. Sharpe, 'Crown, parliament and locality: government and communication in early Stuart England', *Eng. Hist. Rev.*, 101 (1986), pp. 329–30.

171. Above, pp. 419–20.

172. Larkin, *Stuart Royal Proclamations*, II, no. 165, pp. 369–70.

173. *Cal. Stat. Pap. Dom., 1638–9*, p. 61: Buxton to Nicholas, 18 Oct. 1638.

174. Quoted in J. Dias, 'Politics and administration in Nottinghamshire and Derbyshire, 1590–1640' (Oxford University, D. Phil. thesis, 1973), p. 355.

175. *Cal. Stat. Pap. Dom., 1636–7*, p. 177, [? Oct] 1636.

hard-working county gentry might have hoped for a mark of reward. Other than the occasional letter of thanks, however, there is no evidence that faithful service was reciprocated by reward. Charles's remarks to Wentworth suggest that he never fully appreciated the anxieties of those who served him.[176] And in his simple expectation that the royal command would meet mechanically with obedience, he lacked the politician's sense of the need to oil the wheels.

One of the most important favours a monarch could bestow was admission to the royal presence, a sight of divine monarchy. It has long been argued that, unlike their predecessor Elizabeth, the Stuarts failed to exploit the potent charisma of personal monarchy through public procession, progresses and displays.[177] Recently it has been suggested that Charles I was particularly at fault in failing to communicate with his subjects, indeed that he 'systematically distanced himself' from them.[178] There were no royal entries during the 1630s, it is argued; the king's progresses were reduced to hunting trips, and Charles restricted the occasions on which subjects might come to court to be touched for the king's evil. The case is marred by some inaccuracy and much exaggeration. Charles did not ignore public ceremony: in February 1632, the diarist William Whiteway records that the king and queen, having invited themselves to dine with the sheriff of London, 'went thither in great estate which the Londoners much esteemed'.[179] As we have remarked in another context, Charles revived the Garter day procession to Windsor and planned a magnificent spectacle for the inauguration of his son.[180] Nor were royal progresses as restricted as has been suggested. That of 1631 took the king and his entourage from Portsmouth to Windsor and Woodstock;[181] in the summer of 1634, in less than six weeks they passed through Hinchinbrooke, Apethorpe, Belvoir, Welbeck, Nottingham and Castle Ashby.[182] The Venetian envoy Gussoni described the king as 'in almost perpetual movement in his journeys and at all times of the year indifferently'.[183] Together with these the long progress to Scotland to be crowned in 1633, the visit to Oxford University in

176. W.S. Knowler (ed.) *The Earl of Strafford's Letters and Despatches* (2 vols, 1739), II, p. 32: Charles I to Wentworth, 3 Sept. 1636; 'the marks of my favour . . . are neither places nor titles, but the little welcome I give to accusers and the willing ear I give to my servants'.
177. Though there has been no real analysis of Tudor success and Stuart failure. I am currently working on *Representations of Authority: Images of Power in England, 1500–1688.*
178. J. Richards, '"His nowe Majestie" and the English monarchy: the kingship of Charles I before 1640', *P&P*, 113 (1986), pp. 70–96, quotation p. 78.
179. BL, Egerton MS 784 (William Whiteway's diary, 1618–34), p. 180, 7 Feb. 1633.
180. Above, pp. 220–22.
181. PRO, C.115/M31/8135: Flower to Scudamore, 25 June 1631.
182. *Cal. Stat. Pap. Dom., 1634–5*, p. 149.
183. *Cal. Stat. Pap. Venet., 1632–6*, p. 363: relation of 13 April 1635.

1636, and the frequent visits to royal dockyards remind us that Charles passed through quite a lot of his country during the decade.[184] And it is obvious, as we shall see, from correspondents that Charles's appearance could draw 'the love and dutiful demonstrations of his subjects in every place'.[185] But it may still remain true that Charles was less than assiduous in cultivating his people in general and his influential subjects in particular. His reserved manner and even awkwardness appear to have distanced him from some of his most loyal ministers and courtiers; few magnates enjoyed the familiar ease with the king that evidently characterized his relations with Pembroke. Apart from the occasional winning gesture, he did not charm his subjects with long speeches of thanks in return for their welcoming addresses. Indeed Charles became more sensitive to the need for such efforts only late in the decade. It was only from 1635 that he began to go out of his way to touch for the king's evil,[186] and not until his return from Scotland at the end of 1641 that he enacted something approaching a formal entry into the capital, tuning the crowd with 'gesture and speech' to a 'renewal of the shouts of welcome'.[187] It may well be that such gestures would have been even more welcome had they been offered earlier, in less desperate times.

There is, however, no shortage of examples of loyal and zealous servants of the crown during the decade of personal rule. In the Marches the Earl of Bridgewater enjoyed scarcely a day of leisure as he attended to his charge and endeavoured to acquire local knowledge of the Marcher counties. In Nottinghamshire, the Earl of Newcastle worked tirelessly to facilitate the levy of taxes and the raising of troops. In Kent, Sir Edward Dering, though in religious matters unsympathetic to the regime, proved an example of careful thoroughness as JP; Sir Walter Covert, a Sussex JP, regularly attended the sessions and worked tirelessly on out of sessions work though he was in his late eighties in the early 1630s.[188] Sir Thomas Jervoise in

184. See, for example, PRO, C.115/M37/8460; Egerton MS 784, pp. 183, 206; *Cal. Stat. Pap. Dom., 1635–6*, p. 535; *Cal. Stat. Pap. Venet., 1629–32*, p. 368. For the progresses of the 1630s, for example, see *Cal. Stat. Pap. Dom., 1631–3*, pp. 119, 128, 134–6, 278, 329, 377, 404; *1633–4*, pp. 176, 260, 492, 504; *1634–5*, pp. 26, 74, 149, 213; *1635*, pp. 237, 324, 330, 360, 420; *1635–6*, pp. 535, 569; *1636–7*, pp. 66, 129; *1637*, p. 316; *1637–8*, pp. 203, 558; and in addition the progresses to Scotland in 1633 and York (to fight the Scots) in 1639.
185. *Cal. Stat. Pap. Dom., 1631–3*, p. 61.
186. Richards, '"His Nowe Majesty"', p. 93.
187. *Cal. Stat. Pap. Venet., 1640–2*, p. 254. See R.M. Smuts, 'Public ceremony and royal charisma: the English royal entry in London, 1485–1642', in A.L. Beier, D. Cannadine and J.M. Rosenheim (eds) *The First Modern Society* (Cambridge, 1989), pp. 65–93. I am grateful to Malcolm Smuts for an offprint of this essay and for helpful discussions of this subject.
188. A. Fletcher, *A County Community in Peace and War: Sussex, 1600–1660* (1975), p. 222.

Hampshire was an energetic deputy lieutenant; as sheriff of Leicestershire, Sir Henry Skipwith was ambitious to be the first sheriff to pay in the whole of the ship money charged.[189] Lower down the administrative and social scale we find men like Hugh Tresse of Offham in Kent who had been, presumably willingly, twice constable of his parish, three times churchwarden and twice surveyor of the highways;[190] William Cooke, constable of Lancashire, was praised by his superiors for all he did to ease their task as local magistrates.[191] Loyal service in other words did not always depend on rewards. It was given both from a genuine sense of duty and from the logic of what Sir Thomas Temple told his son – 'the old saying is true that the King hath long ears'.[192] The success of ship money, the Book of Orders and even the militia are evidence of considerable efforts by local officials, in the face of a multitude of difficulties, to comply with the king's requests and execute his commands. Compliance, however, is not the same as satisfaction. And in addition to those positively alienated by religious policies or extraordinary levies, there were probably many more JPs and deputies disgruntled by increasing business and mounting burdens for which there were no corresponding rewards.[193] How many there were and how disgruntled is the most difficult question to answer.

Historians of the English 'county communities' have left us with very different impressions of the mood in the shires during the decade of personal rule. In Professor Everitt's Kent and Suffolk, discontents over ship money and religion appear to have fused into a united opposition to the king.[194] In Mr Clark's Kent, indeed, 'there was,' or so the author alleges, 'a unanimous feeling that Charles had succeeded in overthrowing the fabric of established political life.'[195] Similarly knighthood fines, ship money, religious policies, overall a programme of 'centralization' over the decade 'inexorably . . . confirmed the alienation' of Underdown's Somerset from the court.[196] Anthony Fletcher's Sussex was also alienated by religious and secular grievances.[197] However, the story of united opposition before 1640 is not

189. *Cal. Stat. Pap. Dom., 1636–7*, p. 439.
190. Kent Archives Office, QSOW1, f.85v.
191. B.W. Quintrell, *Proceedings of the Lancashire Justices of the Peace at the Sheriff's Table during Assize Week, 1578–1694* (Record Society of Lancashire and Cheshire, 121, 1981), p. 20.
192. Temple of Stowe MSS, Box 8, STT 2326, 7 Aug. 1631.
193. See, for example, J.S. Morrill, 'Sir William Brereton'; *idem, Cheshire, 1630–1660: County Government and Society during the English Revolution* (Oxford, 1974), pp. 22–30.
194. A. Everitt, *The Community of Kent and the Great Rebellion, 1640–60* (Leicester, 1966), pp. 56–68.
195. Clark, *English Provincial Society*, p. 381.
196. D. Underdown, *Somerset in the Civil War and Interregnum* (Newton Abbot, 1973), p. 20.
197. Fletcher, *County Community*, ch. 12.

universally told.[198] Dr Quintrell's Essex, for all its reputation for puritanism, co-operated vigorously in enacting many governmental policies and even emerged as one of the better ship money payers.[199] In Nottinghamshire there was, we are told, little opposition to knighthood fines or ship money or even, at the end of the decade, to the levies of troops for the Scots war.[200] In Cheshire Dr Morrill has documented the growing distrust of the central government and the 'resentment' expressed by Sir William Brereton and others at ship money and other exactions, but he has also acknowledged that many government programmes were 'widely implemented locally' and that the gentry were 'remarkably restrained in expressing their opposition'.[201] Overall, Dr Morrill suggests, the successful collection of ship money and yet the general opposition of the provinces in 1640 indicates that it was the Scots war that was really the turning point in the alienation of the localities from the centre.[202] The latest local study, of Warwickshire, supports the suggestion. Though there were discontents, even 'cumulative bitterness', 'most of the county paid up and kept quiet throughout the 1630s'.[203] 1638 marked the watershed in Warwickshire, though there was no sign of an open opposition movement before 1640.

For the most part, of course, the feeling in any county, especially prior to the Scots war, is hard to characterize, and has to be gauged from often enigmatic comments and still more unrevealing silences. More cautious than many, Dr Hughes writes that 'it remains impossible to make definitive pronouncements about the nature of political life during the 1630s or to answer questions concerning provincial attitudes to Charles I's government during that enigmatic decade.'[204] Indeed to think in terms of a county response, as recent historiography has cautioned us, may be more misleading than helpful, when counties by no means spoke with one voice and the interests of and loyalty to family and region were more powerful than those to the shire. When we write about reactions to the personal rule, then, we are on safest ground when we identify individuals and groups. Later we shall look at some of the more clearly articulated attitudes to the

198. Cf. *ibid*, pp. 239–43.
199. B.W. Quintrell, 'The government of the county of Essex, 1603–1642' (London University PhD thesis, 1965), pp. 61, 67, 121, 267, and *passim*.
200. A.C. Wood, *Nottinghamshire in the Civil Wars* (Oxford, 1937), p. 11; cf. Dias, 'Politics and administration'.
201. Morrill, *Cheshire*, p. 22.
202. J.S. Morrill, *The Revolt of the Provinces: Conservatives and Radicals in the English Civil War, 1630–1650* (1976), pp. 28–31.
203. A. Hughes, *Politics, Society and Civil War in Warwickshire 1620–1660* (Cambridge, 1987), p. 112.
204. *Ibid.*, p. 99; cf. A. Hughes, 'Local history and the origins of the civil war', in R. Cust and A. Hughes (eds) *Conflict in Early Stuart England* (1989), pp. 224–53.

government of the 1630s, to Charles I himself, and to the absence of parliaments; and we shall examine the question of opposition to the regime. Before we do, it will be instructive to examine the responses of some of those smaller communities – the cities and towns of England – to the government of personal rule. For though they too contained different interest groups and men of different persuasions, (at least in official matters) they often spoke collectively as a corporation. Compared with the history of the counties, however, there has still been comparatively little research done on the cities and towns in the seventeenth century. In recent writings on early modern urban history surprisingly little attention has been paid to politics and relations with the central government. In the case of the best documented city, the capital, the two leading authorities are in strong disagreement. Where Professor Pearl stressed the co-operation between the city magistracy and the crown and argued that a municipal revolution was needed to break the link between them in 1640, Robert Ashton charts the developing tensions between the city and the court that in his view made London's parliamentarian sympathies in 1642 a logical outcome of earlier developments.[205] Though the claim for something like a metropolitan high road to civil war remains unconvincing, Ashton presented important evidence of the dissatisfaction of interest groups in the city with royal interference in trade, the incorporation of craft organizations and the attempt to establish a corporation of the suburbs.

For the provinces we have few studies of depth. Those we have invite no simple generalization. Newcastle, for example, appears to have been characterized more by internal divisions than by a corporate voice. The city was divided between an increasingly oligarchic inner ring of merchants and those who resented their monopoly, and also by religious differences. It was the puritan faction which was most alienated from the central government, even to the point of welcoming the Scots in 1640.[206] Religion also appears to have been the major factor in the growth of urban opposition in Norwich, Canterbury and in Gloucester where, according to Mr Clark, 'by the mid 1630s . . . the city's attitude towards the crown was one of sullen hostility'.[207] And in Northampton, Colchester and Salisbury it may well be that it was those of strong puritan convictions who distanced the cities from

205. V. Pearl, *London and the Outbreak of the Puritan Revolution* (Oxford, 1961); R. Ashton, *The City and the Court* (Cambridge, 1979).

206. R. Howell, *Newcastle upon Tyne and the Puritan Revolution* (Oxford, 1967), pp. 62, 99, 116ff and *passim*.

207. J. Evans, *Seventeenth Century Norwich* (Oxford, 1979), ch. 3 and pp. 102–3; P. Clark, 'Thomas Scott and the growth of urban opposition to the early Stuart regime', *Hist. Journ.*, 21 (1978), pp. 1–26; *idem* '"The Ramoth Gilead of the good": urban change and political radicalism at Gloucester, 1540–1640', in P. Clark, A.G.R. Smith and N. Tyacke (eds) *The English Commonwealth 1547–1640* (Leicester, 1979), pp. 167–88.

the court.[208] Clarendon went so far as to suggest that a 'factious humour . . . possessed most corporations' and led them to oppose the king.[209] Whilst evaluation of his generalization must await further research, there can be no denying the mounting tensions in the cathedral cities of England during the 1630s, where age-old jurisdictional disputes between the corporation and close were, as we saw, sharpened by Laud's and Charles's emphasis on clerical power. Cities such as Chichester whose charter was altered to end the mayor's jurisdiction over the close, or Oxford where the town lost considerable power to the university harboured major grievances.[210] But again such rivalries are a reminder that cities were an amalgam of interests – clerical and lay, elite and popular – only some of which were alienated by particular royal policies, which makes for complications when one endeavours to assess an overall civic response to the personal rule. In Newcastle, for example, there was no 'direct . . . connexion in the 1630s, between the puritans and the various manifestations of civic discontent'.[211] And in Chester, for all the typical clash between city and cathedral, the interests of a small clique who wished to preserve the privilege of the Company of Merchants ensured close relations with the court, right up to the civil war.[212]

In many towns, as indeed in London, it was only events that occurred after 1640 that set the corporations in opposition to the king – and then often as a consequence of a coup within the city. Before such occurred, the necessary interactions of city and court, for all the tensions normal in such relations, precluded simple alienation and antagonism, because local communities had 'to call upon the state to help it perform necessary services or cope with its own internal problems, including perhaps social rifts and political divisions'.[213] Whilst the cities were highly jealous of their independent jurisdictions and the government was determined to implement certain orders, we should not assume that conflict was the inevitable or necessary outcome. Some royal policies were clearly of special benefit to the towns – most obviously peace, which greatly expanded trade, but also programmes like the Book of Orders which helped to tackle problems that hit urban communities most acutely.[214] Dorchester, Salisbury and

208. Clark, '"Ramoth Gilead of the good"', p. 187.
209. Clarendon, *History of the Rebellion*, II, p. 470.
210. Above, pp. 398–9; PRO, PC 2/51/292.
211. Howell, *Newcastle*, p. 116.
212. A.M. Johnson, 'Politics in Chester during the civil war and interregnum', in P. Clark and P. Slack (eds) *Crisis and Order in English Towns* (1972), pp. 204–36.
213. Sacks, 'Corporate town and the English state', p. 70.
214. See R.W.K. Hinton (ed.) *The Port Books of Boston, 1601–1640* (Lincolnshire Record Soc., 50, 1956), pp. xxxv, xlvi.

other towns had already embarked on schemes for setting the poor on work, which were aided by Conciliar support.

Such instances of concurrence and mutual interest need to be placed in a cocktail with the burdens of taxes and levies and interfering orders – such as that to the mayor of Reading to remove the unhandsome 'shambles' in Broad Street, or that to Chester to erect a waterworks.[215] How potable or bitter the mix was it is not yet possible to say, and may never be possible to ascertain. But the unusually rich records allow us a close look at the effects of the personal rule on the western and northern capitals – on Bristol and on York.

Case studies: Bristol

Bristol in the seventeenth century was the primary city of the realm outside London. Its geographical position had placed it perfectly to exploit the benefits of the Atlantic trade; the city was surrounded by fertile arable land that provided a food supply. And life for the citizens of Bristol, even the humbler, was probably more comfortable and more protected than almost anywhere in England. Bristol maintained a grain supply; it subsidized food in time of shortage; it received from its wealthy citizens munificent charitable gifts for the relief of the poor. It also kept its streets clean and paid its municipal workers well.[216] (The rakers who received £72 per annum may be evidence that in centuries before our own dustmen were paid more than dons.)[217] During the unstable years of the late 1620s, the burgesses ensured a strict watch and the city was able to set out ships at its own expense to guard its merchant vessels in the Irish seas.[218] The wars of the 1620s, however, imposed heavy financial burdens on the town – and, perhaps worse, the unwelcome presence of Irish troops. In August 1628 it was costing the city £17 10s. a day to feed the unruly soldiers and £140 was needed to provision those bound for Ireland.[219] It is not surprising therefore that the corporation voted to enter in the register book of the city 'there to remain for ever' the Petition of Right that promised to secure the city from such burdens in the future.[220] Though the 1630s continued to present the tiresome interference of royal commissioners and other intrusions, it is nonsense to argue that the end of war 'yielded

215. *Cal. Stat. Pap. Dom., 1633–4*, p. 197; PRO, PC 2/44/213.
216. Bristol Record Office, 04273 (1) ordinances, ff.64, 65.
217. Bristol Common Council Books, 3, f.10.
218. *Ibid.*, ff.4v, 6v.
219. *Ibid.*, ff.6–6v; cf. D.M. Livock (ed.) *City Chamberlains' Accounts in the Sixteenth and Seventeenth Centuries* (Bristol Record Soc., 24, 1966), pp. xxiv, 105, 111, 123, 128.
220. Bristol Common Council Books, 3, f.6v.

them only minimal relief'.[221] The prosperity of the 1630s probably benefited Bristol, whose economy was bound up with trade to Spain, more than any other city. Moreover, unlike other cities, Bristol appears to have been little disturbed by religious divisions. Though it was an old Lollard centre and is sometimes thought of as a puritan stronghold, the citizens of 'several parishes' were in arrears with payments to the lecturers.[222] Bishop Coke reported very favourably in 1633 on his see and appears to have maintained good relations with the aldermen; the corporation presented him periodically with generous gifts as tokens of their esteem and placed importance on their diocesan's approval of the city preachers and lecturers.[223] Evidently the city also took pains to maintain its churches, which Sir William Brereton thought some of the 'fairest' he had seen and which a group of soldiers described as 'richly adorned and sweetly kept'.[224]

Ship money sent some ripples through the calm of the western capital. From the first writ the city became involved in a rating dispute. But the quarrel appears to have been with the sheriff and, typically, while delegates were sent to the Council to plead the city's case, the disputed sum was paid.[225] However unwelcome, the burden of ship money on the citizens was lightened in Bristol by the Common Council's decision to meet some of the cost by disbursements from the city coffers: of the £1,200 assessed in 1635, £200 was paid by the city funds, of the £800 in 1636, £150.[226] Ship money appears to have aroused no widespread opposition from a city that could often see the ship money fleet in adjacent seas.

Such disputes as arose appear rather to have emerged from what were seen as assaults on civic privileges – or at least the privileges of powerful interest groups. Seventeenth-century Bristol was, as it is today, perhaps the most self-consciously proud of its independence of all the provincial capitals: the appointment in the 1630s of an archivist to sort the city records is only one instance of a strong civic pride.[227] It is therefore understandable that in November 1639 a dispute arose, over the city's election of a chamberlain, that might have led to a major clash. In October the Common Council elected William Chetwyn and immediately received from Charles I (who had received

221. As does Sacks, 'Corporate town and the English state', p. 77.
222. Bristol Common Council Books, 3, f.16v.
223. *HMC Cowper, II*, p. 29.
224. E. Hawkins (ed.) *Travels in Holland, the United Provinces, England, Scotland and Ireland by Sir William Brereton* (Chetham Soc., 1, 1844), p. 178; L.G.W. Legg (ed.) *A Relation of a Short Survey of Twenty-six Counties, Briefly Describing the Cities . . . Observed in a Seven Week Journey* (1904), pp. 92, 94.
225. Bristol Common Council Books, 3, ff.56–56v.
226. *Ibid.*, ff.64, 74.
227. *Ibid.*, f.41.

false information about the candidate, probably from his rival) a letter rebuking them for 'an overhasty and precipitate election'. In his place, the king recommended the defeated candidate, Ralph Farmer, 'a man not unknown to yourselves and by many of you much desired'.[228] The councillors obeyed the royal order but also petitioned Charles informing him that Farmer, who had not even been a freeman at the time of the election, had abused both Chetwyn (who was long known to them) and the king in an effort to promote himself.[229] Charles replied, leaving them free to make their choice: Chetwyn was re-confirmed in his post. The instance is typical of Bristol's relations with Whitehall during the decade of personal rule. Another example is that of the differences between the city and the Council over wharfage dues. These had been levied on imported goods at the order of the Common Council acting on behalf of the Society of Merchant Venturers who dominated the city magistracy. In the 1630s, acting on a complaint, the Council set up a commission to investigate by what right the duties had been levied and so threatened the Merchant Venturers' finances and jurisdiction. As the issue led to wrangles between the company and the commissioners, the city astutely sent petitions to the king, which ultimately resulted, in 1639, in a new charter that confirmed and enhanced the Merchants' privileges.[230]

Far from taking a 'localist' stance against the centre, in other words, the city appealed to friends at court (we recall they paid Weston a pension) to settle local problems. Not all elements in the city, however, had equal access to the ear of those in authority. The interests of the Merchant Venturers were by no means always synonymous with those of the city's craft-workers, who often had no powerful voice among the corporation.[231] So no powerful city support was offered to the Bristol soapmakers who were effectively put out of business by the creation of the Westminster company. They were left to appoint their own delegates to go to London on their behalf – and failed to secure a successful response to their petition: in 1637 Juxon and Cottington ordered that of the eleven Bristol soap houses only four should be permitted to continue manufacturing, and only 600 tons.[232] Such cases remind us that city governments often represented factional interests rather than the civic community as a whole. But at least as far as the relations between local and central governors went, communication

228. *Ibid.*, f.96; cf. Sacks, 'Corporate town and the English state', p. 82.
229. Bristol Common Council Books, 3, ff.96v, 99–99v.
230. *Ibid.*, f.81; *Cal. Stat. Pap. Dom., 1637–8*, pp. 23–4; Sacks, 'Corporate town and the English state', pp. 78–80.
231. Sacks, 'Corporate town and the English state', p. 92.
232. H.E. Matthews (ed.) *Proceedings, Minutes and Enrolments of the Company of Soapmakers, 1562–1642* (Bristol Record Soc., 10, 1940), pp. 201, 210.

between Bristol and Whitehall remained open and relations good. The wars with Scotland prompted some discontent; but not a failure of co-operation. Though they had little reason to fear the Scots, Bristol responded promptly to the Council's request, in April 1640, for 200 men armed with pikes and bandoleers.[233] No less promptly it dispatched the town clerk to London to complain and 'settle some way, if it may be, for the present and especially for the future, for the ease of this city in levying land forces, being unusual and rare in port towns who are to furnish seamen and mariners upon occasion of service'.[234] It was again a typical combination of obedience and appeal – but this time the grievance was to form the central tenet of a petition also to the Short Parliament.[235]

Case studies: York

York was not only the northern capital of the realm; it was the seat of the Council of the North and centre of the northern province, with its own archbishop. The north had traditionally been associated with disorder, and even in the more peaceful seventeenth century the city appears to have been a quarrelsome place where civic order was maintained with difficulty. There were sharp quarrels between the magistrates, several instances of constables being abused and women fighting in the streets.[236] Attempts to maintain standards, of environment and behaviour, encountered difficulties: indictments for failing to repair or cleanse the public ways appear frequently in the records, as do those for illicit games of 'shovel groat' played in alehouses late into the night. The justices of the peace, however, appear to have been dedicated and hardworking. Civic orders compelled them to be present to perform their duties, and fined absentees.[237] The city too had undertaken initiatives to tackle important social problems in advance of the Council's own prompting. In 1629 monthly sessions had been ordered and the magistrates anticipated the Book of Orders by measures for enrolling apprentices and providing poor relief.[238] Civic feasts were abandoned so that the money might be spent on the poor and a special fund for lame soldiers, mainly victims of the recent wars, was established.[239] By 1632, quite exceptionally, the reserve fund was

233. Bristol Common Council Books, 3, ff.100v, 102.
234. *Ibid.*, f.102.
235. *Ibid.*, f.102v.
236. York City Archives, F7, quarter sessions minutes, 1638–62, for example pp. 21–2, 39, 47, 64.
237. York House Books, 35, f.125.
238. *Ibid.*, ff.68v, 81v, 86, 90, 90v, 91.
239. *Ibid.*, f.80.

healthy enough for the city to abate the poor rate.[240] During the early 1630s, York was engaged in sending delegations to London for the renewal of its charter. The aldermen responsible 'found it a business very tedious and we well perceive will be also very chargeable'.[241] But the charter was renewed and the privileges of the city preserved. The relations between the corporation and the Council of the North seem generally to have been harmonious. There were disputes over the jurisdiction of lieutenancy between the vice-president and the mayor, and more seriously quarrels over their precedency regarding seats in the cathedral.[242] But for the most part these were settled without contention by Wentworth, who combined a firm assertion of the powers of the king's representative in the north with expressions of love for its primary city. The gifts sent to him at the manor house by the corporation suggest that some affection was reciprocated.[243]

Two visitations dominated the life of the city during the early years of the personal rule. The first was the plague of 1631, which appears to have afflicted York more than other parts of the country. In August Wentworth was sending detailed orders and asking the mayor and aldermen to report daily on their implementation to halt the spread of infection.[244] The other, happier, arrival was that of Charles I in 1633. The king's visit, on his progress to be crowned in Scotland, was preceded by months of planning in York. The highways of the city were repaired and improved; the streets were cleaned. Precedents of royal visits were examined and a silver bowl was commissioned, to be presented as a gift. The recorder prepared a speech 'expressing the great joy that all the citizens thereof do conceive at his Majesty's entrance and to show forth the necessities of the city occasioned for want of a navigable river'.[245] The brief nicely points up the importance of the occasion, for the visit was clearly seen to present practical opportunities as well as an occasion for celebration, and the city determined to take advantage of them. On 3 June 1633 a committee of aldermen was appointed to prepare maps and plans of the River Ouse with a case for the work they deemed necessary, ready to present to the king.[246] The city's 'little businesses' could hardly have had a bigger stage. The description of the royal visit fills four folios of the city's house books. It was a rainy day, as so many special occasions in England are. But the weather did not spoil the elaborate festivities.

240. *Ibid.*, f.168.
241. *Ibid.*, f.107.
242. *Ibid.*, ff.101v, 218; above, pp. 396, 498–9.
243. For example *ibid.*, f.111.
244. *Ibid.*, f.115v: Wentworth to mayor, 31 Aug. 1631.
245. *Ibid.*, ff.193, 198v–201.
246. *Ibid.*, ff.207–207v.

38 The King's Manor, York. The royal arms commemorate the residence of Charles I there in 1633.

The royal arms were raised above the entrance to Charles's lodgings, the residence of the Lord President, from that day to this known as the King's Manor (see Figure 38). The mayor was knighted and the recorder too, whose speech had skilfully blended praise of the king, pride in the city's antiquity and the plea for a restoration of its former glory through the project to render the Ouse navigable.[247] Within weeks of the king's visit the city sent Wentworth a petition to the same effect to forward to his majesty.[248]

The years after Charles's visit saw the first outburst of what was to be a long quarrel between the mayor and the archdeacon of the cathedral over the precedency of seating in church, and over the claim of the dean and chapter to exercise the authority of justices within the city.[249] As with Bristol, however, the city appealed to Justice Hutton, to the Lord Keeper, and ultimately to the king, and, at least in the first case, were vindicated.[250] Jurisdictional disputes between city and close

247. *Ibid.*, ff.208–11.
248. *Ibid.*, ff.214–214v.
249. *Ibid.*, ff.218v, 242v–243.
250. *Ibid.*, ff.218v, 219v–220, 242v–243.

continued, but there is no direct evidence that they marred relations between the corporation and the crown. York was quick to publish the Book of Sports (which it evidently did not regard as a licence to defamation of the sabbath) and was active in executing the Book of Orders and improving the militia.[251] And although they planned to appeal against it the aldermen also responded swiftly to the first writ of ship money.[252] The record shows that for the city (as for the Privy Council) ship money imposed the greatest labour of the decade and occasioned more letters and directives from Whitehall than any other business. But ship money was paid and York was not one of those places that were slow to assess or return payment. Its own complaints about Dunkirkers may have fostered an appreciation of the need for a stronger navy.[253] A potentially more contentious issue for York appears to have been Charles I's decision to admit maltsters into a corporation. For York claimed by the charter granted by Elizabeth the power of the city to appoint maltsters and the right of the citizens to brew their own beer.[254] Similarly in 1639 anxieties concerning their rights led York to send a delegation to London to ensure that nothing prejudicial to the city was contained in the new charter being prepared for Hull.[255]

The Scots war replaced these chimeras with more pressing problems. In addition to the vast burden of providing money, soldiers, weapons and supplies, the war involved the expenses (repairing highways, supplying the tipstaves with ceremonial coats) of a second visit by the king.[256] Though the circumstances – Charles's setting up camp for a war against the Scots rather than a progress to be crowned their king – could not have been more different, the second visit was treated not unlike the first. Because the warning came more suddenly, preparations could not be as careful. The presence of so many soldiers also fostered a sense of insecurity and necessitated a watch day and night.[257] But the city presented a gift to the king as before, delivered a speech of even more extravagant praise of his rule and re-enacted celebrations and ceremonies in a manner very close to those of 1633. The season this time being March, a Maundy service was conducted by the bishop of Winchester and the king's almoner washed the feet of thirty-nine poor men, who received gifts of cloth and a purse. Afterwards, the king touched many to cure them of the king's evil

251. *Ibid.*, f.238. York had been quite strict about sabbath observance, see F.7. See also House Books, 35, ff.106, 111, 117v, 158, 169, 174v, 179v, 190v.
252. *Ibid.*, ff.253, 259–60.
253. *Ibid.*, f.79.
254. *Ibid.*, f.332, 26 May 1637. Cf. f.350.
255. York House Books, 36, f.18.
256. *Ibid.*, ff.21, 21v.
257. *Ibid.*, ff.22–22v.

and gave a purse of £60 to the city's poor and prisoners.[258] Clearly the king had come to set up his temporary headquarters in his loyal capital of the north and appreciated the need to reward and foster that loyalty. As we shall see in more detail, however, the events of 1639 were to bring about a change of attitude. There is – perhaps significantly – little in York's house books about the Scots war. But it cost York dearly: by the summer of 1640 the city was raising several loans and trade was obviously disrupted.[259] When the third visit of Charles was expected (after the first campaign had come to naught) in August 1640 the aldermen met 'to consider whether it be fit to present his Majesty with a gift or not'.[260] Other irritations had come to the surface: the city sent a petition to the Short Parliament against the claims of the bishop and his chancellor to act as justices of the peace and in February 1641 it was to protest to the Long Parliament against the undue powers of bishops and ecclesiastical courts.[261] This obvious civic discontent at clerical pretensions, however, did not mean that the city was alienated from Charles I and his government. In August 1641 the mayor feasted the assize judges arriving on their circuits despite some fear that he might be questioned by parliament for so doing.[262] York also petitioned for the preservation of a court (like that of the Council of the North) in the city and in November, when Charles arrived for a fourth time, greeted him with a purse worth £100.[263] York was to be loyal to the king.

If the records of the northern and western capitals may be our guide, it would seem that though there was fierce pride in civic rights, a determination to protest at assaults on privileges and, most important, tensions between lay and secular jurisdictions, lines of communication with the Council and king were open and frequently employed, as was traditional, to secure redress of grievances and confirmation of rights.[264] There was no breakdown in relations between these cities and the central government during the personal rule.

258. *Ibid.*, ff.28–31.
259. *Ibid.*, f.45v.
260. *Ibid.*, f.46.
261. *Ibid.*, ff.41, 55.
262. *Ibid.*, f.59.
263. *Ibid.*, ff.51v, 62.
264. Cf. Bond, *The Chamber Order Book of Worcester*; and M. Weinstock (ed.) *Weymouth and Melcombe Regis Minute Book, 1625–60* (Dorset Record Soc., 1, 1964).

XI
'ITCHING EARS TO HEAR ANYTHING AGAINST THE COMMONWEALTH'? CENSORSHIP, CRITICISM AND CONSTITUTIONALISM

Censorship of the press

It may well be argued that the official records of the cities are not the sources where we would expect to find expressions of opposition, discontent or disenchantment. The very dependence of the corporations upon the crown for their charters, the maintenance of their privileges and the rectification of their grievances dictated, it may be said, a loyal address to the king. Such strictures can be taken too far, for we do encounter instances of obvious irritation and defiance in official records (Bristol even refused crown commissioners access to its records!),[1] and we are not incapable of detecting resentment even when it is more covert or veiled. Yet official documents need to be read in the context of more private expressions of opinion and more informal revelations of feeling which we are used to gleaning from diaries, private note-books, the correspondence of friends, and reports of words spoken. We shall endeavour to elucidate perceptions of and attitudes to the government of the personal rule from just such materials. Before we turn to them, however, we must encounter a problem to which historians have drawn much attention or – to rephrase without the underlying assumption – a question: that of censorship.

Some, notably Christopher Hill, argue that in the early seventeenth century censorship was widespread and similar in its effects to that of Eastern Europe in the twentieth century; whole undercurrents of opposition and heterodoxy which gushed forth in the 1640s could find no outlet during the pre-civil-war decades.[2] Others, like Annabel

1. D.H. Sacks, 'The corporate town and the English state: Bristol's "little businesses", 1625–1641', *P&P*, 110 (1986), pp. 79–80.
2. C. Hill, 'Censorship and English literature' in C. Hill, *Collected Essays, I: Writing and Revolution in Seventeenth Century England* (Brighton, 1985), pp. 32–71.

Patterson, whilst accepting the premise that censorship was widely practised, draw attention to the capacities of writers (especially, but not only, playwrights) to circumvent it, by a coded discourse which conveyed criticisms to those schooled in reading its cyphers – practices that may even have been tolerated by authority provided their 'functional ambiguity' never simplified into outright opposition.[3] Most recently the assumptions about widespread censorship have been subject to persuasive criticism. Blair Worden has reminded us that the mechanisms for censorship were unsophisticated and largely ineffective and argues that too much emphasis has been placed on it as a limit to literary freedom.[4] Professor Marcus concurs: 'only relatively blatant attacks tended to attract censorship'.[5] Most radically, Dr Lambert has criticized the 'mistaken premise' underlying most work on censorship: 'there never was any intention or attempt on the part of James I or Charles I to "suppress all criticism".'[6]

One of the problems with censorship is that of definition. We may consider censorship in terms of the institutions of control and punishment; but more broadly we may gather under the term all limitations, whether real, felt or imagined, to the free expression of opinion, and the institutions, cultural practices and even psychology determining those limitations. We shall consider both the narrower and broader meanings, incorporating self-censorship, so that before we turn to listen to what was said about the personal rule, we may form some idea of what people felt able to say.

Efforts were made during the 1630s to control the printing press. Such restrictions were not new. The machinery of regulation was erected by the Elizabethan injunctions of 1559 and the Star Chamber decrees of 1566 and 1586. These provided for the licensing of books by ecclesiastical commissioners and Privy Councillors, made the Stationers' Company accountable to the Council and limited the numbers of presses and the apprentices taken by master printers. In 1613 these regulations were supplemented by a grant of authority to the ecclesiastical commissioners to search for prohibited books.[7] Beyond that, everything printed was subject to the laws of treason and seditious libel, and there were precedents of harsh punishments of

3. A. Patterson, *Censorship and Interpretation* (Madison, Wisc., 1984).
4. B. Worden, 'Literature and political censorship in early modern England', in A.C. Duke and C. Tamse (eds) *Too Mighty to be Free* (Zutfen, 1988), pp. 45–62. I am most grateful to Blair Worden for sending me a copy of this important essay in advance of publication.
5. L. Marcus, *The Politics of Mirth* (Chicago, 1986), p. 178.
6. S. Lambert, 'The printers and the government, 1604–1637', in R. Myers and M. Harris (eds) *Aspects of Printing from 1600* (Oxford, 1987), pp. 1–29, quotation p. 1. I am grateful to Sheila Lambert for a copy of this essay and for discussions of this question.
7. See P. Olander, 'Changes in the mechanism and procedure for control of the London press, 1625–37' (Oxford University, B. Litt. thesis, 1976), chs 1, 2.

those who breached them: in 1590 John Udall was sentenced to death for writing against the bishops, and died in prison.[8] After Elizabeth's reign, however, a new genre of printed work emerged to plague the government. The newssheets or corantos sprang up during the 1620s to satisfy the appetite for news of the uncertain events abroad, as the Thirty Years War ended two decades of peace. They were popular and sold cheaply. For the most part, these 'weekly Avisoes' and catalogues of 'remarkable occurrences' were factual. But in their observations on, for example, the refusal of Aragon and Catalonia to contribute to the king of Spain's military campaigns, they could initiate some dangerous reflections.[9] More generally, the narrative of Habsburg victories and popish threats carried an implied criticism of English neutrality, as later the account of Swedish successes presented an unhappy contrast to recent English failures and withdrawal from European engagement.

Charles I early showed concern about the corantos. On 1 February 1629 Secretary Dorchester wrote to the warden of the Stationers' Company to remind him of the king's request that no news be published without obtaining a licence.[10] The king's express will, he wrote, was that 'hereafter none do presume to print or publish any matter of news, relations, histories, or other things in prose or in verse that have reference to matters and affairs of state without the view, approbation and licence' of Rudolph Weckerlin, then secretary to Dorchester and to the Council. It is clear that the order had little effect: corantos still circulated. In 1632, the king himself, acknowledging the failure of Dorchester's directive, wrote personally to the Stationers' Company complaining that despite earlier injunctions, the 'promiscuous' publishing of corantos and pamphlets 'unfit for popular view and discourse' continued unabated.[11] Indeed they appear to have been avidly and widely read. Sent from London they circulated among the provincial gentry, like the Barringtons of Essex.[12] Newsmongers assumed they were read; in January 1632 Sir Gilbert Gerard apologized to Thomas Barrington that he had no other news 'but what you may find in the Swedish intelligencer or the last new currant'.[13] Sir Henry Herbert, who kept Viscount Scudamore abreast of the latest gossip, told him that 'the corantos of this time are like the Thames at a full water, or a spring tide rather, with this difference that the one monthly

8. See W. Prothero (ed.) *Select Statutes and Other Constitutional Documents of the Reigns of Elizabeth and James I* (Oxford, 1913), pp. 442–3.
9. See *The Continuation of our Foreign Avisoes* (1631, STC 11178), p. 7.
10. Berkshire Record Office, Trumbull MS XVIII, f.104.
11. Trumbull MS XIX, f.16, 30 Jan. 1632.
12. A. Searle (ed.) *Barrington Family Letters, 1628–32* (Camden Soc., 4th series, 28, 1983), pp. 220–2.
13. *Ibid.*, p. 224.

the other weekly overflows'.[14] In October 1632 the Privy Council issued a decree against them in Star Chamber, prohibiting all stationers, printers and booksellers from publishing or selling gazettes or pamphlets of news from foreign parts.[15] John Flower, the newswriter, reported the ban and devoted his letter to foreign news.[16] After 1632, we hear little of the corantos for some time, though whether on account of the ban or because the market for foreign news diminished with the death of the hero of the headlines, Gustavus Adolphus, it is hard to say. What is certain is that the government remained sensitive: in October 1634 the Council ordered that no almanacs should be printed without licence,[17] despite the fact that 'the majority of . . . early Stuart almanacs . . . were deferential in tone' or politically quiescent.[18] It may be that news and discomforting comment was being purveyed through a different medium. For Edward Rossingham told Scudamore that one Bucar, the author of an almanac of the preceding year, was fined £100 for publishing dangerous matter against the state 'and for making the common people believe that there would be alteration and change in religion'.[19]

Such occurrences strengthened the case of those who argued that the government suffered from adverse publicity. In 1634 George More and Walter Waldner petitioned the king for the grant of a licence to, in effect, edit an official pro-government newspaper.[20] Arguing that those desirous of news usually consulted the gazettes 'whereby untruths and rumours prejudicial to the government were dispersed throughout the Kingdom', they advocated in addition to the examination and 'reform' of all publications, that 'a means be provided ad faciendum populum, to divulge such reports as upon occasion may tend to the good of His Majesty's service'. The committee of the Council took up the recommendation that all news gazettes be viewed and vetted but, perhaps significantly, no official propaganda organ, such as Richelieu's *Mercure* or *Gazette*, appeared in England.[21]

After the early years of the 1630s, it was the religious publications and polemics that caused the regime the greatest concern. Certainly we must include in that category William Prynne's *Histriomastix* which

14. PRO, C.115/N3/8549, 23 June 1632.
15. PRO, PC 2/42/224, 17 Oct. 1632.
16. PRO, C.115/M32/8199; cf. C.115/M30/8090.
17. *Calendar of State Papers Domestic* [*Cal. Stat. Pap. Dom.*], *1634–5*, p. 270.
18. B. Capp, *English Almanacs, 1500–1800* (1979), p. 71.
19. PRO, C.115/M36/8439, 31 Oct. 1634. Mr 'Bucar' was probably the astrologist John Booker who predicted the death of Gustavus Adolphus and who afterwards was appointed a licenser of books; see *Dictionary of National Biography* [DNB].
20. *Cal. Stat. Pap. Dom., 1634–5*, p. 418. More's father was lieutenant of the Tower of London.
21. *Ibid.*, p. 418; cf. W.F. Church, *Richelieu and Reason of State* (Princeton, 1972), pp. 340–4.

was published late in 1632, a puritan diatribe against the stage and players and, it was charged, a specific attack, under the index reference 'women actors, notorious whores', on Henrietta Maria, who regularly performed in plays.[22] In the course of his denunciation of the theatres as the epitome of Antichrist, Prynne drew an analogy between the Caroline court and that of the Roman emperor Nero who was murdered 'to vindicate the honour of the Roman empire which was . . . basely prostituted' by his viciousness.[23] Whether Prynne consciously made the connection or not, it certainly confirmed Laud's and the king's natural tendency to associate puritanism with sedition. Prynne was tried for seditious libel and lost his ears in the pillory.[24] It did not escape Laud's notice that in 1630 *Histriomastix* had received a licence from Archbishop Abbot.[25] Immediately therefore on succeeding to the see of Canterbury in 1633 he replaced Abbot's chaplains by his own agents William Bray, Thomas Weeks and Samuel Baker, all of whom were to face charges in the Long Parliament.[26] These would, he hoped, more effectively police the order he had issued as bishop of London that the Stationers' Company should print licences in all the books they published and in general tighten Abbot's laxness.[27]

Some historians would claim that his hope was fulfilled. And there were contemporaries who clearly felt the sharpness of the wind of change. A correspondent of the puritan *émigré* John Winthrop lamented in 1636, 'our presses formerly open to truth and piety are closed up against them both of late'.[28] Later, Prynne, Burton and Bastwick were to claim that Laud succeeded in censoring all orthodox Calvinist works, while licensing Arminian and popish books.[29] The claim is erroneous on several counts. For one, as we have argued, Laud tried fairly to enforce the royal prohibition on publishing on controversial points of religion.[30] Secondly, he had only very limited success in controlling the circulation of any books. Even licensing proved ineffectual. St Francis de Sale's *An Introduction to a Devout Life* was brought to the archbishop's chaplain, licensed by him subject to the

22. W. Prynne, *Histrio-Mastix: The Players Scourge* (1633, STC 20464).
23. *Ibid*., p. 852.
24. British Library [BL] Add. MS 11764, ff.8vff; Bodleian, Tanner MS 299, f.123; J. Bruce and S.R. Gardiner (eds) *Documents Relating to the Proceedings against William Prynne in 1634 and 1637* (Camden Soc., new series, 18, 1877). See also, Patterson, *Censorship and Interpretation*, pp. 105–7.
25. S.R. Gardiner, *History of England from the Accession of James I to the Outbreak of the Civil War, 1603–1642* (10 vols, 1883–4), VII, p. 328.
26. Olander, 'Control of the press', p. 70.
27. F.B. Williams, 'The Laudian imprimatur', *The Library*, 5th series, 15 (1960), pp. 96–104.
28. *The Winthrop Papers* (Massachusetts Hist. Soc., 4th series, 6, Boston, 1863), p. 422.
29. Tanner MS 299, ff.156–156v. Cf. N. Tyacke, *Anti-Calvinists: The Rise of English Arminianism* (Oxford, 1987), p. 184.
30. Above, pp. 296–7.

purging of 'divers passages therein tending to popery' and entered in the Stationers' Company register in February 1637. Nevertheless when the book was published, it was discovered to be 'corrupted and falsified by the Translator and Stationer, who between them inserted again the same popish and unsound passages'.[31] The book was called in by proclamation – but not before several hundred copies had been dispersed.[32] Similarly William Barles, an acknowledged recusant, was prosecuted in Star Chamber for passages in his book referring to the blessed Virgin Mary.[33] More worrying to the archbishop was the growing number of puritan and separatist tracts which were emanating from clandestine printing houses in England or, as Proctor informed Bishop Wren, were being illicitly imported from Holland.[34] Publishers and booksellers, defying orders against importing books, sold thousands of Geneva bibles, which had been disapproved of since James I's time.[35] Presbyterian works by John Bastwick (the *Flagellum Pontificiis*) and by William Ames, rector of the university at Franeker, appeared, in order to challenge the very foundations of episcopacy.[36] The High Commission stepped up its campaign, ordering a search for illicit books in places formerly exempt, but with little success. Printers like Michael Sparke continued in business even after censure and imprisonment.[37] Prynne continued to write and get published, whilst in the Tower, attacks on the Book of Sports and the episcopacy (*A Breviate of the Prelates Intolerable Usurpations* for example).[38] Moreover it has been estimated that in 1636–7 he published at least ten books as well as the *News from Ipswich*, for which he was tried and punished again in 1637.[39] The outburst of polemic which led commentators to speak of a war between the bishops and the puritans also led Laud to his most systematic endeavour to regulate the trade in books: the infamous Star Chamber decree of 1637.[40]

The decree of 1637, it has been said, reads like a statute, and was clearly intended to strengthen the ecclesiastical commissioners' jurisdiction over the press which had hitherto rested on letters patent.[41]

31. *Cal. Stat. Pap. Dom., 1637*, p. 78; J.F. Larkin (ed.) *Stuart Royal Proclamations, II: Proclamations of Charles I, 1625–1646* (Oxford, 1983), no. 238, pp. 557–8.
32. Larkin, *Stuart Royal Proclamations, ibid.*; *HMC De Lisle and Dudley VI*, p. 102.
33. Bodleian, Rawlinson MS C.827, 13 Charles I.
34. Tanner MS 68, ff.9v–10.
35. H. Carver, 'Archbishop Laud and the scandalous books from Holland', in *Studia Bibliographica in Honorem Herman de la Fontaine Verwey* (Amsterdam, 1966), p. 46; *Cal. Stat. Pap. Dom., 1637–8*, p. 365; C. Holmes, *The Eastern Association* (Cambridge, 1975), p. 9.
36. Olander, 'Control of the press', p. 99.
37. *Ibid.*, pp. 92, 96.
38. W. Prynne, *The Lord's Day the Sabbath Day* (2nd edn, 1636, STC 20468); *A Breviate of the Prelates Intolerable Usurpations* (1637, STC 20454).
39. Olander, 'Control of the press', p. 104; see below, p. 759.
40. Above, p. 360.
41. Olander, 'Control of the press', p. 171.

Announcing its intent to prohibit all 'seditious, schismatical or offensive books', the decree endeavoured to plug the loopholes in the existing codes of censorship.[42] The number of licensed printers was reduced to twenty and the names of those approved were added to the decree. The number of apprentices was also restricted. The authorized printers were placed under a bond of £300 to publish only licensed books; harsh punishments, the pillory and the whip, were prescribed for those who printed without authority, and carpenters were ordered to report to the government any press that they were asked to build. The arrangements for licensing books were extended and refined: law books were to be reviewed by the Lord Chief Justice, historical works by the secretaries of state, heraldic by the Earl Marshal and all others by the archbishop. Licences were required now for ephemeral works, such as ballads, where before the Stationers' Company had been left to their discretion. Books that had previously been granted a licence were to be relicensed on each publication to ensure that the text had not been tampered with. Most important were the controls on imported books, of which a catalogue was to be presented by the booksellers to the archbishop of Canterbury or the bishop of London. The import of books in English was prohibited and no books were permitted to enter the country except via the port of London where searchers appointed by the ecclesiastical commissioners, rather than the Stationers' Company, were granted extensive powers of inspection. In particular, all 'dry vats, bales, maunds, or other fardels' were to be carefully searched.[43]

The measures appear wide-ranging and thorough, and some have taken them as evidence of an absolutist regime's draconian dictate to stop all criticism.[44] We need therefore to appreciate that there was little new in the decree, which rather subsumed and systematized than innovated – even the authorization of imported books had first been required in 1624.[45] The only truly novel provision was that forbidding the importation of English books and that, Laud was to claim, was motivated as much by a desire to protect the native printing industry and a fear 'that by little and little printing would quite be carried out of the kingdom', as by censorship.[46] That may have been more than special defence pleading, for other aspects of the decree clearly reflected

42. E. Arber (ed.) *A Transcript of the Registers of the Company of Stationers of London* (5 vols, 1875–94), IV, pp. 528–36: prints the decree.
43. *Ibid.*, *passim* and Clause VI, p. 530.
44. Hill, 'Censorship and English literature', p. 37.
45. Olander, 'Control of the press', p. 174.
46. *The History of the Troubles and Trial of William Laud* (1695), p. 350. Though Laud was clearly defending himself, his argument should not be discounted. Cf. Lambert, 'Printers and the government'.

pressure from the printing industry. The journeymen wanted restrictions on the number of apprentices. And, as Dr Lambert has demonstrated, limitations on the number of presses (in 1637 as in 1586) 'was prescribed at the desire of the Stationers' Company, rather than being imposed by government'.[47] In 1630 Abbot had authorized only twenty printers and required them always to put their name to their work, while Laud had tolerated twenty-four for several years.[48] Even after the abolition of Star Chamber in the 1640s, the Stationers, desirous to protect their privileged monopoly, were still urging a restriction of the number of presses.[49]

Secondly the effectiveness of the decree should not be exaggerated. There were numbers of ruses that it was impossible to police. Additions to books after they had been licensed continued.[50] One of Prynne's printers had in his press a letter 'C' which turned one side there 'appeared a pope's head, and then turn it another way and there appeared an army of men and soldiers'.[51] Control of imports was never more than a pious hope. Agents continued to ply between Amsterdam and Norwich selling cheap copies of prohibited books, and even the customs officers could not be relied upon.[52] Information presented against them in 1639 shows that though they were supposed not to process parcels of books from abroad until a chaplain of the bishop was present, 'yet they open them themselves taking out what they please and let the rest pass'.[53] Together with imports, the combination of running presses, set up and moved on quickly, guaranteed the flow of puritan polemic. As Christopher Dow put it, 'Mr Burton knows well enough how to get books printed in spite of authority'.[54] He was not the only one: John Lilburne continued to publish despite the decree, and both Catholic and predestinarian and Presbyterian books circulated as they had throughout the decade.[55] Fewer catechisms appeared after 1637, but as Dr Green demonstrated, these seldom reveal strong partisan convictions.[56] In general the licensing system

47. Lambert, 'Printers and the government', p. 2.
48. *Ibid.*, pp. 3–5. Some claimed that there were more presses after the decree than before (Olander, 'Control of the press', p. 190).
49. Lambert, 'Printers and the government', p. 11.
50. *Cal. Stat. Pap. Dom., 1635–6*, p. 75.
51. *Cal. Stat. Pap. Dom., 1637*, p. 174.
52. Tanner MS 67, f.209; *Cal. Stat. Pap. Dom., 1637–8*, p. 365; *1636–7*, p. 427.
53. *Cal. Stat. Pap. Dom., 1638–9*, p. 258.
54. C. Dow, *Innovations Unjustly Charged upon the Present Church and State* (1637, STC 7090), p. 43.
55. Olander, 'Control of the press', p. 190. Henrietta Maria imported devotional books for members of her household (Tanner MS 70, f.89).
56. Olander, 'Control of the press', p. 193, appendix; I. Green, '"For children in yeeres and children in understanding": the emergence of the English catechism under Elizabeth and the early Stuarts', *Journ. Eccles. Hist.*, 37 (1986), pp. 397–425; I am grateful to Ian Green for helpful discussions about censorship and religious publications.

was frequently circumvented or ignored.[57] As a historian of censorship concluded, 'censure by the authorities . . . failed to thwart publishing by those who were bent on opposing the authorities'.[58] Laud's chaplain Peter Heylyn's verdict on the decree was terse: 'good laws are of no effect without execution'.[59]

Ironically, the attempt at more effective censorship may even have been counter-productive. For, as we know, where there is a market, there will always be a supply; demand unsatisfied by official printers may have stimulated an increase in the unauthorized organization of publication and distribution. Such was Gardiner's belief: 'the appetite for unlicensed literature was too strong to be thus baulked. Clandestine presses continued to pour forth pamphlets to be read by admiring and increasing crowds. Laud's attempt to silence his accusers only added fresh zest to the banquet of libel and invective.'[60] It is a judgement credible enough to those of us who from experience of the famous trials of the twentieth century know that censorship whets curiosity. Contemporaries were no less aware of the Lady Chatterley factor: in 1632 P. Matthieu had prognosticated that 'Princes deceive themselves when they grow passionate to abolish books which displease them; prohibition adds desire and difficulty maketh good the curiosity.'[61] By 1638 it was said that six more printing houses were in operation than had existed before the decree;[62] in October the twenty licensed printers complained that 'since this order abuses are increased rather than reformed': there were, they claimed, thirty-four printers at work in breach of the decree.[63] Sir John Lambe confirmed their complaints; many, he told Laud, printed 'by connivancy'.[64] One, Barret, claimed that he had not even heard of the decree – and despite the punishments threatened received only a £100 fine.[65] Indeed, though others were caught printing illicitly 'no one was ever whipped through the streets of London for breach of the decree of 1637'.[66] In the customs houses, too, officers were still coming across copies of Prynne, Burton, George Walker's work on the sabbath, books against ceremonies, and even a manuscript of a Brownist.[67] The Scots war, of course, opened a postern gate through which Presbyterian propaganda poured.[68]

57. See Williams, 'Laudian imprimatur'.
58. Olander, 'Control of the press', p. 194.
59. P. Heylyn, *Cyprianus Anglicus or the History of the Life and Death of William Laud* (1668), part II, p. 341.
60. Gardiner, *History of England*, VIII, p. 235.
61. P. Matthieu, *Unhappy Prosperitie* (1632, STC 17666), pp. 77–8.
62. Tanner MS 33, f.32.
63. Tanner MS 67, f.39.
64. *Ibid.*, f.46.
65. Rawlinson MS C.827, under 22 Nov., 13 Charles I.
66. Lambert, 'Printers and the government', p. 17.
67. Tanner MS 67, f.209.
68. Cf. below, pp. 816–19.

It may have been the failure to stem the tide of puritan polemic and a growing awareness that he was in danger of losing the argument by default that led Charles I, in the last years of the personal rule, to reconsider the establishment of an official government reporter. In 1638, Nathaniel Butler and Nicholas Bourne petitioned for the right to the sole printing of histories and news from foreign parts. The king agreed to their request, subject to their payment of £10 per annum towards the costs of repairing St Paul's. They were then granted 'the imprinting of all relations of accidents, occurrences and other things of that nature within any his Majesty's dominions', in addition to the sole right to print a gazette, which was to be reviewed by a secretary of state and sold for no more than 2d.[69] It was now seen to be important to communicate to a popular audience an official account to offset false rumours: in 1639 the Council proceeded against one Walkley, a bookseller, who in contravention of Butler's and Bourne's monopoly, had printed a list of the officers appointed for the expedition to Scotland.[70] Yet with the puritans' networks with Holland now reinforced by the influx of propaganda from Scotland, any last remnants of censorship collapsed. The abolition of Star Chamber in 1641 ended the institutional regulation of the press; as the pamphlet literature evidences, attempts to censor by the parliaments of the 1640s and the armies of the 1650s met with limited success.

If the Star Chamber decree failed like its predecessors, that is not to say there was no control, and more importantly no sense of control, over what was published and written. The threat of severe punishment should not be underestimated. An awareness of governmental sensitivity led some to abandon projects and others to submit them to those in high places for official scrutiny. Evidently Brooke's projected treatise against predestination, concerning which Laud had expressed reservations, never went to press.[71] Lord Herbert submitted drafts of his account of the recent war with France to Secretary Coke for his appraisal. Coke advised him that some passages, attributing the origins of the conflict to quarrels between Buckingham and Richelieu, 'cannot but reflect upon the honour of King and State and ought not to be published'. Rather, he advised, 'such a character [was] to be made of the proceedings as may agree with the wisdom and honour of the King'.[72] Twysden informs us that many in Kent wondered whether Selden's *Mare Clausum* had not been issued purely as propaganda for ship money and suspected that answers to the treatise were prohibited.[73] There were those advising the Council in 1637 to review

69. PRO, SO 1/3, f.110, 20 Dec. 1638; *Cal. Stat. Pap. Dom., 1638–9*, p. 182.
70. PRO, PC 2/50/271, 17 April 1639.
71. *Cal. Stat. Pap. Dom., 1629–31*, pp. 384–5, 396, 404; W. Scott and J. Bliss (eds) *The Works of William Laud* (7 vols, Oxford, 1847–60), VI, part 1, p. 292.
72. Melbourne Hall, Coke MS 38; see the summary in *HMC Cowper I*, p. 398.
73. Kent Archives Office, Twysden MS U47/47, Zi, pp. 193–4.

Justus Lipsius's 1619 edition of Tacitus to expunge seditious passages;[74] in 1639 Charles I himself altered passages on church government in Bishop Morton's sermon before it was printed.[75] The effect of these incidents and rumours, their consequences for self-censorship, are extremely hard to gauge – not only in the seventeenth century but in any society. England in the 1630s was not a country in which men were free to publish or read what they saw fit. Nor, however, was it a realm in which all criticism and dissent were stifled.

This was not only due to ineffective censorship. In early modern England, for all the concern with order and hierarchy and orthodoxy, disorder, inversion and dissent were not only tolerated, but authorized. Social customs and practices such as Christmas revels, May day, 'barring out' in schools and 'lords of misrule' functioned as safety valves; they were devices through which criticism could be expressed and contained.[76] Other such devices include the writing of histories and the theatre. With these last the claim for freedom of expression may seem untenable. There is no shortage of examples of historians or playwrights punished for ill-advised references or allusions to controversial events: Middleton and Jonson, Hayward and Raleigh for instance. But such cases were usually of transparent topicality and may have been prosecuted for that reason: that is for abusing the acknowledged licence of play to comment and criticize provided that it did so indirectly and obliquely - what Annabel Patterson has called the 'cultural bargain between writers and political leaders'.[77] Certainly the public stage during the 1630s did not shrink from criticism: the plays of the decade, especially those of Thomas Nabbes and Richard Brome, have recently been described as 'opposition drama'.[78] Moreover, even playwrights such as Thomas Middleton, with a long history of brushes with the censor, continued to be staged – and (like Brome) at court as well as in the public playhouses.[79] The political engagement of drama, poetry and indeed of histories – an engagement we have only just begun to appreciate – suggests perhaps that even in the 1630s the codes of censorship still embraced authorized modes of dissent.[80]

74. *Cal. Stat. Pap. Dom., 1637–8*, p. 71.
75. *Cal. Stat. Pap. Dom., 1639–40*, pp. 212–13.
76. For a brilliant example, see K.V. Thomas, *Rule and Misrule in the Schools of Early Modern England* (Reading, 1976).
77. Patterson, *Censorship and Interpretation*, p. 7. New Historicist critics would argue that this 'cultural bargain' neutralized the threat of dissent.
78. M. Butler, *Theatre and Crisis, 1632–1642* (Cambridge, 1984).
79. See K. Sharpe, *Criticism and Compliment: The Politics of Literature in the England of Charles I* (Cambridge, 1987), pp. 34–9.
80. I plan to work on the politics of histories from the mid-sixteenth to the end of the seventeenth centuries. See K. Sharpe, *Politics and Ideas in Early Stuart England* (1989), pp. 36–8, 41–4.

The control of private papers and archives

More revealing perhaps than the censorship of published books and newssheets was the government's concern to exercise control over private libraries and collections of manuscripts, especially those of historical records and legal precedents. In early Stuart England, the appeal to precedents in politics was all but universal. Precedents were varied and might be manipulated, or at least carefully selected, but they undoubtedly authorized arguments and actions, not least because the common law of England was itself unwritten and based on precedent. Because precedents legitimized, all sought to have access to them and to appropriate them, as today politicians seek and claim the support of statistics. Therefore the libraries and scholars – lawyers and antiquaries – that were the storehouses and custodians of precedents were important political institutions and figures. The parliamentary debates of the 1610s and 1620s, sometimes over major questions of prerogative and law, demonstrated that precedents did not consistently favour any one – king, councillor or critic of royal policy. Antiquaries like Sir Robert Cotton indeed could supply precedents to support different sides of an argument, and his library was placed at the service of Privy Councillors, MPs and scholars alike.[81] James I, no innocent when it came to appreciating the importance of historical argument, kept a watchful eye on those – as well as Cotton, John Selden and Sir Edward Coke – whose libraries, and memories, were potential arsenals of precedents. Charles I, always less inclined than his father to participate in political arguments, appears from the beginning to have been more determined to control them. Though his counsel was sought by some within the Privy Council in 1627, perhaps by the king himself, Cotton was evidently thought to be too unreliable in terms of the other company (men like Sir John Eliot) he kept. In 1630, suspecting that Cotton's library had provided ammunition to those who framed the Petition of Right, the king ordered the closure of the finest repository of medieval and contemporary records in England. Cotton himself was confined, awaiting prosecution in Star Chamber, for having distributed from his collection a pamphlet which scandalized the government by implying its contemplation of tyrannical measures. The Privy Council appointed one of its clerks, Sir William Boswell, to prepare a catalogue of all the manuscripts in the Cottonian collection and to investigate which were out on loan. The catalogue was still

81. See K. Sharpe, *Sir Robert Cotton 1586–1631: History and Politics in Early Modern England* (Oxford, 1979).

being prepared and the library was still sealed in 1631 when Cotton died, allegedly of grief.[82]

The following year governmental attention turned to Sir Edward Coke. On 24 January 1631 the Earl of Holland informed Secretary Dorchester that Charles I required that a book being written by Coke should be sent to the Lord Keeper for his inspection, for 'the King fears somewhat may be to the prejudice of his prerogative for he is held too great an oracle amongst the people and they may be misled by anything that carries such an authority'.[83] Coke was, accurately, rumoured to be ill, so Holland urged Dorchester to enquire into his health, 'and if he be in any present danger that care may be taken to seal up his study if he dies where such papers are as use may be made of them for his Majesty's service and some suppressed that may disserve him'. Coke did not die in 1631, but even before his demise in 1634, his papers were impounded. In April 1632 Sir Thomas Barrington told his mother, 'Sir Edward Coke hath his papers seized by reason of a report that he is about a book concerning Magna Carta and is likely to incur some trouble.'[84] Another newswriter reported 'sackfulls' of manuscripts being removed from Stoke Poges (Coke's retirement residence) – among them commentaries on Magna Carta.[85] In 1633 the king evidently considered calling in Coke's published and circulated writings. In March the Council announced that the king had heard that

> the reports of Sir Edward Coke and his commentary upon Littleton contains many things not to be approved by which students in the law are drawn into erroneous opinions and the same are also vouchsafed by some lawyers in their pleading whereupon unnecessary disputes and other inconveniences must needs follow, for redress whereof his Majesty sitting this day in Council was pleased to command Mr Attorney General who attended them to peruse the said reports and commentary . . . and to make a collection of such things as they found requisite to be purged and reformed in the same.[86]

The following summer, on 3 September, the long-ailing Sir Edward died. His study in the Inner Temple had been sealed in August, and one of his sons, Roger, later claimed that while Coke lay on his deathbed Windebank was sent to ransack the house in Stoke Poges.[87] Rossingham confirms the story: writing to Scudamore on 29 August

82. *Cal. Stat. Pap. Dom., 1629–31*, p. 305; PRO, PC 2/41/99; C.115/M31/8119; Sharpe, *Sir Robert Cotton*, pp. 80–2, 145. Selden's papers were also seized.
83. *Cal. Stat. Pap. Dom., 1629–31*, p. 490.
84. Searle, *Barrington Letters*, p. 237.
85. PRO, C.115/M36/8431: Rossingham to Scudamore, 29 Aug. 1634, reporting events of two years before.
86. PRO, PC 2/42/536.
87. Gardiner, *History of England*, VII, p. 360.

he told the envoy that all Coke's chambers at the Inn had been locked, his old servant imprisoned and his house searched, trunks being broken open in the anxiety not to miss documents.[88] Only the private papers were restored. In 1640 Coke's son was to raise the matter in the Long Parliament and the House of Commons opened an enquiry being 'very desirous to recover these manuscripts as supposing they contain many monuments of the subject's liberties'.[89] They ascertained that they had come into the king's hands with the papers of Noy, to whom Secretary Sir John Coke had delivered Edward Coke's manuscripts.[90] The collection never came to light.

The seizure of Cotton's and Coke's collections were the biggest swoops made by the government in their determination to control papers of importance (either value or threat) to the state; but there were others. In 1632 the Council searched the papers of Sir Miles Hobart who had been involved in the parliamentary fracas of 1629.[91] Early in September 1634 the study of Attorney-General Noy, who died within days of Coke, was also sealed; his papers were perused and, it was said, 'such as the state may have any use of shall be taken'.[92] Noy, however, cheated his searchers from the grave: he had burnt his 'choicest notes' and in particular his personal index of the records – not out of political considerations but because 'Mr Noy meant not that any succeeding lawyer should eclipse him by his own books. Let them study as he had done'![93] In general, the Council appears to have been increasingly concerned to acquire and preserve all 'official' records and to change the habit of ministers regarding them as private property. On the death of Secretary Dorchester, for example, they ordered an inventory of his manuscripts;[94] in 1635 Sir Noel de Caron's papers were searched for official papers belonging to the king;[95] the clerk John Dickinson's papers were ordered to be brought to the Council in 1636;[96] in 1639 Nicholas was pursuing copies of the Privy Council letters 'the originals whereof were burnt when the old Banqueting House was fired'.[97]

88. PRO, C.115/M36/8431. See Lambeth Palace MS 943, p. 369 for a note of the papers in Coke's trunk brought to Bagshot and opened at the king's command on 9 September 1634 and p. 371:'A catalogue of Sir Edward Coke's papers'.
89. *HMC Cowper II*, p. 266.
90. *Ibid.*, p. 268.
91. PRO, PC 2/42/139.
92. PRO, C.115/M36/8432: Rossingham to Scudamore, 2 Sept. 1634.
93. *Ibid.*, It is to be hoped that scholars do not follow his example.
94. *Cal. Stat. Pap. Dom., 1631–3*, p. 396.
95. PRO, PC 2/44/452, 4 March 1635.
96. *Cal. Stat. Pap. Dom., 1635–6*, p. 172, 20 Jan. 1636.
97. *Cal. Stat. Pap. Dom., 1638–9*, p. 341: Nicholas to Mrs Cary, 21 Jan. 1639. Her father had been clerk to the Council; it is interesting to note that he was believed to have taken papers home.

Attitudes to records are never apolitical and certainly were not in the 1630s. In February 1633, learning that Sir John Borough, Keeper of the Tower records, had permitted prisoners in the Tower to examine documents, the Council prohibited all such access, considering 'how unfit it is that persons so ill affected to his Majesty's service should have liberty to peruse the said records'.[98] This enheightened sensitivity to access to 'official' records was displayed again the following year when the Keeper of the records was asked to take an oath swearing to conceal records from all but Privy Councillors and: 'if you shall know of any private person or persons that have embezzled or do detain any such papers or records which belong unto his Majesty, you shall do your best to recover the same.'[99] In 1635 the Council took action to ensure the safe preservation of what was now emerging as an official but secret archive. It having come to the Council's attention that there was a vault containing combustible materials beneath the record repository in the Tower, they evicted one Jefferson, the owner of the house, and made the rooms vacated over to Borough as offices – 'also the Garden Place for airing the records as occasion shall require'.[100]

Clearly the government was anxious to conserve its own arsenal of legal precedents and deny the benefits of them to others. The importance of such materials was soon powerfully brought home. In the ship money trial, the outcome to a large extent hung on the weight of precedent. In June 1637, while the issue was *sub judice*, the Council ordered a search of the Lincoln's Inn study of Oliver St John, counsel to Lord Saye in his challenge to the tax, and subsequently Hampden's principal defence.[101] A newswriter reported that the messenger took away notes on ship money and records concerning the forests.[102] St John's papers were evidently later returned.[103] But after the trial, a search was made of one Claxton's home for a copy of Justice Croke's judgment, which the Attorney took away to compare with others.[104] During the Scots war, such searches for sensitive material were to become frequent. If precedents were to decide the legality of royal policies, the king and Council were clearly acting to ensure that they were stacked on their side.

98. PRO, PC 2/42/419, 1 Feb. 1633.
99. PRO, PC 2/43/6.
100. PRO, PC 2/44/592.
101. PRO, PC 2/48/37, 16 June 1637; W.S. Knowler (ed.) *The Earl of Strafford's Letters and Despatches* (2 vols, 1739), II, p. 85: Garrard to Wentworth, 24 July 1637.
102. *Cal. Stat. Pap. Dom., 1637*, p. 237.
103. *Ibid.*, p. 252.
104. *Cal. Stat. Pap. Dom., 1638–9*, p. 517.

The king and his judges

There are some grounds for concurring with contemporaries who felt, and historians who maintain, that the same holds true of the king's relations with his judges. There is no reason to doubt Charles's belief in his duty to govern in accordance with the common law. Nor should we be cynical about his tendency to consult his judges over any doubtful course: be it potentially contentious (whether the Petition of Right proscribed all imprisonment without cause shown),[105] problematic (the legality of requiring foreign residents to have a visa)[106] or uncontroversial (the taking of fee deer).[107] But Charles's respect for the law went hand in hand, as did everyone else's, with an interpretation of the law. As the debate on the Petition of Right had revealed, Charles believed that the law respected the needs of government, that it had been evolved to support not to impede a dutiful king's capacity to govern. In thinking so, Charles did not differ from his father; and the language of those MPs and common lawyers who spoke of the symbiosis of law and prerogative may have persuaded him that his views did not differ from his subjects'.[108] On occasion, however, as in the wars of the 1620s, many had appealed to the law against the demands of the government. In such a case (because his duty to defend his people was at stake), though there were lawyers ready to endorse these complaints, Charles could only conclude that their interpretations of the law were wrong. As the king was to say, in response to Yorkshire's petition against billeting in 1640, in accepting the Petition of Right it had never been 'in the thought of his Majesty to divest the crown of that necessary power without which it is impossible for armies to march'.[109]

While remaining strictly within the bounds of the law then, Charles was not averse to applying some pressure to see that the law did not disfavour the government. In the first instance judges whose opinions proved consistently unpalatable were dismissed or suspended. In 1630 Charles inhibited Sir John Walter from sitting in court (though significantly he did not remove him) on account of Walter's expressed reservations about the trial of Sir John Eliot and others who, he thought, might have been covered by parliamentary privilege. The king heavily pressured all his judges in his efforts to deny the MPs

105. *Cal. Stat. Pap. Dom., 1628–9*, p. 142; cf. p. 95.
106. *Cal. Stat. Pap. Dom., 1637–8*, p. 203.
107. See Larkin, *Stuart Royal Proclamations*, II, no. 42, p. 90.
108. Cf. J.G.A. Pocock, 'The Commons debates of 1628', *Journ. Hist. Ideas*, 39 (1978), pp. 329–34; see also, P.G. Burgess, 'Custom, reason and the common law: English jurisprudence 1600–1650' (Cambridge University, PhD thesis, 1988).
109. *Cal. Stat. Pap. Dom., 1640*, pp. 595–7.

habeas corpus and to retain them at his pleasure.[110] Justice Heath who had co-operated in their prosecution was in his turn given several indications of the royal displeasure before his dismissal in September 1634. In July 1634 Rossingham informed Scudamore that the chief justice had been 'chidden' for his non-compliance in a recent case of extortion and had been warned that he would be removed from the Common Pleas if he did not mend his ways.[111] In September his removal was announced for something he had done when Attorney-General, but what his sin was, Rossingham thought, 'we are not like to know'.[112] Some have speculated that Heath's reputation as a puritan was his downfall;[113] others more convincingly attribute it to his mis-handling of London's charter for Londonderry.[114] Whatever the case, for all his staunch upholding of the prerogative in the trials of Eliot, Chambers, Leighton and Prynne, he had evidently displeased the king. Though Wentworth secured the transfer of justice Denham from the northern circuit,[115] the suspensions of Walter and Heath were the only actions taken against judges during the 1630s – a small number of incidents compared with, say, the 1550s or the later Stuart decades.[116] After 1634, with the removal of Heath (who was permitted to practise as a king's serjeant) Sir John Finch was appointed Lord Chief Justice and Sir John Bankes succeeded as Attorney on the death of William Noy.[117] Both evidently proved more sympathetic to the king, though it is worth remembering that Finch was a strict Calvinist (and friend of Laurence Chadderton)[118] whilst Bankes had denied the authority of the king's command to breach parliamentary privilege and was kept in office still in 1643; both were lawyers of immense learning, and probably chosen for that before other considerations.[119] Whilst there may be something in the suggestion that after Hampden's case closer care was taken over legal appointments, politics do not seem to have

110. Gardiner, *History of England*, VII, pp. 88–90; T.G. Barnes (ed.) *Somerset Assize Orders 1629–40* (Somerset Record Soc., 65, 1959), p. xxi. For a full account of the prosecution of the MPs, see L.J. Reeve, *Charles I and the Road to Personal Rule* (Cambridge, 1989), ch. 5; and D.S. Berkowitz, *John Selden's Formative Years* (Washington, 1988), ch. 12.
111. PRO, C.115/M36/8426.
112. PRO, C.115/M36/8435: Rossingham to Scudamore, 26 Sept. 1634.
113. J. Reeve, 'Sir Robert Heath's advice for Charles I in 1629', *Bull. Inst. Hist. Res.*, 59 (1986), pp. 221–2; see also Somerset Record Office, Phelips MS DD Ph/219, f.68.
114. T.G. Barnes, 'The cropping of the Heath', paper read at the Royal Historical Society, December 1986.
115. W.J. Jones, *Politics and the Bench: The Judges and the Origins of the English Civil War* (1971), p. 137.
116. *Ibid.*, p. 39.
117. *Cal. Stat. Pap. Dom., 1634–5*, p. 221.
118. See W.R. Prest, 'The art of law and the law of God: Sir Henry Finch 1558–1625', in D. Pennington and K. Thomas (eds) *Puritans and Revolutionaries* (Oxford, 1978), pp. 94–117.
119. *DNB*; Jones, *Politics and the Bench*, ch. 2; G. Bankes, *The Story of Corfe Castle* (1853), p. 58.

been to the fore: Sir Charles Caesar secured the mastership of the Rolls in 1639 for being the highest bidder.[120]

The right of a government to appoint judges whom it regards as sympathetic to its programmes, within the parameters of the law, is one we grant to modern democratic regimes. More insidious, perhaps, was the pressure Charles at times put on his judges once they were appointed. In August 1629, to take an example from the beginning of the personal rule, a furore took place in London. The king expressed his surprise, in a letter sent by Secretary Coke to the Lord Chief Justice of the King's Bench, that the judges had deemed the offence a riot not a capital crime; he asked them to consider whether 'if our laws admit no other proceedings against malefactors' government and the protection of men's lives and estates could be preserved.[121] The letter was a heavy hint to the bench of the king's expectations of them, and the first of many. In February 1632 Charles wrote to enquire of his judges whether he might establish a court of the palace of Westminster with jurisdiction over an area within twelve miles of the palace. The king noted that he had written concerning the matter before and expected 'speedily a plain answer from them by the Attorney General, not thinking it fit to give over much way to the disputing of so high a point of his prerogative'.[122] There were more direct and particular royal interventions. On 4 December 1634 Charles sent a signed letter to the barons of the Exchequer asking them to help one John Lisle in his dispute with Sir Sutton Coney, who claimed land given to Lisle.[123] In 1635 when the judges of the Common Pleas were hearing the case of one Dr Pecke concerning title to the rectory of Lyminge in Kent, Charles wrote to tell them that Pecke's title should be maintained.[124] In August 1637, as we shall see, Lord Keeper Coventry had occasion to check the king's attempts to interfere in a case in Star Chamber.[125] As well as this leaning on the judges, Charles (like his father) attempted also to put a stop to prohibitions which challenged the jurisdiction of the prerogative courts. On 6 May 1631 he appointed a commission of Privy Councillors to search the records and settle disputes concerning jurisdiction 'that all our subjects may receive the benefit of speedy and effectual justice'.[126] The king was present when they met.[127] And the

120. Jones, *Politics and the Bench*, p. 38; *Cal. Stat. Pap. Dom., 1638–9*, p. xxvi.
121. Coke MS 37: Coke to Lord Chief Justice of King's Bench, 9 Aug. 1629, calendared in *HMC Cowper I*, p. 390.
122. PRO, SO 1/2, f.82v; see *Cal. Stat. Pap. Dom., 1631–3*, p. 266.
123. PRO, SO 1/2, f.201.
124. *Ibid.*, f.241v; *Cal. Stat. Pap. Dom., 1635*, p. 471.
125. Coke MS 56: Coventry to Coke, 8 Aug. 1637; below, p. 678.
126. Huntington Library, Ellesmere MS 7928; Birmingham Library, Docquets of Letters Patent, Coventry MS 602204/229.
127. PRO, PC 2/42/456.

newswriters may have been right to suspect that the king having denounced prohibitions *de iure*, the outcome of the commission's work was a foregone conclusion:[128] John Pory even thought its purpose was 'in time to draw appeals from all Courts to the Council board'.[129]

If, however, Charles I went beyond proprieties in his efforts to influence legal decisions, it is by no means clear that he was always effective. Nor is it at all obvious that the judges were, as the Long Parliament charged in 1640, but ciphers. We do know that Attorney Heath attempted to enter illegally a judgment in the court record to show that the judges had delivered a binding precedent for indefinite imprisonment for reasons of state. Dr Guy has shown that the revelation of his deviousness influenced the course that led to the Petition of Right.[130] But it is not clear that Heath acted on royal instructions;[131] he did not hesitate to cross the king's wishes in other matters; and, most importantly here, it was the other judges who prevented Heath from getting away with his sleight of hand. Many of the judges of the personal rule emerge with impeccable records of integrity. In January 1631, for example, Lord Chief Justice Hyde resigned his recordership of Bristol because a *quo warranto* was being brought against the city in the court where he sat and he rightly wished to avoid a compromising conflict of interest; instead he recommended to them as counsel William Noy, who had taken a firm stand for the liberty of the subject in 1628.[132] Similarly when offered a New Year's gift by Sir Richard Wiseman, Lord Keeper Coventry checked before accepting to see whether the donor had any case depending in the common law courts which he was hoping to facilitate by this favour.[133] This integrity extended to politics. Justice Yelverton, who proudly proclaimed his puritanism in defending Smart's resistance to religious ceremonies at Durham, advised that though it was against the law to do less than commanded, those who insisted on more could themselves be indicted at the assizes.[134] In 1634 when the new soap company sought a proclamation to prohibit people making their own soap, Attorney Noy (who never shrank from criticisms of policies he thought ill-conceived or of doubtful legality) ruled such against law and vowed he would

128. T. Birch (ed.) *The Court and Times of Charles I* (2 vols, 1848), II, pp. 218–21: Pory to Puckering, 24 Jan. 1633.
129. *Ibid.*, p. 112: Pory to Puckering, 12 May 1631.
130. J.A. Guy, 'The origins of the Petition of Right reconsidered', *Hist. Journ.*, 25 (1982), pp. 289–312; J. Reeve, 'The legal status of the Petition of Right', *Hist. Journ.*, 29 (1986), p. 263.
131. A point made by R. Lockyer in *The Early Stuarts: A Political History of England, 1603–42* (1989), p. 225. Cf. Berkowitz, *John Selden*, pp. 146, 152.
132. Bristol Record Office, Common Council Books, 3, f.23.
133. Rawlinson MS C.827, under June, 14 Charles I.
134. G. Ornsby (ed.) *The Correspondence of John Cosin* (2 vols, Surtees Soc., Durham, 1869–72), I, p. 155.

never pen it while he lived.[135] Judge Bramston in 1639 refused to detain in prison some ship money recalcitrants while the recorder prepared his case, saying 'And would you have those poor men lie in prison till then that you are provided of your argument, no they shall not . . .'.[136] In the spring both the king's Solicitor and Attorney advised Charles that those who refused to serve in his wars against the Scots could not be detained for that refusal.[137] Lord Keeper Coventry felt quite free to tell the king that the royal desire to cancel and erase the Star Chamber record of the proceedings on Pell *v.* Bagg could not be met because the crown did not have the right to prejudice the interests of a private party in a court of law. As for the erasure of the record, Coventry told Coke, 'I have, ever since I served his Majesty at the Seal, constantly avoided all cancellation of Star Chamber records as matter of high consequence.'[138]

These were not just isolated incidents of individual independence. As a bench too the judges were far less the willing agents in royal programmes than they are often presented. And the importance of their reputation for judicial independence and honesty was appreciated by Privy Councillors as well as the judges themselves. A charge that Finch had been given £500 in connection with the case of Ogle *v.* Stroud, though denied by Ogle himself, 'yet because the scandal lighteth on the said Lord Chief Justice' was investigated 'for the honour of justice'.[139] The king and Council did at times endeavour to persuade the judges of the need for the law to be the support of government. And it would seem that different appointments and different courts carried different expectations, of which the judges themselves were cognizant. So in the trial of Stephens in the Exchequer chamber for failure to pay his knighthood fine, Baron Denham remarked, 'as the Lord Keeper in this place the other day told my Lord Chief Baron, that whereas formerly he had been a great practiser of the common law, now he must forget that and apply himself to another law, the records of the Exchequer.'[140] But by the same token, the judges of the common law courts were quick to check any intrusion into their

135. *DNB*; PRO, C.115/M36/8426: Rossingham to Scudamore, 11 July 1634 (Noy died on 9 August). On Noy, see Jones, *Politics and the Bench*, pp. 92–5 and *idem*, '"The Great Gamaliel of the Law": Mr Attorney Noy', *Hunt. Lib. Quart.*, 40 (1977), pp. 197–226.
136. BL Add. MS 11045, f.33: Rossingham to Scudamore, 2 July 1639; cf. *The Autobiography of Sir John Bramston KB* (Camden Soc., old series, 32, 1845), pp. 68, 77–80.
137. R. Scrope and T. Monkhouse (eds) *State Papers of Edward, Earl of Clarendon* (3 vols, Oxford, 1767–86), II, pp. 38, 45.
138. Coke MS 56: Coventry to Coke, 8 Aug. 1637; Gardiner, *History of England*, VIII, pp. 89–90.
139. Coke MS 53: note of 1 May 1636 on dorse of Van Dyck to Coke, 16 April 1636. See *HMC Cowper II*, p. 115.
140. BL Add. MS 11764, f.92v.

jurisdiction or challenge to the law they practised. In 1631, for example, they spiritedly contested the claims of the Earl Marshal's court (albeit they were backed by the Lord Chamberlain and most probably the king) and stood staunchly for the authority of King's Bench 'being as they affirm, the highest and ancientest next the parliament as where . . . all the Kings were wont to sit in person, and where all the subjects in England . . . are tryable for goods, land and life'.[141] Prohibitions, whereby cases in prerogative courts were removed on petition to common law courts, continued despite the king's dislike of them. Indeed even in the most politically sensitive of cases the judges could display considerable independence. They refused to subscribe to the forced loan despite Charles's threat in a fit of temper to 'sweep all their benches'.[142] They bailed the merchant Richard Chambers, against the king's wishes, because the insolent words he was alleged to have spoken at the Council table did not appear on the return.[143] When, after the dissolution of the parliamentary session of 1629, Charles asked the bench what offences he might charge the miscreants with that were not covered by parliamentary privilege, he received only an equivocal answer. Even when they were pressed by the king they stood firm: 'until the particulars of the fact do appear we can give no directer answer than before'.[144] A proper countenancing of the judges was one of Heath's suggestions to the king for a more effective government and more harmonious relationship with his people.[145]

It has been suggested that 'the judges became more careful and obedient as the 1630s progressed'; and the ship money trial has often been cited as evidence of their final capitulation to the wishes of the government.[146] But, as we shall see, as well as those who found for Hampden, several of the judges who gave judgment in favour of the king did so on technical grounds, making it clear that they would not have upheld the legality of *taxation* (as opposed to a demand for a service) outside of parliament.[147] As Gardiner pointed out, there were good reasons other than self-interest why the judges in the 1630s generally inclined to support the king, and in particular gave judgment for ship money. Even Finch's tone, Gardiner acknowledged, was not that of 'the mere time server that he is generally reckoned'.[148] Such

141. Birch, *Court and Times of Charles I*, II, p. 97: Mede to Stuteville, 27 Feb. 1631.
142. R. Cust, *The Forced Loan and English Politics* (Oxford, 1987), pp. 54–5.
143. B. Whitelocke, *Memorials of the English Affairs* (1682), p. 11.
144. PRO, SP 16/141/44; see also, *Autobiography of Bramston*, pp. 49–54. Cf. Reeve, *Charles I*, pp. 120–1.
145. PRO, SP 16/178/3.
146. Jones, *Politics and the Bench*, p. 137.
147. *Ibid.*, p. 123; below, p. 724. Though Finch and Berkeley made large claims for the prerogative, most of the judges who found for the crown did so on narrow rather than broad grounds. See below and Jones, *Politics and the Bench*, p. 127.
148. Gardiner, *History of England*, VIII, pp. 95, 278–80.

observations still require further consideration and development. It may be, as Professor Jones has suggested, that rather than the judges' judgment, it was the King's habit of asking for and their giving judicial opinions in camera that caused most concern.[149] For whilst Sir Edward Coke had earlier affirmed a resolution of the judges to be of an authority 'next unto the court of parliament', in the political circumstances of the 1630s such pronouncements were feared as challenges to parliament. 'It was as though men had come to fear that a novel concept, that of King and Judiciary, was on the threshold of replacing that . . . of King and Parliament.'[150] Certainly some thought the judges' extra-judicial opinion on ship money their 'greatest crime' and it was undoubtedly this that led to the impeachment of the judges and condemnation of extra-judicial opinions in the Long Parliament.[151] The historian should not, however, let the politics of 1641 stand as a judgement on the quality or integrity of the Caroline bench.[152] Bankes was kept in office in the 1640s; the death of Lord Keeper Coventry was 'generally lamented';[153] Finch has been characterized by Gardiner and Barnes as a pillar of justice and mercy.[154] Overall there were sound legal arguments for the king's actions during the decade of personal rule, whatever the political wisdom of royal courses. We should not then assume that the judges who supported the king did so out of interest, fear or sycophancy. As the historian of the Caroline bench concluded, 'Charles I's judges were neither dishonest nor particularly subservient.'[155]

The Star Chamber

A dark cloud has hung over the history of the Caroline jucidiary blackening the reputation of the bench and the government, obscuring

149. Jones, *Politics and the Bench*, pp. 50–1; Whitelocke, for one, disapproved; see *Memorials of English Affairs*, p. 13.
150. Jones, *Politics and the Bench*, p. 20.
151. *Ibid.*
152. J.P. Kenyon (ed.) *The Stuart Constitution* (2nd edn, Cambridge, 1986), pp. 104–6; Jones, *Politics and the Bench*, p. 138. See also note 155.
153. A.B. Grosart (ed.) *The Lismore Papers* (10 vols, 1886–8), V, p. 121. Bankes was not impeached until after the outbreak of the civil war.
154. Barnes, *Somerset Assize Orders*, p. xxxii.
155. Jones, *Politics and the Bench*, p. 147. Dr J.S. Hart argues that the petitions to the House of Lords in 1641 offer evidence of a failure of justice in the 1630s ('The House of Lords and the reformation of justice, 1640–43', Cambridge University PhD thesis, 1985). His valuable argument, however, is weakened by the absence of such petitions in the Short Parliament, by a too uncritical acceptance of their cases and an insufficient study of the political context of 1641. As he notes, many cases arose, ironically, from the abolition of Star Chamber and the collapse of the Privy Council. Interestingly, few arose from ship money disputes.

any clear perception or study: the myth of Star Chamber has enveloped that court and spread through the subsequent centuries of historiography. The very words have become a synonym for secret, arbitrary and tyrannous legal procedures, disregard of human rights and cruel punishments.[156] Students have tended to think of Star Chamber as the early modern equivalent of the Gestapo or KGB, Latin American trials, Middle Eastern tortures and mutilations, or some grisly combination of them all.[157] Whilst scholarship has elucidated the origins of the court and its role and function in Tudor England,[158] the Caroline Star Chamber remains associated with cruelty and totalitarianism – an instrument, as John Rushworth (who printed many of the most notorious cases) described it, to retain the English in a 'slavish condition'.[159] Yet for all the historian's diatribes and denunciations, Star Chamber, as has recently been demonstrated, was a popular court with litigants – so much so that in 1596 the pressure of business necessitated measures to expedite its procedures (measures which failed).[160] For though the best-known function of the court, and certainly one of importance to Henry VII in his statutes of 1487 and 1495, was dealing with threats to the monarchy and law and order of the realm, increasingly during the Tudor century most of the cases were brought by private plaintiffs rather than by the crown. The numbers of private cases continued to rise well into the 1620s. Though usually and not inaccurately called a prerogative court, Star Chamber was after all very much part of the common law, and indeed a court to which plaintiffs often resorted to sustain rights denied them elsewhere. In the words of Professor Barnes (who is preparing the definitive study): 'the High Court of Star Chamber was . . . fixed solidly in the firmament of English judicature, administering the historically founded yet changing Common Law by a procedure different from that of the Common Law though acceptable to the common lawyers and sanctioned by the judges of the Common Law Courts'.[161]

156. *Oxford English Dictionary*.
157. Cf. T.G. Barnes, 'Star Chamber mythology', *American Journal of Legal History*, 5 (1961), pp. 1–11.
158. See, for example, J.A. Guy, *The Cardinal's Court: The Impact of Wolsey in Star Chamber* (Hassocks, 1977); *idem*, *The Court of Star Chamber and its Records in the Reign of Elizabeth I* (1985).
159. J. Rushworth, *Historical Collections*, II (1680), p. 475. It is a mark of the overall bias of Rushworth's *Collections* that, whilst he weaves the most contentious and political cases into a narrative, the more typical are left to an appendix in vol. III.
160. J.P. Kenyon, *The Stuart Constitution* (Cambridge, 1966), p. 117; see also T.G. Barnes, 'Star Chamber litigants and their counsel', in J.H. Baker (ed.) *Legal Records and the Historian* (1978), pp. 117–28. These build on the pioneering work of the Rt Hon H.E. Phillips, 'The court of Star Chamber' (London university, MA thesis, 1939) and 'The last years of the court of Star Chamber, 1630–41', *Trans. Royal Hist. Soc.*, 4th series, 21 (1939), pp. 103–31.
161. T.G. Barnes, 'Due process and slow process in the late Elizabethan and early Stuart Star

One of the contemporary counsellors at the court made large claims for it that could not be more different from its historical reputation. William Hudson's 'A Treatise of the Court of Star Chamber' was evidently penned in the 1610s and presented to John Williams on his accession to the great seal in 1621.[162] The jurisdiction of the court, he claimed, did not impede but supplemented the common law. Star Chamber dealt with those who abused the law (like the minister who locked the parishioners out of his church and cited Magna Carta as his justification)[163] and those who corrupted its courses (like those who filed a false charge of buggery against one Ashley in order to seize his lands).[164] With Privy Councillors and peers on the bench, Star Chamber, Hudson boasted, had the most learned judges of the realm: 'the court is not only always replenished with nobles, dukes, earls and barons . . . but also with reverend archbishops and prelates, grave counsellors of state, just and learned judges, such composition for justice, mercy, religion, policy and government that it may be well and truly said that mercy and truth have kissed each other.'[165] The jurisdiction of the court, Hudson observed, ranged widely – over perjury, fraud and contempt, none of which had been mentioned in the statute of 3 Henry VII which some saw as the foundation of the court.[166] The court dealt traditionally with breaches of royal proclamations and there the assize judges (in Henry VIII's reign also the JPs) came to hear their charge from the Lord Keeper.[167] In addition its jurisdiction historically embraced controversies between foreign merchants and Englishmen, matters testamentary, contested jointures, differences between corporations and abbots, and criminal cases ranging over treason, felony, forgery, perjury, riot, unlawful assembly, forcible entry, fraud, libel, conspiracy and false accusation.[168] More generally and vaguely, the court, 'by the arm of sovereignty punisheth errors creeping into the commonwealth which otherwise might prove dangerous',[169] under which head Hudson cited the regulation of excessive building ('that horrible mischief'), troublesome individuals, partial or corrupt officials, negligent magistrates. With such matters,

Chamber', *American Journ. of Legal Hist.*, 6 (1962), pp. 221–49, 315–46; quotation p. 224.

162. Ellesmere MS 7921: note by J[ohn] E[vans] to Bridgewater. See also T.G. Barnes, 'Mr Hudson's Star Chamber', in D.J. Guth and J.W. McKenna (eds) *Tudor Rule and Revolution* (Cambridge, 1982), pp. 285–308.
163. Ellesmere MS 7921. f.2.
164. *Ibid.*, f.9v.
165. *Ibid.*, f.22.
166. *Ibid.*, f.33.
167. *Ibid.*, f.35.
168. *Ibid.*, f.37 onwards.
169. *Ibid.*, f.81.

he regarded the court as playing a special and essential role of benefit not only to the government but the whole commonweal.[170]

> Infinite more are the causes usually punished in this court for which the law provideth no remedy in any sort or ordinary course, whereby the necessary use of this court to the state appeareth. And the subject may as safely repose themselves in the bosom of those honourable lords . . . as in the heady current of burgesses and meaner men which run too often in a stream of passion after their own or some private man's affections.[171]

Hudson also praised the 'conveniency' of the 'certain course and form of proceeding' in the court and dispels the myth that it acted arbitrarily or precipitately.[172] Indeed care was taken, he maintained, to ensure that all parts of the trial process were fair and scrupulous. After the plaintiff had filed his bill, the defendant was given eight days to frame his answer, with the advice of counsel, but if the matter were weighty or the bill contained, say, matter of title which could not be answered without evidence, then longer was allowed. The court then proceeded to examination of witnesses, with the defendant still having the right to demur on account of irregularity which, if upheld, led to the defendant's dismissal with costs. Once the case came to court, to prevent excessive interrogation of the defendant the plaintiff was given only four days to put in the articles of examination which were not to exceed fifteen, each containing no more than two questions. After the examination, the defendant had the opportunity to amend his answer before signing, but the plaintiff could administer his interrogatory only once – 'for although after he hath seen the examination he could clear the cause by asking one question, yet shall he not have that advantage'.[173]

In certain state cases, a more expeditious procedure was employed: that of *ore tenus*, whereby the Attorney-General prosecuted orally against a defendant confessing, or, refusing to answer, taken as confessing (*pro confesso*). Hudson acknowledged that some criticized this proceeding 'as seeming to oppose the Great Charter', but vigorously defended it, 'by reason that there is no judicial proceedings nor complaints exhibited whereunto the party charged . . . hath more space given him to answer or liberty to advise with counsel'.[174] Though such a course, he believed, should be used only infrequently, Hudson

170. *Ibid.*
171. *Ibid.*, ff.85v–86.
172. *Ibid.*, f.97.
173. *Ibid.*, ff.121–7, quotation f.126v; cf. Barnes, 'Due process and slow process', pp. 227–31.
174. Ellesmere MS 7921, f.98.

justified the procedure as today governments might defend their dealings with terrorists: 'for when some dangerous person attempts some unusual and perhaps desperate intentions which in short time may be very like to endanger the very fabric of the government', they are 'privately examined without oath'.[175] If one so taken denied the accusation he could not be prosecuted *ore tenus* and the court had to proceed to witnesses' depositions in the usual way. Only if confession were made, and subsequently acknowledged in court, could the trial by *ore tenus* proceed.

Hudson singled out much else for praise: the clerk of the Council kept the court's records and no subordinate clerk was permitted to take examination.[176] And unlike common law courts, he maintained, the process was cheap and open to all. The beggar as well as the king could sue there 'for many of the most indigent people have done in times past and severe punishments have been inflicted upon most eminent men for wrong done to those which were miserable poor'.[177] He regretted that the court no longer acted as it had in other areas, such as mediating over disputed land titles where it might bring 'more sufficient jurors' and 'less corruption' to cases than was encountered elsewhere.[178] Hudson had few criticisms – he thought the fines too high and not used to best effect.[179] In most respects he had nothing but good to say for the purpose, personnel and procedure of the court of Star Chamber that came, as he put it, nearer to the Roman senate than any other.[180]

As a counsellor of the court, Hudson was undoubtedly an interested party. He ignored the arguments of those who protested that because its judges were bishops and Privy Councillors, the court confused judicial with executive roles. He claimed for Star Chamber the redress of wrongs which were more often the business of the Court of Requests. But his knowledge of court procedure was unrivalled and in many respects his claims were not unreasonable. Star Chamber was a common law court that proceeded by written process in a manner similar to the courts of Chancery, Exchequer, Requests and Wards and Liveries. Theoretically at least the written procedures facilitated business and enabled the judges (especially the Privy Councillors who had little time to spare) to get through business in only two days of sitting each week in term.[181] Interrogatories once drawn up were administered by

175. *Ibid.*
176. *Ibid.*, ff.23–5.
177. *Ibid.*, ff.99v, 107v.
178. *Ibid.*, f.38.
179. *Ibid.*, ff.22–3. He also thought that bills were too long (f.115).
180. *Ibid.*, f.9v.
181. T. Powell, *The Attorney's Academie* (1630, STC 20164a), pp. 173ff; T.G. Barnes, 'The archives and archival problems of the Elizabethan and early Stuart Star Chamber',

impartial examiners, and all depositions by witnesses were taken in secrecy, so none could be swayed by what others had claimed. All the papers – examinations and proofs – were available to both sides for the trial where both had counsel to argue the points of law. Those convicted could appeal through counsel at the end of term. In practice, Professor Barnes has shown, the sheer mass of paper, 'the ever-growing bulk of almost all the instruments of procedure, bills, answers, demurrers, interrogatories and depositions' considerably slowed the proceedings and so may have made the court become less attractive to some for suits of damages.[182] And Lord Keeper Coventry for one, recognizing the problem, endeavoured to reaffirm the limitations on the length of interrogatories.[183] But attempts to speed up fell before a strict stand on 'due process'. Far from dispensing summary justice, as Lord Keeper, Coventry was 'second to none in assuring procedural rights even if slow procedure was the concomitant'.[184] As for *ore tenus*, contrary to the impression often given it was used only sparingly, even in the 1630s. Mr Phillips has counted twenty-eight such cases for the whole of Charles's reign and observes that the infamous cases of Leighton, Prynne and Lilburne were not among the number.[185] Far from the trembling victims of an arbitrary jurisdiction, it has been argued, defendants in Star Chamber had advantages 'which were not yet enjoyed by defendants in criminal actions in common law courts: the right to counsel and the right to call witnesses to give testimony on oath on the defendant's behalf'.[186] If such is the verdict of scholarship in general, we must turn to see how it is borne out by the records of the Caroline Star Chamber in particular.

First, however, the reference to Star Chamber records must not pass without comment. For whole classes of documents relating to the court have disappeared and the official records of proceedings of Star Chamber in the Public Record Office end with the beginning of Charles I's reign.[187] Rushworth evidently had access to the order and decree books at the time of compiling his *Historical Collections* and, though his narrative and commentary can distort a reading of them, he also presents us with some 172 cases.[188] In addition there are numerous other documents of more or less official status: treatises on jurisdiction

Journ. Soc. Archivists, II, 8 (1963), pp. 345–9, p. 345. Cf. *idem*, 'Mr Hudson's Star Chamber' and J.A. Guy, *The Court of Star Chamber and its Records* (1985), p. 6 and *passim*.

182. Barnes, 'Due process and slow process', p. 233.
183. *Ibid.*, p. 322.
184. *Ibid.*, p. 346.
185. *Ibid.*, p. 231; Phillips, 'Court of Star Chamber' (MA thesis), p. 35; cf. p. 31.
186. Barnes, 'Star Chamber mythology', p. 9.
187. Barnes, 'Archives of Star Chamber', p. 360.
188. *Ibid.*; see my note 159.

and procedure,[189] the Star Chamber register's rough minute book of hearings for May 1636 to June 1638,[190] notes of cases for 1625–8 in the Lansdowne collection,[191] for 1632 in the Rawlinson manuscripts,[192] 'Les Reportes del Star Chamber Regnante Carolo' in the Yelverton papers,[193] cases for 1633 and 1634 in Additional and Harleian manuscripts,[194] notes on cases for 1638 in the Hargrave manuscripts,[195] as well as a book of 'Cases in the Star Chamber during the reign of Charles I by an eminent practicer in that court, formerly a member of Grays Inn', in Harvard Law Library.[196] Where most of these are anonymous, we may add extensive private notes of Star Chamber proceedings (especially from 1630 to 1635) heard by the Earl of Bridgewater,[197] case notes by the Earl of Huntingdon,[198] and many careful and detailed notes taken by the Secretaries Coke and Windebank which are scattered through the state papers.[199] These, and doubtless other, documents await the full analysis that may enable us, even in the absence of the official records, to piece together the history of the Caroline Star Chamber.[200] But even a preliminary perusal will be sufficient for us to argue that the harsh judgements on the court, drawn from a few isolated and misunderstood causes, cannot be sustained by the evidence of its normal business and procedure.

A glance at the causes that came before the court is sufficient to dispel the myth that Star Chamber was primarily an instrument of the state rather than a court of justice. By far the majority of cases in the Star Chamber were brought by private plaintiffs rather than the Attorney-General, and of these last still fewer were official prosecutions, the Attorney often acting on relation.[201] To take the period 1603–25, for example, of 8,228 identifiable actions, the Attorney brought information in nearly 600; but of those, only 52 can be identified as *pro rege* – a figure which is well under 1 per cent of the total. Even when one turns to the cases that came to hearing the

189. See BL, Harleian MS 6448; also *Star Chamber Cases* (1630, STC 6056).
190. Rawlinson MS C.827.
191. BL, Lansdowne MS 620.
192. Rawlinson MS A.128; see S.R. Gardiner (ed.) *Reports of Cases in the Courts of Star Chamber and High Commission* (Camden Soc., new series, 39, 1886).
193. BL Add. MS 48057 (formerly Yelverton MS 63).
194. BL Add. MS 11764, ff.42, 117 (at back); Harleian MS 4022.
195. BL, Hargrave MS 404.
196. Harvard University Law School Library L. MS 1128: 'Reports of cases in the Star Chamber . . .'
197. Ellesmere MSS 7878–916.
198. Huntington Library, Hastings MSS, Legal Boxes 5, 7, 8.
199. In addition, transcripts and notes in Tanner MS 299; Bodleian, Ashmole MS 394. I have used all the above.
200. Professor Barnes is currently completing such a study.
201. As described by Hudson, Ellesmere MS 7921, f.107v; Barnes, 'Star Chamber Litigants', p. 9.

proportion of official prosecutions for the Jacobean period is only about 3 per cent.[202] Star Chamber was largely used by private plaintiffs as a support to other actions in common law courts, usually 'to mount a collateral attack, either to shore up or cross an action in another court, in furtherance of a large-scale strategy of litigation with the objective of winning a substantial prize' – usually property.[203] There can be no doubt that the Caroline period saw some change in this balance. In large part this was due to an *overall* decline in business; procedural tardiness rendered the court less attractive and led to a steady drop in the number of actions from the early years of James I. But over the Caroline period and still more the 1630s the number of bills fell sharply from nearly 800 per annum to only 300.[204] The likeliest explanation is Coventry's orders barring common informers from the court and bills relating to offences under penal statutes. But the delays in the court were exacerbated by some of the famous state trials and may have further dissuaded the opportunist litigant from pursuing damages in Star Chamber: it is surely no accident that only twenty-seven cases were heard in 1637, the year of the notorious trials of Bishop Williams and Prynne, Burton and Bastwick.[205]

During the 1630s the proportion of bills brought by the Attorney increased. But it never exceeded 18 per cent and on average remained at between 8 and 12 per cent.[206] To translate percentages into some examples, of some 100 cases heard by the Earl of Bridgewater between 1630 and 1635, the Attorney was plaintiff in 22, of which perhaps half were cases where he was acting on relation.[207] Of the 239 cases listed by Mr Phillips for the period February 1632 to October 1640, 85 were prosecuted by the Attorney, of which at least 16 were on behalf of another plaintiff, for example Lord Wentworth on account of his absence in Ireland.[208] Interestingly only 16 cases were heard *ore tenus*, and in only three (including Prynne's second and Lilburne's trials) did the court proceed *pro confesso*.[209] The statistics indicate that even during the decade when business was declining and official cases taking up more time, Star Chamber was not first an organ of the state, but, as Hudson claimed, a tribunal for justice. Indeed a popular tribunal, for many of the plaintiffs were of low social status; the Attorney-General himself acted on relation for men like Philip Jacobson an ironmonger;

202. Barnes, 'Star Chamber litigants', pp. 9–13.
203. *Ibid.*, p. 15.
204. Barnes, 'Due process and slow process', p. 331. See graph, p. 330.
205. *Ibid.*, p. 335; cf. H.E. Phillips, 'Last years of the court of Star Chamber', p. 111.
206. Barnes, 'Due process and slow process', pp. 330–2.
207. Ellesmere MSS 7878–916.
208. Phillips, 'Court of Star Chamber' (MA thesis), appendix 4.
209. *Ibid.*

and in general consideration for humble folk characterized the court's practice.[210]

The cases brought by private plaintiffs ranged widely over riot, combination, forgery, conspiracy and perjury. Most, as with the common law courts, concerned property – violent entry, conspiracy to defraud, forgery of deeds, embezzlement of money – or violations of the person by assault, rape or false defamation. Robert Cremer, for example, brought an action against Sir Hamon L'Estrange for corrupting and altering the copy of a court roll to his disadvantage, being a copyholder in L'Estrange's manor of Heacham.[211] In many cases suitors were seeking redress of wrongs done to them by legal authorities, magistrates or private men in other courts. In 1636, Lightfoot and Hudson brought an action against Jackson and Thurbor for 'presenting them of incontinency which depends in the Arches';[212] Thomas and Robert Remmington filed suit against John Allen, John Jepson and others for falsely presenting them as 'barettors' (vexatious litigants) in order to exact revenge for the plaintiffs' prosecution of the defendants for frequenting an unruly alehouse on the sabbath.[213] One Fawcett brought an action against a JP who had whipped him without due cause;[214] Escott prosecuted Masters for partiality in his exercise of office as justice of the peace.[215] In 1638 Sir Edward Seabright used the court to clear his name, having been falsely charged with the heinous crime of raping his nieces (one being under ten years of age) by their father who sought by Seabright's disgrace and punishment to receive his estates.[216] In such cases Star Chamber in the seventeenth century continued what Henry VII had endeavoured: to provide an appeal beyond and corrective to the sometimes partial justice dispensed by JPs inhabiting a society of local interests, factional alignments and ties of family and friendship. It is evident that Star Chamber was seen to function by the victims of partial justice as an important forum of redress.

This function appears to have been as vital to the judges of the court, in their hearing both private and official cases. The judges, members of the Privy Council, seemed particularly sensitive to cases of the illicit exercise of authority, such as that of Southern *v.* Anson in April 1638, 'for oppression of poor people by colour of order of [the] Council board'.[217] Though in cases where sheriffs, JPs or constables were

210. *Ibid.*, case no. 277, appendix 4.
211. Ashmole MS 394, f.53, 21 Oct., 16 Charles I.
212. Rawlinson MS C.827, 3 Feb. 1637.
213. Lansdowne MS 620, f.1.
214. *Ibid.*, ff.39–40.
215. BL Add. MS 48057, f.71v.
216. Hargrave MS 404 (at back), 14 Nov. 1638.
217. Rawlinson MS C.827, 13 April, 14 Charles I.

clearly exercising their proper jurisdiction the court was there to uphold them and punish their detractors (as they did the abusers of the sheriff of Carmarthen), judges did not hesitate to check the excessive use of magisterial authority.[218] In Fawcett's case, for example, the JP in question, one Grice, claimed that he had whipped him as a saucy fellow who was known as a sabbath breaker and keeper of an unlicensed alehouse. But this defence did not satisfy Coventry, who adjudged that 'it is not to be enquired now what causes Grice *might have* to send him to the house of correction, but for what he sent him'; and 'because sauciness was not cause sufficient' in law, Grice was fined and Fawcett awarded damages.[219] Justice Richardson's denunciation of the JP was more explicit and outspoken: 'This whipping is oppression which is when wrong is done to a man under colour of authority and yet against the laws.'[220] When Sir Thomas Jenkinson, a JP of Suffolk, was brought before Star Chamber on a similar charge, for whipping two women without due cause, 'it was greatly blamed by the court because it subverted all justice'. Jenkinson was put out of the commission.[221] In the course of hearing such cases, the Lord Keeper at times delivered opinions or rulings which deserve to rank with the Petition of Right as safeguards of the liberty of the subject. Coventry's ruling, for example, that 'if there be no felony *in facto* a constable cannot justify the breaking of the house for suspicion' supported personal rights that are not guaranteed to us today.[222] Indeed so open was Star Chamber to humble men who sought redress against wrongs perpetrated by their betters that on one occasion Charles I had to intervene on behalf of one of his peers. One John Burges planned to prosecute Lord Willoughby in Star Chamber for assault after the JPs had refused to take up his case. Burges was unhurt and had provoked Willoughby by 'saucy words', so the king intervened by sending a signed letter (entered in January 1634) stating that 'although we are willing that all our subjects should find our court of justice open to all men alike, yet when a man of mean quality shall prosecute against a nobleman for an offence of passion and heat only and that provoked by ill words . . . it is not reasonable to give way to every man's will'.[223] The unusual intervention and justificatory tone suggest that Burges might have emerged from litigation the victor.

Star Chamber also took special cognizance of abuses of the subject by officials acting in the name of the government. At the trial of

218. Lansdowne MS 620, ff.47v, 70.
219. *Ibid.*, ff.39–40.
220. *Ibid.*, f.40.
221. *Ibid.*, f.60v.
222. *Ibid.*, f.69.
223. PRO, SO 1/2, f.162v. The prohibition appears to have been effective.

George Mynne and Richard Dawe (for demanding illegal fees under colour of their offices as clerks of the Hanaper), Heath thought it appropriate that the court should oppress those who would oppress the king's subjects.[224] The Lord Privy Seal, Manchester, echoed the same sentiments at the prosecution of Thomas Helliard and others for abusing their warrant for digging saltpetre (as was often complained of): 'the King's service', he opined, was 'never better performed than when the guilty ministers thereof are punished'.[225] In 1634 the judges inclined to deal harshly with those prosecuted for counterfeiting farthing tokens, not least because it was the poor who used them as currency and were left with the counterfeits – 'and so', as Justice Jones put it, 'poor people like to be undone'.[226] We should not be surprised to see the judges and Privy Councillors in Star Chamber employing the language of, or acting in accordance with, the paternalism that informed Caroline social policy. Nor is it romantic to argue that Star Chamber was a court concerned with justice for the poor and humble as well as rich and powerful. For not only do contemporaries (such as the author of *Star Chamber Cases*, 1630) give us warrant to do so, traditional notions of justice and considerations of order dictated that, as Coventry put it, 'the justice of this court has been to let justice flourish in her proper colours'.[227]

What then of the official cases prosecuted by the Attorney in which the king and council had an interest? Did justice there flourish in her proper colours? Many of the cases prosecuted by the Attorney might also be categorized as prosecutions for the public benefit, in particular some of those that arose from breach of royal proclamations. Professor Barnes has identified 175 such actions brought of which about 40 came to trial, and characterized them as 'for essentially fiscal ends'.[228] This is too simplistic, for among them we find cases against offenders charged with the corrupt manufacture of goods – the false dyeing, so as to increase the weight, of cloth,[229] selling inferior iron as if it were 'good steel',[230] vending a mixture under the false description of pure beaver;[231] mixing silk with 'rotten wool' or hailshot with cochineal.[232] Such misdemeanours were not purely prosecuted for fines; they were treated as a 'great abuse' by the court which endeavoured to give teeth to the Council's programme to enforce regulations and standards of

224. Harleian MS 4022, f.54.
225. BL Add. MS 11764, f.8.
226. Harleian MS 4022, f.3.
227. Lansdowne MS 620, ff.1–3.
228. Barnes, 'Due process and slow process', p. 335.
229. Ellesmere MS 7880.
230. Ellesmere MS 7883.
231. Rawlinson MS C.827, 18 April, 14 Charles I.
232. *Ibid.*, 24 April, 14 Charles I.

manufacture. As was said in the case of the corrupt manufacture of gold and silver hatbands (using copper!): 'fraud is a common hurt to the weal public and that in all manufactures from the great commodity cloth to the meanest, fraud is so much used tending to the destruction of the whole trade of the Kingdom . . .'.[233] Other prosecutions were directed as much at offenders against the commonweal as against the king: those against Sir Anthony Roper and others for depopulation, against Richard Foley for engrossing iron, enhancing the price and destroying woods, of Charles Francks for transporting gold and silver out of the realm, or of Norton 'for exact [ing] sums of money from subjects and converting it to his own use being collected for ship money'.[234] There are of course more obviously fiscal motives behind some prosecutions for breach of proclamations – like that against dressing meat in Lent. Others, however, are not easily categorized: actions against those who built without licence can be seen as motivated by the desire for fines or (and) a concern about the overcrowding of London; prosecutions of gentry residing in the capital sprang from a determination to reinvigorate local government rather than a plot to tax the gentry.[235] Indeed it was precisely earlier precedents of such prosecutions that Hudson praised as necessary corrections of 'errors creeping into the Commonwealth'.[236]

It is the few *clearly* political cases for which Star Chamber is most infamous: the prosecutions of Walter Long, Richard Chambers and others after the parliament of 1629, of David Foulis for his attack on Wentworth, of Bishop Williams, of Alexander Leighton, of Prynne in 1633, and of Burton and Bastwick in 1637 for libel. Such cases are of great importance and we must return to them. But these must be seen in context. Perjury, libel and scandalous words and behaviour were common offences prosecuted by both private plaintiffs and the Attorney and were generally uncontentious.[237] In 1633 when he was tried for *Histriomastix* Prynne received the same sentence from the staunchly Protestant Sir John Coke as from Lord Cottington, and evidently little public attention or sympathy.[238] Nor was there then any denunciation of Star Chamber as an agent of a tyrannous regime. Secondly, concerning the charge in the most notorious trials – libel for one – the judges, far from desiring to extend the jurisdiction of the court, were opposed to a Star Chamber monopoly of prosecutions. In 1628, at

233. Rawlinson MS A.128, f.2.
234. Rawlinson MS C.827, quotation, 8 May, 14 Charles I.
235. See above, pp. 414–17.
236. Ellesmere MS 7921, f.81.
237. See *Star Chamber Cases* (1630), pp. 1, 35. The author specifically mentions the right of bishops to sue in the court against slanderers.
238. Tanner MS 299, ff.127–30; Gardiner, *History of England*, VII, p. 334.

the trial of Moseley and others for libelling the Duke of Buckingham, Coventry specifically delivered the opinion, 'that there came some hurt to the common wealth by this way that the Star Chamber had of late had assumed to them the punishment of libels for hereby it is come to pass that people think that libels are punishable in no other place'; he recommended the old practice of prosecution in courts leet.[239] Most importantly, we must question the assumption that in the more political cases proper legal procedures were bent or laid aside. This is not to say that in all cases there were no departures from the rules and ideals described by Hudson: the numbers of articles (which were supposedly restricted to fifteen) and questions (similarly to two) increased. In 1632, Alleyn expressed to Secretary Coke his concern over 'the multitude of questions (as ten or twelve almost in every interrogatory) where there should be but four by the order of that honourable court'; Charles I himself ordered the shortening of bills and answers.[240] Still Henry Sherfield was presented with an interrogatory of thirty-five pages.[241] Yet, as much as a problem, this may suggest what other evidence confirms: the fastidious scrupulousness of the judges at all stages of the trial.

Private case notes offer striking testimony to the efforts taken to ascertain the facts of a case. In the trial of Sir William Faunt for questioning the Earl of Huntingdon's exercise of his lieutenancy, twenty-four witnesses were examined and detailed enquiries were made into local military rates since Elizabeth's reign, the materials and equipment purchased, the extra sums raised in the 1620s and monies levied for comparable purposes in Derby, Lincoln and Northampton.[242] To take another example, in the case between the Reverend Thomas Pestell, incumbent of Packington Leicestershire, and Joseph Johnson *et al.*, no fewer than forty-seven interrogatories were taken in order to get at what instigated an act of violence.[243] Considerable time was expended by the court in the difficult case of Lord Chandos *v.* Jane Bayly where the plaintiff charged the defendant with a pretended marriage to disinherit Chandos of his lands.[244] The records of the court show a concern with legal proprieties at all stages, the official who compiled the notes in Rawlinson MS C.827 paying special attention to legal points. When the sitting of the court (and its distinction from a meeting of the Council) was signalled by the laying of a cloth on the

239. Lansdowne MS 620, ff.50v–51.
240. Coke MS 41: Henry Alleyn to Coke, 9 May 1632, calendared in *HMC Cowper I*, p. 457; Lansdowne MS 620, f.14; Barnes, 'Due process and slow process', pp. 322–7.
241. Hampshire Record Office, Sherfield MS XXV, Book F, probably small pages, when clerks got paid by the page.
242. Hastings MSS, Legal Box 7.
243. *Ibid.*, Legal Box 5.
244. Rawlinson MS C.827, 20 Oct., 13 Charles I.

table, the chamber was cleared of footmen, servants and any except the judges and parties to the case.[245] State trials were subject to the same careful procedures. When Sir Thomas Wiseman was tried in 1639 for scandalous words against the Lord Keeper, Coventry was obliged to absent himself from the chamber because he was involved in the proceedings.[246] Even in a case of treasonable words, Heath reminded the judges that 'the rule of Star Chamber is where the defendant denies not to convict upon the testimony of a single witness'.[247] Coventry, as we saw, even told Charles that the king could not intervene in the court's proceedings to the prejudice of a litigant – 'if it should be done it will be a precedent of a very ill consequence and will much weaken the honour and estimation of the justice of that court'.[248] Indeed it was in the more political cases, Professor Barnes observed, that the court was most 'careful to provide ample opportunity for the defence to put its case at length'. Accordingly the trials of Leighton, Prynne and Williams were the longest.[249]

In fact, especially in the most celebrated cases, the scrupulousness of the judges stood in marked contrast to the behaviour of the defendants. Sir John Eliot in 1629 refused to recognize the jurisdiction of the court in his case.[250] Alexander Leighton, who drew up his own answer to charges without the advice of counsel, railed against the court and described kneeling in church as the tail of the dragon and the surplice as 'the rag of the whore'.[251] John Lilburne refused to answer on oath.[252] Prynne, Burton and Bastwick, as we shall see, repeatedly abused the court, refusing to make an answer according to form, and then finally submitting an abusive response.[253] Lesser contempts of court are today treated seriously; in the localities of early Stuart England contempts of JPs usually earned offenders a whipping. It is rather the severity (and nature) of the punishments meted out by the court in these trials than the punishment of contempts itself that horrifies us – and understandably so. Yet attitudes to 'acceptable' or 'civilized' modes of judicial punishment are, as Middle Eastern practice and revivals of the death penalty in America show, culturally determined. As Professor Kenyon astutely reminds us, 'in the absence of a prison system all seventeenth-century courts had to impose fines, corporal punishments or public

245. See PRO, PC 2/43/444.
246. Rawlinson MS C.827, 1 and 6 June, 14 Charles I.
247. *Cal. Stat. Pap. Dom., 1627–8*, p. 69.
248. Coke MS 56; above, p. 661.
249. Barnes, 'Due process and slow process', pp. 334, 346.
250. See PRO, SP 16/143/5.
251. Rawlinson MS C.839, esp. f.12.
252. Rushworth, *Historical Collections*, II, p. 465.
253. Below, pp. 758–62.

penance: this was especially so of Star Chamber which could not impose the death penalty.'[254]

The punishments also need to be seen in context. The large fines (of £10,000 for example) were usually imposed as examples *pour décourager les autres*. Most of them were either mitigated or paid in instalments (sometimes over a long period) or both; not a few were pardoned altogether.[255] When he petitioned to have his own fine reduced George Faunt mentioned that many others had been reduced from thousands to hundreds.[256] The evidence of payments in the receipt books of the Exchequer and lists of mitigations in the state papers bear him out.[257] The city of London probably paid only £12,000 of the massive fine of £70,000 imposed on it in 1635; Henry Foulis had £500 of his £5,000 fine remitted; William Wiseman had his fine of £2,000 (for destroying corn) mitigated by £500; Lord North was pardoned his £10,000 fine; the whole of the fines on James Maxwell and Sir Richard Wiseman who had slandered the Lord Keeper were pardoned.[258] As an earlier historian of the Caroline Star Chamber concluded, the 'tendency was in the direction of leniency'.[259] Nor were the Star Chamber judges 'delighted with blood'.[260] John Glascock who slandered the government and was questioned in Star Chamber was pardoned because he had been drunk at the time.[261] Of 236 known judgments of the court between 1630 and 1641 only 19 involved sentences of corporal punishment.[262] Several of these have passed without historical comment and drew little notice at the time. Offenders counterfeiting the Earl of Dorset's signature or posing as agents of the Council were sentenced to lose their ears;[263] the papist William Pickering was whipped and mutilated 'for speaking and publishing lewd and insolent speeches'.[264] Such crimes, however, were considered, by most, serious offences and in a society where unmarried mothers and vagrants were routinely whipped until bloody even these punishments attracted no more than the interest afforded by the macabre spectacle of the victims' suffering. In other courts the victims might even have fared worse: at least one judge thought Leighton could have been tried for treason (and so

254. Kenyon, *Stuart Constitution* (1966), p. 118; cf. Barnes, 'Star Chamber mythology', p. 7.
255. Phillips, 'Court of Star Chamber' (MA thesis), pp. 130–6; *idem*, 'Last years of the court of Star Chamber', p. 119.
256. *Cal. Stat. Pap. Dom., 1637–8*, p. 126; *HMC Cowper II*, p. 255; cf. Harleian MS 1012, f.67v.
257. Gardiner, *History of England*, VII, p. 148 and note 1.
258. PRO, SP 16/461/95.
259. Phillips, 'Court of Star Chamber' (MA thesis), p. 137.
260. Rushworth, *Historical Collections*, II, p. 475.
261. *Cal. Stat. Pap. Dom., 1638–9*, p. 596.
262. Phillips, 'Last years of the court of Star Chamber', p. 118.
263. Rawlinson MS C.827, Jan., 12 Charles I; 8 June, 14 Charles I.
264. Phillips, 'Last years of the court of Star Chamber', p. 122.

hanged, drawn and quartered), whilst those who, like Prynne, failed to plead at common law had heavy weights tied to them until they pleaded or died, whichever came the sooner.[265] What did arouse some concern during the 1630s were the sentences of mutilation passed on gentlemen, as opposed to common miscreants. Interestingly, the court itself was more sensitive to this than has been noticed. Leighton, for one, was sentenced to 'be whipped . . . unless he could be proved a gentleman'.[266] When William Prynne received sentence for the publication of *Histriomastix*, Attorney Heath expressed his sorrow 'that the pillory and loss of ears should fall on a gentleman and a scholar, but there is an example in Leighton'.[267] After the first stage of the gruesome sentence had been carried out, 'the rest of his punishment [was] at the intercession of the Queen respited'.[268] Significantly, though they were unusual for victims of their status, neither Leighton's nor Prynne's sentences attracted much comment. It was not until Prynne's second mutilation, along with a clergyman (Burton) and a doctor (Bastwick) that the court gained its reputation for cruelty – and then the reasons owe more to the political and religious climate than to changed sensibilities concerning physical punishment. The next year, Sir Richard Wiseman's loss of his ears and whipping for accusing the Lord Keeper of corruption failed to make the headlines.[269]

Why then was the court so unpopular that it was abolished in 1641? If the answer still remains elusive, it may be because the question itself contains an inappropriate assumption. For originally the members of the Long Parliament appear to have intended the reform of the court, and it may be that abolition was steamrollered though by a minority in the frenzied politics of 1641.[270] Professor Kenyon suggested that 'the most important single cause of Star Chamber's unpopularity was the rôle it was called upon to play . . . in the enforcement of the King's fiscal and social policies', through punishing breaches of proclamations.[271] Doubtless there is something in this, though there was nothing novel about Star Chamber's jurisdiction in such cases, nor sufficient evidence to indicate that the enforcement of essentially conservative policies, though irksome to some, was broadly unpopular. Moreover, the heaviest concentration of such cases of fiscal exploitation came in the mid-1630s; towards the end of the decade other distractions and considerations led the Council to withdraw, or cease to enforce,

265. Phillips, 'Court of Star Chamber' (MA thesis), pp. 157–8, 160.
266. Rawlinson MS C.839, f.13v.
267. Tanner MS 299, f.128v.
268. Rawlinson MS D.392 [at end]: unfoliated courtier's diary, Aug. 1634.
269. Rawlinson MS C.827, 6 June, 14 Charles I; cf. Jones, *Politics and the Bench*, pp. 105–6.
270. Phillips, 'Last years of the court of Star Chamber', pp. 104–6.
271. Kenyon, *Stuart Constitution* (1966), p. 119.

many regulatory orders.[272] The issuing of general decrees by the court in a period of no parliaments may be of significance. In 1633 the court issued decrees against engrossing victuals and for setting prices of hay;[273] on 10 May 1633 it published a decree regulating the manufacture of soap, in pursuance of a censure in the court.[274] And on 11 July 1637, of course, Star Chamber issued the famous decree governing printing. This certainly stirred that legally minded gentleman Sir Roger Twysden, but he was exercised not by the censorship it imposed but by the nature and status of the decree itself. For some, he comments, believed that if such decrees became regular, they would render parliamentary legislation redundant.[275] We cannot know how many shared Twysden's constitutional misgivings about the decrees, most of which were uncontentious. But it may be that in this respect Star Chamber was regarded in 1641 as a jurisdiction that should be checked.

The most convincing explanation of the court's demise in 1641 is its association with the Laudian episcopacy, and more particularly with the trials of Bishop Williams, John Lilburne and especially Prynne, Burton and Bastwick. The presence of bishops as judges need not have been a cause of contention: Hudson had praised the court for the 'reverend archbishops and prelates' who sat there.[276] During Charles's reign, however, because more bishops were Privy Councillors, there were three sitting as judges in Star Chamber where only one had sat in Elizabeth's reign. It may have been this that encouraged cases like that brought by one Allen, minister of Sudbury, against his parishioners because they had refused to take the sacrament kneeling.[277] Nor was the defence of episcopal authority by Star Chamber in itself remarkable: the author of *Star Chamber Cases* mentioned the right of bishops to prosecute in the court against those who slandered them.[278] In Elizabeth's reign, John Udall and others were prosecuted there for attacks on the episcopacy. It was the association specifically with Laud that damned Star Chamber in the eyes of the hotter sort of Protestants. In reality, the court never became a secular arm of a Laudian church triumphant: puritans such as Ignatius Jordan found justice there against their detractors;[279] Catholics were examined there for passages in books referring to the blessed Virgin.[280] With a heterogeneous bench

272. Barnes, 'Due process and slow process', p. 335.
273. Rushworth, *Historical Collections*, II, pp. 197–8.
274. *Ibid.*, III, appendix, pp. 109–15.
275. Twysden MS U 47/47 Zi, p. 199.
276. Ellesmere MS 7921, f.22.
277. Gardiner, *Reports of Cases in Star Chamber and High Commission*, pp. 72–3.
278. *Star Chamber Cases* (1630), p. 35.
279. Lansdowne MS 620, f.47v.
280. Rawlinson MS C.827, 3 May, 13 Charles I.

of judges, the court was not inclined to support any narrow religious interest; Laud's long speech at Prynne's trial, justificatory in tone, suggests his own sense of a need to persuade.[281] But whatever the reality, the martyrdom of the puritan trinity in 1637, especially coming after milder punishments for libelling secular Councillors, 'besmirched' Star Chamber with the red dye of the ecclesiastical hierarchy. The sudden reaction against Star Chamber went hand in hand with mounting vitriol against the Caroline episcopacy.

Fear of the censor?

Star Chamber was one of the organs for punishing and controlling too free expressions of opinion. Whilst the incidents of trials for words written or spoken were few and concerned explicit libels, it may be argued that the awareness of these cases and the fear of offending affected all that men and women said or wrote, as well as published. In 1639 Sir Henry Wotton wrote to his nephew, closing his letter, 'my lodging is so near the Star Chamber that my pen shakes in my hand'.[282] Even in less troubled times, John Holles, Earl of Clare had advised his son Denzil not 'to put yourself into any man's courtesy under the witness of your own hand, especially to be a critic in state matters'.[283] Sir William Spring told John Winthrop in April 1636 'Neither is the time with us here so free and sure to us as that I dare write you what I think and would you knew.'[284] Even some within the circles of the court found it best to burn their papers at times.[285] Important reminders though such fragments are that early Stuart correspondents did not feel free to write or say anything, it is to go too far to erect on a few bricks an edifice of censorship, as if it towered over the communication of news and opinion, gossip, criticism and opposition. Christopher Hill has recently argued, as part of a larger claim for widespread censorship, that 'men feared that private letters were liable to be intercepted and read'.[286] The Barringtons evidently did in 1628–9; in 1639 Ashburnham asked Nicholas to warn his brother to be careful what he wrote: 'I am informed that all letters are opened.'[287] If his information was exaggeration it was not falsehood:

281. T. Hargrave, *A Complete Collection of State Trials* (11 vols, 1767–81), I, p. 486; above, p. 289 note 107.
282. Patterson, *Censorship and Interpretation*, p. 209.
283. P. Seddon (ed.) *Letters of John Holles, 1587–1637, II* (Thoroton Soc., Nottingham, 1983), p. 314.
284. *Winthrop Papers*, VI, p. 551.
285. For example, BL, MS Loan 29/172, f.151: Conway to Garrard, 24 July 1637; PRO, C.115/M35/8388: Pory to Scudamore, 17 Dec. 1631.
286. Hill, 'Censorship and English literature', p. 38.
287. *Ibid.*, p. 37; *Cal. Stat. Pap. Dom., 1639*, p. 274.

Henry Mildmay's letters to his wife were opened, and in 1639–40 mail to and from Scotland was intercepted in the Council's efforts to identify the Scots' English puritan collaborators.[288] We do the same today in the war against terrorism, yet most of us do not live in fear of our mail being tampered with. And nor did most seventeenth-century Englishmen. 'Commit this to the flames' may often have been the advice accompanying an indiscreet missive, but the counsel was often given to add sauce to the indiscretion or extra value to the correspondent, much as the modern gossip who insists that his valuable secrets (promiscuously spread) be divulged to none.

Whatever the fear, no one was prosecuted in Star Chamber for opinions expressed in correspondence. There were many hazards to letter writing in seventeenth-century England – weather, poor roads, untrustworthy messengers, highwaymen – but for those who corresponded with trusted friends the risk of being questioned for a letter did not loom large. For all sorts of reasons better than censorship few (not none) expressed treasonable sentiments in their letters or speeches, yet there is no shortage of barbs and critical reflections at individual ministers or on governmental policies. If too much may be made of the fear of interception, some recent contentions about Conciliar endeavours to stifle discussion seem to lack any foundation. For example it is claimed that Charles's proclamations ordering the gentry to leave London were an attempt to prevent their meeting to form a community of dissent,[289] but the proclamations only applied to the vacation time, which arguably was the period of least spicy gossip. Moreover, Gardiner suggests, Charles's building of a portico at the west end of St Paul's cathedral was planned in part to accommodate the gossipers and newsmongers who were ousted from the nave – scarcely the gesture of a monarch who wished to stifle discussion.[290] There was no concerted campaign during the personal rule to police correspondence, debate or the gathering of friends. And there was certainly no shortage of news and gossip passed across the capital and out from London to the provinces.

Newsletters and politics

It is not easy to weigh newsletters as evidence of reactions to the regime, or even more vaguely of a 'mood', until we know more about

288. *Cal. Stat. Pap. Dom., 1639*, p. 295.
289. T. Cogswell, *The Blessed Revolution: English Politics and the Coming of War, 1621–1624* (Cambridge, 1989), p. 34; Butler, *Theatre and Crisis*, p. 118.
290. Gardiner, *History of England*, VII, p. 308. Cogswell notes the importance of Paul's Walk (*Blessed Revolution*, p. 24).

the professional newsmongers, their own sources, their relationships with the clients who hired their services and the extent to which in any individual case what was sent was finetuned to what the recipient wanted to know. Where the more personal correspondence of families and friends is concerned, our own experience must suggest that the most sensitive and indiscreet observations were communicated in person rather than on paper. And in weighing the reception of news, its role in shaping as well as reflecting views, we face greater problems still: the extent to which isolated titbits were woven into a narrative, their relationship to personal experience and prejudice, and the sophistication of the recipient. However, a recent account, evidently unconcerned by some of these difficulties, has made large claims for the importance of newsletters in the formation of a political consciousness.[291] What divers news correspondence had in common, Dr Cust argues, 'was a continuing stress on conflict which counterbalanced the emphasis on consensus' found in political rhetoric.[292] News, he maintains, helped to shape the antagonistic concepts of 'court' and 'country', developed the latter into the beginnings of an ideology of opposition and so 'contributed to a process of political polarization in the early seventeenth century'.[293] It may be significant that Dr Cust's arguments are drawn primarily from the evidence of the 1620s and that, despite his broader claims, almost no cases are cited from the 1630s.[294] For it may be that the newsletters of the 1620s reflected the considerable divisions (within the government as well as across the country) of that decade of unharmonious parliaments, political tensions arising from Buckingham's hegemony and the wars. It is hard to be sure whether the relative absence of documented conflict in the letters of the 1630s owes more to the absence of parliaments (which had brought some provincial gentry to and from London frequently) or to a lowering of the political temperature after 1629. The revival, however, of such correspondence from 1639 is suggestive. What we can say of the intervening years, from the dissolution of parliament to the military preparations for the war against the Scots, is that though there was plenty of news, it does little to support the claims that it fostered a perception of politics as polarized between 'court' and 'country'.

In the case of 'professional' newsletters, it is not clear how they could so function. For the professional newswriters, like John Pory or Edward Rossingham, clearly depended upon court contacts for what

291. R. Cust, 'News and politics in early seventeenth century England', *P&P*, 112 (1986), pp. 60–90.
292. *Ibid.*, p. 75.
293. *Ibid.*, p. 87.
294. I am grateful to Richard Cust for discussions of this anomaly.

they learned beyond the common report of the corantos, indeed they literally had 'friends at court'.[295] Similarly those in the country, like Sir Robert Harley, relied on reporters, like Viscount Conway or the Reverend George Garrard, who operated on the fringes of the court and in the broader sense were part of its orbit.[296] This is not to say that there was no hint of criticism, discontent or satirical edge in the newsletters of the decade. Yet with few exceptions the news correspondence of the 1630s seldom employed the language of polarization and often purveyed information with minimal gloss or comment. When, for example, we turn to the newsletters sent to the Warwickshire gentleman Sir Thomas Puckering by John Pory, John Beaulieu, Sir George Gresley and Captain Edward Rossingham, we encounter a wealth of detailed report of foreign affairs, court faction, the vying for place, indelicate remarks about individuals, words allegedly spoken by the king.[297] But while Pory (the most evident 'authorial presence') seems sympathetic to Bishop John Williams and Rossingham sceptical of the efficiency of the ship money fleet, the letters report the impositions of knighthood fines, predictions of another parliament and refusals to pay ship money without comment.[298] Sir George Gresley, who when he came up to London resided at Essex House, did refer in 1629 to 'our parliament men' (he had been MP for Newcastle under Lyme in 1628);[299] Rossingham could jest that the court was scarcely the best audience for a sermon on virginity,[300] but it would be difficult from such occasional comments as these to discern the newswriters' own political attitudes or sympathies. Nevertheless the information they provided was keenly awaited – and collated – by recipients. Sir Thomas Puckering not only employed several reporters, he purchased separates and criticized his correspondents if their dispatches turned out to be inaccurate. He also shared the service and his information with Warwickshire neighbours, Sir Thomas Lucy and Lord Brooke.[301]

295. Pory often referred to his sources. On one occasion, for example, he noted that his information has been gleaned from 'another courtier, but of greater quality, and more intimate' (Birch, *Court and Times of Charles I*, II, p. 187). Elsewhere, he observed that he had been informed of events 'by the clerk of the entries of the Star Chamber' (*ibid.*, p. 195). On Pory, see W.S. Powell, *John Pory, 1572–1636: The Life and Letters of a Man of Many Parts* (Chapel Hill, NC, 1977), a volume that has a microfiche supplement of several of Pory's letters. For more information concerning Pory's sources, see PRO, C.115/M35/8385, 8386, 8387. Rossingham was Pory's successor in conveying court news to the likes of Sir Thomas Puckering. He knew Wentworth, Sir John Digby and Sir Thomas Edmondes (Birch, *Court and Times of Charles I*, II, p. 228).

296. BL, MS Loan 29/172.

297. On Puckering, see A. Hughes, *Politics, Society and Civil War in Warwickshire, 1620–60* (Cambridge, 1987), pp. 46, 59, 74–5, 90.

298. Birch, *Court and Times of Charles I*, II, pp. 195, 254 and *passim*.

299. *Ibid.*, p. 7.

300. *Ibid.*, p. 231.

301. *Ibid.*, p. 212; Hughes, *Politics, Society and Civil War*, pp. 59–90.

Similarly the Reverend Joseph Mede from his study at Christ's College, Cambridge evidently pieced together news from Pory with other materials sent or reported to him, and forwarded his own collage to Sir Martin Stuteville his kinsman of Dalham, Suffolk.[302] It is not possible to determine what effect news had on Puckering's or Stuteville's perception of their world, but their hunger to receive it and the detailed information of passages foreign and domestic sent is proof that they did not inhabit an insular, provincial world bounded by only local concerns.

It is important to note that the news service attracted not only country clients. The Earl of Huntingdon employed Rossingham,[303] and the largest surviving collection of (several hundred) newsletters for the 1630s owes its existence to Sir John Scudamore's need to be kept informed during his retirement in Holme Lacy, Herefordshire and, after 1634, his embassy to Paris.[304] A team of informants kept Scudamore abreast of events: as well as the professionals John Pory, John Flower,[305] and Edward Rossingham,[306] the antiquarian scholar Ralph Starkey,[307] the courtier John Burgh,[308] Sir Henry Herbert, Master of the Revels,[309] and Sir John Finet, Master of Ceremonies penned him regular dispatches.[310] Scudamore was sent a weekly packet of detailed foreign news, the victories and defeats in Germany and the Low Countries, French manoeuvres, even news from New England.[311] Home news comprised the latest court appointments, deaths and marriages, masques and progresses and stories of jars between individuals and factions, as well as reports of political initiatives such as knighthood fines or the Book of Orders (which was enclosed with one dispatch). Rumours around the court and city (of another parliament), scandal (the pregnancy of Mrs Villiers), tragedy (the account of the vice-chancellor of Cambridge University hanging himself) and prurient gossip (the discovery of a witch with a bizarre 'anal growth')[312]

302. Birch, *Court and Times of Charles I*, II, pp. 84, 86.

303. For example, Hastings MSS 9597, 9598.

304. The hundreds of letters in PRO, C.115/M, N are at least as rich as the Chamberlain to Carleton letters of James I's reign, though they have been little used. We need a published edition.

305. See Flower's list of charges for his obtaining copies of letters and proclamations to forward with news: PRO, C.115/M30/8104.

306. These 1630s letters are (as well as in PRO, C.115/M36) in BL Add. MS 11045. On Rossingham, see *HMC De Lisle and Dudley, VI*, pp. 120, 171, 236, 318, 320.

307. On whom, see Sharpe, *Sir Robert Cotton*, via the index.

308. PRO, C.115/N4. He *may* be John Borough.

309. PRO, C.115/N3.

310. PRO, C.115/N8; not surprisingly, these letters show an obsession with ceremonial matters at times, but also reveal political attitudes.

311. Weckherlin also referred to his weekly duty of writing to Scudamore (PRO, C.115/M37/8474).

312. For the last point, see PRO, C.115/M36/8426.

added spice to the regular diet of hard news, including (alleged) verbatim speeches of the king and his ministers gleaned from 'an ancient Exchequer man' or even the Lord Treasurer himself.[313] Scudamore's correspondents occasionally ventured a reflection or indulged an indiscretion: the chiding of Justice Heath,[314] the hostility to the new soap,[315] a view of the ship money trial.[316] Flower forwarded a book that had been called in;[317] Pory advised that all his letters be committed 'to the safest Secretary in the world, the fire'.[318] But for all the acknowledgement that there were 'many itching ears to hear anything against the church or commonwealth', there was little gloss placed on the material by the professionals, whilst Herbert and Finet wrote very much from the perspective of the court.[319] Evidently those like Pory and Rossingham functioned as a seventeenth-century Reuters, purveying information with minimal slant to patrons and purchasers of different situations and persuasions.[320] The widespread dissemination of such information was, as has been argued, undoubtedly crucial in keeping news circulating from (and through) the entrepôt of London during a decade of no parliaments. But that such news served to polarize the realm or foster an oppositionist stance must remain at best a conjecture, which the evidence we have would seem to undermine.[321]

If the semi-public status of the professional newsletters dictated reports rather than comment, we might expect more revelation from the 'private' correspondence of families and friends. At times such correspondence turns out to be less 'private' than we might at first have thought. The Reverend Garrard, who corresponded frequently not only with Wentworth but with Viscount Conway and others, we discover, derived the news he purveyed largely from Pory whose death he reports in 1635.[322] Nor was he averse to making public letters he had been specifically asked to keep to himself. Conway, who always asked that his indiscreet missives be burned, teased Garrard, 'you show them to my Lord Deputy, peradventure to other statesmen'.[323] The two evidently sustained a railing and satirical

313. PRO, C.115/M35/8385, 8386.
314. PRO, C.115/M36/8426.
315. PRO, C.115/N3/8154.
316. PRO, C.115/M24/8617.
317. PRO, C.115/M30/8153.
318. PRO, C.115/M35/8388.
319. PRO, C.115/M36/8438.
320. Pory may have had an 'office'; he asked for replies or requests to be sent to a shop owned by Nathaniel Butler (PRO, C.115/M35/8387).
321. Indeed, the contrary suggests itself, as many of the newswriters were connected both with the court (and its puritan peers) *and* the country.
322. See Knowler, *Strafford Letters*, I, p. 467: Garrard to Wentworth, 3 Oct. 1635.
323. See BL, Loan MS 29/172, ff.108, 109, 110–11.

correspondence which mixed serious news, reflection and criticism with mirth and insults. In September 1635, for example, Garrard passed on with praise of Brownrigg for being 'no Arminian', news of ship money, criticism of rating and rumour about Cottington's bid for the Treasury, a (probably ribald) song about the lords and ladies of the town, closing with the remark that having put on too much weight he consoled himself that he was still lighter than the 13-stone Lady Salisbury![324] Would that we had the letters which Garrard prudently burnt. Conway's own correspondence with his family, the puritan Harleys of Brampton Bryan, combined – in a mixture that might assault some assumptions – godly exhortation, denunciation of puritans, foreign and court news, reflections on religion and law together with a humour that could descend to vulgarity.[325] Quite how Conway's correspondence helped to shape the view of the world in Brampton Bryan it is hard to say: the latest research on the Harleys stresses the importance of news to the family but offers no analysis of the images it communicated or helped to foster.[326] We have few letters of Lady Brilliana before the outbreak of the Scottish troubles and little evidence of her reactions to the personal rule.[327]

Most of the gentry correspondence of the 1630s is no more yielding. The Clifton correspondence, for example, contains letters of foreign news and court gossip, often what the writer had heard at the Exchange, but is dominated largely by family and local business. We find, similarly, only fragments in the papers of Sir Thomas Jervoise or Sir Edward Dering amidst volumes of papers connected with their pragmatic execution of local office. John Savage's letters to the Earl of Bridgewater kept the Lord President of the Marches up to date with deaths, the change of places and *causes célèbres* like the soap patent, but until 1639 there is little in Bridgewater's papers of national political comment. The same is true of the correspondence of Thomas Smyth of Ashton Court, which, after the death of Buckingham, contains less of national news and observation, and of the Temple papers which yield riches for the historian of political attitudes only with the commencement of Sibthorpe's letters in 1639 to Sir John Lambe, commissary to the archdeacon of the Temples' county of Buckinghamshire.[328]

324. *Cal. Stat. Pap. Dom., 1635*, p. 385: Garrard to Conway, 18 Sept.
325. For example, BL, Loan MS 29/172, f.117: 'like the late Marquis of Winchester the first night he was married, I do not know at which end to begin'!
326. J. Eales, *Puritans and Roundheads: The Harleys of Brampton Bryan and the Outbreak of the English Civil War* (Cambridge, 1990), pp. 84–95; cf. J. Levy [Eales], 'Sir Robert Harley KB (1579–1656) and the "character" of a puritan', *British Library Journ.*, 15 (1989), pp. 134–57. I am grateful to Jackie Eales for a copy of this book and article in advance of publication.
327. See below, p. 845.
328. Temple of Stowe MSS, STT 1876–94.

Even though often at court, Henry Oxinden sent home little political news to his family before 1637.[329] Sir Thomas Knyvett's reports were sent in that 'light hearted tone' that makes it hard to hear the attitude expressed.[330] He praised St John's speech for the subject in the ship money trial, but also the king's willingness to let the case be argued.[331] And whilst he contrasted politicians of disturbed consciences with honest men who slept well, the world of the court clearly drew and fascinated him, as he attended a masque and wrote of the queen who 'dazzles all men's eyes that look on her'.[332]

The Barringtons of Masham in Essex were not likely to be sympathetic to the Caroline regime; their correspondence reflects a worry about Charles's soundness on religion, fear of Spain, concern about the dissolution of the 1629 parliament and a thinly veiled disgust at scandals such as the trial of Castlehaven. But though a former loan refuser, Sir Thomas Barrington reported the imposition of knighthood fines without comment.[333] The most explicit denunciations of the secular government of the 1630s are undoubtedly found in the Holles letters. From his praise of the 'poor state martyrs' of the parliament of 1629,[334] through his doubts about the legality of knighthood fines,[335] his attack on the Star Chamber and Exchequer ('from which two omnipotencies libera nos Domine', he prayed), and support for Bishop Williams,[336] the Earl of Clare vilified the court and the government. 'Law being laid aside,' he rhetorically asked his son Lord Haughton, 'what bounds can be set to will and power?'[337] Why, even the lawyers answered 'power may do what it list' – and commissions against depopulation and unlicensed building proved them right.[338] That Holles was summoned before both must not pass without comment.[339] For his correspondence undoubtedly echoes at all points with *personal* grievances and indeed a sense of general paranoia about his standing with the king. Certainly the sufferings of his son Denzil Holles contributed something to Clare's sense that the prisoners of 1629 were 'martyrs'; being questioned in 1629 for his role in circulating a seditious

329. D. Gardiner (ed.) *The Oxinden Letters, 1607–1642* (1933); and see *idem*, p. 130.
330. B. Schofield (ed.) *The Knyvett Letters, 1620–1644* (Norfolk Record Soc., 20, 1949); E. Cope, *Politics without Parliaments, 1629–40* (1987), p. 141.
331. Schofield, *Knyvett Letters*, p. 91.
332. *Ibid.*, pp. 75, 96.
333. Searle, *Barrington Letters*, p. 132.
334. P. Seddon (ed.) *Letters of John Holles, 1587–1637*, III (Thoroton Soc., 36, Nottingham, 1986), p. 393.
335. *Ibid.*, p. 415.
336. *Ibid.*, pp. 468, 488, 496.
337. *Ibid.*, p. 395.
338. *Ibid.*, pp. 400–1.
339. See P. Seddon (ed.) *Letters of John Holles, 1587–1637*, I (Thoroton Soc., 31, Nottingham, 1975), introduction; *DNB*.

pamphlet enhanced his worries about the law; his ejection from the commission of the peace and failure to secure the posts he had sought assisted a celebration of country honesty over the corruptions of office; close friendship with Williams coloured sympathy for the bishop's fate; and his condemnation of Wentworth's proceedings as 'bloody and tyrannical' owed much to his blaming the Lord Deputy, his son-in-law, for the death of his daughter whom her husband had allowed to travel when she was pregnant.[340] His personal interests and experiences, of course, do not undermine the broader import of Clare's criticisms of the government's religious and legal position. On the other hand there can be no doubt that he avidly sought to reingratiate himself with Charles and had the king to stay with him in 1633 (unfortunately a part of his house collapsed during the visit).[341] Clare's descendant, Gervase Holles, who penned a history of the family during the 1650s, had no doubt that despite his 'disobligations and discontentments', Clare 'had he lived to these unhappy times', would have sided with the king, 'for he was so fine a son of the Church of England'.[342] To such speculation we should not give great weight. More worthy of attention, shortly before his death Clare was denouncing 'those hot headed Bethsemites', Prynne, Burton and Bastwick, 'that so presumptuously will peep into the art of our government'.[343] Even his criticism of the regime may not (by 1637) have developed into opposition. But in its outspoken discontent Clare's correspondence offers an almost unique source of gentry alienation and grievance during the personal rule. For the most part, as Professor Hibbard concluded, 'Gentry correspondence before the latter part of 1639 is . . . very restrained in political comment.'[344]

Diaries and memoirs

Correspondence, it has recently been asserted, is not the place where we should expect to find the frankest commentary on the news. Rather in private memoirs and diaries 'it is possible to see the news being both recorded and discussed'.[345] In private diaries, it is claimed, we find the expressions of doubts and misgivings, supportive of the suggestion 'that news encouraged contemporaries to view politics in terms of

340. Seddon, *Letters of Holles*, I, p. lxxii; *Letters of Holles*, III, p. 477; cf. G. Holles, *Memorials of the Holles Family*, ed. A.C. Wood (Camden Soc., 3rd series, 55, 1937), pp. 107–10.
341. Seddon, *Letters of Holles*, III, p. 455.
342. Holles, *Memorials of the Holles Family*, pp. 107–8.
343. Seddon, *Letters of Holles*, III, p. 520: Clare to Sir Gervase Clifton, 25 May 1637.
344. C. Hibbard, *Charles I and the Popish Plot* (Chapel Hill, NC, 1983), p. 88.
345. Cust, 'News and politics', p. 83.

conflict'.[346] We are fortunate that a number of diaries have survived for the decade of personal rule. Before we turn to them, we must note that diaries as a source pose generic problems that some of their recent interpreters have failed to consider. The puritan habit of note-taking at sermons and of spiritual self-examination led to more puritans keeping diaries than those of less intense personal piety. More generally perhaps the keeping of a private diary reflects personality types and characteristics – be it a certain paranoia, a quest for ordering, a search for the self, a sense of isolation and alienation; to such types the diary may often be an outlet for anxiety of which those more confident of their place in the world feel no need. Though the memoir or diary offers enticingly approachable and rich evidence, as those of Laud or D'Ewes remind us, they may be more revealing of individual personality than of public affairs or perceptions.

D'Ewes's *Autobiography* is one of those historical documents so well known that it has not been properly studied – in the context of D'Ewes's letters, associations and actions and of his purposes in writing it.[347] The date of compilation itself presents problems, for though the author refers specifically to writing in 1637 and 1638 it is evident from forward predictions that it was rewritten later.[348] The death of Buckingham whom he regarded as 'the main cause . . . of the aversion of hearts between the King and his subjects and of the other mischiefs in church and commonwealth' raised his hopes for better times.[349] In January 1629 Charles I sent a 'very gracious message' to the House of Commons regarding his desire to have tonnage and poundage legally which might have made for a successful parliament.[350] On 3 March, however, parliament was precipitately dissolved – 'The most gloomy, sad and dismal day for England that happened in five hundred years last past.'[351] D'Ewes did not blame the king for the precipitate dissolution; 'divers fiery spirits in the House of Commons were very faulty and cannot be excused'.[352] More menacingly, he feared the ungodly had planned the disruption. The following months were to confirm his fears. During the early 1630s D'Ewes observed with sadness the death of Gustavus Adolphus and the precarious condition of Protestantism abroad, and the spread of Anabaptist tenets (under a 'new invented and false name of Arminians') at home.[353] As

346. *Ibid.*, p. 87.
347. This is currently being remedied by Peter Salt of Sidney Sussex College, Cambridge.
348. J.O. Halliwell, *The Autobiography and Correspondence of Sir Simonds D'Ewes* (2 vols, 1845), I, introduction, p. 402; II, pp. 49, 85, 100, 102, 130.
349. *Ibid.*, I, p. 380.
350. *Ibid.*, p. 399.
351. *Ibid.*, p. 402.
352. *Ibid.*
353. *Ibid.*, II, pp. 64, 83.

he worked away on his records and edition of Fleta, too, some of the initiatives of the Caroline government struck him as of dubious legality.[354] The proclamation ordering the gentry to leave London (which moreover led D'Ewes himself to depart Islington) he thought 'took away men's liberties at one blow'.[355] There were to be other assaults on the citadel of freedom. The second writ of ship money earned a memorable entry in D'Ewes's diary for 1635: 'At home the liberty of the subjects of England received the most deadly and fatal blow it had been sensible of in five hundred years last past.'[356] 'What,' he asked his diary, 'shall free men differ from ancient bondsmen and villeins . . . if their estates be subject to arbitrary taxes . . . ?'[357] The most religious and honest men spoke against it, he noted, as the concern for law fused in his mind with fears of innovation in religion. For already by 1634 D'Ewes's personal happiness was disturbed by 'the general hatred of truth and piety at home' which 'filled my soul with frequent sorrow'.[358] Ceremonies were pressed upon tender consciences by those like Laud and Wren who 'called themselves Protestants', but who plotted 'the ruin of the truth and the gospel' through profanation of the Lord's Day, idolatry, and suspension of the godly.[359] Evidently he did not yet blame the king for the ills of the realm. He even hoped that ship money would be legally settled on the crown.[360] But by 1637 D'Ewes believed a parliament was necessary so that the prince might see the truth and 'the distempers of church and commonwealth' be checked before they 'grow into incurable diseases'.[361]

Undoubtedly D'Ewes's *Autobiography* stands as a powerful condemnation of the government by an antiquary of massive legal learning and puritan inclination. Interestingly, however, it has recently been argued that it paints a picture blacker than D'Ewes's perception at the time and suggests that retrospect was colouring the memory with darker hues.[362] For in the 1630s, as well as being a diligent ship money sheriff, D'Ewes remained close to the Catholic Earl of Arundel, Bishop White (who had defended Montagu) and even Laud's vicar-general, Nathaniel Brent.[363] Such associations remind us not to under-

354. *Ibid.*, p. 437.
355. *Ibid.*, p. 79.
356. *Ibid.*, p. 129.
357. *Ibid.*, p. 132.
358. *Ibid.*, p. 110.
359. *Ibid.*, pp. 113–14.
360. *Ibid.*, pp. 131–2.
361. *Ibid.*, p. 133.
362. I owe this information to Peter Salt's paper, 'The political career of Sir Simonds D'Ewes', delivered at the Institute of Historical Research.
363. *Ibid.* He was a diligent ship money sheriff; see J.S. Morrill, *The Revolt of the Provinces: Conservatives and Radicals in the English Civil War, 1630–1650* (1976), p. 25.

play the more moderate passages beneath the sensational in the diary: D'Ewes's respect for 'a virtuous and learned papist',[364] his denunciation of a minister for failing to catechize 'contrary to his duty and the canons of our church';[365] or suspicion that some puritan exiles held 'strange and dangerous opinions'.[366] His reaction to the Scots war is not well documented but by 1640 he knew there would be 'great use of moderate spirits' in parliament, and determined to be one, to assist co-operation between the Commons and the king.[367] Whatever his position in 1640, D'Ewes was clearly less alienated from the regime than he had been in the 1620s when he confided to his diary a longing for rebellion.[368]

D'Ewes's *Autobiography* is perhaps most important for its demonstration of how worries about religion could lead a 'political conservative' to large anxieties about the state as well as church.[369] 'I have ever maintained obedience to the magistrate,' we hear him agonizing '*and* that the conscience ought not to be enforced.'[370] We are now able to see how the same potentially radical fusion occurred in the minds of the godly of lesser social standing and learning, both in the capital and in the provinces. The London turner, Nehemiah Wallington, may have been, as Paul Seaver argues, more disturbed by the conspiracy of papists and prelates to bring in popery than by Charles I's secular enactments, but ultimately the secular and religious realms could not be so separated in his mind.[371] The Book of Sports which God damned by His judgment on sabbath-breakers was after all issued by authority; Prynne was vindictively pursued by the king's Attorney and archbishop; Star Chamber (before which Wallington himself was summoned) which tried the puritan martyrs was an instrument of state. To the absence of parliaments, Wallington attributed the oppression of the subject by patentees and (revealing his metropolitan priorities) 'in paying of money for new corporations'.[372] By 1640 such thoughts had so blended with his horror at idolatry and popery that his 'trust in the fundamental soundness of the Stuart monarchy' had been eroded.[373] He may even have been sympathetic at the time, in 1640 when he

364. D'Ewes, *Autobiography*, II, p. 113.
365. *Ibid.*, p. 102.
366. *Ibid.*, p. 116.
367. *Ibid.*, p. 243: D'Ewes to the Earl of Worcester, 1 Oct. 1640.
368. I owe this point to D. Hirst, *Authority and Conflict, 1603–1658* (1986), p. 78.
369. Morrill, *Revolt of the Provinces*, p. 32.
370. D'Ewes, *Autobiography*, II, p. 113.
371. N. Wallington, *Historical Notices of . . . the Reign of Charles I, 1630–46*, ed. R.J. Webb (2 vols, 1869); P. Seaver, *Wallington's World: A Puritan Artisan in Seventeenth Century London* (1985), p. 158.
372. Wallington, *Historical Notices*, I, p. 120.
373. Seaver, *Wallington's World*, p. 161.

was compiling his *Historical Notices*,[374] to ideas of covenants between subjects and sovereigns which bound monarchs to 'conditions agreed upon between the prince and the people', and to the right of revolution in order to uphold the contract.[375] Such was the radical potential of puritanism (which historians have wrongly downplayed in recent years) in early Stuart London.

The diary of Robert Woodforde, the Northamptonshire attorney, indicates that it was not confined to the hot-house of the capital.[376] Woodforde's politics were not as extreme as those of Wallington. Though he spent quite a lot of time in London, it may be that his provincial circles were less tainted by radicalism; it may also be of significance that his diary ends in 1641 when events were only just beginning to place earlier experiences and thoughts in a more radical context. In terms of his actions, as his discomforted exegete recently acknowledged,, Woodforde made an 'apparently passive and obedient progress through these years' (1637–41) which his diary covers.[377] But whatever his outward conformity and efforts at discretion, Woodforde's reflections and prayers surpassed criticism of the regime and moved towards libel and treason. His abhorrence of altars, sabbath breachers, drinkers (though he himself drank heavily), Arminians and 'base ceremony and superstition' we are familiar with among his puritan brethren.[378] But, for all the recent emphasis on puritan conformity, we read how dislike of canonical prayers and maypoles could lead a figure like Woodforde to pray for the emigrants to New England,[379] pray against 'the wicked bishops their hierarchy'[380] and even pray for the king's as well as queen's conversion.[381] As with D'Ewes and Wallington, political discontents fused with religious fears. Woodforde aided his county's arguments against the forest eyres;[382] he praised St John's speech against ship money at Hampden's trial – 'The lord ease us of this great and heavy tax.'[383] He recorded the resistance of the women who defended their homes with pitchforks as the constables came to distrain their goods for failure to pay.[384] He met with those who came

374. *Ibid.*, p. 152.
375. *Ibid.*, p. 161.
376. New College Oxford MS 9502 (Woodforde's diary).
377. J. Fielding, 'Opposition to the personal rule of Charles I: the diary of Robert Woodforde, 1637–1641', *Hist. Journ.*, 21 (1988), pp. 769–88, quotation, p. 783. This disappointing discussion fails to exploit the riches of the Woodforde diary.
378. Woodforde's diary, entry for 9 July 1638, and *passim*.
379. *Ibid.*, 31 March 1638.
380. *Ibid.*, 22 July 1638.
381. *Ibid.*, 1 Feb. 1638, 11 April 1639, 11 Aug. 1640.
382. *Ibid.*, 18 Sept. 1637.
383. *Ibid.*, 17 Jan. 1638.
384. *Ibid.*, 18 Sept. 1638.

from Scotland with approval of their assemblies there.[385] Though he clearly had deep suspicions of the king himself, they were somewhat allayed by a private tour of the royal apartments during which Woodforde was relieved to see pictures representing the four gospels in the king's bedchamber. 'Lord bless the King's majesty,' he prayed, 'and make him a nursing father to the Kingdoms.'[386] But if direct experience made him, as he wanted to be, less despairing of the king, it made it all the more obvious that Charles was misled – by his wife, false preachers and papists who plotted to undermine true religion. The Scots war exacerbated his fears of plots, by papists at home and the French abroad.[387] He prayed to the Lord that a parliament might 'prevent the plots of thine adversaries'.[388] After it met the pace of events outran his time to record so many 'providences'.[389] Though a legal practitioner, Woodforde's language seldom resonates with the discourse of the law. His politics were those of a puritanism that always tended towards perceiving 'a conflict between two opposing ideals of the commonwealth, which corresponded to the familiar dichotomy between Christ and Antichrist'.[390] In the puritan world-view was always the potential to associate the figures of authority with the degenerate.

How many took that step it is not possible to determine. But that godliness did not *necessarily* lead to the pondering of radical choices during the 1630s is suggested by other diaries and compilations. The incumbent of Santon Downham, Suffolk, John Rous, for instance, was extremely well informed of events during the personal rule – through newsletters, separates, from rumour and conversation – and evidently concerned at some developments. He heard of English people going to mass at the queen's chapel;[391] he acquired a copy of the Arminian *God's Love to Mankind*;[392] he noted Wren's suspensions of those who would not conform to ceremonies;[393] he collected satires on 'the new churchman'.[394] Yet though he 'returned' to Geneva in 1633, possibly on a mission of piety,[395] there is nothing in the diary to indicate a strong antagonism to the bishops – indeed he thought

385. *Ibid.*, 3 Sept. 1639.
386. *Ibid.*, 9 Oct. 1638.
387. *Ibid.*, 22 March 1639.
388. *Ibid.*, 13 Dec. 1639.
389. See *ibid.*, 14 April 1640.
390. Fielding, 'Opposition to the personal rule', p. 778.
391. M.A.E. Green (ed.) *The Diary of John Rous, Incumbent of Santon Downham, Suffolk, 1625–1642* (Camden Soc., old series, 66, 1856), p. 49.
392. *Ibid.*, p. 79; see above, p. 296.
393. *Ibid.*, p. 80.
394. *Ibid.*, p. 78.
395. *Ibid.*, p. 73.

Leighton's attack on them a mistake. [396] Sherfield, he believed, might have escaped question had he ordered a glazier to remove the offending glass rather than committing vandalism with his staff.[397] Such reflections, together with his dispassionate account of the censure of Prynne, Burton and Bastwick, may suggest that in general his failure to comment on what he recorded owes less to censorship that to a moderation that only the events of 1642 tilted to a degree of partisanship.[398]

In John White's godly city of Dorchester, we find two lay puritan diarists whose religion had not obviously led them into radical politics in the 1630s. William Whiteway wrote with sympathy of Leighton who endured his sufferings 'patiently',[399] and of Sherfield against whom Neile and Laud, he noted, spoke 'most bitterly'.[400] Sabbath breaking and May games caused him great upset; he applauded those like Sir Arthur Hopton who spoke out against them, or refused to read the Book of Sports;[401] he recorded the death of a young man killed while sporting on the sabbath and that of a reveller felled by a maypole at Glastonbury.[402] Yet Whiteway donated money to St Paul's, and in his reflections on politics appears far from disturbed by events.[403] Forest fines he positively approved because the eyre proceeded against papists who he believed conspired to ruin the woods so as to weaken England's defences;[404] ship money he records as paid with 'much grudging' but as financing a fleet that made the French and Dutch envious.[405] Having given thanks for Charles I's recovery from smallpox he was proud to have seen the king and queen dine at Whitehall.[406]

Whiteway's diary ends in 1634, before perhaps the years that might have caused him most discomfort. That of his colleague Dennis Bond, woollen draper, bailiff and, in 1635, mayor of Dorchester, continues into the 1640s and 1650s, when he sat as a member of Cromwell's Council of State. The burdens of the war years of the 1620s ('soldiers billeted perforce') and the loan had clearly made him doubt the legitimacy of government measures.[407] In the 1630s, however, he is silent on the compositions for knighthood and ship money – 'a

396. Cope, *Politics without Parliaments*, p. 72.
397. Green, *Diary of Rous*, p. 70.
398. As Cust implies in 'News and politics', p. 85.
399. BL, Egerton MS 784, p. 159.
400. *Ibid.*, p. 180.
401. *Ibid.*, pp. 185, 189.
402. *Ibid.*, pp. 202, 207.
403. *Ibid.*, p. 215. He gave 2s. 6d.
404. *Ibid.*, p. 208.
405. *Ibid.*, pp. 216–17.
406. *Ibid.*, p. 213.
407. Dorset Record Office, D 413/Box 22 (Dennis Bond's diary), p. 46. (There is also a typescript of the diary – MS D 53.)

taxation upon the sea coast for the setting out of a fleet' – perhaps because though he paid £18, as a merchant he could appreciate the need for a navy.[408] Puritan sympathies underlay his marking the planting of New England in 1629 and the victories of the Swedish monarch in the 1630s.[409] He was unsympathetic to the collections for St Paul's – especially as men were 'inforced to give by the active clergy'.[410] But what made the greatest impact on Bond was the punishment of Prynne, Burton and Bastwick. It is important to note therefore that he probably knew little of the offences or individuals (he makes no mention of Prynne's earlier suffering and 'Dr Basquet' suggests ignorance rather than licence in spelling). He may have been present at their suffering, for his entry is unusually detailed in its observation; but present or merely well informed by others, Bond was much struck that 'they were wonderful patient and carried themselves so meekly and resolutely that all the beholders except some ruffians . . . shed many tears'.[411] Bastwick's prayer from the pillory that the gospel might not be taken from the people may have struck a chord of anxiety in Bond himself. And it may be that his entry for the following year signals a new expectancy of some divine intervention in the world: 'This year the 15 December was seen throughout the whole Kingdom the opening of the sky for half a quarter of an hour.'[412] He records the first Scots campaign without comment, but it seems that mounting religious anxieties coupled with remembered grievances of the earlier wars led him to refuse men and money in 1640.[413]

Though the spectrum of political radicalism they project requires a reassessment of a supposed puritan conformity, we would expect that puritan diaries in general air disquiet over the enforcement of canonical practices – and even the authorities of enforcement. What of those of less godly and more secular priorities? What may we learn about perceptions of the personal rule from the diaries that have survived of lawyers and provincial gentlemen, JPs, scholars and ministers? Dr Morrill recently presented the diary of a figure he describes as 'a paradigm of the pure country squire'.[414] William Davenport of Bramall Hall, Cheshire, though he may not have often journeyed to London, did not want for news.[415] He kept a commonplace book in

408. *Ibid.*, p. 47.
409. *Ibid.*, pp. 46–7.
410. *Ibid.*, p. 47.
411. *Ibid.*, p. 48.
412. *Ibid.*, p. 52.
413. *Ibid.*, p. 53.
414. Morrill, *Revolt of the Provinces*, p. 20.
415. J.S. Morrill, *Cheshire 1630–1660: County Government and Society during the English Revolution* (Oxford, 1974), pp. 21–2; *idem*, 'Sir William Davenport and the "silent majority" of early Stuart England', *Journ. Chester. Arch. Soc.*, 58 (1974), pp. 115–30.

which he copied from separates, and entered stories that were doing the local rounds. During the 1620s he was clearly fascinated and probably incensed by the figure of the Duke of Buckingham and this led him to more general criticism of an immoral court ruled by favourites and (later) tainted by the scandal of Castlehaven's crimes of rape and sodomy.[416] Morrill depicts him as a figure who always 'concentrated on those issues which concerned personalities' and, while disenchanted with the court and crown, not one whose disillusion amounted to an ideology of opposition.[417] Despite an attempt by others to drag him into more committed ranks, this assessment of Davenport and his diary remains basically, if not completely, convincing.[418] He was aware of broader issues and grievances and betrays his own discontents at them: the fiasco of the Ile de Rhé cast shame on his beloved country;[419] the commission for knighthood which came to Cheshire in May 1631 he thought a 'strange commission'; ship money a 'great tax'.[420] But he entered too a poem of loyal address to 'the King's most excellent majesty my dread sovereign', and seems to have combined that loyalty, quite conventionally, with suspicion of corrupt or amoral courtiers.[421]

Sir Humphrey Mildmay of Essex would certainly seem to support the claim that the provincial squirearchy even when they lived closer to the centres of power were far from preoccupied with national political issues. 'Public events,' writes one of his biographers, 'are the least concern of Sir Humphrey's journal.'[422] Mildmay, a JP, then sheriff of his county, was certainly not deprived of news: he received many letters and his London friends often turned up at his Danbury home with their gossip; while he returned their visits by spending nearly half the year in the capital.[423] Mildmay did not pass the decade of personal rule without irritants. Over the forest eyres, he thought the king's Solicitor did 'play the devil contra the country';[424] ship money posed him so many difficulties during his year as sheriff that he was forced to use private agents to collect the money, borrow to make up the shortfall and wait four years (from 1635 to 1639) to get his final acquittance.[425] But he had no quarrel with authority. Star Chamber he

416. Chester Record Office, CR 63/2/19.
417. Morrill, *Revolt of the Provinces*, pp. 20–1.
418. Cust, 'News and politics', pp. 81–3.
419. Chester Record Office, CR 63/2/19, ff. 62v–63.
420. *Ibid.*, ff.72v, 80.
421. *Ibid.*, f.78.
422. P.L. Ralph, *Sir Humphrey Mildmay: Royalist Gentleman* (New Brunswick, NJ, 1947), pp. 145–6; cf. H.A. St J. Mildmay, *A Brief Memoir of the Mildmay Family* (1913), p. 78. The diary of Mildmay from 1633 is in Harleian MS 454.
423. Ralph, *Mildmay*, pp. 16, 26, 68.
424. *Ibid.*, p. 147.
425. *Ibid.*, pp. 74–81.

held 'for the good of the commonwealth'.[426] Mildmay's antagonism was reserved for the likes of those whose diaries we have been examining: the puritans. He was by no means without piety. Mildmay took notes on the many sermons he heard, praising the 'learned'; he liked to socialize with the clergy; he exercised Christian charity, visiting his servants when they were sick.[427] But a man alienated by fasts and 'prating', a lover of plays and heavy drinking who liked to see a cleric also in his cups, Mildmay had nothing in common with the Essex 'godly'.[428] He was evidently attached to the Anglican church and its ceremonies and antagonized by the demeanour of Prynne and others, whom he came to suspect of treasonable dealings with the Scots.[429] Whatever appetite he may have had for reform of the commonweal, Mildmay could not walk the same path with the Earl of Warwick or 'Mr Pimp'.[430] Far north in Yorkshire, Sir Hugh Cholmley also passed the years before the Scots war plagued his county in happy content as JP and deputy lieutenant, living in 'as handsome and plentiful fashion at home as any gentleman' – with three or four strangers at his table, and the poor fed at his gate.[431]

By no means all enjoyed country cheer during the 'halcyon days' of the 1630s, showing only minimal engagement with the course of public affairs. Walter Yonge of Colyton in Devon kept a detailed calendar of happenings, fantastic and public, at home and abroad. He was of godly sympathies during the 1630s, for he noted the flourishing of New England, the 'pious' purposes of the feoffees and the blocks to sound religion placed by ceremonies, the Book of Sports and the silencing of preachers.[432] Yet he could praise Laud for his clemency to Leighton, and record the trial of Prynne and company without comment.[433] Perhaps more noteworthy are the veiled comments of the former student of the Middle Temple on the legal cases of the decade. For already by 1629 the removal of the gaoled MPs from one place to

426. *Ibid.*, p. 150.
427. *Ibid.*, pp. 22–4, 33, 109, 118.
428. *Ibid.*, pp. 22–4, 47, 53, 67, 101, 133, 167–8; Mildmay, *Memoir of the Mildmay Family*, pp. 80, 89. (It is worth underlining at this point, since Fielding passes over it, that Woodforde was also given to much over-indulgence in drink.)
429. He described Prynne's as a 'wicked cause' (Ralph, *Mildmay*, p. 149) and disliked the Earl of Warwick (p. 161). During the 1640s, he found comfort in reading Hooker, Andrewes, White and Heylyn (*ibid.*, p. 212).
430. *Ibid.*, p. 156. Intriguingly, he shared this joke with his friend Isaac Dorislaus, on whom see *DNB* and K. Sharpe, 'The foundation of the chairs of history at Oxford and Cambridge: an episode in Jacobean politics', in *History of the Universities, II* (1982), pp. 127–52.
431. *The Memoirs of Sir Hugh Cholmley* (1787), p. 56. He was to be active in mustering men for the Scots war (p. 59) but quarrelled with Strafford and refused ship money in 1640. Ultimately, he declared for the king.
432. BL Add. MS 35331 (Walter Yonge's diary), ff.39, 51, 52v.
433. *Ibid.*, ff.56v, 57.

another to deny them habeas corpus he thought against the law, or as he put it more discreetly 'sic eluditur lex'.[434] In 1633 he noted royal disfavour towards those who had spoken in Star Chamber for Sherfield; the ship money judges he categorized simply as 'pro patria' and 'pro rege'.[435] The oath Charles I required in 1638 he explicitly denounced as 'crossing' the Petition of Right and a threat to subjects' 'propriety in their goods', which may have been a decisive point in his alienation from the regime.[436] Certainly he was not alone in his view that legal proprieties were breached. Bulstrode Whitelocke, later Keeper of the Great Seal for the Republic, recalled his unease during the general 'happiness' of the 1630s about Charles's consulting in advance with his judges and his firm opinion of ship money that 'because it was imposed without assent of parliament . . . it was unlawful'.[437] In Kent, Sir Roger Twysden, an antiquary with a vast knowledge of English law and precedent, became increasingly preoccupied with constitutional issues and grievances – such as the legal status of Star Chamber decrees or the orders to keep watch and man beacons.[438] Most of all he was troubled by ship money. He doubted the legality of the writs; the answer of the judges to the king's query concerning his right to it he regarded as 'ambiguous' and no foundation for future levies. A challenge in the courts he believed the necessary way for the English 'to vindicate their liberties'.[439] Even in the future stronghold of royalism, the University of Oxford, reservations about the legality of Conciliar measures were acknowledged and aired. Thomas Crosfield, fellow of Queen's, was in general much in sympathy with the ecclesiastical and secular authorities. He thought the Book of Sports too much 'exagitated by precise men'; he lauded the beautifying of churches.[440] He had no regrets about the suppression of the corantos' 'idle discourse'; he could see sense in the king's foreign policy and the 'good use' to which ship money was put.[441] But over knighthood fines he understood why 'some lawyers stand and question quo iure hoc requisitur', and why some 'fear his Majesty will bring his subjects under the like servility that Spain hath them'.[442] The cloisters of

434. *Ibid.*, f.31. See Reeve, *Charles I*, ch. 5, for the best account of these proceedings.
435. BL Add. MS 35331, ff.54, 68v.
436. *Ibid.*, f.72v.
437. Whitelocke, *Memorials of English Affairs*, pp. 13, 22.
438. Twysden MS U 47/47, Z1, 2; see also, L.B. Larking (ed.) 'Sir Roger Twysden's journal', *Archaeologia Cantiana*, 1 (1858), pp. 184–214; and J.M. Kemble (ed.) *Certaine Considerations upon the Government of England by Sir Roger Twysden* (Camden Soc., old series, 45, 1849). This work was not begun until 1639.
439. See K. Fincham, 'The judges' decision on ship money in February 1637: the reaction of Kent', *Bull. Inst. Hist. Res.*, 57 (1984), pp. 230–7.
440. F.S. Boas (ed.) *The Diary of Thomas Crosfield* (1935), pp. 68, 74.
441. *Ibid.*, pp. 60, 75, 81.
442. *Ibid.*, p. 47. Crosfield's diary reminds us not to make simplistic connections between religious and constitutional positions, perhaps especially in a decade of no parliaments.

Oxford had not deafened Crosfield's ears to the noise of political debate.

The few surviving diaries offer invaluable insights into the reactions of some articulate men to the decade of personal rule. They reveal, as well as rural content, anxieties, criticisms and grave misgivings. For the most part, however, these are articulated, even in the privacy of the diarists' study, within a context of loyalty to the king; few before 1638 appear to have constructed their experience into an ideology of opposition – though the more committed puritan was easily inclined to place events in a narrative provided by his soteriology. Whether puritan or not, all diaries construct a narrative, and so systematize experience: Yonge drew up an index to his and may, like D'Ewes and Twysden, have written parts retrospectively and in the light of later experiences. What we have to try to gauge (albeit impressionistically) are the feelings of the gentry and where possible the middling and lower orders who did not write up their experiences and responses into a text, but who responded both to particular measures and, perhaps, to the course of events in general. There is no shortage of contemporaries who offer to generalize about the feelings of their fellow countryfolk, or circles of acquaintance. Nehemiah Wallington claimed that all 'the holy people of the lord seeing idolatry, superstition and all manner of profaneness are grieved, but they know not what course to have it reformed'.[443] Some who wrote with hindsight after the outbreak of civil war would detect a prescience of impending crisis. Others, from the later experience of bloodshed and strife, wrote nostalgically of the experience of personal rule.

More illuminating than these retrospective visions are the strictly contemporary comments on the mood of the times. At the beginning of the decade few doubted that a gulf of misunderstanding had opened between the king and his subjects: some prognosticated doom.[444] By 1630 Secretary Dorchester believed there had been an alteration 'all to the better in settling the disquiet of men's minds after the heats kindled by the disorders of the last parliament'.[445] Sir Robert Pye was less confident, praying for 'a true understanding betwixt the King and people'.[446] By 1633, however, there was the beginning of a sense of better times, such that even Bulstrode Whitelocke thought most were 'feeling more sympathy with royalty and generously ascribing past misgovernment to the pernicious influence of favourites'.[447] Charles's journey to York the summer of that year turned out to be a lap of

443. Wallington, *Historical Notices*, p. 28.
444. See *HMC Kenyon*, p. 37.
445. *Cal. Stat. Pap. Dom., 1629–31*, p. 203: Dorchester to Fleming, 3 March 1630.
446. *Cal. Stat. Pap. Dom., 1631–3*, p. 296: Pye to Vane, 28 March 1632.
447. R. Whitelocke, *Memoirs Biographical and Historical of Bulstrode Whitelocke* (1860), p. 88.

honour. As we saw, the mayor welcomed him with praise of his 'eminent virtues, sublime gifts and illuminations' which 'fill not only this city, this Kingdom but the whole universe with splendour'.[448] More revealingly, the ordinary people flocked to the king on his passage to and from Scotland, and on his return into London he 'was received at the waterside with multitudes of people and the greatest acclamations of joy'.[449] The birth of his second son crowned the progress. Capturing the mood, Edmund Bolton quoted to Coke from Seneca, 'optimus civitatis status sub rege iusto', concluding 'consequently the state of our country is happy'.[450] The Gloucestershire lawyer Robert Powell was led to a celebratory piece comparing the life of King Alfred with that of 'the Constantine and Carolus Magnus of our age'.[451] The people were cheering and the bells ringing for Charles five years after the dissolution of his last parliament.

A longed-for parliament?

What then of parliaments during the years when they were not called? If seventeenth-century Englishmen attached importance to parliaments – as they undoubtedly did – how did they react to a period in which the representative assembly of the realm was not called? Somewhat to her surprise, Professor Cope found few demands for a parliament in the gentry correspondence of the 1630s.[452] The royal proclamation against spreading false rumours about the resummoning of parliament may help to explain this, but it by no means prohibited mention of parliaments – either at court or in the country. In his quarrel with the Earl of Huntingdon, Sir William Faunt threatened to complain to parliament about the Lord-Lieutenant's taxation of the county.[453] Windebank, in his memorandum on a proposed national contribution for the Palatinate, acknowledged the popular fear that it would inhibit the recall of parliament 'which is generally and passionately longed for'.[454] The assembly of parliament in Scotland in

448. York City Record Office, House Books, 35, ff.208–11; see above, p. 640.
449. Coke MS 46: Windebank to Coke, 25 July 1633.
450. Coke MS 49: 29 Aug. 1634. 'The best condition of a commonwealth is under a just king'.
451. R. Powell, *The Life of Alfred . . . Together with a Parallel of our Sovereign Lord King Charles* (1634, STC 20161), p. 88.
452. E.S. Cope, 'Public images of parliament during its absence', *Legislative Stud. Quart.*, 7 (1982), pp. 221–34. I am grateful to Esther Cope for sending me an offprint of this helpful article.
453. Hastings MSS, Legal Box 5.
454. Bodleian, Clarendon MS 5, no. 321; on 29 July the Venetian envoy reported that the voluntary contribution for the Palatinate 'seems to have aroused fresh murmurs among the people that it is not proper to disburse money by any other way than that of

1633, it was said, stirred the desire for one in England.[455] At the assizes in Kent some aired the belief that the legality of ship money, rather than being put to the judges, should have been heard 'in parliament'.[456] Significantly, however, the same spokesmen 'confessed the last parliament had been much to blame in their carriage towards his Majesty'. The comment, recalling D'Ewes's and others' denunciation of the 'fiery spirits' of 1629, may bear witness to a broader feeling that Charles had been wronged and could not be expected to summon another session hastily.[457] Many in the country, in other words, may have concurred with those at court who advocated a period of healing so that the next parliament might be more productive. By corollary, it seems too that few believed another parliament would not meet. An anonymous newsletter of November 1631, for example, reported that 'people think we shall have a parliament . . . of which there is no great unlikelihood'.[458] Pory had heard the same rumour; and the next year again predicted a parliament on the death of the Elector Palatine.[459] Hamilton's expedition to Sweden fuelled the expectation, as did the birth of the prince, on which occasion the Venetian ambassador observed it was customary for a parliament to vote subsidies.[460] At the end of 1633, Flower's newsletter referred to the 'great talk' in the city 'of a parliament', though he doubted it.[461] Throughout 1635, with the foreign situation becoming more unsettled, and on the death of Weston, expectations of a parliament increased.[462] Sir Arthur Hopton thought Spain 'presumed too much on the small correspondency between his Majesty and his parliaments'.[463] The failure of Arundel's mission and talk of an alliance with France seemed to bring an assembly nearer: in March 1637 John Browne was granted the clerkship of parliament which had been vacant since 1633.[464] At the same time,

parliamentary ordinance' (*Calendar of State Papers Venetian* [*Cal. Stat. Pap. Venet.*], *1632–6*, p. 131).

455. *Cal. Stat. Pap. Venet., 1632–6*, p. 87.
456. Twysden MS U 47/47, Zi, p. 201.
457. Cf. E. Hyde, Earl of Clarendon, *The History of the Rebellion and Civil Wars in England*, ed. W.D. Macray (6 vols, Oxford, 1888), p. 84.
458. *Cal. Stat. Pap. Dom., 1631–3*, p. 193; cf. *Eikon Basilike* (1876 edn) p. 1.
459. Birch, *Court and Times of Charles I*, II, pp. 143, 151, 207; PRO, C.115/M35/8387.
460. *Cal. Stat. Pap. Venet., 1629–32*, pp. 545, 567; cf. PRO, C.115/M35/8386, in which Pory tells Scudamore that Weston was openly saying another parliament would meet 'for certain', 17 December 1631. See also, *HMC Denbigh, V*, p. 8: Nicholas to Fielding, 13 Dec. 1631.
461. PRO, C.115/M31/8166: Flower to Scudamore, 28 Dec. 1633.
462. Sheffield Central Library, Wentworth MS WW/6, ff.167ff; *Cal. Stat. Pap. Venet., 1632–6*, p. 351.
463. BL, Egerton MS 1820, f.225, 'I refer it to your lordship's consideration whether it would not be a good occasion to call a parliament' (Hopton to Cottington, 30 Dec. 1632). It is as important to note the recipient of this letter as the author.
464. *Cal. Stat. Pap. Dom., 1636–7*, p. 534.

however, other developments seemed to some to push parliaments further off, or even sound their death knell. Correr, the Venetian envoy, reporting in February the judges' declaration on ship money, felt sure that 'at one stroke it roots out for ever the meeting of parliament'.[465] Whatever its truth, his perception came to be shared, as ship money became an annual levy, and rumours of parliament fell silent – until the crisis of the Scots revived them. But until 1637, with scarcely a year passing without the rumour of an assembly being leaked from court and circulated around the country, perhaps few had as yet come to believe that the king or Council was rigidly opposed to them.

There was no real reason for them to believe so, for rumours in this case, as so often, were based on reality. The French ambassador advised Richelieu in August 1629 that despite recent events most Councillors were committed to parliaments, and the comments of ministers and courtiers bear him out.[466] Secretary Dorchester indeed believed the punishment of Eliot and others in King's Bench promised a more moderate and successful meeting in the future when 'the king may meet his people with assurance that they will never transgress in the point of due respect and obedience'.[467] Lord Treasurer Weston himself said a parliament was to be called in 1631.[468] In 1632 Hopton advised Cottington that the time for one was propitious, 'and once a good parliament, and ever a good parliament'.[469] Sir Francis Nethersole petitioned Charles to call one in 1633;[470] Lord Keeper Coventry pressed for one that autumn;[471] in January 1634 Dury told Roe that there were pressures for a parliament 'from which neither the Lord Treasurer nor the Archbishop of Canterbury showed themselves averse'.[472] None of these court commentators expected eleven years of non-parliamentary rule, nor spoke as though parliaments were anathema. Indeed after a successful session in Ireland in 1635 Wentworth clearly believed they might soon and successfully reconvene in England: for 'howbeit the peccant . . . humour be not yet wholly purged forth yet do I conceive it in the way, and that once rightly corrected and prepared we may hope for a parliament of a sound constitution indeed'.[473]

465. *Cal. Stat. Pap. Venet., 1636–9*, p. 153.
466. PRO, 31/3/66, ff.136–7.
467. *Cal. Stat. Pap. Dom., 1629–31*, p. 203.
468. Above, note 460.
469. Egerton MS 1820, f.225. His sentiments are close to those of Charles I himself (Knowler, *Strafford Letters*, I, p. 365).
470. *Cal. Stat. Pap. Dom., 1633–4*, p. 148.
471. Knowler, *Strafford Letters*, I, p. 141: Cottington to Wentworth, 29 Oct.
472. *Cal. Stat. Pap. Dom., 1633–4*, p. 417.
473. Knowler, *Strafford Letters*, I, p. 419: Wentworth to George Butler.

Ultimately, of course, the decision to call a parliament rested with the king, whose attitude we have to deduce from fragments. We do know that as a young monarch Charles had shown no aversion to parliaments. In 1628 in a proclamation for a fast he used language about them as strong as any claims that MPs might have made themselves: 'The High Court of Parliament,' it declared, 'is that Great Council which is the representative body of his whole Kingdom to consult, debate and conclude of those weighty matters which concern the glory of God, the honour of the King, the safety of his Kingdoms and the support of his friends and allies.'[474] Châteauneuf was persuaded that despite Buckingham's counsel to emancipate himself from them, Charles was committed to parliaments. It may be that our best clue to the king's views lies in his own words of 1629, that another session would be recalled 'when our people shall see more clearly into our intents and actions'.[475] Despite the rumours in 1632 he clearly decided the time was not ripe: the Venetian envoy's sense that Charles was opposed to a recall is supported by his deletion of references to a parliament from Nethersole's draft letter for a Palatinate collection.[476] In 1633 Cottington hints that the king was angered by Coventry's pressing one.[477] Yet it seems likely that in negotiating a French alliance, Charles recognized the need to recall a parliament, and it may be closest to the truth to suggest, as courtiers appeared to believe, that a sense of time and circumstance governed Charles's plans rather than an unbending hostility to parliaments. There is more of a sense of the need for tactics than an antagonism in the king's advice to Wentworth on his calling the Irish parliament: 'they are of the nature of cats, they ever grow curst with age, so that if you will have good of them put them off handsomely when they come to any age, for young ones are ever more tractable . . . Nothing can more conduce to the beginning of a new than the well-ending of the former parliament.'[478] Like Wentworth, Charles was all too aware that the last parliament in England had not ended well. Like Wentworth he was waiting for the peccant humour to be purged. In the *Eikon Basilike* he was to say that 'by forbearing to convene [them] for some years', he 'hoped to have extinguished' those 'distempers'.[479]

474. Larkin, *Stuart Royal Proclamations*, II, no. 89, pp. 193–4.
475. Above, p. 57.
476. *Cal. Stat. Pap. Venet., 1629–32*, pp. 183, 629; Clarendon MS 5, no. 315.
477. Knowler, *Strafford Letters*, I, p. 141.
478. *Ibid.*, p. 365, 22 Jan. 1635.
479. *Eikon Basilike*, p. 1.

Criticism and counsel

The absence of parliaments removed an important and traditional forum for the expression of criticism. Wentworth's rule that he would not criticize the crown in his capacity as a local governor should alert us to just how important the removal of a legitimate platform of criticism might have been.[480] But the absence of parliament did not mean that during the 1630s Englishmen could not voice discontents. From within the circles of the court itself, criticism was traditional; the idea of counsel, central to the system of personal monarchy, licensed criticism as well as praise of the king. We have begun to see that even in the literature that was most courtly – what is often labelled 'Cavalier' drama and poetry, or masques – we may discern tones of irony, ambivalence and dissent as well as a language of celebration. And plays performed at court could be quite explicit in voicing anxieties about the style of government as well as particular policies.[481] Massinger's *Emperor of the East*, for example, satirized projectors and criticized those who 'roare out: All is the King's, his will above his laws',[482] while Shirley's *The Grateful Servant* savagely lampoons deceitful and corrupt ministers and boldly reminds rulers:

> . . . nor is there Magicke
> I'th person of a King that plays the Tyrant,
> But a good sword can easily uncharme it.[483]

Nor were discontents and criticism confined to the licensed laboratory of playing; they were clearly articulated in courtiers' correspondence with each other, with friends in the country and in addresses to the king.[484] The propositions submitted by Sir Robert Heath to Charles I in 1629, for making the king loved and dispelling popular fears, clearly demonstrate that the King's Attorney-General thought much was amiss and was not afraid to say that much of the blame rested with the government.[485] Archbishop Ussher of Armagh did not hide, in a letter to Secretary Coke, his strong disapproval of a too autocratic style of

480. See Knowler, *Strafford Letters*, I, p. 33 and in general, D. Hirst, 'Court, country and politics before 1629', in K. Sharpe (ed.) *Faction and Parliament: Essays on Early Stuart History* (Oxford, 1978), pp. 131–2.
481. See Butler, *Theatre and Crisis* and Sharpe, *Criticism and Compliment*.
482. P. Massinger, *The Emperor of the East* (1632, STC 17636), sigs C.2v, C.3v; cf. W. Davenant, *The Cruel Brother* (1630, STC 6302), p. 133: 'the commonwealth hath been so crush'd with . . . such patents'.
483. T. Shirley, *The Grateful Servant* (1630, STC 22444), p. 54.
484. The author of *Micrologia* (1629, STC 17146) described the actor's role as that of one who brought 'enormities in public view' (sig B.3v). The author of *Augustus* (1632, STC 957) even suggested that such criticism was less dangerous than silence (p. 149).
485. J. Reeve, 'Sir Robert Heath's advice for Charles I in 1629', *Bull. Inst. Hist. Res.*, 69 (1986), pp. 215–24.

kingship. 'I see,' he complained without any sense that Coke might be provoked by his misgivings, 'sometimes there is so much made of his Majesty's letters that there must be no dispute made of them; simple obedience they say is required, and not inquiry into the legalness of the command.'[486] As we have seen, in July 1629 Judge Yelverton endorsed the controversial sermon of Peter Smart against ceremonies with a declaration of his own dislike of singing and organ playing ('which he termed "whistling"'), a denial of the bishops' authority to order them, and a statement that he 'had always been accounted a puritan and thanked God for it'.[487]

Such outspokenness in contemporary politics has been known to cost a seat in the cabinet. And those historians predisposed to deny the possibility of criticism in Caroline England are quick to point to the fortunes of Bishop Williams and Attorney Heath. But, as well as pondering the complexities of these cases, we should recall that the elevation of Noy, Digges and Wentworth offers evidence that Charles I did not necessarily regard criticism as disloyal. Nor did Noy or Wentworth feel that their promotion stifled their free expression of opinion. It was Noy who organized the farcical antimasque of projectors that satirized royal patentees in the Inns of Court's entertainment, *The Triumph of Peace*;[488] Wentworth expressed his 'wish' that some of the projectors 'were hanged'.[489] Earl Marshal Arundel was clearly opposed to the soap patent and would not brook the efforts of others to persuade him to support it.[490] There is no evidence that in those cases the outspoken suffered disfavour for their frankness. Sir Thomas Roe, who during the 1630s was often implicitly and at times explicitly critical of royal foreign policy, was appointed in 1636 to the chancellorship of the Order of the Garter, a post to which Charles attached importance. Roe too reminds us that in this context the court should not be too narrowly defined, and that as well as ministers freely exchanging views with relatives or friends, there were correspondents in and on the fringes of court society who passed quite uncomplimentary judgements on their milieu. Criticism of the insincerity of courtiers was such a commonplace that John Nicholas could even tease his son Edward, the clerk to the Admiralty, about it.[491] More specifically Sir Henry Herbert, Master of the Revels, took a clearly moralistic tone in contrasting the court's pleasures at Newmarket with

486. *HMC Cowper I*, pp. 438–9: Ussher to Coke, 10 Aug. 1631.
487. Ornsby, *Correspondence of Cosin*, pp. 155–7; *Cal. Stat. Pap. Dom., 1629–31*, p. 15; above, pp. 330, 662.
488. Sharpe, *Criticism and Compliment*, p. 222.
489. Knowler, *Strafford Letters*, II, p. 117; cf. p. 77 and Wentworth MS WW/10, ff.85–7.
490. Knowler, *Strafford Letters*, I, p. 363.
491. *Cal. Stat. Pap. Dom., 1638–9*, p. 615.

the lot of 'many a good Christian in prison and elsewhere' who 'is not allowed so much to keep soul and body together as one of these horses'. 'I am not,' he affirmed, 'in charity with the excess of expense' and he was no more in sympathy with the complacency such pleasures betrayed – 'I could wish our thoughts did cross the water a little more'.[492] The Reverend Garrard could not resist exposing the foibles of the court in which he was so well connected, in his regular correspondence with Wentworth, Conway and others, and in denouncing particular measures his language was anything but discreet or restrained.[493] Projects he thought a disease bred by the 'discontinuance of parliaments'; on the first writ of ship money 'I tell my Lord Cottington that I had rather give and pay ten subsidies in parliament than ten shillings this new old way of dead Noy's.'[494] Though he burnt some of his papers 'upon fear of coming before the Council table', there is no evidence that Garrard was summoned, but clear indication that he did not muzzle his tongue: in 1639 he was to observe that an ass had been appointed Master of the Rolls.[495] Passed among courtiers, and more broadly, the letters of Herbert and Garrard suggest that currents of criticism ran through the court and capital, to feed and join with other streams of complaint in the country, ensuring that the absence of parliaments did not cause the flow of grievances to run dry.

Riot

At the other end of the social spectrum to the court, popular discontent had a long-established form of expression: riot and demonstration. Popular uprisings present difficulties to the historian of popular politics or responses to government: they may be occasioned more by economic desperation than ideology or political discontent, and more by local grievances than objections to central government. Often it is impossible to disentangle the twine of grievances. But historians of Tudor rebellions have ventured a categorization of uprisings, and have identified in movements such as the Pilgrimage of Grace and Kett's rebellion popular demonstrations against government policies as well as economic problems.[496] A report on the 1630s would have to return

492. PRO, C.115/N3/8548: Herbert to Scudamore, 2 March 1632.
493. For his abhorrence of masques ('Oh, that they would give over these things . . .') see Knowler, *Strafford Letters*, I, p. 176.
494. *Ibid.*, p. 357; II, p. 55.
495. BL, Loan MS 29/172, f.151; *Cal. Stat. Pap. Dom., 1638–9*, p. 621: Garrard to Conway, 28 March 1639.
496. See P. Williams, *The Tudor Regime* (Oxford, 1979), chs 10, 11; *idem*, 'Revolution and rebellion in early modern England', in M.R.D. Foot (ed.) *War and Society* (1973), pp. 225–40; M.E. James, 'Obedience and dissent in Henrician England: the Lincolnshire rebellion, 1536', *P&P*, 48 (1970), pp. 3–78; C.S.L. Davies, 'Révoltes populaires en

the absence of political protests such as these. Uprisings there were from the beginning of the decade. The subsistence crisis of 1629–30 led to many acts of violence and corn riots, but the hostility of the desperate crowds was directed against local engrossers of corn rather than a government whose policies were directed at sustaining the 'just price' and supply which the rioters demanded.[497] Outbursts of revolt also took place in the forests and the fenlands during the decade of personal rule. In 1631, a band led by Captain 'Skimmington' levelled enclosures in the forests of Dean, Gillingham and Braydon, the greatest disturbances taking place at Feckenham in Worcestershire.[498] These were once interpreted as violent popular reactions to the royal programme of disafforestation. An important revaluation, however, has demonstrated that the riots were directed less against the crown than against the gentry who by enclosing woodland drove the landless poor from forests which in the form of waste wood, free pasture and pockets of cultivatable common had provided a bare subsistence.[499] The Council proceeded harshly against the 300 rioters who, armed with spades, had torn down the enclosure in Feckenham forest; but royal policy did not cause the riots, which continued into the 1640s.[500] Indeed while continuing to stimulate a long-term trend to larger units of production of iron, the Caroline government endeavoured to provide some livelihood for those who lost the benefits of the common.[501] The rioters with their spades expressed a class hostility to improving landlords who had breached custom and the (idealized) values of paternalism. Peter Simon, the curate of Newland, who was examined for inciting the disturbances, evidently upheld the authority of princes but preached the equality of other men.[502]

The story of the fenland disturbances is a similar tale. The long-term programme of improvement by drainage schemes, like all improvements, had produced its victims – those who had scratched a living from the reed, fowl, fish and grazing of the bog. From 1603 the stinting of pasture rights was reducing the number of cottagers and the acceleration of the drainage schemes threatened more.[503] Though,

Angleterre, 1500–1700', *Annales*, 24 (1969), pp. 24–59; A.J. Fletcher, *Tudor Rebellions* (1983).

497. See above, pp. 464–5.
498. B. Sharp, *In Contempt of all Authority: Rural Artisans and Riot in the West of England, 1586–1660* (Berkeley, 1980), ch. 4; *Cal. Stat. Pap. Dom., 1631–3*, pp. 36, 289; Egerton MS 784 (William Whiteway's diary, 1618–34), p. 163.
499. Sharp, *In Contempt of all Authority*, pp. 143–5, 250.
500. *Cal. Stat. Pap. Dom., 1631–3*, p. 289; Sharp, *In Contempt of all Authority*, ch. 8.
501. Sharp, *In Contempt of all Authority*, pp. 143, 203.
502. *Cal. Stat. Pap. Dom., 1631–3*, p. 36.
503. See R.B. Manning, *Village Revolts: Social Protest and Popular Disturbances in England, 1509–1640* (Oxford, 1988), pp. 174–5; K. Lindley, *Fenland Riots and the English Revolution* (1982), ch. 2.

again, the king attempted to endow those so deprived of common with a few acres of their own and though, clearly, foreigners thought the reclaimed land a good bet, the fenlanders were not appeased. As the drainers of Hatfield Chase complained, 'The people of the country will not pay any considerable rent for what they say have been their commons', though they had been allowed proportions in lieu and though French tenants tendered for the land.[504] There were riots in the fens north-east of the River Witham in June 1636 and in the West Fen in August;[505] 200 assembled in June 1637 in the Whelpmore Fen near Ely to destroy the drainers' ditches – but did no hurt to men or goods;[506] the winter of 1638 saw another riot in Norfolk.[507] In some instances, the protesters clearly had a notion of their legal rights.[508] Vermuyden feared that lawsuits in the fens could cost more than the value of the land; and Margaret Kirby (presumably the wife of the drainer) claimed that many of the commoners of King's Sedgemoor refused to treat about draining until they had been a commission under the Great Seal.[509] But as this episode nicely indicates, neither the hostility nor sense of legality of the fen dwellers was directed against the king. Indeed when in 1638 Edward Powell led a riot proclaiming 'the losing of the fens would be the losing of their livelihoods', he won the support of the crowd by assuring them that he had access to the king, who was on their side: 'They are told,' Bishop Wren reported, 'that the King at Newmarket leaned on his shoulder and wept when he heard his relation'.[510] Fen riots then were very much in the tradition of an appeal to a benign king as the custodian of custom rather than incipient rebellion against government.

As well as those in the forests and fens there were other sporadic risings during the 1630s. In 1631 a riot broke out in Fleet Street.[511] In the summer of 1634 miners from Baslow gathered to present a tumultuous petition to the Earl of Newcastle.[512] But their demonstration appears to have been less political and their protest less violent than those of their successors in recent times. Not until the later 1630s and 1640 when troops recruited for Scotland were roaming the country were there outbreaks of iconoclasm and riots which may

504. *Cal. Stat. Pap. Dom., 1637*, p. 195.
505. *Cal. Stat. Pap. Dom., 1636–7*, pp. 32, 98.
506. *Cal. Stat. Pap. Dom., 1637–8*, p. 503.
507. *Cal. Stat. Pap. Dom., 1638–9*, p. 299.
508. Cf. C. Holmes, 'Drainers and fenmen: the problem of popular political consciousness in the seventeenth century', in A. Fletcher and J. Stevenson (eds) *Order and Disorder in Early Modern England* (Cambridge, 1985), pp. 166–95.
509. *Cal. Stat. Pap. Dom., 1637–8*, p. 12; *1637*, p. 278.
510. *Cal. Stat. Pap. Dom., 1638–9*, p. 301.
511. *Cal. Stat. Pap. Dom., 1629–31*, p. 33.
512. *HMC Cowper II*, p. 60.

have expressed ideological opposition as well as that indiscriminate hooliganism that has always been a feature of the common soldiery.[513] Before then, the effectiveness of policies to secure food supplies, the absence of a trade crisis, most of all perhaps traditions of deference and conservative popular ideals that had not yet been shattered, ensured that even a decade of unusual taxes and levies remained relatively free of violent popular protest.[514] The grievances catalogued by those who pulled down hedges, parks and chases in 1635 – depopulation, decay of tillage, the subdivision of lands and houses, the decay of hospitality occasioned by the gentry's flocking to London – far from an agenda of opposition reads like a copy of the Privy Council's own list of social problems to be resolved.[515] As the latest study of village revolts concludes, 'On the eve of the Civil Wars, the forms of popular protest remained largely devoid of political content and employed rituals usually derived from the traditional expressions of popular justice'.[516] In 'vainly attempting to restore a lost world which may never have existed', they were perhaps in reality as well as perception more in tune than discord with the policies of the king and Council.

Responses to the regime

Between courtly criticism and popular demonstration lies the most interesting and difficult area for the historian of attitudes to the government of the personal rule. In the case of the gentry and substantial freeholders, for most of whom we have neither diaries nor correspondence, we are often studying men who as JPs, sheriffs and constables were agents as well as subjects of the king's government in the shires. Their dual roles clearly present a problem. When service was a duty and a desired route to local supremacy, we cannot simply deduce from willingness to execute office an enthusiastic support for the measures of the king and the Council. On the other hand, active execution of royal orders suggests that the magisterial class in general was not alienated by the regime. The same complexity underlies the successful collection of levies and taxes: payment does not indicate endorsement or willing acceptance of the measure; Sir Philip Warwick, no hostile commentator, believed that most considered knighthood

513. See below, pp. 908–9.
514. Buchanan Sharp describes 'most food riots' as 'extreme forms of petitioning' (*In Contempt of all Authority*, p. 42). See Fletcher and Stevenson, *Order and Disorder*, introduction; and the important essay by John Walter, 'The social economy of dearth in early modern England', in J. Walter and R. Schofield (eds) *Famine, Disease and the Social Order in Early Modern England* (Cambridge, 1989), pp. 75–128.
515. *Cal. Stat. Pap. Dom., 1635–6*, p. 22.
516. Manning, *Village Revolts*, pp. 318–19.

fines illegal.[517] Yet the failure of the benevolence and the collapse of ship money in 1640 indicates that consensus was essential to the payment of taxes. The thorny question of responses to the regime, then, must lie somewhere between the outspoken words of a few and the compliant actions of most. If we would be wrong to read every act of co-operation as support for the government, it would be misguided to interpret each denunciation or gesture of resistance as one voice of a hidden chorus of opposition. With such cautionary remarks in mind, we must endeavour to evaluate the levels of disaffection and the extent to which it undermined the effectiveness – or even survival – of personal government.

To almost every governmental measure we can find evidence of critical reaction and even principled objection. A churchwarden of Pluckley in Kent refused to take an apprentice and continued in his obstinacy even when he was offered money as an inducement to take a boy. 'His answer was he would receive one in a legal manner but would not express what conditions he expected.'[518] Whilst his claim that most felt as he did is not sustainable, it is clear that he was not alone. The attorney Thomas Trevelyan was summoned by the Privy Council to explain his refusal to take an apprentice and Thomas Conisby was prosecuted in Star Chamber for having 'said he had viewed the statutes and could there find no warrant to enforce any man to take a prentice'.[519] As well as the famous case in Shropshire when Corbet invoked the Petition of Right against Bridgewater's assessment for the muster master, there are several recorded protests against orders for musters and militia rates.[520] Essex responded to an order for twelve bandsmen to keep watch at Tilbury by asserting that they were 'no way liable to that charge'.[521] Captain J. Prust, muster master of Dorset, told the Council that he had received no money in over two years, 'the country alleging that there is no law for any such taxation'.[522] In Northamptonshire, the Earl of Exeter reported those who refused to pay the rates 'inclined to oppose the service by the instigation of John Waters, a most seditious refractory attorney who stands upon the letter of the law'.[523] Sir Arthur Haselrig in Leicestershire refused to pay for a muster master because the demand was not 'justified';[524] alderman Thomas Atkin questioned the very legality of the commission of

517. P. Warwick, *Memoirs of the Reign of King Charles I* (1701), pp. 48–9.
518. *Cal. Stat. Pap. Dom., 1633–4*, pp. 88–9: Dering to Council, 5 June 1633.
519. PRO, PC 2/43/71; Harleian MS 4022, f.11v.
520. Above, pp. 496–7.
521. *Cal. Stat. Pap. Dom., 1639*, p. 115.
522. *Cal. Stat. Pap. Dom., 1629–31*, p. 451.
523. *Cal. Stat. Pap. Dom., 1631–3*, p. 278.
524. Hastings MSS, Legal Box 5.

lieutenancy.[525] In Hull one Johnson defiantly proclaimed in 1634 that he would 'sell old soap in despite of any man; he will maintain and justify it; [he] cares for none who . . . question him'.[526] In East Smithfield illegal soap boilers 'squirted scalding liquor' at the constables 'and in contemptuous manner affirmed that they there boiled soap and would boil soap and threatened to kill whoever should enter'.[527] A 'tumult' greeted the demand for payments to St Paul's at Colchester, where the recalcitrants were said to invoke Diana, the protectress of slaves.[528] Forest and knighthood fines met with some legal challenges. In Northamptonshire it was said that twenty or thirty gentlemen vowed to leave their seats in Rockingham forest rather than suffer 'slavery'.[529] In Warwickshire, William Purefoy 'believed himself not legally liable to be fined' for distraint of knighthood.[530] Edward Stephens of Little Sodbury, Gloucestershire brought an action against his fine to court – an attempt, Baron Davenport described it, to 'take away a right from the King which pertains to him by the common law'.[531] Thomas Askham of Nottinghamshire refused to compound, saying that if he were summoned to Whitehall to answer 'he knew the way well enough . . .'.[532]

In addition to these challenges to particular enactments, there were more general critiques and denunciations of the government. In August 1631, Edmund Callow of Somerset in the course of a conversation with Thomas Powlett declared that the king 'went about to undo his Kingdom' and when rebuked insisted 'why so he doth'.[533] In 1637 one Chaloner said 'he hoped to be in the head of an army in this Kingdom to suppress the new levies of money and to punish the inventors'.[534] A paper found in Lincoln's Inn in 1638 alleged that two in three exclaimed against the government, and the 'enormities' it had perpetrated since the last parliament and which would only be reformed by another.[535] Sir Henry Anderson of Yorkshire determined to present his critique of the government directly to the king and, procuring access though the Earl of Holland to His Majesty, 'he made

525. Bodleian, Bankes MS 42/63.
526. *Cal. Stat. Pap. Dom., 1634–5*, p. 137.
527. *Cal. Stat. Pap. Dom., 1636–7*, p. 157.
528. *Cal. Stat. Pap. Dom., 1631–3*, p. 410.
529. P.A.G. Pettit, *The Royal Forests of Northamptonshire: A Study in their Economy, 1558–1714* (Northamptonshire Record Soc., 23, 1968), p. 93.
530. Hughes, *Politics, Society and Civil War*, pp. 102–3.
531. Tanner MS 288, f.90; H. Leonard, 'Distraint of knighthood: the last phase, 1625–41', *History*, 63 (1978), pp. 29–30.
532. J. Dias, 'Politics and administration in Nottinghamshire and Derbyshire, 1590–1640' (Oxford University, D. Phil. thesis, 1973), p. 349; see also p. 373.
533. *Cal. Stat. Pap. Dom., 1631–3*, p. 132.
534. PRO, C.115/N4/8615: J. Burgh to Scudamore, 17 May 1637.
535. *Cal. Stat. Pap. Dom., 1638–9*, p. 89.

a most parliamentary speech, disliking the ways they went in these times, dissuading the King wholly from the further taking of ship monies and moving his majesty to return to the old way of parliaments.'[536] The Earl of Warwick too told Charles I frankly that his tenants, accustomed to the milder rule of Elizabeth and James, could not be reproved for their opposition to new levies;[537] the Earl of Danby wrote a letter informing the king of the people's discontents at measures which breached the laws.[538]

Legal and constitutional opposition?

Such instances make it clear that there was neither universal contentment nor consensus during the 1630s. They offer evidence of dissent, indeed examples of men (and women) opposing government policies. But should they lead us to talk of '*an* opposition' to the personal rule? Recent controversies over the use of this term in early Stuart historiography have revolved around larger issues than mere semantic quibbles. The question still remains, given the undoubted evidence of dissent: does it add up to a group or ideology, usually called the 'Country', to 'a certain set of ideas about the English constitution'?[539] The context of some of the examples I have reviewed might lead us to doubt whether fundamentally different views of the polity informed acts of defiance. Those, for example, who refused to pay Captain Prust his fee acknowledged that he 'ought to be paid';[540] John Potkins who refused an apprentice was anxious that the business did not 'breed great wrong to this King' as well as kingdom;[541] the Lincoln's Inn papers referred to Charles himself as 'temperate'.[542] Most of all, the address of Anderson and the Earls of Danby and Warwick to the king remind us that criticism and dissent still operated through the traditional modes of petition and counsel which, all agreed, were central to the system of monarchy. Even Charles I could appreciate that 'to give the crown uncongenial counsel is far from having an allegiance to . . . "the

536. Knowler, *Strafford Letters*, II, p. 56: Garrard to Wentworth, 23 March 1637.
537. *Cal. Stat. Pap. Venet., 1636–9*, p. 124.
538. *Ibid.*, pp. 110–12.
539. See R. Zaller, 'The concept of opposition in early Stuart England', *Albion*, 12 (1980), pp. 211–34, quotation p. 212; R. Cust and A. Hughes (eds) *Conflict in Early Stuart England: Studies in Religion and Politics, 1603–1642* (1989; via index) and my remarks in *Faction and Parliament* (2nd ed, 1985), preface. The following discussion owes much to the recent debates over 'revisionism', both in print and, as importantly, in conversation.
540. *Cal. Stat. Pap. Dom., 1629–31*, p. 451.
541. *Cal. Stat. Pap. Dom., 1633–4*, pp. 88–89.
542. *Cal. Stat. Pap. Dom., 1638–9*, p. 89.

opposition"'.[543] Though at times he reacted with anger, Charles took Warwick's 'long importunity' with good grace; 'his countenance remained smiling and composed' and he even ventured an ironic jest.[544]

The recalcitrants who might seem best to qualify as a constitutional opposition are those who invoked the law in their stand against demands and measures. But legal objections should not be equated simply with constitutional opposition to the government. In his speech in defence of Stephens in the Exchequer, for instance, Sir Edward Littleton questioned whether a man not personally summoned to be knighted had a legal obligation to pay a fine for failure to attend, but he did not question the legality of the knighthood fine. Quite the contrary, he affirmed it: 'for mine own part if I should question the thing in general I should speak against mine own knowledge, for I know it and I think none who understand it doubt it. But it is an ancient and undoubted right of the crown of England for the King by a writ to command the subjects of this realm to take upon them the order of knighthood.'[545] Stephens's plea and Littleton's defence questioned, as the king's counsel put it, the 'form' not the 'substance'.[546] It would be naive to separate them totally or fail to see that demonstrating the invalidity of forms is an obvious strategy in arguing a legal case. But Littleton's speech, coming from a lawyer who had ardently supported the Petition of Right, suggests that Stephens's case cannot simply be taken as a stand for the subject against the prerogative.

This has wider import, for in the early modern period the law and courts were not regarded only, or perhaps primarily, as an arena of contest and dispute, but as a forum for reconciliation and settlement. Litigants did not just 'use' the law as a weapon; they appealed to the law as an arbitrator.[547] As John Pocock has reminded us, the law was a common language in the seventeenth century, one shared by kings, ministers and subjects. Because all adhered to the belief that law and prerogative contained and complemented each other, the concept of a legal opposition to the crown is problematic. Those who went to the courts in the 1630s – Charles I among them – hoped that the law would foster agreement not promote difference. This is not to deny that within the shared discourse of the law there were many disagreements,

543. J.C.D. Clark, *Revolution and Rebellion: State and Society in England in the Seventeenth and Eighteenth Centuries* (Cambridge, 1986), p. 134. We badly need a study of the notion of counsel in early modern Europe.
544. *Cal. Stat. Pap. Venet., 1636–9*, p. 124. Charles wryly observed that he hoped the earl (and his willingness to sacrifice his goods for His Majesty) 'would be an example to others'.
545. Tanner MS 288, ff.91–91v.
546. Cf. Leonard, 'Distraint of knighthood', p. 31 and J.P. Cooper, *Land, Men and Beliefs* (1983), pp. 29–30.
547. See Sharpe, *Politics and Ideas*, pp. 40–1.

but differing interpretations did not in the early Stuart decades undermine belief in a common agreed code, nor did they fall into neat patterns of governmental interpretations and other readings. Notes among the papers of the Temple family of Stowe, who served Charles I as JPs, deputy lieutenants and sheriffs, throw interesting light on how tensions could still be contained by an agreed body of law. The notes, of uncertain date, pose the question of the response of a subject to a prince acting against his own laws on pretence of necessity or reason of state. The answer is clear and conservative:

> As the law has set the King's person and private actions above the censure and reach of any but God Almighty so has it excellently provided that none of his public acts in his public capacity are valid but what are legal and the execution thereof [is] committed to those who are sworn neither to counsel nor act but according to law and are answerable for the same if they do otherwise.

Though resistance to authorized command was forbidden, legal challenge was part of, even a 'support of government'. Necessity was acknowledged, but 'every subject hath liberty to bring his action to try whether the necessity were real or no . . . and therefore there is no occasion for prince or people to strain or exceed the law.'[548] In 1638, after nine years of personal rule, the Earl of Huntingdon reaffirmed the symbiosis of law and government. The common law, he told the Leicestershire gentry, 'is the subject's birthright'; 'by the common law every man eats the fruit of his own olive tree and drinks the wine of his own grapes'. Yet, he continued, the law 'is a dumb magistrate, but the magistrate is lex loquens, a speaking law'.[549] In their partnership lay the 'excellency' of the English law over the civil codes of other realms.

If belief in the harmony of that partnership was all but universal, there were some who wished to make greater claims for authority. When the judges delivered their judgment on the ship money case, Thomas Harrison, a vicar from Creake, Northamptonshire, upbraided Justice Hutton, who had found for Hampden. Hutton, he argued, in fostering sedition was guilty of treason. 'We are not to question the King's actions,' he asserted, 'they are only between God and his own conscience.' In the proceedings in King's Bench against Harrison, Lord Chief Justice Finch asked him 'Do you not think that the King may govern his people by the common laws?' 'Yes,' Harrison replied, 'and by something else too.'[550] Whatever his fears for the stability of the

548. Temple of Stowe MSS, Miscellaneous Legal Box, 5.
549. Hastings MSS, HAM Box 26. Cf. Bridgewater's notes, Ellesmere MS 7920.
550. Tanner MS 299, ff.171v–174; cf. Rawlinson MS C.169, ff.340–51.

commonweal in 1628, Charles I himself never claimed that 'something else'. Indeed in the midst of the proceedings against Harrison, Attorney Bankes intervened to 'let your lordships know that yesterday I had express command from his Majesty to be present this day with the rest of the King's counsel to inform against this man and to tell your lordships that he protests a detestation of the fact and willeth that your lordships give severe censure'.[551] Harrison was fined, imprisoned and made to appear in all the courts of Westminster with a paper on his head announcing his fault. Like James I in Cowell's case, Charles publicly affirmed his commitment to the common law. It is noteworthy, however, that in a crisis others were to repeat ideas that had informed Harrison's injudicious outburst. Among Twysden's papers in Kent we find a copy of a letter from the 'principal gentlemen' of Herefordshire to their MPs in the Long Parliament concerning the issues of law and prerogative and the quarrels between king and parliament. Traditionally, they reassert the principle of unity but add that 'if any should have the power of binding it would rather be thought the King than the Commons, for we find in the statute books that those charters and other acts . . . are yet there entered as proceeding from the free grace and favour of the Prince. All the law we have is either mediately or immediately from him.'[552] Even during the 1630s, the Venetian envoy believed, many were accommodating themselves to measures they might once have questioned, on the grounds that their security necessitated them.[553] Clarendon recalled the 1630s as a decade when 'wise men thought it a time wherein those two unsociable [as by the time of writing they had come to be] adjuncts which Nerva was deified for uniting *imperium* et *libertas* were as well reconciled as is possible.'[554]

We cannot endorse Clarendon's assessment without an investigation of what has been described as the constitutional *cause célèbre* of the personal rule. And in order to understand the ship money case, we shall need to consider the doubts and reactions the levy provoked. Once we have clarified some of the misunderstanding that still surrounds them, ship money and the Hampden case offer us a case study in the nature and extent of dissent and illuminate the broader issue of opposition to the government of the 1630s.

Though ship money was paid, there is evidence of resistance from the beginning. Most merely protested inability or contested the fairness of their assessment, but there were broader implications behind

551. Tanner MS 299, f.173.
552. Twysden MS U 47/47, Z2, p. 149.
553. *Cal. Stat. Pap. Venet., 1632–6*, p. 397. He writes on 13 June at the time France has just declared war.
554. Clarendon, *History of the Rebellion*, I, p. 96.

other refusals. The inhabitants of Tiverton told the Privy Council that they could not pay ship money because they had not been reimbursed their payments for billeting soldiers.[555] The constables of Tintinhull hundred in 1635 informed the sheriff that Sir Robert Phelips had observed they were not a maritime province, an argument which he would be taking up with the Council.[556] Others raised the same objection, which became more common as it emerged that ship money would be a regular levy.[557] There are several examples of non-cooperation, the need to distrain to exact payment, violent resistance against the bailiffs and flight to escape the charge. Doubtless in many cases a simple reluctance to pay a new levy was more to the fore than considerations of constitutional proprieties. The Cambridge brewer worth £4,000 a year who purchased a place as servant to the university in the hope of securing exemption belongs more with the modern businessman and his tax shelter than with the champions of constitutional resistance to arbitrary taxation.[558] As we have seen, many who protested their inability or the inequity of their rate were not principled opponents of the levy: 'the ship money,' Bridgewater was told, 'is not so much murmured against as the manner of the taxing.'[559] However, from the first writ there was a hard core opposed to the charge on principle and convinced that it was illegal, or of doubtful legality. In January 1635 the mayor of London consulted lawyers, who informed him that no such tax could be imposed but by parliament.[560] In December Denzil Holles refused.[561] William Strode of Somerset, distrained of a cow for non-payment, recovered it by writ of replevin and sued the constable.[562] A Nottinghamshire attorney John Coude declared distraint illegal and persuaded his countrymen not to pay; Richard Bingegood, 'a turbulent person and full of law', threatened to arrest the constable who went to distrain his goods.[563] Amidst the atmosphere of uncertainty about the legality of the levy and the sheriffs' and constables' power of distraint, some, like the freeholders of Northamptonshire, sought redress of the grievance through the traditional process of a petition 'to the honourable bench', in the hope that the county magistrates might exercise influence with the Council.[564] Others thought the

555. *Cal. Stat. Pap. Dom., 1634–5*, p. 424.
556. *Cal. Stat. Pap. Dom., 1635*, p. 119.
557. *Ibid.*, p. 146; *Cal. Stat. Pap. Venet., 1636–9*, p. 99.
558. *Cal. Stat. Pap. Dom., 1635*, p. 372.
559. Above, pp. 574–83. Ellesmere MS 6976.
560. *Cal. Stat. Pap. Venet., 1632–6*, p. 314.
561. *Cal. Stat. Pap. Dom., 1635*, p. 523.
562. *Cal. Stat. Pap. Dom., 1636–7*, p. 205. He claimed, however, that his action was opposed to the rate not the principle (*ibid.*, pp. 400–1). Strode, like Holles, was one of the MPs from 1629 whom Charles had sought to punish in Star Chamber.
563. *Cal. Stat. Pap. Dom., 1637*, pp. 253, 279.
564. Northamptonshire Record Office, Montagu MS 27, f.23.

solution was only to be had through a legal judgment. In June 1636, the merchant Richard Chambers, who had earlier led the merchants' resistance to tonnage and poundage, commenced an action against Sir Edward Bromfield, mayor of London, who had gaoled him for his ship money default. But when the action came to King's Bench the judges would not hear the case, Justice Berkeley arguing 'that there was a rule of law and a rule of government, and many things which might not be done by the rule of law might be done by the rule of government'.[565] The matter, however, did not stop there. Later the same year Viscount Saye and Sele, who had been endeavouring to force a case for some time, filed a suit against a constable for distraining two oxen on his manor of Brumby, Lincolnshire, for Saye's ship money default. His case was that the constable's plea that he acted by the king's writ was invalid because the writ was not a sufficient warrant. The case was set to be heard in Hilary term 1637.[566]

As well as Saye's case, the Earl of Warwick sought audience with the king and aired his misgivings about the legality of ship money.[567] And a remonstrance against the tax, declaring it against Magna Carta, the Petition of Right and fundamental law, was prepared, 'intended to have been presented by a private hand unto his Majesty'.[568] Those opposing the levy were claiming the name of 'patriots'.[569] Rumours were spreading that the king would abandon the tax and call a parliament.[570] In the face of these challenges, Charles I saw the need to settle the doubts. On 2 February 1637, he wrote to the judges explaining the origin, purpose and general success of ship money. But acknowledging that some 'out of ignorance' challenged it and 'foreseeing . . . that from hence divers suits and actions' would follow, he posed a question:

> When the good and safety of the Kingdom in general is concerned, and the whole Kingdom in danger whether may not the King by writ under the Great Seal command all the subjects of this Kingdom, at their charge to provide and furnish such number of ships with men, victual and munition . . . for the defence and safeguard of the Kingdom from such danger and peril, and by law compel the doing thereof in case of refusal or refractoriness?
>
> And whether in such cases is not the King the sole judge . . . of the danger . . . ?[571]

565. Rushworth, *Historical Collections*, II, p. 323.
566. N.P. Bard, 'The ship money case and William Fiennes, Viscount Saye and Sele', *Bull. Inst. Hist. Res.*, 50 (1977), pp. 177–84; Rawlinson MS C.96.
567. *Cal. Stat. Pap. Venet., 1636–9*, p. 124.
568. Rushworth, *Historical Collections*, II, p. 359.
569. PRO, C.115/N8/8801: Finet to Scudamore, 11 Feb. 1637.
570. Birch, *Court and Times of Charles I*, II, p. 275: Rossingham to Puckering, 7 Feb. 1637.
571. PRO, PC 2/47/179; Gardiner, *History of England*, VIII, pp. 206–7.

To both questions on 7 February all twelve judges replied in the affirmative. A week later it was ordered that the ruling should be entered in the courts and publicized by the justices of assize on their circuits, 'that all men may take knowledge thereof and inform themselves, as this case shows, that justice and sovereignty kiss each other'.[572]

We cannot say in what way the country 'took knowledge' from the report of the judges' answer. But a fascinating account, among Sir Roger Twysden's manuscripts, offers an illuminating glimpse of one locality's response. In Kent, the justices of assize dutifully reported the king's question and the judges' answer – at which Twysden 'did in my conceit see a kind of dejection' in the faces of the auditories. After the assizes, he tells us, the gentry in their country houses further reflected on what they had heard: 'Some held my lord keeper's speech very moderate, that more could not be hoped for from a prince than in causes of weight to proceed by the advice of his judges and that the declaration the judges had made was fully to the point and by that the King had full right to impose it'. However, 'others argued far differingly that it could not but be expected that a just King would take counsel of his judges in a case of this weight, the greatest was ever heard at a common bar in England, that in a judgement that not only may but doth touch every man in so high a point, every man ought to be heard and the reasons of every one weighed, which could not be but in parliament.'[573] Such men argued that before in 1588 and in the reign of James I ship money had been a voluntary levy, not 'this way which was compulsory'. They considered and cited, according to Twysden, Fortescue, Philip de Comines, Giovanni Villani, Pasquier, Guicciardini, Baptista Adriana 'and other approved histories too long to relate', to show the limits to royal authority.[574] Clearly the report of the judges' answer provoked an important debate. But the account must be used with more caution than is displayed by its recent editor.[575] For the erudition of the discussion is more likely to belong to Twysden's learning and later compilation than to the immediate responses of the Kentish gentry. Twysden may himself on his way home from the assize have 'had by the way some speech with judge Weston', but it is not clear that he was privy to the reflections of others.[576] Evidently little was said at the assizes and the later reflections in country houses across the county may be based on little more than his own contemplations and imagination. 'No man will doubt,' he writes revealingly, 'but these thoughts and many more passed in men's minds that shall

572. Rawlinson MS C.827: Lord Keeper's charge, 14 Feb. 1637.
573. Twysden MS U47/47, Z1, p. 201; Z2, p. 108.
574. Twysden MS U47/47, Z2, p. 109.
575. Fincham, 'The judges' decision on ship money'.
576. Twysden MS U49, f.19.

understand this was the greatest cause according to the general opinion of the world was ever heard out of parliament.'[577] Whomsoever's views they articulate, however, Twysden's notes exposed problems left unanswered by the judges' response to the king, for while all concurred 'that presupposing the whole Kingdom being in danger . . . in such a case the King might [tax]', the mere 'affirmation of a necessity could not be held to be one'.[578] More personally, he observed, 'This answer ambiguous in itself referring all to such a case as was there put and such danger, and spoke only of raising ships etc. in time of danger not money'. Accordingly it 'did not give the satisfaction was expected'.[579]

Certainly it did not satisfy Viscount Saye. By the time his case came to a hearing in King's Bench the judges had received and responded to the king's question. The court therefore decided 'ne voile granter a voier al tryall sur cest issue quia matter de grand consequence inter le Roy et subiect . . .'.[580] The king's hope that the matter was now settled, however, soon proved false. There were reported to be 'many hundreds of defaulters in every county', and from Northampton Sir Robert Banaster specified that the judges' answer had 'prevailed . . . little'.[581] Saye too was determined to press a case. Probably acting as his uncle's agent, Saye's nephew, Sir Peter Temple, sheriff of Buckinghamshire, in the summer of 1637 returned a list of ship money recalcitrants with the name of John Hampden in first place. On this occasion, either confident after the judges' opinion, or because he sought to cut the ground from under refusers, the king permitted the case to come to law. On 11 August a writ of *scire facias* was issued against John Hampden for his failure to pay his ship money assessment of 20 shillings.[582]

Hampden's case is still grossly misrepresented in the textbooks of English history as a trial between the common law and the royal prerogative. All too often the simple statement that the judges decided seven to five 'for the king' has glossed over the complexities of the issues and the judges' individual decisions.[583] In the first place, Hampden's counsel, Oliver St John neither denied the king's powers to act in an emergency nor his right to define what constituted a threat; therefore he did not directly challenge the king's authority to issue writs

577. Twysden MS U47/47, Z2, p. 110.
578. *Ibid.*, p. 109.
579. *Ibid.*, Z1, p. 70.
580. Rawlinson MS C.96 (reports in King's Bench), Hilary term, 12 Charles I. 'To not permit this issue to go to trial because a matter of great consequence between the king and the subject'.
581. PRO, SP 16/363/34; *Cal. Stat. Pap. Dom., 1636–7*, p. 471.
582. Bard, 'The ship money case', pp. 181–3.
583. BL Add. MS 34324, f.284.

commanding subjects to provide a ship – though he might have done so since John Borough appears to have found no examples of a national demand after 25 Edward III, when tonnage and poundage was granted to the crown for defence of the narrow seas. Instead, perhaps in order to circumvent the judges' recent ruling, St John questioned not the power but the means and forms by and through which the king had exercised it. The king, St John argued, quite uncontentiously, could not levy any money from subjects outside parliament except in a dire and immediate emergency, as when the realm was invaded. No such danger was specified in the ship money writ which was issued six months prior to the fleet being prepared – time enough for a parliament to be summoned and grant a subsidy. Ship money therefore was not exempt from the normal compulsion the king was under to call a parliament; it was an unparliamentary tax.[584]

The king's Solicitor, Edward Littleton, was first to speak for the crown. Because St John had not questioned the king's emergency power he had no need to defend it. Acknowledging that the king had no right to request ship money except in an emergency, he concentrated on arguing that the situation had not permitted the delays which a parliament would have occasioned: the issuing of writs for an election; waiting forty days before it could meet and perhaps some weeks more before it commenced business.[585] Robert Holborne, Hampden's other lawyer, countered that the writ of 1635 on which his client had defaulted had made no mention of imminent danger. Then, sensing that the case might proceed on technicalities and desirous of engaging wider principles, he asserted: 'by the fundamental laws of England, the King cannot, out of parliament, charge the subject – no not for the common good unless in special cases', even though he might judge the danger imminent. The absolute right of the subject in his property excluded the monarch's discretion to define imminent danger.[586] Fired by Holborne's appeal to principle, Attorney Bankes eschewed Littleton's narrow stand to champion the royal prerogative. The king, he argued, 'is the first mover among these orbs of ours, and he is the circle of this circumference . . . He is the soul of this body whose proper act is to command.'[587] The law of nature, as well as the laws of England, endowed the crown with the prerogative to defend the realm and to command the aid of the subject; it trusted the king with the exercise of that power and 'where the law doth trust we ought not to distrust'. The means through which the king exercised his powers

584. Hargrave, *State Trials*, I, pp. 515–44; see the helpful extract in S.R. Gardiner (ed.) *Constitutional Documents of the Puritan Revolution* (Oxford, 1906), pp. 109–15.
585. Hargrave, *State Trials*, I, pp. 544–62 (over three days).
586. *Ibid.*, pp. 562–86 (he argued over four days); quotation p. 565.
587. *Ibid.*, pp. 586–608 (over three days); quotation p. 610.

were no less outside others' scrutiny than the powers themselves.[588] As the speeches of counsel ended, it was evident that both narrow and broad questions had been raised: the lofty principles of prerogative, law and parliament, and the technical matters of the form of exercise of agreed authority. 'The Court was thus presented with two arguments couched in moderate, and two in extreme, forms.' It was how they responded to the *four* positions that divided the bench in their judgments.[589]

While the judges deliberated and consulted the records, those present, and newsmongers who had heard reports, began to form their own judgements. There was a widespread appreciation of the king's willingness to have the case heard and a recognition that the stakes were high. As the Venetian envoy Zonca reported, 'if they are wrong, they will pay without further objection, and if they show they are right, they hope his Majesty will revoke those orders.'[590] News of the arguments on both sides was eagerly awaited. Most commentators appear to have thought, as the Earl of Leicester was informed, that St John (who we recall had steered away from the wider issues) had 'said as much . . . for the subject as could be expected'.[591] Littleton's boast that he could 'blow off most of that' came close to hubris, for few thought he spoke well.[592] Hawkins, Leicester's estate manager, predicted that if Holborne matched St John and the Attorney performed no better than the Solicitor, 'the matter will be left more doubtful than it was at first'.[593] Holborne evidently researched well but articulated his case poorly, or as Burgh put it in a newsletter to Scudamore, he 'expressed much pains and reading, only he wanted good elocution, for he hath an imperfection in his speech'.[594] Even after Bankes had concluded, it was reported that 'men's judgements do yet much differ . . . some thinking that satisfaction is given, others otherwise'.[595] Whatever some hoped, Burgh predicted a decision for the crown.

The judges (who gave their opinions over the course of the next six months) concurred on a number of basic points. Their general view was that for ordinary defence the king must expend his own revenues or go to parliament; in the case of emergency most agreed he was sole judge of the danger and bound to take measures to avert it – Croke

588. Quotation p. 591.
589. D.L. Keir, 'The case of ship money', *Law Quart. Rev.*, 52 (1936), pp. 546–74, quotation p. 560.
590. *Cal. Stat. Pap. Venet., 1636–9*, p. 332, 4 Dec. 1637.
591. *HMC De Lisle and Dudley, VI*, p. 132: Hawkins to Leicester, 9/19 Nov. 1637.
592. *Ibid.*
593. *Ibid.*, p. 136, 30 Nov. 1637.
594. PRO, C.115/N4/8619, 5 Dec. 1637. Burgh himself wanted good spelling – he called him 'Oldborne'.
595. *HMC De Lisle and Dudley, VI*, p. 139: Hawkins to Leicester, 21 Dec. 1637.

alone venturing a different view, in part to draw back from it.[596] All too accepted that the common law prohibited taxation without consent – though some were to claim it did not apply to the defence of the realm. Agreement on the basic points of law, however, still left room for judgments quite different in tone and implication. Taking their cue from Bankes, Justices Berkeley, Crawley, Vernon and Finch chose to counter Holborne's arguments by making strong claims for the prerogative. Acts of parliament, they argued, could not take away the royal power requisite for the defence of the realm. 'The law,' Sir Robert Berkeley asserted, 'knows no such King-yoking policy. The law is of itself an old and trusty servant of the King's; it is his instrument or means which he useth to govern his people by.'[597] Against, as they saw it, such extravagant claims, Hutton and especially Croke took a stand. There could be, Croke opined, no legal charge on the subject whatsoever except in parliament, which in the event of danger was to judge the threat and the remedy. Whilst in the event of a present threat the king might call upon men's persons, 'no necessity can procure this charge without a parliament'.[598] Despite this rhetoric on both sides, their judgments may well have been based on less theoretical considerations. The other judges eschewed the questions of principle. Baron Weston, who delivered his opinion first, conceded the need in normal circumstances to consult a parliament, but found for the king because the law did not bind the king to call a parliament in executing his duty to protect the realm. And Trevor, Jones, Denham, Bramston and Davenport confined themselves to two more technical questions: whether the king could use his powers to ward off apprehended, as well as immediate, danger; and whether he had executed his authority by due means.[599] This last point revolved around the distinction in the crown's case between a service and a tax.[600] Because Bramston and Davenport could not see how Hampden was to perform the *service* demanded by the writ and because the writ of *scire facias* sent him on his default was a procedure for levying *debt*, they gave judgment against the king.[601] So a bench unanimous on some points, and divided perhaps nine to three on the larger questions, gave a final verdict by the narrowest majority.

596. Keir, 'Case of ship money', pp. 562–4; on Croke, see S.R. Gardiner, *Notes on the Judgement Delivered by Sir George Croke* (Camden Miscellany, 7, 1875).
597. Hargrave, *State Trials*, I, p. 625.
598. *Ibid.*, p. 641.
599. Keir, 'Case of ship money'; on Jones, see H. Parker, *The Case of Ship Money Briefly Discoursed* (1640, STC 19215), p. 29.
600. Parker denies the distinction (*Case of Ship Money*, pp. 40–2).
601. See C. Russell, 'The ship money judgements of Bramston and Davenport', *Eng. Hist. Rev.*, 77 (1962), pp. 312–18. Bankes appears to have foreseen this problem (Hargrave, *State Trials*, I, p. 608).

Contemporary observers appear to have been more sensitive to these fine distinctions than most historians have been. The Earl of Holland made the count seven against five.[602] The Earl of Stirling, sending news of the case to the Marquis of Hamilton in Scotland, informed him that 'his Majesty hath prevailed . . . having had eight voices of twelve';[603] the Venetian ambassador reported the final formation as seven to four with one neutral;[604] Bulstrode Whitelocke's recollection was that only Croke and Hutton argued against the king.[605] Burgh told Scudamore that Justice Hutton had been 'absolutely for the subject'; Jones, however, 'inclined much that way but concluded for the King'.[606] Robert Woodforde, attorney though he was, was even more puzzled by the opinion: 'Judge Jones fluttered in his argument meteor-like flying between heaven and earth and yet in the end concluded against Mr Hampden.'[607] One astute commentator clearly discerned the difficulties and a possible outcome: 'It is doubted that there will not be unanimity in the vote of the judges concerning the King's absolute right; but perhaps they may agree in condemning Hampden for this time as having been defective in his plea but without voting concerning the merits of his cause.'[608]

Having lifted the obfuscating haze of Whig myth, we must consider the importance of Hampden's case for ship money and more broadly for the history of the personal rule. Certainly the judges' opinions were widely circulated and well known.[609] The Exchequer chamber was crowded, with evidently some relatively humble folk in the public gallery. One reporter confessed that Judge Trevor's 'voice was so low that I could not hear his argument but now and then'.[610] The less sophisticated concerned themselves little with fine points. William Sancroft informed his brother that 'when any one gave for the country tis strange how he was hummed and applauded, and how slighted if for the King'.[611] In the countryside, some who believed what they wanted to were claiming that the most honest judges had not thought ship money lawful.[612] In the homes of the nobility and gentry the arguments were pondered carefully. Twysden perceptively noted, for

602. Scottish Record Office, Hamilton MS GD 406/1, 374: Holland to Hamilton, 13 June [1638].
603. Hamilton MS 593, 12 June 1638.
604. *Cal. Stat. Pap. Venet., 1636–9*, p. 426, 25 June 1638.
605. Whitelocke, *Memorials of the English Affairs*, p. 24.
606. PRO, C.115/N4/8625, 3 May 1638.
607. New College Oxford, MS 9502 (Woodforde's diary), 28 April 1638.
608. PRO, SP 16/386/88.
609. Copies of the arguments of St John, Bankes, Littleton and Holborne are in the Hastings MSS, and there are extracts and summaries in numerous collections.
610. Rawlinson MS C.169, f.79.
611. Tanner MS 70, f.164.
612. *Cal. Stat. Pap. Dom., 1637–8*, p. 561.

example, that at the trial of Prynne, Burton and Bastwick, Laud explained that he had omitted prayers for the navy, 'the King having neither then nor now any declared enemy'. This, he claimed, 'made much discourse how the King could have any necessity that had no enemy'.[613] His notes suggest that it was the narrower issue of the case rather than the rhetoric of law and prerogative that engaged Twysden. Among the papers of the Earl of Huntingdon we find a detailed examination of the case.[614] On the dorse of the transcripts of the judges' arguments are listed (whether by Hastings himself or not we cannot be sure) 'certain necessary queries upon the perusal of these arguments'. The author raised a series of questions that the court had not considered: whether as many ships had been built as there were counties, whether each county had been informed which was its vessel, whether the monies collected equalled exactly that expended on the fleet, and whether at the end of six months the ships were returned to the counties that set them out. Such questions betray strong doubt about the key claim that the ship money writ was a demand not for a tax but for a service. Furthermore, the author reflected on whether a parliament, 'though a great body and so slow of motion', might not have been called to provide for the safety of the realm between the first hatching of the project and 10 March 1636. Was there each year a sudden new danger that could not stay the summoning of a parliament? Evidently there were some for whom Hampden's case had not been a final 'determination of the right'.[615]

The judges were less troubled. Hutton, who explained to Wentworth that he had given judgment against the king because the writ had shown no imminent danger, believed that once the verdict had been given, *all* the judges were bound by it.[616] Like a good lawyer, he was even able to appreciate that Finch had argued his case well.[617] Bulstrode Whitelocke was also impressed by the forensic standards: 'The arguments,' he writes in his *Memorials*, 'both at the bar and the bench were full of rare and excellent learning.'[618] Though none ventured the charge at the time, it was to be claimed in 1640 that the judges had been cajoled. Sir John Strangeways in the Long Parliament made the sinister observation that the judges who found for Hampden held their patents 'quam diu se bene gesserint', while those who gave

613. Twysden MS U 47/47, Z1, p.204.
614. Hastings MSS, ship money box: book of transcripts of judges' 'opinions'.
615. *Cal. Stat. Pap. Dom., 1637–8*, p. 566. See also *1640*, p. 308; BL Add. MS 11045, f.43; below, p. 729.
616. Knowler, *Strafford Letters*, II, pp. 177–8, 13 June 1638.
617. *Ibid.* Croke also praised those he disagreed with for having argued 'so learnedly and well' (Hargraves, *State Trials*, I, p. 638). Only those possessing no acquaintance with the law will be surprised at the willingness of one side to praise the other.
618. Whitelocke, *Memorials of the English Affairs*, p. 24.

judgment for the crown served 'durante bene placito'.[619] But neither the nature nor the date of the judges' appointments simply explains their verdict. And at a time when it was not necessarily to their advantage to do so, they denied that they had bowed to official pressure.[620] 'Divers of them', notably Croke, 'confessed my Lord Keeper did fairly solicit them, but neither with promises nor threats'. Each claimed to have acted on his conscience, and each, at the time of the trial, was prepared to accept that others did.[621] As Justice Jones said to Croke, 'Brother, we sit next one another, ancient judges, though different in opinion. I speak out of my conscience, as you have spoke out of yours; so though there be variety of opinions, yet conscience is the same.'[622] There is no need to doubt it, or to question that in the most difficult case they had faced, the judges delivered what they thought good law. For Sir Philip Warwick, who denounced knighthood fines as illegal, harboured no such doubts about ship money;[623] Sir Thomas Roe always thought the writ issued 'secundum legem et consuetudinem Angliae'.[624] Albeit by a narrow margin, the judges had borne him out.

Clarendon, writing after the event, could not describe the case as a victory for the crown. Rather he maintained the 'judgement proved of more advantage and credit to the gentleman condemned . . . than to the King's service'.[625] Before the trial, he believed, many had paid willingly, 'pleasing themselves with doing somewhat for the King's service as a testimony of their affection, which they were not bound to do'. After the judgment, required now to pay by law, they were disturbed – not least by the 'apothegms of state urged as elements of law' in the speeches of Finch, Berkeley and others. There may be something in Clarendon's suggestion. John Burgh had expressed his opinion that it had been better that the ship money had not come to law, for if judgment went for the king, 'then it will be as a perpetual case and law and may for ever be continued and by the same reason the King may levy upon the people what monies he pleases'.[626] Twysden overheard speech to the same effect: before it came to law, ship money was but an irritant, a 'grating on the liberty of the subject'. But 'if the tax were adjudged legal' it 'made the King more absolute than either

619. Coke MS 64: paper endorsed 6 Nov. 1640; *HMC Cowper II*, p. 263.
620. See Keir, 'Case of ship money', p. 548.
621. BL Add. MS 11045, f.134; for the judges' response to the charges, see Tanner MS 65, ff.17–19.
622. Hargrave, *State Trials*, I, p. 665.
623. Warwick, *Memoirs*, pp. 51–3.
624. *Cal. Stat. Pap. Dom., 1634–5*, p. 338. 'According to the law and custon of England'.
625. Clarendon, *History of the Rebellion*, I, pp. 86–7.
626. PRO, C.115/N4/8619: Burgh to Scudamore, 5 Dec. 1637. It is worth emphasizing that Burgh was writing to an 'Arminian' courtier.

France or the Great Duke of Tuscany'. None, he felt, 'could expect a parliament but on some necessity not now imaginable'.[627] It was perhaps similar reflection that led Saye and Warwick to contemplate emigration to America.[628] Far from fostering acquiescence, Clarendon believed that Hampden's case created a more determined opposition. Perceiving it now as a matter of principle many 'thought themselves bound in conscience to the public justice not to submit'.[629]

Traditionally it has been argued that Hampden's case heralded the collapse of ship money payment. There can be no doubt that the trial impeded the collection. In the summer of 1637, William Walter, sheriff of Oxford, told the Council that ship money was coming in slowly: 'and why it comes so is because I find many harbour an opinion that this cause is depending in trial at the suit of some of their neighbours and they will first see the issue of that'.[630] If the writ of 1636 encountered such problems half-way through the year, that of 1637, issued as the case was finally about to be heard, got off to a bad start. The sheriff of Hertfordshire confessed in February that he could not secure the necessary co-operation in making assessments, 'the general vote of the county being they would first hear what was determined at London'.[631] The opinions of the judges who found for Hampden exacerbated the delays and strengthened the resolve of those firmly opposed to payment. Harrison's anger at Judge Hutton stemmed not least from observing the impact of his judgment in Northamptonshire where, echoing the judge's words, he maintained, 'The people go on more and more in their stubborn refusing the paying of ship money . . . and Mr Justice Hutton . . . hath given the people such encouragement to their disobedience.'[632] Several sheriffs lend support to Harrison's claims. William Boteler in Bedford encountered in May 'so sudden and so general a backwardness';[633] Sir Francis Thornhagh, sheriff of Nottingham, told Nicholas: 'The argument of Judge Croke and Hutton against the King for this ship money have made men more backward than they would have been.'[634] Laud was as pessimistic; as a consequence of the judgments against the king, he wrote to Wentworth, 'the faction are grown very bold . . . the King's monies come in a great deal more slowly than they did in former years and that to a very consider-

627. Fincham, 'The judges' decision on ship money', p. 236.
628. Hirst, *Authority and Conflict*, p. 179.
629. Clarendon, *History of the Rebellion*, I, p. 87
630. *Cal. Stat. Pap. Dom., 1637*, p. 169, 6 June.
631. *Cal. Stat. Pap. Dom., 1637–8*, p. 244, 10 Feb. 1638. Evidently there was no such problem in Chester where Cholmondeley reported 'The service has gone on without murmur or reluctancy' (*ibid.*, p. 265, 18 Feb. 1638).
632. Rawlinson MS C.169 ff.340ff.
633. *Cal. Stat. Pap. Dom., 1637–8*, p. 432, 13 May 1638.
634. *Ibid.*, p. 443, 18 May 1638.

able sum'.[635] Some evidently thought Charles would drop both the case and the tax on hearing Hutton's argument.[636] It is not surprising that with such hopes in the air and final judgment still pending, many clung to their purses.

Once the final verdict was known, however, the situation was changed. Nicholas thought the business now settled: 'The judgment for the ship money,' he told Captain Pennington to whom the outcome was of some importance, 'is now given for the King and so entered, and the business goes on well and quietly.'[637] If his enthusiasm glossed over some complexities, it was not wide of the mark. For though some appealed to the arguments of Croke and Hutton, or as in Oxford awaited a further trial 'the next term, not conceiving the last to be a determination of the right', most evidently paid up.[638] The figures tell the story. By the end of April 1638 payments on the writ of 1637 were £28,355 down on those of the previous year; by June they had worsened to nearly £32,000 below.[639] By the end of August, however, there had been a substantial improvement: the £122,578 paid was now only £21,464 short of the previous year's total at the same time and by the end of the year the figure had fallen to £19,000.[640] Overall, as we have seen, the final total paid was still 90 per cent of that demanded. The payments cannot be taken as evidence of willingness. But after the delays of the preceding months, they may be interpreted as a demonstration of the respect for the law. If the law did not always resolve as men wanted, yet a legal decision was binding. Non-payment continued, and even increased, with the additional burdens.[641] Expressions of opposition to ship money, however, were confined to either drunken denunciations or to the quite legitimate observation of the limitations to the judges' endorsement of the levy. Rossingham for one had noted that the decision had not underwritten an annual demand, while a lawyer, Mr Peard, was to argue ingeniously in 1640 that a refuser could not be gaoled until a writ of *scire facias* had been issued requiring explanation for failure to pay.[642] Respect for the law meant that, for most, the matter had been resolved – at least until a parliament might legislate otherwise.

The case of ship money, then, supports the suggestion that while there was a hard core of committed recalcitrants, wider doubts about

635. *Works of Laud*, VI, part 2, p. 524, 14 May 1638.
636. *Cal. Stat. Pap. Dom., 1637–8*, pp. 520, 561, 566.
637. *Ibid.*, p. 523, 20 June 1638.
638. *Ibid.*, p. 566.
639. *Cal. Stat. Pap. Dom., 1637–8*, pp. 387, 488.
640. *Ibid.*, p. 595; *1638–9*, p. 295.
641. Above, pp. 592–3; below, pp. 809–11, 899–902.
642. BL Add. MS 11045, f.43; *Cal. Stat. Pap. Dom., 1640*, p. 308.

the legality and still wider reluctance to pay a novel charge, it is perhaps inappropriate to talk of a widespread constitutional opposition to the regime. Many appear to have recognized that while ship money strained the partnership of prerogative and law, it did not break it. Counsel on both sides appreciated that their opponents had a case and that the king had been gracious in having it heard. Twysden's, Saye's and Warwick's despair surely comes from a recognition that the government had been shown to be acting *within* the law. And as yet few, if any, were prepared to challenge the law and constitution that had found for the king. In the absence of an alternative ideology, the solution to undesirable courses was petition, persuasion or violent resistance. Since none seriously contemplated the last, whatever their disgruntlement, opposition was confined to traditional courses of appeal, protest and counsel.

XII
'FACTIOUS AND SCHISMATICAL HUMOURS': PURITANISM AND OPPOSITION

The conformity of the godly?

Laud's reference to 'the faction' that opposed ship money reminds us that he at least believed that there was one coherent group with an ideological bond that separated them (as his language suggests) from the commonweal. Quite simply, Laud connected the hard-core opposition to ship money with the puritans. It was for the archbishop a natural connection: the puritans, he believed, in refusing to be obedient to the church ultimately undermined the state. In recent historiography it has been the consensus that Laud's perception manifested his paranoia, indeed that, more dangerously, through that paranoia he helped to create an opposition from a group that had quiescently lived within the bosom of the church and state.[1] It is now orthodox to dismiss Hill's and Walzer's identification of a revolutionary puritanism and even to play down the differences between puritans and Anglicans over (as well as theology) questions of liturgy, ceremony and church government.[2] The puritans, it is said, were, give or take a few differences, loyal members of the Church of England – and often, as magistrates, pillars of local society. 'By the 1620s,' Professor Collinson writes, 'puritanism was a socially respectable movement with deep roots and its leaders were among the . . . elite.'[3]

1. P. Collinson, *The Religion of Protestants* (Oxford, 1982); N. Tyacke, *Anti-Calvinists: The Rise of English Arminianism, circa 1590–1640* (Oxford, 1987). This view is also held by Conrad Russell, see *The Times Literary Supplement* August and September 1987, pp. 899, 925, 955, 987.
2. M. Walzer, *The Revolution of the Saints* (1966), a brilliant book for all its problems. For C. Hill, see *Society and Puritanism in Pre-Revolutionary England* (1964); *Puritanism and Revolution* (1965); *The Collected Essays II: Religion and Politics in Seventeenth Century England* (Brighton, 1986).
3. Collinson, *The Religion of Protestants*, p. 149.

Such scholarship has valuably demonstrated that *simple* polarities between 'Anglican' and 'puritan' cannot be sustained, that bishops, and even archbishops like Grindal and Abbot held views close to those of the puritans on many issues and were not inclined rigidly to enforce against them the canons and injunctions of the church. But the revisionism has gone too far. For differences there were, and whatever the individual preferences of bishops, or even archbishops, at particular times, the Church of England had a clearly prescribed liturgy. Moreover, surplices, rings in marriage, the sign of the cross in baptism and kneeling at communion were enjoined by the canons and articles of the church and required by Elizabeth I and her successors. Not to adhere to them was therefore to disobey the monarch, and to be guilty of political dissent as well as nonconformity. For, as Hooker maintained, membership of the Christian commonwealth of the Church of England and citizenship in the commonwealth of the realm were one and the same. The puritans, he argued, 'by following the law of private reason where the law of public should take place . . . breed disturbance'.[4] Conscience could be no defence for contesting with authority in church or state. Hooker of course was responding to a challenge rather than simply describing a reality. It may be that the strongest rulers in early modern England were those who knew when not to press a point, when to turn a blind eye, and that James I's 'finest achievement was the establishment of a religious détente', secured by not standing on the letter of the ecclesiastical law.[5] Yet this is far from indisputably the case. Elizabeth I, who had sought above all a peaceful religious settlement, still endeavoured rigorously to enforce the injunctions and Act of Uniformity. On matters of liturgy and church government, James I too, especially when faced with puritan pressure, could take a tough line. Charles's obsession with order and uniformity was a marked difference of style, but his determination to enforce conformity was by no means unprecedented.

The question remains, was it foolhardy? Did Charles I and Laud by an over-rigid insistence on conformity create the threat they had imagined and drive puritans from the church into separatism and political radicalism? To some historians, the very fact of the civil war provides a quick and easy answer. But it is far from clear that the conflict and alignments in 1642 owed much to the religious disagreements of the 1630s and far from obvious that Charles I and Laud were

4. Quoted in D. Little, *Religion, Order and Law* (Oxford, 1971), p. 163. Walzer is interesting on the tendency of the puritans to use less organic imagery (*Revolution of the Saints*, ch. 5).

5. J.P. Kenyon's phrase (*The Stuart Constitution*, 2nd edn, Cambridge, 1986, p. 115) aptly sums up the thesis of Collinson, *The Religion of Protestants*, Tyacke, *Anti-Calvinists*, and K. Fincham and P. Lake, 'The ecclesiastical policy of King James I', *Journ. Brit. Stud.*, 24 (1985), pp. 169–207.

wrong to regard the puritans as a canker rotting the church from within which had to be cured.

Let it first be said that by no means all of godly persuasion were bent on undermining the established church. Lucy Downing, we recall, explained to John Winthrop that, for all that some things were wanting, 'Christ and the word of reconciliation' were as much maintained 'as hath been known in England'.[6] In *The Saints Sure and Perpetual Guide* (1634) Robert Bolton, a puritan preacher of Northamptonshire, could still express his pride that 'our church in that most exquisite and worthy confession of faith contained in the articles of Religion doth hold and profess all substantial points of divinity'.[7] Emmanuel Downing expressed evident dismay in November 1637 at the assaults on the 'the holy book of Common prayer'.[8] In his manual for spiritual self-examination, *The Heavenly Academie*, Francis Rous counselled his brethren not to 'make little errors great' nor 'condemn the wheat' in the church 'for the tares'.[9] Many of the gentry of godly inclination were anxious to maintain the church and, as Professor Fletcher reminds us, 'it was quite possible for a puritan minister to conform to the prescribed ceremonies, without compromising his fundamental religious stance'.[10] That admitted, nonconformity was frequently neither quiescent nor confined to the individual conscience. Not only did puritan ministers, like Harley's at Brampton Bryan, omit parts of the Prayer Book and ceremonies, the godly obstructed those who chose to conform.[11] Matthew Nicholas was accused of being tainted by the beast for preaching in his surplice;[12] Humphrey Ramsden of Northamptonshire was maligned and accused for a drunkard for his love of 'those ancient ceremonies used in the primitive church'.[13] Cosin, attacked by Smart in 1628, was maligned again in 1634 for his liturgical preferences by James Hambleton.[14] Protest against ceremonies was not confined to verbal abuse. In Norwich, Daniel Weymond and others, dismayed at the appearance of rails in their church, proceeded to disrupt the entire service: they opened the door and walking in front, behind and around the minister, demeaned themselves 'in most undecent, profane and

6. *The Winthrop Papers III, 1623–1649* (Massachusetts Historical Soc., Boston, 1943), p. 278.
7. R. Bolton, *The Saints Sure and Perpetual Guide* (1634, STC 3248), for example, p. 129.
8. *The Winthrop Papers* (Massachusetts Hist. Soc., 4th series, 6, 1863), p. 48. Since he referred to the Scots' 'outrages', there is no reason to believe that this letter is ironic.
9. F. Rous, *The Heavenly Academie* (1638, STC 24341), p. 165.
10. A.J. Fletcher, *A County Community in Peace and War: Sussex 1600–1660* (1975), p. 73.
11. J.T. Cliffe, *The Puritan Gentry: The Great Puritan Families of Early Stuart England* (1984), p. 28.
12. *Calendar of State Papers Domestic* [*Cal. Stat. Pap. Dom.*], *1636–7*, p. 555.
13. *Cal. Stat. Pap. Dom., 1638–9*, p. 587.
14. W.H.D. Longstaff (ed.) *The Acts of the High Commission Court within the Diocese of Durham* (Surtees Soc., 34, 1858), p. 77.

unseemly manner' – to the dismay of the congregation.[15] A group at Colchester opposed to services conducted according to the Book of Common Prayer disrupted them by firing shots in church.[16]

Though the respectable godly were themselves hostile to conventicles, the gap between such nonconformity and separatism was not always as great as some recent historiography has suggested. Some who denounced ceremonies did so specifically to draw off their auditories to separate worship. One Pearne of Wilby in the diocese of Peterborough denounced the popery rife in the land, as he suspended parts of the service.[17] Elizabeth and James Andrewes of Cambridge held private services (for fifteen or more) in their homes, claiming they knew no law that questioned it.[18] In Welling a petition was circulated to dissuade communicants from going to the rails.[19] A group at Colchester who attended only the sermon tried to persuade others to boycott the service;[20] in Northamptonshire one Mr Marston dispensed forbidden catechisms, while one Cranford, having acquired a certificate of his conformity 'which he hath seldom or never practised since', drew to his afternoon service the 'factious' of other parishes.[21] In *A Letter . . . to a Lady* (1634), Sir Humphrey Lynde referred to 'the wine office where I and many of our learned and zealous brethren meet often about a further reformation of religion in desiring that not so much as a rag of popery may remain in the House of the Lord; neither bells nor organs, rochets or mitres, square caps or surplices, cross or image'.[22]

We do not know how many such meetings took place, but the instances of separatism reported were enough to vindicate Laud from completely unfounded paranoia. As early as 1631, Bishop Hall reported 'eleven several congregations of separatists' in London 'with their idly pretended pastors who meet together in brewhouses every Sunday'.[23] From Kent, Edward Dering was alarmed enough to write to Laud about the separatist sect led by Fenner which denied any covenant between God and man, denied that England had either a true church or true ministry and rejected parts of the apostles' creed as anathema to the faith.[24] In 1637 Giles Creech of St Giles in the Fields informed the government that there were in London sects of familists

15. Bodleian, Tanner MS 68, f.104.
16. Tanner MS 70, ff.107–9.
17. *Cal. Stat. Pap. Dom., 1633–4*, pp. 297–8.
18. Tanner MS 65, ff.67–73.
19. Huntington Library, Temple of Stowe MS STT 1891: Sibthorpe to Lambe, 7 June 1639.
20. Tanner MS 65, ff.69–73.
21. Temple of Stowe MS 11, STT 1880.
22. H. Lynde, *A Letter . . . to a Lady* (1634, STC 17093), sig. A3.
23. *Cal. Stat. Pap. Dom., 1631–3*, p. 74: Hall to Laud, 11 June 1631.
24. Kent Archives Office, Dering MS U 350/C2/54: draft letter to Laud, 20 Jan. 1636.

of the mount who denied the Resurrection and maintained that all property should be held in common; his list of members included a bookseller and official at the customs house.[25] In addition, he reported a group of 'essensialists' who held there was no sin at all and cited one Lockey, a tailor of Lime Street, who, proclaiming there was no evil, attracted (we will not be surprised to learn) a considerable following: 'he hath many meetings up and down'.[26] The Earl of Bridgewater, a patron of the godly, informed in 1639 against a conventicle in Blodwell, Shropshire.[27] Such instances and informations clearly aroused the fear – in those of quite different sympathies to Laud – of a sectarian, antinomian challenge to all social and moral order: the vision of Munster. What distinguished Laud himself was his inclination to suspect it was more widespread than it was and to elide a distinction between the godly and the extreme separatists. But, as Professor Hirst shrewdly comments, 'Laud's suspicions were not without foundation.'[28] For though few elected to 'separate absolutely' from the established church, they did constitute informal groups which plotted to undermine it from within.[29] Robert Woodforde, the Northampton attorney, could not resolve to 'separate because of some imperfections',[30] but he met with separatists and notes that they prayed for the overthrow of the 'Antichristian power that is amongst us'.[31]

If nonconformity was never far from, indeed in a way constituted a form of, separatism, it also slid easily into an opposition to the government of the church.[32] From rejection of the canons of the church it was not a big step to a questioning of the authority of those who enforced them. The puritans, Anthony Fletcher puts it, 'were content to tolerate the institution of episcopacy so long as it did not press too hard upon their consciences', as long as, that is, the ordinances of the church were not, as under Abbot they often were not, enforced.[33] Once they were upheld, even so-called 'moderate' puritans were led to challenge the church hierarchy. Samuel Ward of Ipswich not only denounced the Book of Common Prayer (and all set prayers) as a confinement of the spirit, he advocated that all churchmen be elected; after suspension and

25. Tanner MS 70, f.181.
26. *Ibid.*, f.182.
27. *Cal. Stat. Pap. Dom., 1639*, p. 417: Bridgewater to Laud, 24 July. He jailed the leader.
28. D. Hirst, *Authority and Conflict: 1603–1658* (1986), p. 72. I have greatly benefited from a fruitful discussion of this with John Morrill, who disagrees.
29. C. Holmes, *Seventeenth Century Lincolnshire* (Lincoln, 1980), p. 41; *The Collected Essays of Christopher Hill* II, pp. 80–1.
30. New College Oxford MS 9502 (Robert Woodforde's diary), 21 June 1639. The date of his doubt ('I am not yet wholly convinced') is worthy of note.
31. *Ibid.*
32. Cf. Holmes, *Seventeenth Century Lincolnshire*, pp. 41–3; A. Hughes, *Politics, Society and Civil War in Warwickshire, 1620–1660* (Cambridge, 1987), p. 79.
33. Fletcher, *County Community*, p. 74.

imprisonment in 1635 he went to Holland where he *may* have been re-ordained by a minister.[34] Robert Woodforde, whilst not committed to separating, employed apocalyptic language in his comments on the hierarchy, praying for the rescue of ministers questioned in High Commission to be freed from 'the paw of the lion', and recording in his diary, 'I prayed against wicked bishops their hierarchy'.[35] Lewes Hughes, the author of *Certaine Greevances* presented to parliament in 1640, proceeded from criticism of popish ceremonies to an attack on bishops to counselling the godly to renounce authority, denying there could ever be a place in the church for the archbishop.[36] A preference for a non-episcopalian church was probably more widespread than the evidence of published invectives against the bishops; doubtless many had hoped from the time of the Elizabethan settlement that the church would develop a more continental direction in church government as well as worship. As Oliver St John had, he said, always regarded the 1559 Prayer Book as a temporary measure,[37] so Leighton tried to claim that Elizabeth I had always preferred and intended the abolition of an episcopal church, which was an obstacle to preaching.[38] The support for the Scots' resistance to the Prayer Book in puritan circles, even among the non-separating Harleys, indicates a widespread willingness, and some enthusiasm, for a Presbyterian church in England.[39]

Resistance to the authority, let alone the institution, of episcopacy inevitably made the puritans political opponents in the eyes of a head of the church who, possibly more than his father, associated the preservation of the crown with the maintenance of ecclesiastical hierarchy. The king and Laud, however, were not alone. In *The Schismatical Puritan* (1630) Giles Widdowes, former tutor to Prynne, cast his title character as one whose tenets led to the 'confusion of church and commonwealth'.[40] Calibut Downing (interestingly a future independent) argued in 1632 that government by lay elders would lead to the

34. *Cal. Stat. Pap. Dom., 1635–6*, p. liv; *Dictionary of National Biography* [*DNB*].
35. Woodforde's diary 2 Sept., 24 Oct. 1637.
36. L. Hughes, *Certaine Greevances Well Worthy the Consideration of Parliament* (1640, STC 13916).
37. I owe this information to Conrad Russell's 'Religion and the origins of the civil war', paper delivered at the Institute of Historical Research, Nov. 1987.
38. A. Leighton, *An Appeal to the Parliament; or Sion's Plea against the Prelacie* (1628, STC 15429), pp. 30, 72. To Leighton, Bancroft was in league with the pope (p. 76) and the service book itself was popish (p. 90).
39. Below, pp. 819–24; *Cal. Stat. Pap. Dom., 1639–40*, p. 401; R. Howell, *Newcastle-upon-Tyne and the Puritan Revolution* (Oxford, 1967), pp. 94–119; J. Eales [Levy], *Puritans and Roundheads: The Harleys of Brampton Bryan and the Outbreak of the English Civil War* (Cambridge, 1990), pp. 110–11.
40. STC 25594, sig. B2. Widdowes defined a puritan as one opposed to the Thirty-Nine Articles, Prayer Book and canons.

destruction of monarchy.[41] In Kilsby Northamptonshire, the vicar, Nicholas Darton, told Windebank, the refractory spoke 'so vile against God, the King and the church and sow sedition . . .'.[42] Dr Pocklington accused them of treason.[43] Again, partisan though they were, those who feared that the puritans threatened the state cannot be dismissed as paranoid. At the most immediate level, the connection between puritanism and the staunchest opposition to ship money was noted by many sheriffs. Mildmay, sheriff of Essex, described the refractory of the county as 'a generation of discipliners, very zealous in all causes that concern the hindrance of his Majesty's service';[44] and a paper of 1638 predicted the most trouble from Essex, Northamptonshire, Gloucestershire and Buckinghamshire, well-known puritan strongholds.[45] What Avihu Zakai has labelled the provocativeness of the godly was not confined to the realm of religion.[46]

More fundamental, however, was the disjuncture between the logic of the puritan faith and the community of the visible church and commonweal on which the theory of order was founded. Ultimately the doctrine of double predestination respected neither prelate nor prince.[47] One Farnam, petitioning for his release from confinement, offered a prayer for Laud, but only on the condition that he was one of God's chosen, 'for it is a sin to pray that the Lord would change his decree'.[48] Pursuing the same logic Henry Greenwood did not stop short of publishing the view that hell was prepared for the ungodly, even the ungodly monarch.[49] If the prince were an idolator or heretic, the author of *Christ's Confession* argued, officers could hold no place

41. C. Downing, *A Discourse of the State Ecclesiastical of this Kingdome* (1632, STC 7156), pp. 15–16.
42. *Cal. Stat. Pap. Dom., 1639–40*, pp. 211–12; cf. *1637*, pp. 257–8. Darton blamed both the 'factious and seditious' and 'the rest' who 'will not . . . be witnesses against them'.
43. *Cal. Stat. Pap. Dom., 1638–9*, p. 534: Pocklington to Lambe, 4 March 1639.
44. *Cal. Stat. Pap. Dom., 1636–7*, p. 229: Mildmay to Dudley Carleton, 13 Dec. 1636.
45. PRO, SP 16/386/88.
46. Hill, *Collected Essays, II*, p. 81. See A. Zakai, '"The gospel of reformation": the origins of the great puritan migration', *Journ. Ecclesiastical. Hist.* 37 (1986), pp. 584–602. I am grateful to Professor Zakai for discussions of puritanism at the Huntington Library in 1985.
47. See Walzer, *Revolution of the Saints*, ch. 8. Bancroft associated the puritans with resistance theories (J. Sommerville, *Politics and Ideology in England, 1603–1640*, 1986, p. 80). Andrewes thought that nonconformity led to schism and predestination to subversion (I owe this point to Peter Lake, 'Lancelot Andrewes, John Buckeridge and avant-garde conformity in Jacobean England', paper read at the Institute of Historical Research). See also Somerset Record Office, Phelips MS 211, f.66v: 'Calvinism doth give licence and occasion for men daily to invent new opinions which . . . beget tumults'; and *Calendar of State Papers Venetian* [*Cal. Stat. Pap. Venet.*], *1628–9*, p. 432.
48. *Cal. Stat. Pap. Dom., 1636–7*, p. 488.
49. H. Greenwood, *Greenwood's Works in Seven Several Translations* (1628 edn, STC 12331), 4: *Tormenting Tophet*, p. 27.

with conscience.[50] Kings, *The Fall of Babylon* declaimed, were lords over men only in so far as they were subjects in the secular polity, not as disciples of Christ's kingdom.[51] Though most did not pursue its logic to revolutionary conclusions, such thinking could, as it had in sixteenth-century France and the Low Countries, forge a revolutionary ideology. Johnston of Wariston's diary offers an excellent illustration of how quickly Calvinism could develop into a revolutionary creed; that he found passages of great enlightenment in Burton and others reminds us how English polemicists could contribute to that development.[52] As Christopher Dow asked, what readier way was there to incite sedition than to suggest that the king, as Burton accused, neglected religion?[53] After 1649, William Purefoy, MP for Warwick, was to claim that he had designed the overthrow of the monarchy ever since his sojourn in Geneva thirty years before.[54] During the 1620s the radical preacher Thomas Scott claimed that 'all judicious puritans hold that it is against conscience to yield obedience to tyrannical and lawless commands as of duty'; Burroughs argued that the people chose their kings and asked 'if the supreme magistrate refuse or neglect that which he ought to do . . . may not the people give power to some other?'[55] Many of the godly gentry who served assiduously as JPs, sheriffs and deputies during the 1630s would have been appalled by these claims. But, alone of the discontents, the puritans had a tradition and ideology of opposition, which provided a broader context for particular grievances and which could, under the pressure of events, formulate a theory of resistance.

The strength of puritanism

In any consideration of puritanism as an opposition movement, the central problem is that of the strength of the puritans – among the propertied classes in particular and across the nation as a whole. Undoubtedly the sympathies of some gentry with the puritan antagonism

50. P.J., *Christ's Confession* (1629, STC 19069), pp. 29, 70.
51. *The Fall of Babylon in Usurping Ecclesiastical Power* (1634, STC 1101), sigs. A 1–2.
52. G.M. Paul (ed.) *The Diary of Archibald Johnston of Wariston, 1632–9* (Scottish Historical Soc., 1st series, 61, 1911); see below, pp. 818–19.
53. C. Dow, *Innovations Unjustly Charged upon the present Church and State* (1637, STC 7090), p. 27; cf. H. Vertue, *A Plea for Peace* (1637, STC 24691).
54. W.M. Abbot, 'The issue of episcopacy in the Long Parliament, 1640–48: the reasons for abolition' (Oxford University, D. Phil. thesis, 1981), p. 66. I am grateful to Bill Abbot for several helpful discussions.
55. Quoted by R. Cust, *The Forced Loan and English Politics, 1626–28* (Oxford, 1987), p. 178, my modernization; Jeremiah Burroughs, *ibid.*, p. 184. James I himself would have accepted passive disobedience of tyrants and lawless commands, but not Scott's right to define them in his terms.

to ceremonies and their desire for further reformation of the church are important in explaining the alienation of men who were leaders of local society and government from the Caroline regime. However, the numbers so disaffected, still more the extent of their alienation, are subjects that await a great deal more research. We must be wary of overestimating their number and especially of assuming puritan family pedigrees. Though the descendant of Henry Hastings, third Earl of Huntingdon, the great patron of Elizabethan puritanism, Henry the fifth earl evidently inherited no antipathy to the ceremonies and liturgy of the Anglican church. The 'beautifying and decoring of the church', he believed, 'all that are of impartial judgement must needs consent unto for the fittingness and decency thereof'.[56] The church, he told the Leicestershire sessions, 'is the place where God's ambassador doth deliver his word unto us and the sacraments, God's greatest seals'.[57] On his travels around England, he admired the handsome cross at Hinchley, Chackley church with its 'much coloured glass' and Rixon church with its organ 'almost as big as the organ in St Paul's'.[58] In his considerable library, Huntingdon had amidst his collection of sermons and theological works, the complete Lancelot Andrewes, Bishop Hall's *Christian Moderation* and Laud's *Conference with Fisher*.[59] Among his mother's collections, inventoried in 1633, we find along with notes on the certain assurance of election, 'notes taken out of Dr Andrewes book of sermons'.[60] It is difficult to recruit Hastings to the ranks of puritan critics for all his family associations. In 1639 he was indignant at those who showed reluctance to go to York to join the king against the Scots.[61]

The Montagus of Northamptonshire offer another interesting case study. Henry, Earl of Manchester, despite the family's godly sympathies, was resolute in Star Chamber in enforcing the law against puritans as well as papists. To his son, who converted to Rome, he explained his faith in terms that fit easily with Clarendon's portrayal of him as a loyal member of the church: 'we build upon Christ not Luther. We renounce all men alike as inventors of our religion and hold only the Apostolical doctrine of the ancient primitive and Catholic church . . .'.[62] His brother, Edward, was evidently no supporter of

56. Huntington Library, Hastings MS 5537: Huntingdon to Sir J. Lambe, 8 Sept. 1634.
57. Hastings MSS, HAM Box 26, see above, pp. 434–5.
58. Hastings MSS, Personal HAP Box 18: 'Observations of things I observed in my journey 22 August 1633 to Engleside'.
59. Hastings MSS, Financial Box 12.
60. Huntington Library, Ellesmere MS 6871.
61. Hastings MS 5549.
62. *HMC De Lisle and Dudley, VI*, p. 44, 20 May 1636; E. Hyde, Earl of Clarendon, *The History of the Rebellion and Civil Wars in England*, ed. W.D. Macray (6 vols, Oxford, 1888), I, p. 69.

Laud's; he may have been uneasy about the suppression of the Kettering lecture.[63] But at least until 1639 he did not articulate that unease or even confide it to his correspondence.[64] During the personal rule, he laboured diligently as a commissioner for knighthood fines and as a local governor. His desire for peace and order even led him to co-operate with his diocesan, Bishop Dee of Peterborough. Godly though he was, Montagu manifested no opposition to the church or state before the outbreak of the Scots war, which he regarded as a punishment on the land for idolatry.[65] Whatever his unease or desire for reforms before then, 'he wanted order in the church and in his household, just as he did in the country and the Kingdom'.[66] Robert Sidney, the Earl of Leicester, descendant of the Elizabethan icon of the puritan cause and ministry, rejected what he called the charge of puritanism. 'I renounce,' he told his monarch, in what Clarendon believed was not just special pleading, 'all but the Christian faith established in the church of England . . . I never had a thought of disobedience or unconformity to any ordnance thereof'.[67] Such statements by descendants of the leaders of Elizabethan puritanism caution us against making assumptions about the inheritance of values.

To urge such caution, however, is not to negate the importance of aristocratic and gentry patronage of puritanism, nor to deny that it could promote opposition to the regime. Sir Robert Harley, for example, offered protection to notoriously nonconformist ministers in Herefordshire and made his family seat, Brampton Bryan 'a centre of zealous puritan worship'.[68] During the 1630s, as well as his contact with Prynne and Burton, Sir Robert visited John Workman, the puritan minister of Gloucester, in the Gatehouse prison and supported the separatist John Stoughton of Aldermanbury at his appearance before High Commission. He was charged with sanctioning the nonconformity of his own incumbent, Stanley Gower, and with maintaining a suspended minister as a schoolmaster.[69] Such associations led, in 1635, to his removal from his office as Master of the Mint. His worries about the dangers of idolatry can only have been raised by the Scots war, in which, he believed, Charles recruited Catholic troops for his army.[70] In the Short Parliament, as well as his staunch advocacy of religious reform and the denunciation of Laudian 'crimes', Harley expressed his

63. E. Cope, *The Life of a Public Man: Edward, First Baron Montagu of Boughton, 1562–1644* (American Philosophical Soc., Philadelphia, 142, 1981), pp. 145, 152.
64. *Ibid.*, pp. 133, 145, 150, 163.
65. *Ibid.*, pp. 134, 154, 163; cf. pp. 206–7.
66. *Ibid.*, p. 145.
67. *HMC De Lisle and Dudley, VI*, p. 355. Leicester was, at the time of his letter in 1640, hoping for the secretary's place, or better, but his letter is still striking. See *DNB*.
68. Eales, *Puritans and Roundheads*, p. 55.
69. *Ibid.*, pp. 62–9; *Cal. Stat. Pap. Dom., 1637–8*, p. 249.
70. Eales, *Puritans and Roundheads*, p. 91.

antagonism to both ship money and the Scots war.[71] A sense that they might be 'experiencing the final phases of the struggle between Christ and anti-Christ' began to permeate the Harleys' perception of politics as of religion.[72]

The most famous puritan magnates of the Caroline era were the Rich family, notably the Earls of Warwick and Holland. Though in his lifestyle far from puritanical in the modern sense of the term, and less than 'godly' in seventeenth-century usage ('a man,' Clarendon claimed, 'of less virtue could not be found out') Robert Rich, Earl of Warwick was the principal patron of the puritans.[73] (See Figure 39.) The many benefices at his disposal he granted to puritan ministers, some zealous in their faith and sectarian inclinations.[74] It was Warwick who gave a place, after he was deprived by Wren, to Jeremiah Burroughs who was later prosecuted for seditious speeches against the king 'as they say about the Scots power to depose'.[75] It was to a large extent Warwick's leadership and patronage that characterized Essex as a puritan county.[76] His half-brother Sir Nathaniel Rich played an important part in sustaining the godly. Nathaniel received tracts from James Forbes at Delft for distribution in England and maintained a correspondence with Prynne, as was revealed by a Council examination in April 1637.[77] Warwick's relatives the Barringtons patronized Nathaniel Ward and Ezekiel Rogers, both of whom were to emigrate to America before the decade was out.[78] Warwick was by no means an outcast from the court and government: he attended Charles I to Dover to receive Henrietta Maria;[79] he officiated at the king's coronation;[80] he escorted ambassadors and danced in court masques;[81] in 1638 he was still exchanging

71. *Ibid.*, pp. 67, 95–7.
72. *Ibid.*, p. 89. Cf. T.T. Lewis (ed.) *Letters of the Lady Brilliana Harley* (Camden Soc., old series, 58, 1854), p. 41.
73. Clarendon, *History of the Rebellion*, II, p. 544.
74. See B. Donagan. 'The clerical patronage of Robert Rich, 3rd Earl of Warwick, 1619–1642', *Proceedings of the American Philosophical Soc.*, 120 (1976), pp. 388–420. Cf. W. Gouge, *The Saints Sacrifice* (1632, STC 12125), epistle dedicatory; and C. Holmes, *The Eastern Association* (Cambridge, 1975), p. 19. See also K. Shipps, 'The political puritan', *Church History*, 45 (1976), pp. 196–205 and *idem*, 'Lay patronage of East Anglian puritan clerics in pre-revolutionary England' (Yale University PhD thesis, 1971), ch. 4.
75. Tanner MS 314, f.180; cf. Holland's letter to Wren about him, Tanner MS 68, f.248.
76. See W. Hunt, *The Puritan Moment: The Coming of Revolution in an English County* (Cambridge, Mass., 1983), *passim*. I am grateful to the late Brian Lyndon for information about the strongholds of Essex puritanism.
77. *Cal. Stat. Pap. Dom., 1633–4*, p. 413; Bodleian, Bankes MS 42/62.
78. A. Searle (ed.) *Barrington Family Letters, 1628–1632* (Camden Soc., 4th series, 28, 1983), pp. 13–14, 129–31.
79. British Library [BL] Add. MS 12496, f.37.
80. C. Wordsworth (ed.) *The Manner of the Coronation of King Charles I of England* (Bradshaw Soc., 2, 1892), p. 12.
81. See S. Orgel and R. Strong (eds) *Inigo Jones: The Theatre of the Early Stuart Court* (2 vols, Berkeley and London, 1973) and PRO, C.115/M35/8390, where Warwick is described as the 'chief' masquer at Lord Goring's entertainment.

New Year's gifts with the king.[82] In Essex, he was a diligent Lord-Lieutenant, and there is evidence of his prompt activity in raising troops for the Scots war.[83] His concern for social order even led him in 1640 to punish those soldiers and rioters who pulled down altar rails in the churches of his county.[84] But Warwick's opposition to the Laudian church was clearly linked to his rejection of secular measures like ship money. His appeal to Charles in 1637 to abolish ship money, call a parliament and to pursue a French alliance against the Habsburgs, the Venetian envoy saw as connected to the issue of religion.[85] Warwick, it has been said, was no born frondeur.[86] He hoped perhaps that the king might be persuaded to reforms by the counsel of parliament. But along with other godly discontents with whom he was closely tied in colonial ventures to Providence and New England – Viscount Saye and Sele and Lord Brooke – Rich stood against many of the policies of the personal rule, and in the elections of 1640 was to be instrumental in securing the return of MPs committed to dismantling them.[87]

Important to the Riches' and perhaps more generally the puritans' relations with the government during the decade of personal rule was the presence of one of their family in the king's counsels. Even less than his elder brother Warwick did Henry Rich, Earl of Holland live according to the moral codes of the godly. His closeness (sometimes rumoured to be intimacy) with the queen made him suspect in some godly circles; his energetic commitment, as chief justice in eyre, to the enforcement of forest laws was seen as an infringement of the liberties of the subject. Holland, however, was the representative of the godly party at court. He lobbied for intervention in Europe against the Habsburg Antichrist. And he does appear to have intervened to protect puritan ministers in trouble: it was, for example, Holland who wrote to Bishop Wren requesting that Burroughs be permitted to resign his benefice and leave for Essex unmolested.[88] Moreover, Holland was the court intermediary for the board of the Providence Island Company which has (with some exaggeration) been characterized as the front for

82. BL, Harley Roll, T2.
83. Essex Record Office, Morant MS D/Y/2/9, ff.335–43 (I owe this reference to the late Brian Lyndon); Bodleian, Firth MS C.4, pp. 597–9.
84. *Cal. Stat. Pap. Dom., 1640*, p. 517.
85. See, for example, his dispatch of 16 Jan. 1637 (*Cal. Stat. Pap. Venet., 1636–9*, pp. 124–5).
86. Hunt, *Puritan Moment*, p. 166.
87. Christopher Thompson's researches, however, have shown that Warwick's colonial ventures were directed more to the Caribbean than New England, the focus of those with more ideological preoccupations. C. Thompson, 'Providence and New England', a paper read at Oxford in January 1974. On Warwick's electoral patronage, see Holmes, *Eastern Association*, pp. 21ff.
88. Tanner MS 68, f.248. Burroughs was later charged with making seditious speeches about the Scots war.

39 *Robert Rich, 2nd Earl of Warwick* by Van Dyck, 1637–8. Though the leading patron of puritanism, and member of the Providence Island Company, Warwick performed in masques and appears here very much the courtier.

a puritan opposition to the crown.[89] Holland's role, for all the superficiality of his personality, was an important one. In 1629, Lionel Sharpe, who had some good advice to give on several matters, reminded Secretary Dorchester (after the quarrels over religion in parliament) how Queen Elizabeth had contained the puritans 'by allowing some great lord to take, as it were, the protection of the party, as Sir Francis Walsingham and Sir Walter Mildmay in the Lower House . . . and two lords, the Earls of Leicester and Essex'.[90] Holland was the nearest the personal rule came to having such a figure, a Leicester, or Jacobean Earl of Southampton.[91] It was especially significant then that at a time when a mediating figure was most needed, Holland fell from favour, and lost (as we shall see) his command against the Scots.[92] His distance in 1640 from the queen and the king meant that the network of the godly he led, no longer earthed to the royal counsels, was all the more drawn to a programme of opposition from outside. As Viscount Conway put it to Laud in a letter analysing the government's difficulties and the opposition it faced, 'The Earl of Warwick is the temporal head of the puritans and the Earl of Holland is their spiritual head, or rather the one is their visible and the other their invisible head . . . not because he means to do good or hurt but because he thinks it is a gallantry to be the principal pillar on which a whole cabal must rely.'[93]

Conway's language should not pass without notice. A cabal is 'a secret or private intrigue of a sinister character formed by a small body of persons'. Certainly the patricians of Caroline puritanism were a tight network: the Riches were related to the Barringtons and the Fiennes, in the East Anglian cousinage of puritanism; Warwick, the Earl of Southampton and Pym dwelt in the same parish in London;[94] Viscount Saye was related to Sir Robert Harley, and Lord Brooke had family links with Brilliana Harley;[95] Sir Henry Wallop of Hampshire was related to Lady Judith Barrington.[96] Terms like the 'caucus', the 'faction' were often used against them by the enemies of the puritans in the country as well as at court. But while historians have begun to uncover evidence of close co-operation among puritan peers in 1640, the full extent and cohesiveness of the puritans' organization during the

89. A.P. Newton, *The Colonising Activities of the English Puritans* (New Haven, 1914); cf. below, pp. 751ff.
90. *Cal. Stat. Pap. Dom., 1628–9*, p. 542.
91. On the godly quest for a successor to Leicester, see S.L. Adams, 'The Protestant cause: religious alliance with the West European Calvinist communities as a political issue in England, 1585–1630' (Oxford University, D. Phil. thesis, 1973). I am grateful to Simon Adams for many helpful discussions.
92. Below, pp. 838–9.
93. *Cal. Stat. Pap. Dom., 1640*, p. 278, 8 June 1640.
94. *Cal. Stat. Pap. Dom., 1637–8*, p. 162.
95. Eales, *Puritans and Roundheads*, p. 61.
96. Searle, *Barrington Letters*, p. 208. Wallop was her brother-in-law.

1630s still awaits further research. The Drydens at Canons Ashby and the Knightleys of Fawsley protected godly ministers but we know little of their politics.[97] From Chichester, Laud was informed in 1634 that 'some puritan justices of the peace have awed some of the clergy into like opinions with themselves'.[98] As the decade neared its close, the JP Edward Burton alerted the archbishop to the activities of the puritans' 'swaying of temporal affairs in open sessions their own way with difference and distinction between other men and those of their own character'.[99] In 1640 their leaders Sir Thomas Pelham and Sir John Stapley held the county in their grip.[100] Though recent studies reveal that wealthy puritan gentry were concentrated in significant numbers only in four counties (Devon, Essex, Northamptonshire and Suffolk) and were a strong presence in Lincolnshire and Warwickshire, the influence that elsewhere could be wielded by a few committedly godly magistrates remains as yet in the realm of conjecture.[101]

What is clear is that Charles and Laud added, in some cases unnecessarily, to the number of those completely out of sympathy with the regime. Here we recall Henry Sherfield. For all his spiritual self-examination and strong godly commitment, Sherfield, as well as being an active magistrate, had conformed to the liturgy – he knelt at communion – and had punished separatists. With more cause than many puritans, he regarded himself as a good member of the church. Some of the judges at his trial appear to have accepted his denial of puritanism and inclined to treat him leniently. After his punishment, however, he was quickly taken up by others of less moderate views. In October 1633, for instance, William Prynne wrote to him, evidently regarding Sherfield as a fellow traveller, for help in his own troubles and trial for *Histriomastix*.[102] Sherfield died shortly afterwards, but he was perhaps already being recruited to the 'faction'. It may be that whilst he rightly recognized the threat some puritans represented to state and church, in his dealings with those like Sherfield, Charles added more moderate men to their ranks.

If the puritanism of the nobility and gentry still awaits further exploration, that of the middling sort, still more of plain folk, remains

97. Cliffe, *The Puritan Gentry*, p. 179.
98. W. Scott and J. Bliss, *The Works of William Laud* (7 vols, Oxford, 1847–60), V, p. 330.
99. Fletcher, *County Community*, p. 241; cf. *Cal. Stat. Pap. Dom., 1639–40*, pp. 386–7: Burton to Dr Bray, 27 Jan. 1640.
100. Fletcher, *County Community*, p. 243.
101. Cliffe, *The Puritan Gentry*, p. 12; Holmes, *Seventeenth Century Lincolnshire*, pp. 41–6; Hughes, *Politics, Society and Civil War*, pp. 64–84. Like all dedicated minorities they possessed an influence greater than their number. As Robert Weldon told Lambe, 'they prevail upon those that are not of their garb' (*Cal. Stat. Pap. Dom., 1637–8*, pp. 191–2). See, too, A. Hughes, 'Thomas Dugard and his circle in the 1630s: a parliamentary–puritan connexion?', *Hist. Journ.*, 29 (1986), pp. 771–93.
102. Above, pp. 345–8; Hampshire Record Office, Sherfield MS XXXIX, 88.

a dark corner of religious history. Were the puritans numerous and strong, or a small and beleaguered minority? The course of events offers ambiguous suggestions: while there were thousands of signatures against the bishops in 1640 and much evidence of anticlericalism, the continued use of the Prayer Book during the 1640s and 1650s, when it was officially outlawed, undercuts assumptions about a widespread nonconformity.[103] If the puritans during the republic failed to establish their godly Commonwealth, Professor Finlayson asked recently, might we not question their supposed strength in the earlier decades of the century?[104] Though suggestive, such attempts to gauge the popularity of puritanism before the civil war by retrospective reading of its consequences are fraught with problems – not least because they underplay the significance of the great upheaval itself. But contemporary commentary poses its own difficulties. There is, for example, no shortage of reports suggesting that puritans gained an easy following or secured control in the parishes. In a sermon of 1637 John Swan lamented

> that man among us who can but show his dislike of the church's hierarchy, traduce the men thereof for unsound intentions, prefer preaching before praying, soar uploft into the high and deep points of predestination, detract from the honour of the house of God and be homely bold in his holy worship shall not want a train to follow after him from parish to parish, from town to town, from city to city . . . yea from one England to another.[105]

Robert Sibthorpe writing to Lambe from Northamptonshire bemoaned his fate 'living in the midst of the faction who are too many and too mighty for me'.[106] Dr John Andrewes, invited by Laud to preach a visitation sermon at Beaconsfield, told the chancellor of Lincoln that 'any other priest in those parts would be better accepted both of the laity and the generality of the clergy and the main reason is because he is not of the new cut, nor any wise inclining to puritanism wherewith the greatest number (both of priests and people) in those parts are foully tainted'.[107] Such comments, however, are often made by those most paranoid about the strength and intentions of the godly. More importantly they need to be placed alongside the despairing letters and

103. J.S. Morrill, 'The Church in England, 1642–49', in Morrill (ed.) *Reactions to the English Civil War* (1982), pp. 89–114.
104. M. Finlayson, *Historians, Puritanism and the English Revolution: The Religious Factor in English Politics before and after the Interregnum* (1984).
105. J. Swan, *A Sermon Pointing Out the Chief Causes and Cures of such Unruly Stirs as are not seldom found in the Church of God* (1637, STC 23515), p. 11.
106. Temple of Stowe MS STT 1880: Sibthorpe to Lambe, 28 April 1639.
107. *Cal. Stat. Pap. Dom., 1634–5*, p. 64.

sermons of puritans who portray a society largely indifferent or hostile to their proselytizing. Of the godly, one preacher said in 1632, 'how few such are to be found . . . every eye spiritually enlightened may clearly see and heartily bewail';[108] the author of *The Fall of Babylon* thought it their lot to be often scoffed at and mocked;[109] Woodforde frequently betrays his sense of isolation in a world that did not share his spiritual commitment.

Between these competing claims, or rather laments, it is hard to discern the breadth of the puritan appeal. Yet there is enough evidence of less partisan colour to suggest that like Laud, Wren, Pierce and others, some historians, perhaps from their own sectarian sympathies, have overestimated the numbers of the godly. Popular courtesy books and manuals for instance show little patience with their cause. In his bestselling collection of moral essays (six editions of the *Resolves* were published in the early seventeenth century) Owen Feltham was clear about how he treated a man who spurned the authority of the church or branded others as reprobates: 'I shall think him one of those whose opinion hath severed his zeal to madness.'[110] The *Divine Poems* of Francis Quarles, secretary to Bishop Ussher, satirize the puritans' bare heads, howling and 'affected graces'.[111] Thomas Nashe, who depended for his living on a feel for the market, joked that if he had entitled a work a sermon, no one would have read it.[112] Even George Wither, no friend of the hierarchy, mocked those 'that howle, or whine or snuffle in the nose'.[113] When we consider attitudes to puritanism, we should never forget the caricatures of the precision represented on the Jacobean and Caroline stage. For given that the theatres played to packed houses and mixed audiences, the ridiculous Zeal-of-the-Land Busy and his like must have been expected to raise a laugh: the figure of self-righteous superiority is an obvious butt for popular humour in any age.

Satirical and comic literature is not the only evidential antidote to the excessive claims made for the godly.[114] Anyone perusing the legal records and justices' notebooks of early modern England, with their

108. R. Bolton, *Mr Boltons Last and Learned Worke of the Last Four Things* (1632, STC 3242), p. 179.
109. *The Fall of Babylon* (1634); Zakai, 'Gospel of reformation'.
110. O. Feltham, *Resolves, Divine, Morall, Politicall* (1628 edn, STC 10756), p. 10.
111. F. Quarles, *Divine Poems* (1630, STC 20533), p. 41.
112. T. Nashe, *A New Discourse of a Stale Subject Called the Metamorphosis of Ajax* (1596), sig. H. 7v. I owe this reference to D. Margolies, *Novel and Society in Elizabethan England* (1985), p. 43. See in general, L.C. Stevenson, *Praise and Paradox: Merchants and Craftsmen in Elizabethan Popular Literature* (Cambridge, 1984).
113. G. Wither, *Britain's Remembrancer* (1628, STC 25899), p. 248.
114. Though see Stevenson, *Praise and Paradox*, and M. Spufford, *Small Books and Pleasant Histories: Popular Fiction and its Readership in Seventeenth Century England* (Cambridge, 1981). See also Massinger's *The Renegado* (1630, STC 17641), sigs. H1v–H2.

frequent references to cases of bastardy, incontinence, drunkenness and debauchery, might be led to doubt the popular appeal of puritanism. And any with experience of the near unrelieved toil of agrarian labour may doubt whether the strict Sabbatarianism of the godly, their assaults on holy days, church ales and parish festivities offered anything to the humble sort. Even in areas known for the efforts of some magistrates to establish models of godliness there is no shortage of evidence of popular resistance. In Dorset, for example, for all that Dorchester was the home of John White, the rector of Holy Trinity and member of the Massachusetts Bay Company, there are multiple presentations in the peculiar court for incontinence, drinking in sermon time and fishing on the sabbath.[115] At Bridport, 'divers of the inhabitants' presented William and John Sands for holding their puppet shows during the day and late at night because they 'cannot keep their children and servants in their houses by reason they frequent the said shows'.[116] Poor Woodforde found to his dismay that in Rugby some enterprising characters set up bear-baiting as a rival entertainment to the preacher and learned that some had been found on the sabbath with prostitutes.[117] Evidently there was a market for secular pursuits even in godly Northamptonshire.[118] The butchers of Towcester kept open shop on the sabbath and Thomas Holliard, charged with 'setting up trunks to play at . . . an unlawful game', evidently expected two teams of men would be prepared to tear themselves away from their devotions.[119] The fact that Northamptonshire villagers were frequently fined for stealing trees from royal forests for maypoles nicely illustrates the limitations to the campaign for sobriety there.[120] In Banbury, the butt of Ben Jonson's humour against the puritan, cakes and ale still marked the festival of perambulation day; and the town's accounts show disbursements for visiting actors.[121] As Henry Sherfield had acknowledged, the puritan drive for a moral reformation was inherently unpopular.[122] Drunkenness, the Earl of Huntingdon reported, was especially a problem in the market towns which were often the centres of godly preaching.[123]

115. Dorset Record Office, P 204, CP 13: Wimborne Peculiar court presentments, 1619–40.
116. Dorset Record Office, quarter sessions orders, 1625–37, ff.272–3.
117. Woodforde's diary, 20 Feb. and 11 March 1638.
118. Woodforde himself attended many 'interludes'.
119. J. Wake (ed.) *Quarter Sessions Records of the County of Northampton I* (Northamptonshire Record Soc., 1924), pp. 28, 63.
120. P.A.J. Pettit, *The Royal Forests of Northamptonshire: A Study in their Economy, 1558–1714* (Northamptonshire Record Soc., 23, 1968), p. 86.
121. E.R.C. Brinkworth, *South Newington Churchwardens' Accounts, 1553–1684* (Banbury Historical Soc., 6, 1964), p. 44; J.S.W. Gibson and E.R.C. Brinkworth, *Banbury Corporation Records* (Banbury Historical Soc., 15, 1977), p. 157.
122. Sherfield MS XXXVIII: speech at sessions, Aug. 1628.
123. Hastings MSS, HAM Box 26.

Indeed the puritan preacher had to contend with myriad competing distractions in his efforts to disseminate the word more widely. Preachers often betray anxiety about the greater appeal of plays over sermons, and the Sabbatarians were as anxious to remove distractions from the word as to check profanity. *Bartholomew Fair*, in this respect, for all its brilliant evocation of locality, was all cities, teeming with sensual delights, worldly and debauched characters all of which contended with the puritan ministry for the souls of the people. The enthusiasm of the commonalty to hear long sermons, and indeed to pay for their preachers, seems no greater than their readiness to obey puritan injunctions to morality and sobriety. While preachers – in Bristol, in the Harleys' corner of Herefordshire and elsewhere – complained that their stipends were not paid, the theatres played to full houses.[124] Among those who attended sermons there appear to have been many for whom the spectacle was the attraction, for the Master of the Revels noted that a visiting French acting company 'had the benefit of playing on the sermon days', implying that the audience for the one would flock to the other.[125] Some went to scoff, like the puppeteers of Bridport who (enacting the script of the puppet Dionysius in *Bartholomew Fair*) followed the preacher home and 'challenged him his sermon' on the way.[126]

The zealous puritans of early Stuart England may have been regarded by the people as the more secularly minded today view the Mormon at the door – with a mixture of fascination and irritation, sometimes as devout men of principle, but often as ludicrous and tiresome. Certainly Richard Baxter tells us that anyone, in his native Kidderminster, gadding to sermons was 'made the derision of the vulgar rabble under the odious name of a puritan'.[127] Sermon-goers at Hatfield in Essex referred to the 'hatred of the world for the people of God'.[128] In Lincolnshire, we are told by the historian of the diocese, 'for every sermon gadder encountered in the visitation records, we find at least a dozen other parishioners who dozed or laughed or farted their way through long hours of obligatory boredom'.[129]

The puritans clearly divided the parishes, and nowhere was the division more visible than their trek to hear a sermon, while others played on the village green. Rather than winning the people by the

124. Bristol Record Office, Common Council Books, 3, f.16v; BL, MS 29/172, f.344.
125. J.Q. Adams (ed.) *The Dramatic Records of Sir Henry Herbert* (New Haven, 1917). p. 61.
126. Dorset quarter sessions orders, f.273.
127. D. Underdown, *Revel, Riot and Rebellion: Popular Politics and Culture in England, 1603–1660* (Oxford, 1985), p. 131.
128. Hunt, *Puritan Moment*, p. 231.
129. H. Hajzyk, 'The church in Lincolnshire, *c*.1595–*c*.1640' (Cambridge University, PhD thesis, 1980), p. 156.

word, it would seem, the puritan ministry was, quite literally, preaching primarily to the converted. In Bere Crocombe, Somerset, in 1636 the churchwardens presented not only nonconformists who refused to bow or wear a surplice, but also the preachers who had gone on for three hours![130] In Warwickshire, the godly had 'lost the initiative to a more overtly conformist strand of Protestantism'.[131] In Herefordshire, the sheriff thought that his countrymen 'if the times would serve . . . would show as little favour to those that they call puritans as any English or Irish papist would do'.[132] The puritans, even in their strongholds in Essex and Northamptonshire, were never more than a well organized, minority sect which failed to win over the commonalty and had only limited success in recruiting the better sort.[133]

It may be too that the belief that puritans might be socially disruptive and politically subversive was not confined to churchmen and magistrates. A commonplace book dating from the mid-1630s (containing excerpts from Bacon and doggerel verse, stories about the Tudors, witty anecdotes, and notes on religious issues) passes from observations on the puritans' rejection of the church and denial of the authority of the magistrate in ecclesiastical matters to note with horror that in Switzerland an Anabaptist cut off his brother's head because he believed God had commanded him.[134] The story of the separatist Enoch ap Evan who axed to death his mother and brother because they knelt in church brought the fears of the zealous sectary closer to home.[135] Ballads suggest indeed that at the lower end of the social hierarchy the puritans were perceived to be a threat to social order, holding like the Anabaptists all in common, including wives. 'The Summons to New England' is especially interesting in its accusations:

Let all that putrifidean sect
I mean the counterfeit elect
All zealous bankrupts punks devout
Preachers suspended rabble rout
Let them sell all and out of hand
Prepare to go for New England
To build new Babel strong and sure
Now called a church unspotted pure.

130. I owe this information to Christopher Haigh's 'The Church of England and its people, 1604–42', paper delivered at the University of Southampton, 25 May 1983. I am grateful to Chris Haigh for many helpful discussions on puritanism.
131. Hughes, *Politics, Society and Civil War*, p. 68.
132. Hirst, *Authority and Conflict*, p. 226.
133. Cf. A. Everitt, *The Community of Kent and the Great Rebellion* (1966), p. 60; *idem*, *Suffolk and the Great Rebellion* (Suffolk Record Soc., 3, 1960), pp. 12, 18–20.
134. Huntington Library MS, HM 1338.
135. P. Studley, *The Looking Glass of Schism* (1634, STC 23403).

Sung to the tune of 'The Townsman's Cap', the ballad continues:

No discipline shall there be used
The law of nature they have choosed
All that the spirit seems to move
Each man may take and that approve
There's government without command
There's unity without a bande
A synagogue unspotted pure
Where lusts and pleasures dwell secure.

Loe in this church all shall be free
To enjoy all Christian liberty
All things made common t'avoid strife
Each man may take another's wife
And keep a handmaid too if need
To multiply, increase and breed
And is not this foundation sure
To raise a church unspotted pure.[136]

The ballad echoes in popular terms the charges of insincerity, excessive zeal, anarchy and debauchery levelled by others. It depicts the puritans too, as had James I and the playwright William Davenant, as a Judaical sect, separated from neighbours whom they deemed unclean. Most importantly the song summons the historian to a reconsideration of one of the most celebrated phenomena of the 1630s, of puritanism and indeed of the Western world: the 'godly' exodus to America.

The 'puritan exodus'?

The history of the puritan migration, the 'puritan hegira', is one of the triumphs of myth over evidence, and of nationalist historiography over research. The textbooks, especially of American history, still tell of a mass exodus of the godly from the shores of persecution to the land of freedom where they could establish a true church and moral commonwealth.[137] The most recent study, however, has deconstructed that orthodoxy, not least by demonstrating that the story has been written from the beginning from the partisan 'eloquent, insistent and self-serving assertions of American Puritan authors'.[138] Professor Cressy

136. Tanner MS 306, f.286.
137. My own A-level American history text was entitled *The History of a Free People*. See C. Brindenbaugh, *Vexed and Troubled Englishmen, 1590–1642* (Oxford, 1976), p. 434.
138. D. Cressy, *Coming Over: Migration and Communication between England and New England in the Seventeenth Century* (Cambridge, 1987), p. 77. Professor Cressy draws on earlier work to challenge the primacy of religious motivation.

argues persuasively that while religious commitments or fears were one of a matrix of motivations that inspired emigration, 'terms like "Puritan migration". . . should be dropped from discussion of seventeenth-century Anglo-American history'.[139] Of the migrants to the New World, those to New England were fewer in number than those who went to the rather less godly Caribbean or Chesapeake. Of the 10,000 ordained ministers of England, only 76 departed for New England during the 1630s and of these a third had been in no trouble with the ecclesiastical hierarchy at home.[140] Many exiles left for New England, as migrants have across the centuries (and as they travelled within England during the troubled decades of the sixteenth and seventeenth centuries) – to better their economic conditions. Unemployment, especially in the cloth trade, led many to depart from the wool towns of East Anglia and Essex.[141] Still others, far from fleeing religious persecution, were convicted criminals slipping away from the law and perhaps the noose – men like Robert Wright, a brewer who was wanted in London 'for clipping the King's coin'.[142] Even with the unquestionable puritans personal factors were weighed in the scales with conscience, John Winthrop himself having seen his career as a lawyer fail before he decided to take ship to Massachusetts.[143] The inhabitants of New England were a motley crew, the colony's governors battling against drunkenness and debauchery in the 1630s much as the magistrates at home.[144]

There is plentiful contemporary testimony to support Cressy's case. As John Endecott wrote to Winthrop of the ship bound for New England from Bristol: 'We have heard of several ungodly carriages in that ship, as first in their way over bound they would constantly jeer at the holy brethren of New England and some of the mariners would in a scoff ask when they should come to the holy land.'[145] While the godly conducted their services they witnessed on shipboard what they had frequently experienced in their parishes, the sight and sound of others singing and carousing.[146] William Whiteway noted in his diary that the year when wheat prices rose by 50 per cent, many left England for America.[147] Even the Suffolk puritan Emmanuel Downing admitted

139. *Ibid.*, p. 106.
140. *Ibid.*, p. 87.
141. *Ibid.*, p. 89 and ch. 3, *passim.*
142. *Ibid.*, p. 99.
143. *Ibid.*, p. 94.
144. *Ibid.*, p. 101.
145. *Winthrop Papers*, pp. 141–2, quotation p. 142; *Winthrop Papers IV, 1638–44* (Massachusetts Hist. Soc., 1944), p. 270.
146. Indeed, they often left to escape the hostility of their neighbours as much as the repression of the authorities. I am grateful to Professor Zakai for discussions of this point. Above, p. 748.
147. BL, Egerton MS 784 (William Whiteway's diary, 1618–34), p. 154.

that many left to pursue their profit; of those emigrating out of religious motives some, he believed, went 'to satisfy their own curiosity in point of conscience, others (*which was more general*) to transport the gospel to those heathen that never heard thereof'.[148] Those who sought to draw more Englishmen across the Atlantic found it essential to press the material as well as spiritual advantages: 'if gentlemen of ability would transport themselves,' Richard Saltonstall wrote from Massachusetts, 'they might advance their own estates' as well as 'propagating the gospel to these poor barbarous people'.[149]

The controversy over the emigration from the diocese of Norwich offers a valuable case study of the complexities of the exodus and the distortions of mythical and partisan historiography. In January 1641 Nehemiah Wallington heard of the Long Parliament's investigation into those forced to flee from the diocese as a consequence of Bishop Matthew Wren's enforcement of the Prayer Book and canonical ceremonies.[150] Some charged Wren with 1,350 persons 'the most being tradesmen considerable and useful persons enforced to leave'; others put the number at 3,000.[151] Wren and his witnesses denied the accusation. He claimed that low wages and the effects of plague on trade had been the drives to exile and pointed out that fewer had departed during his episcopate than under his predecessor Corbet, who had not been diligent in enforcing conformity.[152] There is sufficient evidence to suggest that his reply to the charge was more than defensive pleading. Years before Wren's indictment, William Allanson had written to Samuel Wright that the puritan aldermen of Norwich were claiming that the unemployment in the city had been caused by weavers being forced to leave through pressures on their conscience, when in reality the plague had forced them to seek a livelihood in Holland.[153] The curate of Great Yarmouth warned Wren that 'some puritanical slir' would be placed on him and that all who had left would be counted as religious exiles.[154] The Long Parliament committee preparing the bishop's impeachment seized on the Norwich port books for 1637–8 to document the numbers of leavers. From the bare figures they concluded 'they were driven over by you' and denied Wren access to them, so depriving him of the chance to point out the reasons the

148. Coke MS 47: Downing to Coke, 12 Dec. 1633; *HMC Cowper II*, pp. 38–9. This implies a more general Christian mission that echoes the Spanish missions of the sixteenth century.
149. *HMC Cowper I*, p. 449: Saltonstall to Downing, 4 Feb. 1632.
150. N. Wallington, *Historical Notices of . . . the Reign of Charles I, 1630–46*, ed. R.J. Webb (2 vols, 1869), I, p. 166.
151. Tanner MS 68, f.332.
152. *Ibid.*, f.338; C. Wren, *Parentilia or Memoirs of the Family of the Wrens* (1750), pp. 101–2.
153. Tanner MS 68, f.147, 8 Oct. 1636.
154. Tanner MS 314, ff.116–17: Matthew Brooks to Wren, 8 May 1641.

migrants had given for their departure.[155] Wren was right to think that the records would have supported his defence. First we know that many of those departing left not for New England but for Holland whither they went for higher wages, or to learn a skill, as much as from religious scruples.[156] Secondly, many of the families emigrating were Walloons and members of the stranger churches, who resisted the injunction to attend their parish services.[157] Most of all, transcripts of the register of passengers departing from Great Yarmouth from 1637 to 1639 appear to bear out some of Wren's claims. The majority were weavers – half were in their teens or twenties, which suggests that economic opportunities were the spur to emigration. Of 109 who departed between Michaelmas 1637 and 1638, only 30 declared a clear intent to 'dwell' – many of them 'on liking'.[158] Others either cited a specific purpose – to better a skill, clear debts, seek employment – or explicitly announced their plans to see friends and relatives, and then return.[159] None of course announced religious scruples as their motivation to their examiners; what the emigrants told customs officials cannot be uncritically accepted. But there is no reason to doubt those like William Howell whose declared intent was to go to Holland for three months and return. Dr Cressy's researches show that there was a return migration from New England 'of several thousand souls during the 1630s and 1640s' including 200 members of the original Winthrop fleet.[160] The lawyer, Thomas Leckford, came back not least because, as he explained, 'I am kept from the sacrament'.[161]

Emigration for religious reasons – from Norfolk as other shires – undoubtedly took place. A puritan pamphlet of 1628, in the form of a letter from Michael Mean-Well to Mathew Mark-Well, outlined all the reasons why those of tender consciences should leave: the distasteful ceremonies prescribed, assertions that Christ died for all men and that all children baptized were saved 'and that our Sabbath is not a divine institution'.[162] In the file of charges against Wren we find a case that though it sounds dramatized in the telling may well have been true in substance. Dr Lushington, one of Wren's appointees, officiating at St Symond's in his preaching requested 'free will offerings' and coming

155. *Ibid.*, ff.114, 116–17, 118.
156. C.B. Jewson (ed.) *Transcript of Three Registers of Passengers from Great Yarmouth to Holland and New England, 1637–9* (Norfolk Record Soc., 25, 1954); see also Tanner MS 433.
157. W.J.C. Moens (ed.) *The Walloon Church of Norwich: its Registers and History* (Huguenot Soc., I, 1887), p. 94.
158. Tanner MS 433.
159. *Ibid.*; Jewson, *Transcript of Three Registers.*
160. Cressy, *Coming Over*, p. 192.
161. *Ibid.*, p. 199.
162. *Cal. Stat. Pap. Dom., 1628–9*, p. 30.

from the pulpit to receive them, he 'elevated them above his head in such manner that it bred offence in many of the parishioners who then went out of the church and one of them accordingly as he then declared openly in the church with his family went to New England'.[163] In the absence of official records of those leaving, still more the impossibility of discerning what finally motivated each migrant to go, we will never be able to conclude how many were *religious* exiles. The 565 who left Essex for the New World during the decade of personal rule had, the historian of the county tells us, plenty of secular reasons impelling them.[164] The largest contingent of Kentish migrants came from known centres of radical puritanism, but also from communities suffering economic hardship. 'It seems likely,' Peter Clark concludes, 'that it was the critical juncture of religious and economic factors which sped many on their way.'[165] In an England in which there were bishops unwilling to enforce conformity and godly patrons, there were many alternatives to emigration for those alienated by the ecclesiastical policies of their incumbent or diocesan.[166] As Dr Cressy maintains, the old assumptions about 'the primacy of puritan concerns in the bulk of the movement to New England' await the support of 'firm evidence'.[167]

The government's attitude to the exodus was ambivalent and changing. On the one hand, the departure of trouble-making schismatics seemed desirable: informed by Laud's report of 1636 that Mr Bridges of Norwich had fled abroad rather than conform, Charles noted in the margin: 'Let him go we are well rid of him.'[168] Laud expressed similar sentiments in his letter to Bishop Bramhall, concerning the puritans who left Ireland: 'Tis great pity the ring-leaders of your nonconformists fell short of New England . . .'.[169] Yet relief at the purging of dissidents from the homeland was accompanied by concern that the colonies were being populated by sectaries and rebels. Emmanuel Downing writing to Secretary Coke tried to assuage the 'causeless fear' that 'a colony planted in a strange land were ever so foolishly besotted as to reject the protection of their natural prince', but in so arguing he acknowledged the fear that motivated the Council to take regulatory action.[170] As early as 1632, the signet office letters for the foundation of the colony of 'Carolana' stipulated that none who were not Protestants

163. Tanner MS 220, f.123.
164. Hunt, *Puritan Moment*, p. 258.
165. P. Clark, *English Provincial Society from the Reformation to the Revolution: Religion, Politics and Society in Kent, 1500–1640* (Hassocks, 1977), p. 372.
166. Wren himself pointed out that, had religion been their only motive, the exiles could simply have gone to another diocese (*Parentilia*, p. 102).
167. Cressy, *Coming Over*, p. 106.
168. *Works of Laud*, V, p. 340.
169. Huntington Library MS 15172 (Bramhall letters): Laud to Bramhall, 27 June 1637.
170. Coke MS 47: Downing to Coke, 12 Dec. 1633.

conformable to the church of England should be permitted to participate in the venture.[171] In February 1634 the Council, announcing its concern at the disaffected who were passing to New England, ordered the stay of all ships until further notice from the Board.[172] Days later they issued instructions requiring certificates from the ports and lists of passengers' names, and ordered that all services on board be conducted according to the Book of Common Prayer.[173] By the end of the year new regulations were drawn up 'for the stopping of such promiscuous and disorderly parting out of the realm', by which none was permitted to leave without having sworn the oaths of allegiance and supremacy and secured a certificate of their conformability from two justices of the peace.[174]

Such actions were of limited effectiveness. Sympathetic ministers and justices could collaborate in circumventing the rules; clerks of the passes and customs officials often, through indolence, permitted those without, or with forged, passports to slip away.[175] Last attempts to close the loopholes were made in 1637 and 1638 when proclamations prohibited the emigration of anyone who had not secured a licence from the commissioners for plantations, with threat of serious punishment on any who conveyed passengers not so licensed.[176] In August 1638, observing that nonconformist ministers were leaving for the Somers Islands and other plantations 'where they take liberty to nourish and preserve their factious and schismatical humors', the Council required all clergy to obtain first the approval of the archbishop of Canterbury or bishop of London.[177] By 1638, however, the government was too preoccupied with the Scots to devote attention to the New World. It may be too that the rising in Scotland – what Sir John Clotworthy called the new 'America' – stemmed the tide of emigrants, who now hoped that the forces of Antichrist would be overthrown at home.[178] The committed godly exiles were not seriously impeded by the Council's efforts at control.

The effect of the exodus and the attitudes to the emigrants of the

171. PRO, SO 1/2, f.92, April 1632.
172. PRO, PC 2/43/502.
173. PRO, PC 2/43/508.
174. Cressy, *Coming Over*, p. 135; PRO, C.115/N9/8852: Rossingham to Scudamore, 9 Jan. 1635.
175. *Cal. Stat. Pap. Dom., 1629–31*, p. 190. Cf. PRO, PC 2/48/287.
176. PRO, PC 2/49/79; J. Rushworth, *Historical Collections* II (1680), p. 409; J.F. Larkin (ed.) *Stuart Royal Proclamations II: Royal Proclamations of King Charles I, 1625–1646* (Oxford, 1983), no. 237, pp. 555–6.
177. PRO, PC 2/49/393.
178. D. Dalrymple, *Memorials and Letters relating to the History of Britain in the Reign of Charles I* (Glasgow, 1766), p. 41; see below, p. 821 and note 362.

puritans who remained at home await further exploration. Some of the sermons delivered by ministers departing betray the unease of the exiles that by no means all the godly understood or sympathized with their action.[179] Michael Mean-Well's letter, with its appeal to Cartwright, Penry and Knox, is as defensive as it is hortatory. While some like Woodforde greatly esteemed the emigrants and held a farewell dinner to bless their voyage, others were outspoken in their doubts and criticisms.[180] Sir Simonds D'Ewes, though anxious about the health of the church, was no warm supporter of the exiles: 'I cannot approve all they do', he told Weckherlin; 'I cannot deny,' he entered in his diary, 'that I think they go a little too far . . . and that there are crept in amongst them some that hold strange and dangerous opinions.'[181] Sir Edward Dering, not without his worries about the church, was even more alarmed about the exiles. Those, he informed Secretary Coke, who left from Rye without passports carried 'wicked packets' overseas; daily, he told Dorchester, enemies to church and state stole overseas through the connivance of the clerk of the passage.[182] D'Ewes's and Dering's reservations speak more generally to the rift between the exiles and those who stayed at home. For those who wrote from England 'told of suspension and harassments, but they did not normally see them as catastrophic'.[183] Indeed the emigration evidences as much the weakness as the strength of radical puritanism in Caroline England. The godly exiles left because they despaired of establishing their Geneva in Albion; significantly, many returned in 1640, when to some events seemed to present the hope of a thorough reformation.

Whilst in puritan soteriology there lay the potential for a radical challenge to authority, the evidence suggests that the committed puritans remained a small band who often felt themselves beleaguered outcasts; unsupported by their neighbours, as well as hounded by ecclesiastical authorities, a few took ship to New England. If puritanism was not popular, radical puritans were a tiny sect, not a large band. From 1637, however, a series of events began to change the climate, to radicalize the moderates and to bring a measure of public sympathy to the cause of the godly. The first of these turned out to be a governmental act of folly: the trial and punishment of William Prynne, Henry Burton and John Bastwick.

179. See T. Hooker, *The Danger of Desertion* (1641).
180. Woodforde's diary for 26 Nov. 1637, 13 Feb. 1638, 31 March 1638.
181. Berkshire Record Office, Trumbull MS XIX, f.118, 29 May 1637; J.O. Halliwell, *The Autobiography and Correspondence of Sir Simonds D'Ewes* (2 vols, 1845), II, p. 116.
182. Coke MS 41, 7 June 1632; *Cal. Stat. Pap. Dom., 1629–31*, p. 190.
183. Cressy, *Coming Over*, p. 236.

The trial of Prynne, Burton and Bastwick

The 1637 Star Chamber prosecution of Prynne, Burton and Bastwick is one of the *causes célèbres* not only of the 1630s but of seventeenth-century English history. The graphic stories of a show trial and gruesome punishments have besmirched the court of Star Chamber and the episcopate and government of Caroline England. Perhaps no other act has been seen to qualify so well for the epithet 'tyrannous' as the mutilation of the puritan martyrs; no other event made such an impression on the public consciousness as their sufferings in the pillory. The power of the basic story, however, has often led to a suppression of the details, details which enable us to see the outline from a rather different perspective.

All three miscreants had appeared before the courts earlier: in October 1628 Henry Burton had been examined by the ecclesiastical commissioners and answered that he believed there was nothing in his works that was repugnant to the doctrine and discipline of the church;[184] in May 1629 he was questioned again.[185] John Bastwick, a doctor from Colchester, was summoned before High Commission in October 1634 and dealt contemptuously with his examiners. His reply to the articles against him was judged to be scandalous and Bastwick was admonished to answer *plene et pane* on pain of a £100 fine. Refusing to enter bond for his reappearance, Bastwick told his inquisitors that he stood before them like St Paul before Nero. On account of his wife's pregnancy the court proceeded leniently and ordered him to appear at the next session by virtue of the bond he had already given.[186] Prynne we know had already appeared in Star Chamber, charged with libel for publishing *Histriomastix*, which scandalized the queen, and implied that it might be lawful to lay violent hands upon a prince. Prynne and his counsel denied the offensive passages and argued that incriminating interpretations were imposed on the text. But there was no disagreement among the judges. Sir John Coke, Attorney Heath, Justice Richardson and the Earl of Pembroke, men of strong Protestant convictions, all agreed with Cottington who branded Prynne a dangerous man and passed sentence that he should have his ears cropped in the pillory. The Earl of Dorset, who had shown leniency to the 'conformable' Sherfield, wanted the 'seditious' Prynne's nose slit too.[187]

184. *Cal. Stat. Pap. Dom., 1628–9.* p. 364.
185. *Ibid.*, pp. 533, 541.
186. *Cal. Stat. Pap. Dom., 1634–5*, p. 269.
187. BL Add. MS 11764, ff.8v–28; J. Bruce and S.R. Gardiner (eds) *Documents relating to the Proceedings against William Prynne in 1634 and 1637* (Camden Soc., new series, 18, 1877); above, pp. 347, 647–8. See D.L. Smith, 'The political career of Edward Sackville, Earl of Dorset, 1590–1652' (Cambridge University, PhD thesis, 1989), pp. 214–20.

Neither his trial nor punishment was the subject of public attention or sympathy. When the Inns of Court atoned for his crimes by staging a public procession and masque in honour of the king and queen, 'nothing is heard of any token of disapprobation'.[188] Prynne, however, was not silenced. After his punishment, incarcerated in the Tower, he wrote in the form of a letter to one of the judges a libel 'and therein scandalised the whole court'. When the Attorney sent for him and asked if he had written it, Prynne defied him by tearing up the paper and throwing it out of the window.[189]

Despite their earlier brushes with authority and Prynne's savage punishment, all three continued to publish vituperative treatises against the church. Burton's sermons published (under the title *For God and the King*) in 1636 attacked ceremonies, altars and the institution of episcopacy. Bastwick followed his Latin *Flagellum Pontificis* with *The Litany of John Bastwick* (1637), a prayer for delivery from the episcopal Antichrist: 'from bishops, priests, and deacons Good Lord deliver us'. 'So far am I from flying or fearing,' he defiantly concluded, 'as I resolve to make war against the beast.'[190] Prynne (in whose study in 1635 was found a libellous sermon against the king)[191] concentrated his assault on the declaration of Sports and in *News from Ipswich* on Bishop Wren, one of those bishops, he charged, intent on snatching the crown from the King to 'set it on their own ambitious pates'. Undoubtedly it was the Council's mounting concern at the attacks on church and state printed in Holland or on clandestine presses in England that prompted action.[192] But it is important to note that many, and even those of godly sympathies, were appalled at the vitriol of these pamphlets. The Earl of Leicester was told by his estate manager that the books contained 'matter foul enough'.[193] One of Winthrop's correspondents, who was contemplating joining the brethren in Massachusetts, described *News from Ipswich* to him as 'a book of extreme bitterness and far enough off from the spirit of Christ, wherein the libeller . . . speaks of the bishops that which the Archangel would not speak unto the Devil', and as a work irreverent towards the king.[194] When infor-

188. S.R. Gardiner, *History of England from the Accession of James I to the Outbreak of the Civil War, 1603–1642* (10 vols, 1883–4), VII, p. 334.
189. BL, Harleian MS 4022, ff.44–5.
190. Gardiner, *History of England*, VIII, pp. 226–7.
191. BL Add. MS 11764, f.20.
192. Articles against Burton were drawn up for prosecution in the court of High Commission (*Cal. Stat. Pap. Dom., 1636–7*, p. 198) and Juxon felt the court needed to do more to check the distribution of pamphlets. Because, however, 'one of these libels contains seditious matter in it', Laud asked Charles I to 'call it into a higher court' (*Works of Laud*, V, p. 338). See Laud's notes on Burton's books, PRO, SP 16/354/176.
193. *HMC De Lisle and Dudley, VI*, p. 105.
194. *Winthrop Papers*, pp. 446–7; also *Winthrop Papers III*, p. 400. The letter is anonymous, but his godly sympathies are clear.

mation was filed against Prynne, Burton and Bastwick in March 1637 there was little indication of support for their cause.

Traditional accounts that make the trial sound like a travesty of justice are themselves a travesty of the truth. According to one author (who demonstrates throughout his account a good knowledge of legal procedure) Bastwick was given twelve days to answer the articles against him, then further time. When the attachment was returned still with no answer, the Attorney desired that, according to the practice of the court, in the absence of an answer the trial should proceed *pro confesso*. Bastwick petitioned for an opportunity to answer and on 28 April was given still more time. On 10 May, several weeks after the initial charge, Bastwick's wife appeared to petition on his behalf. The court permitted her petition to be read. A week later, with still no answer returned, the Attorney requested a day for a hearing *pro confesso*. At last, in June, Bastwick put in an answer, but it was so abusive that the Council ordered the Solicitor to ascertain what lawyer had helped to draw it. Meanwhile, on 5 May, Prynne had appeared to answer his charges. His petition was read – though it was scandalous – because the court was anxious to satisfy all of the justice of the proceedings. Burton, called on 2 June, refused to answer any interrogatories.[195] Contemporary observers at this stage did not mask their impatience. Burgh told Viscount Scudamore that the defendants had not put in an answer 'for they have drawn their answer themselves but of that length . . . and so contrary to the formality and proceedings of that court, being rather a justification or book, full of citations of Scripture and writers, than orderly and modest, that their counsel, upon just reason, refused to set their hands unto it'.[196] The failure to answer in due form, however, was not in professional men, one himself a lawyer, a sign of ignorance. 'They are desperate mad factious fellows,' Burgh predicted in his second missive on the trial, 'and covet a kind of puritanical martyrdom or at least a fame of punishment for religion.'[197]

On 14 June proceedings *pro confesso* commenced against all three. Prynne immediately entered an objection to the presence of bishops as judges – though there were no legal grounds for his objection – and now offered an answer. The court rejected it not least because his counsel had refused to sign it. Still at this stage, however, an opportunity was given them: 'the court offers to hear their counsel or themselves if [they] keep within bounds of modesty and the rules of the court'.[198] Cottington hinted that a plea for mercy might have been

195. Bodleian, Rawlinson MS C.827, under dates cited.
196. PRO, C.115/N4/8614, 3 May 1637.
197. PRO, C.115/N4/8615, 17 May 1637.
198. Rawlinson MS C.827, 14 June 1637.

expected rather than a display of impudency. The Lord Keeper echoed him: 'This is a place where you should crave mercy and favour . . . and not stand upon such terms as you do'.[199] With no such plea made, the court proceeded. Justice Bramston (whose judgment for Hampden showed him to be no sycophant to the crown) decreed that the offence might justly be taken *pro confesso* 'by the rules of this court' and of all other courts.[200] On 30 June, Star Chamber summoned the three for sentence. One more time the Lord Keeper invited them to speak in their defence, provided they kept within the bounds of modesty. The offer was abused. Prynne, riled by Finch's reference to his cropped ears, responded that the justice should be glad to have them; he then urged the court to hear a cross bill against the prelates – 'a bold presumption of wretched men' a newswriter called it.[201] Burton accused the court of not giving him a hearing; Bastwick compared their cause against the prelates with a duel, and branded the bishops as cowards. Coventry, perhaps trying one last time, suggested they would be better off seeking clemency than clamouring against the judges. The court, led by Cottington, proceeded to the sentence of whip, pillory and mutilation.[202] Windebank noted that though Laud had spoken for two hours (the archbishop had drawn up 27 pages of notes during the proceedings), 'The Lord Treasurer [Bishop Juxon] and archbishop Laud did not join in the sentence.'[203] Throughout the trial the judges' concern to be just, even their preparedness to be patient, in the hope of obtaining a formal answer appears in marked contrast to the defendants' stonewalling and insolent behaviour. There is more than a suggestion that an acknowledgement of fault and petition for mercy might have mitigated their punishment: one John Fathers believed they might even have been dismissed had they recanted.[204] It may be that as the Council determined to set an example that would discourage libellous publishing, Prynne and his co-defendants actually sought 'puritanical martyrdom' for their cause. In November 1630 when Alexander Leighton had escaped before his ordeal there had been disappointment in some godly circles, for 'they had hoped his suffering would have

199. *Ibid.*; J. Bastwick, *A Brief Relation of Certain Passages in the Star Chamber* (1640, STC 1569), p. 14. It is worth recalling that Finch was a Calvinist. See W. Prest, 'The art of law and the law of God: Sir Henry Finch (1558–1625)', in D. Pennington and K. Thomas (eds) *Puritans and Revolutionaries: Essays in Seventeenth Century History presented to Christopher Hill* (Oxford, 1978), p. 116.
200. Rawlinson MS C.827, 14 June 1637.
201. *Ibid.*; see Tanner MS 299, ff.136–139v for their answer; PRO, C.115/N4/8614. The cross bill is in Tanner MS 299, ff.148–60.
202. Tanner MS 299, ff.136–139v.
203. *Cal. Stat. Pap. Dom., 1637*, pp. 214–19.
204. *Cal. Stat. Pap. Dom., 1637–8*, p. 296. John Fathers was vicar of St Stephen's, Cornwall.

been a great glory for the truth'.[205] Prynne, Burton and Bastwick did not waste their 'opportunity'.

In the dock the defendants had proved reluctant to answer. In the pillory they were eloquent and well rehearsed. It was indeed powerful eloquence. Approaching the three pillories set up for their torture, Burton compared them to the three crosses at Calvary and (implicitly of course) his sufferings to those of Christ. Emulating his Saviour's language, Burton proclaimed this his wedding day; asked by sympathetic bystanders if he needed water, he replied that he had the water of life. Bastwick delivered a homily from the pillory: 'Be not ye discouraged at their power, neither be affrighted though we suffer; do not you determine to turn from the ways of God, but go on and fight against Gog and Magog.' Prynne took his turn to rail again against the court and the episcopate, observing that in the days when bishops claimed their power *iure divino* 'libelling against prelates' was now worse than libelling kings. Against these false priests who usurped royal authority as well as abused the people, Prynne claimed he had stood.[206] With all the demagogue's brilliant rhetorical devices of involving the audience, he exclaimed: 'It is for the general good and your liberties that we have engaged our own liberties.'[207] Even as they addressed the crowd, the executioner set about his grisly work. When he cut off Burton's left ear

> though he cut it deep and close to the head in an extraordinary manner yet this champion never moved nor stirred for it. And the temples and head arteries being cut so as the blood came streaming down on the scaffold which divers persons standing about the pillory dipped their handkerchiefs in as in a thing most precious, the people giving a mournful shout and a compassionate crying for the chirugeon whom the crowd and other impediments for a time kept off, that he could not come to staunch the stream of the blood, this patient all the while held his peace, holding up his hands and said be content, it is well, blessed be God . . .[208]

If the description of the scene seems to draw on martyr narratives, it was clearly meant to. The author's reference to 'holy Mr Burton that did suffer for the Lord Jesus Christ' informs us that we are reading hagiography as well as history.

The reality was a little short of an apotheosis. At their show of 'brazen audacity', the Venetian envoy Correr reported, 'the wisest were

205. *Cal. Stat. Pap. Dom., 1629–31*, p. 383.
206. Tanner MS 299, ff.140–6.
207. *Ibid.*, ff.142v–143.
208. *Ibid.*, f.146.

disgusted'.[209] The newswriter Rossingham described very different reactions: 'some wept, some laughed and some were very reserved'.[210] Some may have gathered, as at public executions, for the spectacle, to poke fun at cranks. But it is clear that by their fortitude in suffering Prynne and his fellows won sympathy. Hawkins, who had not been sympathetic to them earlier, told Leicester how they endured their sentence 'with the most undauntedness that hath been seen'.[211] John Finet, Master of Ceremonies, told Scudamore that all three had suffered 'with that obstinacy (I dare not say resolution) as moved the numerous multitude of beholders to compassion . . . and almost to commotions after their several unsettled dispositions and affections'.[212] Correr agreed that 'the senseless people . . . had compassion on them'.[213] Some dipped their handkerchiefs in their blood, prompting Kenelm Digby, recently converted to Rome, to tease Conway – 'You may see how nature leads men to respect relics of martyrs.'[214]

As they were led off to prisons in different corners of the land, Prynne, Burton and Bastwick, 'mightily courted by the people', were followed as if on a triumphal procession.[215] As Prynne headed north and the news of the pillory spread, he was feasted at Barnet, St Albans and Chester. The Council now realized that what had been intended as an example had been badly mismanaged, indeed had backfired. In September the Attorney-General headed an enquiry into the events that had occurred as the martyrs had been taken to prison.[216] The Council summoned several who had offered support along the way; the citizens of Chester were punished for 'Prynne's entertainment'.[217] The Council acted nervously and defensively. Charles vindictively and speedily confiscated Prynne's lands in Somerset for his default of his fine.[218] Laud expressed his annoyance that Burton and his fellows had been allowed to preach from the pillory.[219] Wentworth, hearing the news, had a deeper sense of foreboding. 'A Prince,' he confided his fears to Laud, 'that loseth the force and example of his punishments loseth withal the greatest part of his domain.'[220]

209. *Cal. Stat. Pep. Venet., 1636–9*, p. 304.
210. *Cal. Stat. Pap. Dom., 1637*, p. 287: Rossingham newsletter, 6 July. The presence of this letter in state papers is evidence of the government's sensitivity to public reaction to the punishment. Cf. Gardiner, *History of England*, VIII, p. 232.
211. *HMC De Lisle and Dudley VI*, p. 115, 6 July 1637.
212. PRO, C.115/N8/8806, 6 July 1637. Does his 'dare not' betray a respect?
213. *Cal. Stat. Pap. Venet., 1636–9*, p. 304.
214. *Cal. Stat. Pap. Dom., 1637*, p. 332.
215. *HMC De Lisle and Dudley VI*, p. 120.
216. *HMC Cowper II*, p. 167; *Cal. Stat. Pap. Dom., 1637*, p. 414.
217. PRO, PC 2/48/359; *Cal. Stat. Pap. Dom., 1638–9*, p. 142.
218. PRO, SO 1/3, f.93v, July 1638.
219. W. Knowler (ed.) *The Earl of Strafford's Letters and Despatches* (2 vols, 1739), II, p. 99: Laud to Wentworth, 28 Aug. 1637.
220. *Ibid.*, p. 119.

Wentworth's sense that the trial marked a critical moment was not over-dramatization. The support for Prynne, Burton and Bastwick does not speak to the existing strength of puritan opposition. Their earlier punishments had attracted no attention; little interest had been taken in their trial. A popular ballad of 1641 even acknowledged they had been tried fairly.[221] Clarendon's recollection that most thought their scandalous writings 'deserved . . . exemplary punishment' was probably close to the truth.[222] What caused offence was the punishment itself, the degradation of a gentleman, a lawyer and a divine, and the brilliance with which the victims manipulated what may have been a mixed crowd. Clarendon's argument that it was widely held that their status should have spared them such barbarities was endorsed by Laud's chaplain, Peter Heylyn. Their punishment, he wrote in his life of the archbishop, 'was a very great trouble to the spirits of many very *moderate and well-meaning men*, to see the three most eminent professions . . . to be so wretchedly dishonoured'.[223]

Heylyn's words should be pondered. It was not only the committed godly who were affected by what many had seen and more had heard of. A witness assured Burton that his suffering would convert many.[224] Isaac Pennington may have been right when he told his cousin, Sir John Pennington (unlike Isaac no puritan) 'these proceedings cause much dejection among many good loyal subjects, make men fly and many more think of providing for their safety in other places.'[225] Dennis Bond, we recall, recorded the occasion at length in his diary of typically brief entries.[226] When a minister in Shoreditch damned all who thought well of the martyrs, several left his church 'for the common people are extremely compassionate towards them'.[227] In their struggle for public support the puritans, through Prynne, Burton and Bastwick, had won a significant battle. John Winthrop was told by his informant Henry Jacie, 'By these devices the prelates hoped to have more prevailed; but it's feared they have lost greatly by it. The poor credit they had with the vulgar is almost quite lost.'[228] The disgrace of gentlemen certainly sharpened the antagonism of the propertied towards the episcopacy. But it was not only the bishops who were tainted. The trial stained as well as the church, the court of Star

221. Tanner MS 306, f.294.
222. Clarendon, *History of the Rebellion*, I, p. 126.
223. P. Heylyn, *Cyprianus Anglicus or the History of the Life and Death of William Laud* (1668), part II, p. 313, my italics.
224. Bastwick, *A Brief Relation*, p. 28.
225. *Cal. Stat. Pap. Dom., 1637*, p. 311, 13 July.
226. Above, pp. 696–7.
227. *Cal. Stat. Pap. Dom., 1637*, p. 311: another Rossingham newsletter (of 13 July) that is in state papers.
228. *Winthrop Papers*, pp. 484–8, p. 487.

Chamber, the judges and the government. The scandal of the offences, the details of the trial, Laud's powerful defence of his churchmanship, were all submerged by the power of spectacle and the hagiographer's pen. Burton was right to vaunt from the pillory that 'this day will never be forgotten'.[229] It was Charles's government in church and state that suffered in 1637. As the Venetian ambassador astutely prognosticated, 'this pest may be the one which will ultimately disturb the repose of this Kingdom'.[230]

229. Bastwick, *A Brief Relation*, p. 27.
230. *Cal. Stat. Pap. Venet., 1636–9*, p. 242.

PART V

'THE FIRST ALARM OF ANY TROUBLE': CHARLES I AND THE SCOTS

XIII
'THE FATAL ADVERTENCY': THE PRAYER BOOK AND THE WAR BETWEEN THE KINGDOMS

1637: The critical year?

The year 1637 appears in many ways to have been the turning point in the history of the personal rule. There were delays in the French ratification of the treaty which were beginning to raise doubts about England's entry into what some hoped would be a crusading war against the Habsburgs. The plague, seen by some as a judgment on the land, impeded the implementation of government policies. Ship money was challenged in the courts. The punishment of Prynne, Burton and Bastwick brought sympathy to the puritans and exacerbated the unpopularity of the bishops. Yet it would be misleading to describe only problems and difficulties. Twelve years into his reign, Charles faced no threats like the papal excommunication against Elizabeth, nor any scandal like the Overbury murder that tainted James I. Where Elizabeth lacked an heir and James had lost his eldest son, leaving the weak younger prince as sole successor, Charles by 1637 had secured, as it must have seemed, the rule of the Stuart dynasty. Gardiner's summary of Charles I's position in the summer of 1637 (an important reminder that Gardiner's Whiggery was never crudely imposed on the evidence) cannot be bettered:

> The King was in the prime of life, in excellent health, devoted to active exercise in the open air, happy in his domestic relations, attentive to business and as attached to the new, thorough principles of government as even Laud or Wentworth . . . Two sons and three daughters set at defiance all ordinary chances in reference to the succession, and the likelihood seemed to be that long ere the father was called away [Charles was thirty-seven] the eldest son, then in his seventh year, would be out of tutelage and that on his father's death he would be fully competent to ascend the throne and carry on

> the government according to what would then be regarded as the settled principles of the English constitution.[1]

The government, Gardiner concluded, was 'now to all appearance at its height of power'. There was discontent, and the rumblings of opposition had been heard. The quiet that greeted Charles on his entry to Oxford suggested that there was little warm enthusiasm for the regime. But with the realm materially prosperous and the law having decided for the crown, there was no general mood of resistance. The continuance of government without parliament seemed 'most likely to be successful'.[2]

The Venetian envoy Angelo Correr carefully weighed the situation in the autumn of 1637 when he prepared his long relation of England for the Doge and Senate. He was not blind to the problems and weaknesses of the country, which he thought too embroiled in disputes over religion and liberties to go to war. He recognized that the people were disaffected by imposts, patents and taxes; he perceived that religious divisions were hardening and that the puritans were gaining adherents; the bishops aroused suspicion and applied 'too hasty medicaments' in their efforts to reform the church; he held out little hope for the Palatinate. Charles, he believed, had changed the principles of government and had embarked on the task – 'the most glorious that a prince ever took up' – of establishing his authority.

> It remains to be seen if he will go on and . . . be able to do by the royal authority what former kings did by the authority of the realm. This is a difficult matter and the more perilous, seeing that if it be true that the estates are perturbed about the two great causes of religion and the diminution of the liberty of the people, he has perturbed both, and will be very fortunate if he does not fall into some great upheaval.

Correr, however, admired the king's qualities, of virtue, valour, and commitment to government. For all the difficulties, therefore, he concluded 'Yet I am persuaded that if his Majesty adopts gentle methods in his government and in religion, he will attain his ends' and be powerful.[3]

English commentators seem in general to have had no sense of imminent crisis or foreboding. In July 1637 Charles told his nephew the Elector Palatine before his departure that 'but for his business he

1. S.R. Gardiner, *History of England from the Accession of James I to the Outbreak of the Civil War, 1603–1642* (10 vols, 1883–4), VIII, p. 221.
2. Cf. *Calendar of State Papers Domestic* [*Cal. Stat. Pap. Dom.*], *1636–7*, preface.
3. *Calendar of State Papers Venetian* [*Cal. Stat. Pap. Venet.*], *1636–9*, pp. 295–308, 24 Oct. 1637. Correr describes the bishops 'restoring in their churches some rules of slight moment which had fallen into desuetude' (p. 304).

was the happiest King or prince in all Christendom'.[4] In September, after the noise of Prynne's punishment had died, Hawkins told the Earl of Leicester he had little to report: 'our times here are so quiet that they yield no occurrence worth the relation'.[5] The record volume of state papers testifies to the quiet progress of normal business behind the noise of occasional controversy. If there was a change of mood in the nation, one astute newswriter thought it might favour the king. On 25 October 1637 John Burgh, in his regular newsletter to Scudamore, echoed Hawkins's apology that there was little worthy of report, then continued:

> All things are at this instant here in that calmness that there is very little matter of novelty to write, for there appears no change or alteration either in court or affairs, for all business goes undisturbedly on in the strong current of the present time to which all men for the most part submit, and that effects this quietness. And although payments here are great (considering the people have not heretofore been accustomed unto them) yet they only privately breathe out a little discontented humour and lay down their purses, for I think that great tax of the ship money is so well digested, (the honour of the business sinking now into apprehension and amongst most winning an affection to it) I suppose [it] will become perpetual. For indeed if men would consider the great levies of monies imposed in foreign parts for the service of the state, these impositions would appear but little burdens, but time can season and form minds to comply with public necessities.[6]

Contemporaries who did not know the future could only, as Correr put it, 'examine future events in the mist of appearances'.[7] Appearances suggested to them that, despite grumblings, the king (if he chose) could go on governing as he had for the last eight years without a parliament. Their perspective should be preferred to that of hindsight, which dooms the personal rule to inevitable collapse.[8] As Gardiner acknowledged, 'How long this state of things would have endured if no impulse had come from without, it is impossible to say'.[9] What is certain is that none predicted in 1637 that the 'great upheaval' which would bring down the government would take place in Scotland.

The full story of the origins of the Scottish rising has recently been

4. *Cal. Stat. Pap. Dom., 1637*, p. 287.
5. *HMC De Lisle and Dudley VI*, p. 125.
6. PRO, C.115/N4/8617.
7. *Cal. Stat. Pap. Venet., 1636–9*, p. 296.
8. As, most extravagantly (and unconvincingly) in T.K. Rabb, 'The role of the Commons', *P&P*, 92 (1981), p. 65.
9. Gardiner, *History of England*, VIII, p. 302.

well told by historians of Scotland.[10] We must, however, tell it briefly here so as better to understand (what is our main concern) its consequences for the regime in England. In some ways the origins of the Scottish troubles began with what might have seemed to be their resolution: with the Jacobean succession and the union of two traditionally hostile kingdoms under one crown.[11] After James VI and I's plans for a total union had been rejected, Scotland and England were left as distinct countries, with separate governments and administrations, different and alien cultures, joined only by the accident of a common monarch. A king of three countries, of course, could at any time reside only in one. In a system of personal monarchy when government worked through a network of personal relationships, the absence of the ruler was a major source of weakness. The history of early modern Europe charts the consequences of such a situation: the absence of Philip II contributed much to the rebellion in the Low Countries; the residence of the kings of Spain in Castile fostered discontent and ultimately rebellion in the other Iberian kingdoms – Aragon, Catalonia and Portugal; Sicily, which never saw its Habsburg rulers, rose in revolt.[12] The difficulties of an absent prince might be ameliorated by the appointment of an overlord or viceroy familiar with the country and trusted by the sovereign; frequent visits by the monarch could also mitigate the sense of distance and isolation. But in the end, in a pre-bureaucratic age there was no substitute for the power of the king's presence, as dispenser of patronage and punishment, as overlord, as the embodiment of the idea of order and, through ceremony and ritual, as the principal actor in the theatre of authority. In early modern Britain, Ireland was (as it has remained) a constant problem for the government at Whitehall; Wales, by contrast, incorporated into the English administration and the seat of the Tudor dynasty which effected that incorporation, emerged from a border land of strife and instability to become a headquarters for the king in the civil war.

The dynastic union with Scotland might have promised similarly to strengthen the crown. It signalled, it seemed, the end of hostilities (James dissolved the garrison at Berwick) and so closed England's

10. For example, D. Stevenson, *The Scottish Revolution, 1637–1644* (Newton Abbot, 1973); M. Lee, *The Road to Revolution: Scotland under Charles I, 1625–1637* (Urbana, 1985); P. Donald, 'The king and the Scottish troubles, 1637–41' (Cambridge University, PhD thesis, 1988), forthcoming as a book. I am grateful to Peter Donald for permission to read his thesis.
11. Cf. Correr's remarks in October, *Cal. Stat. Pap. Venet., 1636–9*, p. 296.
12. Cf. J.H. Elliott, 'The king and the Catalans, 1621–40', *Camb. Hist. Journ.*, 11 (1955), pp. 232–52. Wentworth advocated a Lord Deputy for Scotland, as Ireland. See Sheffield Central Library, Wentworth Woodhouse MS 10, ff.13–15.

vulnerable northern gate.[13] It meant too that the traditional enmity between the English and the French might be softened by the dynastic links between the French crown and the Stuarts. On the other hand, 1603 robbed the Scots of their king, who was drawn by considerations of wealth and power to make his permanent seat of government in London. Under James this may never have loomed large as a problem. When he succeeded to the English throne, James had been king of Scotland for thirty-five years. He had ruled there successfully; he had established a network of relationships; he was known in Scotland as a Scot. James may have astutely foreseen the future difficulties for his successors; he pressed for a full union of trade, law and government to resolve the potential problem of ruling the two kingdoms. But for himself distance and absence were not major impediments. He returned only once to his native country; for the rest, as he boasted (not unreasonably), he governed Scotland with his pen.[14] He could do so because those who governed on his behalf knew well the monarch who was writing. James's boast passed over some difficulties. The king's support for episcopal government, his desire to bring the Scottish kirk more into line with the Church of England, his campaign to secure and enforce the five articles of Perth (enshrining some Anglican rites, including kneeling) aroused hostility and opposition.[15] But not least because he had a political feel for the sensibilities of his native countrymen, James knew when not to press a point too far and so was able to enact unpopular measures in principle without arousing widespread antagonism. Scotland was quiet and peacefully governed by James I of England as it had been when James VI had occupied his throne in Edinburgh.

James's reign as king of both countries, however, exacerbated the difficulties for his successor. In Scotland the absence of the monarch removed the keystone from the edifice of government, for all James's boasts. Without the king, the court ceased to fulfil its vital function as

13. Lambeth Palace MS 943, pp. 687–8. The author of this manuscript observed that James I was 'so transported with faciam eos in gentem unam', as he would not endure any 'footsteps of hostility', whereas it was 'the practices of the most prudent persons and times, having under their dominion several nations, not so much to study how to make them one as so to alloy and temper one by the other as might contain both in due obedience'.

14. See M. Lee, *Government by Pen: Scotland under James VI and I* (Urbana, 1980).

15. J. Row, *The History of the Kirk of Scotland: 1558–1637*, ed. D. Laing (Edinburgh, 1842), pp. 225–338. Row's is, of course, a Presbyterian critique of James VI's policies, but his catalogue of James's injunctions, not least his order in 1625 that Easter communion be taken kneeling, is an important reminder that James was pressing on with his policy to bring the kirk into line with the Church of England. It is difficult to speculate as to what would have happened had he lived longer. I am not persuaded by Professor Russell's recent suggestions that James was inclined to leave well alone. The difference between James and Charles here was, as often, one of style more than policy. That does not mean it was not a crucial difference.

a nexus of communication to and from the ruler; as David Stevenson put it, after 1603 there is a sense in which Scotland was all country and no court.[16] In England, the Scottish confidants in the bedchamber, who linked the king to the families who governed Scotland in his absence, drew hostility from English courtiers who envied their influence and aspired to their places. The charge that Scots controlled the king was voiced in gentry correspondence and in parliament. The dynastic union of 1603 sharpened English contempt and hatred for the Scots; the prospects for cultural or political union became more unlikely as envy of the Scots' proximity to the king enhanced English jingoism.[17] James's policy and appointments were more balanced than the discontented were prepared to allow. He divided Privy Chamber appointments equally between English and Scots; he placed young men of both nations in the entourage of his son, Prince Henry. Henry, as his *Barriers* and masques represent him, was to be the heir of British kings, the embodiment of English and Scottish heritage.[18] But the dominance of a Scottish bedchamber favourite, Robert Carr, Earl of Somerset, overshadowed all. More importantly, when Prince Henry died tragically young in 1612, his successor as Prince of Wales was a boy who had left Scotland at three years of age and who had already perhaps become estranged from his father.

Charles's relationship with his father and adolescent development has not been sufficiently studied as a chapter in Scottish history. Yet Charles's distance from James and apparent distaste for his father's Scotch familiarity separated the prince from the centre of Scottish influence at the English court – the entourage in the royal bedchamber.[19] From 1621, he was to join with George Villiers in wresting control of it from the Scots who had been entrenched since 1603.[20] Charles was by no means completely estranged from the country of his birth. He retained many Scots in his household, as prince and king; he could write and spell perfect Scots; he may even have spoken with a Scottish accent.[21] But his personal style and tastes were far removed from those

16. Stevenson, *The Scottish Revolution*, p. 324.
17. For the political reality behind the rhetoric, see N. Cuddy, 'The revival of the entourage: the bedchamber of James I, 1603–25', in D. Starkey (ed.) *The English Court from the Wars of the Roses to the Civil War* (1987), pp. 173–225. See also, B. Levack, *The Formation of the British State: England, Scotland and the Union, 1603–1707* (Oxford, 1987), ch. 2.
18. See R. Strong, *Henry, Prince of Wales, and England's Lost Renaissance* (1986), p. 141; and T.V. Wilks, 'The court culture of Prince Henry and his circle, 1603–1613' (Oxford University, D. Phil. thesis, 1988).
19. We recall Burnet's remark that Charles was offended by James's 'light and familiar way'.
20. Cuddy, 'Revival of the entourage', pp. 222–4.
21. The letters in the Hamilton MSS in the Scottish Record Office and signet letters to Scotland testify to his spelling in Scotch when occasion suggested it. See also, P. Thomas, 'Charles I: the tragedy of absolutism', in A.G. Dickens (ed.) *The Courts of Europe* (1977), p. 195.

of his northern kingdom as well as contrary to those of his father. The elaborate ceremony of the Spanish court that attracted Charles was the polar opposite to the casual informality of that at Edinburgh; as the king's taste for elaborate religious ritual clashed with the simplicity of the kirk. The king of Scotland who succeeded James VI in 1625 was a Scottish king by title only.

Until he was crowned in Edinburgh, there was a sense in which he was not even that. The Scots expected to see their new king come to be crowned soon and Charles, recognizing the importance of an early visit, evidently hoped to fulfil their expectation. In October 1625, sending to Scotland an order that poor beggars should be assigned a parish, the king expressed his intention to come north for his coronation soon.[22] Plague, war with Spain then France, military failure, impoverishment and quarrels with parliaments all frustrated that intention. In July 1628 Sir William Trumbull informed a correspondent that Charles would go to Edinburgh that summer.[23] This was more than speculation, for the Earl of Mar acquainted the Marquis of Hamilton with the plans: 'the King's majesty is resolved god willing to honour this his ancient and native country with his royal presence about the hinder end of August next'.[24] God was not willing: at the hinder end of August, the Duke of Buckingham's assassination and the subsequent campaign to relieve La Rochelle obstructed any such progress.[25] The promised visit was not abandoned: in November 1631 Cottington informed Hopton, ambassador to Spain, of the royal preparations to go north the following spring.[26] But in Scotland the promises were wearing thin. On 6 October 1632 Lord Drummond, writing to the Earl of Morton, betrays the dissatisfaction and the king's sensitivity to it: Charles, he reported, was now 'fully resolved to see Scotland this next spring and is offended if any seem doubtful of it'.[27] On this occasion the royal resolution held firm. The journey to Edinburgh in May may be an indication of Charles's confidence that the government of England was back on sound tracks. As far as Scotland was concerned, eight years had elapsed since their new monarch had succeeded, and it was over fifteen years since a king of Scotland had stood on Scottish soil.

In the years between Charles's succession and progress to his coronation much had happened to which hindsight would attribute great

22. National Library of Scotland, Advocates' MS 33.7.11.
23. Berkshire Record Office, Trumbull MS XVIII, f.117.
24. Scottish Record Office, Hamilton MS GD 406/1, 100, 15 July 1628. Cf. *Cal. Stat. Pap. Venet., 1628–9*, p. 190.
25. *Cal. Stat. Pap. Venet., 1628–9*, p. 294.
26. British Library [BL], Egerton MS 1820, f.100.
27. National Library of Scotland MS 83 f.41, 6 Oct. 1632.

importance. The king embarked immediately on a number of reforms of state and church which though well intentioned and not without sense were, as often with Charles, enacted with excess haste, inadequate explanation and insufficient sensitivity to the suspicions of others. His separation, for example, of the Court of Session and the Privy Council, though it had some administrative advantages, appeared to be an assault on the authority of the Council, which was, as a consequence, deprived of legal experts. More dangerously, because he had to effect the measure before his twenty-fifth birthday in November 1625, Charles, on 12 October, hurried through an Act of Revocation, by which he appeared to go beyond the customary claim to resume lands alienated during his minority and to re-annex to the crown all church lands fallen into the hands of laymen since 1540. The king's intents were far more moderate than the language of his act. He desired, as in England, to make greater provision for the clergy out of the teinds and to reduce the power of the nobility who through their possession of tithes could exercise undue authority over the gentry.[28] But the measure raised the spectre of an assault on property rights and 'bred great fear of an altercation to come'.[29] No less did Charles's evident determination to enhance the prestige and power of the bishops and clergy. In 1626 he made John Spottiswood, archbishop of St Andrews, president of the Exchequer and ruled that he should have precedency of the Chancellor; he appointed bishops to various commissions (for the Exchequer, for grievances); he added bishops and the most suitable clergy to the commissions of the peace. Frustrating the hopes of many, he issued a proclamation commanding the observation of the articles of Perth, and sent personal instructions for kneeling at communion. Already by the end of 1626, writes the historian of Caroline Scotland, 'the net result of Charles' activity was that he had seriously jeopardised his chances of ruling Scotland successfully. It was painfully apparent that he had little knowledge of his ancestral kingdom.'[30]

That his knowledge was little was not entirely the fault of the king. With the death of the Marquis of Hamilton weeks after that of James I the vital links between Edinburgh and London were severed. A glance at the list of bedchamber and privy chambermen is enough to reveal that there were Scots close to Charles at court; he added to their number on the Council the secretary for Scotland, Sir William Alexander. But in most cases these figures were by now Anglicized Scots who

28. Lee, *Road to Revolution*, ch. 1. I am grateful to Maurice Lee for showing me the typescript of this book ahead of publication and for many helpful discussions. Stevenson, *The Scottish Revolution*, pp. 33–40.
29. Row, *History of the Kirk*, p. 341.
30. *Ibid.*, pp. 340–3; Lee, *Road to Revolution*, pp. 36, 62–4.

had had little if any direct contact since 1603 with their country. As for Scottish visitors to England, the elaborate formality of the new arrangements instituted by Charles ostracized and alienated them. Charles therefore during his early years depended for information and counsel on a group of bishops in Scotland. Deprived of the normal channels of communication, the malcontents were compelled to come south to appeal directly to the king. As a result of these consultations, Charles came to place his trust in one of the delegates, William Graham, Earl of Menteith, who from 1628 became the king's principal adviser on Scottish affairs. Under Menteith's guidance, it has been persuasively argued, despite the strains of war, a new era of better understanding began.[31] Suspicions of the new monarch, however, had already been excited; just as important, the growing gap between the two nations had not been, perhaps could not be, bridged. In 1628, doubtless as much for political as military reasons, there was discussion of a scheme for a union of arms, rather like that Olivares devised to forge bonds between the various kingdoms of Spain.[32] With the end of the war, another enterprise in which the two kingdoms were to join was high on the king's agenda.

We have glanced at the scheme, cherished by Charles himself, to erect a society for the fisheries of Great Britain.[33] Hitherto, however, we have paid little attention to a dimension announced by its title. Though the enterprise was motivated principally by the need to promote shipping, strike back at the Dutch and bring profit to the royal coffers, it was further attractive as a co-operative venture which might bring together as adventurers the leading subjects of Charles's Scottish and English kingdoms. As the Earl of Carlisle reported it to Morton on 16 July 1630, the design was intended for 'the general profit of this whole island'.[34] Months later, in November, a commission was directed by the king to Morton, Menteith, Hamilton, Roxburgh, Alexander and others to consider proposals for the raising of capital and building a fleet; their brief was similar to that granted to the English commissioners with whom the Scots were to collaborate.[35] In addition, Sir William Alexander was sent separate instructions to treat about the matter with the Privy Council in Edinburgh.[36] High profits were mentioned – £165,000 in the first year – and an enthusiastic response was anticipated. The Scots, however, imme-

31. Lee, *Road to Revolution*, chs 2, 3. Stevenson, *The Scottish Revolution*, pp. 17–20.
32. *Cal. Stat. Pap. Dom., 1625–49*, pp. 241–2. See also Stevenson, *The Scottish Revolution*, pp. 33–4.
33. Above, pp. 250–52.
34. National Library of Scotland MS 82, no. 18, 16 July 1630.
35. Advocates' MS 31.2.16.
36. *Ibid.*, ff.23v–25v.

diately objected to the basic principle of the scheme: the erection of a common British fishing industry. The lochs, islands and seas off the coasts of Scotland, they protested, were open only to Scots.[37] In a letter to the Council in October 1631, Charles attempted to assure them that Scots privileges would not be violated, but the Scots insisted on an absolute exclusion of the English from, as they put it, what God had given them, their fishing waters.[38] The king refused to reserve any territories 'which may be a hindrance to this general work which may so much import the good of all our kingdoms'.[39] Discussion dragged on for months, propositions and objections manifesting the suspicion the Scots and English harboured concerning the contribution of the other. In particular the establishment of a government for the company gave rise to a multiplicity of questions and difficulties. The Scots commissioners asked whether the numbers from each country would be equal and whether all participants would be naturalized in England. They objected that Scottish law prohibited the trial of a Scot outside his country; they wished to entrust the committee with no executive power and to refer all appeals arising to the Councils of the separate kingdoms, 'so as the chief power may be kept in equal balance betwixt the kingdoms'.[40] Such issues prolonged negotiations for months longer as articles, objections and counter-articles passed between Edinburgh and London. In the end, as efforts were made to draw up a constitution, the central problem became clear: there could be no common signature for both the kingdoms because they were not united, but had their own chancellors, registers and seals, indeed their separate laws and government.[41] The fishing project reminds us, as it did contemporaries, that the dynastic union of 1603 had done nothing to bring the two countries together.

The king of Scotland's coronation

The royal visit of 1633 did little to forge closer bonds. Charles must have appeared less than eager to reach his northern realm. The king departed from Whitehall on 8 May 1633, only to spend the next five nights at the royal lodge at Theobalds. Leaving Theobalds the party travelled to another royal house, Royston, thence to Huntingdon where the king lodged 'at the sign of the George'. Passing into

37. *Ibid.*, f.26.
38. *Ibid.*, ff.28–30.
39. *Ibid.*, f.37.
40. *Ibid.*, ff.56v–57: 'Matters in difference betwixt the English and Scots commissioners concerning the fishing'; also ff.62v–63.
41. *Ibid.*, f.65; cf. Levack, *Formation of the British State*, chs 1, 6.

Lincolnshire, the train reached Newark on the 18th, where the king was royally feasted by the Earl of Exeter. On the 20th he lodged at Worksop manor, one of the Earl of Arundel's seats, and while there was entertained by the Earl of Newcastle at his neighbouring Welbeck House. The occasion is famous for the masque-like entertainment devised by Ben Jonson; but the court diarist was obviously less than appreciative and more impressed by the food. 'The King was royally feasted at Welbeck House at the Earl of Newcastle's where was a standing banquet *after dinner* amounting to the value of seven hundred pound and after that in the outer court there was a speech made to the King, then a marriage between an exceeding tall wench and a very low dwarf with quintance [quintain] and dancing'.[42] Thursday the 23rd saw the progress reach Pontefract and the Earl of Kingston's residence. Setting off the following morning they gained York where, on this first of many visits, Charles feasted with the mayor and archbishop; from there on to Ripon and Richmond where the king exhibited a rare sense of the common touch: 'at this town there was brought to the King a woman who had four children at a birth, all boys . . . to the woman the King gave four pounds'. By the end of the month, the royal party came to Auckland where they paused at the bishop of Durham's house before preparing to enter the city the next day. On 1 June Charles rode into Durham in state attended by the high sheriff and 140 men. Newcastle was the next port of call. Again Charles made a state entry, supped with the mayor whom he knighted and, indulging his interests, went by barge to see the ships anchored there. This proved to be a less happy moment: when the naval guns were fired in the king's honour, one exploded, killed three men and wounded several more. Safe, however, the king travelled the twenty-six miles to dinner at Alnwick, before completing the last eight miles over English soil to Berwick. Berwick had marked the border between the two once hostile nations, and it is revealing that the court diarist paused to reflect on past conflicts, observing that the city was 'walled round so politickly that if it were furnished with victuals and ordnance it were not to be won'. The writer cannot have known how soon his words would be proved false. But the symbolic importance of the border was important to him, as it must have been to all the party. For here the ministers and officers of the royal household of England surrendered their places and jurisdiction to their counterparts in Scotland.[43]

Well over a month had elapsed since the king's departure when he stood on the Scottish ground of Dunglasse on 12 June. He was to

42. Bodleian, Rawlinson MS D.49: 'The jesse [gests] of the progress to Scotland', ff.4–6.
43. *Ibid.*

remain in Scotland no longer than it had taken to get there.[44] After visiting the Earl of Winton at Caton on the 13th, and the Earl of Morton at Dalkeith the following day, Charles made Edinburgh on the 15th, where he lodged at his royal palace of Holyrood, which he had last seen before he could walk. Now he entered in state with all the lords of Scotland before him and those of England after him, to a welcoming volley (this time without mishap) of cannon fire.[45] In the celebrations and pageants that greeted their king, the Presbyterian Scots emulated the elaboration and mythological tableaux that London had erected for James on his entry as king of England thirty years before:

> coming to the first gate there appeared very gorgeously attired . . . three angels and made a speech, then an angel came down in a cloud and gave the King the keys of the city gates and then at the next gate was another speech made with signs of peace and war and then in the high street was a conduit which ran with sack, claret and white wine and upon Bacchus and his wild crew drinking wine in bowls and healths in glasses, throwing the glasses up into the air, crying welcome King Charles. A little further in the same street was Parnassus Hill stuck about with green boughs whereon were the nine Muses which made another speech to the King. On top of this hill was a spring which also ran with wine, a little lower a curtain being drawn there appeared from the breast upward the pictures of all the kings which have been kings of Scotland to the number of 107 . . .[46]

A monarch who took so much trouble over his masques at Whitehall must have felt very much at home.

Three days after these mythological festivals of welcome, the king rode to chapel with the lords of Scotland for his coronation. The service was held at Holyrood chapel where, in accordance with royal orders, the service was conducted according to Anglican rites. The table was set like an altar, with candles and a basin, with a tapestry behind 'wherein the crucifix was curiously wrought'.[47] The archbishop of St Andrews presided with other bishops in 'white rochets and white sleeves and loops of gold having blue silk to their foot'.[48] The

44. The Venetian envoy reported that the king was expected to remain a year (*Cal. Stat. Pap. Venet., 1632–6*, p. 53).
45. Rawlinson MS D.49; see also Advocates' MS 15.2.17: 'The order of K. Charles entring Edinburgh in state'.
46. Rawlinson MS D.49.
47. J. Spalding, *Memorials of the Troubles in Scotland and England, 1625–45* (Spalding Club, Aberdeen, 1850), p. 36.
48. *Ibid.*, pp. 35–6.

only concession to the kirk wearied the English, the court reporter observing that the king heard 'such sermons that he was four hours in the church'.[49] By contrast, the occasion was a shock to the Scots. The contemporary historian of the kirk, John Row, described the dismay of his countrymen that 'such rites, ceremonies and forms . . . should be used in this reformed kirk'; the bishops' habits and bowing to the altar 'bred great fear of bringing in popery' and caused great offence.[50] The service may not have been the only cause of offence that day. After his coronation Charles returned with the crown and sceptre of his kingdom to his palace, where he dined privately. In the city bonfires were prepared for a night of revelry. It may be that on this of all days Charles's desire for privacy, or weariness, should have been overcome. Fortunately there was another occasion. Two days later the king rode to the parliament house with forty lords and barons 'which was a royal show'. The show lasted ten days, punctuated by a magnificent feast given by the merchants and a football match played between barons and gentlemen. Charles left Edinburgh on the 28th and after a quick visit to Stirling, commenced his return to Whitehall.[51]

The royal chronicler, impressed by the royal feast, with the merchants in their white satin doublets, black breeches and gold chains, had nothing to say about the politics of the parliament or visit. Another diarist, certain of the general outline, felt little need to record details. 'The King went into Scotland, was royally received, all things propounded in parliament granted, the clergy conform.'[52] The silence and brevity are both revealing and conceal a great deal. Charles indeed succeeded in obtaining the legislative ratification of the religious articles and revocation, a statute authorizing the monarch to prescribe clerical dress and the vote of a substantial subsidy. But the political costs had been high. Petitions about the disordered state of the kirk and protests against the royal prescription of apparel were entered; measures passed by narrow votes, accompanied by the unseemly spectacle of the king scribbling notes on the dissidents.[53] Rumours circulated that undue pressure had been applied and voting had been fixed; Lords Lindsay and Loudoun had their patents for earldoms revoked for obstructing royal wishes. The new tax – the two in ten –

49. Rawlinson MS D.49.
50. Row, *History of the Kirk*, p. 362; Spalding, *Memorials of the Troubles*, p. 36. See also J.S. Morrill (ed.) *The Scottish National Covenant in its British Context* (Edinburgh, 1990), pp. 2–3.
51. Rawlinson MS D.49.
52. Rawlinson MS D.392 [at end], entry for May 1633.
53. J. Rushworth, *Historical Collections*, II (1680), pp. 178–84; Lee, *Road to Revolution*, pp. 131–4; Gardiner, *History of England*, VII, pp. 286–9; Row, *History of the Kirk*, p. 367.

angered the moneyed classes. This was not the atmosphere of a coronation state visit.[54] When Charles left Edinburgh, he left a city which harboured resentments and worries about the future.

There is no indication that the king or English Council regarded the progress as anything other than a spectacular success. Charles had enjoyed the adulation of the crowds and the Councillors with him at Berwick had told their colleagues in London that 'his Majesty's satisfaction hath appeared in his cheerful and daily conversing amongst them in so princely and gracious manner that the memory thereof will remain in men's hearts'.[55] The Venetian envoy heard that the king had expressed himself 'highly delighted with the affection which . . . surpassed all belief'.[56] After the coronation in Edinburgh, hundreds came to be touched for the king's evil.[57] On his return to London multitudes came to greet him at the waterside.[58] Charles may have felt at last that he was understood by his subjects. As for Scotland, the Council in England, which had no jurisdiction over the northern kingdom, knew nothing except from the informal correspondence of those who accompanied the king. And despite the protests and close votes, the king and his entourage were evidently well satisfied with the outcome of the parliament. Secretary Coke reported 'much satisfaction to his Majesty in every point';[59] the newswriter Flower had heard all passed according to expectation, the king succeeding in making the kirk more conformable to the church in England.[60]

Though hindsight would dismiss such comments as naive, blind optimism, their unanimous sense of achievement is so remarkable that we must endeavour to understand it. Though he had had to cajole and manoeuvre, Charles had seemingly got his way and established by law the programme his father had endeavoured to enforce sporadically. Though the complaints of the disgruntled had been voiced – as they had by Melville and others in James's time – the king had witnessed the love of his people. The short sojourn in Scotland had not been sufficient to impart any understanding of the difficulties royal orders encountered or of the depth of the misgivings muttered as the bonfires of celebration crackled. After the fall of Menteith, in 1633, Charles had no trusted adviser familiar enough with Scotland and willing to temper

54. Gardiner, *History of England*, VII, pp. 288, 293.
55. *Cal. Stat. Pap. Dom., 1633–4*, p. 94; also Melbourne Hall, Coke MS 46 and PRO, C.115/M31/8155.
56. *Cal. Stat. Pap. Venet., 1632–6*, p. 122, 8 July 1633.
57. Advocates' MSS 33.2.26; 15.2.17, f.23. Contrary to the argument of J. Richards; see above, pp. 630–31.
58. Coke MS 46: Windebank to Coke, 25 July 1633.
59. *Cal. Stat. Pap. Dom., 1633–4*, p. 126: Coke to Windebank, 2 July 1633.
60. PRO, C.115/M31/8155, 8156.

his sense of triumph.[61] As the king journeyed back to England, it was with thoughts of following on a success.

The Prayer Book and the canons

Charles, as always, acted precipitately. On 8 October he wrote to Bishop Wedderburn of Dunblane, dean of the chapel royal, enclosing articles for the better ordering of services at Holyrood. The king enjoined that the dean should officiate in whites, that the communion should be taken kneeling, that prayers should be held twice daily and generally that all should be conducted according to the English liturgy, 'till some course may be taken for making one that may fit the custom and constitution of that church'.[62] The next year in May, the Lords of the Sessions received personal instructions from Charles to repair to chapel twice a year in order to take the sacrament.[63] More importantly, prompted by what he had seen amiss and by the advice he had received in Edinburgh, Charles wrote to his Scottish bishops, urging them to draw up a Book of Common Prayer and canons 'for the uniformity of the discipline' of the kirk.[64] The bishops worked quickly. By February 1635, the book of proposed canons was sent to Laud and Juxon, together with a draft of the new Prayer Book to Laud and Wren.[65] The bishops mentioned no obstacles nor prognosticated any difficulties. The acceptance of the English book and 1562 articles by the Irish convocation in 1634 fed the hope of a uniform liturgy for all three British kingdoms.[66]

Some in Scotland, however, appreciated that the calm was deceptive. At the end of January 1634 Sir Robert Jackson and the minister Gilbert Durie had written to Sir John Coke expressing their fears that the country might by the influence of some 'turbulent malcontents amongst us burst forth 'ere long into a more raging storm'.[67] Bishop Juxon himself predicted an initially hostile response, for all that he believed time would settle the business. The canons, he punned with

61. See Lee, *Road to Revolution*, pp. 119–27.
62. National Library of Scotland, Wodrow MS LXVI, f.19; D. Laing (ed.) *The Letters and Journals of Robert Baillie, 1637–1662* (3 vols, Bannatyne Club, Edinburgh, 1841–2), I, pp. 421–2.
63. D. Dalrymple, *Memorials and Letters relating to the History of Britain in the Reign of Charles I* (Glasgow, 1766), p. 1.
64. Gardiner, *History of England*, VIII, p. 307.
65. *Ibid.*, p. 309.
66. P. Heylyn, *Cyprianus Anglicus or the History of the Life and Death of William Laud* (1668), part II, p. 257.
67. Coke MS 47, 31 Jan. 1634. One is tempted to speculate on the contacts Coke made on his visit. They wrote at the time of the proceedings against Lord Balmerino for his supplication against royal policy. See Gardiner, *History of England*, VIII, pp. 293–5.

Bishop Maxwell, 'per chance at first will make more noise than all the cannons in Edinburgh castle; but when men's ears have been used a while to the sound of them, they will not startle so much at it, as now at the first, and perchance find them useful for the church'.[68] Though the canons, enjoining east end tables, kneeling and confession, undoubtedly offended, Juxon may have been right that time might have won their acceptance. What caused more immediate and more widespread offence was their imposition by royal fiat, without the consultation of the clergy. Clarendon's belief that this was the 'fatal advertency' was shared by Heylyn, who thought the orders might have been issued as injunctions by virtue of the royal supremacy.[69] Issued as they were purely by royal decree, the canons announced that the kirk was to be governed, without consultation, from England by a king who was quite conspicuously all too English and by English bishops. They aroused in advance fears concerning what was to follow, for the canons required obedience, on pain of excommunication, to a Prayer Book that was as yet not completed.[70]

By the autumn of 1636, the new book was ready. It was the work of Scottish bishops (principally Wedderburn of Dunblane) who had gone to some lengths to remove from the English Prayer Book terms and phrases like 'priest' which offended the Presbyterian Scots. Wedderburn had also advised the omission of 'and take and eat this in remembrance that Christ died for thee', in order to prevent the objection that the book implied a merely commemorative (Zwinglian) communion, rather than the real spiritual presence adhered to by the Scotch Calvinists.[71] It is indicative of the overall response that this good intention was the mother of ill consequence: the removal of the words, far from appeasing, nurtured the suspicion that it enshrined the papal doctrine of the real presence. The historian of the Prayer Book has demonstrated that nothing in it was Catholic, nor even English; 'provided that the merits of the book received serious attention', it might even have proved acceptable.[72] But before it had even appeared rumours circulated that it added to the English liturgy 'sundry more popish rites'.[73] By the time it was finally published in the spring of 1637 rumour had already damned it as the mark of the Beast.

68. Wodrow MS LXVI, f.36, 17 Feb. 1636.
69. E. Hyde, Earl of Clarendon, *The History of the Rebellion and Civil Wars in England*, ed. W.D. Macray (6 vols, Oxford, 1888), I, p. 138; Heylyn, *Cyprianus Anglicus*, II, p. 283.
70. The canons as printed in 1636, with Charles I's preface enjoining obedience 'by our prerogative royal', dated 23 May 1635 are in W. Scott and J. Bliss (eds) *The Works of William Laud* (7 vols, Oxford, 1847–60), V, pp. 583–606.
71. Gardiner, *History of England*, VIII, pp. 310–12; G. Donaldson, *The Making of the Scottish Prayer Book of 1637* (Edinburgh, 1954).
72. Donaldson, *Prayer Book*, p. 71.
73. Gardiner, *History of England*, VIII, p. 313. Some had walked out at readings of the book before the Edinburgh riots (Stevenson, *The Scottish Revolution*, p. 59).

At least as damaging, it was seen as an English imposition and in particular the work of the archbishop of Canterbury, a claim repeated by generations of historians who have referred to 'Laud's liturgy'.[74] In 1640 Laud was charged with devising the orders enjoining vestments, the canons and the Prayer Book. In the latter case, during the revisions, it was said, popish innovations were 'surreptitiously inserted by him without the King's knowledge and against his purpose'.[75] At his trial Laud was to deny the charge: he exercised no authority in Scotland; the Prayer Book, he maintained, was the handiwork of the Scots and the king.[76] It may be thought that he protested too much. Laud played an important role in the coronation visit of 1633 and was made a Privy Councillor of Scotland: he communicated frequently with the bishops, sending instructions about dress, preaching and the liturgy.[77] Charles also entrusted him with reviewing the canons and the Prayer Book.[78] However, there is a basic truth in Laud's defence. When he reported to Wedderburn that the king disliked his omission of part of the liturgy in the chapel royal, Laud gave the impression, sustained by other correspondence, that he was acting as royal secretary and counsellor.[79] Certainly Charles knew his own mind: he sent personal instructions concerning the liturgy, for one insisting on the retention of those saints' days that were in the English book.[80] Though it suited the Covenanters to deny it, the new Prayer Book for Scotland was as much the king's as Laud's. But it was, still more, the Scottish bishops' book. Laud's claim that his own inclination to introduce to Scotland the English Prayer Book had been overridden by the advice of Scottish bishops need not be doubted.[81] During the years the new book was in preparation, Bishop Maxwell travelled frequently between Edinburgh and London, relaying recommendations. In April 1635, Bishops Spottiswood of St Andrews, Lindsay of Glasgow, Lindsay of Edinburgh and others reported their labours nearing a close, adding that 'They could wish for a full conformity in the church but . . . this must be the work of time'.[82] The next spring they pressed the need for changes to the English book, and, it would seem, Charles

74. Baillie thought it reduced Scotland to a 'pendicle' of the diocese of York (Laing, *Letters and Journals of Baillie*, I, p. 2). For Laud's liturgy, see most recently W. Makey, *The Church of the Covenant* (Edinburgh, 1979), p. 17.
75. See Huntington Library, Ellesmere MS 7001, for Blair's charges against Laud.
76. See Lambeth Palace MS 943, pp. 659–67: 'The true narrative concerning the Scottish Service Book'.
77. Lee, *Road to Revolution*, ch. 4; Wodrow MS LXVI, ff.23, 25, 27, 32, 34.
78. Wodrow MS LXVI, f.36; *Cal. Stat. Pap. Dom., 1636–7*, p. 260.
79. Wodrow MS LXVI, f.25, 6 May 1634.
80. *Ibid.*, f.19: Charles I to Bishop of Wedderburn, 8 Oct. 1633; Rushworth, *Historical Collections*, II, p. 343.
81. *Works of Laud*, III, pp. 426–9.
82. Donaldson, *Prayer Book*, pp. 42–54; *Cal. Stat. Pap. Dom., 1635*, p. 4.

and Laud accepted and incorporated them.[83] Though Heylyn claimed Laud effected final alterations, it may be that he erroneously attributed to the archbishop's mind notes found on the drafts in his hand.[84] As Professor Donaldson concluded after exhaustive examination of the compilation, 'the responsibility for the chief characteristics of the book of 1637 belongs to the Scottish bishops and not to the King or Laud.'[85]

Laud himself in an important, unpublished and neglected letter both endorses that conclusion and lays a measure of blame on the Scottish bishops for the subsequent troubles. Albeit writing after the event, he claimed to have had a sense of the potential opposition to which the bishops had proved insensitive. Writing to Bishop Bramhall of Derry early in September 1639, he reflected:

> to live in the midst of Scotland and not to discover the grounds of these tumults argues either extreme obstinacy or too imperious a disposition to involve the state. But it is true too that some of them did discover enough, and were most right in their judgements concerning a remedy. And if the advice which they gave might have been followed in time things had never come to the difficulty in which they now are.

For all the defence, there is a surprising ambivalence in Laud's support for the bishops – as there was in his view of their campaign to recover their rights. 'I must further tell you,' he confided, 'that when I saw this beginning (and it was full two years at least before anything brake out) though I could not advise them altogether to neglect and forsake the church's right: yet I did seriously and frequently both by letters and otherwise, as I had occasion to meet them, counsel them to be very careful what they did and how they demeaned themselves . . . that they should be very moderate in the prosecution and temper themselves from all offence. But I doubt this counsel of mine was not followed so well as it ought to have been.'[86] Laud appreciated that the troubles stemmed not only from the Prayer Book. He recognized that the bishops had alienated powerful figures and so sharpened the 'natural propension of that nation against episcopacy'. By raising the bishops to new heights of power, by appointing nine to the Council, by elevating Spottiswood to the chancellorship, by taking measures to augment their incomes, Charles exacerbated the old distaste of the aristocracy for the episcopate and evoked fears about the security of church

83. *Works of Laud*, III, p. 356; Donaldson, *Prayer Book*, pp. 52–9.
84. Donaldson, *Prayer Book*, p. 80; Heylyn, *Cyprianus Anglicus*, II, pp. 305–6.
85. Donaldson, *Prayer Book*, p. 78.
86. Huntington Library MS, HA 15172, (Bramhall letters): Laud to Bramhall, 2 Sept. 1639; cf. *Works of Laud*, III, pp. 428–9.

property that had come into lay hands.[87] The knowledge that the Prayer Book was largely the work of Scottish bishops would have done little to commend it. Rather that knowledge placed the book in a longer history of struggles between episcopacy and presbytery which had been fought since the Reformation. As John Leslie, Earl of Rothes put it, 'the high presumption of bishops intending so great alteration on the public worship of God without warrant in law and consent of the church cannot be so well understood as by a . . . full and large information of our Reformation'.[88]

In response to a royal letter of October, on 20 December the Council issued a proclamation requiring that all services be conducted according to the new Prayer Book, two copies of which were to be purchased by every parish church by Easter.[89] Not until May did the book reach Scotland.[90] The bishop of Edinburgh was the first, on 16 July 1637, to order its use the following Sunday. Charles, it is important to observe, evidently had no sense of foreboding of the famous scene that was to ensue.[91] He presumably did not know that several people had walked out during the reading of the book at various synods in May.[92] In the words of Professor Lee, 'Charles had been given no reason to anticipate a serious reaction. After all, the canons had been accepted, the English Prayer Book had been used in the chapel royal for twenty years, and he had no reason to suppose that people would regard as popish anything endorsed by his bishops'.[93] The bishop of Ross had been using the new book at Ross since 1636.[94] But it was Charles's mistake to equate the judgement of the bishops with the mood of the church and nation. As Heylyn noted, the Prayer Book, *unlike* the articles of Perth, was never presented for consideration to the kirk or an Assembly;[95] when Charles spoke of 'having taken the counsel of his clergy', he meant only the bishops.[96] As the Earl of Roxburgh was to tell Hamilton, broader consultation might well have prevented mischief: 'a timely and careful foresight facilitates many difficulties'.[97]

87. Lee, *Road to Revolution*, pp. 163–4; Clarendon, *History of the Rebellion*, I, pp. 115–17, 137; Stevenson, *The Scottish Revolution*, p. 27.
88. J. Leslie, Earl of Rothes, *A Relation of Proceedings Concerning the Affairs of the Kirk of Scotland*, ed. J. Nairne and D. Laing (Bannatyne Club, Edinburgh, 1830), p. 41.
89. *Register of the Privy Council of Scotland, VI, 1635–7*, pp. 336, 352–3.
90. Gardiner, *History of England*, VIII, p. 313.
91. Lee, *Road to Revolution*, pp. 204–5.
92. Stevenson, *The Scottish Revolution*, pp. 59–60.
93. Lee, *Road to Revolution*, p. 205.
94. Spalding, *Memorials of the Troubles*, p. 86.
95. Heylyn, *Cyprianus Anglicus*, II, p. 307.
96. Gardiner, *History of England*, VIII, p. 312; cf. C. Carlton, *Archbishop William Laud* (1987), p. 156.
97. Hamilton MS 382, 28 July 1637.

The troubles

When on 23 July the dean of St Giles (recently elevated and reconstructed to be the cathedral church of the new diocese of Edinburgh) commenced the service according to the Prayer Book, there were immediately cries of 'the mass is entered among us'. Noise and confusion mounted, a stool was thrown at the dean and according to one 'True Relation of the "Broil"', the bishop shat himself through fear for his life as the mob hurled stones at his carriage.[98] All the evidence points to the riot being orchestrated, whatever the truth of the alleged meeting in June. The Earl of Roxburgh informed the Marquis of Hamilton that the outburst had occurred 'upon the apprehension of the reading of the service book before ever it was opened or word read or spoken'.[99] The rioters were mostly common folk (large numbers of them women), 'two thousand of the baser sort of people', as Cosin described them adding 'but set on, as it is thought by others'.[100] The riot was not spontaneous, but 'the chosen occasion for a demonstration by a powerful opposition which was already organised into something little short of conspiracy'.[101]

The following day the Scottish Privy Council convened. It was a divided body: nine bishops sat alongside noblemen who had little sympathy for them. But a riot could not be treated lightly. The Council arrested several ringleaders and ordered the protection of ministers who conducted services according to the new rites; but, on Spottiswood's advice, order to use the book was suspended, pending royal instructions.[102] Accusations and recriminations were quickly exchanged: the nobility blamed the bishops for having paid no attention to popular feeling; the bishops accused the nobles, and Lord Treasurer Traquair in particular, for failing to support them. Over the following days and weeks petitions and protests revealed the depth of resentment. A petition of ministers described the book as a plot to destroy the kirk and raise the episcopacy.[103] The Earl of Buccleuch told the Earl of Morton in August, 'I perceive as great discontentment in all sorts of people both of the best and meanest quality because they all apprehend it will subvert that service of God . . . and discipline

98. 'A Brief and True Relation of the Broil which fell out on . . . the 23rd July 1637', appendix to Leslie (Rothes), *Relation of Proceedings*, pp. 198ff; Gardiner, *History of England*, VIII, p. 314.
99. Hamilton MS 382.
100. G. Ornsby (ed.) *The Correspondence of John Cosin* (2 vols, Surtees Soc., 52 & 55, 1869–72), I, pp. 220–1: Cosin to Mede, 4 Aug. 1637.
101. Donaldson, *Prayer Book*, p. 83.
102. *Register of the Privy Council of Scotland, VI, 1635–7*, pp. 483–4; Gardiner, *History of England*, VIII, p. 316–17.
103. National Library of Scotland, Denmilne MS XII, 5.

lawfully established . . . being enjoined without the universal consent of the Kirk.'[104] Suggesting that a large part of the problem was a failure of consultation and information, Buccleuch closed saying that 'it is possible that neither his sacred Majesty nor the greatest part of the Lords of his Majesty's Privy Council do well know the errors of it'. The Council in fact wrote to Charles to tell him of the general discontent; a second riot in Edinburgh in September corroborated their report.[105] The king, however, announced his determination to have the book enforced: 'I mean to be obeyed.'[106] Ordered to leave Edinburgh on pain of the crime of rebellion, the petitioners threatened to bring the bishops to trial. The struggle had rapidly transcended the issue of the Prayer Book; it was becoming a question now of the nature of the kirk and the king's authority over church and kingdom.

The Scots, especially the aristocracy, were not yet committed to rebellion. On 2 November, Rothes, one of the organizers of the resistance, excused himself to Balcarres, that 'for all the false suggestions given out by some I dare say there is nothing either yet done or intended that is not legal and submisse.'[107] Hitherto, the protesters were proceeding by supplication. Evidently some were hoping 'that those Scottish men that are about the King will . . . move his Majesty that we be no more troubled in the government of our Kirk'.[108] Traquair was hinting in October, as the petitioners elected representatives, that it might be best to conciliate.[109] Such has been the verdict of historians: that Charles fatally opted for confrontation when he might have preserved his authority, and that of the bishops, by compromise. The verdict expresses at one level a simple truth; at another level that truth is not so simple. Having issued the Prayer Book, it is not easy to see how Charles could have withdrawn it without in effect acknowledging that he had no authority as head of the church in Scotland. The petitioners' moves to bring the bishops to trial and the demand for their removal from the Council presented a challenge to his kingship to which he could not accede. Secondly, it is not clear that the withdrawal of the Prayer Book would have appeased the protest. A document among the papers of Sir John Coke at Melbourne Hall, endorsed 'the paper sent to your honour by my Lord Stirling', reveals that Stirling for one believed the rebels were bent on removing the

104. National Library of Scotland MS 79, f.54: Buccleuch to Morton, 21 Aug. 1637.
105. Laing, *Letters and Journals of Baillie*, I, p. 451.
106. Hamilton MS 385, 25 Aug. 1637: cf. Gardiner, *History of England*, VIII, pp. 319–21.
107. Advocates' MS 29.2.9, f.100, 2 Nov. 1637.
108. *Cal. Stat. Pap. Dom., 1637–8*, p. 20: Robert Innes to Windebank, 14 Dec. 1637.
109. Hamilton MS 1011, 19 Oct., printed in P. Yorke, Earl of Hardwicke, *Miscellaneous State Papers* (2 vols, 1778), II, p. 95.

canons and the High Commission as well as the Prayer Book.[110] Viscount Conway told Harley that as well as the removal of the Prayer Book 'I think they do desire alterations in some other things.'[111] Hawkins wrote to the Earl of Leicester of Scotland, that the people 'being now stirred will not be contented without satisfaction in some other particulars'.[112] One preacher was to blame all the 'trash and trumpery' in the book on the introduction of bishops into the kirk.[113] Such statements remind us of the limitations to James's success in bringing the kirk into closer conformity with the church. They also suggest that a compromise over the Prayer Book would also have led to the dismantling of what James as well as his son had worked for.[114]

Charles therefore stalled. Refusing a formal response to the petitioners while riots raged in Edinburgh he issued a proclamation, on 7 December, announcing his abhorrence of popery and fidelity to the religion and laws of Scotland.[115] If the intention had been to assuage the discontent, it did not succeed. Lord Loudoun used the royal declaration as an excuse to renew the petitions against all innovations.[116] He and others addressed the Council, formally requesting that the bishops be withdrawn from their places on it. Traquair, going to London to report on the state of affairs, confided his despair to Hamilton: 'It would be as easy to establish the missal in this kingdom as this service book.'[117] The Lord Treasurer's advice to the king – to withdraw the book and the canons – was not taken. Charles sent him back to enforce it.[118] While Traquair had been journeying south, however, the petitioners had been organizing. Sir John Finet heard of 20,000 nobles, gentlemen and ministers drawing together 'in and about Edinburgh . . . for preservation of their old constitutions'.[119] When on 19 February 1638 a royal proclamation was read defending the book and threatening the petitioners with 'high censure', the protesters responded by drawing up a Covenant for the defence of the religion to which all would subscribe and stand united, in defiance of those

110. Coke MS 59. By March 1638, these were certainly demands that Traquair reported to Charles (Denmilne MS XII, 31).
111. BL, Loan MS 29/172, f.178, 12 Jan. 1638.
112. *HMC De Lisle and Dudley, VI*, p. 136, 30 Nov. 1637.
113. Bodleian, Tanner MS 67, f.28: sermon preached at St Giles, July 1638.
114. Bulstrode Whitelocke saw the conflict in terms of the longer story of the struggle between episcopacy and Presbyterianism (B. Whitelocke, *Memorials of the English Affairs*, 1682, p. 28); cf. Stevenson, *The Scottish Revolution*, p. 47.
115. Denmilne MS XII, 16; *Register of the Privy Council of Scotland, VI, 1635–7*, p. 546.
116. Denmilne MS XII, 19.
117. Hamilton MS 982, 26 Feb. 1638.
118. Gardiner, *History of England*, VIII, pp. 326–8; Donald, 'The king and the Scottish troubles', pp. 45–6.
119. PRO, C.115/N8/8815: Finet to Scudamore, 24 Jan. 1638.

who would cast on them 'the foul aspersions of rebellion'.[120] The Covenant, in some 4,300 words, condemned Arminianism, enjoined an oath of commitment to Calvinism and claimed that Presbyterianism was the only legitimate government for the kirk. More radically still, it asserted the supremacy of parliamentary statute and questioned the king's authority and exercise of government. Yet within days, often amid scenes of emotion and hysteria, the Covenant was being signed by ministers and people. John Burgh was quick to write to Scudamore: far from quieted, the 'stir' in Scotland was 'rather seeming to burst out into a flame unless speedy prevention quench it'.[121] The minister David Mitchell described the bond to Dr Lesley, bishop of Raphoe, as 'a mutual combination for resistance' and expressed his suspicion that 'when all shall be discharged, service-book, canons and High Commission, they will not rest there; there is some other design in their hearts'. 'There is,' he lamented, 'nothing expected here but civil war.'[122]

During the spring, as the Covenanters took hold in Scotland, the king reviewed his position. Woodforde recorded 'the business of Scotland' as 'much talked on' but 'what the issue of it will be none know'.[123] Charles recognized now the need to make concessions; he was prepared to lay aside the Prayer Book and the canons and modify the role of High Commission.[124] But he could not negotiate until the Covenanters had dismantled what was becoming, in effect, an alternative government. It is not clear whether Charles expected success. When, as he had promised in February, he dispatched Hamilton to Scotland on 16 May Charles sent him with two alternative sets of instructions: one to announce a demand for the disbandment of the Covenant; the other a vaguer exhortation to obedience.[125] It may be that, not being certain of the mood in Edinburgh, the king had to entrust his delegate to gauge it on his arrival. Hamilton reached Scotland, on what was to be the first of three diplomatic missions, on

120. Denmilne MS XII, 29; *Register of the Privy Council of Scotland, VII, 1638–43*, pp. 3–4; Gardiner, *History of England*, VIII, p. 328.
121. PRO, C.115/N4/8623, 14 March 1638. On the Covenant, see M. Steele, 'The "Politick Christian": the theological background to the National Covenant', and E.J. Cowan, 'The making of the National Covenant', in Morrill, *The Scottish National Covenant*, pp. 31–67, 68–89.
122. Dalrymple, *Memorials and Letters*, pp. 36–7, 19 March 1638.
123. New College Oxford MS 9502 (Woodforde's diary), 27 April 1638.
124. For a detailed narrative of these weeks, see Donald, 'The king and the Scottish troubles', pp. 68–74; on the Covenant, see Gardiner, *History of England*, VIII, p. 342–3. The text is in A. Peterkin, *Records of the Kirk of Scotland* (Edinburgh, 1828), pp. 9–13.
125. Stevenson, *The Scottish Revolution*, p. 89; Donald, 'The king and the Scottish troubles', p. 74; Gardiner, *History of England*, VIII, pp. 342–3; G. Burnet, *The Memoirs of the Lives and Actions of James and William, Dukes of Hamilton* (1677), p. 50; Laing, *Letters and Journals of Baillie*, I, p. 85.

4 June. The news he had to report could hardly have been worse. The Covenanters were now threatening to summon a parliament and assembly on their own authority, if the king did not grant them. In addition to the abolition of the Prayer Book and canons, they now demanded the suspension of the articles of Perth and emasculation of the authority of the bishops.[126] Seditious sermons were preached daily – 'There is nothing,' he wrote to Laud, 'but confusion amongst us and I not able to help it.'[127] Far from hoping to secure the surrender of the Covenant, Hamilton reported many now of the king's own Council (including his advocate) come out in support of it. Only force could now break the Covenant. In such circumstances, the marquis could see no point in publishing the king's declaration until Charles was prepared to enforce it.[128]

The road to war

Charles appears to have been as unsurprised by the report as he was resolute. The issue now was what he had always suspected: that of obedience to his authority. 'So long as this Covenant is in force,' he explained to Hamilton, 'I have no more power in Scotland than as a Duke of Venice, which I will rather die than suffer.'[129] Because therefore he accepted Hamilton's counsel that 'not anything can reduce that people to their obedience but only force', the king prepared for battle: artillery was commissioned, arms ordered from Holland, and a fleet organized to sail to Firth.[130] Hamilton, the king now instructed to play for time while he gathered strength. [131] Though he began to prepare for war, Charles did not neglect the strategic importance of continued diplomacy: in particular, as he confided to Hamilton, driving the Covenanters to extreme and blatantly illegal measures (like calling a parliament without royal authority) might more clearly reveal them as traitors and erode their support.[132] On 28 June therefore Charles issued from Greenwich a declaration proclaiming his com-

126. Hamilton MSS 10485, 10486: Hamilton to Charles I, 7 and 9 June 1638; S.R. Gardiner, *The Hamilton Papers, 1638–50* (Camden Soc., new series, 27, 1880), pp. 3–8.
127. Hamilton MS 553, 7 June 1638.
128. Hamilton MS 10775: Hamilton to Charles I, 15 June 1638; Gardiner, *Hamilton Papers*, pp. 9–10. See also Hamilton MS 10488.
129. Hamilton MS 10492: Charles I to Hamilton, 25 June 1638; see also, Burnet, *Memoirs of the Dukes of Hamilton*, p. 60.
130. Hamilton MS 10484: Charles I to Hamilton, 10 June 1638; Hamilton MS 10490, 20 June 1638; Burnet, *Memoirs of the Dukes of Hamilton*, p. 59.
131. Hamilton MS 10484. Hamilton regarded this as almost impossible, see Hamilton MS 10491, 24 June 1638; Gardiner, *Hamilton Papers*, pp. 14–16.
132. Hamilton MS 10492: Charles I to Hamilton, 25 June 1638; Burnet, *Memoirs of the Dukes of Hamilton*, p. 60.

mitment to the Protestant religion and his preparedness to consider what an Assembly or parliament might propose.[133] When it was read on 4 July in Edinburgh, the Covenanters immediately entered a protestation that the bishops could have no place in any such assembly, but were rather to be tried there for their crimes.[134] Hamilton set off for England, convinced now that 'confusion and ruin' threatened his country, and concerned that the Scots were 'said to intend the invading of England'. What he learned after meeting with the king induced no optimism. 'My heart is broke,' he confessed, arriving at Theobalds, '. . . since I can see no possibility to save our master's honour . . . or the country from ruin.'[135]

Hamilton returned to Scotland on 10 August, planning to divide and, if not rule, conduct a holding operation. But he encountered a situation worse than he had left: the Covenanters were now insisting the bishops be deprived of their votes, and were even beginning to levy men.[136] So grave was his position that Hamilton felt the need to confer again with the king. On 17 September he was able to announce in Edinburgh substantial royal concessions. The king, on advice, offered to withdraw the book, the canons, High Commission and the articles of Perth and to revoke them entirely if parliament so expressed itself. Furthermore, the king agreed to limitations on the power of the bishops so as to make them more responsible to the Assembly.[137] In addition, in order to cut the ground from under the Covenanters, Charles proposed a bond of faith (based on the National Covenant of 1580) by which signatories would swear to stand by the king for the promotion of true religion.[138] The concessions were real and it is far from clear that Charles was here only playing for time. As quarrels raged about the constitution of a forthcoming Assembly, he urged Hamilton to convince the ministers 'what a wrong it will be unto them . . . if there must be such a number of laics to overbear them'.[139] But it may be too that rather than being sanguine that they would be accepted, Charles proposed terms the refusal of which would expose the Covenanters' disobedience of authority and create a party.[140] If this

133. Denmilne MS XII, 65.
134. Hamilton MS 558: Hamilton to Laud, 4 July 1638; Gardiner, *History of England*, VIII, p. 346.
135. Hamilton MS 718: Hamilton to [?], July 1638.
136. Burnet, *Memoirs of the Dukes of Hamilton*, p. 69; see too Hamilton MS 677: archbishop of St Andrews to Hamilton, 9 Aug. 1638.
137. Burnet, *Memoirs of the Dukes of Hamilton*, pp. 71–2; Peterkin, *Records of the Kirk*, pp. 79–81.
138. Gardiner, *History of England*, VIII, pp. 363–4.
139. Burnet, *Memoirs of the Dukes of Hamilton*, p.74, 9 Sept. 1638.
140. Baillie noted that the king's concessions 'make us tremble for fear of division'; see Laing, *Letters and Journals of Baillie*, I, p.103.

were the case, his suspicions were soon vindicated. When the Councillors, having signed the king's Covenant, proclaimed the royal concessions and the conventions of an assembly and parliament, the Covenanters entered a protestation, rejecting the bond of faith and the proposed limitations of the episcopacy, referring their future to the forthcoming Assembly.[141] Hamilton knew what it meant: 'my chief end and next endeavour', he reported on 24 September, 'must be to preserve episcopacy, which is a task of greater difficulty than can be imagined', especially since he enjoyed little support: 'too many of our number inclines in their hearts the puritanical way and totally for the abolishing of episcopacy'.[142] Charles was less pessimistic about the breadth of opposition to episcopal government. But he concurred with his minister that those who plotted to bring the bishops down were the enemies of monarchy as well.[143] There was nothing to be hoped from the Assembly. The very day after it convened, the marquis informed his monarch: 'truly Sir my soul was never sadder than to see such a sight, not one gown amongst the whole company, many swords but many more daggers . . .'. The commissioners, some illiterate, all 'most rigid and seditious Puritans' filled him with despair: 'what then can be expected but a total disobedience to authority if not a present rebellion?'[144] When the Assembly moved quickly to indict the bishops, Hamilton announced it dissolved. From then on, the measures taken by the Assembly, which continued to sit, were the treasonable actions of a body with no legal authority. The Covenanters, in effect, had issued a 'declaration of war' (as Gardiner commented 'it was nothing less'). It was on preparations for the war rather than negotiations that energies in England were now focused.[145]

Charles had been considering the military option at least since June, not least because Hamilton (and the Earl of Stirling) could see no alternative.[146] Learning from Juxon that £200,000 could be spared from the Exchequer, Charles announced his resolve to come north in person at the head of an army.[147] Hamilton warned of the Covenanters' strength – 'believe me it will be a difficult work and bloody' – made strategic suggestions and counselled the king, while negotiations continued, to prepare discreetly and quietly.[148] Charles kept the

141. Peterkin, *Records of the Kirk*, pp. 84ff; Hamilton MS 564: Hamilton to Laud, 24 Sept. 1638; Gardiner, *Hamilton Papers*, pp. 26–32: Hamilton to Charles I, 24 Sept. 1638.
142. Gardiner, *Hamilton Papers*, p. 31; Hamilton MS 565: Hamilton to Laud, 27 Sept. 1638.
143. Burnet, *Memoirs of the Dukes of Hamilton*, p. 82: Charles I's letter of 20 Oct. 1638; Gardiner, *Hamilton Papers*, pp. 37–40: Hamilton to Charles I, 5 Oct. 1638.
144. Gardiner, *Hamilton Papers*, pp. 59–60: Hamilton to Charles I, 22 Nov. 1638.
145. Gardiner, *History of England*, VIII, p. 364. See Hamilton MS 326: Hamilton to Charles I, 27 Nov. 1638.
146. For Stirling, see Hamilton MS 593: Stirling to Hamilton, 12 June 1638.
147. Hamilton MS 10490.
148. Hamilton MSS 10488, 10491.

business very much to himself. Though he communicated 'the generals of the business' to the foreign committee, the English Privy Council was only apprised of the situation in Scotland on 1 July, when he pressed the necessity of preparing for war.[149] After all they had seen or heard of the success of the coronation visit, the Councillors, not privy to Hamilton's dispatches of despair, may not have grasped the gravity of the situation. The committee appointed to advise on the Scottish crisis divided, Arundel, Cottington and Windebank inclining to war, Vane and Coke urging caution, given the difficulties they anticipated in raising men and supplies.[150] It may be that none expected actual conflict. Windebank writing to Hopton in Spain in September informed him that though as yet there was no firm news from Hamilton, 'yet doubt not all will be well'.[151] Charles had by now decided otherwise. As Hamilton returned to Scotland on the 17th, the king ordered the transportation of military supplies from the Tower to Hull.[152] And with the failure of royal concessions to settle, preparations were accelerated.[153] Hamilton advised the fortification of Berwick, Carlisle and Newcastle; swords and pikes began to arrive from the Low Countries; Richard Delamain, 'a professor of the mathematics', was called in to advise on fortifications.[154] Though he was critical of the tardiness in England and fearful about a shortage of money, Hamilton began to take heart that 'whensoever his Majesty shows himself like himself . . . his mad people will find their own weakness'.[155] Windebank was even more confident that 'the work will be done very shortly, for I think there will be no man so mad when the King's army is in the fields to hazard both their life and estate.'[156] When in January 1639 the Council committee advised that the king go to York in the spring at the head of an army of 30,000, it was probably still hoped that he would treat from strength rather than engage in battle.[157]

English perceptions

Increasingly the buzz of rumour about the Scottish troubles could be heard around the country. Writing from hindsight, Clarendon stressed

149. Hamilton MS 423: Windebank to Hamilton, 24 June 1638; W.S. Knowler (ed.) *The Earl of Strafford's Letters and Despatches* (2 vols, 1739), II, p. 181.
150. Knowler, *Strafford Letters*, II, pp. 185–6: Northumberland to Wentworth, 23 July 1638.
151. Bodleian, Clarendon MS 14, no. 1136.
152. Hamilton MS 10796: Vane to Hamilton, 17 Sept. 1638.
153. *Cal. Stat. Pap. Dom., 1638–9*, p. 160.
154. For example, Hamilton MS 572; Bodleian, Bankes MS 54/81, 9 Oct. 1638: warrant to Delamain. See above, p. 182.
155. Hamilton MSS 575, 581: Hamilton to Laud, 16 Nov. and 26 Dec. 1638.
156. *Cal. Stat. Pap. Dom., 1638–9*, p. 63: memorandum of 20 Oct. 1638.
157. See A. Collins (ed.) *Letters and Memorials of State Collected by Sir Henry Sidney* (2 vols, 1746), II, pp. 578–9.

the importance of the news: 'this was the first alarm England received towards any trouble, after it had enjoyed for so many years the most uninterrupted prosperity'.[158] Strictly contemporary accounts, however, do not suggest that there was an immediate apprehension of a crisis – or even an immediate concern about the northern news. Some did have an early sense of foreboding. Sir Peter Middleton confided to Wentworth in March his fears about the state of affairs in Scotland;[159] Sir Edward Stanhope expressed his conviction that the business could not be settled peacefully without the king's yielding 'far beneath sovereignty'.[160] On the other hand, Lords Clifford, Fielding and Goring were all optimistic that either negotiations would resolve the difficulties or the opposition would dissolve.[161] The Earl of Morton thought that before December the English had shown little interest in his country: 'Hitherto,' he wrote to Hamilton, 'only the Scotsmen at court were inquisitive how business stood there, now the great ones . . . are most anxious to listen after news'.[162] Further away from Whitehall, at least one informant believed that those most ignorant of events were most apprehensive, 'for there is less fear of the Scots at Newcastle than at Nottingham and less at Berwick than at Newcastle'.[163] There was little in the newsletters and few in the country appear to have developed any sophisticated understanding of the issues. 'An answer to a gentleman of Norfolk who sent to know of the Scottish business' explained that even the usual informants could cast little light: 'the truth is we here consider the Scotch affairs much after the rate that the country people do the moon. Some think it no bigger than a bushel and some too wise imagine it a vast world . . . the first would make us too secure, the other too fearful . . . I confess I know not how to meet them in the middle.'[164] The writer, for all his disclaimer, ventured a perceptive observation: 'I should believe the question to be rather a King and no King than a bishop and no bishop,' he closed; 'I think their quarrel to the King is that which they have to the sun, he doth not warm and visit them as much as others.'[165]

There is little in such comments to support the fears articulated by Hamilton and the Earl of Northumberland that the English might be more inclined to join with the Scots than to fight them.[166] Nor is there

158. Clarendon, *History of the Rebellion*, I, p. 149.
159. Wentworth Woodhouse MS 10, ff.192–3.
160. Knowler, *Strafford Letters*, II, p. 236, 13 Nov. 1638.
161. Coke MS 58: Clifford to Coke, 3 Aug. 1638; Hamilton MS 543: Goring to Hamilton, 4 Dec. 1638.
162. Hamilton MS 464, 29 Nov. 1638.
163. Nottingham University Library, Clifton MS C1/C, 235: Thomas Hutchinson to Clifton, 26 April 1638.
164. Bodleian, Ashmole MS 826, f.103; Tanner MS 67, ff.53–53v.
165. Tanner MS 67, f.53v.
166. Hamilton MS 327: Hamilton to Charles I, 20 June 1638.

strong evidence that many in England were quick to identify with the Scots' attack on episcopacy. Robert Woodforde reacted to the news of war with his usual combination of prayer and self-interest. He prayed 'Lord prevent the evil that hangs over the kingdom'; he worried that in wartime creditors would call in their loans while his land decreased in value.[167] Sir Edward Montagu, whose religious preferences were to loom large in his allegiance in 1642, promised Secretary Coke in 1638 that he was ready to venture his life and all he had to support the king.[168] According to Robert Baillie, the Covenanters themselves were disappointed by the response from England: 'The hope of England's conjunction . . . was but small; for all the good words we heard long ago from our friends, yet all this time, when their occasion was great to have kythed their affection both to us and their own liberty there was nought among them but a deep either sleep or silence.'[169] Until the war began in earnest and, more importantly, Scottish propaganda pamphlets flooded into England, most Englishmen knew nothing of the Covenanters' cause or still viewed them with the contempt the English had long felt for the Scots.[170] One thing they did expect as the seriousness of the situation dawned. As the news of the abortive assembly and Scots demands percolated south, Sir Thomas Peyton felt 'Certain this is, that they will bring forth a parliament here in England: for whether the King comply or confront their demands, it is thought they will be such as the King will answer with the voice of the whole kingdom . . .'.[171]

Mobilization for war

The preparations for war had already begun to involve the whole kingdom. In July 1638, the precedents having been searched, the king was informed that he might command all holding offices or lands in the border parts to repair thither well arrayed to defend the realm, and that he might require the towns of Berwick, Carlisle and Newcastle to fortify and furnish themselves with munitions at their own charge.[172] The hope fading that such military display, together with a naval

167. Woodforde's diary, 28 Nov., 14 Dec. 1638.
168. Northamptonshire Record Office, Montagu MS III, f.221, 18 April.
169. Laing, *Letters and Journals of Baillie*, I, p. 219.
170. Jenny Wormald has graphically demonstrated that contempt in 'James VI and I: two kings or one?', *History*, 68 (1983), pp. 187–209. For equally graphic Caroline examples, see E. Hawkins (ed.) *Travels in Holland, the United Provinces, England, Scotland and Ireland by Sir William Brereton* (Chetham Soc., 1, 1844).
171. D. Gardiner (ed.) *The Oxinden Letters, 1607–1642* (1933), p. 142: Peyton to Henry Oxinden, 26 Nov. 1628.
172. Coke MS 58, 1 July 1638.

blockade, might 'in time subdue them without an army', escalating preparations began to have a wider impact on the country.[173] In September, the Council meeting at Oatlands resolved on supplies for an army of 12,000 foot and 400 horse and prepared a proclamation banning the export of horses.[174] By November orders were sent to lord-lieutenants requiring them to see the 'spare men' of the militia exercised, furnished and organized into bands in readiness for action.[175] Hamilton's relation to the Council on 15 January started the new year with a flurry of activity.[176] With the advice of the marquis, Charles planned a four-pronged attack: the Marquis of Huntley was to strike from the north, the Earl of Antrim to land troops in Argyleshire, Wentworth's men were to move on Edinburgh from Clyde, while the king led an army from his base at York.[177] Sergeant Major Astley was commissioned to inspect the defences of York, Newcastle and Berwick.[178] The Council resolved to raise an army of 30,000 (24,000 foot, 6,000 horse) from the trained bands, sparing the northern counties whose militia were needed as a reserve.[179] On 18 January Charles asked his Secretary of State Windebank to look into the Henrician precedents and prepare a letter to all noblemen, gentry and corporations announcing the king's going to York and inviting them to offer their aid.[180] A proclamation ordered all those nobles with houses in the north who still remained in London to leave 'for the defence and safeguard of those parts'.[181] During January and February letters were dispatched to lord-lieutenants specifying the numbers of foot and horse which they were to contribute and exercise weekly: 500 from Norfolk for example, 550 from Essex and 1,000 from Hampshire.[182] The size of the army and scale of the demands were unknown in living memory. The soldiers who joined Mansfeldt's hapless expedition in 1624 or the fleets to Cadiz or Rhé were fewer in number and, more importantly, conscripts rather than trained bandsmen. The call to arms for a war on British soil had not been heard since the 1550s.

Not surprisingly, therefore, many problems were encountered in the

173. *Ibid.*
174. Coke MS 59, 10 Sept. 1638; cf. York Record Office, York House Books, 36, f.18v. There was a European shortage of horses, see P. Edwards, *The Horse Trade in Tudor and Stuart England* (Cambridge, 1988). Nobles were give priority of purchase at fairs; see PRO, PC 2/50/149.
175. Hampshire Record Office, Herriard MS XLIV/23/18.
176. Gardiner, *History of England*, VIII, pp. 382–3.
177. *Ibid.*, pp. 351–6; IX, p. 1.
178. *Cal. Stat. Pap. Dom., 1638–9*, pp. 291, 349–50, 383–5.
179. *Ibid.*, pp. 323, 337.
180. *Ibid.*, p. 327.
181. J.F. Larkin (ed.) *Stuart Royal Proclamations II: Royal Proclamations of King Charles I, 1625–46* (Oxford, 1983), no. 276, pp. 648–50.
182. PRO, PC 2/50/161; Bodleian, Firth MS C.4, pp. 604–6; Herriard MS 027/2.

endeavours to assemble an army of well-equipped men at York by April. In the first place the aristocracy to whom the king had issued a personal summons had become a civilized class after a century and more of peace and so, even when willing, were not always equipped to respond. Of the 115 peers who received the royal call, only 17 returned excuses; 77 promised contributions or attendance, but few were able to offer horse.[183] Lord Arundel of Wardour for example offered money, excusing himself that he had already given his horses to the king being now eighty years old and unfit to serve, and 'also living in a peaceable estate where no man would have expected such a commotion'.[184] The Earl of Bridgewater was unlikely to have only been making excuses when he responded to Secretary Coke in February: 'I find it extreme hard to get horses and I believe it will be impossible to have arms ready'.[185] Certainly the arms in his own possession – listed as 'past wearing', 'past use', 'rusty' – were likely to be of little service.[186] And, as he informed Holland, new ones could not be made soon enough, nor was there in the European situation easy or quick access to supplies from abroad.[187] Bridgewater offered money in lieu, but his offer was refused.[188] He therefore asked to purchase arms from the royal store.[189] Notwithstanding all his difficulties, through strenuous efforts he had some horse and men ready by mid-March, only to find that the money he had originally offered was now demanded. He protested: 'I cannot expend and disburse my monies and have them ready lying by me. I have no mint nor spring out of which monies may flow into my purse or chest, therefore I know not what answer to make to this unexpected message.'[190] Uncomfortingly, Bridgewater was told to pay £1,000 and sell his horses.[191] Other noblemen were caught unprepared. The Earl of Kingston told Sir Gervase Clifton that he had two old suits of armour which he hoped 'with a little cost may be made good curiashiers à la moderne'.[192] One he offered to Clifton with the probably optimistic claim that, though old, it was better than 'any of these new which be unable to resist a paper bullet'. Kingston felt sure that once action commenced, the 'fashion' of arms would be irrelevant. His comments nicely point up how the English aristocracy had become the

183. See P. Haskell, 'Sir Francis Windebank and the personal rule of Charles I' (University of Southampton, PhD thesis, 1978), ch. 9; appendix J, 'Response of the lay peers to the king's summons to York, 1639'. See also, *Cal. Stat. Pap. Dom., 1638–9*, p. 516.
184. *Cal. Stat. Pap. Dom., 1638–9*, p. 475.
185. Ellesmere MS 6598, 12 Feb. 1639. He 'wanted' to provide twelve.
186. *Ibid.*, no. 6503; on the attempt to obtain arms and the shortage, see Ellesmere MS 7429.
187. Ellesmere MS 6601.
188. Ellesmere MS 6600.
189. Ellesmere MS 6601.
190. Ellesmere MS 6604: Bridgewater to Coke, 14 March 1639.
191. Ellesmere MS 6605.
192. Clifton MS 290, 1 March 1639.

anachronistic exceptions in a European age of the modernization of military tactics and equipment.[193] As Lord Brudenell reflected, 'long peace' had made the realm 'much unprovided for such action'.[194]

If the nobility faced difficulties responding to the royal call, these were nothing beside the problems in providing supplies and recruiting the bandsmen in the counties. Yorkshire responded promptly to the demand for men to rendezvous at York. The vice-president of the Council of the North protested the disproportionate burden laid on them, but hoped it would be 'an example of loyalty and obedience to other counties'.[195] From most shires, however, came complaints about difficulties many of which appear to have been genuine. Norfolk found such difficulty providing horses and armour that even the diligent Lord Maltravers asked the Council for more time, acknowledging the shortage of arms to be 'the common despair of us all'.[196] The Kentish men had to make do with 'muskets having no touch holes' and 'pikes . . . so rotten as they were shaken . . . all to pieces'.[197] This was a national problem: the old weapons used at the musters were ill suited for the war, and it was too late to acquire new. Sir Thomas Morton writing from Durham explained to Windebank that though many men were arriving with defective weapons they offered 'excuse that they could get none for money'; even those who had purchased from the royal stores had come with their pikes too short. Given the urgency, 'the inspectors could not but allow of them'.[198]

Selecting and transporting the bandsmen presented as many problems. Local gentlemen used pressure to secure exemption for their tenants;[199] Captain Boswell of Hampshire, acting on the deputies' instructions, tried to spare married men whose dependants might be thrown on parish relief in the event of their death.[200] Much to Hamilton's despair the Council itself permitted the counties to substitute others for the trained men when there was just cause.[201] For as a consequence, in Kent and Hampshire, the trained bandsmen hired others to fill their places – often the lower orders of society, criminals, beggars and drunks.[202] Hamilton believed the deputy lieutenants took such advantage of the clause that among one contingent 'there is hardly

193. See G. Parker, *The Military Revolution: Military Innovation and the Rise of the West, 1500–1800* (Cambridge, 1988).
194. *Cal. Stat. Pap. Dom., 1638–9*, p. 466.
195. Coke MS 60: Osborne to Coke, 26 Jan. 1639.
196. Tanner MS 177, f.24.
197. BL Add. MS 11045, f.12; *Cal. Stat. Pap. Dom., 1639*, p. 49.
198. *Cal. Stat. Pap. Dom., 1638–9*, p. 564.
199. For example, Herriard MSS F.9, E.77.
200. Herriard MS F.9.
201. Firth MS C.4, p. 612; Hamilton MSS 11144, 1213.
202. For Hampshire, Herriard MSS; for Kent, see Kent Archives Office, Twysden MS U 47/47/01, f.14.

any trained men'.[203] The Earl of Devonshire apologized to Coke that the troops he sent up had not been exercised in three months; 'the need thereof being every day more apparent than ever'.[204] In the Marches, Captain Thomas Williams admitted to Bridgewater that the men he had levied 'are all given to drink', with the (not entirely happy) exception of William Pitchford who though 'given much to drinking . . . of late hath left off'.[205] Two further problems compounded the difficulties: money to pay the bands was in short supply or came slowly, and the appointment in some cases of foreign captains and officers intensified the troopers' discomfort at marching out of home territory.[206] The Reverend Garrard told Wentworth that the troops conscripted to man Hamilton's fleet embarked very unwillingly.[207] The decision to send 30,000 men to York within three months presented a multitude of problems.

Both at the centre and in the localities many worked hard to overcome them. The Council sent to Holland for 8,000 muskets;[208] supplies of foreign saltpetre were arranged – evidence of the limited success, for all their unpopularity, of the petremen's destructive digging.[209] Some able to teach the arts of gunsmithing and making armour were sent north.[210] Artillery and engineers were transported from the Tower to Newcastle and Hull; according to Sir John Heydon, lieutenant of the ordnance, 'a far greater proportion of munition and of all other provisions belonging to a train of artillery than within the memory of any man . . . was ever known to have been issued out of [the] magazine in the Tower.'[211] Professsional soldiers were called back from Holland and Germany to instruct raw recruits.[212] In the counties, some deputies, not all known for their industry, devoted themselves energetically to the war effort. Sir Henry Slingsby, deputy of Yorkshire, who admitted his inclination to idleness, tells us that amid the 'extraordinary preparation that was made for this war' he 'did perform

203. Hamilton MS 1213: Hamilton to Vane, 18 April 1639.
204. *HMC Cowper II*, p. 228, 22 May 1639.
205. Ellesmere MS 6602, 8 March 1639.
206. For example, *Cal. Stat. Pap. Dom., 1638–9*, p. 557; Hamilton MS 690; and see Bristol Record Office, Smyth of Ashton Court MS 30674/132a: Pembroke to Poulett, 7 March 1639.
207. Knowler, *Strafford Letters*, II, p. 351, 20 May 1639.
208. Coke MS 59: Astley to Coke, 6 Oct. 1638; calendared in *HMC Cowper II*, p. 196. On the scale of imported arms, see E.J. Courthorpe (ed.) *The Journal of Thomas Cunningham* (Scottish Historical Soc., 3rd series, 11, 1928), p. 53.
209. PRO, PC 2/50/233.
210. PRO, PC 2/50/35, 49. The Dutch engineer Thomas Rudd would not budge until he had had his five years' arrears of pay (*Cal. Stat. Pap. Dom., 1638–9*, p. 515) – a nice comment on the dangers of such credit.
211. Coke MS 61: Heydon to Coke, 18 April 1639; calendared in *HMC Cowper II*, pp. 221–2.
212. PRO, 31/3/71, f.111.

most diligently'.[213] He was probably not exceptional. Tichborne and Jervoise in Hampshire laboured hard to select and convey well-armed troops. And, importantly, some who had voiced criticisms of the Caroline regime were among the most active. In Essex, for example, the Earl of Warwick as Lord-Lieutenant responded swiftly and efficiently to the demand for men, as did the future parliamentarian leader Sir Thomas Barrington as deputy.[214] As a result of their labours the 1,500 men required of the county, with coat and conduct money, rendezvoused at *The Lion* in Kelvedon on 1 April 1639.[215] The Essex and Cambridgeshire troops were found to be among the best of those sent to York.[216] That an army estimated in May at 28,000 was at the king's disposal in a short time is no small tribute to the continuing co-operation of the county gentry.[217]

The military odds

Historians have been disdainful of the army that marched to Berwick in May 1639, and it is not difficult to see why. Those sent were a very mixed band; many of those reluctantly pressed ran away – sometimes with the county arms supplied to them.[218] Robert Sibthorpe thought the king in a 'lamentable case . . . so hazarded by the desertion of those who should defend him'.[219] Several commentators were pessimistic, at times even despondent, about the condition of the troops and arms that were transported north.[220] One joker of Christchurch, Dorset said that the king had taken off to war men 'more fit to use such weapons as these, laying his hands upon . . . his members'.[221] Hamilton could less afford to jest. In April he surveyed the ranks of those who were to board his fleet: poorly victualled and inexperienced, they presented 'never a corporal or a soldier that ever had a musket in their hands till

213. D. Parsons (ed.) *The Diary of Sir Henry Slingsby* (1836), p. 14.
214. Firth MS C.4, pp. 597–9.
215. *Ibid.*, p. 614.
216. Hamilton MS 939: Hamilton to Windebank, 23 April 1639. He added 'I hear by our officers that they found best respect from the Lord Lieutenant and deputy Lieutenants of those shires'. It is worth emphasizing that both were known strongholds of puritanism.
217. BL Add. MS 11045, f.20: Rossingham to Scudamore, 23 May.
218. See Smyth of Ashton Court MS C 61/4; Firth MS C.4, pp. 624–5; Larkin, *Stuart Royal Proclamations*, II, no. 281, pp. 667–9; PRO, PC 2/51/58; Huntington Library, Temple of Stowe MS 11, STT 1893.
219. Temple of Stowe MS 11, STT 1893: Sibthorpe to Lambe, 17 June 1639.
220. For example, Hamilton MS 938; *Cal. Stat. Pap. Dom., 1638–9*, p. 557; *1639*, pp. 33, 49. Wentworth counselled delay because he believed the king's forces would not be trained and ready. See also Countess of Westmorland to Windebank, 6 May 1639 in P. Hardwicke, *Miscellaneous State Papers* (2 vols, 1778), II, p. 128.
221. *Cal. Stat. Pap. Dom., 1639*, p. 404.

their coming to Gravesend'; some among their colonels were 'no ways able to endure the sea' so, he lamented, 'I shall have a regiment of undisciplined men without commanders.'[222] If such men were put into action, he frankly told Charles I, 'we may receive an affront'.[223] Sir Henry Vane apologized for the want of victuals and good officers; the misguided decision to allow the localities to substitute men for the trained bands meant that as well as receiving raw troopers, the marquis could not 'now find sergeants amongst the whole number able to instruct the rest'.[224] Wentworth's fear that a war might be engaged before England was properly prepared was proving all too real, it seemed.[225] As the signet clerk Edward Norgate said to Windebank's secretary at the end of May, while the king was on his way to join his army: 'I think none who love him but must wish the army ten times doubled, and those fifteen times better accommodated.'[226]

Such pessimistic testimonies, however, are only one side of the account; and it has been too little noticed that by no means all contemporaries echoed them. Heylyn, for example, (even with here the benefit of hindsight) described the force as 'the best for quality of the persons, completeness of arms, number of serviceable horse and necessary provision of all sorts that ever waited on a King of England to a war with Scotland'.[227] Clarendon endorsed his judgement, albeit in less extravagant language.[228] In less despondent moments, the officers could see the potential in their recruits too. Hamilton described the 'bodies of men' as 'extremely good, well clothed and not badly armed as I feared';[229] Vane, writing from York, was pleased that 'the foot and horse that are come up are very good and the men full of courage'.[230] The discrepancy between accounts may in part be explicable by time. Throughout history officers have made fine soldiers of the most unpromising raw material, and it would appear that between the call for troops in January and the early days of June something of a more effective, a more disciplined and better trained fighting force was forged. Colonel Gage had predicted that if the army could maintain a defensive posture at Berwick until the men were taught use of their arms, and if commanders were resolved, the rank and file 'will fall

222. Hamilton MS 11144.
223. Gardiner, *Hamilton Papers*, pp. 73–5.
224. Hamilton MSS 1207, 1213.
225. Knowler, *Strafford Letters*, II, pp. 300–1: Wentworth to Windebank, 20 March 1639; and J. Nalson, *An Impartial Collection of the Great Affairs of State from the Beginning of the Scotch Rebellion in 1639 to the Murder of Charles I* (2 vols, 1682–3), I, pp. 209–11.
226. *Cal. Stat. Pap. Dom., 1639*, p. 248.
227. Heylyn, *Cyprianus Anglicus*, II, p. 360.
228. Clarendon, *History of the Rebellion*, I, p. 151.
229. Hamilton MS 11144.
230. Hamilton MS 1190, 12 April 1639.

bravely on how raw so ever they be'.[231] A letter from the camp at Berwick suggests that conditions there were harsh: there was a shortage of hay for bedding and, apart from the officers who slept in tents, the troops slept on the bare, damp ground. Beer was scarce, a crisis when the water of the Tweed was too salt to drink. As for the bread baked at Newcastle, it was often mouldy when it arrived. Not surprisingly, several of the soldiers had fallen ill: 'if they were not hardy, it were enough to perish them,' the newsletter concluded. Yet such discomforts (the poet Thomas Carew remembered vividly the 'cold nights out by the banks of Tweed') may also have functioned like a rudimentary basic training, hardening constitutions, fostering a sense of community.[232] Certainly discipline was maintained. Soldiers guilty of breaches of discipline were tied on a sharp-backed wooden horse with a heavy musket tied to each leg. Understandably they were 'kept in good order and little or no pillage done, though the Scottish cattle and sheep in abundance lie just over them'.[233]

The troops evidently received some military training during these weeks: Savile's men were praised as 'most neat in making their trenches'.[234] And those officers who had expected little began excitedly to note the improvements in their charges. In May a captain reported to Vane with pride that his men were 'in health and in heart and begin to handle their arms pretty well, and I may say we are all of one mind free of mutiny and discontent and all of them with patience endure more than I will express without repining'.[235] There is a growing camaraderie between officer and men discernible in Captain Hamilton's dispatches. Time, shared hardship, training, perhaps too the tenseness bred of inactivity, were combining to produce that other necessary quality of a good soldier: the right attitude. In this regard Hamilton had always been confident that though they had come up 'not without grudging', 'I am not too much troubled with it, for I do not doubt so to incense them against the rebels.'[236] Norgate thought the men courageous enough 'as brave in courage as in clothes'; Captain De Vic reported them 'willing to be put on any service'.[237] In April Colonel Fleetwood, though he would have desired greater numbers, could yet boast that 'if we fight them it will be the bloodiest battle that ever was. For we are resolved to fly in the very face of them; our

231. Clarendon MS 15, no. 1200: Gage to Windebank, 5 March 1639.
232. Rawlinson MS B.210, ff.36ff: copy of a letter from the camp at Berwick; R. Dunlap (ed.) *The Poems of Thomas Carew* (Oxford, 1949), p. 86.
233. Rawlinson MS B.210, f.36 onwards.
234. *Ibid.*
235. Hamilton MS 1197: Captain Sir J. Hamilton to Vane, 14 May 1639.
236. Hamilton MS 1213: Marquis of Hamilton to Vane, 18 April 1639.
237. *Cal. Stat. Pap. Dom., 1639*, pp. 12, 166.

spirits are good if our skill be according.'[238] Whatever their earlier attitude, there is no evidence of any sympathy with the Scots among the men. Many of the anti-Scots ballads popular in 1640 owed something to the campaign of 1639, as well as to traditional national hostility.[239] At the camp, the soldiers infested with lice liked to joke: 'every louse they kill they call a Covenanter and brag how many Covenanters they kill of a day.'[240] Thomas Windebank told his cousin that during a 'cold, wet and long time of living in the field', he and the soldiers had 'kept ourselves warm with the hopes of rubbing, fubbing and scrubbing those scurvy, filthy, dirty, nasty, lousy, itchy, scabby, shitten, stinking, slovenly, snotty-nosed, logger-headed, foolish, insolent, proud, beggarly, impertinent, absurd, grout-headed, villainous, barbarous, bestial, false, lying, roguish, devilish . . . damnable, atheistical, puritanical crew of the Scotch Covenant'.[241] By now the rabble had become a nationalist army 'in hope of fight which they extremely desire'.[242] The king himself could write that he would lead an army of 20,000 men 'in notable good condition, pressing hard to see the face of their enemies'.[243]

Skirmish and negotiation

As a fighting force the troops were never put to the test. By the time Charles reached Berwick, his military strategy had collapsed: Aberdeen had fallen, the Covenanters were in control of Scotland and the hopes of resistance from within, fostered by Hamilton, had floundered.[244] Charles's plan 'to force them to obedience . . . by stopping of their trade' (which Baillie acknowledged might have worked) required more time than Hamilton, off the Firth of Forth, had provisions for.[245] The attempt to enforce the royal will upon the Scots now depended on the outcome of an engagement between two forces – Colonel Leslie's Covenanters and those assembling under the king's banner. At the

238. Ashmole MS 800, ff.50–51v, 5 April 1639.
239. Below, pp. 903, 912–13.
240. Rawlinson MS B.210, f.36ff.
241. *Cal. Stat. Pap. Dom., 1639*, p. 341. Those who read the *Sun* during the Falklands campaign can appreciate the significance of this sort of jingoistic abuse.
242. *Cal. Stat. Pap. Dom., 1639*, p. 243.
243. BL Add. MS 11045, f.27.
244. Peterkin, *Records of the Kirk*, I, p. 196; Gardiner, *History of England*, IX, pp. 1–5; Hamilton MSS 10533, 1150, 1190, 1199.
245. Burnet, *Memoirs of the Dukes of Hamilton*, p. 136 (Charles I to Hamilton, 26 May 1639); Hamilton MS 10550; Laing, *Letters and Journals of Baillie*, I, p. 207. See the narrative of the campaign in Hamilton MS GD 406, M1/90: the narrator observes that 'we stopped all trade and fishing by sea'. But Hamilton realized a blockade would not quickly be effective (Gardiner, *Hamilton Papers*, p. 78).

beginning of May there was growing uncertainty about the risk of such an encounter. Verney believed the men were too few and inadequate for the fight.[246] This was not least on account of rumours of the rebels' strength. There was, however, little accurate knowledge of their number or quality. The Earl of Leicester was told they were 'considerable' and could be quickly mobilized, but that no more detailed account could be given: 'they are extremely undervalued by some here among us and as much overvalued by others.'[247] Estimates of the Scottish army ranged from 13,000 to 20,000, making calculations of the military odds nigh impossible:[248] 'many complain in their letters,' Rossingham told Scudamore, 'that the condition of the Covenanters are concealed from our army almost as much as if Scotland were in the Indies.'[249] The Scots, by contrast, appeared to know all too much of the English plans, Leslie moving the site of their rendezvous so as to abort the king's efforts to send ahead and draw men off from their officers.[250] The psychological battle was being lost before any physical encounter. There was no physical encounter. When on 3 June the Scots breached the king's order to keep their army ten miles from the border, Holland was sent with 300 horse and 3,000 foot to repel them. Believing that the Scotch forces far outnumbered his own, having marched to Kelso, Holland ordered a retreat. It was the nearest the first bishops' war came to a battle.

Contemporaries as well as historians defended Holland's decision. Sir Henry Slingsby explained, 'we could not assault them as we were, our foot being so far behind'.[251] But we should not assume that a battle would have routed the English. Though evidence of Leslie's army varied, it was less numerous and less well equipped than feared. Lord Fielding felt sure they did not exceed 13,000 'and those disagreeing and jarring among themselves'.[252] Captain Pennington too was convinced that they were 'not so potent or strong as they brag of'.[253] Later it was discovered that the Covenanters were 'indifferently armed, some of the musketeers having fowling pieces instead of muskets' or spears instead of pikes.[254] It was probably the case, then, that Charles had numerical superiority and suffered no disadvantage in equipment or supplies. The men were prepared: 'upon the first intimation of the

246. H. Verney (ed.) *Letters and Papers of the Verney Family* (Camden Soc., old series, 56, 1853), pp. 228–9.
247. *HMC De Lisle and Dudley, VI*, pp. 166–7: Sir J. Temple to Leicester, 29 May 1639.
248. Hamilton MS 844; Rawlinson MS B.210; BL Add. MS 11045, f.25.
249. BL Add. MS 11045, f.22, 28 May 1639.
250. Hamilton MS 844.
251. Parsons, *Diary of Sir Henry Slingsby*, p. 35.
252. Hamilton MS 844: Fielding to Hamilton, 1 June 1639.
253. *Cal. Stat. Pap. Dom., 1639*, p. 210.
254. BL Add. MS 11045, f.31.

Scots' approach', Norgate wrote, 'and their dislodging and new camp upon the face of the enemy, they cast up their caps with . . . shouts and signs of joy'.[255] 'They all,' according to a report from the camp, 'with a unanimous consent do often express their willingness to go on and fight . . . the chiefest motive thereto being their true love to our Prince'.[256] It was not only proud English commanders who would have placed odds on that enthusiasm on the battlefield. At least according to Rossingham, it was 'verily believed by those which were in the Scots army that if we had come to blows, we should have beaten them'.[257] Kelso may have seen the unnecessary loss of an opportunity. Several commentators concur that the English heard far too late of Leslie's approach.[258] The scouts gave no warning of their march until they were five miles from Holland's quarters and 'were almost entrenched'. Instead of crossing in the cool of the night, the English were forced to wade over the Tweed in daytime when it was so hot that some fainted. The footmen, weary of drawing the cannon, lagged behind the horse. Holland believed he saw 4,000 men, but some told him of 3,000 in ambush, and scouts claimed 10,000 and 15,000.[259] Captain Dymoke thought they had been frightened by 'apparitions', or by bands of peasants marching in the rear with but pitchforks. He regretted they had not come to blows.[260]

Whether Holland should have ordered the retreat was (and perhaps is) a matter for debate. The consequences of his decision, however, are clear. 'I was at court the next day,' our narrator writes, 'and I find this doth a little trouble the English that they retreated or rather that our forces were not set the night before . . . and that our intelligence is so poor that the enemy is on our backs 'ere we know it.'[261] One can almost hear the despair that 'they know everything to the King's disservice and we so studiously and exquisitely ignorant'.[262] The real possibility of a quick victory, which Colonel Gage and others had hoped for and which shortage of supplies necessitated, had passed, and with it all the advantages of surprise.[263] A newsletter mournfully recounted that 'men of good judgement say that if his Majesty would have taken his advantages to punish their insolencies, he might have

255. *Cal. Stat. Pap. Dom., 1639*, pp. 242–3; Gardiner, *History of England*, IX, pp. 22–3.
256. Rawlinson MS B.210, ff.36ff.
257. BL Add. MS 11045, ff.31–2: Rossingham to Scudamore, 25 June; cf. *Cal. Stat. Pap. Dom., 1639*, p. 282.
258. For example, *Cal. Stat. Pap. Dom., 1639*, p. 272; Parsons, *Diary of Sir Henry Slingsby*, p. 34; Rawlinson MS B.210.
259. Hamilton MS M1/90; Rawlinson MS B.210.
260. *Cal. Stat. Pap. Dom., 1639*, pp. 367–70: Dymoke to Windebank, 5 July.
261. Rawlinson MS B.210, ff.36ff.
262. *Cal. Stat. Pap. Dom., 1639*, p. 272.
263. Clarendon MS 15, no. 1200.

marched to Edinburgh and bred such confusion amongst them as that the common people must of necessity have deserted their nobility.'[264] As for the English soldiers, with the excitement of impending conflict removed, they 'sank into listless dissatisfaction' and a sense of shame. There was no other option than the resumption of negotiations.[265]

Rumours of negotiations had begun to circulate as the troops prepared to give battle; there were those pressing the king, even at the eleventh hour, 'to lay hold of every overture for peace'; the Covenanters were making private soundings about the possibilities of an accommodation.[266] After the abortive skirmish at Kelso, the Scots, themselves anxious not to engage, immediately pursued a peace. At a hint, some suggested, of one of the king's servants that they should petition his master and all would be granted that they desired, the Covenanters sent Dunfermline to the king with propositions for a treaty.[267] Hamilton and Laud advised he be heard. Charles refused to negotiate until his proclamation outlawing the rebel leaders as traitors had been read.[268] The Scots complied – by reading it in private – and commissioners for the treaty were appointed.[269] The Covenanters demanded the ratification of the Assembly and parliament, the freedom of kirk and parliament to determine all at issue and punishment of those incendiaries who had sparked the troubles. Charles replied 'with great temper and patience' but also frankly: 'your propositions are a little too rude; they are as much as to say give us all we desire'.[270] With the king's army still being strengthened by contingents arriving at Berwick, and news of Montrose's defeat at Aberdeen, the Scots were prepared to make some concessions.[271] On 18 June articles were agreed whereby the forces of both sides were disbanded and royal castles were restored.[272] Charles refused to ratify the acts of the 'pretended Assembly' at Glasgow (a phrase which nearly terminated negotiations), but agreed to refer all matters to a future Assembly and a parliament to be summoned in August.[273]

There were mixed reactions to the settlement. The Earl of Arundel was congratulated on the success which promised the joy of long

264. BL Add. MS 11045, f.45, 13 Aug. 1639.
265. Gardiner, *History of England*, IX, p. 30; *Cal. Stat. Pap. Dom., 1639*, pp. 367–70.
266. *Cal. Stat. Pap. Dom., 1639*, p. 123: Countess of Westmorland to Windebank, 6 May; PRO, 31/3/71, ff.71v, 74v; *Cal. Stat. Pap. Dom., 1639*, p. 138.
267. *Cal. Stat. Pap. Dom., 1639*, p. 288; Nalson, *Impartial Collection*, I, pp. 232–40.
268. Advocates' MS 19.1.17, f.1v; Burnet, *Memoirs of the Dukes of Hamilton*, p. 140. For the proclamation, see *Cal. Stat. Pap. Dom., 1639*, p. 77; Gardiner, *History of England*, IX, p. 36.
269. C.S. Terry, *The Life and Campaigns of Alexander Leslie, Earl of Leven* (1899), p. 76.
270. *Ibid.*, pp. 78–9; *Cal. Stat. Pap. Dom., 1639*, pp. 299–300, 307.
271. Stevenson, *The Scottish Revolution*, p. 155; *Cal. Stat. Pap. Dom., 1639*, p. 319.
272. Advocates' MS 19.1.17, f.11.
273. *Ibid.*, ff.4–5; *Cal. Stat. Pap. Dom., 1639*, p.313; BL Add. MS 11045, f.31.

peace;[274] Norgate reported 'great joy' at Berwick 'for the hope of a friendly end and fair accommodation'.[275] Others were much more doubtful of the stability of (and less joyful at) the treaty. One informant in the army told a friend in London that there was widespread suspicion of the Scots' intentions: 'we all believe that they did not call together so great an army . . . for so slight a cause'.[276] One preacher delivered a stinging sermon declaring that 'it had been much better all the rivers should run with blood than that the King should have made such a dishonourable peace'.[277] Many, Whitelocke recalled, agreed that it was dishonourable so to conclude when the king had assembled a brave army.[278] But official panegyric made a virtue of pacifism, celebrating a victory without a battle. So Abraham Cowley commemorated the treaty in an ode to the king:

Other by war their conquests gain
You like a God your ends obtain
Who when rude chaos for his help did call
Spoke but the word and sweetly ordered all.[279]

The war and the localities

Though a battle had not been fought, English society had been mobilized for war on a massive scale and all, as it now appeared, unsuccessfully, fruitlessly and needlessly. The burdens and hardships inflicted by the war on the localities should not be underestimated. The levying of men, in numbers far in excess of the 1620s, presented a myriad of difficulties. Essex was asked to contribute 1,100 trained men and find a further 400 untrained; the 1,000 men requested from Hampshire may have constituted at least 1 per cent of the adult male population.[280] When we focus more closely, we see that the impact on some villages and communities was still worse. Fifteen men were picked to go from the small village of Hursley in 1639.[281] The burden too was unevenly distributed. Captain Richard Jervoise may have been favoured by his relative in being asked for only a dozen men from his company of over

274. Arundel Castle letter book, no. 378: B. Gesler to Arundel, 6 July 1639.
275. *Cal. Stat. Pap. Dom., 1639*, p. 330.
276. Cambridge University Library, Buxton MSS, Box 97, 12 June 1639.
277. BL Add. MS 11045, f.38: Rossingham to Scudamore, 16 July 1639.
278. Whitelocke, *Memorials of the English Affairs*, p. 29.
279. Quoted in C.V. Wedgwood, *Poetry and Politics under the Stuarts* (Cambridge, 1960), pp. 55–6.
280. Firth MS C.4, pp. 611–16; Herriard MS 027, file XLIV, 2, 3. The population of Hampshire was somewhere between 90,000 and 110,000 in the 1630s. See J. Taylor, 'Population, disease and family structure in early modern Hampshire with special reference to the towns' (University of Southampton, PhD thesis, 1980), p. 226.
281. Herriard MS 027, file XLIV, 4.

a hundred; for some had to contribute a quarter, and 200 of Captain Doddington's 762 were selected to march north.[282] Selection from the bands was an invidious task for even fair-minded deputies, when local communities tried to protect their inhabitants and powerful figures applied pressure to get their servants excused. William Forde for instance wrote to Sir Thomas Jervoise asking him to exempt his son's bailiff, reminding him that 'a good bayley is of much value to a poor gentleman that hath great doings in county business'.[283] By no means all officers were fair-minded. On 24 March 1639 one Dalmes complained to Jervoise that a parson with whom he had recently been in conflict was conspiring to have his supporters picked by the captain for the Scottish service.[284] In a famous case that ended up at the Council Board, the Northamptonshire constable George Plowright was chosen for Scottish service by the deputy with whom he had contested over ship money and against whom he had a suit in Star Chamber pending.[285] The politics of revenge and favour may well have characterized the selection in many other cases.

The Council's permission to appoint substitutes for trained men opened the recruitment to further inequity and corruption. Those who avoided the draft must often have been those who could afford the expense of a hired replacement. That expense was not inconsiderable: Twysden records that in Kent each soldier, paid and equipped, cost £7, so what with maintaining them several days at 12d. a day until they marched north 'and all other expenses rated, the 1,000 men . . . required cannot be thought to have parted thence for less than £7,000 if not £8,000, which was defrayed by particular purses'.[286] Coat and conduct money cost each lathe of Kent £300 and the supply of magazines, powder, match and bullet still more.[287] Essex levied £2,000 on the county in March 1639 to pay for its troops;[288] the conduct of its soldiers cost Chester over £500, and even the hundred of Macclesfield nearly £200.[289] Worcester had to raise the equivalent of four fifteenths.[290] These were charges equal to, if not in excess of, ship money. The counties were evidently not sanguine that the Council's promises that the sums would be repaid 'out of the Exchequer . . . as

282. *Ibid.*, file XLIV, 5, 12.
283. Herriard MS F.9.
284. *Ibid.*, 24 March 1639.
285. See Temple of Stowe MS 11, STT 1582–3; Coke MS 61; see V.L. Stater, 'The Lord Lieutenancy on the eve of the civil wars: the impressment of George Plowright', *Hist. Journ.*, 29 (1986), pp. 279–96.
286. Twysden MS U 47/47/01, 8.
287. *Ibid.*
288. Firth MS C.4, p. 606.
289. Chester Record Office, CR.63/2/6, ff.63v, 65v.
290. S. Bond (ed.) *The Chamber Order Book of Worcester, 1602–1650* (Worcestershire Record Soc., new series, 8, 1974), p. 328.

on former occasions' would be fulfilled.[291] In addition there were other, less visible costs imposed by war. Purveyance rights were exploited, especially to commandeer carts for the transport of supplies across the length of England. Nottinghamshire, for example, was asked for an extra thirty carts, each with four able horses, in June 1639.[292] When the deputies pleaded the county's poverty, the demand was reduced to twelve – an imposition which still caused difficulties. Hampshire in July protested at the excessive charge to the county of timber carriage.[293] In Kent the purveyance of carts led to resistance, when the levy imposed by JPs to make up the difference between the real cost and the king's price 'was denied by many to be paid'.[294] Refusals to pay military charges occur much more frequently in the sessions records of the North Riding for 1639.[295] And across the country the war added sudden charges to what we have seen were already mounting local rates, taxes and expenses. The campaign of 1639 may have made costs that had been just bearable quite suddenly intolerable.

In 1639, however, financial grievances were not those most loudly or frequently heard. The greatest concern of the English localities during the spring and summer of that year was their security and defence. Since 1635 the Privy Council, not without reason, in letters ordering musters and in writs for ship money, had reiterated the potential threats to England, in the volatile European circumstances that ensued on the French entry into the Thirty Years War. Such warnings had not fallen on deaf ears. When therefore the Scots war led to requests – for the first time – for the withdrawal of troops from the trained bands, the responses across the country expressed considerable anxiety. At York where there was little to fear from foreign attacks, the request to march the trained bands to the rendezvous camp was promptly countered by a petition to the king from the deputies and colonels. Reminding His Majesty that the request was unprecedented, they urged him to consider the danger the county might be in 'when those forces shall be totally drawn from us which, as we conceive, are and have always been settled among us for our defence at home'.[296] The vice-president of the Council of the North backed the petition: the contribution of three regiments, he pointed out, meant the removal of half the gentry and justices, leaving the county in a weak condition for

291. *Cal. Stat. Pap. Dom., 1638–9*, pp. 582–3.
292. Clifton MS C1/C, 382.
293. Rawlinson MS D.666, ff.85–85v.
294. Twysden MS U 47/47/01, 10.
295. J.C. Atkinson (ed.) *Quarter Sessions Records* (North Riding Record Soc., 4, 1886), p. 121.
296. York House Books, 36, f.24; Coke MS 60: petition of 10 Jan. 1639; *Cal. Stat. Pap. Dom., 1638–9*, p. 305.

both its defence and government.[297] Almost all shires echoed these fears: the deputies of Cambridgeshire protested that they were asked to provide half their trained men;[298] in Norfolk, fears that the county's horse might be sent to Scotland caused such resentment that Maltravers had to reassure them that their exercise was only a routine precaution.[299] The deputies of Pembrokeshire replied boldly to the Council that in the Marches the trained bands were at the minimum strength needed to defend the county so no man could be spared.[300]

Coastal counties felt especially vulnerable, and not without cause. In March the mayor of Plymouth reported that fifty-six sail had been seen off Newhaven; sixteen more were sailing from Holland and it was rumoured that France was preparing a larger fleet at Brest and recruiting sailors at La Rochelle.[301] These were not the circumstances, as Cornwall, Kent and Dorset explained, in which coastal shires felt happy to send their militiamen to a remote part of Britain to fight for a little-comprehended cause.[302] Hampshire was quite explicit about its reservations. On 16 May the deputies addressed the Lord-Lieutenant: 'we do . . . beseech your lordship if it may be to spare the going of these men. Our county is a maritime port and in as much danger of an invasion by a foreign enemy as any part of the kingdom'.[303] Even when Hampshire's forces were assembled entire, they continued, they were scarcely adequate for the county's defence. That nearly 1,200 men were being taken from eight regiments totalling 4,691 was clearly a cause for consternation.[304] As Richard Norton put it to his fellow deputy Jervoise, on receiving the order for the levies, 'the cause is very weighty and requires a great deal of mature deliberation'.[305] The mayor of Plymouth was blunt: 'we conceive . . . that there is cause rather to send forces to us than to draw any from us'.[306] The requisitioning of county arms added to all those worries. County weapons were taken by the soldiers conscripted and 'borrowed' from the trained bands for the troops at York. The king's promise that they would be restored clearly inspired little confidence: Lindsey told Windebank of the many county petitions against the removal of weapons, and the difficulty encountered in persuading the counties to part with them.[307]

297. Coke MS 61: Osborne to Coke, 1 March 1639.
298. *Cal. Stat. Pap. Dom., 1639*, p. 29.
299. Tanner MS 177, f.124v.
300. PRO, PC 2/50/388.
301. *HMC Cowper II*, p. 215; *Cal. Stat. Pap. Dom., 1638–9*, p. 563.
302. Twysden MS U 47/47/01, 9; *Cal. Stat. Pap. Dom. 1640*, p. 55.
303. Herriard MSS, Box 027, file XLIV, 19. For Portsmouth's fears, see Denmilne MS XII, 68.
304. Herriard MS 027, XLIV, 12.
305. *Ibid.*, XLIV, 3.
306. *Cal. Stat. Pap. Dom., 1638–9*, p. 563.
307. *Cal. Stat. Pap. Dom., 1639*, p. 19; Firth MS C.4, p. 612.

Nor were the promises kept. When Cambridgeshire and Essex complained that their county arms had not been returned to them, the Council responded by ordering them to purchase replacements at their own cost.[308] The fears of the counties for their security in 1639 need not be interpreted as excuses. There were real reasons for concern at the weakening of the already unsatisfactory militia forces on which the defence of England depended.

The removal and transport of troops also brought back some bad memories of the 1620s, which exacerbated the feeling of insecurity. Wandering soldiers, many hired conscripts, sometimes ill-fed, often disgruntled, threatened local order and fostered fears of theft, pillage and assault. In May complaints were heard from Hampshire that 'lewd practices are daily multiplied . . . and the country [is] more subject to rapine and spoil than at other times'.[309] Through the summer, as the troops were disbanded and were left to drift back to their localities, problems multiplied. The French ambassador observed that many soldiers were owed allowances that were retained by their conductors and so were left to find a livelihood by whatever means they could; in August the Council instigated an enquiry into the abuse.[310] That the men had camped within sight of the enemy but not tasted action if anything exacerbated their belligerence and the menace they presented. For the communities through which they passed, as well as for the soldiers themselves, 1639 had been a year in which they had suffered the hardships of preparing for war, without the satisfaction of having routed the ancient enemy.

Perceptions and propaganda

The year 1639 marked a yet more important change in the localities of England: a shift in perception, the onset of worries about the government of church and state. For though it commenced as a little-understood rising in a distant kingdom for which the English had little respect, the Scottish crisis began to be debated and in turn prompted the discussion and contemplation of questions of import for English, as well as Scottish politics. Scottish declarations and propaganda, countered by royal proclamations and explanations, brought the issues of church government, the nature of authority and obedience, even the right of resistance into the forum of public debate. The Covenanters' propaganda fuelled fears in England and prompted English men and

308. PRO, PC 2/50/486; PC 2/51/58, 98; Smyth of Ashton Court MS 36074/56: 'the most of the arms were embezzled, pawned or spoiled'. See PRO, PC 2/51/70.
309. Herriard MS, Box 13, 8 May 1639.
310. PRO, PC 2/50/606; Firth MS C.4, p. 622; Huntington Library, Hastings MS 4271.

women to see their own experience as part of a more menacing plot. Wandering soldiers with their half-truths and rumours communicated a highly simplified version of events to the communities where the mobilization for war heightened political consciousness. Together with the very real worries about the Habsburgs and the French, or Dutch and pirate shipping, the Prayer Book rebellion and the 'bishops' war' induced fears of conspiracy and instability. These in turn became self-fulfilling, destabilizing a regime which still in 1639 sufficiently enjoyed the co-operation of the gentry and people to raise a large army to fight to sustain it against a foe.

From the beginning the Scottish crisis saw a contest for support – and for support not only within Scotland. Increasingly from their first statement of the 'Reasons why the Service Book Cannot be Received', through their 'Reasons for the Lawfulness of the Subscription of the Confession of Faith', the Covenanters appealed to the king's English subjects, as well as to fellow Scots who had as yet to be won to their cause.[311] The *Short Relation* of July 1638 introduced a more direct address to England, as the crisis loomed.[312] With the inevitability of conflict dawning, and the king beginning to publish his own version of events, a propaganda war was waged in the van of the armies. Rothes replied to the king's proclamation of February, justifying taking up arms against the Covenanters, with a remonstrance asserting their liberty to determine their own religion and affairs, and a statement of their own reasons for arming in their defence.[313] They may also have been behind the circulation of a forgery, on the very eve of battle: a copy of an alleged speech by the Duke of Lennox to the king, arguing that the Scots were basically loyal and dissuading him from belligerent courses.[314]

We must turn to examine the religious and political debates initiated by this propaganda.[315] But it is important first to appreciate that, even though it was illegal, it was widely distributed and read. There is more than a cause for suspicion that the puritans had their own distribution

311. Wodrow Quarto MS XXIV, ff.36–64; *Reasons for which the Service Book ought to be Refused* (Edinburgh, 1638, STC 22037); Denmilne MS XII, 32; see *The Confession of Faith of the Kirk of Scotland* (1638, Edinburgh, STC 22026).

312. Donald, 'The king and the Scottish troubles', p. 167. See *A Short Relation of the State of the Kirk of Scotland . . . to our Brethren in the Kirk of England* (1638, Edinburgh, STC 22039).

313. Donald, 'The king and the Scottish troubles', p. 210. See, *The Remonstrance of the Nobility* (1639, Edinburgh, STC 21907). Denmilne MS XII, 58, 25 April 1639. This pamphlet takes up the idea of justifiable resistance led by the inferior magistrate. Cf. STC 21909.

314. Rawlinson MS D.361, f.69v: a speech said to be delivered by the Duke of Lennox. BL, Harleian MS 4931, f.35 rightly describes it as 'a feigned thing made and scattered abroad'.

315. Below, pp. 816–20, 902ff.

networks and connections in Scotland. Smart had published with Scottish presses, and it may be that several of the diatribes against the bishops were printed in the northern kingdom.[316] Robert Woodforde was shown journals of the proceedings of the Assembly and other pamphlets;[317] Oliver St John's papers include a copy of the 'Reasons Why the Service Book Cannot be Received';[318] and Walter Yonge not only took a wide interest in the events in Scotland, he evidently knew well the 'Short Relation of Passages Lately Fallen Out' there.[319] Though sinister, this complicity is not surprising. Perhaps more important is the interest taken in Scotch propaganda by those of no ardent puritan conviction: the Temple family archives, for example, contain copies of Scottish protestations;[320] the Earl of Bridgewater was clearly well informed of arguments on both sides,[321] and the Earl of Huntingdon purchased copies of the Scottish Prayer Book, and speeches and declarations by both the king and the Covenanters.[322] The Covenanters were out to reach a wider audience; and especially perhaps to undermine support for the king on the border. On 16 February 1639 the mayor of Newcastle reported to Windebank that books were being brought into the city from Scotland and 'the same night divers of the same books were scattered abroad and cast in at the doors and shop windows of several people' [323] He ordered the town's ministers to instruct the people not to be misled. There was evidently a similar tale to tell at Carlisle, where the mayor seized distributors of Scots pamphlets.[324] And the distribution network of course had its agents in London, where the government perpetrated dawn raids on booksellers and distributors, including one Samuel Vassall who specialized in Scottish and English opposition literature.[325]

Eventually, Charles I saw the need to counter the Scots propaganda.[326] In February, a royal proclamation ordered any subject who received libellous pamphlets from Scotland to deliver them to a JP.[327] In March a number of warrants were issued to search the houses of

316. For example, P. Smart, *The Vanity and Downfall of Superstitious Popish Ceremonies* (Edinburgh, 1628, STC 22643); *A Sermon Preached in the Cathedral Church of Durham* (1628, STC 22640–7).
317. Woodforde's diary, 5 Feb., 3 Sept. 1639.
318. Bedfordshire Record Office, St John of Bletsoe MS DDJ 1409; cf. 1364; see also *Cal. Stat. Pap. Dom., 1638–9*, pp. 554–5.
319. Donald, 'The king and the Scottish troubles', pp. 153–5.
320. For example, Temple of Stowe MSS, Box 9.
321. Ellesmere MSS 7726, 7727, 7731–2.
322. Hastings MSS, Financial Boxes 12, 13; see also Parliament Box 3.
323. *Cal. Stat. Pap. Dom., 1638–9*, p. 473.
324. *Ibid.*, p. 551.
325. *Cal. Stat. Pap. Dom., 1639*, p. 525; cf below, p. 820. For Vassall, see too Gardiner, *History of England*, VII, P. 167. He refused to pay an imposition on currants.
326. BL Add. MS 11045, f.1.
327. Larkin, *Stuart Royal Proclamations*, II, no. 280, pp. 662–7.

those known to have correspondents in Edinburgh. 'All the letters from Scotland,' Rossingham informed Scudamore, 'have been broken up by the state of the late weeks to discover the Scotch abettors'.[328] Scotch posts were stopped and searched to check the flow of illicit material, and in April the 'libellous' pamphlet, 'An Information from the Estate of the Kingdom of Scotland to the Kingdom of England', was ordered to be burnt.[329] Negative measures, however, were of little use without an alternative royal account of events. As it became clear that the Scottish troubles were attracting wide interest, the king began to see the need to appeal to his English, as well as his Scottish, subjects in drafting his proclamations and declarations. From early on, Charles had stressed to his Scottish Councillors and ordered to be placed on record, his determination to live and die in the reformed religion.[330] But not until February 1639 did he feel the need to explain himself to his English subjects. On 27 February Charles issued a declaration 'to inform our loving subjects of Our Kingdom of England of the seditious practice of some in Scotland . . .', explaining his attempts to appease the disorder and the Scots' desire, under the pretence of religion, to challenge monarchical government.[331] But by February 1639 the Scots had for months been denouncing the Prayer Book as popish, and even casting aspersions on the king, in order as Charles put it, 'to pervert our good people from their duty'. The king had entered the propaganda war too late. His *Large Declaration*, drafted by Balcanquhall and distributed at Easter, containing a full and detailed narrative of the troubles, convincingly highlighting the illegalities of the Covenanters' measures, should certainly have been issued earlier.[332] Rossingham thought its publication three months earlier might well have been effective.[333] Others stressed the need for a gazette to expose the cruelty of Scottish leaders so as to undermine any sympathy they had gained. By the time it was contemplated, the armies were on the march.[334]

Religious issues of course were central to the pamphlet debate of 1639. It is important to recall that after 1628 in England the public discussion of controversy had been muted and that before the trial of

328. PRO, C.115/N9/8854, 5 March 1639.
329. BL Add. MS 11045, f.1.
330. For example, Denmilne MS XII, 16; *Register of the Privy Council of Scotland, VI, 1635–7*, p. 546; Denmilne MS XII, 65. See also, Peterkin, *Records of the Kirk*, I, pp. 70–1; Hamilton MS 10781.
331. See above, note 327.
332. [W. Balcanquhall] *A Large Declaration Concerning the Late Tumults in Scotland* (1639, STC 21906); Rushworth, *Historical Collections*, III, pp. 1018–39. Burnet said Charles I himself revised it (*Memoirs of the Dukes of Hamilton*, p. 116).
333. BL Add. MS 11045, f.1; but see Coke MS 60: W. Radclyff to Coke, 26 March 1639 (*HMC Cowper II*, pp. 216–17).
334. *Cal. Stat. Pap. Dom., 1639*, p. 233; cf. PRO, PC 2/50/271.

Prynne, Burton and Bastwick there was no evidently broad public interest in puritan polemics. The Scots' religious grievances, however, were presented not as those of a party, but a nation, and a nation of whose loyalty and fidelity to the crown there had been much report from the king's coronation visit of 1633. The importance of Scottish polemic, coming at a time when the ecclesiastical hierarchy had just become associated with savagery, cannot be overestimated. In their *Reasons* for refusing the Service Book, the Covenanters were careful to demonstrate that ceremonies (such as the ring in marriage and the cross in baptism) were popish and to claim that the English Prayer Book was largely detested by the English people.[335] The pamphlets exchanged between the Covenanters and Aberdeen recalled the dispute concerning salvation and the rifts between the clergy that had been a characteristic of English religious life in the years after the Montagu affair.[336] Soon the rhetoric of Arminianism and popery was transformed into the discussion of more fundamental issues: the location of authority in religious matters, and in particular the role of the bishops. The Scots insisted that this was not a purely indigenous debate, not least because they blamed the English episcopacy, along with their own, for the popish mass book imposed on them. Scotch propaganda such as their *Information to All Good Christians* stressed their need to preserve themselves from the popish plots of the English prelacy.[337] Preachers came over the borders 'preaching strange doctrine, inveighing against bishops and praying for the good cause of the Covenanters'.[338] The bishops became, in the Venetian ambassador's words, 'the crux of this dispute'; and others in England began to refer to the conflict as *bellum episcopale*, merging the issue in Scotland with those thought to be the protagonists of war in England.[339] Charles himself appreciated that debates about religion and church government in one of his kingdoms could not but have resonance and significance in the others. As early as November 1638, he had advised Hamilton that 'I should not be thought to desire the abolishing of that in Scotland which I approve and maintain in England': the five articles of Perth, ceremonies and the episcopacy.[340] 'We would not,' the king announced in his declaration of the following February, 'have them, *or any of our other subjects*, think that we can or will permit episcopal government . . . to be abolished, seeing it is known to the whole civil state, and most consonant to monarchical government.'[341] But, as the royal language

335. St John MS, 1409.
336. Spalding, *Memorials of the Troubles*, pp. 95–7.
337. *An Information to All Good Christians within the Kingdom of England from the . . . Kingdom of Scotland* (1639, Edinburgh, STC 21905); Rushworth, *Historical Collections*, II, pp. 798ff.
338. *Cal. Stat. Pap. Dom., 1638–9*, p. 385: Astley to Windebank, 30 Jan. 1639.
339. *Cal. Stat. Pap. Venet., 1636–9*, p. 541; Temple of Stowe MSS, Box 11, STT, 1890.
340. Hamilton MS 10520, 12 Nov.
341. Larkin, *Stuart Royal Proclamations*, II, p. 665.

betrays, the denunciations (and defences) *had* led subjects to think about the institution of episcopacy and the bishops' blame for the perceived ills of the church. And it was not only the Scots who had been prompted into such contemplations.

The debate over religion and church government was also a debate over political authority, when the king was head of the church and hierarchy in the church and in the state were mutually supporting and interdependent. The very formation of the Covenant to eradicate popery and preserve the 'true religion' was, as Charles claimed, a direct assault on his sovereignty. Its justification Hamilton thought articulated tenets 'so dangerous to monarchy as I cannot yet see how they can well stand together'.[342] It is not difficult to see why he thought so. In answering the charge that the Covenant breached a statute against the formation of bonds (of 1585), the Scots argued that some things were above the letter of the law, recalling that Esther had broken the law in order to save her people.[343] The renewal of superstition they claimed as due grounds for abrogating the articles of Perth, even though these had been ratified by parliament. When Hamilton tried to have the Covenant rescinded, the Covenanters protested and through the debates, Leslie claimed, the people were led 'to examine and consider what they were urged to obey and not to render such unlimited respect as they were wont to those that were set in public places'.[344] It is certain that some were led by the arguments into more radical reflections. Baillie recorded in the winter of 1638–9, for instance, that he was stimulated to ponder the issue of subjection and to read Bishop Bilson's justification of resistance, with revolutionary results: 'I was lately in mind that in no imaginable case, any prince might have been opposed. I incline now to think other ways.'[345]

Johnston of Wariston, though never like Baillie a moderate, also went through a self-education in radical theory during the course of the debates over the Prayer Book and its enforcement. He began as early as November 1637 to study the royal prerogative, and started to ponder the application of the 143rd Psalm:

> for the enemy hath persecuted my soul; he hath smitten my life down to the ground; he hath made me to dwell in darkness, as those that have been long dead.[346]

342. Hamilton MS 10488: cf. Hamilton MS 556. Recent commentators agree with him. See the essays by Steele and Cowan in Morrill, *The Scottish National Covenant*, and above, note 121.
343. Denmilne MS XII, 32.
344. Leslie (Rothes), *Relation of Proceedings*, p. 124.
345. Laing, *Letters and Journals of Baillie*, I, p. 115.
346. G.M. Paul (ed.) *The Diary of Archibald Johnston of Wariston, 1632–39* (Scottish Historical Soc., 1st series, 61, 1911), p. 275.

By February he was reading the literature of the Dutch Calvinists' resistance to the king of Spain and Popolinière on the history of the civil war in France.[347] A reading of Beza and Arnisaeus helped him to draw up the *Protestation* and subsequent polemic; the writings of Buchanan and Burton and Prynne brought theoretical reflections very much back to the situation in Scotland – and England.[348] By January 1639 Wariston was contemplating a new version of the Protestation, and in preparation he extracted arguments in defence of resistance from Buchanan, Knox and Althusius, the Dutch author of *De Iure Majestatis* and advocate of popular sovereignty.[349] All this radical intellectual pedigree underlay the Covenanters' explanation of their reasons for taking up arms, penned in April. For there they dismissed absolute sovereignty as absurd, denied any power in the magistrate that opposed God, decreed that princes ruled for the people (not vice versa), stressed the contract between king and subject which bound the former as well as the latter, and justified resistance from biblical texts and the writings of reformed divines.[350] Drawing on the post-Calvinist doctrine of resistance led by the 'inferior magistrate', they distinguished the unlawful resistance of the individual from the legitimate resistance of those in higher positions who acted for the whole body of the realm. Such arguments had not been aired since the sixteenth century; in an England that avoided the religious conflicts of her neighbours they had then circulated only among elite circles in Latin.[351] Now these ideas were the talk of the town, and their implications did not pass unnoticed. As the Venetian envoy astutely put it, the Scots sought to lay down the foundations for a democratic state like that of the Dutch.[352]

The effects of these radical debates on the English political consciousness, if hard to document in detail, are impossible to deny. The Covenanters were at pains to persuade their English audience that Scottish struggles were struggles for English liberty too. Baillie claimed that justificatory declarations like the *Remonstrance* of February 1639 won the Covenanters much English sympathy.[353] Certainly the Caroline government was sensitive to the danger that they might. As early as July 1638 Laud believed the Scots were plotting to get a parliament

347. *Ibid.*, pp. 310, 324.
348. *Ibid.*, pp. 314–19, 345, 373.
349. *Ibid.*, p. 408. See now Cowan, 'The making of the National Covenant'.
350. Denmilne MS XII, 58.
351. See J.H. Salmon, *The French Religious Wars in English Political Thought* (Oxford, 1959); J.E. Phillips, 'George Buchanan and the Sidney circle', *Hunt. Lib. Quart.*, 12 (1948), pp. 23–56.
352. *Cal. Stat. Pap. Venet., 1636–9*, p. 536.
353. Laing, *Letters and Journals of Baillie*, I, pp. 188, 199, 219, 226 (albeit it was not translated into the aid he had hoped for).

called in England.[354] In *The Duty of All True Subjects to Their King* (1639) Henry Peacham, observing that the enemy by libels and letters sought to undermine the commonweal from within, endeavoured to counter the Scots' arguments. His reassertion of the duty of obedience, his emphasis on the divinity of kings, were his antidotes to the danger of tumults arising from pretence of conscience. His catalogue of rebels who had been damned by God's judgments attempts to undercut the biblical and historical justifications of resistance.[355] Evidently it was feared that Scotch propaganda was permeating far down the social scale and into the provinces, for in Essex Maynard was worried about its influence on the conscripted soldiers.[356] The archives reveal that the government's fears were not misplaced. Scottish pamphlets were being collected and distributed by those who were already avid readers of English opposition literature. John Bartlett, the stationer, added Scottish news to his stock of works by Prynne, Burton and Bastwick.[357] As well as the *Scottish Scout*, letters from Edinburgh and other Scottish pamphlets, Mr Vassall's confiscated papers included the censure of John Williams, bishop of Lincoln, a remonstrance against ship money, and the king's letter inviting his Catholic subjects to contribute to the Scottish campaign in the north.[358] Similarly Robert Maude, questioned concerning his possession of Scottish libels in 1639, answered that he had had them from one Lander who also passed to him a remonstrance against ship money.[359] It was precisely such juxtapositions of English discontents with Scottish propaganda that were, literally, to revolutionize English political thinking. Even in 1639 Scottish charges of popery and challenges to authority began to place what had been seen as irritants and grievances into a narrative that threatened sinister developments which would need to be checked. As Bulstrode Whitelocke recalled, this was precisely the Covenanters' intention: 'Their remonstrances, declarations and pamphlets were dispersed, and their emissaries and agents insinuated into the company of all who were any way discontented, or galled at the proceedings of the state of England.'[360] The French ambassador, perhaps reflecting on his own country's past, was quick to see the Scotch pamphlets distributed in England as 'fort dangereux pour cette monarchie'.[361]

354. Donald, 'The king and the Scottish Troubles', p. 165.
355. H. Peacham, *The Duty of All True Subjects to their King* (1639, STC 19505), p. 34 and *passim*. See also, H.Valentine, *God Save the King* (1639, STC 24575).
356. N.Tyacke, *Anti-Calvinists: The Rise of English Arminianism c.1590–1640* (Oxford, 1987), p. 238.
357. *Cal. Stat. Pap. Dom., 1637–8*, p. 27.
358. *Cal. Stat. Pap. Dom., 1639*, p. 525.
359. Bankes MS 52/24.
360. Whitelocke, *Memorials of the English Affairs*, p. 28.
361. PRO, 31/3/71, f.23.

It was not the Scots alone who were to press the connection between their cause and the ills of England. The puritan attacks on the government in church and state had been hotting up from 1636 with the pamphlets against episcopacy and manoeuvres to have ship money tested at law. There were several contemporaries, not all of them extreme in their views, who saw that the Scots war presented the discontented godly with an opportunity they were desperate to seize, not least because they were failing to secure widespread support at home. In April 1638, a newsletter incisively suggested that the Scots troubles had rescued the puritan leaders from an emigration to which they were being driven by their isolation at home. Some, he reported, tried to drum up a petition to the king

> for removal of such grievances as they labour under, but there cannot be gotten above two of the nobility that will join in this business; you may guess who they are; so as they conceive it but folly of themselves to push whereas the rest have declared they will not join in it; but however they are resolved not to abide here, being indeed such a light as must suffer extinguishment if it abide in this so dampish an air . . . I hear . . . that they hope to find an America in Scotland.[362]

There was evidently quite a traffic of visitors from English godly circles to Edinburgh;[363] when the proclamation condemning the Scots as traitors was read at Exeter and St Paul's the puritans kept their hats on.[364] Some puritan enthusiasts like John Fenwick, the Newcastle merchant, went north to subscribe the Covenant.[365] Hamilton began to fear that such mutual correspondence not only radicalized the committed members of the faction, but more generally weakened the spirit of the English for the fight. 'I am afraid,' he wrote to the king concerning the English attitude to a war, 'they will not be so forward in this as they ought, nay that there are so many malicious spirits amongst them that no sooner will your back be turned but they will be ready to do as we have done here which I will never call by another name than rebellion.'[366]

Even beyond puritan circles, the Scots war and the debates it generated transformed the perceptions of events and the language and taxonomy of politics. Henry Spendlow, the minister of St Martin's in

362. Dalrymple, *Memorials and Letters*, p. 41. Dr Donald has identified the author as Clotworthy ('The king and the Scottish troubles', p. 184). The two nobles were probably Brooke and Saye, or possibly Warwick.
363. *Cal. Stat. Pap. Dom., 1638–9*, pp. 337, 385, 554–5; Donald, 'The king and the Scottish troubles', ch. 3.
364. *Cal. Stat. Pap. Dom., 1639*, p. 160; PRO, C.115/N9/8854.
365. *Cal. Stat. Pap. Dom., 1638–9*, p. 337.
366. Hamilton MS 327: Hamilton to Charles I, 20 June 1638.

Norwich, for example, rebuked those who failed to come up to the rails for communion, saying they were 'as ill as rebels and Scots and so he accounted them'.[367] At York, name calling – shouting 'Puritan!' for instance – suggests that the issues were sharpening divisions in the city.[368] In Newcastle the puritan contingent 'were drawing strength and encouragement from over the border'.[369] In Northamptonshire, the letters of Robert Sibthorpe reveal a society clearly polarizing along religious and political lines.[370] When he expressed his hopes for peace in Scotland, Sibthorpe did so from a lucid perception of its implications for England: 'for otherwise,' he told Sir John Lambe, 'I and such as I am . . . must expect little peace . . . if bellum episcopale as they say some style it be not ended and rebellio puritannica for I know it may be truly styled be not subdued.'[371]

Particular events brought the conjunction between Scottish and English affairs into sharp focus. In April the refusal of the city of London to lend the king money for the campaign (though motivated as much by doubts about the financial security as by politics) Windebank believed 'a dangerous consequence' to the king's affairs, in setting an example of non-cooperation.[372] The next month the aristocratic leaders of the malcontents, probably already in contact with the Covenanters, took the occasion to make a constitutional stand when Charles required the nobility and gentry assembled at York to take an oath of allegiance. For Lords Saye and Brooke refused it, protesting that it was unconstitutional to enforce the swearing of an oath not approved by parliament.[373] The French ambassador immediately appreciated the significance of their example. 'Ces milords sont estimés gens d'esprit puritains et désireux de Parlement'. Their imprisonment, he predicted, would cause a stir.[374] It was an accurate forecast: Woodforde soon heard about the confinement of 'the godly and gracious Saye';[375] Garrard told Wentworth, 'Tis our whole discourse here, notning else is spoken of';[376] Vane informed Hamilton that the prisoners 'in the court and this town are held the greater

367. Tanner MS 220, f.119.
368. See York Record Office, York MS F.7, f.39 and other references.
369. R. Howell, *Newcastle-upon-Tyne and the Puritan Revolution* (Oxford, 1967), p. 107; cf. pp. 92ff.
370. Temple of Stowe MSS, Box 11, esp. STT 1876–94.
371. *Ibid.*, no. 1890.
372. V. Pearl, *London and the Outbreak of the Puritan Revolution* (Oxford, 1961), p. 98.
373. *Cal. Stat. Pap. Dom., 1639*, pp. 67–8; Gardiner, *History of England*, IX, pp. 11–12. See R. Scrope and T. Monkhouse (eds) *State Papers Collected by Edward, Earl of Clarendon* (3 vols, Oxford, 1767–86), II, p. 45. The oath is in Harleian MS 4931, f.38. For a London merchant's refusal to swear the oath of allegiance, see Advocates' MS 7.1.19.
374. PRO, 31/3/71, ff.63–4.
375. Woodforde's diary, 25 April 1639.
376. Knowler, *Strafford Letters*, II, p. 351, 20 May 1639.

martyrs'.[377] As it turned out it was the king's authority that suffered. For advised that they had committed no act of illegality in their refusal, Charles was compelled to allow Saye and Brooke to retire to their homes.

The Scots' resistance galvanized the recalcitrants across England and led others who had conformed into the ranks of opposition. One chronicler of the Scottish troubles claimed that 'the people in England in general abhorred that wicked war as a design to enslave both nations and loved the Scots as brothers prosecuted by that same wicked power'.[378] Though the claim is more extravagant wishful thinking than reality, it is not entirely without foundation. Twysden records that though they at first appeared sinfully rebellious, the Scots'

> standing on the liberties the laws they were born under did allow them . . . made many observe that at the same time both England and Scotland did by several ways seek to vindicate their liberties, England by referring the case to the judges, Scotland by a more tumultuous way and it was generally hoped the stirs in Scotland might make the King look with a more favourable eye on England.[379]

Others not only made the connection but took courage from it to deliver a warning to the government. One John Alured in Nottinghamshire went about saying that the Scots would reform the land with a parliament and make the king renounce taxes;[380] the chief constable of Northamptonshire cautioned that ship money might raise a stir like that in Scotland.[381] The Venetian ambassador began to think that the mounting resistance to ship money followed the developments in Scotland.[382]

In practice then as well as perception, English affairs became entwined with the Scottish troubles and Scotland's resistance began to dominate English politics. The Earl of Northumberland told Coke in June 1639: 'The north is now the scene of all our news; we look after little but

377. Hamilton MS 1207, 28 April 1639.
378. Advocates' MS 32.4.8.
379. Twysden MS U 47/47, Z1, p. 142.
380. *Cal. Stat. Pap. Dom., 1637–8*, p. 558.
381. *Ibid.*, pp. 560–61. See also BL Add. MS 11045, ff.1, 7.
382. *Cal. Stat. Pap. Venet., 1636–9*, p. 430; cf. H. Parker, *The Case of Ship Money Briefly Discoursed* (1640, STC 19215), p. 28. No wonder Windebank told Hamilton he strove to interrupt 'that dangerous intelligence which is too notoriously held between the ill affected of both nations' (*Cal. Stat. Pap. Dom., 1638–9*, p. 593). Valentine wrote significantly that the king's enemies at home were 'entered into a *Covenant* against him' (*God Save the King*, p. 35).

what comes from thence.'[383] In a letter to the Earl of Bridgewater, John Castle reported the news that 'the theatre for these kingdoms has now for a good while been chiefly placed at Edinburgh'.[384] His metaphor was apt. The drama of politics was now no longer directed by the king and framed within a proscenium arch of order at Whitehall. Others were taking the lead, speaking a very different language, acting new parts which were far removed from the ideals represented at court. The order of masque was giving way to confusion; some began to perceive it could only end in tragedy. A newsletter from the camp at Berwick scripted the plot that the nation was soon to enact: 'the contempt of religion brings discord and confusion, treadeth virtue underfoot, giveth authority unto vice and soweth quarrels and dissentions amongst men . . . and in the end open and civil wars'.[385]

383. Coke MS 62, 6 June 1639 (not in calendar). Cf. Hamilton MS 815: Hamilton to Vane, 17 May 1639, 'the North is now the seat of all the news . . .'.
384. Ellesmere MS 7809, 24 Oct. 1639.
385. Rawlinson MS B.210, ff.36.ff.

XIV
'A VERY ILL TIME': FOREIGN AFFAIRS, FACTIONS AND FEARS

'A more obliging way' to *Spain*

The Prayer Book rebellion and war in Scotland became the focus not only of British affairs. When Castle wrote to tell the Earl of Bridgewater that the theatre of affairs was now placed in Edinburgh, he concluded by observing that the audience was not only British but international: 'what should be acted there has been the expectation of all the princes in Christendom who are to frame the scene of their own interests accordingly.'[1] He did not exaggerate. The Scottish crisis rearranged the position of England and consequently of other actors on the diplomatic stage; and it redirected the course of English foreign policy in a manner that was in turn to have serious consequences for domestic politics too. From 1637 Charles's problems at home and abroad not only became inseparable: each began to complicate and exacerbate the other, tying the king in the knot that they formed.

Though the delays at Paris had begun to create unease, Charles I, when the Prayer Book was first used in St Giles's in the summer of 1637, was still hopeful of the French alliance and intent on putting his nephew to sea at the head of a fleet. Sir John Finet, indeed, was expecting at the end of June 'our King and that of France . . . instantly to declare and execute both by sea and by land for their confederation offensive and defensive against the house of Austria'.[2] The diet at Hamburg to which Richelieu had referred the treaty for ratification by French allies (the Dutch, the Swedes and the princes) was scheduled for the summer of 1638.[3] However, over the course of the year between

1. Huntington Library, Ellesmere MS 7809, 24 Oct. 1639.
2. PRO, C.115/N8/8805: Finet to Scudamore, 13 June 1637.
3. S.R. Gardiner, *History of England from the Accession of James I to the Outbreak of the Civil War, 1603–42* (10 vols, 1883–4), VIII, pp. 375–6.

the riot at Edinburgh and the Congress at Hamburg, the tide of English foreign policy was turned and a sea change reoriented England once again from belligerent to pacific courses and from France towards Spain.

In the first place the Scotch imbroglio increasingly rendered it unlikely that England would be able to contribute the ships and men agreed in the French treaty. By corollary it also virtually guaranteed English neutrality and removed the fear in France and Spain that English forces might be secured by the one against the other. In August, the Venetian ambassador Correr, reporting to the Doge and Senate on the news from Scotland, commented on the sudden shift of perspective that ensued: 'how little occasion they have here to think of foreign affairs!'[4] Though news in October of the surrender of Breda made the French alliance still more inviting, Correr began to doubt it: 'Their chief attention is now directed to Scottish affairs . . .'.[5] As attempts to settle affairs in the north came to naught, the realization grew that England might long be embroiled in intestine struggles. By the summer of 1638 Windebank, informing Hamilton of the latest developments in the old plan for a joint restoration of Lorraine and the Palatinate, closed his letter with the realistic sense that 'we have reason in the first place to look to the fire in our own bowels'.[6] As a letter to the Scots explained in July: 'all designs foreign receive a stoppage until it be seen wherein yours will determine'.[7]

To an extent the French treaty was the first casualty of the Scots troubles. As early as September 1637 the Venetian envoy was reporting that an alliance with France was 'now only mentioned under the breath'.[8] Among English Councillors there was more optimism. Windebank was expecting Bellièvres to conclude in December.[9] But the French were now delaying, waiting on events, and relations were beginning to sour. Coke voiced the frustration of others when he pointed out that 'if the French were as eager . . . as the English . . . the world would not have occasion to stand waiting'.[10] The formalities were maintained: Roe was dispatched to Hamburg with power to promise concessions to the Dutch to bring them in. Leicester, however, began to express his anger that what had been promised was not

4. *Calendar of State Papers Venetian* [*Cal. Stat. Pap. Venet.*], *1636–9*, p. 259.
5. *Ibid.*, p. 288, 16 Oct. 1637.
6. Scottish Record Office, GD 406/1, Hamilton MS no. 423, 25 June.
7. D. Dalrymple, *Memorials and Letters Relating to the History of Britain in the Reign of Charles I* (Glasgow, 1766), p. 41. The author of this letter has been identified as Sir John Clotworthy. See above, p. 821, note 362.
8. *Cal. Stat. Pap. Venet., 1636–9*, p. 274.
9. R. Scrope and T. Monkhouse (eds) *State Papers Collected by Edward, Earl of Clarendon* (3 vols, Oxford, 1767–86), II, p. 5.
10. *Cal. Stat. Pap. Venet., 1636–9*, p. 323.

being fulfilled: 'whosoever treats in France,' he half-defended himself to Windebank, 'shall meet with dark passages enough'.[11] He was also becoming more suspicious of their plans, as French troops marched into Picardy – 'if at this time they meddle too much with Flanders,' he cautioned, 'I think his majesty will have some reason to take it unkindly.'[12] There were other causes of suspicion and things to take unkindly. From the beginning of the Scottish trouble, Charles I and several of his ministers began to think that the French fomented the resistance there. The French were old allies of the Scots, and only recently friends with England. Even in 1631 the Venetian envoy had noted the English concern that France had a strong party in Scotland.[13] By the summer of 1638 Hamilton was warning his master that the Gauls had not forgotten the events at Rhé and La Rochelle and were not without links with the Covenanters.[14] The Earl of Leicester was briefed to investigate, but found no definite evidence.[15] Still the suspicions of French and Dutch aid (later to be confirmed) grew to obstruct the finalization of the Anglo-French treaty and to incline the king to hearken to other voices.[16]

Since Arundel's return Charles had dismissed the overtures of the Habsburgs. Within a few short weeks of the outbreak of rebellion in Scotland, however, the Habsburg option was back on the table. As the foreign committee saw that the French treaty was in limbo and that domestic preoccupations impeded military action, the only alternative course for the recovery of the Palatinate appeared to be the resumption of diplomatic negotiations with Spain.[17] The Habsburgs' losses and defeats raised hopes that they might be ready to offer better terms. But there was really no alternative. The Privy Council was unanimous that diplomacy was preferable to war: 'seeing the uncertainty of the alliance with the most Christian which he has not yet signed and the allies not ratified and with Scotland so disturbed'.[18] The expected arrival of the Duchess of Chevreuse and the Queen Mother in the winter (though not welcome to Charles) further distanced England from Richelieu and smoothed the way for negotiation with Spain, to whose cause Marie de Medici was committed.[19] In February 1638 it was decided to send Hopton back to Spain as ambassador.[20] Lord Aston himself seemed

11. A. Collins (ed.) *Letters and Memorials of State Collected by Sir Henry Sidney* (2 vols, 1746), II, p. 547, 11/21 May 1638.
12. *Ibid.*
13. *Cal. Stat. Pap. Venet., 1629–32*, p. 523.
14. Hamilton MS 327, 20 June 1638.
15. Collins, *Letters and Memorials*, II, p. 562: Leicester to Windebank, 29 June/11 July 1638.
16. Below, pp. 829, 833.
17. See *Cal. Stat. Pap. Venet., 1636–9*, pp. 269, 289.
18. *Ibid.*, p. 294, 24 Oct. 1637.
19. *Ibid.*, p. 276; *Clarendon State Papers*, II, p. 2.
20. *Cal. Stat. Pap. Venet., 1636–9*, p. 374.

surprised and uncertain what change had taken place since the cold war of the winter of 1636–7. Hopton's coming, he told Windebank, would signal to Madrid that His Majesty had 'changed his resolutions and intends to go a sweeter and more obliging way with them'.[21] Friendlier relations were indeed being re-established with the Habsburgs – and not only with Madrid. At Brussels the Princess Phalsburg had taken up the negotiation of the exchange of the Palatinate and Lorraine.[22] In October, Gerbier came from the Low Countries with details of the proposals.[23] In Vienna, John Taylor was anxious to oil the wheels. Scolded in March for his excessive optimism about imperial friendship, he felt triumphantly vindicated at the news of Anglo-Spanish rapprochement. Though the French treaty was still formally in progress, Taylor sensed that the Scots war had all but put paid to it.[24] In May he felt able to reiterate his old advice: 'take heed,' he wrote to Windebank, 'you do not more harm unto yourselves by advancing the greatness of France and Holland . . .'.[25]

The reopened Spanish negotiations soon encountered the same difficulties as the French treaty. On 5 June Hopton, recently arrived in Spain, wrote to Windebank that at a recent audience with Olivares, the Condé Ducque had asked 'many questions' about the troubles in Scotland.[26] Spain's interest, Hopton knew, still lay in recruiting Irish troops and in securing the support of the English fleet, and the mounting crisis in Scotland made it apparent that Charles would be unable to spare either.[27] Even Taylor, after his initial enthusiasm, began to see the clouds of Scotland darken across his dream. News of the Scots' resistance, he wrote in August, was plentiful in Prague and Vienna; he hoped the Scots would settle soon for 'it doth hurt abroad'.[28] Neither Hopton nor Taylor progressed far with their negotiations and both blamed the Scots for their frustrations. They 'took a very ill time', Hopton wrote to Cottington.[29] Taylor, as usual, was more extravagant: the devil had raised the Scots, he protested to Windebank, to rob Charles of the greatest renown that might have come to him – presumably the satisfaction of restoring the Palatinate.[30] Over-dramatic and over-optimistic as he was, Taylor was not entirely wrong. As the more cautious and astute Hopton realized, Spain still desired England's

21. Bodleian, Clarendon MS 14, no. 1073: Aston to Windebank, 3 April 1638.
22. *Clarendon State Papers*, II, p. 16.
23. *Cal. Stat. Pap. Venet., 1636–9*, p. 457.
24. Clarendon MS 14, no. 1069: Windebank to Taylor, 30 March 1638.
25. *Ibid.*, no. 1084.
26. *Ibid.*, no. 1098.
27. Cf. *ibid.*, nos 1105, 1113.
28. Clarendon MS 14, no. 1117, 3 Aug. 1638.
29. Clarendon MS 15, no. 1195, 28 Feb. 1639.
30. *Ibid.*, no. 1199: Taylor to Windebank, 2 March 1639.

friendship but believed now they could have it without needing to purchase it.[31] England had nothing to bargain with now its fleet was committed and its domestic peace shattered.

With preparations for the campaign against the Scots as their first priority, the king and Council during the early months of 1639 reverted to playing off France against Spain whilst staying out of any European engagements. Leicester continued to advertise the French of his master's favours to them, and even recovered at times an optimism that 'this state is really and fully resolved to conclude and join with us'.[32] In England, the French ambassador, Bellièvres, was not ignorant of the rapprochement between England and the Habsburgs, nor of the fact that Spain was stirring rumours that France aided the Scots.[33] His brief, however, was if possible to obtain the levies of Scottish and Irish troops which had been promised in 1637.[34] Charles's negotiations with Brussels and Madrid also caused him concern, especially as his intelligence told him that most of the English Council was behind them.[35] If the treaty with England was floundering, it was essential to ensure England remained in impotent neutrality, unable to assist the Habsburgs. Conveying to Richelieu his fear that if Scotland were to settle, England might now plot against France, Bellièvres advised the cardinal to encourage the Covenanters and renew the 'auld alliance'.[36] By the summer, the French envoy was in correspondence with Leslie and Argyle, manoeuvring for their assistance with the recruitment of troops for French armies.[37] The fears of French dealings with the rebels had become a reality.

During the same months, Charles was explaining to Philip IV that his treating with France was but form and contained nothing of disadvantage to the Habsburgs.[38] For all the disingenuity of that claim, it suited Spain to listen. The strength of their enemies once again pointed up the advantage of England's friendship, especially when the defeat of Bernhard of Weimar closed the Rhine valley to Spanish troops, and left the Channel the only route to the Low Countries.[39] The mounting French threat to Flanders compounded their problems. In February moves towards a reconciliation were made in earnest. The

31. *Ibid.*, no. 1203: Hopton to Windebank, 9 March 1639.
32. Collins, *Letters and Memorials*, II, p. 605, 25 Aug./2 Sept. 1639.
33. PRO, French transcripts, 31/3/71, ff.11–11v, 36.
34. Above, pp. 526–30.
35. PRO, 31/3/71, f.85. Most of the English Privy Council, he noted, received Spanish pensions. This had been the case in James's reign too.
36. *Ibid.*, ff.85, 95.
37. *Ibid.*, f.108.
38. H. Lonchay (ed.) *Correspondance de la cour d'Espagne sur les affaires des Pays Bas au XVII siècle, III* (Brussels, 1930), p. 288, no. 843.
39. See Gardiner, *History of England*, IX, p. 57.

Cardinal Infant liaised with Philip IV over the dealings with England. Whilst there could be no question of the Electoral dignity being surrendered, he thought that Bavaria might be compensated for the surrender of his land in the Palatinate, and that faced with the Scots troubles, England might be disposed to accept such a compromise and ultimately come to the Habsburgs' aid.[40] From Brussels the Princess Phalsburg now formally proposed that the Elector Palatine be restored to his dignity and estates in return for English aid in bringing the allies off from France and effecting a peace.[41] In the circumstances the propositions were not unattractive, especially when the Cardinal Infant was also making vague noises to an English colonel in his service that troops might be found to aid Charles against the Scots.[42] In England there were those advising acceptance. The Duchess of Chevreuse was pressing a Habsburg marriage alliance, and the queen (under her influence) was said to find the terms 'most acceptable'.[43] Charles therefore in March instructed Hopton to treat privately in Spain concerning the Phalsburg proposals.[44] What Hopton reported raised little hope. The letters he had from Vienna and Brussels inclined him to think that the Spaniards were 'juggling', and were too 'adoring of the golden calf' of Bavaria to be sincere.[45] On the Spanish side, as on the French, there seemed little cause for optimism.

In May 1639, as the armies were marching to Berwick, Windebank weighed up the foreign situation in position papers sent north to the king. The French ambassador had been protesting at the treating at Brussels. To suspend it, however, Windebank argued, would be for the king to cast himself entirely on the French 'and what sure foundation you can have there, considering how you have been used in a treaty now above two years, I most humbly submit to your Majesty's wisdom'.[46] On the other hand, acceptance of the propositions from Brussels would almost certainly put an end to any hopes of negotiations at Hamburg:

> Whereof though there be little good to be expected, yet if it be once known your Majesty hath deserted it, beside your being on the other side cast wholly upon the Spaniard (and what sure foundation can be expected there so many years' experience of their amusing treaties shows) your Majesty will bring yourself into jealousy with

40. Lonchay, *Correspondance*, p. 292, no. 857, 27 Feb. 1639; cf. *ibid.*, p. 280, no. 815.
41. *Clarendon State Papers*, II, pp. 16–17.
42. *Ibid.*, p. 21: Colonel Gage to Mr George Gage, 5 Feb. 1639, Brussels; cf. p. 23.
43. *Cal. Stat. Pap. Venet., 1636–9*, pp. 523, 543.
44. Clarendon MS 16, no. 1212: instructions to Hopton, 26 March 1639. See also *Clarendon State Papers*, II, p. 23: instructions to Colonel Gage, 5 Feb. 1639.
45. Clarendon MS 16, no. 1219: Hopton to Windebank, 6/16 April 1639.
46. *Clarendon State Papers*, II, pp. 48–50: Windebank to Charles I, 31 May.

> the French and the Hollanders and most of the Protestant party, whereof as your business now stands in Scotland you have little need.[47]

If the advice was pessimistic, it was also astute and frank: England could place no trust in either party, nor with its current difficulties could it afford to alienate either. All diplomacy waited on the settlement of Scotland.

Rumours of a negotiated settlement had begun to circulate even as the troops prepared to give battle. Bellièvres reported the progress of talks throughout June and on 7 July announced a peace settlement.[48] By the end of the month, Windebank at last felt sure enough of the end of hostilities to report it to Hopton.[49] To England's envoys in France and Spain it was especially welcome news: England would once again be courted by all sides. The Treaty of Berwick, however, did not see a simple return to pre-war diplomacy. During the months of the Scots troubles, England had turned back to the Habsburgs. Bellièvres, perceiving the dangers for France, determined to court the Elector Palatine, who arrived in England in August, and to try to win back the queen.[50] In Spain, the news of the peace prompted Olivares into proposing new terms, which Hopton considered worth heeding.[51] Spain's need of English friendship could not be doubted: during the summer of 1639 Olivares had to hire English merchant ships to defend the coasts of Biscay against the French and the Dutch.[52] With Scotland settled, he sought a greater favour, for which he was prepared to make concessions. A large fleet had been fitted at Corunna to convoy to Flanders an army of 10,000 troops with money and supplies. Knowing it was vulnerable to attack in the Channel, the Condé Ducque sought an English escort to ensure the safe arrival of his ships. Charles I instructed Pennington to protect them.[53] Events, however, ran faster than diplomacy.

On 8 September, as the Spanish fleet came into the Channel, it was attacked in the straits of Dover by a Dutch fleet under the command of Tromp. The Spaniards were forced to put into the Downs for safety and shelter. Charles I saw the unexpected event as an opportunity from which to extract full advantage. For though he had offered to protect Spanish shipping, by the terms of the agreement, England claimed, the

47. *Ibid.*, p. 49.
48. PRO, 31/3/71, f.85.
49. Clarendon MS 17, no. 1271.
50. PRO, 31/3/71, f.98, 8 Aug. 1639.
51. Clarendon MS 17, no. 1285, 17/27 Aug. 1639.
52. Nottingham University Library, Clifton MS Cl/C 678; Gardiner, *History of England*, IX, p. 57.
53. Gardiner, *History of England*, IX, pp. 58–9.

Spaniard should have asked leave to come into any English port and then docked with no more than eight vessels – not the fleet of sixty that was now at Dover.[54] With Tromp lying in wait for the ships, the Spanish ambassador Cardenas was summoned and informed that England would require more from Spain on behalf of the Palatine and a payment of £150,000[55] – 'little enough', as Windebank put it to Hopton, 'for the saving of Flanders'.[56] Otherwise, he was threatened, England would remain neutral and leave the Spanish ships to their fortunes. During the tense days that ensued and an answer was awaited, the French entered negotiations too. Gaining Henrietta Maria, as he believed, to his side, Bellièvres endeavoured to get Charles to permit the ruin of the Spanish fleet at the hands of the Dutch and so weaken the Habsburgs in Flanders.[57] The king responded by reminding the French envoy that Spain was also making attractive offers: in return for assistance to the French and Dutch, he required that Richelieu place the Elector Palatine at the head of the army of Bernhard of Weimar, who had died whilst leading his troops across the Rhine in June.[58] Charles in other words had put his favour and the fate of the fleet out to auction (would it have become a Dutch auction?). He gave Bellièvres fifteen days to respond to his demands, before concluding; Spain was granted similar terms.[59] While he waited, Pennington, captain of the English ships that were holding the ring in the Downs, anxiously sought instructions on how to deal with the clash when it came. Northumberland confessed his ignorance: 'I am very sorry that I cannot send you more clear and particular instructions . . .'; he had pressed the king, but could get no answer.[60] Charles was not indecisive; he was waiting on the best bid.

While he waited, Tromp decided to act. Quite probably with Richelieu's support, he attacked. On 11 October after a fight in the Downs, the Spanish fleet was routed, many vessels were sunk or run ashore and Spanish sailors and soldiers were forced to flee across English soil.[61] The English fleet stood by, powerless and helpless. What had looked like a splendid opportunity for the reassertion of England's capacity to tip the balance of power had turned into a disastrous demonstration of her weakness. Writing from Brussels

54. British Library [BL] Add. MS 11045, f.55: Rossingham to Scudamore, 17 Sept. 1639.
55. See Clarendon MS 17, no. 1296.
56. *Clarendon State Papers*, II, pp. 71–6, 29 Sept. 1639, quotation p. 74.
57. PRO, 31/3/71, ff.114–16, 9 Oct. 1639.
58. *Ibid.*, ff.116v, 118v; Gardiner, *History of England*, IX, p. 63.
59. PRO, 31/3/71, f.117.
60. *Calendar of State Papers Domestic* [*Cal. Stat. Pap. Dom.*], *1639*, p. 538: Northumberland to Pennington, 30 Sept. See also *ibid.*, p. 538: Thomas Smith to Pennington.
61. Gardiner, *History of England*, IX, pp. 67–8. See also, *A New Spanish Tragedy* (1639, Bodleian, Wood, 401/137).

within days of the disaster, Count Leslie, who had held out high hopes of negotiations with the Habsburgs, informed Windebank, 'now the fleet is lost, I fear a fatal blow for the peace of Christendom . . . I do assure you his Majesty's reputation suffers extremely'.[62] Hopton concurred.[63] Though neither Madrid nor Brussels formally blamed England (Philip IV specificially argued the need to mask their resentment) they had received powerful confirmation of their long-held suspicion that Charles was unable to offer them effective assistance.[64] The foreign committee in England was paralysed into uncertainty by its recognition of the nation's weakness. They did not know how to respond to the attack.[65] For if they demanded reparation of the Dutch and were refused, honour would necessitate a war 'and in what estate his Majesty is to enter into a war,' Windebank explained candidly to Hopton, 'considering the disorders of Scotland and the straight union between the crown of France and the States . . . is not hard to determine.'[66] Windebank coupled England's international and domestic crises at the close of 1639. Tromp's action was, to say the least, bellicose and underlined the threat of Dutch sea power to England; the close union between France and the United Provinces (and the easy defeat of the Spanish) revealed the distance that had opened between England and the allies since the Scotch troubles and re-emphasized the vulnerability of Flanders. Distance turned into hostility with the news early in December that Richelieu had ordered the arrest of the Elector Palatine who had been travelling in disguise through France en route to Breisach.[67] At home, the Scots were stirring – with French and Dutch encouragement and help.[68] During December Loudoun came from Scotland to request assistance from Bellièvres; the envoy informed his master that the Scots were going to insist on a commercial settlement with England that would favour the French, and that they would demand as well as a Scottish ambassador to Paris places on the English Privy Council for Scots who might represent French interests.[69] With problems mounting again in Scotland there was little that Charles could do. Northumberland

62. Clarendon MS 17, no. 1314, 28 Oct. 1639.
63. *Ibid.*, no. 1318, 6/16 Nov. 1639.
64. Lonchay, *Correspondance*, III, p. 351, no. 1040: Philip IV to Cardinal Infant, 29 Nov.; Clarendon MS 17, no. 1323.
65. *HMC De Lisle and Dudley, VI*, p. 196; Clarendon MS 17, no. 1323.
66. Clarendon MS 18, no. 1351, 7 Feb. 1640.
67. Gardiner, *History of England*, IX, p. 70.
68. The University of Leyden wrote to express support for the Scots' struggle for liberty (National Library of Scotland, Denmilne MS XII, 36). Dutch ministers also attended the Glasgow Assembly; see National Library of Scotland, Wodrow Octavo MS XXVII, f.106. On France, see M. Avenal (ed.) *Collection de documents inédits: lettres, instructions diplomatiques et papiers d'état du Cardinal Richelieu, IV* (Paris, 1861), p. 688 and note.
69. PRO, 31/3/71, ff.136, 140–140v.

advised Leicester that he thought England compelled to 'remain quiet towards foreign parts, and intend [attend] only our troubles at home'.[70] 'The truth is,' he wrote at Christmas, 'we think so much upon reducing Scotland to obedience that other matters of no less importance are wholly neglected.'[71]

The breakdown of the peace

The breakdown of the Treaty of Berwick originated in the peace itself. Though the generalities had been agreed, the crucial details had been left unresolved.[72] An Assembly of the kirk and a parliament were to be called, but there had been no discussion of their composition. The Scots had aired many grievances in the king's tent at Berwick that had not been comprehended in the terms of pacification.[73] It did not take long for the cracks to appear from beneath the paper. On 22 June, Secretary Coke wrote from the border to his partner Windebank to inform him that the Covenanters were talking as though they had 'condescended' to the peace.[74] When the treaty was proclaimed at Edinburgh, it met with an immediate protest at the phrase 'pretended Assembly' (to describe that of Glasgow) and the Scottish commissioners (perhaps sensing they had done too little) began to draw up and circulate a list of what they claimed had been orally agreed though not included formally in the treaty. Before the month was out Edward Norgate for one could see the way things were drifting: 'We hear,' he told Robert Reade, 'these people are as ready to relapse into their former disobedience as the devil can wish.'[75] The very next day bore him out. On 1 July the king published his proclamation ordering elections to the forthcoming Assembly and summoned all archbishops and bishops to take their places there.[76] The Covenanters immediately objected to the writs issued to the bishops, whom they clearly regarded as already outlawed. Traquair's coachman was beaten, and riots broke out on the streets of Edinburgh.[77] Already Charles was faced with the decision whether to give way or resume preparations for war; or as Hamilton asked, 'whether it be fit to give way to the madness of the

70. *HMC 3rd Report*, p. 78, 28 Nov. 1639.
71. *Ibid.*, p. 79, 26 Dec. 1639.
72. Cf. C.S. Terry, *The Life and Campaigns of Alexander Leslie* (1899), p. 83.
73. National Library of Scotland, Advocates' MS 19.1.17, ff.7, 13; G. Burnet, *The Memoirs of the Lives and Actions of James and William, Dukes of Hamilton* (1677), p. 143. See P. Donald, 'The king and the Scottish troubles, 1637–41' (Cambridge University, PhD thesis, 1988), p. 265.
74. *Cal. Stat. Pap. Dom., 1639*, p. 340; Burnet, *Memoirs of the Dukes of Hamilton*, p. 143.
75. *Cal. Stat. Pap. Dom., 1639*, p. 355, 30 June.
76. A. Peterkin, *Records of the Kirk of Scotland* (Edinburgh, 1828), p. 230.
77. Gardiner, *History of England*, IX, p. 45; Advocates' MS 19.1.17, f.13.

people, or of new to intend a Kingly way'.[78] The choices presented by the marquis were both unpalatable to the king: 'whether to permit the abolishing of episcopacy, the lessening of kingly power in ecclesiastic affairs . . . and to expect better . . . or to call a parliament in England and to leave the event thereof to hazard and their discretions and in the interim Scotland to the government of the Covenanters'. Hamilton advised giving way, and Charles, for the time, followed his counsel. Persuaded that he might reintroduce the bishops when he had regained control, the king settled for a compromise. He instructed Traquair who was going as his commissioner to the Assembly to ensure that bishops' rents and lands were preserved inviolate and to secure for the king the right to choose the ministers who would take their places.[79]

The assault on the bishops proved to be not the only difficulty. When he reached Scotland, Traquair found the terms of the Treaty of Berwick violated by the Covenanters.[80] Charles himself remonstrated with Rothes over the Covenanters' failure to disband their forces and restore his supplies, the unlawful pressure they exerted on their countrymen to sign the Covenant, and their interference in the elections to the Assembly.[81] Windebank proved a master of understatement when he told Hopton that 'our business of Scotland since the Pacification hath met with some difficulties'.[82] A second campaign was already being discussed when the Assembly convened on 12 August.[83] Within days, it voted to abolish episcopacy and enforce the subscription of the Covenant.[84] The parliament, from which the bishops were now banned, looked certain to ratify the Assembly and condemn episcopacy as unlawful. Such courses threatened Charles's only remaining hope of future restoration and raised dangerous implications for the government of his other kingdoms that he could not ignore. On 1 October he wrote personally to his Scottish Council, to correct their mistaken notion that they might agree to a parliamentary statute for the illegality of episcopacy. They might, he instructed them, give way to the condemnation of bishops as antagonistic to the constitution of the kirk, but not endorse any declaration that they were 'unlawful' for 'absolutely unlawful in one church cannot be lawful in another of the same profession of religion . . . therefore if I do acknowledge or

78. J. Nalson, *An Impartial Collection of the Great Affairs of State from the Beginning of the Scotch Rebellion in 1639 to the Murder of King Charles I* (2 vols, 1682–3), I, pp. 242–5: Hamilton to Charles I, 8 July 1639.
79. Hamilton MS 809: Charles I to Hamilton, 17 July 1639; Burnet, *Memoirs of the Dukes of Hamilton*, pp. 144, 148–9.
80. Burnet, *Memoirs of the Dukes of Hamilton*, p. 156.
81. Denmilne MS XII, 55.
82. *Clarendon State Papers*, II, p. 66, 6 July 1639.
83. BL Add. MS 11045, f.46: Rossingham to Scudamore, 13 Aug. 1639.
84. See Peterkin, *Records of the Kirk*, pp. 241–72; Collins, *Letters and Memorials*, II, p. 604.

consent that episcopacy is unlawful in the Kirk of Scotland . . . it may be by some probably inferred that the same calling is acknowledged by us to be unlawful in any other churches in our dominions'.[85] Charles warned them he would not permit the rescinding of any acts in favour of episcopacy – acts, as he explained them to Traquair, 'which our fathers with so much expense of time and industry established, and which may hereafter be of so great use to us'.[86] The king was not ignorant of the probable consequence of his stand: 'though it should perhaps cast all loose . . . yet we take God to witness that we have permitted them to do many things in this assembly for establishing of peace contrary to our judgement, and if on this point a rupture happen we cannot help it, the fault is on their part which one day they will smart for'.[87]

The king's worst fears were duly confirmed. The parliament proposed bills outlawing episcopacy, and ordered that the command of Scottish castles be entrusted to Scottish subjects.[88] The news quickly spread that war would ensue. On 24 October John Castle informed the Earl of Bridgewater of what had taken place in the northern kingdom: 'The point at which his Majesty takes displeasure is their peremptory proceeding to confirm by parliament the act they made in the late Assembly for abolishing of the episcopacy which his Majesty will not assent unto.'[89] This, he added, made most at court believe 'that we shall enter into a new war'. If there were still any room for doubt, the events of the next week dispelled it. For when on 31 October Traquair announced the prorogation of the parliament until March, they argued (staking out a claim that was later to be made in England) that a royal prorogation was invalid without the consent of parliament itself.[90] The parliament, having established a standing committee to make appointments between sessions, continued to sit.[91] Northumberland felt sure that 'This must needs be so offensive to the King that I do not see how a war can possibly be avoided.'[92] The Scots dispatched Dunfermline and Loudoun as commissioners to present their demands to the king.

85. Hamilton MS 1031. Such was not only the king's perception. As Sir James Douglas put it to Windebank: 'Episcopacy orthodox in England, heretical in Scotland. Lord God have mercy on my soul' (*Cal. Stat. Pap. Dom., 1639*, p. 454). See also BL Add. MS 11045, f.68.
86. Burnet, *Memoirs of the Dukes of Hamilton*, pp. 158–9: Charles I to Traquair, 1 Oct. 1639.
87. Hamilton MS 1031.
88. Gardiner, *History of England*, IX, p. 54.
89. Ellesmere MS 7809.
90. Gardiner, *History of England*, IX, pp. 54–5; see St John's speech in the Short Parliament on 20 April 1640 in E. Cope (ed.) *Proceedings of the Short Parliament of 1640* (Camden Soc., 4th series, 19, 1977), p. 163.
91. BL Add. MS 11045, f.61.
92. *HMC De Lisle and Dudley, VI*, p. 201: Northumberland to Leicester, 7 Nov. 1639; cf. Hamilton to Roxburgh, 8 Nov. 1639 (Hamilton MS 932).

They desired the nomination of the Lords of the Articles, the Lords of the Session, judges and all major officers – demands to which if the king acceded, the newswriter Rossingham told Scudamore, 'all his civil power in that kingdom as well as his ecclesiastical would be utterly abolished'.[93] The foreign committee now unanimously gave Charles the same advice: if he gave in to the Covenanters, he would be no more king of Scotland than of China.[94] Loudoun was not given audience. Instead of negotiation, Charles sat with his committee for Scottish affairs to prepare for war. And with the advice of his Council he resolved at last on calling a parliament so as to explain his needs and secure, as he hoped, the finances for his campaign.[95]

Factions and fears

The Scots war and the reorientation of foreign policy it instigated had important consequences for factional alignments and the balance of power at court. From the death of Weston in 1635, as we have seen, no one figure dominated the king's counsels. Laud emerged as a trusted adviser on secular as well as religious affairs and even joined the foreign committee. Yet he exercised little sway in foreign policy, in part because his isolationist instincts did not accord well with the events of the mid-1630s. The collapse of the Spanish negotiations, the Peace of Prague and the rapprochement with France advanced the queen's party – especially the Earl of Holland – which had long advocated a French alliance against the Habsburgs. The queen's group and Laud coexisted in uneasy tension. Laud's lack of enthusiasm for the war, and his sustained attack on the proselytizing by Catholics within the queen's entourage, set him at odds with Henrietta Maria. The two factions vied for power. In domestic affairs Laud pulled off a triumph, obtaining the Lord Treasurership for his client, Bishop Juxon. In foreign affairs, however, the queen's party had the upper hand – not least because, with the failure of Arundel's mission to Vienna, the old Spanish faction all but disintegrated. Personal factors as well as ideological considerations aligned others in one or other of the camps. Cottington, one of the leading Hispanophiles of the earlier 1630s, went over to the queen out of hostility to Laud as much as genuine conversion to the French cause. Wentworth's friendship with Laud and rivalry with Holland as well as his opposition to war against the Habsburgs was enough to make the queen (who was evidently in

93. BL Add. MS 11045, f.82, 17 Dec. 1639.
94. *Ibid.*, f.81, 9 Dec. 1639.
95. *Clarendon State Papers*, II, p. 81; BL Add. MS 11045, f.81v.

awe of him) brand him as an enemy. For all the religious diversity of its members, the queen's party was the champion of a war against the Habsburgs, long desired by the puritans. Wentworth and Laud feared the consequences of rupturing the peace.[96]

The Scots war radically rearranged the constituency of the factions and readjusted the balance of power between them. In the first place, the crisis of the north, in putting paid to the French alliance, helped to restore a Spanish faction. The renewed negotiations with the Habsburgs and the suspicions of French aid to the Scots, as well as the need for peace, reoriented many towards Spain from 1638 onwards and strengthened the opponents of the queen's faction. By July 1639 Bellièvres reported that most of the Council (which months earlier was behind the French treaty) were now inclined to Spain and receiving a Spanish pension; Windebank he believed rose to greater prominence as leader of the party.[97] Even the queen, under the influence of her mother and the Duchess of Chevreuse, had turned against France and so liberated others to air reservations about the French treaty which they had silenced out of respect for her.[98] Though the French envoy began to woo Henrietta Maria back, a Spanish faction had re-coalesced, recruited the 'pacifists' and grown in favour with the king, who was piqued at the French delays in concluding a treaty and suspicious of their dealings with the Covenanters.[99] In November, Northumberland told Leicester (who pinned his hopes for high office on the French treaty) the bad news: that even if the treaty could be revived 'you may imagine how hard a matter it will be at this time to bring us to that resolution, especially now when Canterbury, Hamilton and [the] Deputy, who are the persons that do absolutely govern, are as much Spanish as Olivares.'[100] The French detention of the Elector Palatine further strengthened the Spaniards and realized Leicester's fears: the queen's suit to promote the earl for the secretaryship vacated by Coke was 'peremptorily' refused.[101]

The war also narrowed and reduced the queen's old party. For what had held together the strange coalition of Catholic favourites and 'puritan followers' within Henrietta Maria's household was a commitment to a French alliance. The end of prospects for the French treaty

96. See above, pp. 537–41.
97. PRO, 31/3/71, ff.85, 141v.
98. *Ibid.*, ff.39, 95v. The Duchess of Chevreuse arrived in England in April 1638 (Gardiner, *History of England*, VIII, p. 378).
99. PRO, 31/3/71, f.114; Collins, *Letters and Memorials*, II, p. 613. Northumberland told Leicester that the king was 'much unsatisfied that the French have kept the treaty all this while in their hands without signing it' (17 Oct. 1639).
100. *Ibid.*, p. 617, 14 Nov. 1639.
101. *HMC 3rd Report*, p. 78: Northumberland to Leicester, 21 Nov. 1639. We recall the king's belief that Leicester was thought to be too pro-French in his negotiating.

therefore made the place of the puritan magnates in the queen's household redundant. Events also distanced them from their erstwhile allies and from Henrietta Maria herself. In the context of the Scottish crisis puritan sympathies began to smack of disloyalty. The Earl of Hamilton for instance was charged with treasonable collusion with the Scots by the queen's Lord Chamberlain and was clearly out of favour with Henrietta Maria in 1639.[102] And Holland attracted suspicion for his good understanding with the Covenanters at the Treaty of Berwick.[103] Francophilia and puritanism were seen to go hand in hand with a too conciliatory attitude to the Scots; the Hispanophiles and Catholics by contrast – Arundel, Cottington and Windebank – had been staunch advocates of force against the rebels.[104] As he inclined to Spain in foreign policy, so Charles increasingly removed his favour from the French faction at home. Not only were Leicester's hopes dashed, the Venetian ambassador heard them 'talk freely at the palace about replacing many ministers suspected of partiality towards the Scots and Dutch'.[105]

As a consequence – a fatal consequence – the queen's party became exclusively identified with Catholicism. From the time of the missions of Panzani and Conn there had been pressure on the queen to lead a devout party at court in the interest of Rome and the Catholic cause in Europe. The manoeuvring for an alliance with France, however, had tempered those pressures. It was the queen's (temporary) conversion to Spain that for the first time made life uncomfortable for her puritan followers: in 1638 the Duchess of Chevreuse tried to convert the Earl of Holland to Rome and Rich, in order not to alienate the queen, had to pretend that he was not averse.[106] After the outbreak of Scottish troubles her own identification of puritanism with rebellion enhanced the queen's tendency to advance her Catholic followers. She bestowed the keepership of the park at Greenwich – much to Holland's discontent – on Harry Jermyn, who also expected to secure the treasurership of the household and was rumoured to be made a viscount.[107] In order to please his father, Sir Thomas Jermyn, Henrietta Maria urged her husband to oust the aged puritan Secretary Coke and promote to his place Sir Henry Vane.[108] On the death of Coventry, she also

102. Gardiner, *History of England*, IX, p. 7; *HMC 3rd Report*, p. 79.
103. B. Donogan, 'A courtier's progress: greed and consistency in the life of the Earl of Holland', *Hist. Journ.*, 19 (1976), p. 344.
104. Above, p. 795.
105. *Cal. Stat. Pap. Venet., 1640–2*, pp. 12, 17. In November 1639, the committee in 'daily attendance' on the king consisted of Laud, Juxon, Hamilton, Wentworth, Cottington, Vane, Windebank and Northumberland.
106. *Cal. Stat. Pap. Venet., 1636–9*, p. 417.
107. Ellesmere MS 7837: Castle to Bridgewater, 9 June 1640. Cf. Ellesmere MS 7819. The expectation proved false.
108. Ellesmere MS 7818: Castle to Bridgewater, 16 Jan. 1640.

used her influence to obtain the Lord Keepership for Finch over his rival candidate, Sir Edward Littleton.[109] A correspondent told John Winthrop of the death of Coventry and retirement of Coke: 'New England in those two is stripped at once of our best friends at the Board.'[110] Religious convictions which had once cut across factional lines were increasingly seen to be the determinants of alliance. Some thought Coke was dismissed for excess of sympathy for the Dutch and the Scots.[111] More particularly, and dangerously, Henrietta Maria was estranging her former, puritan followers and forming a unified Catholic faction at the time she was rising to her greatest influence and power.

The influence of the queen's faction did not go uncontested. The power of the queen's Catholic party was ardently opposed by Laud. Laud and Wentworth endeavoured to block the appointment of Vane and keep Sir John Coke in office.[112] From the spring of 1639, when against his advice England had prepared for war against the Scots, Wentworth had sent detailed letters of advice on the conduct of the campaign.[113] His determination to see the Covenanters routed as rebels and his devotion to the king's cause could not be doubted. 'If,' he wrote prophetically in May 1639, 'the cause require [I will] lay down my life in pursuit of his Majesty's commands and service.'[114] At a time when other Councillors appeared perhaps less enthusiastic for the fight, Wentworth's zealous commitment began to make an impression on his master. The Lord Deputy had for long been wanting to go to England to conduct his case against Adam Loftus, whom he had dismissed from his office as Chancellor of Ireland.[115] By the summer he had the king's permission to come over. The news of his coming gave rise to widespread speculation about the purpose of his visit and his place in the king's Council. On 18 August Robert Hobart told his kinsman John Hobart: 'there have been a speech that the Deputy of Ireland was sent for to come hither, which was thought to be for employment against Scotland, but when I was ready to seal up my letter one did confidently [say] he shall be Lord Treasurer here, for he is thought to be the likeliest and fittest man to fit and serve the King's

109. Ellesmere MS 7819.

110. *The Winthrop Papers* (Massachusetts Historical Society, 4th series, 6, 1863), p. 167, or *Winthrop Papers IV* (Massachusetts Historical Soc., 1944), p. 258. Though Finch had a Calvinist upbringing, he was evidently not seen as sympathetic to the exiles.

111. PRO, 31/3/71, f.114v, where he appears as 'Mr Kocke le premier Secrétaire'.

112. Ellesmere MSS, 7818 7819; Melbourne Hall, Coke MS 59; Clarendon, *History of the Rebellion*, I, p. 165.

113. Coke MS 61, esp. Wentworth to Vane, 30 May 1639.

114. *Ibid.*

115. Gardiner, *History of England*, IX, p. 77.

occasions.'[116] The rumour that Wentworth was coming for more than his personal affairs was confirmed by those in the highest places. Northumberland wrote to express his pleasure that Wentworth was coming back: 'wise and faithful counsels,' he told him, 'were never more needful than at this time.'[117] Wentworth arrived on 22 September and was immediately taken into the king's confidence, and appointed to the committee for Scottish affairs.[118] The Venetian envoy described him in November as the minister 'whom the King trusts more than anyone else'.[119] In December, Wentworth was made Lord-Lieutenant of Ireland – a sign perhaps that he would not be returning imminently; the next month he received his long-awaited patent for the earldom of Strafford.[120] Speculation again mounted that he would take the white staff as Treasurer.[121] The Scots began to see Strafford with Laud as their greatest enemy, or oppressor (as they put it) of their liberties and religion.[122] The man so often wrongly described as a leading figure in the personal rule had now at last taken his place as the king's principal adviser.

The queen was not happy at Wentworth's return. No friend to France, indeed sometimes described (wrongly) as Spanish, and rigorous in Ireland against recusancy, Wentworth added formidable weight to Laud's faction. A friend of Cottington and Northumberland, both of whom the queen had courted, the Lord Deputy appeared more than ever to be the obstacle to her bid for power. The two groups vied for supremacy. Wentworth tried to persuade Charles that he could not do his best in Ireland if Secretary Coke were removed from his place; Laud promoted Roe for the secretary's place.[123] On that occasion the queen won and Vane obtained the office. But Wentworth had his revenge: when he was elevated to his earldom, he also took the subsidiary title of Baron of Raby – the estate of which was in Vane's family possession.[124] Court gossips noted the outright hostility between the two groups. Sir Richard Cave informed Roe: 'The court . . . is divided into a double faction. The Lieutenant of Ireland goes on still in a close high way; Sir Henry Vane marches after him in a more open posture . . . fiery feud

116. Bodleian, Tanner MS 67, f.126; cf. *HMC Cowper II*, p. 241 and *Cal. Stat. Pap. Venet., 1636–9*, p. 577.
117. W. Knowler (ed.) *The Earl of Strafford's Letters and Despatches* (2 vols, 1739), II, p. 380, 11 Aug. 1639.
118. Gardiner, *History of England*, IX, p. 74.
119. *Cal. Stat. Pap. Venet., 1636–9*, p. 595.
120. Ellesmere MS 7815: Castle to Bridgewater, 24 Dec. 1639.
121. *HMC De Lisle and Dudley, VI*, p. 204; *HMC 3rd Report*, p. 77.
122. See *The Intentions of the Army of the Kingdom of Scotland Delivered to their Brethren of England* (1640, Edinburgh, STC 21919).
123. Ellesmere MS 7819. See too M.B. Young, *Servility and Service: The Life and Work of Sir John Coke* (1986), p. 263.
124. Clarendon, *History of the Rebellion*, I. p. 197.

there is between them.'[125] The king evidently tried to reconcile the parties: he called Hamilton and Wentworth together and urged them to be friends 'seeing they were persons that he meant to trust with most of his business'.[126] Wishing to retain his freedom of manoeuvre, he appointed a new committee to attend him daily, consisting of Laud, Juxon, Wentworth, Cottington, Windebank, Hamilton and Vane. But relations were by no means harmonious: the puritan peers had lost their power base and Wentworth had made an enemy of the queen. Both, as Clarendon was to observe with the benefit of hindsight, 'afterwards produced many sad disasters'.[127]

The spectre of popery

The ascendancy of the queen's faction, and more especially of the Catholics within her entourage, undoubtedly fostered a fear that began to seize the nation in 1639: a suspicion of popish plots and a fear of a Catholic invasion or rising. Circumstances combined to provide a fertile ground for anxiety. The uncertain situation in Europe, the escalation of the war between Habsburg and Bourbon and England's strategic position in the midst of the contending parties made the military threat from without all too real. England's withdrawal from the French alliance and the desired war against the Habsburg Antichrist and Charles's rapprochement with Spain seemed to signify the work of popish counsels close to the king. The re-formation of a Spanish faction and the visible power of the queen completed for many the jigsaw of a conspiracy. From 1638, Scottish propaganda had represented the war as promoted by papists and crypto-papists; and characterized the assault on the Protestantism of the kirk as a prelude to the eradication of orthodoxy in England. At home as well as abroad, some began to see the realm in the grip of a popish conspiracy. The growing conviction of conspiracy was constructed on false observations and fears. The French alliance had foundered more on Richelieu's than Charles I's lack of enthusiasm for it; Laud was as staunch an opponent of the queen's proselytizing as any at court. But anxieties are not always born of an accurate evaluation of events. A latent fear of Catholic plots was the bequest to early Stuart Englishmen of the Armada and Gunpowder Plot. It needed little to trigger that fear.

Isolated episodes throughout the years of personal rule show that this latent fear was never far below the surface of the nation's

125. *Cal. Stat. Pap. Dom., 1639–40*, pp. 435–6, 7 Feb. 1640.
126. Collins, *Letters and Memorials*, II, p. 614: Countess of Carlisle to Leicester, 17 Oct. 1639.
127. *HMC 3rd Report*, p. 78; Clarendon, *History of the Rebellion*, I, p. 197.

consciousness. In 1631, for example, when the Spanish ambassador to London, Necolalde, took lodgings in an area inhabited by many English Catholics, the Venetian envoy heard 'everyone . . . talking about it, putting interpretations on it which correspond with the intrigues which the Spaniards have always carried on in this kingdom'.[128] Two years later, one Henry Sawyer, a mole-catcher from Huntingdonshire, was examined by the Council for saying that when the king went to Scotland to be crowned, the Catholics would rise up against the Protestants.[129] Rumour spread the same year of a papist rising planned at Lady Digby's house at Gothurst in Buckinghamshire.[130] In London, the comings and goings of English Catholics to the queen's masses presented the very visible confluence of English recusants, powerful Catholic magnates and representatives of Catholic powers on which fears of a fifth column mushroomed. In 1634 some apprentices talked of pulling down the chapel at Somerset House.[131] Stories of conversions, swelled by report beyond all proportion, spread from the capital to the country. In Suffolk one William Watling had come to believe by 1634 that 'the King . . . hath a wife and he loves her, and she is a papist and we must be all of her religion'.[132] The arrival of Conn confirmed all these fears. Puritans spread the story that the papal agent had formulated a plot with the king's confessor.[133] Several Councillors feared that 'this novel and free revival of confidential relations with the Holy See . . . will serve to turn utterly upside down the quiet of the people'.[134]

Before 1637, however, such reports were occasional and isolated. The trial of Prynne, Burton and Bastwick may have been something of a turning point, for in his speech Laud voiced his concern that they kindled fears in men's minds of popish plots.[135] Certainly over the course of the next months, the suspicions of papists had become so strong that the king felt compelled to take remedial action: Conn was ordered to leave and the justices of assize were instructed to counteract the false report that Catholics were officially protected and the king himself a convert.[136] But the mounting Scottish crisis fed the suspicions in several ways. News of the Scots' resistance inspired incidents and stories of a determined Protestant stand in England. Marmaduke Lloyd

128. *Cal. Stat. Pap. Venet., 1629–32*, p. 530.
129. *Cal. Stat. Pap. Dom., 1633–4*, p. 26.
130. *Ibid.*, p. 73.
131. *Cal. Stat. Pap. Dom., 1634–5*, p. 22; above, pp. 304–5.
132. Tanner MS 70, f.125: examination of William Watling.
133. *Cal. Stat. Pap. Venet., 1636–9*, p. 120.
134. *Ibid.*, p. 39.
135. T. Hargrave, *A Complete Collection of State Trials* (11 vols, 1776–81), I, p. 487.
136. *Cal. Stat. Pap. Venet., 1636–9*, pp. 419, 543; *Cal. Stat. Pap. Dom., 1639*, p. 77; Bodleian, Rawlinson MS B.243, f.18v.

reported one such tale to the Earl of Bridgewater, who was alarmed enough to forward an account to Secretary Coke. A young gallant riding from Bristol into Monmouthshire met a woman who begged alms of him. He promised a shilling (a handsome benefaction) if she would kneel and worship the cross on it. The poor woman preferred her Protestantism to her prosperity and declining, replied 'she would never kneel nor worship the cross'. The young man drew his sword and killed her.[137] We have more than a sense that the story is apocryphal or embellished. But such tales were becoming current. The arrival of the Queen Mother in October, at the height of the Scottish troubles, could not have been more untimely. Laud had 'great apprehensions' about it;[138] Robert Woodforde, hearing the news, could only resort to prayer: 'Lord preserve and keep this kingdom.'[139] By the end of the year the decision to fight the Scots and the arming of local society appeared to mark the triumph of papist counsels – especially when the queen called upon the Catholics to fast on Saturdays so as to contribute to the campaign in the north.[140] Though the pope saw the dangers and moved to prohibit Catholics offering troops or money for the expedition, the queen's injunction served to associate the war with the rising prominence of her faction at home.[141] When Henrietta Maria also acted to promote a Spanish match for her daughter it was as though the last bead were threaded on the rosary. For as the army marched, the Duchess of Chevreuse was seen to lead the princess to mass.[142]

After the long years of peace amid a Europe in crisis, the war against the Scots excited fears of imminent instability, and even Armageddon. There was a sense of foreboding in gentry circles. Lord Montagu feared that if they fell to blows with the Scots 'it would be the heaviest plague that ever fell upon England'.[143] We can hear Sir Henry Slingsby working out profound worries in his diary: 'These are strange, strange spectacles to this nation in this age that have lived thus long peaceably without a noise of shot or drum and after we have stood neutrals and in peace with all the world besides hath been in arms and wasted with it, it is I say a thing most horrible that we should engage ourself in a war one with another and with our own venom gnaw and consume ourself.'[144] Slingsby could only explain it

137. Coke MS 58, 9 July 1638; cf. *HMC Cowper II*, p. 188.
138. W. Scott and J. Bliss (eds) *The Works of William Laud* (7 vols, Oxford, 1847–60), III, p. 230. The watermen called the 'extreme wet and windy weather' of her arrival week 'Queen Mother weather' (p. 231).
139. New College Oxford MS 9502 (Woodforde's diary), 2 Nov. 1638.
140. BL Add. MS 11045, f.9: Rossingham to Scudamore, 2 April 1639; BL, Harleian MS 4931, ff.31, 32–3.
141. *Clarendon State Papers*, II, p. 44.
142. *Cal. Stat. Pap. Venet., 1636–9*, p. 543.
143. *HMC Buccleuch-Whitehall*, III, p. 379.
144. D. Parsons (ed.) *The Diary of Sir Henry Slingsby* (1836), p. 10.

by reference to the irrational. There was a prophecy, he recalled, that after the Saxons and Normans, England would be conquered by Scots. Was that now to be fulfilled?[145] What Slingsby had read in prophecy, others were to interpret from natural portents. Many, shocked by the outburst in Scotland, found their only explanation in the operation of some uncontrollable supernatural force which assaulted the commonweal. James Douglas expressed to Windebank his perception that 'doubtless there is some supernatural disposition makes their people incensed without any reason'.[146] Natural phenomena duly obliged to confirm his impressions. The winter of 1638–9 evidently witnessed freak storms, which contemporaries were quick to read as signs. In his diary for December 1638, for example, Dennis Bond of Dorset recorded: 'This year the 15 December was seen throughout the whole kingdom the opening of the sky for half a quarter of an hour.'[147] Weeks later Henry Hastings described to the Earl of Huntingdon another strange natural occurrence, in language of powerful significance:

> about a week since at eight of the clock at night some clouds being dispersed . . . seemed to the beholders like men with pikes and muskets, but suddenly the scene being changed they appeared in two bodies of armed men set in battalion, and then a noise was heard and sudden flashing of light seen and streaks like smoke issuing out of those clouds.[148]

Hastings's military language is visionary; it articulated the anxiety of a critical expectation: an expectation that not only England and Scotland would soon be at war, but perhaps too that the realm was preparing for some bigger battle. There is an apocalyptic tone to Hastings's description. In a society used to interpreting natural phenomena as signs of God's intervention, the vision appeared to announce some imminent cosmic struggle. Perhaps in that year 1639 when, according to Lady Harley, 'many are of the opinion that Antichrist must begin to fall', that 'sudden flashing of light' seemed to portend the last days.[149] Admiral Northumberland's secretary sensed the nation's fear as the armies were being prepared. 'The last great lightning,' he told Captain Pennington, 'has done a world of mischief all over England, and the people are generally so molested with predictions and rumours of supposed visions, as if they were all struck with a panic fear.'[150] The

145. *Ibid.*, p. 11.
146. *Cal. Stat. Pap. Dom., 1638–9*, p. 507.
147. Dorset Record Office, D 413, Box 22, p. 52.
148. Huntington Library, Hastings MS 5558: Hastings to Huntingdon, 3 Feb. 1640.
149. T.T. Lewis (ed.) *Letters of the Lady Brilliana Harley* (Camden Soc., old series, 58, 1854), p. 41.
150. *Cal. Stat. Pap. Dom., 1638–9*, p. 361.

Privy Council reacted nervously to the tense atmosphere: provost marshals were ordered to police the counties, punishing vagrants and such as 'in times of suspicion and trouble may by tales and false rumours distract the people's minds'.[151]

In some parts of the realm panic had placed local society in a state of alert, which in turn exacerbated the fear of imminent instability. Robert Woodforde recorded that 'the time in the apprehension of all seems to be very doubtful and many fears we have of dangerous plots by French and papists.'[152] His native Northamptonshire exhibited great paranoia. In April 1639 Robert Sibthorpe told Sir John Lambe that the town of Kettering had set up eight watchmen as a guard day and night, at the prompting of a prominent local magistrate, Mr Sawyer. Sawyer also came to church 'attended with half a dozen men with swords by their sides and pistols under their cloaks or coats beside his three rapier staves for himself. . . and the clerk's son watcheth upon the battlements (together with some others)'. The community was clearly on the edge of its nerves. 'Upon Sunday last,' Sibthorpe went on, 'was discovered three or four horsemen coming towards the town who indeed were for York, and came down, gave the alarm and the watch seized them.' The strangers turned out to be only messengers, 'yet this hath made so great a noise in the country that Kettering fair was but a little one (which useth to be great) on Maundy Thursday, people fearing . . . to be surprised in that town which is so afraid of itself'.[153] Sibthorpe's conviction that it was all a 'causeless fear' did not soothe the anxiety. Rumours circulated of a popish plot to set Kettering on fire, and Sawyer strengthened the watch.

The absence of the king in the north had contributed to the mood of instability, and his return might have helped to cool the political temperature, had not other events conspired to keep it high.[154] On 8 August George Weckherlin reported from London to Coke that 'Great contentment brought his Majesty's safe return to all the inhabitants here (as their bonfires did testify). But much displeasure was caused to some that saw his Majesty come in the said Queen Mother's coach.'[155] All was far from harmonious. Charles, disgruntled at their lack of support for his campaign, refused the city's welcoming present of

151. Bodleian, Firth MS C.4, p. 596.
152. Woodforde's diary, 22 March 1639. Unfortunately for Charles I, he did not appear to identify the two. It was still the Spanish who were regarded as the Catholic bogy. Perhaps this was not least because France, for all its Catholicism, could be seen as championing the Protestant cause abroad.
153. Huntington Library, Temple of Stowe MSS 11, STT 1876, 12 April 1639; STT 1880, 28 April 1639.
154. Cf. Hamilton MS 811.
155. Coke MS 63: Weckherlin to Coke, 8 Aug. 1639 (calendared in *HMC Cowper II*, p. 239).

£10,000.[156] News was already spreading that the peace might be short-lived. Worse still, the king returned virtually as a large Spanish fleet was sailing towards Dunkirk, exciting fears of a Catholic invasion. As the convoy approached, some alleged that the ships were 'set out by persuasion of the prelates and papists of England to come and subdue the protestations of their enemies, as well in England as in Scotland or Ireland'.[157] There were said to be 20,000 men on board – ready, it was feared, to renew the enterprise of 1588.[158] Even the less catastrophic denouement and rout of the Spaniards left anxieties in their wake. Reports of the dog-fight at sea were exaggerated out of all proportion: thousands were said to have been slain and the Spaniards, out of ammunition, were alleged to have fired gold and silver from their cannon.[159] From such wealth, it was feared, another attack might easily be mounted. A ballad called *A New Spanish Tragedy* therefore closed with a prayer:

> But to conclude my ditty
> I think there have not been
> Since eighty-eight the like sea-fight
> Near unto England seen
> The Lord preserve our gracious King.[160]

Fears and events had begun to push each other into a crescendo of national paranoia. It was not the best atmosphere in which to prepare a second campaign against the Scots or to ask the first parliament in more than a decade to finance it.

156. *Ibid.*
157. J. Spalding, *Memorials of the Troubles in Scotland and England, 1624–1645* (Aberdeen, 1850), p. 240.
158. R. Clifton, 'The fear of Catholics in England, 1637–1645' (Oxford University, D. Phil. thesis, 1967), pp. 56–7. D'Ewes had thought in 1605 that a Spanish fleet was ready to aid the Gunpowder plotters (p. 58).
159. L. Price, *A New Spanish Tragedy* (1639, STC 20318).
160. *Ibid.*

PART VI

'THE CROSS HUMOURS OF THE PEOPLE'?: THE END OF PERSONAL RULE

XV

'A BED OF RECONCILIATION'? THE SHORT PARLIAMENT

Origins and elections

On 12 August 1639 the Venetian ambassador reported that Charles I had decided to summon a parliament.[1] His information, though wrong, is revealing. By the autumn of 1639 it was beginning to be clear that the Treaty of Berwick would not hold; and it was beginning to be felt that a second campaign to reduce the Scots would necessitate the assistance of a parliament. The first campaign had been, if abortive, still expensive. The Exchequer was empty, Hawkins told Leicester, and the revenue anticipated for the next two years.[2] Charles in fact had raised nearly a quarter of a million pounds on anticipated revenue and had again sold or pawned jewellery in order to raise funds quickly for his army at Berwick.[3] Perhaps more importantly, the calculation had been made in March that to keep an army in the field for a year would cost over £935,000.[4] Even with the considerable improvements in royal revenues during the 1630s, such sums were beyond the king's means. On the other hand, the situation in Scotland had developed into an open challenge to royal authority which could not be ignored. On 27 November, Traquair arrived from Edinburgh to report the state of affairs to the committee for Scotland.

All concurred now that the king must enforce obedience, but there were differences about how he might finance a campaign. Some advocated an excise; others suggested that the counties should be required to raise men at their own charge.[5] These proposals 'met with so many

1. *Calendar of State Papers Venetian* [*Cal. Stat. Pap. Venet.*], *1636–9*, p. 563.
2. *HMC De Lisle and Dudley, VI*, p. 212, 12 Dec. 1639.
3. *Calendar of State Papers Domestic* [*Cal. Stat. Pap. Dom.*], *1639–40*, p. 393; *1639*, p. 402.
4. *Cal. Stat. Pap. Dom., 1638–9*, p. 637.
5. See S.R. Gardiner, *History of England from the Accession of James I to the Outbreak of the Civil War, 1603–42* (10 vols, 1883–4), IX, p. 75.

weighty objections' that discussion of them did not proceed far. On the other hand the recourse to a parliament appeared to some 'at first impracticable at this time, it being unlikely that a parliament would furnish supplies in time and in proportion answerable to this present exigent'.[6] The deadlock was broken by Wentworth, now seen as the king's principal minister. The Lord Deputy argued forcefully 'that there was no way to bring them to their duty and for his Majesty to re-establish his authority and power . . . but the way of an effectual war, and no war to be made effectually but such a one as should grow and be assisted from the high counsel of a parliament'.[7] He urged the need 'to communicate these great affairs' to the king's 'good subjects'; he was confident that they would respond with supply.[8] Laud and Hamilton supported him, and the meeting was won over.[9] Those 'most averse to parliaments', Northumberland told Leicester, 'did now begin to advise the King's making trial of his people in parliament before he used any way of power'.[10] The final doubters were persuaded by a saving clause.[11] Accordingly, as Laud recorded in his diary, at the full Council meeting of 5 December, 'a resolution voted at the Board to assist the King in extraordinary ways if the parliament should prove peevish or refuse'.[12] The king was thus also 'soon gained'. After all the rumours, the decision was announced within days. The French ambassador had no doubt that Charles intended to hold a parliament 'à sa mode', nor that if his plans succeeded it might make him more absolute than any of his predecessors had been.[13] Those in the country who received the news of the assembly with joy had quite other expectations.

The warrant for issuing the writs for a parliament went out on 12 February, summoning an assembly for 13 April. As the French ambassador had predicted, it was decided that Wentworth should meet with the Irish parliament first – not least in the hope that it might set a happy example to its English successor.[14] There was much labouring for places in the first parliament for eleven years and keen competition for seats. Candidates could not afford to be complacent. Robert Reade

6. A. Collins (ed.) *Letters and Memorials of State Collected by Sir Henry Sidney* (2 vols, 1746), II, p. 623: Northumberland to Leicester, 12 Dec. 1639; R. Scrope and T. Monkhouse (eds) *State Papers Collected by Edward, Earl of Clarendon* (3 vols, Oxford, 1767–86), II, p. 81.
7. Huntington Library, Ellesmere MS 7814: Castle to Bridgewater, 6 Dec. 1639; *Cal. Stat. Pap. Dom., 1639–40*, p. 158.
8. British Library [BL] Add. MS 11045, f.81: Rossingham to Scudamore, 9 Dec. 1639.
9. W. Scott and J. Bliss (eds) *The Works of William Laud* (7 vols, Oxford, 1847–60), III, p. 233.
10. Collins, *Letters and Memorials*, II, p. 623.
11. *Clarendon State Papers*, II, p. 81: Windebank to Hopton, 13 Dec. 1639.
12. *Works of Laud*, III, p. 233.
13. PRO, French transcripts, 31/3/71, f.154, 22 Dec. 1639.
14. *Ibid.*, f.154v.

warned his cousin Thomas Windebank that 'there is much bandying for places that for aught I see we who were made sure at first of burgess ships are as likely to miss them as others, men not being able to perform what they promise'.[15] The Council drew up its own list of burgesses it wished to see nominated in the government interest.[16] Letters were sent, as soon as the writs went out, to various towns, as Hamilton told Laud, 'to keep themselves free till some friends are nominated'.[17] There was much lobbying. Sir Gervase Clifton's support was sought by Thomas Hutchinson and Robert Sutton in Nottinghamshire;[18] Sir John Harpur asked for Coke's backing in Derbyshire;[19] in Northamptonshire Robert Woodforde's voice was entreated for Sir Christopher Hatton.[20] Seeking support at the hustings was by no means novel. But gentry correspondence betrays a greater sense of uncertainty and of the need to prepare more carefully for the campaign than is evident in earlier Stuart elections.[21] Henry Hastings, for example, stressed to the Earl of Huntingdon the importance of timing and the disadvantage they were under having delayed announcing their support. In Leicestershire Sir Arthur Haselrig began his campaign early. 'By their persuasions and taking away some voices who are already engaged,' Hastings wrote, 'my Lord Ruthen and Sir Arthur have gained much advantage in time, we playing but an after game our work being to persuade men from what they have already promised.'[22] Sir Walter Pye in Herefordshire advised Sir Robert Harley that though opposition to their candidacy was not expected, 'I think it just for us to bring such a number of freeholders with us as may not only secure us but destroy [any] subterfuge.'[23] He made provision for the entertainment of the voters at Hereford on the night before the hustings. Not only were similar elaborate preparations being made around the country; some were resorting to what were, to say the least, dubious courses. Concern was to be expressed at the use of bribery during the campaigns;[24] in Essex, the Earl of Warwick recruited puritan preachers

15. *Cal. Stat. Pap. Dom., 1639–40*, p. 474, 20 Feb. 1640.
16. *Cal. Stat. Pap. Dom., 1640*, p. 4.
17. *HMC De Lisle and Dudley, VI*, p. 236.
18. Nottingham University Library, Clifton MS Cl/C 684: Kingston to Clifton, 16 Dec. 1639; cf. nos 237, 429.
19. Melbourne Hall, Coke MS 64: Harpur to the younger Coke, 31 Dec. 1639.
20. New College Oxford MS 9502 (Woodforde's diary), 5 March 1640.
21. On the elections in general, see J.K. Gruenfelder, 'The elections to the Short Parliament, 1640', in H.S. Reinmuth Junior (ed.) *Early Stuart Studies* (Minneapolis, 1970), pp. 180–230; and J.K. Gruenfelder, *Influence in Early Stuart Elections* (Columbus, 1981), pp. 183–202.
22. Huntington Library, Hastings MS 5557, 13 Jan. 1640.
23. BL, MS 29/172, f.254, 10 Feb. 1640; cf. f.265.
24. See, for example, J.D. Maltby (ed.) *The Short Parliament Diary of Sir Thomas Aston (1640)* (Camden Soc., 4th series, 35, 1988), p. 77; *Cal. Stat. Pap. Dom., 1639–40*, p. 609.

like Stephen Marshall to canvass from the pulpit for his candidates, and even instructed the captains of the trained bands to threaten any who failed to vote for the godly Sir Thomas Barrington and Harbottle Grimston.[25] The keen desire to get elected was leading to some rather ungentlemanly practices.

The elections to the Short Parliament reveal the first cracks in the ideal model of parliamentary selection in early modern England that Professor Kishlansky constructed in his recent analysis.[26] The guiding principles of honour, harmony and community assent in the selection of local elites (the 'natural' choice) can still be found in the spring of 1640. In Somerset, for example, on 24 March, Sir John Coventry, Sir Ralph Hopton and Thomas Smyth signed an agreement:

> It is this day agreed between us . . . that we will proceed no further in labouring for voices to be knights of the shire, and that we will and do disengage the freeholders from any promises made unto us or either of us to that purpose, and do leave them at liberty to choose such gentlemen of worth as they shall think fit. And we promise each to other that neither [i.e. none] of us will be present at the election of the said knights nor use any endeavour for the obtaining that place, desiring also that our friends will as much as in them lieth make known and publish this our agreement and also endeavour that this agreement be on all sides observed.[27]

Smyth kept to the pact, telling one would-be supporter that he had 'wholly cast myself upon a free election . . . I never asked a voice of any of my own kindred'.[28] Yet it is clear that he was struggling to maintain old codes that were being challenged. In Kent too those old friends Sir Edward Dering and Sir Roger Twysden, for all their desire for co-operation, found themselves falling out, and in the end opposing each other for the senior seat.[29] Whether the gentry used to codes of honour liked it or not, elections to parliament were becoming a political contest – and a contest that could erode traditional loyalties. Sir Edward Phelips lamented to Smyth that 'I scarce yet know how firm my own quarter stands to me they having been so over laboured on all sides in my absence.'[30] What he heard suggested that across all England, the elections 'are like to produce great factions'.

The breakdown of traditional practices is well illustrated by events

25. C. Holmes, *The Eastern Association in the English Civil War* (Cambridge, 1975), pp. 21–4.
26. M. Kishlansky, *Parliamentary Selection: Social and Political Choice in Early Modern England* (Cambridge, 1986).
27. Bristol Record Office, Smyth of Ashton Court MS 36074/49, 24 March 1640.
28. *Ibid.*, 36074/133 b.
29. Kishlansky, *Parliamentary Selection*, pp. 130–2. See also, Kent Archives Office, Dering MS U 350, C2/73.
30. Smyth of Ashton Court MS AC/C.58/9, 29 Jan. 1640.

in Gloucestershire. On 24 March John Allibond explained to Heylyn what had happened. Normally in the county, the general accord of the gentry swayed the plebeians and settled the election of MPs; accordingly at the last assizes Sir Robert Tracy and Sir Robert Cooke had been nominated and were expected to co-operate with each other in the smooth progress to their final election. On the evening before the election day, Tracy fell ill, but confident of the arrangements, felt no concern at being absent for the shout. However, 'on Wednesday morning, when it was generally expected that the election should be a matter of ceremony and formality . . . suddenly there was set up, and forcedly as he pretends, Mr Stephens of Eastlington for opposing of the ship money in which cause he had suffered, having been put out of the commission of the peace.'[31] Faced with this unexpected intrusion, Tracy's side proceeded as had been agreed and nominated Cooke for the second place. In breach of their gentlemen's agreement, however, some of Cooke's tenants backed Stephens. Cooke professed his surprise and sincerity, claiming he had dealt with his men – as far as they could be dealt with. Allibond was not convinced: 'Heu fidem puritannicum' was how he interpreted the apostasy. Tracy did not let the challenge pass; he rescued himself from defeat by using his influence with the sheriff, a kinsman, to adjourn to poll to Winchcombe, where Stephens could not gather his support in strength. But the assault on custom sent shock waves through the county gentry and raised the suspicion that 'there is a kind of cunning underhand canvass of this nature the greater part of the kingdom over . . . '.[32] Farther north, at Chester, John Werden disliked the behaviour exhibited by the rival candidates: 'I am sorry in my heart,' he told Sir Thomas Smyth, 'to see the preparations of discord . . . all joined in their own profit where there was a bare pretence of a public good.'[33] In the change in electoral behaviour Werden foresaw in microcosm that shift from community to contest that was to be the legacy of political revolution.[34]

If the sharpening of gentry competition eroded custom and harmony, it also presented a challenge to norms of social deference. More contests, perhaps still more an atmosphere of contest, meant the involvement of ordinary freeholders in an important moment of the political process. As Professor Hirst has demonstrated, the franchise in early Stuart England was relatively open and wide.[35] Though for most of

31. *Cal. Stat. Pap. Dom., 1639–40*, pp. 580–1: John Allibond to Heylyn, 24 March 1640.
32. *Ibid.*, p. 581.
33. *Ibid.*, p. 590. The calendar has him as Thomas Murden, but see J.S. Morrill, *Cheshire 1630–1660: County Government and Society during the English Revolution* (Oxford, 1974), p. 32.
34. K. Sharpe, *Politics and Ideas in Early Stuart England* (1989), pp. 63–71.
35. D. Hirst, *The Representative of the People?: Voters and Voting in England under the Early Stuarts* (Cambridge, 1975).

the early seventeenth century few elections were contested, in those that were often quite humble folk could exercise a choice. In the spring of 1640 there was in some shires considerable popular interest in the elections, and beyond that perhaps a politicization of the commonalty as rival candidates appealed for their support. During preparations for the elections in Norfolk Sir Thomas Wodehouse described to John Potts the contest to gain support from outside the community of gentry: 'It is likely that there will be the greatest noise and confluence of men that ever have been heard or seen . . . for never do I think there was such working and counterworking to purchase vulgar blasts of acclamation.'[36] Ballads and doggerel verse offer some insight into the process through which the contest was translated into the popular consciousness. In Lincolnshire, popular grievances blended with personal rivalries in the poem of advice that circulated at the hustings:

Choose no ship sheriff nor court atheist
No fen drainer nor church papist
But if you'll scower the pope's armoury
Choose Dallison and Dr Farmoury . . .

respectively recorder of the town and chancellor of the diocese.[37] At Canterbury where Laud's Chancellor Dell stood, verses were distributed:

If you choose Dell, you do well
But if you'll do your King and country good,
I hope I am understood.[38]

Not all ballads were so localized or partisan. A 'Song on the occasion of parliament' which looked forward to the reform of the law, the abolition of patents and the end of ship money, counselled moderation to all electors:

Both papist shun and puritan
For fear of their infection.[39]

Yet whether specifically partisan or not, popular song and verse were echoing the personal quarrels of the gentry candidates and rehearsing in simplified form the issues that had begun to divide them.

How far then were the elections of the spring of 1640 characterized by fundamental and divisive issues – by profound disagreements about the government and constitution of church and state? Stephens's surprise candidacy in Gloucester clearly owed much to his reputation

36. Bodleian, Tanner MS 67, f.189.
37. BL Add. MS 11045, f.99: Rossingham to Scudamore, 20 March 1640.
38. *Ibid.*, f.99v.
39. BL, Harleian MS 4931, f.39.

as an opponent of ship money.[40] The mayor of Sandwich advised Nicholas that his efforts to secure him a seat had failed on account of Nicholas's being lampooned as a papist.[41] In Northamptonshire, the cry of 'Away with deputy lieutenants!' spoke to at least local issues of authority and its exercise.[42] Henry Hastings told the Earl of Huntingdon that in Leicestershire 'the county in general take the same exception against Sir Henry Skipwith which in Derbyshire they do against Sir John Harpur, which is that he is a courtier and hath been sheriff and collected the ship money and that he lives out of the county and those things are privately urged by his opposers to the freeholders and work much to his disadvantage'.[43] Issues there were and they were beginning to rank men into sides. In Kent Sir Edward Dering was told that his enthusiastic service in the collection of knighthood fines would affect his chances at the poll.[44] A reputation for opposition to unpopular royal policies obviously helped some candidates. Hamilton told Leicester that 'burgesses and knights are chosen in many places such as discover the cross humours of the people'.[45] The Venetian envoy heard that in many parts of the country 'choice has fallen upon not only puritans but those who in the past have shown much boldness in opposing the King's decrees'.[46] Windebank was frankly pessimistic in his letter to Hopton: 'the elections have been very tumultuary and with much opposition to all that have relation to the court'.[47]

So badly did some observers believe things had gone that doubts were raised about whether the parliament would ever meet. In January Sir Edward Phelips confided to Thomas Smyth that 'the fame of the Robins of the West hath I believe reached the King's ear for I have heard divers Privy Councillors discourse of them and truly if necessity do not overtake balance these proceedings may probably alter the King's former resolutions for a parliament.'[48] By March, the Venetian envoy had heard that some ministers, suspecting that immoderate MPs were being chosen, were considering a postponement of the parliament.[49] Northumberland confirmed his story. 'The elections that are generally made,' he informed Leicester, 'give us cause to fear that the parliament will not sit long; for such as have dependence on the court

40. *Cal. Stat. Pap. Dom., 1639–40*, p. 580.
41. *Ibid.*, p. 561.
42. Bodleian, Bankes MS 42/55. The dispute that produced the outburst stemmed from local quarrels over the press, cf. above, p. 810 and note 285.
43. Hastings MS 5557.
44. A. Everitt, *The Community of Kent and the Great Rebellion* (Leicester, 1966), p. 74.
45. *HMC De Lisle and Dudley, VI*, p. 236.
46. *Cal. Stat. Pap. Venet., 1640–2*, p. 25.
47. Bodleian, Clarendon MS 18, no. 1368, 27 March 1640.
48. Smyth of Ashton Court MS C.58/9, 29 Jan. 1640.
49. *Cal. Stat. Pap. Venet., 1640–2*, p. 27.

are in divers places refused and the most refractory persons chosen.'[50] Such fears, however, were out of all proportion to reality. On the broadest calculations of the numbers of contested elections, below a quarter ended in a poll.[51] In the remaining cases, names of long-established families emerged, as they always had, by consensus in the political community. In Kent, for instance, New Romney returned a Godfrey as they did traditionally; Rochester elected Sir Thomas Walsingham for the sixth time.[52] In Sussex, though the 'obvious' choice, Sir Thomas Pelham, felt uneasy enough on this occasion to spend lavishly on entertaining the freeholders, there were no surprises.[53] The struggle in Norfolk was personal and familial rather than ideological.[54]

Issues reared their heads in the elections to the Short Parliament to challenge customary procedures and choices. But for the most part they were interpreted and discussed in a local context and, whatever had been predicted, local men were chosen. Those who went up to Westminster in April were not a new class of radicals bent on assaulting the king's government. Many like the diligent ship money sheriff Sir Thomas Chicheley, chosen for Cambridgeshire, were magistrates or officers who had actively co-operated with the regime.[55] Clarendon recalled that 'notwithstanding the murmurs of the people against some exorbitancies of the court', 'the general composure of men's minds in a happy peace and universal plenty over the whole nation . . . made it reasonably believed . . . that sober men and such as loved the peace and plenty they were possessed of, would be made choice of to serve in the House of Commons'.[56] Moreover 'the general aversion over the whole kingdom to the Scots and the indignation they had at their presumption in their thought of invading England, made it believed that a parliament would express a very sharp sense of their insolence and carriage towards the King, and provide remedies proportionable.'[57]

The hopes of a parliament

As was usual with meetings of parliament, MPs came up to Westminster to present the grievances of their localities and to hear the king's case for supply. Less typically, several petitions of grievances,

50. Collins, *Letters and Memorials*, II, p. 641.
51. See Hirst's tables, *Representative of the People?*, appendix 4.
52. Everitt, *Community of Kent*, pp. 74–5.
53. A. Fletcher, *A County Community in Peace and War: Sussex 1600–1660* (1976), p. 243.
54. Holmes, *Eastern Association*, p. 24.
55. I owe this point to Dr Mark Wittow.
56. E. Hyde, Earl of Clarendon, *The History of the Rebellion and Civil Wars in England*, ed. W.D. Macray (6 vols, Oxford, 1888), I, p. 171.
57. *Ibid.*

especially from the godly counties, were sent up to await the members on their assembly. The freeholders of Northamptonshire bemoaned the troubles to their consciences through innovations in religion, and the late exaction of ship money, forest fines and the costs of war – 'army money, waggon money, horse money, conduct money'. They pressed for annual parliaments to prevent the like inconveniences in the future.[58] Essex added to the list the vexations of ecclesiastical courts, and the costs of impositions and monopolies 'the undoing of many and the heavy grievance of all'.[59] Hertfordshire claimed that in consequence of 'exactions and excommunications for small causes', many poor people had been forced to flee their dwellings. They presented the 'manifest abuses of feodaries and escheators', the 'encroachments of purveyors', and urged that the legality of ship money be re-examined.[60] The freeholders of Suffolk complained that their charge 'is so unsupportable as we are not able to stand under the burden thereof'.[61] There may well have been other petitions which have not survived.[62] Certainly there is other evidence of local preoccupations and discontents. The commonalty of Newcastle petitioned the town's mayor to instruct the MPs going to Westminster 'to maintain the orthodox faith of our church', 'to stand out for the liberties and freedom of the subjects which is principally in the maintenance of Magna Carta and the other fundamental parliamentary laws' and in particular to lobby for the abolition of monopolies on tobacco, starch and – of particular local concern – coal and salt.[63] John Davenport's (of Whatcote, Warwickshire) list of things amiss and desiderata included regulation of timber consumption, the end of writs for debts under 40s. and – surely a naive optimism in the powers of parliament – a reduction in the number of sparrows which ate his grain![64] Commonly repeated religious and secular grievances leave us in no doubt that, for all the surface calm, resentments had built up in the localities and that a parliament was now expected to redress them. But it is important to appreciate too that petitions were couched in no new radical language; they were phrased in the conventional discourse of appeal to an assembly in which the king, Lords and Commons would meet together for the good of the commonweal. The Hertfordshire freeholders for

58. PRO, SP 16/450/25, printed in E. Cope (ed.) *Proceedings of the Short Parliament of 1640* (Camden Soc., 4th series, 19, 1977), p. 275. See also p. 234.
59. Harleian MS 4931, f.41; Cope, *Proceedings of the Short Parliament*, pp. 275–6.
60. Harleian MS 4931, f.42; Cope, *Proceedings of the Short Parliament*, pp. 277–8.
61. Tanner MS 67, f.174, not printed in Cope. Dr Jamie Hart notes the absence of petitions to the Lords, which he ascribes tentatively to a belief that the session would be longer. See J.S. Hart, 'The House of Lords and the reformation of justice, 1640–43' (Cambridge University, PhD thesis, 1985), p. 25.
62. See BL, MS 29/172, f.251: 'Queries sent to parliament'.
63. *Cal. Stat. Pap. Dom., 1639–40*, p. 601.
64. *Ibid.*, p. 599; cf. York Record Office, York House Books, 36, f.41; Bristol Record Office, Common Council Books, 3, f.102v.

example specifically presented religious innovations that violated 'the proclamations of . . . our most gracious sovereign King Charles' as well as acts of parliament; and they instructed their members 'to advance by your allowance this our most humble petition to our most gracious sovereign and to the upper house of parliament'.[65]

Popular ballads again underline the popular expectation not that parliament would stand in antagonistic opposition to the crown, but that it would counsel a just king and co-operate with him in a programme of reform and renewal that might strengthen the realm for a victorious war against the Scots. A song on the occasion of recalling parliament looked forward to harmony rather than contest. Predicting that the meeting might open a good king's eyes to those who had abused his grace, the refrain continued:

But our good King pleased, we shall be eased
From projects and ship money
The Scots beside do reveal their pride
And vow they will be bonny. . . .

God grant the King accept each thing
Both houses shall present him
No doubt it then but they again
Most freely will content him.[66]

The *Exact Description of the Manner How His Majesty and His Nobles went to the Parliament, on Monday, the 13th day of April 1640* was titled 'to the comfortable expectation of all loyal subjects'. The ballad took heart from the sight of 'our loyal King', 'our gracious King, our Charles the great / our joys sweet compliment' and his son 'that hopefull lad / whose sight made all true subjects glad'. Its tone was confident optimism for a good session:

For we may be assured of this
If anything hath been amiss
Our King and State will all redress
In this good parliament.[67]

The king's business or the country's?

The king's desires were simple and immediate; Charles had agreed to a parliament on the strength of the argument that it would grant

65. See above, note 60.
66. Harleian MS 4931, f.39.
67. *An Exact Description of the Manner how his Majesty and his Nobles went to the Parliament* (1640, Bodleian, Wood 401/138); see also H. Rollins, *Cavalier and Puritan* (New York, 1923), p. 78.

subsidies for the war. Despite some rumours about the machinations of the ill-affected, he did not doubt (Vane told Roe) 'the particular content he shall reap therein'.[68] Indeed though there were evidently some early thoughts of dealing with the likely recalcitrants in advance (Laud annotated Henry Neville's advice to James I on the Addled Parliament), no such plans were felt necessary.[69] Charles's optimism was greatly strengthened by the success of the parliament that convened in Ireland in March. Four subsidies were voted, and more importantly a resolution that the parliament would, if need be, grant further to the utmost of their ability: 'which,' Wentworth boasted to Hamilton, 'being done with so universal an alacrity and with entire purpose to perform accordingly if his Majesty's affairs really and justly need it . . . I do seriously judge to be better than if they had outright given ten subsidies.'[70] Some years earlier Wentworth had expressed his hope that successful parliaments in Ireland might soon be emulated in England.[71] Now he hoped an English assembly might follow the example of the Irish to defeat the Scots. Telling the marquis that he would find him in London before the parliament convened, he reflected: 'if those there do but follow the path these have trod out before them, his Majesty will have the Earl of Argyle and the rest of them [the Covenanters] very good cheap.'[72] Hamilton passed on the good news to Leicester. Laud, however, could not allay his doubts and fears that a parliament would 'the very first day of their sitting' embark on his destruction.[73]

On the day the parliament assembled, 13 April, Charles probably believed that he had the ace up his sleeve that would ensure the run of the cards. Perhaps with bad political judgement, he opted to say little. Announcing that 'There was never King had a more great and weighty cause to call his people together', he handed over to his Lord Keeper to explain in full 'the particulars'.[74] The newswriter Rossingham seemed a little surprised that the royal speech was 'very short', on this the occasion of the first parliament in eleven years.[75] Finch, however, addressed the houses at some length. His encomium of the king was matched by some flattery of the parliament which was, he reminded his auditories, 'the general, ancient and greatest counsel of this

68. *Cal. Stat. Pap. Dom., 1639–40*, p. 477, 21 Feb. 1640.
69. *Ibid.*, p. 329. See T. Moir, *The Addled Parliament of 1614* (Oxford, 1958).
70. Scottish Record Office, GD 406/1, Hamilton MS 803, 24 March 1640.
71. W. Knowler (ed.) *The Earl of Strafford's Letters and Despatches* (2 vols, 1739), I, p. 419; see above, p. 704.
72. Hamilton MS 803, see *HMC De Lisle and Dudley, VI*, p. 242.
73. BL Add. MS 11045, f.82. See *Cal. Stat. Pap. Dom., 1639–40*, p. 460: Laud to Roe, 14 Feb. 1640.
74. Cope, *Proceedings of the Short Parliament*, p. 115.
75. BL Add. MS 11045, f.109.

renowned kingdom', whose members came 'all armed with the votes and suffrages of the whole nation'.[76] In them, the king would, 'sequestering the memory of all former discouragements in preceding assemblies', place his confidence and his trust. Danger knocked at the gates of the commonwealth. The Scots – here he pandered to English prejudice – had enjoyed all the fruits of union with England: 'They participated of English honours [debased 'em, we hear some mutter]. The wealth and revenues of the nation they shared in' [aye and too much].[77] But what they should have repaid with loyalty and obedience they countered with insolence and rebellion, such that 'no true English . . . heart' could not but spurn it as 'foul and horrid treason'. Those who challenged England, however, always found it of 'too tough a complexion and courage' to master, and so it would be now.[78] The king had reluctantly decided to resist the threat by force. The Irish parliament had opened their purses with cheer. But money was desperately needed – not because Charles had been extravagant with 'unnecessary triumphs or sumptuous building', but because having financed a campaign the last summer at his own charge, the coffers were empty and the charge of an army 'must needs amount to a very great sum'. A parliament had been called therefore 'for the common preservation' of the realm. There was no time to be lost.[79] The 'bleeding evils' that menaced the realm could stay for neither debate nor delay; the Scots took advantages of time 'to frame their projects with foreign states'. The Commons accordingly were asked 'that you will for a while lay aside all other debates, and that you would pass an act for such and so many subsidies as you in your hearty affections to his Majesty and to the common good shall think fit'. Grant of subsidy, Finch told them, would not terminate the session. Later, just grievances would be heard and redressed. Moreover, the king himself, to end one dispute, had caused a bill to be drafted to legalize tonnage and poundage, acknowledging that he had collected it *de facto* rather than by right. But, first, provision for the army was an urgent priority: preparations were already in hand and the campaigning season was upon them. The 'straightness of time' required action not words.[80]

At the end of Finch's speech, Charles – unexpectedly, perhaps – rose again, and produced a letter from the Covenanters to the king of France requesting his aid. The superscription powerfully made the point – had the drama of this denouement been carefully stage-managed? In an address that treasonably denied Charles's authority,

76. Cope, *Proceedings of the Short Parliament*, p. 115, see pp. 115–21.
77. *Ibid.*, p. 117; my asides the product of an undergraduate diet of Carlyle's *Cromwell*.
78. *Ibid.*, p. 118.
79. *Ibid.*, pp. 119–20.
80. *Ibid.*, pp. 120–1.

the letter to Louis was headed 'Au Roi' as though he were their king.[81] Two days later, the election of Serjeant Glanville as speaker provided the usual occasion for exchange of compliment and reiteration of the harmony of prerogative and law, recently reaffirmed in the king's acceptance of the Petition of Right. Not all, however, believed the opening augured well. Rossingham summarized Finch's speech for Viscount Conway, then added: 'I perceive by the parliament manner that the King's speech and that of the Lord Keeper gave little hope of a continuing parliament; not one word of the ship money when the Lord Keeper spoke of the act of tonnage and poundage, which they expected.'[82] As matters passed from formalities to business, there was a sense of urgency on all parts – but no consensus about what should take priority in what looked likely to be a brief session.

The differences that were to bedevil the Short Parliament became apparent on the very first day of business. Windebank moved quickly on the morning of 16 April to press the government case. He reminded the house of the Covenanters' letter, adding now that an examination of Loudoun, the Scots commissioner confined in the Tower, had yielded his acknowledgement of its authenticity.[83] Harbottle Grimston, MP for Colchester and a known client of the Earl of Warwick, rose to answer and draw the attentions of the house to other concerns. Recognizing the great cause of which the secretary had spoken, he argued that there was also 'a case here at home of as great a danger': the threat to liberty and property and the assault on the church. It was for the house to decide whether internal or external ills were more threatening, but, Grimston reminded them, 'it is impossible to cure an ulcerous body unless you first cleanse the veins', whereas the body once healthy, external sores would 'fall away of themselves'.[84] The opening two speeches had laid out two agendas – both in the name of the good of king and people. The Commons would have to decide which would have first claim on their time. The third speaker of the day had already begun to sense the destructive implications of Grimston's programme, and endeavoured to moderate. Sir Benjamin Rudyerd, a client of the Herberts, had since the 1620s been a leading voice for moderation and reconciliation. Now again he took up his familiar role and lines. Parliament, Rudyerd reminded his fellows, had

81. *Ibid.*, pp. 121–2. This may be an instance of the brilliant sense of the theatricality of the moment that Charles learned to use to effect rather late and, of course, most effectively at his execution.
82. *Cal. Stat. Pap. Dom., 1640*, pp. 32–3. This letter repays comparison with Rossingham's to Scudamore, for to Conway he ventures more reflection on the mood of the house.
83. Cope, *Proceedings of the Short Parliament*, p. 134. On Loudoun's confinement for signing the letters to the king of France, see Gardiner, *History of England*, IX, p. 97.
84. Cope, *Proceedings of the Short Parliament*, pp. 135–7; cf. Maltby, *Aston Diary*, p. 3.

not recently been blessed with fortune, 'but the happy success of this parliament seems to be the general power of all'. A door, he went on, 'is . . . now opened to us of doing good': the parliament might be what it should be, a 'bed of reconciliation' between king and subjects. To be so it was important for them to 'look on the king's occasions' and then turn to the redress of grievances, rather than to act precipitately and jeopardize the future of parliaments. 'I would desire nothing more,' he closed, 'than that we proceed with such moderation as the parliament may be the mother of many more happy parliaments . . .'.[85] Where Rudyerd had pointed to the drawbacks of dissatisfying the king, Sir Francis Seymour, another veteran of the parliaments of the 1620s, raised the undesirability of offending the country that had chosen them, through shelving their just grievances. A parliament, he echoed Tully, 'is the soul of the commonwealth, wherein his Majesty may hear and see all the grievances of his subjects': the censure of MPs in inferior courts, the liberties taken by papists, the shortage of able preaching ministers, excessive claims for the prerogative and the invasion of the property of the subject. Despite Rudyerd's plea, Seymour, as Sir Thomas Peyton put it to Henry Oxinden, was saying much the same as Grimston. The Commons could not do the king's service by 'neglecting the Commonwealth'.[86]

Was there then a course the Commons could follow that would advance the king's pressing concerns as well as their own? Sir Henry Vane may have cleverly attempted to reveal one: he advised a committee for grievances leaving the full house free to deal with supply and thereby 'he hoped the King and country would receive content'.[87] The speaker who next rose spoke briefly but scuttled Vane's strategy. John Pym, a client of the Earl of Bedford, had risen to prominence in Charles's last parliament as the spokesman for the godly. In his first speech of the new session he was to dominate he insisted 'that for a committee of grievances it was to be the whole house, for not any subcommittee must conclude the house'.[88] Between Windebank's and Grimstone's programmes a choice of priority would have to be made.

We have a sense from the proceedings that the tactics for the next day had been carefully worked out so as to make the election of priorities a foregone conclusion. First thing on the morning of 17 April the speaker dutifully reported to the Commons the heads of the king's and Lord Keeper's speeches.[89] Francis Rous, who had spoken forcefully in 1629, seized the initiative with what was evidently a fully

85. Cope, *Proceedings of the Short Parliament*, pp. 138–40; Maltby, *Aston Diary*, pp. 3–4.
86. Cope, *Proceedings of the Short Parliament*, pp. 140–2; Maltby, *Aston Diary*, pp. 4–5.
87. Cope, *Proceedings of the Short Parliament*, p. 143.
88. *Ibid.*, pp. 143–4, perhaps a brilliantly prescient tactical motion.
89. The best account is in Maltby, *Aston Diary*, pp. 6–7.

prepared speech on religious and secular grievances: the flirting with Rome and the denigration of the godly, the abuses of monopolies and ship money.[90] John Pym, in what may have been the staged main act after a warm-up, followed with a detailed, two-hour-long analysis of the subjects' grievances under three heads – those against parliament, those against Protestantism and those against property. In emotive language Pym raised the matter of the precipitate dissolution of the last assembly that had stifled 'our last sighs and groans to his Majesty', and the examination and imprisonment of the MPs – 'a death to a good subject' no less than it had been to Sir John Eliot. He catalogued the papists elevated to high places, popish books published and ceremonies countenanced and enforced by bishops and ecclesiastical courts. Finally he listed the 'many grievances' of tonnage and poundage exacted without parliament, knighthood and forest fines 'forced against law', monopolies 'whereof we have a multitude', and ship money levied 'without any colour of law at all'. For all his claim to advance the king's business, Pym's was a comprehensive assault on the programmes of the personal rule, and one which laid the blame very close to the king's door. 'That the Lords of the council should countenance these things,' he declaimed, 'is a very great grievance', one occasioned by the intermission of parliaments. All these ills and distempers, he argued, 'disabled us to administer any supply until they be redressed'.[91] When Pym sat down, as if on cue the MPs of Northamptonshire, Middlesex and Suffolk presented their counties' petitions of grievances. Sir John Hotham 'thought good to fall on the preparation of them the next day'.[92] Almost without a decision, let alone a dissentient voice, the Commons, without any general intent of lessening the king's power, had embarked on the course that, as Rudyerd had admonished, would produce their early dissolution.[93]

The next day, Saturday the 18th, as further petitions were presented from Hertfordshire, Essex and Norwich, the house constituted itself as a committee of the whole for grievances, with Harbottle Grimston in the chair, and proceeded to investigate the circumstances of the 1629 dissolution.[94] When they reconvened on the Monday, Sir Edward Herbert, Solicitor-General, attempted to check the immoderate lan-

90. Cope, *Proceedings of the Short Parliament*, pp. 145–8, a speech which appears to have been a script.
91. *Ibid.*, pp. 148–57, 254–60; Maltby, *Aston Diary*, pp. 8–10.
92. Cope, *Proceedings of the Short Parliament*, p. 157. Hotham, as MP for Beverley in Yorkshire, doubtless had come up instructed to end many grievous burdens the war had imposed on his county.
93. Mr Rigby closed the debate by urging the house that any loss the king might suffer from the reform of grievances 'may be supplied by a constant revenue to be settled by us' (Maltby, *Aston Diary*, p. 11). Evidently, he (and perhaps most MPs) thought that proceeding to a discussion of grievances need not be inimical to the king's interests.
94. Cope, *Proceedings of the Short Parliament*, pp. 158–62.

guage and claims made by some: their questioning the royal power of dissolution, he pointed out, 'manifestly trenched upon the prerogative'. Ignoring his counsel, however, Oliver St John rejected the request to examine precedents. Anxious perhaps about the present as well as past deployment of the royal prerogative of dissolution, he boldly opined: 'that the King called Parliaments by his Great Seal and not by bare command of word, and therefore he held it might not be adjourned with a bare command, nay he said it was a question whether the Great Seal could adjourn it, for the court must adjourn itself'.[95] If his anxiety was prescient, it was not misplaced. The following day after noon the Commons were summoned, unusually, to the Banqueting House where, with the king present but silent, the Lord Keeper addressed them on behalf of His Majesty. Lest they had not from his opening speech grasped the urgency of the king's needs, Finch spelled them out. The king's army was 'now on foot and marching and that the charge of it amounted to £100,000 monthly which was more than he could furnish out of his own coffers'. Without immediate parliamentary support, all the expenditure and preparation made would be wasted. A full supply was neither expected nor demanded: 'only so much as might keep the design on foot from being lost'. That once granted, the house could return to its grievances with the king's blessing. As for ship money, which had exercised so many speakers and about which he had said nothing before, Finch assured them that the king never intended that it become an annual tax or private benefit to the crown; he sought only that 'he might be able . . . to defend us with safety and honour'. Charles, therefore, asked for the trust of his subjects that he acted out of love for his people. He asked of the Commons that they – like his Irish parliament – should show their trust and affection in a speedy grant of supply; and of the Lords 'that they should give their assistance'.[96] After a frustrating start as far as the crown was concerned, the Lord Keeper's speech was an attempt to turn the tide. But, ironically, it flung the parliament into the destructive whirlpools of privilege and procedure.

On 23 April, two days after the Lord Keeper's address, the Commons met as a committee to consider the king's business. Rudyerd attempted to steer the discussion to the new course. 'Trust him that he may trust us,' he counselled. For though the commonwealth was a 'miserable spectacle', they had 'the King's word for redress which as it was sacred so likewise inviolable and therefore wished the house to

95. *Ibid.*, p. 163.
96. *Ibid.*, pp. 164–7. Aston underlines the sense of unusualness and the power of majesty; 'afternoon attended the king and the Keeper made a speech. The king in person' (Maltby, *Aston Diary*, p. 25).

bring things to a happy conclusion'.[97] After the pause that followed, Sir Ralph Hopton undercut him. A servant who paused to pull out a thorn, he observed, that he might more swiftly progress, advanced rather than impeded his master's service. 'He said we had many thorns to pull out before we were able to serve the king . . .' and went on to list them.[98] Perhaps because his metaphors were so effective, Hopton's argument won the day. Sir Francis Seymour appreciated the king's needs as well as the country's grievances, 'which put him in a great strait'; but recalling the 'false gloss' placed on the Petition of Right, he thought 'we have cause to fear the worst', and urged that grievances should come first.[99] Sensing the support for such a course, Vane reminded them that 'the work of the day was a supply' and hinted that if it did not come first, the parliament might be dissolved.[100] Strafford's secretary, Sir Philip Mainwaring, supported him, but Pym felt confident enough to urge that the question be put whether grievances should have the precedence over supply. Just for good measure he reminded the house (perhaps fleetingly flashing some cards up his sleeve) that the king had neither confided in them nor sought their counsel for the Scots war.[101] The Commons voted for a conference with the Lords to present their grievances. It looked as though it would be some time before they returned to the king's business.

Time was what Charles I did not have. On the very day the Commons resolved to proceed with their grievances, the Earl of Northumberland wrote to Leicester in Paris: 'The year is now so far spent that [the king's] present occasions cannot admit of so long a delay as must of necessity be suffered while these grievances are preparing.'[102] Northumberland's son Henry Percy believed that it would sound the death knell of the parliament. 'We seem,' he wrote, also on the 23rd, 'to be very averse from those things that are necessary for the honour of the king and good of our country and particularly we have this day declined the supply of the king and have resolved the grievances shall take place, wherefore the king resolved to dissolve us tomorrow. They are in Council now but it is to confirm the king's sense by the vote of the Council.'[103] If Percy's information was correct, the Council meeting must have voted for, and persuaded

97. Cope, *Proceedings of the Short Parliament*, pp. 169–70. A speech, Aston records, followed by 'a long pause, no man speaking' (Maltby, *Aston Diary*, p. 36).
98. Cope, *Proceedings of the Short Parliament*, p. 170.
99. *Ibid.*, pp. 170–1.
100. *Ibid.*, pp. 171, 173; Maltby, *Aston Diary*, p. 39.
101. Cope, *Proceedings of the Short Parliament*, p. 173. It may be significant that Pym had not raised this important point in his speech concerning grievances on the 17th. See below, p. 873.
102. *HMC De Lisle and Dudley, VI*, p. 254.
103. *Ibid.*, pp. 251–2.

Charles to, one last try. It was probably on the advice of his Council that the next day Charles decided upon a direct appeal to his peers. Speaking personally, he informed the upper house that the Commons had voted to pursue their grievances 'and so put the cart before the horse'. If there were time for debates, he continued, they might be tolerated, but 'the necessities are so urgent that there can be no delay'. Vowing to make good his promises concerning redress of abuses, Charles insisted that he must be trusted and urged the peers on their honour not to join the Commons 'but leave them to themselves'.[104] With a promising expedition that contrasted with the Commons, the Lords went into committee to discuss the king's message. The king's cause did not lack powerful spokesmen. Strafford underlined the seriousness of the Scots threat; the Earl of Dorset feared they would 'gladly change soils with us'. Viscount Saye opposed them on a number of counts: he urged unity between the houses, pressed the Commons' jurisdiction in matters of supply and claimed that 'it is not in the intentions of the H[ouse] of C[ommons] to leave [the] King in a desperate estate'. Whilst Bristol and Southampton, more equivocal, suggested renewed discussion with the Commons, none joined Saye in rejecting the king's request for their assistance. By majority vote the house resolved 'that his Majesty's supply shall have precedency . . . before any other business be treated of'.[105] On the next day, Saturday the 25th, the Lords desired the Commons to meet with them in the Painted Chamber. There the Lord Keeper summarized the king's speech, stressed the real emergency ('the Scots had pitched their tents up at Dunse') and communicated the Lords' resolution for supply together with their assurance that 'afterwards they would freely join with the House of Commons in anything for the common good'.[106]

Finch was careful to explain that the Lords 'would not meddle with supply as appertaining properly to the House of Commons'. They merely gave advice for the good of the kingdom. But his distinction did not satisfy those who discussed the resolution on the 27th. Sir Walter Earle took great umbrage at the 'trenching upon the liberty of Parliament' (*sic*), and Pym, seizing an opportunity, described it as a 'danger . . . of much consequence'. Though Rudyerd, continuing his tireless endeavours to conciliate, won some support, the house decried the violation of its privileges and resolved to secure redress.[107] Far from speeding supply the king's appeal to the Lords had pushed

104. Cope, *Proceedings of the Short Parliament*, pp. 69–70.

105. *Journal of the House of Lords, IV*, pp. 65–7; Cope, *Proceedings of the Short Parliament*, pp. 69–71, 79–80.

106. Cope, *Proceedings of the Short Parliament*, pp. 176–7; Maltby, *Aston Diary*, pp. 63–5.

107. Cope, *Proceedings of the Short Parliament*, p. 177–80. Peter Ball denied the breach of liberty.

another grievance to the top of the agenda. To those engaged in getting the troops prepared, the seemingly obstructive behaviour of the Commons was as baffling as it was frustrating. 'There are many wise men of the House of Parliament,' John Nicholas wrote to his son, 'and it is strange to me that they supply not his Majesty's wants and then seek ease of grievances.'[108] Vane could tell Conway only that things were coming to a head: 'some days will give a clear light of their intentions'.[109] On 29 April, however, having made a forceful representation of their anger to the Lords, the lower house returned to the discussion of grievances, under Pym's three heads. It is significant that, for all their discontents, they were more divided over religious matters, especially the placing of the communion table, than over other grievances.[110] Here it was far from obvious that Pym could carry the house. But meanwhile time was passing with no progress on the king's business. Charles I therefore attempted yet another strategy. His hope of applying pressure for supply through the upper house having failed, he sent on 2 May a message which Vane read to the Commons: 'That his Majesty had often told us of his danger and yet had received no answer at all; he doth now again require a present answer of his supply and promises all that before he promised, adding that a delay was every way as destructive as a denial.'[111]

The direct message at least had the immediate effect of concentrating the house on the question of supply. Pym, perhaps sensing the possibility of some resolution, tried to focus the house on the jurisdictional dispute with the Lords, but the Commons went into committee on the king's message, 'which was to be debated for answer'.[112] Sir Francis Seymour even moderated his earlier stance to offer a compromise and route round the impasse: 'that if he had satisfaction for ship money he should trust the king with the rest'.[113] Vane saw the opportunity Seymour's motion presented. 'He approved of Sir Francis Seymour's motion hoping that this day should produce some good effect' and, attempting to win the wavering, concluded 'that if a rupture should happen, he did believe that the country would not thank us'.[114] Pym, beginning to fear that Seymour spoke for many, intervened to check progress towards a compromise. 'The taking away of ship money he

108. *Cal. Stat. Pap. Dom., 1640*, p. 74, 27 April.
109. *Ibid.*, 28 April.
110. Maltby, *Aston Diary*, pp. 85–109, esp. pp. 88–93.
111. Cope, *Proceedings of the Short Parliament*, pp. 187–8.
112. *Ibid.*, p. 188.
113. *Ibid.*, p. 189. Seymour 'said that he perceived the [king's] message could receive no delay'. Rossingham reported the king's message 'put all other business aside' (BL Add. MS 11045, f.114).
114. Cope, *Proceedings of the Short Parliament*, p. 189.

said were not enough', when the realm was oppressed with other military charges for a war entered into without their counsel.[115] Pym had support: Strode and Earle stressed the importance of religious grievances; Kirton expressed concern about other threats to property; Sir John Hotham, MP for Beverley in Yorkshire, understandably drew attention to the military charges that had especially burdened his county. But Pym's invitation to investigate the causes of the war found no takers and there were several ready to follow Seymour down the path of compromise.[116] It was far from clear which way the house would go. Solicitor Herbert described them as 'much divided'.[117] Yet the Privy Councillors clearly felt that it was worth gambling on a positive reaction to the king's message. They pressed to have it put to the question whether the house would supply. Given the lateness of the hour, however, the 'absolute answer' was deferred.[118]

Vane spent the rest of the weekend closeted with the king. Seeing that Seymour's compromise had won support from the back benches, he turned it into a concrete proposal which on Monday the 4th he presented to the house. In exchange for an immediate vote of twelve subsidies the king would surrender ship money and prolong the session to hear other grievances.[119] It may be that the strategy took the malcontents by surprise. Seymour had to back-pedal somewhat to reject an offer he thought he could not take to the country.[120] Some, like Sir Nevile Poole, Sir Gilbert Gerard, Oliver St John and Sir Robert Cooke, wanted other grievances and charges placed in the bargain. But as well as government spokesmen there were MPs prepared to accept the deal: predictably Rudyerd, also Falkland, Hyde, and evidently Sir Peter Heyman (who had been imprisoned after 1629).[121] Sir Henry Slingsby 'urged the grace of the king in his offer of remitting ship money'.[122] The discussion, however, got bogged down in a debate over whether any such bargain could be struck before the house had determined the legality of ship money, and whether, if the

115. *Ibid.*, p. 190. Pym appears ruffled in the version reported by Aston. He raised the stakes by raising the issue of the king's prerogative of peace and war but, aware of the danger of alienating the house, put it, 'we ought not to desire it, but if his Majesty please to satisfy us of the causes of this war . . .' (Maltby, *Aston Diary*, p. 123).
116. Cope, *Proceedings of the Short Parliament*, pp. 190–3, 206–8; Maltby, *Aston Diary*, pp. 121–7.
117. Cope, *Proceedings of the Short Parliament*, p. 191. He pressed the need for a 'direct answer', precisely what Pym could not afford.
118. *Ibid.*, pp. 192–3.
119. *Ibid.*, p. 193. The version in Aston's diary (p. 128) makes it clearer that Vane's proposal was intended to out-manoeuvre those relying on a delay to the king's message.
120. Cope, *Proceedings of the Short Parliament*, p. 195.
121. Maltby, *Aston Diary*, pp. 128–44.
122. Cope, *Proceedings of the Short Parliament*, p. 196, though the version in Aston conveys a different sense (Maltby, *Aston Diary*, p. 140). As Slingsby was called to the bar, the version in Cope seems closer to his meaning.

levy were legal, the king could be held to the deal. Confusion ensued over the procedural order of questions and business, so that it was impossible, as Herbert put it, to 'offer anything agreeable to all sense of the house'.[123] One diarist suggests that, clearly perceiving that their choice now lay between agreeing to the compromise or facing a dissolution, a considerable party was inclined to accept. Others, sensing the drift, saw the house 'to be so far yielding that they were not willing to put it to vote, fearing lest it might be carried for the king'.[124] In the event, though they had sat from 7 a.m. till 6 p.m., nothing was resolved and the house adjourned to the next day.[125] Charles, as Sir Thomas Aston noted in his parliamentary diary, had warned that any further delay would be seen 'as good as denial'.[126] And at least one official government source in the Commons reported that the proposed compromise was unlikely to receive assent: 'the sense of the House was that not only ship money should be abolished but also all military taxes and other taxes for the future by what name or title soever . . . should be provided against before that twelve subsidies were granted'.[127] There seemed little to be gained from still further procrastination.

The dissolution

The following day, 5 May, Charles summoned the House of Commons to the Lords, and dissolved the parliament. In his speech, he carefully exonerated the Lords from blame; he rehearsed his offers to the Commons; as he had in 1628 and 1629, he attributed the misunderstanding not to the whole house, but to 'some cunning and ill affectionate men' who had disrupted it.[128] Given his repeated warnings that time was pressing and delay akin to denial, we may not need to seek for any explanations for the dissolution other than that. The king's declaration of the causes which moved him to terminate the session fairly accurately traced the history of those three short weeks and reiterated his final speech.[129] At another level, however, the timing and circumstances of the dissolution call for comment. For arguably more

123. Maltby, *Aston Diary*, p. 134.
124. Cope, *Proceedings of the Short Parliament*, p. 243; cf. Maltby, *Aston Diary*, p. 144. See Clarendon, *History of the Rebellion*, I, p. 180.
125. *Cal. Stat. Pap. Dom., 1640*, p. 40.
126. Maltby, *Aston Diary*, p. 144.
127. *Cal. Stat. Pap. Dom., 1640*, p. 40.
128. Cope, *Proceedings of the Short Parliament*, pp. 197–8.
129. *His Majesty's Declaration to all his Loving Subjects of the Causes which Moved Him to Dissolve the Last Parliament* (1640), BL, E.203.1; see too *Bibliotheca Regia or the Royal Library* (1659), pp. 430–8.

progress had been made in the latter than earlier days of the parliament towards a compromise. And whilst the twelve subsidies floated by Vane appear not to have won widespread assent there is no reason to believe that this figure had been intended as a sticking position. Temple later commented to the Earl of Leicester that Vane had the king's approval to drop his demand to eight subsidies, but that he stood on twelve 'and never came lower'.[130] In the Commons, one diarist recorded that 'it was feared' the house 'would have yielded to have given six subsidies', but that the parliament broke first.[131] Though neither was sufficient, the gap between eight and six was difficult neither to bridge nor resolve; there was clearly a sense that Vane's proposition was a negotiating stance.[132] It should not have spelled the end. Nor need the disagreements about other grievances have been fatal to the working out of a compromise. On the day the MPs began to ride home, Northumberland explained to Viscount Conway (then at Berwick) that the king had offered to rescind ship money in return for subsidies but that the Commons had sought to throw military charges and religious innovations into the bargain. Even those demands in themselves he thought not destructive: 'had they been well advised I am verily persuaded they might in time have gained their desires'. But, he added, 'they in a tumultuous and confused way went on with their businesses which gave so great offence to his Majesty that this morning he had dissolved the parliament'.[133]

What were those businesses that excited the king's offence? Charles's decision to summon the speaker to the upper house for the dissolution provides a clue that he might have feared a re-enactment of 1629, when, we recall, Eliot's resolutions had been read after Black Rod had knocked at the door.[134] A correspondent of John Winthrop confirms our suspicion when he reports the end of the parliament, on 13 May, explaining that the speaker had been called to the Lords 'to make sure

130. *HMC De Lisle and Dudley, VI*, p. 387. Temple reports Strafford's analysis of the breaking of parliament. The personal hostility between him and Vane is obviously important here, but should not discount his explanation, not least because, even at his trial, on this matter the Commons believed him. Cf. Clarendon, *History of the Rebellion*, I, p. 182.
131. Cope, *Proceedings of the Short Parliament*, p. 244.
132. Though six or seven subsidies would have been a poor exchange for ship money, the other advantages of being seen to work with parliament might have made it worth while. Sir William Savile claimed his native Yorkshire would have voted any number to be rid of ship money (*Cal. Stat. Pap. Dom., 1640*, p. 154).
133. *Ibid.*, pp. 114–15, 5 May.
134. Cope, *Proceedings of the Short Parliament*, p. 197. The speaker pretended he was unwell, but was in the Lords when the Commons were summoned (*Cal. Stat. Pap. Dom., 1640*, p. 116). See I.H.C. Fraser, 'The agitation in the Commons, 2 March 1629 and the interrogation of the leaders of the anti-court group', *Bull. Inst. Hist. Res.*, 30 (1957), pp. 86–95.

he should not go into the nether house to prevent the house from protesting against the war, ship money and conduct money'.[135] Ship money and military charges had been declaimed as grievances from almost the first day of the session; it was the decision to go to war, the sufficiency of the king's causes, the appropriateness of entering a conflict without parliamentary counsel that had begun to raise more sensitive matters in recent days. Endeavouring to explain the dissolution, John Nalson heard some suggest that Charles had received intelligence that a party (in league with the Scots) was about to demand a full enquiry into the causes of the war.[136] Hearsay is supported by firm evidence. On 5 May John Johnston informed John Smith that the parliament was about to petition the king to reconcile with the Scots.[137] It is certain that leaders of the house were in touch with the Scots commissioners, who had asked for their assistance in distributing their declaration in England.[138] Evidently the government received information that it had been planned to bring the Scots declaration of their grievances before the Commons on 5 May and that Pym had been primed to speak to them, pointing up the afflictions common to English and Scottish subjects.[139] The intelligence probably led to a hastily convened Council meeting and decision to dissolve the parliament, for Charles was later to remind his committee that they had counselled him to put an end to the session.[140] His statement that he did not doubt the loyalty of most members is also corroborated by a search for precedents within days of the dissolution to ascertain whether the same MPs could be resummoned to Westminster without recourse to new elections.[141] Everything points to the suggestion that the Short Parliament was broken by the fear of a conspiracy. It would not be the last time that the hopes of a harmonious settlement foundered on such fears.

Contemporaries were quick to pass their verdict on this addled parliament and in some cases to attribute blame. There was a general sadness – and fear – at the dissolution, on all parts. Brampton Gurden wrote to Winthrop 'we are here in a very hard condition in regard our

135. *The Winthrop Papers* (Massachusetts Historical Soc., 4th series, 6, Boston, 1863), p. 565, or *Winthrop Papers IV* (Massachusetts Historical Soc., 1944), p. 235.
136. J. Nalson, *An Impartial Collection of the Great Affairs of State from the Beginning of the Scotch Rebellion in 1639 to the Murder of King Charles I* (2 vols, 1682–3), I, p. 343.
137. *Cal. Stat. Pap. Dom., 1640*, p. 119. The letter is endorsed 'Scottish letter intercepted'.
138. *Ibid.*, pp. xvi–xvii, 140–1.
139. *Ibid.*, p. 144: information for the government. The information reports that the Scots *Declaration to the English* was planned for discussion on 7 May, but brought forward to 5 May. See also pp. 140–1, 153–4. Pym's earlier allusion to the general questions of the war suggest that some such manoeuvre may have been planned from the start.
140. Ellesmere MS 7849.
141. Ellesmere MS 7834: Castle to Bridgewater, 15 May.

parliament is dissolved';[142] George Wyllys heard that England was 'full of fears generally' at the news.[143] At the other end of the spectrum of religious sensibilities, Richard Holdsworth, archdeacon of Huntingdon, was 'in as sad thoughts for the breaking up of the parliament as any man living';[144] Windebank agreed 'this is a very great disaster'.[145] Explanations of what had gone wrong greatly differed. Governor John Winthrop of Massachusetts was assured that 'it comforteth the hearts of honest men of both houses that they yielded not to give a penny to help the King in his intended war against the Scots'.[146] On the government's part Windebank justified the regrettable dissolution: 'there was,' he explained to Hopton, 'no other way and his Majesty hath wherewithal to justify himself to God and the world that the fault is not his, having offered redress of all their grievances and particularly . . . the shipping money.'[147]

But between these stark poles there was a range of reactions which suggests both that contemporaries did not see the parliament as ruined by inevitable ideological differences and that they had not yet formed into clear political camps. Even Wentworth, as the Earl of Leicester was informed, laid the blame for the breaking of parliament less on the Commons than on the conduct of Vane and Windebank who evidently (in his view wrongly) told Charles there was no hope the Commons would supply.[148] On the other hand, in the country (as well as at court) there was some sense that the Commons at least in part had themselves to blame for their failure. Hugh Cholmley, an MP for Yorkshire, believed the king 'ill advised' in breaking with the parliament, but others were more apt to point to how little it had acted.[149] Dennis Bond and William Bribey recorded its passing 'and nothing done';[150] Hawkins sounded frustrated at business getting bogged down in the jurisdictional dispute and feared such wasted time would lose the whole opportunity of the parliament.[151] Bishops Bridgeman and Cosin christened it a 'non-parliament'.[152] Sir Henry Slingsby observed that the parliament had sat for three weeks 'without having anything done

142. *Winthrop Papers*, 6, p. 565; *Winthrop Papers IV*, p. 235.
143. *The Wyllys Papers, 1590–1796* (Connecticut Historical Soc., Hertford, 21, 1924), pp. 11–12.
144. Lambeth Palace MS 943, p. 599.
145. *Clarendon State Papers*, II, p. 84.
146. *Winthrop Papers*, 6, p. 565; also *Winthrop Papers IV*, pp. 235, 243.
147. Clarendon MS 18, no. 1382.
148. *HMC De Lisle and Dudley, VI*, p. 387; cf. note 130, above. Wentworth's tactics had worked in the Lords, see J.P. Cooper, *Land, Men and Beliefs* (1983), p. 198.
149. *The Memoirs of Sir Hugh Cholmley* (1787), p. 60.
150. Dorset Record Office, D 413, Box 22, f.52; *Wyllys Papers*, pp. 11–12.
151. *HMC De Lisle and Dudley, VI*, pp. 256–7.
152. G.T.O. Bridgeman, *History of the Church and Manor of Wigan*, part II (Chetham Soc., new series, 16, 1899), p. 432.

to content either King or country'.[153] Sir Thomas Peyton was blunt: 'this great Council dissolved' he told Henry Oxinden, 'because it was so long a resolving.'[154] Popular attitudes also appear to have been more mixed than has been claimed. Though the 'hearts of good people were much dejected' and though the apprentices were to attack Laud's London residence, blaming the archbishop for the dissolution, ballads suggest a greater popular sympathy for the king (and less for the Commons) than we might have supposed.[155] On the eve of the parliament, popular verses had urged them not to grudge money to suppress the Scots rebellion 'against a King so mild and gracious'.[156] At its close, the lines addressed 'To the House of Commons at their rising from the last session of parliament' are sharp in their criticism.

> You that will question your King's power below
> If you come there will you the heaven's King, so
> Do not aspire, you may take up your rest
> Safer beneath than in the eagle's nest
> Doth clemency offend you, will you harm
> And pluck the sun from heaven that keeps you warm
> Nor Kings nor Bishops please, what have we got
> An outside English or an inside Scot.[157]

Taking up the theme of factional conspiracy, the poem moves to condemn a parliament that through inactivity squandered the opportunity of a successful session:

> If factions thus our country's peace distracts
> We may have worlds of parliaments, no Acts
> Ill-ended sessions, though 'twas well begun
> Too much being spoken made too little done
> Thus factions thrive, Puritanism bears sway
> Nought must be done but only Saye [*sic*]
> Stoop down you barren headed hills confess
> You might be fruitful if you would be less.

Clarendon, who was able with hindsight to see the crucial importance of the three weeks in the spring of 1640, concurred with those who argued that the chance for harmonious settlement was lost through mismanagement by the government and the machinations of a few in the Commons. For in general, 'it could never be hoped that more

153. D. Parsons (ed.) *The Diary of Sir Henry Slingsby* (1836), p. 48.
154. D. Gardiner (ed.) *The Oxinden Letters, 1607–1642* (1933), p. 173.
155. Woodforde's diary, 5 May; below, p. 906.
156. Rollins, *Cavalier and Puritan*, p. 86.
157. Tanner MS 306, ff.290–290v. See also M.A.E. Green (ed.) *The Diary of John Rous, 1625–1642* (Camden Soc., old series, 66, 1856), pp. 88–90. Rous copies this ballad.

sober and dispassioned men would ever meet together in that place or fewer who brought ill purposes with them'.[158] On balance, the evidence suggests that he was right. That is not to deny that the Commons were determined to secure redress of pressing grievances. Not least, as many speeches reaffirm, most MPs had a strong sense of their responsibility to their constituents and of their accountability to them on their return. The recently printed journal of the Cheshire MP Sir Thomas Aston also evidences more than other sources we have 'the deep sense of grievance and profound mistrust' which may have begun to colour perceptions of the king as well as his ministers.[159] Speakers did not hesitate to question the legality of governmental levies and courses; nor in some cases to express their discontent that, almost unprecedentedly, the king had embarked on a war without first seeking their counsel. Oliver St John ventured to attribute the problems of the realm generally to the personal rule: 'the intermission of 11 years hath brought all this'.[160] Yet for all that, the debates convey the impression of moderate men who were not fundamentally antagonistic to the king's government. Even when debating the detested ship money, the tone was far from radical. When George Peard, a Middle Temple lawyer, referred to the tax as 'an abomination', he was compelled to confess himself sorry for his language.[161] And whilst some strongly denounced its illegality and more were inclined to believe them, 'yet in this whole discourse about this ship money,' Rossingham told Conway, 'they used these words, saving the judgement of the reverend judges, which judgement they would not declare to be against law till the King's counsel should be heard to argue it in the House of Commons.'[162]

Perhaps of still more significance, religious issues do not appear to have loomed largely – or at least destructively – in the Short Parliament.[163] Despite the speeches of Pym, Seymour and Rous outlining religious innovations, the opinion of the house was that 'they would trust his Majesty to give them time to sit for the redressing of them' at a later date.[164] As we have seen, the 4th of May when Vane's offer was on the table saw a crucial day's debate when things could have gone either way. One puritan newswriter thought the house inclining to

158. Clarendon, *History of the Rebellion*, I, pp. 179–84, quotation p. 183.
159. Maltby, *Aston Diary*, p. xiii. Aston became a Royalist.
160. *Ibid.*, p. 58.
161. Cope, *Proceedings of the Short Parliament*, pp. 172–3.
162. *Cal. Stat. Pap. Dom., 1640*, p. 109, 30 April. Cf. Maltby, *Aston Diary*, pp. 138–9.
163. Cf. Gardiner, *History of England*, IX, p. 112, despite his emphasis on religion. Cf. M. Stieg, *Laud's Laboratory: The Diocese of Bath and Wells in the Early Seventeenth Century* (1982), p. 21.
164. BL Add. MS 11045, f.114; cf. Maltby, *Aston Diary*, pp. 87–95. Sir Neville Poole was tired of the religious debate; 'Enough of this already, moves to waive the rest.'

agree, despite Pym's protests concerning wider issues.[165] There is an impression of Pym's struggling for the support of the back benches in the parliament. And it may be that if the Council had earlier seized the initiative and proposed a bill of concessions in return for subsidies, along the lines of Vane's eleventh-hour proposal, it might have obtained supply.[166] We cannot finally conclude what the outcome of the Short Parliament would have been had it sat longer.[167] We do know who the king blamed for its failure: days after the dissolution a search was ordered of the houses of the Earl of Warwick, Lords Saye and Brooke and Pym, Hampden and Sir Walter Earle.[168] All were suspected of dealings with the Scots; in addition, papers concerning Mainwaring's sentence in 1629 and petitions of silenced ministers were seized.[169] Pym burned other petitions.[170] There may well have been something to Sir William Calley's suspicion that the dissolution had been 'occasioned by some violent froward heads . . .'.[171]

The Convocation and the canons

The 5th of May was not quite the end of the Short Parliament. Synonymously with the summoning of the Lords and Commons Charles had, customarily, issued a commission for the assembly of a Convocation of the clergy. Moreover for the first time since 1606 he had granted it a licence to draw up canons for the direction and government of the church.[172] During the course of the parliament's short life, the Convocation had embarked on its work. Promptly, while the Commons prevaricated over supply, the clergy on 22 April voted six subsidies to the king. To those with pressing religious grievances, the commission to the Convocation was a cause of concern. In 1629, Pym and others had endeavoured to assert the authority of parliament in religious matters, an authority that an independent commission to Convocation appeared to threaten. After a decade of heightened tension in lay–clerical relations, there was no inclination to yield anything to the clergy – still less to a body dominated by an

165. D. Hirst, *Authority and Conflict* (1986), p. 189.
166. Cf. G.E. Aylmer, *Rebellion or Revolution?: England 1640–60* (Oxford, 1986), p. 13.
167. Cf. Cope, *Proceedings of the Short Parliament*, p. 9.
168. *Winthrop Papers*, 6, p. 565; *Cal. Stat. Pap. Dom., 1640*, p. 152.
169. *Cal. Stat. Pap. Dom., 1640*, p. 152.
170. BL Add. MS 11045, f.116.
171. *Cal. Stat. Pap. Dom., 1640*, p. 144.
172. *Cal. Stat. Pap. Dom., 1639–40*, p. 472, king's writ, 20 Feb. 1639. See also E. Cope, 'The Short Parliament and convocation', *Journ. Eccles. Hist.*, 25 (1974), pp. 167–84. The account that follows is based on my own researches, but I am grateful to Julian Davies for the opportunity to compare mine with his important chapter.

ecclesiastical hierarchy which some dismissed as unorthodox.[173] On 21 April Sir Walter Earle, who had urged the house to give religious grievances priority, suggested that the Commons investigate the commission granted to Convocation;[174] Pym seconded him by asserting the following day that no actions of Convocation could bind the laity.[175] Some MPs even 'desired that some committee chosen might go to the Lords and desire them to join with the House of Commons in petition to the King to stop the proceedings of the Convocation'.[176] The Lord Keeper's speech and the king's demand for a speedy account of his business turned attention away from the problem. But it may be that Charles had already begun to consider prolonging the Convocation in the event, growing in likelihood, of an early dissolution of the parliament: notes in the state papers dated in April appear to be concerned with such a question.[177]

Whether planned in advance or not on the dissolution of the parliament, the king, having consulted his judges, issued a new commission authorizing the Convocation to proceed with its work.[178] It has been suggested that Charles's motive was largely financial: with the army assembling and the Commons having failed to supply, any financial aid was desperately sought after. Finance, however, may not have been the only, or even the first consideration. In issuing the commission to draw up new canons, Charles appears to have been continuing his policy of trying to secure a peace in the church.[179] Early in April Rossingham reported to Scudamore that the king had ordered that the new canons should in no way overturn those of 1604, nor the Thirty-Nine Articles, nor alter the liturgy of the church, but that they should be directed against papists and Jesuits on the one hand and 'factious puritans' on the other.[180] In the spirit of his master, Laud, according to Heylyn, attempted to settle some of the religious differences in the parliament by suggesting that leading MPs and clergy consult together to resolve them.[181] When the parliament broke before any such

173. The list of those appointed to draw up the canons is in Nalson, *Impartial Collection*, I, p. 364.
174. Cope, *Proceedings of the Short Parliament*, p. 164.
175. *Ibid.*, p. 168.
176. *Ibid.*; cf. pp. 175, 181; Maltby, *Aston Diary*, p. 52; BL Add. MS 11045, f.136; Nalson, *Impartial Collection*, I, pp. 364–5.
177. *Cal. Stat. Pap. Dom., 1640*, pp. 24–5.
178. Cope, 'Short Parliament and Convocation', p. 177; Gardiner, *History of England*, IX, pp. 142–3. The Convocation sat with its own full agreement. See Dering MS U 350/C.2, 47: H. Hammond to Dering, 16 May.
179. As the prefatory declaration makes clear, see *Works of Laud*, V, part 2, pp. 609–13. See Charles I to Laud, 17 May, *Cal. Stat. Pap. Dom., 1640*, p. 175 and *ibid.*, p. 149.
180. BL Add. MS 11045, f.105, 2 April.
181. P. Heylyn, *Cyprianus Anglicus or the History of the Life and Death of William Laud* (1668), part II, p. 396.

proposal could bear fruit, Laud expected that the Convocation would be dissolved too.[182] The assembly unprecedentedly continuing, however, he sought to lead them to promulgate a body of canons that might allay fears of popery and superstition, redress some grievances, and so provide for the peace of the church.

Several of the seventeen canons took up criticisms of the church and its hierarchy.[183] They proscribed vexatious citations into ecclesiastical courts; they limited the use of excommunication; they ordained that the proceeds of all commuted penances should be donated to charitable uses. They reaffirmed the need for the clergy to be free of any scandalous carriage or conversation; they recommended, perhaps in response to the complaints against Wren's visitational exuberance, that one common book of visitation articles be drawn up – for use throughout the dioceses and parishes of England. The canons were resolute in their condemnation of popery and Socinianism. The second required that the names of all over twelve years of age who did not go to church to take communion be returned as recusants whose continuing delinquency would result in excommunication. Bishops were enjoined to present to the assize judges (and to send into Chancery annually) all presented to them for recusancy, or marrying, burying and baptizing by other than Anglican rites. Although similar anathemas and proceedings were announced against sectaries (Brownists and familists were named in particular), the Convocation seems to have sought a form of words that would not unnecessarily antagonize tender consciences. So the requirement instituted in the directions of 1629 that all lecturers should conduct divine service before preaching was moderated by the injunction (from the 56th canon of 1604) that twice a year preachers should administer the sacraments and preach on the lawfulness of ceremonies. Canon VII, a declaration concerning some rites and ceremonies, which resounds with the moderation often expressed and practised by Laud, drew back from the excesses of some enthusiastic high churchmen of the personal rule. Announcing that it was '*generally to be wished* that unity of faith were accompanied with uniformity of practice in the outward worship and service of God', the canon turned to the contentious issue of the position of the communion table.[184] Following Laud's preferences, rather than the king's, the canon decreed the position under the east window as 'in its own nature indifferent'. Whilst insisting on rails to preserve the table from profanation, the canon

182. Gardiner, *History of England*, IX, p. 142. Laud, however, clearly believed in the right of the bishops and clergy to legislate for the church: see *Cal. Stat. Pap. Venet., 1636–9*, p. 156. Williams agreed: see Hastings MSS, Parliamentary Box 1. Cf. Sir Edward Coke's view: *Cal. Stat. Pap. Dom., 1633–4*, p. 344.

183. *Constitutions and Canons Ecclesiastical* (1640), BL, E.203.2. These are also printed in *Works of Laud*, V, part 2, pp. 607–33.

184. *Works of Laud*, *ibid.*, pp. 624–6; cf. above, pp. 333ff.

(more moderate than the metropolitical order) left the position during communion time to the decision of the individual bishop. No north–south placing was enjoined, nor coming up to receive communion; and pains were taken to clarify that even when the table was placed, as was deemed fit, at the east, no sacrifice was implied. It was a statement 'studiously moderate' which gave Elizabeth's injunctions 'the force of canonical law'.[185]

Two other canons, which were to cause a furore, were probably drawn up in the same spirit of conservatism and moderation. The first reasserted the royal supremacy over the church and the divine right of kings in the face of the Scots resistance. Though 'aid and subsidy' were decreed to be due to kings by the law of God, yet the first canon announced, 'subjects have not only possession of but a true and just right, title and property . . . in all their goods and estates, and ought so to have'.[186] Prerogative and property, it was reiterated, 'mutually go together'. The second, Canon VI, devised at Charles's specific request, enjoined an oath for the preventing of all innovations in the doctrine and government of the church. Intended to 'secure all men against any suspicion of revolt to Popery', the oath required all clergy to swear that they approved 'the doctrine and discipline, or government established in the Church of England, as containing all things necessary to salvation' and they would not consent to alter 'the government of this church by archbishops, bishops, deans and archdeacons etc . . .'.[187] Charles clearly hoped that the canons, as he declared in his confirmation of them, would allay fears and correct misunderstandings about his religion. After the book was signed, on 29 May, by fourteen bishops and eighty-nine clergy, the king ordered 17,500 copies to be distributed.[188]

The royal optimism was not entirely groundless. As even the nonconformist Dr Gardiner could acknowledge, the canons 'were not wanting in that reasonableness which has ever been the special characteristic of the English church'.[189] Moreover, though the committee that worked on drawing them up consisted largely of archdeacons and procurators, such differences as emerged do not trace neat party lines within the church. The Calvinist Bishop John Davenant of Salisbury saw no objections that could be made to them. 'In my poor judgement,' he opined, 'there is not one of them wherein full satisfaction may not be given to any man who is not unwilling to be satisfied.'[190]

185. *Works of Laud*, V, pp. 624–6; W.H. Hutton, *William Laud* (1895), p. 93.
186. *Works of Laud*, V, part 2, p. 614.
187. *Ibid.*, pp. 623–4.
188. *Cal. Stat. Pap. Dom., 1640*, pp. 232, 257.
189. Gardiner, *History of England*, IX, p. 143.
190. *Cal. Stat. Pap. Dom., 1640*, p. 642: Davenant to Laud, 28 Aug. Despite the recipient, there is no reason to doubt the sincerity of this letter, which Dr Foster should have

Two who refused to subscribe the canons were men of quite different sympathies: Bishop Godfrey Goodman of Gloucester and Richard Holdsworth, archdeacon of Huntingdon and president of Sion College. Goodman, whom Panzani and others (including Sir William Hamilton, the English agent at Rome) thought inclined to Rome, declined to take the oath – probably, as Laud suggested, precisely because it jarred with his popish predilections.[191] Holdsworth's objections were several. He had (he was later to claim) opposed the continuance of the Convocation in the first place; he advised against the first canon (on royal authority) until the judges had been consulted; he thought the canon against popery insufficiently strict; and he feared that the seventh amounted to a recommendation of 'these new taken up ceremonies' of turning to the east and bowing to the altar, which he believed should be left to conscience rather than prescribed.[192] Though others (Laud himself among them) shared Holdsworth's doubts about the prolongation of Convocation, 'there was certainly no identifiable Calvinist opposition within the house' and little evident disagreement to the canons. Even Bishop John Williams endorsed them.[193]

The outcry that was heard over the following months then, could not have been anticipated. Some objections to the canons were, of course, predictable. Nehemiah Wallington listed the 'cursed book' as another of the 'snares for the poor children of God', and may have begun to draft a tract against them.[194] Harbottle Grimston, another devotee of the obvious pun, began to wonder whether the canons were intended 'to blow up the Protestant religion'. (See Figure 40.)[195] In general, however, it was the oath (devised against popery) that excited the most concern, and not only among the circles of the godly.

The sworn commitment to uphold the government of the church was of course anathema to those who had since its very foundation campaigned for a reformation on continental lines. 'A Treatise concerning the new Oath' questioned the distinction of bishops and dismissed archdeacons as 'a grievance and burden . . . to the commonwealth'.[196] Petitions from Northamptonshire and London clergy raised 'exceptions' which rehearse puritan objections to the hierarchy:

pondered. Cf. A. Foster, 'The function of a bishop: the career of Richard Neile, 1562–1640', in R. O'Day and F. Heal (eds) *Continuity and Change: Personnel and Administration of the Church of England, 1500–1642* (Leicester, 1976), p. 52.

191. See *HMC Cowper II*, p. 256; *Dictionary of National Biography*.
192. Lambeth Palace MS 943, p. 599.
193. The phrase is from Julian Davies's *The Caroline Captivity of the Church* (forthcoming).
194. P. Seaver, *Wallington's World: A Puritan Artisan in Seventeenth Century London* (1985), pp. 51, 205. Cf. N. Wallington, *Historical Notices of . . . the Reign of Charles I, 1630–46*, ed. R.J. Webb (2 vols, 1869), II, p. 28.
195. W. Abbott, 'The issue of episcopacy in the Long Parliament, 1640–48' (Oxford University, D. Phil. thesis, 1981), p. 68.
196. Bodleian, Rawlinson MS D. 353, f.148.

This Canons ſeal'd, well forgd, not made of lead,
Give fire, O noe 'twill breake and strike vs dead.
That I. A. B. doe ſweare that I doe approve the Doctrine and Diſcipline or Government eſtabliſhed in the Church of England, as containing all things neceſſary to Salvation; And that I will not endeavour by my ſelfe or any other, directly or indirectly to bring in any Popiſh Doctrine, contrary to that which is ſo eſtabliſhed: Nor will I ever give my conſent to alter the Government of this Church, by Archbiſhops, Biſhops, Deanes, and Arch-Deacons, &c. as it ſtands now eſtabliſhed, and as by right it ought to ſtand: Nor yet ever to ſubject it to the uſurpations and ſuperſtitions of the Sea of Rome. And all theſe things I doe plainly and ſincerely acknowledge and ſweare, according to the plain and common ſence, and underſtanding of the ſame words, without any equivocation or mentall evaſion, or ſecret reſervation whatſoever. And this I doe heartily, willingly and truly, upon the faith of a Chriſtian: So help me God in Ieſus Chriſt.
oath
Prime, lay the Trayne, thus you must mount, and levell,
then ſhall we gett the day. but freind the Devill.
Turne, wheele about, take tyme, and stand your ground,
this Canon cannot faile, but tis not ſound,
Feare not, weel cast it, tis a deſperate caſe,
weel ſweare it, and enjoyne it, but tis baſe,
The Mettalls brittle, and tis ram'd ſo hard,
with an Oath &c: that hath fowly marr'd
All our deſignes, that now we have no hope
but in the ſervice of our Lord the Pope,
Diſsolve the Rout, each man vnto his calling
which had we kept, we had not now beene falling

40 *A Satire against Archbishop Laud* by Wenceslaus Hollar, 1640. Echoing the familiar pun about the controversial canons, Laud's canon explodes in his own face.

whether any settled discipline was necessary, whether doctrines that enabled Arminians to claim orthodoxy could be regarded as established, and whether oaths of such a sort were legal.[197] Behind such questions lay, as they admitted, a desire to *alter* the church in some points rather than swear to sustain it.[198] But others, not obviously alienated from the church, had scruples about an 'Etcetera' which embraced they knew not what. Martin Blake, for example, the conformist vicar of Barnstaple in Devonshire, wanted to take the oath with an explication to limit its vagueness, but the injunction to swear it plainly left him not knowing what to do. He prayed that 'our dear sovereign might remove it'.[199] Isaac Bedford consulted his cousin Thomas, a minister at Plymouth. 'I pray you', he wrote in July, 'satisfy me in these quarrels concerning the new oath and canons what you and other ministers about you do conceive, for I and many others that allow of the government of the church by bishops, yet do desire to be satisfied if whether it be lawful to take an implicit oath with an Etc., when there may be doubt of how much is signified.'[200] For one thing, Bedford wondered whether this new oath did not subvert the oath of supremacy, in denying the king's own authority ever to alter the government of the church. Though he had doubts about the role of High Commission and archdeacons, Bedford was willing to swear allegiance to the doctrine and discipline or government of the church; it was the unspecificity and form of the oath that most bothered him – 'for my conscience tells me that the substance is good'.[201] Others of moderate disposition shared his scruples: Richard Baxter, who as assistant minister at Bridgnorth in Shropshire was as yet by no means hostile to the church, recalled the etcetera oath as 'the first thing that threatened me'.[202] Queries from Kent, Devon and Norfolk evidenced the breadth of such unease.[203] Again some staunch Calvinists were happy to support the oath. Some of tender conscience in Northamptonshire were referred to John Prideaux;[204] Davenant told his clergy that it 'cannot trouble any man's conscience'.[205] But as it became clear that many were troubled, not least by the novelty of an oath binding clergy already beneficed, Laud was advised by Dr Sanderson to further explain

197. Harleian MS 4931, ff.56, 101; Tanner MS 65, f.42.
198. For example, Harleian MS 4931, f.56.
199. Tanner MS 65, f.199. His misgivings were shared by the Earl of Bath and Devonshire gentry who petitioned against the oath. See *Clarendon State Papers*, II, p. 116.
200. Tanner MS 285, f.66.
201. *Ibid.*
202. N.H. Keeble (ed.) *The Autobiography of Richard Baxter* (1974), p. 21.
203. Harleian MS 4931, ff.58–60.
204. *Cal. Stat. Pap. Dom., 1640*, p. 381.
205. I owe this information to Dr Julian Davies. Cf. *Cal. Stat. Pap. Dom., 1640*, p. xxi.

or suspend it.[206] The oath was abandoned in September, a month before the deadline by which it was supposed to have been sworn.

The etcetera oath may have been intended to bind men in England, as did the Covenant in Scotland, in defence of a church defined by canons to which all moderate men could subscribe.[207] If so, like the Book of Sports before, it not only failed of its purpose, the settling of dispute; it fuelled fears that as yet unspoken alterations were planned in the church to which English subjects were being asked to swear fealty, as the Scots had been earlier required to swear obedience to a Prayer Book they had not seen. Scots propaganda in the spring and summer of 1640 continued closely to identify the threats that menaced England as well as the northern kingdom. Two thousand copies of *An Information from the Estates of the Kingdom of Scotland to the Kingdom of England* were sent south in March and April.[208] Rather than doing the king's business, the Short Parliament and Convocation had played into the hands of the Scots. Thomas Peyton had a sense that things had greatly changed for the worse. He wrote the day after the dissolution to Henry Oxinden:

> And now some say we are where we were, but I think we are worse; for what grievances soever the subject thought themselves molested with, and therefore would resist them, this striving with the King could be thought but the act of private men till now it is in parliament made the act of the third estate. And there I think the King suffers in the honour of his government among neighbouring princes who may privately rejoice to see distractions breed in so flourishing a kingdom . . . for this cause it had been better the Parliament had never been.[209]

206. Nalson, *Impartial Collection*, I, p. 496. I owe this point to John Morrill.
207. Gardiner, *History of England*, IX, p. 146.
208. STC 21916; See J. Spalding, *Memorials of the Troubles in Scotland and England, 1624–45* (Aberdeen, 1850), pp. 257–8.
209. Gardiner, *Oxinden Letters*, p. 173, 6 May.

XVI
'WHO ENTERS THE NORTH FIRST WILL CARRY IT': THE RENEWAL OF HOSTILITIES, THE BURDENS OF WAR AND THE CONSEQUENCES OF DEFEAT

The second campaign

The preparations for the second Scots war commenced within weeks of the peace that ended the first without a battle. This was not only a consequence of the instability of the Treaty of Berwick which, as was quickly discovered, promised little prospect of a lasting settlement. In the aftermath of the fiasco at Kelso there was also a sense that a battle, if entered, might have been won.[1] By mid-August, in fact, it was common news that if the Scots did not fall into line, the king would mount a second enterprise – confident that a smaller force would bring the Covenanters to submission.[2] During the autumn, on both sides, military preparations took over from negotiation: the Scots began to order musters; Charles placed a large magazine of ammunition in Edinburgh Castle.[3] In December the committee for Scottish affairs counselled the resumption of hostilities and a parliament to finance it.[4] Though the Treasury was exhausted by the cost of the former expedition, and Northumberland was pessimistic about the willingness of the parliament to supply, Charles ordered moneys to be taken up on credit in anticipation of subsidies.[5] Pikes and muskets were ordered.

1. Rossingham wrote to Scudamore on 13 August to report that the Scots army was discovered to be devoid of officers and weapons: 'I have heard many men of good judgement say . . . his Majesty . . . might have marched to Edinburgh' (BL Add. MS 11045, f.45).
2. *Ibid.*, f.46.
3. *Ibid.*, ff.52, 68.
4. A. Collins (ed.) *Letters and Memorials of State Collected by Sir Henry Sidney* (2 vols, 1746), II, p. 623. Above, pp. 851–2.
5. *HMC 3rd Report*, p. 79; BL Add. MS 11045, f.81v.

The Council of War, as it had now become, began to sit three times weekly to organize the campaign.[6]

In the early New Year of 1640, Lord Ettrick advised Charles not to give his rebellious countrymen the advantage of delays. But in preparing for war he urged the king to provide experienced commanders and all necessaries, sparing no cost.[7] If the counsel were sound it was not easy to follow. Northumberland doubted whether 'less than a million a year' would defray the expense and reflected 'God only knows how this money will be gotten.'[8] Charles, however, had already made enquiries as to whether the duty of border service had ended with his succession (to the thrones of Scotland and England):[9] he resolved to raise an army of 35,000 once again from the trained bands of the counties.[10] The letters were sent down to the counties in March amid the more peaceful campaigns for elections to parliament.[11] Some were still hoping for a settlement: the king heard the petitioners from Scotland in the presence of his committee for one and a half hours; but, Rossingham informed Scudamore, 'there is little appearance of an accommodation and it is visible we make great preparations for war'.[12] Recalling the problems of the spring the Council issued instructions that 'in the liberty given to charge men to serve in the place of trained soldiers, there be not any rewards or money taken';[13] Northumberland gave notice of his intention to send agents to inspect the bandsmen selected; Strafford prepared to raise 8,000 foot.[14] The Venetian ambassador was impressed by the expedition: 'military preparations,' he informed the Doge and Senate at the end of the month, 'increase marvellously.'[15]

Before its outcome was known, the Short Parliament began to impede this progress. During the elections there was sharp criticism of the lieutenancy and denunciation of martial law and coat and conduct money as illegal. The deputies of Northamptonshire were threatened with prosecution in the forthcoming parliament;[16] those of Hertfordshire, hearing the Petition of Right invoked, were either

6. *Calendar of State Papers Domestic* [*Cal. Stat. Pap. Dom.*], *1639–40*, pp. 134, 188.
7. *Ibid.*, p. 373, 25 Jan.
8. *HMC De Lisle and Dudley, VI*, pp. 219–20: Northumberland to Leicester, 2 Jan. 1640.
9. *Cal. Stat. Pap. Dom., 1639–40*, p. 47: Charles I to Sir John Bramston, 20 Oct. 1639.
10. *HMC De Lisle and Dudley, VI*, p. 219.
11. J. Nalson, *An Impartial Collection of the Great Affairs of State from the Beginning of the Scotch Rebellion in 1639 to the Murder of King Charles I* (2 vols, 1682–3), I, p. 377.
12. BL Add. MS 11045, f.97v, 8 March 1640.
13. Chester Record Office, CR.63/2/6, ff.74v–75, 26 March 1640.
14. Nalson, *Impartial Collection*, I, p. 377; Scottish Record Office, GD 406/1, Hamilton MS 803: Wentworth to Hamilton, 24 March.
15. *Calendar of State Papers Venetian* [*Cal. Stat. Pap. Venet.*], *1640–2*, p. 30, 30 March 1640.
16. *Cal. Stat. Pap. Dom., 1640*, p. 25.

unable or unwilling to extract press money from the county.[17] Once the parliament was sitting, military preparations were obstructed by the absence of many deputies (who still succeeded in obtaining seats, in some cases no doubt because they behaved 'with moderation to the country' in exercising royal orders).[18] In Yorkshire Sir Edward Osborne complained that the want of deputies brought all to a halt.[19] On 26 April, becoming aware that the problem was general, the Privy Council commanded lord-lieutenants to their counties to oversee the raising and transport of troops.[20] Such inconveniences were the price the king and Council had been prepared to pay for what, it was hoped, would be the means to pay the troops, now assembling for their county rendezvous on 10 May.

The dissolution of the parliament without the desperately needed subsidies confirmed all the worst fears Northumberland had harboured since the autumn. Writing to Leicester, two days after the MPs were dismissed from Westminster, he announced with audible despondency the king's intention to press on levying an army of 30,000 – 'as yet I cannot learn by what means we are certain to get one shilling'.[21] To Conway, he was even more willing to admit defeat: 'We have engaged the king,' he admitted, recalling the Council's promise of the winter, 'in an expensive occasion without any certain ways to maintain it . . . our designs of raising this great army are likely to fail'.[22] Neither the king nor the Council was so ready to concede failure. From Council debates emerged the decision not only to pursue the war but to wage an offensive campaign which might quickly mobilize the troops, surprise the Covenanters, and avoid the expenses of a long war of attrition.[23] Shortage of money, however, necessitated some delay: the day parliament dissolved, the Council issued letters that the troops ordered for 10 May would not now be required nor enter the king's pay until 10 June.[24] The postponement, as we shall see, not only exacerbated the fiscal burdens on the counties, it threw local society into disorder as troops, left idle and unpaid, began to mutiny.[25] The second campaign was scarcely off to the start that Ettrick had advocated when he pressed the importance of satisfying the soldiers as the greatest inducement to their fidelity and courage.

17. *Ibid.*, p. 44.
18. *Ibid.*, p. 25.
19. *Ibid.*, p. 34.
20. *Ibid.*, p. 71.
21. Collins, *Letters and Memorials*, II, p. 652, 7 May 1640.
22. *Cal. Stat. Pap. Dom., 1640*, p. 179, 18 May.
23. *Ibid.*, pp. 112–13: Vane's notes on the committee for Scottish affairs, 5 May 1640. See too, *HMC Cowper II*, pp. 253–4.
24. Nalson, *Impartial Collection*, I, p. 486.
25. Below, pp. 905–9.

The dissolution of the Short Parliament, as it starved the soldiers of supply, also robbed them of that other important sustenance of armies: spirit. Conversely the Covenanters, who English military intelligence indicated were but poorly equipped and facing similar problems of supply, took heart from 'the disorders of our parliament'.[26] Loudoun returned to Scotland with assurances of the friendship of many in England to their cause.[27] Windebank observed with bitterness that 'they have too much encouragement by the unhappy rupture of the parliament who have clearly discovered they like their courses so well that they would contribute nothing towards their suppression.'[28] The city proved no more accommodating. Not least because with the failure of subsidies, the government presented a poor security risk, the mayor and aldermen hedged when requested to return the names of wealthy citizens who might advance a loan to the king.[29] In parts of the country too, the parliament's failure to supply was interpreted as, in some ways, invalidating the campaign and legitimizing non-cooperation. Though troops were still gathering and many were ready to march, the Council had no choice but again to delay. On 26 May Windebank had to break the news to Conway who commanded the horse at Newcastle: 'the day of the rendezvous is again put off from 1 June to 1 July and we are using all the means we can to raise money against that time'.[30] The delay threatened the disintegration of the army. As Sir William Pelham protested to Conway, Sussex had raised its contingent of 200 men ready for 1 June; now they were put off to 1 July; if they remained gathered, being taken from their employment, they would demand pay which the country could not afford; if allowed to disperse they could not easily again be brought together.[31] It was a problem presented to most counties.

June and July were critical months for the campaign, as the Council frantically tried to raise loans from home and abroad for the army.

26. *Cal. Stat. Pap. Dom., 1640*, p. 215; Castle told Bridgewater in June that one man in London was asking whether it was safe for them to embrace the war when parliament had not favoured it, whether the Scots were actually rebels and whether they could safely fight without knowing the cause of conflict (Huntington Library, Ellesmere MS 7838). Castle believed that the king's declaration explaining the dissolution of the parliament should have been 'put abroad immediately upon the dissolving'.
27. Nottingham University Library, Clifton MS Cl/C 687; J. Spalding, *Memorials of the Troubles in Scotland and England, 1624–45* (Aberdeen, 1850), p. 320; S.R. Gardiner, *History of England from the Accession of James I to the Outbreak of the Civil War, 1603–42* (10 vols, 1883–4), IX, p. 168; see P. Donald, 'New light on the Anglo-Scottish contacts of 1640', *Bull. Inst. Hist. Res.*, 62 (1989), pp. 221–9.
28. *Cal. Stat. Pap. Dom., 1640*, p. 127: Windebank to Conway, 7 May.
29. V. Pearl, *London and the Outbreak of the Puritan Revolution* (Oxford, 1961), pp. 100–2; Ellesmere MSS 7838, 7849; Gardiner, *History of England*, IX, p. 98; R. Ashton, *The Crown and the Money Market, 1603–40* (Oxford, 1960), p. 180.
30. *Cal. Stat. Pap. Dom., 1640*, p. 219.
31. *Ibid.*, p. 263.

A forced loan was considered; a debasement of the coinage was debated.[32] The king negotiated with the merchants who protested against a debasement, using the threat of clipping his coin as a bargaining counter.[33] He even considered seizing the bullion in the Tower.[34] In the end, the city remaining stubborn in its refusals, Charles was thrown back on to the customs farmers.[35] Through all the delays Northumberland's pessimism rose into a crescendo of despair. 'I know not what to think of our army,' he wrote to Leicester who had begun to serve as a confessor. 'The men that are pressed run so fast away and are so mutinous that I doubt we shall want a very great part of our number; and those that remain will be readier to draw their swords upon their officers than against the Scots.'[36] 'We are,' he lamented, 'in a most wretched and beggarly condition'.[37] As late as July Northumberland was uncertain whether he would be needed in the north.[38] Newswriters and others echoed his doubts: for all the rumours of the king leading the army, John Castle told Bridgewater, 'I believe no such matter', considering 'the nobility were brought low enough by the last journey'.[39] In Nottinghamshire the Earl of Kingston assured the soldiers 'they should have no cause to fight this summer'.[40] There was good ground for pessimism, for the fiscal crisis was compounded by other problems. In June the judges ruled that martial law could not be legally executed in England except where an army was camped in the face of the enemy.[41] Given the mood of the conscripted soldiers, Conway believed that 'if martial law cannot be executed it is all one as if the troops were disbanded'.[42] Attacks on the money wagons led to a decision not to pay the soldiers in advance, which in turn fostered more unruliness.[43] Everything was pointing to the dissolution of the army through want of pay and lack of discipline. 'How his Majesty,' Castle pondered, 'will be able . . . either to make a peace or to prosecute the war God Almighty knows.'[44]

32. *Ibid.*, pp. 376, 465; Ellesmere MS 7844.
33. *Cal. Stat. Pap. Dom., 1640*, p. 534.
34. R. Scrope and T. Monkhouse (eds) *State Papers Collected by Edward, Earl of Clarendon* (3 vols, Oxford, 1767–86), II, p. 87.
35. Gardiner, *History of England*, IX, p. 174.
36. *HMC De Lisle and Dudley, VI*, p. 285, 18 June 1640.
37. *HMC 3rd Report*, p. 81, 28 May 1640.
38. Collins, *Letters and Memorials*, II, p. 657; *HMC 3rd Report*, p. 81.
39. Ellesmere MS 7837, 9 June 1640. Castle's newsletters provide an invaluable comment on the mood during the months of preparation for war.
40. Clifton MS Cl/C 687, July 1640.
41. Lambeth Palace MS 943, pp. 695–6: Conway to Laud, 8 June 1640.
42. *Cal. Stat. Pap. Dom., 1640*, p. 352: Conway to Strafford, 28 June. Conway had told Laud, 'I do not think fit the lawyers should deliver any opinion for if the soldiers do know that it is questioned, they will decide it by their disobedience'; see note 41, above.
43. *Ibid.*, p. 497.
44. Ellesmere MS 7843: Castle to Bridgewater, 1 July 1640.

By the summer, however, the need for the army had become even more apparent – not as an offensive force against the Scots but as a defence in the increasingly likely event of their invasion of England. From the end of June, Conway was expressing his concern about the possibility of a Scottish incursion and in particular about the vulnerability of Newcastle.[45] He presented plans to fortify the city by raising an imposition on the inhabitants, but in 'these distempered times' Northumberland thought it ill-advised.[46] By the beginning of August, Windebank and Vane had come to accept that the Scots were preparing to invade.[47] If the expectation of a friendly reception in England provided encouragement, their own problems added the spur of necessity. In June, it was reported that the Covenanters were also desperate: 'they must either change for fresher pastures this side of Tweed or famish on their own'.[48] In July, finding difficulty in obtaining money and provisions for his army, Leslie successfully argued the case for invasion.[49] Rumour was circulating by the beginning of August that they would cross the border and were already marching; Castle believed it all too likely, 'especially if their infinite necessity be considered together with the opportunity to serve themselves of the present distempers of our people, whose humours are in motu fluido'.[50] By now the inevitability of invasion and battle was widely accepted at court. Time and expedition were now matters of survival; as the Marquis of Douglas had predicted in the spring, when he had foresight of the Covenanters' plans: 'it seems who enters the north first will carry it.'[51]

Urgency added frantic desperation to the efforts to gather an army. In mid-August when the Scots marched, issuing ahead of them a justificatory declaration inviting the English to join them in an appeal to another parliament,[52] still one-third of the English troops – and much of their arms supply – had not gone up to York.[53] At Newcastle, Conway was not sanguine of the recruits sent to him: 'I am teaching,' he told the Countess of Devonshire, 'cart horses to manage and making men that are fit for Bedlam and Bridewell to keep the ten commandments.'[54] At York Sir Edward Osborne could offer little

45. *Cal. Stat. Pap. Dom., 1640*, pp. 297–8: Conway to Northumberland, 14 June.
46. *Ibid.*, p. 363: Northumberland to Conway, 30 June 1640.
47. *Ibid.*, pp. 549, 558.
48. Ellesmere MS 7837: Castle to Bridgewater, 9 June 1640.
49. Gardiner, *History of England*, IX, pp. 181–2.
50. Ellesmere MS 7847: Castle to Bridgewater, 8 Aug. 1640.
51. *Cal. Stat. Pap. Dom., 1640*, pp. 198–9.
52. *The Intentions of the Army of the Kingdom of Scotland Declared to their Brethren of England* (1640, STC 21919); cf. Spalding. *Memorials of the Troubles*, pp. 321–9; Ellesmere MS 7847: Castle to Bridgewater, 8 Aug. 1640.
53. *Cal. Stat. Pap. Dom., 1640*, p. 609.
54. *Ibid.*, pp. 230–1.

more cause for optimism: 'I doubt extremely our forces are not now in so ready a condition as they were last year, very many arms being lost in that expedition and none to be bought ever since for supply of defects.'[55] The pragmatic Windebank, as often, understated the frenetic activity in which he was engaged: 'we are busy,' he assured Conway.[56] Sir Nicholas Byron exhibited no such restraint. 'We are here,' he wailed to Vane, 'and in every place in such distraction as if the day of judgment were hourly expected.'[57] The odds did not seem good. On 18 August the Scots were heard to be approaching with 30,000 foot and 3,000 horse; the English forces were reckoned at 14,000 and 2,500 'and they most of them mutinous and discontented'.[58] Hasty decisions were made. On 19 August orders were issued to lord-lieutenants of the midland and northern counties to call out the trained bands;[59] the following day a royal proclamation summoned all 'of what state or condition soever, who hold of his Majesty by grand Sergeanty . . . or Knight service' to appear at Newcastle furnished by 20 September;[60] another proclamation dated 31 August required all lord-lieutenants south of the Trent to put in readiness not only the trained bands, but also the spare men and 'all other persons, that are able, either in body or estate, to do service' for 'the defence of the public'.[61] Most importantly, Charles decided to go to York himself to command his army.[62]

For all the talk of English sympathy with the Scots, the king's journey north rescued the situation from disaster and despair. By the end of August, John Castle was writing not of the inevitability of defeat without a battle, but of men fired for a fight.[63] Charles set off for Newcastle on the 28th as the rebel army advanced to Alnwick. 'The trained bands of the Northern Counties are ordered with all expedition to come after his Majesty to Newcastle,' Castle told the Earl of Bridgewater, 'and they say they begin to march with a great deal of cheerfulness and resolution against the Scots.'[64] Reminding us of the powerful effect still of the royal presence, he observed: 'All the

55. *Ibid.*, p. 585.
56. *Ibid.*, p. 619.
57. *Ibid.*, p. 617, another reminder that apocalyptic language and perception were not the preserve of the 'godly'.
58. Ellesmere MS 7851: Castle to Bridgewater, 18 Aug.; cf. Ellesmere MS 7849, 15 Aug.
59. *Cal. Stat. Pap. Dom., 1640*, p. 603.
60. J.F. Larkin (ed.) *Stuart Royal Proclamations II: Royal Proclamations of King Charles I, 1625–46* (Oxford, 1983), no. 312, pp. 731–2; cf. Ellesmere MS 7873 and National Library of Scotland, Denmilne MS XIII, 13.
61. Larkin, *Stuart Royal Proclamations II*, no. 313, pp. 732–4.
62. Ellesmere MS 7851: Castle to Bridgewater, 18 Aug. This had been mooted since early August; see Ellesmere MS 7848.
63. Ellesmere MSS 7852, 7853: Castle to Bridgewater, 22 and 24 Aug.
64. Ellesmere MS 7856, 29 Aug.

north since his Majesty's coming are fallen to a better devotion . . . the King's harangue was so princely and so pathetic [Charles had learned the art of oratory that was to serve him so well, even beyond the grave] that it moved tears in many gentlemen that heard it who before were of another kind of temper.'[65] Vane was lifted enough to believe that if the king's presence could unite the English, he would 'less apprehend anything the rebels can do'.[66] By the time Charles reached York, the Scots had crossed the Tweed. Strafford, in command of the campaign, far from alarmed, thought it gave the king the advantage. 'I am not sorry the Scots are come in,' he frankly told Hamilton, 'Newcastle now safe, and certainly it will give his Majesty many great advantages which might have been disputed had we been the aggressors.'[67] Sir Thomas Jermyn was also sanguine. Estimates of the Scots army, he noted, had varied from 14,000 to 30,000 and Conway at Newcastle had only 15,000 foot and 2,000 horse. But if Yorkshire held firm to the king, he was still confident of 'a good end',[68] for by the time the Yorkshire troops were joined with the king's men, the combined force would total 25,000 infantrymen and 2,500 cavalry, 'an army which might promise itself (if the English be not degenerated) good success against a greater than is like to oppose it'.[69]

In principle, Jermyn may have been right. But the military odds were not just a matter of numbers. In the race for the north, the king had been endlessly delayed by lack of funds; and despite a final sprint he had come up just too late.[70] While Charles's combined forces almost certainly equalled the Scots, his army was divided, one part with Conway at Newcastle, the other with the king himself at York. If the Covenanters crossed the Tyne before the king's men joined Conway, they could divide and weaken the English forces and attack Newcastle from the unfortified southern side. Conway was instructed at all costs to hold the Scots back until the king's army reached him.[71] On the 28th, however, they crossed the river at Newburn ford, some four miles west of Newcastle. Conway sent a third of his troops to meet them, leaving the remainder to guard the city for the better defence of which he had in vain made efforts and pleas. At Newburn the small English force was routed, and forced to flee before Scottish cannon fire. Conway made a decision to march south to join with the king's

65. *Ibid.*; cf. *Cal. Stat. Pap. Dom., 1640*, p. 630; Hamilton MS 1231.
66. *Cal. Stat. Pap. Dom., 1640*, pp. 620–1: Vane to Windebank, 23 Aug.
67. Hamilton MS 1231, 24 Aug. We note the important disclaimer.
68. Bodleian, Tanner MS 65, ff.100–100v: Sir Thomas Jermyn to Sir Robert Crane, 20 Aug.
69. *Ibid.*, f.100v.
70. Ellesmere MS 7855; P. Hardwicke, *Miscellaneous State Papers* (2 vols, 1776), II, p. 147: minutes of committee, 16 Aug.; *Clarendon State Papers*, II, pp. 90, 92.
71. *Clarendon State Papers*, II, p. 107; Gardiner, *History of England*, IX, pp. 191–3.

army and so left Newcastle to be occupied by the Scots.[72] A minor skirmish, the battle at Newburn was to be the only engagement of the war. But as John Nalson was soon after to appreciate, 'This little disaster proved of fatal consequence . . .'.[73]

The English soldiers proved to be of little effect at Newburn. 'No sooner did the Scottish cannon begin to play but they, struck with fear, threw down their arms and ran away.'[74] Vane reported sadly to Windebank how, by careful placing of their artillery, the Covenanters had beaten the English infantry out of their inadequate defence works, adding 'the truth is our horse did not behave themselves well for many of them ran away and did not second those that were first charged'.[75] In the wake of various post-mortems, Conway felt the need to justify himself. In his narrative of his conduct in the action at Newburn, he explained the defeat in terms of long-term failings and inadequacies in preparing for the whole campaign. Money had not been forthcoming; his troops, arriving not as promised in May, but in July and August, were raw and unready for fight. The shift from an offensive to defensive strategy had thrown him on the disadvantage. At Newburn, the low ground and minimal fortification had exposed the English, leading him to favour a retreat and return to Newcastle. Strafford, however, ordered an engagement. Once lost, Conway concluded that Newcastle too was indefensible, being unfortified on 'the bishopric side'. Fearing the unnecessary loss of men, therefore, he had led his troops towards Darlington, and left Newcastle to the Covenanters.[76] In retrospect, as he narrated it, it all seemed the inevitable denouement of a year's shortcomings: 'Now,' he concluded 'upon the whole matter it may easily be judged whether the two actions of the retreat at Newburn and quitting Newcastle were the causes of our losses, or the effects of ill-grounded designs: to make a war without means, to go on with it, and to begin it at sea thereby giving the Scots a pretext to attempt us by land before we were able to resist them.'[77]

Historians have tended to concur with Conway's analysis, and to write of the defeat as the inevitable consequence of attempting to fight a war with an untrained, ill-supplied, unwilling ramshackle of an army, and without the co-operation of the nation. Such verdicts are too simplistic. The king had devised a military strategy against the

72. Gardiner, *History of England*, IX, pp. 193–5; *Clarendon State Papers*, II, pp. 99–110; Ellesmere MS 7857.
73. Nalson, *Impartial Collection*, I, p. 425.
74. G. Burnet, *The Memoirs of the Lives and Actions of James and William, Dukes of Hamilton* (1677), p. 173.
75. Hardwicke, *State Papers*, II, p. 162, 29 Aug.
76. *Clarendon State Papers*, II, pp. 99–110.
77. *Ibid.*, p. 110.

Covenanters in all his three kingdoms. And despite his difficulties, Charles did for the second time in just over a year assemble a large army in the north. And while it *may* be that those men recruited, unlike the infantry of the first campaign, from south of the Humber, were less imbued with spirit for the fight, it would be wrong to dismiss the force when contemporaries did not.[78] Even after Newburn, Vane could write of the troops at York, who had followed the king, that

> Braver bodies of men and better clad I have not seen anywhere for the foot. For the horse, they are such as no man that sees them by their outward appearance but will judge them able to stand and encounter with any whatsoever. Sure I am that I have seen far meaner in the King of Sweden's army [he had been ambassador in 1632] do strange and great execution; and by the report of all they are far better than those they are to encounter, being but little nags most of them.[79]

The army was well backed by artillery and supplies. Vane's evaluation is supported by a muster book of the king's army in the Cottesloe manuscripts at the National Army Museum, which suggests a well ordered force of over 17,000 foot and 2,500 horse complete with artillery and supported by surgeons, doctors and apothecaries.[80] As for Conway's force at Newcastle, the Scots themselves testified that when they entered the garrison 'there was found abundance of bread, wine, beer, beef, victuals and all sorts of good provision'.[81] By contrast, the Covenanters were in no good condition. Despite their victory at Newburn ford, they were, as Robert Baillie admitted, 'in great straits': 'All our victuals were spent; all the country had fled with all they could carry: if Newcastle had but closed their ports we had been in great hazard of present disbanding.'[82] The strategic position of the Scots army was certainly far from secure: barred of supply by sea and cut off by the garrison at Berwick, they were placed in a desperate position for another engagement. Sir John Byron believed that if Newcastle had held *another twenty-four hours*, the Scottish forces would have disbanded; once in the city, by contrast, they enjoyed plentiful supply,

78. See Gardiner, *History of England*, IX, pp. 158–9.
79. Hardwicke, *State Papers*, II, p. 172: Vane to Windebank, 11 Sept.
80. MS of Lord Cottesloe, photograph in National Army Museum. I am most grateful to Dr Ian Roy for a copy of this MS and for a helpful discussion of the condition of the king's army.
81. Spalding, *Memorials of the Troubles*, p. 337; cf. D. Laing (ed.) *The Letters and Journals of Robert Baillie, 1637–1662* (3 vols, Bannatyne Club, Edinburgh, 1841–2), I, p. 257; *Clarendon State Papers*, II, p. 98.
82. Laing, *Letters and Journals of Baillie*, I, p. 259.

access to the sea and a base from which to move on Durham.[83] If Byron and Baillie were right, the failure of the second Scots war was less the failure of an entire campaign – for all its problems – and more the strategic failure to fortify Newcastle, perhaps even simply a final failure of nerve on Conway's part. On the 29th Vane expressed the view that Newcastle could hold out for only *two* days so it may be that when he marched from the city that very day Conway gave up too early.[84] Rather than the inevitable outcome of events, Newburn may have been one of those historical battles decided by twenty-four hours. But whatever the causes, the consequences of defeat were truly to reverberate through history.[85] For as the Council discerned, the long campaign that would have to be mounted to remove the Covenanters from Newcastle required the subsidies of a parliament – what would turn out to be the longest and most revolutionary parliament in English history.[86] The invasion of the Scots meant that the problems Charles faced in his two kingdoms were now, quite literally, inseparable. In the victory at Newburn on 27 August the Scots 'set their first seal upon the civil conflict which deluged England for so many years with blood'.[87]

The British problem in European context

Preparations for the second Scots war not only overrode all other business at home; the effort to secure aid against the rebel Covenanters also became the all but exclusive purpose of diplomacy and foreign policy. It might be thought that after the humiliating fiasco in the Downs, the Dutch assault on the Spanish fleet under the king's very eyes, England would no longer carry the weight to conduct a foreign policy. The resurgence of the Scottish troubles and the inevitability of renewed war between the kingdoms of Britain made it unlikely, to say the least, that Charles could use the counter of his military assistance to bargain with any. However, the episode in the Downs had made even clearer to Madrid Spain's naval weakness and desperate need of English maritime protection.[88] Since the fall of Breda, Spanish communications

83. *Cal. Stat. Pap. Dom., 1640–1*, p. 93: Byron to Lord Edward Newburgh, 24 Sept.; R. Howell, *Newcastle-upon-Tyne and the Puritan Revolution* (Oxford, 1967), ch. 4, esp. pp. 140–1.
84. Hardwicke, *State Papers*, II, p. 162.
85. See E. Hyde, Earl of Clarendon, *The History of the Rebellion and Civil Wars in England*, ed. W.D. Macray (6 vols, Oxford, 1888), I, pp. 189–90.
86. Hardwicke, *State Papers*, II, pp. 168, 179: Vane to Windebank, 13 Sept.; *Cal. Stat. Pap. Dom., 1640–1*, p. 74: Vane to Windebank, 18 Sept.
87. J.H. Wiffen, *Historical Memoirs of the House of Russell* (2 vols, 1833), II, p. 176.
88. A.J. Loomie, 'Alonso de Cardenas and the Long Parliament 1640–48', *Eng. Hist. Rev.*, 97 (1982), pp. 289–307, p. 291; cf. H. Lonchay (ed.) *Correspondance de la cour d'Espagne sur les affaires des Pays Bas au XVII siècle, III* (Brussels, 1930), p. 351, no. 1040.

with Flanders had been exclusively dependent on the passage by sea, making English amity more imperative than ever; with the French treaty all but abandoned, England and Spain had resumed negotiations. Far from abandoning them, in the wake of the Downs the Spanish agent in London, Cardenas, was instructed to represent to Charles the threat posed to England by the Dutch and to negotiate for a closer alliance.[89] Perceiving Charles's difficulties with the Scots, Olivares also came to see the moment as propitious for concluding an alliance. In March 1640 he resolved to send a special envoy to England to proffer proposals for a treaty of marriage between Prince Carlos and the Princess Mary, hoping thereby, as he argued in the Council of State, 'to negotiate a breach between England and Holland, totally restore our fortunes in relation to France, and simultaneously restore the King of England's fortunes in Scotland, without his having to call parliament'.[90]

The Earl of Northumberland expected little from any negotiations. 'We are so set upon the reducing of Scotland,' he told Leicester, 'as till that be effected we shall not intend the re-establishing the broken estate of Europe; nor can I persuade myself that a confederation with us will be much sought by any of our neighbours at this time.'[91] But despite his pessimism, the European situation was still too delicately balanced to leave England out of account. While the Scottish crisis had emasculated England, it also offered an opportunity to those who wished to secure her friendship and navy. The Scots trouble could not be relied upon to last indefinitely; once at peace again England could tip the scales decisively. Accordingly, the French were still making overtures to Charles in the spring of 1640, despite having virtually placed the Elector Palatine in custody.[92] Indeed 'it is believed and reported', Thomas Smyth was informed, 'that the French King doth keep him in durance the longer, hoping to bring our King to conditions of entering into a firm league with the French and the States against the Emperor and the King of Spain, and they say that the French offers to maintain twice as many as our King shall and to make the Prince Elector general of them all and so to send him into Germany strong to regain his own country.'[93] By 1640, however, French propositions cut little ice with Charles: he was incensed at their detention of his

89. Bodleian, Clarendon MS 17, no. 1321: Colonel Gage to Windebank, 9 Nov.; Gardiner, *History of England*, IX, pp. 89–90.
90. J.H. Elliott, 'The year of the three ambassadors', in H. Lloyd-Jones, V. Pearl and B. Worden (eds) *History and Imagination* (1981), pp. 165–81; quotation from Archivo General de Simancas, Estado, legajo, 2521 (p. 171).
91. *HMC 3rd Report*, p. 80, 14 Feb. 1640.
92. PRO, 31/3/72, *passim*; Ellesmere MS 7812; Collins, *Letters and Memorials*, II, p. 642; *HMC 3rd Report*, p. 78; Gardiner, *History of England*, IX, pp. 70, 89.
93. Bristol Record Office, Smyth of Ashton Court MS 36074/136b: Baynham Throckmorton to Thomas Smyth, 11 Feb. 1640.

nephew; he was convinced they supported the Covenanters; after the battle of the Downs he was even more suspicious of their alliance with the Dutch and combined naval power. Moreover, rumours were filtering to England that, crushed by the burden of war taxation, a great part of France was on the brink of rising in rebellion.[94] Aerssons, the Dutch envoy, coming to explain Tromp's action and propose a marriage alliance with the house of Orange also received short shrift. Though meeting with little success, the French and Dutch could not, after the Downs, cease to try to woo England into an alliance that might finally bring down the Habsburgs.[95] For it was known in Paris and the Hague that 'a great don' from Spain was imminently expected, with propositions that might draw Charles into a maritime treaty with Madrid.[96]

As the Marquis Virgilio Malvezzi was leaving Spain, the elections were taking place for the Short Parliament. Its outcome was of obvious European as well as British importance; as Northumberland put it, the Spaniards and others 'would be glad to see the issue of the parliament and how we shall be able to master our great designs for this next summer before they conclude anything with us'.[97] Malvezzi was coming with instructions to offer an offensive and defensive alliance by the terms of which Spain would offer Charles 8,000 troops for his war against the Scots in exchange for the assistance of his fleet and a declaration of war against France and the United Provinces.[98] While the Commons prevaricated, Malvezzi worked with the Marquis de Velada and the Duchess of Chevreuse to promote a Spanish match.[99] He did not lack support. Castle observed 'with what extraordinary affection and desire the Queen's Majesty here affecteth a reciprocal marriage betwixt her children and the children of her sister' and announced her a principal supporter of the alliance.[100] Strafford arranged the appointment of Cottington, Windebank, Vane and Northumberland as commissioners to negotiate;[101] by the end of April a treaty in Spain was 'considered a certainty'.[102] On 5 May, as we know, the Short Parliament was dissolved, without having voted supply. Northumberland could not but wonder 'what will the world judge of us abroad', continuing a war against the Scots 'not knowing

94. *Ibid.*
95. Gardiner, *History of England*, IX, p. 89.
96. Smyth of Ashton Court MS 36074/136b.
97. Collins, *Letters and Memorials*, II, pp. 637–8: Northumberland to Leicester, 20 Feb.
98. *Cal. Stat. Pap. Venet., 1640–2*, p. 31; Elliott, 'Year of the three ambassadors', pp. 172–3; *Clarendon State Papers*, II, p. 83.
99. *Cal. Stat. Pap. Venet., 1640–2*, p. 42; Clarendon MS 18, no. 1386.
100. Ellesmere MS 7830: Castle to Bridgewater, 9 April.
101. PRO, 31/3/72, ff.141–141v, 17 May 1640.
102. *Cal. Stat. Pap. Venet., 1640–2*, p. 42: Contarini, envoy in Spain, to Doge, 5 May.

how to maintain it for one month?'[103] Answering his own rhetorical question, he told Leicester 'all nations think us in that desperate condition at home that they neither desire nor consider our friendship'.[104] Once again he was excessively negative. The dissolution of parliament was seen in Madrid as an opportunity – to make England dependent on Spanish aid.[105] Moreover, Philip IV, convinced that the English puritans and parliament plotted to overthrow Charles, feared the likely consequences for his own affairs. It was of the first importance to Spain, he instructed Velada and Malvezzi, 'that we do not lose that King [of England] for, should that country become a republic, I have no doubts that I will lose my province of Flanders'.[106]

At a meeting on 8 May, Charles, more than ever aware of the need for Spanish money, commended the Spanish negotiations to his commissioners.[107] Three days later Strafford paid a visit to Velada and offered, in return for a loan of £300,000, to commit England, as soon as the Scots were suppressed, to a war against the Dutch.[108] The secret negotiations resulted in a draft treaty whereby for the 1.2 million ducats requested, England agreed to protect Spanish commerce, convoy men and money to Flanders, succour Dunkirk in the event of an attack, supply Irish troops to Spain and break with the Dutch after the Scots war.[109] Joachimi, the Dutch envoy, was understandably concerned and manoeuvred to block the negotiations.[110] Strafford's committee, however, was entirely pro-Spanish. Only Hopton, writing from Madrid, counselled caution. He reminded Windebank that given Spain's poor fleet, in a naval war against the French and Dutch, England would stand alone. More particularly, in the immediate circumstances, he feared the Spanish negotiations could drive the French and Dutch to ally with the Covenanters. 'It imports much more,' he admonished, 'to get no enemies than some friends.'[111]

Before the draft articles reached Madrid, their value (at least to England) was gravely called into doubt. In June the kingdom of Catalonia rose in open revolt, and so plunged Philip and Olivares into a civil war within the Iberian peninsula that mirrored Charles's in

103. Collins, *Letters and Memorials*, II, p. 652: Northumberland to Leicester, 7 May.
104. *Ibid.*, pp. 654–5, 4 June.
105. Elliott, 'Year of the three ambassadors', p. 174.
106. Philip IV to Malvezzi, 25 June, Archivo General de Simancas, Estado, 2575, quoted in Loomie, 'Cardenas and the Long Parliament', p. 292.
107. *Cal. Stat. Pap. Venet., 1640–2*, p. 45; Clarendon MS 18, no. 1382.
108. Elliott, 'Year of the three ambassadors', p. 175.
109. Clarendon MS 18, no. 1383; *Clarendon State Papers*, II, pp. 84–5. See also, Clarendon MS 18, no. 1386: Windebank to Hopton, 27 May.
110. *Cal. Stat. Pap. Venet., 1640–2*, p. 46.
111. *Clarendon State Papers*, II, p. 86: Hopton to Windebank, 15/25 June.

Britain.[112] Windebank began to doubt the likelihood of Spain's being able to find the money to aid the king's campaign against the Scots.[113] Strafford, if only because he had no choice, persisted with negotiations through August for a loan of (now only) £50,000 but before anything could come of it, the defeat at Newburn had made it redundant.[114] All the Lord Deputy had gained was the odium of those who had discovered his dealings with the Habsburgs and who, in the context of the fears and suspicions of 1640, attributed to those negotiations the darkest and most sinister of motives.

The crisis in the counties

With their desperate problems in mounting the second campaign against the Scots without adequate supply, the king and Council did not struggle alone. No sooner, it must have seemed, had the soldiers sent north in the summer of 1639 made their way back to their localities, peace being proclaimed, than once again the shires of England were called upon to provide men and money for another war. The Council determined to compose an army of 30,000 (the trained bands of the realm in total were only 79,000) and sent letters to the counties in March detailing the number they were to have pressed, supplied and ready to go north.[115] The soldiers pressed, either bandsmen or substitutes, were to be lent the county arms and maintained at the county's expense until they entered royal service.[116] The demands met with immediate opposition. Threatened with being reported to the forthcoming parliament, many deputy lieutenants feared to press men or levy coat and conduct money.[117] Those of Dorset refused the Earl of Suffolk's request for 600 soldiers from the trained bands 'saying they never knew the train to march out of their county'.[118] To the Short Parliament came petitions and protests about military burdens and charges ('army money, wagon money, horse money, conduct money').[119] Several attacked the whole system of impressment;[120] Sir John Hotham protested that military costs in his

112. See Elliott, 'Year of the three ambassadors', p. 176 and *idem*, *The Revolt of the Catalans* (Cambridge, 1963).
113. *Clarendon State Papers*, II, p. 87: Windebank to Hopton, 24 July.
114. Gardiner, *History of England*, IX, p. 184.
115. *Cal. Stat. Pap. Dom., 1640*, p. 98; Chester Record Office, C.63/2/6, f.73v: a list of men to be pressed.
116. *Cal. Stat. Pap. Dom., 1640*, p. 55; Chester Record Office, C.63/2/6, ff.74v–75.
117. Above, p. 886.
118. *Cal. Stat. Pap. Dom., 1640*, p. 55.
119. Above. p. 859; Gardiner, *History of England*, IX, p. 115.
120. E. Cope (ed.) *Proceedings of the Short Parliament of 1640* (Camden Soc., 4th series, 19, 1977), pp. 190, 209, 257–8.

county (Yorkshire) had amounted to £40,000 in the previous year alone.[121]

It was against this background of local antagonism and protest that Charles decided, after the dissolution of parliament, to continue the war. There can be no doubt that speeches in parliament denying the legality of press money and other charges transformed the mood in the localities.[122] The Hampshire deputies (charged with raising 1,300 men) reported that while some parts of the county co-operated, 'others are altogether averse'.[123] The Norfolk deputies met with opposition to coat and conduct money and wrote to the Council to ask how they might proceed with those who refused the press.[124] The Earl of Exeter had to report that the west division of Northamptonshire refused any money;[125] Essex paid only a quarter of the £2,400 it was charged and several deputies refused to sign coat and conduct warrants.[126] As a consequence, on 22 May, the lord-lieutenants presented a rather patchy response on their progress towards providing troops. Suffolk and Leicestershire, for example, had responded well.[127] But Bedfordshire and Shropshire had come up with little money, as had Southwark and Guildford in Surrey.[128] As Conway told Strafford, 'the army which should have come hither by this time doth move slowly'.[129] It was moving so slowly that before the end of May the Council postponed the rendezvous from 1 June to 1 July. This only had the effect of penalizing the most compliant counties, who were now faced with supporting the pressed men for a month at their own charge.[130] Windebank reported the southern and western counties, those most remote from the conflict, as most refractory.[131] Coryton complained of mustering 1,400 soldiers weekly in Cornwall;[132] from Cambridgeshire and Suffolk came reports of indiscipline;[133] on 17 June, the pressed men of Dorset murdered their lieutenant, Mohun.[134]

As with the previous campaign, the levying of men disrupted as well as burdened county society. There were fears for local security as the

121. Cope, *Proceedings of the Short Parliament*, p. 192.
122. Rossingham reported a refusal by deputies to sign coat and conduct warrants 'which has been in practice much more than time out of mind' (*Cal. Stat. Pap. Dom., 1640*, p. 155).
123. *Ibid.*, p. 152.
124. *Ibid.*, p. 161.
125. *Ibid.*, p. 195.
126. *Ibid.*
127. *Ibid.*, p. 204.
128. *Ibid.*, pp. 205–6.
129. *Ibid.*, p. 214, 25 May.
130. See above, p. 888.
131. *Cal. Stat. Pap. Dom., 1640*, p. 301: Windebank to Conway, 15 June.
132. *Ibid.*, p. 372.
133. *Ibid.*, p. 336; cf. Bodleian, Bankes MS 42/36.
134. *Cal. Stat. Pap. Dom., 1640*, pp. 316, 333.

county arms (well below their former complement as a consequence of the last campaign) were handed to the conscripts.[135] Francis Basset complained of a shortage of labour in Tehidy. 'I cannot,' he wrote to Nicholas, 'get men half sufficient either for my tillage for next year or to thresh and make the best profit of what I have of the last.'[136] At the summer assizes, while the judges defended the king's powers to conscript, there were petitions presented by the Grand Juries against compelling men to serve in the army, and against coat and conduct money and ship money, which the constables, distracted by their military duties, were still charged to collect.[137] Continued delays in marching the conscripts added a bitter outcry against the billeting of unpaid and unruly troops.[138] Yorkshire was the county worst hit. The inhabitants of Doncaster protested that they were 'sore over-burdened and charged with carriages in this expedition . . . by reason the said town is situate upon the roadway and a multitude of teams is used now in this expedition northwards'.[139] Outbreaks of plague compounded their difficulties, and efforts by the Council to force other wapentakes to share the costs only multiplied the complaints.[140] With an army of 19,000 (as well as the trained bands) quartered on them, Yorkshire was forced to levy high rates, which led some of Sir Henry Slingsby's tenants to doubt whether they could pay their landlord's rents.[141] Men, Slingsby recalled, were 'at a stand what course to take'.[142] The gentry took the lead and presented at the assizes a petition in which they claimed to have expended £100,000 in military charges the last year and declaimed against the illegality of the billet. To recover from their costs, they estimated, would take them twenty years. The Yorkshire petitioners called for a parliament to relieve them.[143] Before they heard of the favourable answer to their plea, Newcastle fell. With the news of a war lost before the army had reached the battlefield it was not only the Yorkshire gentry who were led to reflect for the second time in a year that 'all this charge hath been to no great purpose, for they did lie idle billeted about York and when they had been at all this charge they were sent home again'.[144]

135. See the petition of the mayor of Boston, *Cal. Stat. Pap. Dom., 1640,* p. 538 and *ibid.*, p. 196; Chester Record Office, CR.63/2/6, f.74v.
136. *Cal. Stat. Pap. Dom., 1640,* p. 458.
137. For example, *ibid.*, pp. 466, 512–13, 523.
138. For example, *ibid.*, p. 500.
139. J. Lister (ed.) *West Riding Sessions Records II: Orders 1611–42, Indictments 1637–42* (York. Arch. Soc. Rec. series, 54, 1915), p. 219.
140. *Ibid.*, pp. 260, 269; cf. pp. 310–11.
141. D. Parsons (ed.) *The Diary of Sir Henry Slingsby* (1836), p. 60.
142. *Ibid.*, p. 61.
143. *Ibid.*; see *Cal. Stat. Pap. Dom., 1640,* pp. 523–4: petition of the gentry of Yorkshire, 28 July.
144. Parsons, *Diary of Sir Henry Slingsby*, p. 60.

The propaganda war

Scottish propaganda concentrated on persuading the English that the war was the unnecessarily belligerent act of a government deeply infected with popery. On the eve of the Short Parliament, the Covenanters had distributed 2,000 copies of their *Information, from the Estaits of Scotland,* which Charles had been so concerned about as to have it burned by the public hangman, as a document 'tending to raise mutiny and sedition in the kingdom'.[145] During the course of the Assembly, the estates of Scotland directed *A Remonstrance Concerning the Present Troubles* . . . 'unto the parliament of England'. Justifying their own petitions, the Covenanters blamed the breakdown of peace on Spanish plots in general and on one prelate in particular who had weighed, they argued, more in royal counsels than the supplications of a loyal nation. They appealed to the Commons to bring such miscreants to justice and to hear the petitions of their brothers who rejoiced with them in their first sunshine of comfort, a parliament.[146] As we have seen, on the day of dissolution the Scots had conspired with leading MPs to bring in a petition against the second campaign. Their endeavour was to end the war with paper before ever a cannon shot had been heard. After the break-up of the parliament, the Scots continued to press the identity of their struggle with the grievances of England, in order to undermine the war effort or force another parliament which might compel the king to make peace on terms that satisfied the Covenanters. Then, as they prepared to march on England in August, they issued pamphlets justifying their plans. *The Intentions of the Army of the Kingdom of Scotland, Declared to their Brethren of England* began with expressions of gratitude that the late parliament had justified their cause.[147] The Covenanters had sought peace, but prelates and papists had blocked their petitions. 'All the designs of both kingdoms,' they announced, 'is for the truth of religion and for the just liberty of the subject.'[148] But in Scotland (as in England) Laud and Strafford – now identified as the twin pillars of evil – sought to suppress them. Petitions were inefficacious, 'these that govern the King's counsels being far from any inclination or intention to satisfy the just desires and grievances of the subject as they have made manifest by breaking up of parliaments in both kingdoms'.[149] It was

145. Spalding, *Memorials of the Troubles*, p. 257; Larkin, *Stuart Royal Proclamations*, II, no. 297, pp. 703–5.
146. *A Remonstrance Concerning the Present Troubles from the Meeting of the Estates of Scotland . . . unto the Parliament of England* (1640, Bodleian, Antiq f Sc 1640 E i).
147. STC 21919; see Spalding, *Memorials of the Troubles*, pp. 321–4.
148. *Ibid.*, p. 323.
149. *Ibid.*, p. 325.

for England to know that far from taking up arms for invasion, the Covenanters came – out of necessity – as friends and brothers, to defend their faith and freedom. The *Intentions* was a complex vindication of the Covenanters' aggressions, with an especially tortuous rationalization of the justification of necessity. A shorter broadside accompanied the pamphlet, simply calling for the evil counsellors who afflicted both nations to be brought to justice in parliament: 'The preservation or ruin of religion and liberties,' the *Information from the Scottish Nation* asserted, 'is common to both nations. We must now stand or fall together.'[150]

The impact of the Scots propaganda in 1640 is hard to gauge. It did not go entirely unanswered. *The Epistle Congratularie of Lysimadius Nicanor of the Society of Jesu to the Covenanters* cleverly satirized the Scots as partners of the dreaded Jesuits in rebellion against divine authority. With heavy irony all the Covenanters' acts are applauded as they strike more and more at sovereignty.[151] At the popular level, too, some ballads and verses suggest that, for all their justificatory propaganda, the Covenanters did not entirely succeed in overcoming the traditional jingoism of the English nor in dispelling suspicions of their true intentions. 'A True Subjects wish for the Happy Success of Our Royal Army preparing to resist the fractious rebellion of those insolent Covenanters . . .' appeals to ingrained prejudices and, against Scottish claims to brotherhood, evokes a crude but powerful nationalism:

> If ever England had occasion
> Her ancient honour to defend
> Then let her now make preparation
> Unto an honourable end
> The factious Scot
> Is very hot
> His ancient spleen is ne'er forgot
> He long hath been about this plot.[152]

Proceeding to a brief verse narrative of the troubles, the poem brands the Scots with rebelling under the cloak of religion against a 'gracious sovereign' who did 'very mildly' grant their legitimate desires. Reminding Englishmen of their treasonable dealings with the French, the poet calls on his readers to 'elevate St George's banner against them',

150. *Ibid.*, p. 330.
151. 1640, STC 5751. The tract compares Colonel Leslie with Loyola! (p. 59). There is also, of course, Charles I's own *Large Declaration Concerning the Late Tumults in Scotland* (1639, STC 21906).
152. 1640, Bodleian, Wood 401/142/2.

And they shall see
How stoutly we
. . . will fight if there occasion be.

Nevertheless, though the pamphlet war was not one-sided, there were many who believed that Scots propaganda at least insinuated doubts about the legitimacy of the war, if it did not evoke outright sympathy. The Venetian envoy reported that the August manifesto circulated 'throughout the kingdom and does great harm',[153] and several echoed Northumberland's and Sir Edward Osborne's fear that 'if Hannibal were at our gates some had rather open them than keep him out'.[154] Godly observers of events, like Woodforde, may well have been led to a radical change of heart by reading Scottish polemic. Where in the winter of 1639 Woodforde had prayed to avert a war, by the summer of 1640 he had 'great expectations of this great business of Scotland', as friends informed him the Covenanters were about to invade.[155] Amongst 'puritanical people', as a correspondent described them to Windebank, the Covenanters' appeal to common grievances struck a chord of harmony.[156] Across the nation at large, however, support for the king's campaign was eroded less by sympathy for the Covenanter than by the collapse of all hierarchy and order that was threatening in the shires.

Even before the débâcle of the Short Parliament, political uncertainty had begun to destabilize local government and society. Ever the barometer of coming storms, the moneylenders were calling in their loans in an atmosphere in which no financial bets were deemed safe.[157] George Wyllys told his son, the governor of Connecticut, that things were so unsettled in England he could not sell any land – except at prices well below its value.[158] There can be no doubt that the collapse of the first parliament in eleven years after only three weeks turned a feeling of instability into a sense of crisis. The examination of Aldermen Geere and Atkins concerning their refusal to co-operate with levying a loan from the most able merchants sent further alarm signals to the city, which entered now a period of hostile alienation from the government.[159] Across the nation, with the parliament dissolved and the troops assembling, 'everyone standeth,' Hawkins

153. *Cal. Stat. Pap. Venet., 1640–2*, p. 70.
154. *HMC De Lisle and Dudley, VI*, p. 292; *Cal. Stat. Pap. Dom., 1640*, p. 585; cf. Hardwicke, *State Papers*, II, pp. 155, 159; *Cal. Stat. Pap. Dom., 1639–40*, p. 503.
155. New College Oxford MS 9502 (Woodforde's diary), 12 Aug.
156. *Cal. Stat. Pap. Dom., 1639–40*, p. 515.
157. BL Add. MS 11045, ff.109–10: Rossingham to Scudamore, 14 April.
158. *The Wyllys Papers, 1590–1796* (Connecticut Historical Soc., 21, Hertford, 1924), p. 9.
159. Bankes MS 42/25.

reported to Leicester, 'at a gaze what will next be done.'[160] From their very different viewpoints, puritans and courtiers alike had a foresight of a major catastrophe. 'The state of things in the kingdom is very doubtful and uncertain,' Robert Woodforde recorded in his diary for May;[161] 'There is a very general unsatisfaction and fear in the hearts of every creature,' the Countess of Carlisle told her brother-in-law, Leicester.[162] Thomas Peyton, we have seen, believed the parliament had done more harm than good and hinted at the onset of conspiracy, violence and universal discontent: 'I cannot meet with any man,' he wrote to Henry Oxinden, 'but knows what will become of these things; so inspired are the more zealous, so ready to execute mischief are the soldiers, so provident are worldly excesses, and generally so wise are become the Commons having received a diffusive knowledge from the dispersed house.'[163]

The summer months added desperation to anxiety, as the Council and the counties struggled to sustain the war effort without funds. Seizure of the bullion in the Mint and rumours of debasement of the coinage threatened a stoppage of all commerce. The distraction of the magistracy, the climate of instability and the fact that parliament had requestioned its legality led to refusals to pay ship money on a scale not seen hitherto. The sheriff of Derbyshire complained that since the parliament, he had been dared to distrain and threatened by refusers.[164] A lawyer, Mr Peard, questioned the legality of imprisonment for ship money refusal; evidently many constables began to be fearful of co-operating in its collection.[165] Confusion at home, Sir Nicholas Byron had come to think, was more to be feared than any designs of the Scots – and his apprehension of political breakdown was widely current at court.[166] Describing the 'desperate condition' to Leicester, Northumberland predicted: 'It is impossible things can long continue in the condition they now are in; so general a defection in this kingdom hath not been known in the memory of any.'[167] John Castle deployed very familiar images to represent a very unfamiliar mood of popular anger and insurrection: 'There is at this time reigning here at Westminster,' he informed the Lord President of the Marches,

160. *HMC De Lisle and Dudley, VI*, p. 260.
161. Woodforde's diary, 12 May.
162. *HMC De Lisle and Dudley, VI*, p. 261.
163. D. Gardiner, *The Oxinden Letters 1607–42* (1933), p. 173: Peyton to Oxinden, 6 May 1640.
164. *Cal. Stat. Pap. Dom., 1640*, p. 269.
165. *Ibid.*, p. 306.
166. *Ibid.*, p. 493.
167. Collins, *Letters and Memorials*, II, p. 654–5, 4 June.

> a disease (which is morbus epidemicus) wherein they that labour of it complain of a stifling at heart and distemper in the head, and there is cause to fear that almost generally through the kingdom the common people are sick of those parts. They labour of a suffocation of their hearts in the duty and obedience they owe to his Majesty's service and commands and they are stricken in the head that they rave and utter they know not what against his Majesty's government . . .[168]

The norms of political life – norms of harmony and deference – were giving way to those heralds of civil war – threat, confrontation and violence. When the East India Company refused to lend money for the army in August, the usually good-humoured Cottington lost his temper. Newly appointed its constable, he threatened the merchants with 'louder language forth of the Tower' and frightened the whole city as a consequence.[169] A microcosm of the divisions in the realm, London's elections for the mayoralty in the autumn of 1640 witnessed the unprecedented breach of the rule of aldermanic seniority and scenes of tumult, as the expected successor, Acton, was challenged for his service to the king.[170] A political squib described London as as much for the Covenant as Edinburgh.[171] In the counties, some praised the Scots as better subjects than the English and welcomed their invasion.[172] Their victory at Newburn – the first on English soil since Otterburn in 1388–appeared so inexplicable that some were indeed led to wonder whether they did not, as they had claimed, have God on their side. The vicar of Rotherham noted that the army fled 'in all haste *on the Lord's Day*' and that 'by the news and noise thereof the people in the several churches in York were terribly affrighted, and many fled out of the churches with confusion in sermon time'.[173]

The mood in 1640 of instability and crisis was compounded by the most widespread and publicly reported acts of violence since the Wars of the Roses. The rumour having spread that the archbishop of Canterbury was responsible for the dissolution of parliament, a mob of 1,200 apprentices headed for Laud's London residence at Lambeth where they thronged at the gate, refusing to budge–to the fright of the local JPs – until 2.30 in the morning.[174] When they discovered that

168. Ellesmere MS 7838, 23 June 1640.
169. Hamilton MS 1231: Strafford to Hamilton, 24 Aug.
170. BL Add. MS 11045, f.122. Rossingham described it to Scudamore: 'this was such a business as there is no precedent for it' (7 Oct.).
171. *Cal. Stat. Pap. Dom., 1640*, p. 612.
172. *Cal. Stat. Pap. Venet., 1640–2*, pp. 73–4; A. Fletcher, *A County Community in Peace and War: Sussex, 1600–1660* (1975), p. 248.
173. C. Jackson (ed.) *The Life of Master John Shaw* (Surtees Soc., 65, 1877), p. 131.
174. W. Scott and J. Bliss (eds) *The Works of William Laud* (7 vols, Oxford, 1847–60), III,

Laud had (prudently) moved into Whitehall, they threatened to return. Sir John Lambe's house was also attacked, prompting Hawkins to write to Leicester that 'I never knew the subjects of England so much out of order'.[175] Even an armed watch placed at Lambeth proved to be little deterrent. True to their promise, the apprentices returned with a force of 3,000; chanting that they would not give up until they had caught 'the fox', they broke open the White Lion prison and released two of their fellows who had been gaoled after the previous affray, and all the other inmates as well.[176] The mayor ordered the city's portcullises to be made serviceable and chains to be placed across the streets as measures of crowd control.[177] So insecure was the court that arms were brought from the Tower to Whitehall and stored under the Masquing House there, in readiness to defend the palace.[178] Still placards continued to urge the abolition of episcopacy and to threaten Laud, Wentworth and the Marquis of Hamilton. Castle knew that such scenes of violence would not be confined to the capital. 'The ball of wild fire that is kindled here,' he wrote, 'will fly and burn (it is feared) a great way off where there will not be so good means to quench it as here under the King's window where his person strikes more terror than the trained bands with their arms.'[179] He was right. Disturbances spread to Southwark and Blackheath – and thence across the country. In May there were riots in the fens, mutinies at Newcastle, and rumours of a rising in Norfolk and the West Country 'where the clothiers have in many places discharged their workfolks because they cannot vent their cloth', especially to London.[180]

As the soldiers were pressed and prepared for the march, more violence exploded. Houses were burned at Aylesbury in an affray that took place between the officers and new conscripts of Buckinghamshire.[181] Norfolk soldiers refused to embark; at Newmarket in Cambridgeshire the men levied beat their officers.[182] Others tied up their captains and threw cudgels at them; Lord Digby wrote with a disturbing feel for the officers' helplessness, as though they were cocks on Shrove Tuesday.[183] Violence and insubordination escalated to murder. It was

p. 84; Ellesmere MS 7833: Castle to Bridgewater, 12 May. See also *Cal. Stat. Pap. Dom., 1640*, p. 150; *Cal. Stat. Pap. Venet., 1640–2*, p. 47.

175. Ellesmere MS 7834; *HMC De Lisle and Dudley, VI*, p. 267.
176. Ellesmere MS 7834: Castle to Bridgewater, 15 May; *Cal. Stat. Pap. Dom., 1640*, p. 167; *HMC De Lisle and Dudley, VI*, p. 272.
177. BL Add. MS 11045: Rossingham to Scudamore, 19 May.
178. Ellesmere MS 7835: Castle to Bridgewater, 18 May. Castle provides the most detailed and vivid account of these events.
179. *Ibid.*
180. *Cal. Stat. Pap. Dom., 1640*, pp. 167, 189, 190; Ellesmere MS 7835.
181. BL Add. MS 11045, f.116.
182. Ellesmere MS 7838: Castle to Bridgewater, 23 June.
183. *Cal. Stat. Pap. Dom., 1640*, p. 333: Sir K. Digby to Viscount Conway, 23 June.

not only the conductor of the Dorset bands who met his death, marching the men to their rendezvous.[184] In Essex and Devon, officers were slain by their subordinates, as the soldiers went on a rampage of pillage and attacks on property.[185] The return of the lord-lieutenants to the counties, more importantly the (illegal) imposition of martial law in July, began to see some check on the outrages. Conway thought that obedience might be secured 'if he that commands hath power to reward and punish'.[186] It was a familiar axiom, but one that was increasingly only prescriptive rather than descriptive. For the complex nexus of command, consent and compliance had fractured, and there were growing suspicions that not all even of the magisterial class would strive to repair it. Attorney Bankes lamented that 'there is met a general remissness and backwardness in the deputy lieutenants and others to whom it appertains to countenance and assist the commanders and officers in punishing and reducing them to conformity'.[187] Amid rumours that some leading puritans in England had conspired with the Scots, Conway recognized that the greatest danger would befall the realm if any emerged to lead the discontented multitude. Conway found reassurance from tradition that it could not happen in England: 'he that fears that any heed can be given to any discontented body here . . . will be afraid like boys and women of a turnip cut like a death's head with a candle in it'.[188] But scarcely had Halloween come and gone before his confidence was shown to be misplaced.

The nature of the violence in the summer of 1640 is revealing of the way in which, in circumstances of inexplicable instability, men seek scapegoats to drive out their troubles. As the apprentices blamed Laud for the dissolution of the parliament, so, in many instances, the soldiers vented their anger at the episcopate and its trappings. From several counties it was reported that the indiscipline of the soldiers was related to religious fears or convictions. At Warminster the conscripts refused to march with their captain because he was alleged to be a papist;[189] those of Sir Jacob Astley's regiment would not fight, they said, against the gospel;[190] a Devonshire lieutenant was murdered because the troops under his command had heard he was popishly affected.[191] As they marched the soldiers committed frequent iconoclasm

184. *Ibid.*, p. 316.
185. *Ibid.*, p. 494; Ellesmere MS 7842, 6 July.
186. *Cal. Stat. Pap. Dom., 1640*, p. 277: Conway to Laud, 8 June.
187. Bankes MS 42/36, 28 June.
188. *Cal. Stat. Pap. Dom., 1640*, pp. 277–8. Familiar reference to the pagan Hallowe'en in a letter to Laud from Harley's brother-in-law is worthy of note.
189. *Ibid.*, p. 281.
190. *Ibid.*, p. 477.
191. *Ibid.*, p. 494.

against that symbol of the church hierarchy, the altar rail. In Staffordshire, Wiltshire, Derbyshire and Essex rails were torn down;[192] at Reading in Berkshire the organ was also smashed.[193] But no fine liturgical discrimination confined the mob's destruction to the rails. At Marsworth in Buckinghamshire the soldiers broke into the church and, as well as breaking the rails and all the glass, tore up the prayer book and the surplice.[194] At Ashford in Kent, a soldier, in a mock ritual of inversion organized by the crowd, put on a cassock and surplice and 'being brought to the pillory by the rabble he was by them accused of being cause of a great many disorders'.[195] Such incidents cannot be simply catalogued as proof of the soldiers' or more broadly popular antagonism to church ornament and clerical dress. The troops had as many secular targets for their violence. Attacks on the Earl of Huntingdon's park, Sir John Coke's grounds, the enclosures at Uttoxeter in Staffordshire, or the house of correction on the road to Selby suggest class revolt against the symbols of privilege and punishment which the collapse of magisterial authority unleashed.[196] The younger Coke described the conscripts in Derbyshire as a lawless band who 'do rob all men they meet as they go straggling through the country without any order or command', threatening to burn whole towns on their return.[197] Attacks on churches in part belong to these indiscriminate assaults on the instruments of control and constraint. But what the iconoclasm suggests too is that the anxiety and tension of war, and still more defeat, had begun to set the match to the tinder of propaganda to ignite a fire of antipopery. It was to be a fire around which would gather a party that would lead a revolution.

Anti-popish hysteria and popular politics

Before the Short Parliament, for all the real concern about the toleration of Catholic worship and the proselytizing of the queen's faction, anti-popery had never reached a pitch of hysteria. In no way did the parliament give a lead to a new wave of persecution. Even Pym, who had banged the anti-papist drum since the 1620s, could speak with moderation and dispassion about the problem in the Commons: 'I

192. *Ibid.*, pp. 477, 522, 585; *HMC Cowper II*, p. 256.
193. BL Add. MS 11045, f.125v.
194. Ellesmere MS 7765.
195. Ellesmere MS 7856: Castle to Bridgewater, 29 Aug.
196. *Cal. Stat. Pap. Dom., 1640*, pp. 449–50; G. Wrottesley (ed.) *The Staffordshire Muster of 1640* (William Salt Arch. Soc., 15, 1894), p. 205; Lister, *West Riding Sessions Records*, II, p. 230. See too B. Manning, *The English People and the English Revolution* (1976), ch. 1.
197. *HMC Cowper II*, p. 258: Sir J. Coke the younger to Thomas Coke, 29 June.

desire', he announced on 17 April, to have 'no new laws made against them, God be thanked we have enough of good old laws, nor a rigid execution of those we have but only so far forth as may tend to the safety of his Majesty'.[198] The dissolution, however, marked a radical new phase. With three Spanish envoys at court, the rumour quickly spread that the parliament had fallen as a result of a Catholic plot.[199] There were more Catholic officers in the army and some alleged that agitators endeavoured to infect the troops with fear of their intentions.[200] The atmosphere was tense. Carrots were thrown at the Queen Mother's coach;[201] some claimed that the king too went to mass;[202] one William Collyer of Bristol knew forty in the city who would swear Charles had converted to Rome.[203] The Council felt the need to act: orders were sent out in May to burn popish books, and in June to deal more severely with recusants, in the hope of quelling the riots.[204] Windebank advised that all foreign priests at court should be expelled – counsel which, had it been taken, could have done much to make the Catholic problem less conspicuous before the convention of the Long Parliament.[205] As it was, the fears festered and spread. The mayor of Norwich informed the Privy Council that he had received a tip-off that the city was to be attacked by 12,000 papists.[206] John Gell of Hopton in Derbyshire heard that the papists of Lichfield had ordered 200 hatchets for a planned massacre of Protestants;[207] Stanley Gower told Harley that in general 'papist houses are so ready for to execute whatsoever plots are hatching', and urged that all their homes be searched.[208] The defeat at Newburn saw disturbances reach a new height. By the autumn the fear of plots, confirmed as it seemed by events, had taken hold of the populace (Londoners petitioned that Catholics should be forced to wear 'distinguishing clothes') and some of the leading gentry, including Pym.[209] It was an inauspicious atmosphere in which the Long Parliament was convened, for hysteria

198. Cope, *Proceedings of the Short Parliament*, p. 150; cf. p. 225. The Commons, for example, made no protest about the privileges enjoyed by Catholics during parliament.
199. R. Clifton, 'The fear of Catholics in England, 1637–45' (Oxford University, D. Phil. thesis, 1967), pp. 77–80.
200. *Ibid.*, p. 89; *Cal. Stat. Pap. Dom., 1639–40*, p. 246; Gardiner, *History of England*, IX, p. 158; Nalson, *Impartial Collection*, I, p. 495.
201. Ellesmere MS 7860: Castle to Bridgewater, 24 Sept.
202. *Cal. Stat. Pap. Dom., 1640*, pp. 192–3.
203. *Ibid.*, p. 272.
204. Nalson, *Impartial Collection*, I, p. 489; *Cal. Stat. Pap. Venet., 1640–2*, p. 52.
205. *Clarendon State Papers*, II, p. 113.
206. J.T. Evans, *Seventeenth Century Norwich: Politics, Religion and Government, 1620–90* (Oxford, 1979), p. 109.
207. J. Dias, 'Politics and administration in Nottinghamshire and Derbyshire, 1590–1640' (Oxford University, D. Phil. thesis, 1973), p. 455.
208. BL, MS 29/172, f.308.
209. Clifton, 'Fear of Catholics', p. 121.

is the solvent of political moderation and compromise. As Anthony Fletcher concluded, in the apprehension of leading MPs that religion and government were being subverted by popish malignants, the English civil war had its origins.[210]

The violence and instability of 1640 not only fed the fear of popery. It also stimulated a powerful reaction that, like the popish scare, was to dominate the politics of the following months: a fear of the many-headed monster, the mob. The dread of a collapse of the social order was never far below the surface of early modern England: the homilies on obedience are texts which as much acknowledge a tense social reality as they prescribe an ideal commonwealth. The very first disturbances in the spring of 1640 quickly triggered deep-seated worries about the stability of social hierarchy. Conway asked anxiously for regular reports on the apprentices' activities; he hoped their riotous assembly would be 'but a Shrove Tuesday business' – contained, that is, within the boundaries of licensed social inversion, which was part of the matrix of social control.[211] But he could not mask his fears; knowing, he wrote to Garrard, that 'there is no trust to be put in the common people; they have neither constancy nor gratitude. They neither requite the love that is bestowed on them, nor continue in their love to anyone.' Hawkins was disoriented by the 'strange manner' in which the soldiers attacked church rails;[212] in Derbyshire the younger Coke read the king's proclamation to the rioters and then, trusting no more in the power of the (even the royal) word, he fled back to defend his house.[213] John Castle, seeing the 'wildfire' he had glimpsed burn across the land could only pray: oh Lord, 'defend this great ship from breaking upon these rocks'.[214] Even Wallington prayed 'the lord keep us from mutiny'.[215] He may have had good cause, for born of the violence of 1640 was a wider suspicion of 'the faction' and a sense of the overriding need to uphold royal authority as the bulwark of property, hierarchy and order. The need to move the Mint for fear of an attack by the mob, the tumults at the mayoral elections, prompted a sharp conservative reaction in the city: 'the gravest citizens were much scandalised at it'.[216] News of rebellions in Catalonia and further riots at home strengthened the party committed to preserve social order before all else, even before tackling the grievances of the realm. When a mob in the autumn broke into the High Commission court in the

210. A.J. Fletcher, *The Outbreak of the English Civil War* (1981), p. xxi.
211. BL, MS 29/172, p. 287: Conway to G. Garrard, May 1640.
212. *HMC De Lisle and Dudley, VI*, p. 318.
213. *HMC Cowper II*, p. 256.
214. Ellesmere MS 7842.
215. N. Wallington, *Historical Notices of . . . the Reign of Charles I, 1630–46*, ed. R. Webb (2 vols, 1869), I, p. 126.
216. *Clarendon State Papers*, II, p. 126.

Convocation House, and ripped down benches and tore up books, one newswriter observed: 'Although there may be some delinquencies sometimes committed in the prosecution of some causes in that court by the iniquity of the subordinate officers, yet for the common people to go about to reform abuses of a court of justice by club law is held no less than a capital crime, and this is the judgement of sober and wise men.'[217] It was a sentiment that many of the propertied were to voice as the mob hurled themselves noisily into the sacrosanct forum of gentry politics.

This conservatism was not just a class phenomenon. Popular patriotism and affection for the king not only endured; in many communities it was reinforced by suspicion of the puritan, fear of the soldiers and hostility to their iconoclasm. Many broken rails, we must recall, were restored at parish expense. In 1640 the parish of Strood in Kent paid to have the royal arms carved in the church.[218] Moreover the Scots invasion and exaction of tribute from English subjects refocused popular feeling on a foreign incursor rather than internal ills. A minor victory at Stapleton, County Durham in September against a band of Scots who had attempted to plunder the house of Thomas Pudsie occasioned the ballad *Good News from the North*.[219] After denouncing the Scots who, taking prize, 'afflict the people in outrageous wise' the versifier concludes:

> I'll daily pray and hourly
> As it doth in my power lie
> To him by whom kings reign; that with success
> King Charles go on and prosper may
> And (having made the Scots away)
> Rule o'er his lands in peace and happiness.[220]

The Scottish occupation of English territory began to stimulate some fundamental rethinking about the course of events over the previous year. A widely circulated letter, purportedly from an alderman of Newcastle to a friend in London, cataloguing the Scots insolence and seizure of money and cattle, reflected back: 'I confess the apprehension of Popery and innovation in religion did trouble us all, but he that should look upon our conditions would scarce believe this the lively remedy. I should have preferred by much to have suffered as a martyr

217. BL Add. MS 11045, ff.129–30: Rossingham to Scudamore, 27 Oct., 3 Nov.; cf. *HMC Cowper II*, p. 262.
218. Above, p. 391; H.R. Plomer (ed.) *The Churchwardens' Accounts of St Nicholas Strood, Part II, 1603–62* (Kent Arch. Soc., Records Branch, 5, 1927), p. 186.
219. Cf. Hardwicke, *State Papers*, II, p. 283, on Captain Digby's minor victory over Sir Alexander Douglas.
220. *Good News from the North* (1640, Wood, 401/134); cf. H. Rollins, *Cavalier and Puritan* (New York, 1923), p. 100.

for my religion than to run the hazard of being a traitor for my country . . .'[221] More important, verses began to blame those, notably puritans, who had been slow to grant the king the aid to repel the rebels but quick to present less menacing domestic grievances. So the lines against the coming of the Scots into England:

Let Puritans rise, let protestants fall
Let Brownists find favour and Papists loose all
Let them damn all the patents that ever was given
And make Prynne a saint, though he never see heaven
Let them prove Madam Purbeck to be without spot
If ere we return, then hang up the Scot. . . .

Let giving of subsidies be so delayed
And at the King's charges let them ever be paid
Though many believe we come for their good
And therefore are loathe we should spend any blood
When ever we come here you must all to the pot
Then too late you will say, let us hang up the Scot.[222]

Another poem, 'A Curse on Ye Scots' not only echoes the king's earlier declarations that the Scots only pretended religious sensibilities as a veil to rebellion, it specifically blames Pym for the present sad plight of England. Rebels, the Scots were a subhuman form inhabiting a territory exiled from civilization and godliness:

Even nature doth ye Scotch men beasts confess
Making ye country such a wilderness . . .

Had Cain been Scot, God would have changed his doom
Not made him wander but confined him home.

Rehearsing the age-old fear that the Scots sought to grasp English wealth, the verses continue:

They wanted food and payment so they took
Religion for their seamstresse and their cook

The poet could not suppress his patriotic anger:

Where is the Stoic can his gall appease
To see his country sick of Pym's disease.[223]

During the very months these ballads were circulating, the verse 'God Have Mercy Good Scot' voiced thanks for the intervention from

221. Berkshire Record Office, Trumbull MS XX, 40, 8 Sept. 1640; cf. Tanner MS 65, ff.110–12.
222. Tanner MS 306, f.292.
223. Tanner MS 465, f.92: 'A Curse on Ye Scots'.

the north that would crush projectors, repress Catholics and strike down 'proud prelates that straddle so wide / As if they did mean the world to bestride'.[224] Amid war, violence at home and instability, England was polarizing – not only the political nation, but those classes traditionally outside it. Two totems had been erected during the course of 1640: one represented fear of Catholic plots; the other a horror of popular insurrection and of a 'fanatical crew' that stirred it.[225] As yet no unbreakable circles had linked arms around each pole. Sir Thomas Knyvett, who could indeed exclaim 'God a mercy good Scot!' for the favour of a parliament that might purge the ill humours of the land, also had his reservations: 'mistress mark the winding up. Scot is not gone yet. Behold I doubt we must be acquainted with Mr Knox as well as Buchanan . . . before we be rid of them.'[226] Others would travel between the totems as events made now one menace, now the other loom larger. But the totems would ultimately convert into military standards, behind which armies would march into civil war. Already some, if they had not quite nailed their colours to those poles, had taken up a position from which they would not budge. Attitudes to the Scots in 1640 proved to be something of a litmus paper of other divisions. While some prayed, with Lady Lee, 'beseech God send us well rid of the Scots' and looked to the parliament of November to 'make a good war', there were others with quite different interests.[227] For the presence of a Scots army in England, for which the king was obliged to pay, precluded an early dissolution. Henry Townshend recognized that the Scots guaranteed the continuance of the parliament.[228] Strafford, in a letter to Sir George Radcliffe, confided his fear that they would make a rod by which the faction would rule over the king – 'to force him to do anything the puritan popular humour hath a mind unto'.[229]

Another parliament?

After the defeat at Newburn, pressure to summon another parliament came from all quarters. On 24 August, even before the engagement, the

224. Copies in BL, Harleian MS 4931, f.80; Denmilne MS XIII, 69; see M.A.E. Green (ed.) *The Diary of John Rous, Incumbent of Santon Downham, Suffolk, 1625–1642* (Camden Soc., old series, 66, 1856), pp. 110–11.
225. The phrase is from *A Whip for the Back of a Backsliding Brownist* (1640, STC 3920).
226. B. Schofield (ed.) *The Knyvett Letters, 1620–44* (Norfolk Record Soc., 20, 1949), pp. 96–7: Thomas Knyvett to wife [Dec. 1640–Jan. 1641].
227. Clarendon MS 19, no. 1457: Lady Lee of Ditchley to Hyde, Nov. 1640; cf. Conway to Garrard, 29 Oct. (BL, MS 29/172, p. 306).
228. J.W. Willis Bund (ed.) *The Diary of Henry Townshend of Elmley Lovett, 1640–1663* (Worcestershire Historical Soc., 1915), p. 18.
229. T.D. Whittaker (ed.) *The Life and Correspondence of Sir George Radcliffe* (1810), pp. 214–21: Strafford to Radcliffe, 5 Nov., quotation p. 219.

gentry of Yorkshire, unable to sustain their burdens, had petitioned for a parliament where they might air their grievances.[230] On the day of the battle, a group of peers and leading MPs from the Short Parliament drew up a petition to present to the king in which they outlined the nation's grievances: military charges, unruly soldiers, innovations in religion, ship money, patents and the menace of popery. Attributing the ills to the intermission of parliaments they asked that one might immediately be summoned at which the authors of the bad counsels and projects that had afflicted the realm might be called to account.[231] In addition, a more popular petition (Spalding claimed it was signed by 7,000) was known to be circulating in the capital, to be sent up to the king at York.[232] Northumberland petitioned against the ravages of the occupying Scots.[233] And in Northamptonshire, Woodforde tells us, some knights and gentlemen of the county met to frame a petition of grievances which Mr Knightley was appointed to take to York.[234] In the English localities a parliament was urgently desired not least to communicate to the king the collapse of order that government demands had brought about. The Covenanters too desired a parliament in England. Since the dissolution of the Assembly in the spring, they had been in league with the leading MPs. In their justificatory propaganda on entering England in August they had called for the resummoning of parliament. On 2 September their London friends forwarded intelligence of their own petition for a parliament and assured them of widespread support for their cause if one were called.[235] Taking their cue, the Scots in turn sent to Charles I on the 4th, asking that their grievances might be treated on, with the advice of an English parliament.[236] Rebel Scots, disaffected English puritan peers and gentry and desperate local governors – whose interests were sharply to diverge over the following months – were united in their plea and demand.[237]

It is important to appreciate that Charles himself may already have been at one with them. As early as 15 August Castle reported the gossip at court that Charles was talking of resummoning a parliament (he had toyed with recalling the old one); and laid a wager – he was a shrewd punter – that there would be one by All Hallowstide, that is 1 November.[238] When, before having received any of the petitions, the

230. *Cal. Stat. Pap. Dom., 1640*, pp. 624–5.
231. *Ibid.*, p. 639; *Clarendon State Papers*, II, p. 94.
232. Spalding, *Memorials of the Troubles*, p. 344.
233. Nalson, *Impartial Collection*, I, p. 440.
234. Woodforde's diary, 15 Sept.
235. Denmilne MS XIII, 28: English intelligence to the Scots army.
236. Hamilton MS 1305; J. Rushworth, *Historical Collections*, III p. 1255.
237. Cholmley points out that the Yorkshire petition prompted Bedford and the other eleven peers (*The Memoirs of Sir Hugh Cholmley*, 1787, p. 62).
238. Ellesmere MS 7849; he added 'which God grant may fall out to be true'.

king, on 1 September, wrote to his Council at Whitehall to ask for their advice about how to check the Scots, he must have been aware that the option of a parliament would be considered.[239] Certainly in response to the royal letter, the Council found itself debating two inseparable propositions: how to raise money and forces to resist a possible Scottish march on London and if possible beat them back over the border, and how to reconcile the king and his people, so as to unite the realm behind a war effort.[240] The Privy Seal, the Earl of Manchester, astutely perceiving the significance of aristocratic disaffection to the regime, advised the calling of a Council of Peers, which in Edward III's reign had raised money for the king's wars. 'The kingdom,' Manchester argued, perhaps with too little sense of the changes since the fourteenth century, 'will follow the peers'.[241] Windebank, Cottington and Arundel supported him – perhaps because as old members of the Spanish faction they had most to fear from a parliament. Other Councillors pressed immediately for a parliament or recognized that it would be the inevitable outcome of a Great Council: Sir Thomas Roe and the Earl of Dorset argued that there was 'no way but to indict a parliament'.[242] Laud and the Earl of Berkshire were sure 'the parliament a consequent' of the Council.[243] Perhaps in recognition of that logic, the meeting was unanimous in advising Charles to call a Council of Peers. It was summoned to York for 24 September.[244] There can be little doubt that Charles fully appreciated the need to summon a parliament too. Though as late as the 18th Vane was claiming that 'I do not find in his Majesty yet any certain resolution for the same',[245] he himself informed Arundel that a Council of Peers would demand a parliament, which could not be avoided.[246] Windebank, writing privately to Charles the day after the Council meeting, put it starkly that the choice would be between a parliament or succumbing to the rebels, for only a parliament could 'sweeten' the money for a war from the people.[247]

Charles had no desire, nor any sense of a need, to succumb to the rebels. He was suspicious of their petition for a peace. And he was far from pessimistic about his prospects in a war – if the money to

239. *Cal. Stat. Pap. Dom., 1640–1*, p. 1: Vane to Windebank, 1 Sept.
240. *Clarendon State Papers*, II, pp. 97–8: Windebank to Charles I, 3 Sept.; Hardwicke, *State Papers*, II, pp. 168–70 (a memorial of the Council's discussions); cf. *Cal. Stat. Pap Dom., 1640–1*, p. 8.
241. Hardwicke, *State Papers*, II, p. 169.
242. *Ibid.*
243. *Ibid.*, p. 170.
244. *Cal. Stat. Pap. Dom., 1640–1*, p. 8.
245. Hardwicke, *State Papers*, II, p. 181: Vane to Strafford, 18 Sept.
246. Arundel Castle letters, no. 380: Vane to Arundel.
247. *Clarendon State Papers*, II, pp. 97–8.

pay the troops was forthcoming. Sensing that he had only narrowly missed a victory, and seeing his forces at York in good order and spirit, Charles, not for the last time, was eager to take his military chance.[248] The Yorkshire bands had come up and those of the midland counties, more aware of the threat they faced after the Scots crossed the Tweed, were known to be on their way. The combined forces would undoubtedly outnumber Leslie's men; there was everything to fight for.[249] The gloomy Vane had also taken good heart at the sight of the force. 'We shall have a gallant army,' he told Windebank, 'We shall have horse and foot sufficient.'[250] 'So as you do provide us monies in time,' he promised his fellow secretary, 'I do not see . . . but that, God being with his Majesty's army, success will follow.' As a corollary, however, he warned 'should there be a failing of monies for these three months no man can foresee the calamities and miseries both to King and state that may thereupon ensue.'[251] Money for another campaign was the king's first priority. To obtain it, he was quite ready to call a parliament.

This was made clear – at least to Windebank – well before the Council of Peers. On 7 September two of the signatories of the peers' petition, the Earls of Hertford and Bedford, appeared before the Council in order to secure support. They argued at the Board that 'the very summoning of a parliament would so win the hearts of the people' as to remedy the king's troubles.[252] Told that the danger could not wait for a parliament and informed of the summoning of the Council of Peers, they urged that such a course should not exclude a parliament. Windebank reported all to the king. Charles, as was his custom with his secretary's clear dispatches, apostiled the letter and returned it: 'Ye may assure them that there is no thought of excluding a parliament.'[253] The king's want of money, his growing realization as the petitions came up of the unlikelihood of obtaining it, his sense, as the Scottish exaction of tribute alienated the northern counties, that the strategic moment was right all combined to clarify his decision.[254] The

248. See *HMC 3rd Report*, p. 82; *Cal. Stat. Pap. Venet., 1640–2*, p. 64; Harleian MS 456: speeches of Charles I; BL Add. MS 11045, f.119; Gardiner, *History of England*, IX, pp. 202–3. See also, C. Russell, 'Why did Charles I call the Long Parliament?', *History*, 69 (1984), pp. 375–83.
249. Gardiner, *History of England*, IX, p. 204.
250. Hardwicke, *State Papers*, II, pp. 173–4; *Cal. Stat. Pap. Dom., 1640–1*, p. 15; Gardiner, *History of England*, IX, p. 201.
251. Hardwicke, *State Papers*, II, pp. 173–4, 11 Sept.
252. *Clarendon State Papers*, II, pp. 110–13: Windebank to Charles I, 7 Sept.
253. *Ibid.*, p. 112.
254. Cf. Gardiner, *History of England*, IX, p. 203; above, p. 915. Though see Clarendon, *History of the Rebellion*, I, p. 211.

day before the Great Council convened, Captain Rossingham heard that Charles had resolved on a parliament.[255]

On 24 September the magnates convened in the dean of York's hall, prophetically as well as symbolically, 'put into the posture of a house of parliament'.[256] The bishop of Peterborough led a few short prayers after which Charles, with perspicacity and eloquence, opened the debate with an announcement that he had issued writs for a parliament to meet on 3 November. Meanwhile he sought their lordships' advice as to how his army might be maintained until it met. Garter King at Arms then read to the company the Covenanters' petitions and remonstrances, Charles interlocuting to explain an article from time to time. One reporter at least was moved at the Covenanters' demands – 'tedious and impertinent, with two worse qualities untruth and impudence . . . None that is or would be a good Christian or subject can hear it without detestation.'[257] After lunch, the Council appointed eight earls and eight barons commissioners to treat with the Scots; then proceeded to the pressing question of money.[258] Charles asserted his confidence that only want of supply had kept him from enforcing his authority on the rebels. He was disinclined to treat with them on any terms other than those of the pacification of Berwick; his honour was at stake.[259] The peers agreed to secure a loan of £200,000 in London on their securities.[260] Over the following days and weeks the loan strengthened Charles's resolve not to give in to the Covenanters' demands for contribution to sustain their army: 'This contribution they have taken against our wills,' he argued, 'shall we now allow it them willingly?'[261] While the Council sat, the commissioners were meeting with the Scots at Ripon. The Covenanters demanded £40,000 a month until a peace was concluded under threat of pillaging the north.[262] The English peers found it a demand hard to swallow. As Lord Maynard put it: 'The giving them anything a hard morsel to digest by any Englishman.'[263] And even Saye thought it dishonourable for the king to buy a peace.[264] It was therefore agreed that the Scots would continue to take £25,000 a month, secured by the bonds of the

255. BL Add. MS 11045, ff.120–21v: Rossingham to Scudamore, 23 Sept.
256. Ellesmere MS 7740: account of proceedings at the Great Council of York.
257. Ellesmere MS 7740. This is to be compared with the usual account by Sir John Borough in Harleian MS 456: 'Minutes of Proceedings of the Great Council of Peers at York . . .'.
258. Ellesmere MS 7740.
259. Harleian MS 456, ff.1v–2, 9v.
260. *Ibid.*, f.6.
261. *Ibid.*, f.27v.
262. J. Bruce (ed.) *Notes of the Treaty carried on at Ripon between King Charles I and the Covenanters of Scotland, AD 1640* (Camden Soc., old series, 100, 1869), p. 22 and *passim.*
263. Harleian MS 456, f.37.
264. *Ibid.*, f.39v.

northern gentry, for two months, and that thereafter all should be referred to the English parliament.[265]

As there were differing opinions on the payment of tribute (Vane for one did not regard it as dishonourable) so there were different perceptions of what had been decided at the Council and agreed by its commissioners for the treaty at Ripon.[266] Bristol and even Strafford were hesitant about re-embarking on war: the Lord-Lieutenant confessed 'he would not answer the success'.[267] The terms of the peace, on the other hand, constituted, as Bristol acknowledged, 'a treaty of the greatest disadvantage . . . since the Conquest'.[268] The king himself was clearly unhappy with it. Throughout the Council discussions his interventions had tended to argue the unlikelihood of an honourable peace and the possibility of victorious war. As the Council came to an end and the treaty commissioners headed for London, Charles looked to his parliament to provide the money that alone was needed to fight it. As he now appreciated, there was 'nothing to be done without a parliament for uniting the affections of the people'.[269]

The news of the resummoning of parliament met with widespread joy. Sir Henry Slingsby recorded the 'great expectation there is of a happy parliament where the subject may have a total redress of all his grievances';[270] Thomas Knyvett, more poetically, expressed his confidence that 'if ever Astraea will appear in her glory in Westminster Hall again', sure the time was to be 'after this purgation'.[271] That joy was shared by the Council and the court. To the Earl of Bridgewater it was 'most welcome' news.[272] Hopton was delighted to hear that a parliament would preserve the king in his due authority and reputation at home and abroad.[273] Hawkins was sure a parliament 'will facilitate all other difficulties'.[274] Northumberland was less sanguine: 'I do believe,' he wrote to Leicester, 'that until we have settled these points that were in agitation the last parliament which were matters of religion, propriety of goods and liberty of person, and peradventure some others, we shall hardly bring the parliament to any resolution that may free us from this army of rebels.'[275] But for the most part courtiers,

265. *Ibid.*, f.53; Gardiner, *History of England*, IX, p. 214.
266. Harleian MS 456, f.43. Vane seems to have become convinced over a few short weeks of the futility of fighting on.
267. *Ibid.*, ff.16v, 55.
268. *Ibid.*, f.57.
269. *Ibid.*, f.37v.
270. Parsons, *Diary of Sir Henry Slingsby*, p. 64.
271. Schofield, *Knyvett Letters*, p. 97.
272. Ellesmere MS 7869: Castle to Bridgewater, 26 Sept.
273. Clarendon MS 19, no. 1449: Hopton to Windebank, 7/17 Nov.
274. *HMC De Lisle and Dudley, VI*, p. 330.
275. Collins, *Letters and Memorials*, II, p. 662, 22 Oct.

even when they recognized that it would be far from plain sailing, looked to a parliament as the best course for strengthening the king and the government. Conway, as he told the Reverend Garrard, knew there would be 'hot work' and that the king's friends would have to argue their case. But he was far from despair: 'arm yourself with zeal,' he counselled, 'and with the sword of eloquence, cut in two the Puritans and chop off the heads of all anti-monarchists but above all give money enough without that there will be no driving the Scots out of Newcastle . . .'.[276] For Conway the parliament about to meet had been summoned not, as the Covenanters desired, to confirm the truce; rather the truce had been made in anticipation of the parliament; 'the cessation of arms which we have made is not out of any fear that we have of them, but partly for want of money, partly for somewhat else and partly that the parliament might make a good war'.[277] Conway articulated the king's mind. Though he knew of the grievances of the realm and sincerely intended a reformation, Charles I rode south from York to open a parliament that he believed (as he had in 1628) would restore his and the nation's honour after military failure and defeat. 'His Majesty', Sir John Coke was told on 3 November, 'is this day gone to parliament, of which there is very great hopes for the settling and ending of all things in peace . . .'.[278]

In his opening speech, Charles displayed what reads like a calm confidence. He had met his last parliament, he told them, speaking at unusual length, to counter what he knew to be the traitorous designs of the Scots 'wherein had I been believed, I sincerely think that things had not fallen out as now we see'. Since then, at his own charges, he had laboured to preserve 'the security and good of this kingdom, though the success hath not been answerable to my desires'.[279] Charles now called upon the assistance of this parliament to provide for the kingdom's safety and well-being by 'first the chasing out of rebels' and 'secondly . . . in satisfying your just grievances'. Money had been raised for the army in the city for just two months; thereafter it was for parliament to sustain it. The king then gave way to Finch, who outlined the history of the Council of the Peers and the treaty at Ripon.[280] With the Scots' invasion unquestionable proof of their insincerity and enmity to England, both the king and Lord Keeper seemed not to doubt that all would unite now against the common foe.

276. BL, MS 29/172, p. 306, 29 Oct.
277. *Ibid.*
278. *HMC Cowper II*, p. 262: Thomas Witherings to Coke, 3 Nov.
279. Ellesmere MS 7757: copy of the king's speech; cf. *Cobbett's Parliamentary History of England*, II (1807), pp. 629–30.
280. *Cobbett's Parliamentary History*, II, pp. 630–6. It was a three-hour speech (BL Add. MS 11045, f.131).

King and Commons, Finch was sure, would together 'steer between the tropics of moderation'.[281] Having outlined the differences with his Scottish subjects – 'rebels' he did not hesitate to call them – Charles addressed the Lords, concluding 'I doubt not, by your assistance, to make them know their duty and to make them return whether they will or no.'[282] The royal language betrays no sense of a new world; the invaders repelled, it would be business as usual. Only one caution he urged on the Commons, 'to make this a happy parliament: that you on your parts as I on mine lay aside all suspicion of one another'.[283]

With a Scottish army in Northumberland, however, removing the option of dissolution, business was not as usual.[284] And that 'suspicion' he referred to, fast spreading like a cancer during the closing months of the personal rule, was not only to overrun Charles's confident hopes. It was to end his life and still for ever the body of a commonweal of shared assumptions and values. In the very first speech of the parliament John Pym, though he could not have known it, sounded the death knell of the old body politic: there is, he told his fellow MPs, 'a design to alter the kingdom both in religion and government. This is the highest of treason . . .'.[285]

281. *Cobbett's Parliamentary History*, II, p. 632.
282. *Ibid.*, pp. 629, 638–9.
283. *Ibid.*, p. 630.
284. See Laing, *Letters and Journals of Baillie*, I, pp. 280–3; T. May, *The History of the Parliament of England which Began November the Third 1640* (1812 edn), p. 70; *Cal. Stat. Pap. Venet., 1640–2*, p. 106; Woodforde diary, 30 Nov. We note that Burgess's sermon on 17 November expounded on the text 'come and let us join ourselves to the Lord in an everlasting Covenant . . .' (Nalson, *Impartial Collection*, I, p. 540).
285. W. Notestein (ed.) *The Journal of Sir Simonds D'Ewes from the Beginning of the Long Parliament to the Opening of the Trial of the Earl of Strafford* (New Haven and London, 1923), pp. 7–11, quotation p. 8.

XVII

EPILOGUE: THE PERSONAL RULE AND THE ENGLISH CIVIL WAR

The Personal Rule and the English Civil War

Recent scholarship has made us aware that when we seek to explain the origins of the English civil war, we must be clear exactly what it is we are trying to explain.[1] In order to understand how two armies were raised, we shall not need to begin our story before the outbreak of the Irish rebellion in October 1641. For before then, whatever the level of political crisis, there is no likelihood that it would have been resolved by civil war. After the Irish rebellion, a decision had to be made whether or not to trust the king with an army to suppress the revolt. When parliament claimed the right to levy and command such forces, a major challenge to an undoubted royal prerogative together with the raising of troops combined to make civil war all but inevitable.

If, however, we take a step further backwards, we find ourselves needing to explain not just how two armies came to be raised, but how two parties had formed behind whose banners the troops would march into battle. And not only how but when. 'There could be no civil war before 1642,' Dr Morrill asserted some years ago, 'because there was no royalist party. The origins of the English civil war are really concerned less with the rise of opposition than with the resurgence of loyalism.'[2] Because, the argument goes, Charles was largely isolated and devoid of support in 1640, the story of the emergence of parties that would ultimately become sides is one that opens with the convention of the Long Parliament in November 1640. There is much to commend such an argument. Over the course of the following two years many who had commenced as vociferous critics of the king

1. Cf. J.S. Morrill, *The Revolt of the Provinces: Conservatives and Radicals in the English Civil War 1630–1650* (1976), p. 1.
2. *Ibid.*

gravitated towards him, as disorder threatened, and ultimately fought for the Royalist cause. Sir Ralph Hopton was one of the king's ardent commanders who had only months before the outbreak of war supported the Grand Remonstrance, that long and harsh indictment of Charles's government, the debate on which divided the House of Commons almost down the middle.[3] By the spring of 1641, the historian, rather like the Venetian ambassador who reported on the parliamentary debates, feels he is in a very different political world. It is a world of changed personalities – only half the king's Privy Councillors in the summer of 1641 had held office the previous autumn. It is a world in which, as the weeks and months passed, events in London and at Westminster ran far ahead of provincial feelings or understanding.[4] It is a world in which the fundamentals and traditions of politics were challenged: 'You have taken the government all in pieces,' Charles accurately put it in a speech to parliament on 15 February.[5] It is a world in which quite novelly, quite against their earlier inclinations and probably still quite against the better judgement of many, parliament began to govern: to call Councillors to answer on oath, to dispense money for the maintenance of the king's and Scots' armies, to issue orders in its own name concerning the liturgy and modes of worship, to demand a say in the appointment of the king's Councillors. In Professor Russell's words, the crisis of 1642 and the crisis of 1640 are 'two separate crises: in one we have to explain the unity of the political nation and in the other we have to explain its division'.[6]

Nevertheless, the two should not be artificially or absolutely separated. For without the disaffection of 1640 it is hard to imagine how a party could have been formed – not only to fight the king but to assault the undoubted prerogatives of the crown. Moreover, the apparent unity of the House of Commons and isolation of Charles I in November 1640 are more apparent than real. That is to say, although all MPs came up to Westminster determined to obtain redress of their grievances and the reform of government, there were from the beginning very different perceptions of the extent and nature of necessary reformation. And whilst few MPs in November were as anxious as was the king to force the Scots to make an 'honourable' treaty, along the lines of the peace of Berwick, anti-Scottish sentiment was by no

3. On Hopton, see F.T.R. Edgar, *Sir Ralph Hopton, the King's Man in the West* (1968).
4. Cf. A. Fletcher, *The Outbreak of the English Civil War* (1981).
5. J. Nalson, *An Impartial Collection of the Great Affairs of State from the Beginning of the Scotch Rebellion in 1639 to the Murder of King Charles I* (2 vols, 1682–3), I, p. 776.
6. Cf. C. Russell, *Parliaments and English Politics, 1621–1629* (Oxford, 1979), p. 426; C. Russell (ed.) *The Origins of the English Civil War* (1971), pp. 1–2.

means wanting in a house populated by MPs some of whom had served in the first campaign. As Professor Russell observed, 'it is no coincidence that Falkland and Sir Frederick Cornwallis long before they were royalist MPs had been anti-Scottish volunteers in the first Bishops' War.'[7] Beyond Westminster, as diaries and gentry correspondence make clear, there were very different attitudes to the Scots which did much to determine domestic political sympathies over the course of the year before a peace was concluded in the autumn of 1641.[8] Gervase Holles, MP for Grimsby, came round to a profound distrust of Pym's brotherly friendliness with the Scots and in April delivered a speech denouncing their designs on England's birthright. 'I fear,' he argued in a thinly veiled criticism of the leadership, 'we have nourished in our bosoms those that will sting us to death.'[9] Together with such different attitudes, there were also among those who met at Westminster and across the country at large very differing levels of concern about the alleged popish threat and very different views about how the Church of England might best be purified. In November 1640, no such differences ranked men into parties. They were differences of emphasis and degree that separated more in potential than in the present. As Professor Kenyon astutely pointed out, the speeches and language of the leader of parliament Pym and the king's chief minister Strafford at the impeachment of the Lord-Lieutenant suggest that 'the ideas of these two great men were almost identical'.[10] Even Charles and Pym clearly expected to find a common ground. Yet, when all that is said, it remains true that a common articulation of shared ideals masked important differences about how they might be restored.[11] Different policies and programmes, different reactions to personalities, different hopes and fears, most of all different degrees of disenchantment with the regime and distrust of Charles I personally characterized the MPs of the Long Parliament in 1640, as they were to divide them in 1642.

Whilst for a few conspicuous individuals we can plot the trajectories of increasing conservatism or radicalization which they followed over the years 1640 to 1642, in the case of the large majority of silent backbenchers we cannot know the moments or issues which were to

7. C. Russell, 'The British problem and the English civil war', *History*, 72 (1987), p. 414. This is rather a different emphasis to Professor Russell's concentration on Charles's isolation in 'Why did Charles I call the Long Parliament?', *History*, 69 (1984), pp. 375–83.
8. For example, compare New College Oxford MS 9502 (Woodforde's diary), and B. Schofield (ed.) *The Knyvett Letters, 1620–1644* (1949); see below, pp. 945–6.
9. *Cobbett's Parliamentary History of England*, II (1807), pp. 771–2.
10. J.P. Kenyon (ed.) *The Stuart Constitution* (Cambridge, 1966), p. 10.
11. Cf. K. Sharpe, *Politics and Ideas in Early Stuart England* (1989), introduction, esp. pp. 20–31, 63–71.

be decisive when it came to making hard choices.[12] However, in order to understand the importance of the personal rule in the story of the civil war, we need to assess the extent to which, by November 1640, Charles's government had fundamentally alienated the political nation, and beyond that the middling sort and commonalty. We shall need to examine the grievances of the realm, and the degree to which they were either novel in their seriousness or intrinsically defied political compromise and settlement. And we shall endeavour to evaluate when or whether the 'intermission of parliaments' was itself the greatest problem; whether the collapse of the personal rule was inevitable from the outset.[13]

It is worth recalling at this point that the members of the Long Parliament were not different men from those who had served Charles over the previous eleven years: as lord-lieutenants, as deputies, sheriffs and JPs. The Sir Edward Dering who was to denounce ship money in 1641 was one of those prominent in his county in 'steering it better'.[14] This is not to say that local governors had applauded the measures enacted by the king and Council. Nor is it to accuse Dering and his like of hypocrisy. A parliament was the proper forum, as Wentworth had explained, for the articulation of discontent at the very policies which as local magistrates MPs had helped to enforce.[15] It is, however, to observe that before 1640 the gentry had not felt so alienated by royal policies as to withdraw their co-operation and that there was nothing necessarily revolutionary about the articulation, after eleven years without an assembly, of numerous grievances in parliament.[16] Although he had a more pressing priority, Charles himself regarded 'satisfying your just grievances' as crucial to the business of parliament.[17] The presentation of county petitions, the briefing of MPs, the speeches airing the country's discontents did not in themselves mark a break; they constituted 'business as usual'. The question remains: did the grievances signify fundamental problems in the body politic that only radical constitutional change could resolve? And were they themselves such that they divided king and parliament so far as to be irresoluble by the normal political processes of mediation and settlement? Or was

12. Even in the latest scholarship there is still a tendency to equate 'the Commons' with a vociferous few; see below, p. 940ff.
13. See *Cobbett's Parliamentary History*, II, pp. 702ff.
14. British Library [BL], Stowe MS 743, f.132. I owe this reference and point to the kindness of Ken Fincham. D'Ewes too had been a fairly diligent sheriff.
15. W. Knowler (ed.) *The Earl of Strafford's Letters and Despatches* (2 vols, 1739), I, p. 33.
16. Cf. G.R. Elton, 'Tudor government: the points of contact, I: parliament', *Trans. Royal Hist. Soc.* (5th series, 24, 1974), pp. 183–200; C. Russell, 'The nature of a parliament in early Stuart England', in H. Tomlinson (ed.) *Before the English Civil War* (1983), pp. 123–50.
17. *Cobbett's Parliamentary History*, II. p. 629.

it less the issues and grievances themselves than what for the moment we shall vaguely call the political climate in which they were discussed that precluded traditional compromise? If business turned out not to be as usual, was it because MPs came to Westminster with unusual business?

Historians of the 1630s have often drawn attention to the number and scale of the financial exactions of the decade, some of dubious legality. In his opening speech on grievances Pym catalogued the complaints that were rehearsed as MPs presented county petitions – against ship money, knighthood and forest fines, new books of rates, patents and monopolies (of soap, salt and beer), fines for depopulation and buildings erected against regulations, military charges of coat and conduct money and for supplying county magazines and so on. A common grievance of the localities, the fiscal exactions were to be listed again in the autumn of 1641 as part of Pym's desperate endeavour to win support. However, for all the novelty of the Caroline levies and county discontent, the financial expedients of the personal rule cannot be held to have contributed greatly to the failure to arrive at a peaceful settlement before 1642. Nor did they play a significant role in the choice of sides. Sir Simonds D'Ewes, Sir Anthony Gell and Sir Philip Parker for example had been diligent ship money sheriffs; Sir Thomas Aston, Sir Francis Seymour, Sir Edward Phelips and Sir Thomas Smyth who denounced the levy were to fight for the king in 1642.[18] Most of those fined for encroachment on the forests became Royalists.[19] As the Short Parliament had suggested, ship money was a grievance that *could* be resolved by the traditional bargain that assemblies of parliament implied.

In the Long Parliament none of the fiscal expedients of the 1630s proved a stumbling block to either the king or the Commons. On his part, Charles acceded to the abolition of ship money and surrendered forest and knighthood fines in the hope of a bountiful supply from the love of his subjects. On their part, many members of parliament were anxious to ensure that the crown was properly supported. In May 1640 Sir Thomas Peyton had suggested that it was less the fiscal burden than the manner of levying taxes and imposts that had aroused opposition. 'With a little more continuance of these annual charges', he told Oxinden, the king 'might have habituated the country, especially had it been managed with equality, that he might have established his own

18. J. Maltby (ed.) *The Short Parliament (1640) Diary of Sir Thomas Aston* (Camden Soc., 4th series, 35, 1988), p. xiv; M.F. Keeler, *The Long Parliament, 1640–41* (Philadelphia, 1954). Few of the 150 ship money sheriffs became Parliamentarians; see E. Cope, *Politics without Parliaments, 1629–40* (1987), p. 107.

19. *Cobbett's Parliamentary History*, II, p. 726; P.A.J. Pettit, *The Royal Forests of Northamptonshire* (Northamptonshire Record Soc., 23, 1968), p. 93.

greatness for ever.'[20] Greatness was still promised in the autumn. When Charles presented his Exchequer accounts and financial estimates to parliament in December, the Commons acknowledged them with thanks, 'saying they doubted not but to raise his Majesty's revenue to such a considerable sum as should maintain him like a great King' – and that without monopolies or other 'pressures upon the people'.[21] Charles would not have been averse to trading prerogative finance for subsidies or a revenue settled by parliament, and Pym since the 1620s had been one of those few MPs aware of the need to tackle the fiscal weakness of the monarchy.[22] If, as has often been pointed out, in this he was untypical of the country MPs who had to account to their constituents for moneys voted, events must soon have persuaded even them that properly maintaining the king – or even the grievances of prerogative finance – were considerably less burdensome than the costs of political disruption. For all that the shires of England felt themselves oppressed by fiscal demands during the 1630s, in the months after the calling of the Long Parliament vastly greater sums were levied and paid. By October 1641 the city of London was reporting that the privileges of immunity from action for debt enjoyed by MPs and their servants had already cost £1 million, far in excess of ship money.[23] Between April and December 1641 the county of Kent paid six subsidies and a poll tax that amounted to perhaps five times its ship money charge.[24] Twysden was to claim that 'the assessments of those times were so immense' that one-third of land value went into paying them.[25] During the war, the weekly assessment alone demanded £35,000 (eight or nine times the annual ship money burden).[26] With the poll tax, the levy of £400,000 to suppress the Irish rebellion, and the 'propositions' or loans and excise, parliamentary levies dwarfed the exactions of personal rule. Moreover, for all the earlier rating disputes and complaints, the assessment, and the £4 million raised in March for an army, were modelled on ship money, each county being charged a lump sum which it was to apportion as it saw fit.[27] It did not require

20. D. Gardiner (ed.) *The Oxinden Letters, 1607–42* (1933), p. 173: Peyton to Oxinden, 6 May 1640.
21. BL Add. MS 11045, f.137: Rossingham to Scudamore, 22 Dec. 1640. Cf. C. Russell, 'Charles I's financial estimates for 1642', *Bull. Inst. Hist. Res.*, 58 (1985), pp. 109–20.
22. C. Russell, 'The Parliamentary career of John Pym, 1621–29', in P. Clark, A.G.R. Smith and N. Tyacke (eds) *The English Commonwealth, 1547–1640* (Leicester, 1979), pp. 147–66, esp., pp. 152–3.
23. D. Hirst, *Authority and Conflict: England 1603–58* (1986), p. 212.
24. Kent Archives Office, Twysden MS U 47/47/01, p. 17.
25. *Ibid.*, p. 22.
26. D.H. Pennington, 'The cost of the English civil war', *History Today*, 8 (1958), pp. 126–33; W. Kennedy, *English Taxation, 1640–1799* (1913); cf. Bodleian, Clarendon MS 17, no. 1338, for examples of comparative impact.
27. Morrill, *Revolt of the Provinces*, p. 59.

the calculation of personal losses in the civil war (Sir Thomas Jervoise's exceeded £13,000) to make the burden of the 1630s seem light.[28] The levies that during the personal rule had spoiled some Christmas pies should not loom large in explanations of political breakdown.

Fiscal levies were only the most tangible of the demands made by the Caroline government of the counties and towns during the decade of personal rule. Over the last thirty years, the historians of the 'county communities' have demonstrated the levels of local resentment at central interference and their work has been synthesized in an important essay which characterizes the English civil war as a revolt of the provinces.[29] Most recently, in notions of 'the country' Dr Cust has discerned an ideology that links the 'opposition' of the 1620s to the parliamentarian cause in 1642.[30] The petitions sent up from the shires with MPs to the Long Parliament, as well the speeches of archetypal county members like Sir John Holland, offer powerful evidence of the county objections to the local impact of ecclesiastical and secular policies, and most particularly their hostility to the military charges consequent upon the Scots wars.[31] Yet, as has been well demonstrated, such local resentments do little to explain the choice of sides in the English civil war. In most counties, it was activist minorities that aligned the shires with the cause of king or parliament.[32] In Lincolnshire of the twenty-three who signed a declaration in support of parliament only nine had held magisterial office during the 1630s.[33] Moreover, as the Long Parliament itself began to take on the tasks of government, indeed to interfere more with the localities than the Caroline regime, it evoked exactly the same country resentments and suspicions of central power encountered by king and Council. In Professor Hirst's words, those 'who had objected to the novel devices of the 1630s soon showed by delays and evasions that being part of a "country" reaction against the crown did not always make them followers of Pym'.[34]

It may be that historians have exaggerated the degree of provincial antagonism to the personal rule *before* 1640. For the early county petitions of grievances, such as those of Dorset and Kent, certainly give prominence to the military burdens which, more than any other, threw local society into turmoil.[35] And it may be revealing that in his

28. Hampshire Record Office, Herriard MS F. 9.
29. Morrill, *Revolt of the Provinces, passim.*
30. R. Cust and A. Hughes (eds) *Conflict in Early Stuart England* (1989), chs 1, 5; R. Cust, 'News and politics in early seventeenth century England', *P&P*, 112 (1986), pp. 60–90.
31. Holland's speech is in Bodleian, Tanner MS 239, f.13.
32. See, for example, A. Hughes, *Politics, Society and Civil War in Warwickshire: 1620–1660* (Cambridge, 1987), p. 132; W. Hunt, *The Puritan Moment: The Coming of Revolution in an English County* (Cambridge, Mass., 1983), ch. 11.
33. C. Holmes, *Seventeenth Century Lincolnshire* (Lincoln, 1980), p. 145.
34. Hirst, *Authority and Conflict*, p. 208.
35. See *Cobbett's Parliamentary History*, II, pp. 652–6.

appeal for support to the counties, the Grand Remonstrance, Pym devoted relatively little space to the programmes of the 1630s – the quest for an exact militia, the Book of Orders, and social policy. Indeed in listing the ills of depopulation and the destruction of timber, the Grand Remonstrance clearly echoed what had been Caroline policy, as the boast that parliament would improve the English herring fishing followed the king's own hopes and endeavours.[36] Provincial grievances, quite simply, did not sustain the political temperature of the Long Parliament. Increasingly they drove a wedge between the parliamentary leadership which had a more urgent agenda and the backbenchers who had come up in November 1640, as they typically did, to press local needs and complaints and be gone. The typical county MP in fact may be exemplified by Thomas Smyth who by February 1641, fearful of the advantage his tenants might take of his absence to cheat him, resolved to return home.[37] By the summer, so many had joined him that the Commons barely constituted a quorum;[38] 'Even that stern radical Sir Arthur Haselrig went home early.'[39] The feeling in the provinces was crucial in the calling of a parliament, but local discontents did little to shape the course of events in parliament once it assembled.

Once scholars were agreed that the political crisis of the mid-seventeenth century was a crisis of the constitution, and that members of the Long Parliament assembled at Westminster to defend the law and constitution against the arbitrary courses of a king bent on erecting absolutism. As we have commented, a Venetian envoy believed that Charles was endeavouring to change the nature of government in England, and some were anxious about the legality of royal measures, still more about the language in which they were defended.[40] May we then still speak of the personal rule as the 'eleven years' tyranny'? Is it right to regard Charles I as a tyrant – or even as a monarch who pursued a novel absolute rule? A young scholar in a recent important if problematic study announced a clear verdict: 'Within the framework of anti-absolutist theories, Charles's rule was indeed tyrannical.'[41] If we

36. S.R. Gardiner (ed.) *Constitutional Documents of the Puritan Revolution* (Oxford, 1906), p. 224, clause 142.
37. Bristol Record Office, Smyth of Ashton Court MS 36074/156b, 26 Feb. 1641. Another paradigm are Derek Hirst's Northamptonshire members who were instructed to secure a bill for the navigation of the River Nene. D. Hirst, *The Representative of the People?: Voters and Voting in England under the Early Stuarts* (Cambridge, 1975), p. 182. Below, pp. 940–41.
38. Cf. Fletcher, *Outbreak of the English Civil War*, p. 70.
39. Hirst, *Authority and Conflict*, p. 207.
40. *Calendar of State Papers Venetian* [*Cal. Stat. Pap. Venet.*], *1636–9*, pp. 295–301; above, p. 770; Maltby, *Aston Diary*, p. 112.
41. J. Sommerville, *Politics and Ideas in England, 1603–1640* (1986), p. 116 and *passim*; cf. my *Politics and Ideas*, pp. 283–8.

must reject such a judgement, it is not least because Charles himself was an exponent of 'anti-absolutist theories' – or, to put it a better way, was committed to the traditional symbiosis of prerogative and law rather than any new theory of state. It is true that at times, especially wartime, the king and some of his ministers used the language of necessity to justify courses which others saw as an affront to the liberties and property of the subject guaranteed by law. But such *ad hoc* justifications of necessary measures were not elaborated into a new theory of sovereignty. They were expressions rather of the difficulties of government in times of crisis or threat of invasion which were characteristic of the *dominium politicum et regale* of early modern England. That model princess Elizabeth had flouted statutes and indeed deployed the county militia for service overseas in, as she saw it, fulfilling her duty to defend her subjects.[42] The Scots were to adopt the argument of necessity in their justificatory propaganda, evidently from the conviction that such an argument was not itself anathema to English thinking. The Long Parliament, of course, was to find in precisely the doctrine of necessity the only defence of actions it too felt compelled to take to protect the commonweal, as it increasingly took on the role of government. The argument from necessity was not, then, the hallmark of a king bent on absolutism, nor did it divide him from his subjects. As the legal cases, especially the ship money trial, evidence, there was little theoretical dispute about the powers Charles claimed; the disagreements were over perceived abuses of authority rather than the nature of authority itself.[43]

No more in practice than in theory can Charles be described as endeavouring to lay the foundations of an absolutism, let alone a tyranny. Certainly the personal rule was not characterized by harsh punishments or repressive measures. There was no single case of execution for treason or crimes of state and few instances of savage sentences.[44] While some of his ministers – Strafford and Laud among them – might have wished at times that Charles and his Council had pursued recalcitrants and brought them to obedience by exemplary punishments, the king did not.[45] And while others advocated measures for greater control – a purge of the magisterial benches, or changes in the nature of local government – Charles resisted them. In his perception

42. As Penry Williams reminds us in *The Tudor Regime* (Oxford, 1979), pp. 395ff.
43. Cf. J.P. Cooper, *Land, Men and Beliefs* (1983), p. 102.
44. G.E. Aylmer, *Rebellion or Revolution? England 1640–1660* (Oxford, 1986), p. 7.
45. We recall Wentworth's remarks on the militia (Knowler, *Strafford Letters*, II, p. 411, and cf. II, p. 119). This is not to argue that Wentworth was ever an 'absolutist'; see above, pp. 133–7. Laud too argued that 'the king's just and legal prerogative and the subject's assurance for liberty and property may stand well together and have so stood for hundreds of years' (quoted in C. Wordsworth (ed.) *The Manner of the Coronation of King Charles I of England*, Bradshaw Soc., 2, 1892, p. lx).

of the English polity and in his policies Charles was not only a conservative; he was also what some in modern politics might refer to as a 'wet', committed to the traditions and norms of English government and suspicious of radical change.[46] As Gardiner himself described the king: 'He had no wish to erect a despotism, to do injustice, or to heap up wealth at the expense of his subjects.'[47] Charles was concerned above all else with order and regulation. But ordered and regulated societies are not necessarily the product of despotic or absolutist governments. Today we regard a measure of regulation as the guarantee of freedom. The seventeenth century regarded order as the *sine qua non* of the survival of the commonweal, as the replication of a divine order, the alternative to which was not only chaos but damnation. Indeed many of Charles's critics would have surpassed, and were far to surpass, the king in their use of authority to secure order and regulation – in the person as well as the polity. Notable among them, of course, were the puritans. In January 1641 the minister John Bankes wrote from Kent to Sir Edward Dering concerning the evils of drink, swearing and whoredom that beset the land. He saw the solution in the establishment of far harsher punishments for moral lapses and in more authority. 'It were not amiss in my opinion that every minister, constable, churchwarden, sideman and overseer of the poor in every parish had the power, in this case, of a justice of peace.'[48] The governments of the 1650s were even to erect the major-generals as moral police as well as local governors. The extent of the authority of government was not the issue that divided men in civil war in 1642, nor even in the Long Parliament. Not until the scheme of bridge appointments (whereby Pym and others would have entered Charles's government) had failed, did the parliamentary leadership launch an assault on the organs of authority. The theoretical constitutional battles over power and sovereignty were more a consequence than a cause of the English civil war.[49]

Yet even if Charles did not strive for absolute government, did his regime during the 1630s represent a threat to the rule of law, which in turn founded an opposition party devoted to preserving the law and constitution against arbitrary courses? Certainly we have encountered in this study those who, questioning the legitimacy of royal or Conciliar orders and demands, appealed to the law and the courts. But it is worth recalling how frequently Charles I did the same. That is

46. I am very grateful to John Kenyon for some discussions of this point.
47. S.R. Gardiner, *History of England from the Accession of James I to the Outbreak of the Civil War, 1603–42* (10 vols, 1883–4), VIII, p. 299.
48. Kent Archives Office, Dering MS U 350/C.2/88, Jan. 1641. The letter is a nice comment on the failure of the puritans to establish their godly commonwealth.
49. Cf. Sharpe, *Politics and Ideas*, introduction; Cooper, *Land, Men and Beliefs*, ch. 5.

to say that far from there being clear groups which we might label 'constitutionalists' or 'absolutists', there were doubts about whether particular courses were compatible with an *agreed* body of law to which all could appeal to arbitrate. As the cases of the 1630s clearly reveal, there were no major disagreements over the law and constitution.[50] Charles I quite genuinely claimed that his 'intention was ever to govern according to the law and not otherwise'.[51] He advised his son that the laws which guaranteed the subjects their liberty 'reserve enough to the majesty and prerogative of any king'; he went so far as to counsel him to remit rather than exact the 'rigour of the laws, there being nothing worse than legal tyranny'.[52] On the other hand, Sir Thomas Peyton believed that as it was lawful for any man to take what he needed to save his life, so 'I think the King may use the goods of his subjects nolentibus volentibus . . . for the conservation of the more universal and general good.'[53] And in his charge against Cosins, the puritan Smart proclaimed: 'surely the laws were made to bind his subjects not the prince himself'.[54] Even in the ship money case the issues were more technical than philosophical, and though the outcome may not have been pleasing, few at the time – or even in the Short Parliament – asserted that it was not good law. Holborne, Hampden's counsel, indeed became a Royalist.

The Long Parliament's critique of arbitrary courses and reversal of the ship money judgment owe more to politics than to fundamentally different perceptions of the law. Where in the 1620s many had supported Sir Edward Coke's claim against James I that only the judges understood the law, in 1641 they impeached the judicial bench for subverting it. What had changed was not so much the position of the judges – most protested they had been left to their consciences and Finch delivered a clear statement of his commitment to the idea 'that the King ought to govern by the positive laws of the kingdom' – as to what in the winter of 1640–1 was acceptable to the political nation, or its representatives in parliament.[55] Certainly in the parliamentary impeachments and trials, most notably of Strafford, politics ran roughshod over the law. Though in making his defence he performed brilliantly, the Wentworth who had spoken so ardently for the Petition of Right had no hard task in exposing the blatant illegalities in his prosecution and conviction for treason. Appealing simply to 'the plain

50. See also P.G. Burgess, 'Custom, reason and the common law: English jurisprudence, 1600–1650' (Cambridge University, PhD thesis, 1988).
51. *Cobbett's Parliamentary History*, II, pp. 755–6.
52. *Eikon Basilike* (1876 edn), pp. 196–7.
53. Gardiner, *Oxinden Letters*, p. 173.
54. Bodleian, Rawlinson MS D.821.
55. See *Cobbett's Parliamentary History*, II, pp. 692–3. Finch was not permitted to defend himself (BL Add. MS 11045, f.137).

letter of the law and statute that telleth us what is and what is not treason, without being more ambitious to be learned in the art of killing', he not only won the respect of unsympathetic observers (not least the lawyer Bulstrode Whitelocke), he demonstrated how thin was the legal case against the Caroline regime, and how little the parliamentary leadership would be constrained by legalities.[56] Lord Digby for one, though he continued to believe Strafford a tyrant, was repelled by the course of the trial: 'we must not,' he urged, 'piece up want of legality with matter of conveniences.'[57] No wonder his speech was ordered to be burned.[58] It is one of the ironies of the politics of the 1640s that the parliamentary governments were undoubtedly to be guilty of the offence of flouting the laws and Petition of Right, when they could not prove the charge against the king or his ministers.[59] But it is also evidence that a stand on the law and constitution as established played little part in the divide of 1642 and perhaps a less important role than we have given it in the opposition of 1640.

Most recently, and perhaps not least as a consequence of the resurgence of religion in our own political conflicts and crises, historians have stressed the centrality of religion in shaping both the opposition to the government in 1640 and the patterns of allegiance in 1642. One scholar has gone so far as to describe the mid-century crisis as England's wars of religion.[60] The thesis has the strength of plausibility. As our own experience has demonstrated, religious commitments are the human convictions and values least susceptible to compromise. Questions of faith are not easily settled by the arguments of reason. And in the realm of religion, matters of seemingly small import most quickly take on more fundamental significance. As the author of *Augustus* claimed and unwittingly predicted in 1634, 'Men are more sensible of the smallest mutations in the church than greater changes in the state and raise more frequent troubles about it'; nothing, he concluded, had more frequently produced rebellion.[61] There can be no doubt that anxiety over what they perceived as the rise of Arminianism and the shift to more ceremony in the liturgy contributed to the failure of the parliaments of the late 1620s. Despite Laud's and the king's efforts to establish peace the issues of doctrine and liturgy continued to concern and divide – for all that there was some lowering

56. *Cobbett's Parliamentary History*, II, p. 747; R. Whitelocke, *Memoirs Biographical and Historical of Bulstrode Whitelocke* (1860), p. 154.
57. *Cobbett's Parliamentary History*, II, pp. 749–53, quotation p. 753.
58. *Ibid.*, pp. 882–3.
59. Cf. Morrill, *Revolt of the Provinces*, p. 52.
60. J.S. Morrill, 'The religious context of the English civil war', *Trans. Royal Hist. Soc.* (5th series, 34, 1984), pp. 155–78; *idem*, 'Sir William Brereton and England's wars of religion', *Journ. Brit. Stud.*, 24 (1985), pp. 311–32. John Morrill argues that the allegiance of the militants was determined by religion.
61. *Augustus* (1632, STC 957), pp. 125–9.

of the temperature. When men and women came to make choices in 1642 religious commitments were often decisive in their alignment.

We should not, however, from such observations be tempted to the simple conclusion that religion provides the key to the crises of 1642 or 1640. In the first case, though the correlations are high they are not unproblematic. Not all Anglicans were Royalists.[62] Of 197 identifiable puritan gentry families in 1643, one-third were not Parliamentarian.[63] Prominent puritan gentry like John Preston, Sir Gervase Cutler and D'Ewes's brother, . . . Richard, were to throw in their lot with the king.[64] The most radical MP in the Commons was the very ungodly Sir Henry Marten.[65] Given that many of the puritan members were also older than their less godly colleagues, as were the Parliamentarians in the civil war by a decade on average the seniors of the Royalists, it is not clear whether their age or religious commitment was of greater importance in their alignment – or how integrally the two factors were connected.[66] It is also essential when we emphasize religious explanations, to define carefully what issues we have in mind. For between November 1640 and the outbreak of civil war the religious issues changed drastically, and may in fine have had little connection with the tensions of the 1630s. The question of doctrine never appears to have loomed large and increasingly to have faded in significance.[67] In January 1641, Agostino, the Venetian ambassador, admitting his bewilderment at the number of different sects in parliament, predicted that the Commons would settle a *new* religion – expected to be that of Calvin – not least because the Scots insisted on their 'abandoning the Protestant'.[68] Nothing, however, was done to reform doctrine before the hostilities. And, revealingly, in neither the county petitions nor charges against 'malignant clergy' do doctrinal issues appear prominent.[69] Only one of twenty-six petitions against the clergy among Dering's papers in Kent mentions Arminianism; there are few references to predestination in some 800 petitions that came in for the

62. Cf. Aylmer, *Rebellion or Revolution?*, p. 31. Cf. Hughes, *Politics, Society and Civil War*, p. 167.
63. J.T. Cliffe, *Puritans in Conflict: The Puritan Gentry during and after the Civil Wars* (1988), pp. 43–5.
64. *Ibid.*, p. 45.
65. Hirst, *Authority and Conflict*, p. 225. Hirst is healthily sceptical of excessive emphasis on religious explanation.
66. Cf. J.P. Kenyon, *Stuart England* (Harmondsworth, 1978), p. 114; cf. R. Howell, *Newcastle-upon-Tyne and the Puritan Revolution* (Oxford, 1967), p. 117.
67. It was little discussed in the Short Parliament, cf. above, p. 876.
68. *Cal. Stat. Pap. Venet., 1640–2*, pp. 117, 133.
69. I. Green, 'The persecution of "scandalous" and "malignant" clergy during the English civil war', *Eng. Hist. Rev.*, 94 (1979), pp. 507–31. Cf. C. Holmes (ed.) *The Suffolk Committees for Scandalous Ministers, 1644–46* (Suffolk Record Soc., 13, 1970), and this in a supposedly godly stronghold.

removing of scandalous ministers.[70] A petition from Surrey (in defence of episcopacy) even applauded what it saw as the Caroline proscription of Calvinism.[71]

As for matters of ceremony and liturgy, the house moved cautiously, perhaps because it was apparent that there was no consensus. A correspondent told John Hobart in January that for all the importance of religion, 'I believe they will go near to leave it as they found it'.[72] Though in April they fined the members of the late Convocation, and drafted bills for stricter sabbath observance and against pluralism, there was no major assault on the Laudian church.[73] Not until September 1641 did the Commons vote orders for the removal of altars, rails and crucifixes, and even then they 'had only a limited impact', as several parishes retained the rails that they had, in some cases, proudly installed at great expense.[74] Still the parliament ordered the retention of the sign of the cross in baptism, and a proposal to alter the Prayer Book was defeated, even in a thin house where the more zealous usually exercised their greatest influence.[75] Though Laud was impeached in December 1640 (and Wren the following summer), partly at the instigation of the Scots, the slow pace of proceedings against him scarcely indicate that pursuit of the archbishop and condemnation of his programmes had a high priority. Sir Edward Dering could even acknowledge that 'his intent of public uniformity was a good purpose though in the *way* of his pursuit thereof he was extremely faulty'.[76] For all the rhetoric against and assaults on the archbishop after the Short Parliament, Laud was not of great importance in the politics of the winter of 1640. In part this was because Charles showed his willingness to desert him, to elevate Williams and Ussher and to promise to restore the church to the primitive purity of Elizabeth's time.[77] In part it was because the issues that had perforce dominated the debates were

70. Green, 'Persecution of clergy', p. 511; Holmes, *Suffolk Committees for Scandalous Ministers*, p. 9.
71. N. Tyacke, *Anti-Calvinists: The Rise of English Arminianism, c.1590–1640* (Oxford, 1987), p. 243.
72. Tanner MS 65, f.234.
73. *Cobbett's Parliamentary History*, II, p. 772. Though cf. J. S. Morrill, 'The attack on the Church of England in the Long Parliament, 1640–42', in D. Beales and G. Best (eds) *History, Society and the Churches* (Cambridge, 1985), pp. 105–24.
74. *Cobbett's Parliamentary History*, II, p. 906; Gardiner, *History of England*, X, p. 14; Cliffe, *Puritans in Conflict*, p. 3; Fletcher, *Outbreak of the English Civil War*, p. 118.
75. *HMC Cowper II*, p. 290; Gardiner, *History of England*, X, p. 15.
76. Above, p. 402.
77. J.O. Halliwell (ed.) *The Autobiography and Correspondence of Sir Simonds D'Ewes* (2 vols, 1845), II, p. 262. See W.M. Abbot, 'The issue of episcopacy in the Long Parliament, 1640–48' (Oxford University, D. Phil. thesis, 1981). For the appointments of Hall, Skinner and Prideaux, see Gardiner, *History of England*, X, p. 41.

less about the Laudian innovations than about the very nature and government of the church – about episcopacy and Presbyterianism.

It was as early as 11 December that the city of London had forwarded to the Commons a petition signed by 15,000 calling for the abolition of episcopal government 'with all its dependencies, roots and branches'.[78] The following February, more forcefully, the Scots commissioners treating in London had drawn up and printed a declaration of their desire to see the removal of the bishops from England as well as the kirk, and explained their desire to see unity of religion between the two kingdoms.[79] Thereafter the position and powers of the bishops overrode most other religious issues. Undoubtedly the episcopal question was connected with earlier religious convictions and with attitudes to the Laudian hierarchy. Some puritans had long desired either a Genevan discipline or bishops greatly reduced in power to the role of pastors in the church; and the East Anglian leadership in the Lords and Commons connected such long-held desires with the adoption by the Long Parliament of the root and branch petition. More broadly the anticlericalism excited by the high-handedness of the Laudians added less-hot Protestants to the ranks of those who wished to see the bishops' wings clipped if not to have them put down.[80] The London aldermen who backed the petition for abolition, it was said, did so because they could not abide the insolence of the prelates.[81] Yet despite these connections and continuums, the episcopal issue effected a realignment of religious positions and groupings that made the ecclesiastical politics of 1641 quite different from that of the 1630s. For many of those who could delight in the removal of the clergy from the commission of the peace, or even accept the expulsion of the bishops from the Lords, balked at the threat to the episcopal office. As early as February 1641 Hugh Pyne had perceived that the episcopal cause 'hath so many advocates and so strong a party in our house'.[82] Sir Henry Slingsby was all for reducing their powers but sharply opposed to their abolition, the programme as he saw it of 'our countrymen that live beyond seas in Holland'.[83] Lord Digby passed in a few weeks from a vitriolic condemnation of the prelates who 'usurp to themselves the grand pre eminence of parliament' to an equally sharp diatribe against their detractors.[84] 'Not a patent, not a monopoly, not the price of a

78. *Cobbett's Parliamentary History*, II, pp. 673–8.
79. Gardiner, *History of England*, IX, p. 296.
80. Above, pp. 392–401. Hall had recognized in 1639 that among the enemies of the bishops were not only Scots and puritan revolutionaries 'but some also of a milder and subtler alloy' (*Calendar of State Papers Domestic* [*Cal. Stat. Pap. Dom.*], *1639–40*, p. xvii).
81. BL Add. MS 11045, f.135.
82. Smyth of Ashton Court MS 36074/139b: Pyne to Smyth, 2 Feb.
83. D. Parsons (ed.) *The Diary of Sir Henry Slingsby* (1836), p. 67.
84. J. Nalson, *Impartial Collection*, I, p. 505.

commodity raised,' he exclaimed in February, 'but these men make bishops the cause of it.'[85] It was the same story outside Westminster. During November and December 1641, seven county petitions in defence of the bishops were presented to parliament, one with 100,000 signatures appended.[86] A remonstrance from Cheshire expressing fears of a desire by some 'to introduce an absolute innovation of Presbyterian government' rejected 'the arbitrary government of a numerous presbytery' in favour of episcopacy.[87] The following spring added expressions of support from Cornwall, Wales, Oxford and Nottinghamshire, but also Somerset, Kent, Herefordshire and Huntingdonshire.[88] It was all a far cry from the discontent with Laud and his supporters.

Indeed, the threat to episcopacy along with the beginning of a breakdown of religious authority conspired over the course of the Long Parliament to bring men, if not into more sympathy with the Laudians, then at least to enhanced suspicion and dislike of Laud's puritan enemies. For one thing the episcopal bench closed ranks. Whatever his disagreements with Laud, or indeed his reputation as a moderate Calvinist, Bishop Williams did not shrink from dismissing the Geneva discipline as 'fit only for tradesmen and beggars'.[89] More generally, the questioning of the nature and government of the church had led some to run ahead of parliamentary decisions and to follow their consciences in a manner that alarmed social conservatives. By March 1641, Thomas Knyvett was expressing to John Buxton his concern that the Book of Common Prayer was being spurned and the church disturbed, all with the countenance of parliament. 'No man,' he wrote, 'fears the power of any ecclesiastical court . . . they have so shaken the former settled government in the church and published no nor yet agreed upon any new that we shall shortly not have so much as the face of a true Protestant Church but all will be in confusion.'[90] 'Geneva print', he feared, bore too much sway. The following months, as the sects began to proliferate, brought many to echo Knyvett's fears. It is revealing that in March, when Dr Chaffin was examined for words against the puritans (he had added to the litany 'from all lay Puritans, and all lay parliament men God deliver me) the vote of the

85. *Ibid.*, pp. 748–9: speech of 9 Feb. Cf. D. Hirst, 'The defection of Sir Edward Dering, 1640–41', *Hist. Journ.*, 15 (1972), pp. 193–208; S.P. Salt, 'The origins of Sir Edward Dering's attack on the ecclesiastical hierarchy, *c.*1625–40', *Hist. Journ.*, 30 (1987), pp. 21–52.
86. Abbot, 'Issue of episcopacy', p. 220; *Cal. Stat. Pap. Venet., 1640–2*, p. 242.
87. Gardiner, *History of England*, IX, pp. 392–3.
88. *Bibliotheca Regia or the Royal Library* (1659), p. 322.
89. Abbot, 'Issue of episcopacy', p. 129.
90. Cambridge University Library, Buxton MSS, Box 97: T. Knyvett to J. Buxton, 16 March.

house, albeit by the narrowest margin, had gone against his punishment.[91] Later in the year after a fracas in Leominster church, some of the local inhabitants laid in muskets, the sheriff reported, to kill the puritans.[92] Preoccupation with the sins of Laud seem already to be part of a lost world.

What perhaps alone served to connect the religious issues of 1640–2 with Laud and the Caroline regime was the fear of popery. John Pym opened his first speech to parliament with his conviction of a papist conspiracy to undermine church and state; and for the next year he laboured, with a large measure of success, to persuade his fellow MPs of its menace and the need to counteract it.[93] From the beginning Pym did not want for those who shared his paranoia. As early as 18 November 1640 Sir Robert Harley reported from committee a recommendation that none should sit in the House of Commons who refused to take the sacrament. 'This,' he announced, 'was intended for the discovery of papists among them', and the committee advised too that some confession of faith, renouncing the pope, should be taken by all former or suspected recusants.[94] Dering rose to support the motion, and coupled the papists (with their Index and Inquisition) with the 'prelating faction' supported by High Commission and the episcopal licensing of books. 'A pope at Rome,' he quipped, 'will do me less hurt than a patriarch may do at Lambeth.'[95] Both, he believed, were equally enemies to the Protestant faith and established church. Sir John Wray, perhaps already a committed Presbyterian, urged the house to wield the axe not just at the branches of popery, but at its roots.[96] None rose in 1640 to question the existence of a popish plot or the endeavours of the committee of inquiry to root out conspirators – like Windebank. Petitions came in complaining of the leniency shown by the government towards papists, and blaming them for the ills of the realm.[97] As the months passed, the paranoia, events and Pym's frustrations all interflowed to raise the levels of fear. The stabbing of Justice Heyward as he was about to deliver a list of the names of Westminster recusants appeared to offer powerful proof of the need for vigilance; a strict guard was placed on the Commons.[98] Alarming stories came from the localities of planned Catholic uprisings; more recusants were

91. *Cobbett's Parliamentary History*, II, p. 722.
92. Hirst, *Authority and Conflict*, p. 209.
93. Cf. Fletcher, *Outbreak of the English Civil War*, p. xxi and *passim*.
94. *Cobbett's Parliamentary History*, II, pp. 669–70.
95. *Ibid.*, pp. 670–1.
96. *Ibid.*, pp. 671–2.
97. See, for example, *ibid.*, p. 765, where the city petition blames the papists for the decay of trade; cf. p. 780; BL Add. MS 11045, f.144.
98. Buxton MSS, Box 97: Knyvett to Buxton, 23 Nov. 1640; BL Add. MS 11045, f.144; cf. f.131.

presented.[99] Clotworthy reported learning of plans for a Catholic Irish invasion.[100] On 3 May (with rumours of the Army Plot circulating) Pym warned of desperate designs against the parliament at home and from abroad: 'that the French are drawing down their forces to the seaside so that there was cause to fear their intent was upon Portsmouth; that divers persons of eminency about the Queen, as by good information appears, are deeply engaged in these plots'.[101] So powerfully did the conviction take hold that the clandestine practices of papists were even deployed in the summer as the explanation for why the parliament had achieved so little reform![102] And in the famous Grand Remonstrance of November Pym unfolded the larger tapestry of grievances, secular and religious, which, he alleged, had been woven by Jesuits, bishops, popish courtiers and prelates acting in concert. By the time of the Remonstrance, some were beginning to doubt the existence of the papist conspiracy and even accuse Pym and others of manipulating it for their own ends.[103] But for the whole of the first session of the Long Parliament, the papist scare dominated the agenda and coalesced the Commons. More than anything else it was the solvent that eroded trust in the king.

As we have seen, however, it was a fear recently born in 1640 and then wholeheartedly entertained only by a minority. Whilst Pym and Earle had since the 1620s identified a conspiracy, whilst the puritans were from the beginning inclined to suspect Laud of popery, it was not until at least 1639 that the fear began to spread widely. The Scots propaganda, the situation abroad, a reorientation of English foreign policy and of the politics of faction all nurtured it. The dissolution of the Short Parliament saw it walk abroad. Yet even in November Pym's revelations may have come as a surprise and cast a retrospective illumination in the light of which the dark plots could be glimpsed.

99. In Derbyshire there were rumours circulating that papists had caused 200 hatchets to be made to massacre Protestants (J. Dias, 'Politics and administration in Nottinghamshire and Derbyshire, 1590–1640', Oxford University, D. Phil. thesis, 1973, p. 455).
100. R. Clifton, 'The fear of Catholics in England, 1637–45' (Oxford University, D. Phil. thesis, 1967), p. 100.
101. *Cobbett's Parliamentary History*, II, p. 776. It is worthy of note that this is one of the first occasions on which the French were implicated in the Catholic threat. The arrival of the Queen Mother, and Henrietta Maria's growing estrangement from the war party, were clearly crucial.
102. See *ibid.*, p. 780.
103. T. May *The History of the Parliament of England which Began November the Third 1640* (1812 edn), p. 77. By the following spring, county petitions explicitly rejected the idea of a plot. As Hertfordshire put it: 'we wish fears and jealousies might not easily be entertained or longer continued amongst you . . . And for plots from papists at home, they are still underground as formerly and with us they are so quiet as we have had no cause hitherto to apprehend any danger from them' (Huntington Library, Ellesmere MS 6945).

The story of the 'conspiracy's' grip on the nation therefore is only to a small extent a tale of the personal rule.[104] As Professor Fletcher has argued, even in 1640 'the majority of . . . members – in the Lords as well as the Commons – had to be convinced of [Pym's] case . . . The deepest irony . . . is that the further parliament plunged into investigating and combating popish conspiracy, the more the plot seemed to become a self-fulfilling prophecy.'[105]

What I have suggested then is that though there were financial complaints against, provincial discontent with, legal and constitutional doubts about, and religious objections to the personal rule, these did not determine the political developments, or even the mood of the first months of the Long Parliament. There were backbenchers who might have wished that their county's grievances had been accorded a more prominent place; many country MPs had expected their petitions of complaints to set the agenda.[106] But not until June were knighthood fines and forest fines declared illegal, not until June was a bill drawn up against the illegality of the ship money that had dominated the last days of the Short Parliament.[107] And not until July were the courts of Star Chamber and High Commission (and the Councils of the Marches and North) abolished. Still, pressing grievances remained untackled – or at least unsettled. Monopolies, coat and conduct money and other military charges were denounced in the house, but not proscribed by statute; the abuses of fen drainers and petremen, of lord-lieutenants and their deputies had lain unattended. Pym had his own agenda, which did not accord with the county MPs' priorities. For a time – not least through fanning the flames of anti-popish hysteria – he managed to carry the house.

Increasingly however there was disenchantment and a widening gap between the leadership and back benches, which reflected the greater gulf between Westminster and the localities. Not only did several – probably like the Northamptonshire MPs once they had secured their

104. Fletcher, *Outbreak of the English Civil War*, p. xix. Caroline Hibbard points out that there was little about a papist plot in the gentry correspondence of 1639 and 'even in 1640–1642 it proved difficult for many of the gentry to accept the radical critique of the court that a popish conspiracy theory represented' (*Charles I and the Popish Plot*, Chapel Hill, NC, 1983, p. 88); cf. Clifton, 'Fear of Catholics', *passim*.
105. Fletcher, *Outbreak of the English Civil War*, p. xxv.
106. Sir John Holland's speech of 9 November (Tanner MS 239, f.13v; *Cobbett's Parliamentary History*, II, pp. 647–9; W. Notestein (ed.) *The Journal of Sir Simonds D'Ewes from the Beginning of the Long Parliament to the Opening of the Trial of the Earl of Strafford* (New Haven and London, 1923), pp. 15–16) seems to be the paradigm of this position. Any still attached to the idea that the civil war represented a split between court and country should read Holland's speech, remembering that he owed his seat at Castle Rising to the patronage of the Earl of Arundel.
107. Cf. Hirst, *Authority and Conflict*, p. 201.

bill for the better navigation of the river Nene – go home.[108] They articulated their discontent at having been patient, only to see promises unfulfilled. 'I am in such a great rage with parliament,' the Yorkshire gentlewoman Margaret Eure wrote to Verney, 'as nothing will pacify me, for they promised us all should be well if my Lord Strafford's head were off and since then there is nothing better but I think we shall be undone with taxes.'[109] In July in the house, Sir Philip Parker posed the dangerous rhetorical question: 'How long have we sat here and how little have we effected? How much time have we consumed and what little have we performed therein?'[110] Other backbenchers began to complain that business had been determined by 'the sole arbitrament of a few individuals'.[111] In the country at large, Guistiniani, the Venetian envoy, believed that 'parliament is losing the great credit which it enjoyed universally since it appears that instead of relief it has brought expenses and discomfort to the people'.[112] The Cheshire gentleman William Davenport copied a poem penned against a man in parliament who waded in the blood of Strafford, brought the bishops down, plotted with the Scots, and sought to make England a republic like the Dutch.[113] Whatever the degree of discontent among the country gentry in the autumn of 1640, by the autumn of the following year it had become focused on the parliamentary leadership, which only recovered authority with the outbreak of the Irish rebellion in October. It is a barometer of the extent to which the political climate of the Long Parliament differed from that of the 1630s.

For both John Pym and Charles I had programmes of greater priority than tackling the provinces' grievances. The king, of course, was most concerned to raise money to pay his army and to push back the Scots. And Pym's agenda was very much determined as well as enabled by the presence of a Scottish army in England and Scottish treaty commissioners in London: the Covenanters who guaranteed the survival of the parliament also required that its leaders represent their interests. At the head of the Scots interests was the head of Strafford. And as a consequence, the impeachment of Strafford and, with less urgency because he was deemed to be less dangerous, Laud was high on Pym's list of priorities too. Months of the first session of the

108. The recess in September, necessitated because the house was scarcely quorate, not only evidences a lowering of the political temperature. MPs returning to their localities went back to a world far removed from the high politics of Westminster. Charles was probably right to believe that the fuller the house, the better his cause was served.

109. Quoted in Hirst, *Authority and Conflict*, p. 208.

110. *Cobbett's Parliamentary History*, II, p. 867.

111. *Cal. Stat. Pap. Venet., 1640–2*, p. 222, 4 Oct. 1641.

112. *Ibid.*, p. 215. By contrast, he thought the people 'display the greatest attachment to the king'.

113. Chester Record Office, CR/63/2/19, f.86.

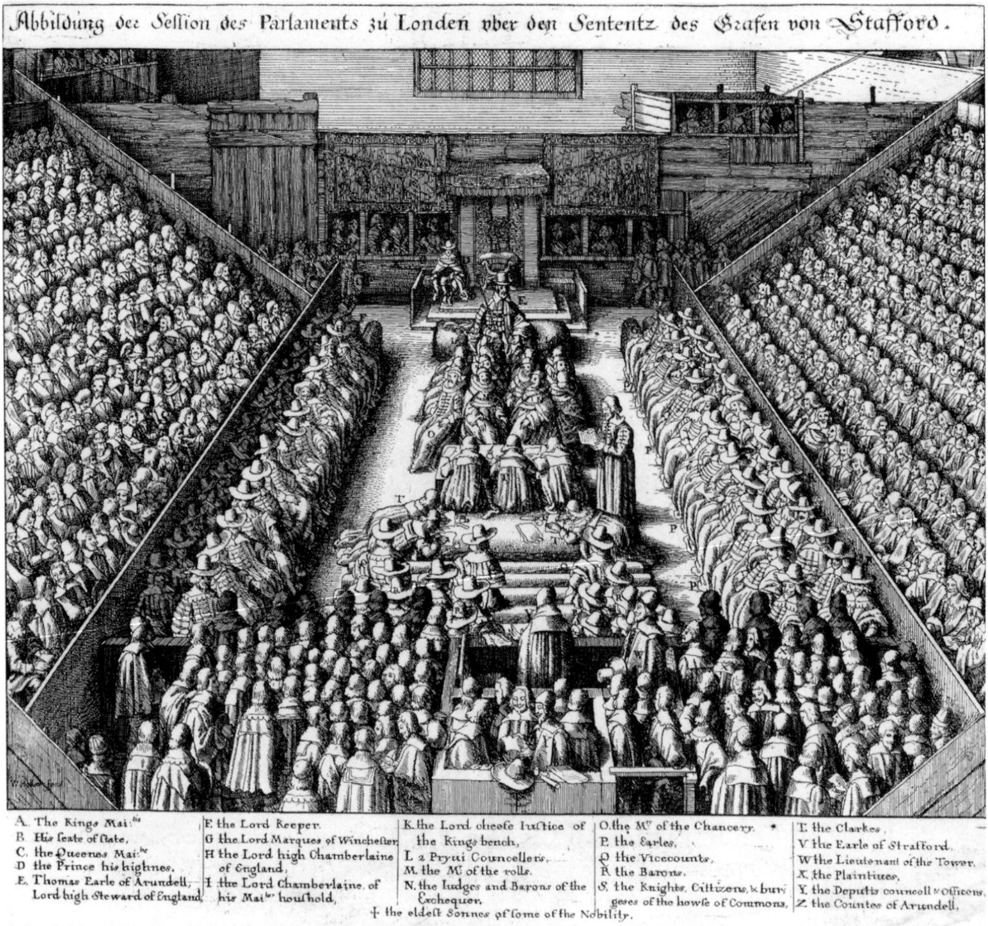

41 *The Trial of Strafford*, etching by Wenceslaus Hollar, 1641. The king and queen observed the proceedings from a private box.

parliament were spent on the pursuit of persons rather than policies. Bishops Pierce, Cosin and Wren, Lord Keeper Finch and the other judges were impeached. Finch and Secretary Windebank were forced to flee in fear of their lives. It was Strafford's trial, however, that consumed time until his execution in May. By November 1640 Wentworth was clearly a widely hated figure. Ballad-mongers sang of 'He who did our laws abuse / And many men misuse', who ruled Ireland with a tyranny that he sought to extend to England.[114] It is worth questioning however the extent to which the English attitude to Strafford in 1640 was indigenous and spontaneous, and the extent to

114. H. Rollins, *Cavalier and Puritan* (New York, 1923), pp. 120ff.: 'The True Manner of the Life and Death of Sir Thomas Wentworth'.

which it was a product entirely of Scottish propaganda and the Scots wars.[115] For Wentworth, a former hero of the 1628 parliament, had featured little in the politics of the 1630s and had not returned from Ireland until the autumn of 1639. He cannot have been widely known to the parliamentary gentry before 1640. Though Irish enemies, Clotworthy and Cork, were brought in as leading witnesses against him, his prosecution was initiated by the Scots, who at Ripon were insisting on the pursuit of those 'incendiaries' who had ruptured the harmony of the kingdoms. Before the Long Parliament convened they sent articles against him, cataloguing his plans to destroy the liberties and religion of Scotland and Ireland and his threats to England, witnessed in his destruction of their last parliament: 'we do,' the Scots commissioners concluded, 'therefore desire . . . that this great incendiary upon these and the like offences not against particular persons but against kingdoms and nations may be put to trial'.[116] Pym took up the 'received information' within days of the parliament's meeting, to indict the Lord-Lieutenant of high treason and carried the Commons through the long weeks of preparing charges and trial.[117] (See Figure 41.) Once again there is a suggestion that his success owed more to Pym's skilful 'management' than to an intrinsic common preoccupation with the earl among the back benches. The Venetian ambassador Agostino may have voiced frustrations he had heard uttered when, reporting the lengthy proceedings that dominated all other business, he observed: 'And so time is spent in vindicating rather than in a profitable economy, all idea of state policy being put aside.'[118] One correspondent of Thomas Smyth's certainly thought the trial 'so tedious a work' and hoped that something more positive might follow from the 'long wearisome time' they spent on the business.[119]

As the trial proceeded the irritation with the time and distraction of the proceedings against Strafford mounted.[120] Thomas Smyth told his friend John Edwards that he was 'wearied out daily with attending my

115. Temple thought that the best way to save Strafford's life would be to hasten the Scots out of England (*HMC De Lisle and Dudley, VI*, p. 368). For the Scots' charges, see J. Spalding, *Memorials of the Troubles in Scotland and England, 1624–45* (Aberdeen, 1850), p. 371.

116. Gardiner, *History of England*, IX, p. 213; Ellesmere MS 7060.

117. *Cobbett's Parliamentary History*, II, pp. 733–5, 11 Nov. 1640. Pym probably knew of Strafford's advice to Charles to charge MPs in league with the Covenanters with treason, and so strategically struck first.

118. *Cal. Stat. Pap. Venet., 1640–2*, p. 101.

119. Smyth of Ashton Court MS AC/C.48/29: Elizabeth Gorges to Thomas Smyth, 2 April 1641.

120. T. May, *The History of the Parliament of England*, p. 64: 'the length of his trial, while two armies at a heavy expense were to be paid and other business at great stand, did divide some impatient people . . . from the Parliament'.

Lord of Strafford's trial which has held since Monday sevennight and is not halfway ended. If he be not more speedily dispatched the kingdom will be undone and I fear we shall have somewhat to do to rid the Scots and bring this parliament to a successful conclusion.'[121] The juxtaposition in Smyth's last clause displays forcefully how potentially closer were MPs like him to the king's priorities than to Pym's.[122] Strafford's trial was also to expose other differences between the leadership and the back benches. During the course of proceedings it became increasingly clear not only that the charge of treason so confidently asserted in November could not be proved, but also (at least to some) that Pym had manipulated the evidence. At the time of presenting the articles against the Lord-Lieutenant Pym had claimed that 'five or six witnesses can depose that he hath advised his Majesty to make use of the Irish army for reducing of England.'[123] He added that there was 'a hundred times as much more evidence' against the earl as was recited.[124] In the event, there turned out to be only one 'witness' – Henry Vane; and his testimony emerged both late (after four interviews) and ambiguously.[125] Lord Digby could not hide his sense of betrayal. The charge, he recalled, 'I was assured would be proved before I gave my consent to his accusation'. Now, he thought, Vane's notes were of use not as proof but only 'to accuse and bring men into danger'.[126] Digby was not isolated; the younger Coke began to doubt whether any charge of treason had been proved, and was greatly disturbed at Pym's desperate shift of tactic from judicial proceedings to an act of attainder which simply declared Strafford guilty: 'ubi non est lex non est transgressio'.[127] Others, as one Taylor put it bluntly, disliked committing murder with the sword of justice.[128]

121. Smyth of Ashton Court MS 36074/156a, 31 March 1641.
122. In contrast to Baillie's too simple belief that the English with the Scots were panting for the legal processes against Strafford and Laud (D. Laing (ed.) *The Letters and Journals of Robert Baillie, I*, Edinburgh, 1841, p. 280).
123. Melbourne Hall, Coke MS 64: 'Articles of the Commons assembled in Parliament against Thomas Earl of Strafford'.
124. *Ibid.*
125. Digby, pointing out that Vane had been examined already 'thrice upon oath', argued that 'he who twice upon oath, with time of recollection, could not remember anything of such a business, might well a third time misremember somewhat . . .', especially when the crucial question was one of the words *here* or *there* (*Cobbett's Parliamentary History*, II, p. 752).
126. *Ibid.*, p. 751.
127. *HMC Cowper II*, pp. 278, 279. The younger Coke, who had spoken against Strafford, grew increasingly disquieted as proceedings developed. 'That nothing concerning religion, after so great a clamour, should be so much as objected to the Earl of Strafford sticks somewhat with me,' he told his father. 'And if his impeachment hath been trained into this length by private practice for private men to work out their own ends and preferments thereupon, their ambition may perchance in the end cost them as dear as it hath done the kingdom.'
128. He was expelled (*Cobbett's Parliamentary History*, II, p. 815).

A party formed against Pym, larger Coke thought than the numbers who voted against the attainder.[129] The execution of Strafford fractured the apparent consensus, greatly reduced the possibility of political settlement and weakened Pym's hold on the Commons. Pym had no choice but to hound Strafford to the grave, for the Scots insisted on his head and relied on Pym and his aristocratic patrons to deliver it: 'the wise English know,' Andrew Honyman wrote to Balcarres with all the menace of a mafia hoodlum, 'that dead dogs bark none.'[130]

The trial of Strafford and Pym's orchestration of it reveal less about the domestic politics of the 1630s than they display the extent to which the Scots influenced the course of the Long Parliament during its first session. Such observations have recently led a leading Stuart historian to argue that the English civil war is something of a misnomer; that the crises of 1642 and indeed of 1640 were the consequence of a 'British problem', of one monarch ruling over multiple kingdoms – England, Scotland and Ireland. Attitudes to the Scots, Professor Russell maintains, provide 'a better predictor of allegiance in the Civil War than any other issue'. By prolonging their treaty negotiations the Scots guaranteed the life of the parliament; in demanding Strafford's life and the abolition of episcopacy they complicated the relations between Charles I and his parliament. They divided the English parliament and polity.[131] There is much of value in this argument and perspective. But we should not herald it as the new explanation for what went wrong. For seen another way, and undoubtedly the way most of Charles's subjects saw it, Scotland was a foreign country; and the problem was less one of the difficulties of multiple kingdoms than the failure militarily to defeat an ancient foe. There was little broad sympathy with the Scots in the 1630s,[132] and such as was manufactured in 1639 and 1640 was soon eroded by the Scots' invasion.[133] Thomas Triplett urged Hyde and his fellow MPs to hurry and rid England of the Scots invaders. There were 'lamentable cries' against them in the north and if parliament were closer, he added, 'you would be troubled by many times more clamouring against the Scots than you have been with

129. *HMC Cowper II*, p. 279; he noted seventy-six opposed to the attainder and 'near 200' absentees; cf. Buxton MSS, Box 97: Knyvett to Buxton, 31 March 1641.

130. National Library of Scotland, Advocates' MS 29.2.9, f.151, 3 March 1641. In the same letter, referring to Pym's speech supporting relief of the Scots, Honyman notes, 'there was a must needs in his speech which language Parliament liked not'.

131. C. Russell, 'The British Problem', p. 408.

132. Sir William Brereton thought them a 'most sluttish, nasty and slothful people', who wallowed in filth (E. Hawkins (ed.) *Travels in Holland, England, Scotland and Ireland by Sir William Brereton*, Chetham Soc., 1, 1844, pp. 102–5). In 1636 Charles I had ordered a reissue of the proclamation regulating the borders – a nice comment on the failure of the nations to grow closer after 1603. Cf. above, pp. 805, 903.

133. Cf. Berkshire Record Office, Trumbull MS XX, 40.

hands against episcopacy'.[134] Even further south there was disquiet about the Scots. Thomas Knyvett for one was appalled at the impudence of the Scots' demands: for instance that they might have half the places on the English Privy Council. 'These proud lousy rogues,' he wrote to Buxton, were 'making no difference between the kingdoms in honour.'[135] When in January a sum was voted for the relief of the Scots, Benjamin Rudyerd reminded the house of the Scots breach of their promise not to plunder and pointed out that their demand for £514,000 was 'more than ever we gave the king at once'. He hinted at the Scots' rising ambitions.[136] Gervase Holles was more explicit. Seeing the Scots 'swell in their demands beyond all proportion', requiring things 'dishonourable for this nation to suffer', he urged his fellows to display the courage of their ancestors and not be dictated to.[137] There were others beginning to express frustrations that 'the demands of the Scots' led to the neglect of 'our own business'.[138] Had it not been for the leadership, settlement with the Scots might well have been secured or forced earlier, with business returning to something more like normal. It was not just the British problem *per se*, but the collaboration between the Covenanters and a faction within England that delayed settlement in both kingdoms.

It was not only alliance with the Scots that distanced Pym and his friends from the country MPs with their localist priorities in the parliament. As is usually the case today, what distinguished the leaders of parliament from the backbenchers was that where the latter looked back home to their shires, the former looked downriver to Whitehall – to office and place in the king's government. It is not necessary to ascribe such desires simply to selfish ambition, for the ambition to serve the commonweal, even to save the state, was (and probably is) a genuine trait of the politician. In 1640 Pym had no doubt that the only way to counteract the popish menace was for men in whom the nation could place its trust to be taken into the king's counsels to offer sound, Protestant advice.[139] There was good precedent, even though it had turned out badly: of whom, Digby asked, had they held out 'better hopes than of the late Mr Noy and Sir Thomas Wentworth', who had been recruited as royal ministers after 1628.[140] It was not only Pym

134. Clarendon MS 19, no. 1472, 18 Dec. 1640.
135. Buxton MSS, Box 97, 16 March 1641.
136. *Cobbett's Parliamentary History*, II, pp. 708–9.
137. *Ibid.*, pp. 771–2; the speech rang with English patriotism and claimed the Scots sought to rob the English of their birthright. (Sir John Wray had felt the need to address this worry: *ibid.*, p. 708.) His concern with the nation's 'honour' at several points echoes Charles I. See Holmes, *Seventeenth Century Lincolnshire*, p. 142.
138. Parsons, *Diary of Sir Henry Slingsby*, p. 65.
139. We recall Pym's speech in the Short Parliament pointing out that the laws against popery were adequate. Above, pp. 909–10.
140. *Cobbett's Parliamentary History*, II, p. 705.

who thought a change of ministers and Councillors might re-establish trust in royal government and greatly lessen the force of disaffection to the regime. From the spring of 1640 some Privy Councillors were aware of a gulf of misunderstanding between the king and powerful subjects, which needed to be bridged. Wentworth advised Laud in May that there 'was nothing of more advantage to the service of the king than at this time to bring in wise and worthy persons to serve his Majesty', adding in particular his recommendation that, not least to secure Northumberland's loyalty, the Earl of Leicester should be brought in.[141] By August the full Privy Council was discussing 'whether it will not be fit to call some of the country nobility to the Board'.[142] The queen was in on the design. At the suggestion of Henry Percy, it was arranged for Henrietta Maria to persuade Charles to employ the Earl of Essex, so as to bring off from the disaffected a popular figure.[143] As Windebank put it frankly to Charles, 'if this lord were taken off, the knot would be much weakened'.[144] More such manoeuvres were under consideration: 'Lords Saye and Brooke another time'.[145] The negotiations went along with the queen's adding her sweet voice (as Finch underlined in his opening speech) to the chorus of peers calling for a parliament.[146] By the time it met the rumours of a translation of places had spread across the country. In Cheshire Davenport had heard that among others the Earl of Bedford would be appointed Lord Treasurer, the Earl of Warwick Secretary of State and the Earl of Hertford Lord Chamberlain.[147] A correspondent of Sir Edward Hyde's, Mr Aylesbury, added to the rumours the Earl of Holland's nomination as Lord Deputy of Ireland.[148] By February 1641, the name of Pym, a trusted friend of Bedford, was widely cited in connection with the chancellorship of the Exchequer; and he, Bedford and Warwick were reported negotiating with the queen in private.[149] The king, for all his evident former scepticism, was prepared to

141. *HMC De Lisle and Dudley, VI*, p. 261.
142. *Cal. Stat. Pap. Dom., 1640*, p. 634.
143. *HMC Cowper II*, p. 272; *HMC De Lisle and Dudley, VI*, p. 368; *Cal. Stat. Pap. Dom., 1640*, pp. 652–3.
144. R. Scrope and T. Monkhouse (eds) *State Papers Collected by Edward, Earl of Clarendon* (3 vols, Oxford, 1767–86), II, pp. 94–5: Windebank to Charles I, 31 Aug. 1640.
145. *Cal. Stat. Pap. Dom., 1640*, p. 652: proceedings of committee of the Council, 31 Aug.
146. *HMC Cowper II*, p. 275; cf. *HMC De Lisle and Dudley, VI*, pp. 365–9; W. Davenant, 'To the queen', in A.M. Gibbs (ed.) *Sir William Davenant: The Shorter Poems* (Oxford, 1972), pp. 139–40; K. Sharpe, *Criticism and Compliment: The Politics of Literature in the England of Charles I* (Cambridge, 1987), ch. 2; *Cobbett's Parliamentary History*, II, p. 631.
147. Chester Record Office, CR/63/2/19, 20 Nov. 1640; cf. Huntington Library, Hastings MS 5534.
148. Clarendon MS 19, no. 1476, 24 Dec. 1640.
149. *HMC Cowper II*, p. 272; Pym is first mentioned towards the end of January (*HMC De Lisle and Dudley, VI*, pp. 366–8: Hawkins to Leicester, 21 Jan. 1641).

entertain the plans not only on account of the promise of a regular and secure revenue, but also to save Strafford.[150]

As we know, nothing in the end came of the scheme. Though the Earl of Southampton was sworn of the bedchamber in January, the bridging appointments were not made.[151] There are various explanations for the failure. Charles I may have insisted on too much; Pym and Bedford may have been unable to assure the supply they wished to obtain; Essex, and perhaps Pym, refused to spare the life of Strafford. Bedford died in May before the hopes had finally faded. What is important to note is that whatever the reasons for the collapse of the scheme, they owe little to the policies of the 1630s, and much to the politics and personal relationships of the spring of 1641 – not least, again, to the Scots, who alone guaranteed Pym's position and who may have obstructed the scheme.[152] Bedford was on good terms with Laud and subscribed liberally to St Paul's; Pym was not preoccupied with the country grievances and was desirous of strong government.[153] Secondly the role of the queen should not pass without comment. For Henrietta Maria's position as intermediary reminds us that the 'bridge appointments' scheme amounted to a re-creation of the queen's old faction of puritan followers – a faction which had dissolved with the Prayer Book rebellion and reorientation of England towards Spain. Holland in particular was endeavouring to recover a place of power which events in 1637 had seemed to promise him.[154] It is worth reflecting whether Pym's fears of a popish plot would have gained so much currency and aristocratic support had the queen's puritan caucus survived and a leading Protestant nobleman been seen to represent the interests of the godly at court. As with so many of Charles's troubles,

150. *HMC De Lisle and Dudley, VI*, p. 368.

151. See E. Hyde, Earl of Clarendon, *The History of the Rebellion and Civil Wars in England*, ed. W.D. Macray (6 vols, Oxford, 1888), I, pp. 280–2, 333–6; C. Roberts, 'The Earl of Bedford and the coming of the English revolution', *Journ. Mod. Hist.*, 49 (1977), pp. 600–16.

152. All the lords involved were those believed to have most intelligence with the Scots (*Clarendon State Papers*, II, pp. 94–5). Hamilton had an important role in securing their appointment as Councillors (*HMC De Lisle and Dudley, VI*, p. 387). There are hints that these English lords displeased the Scots in Baillie's account. Baillie reports that they began to be less supportive of the Scots: 'all began to turn their note', leading many to think 'it was rash impudence so soon to put these men in possession of the honours which some of them were thought alone to seek' (Laing, *Letters and Journals of Baillie*, I, pp. 304–6). This requires further examination.

153. J.H. Wiffen, *Historical Memoirs of the House of Russell* (2 vols, 1833), II, p. 170; Clarendon, *History of the Rebellion*, I, pp. 241. 334; Russell, 'Parliamentary career of Pym'.

154. Cf. B. Donogan, 'A courtier's progress: greed and consistency in the life of the Earl of Holland', *Hist. Journ.*, 19 (1976), p. 344.

the problem of disgruntled magnates and the politics of place really began after 1638.[155]

Whatever the causes of the failure to alter the king's counsellors, the consequences of that failure are clear: the beginnings of a shift from traditional to radical remedies to cure the ills of the realm. After the death of his patron, Bedford, and the end of his bid for office, Pym's own position – perhaps he feared his life – was threatened. The king, he knew, blamed him for the spilling of Strafford's blood and Charles was not a monarch who lightly forgave or forgot a grudge. Pym was driven more to depend on his power base in the north, the Scots army, and in the Commons. As Professor Hirst observes, the constitutionalist reforms were only in the summer 'at last given focus by a leadership whose own hopes of office had been dashed and which was now fearful of a royal counter-attack'.[156] Strong government seems less attractive when one is not only not a part of it but under threat of being a victim of its power. After the spring of 1641, John Pym, like the political situation generally, was radicalized and, almost necessarily, committed to more radical courses to ensure his own as well as the country's security. By the autumn, the Venetian envoy was observing that the few MPs in charge during the parliament's recess were 'called upon *for their own safety's sake* to continue boldly in the course' which they began.[157] The Grand Remonstrance owes as much to Pym's desperation as to his conviction.

John Pym in fact may have been a microcosm as well as agent of political change. During much of the 1620s his commitment to the proper funding of royal government and his concern with administrative efficiency might have qualified him to be a prospective candidate, like Wentworth, for royal office. Even the fear of Arminianism which, it has been claimed, gripped him from 1626, did not deter him from his wish to see the crown strengthened. Pym exemplified in his person that commitment to unity which was itself the cement of the English polity.[158] Despite the story that he contemplated emigration, Pym throughout the 1630s never spoke out against Charles's government, nor does he appear as a refuser of ship money or other levies. Whilst he was active as treasurer of the Providence Island Company, he continued to serve as a receiver of crown land revenues.

155. See J. Adamson, 'The baronial context of the English civil war', *Trans. Royal Hist. Soc.*, 5th series, 40 (1990), pp. 93–120. I am most grateful to John Adamson for sending me a copy of this important paper in advance of publication. It is worth noting that in 1638 Lords Russell and Herbert held the royal train at the Garter procession (PRO, LC 5/193, f.154v).

156. Hirst, *Authority and Conflict*, p. 201.

157. *Cal. Stat. Pap. Venet., 1640–2*, p. 244.

158. Russell, 'Parliamentary career of Pym'.

If he harboured misgivings about the king's government of the state as well as the church, perhaps like Wentworth he regarded it as inappropriate to air them outside parliament.[159] Though by 1640 he was clearly anxious about the growing hold of popery – not least at court – his bid for power showed that he was neither, for the most part, fundamentally opposed to Charles's government nor believed it beyond reformation. It was the experience of the Long Parliament – the evidence of the king's willingness to use force to free Strafford, but as important his own experience of vulnerable isolation – that transformed his position and perception, converting him from the champion of strong monarchical rule to the architect of parliamentary government.[160]

The experience of that unprecedented long session of parliament more generally transformed perceptions at Westminster. Because of their very different circumstances, it is dangerous to read too much from the politics of 1641 as an accurate comment on, or even on perceptions of, the politics of personal rule. Indeed it is from the early months of the Long Parliament that we can begin to trace the myths that have obscured the story of the 1630s. For in the first place the parliament provided another arena in which private battles could be fought, with more regard to victory than scrupulousness in the use of evidence. So Faunt's petition against the Earl of Huntingdon, Corbet's against Bridgewater, Smart's against Cosin, the Beckington parishioners against Pierce presented what was often at best a selective account of old quarrels, and in some cases played very much to the gallery.[161] The compilation of charges could descend to muck-raking. Windebank and Finch both doubted the possibility of a fair trial despite being convinced of their capacity to defend themselves if examined fairly.[162] The impeachment of Wren suggests that their fears were well placed. When the churchwardens of St Edmunds gave evidence that the bishop had laid visitation charges on them of 13s. 4d., the 'sum not being accepted they were sent away to give in more full account'.[163] Documents were denied to Wren, for his defence, while they were manipulated to enhance the appearance of his guilt.[164] Some, alleging that he had purloined money from churches, frankly admitted 'the which not being able to prove we only offer to the consideration of

159. Cf. S.R. Brett, *John Pym, 1583–1643* (1940), p. 135 and ch. 6.
160. See *Cal. Stat. Pap. Venet., 1640–2*, pp. 148, 147, 220.
161. See Ellesmere MSS 7670, 7688, 7689, 7693, 7695; Coke MS 64; *Cobbett's Parliamentary History*, II, pp. 725ff.; Rawlinson MS D.821, f.4; Smyth of Ashton Court MS 36074/139a.
162. Tanner MS 65, f.226; *Cobbett's Parliamentary History*, II, pp. 682–5, 686–9, 694.
163. Tanner MS 290, f.108; cf. Tanner MS 68, *passim*.
164. Above, pp. 753–4.

the house'.[165] Proof now was less important than politics. Many, it was said, were afraid to speak in Wren's defence.[166] A core of fact was spiced with rumour, hearsay and malice in making a case. In one debate it was even alleged that the Northamptonshire gentleman Francis Nichols had been harassed for five years by High Commission, only for wearing his hat at a sermon, when in truth he was summoned for attending conventicles![167] In Laud's and Strafford's trials we see the most obvious distortions and manipulation in the name of a case – not least perhaps in identifying them throughout as the king's principal ministers. To write the history of the 1630s, as so often it has been written, from the debates and impeachment speeches of 1641, is to look not at the object but at the image already distorted. It is to deliver the judgment having heard only the case for the (not always scrupulous) prosecution.

This is absolutely not, as I trust is clear, to argue that all was harmony and content in the England of the 1630s: we have seen that it was not. But it is to suggest that discontents were not yet seen as beyond resolution by the normal political procedures. Historians of the counties often comment on the remarkable degree of stability still evident in 1639; even Warwick and Barrington actively co-operated with royal orders.[168] For all the grievances most MPs, far from thinking of radical upheavals, thought only of moderate reforms. In his speech in support of the bill for holding frequent parliaments, George Digby, MP for Dorset, sketched a picture of England which was far from monochrome.

> Take into your view Mr Speaker, a kingdom in a state of the greatest quiet and security that can be fancied; not only enjoying the calmest peace itself, but, to improve and secure its happy condition all the rest of the world at the same time in tempests, in combustions, in uncomposable wars. Take into your view, sir, a king, sovereign of three kingdoms . . . a king, firm and knowing his religion, eminent in virtue; a king that hath in his own time, given all the rights and liberties of his subjects a more clear and ample confirmation, freely and graciously (I mean in the Petition of Right) than any of his predecessors . . . This is one map of England, Mr

165. Tanner MS 220, f.124.
166. Tanner MS 68, f.340.
167. J.T. Cliffe, *The Puritan Gentry: The Great Puritan Families of Early Stuart England* (1984), p. 194.
168. For example, B. Coward, *The Stanleys, Lords Stanley and Earls of Derby, 1385–1672* (Manchester, 1982), p. 162. Cf. V. Stater, 'The Lord Lieutenancy on the eve of the civil wars: the impressment of George Plowright', *Hist. Journ.*, 29 (1980), pp. 279–81, 290–6.

> Speaker. A man, sir, that should present unto you now a kingdom groaning under that supreme law which salus populi periclitata would enact; the liberty, the property of the subject fundamentally subverted, ravished away by the violence of a pretended necessity; a triple crown shaking with distempers; men of the best conscience ready to fly into the wilderness for religion. Would not one swear that this were the antipodes to the other? And yet let me tell you Mr Speaker this is a map of England too and both at the same time but too true.[169]

Digby went on to ascribe the people's enslaving to the ship money judgment. His reference to a 'triple crown shaking' takes us back to the same year as Hampden's case.[170] Was it, then, only from the hindsight of 1640 (or 1639) that Digby saw the intermission of parliaments from 1629 as the cause of the nation's ills? And if so was he typical of the backbenchers' perceptions of the decade of personal rule? If those who had served the king in the localities had become sufficiently discontented and distrustful by 1640 to permit the designs of Pym and the Scots to take priority over the demands of the king, how and when had that come about? Two legally minded observers and critics of the regime were both clear in their answer. In *Certain Considerations* upon the nature of government, Sir Roger Twysden dated the rise of an opposition to the regime from the outbreak of the Prayer Book rebellion in Scotland.[171] Bulstrode Whitelocke concurred. Though even after the first session of the Long Parliament, he thought, 'the calm was not quite blown over', it was the Scots rising that 'was the fountain from whence our ensuing troubles did spring'.[172]

Such too must be the conclusion of our own investigation. If, as Professor Russell put it, 'revenue, local government, patronage, religion and war' were the areas of difficulty for Charles's government, it was after 1637 that they threatened the stability of the personal rule.[173] It was after the Prayer Book rising that the city financiers called in their loans, invested abroad and created a climate of economic instability which in turn exacerbated political uncertainty. It was after the military failure of the first Scots campaign that Charles faced a fiscal crisis.[174] It was after 1638 – perhaps not until 1640 – that the government lost the active co-operation of the county magistracy

169. *Cobbett's Parliamentary History*, II, p. 703.
170. Cf. *HMC De Lisle and Dudley, VI*, p. 393: Temple to Leicester, 24 March 1641.
171. J.M. Kemble, *Certain Considerations upon the Government of England by Sir Roger Twysden* (Camden Soc., old series, 45, 1849), p. 145.
172. B. Whitelocke, *Memorials of the English Affairs* (1682), pp. 25–6, 45.
173. Russell, *Parliaments and English Politics*, p. 418.
174. F.C. Dietz, *English Public Finance, 1558–1641* (New York, 1964), p. 287.

in executing its orders and commands. And it was after 1638 that anxieties about religious change began to escalate into a fear that the government, and perhaps even the king, were popishly affected.

It may be argued that a regime that collapsed under a foreign threat, a propaganda campaign and a military failure was already moribund; that the will to shore up the government was lacking in those discontented at fiscal demands and royal policies. But there are few eras of history – no, not even the golden days of Elizabeth I – when such disaffection is not in evidence. 'Country' sentiments and criticisms were, and still are, a necessary and healthy aspect of the *mundus politicus*. Far from being intrinsically weak in 1637, Charles's government appears to have been rather stronger than in the 1620s or than that of his immediate predecessors, or successors – Cromwell and Charles II.[175] As Professor Cope concedes, writing of the peers' petition for a parliament: 'Although some of the grievances cited in the petition were long-standing most either stemmed directly from the events of 1639–40 or were aggravated by those events'.[176] There was nothing then inevitable about the downfall of the personal rule. Indeed when we glimpse back over our story, we can see how things might well have unfolded differently. What if Charles's army had made it north a few days earlier or Newcastle had held a day longer: would the Scots forces have disbanded? What if in the first campaign the armies had come to blows and England secured victory? Had Richelieu signed the treaty offensive and defensive and Charles had entered a confederacy against the Habsburgs as a champion of Protestantism, would the popish scare have lost the force of conviction? And if Lindsey's or Northumberland's fleet had achieved a dramatic success would the sting have gone out of the opposition to ship money?

It is suggestive that so many of our questions concern matters foreign and military. Those who have written the history of the 1630s from far down the road of later English developments have undoubtedly underestimated the degree to which foreign considerations were the motor of events in England rather than an insignificant trailer to the drive of English – or even British – history. Even in 1641 Charles hoped the marriage of his daughter to the Prince of Orange might win him assistance in removing the Scots and regaining the upper hand.[177] But in matters both foreign and domestic, and not least because each complicated the other, the year 1637–8 marked a turn

175. For an interesting comparison with Cromwell, see Hirst, *Authority and Conflict*, p. 333. Cromwell lamented in 1658 'if only the nation would be content with rule'! (*ibid.*, p. 352).

176. Cope, *Politics without Parliaments*, p. 197; cf. C. Holmes, *The Eastern Association in the English Civil War* (Cambridge, 1975), p. 24.

177. *Cal. Stat. Pap. Venet., 1640–2*, pp. 106–8.

of the tide. The ship money case, the trial of Prynne, Burton and Bastwick and the plague at home occurred amidst the Scots rebellion, new negotiations with Spain and the collapse of the French alliance. Events began to combine to turn particular grievances into distrust and turn disaffected magnates into a potential leadership of opposition.

After 1637, observers noted a change in the king too. The Venetian envoy reported that he gave up hunting and, as if the outward visage of the body politic, 'his very face clearly betrays the passions within'.[178] Almost alone at the centre of all the overlapping circles, English, Scottish and continental, was the king himself. Charles I has been the central actor in our story: should we then close our investigation of his very personal rule by attributing to his person the troubles of 1637, 1640 and 1642? Professor Russell believes that we should. For in all his situations Charles manifested the 'same imaginative blindspots' and acted from 'the same convictions'.[179] Certainly Charles Stuart, unlike his father, was no politician, but a man (to recall Burnet) of profound conscience and deep principle. Honour and order (his own and the commonweal's) were the principles he held to throughout – in 1638 when he refused to accept the Covenant, as a decade earlier where our story began as it ends with military failure and Charles's determination to recover his honour.[180] Still in 1640 he doubted not that a parliament would be 'sensible of the honour of his Majesty and the nation'.[181] Not the last to believe that what was for men's good mattered more than what pleased, he paid little attention to the art of persuasion, following the *Counsellor of Estate*'s axiom that 'it shall suffice' the ruler 'that those things which he ordains or commands may be good and profitable to the public'.[182] Whatever his deficiencies in those arts of politics – manoeuvre, management, compromise – Charles, convinced that he pursued courses for the good of the commonweal, held to 'convictions' when a politician might have surrendered them. He did not always do so out of ignorance of the consequences or the risks. He believed some principles worth adhering to whatever the political repercussions.[183] And, well, he may even have been right.

178. *Cal. Stat. Pap. Venet., 1636–9*, p. 435.
179. Russell, 'The British problem', p. 410.
180. *Cal. Stat. Pap. Dom., 1639*, p. 123: Countess of Westmorland to Windebank, 6 May. Charles, she reported, would not 'suffer in point of honour' to settle with the Scots.
181. *Clarendon State Papers*, II, p. 81.
182. P. Bethune, *The Counsellor of Estate* (1634, STC 1933), p. 79.
183. Professor Russell argues that it was Charles's tragedy that he got what he wanted. But it appears to me that Russell simultaneously accuses him of being both too rigid and not rigid enough ('The British problem', pp. 246–51).

INDEX

References in *italic* are to illustrations.

Other than in the entry under his name, Charles I is referred to as C.

Kevin Sharpe was educated at Oxford and is now Reader in History at the University of Southampton. Among his books are *Politics and Ideas in Early Stuart England* (1989) and *Criticism and Compliment: The Politics of Literature in the England of Charles I* (1987). He has been a visiting fellow at the Institute for Advanced Study, Princeton, the Stanford Humanities Center, the Henry E. Huntington Library, California, and the Humanities Research Centre, Canberra.